A HANDBOOK OF Contemporary Soviet Psychology

A HANDBOOK OF Contemporary Soviet Psychology

Edited by

MICHAEL COLE · IRVING MALTZMAN

Foreword by A. N. Leont'ev, A. R. Luria, and A. A. Smirnov

BASIC BOOKS, INC., PUBLISHERS

NEW YORK • LONDON

The chapters of this volume
have been translated from the Russian by
Rosa Glickman, David G. Nichols,
Elka Schuman, and Lynn Solotaroff.

Library of Congress Catalog Card Number: 68–54138
Manufactured in the United States of America
Designed by Sophie Adler

FOREWORD

A. N. Leont'ev, A. R. Luria, A. A. Smirnov

IN THIS *Handbook of Contemporary Soviet Psychology,* Soviet scientists, each eminent in his field, present a broad, comprehensive view of the main lines of development and the chief advances of Soviet psychological science. In addition, the American editors have supplied a historical introduction and notes and have organized the volume in such a way as to give the Western reader a clear perspective on Soviet psychology and to allow him to follow up the lines of research reported in the various chapters.

This handbook is an unprecedented achievement, in scope and depth, in an area in which scientific communication has been, to say the least, inadequate. In 1959–1960, a two-volume work, entitled *Psychological Science in the U.S.S.R.,* was published, in Russian, in which leading Soviet psychologists surveyed for their colleagues the accomplishments and direction of their science. This Russian work, edited by, among others, the authors of this Foreword, has served as the basis and point of departure for the present work.

The Russian work represented such fields of psychology as general psychology (its main divisions), physiological psychology, problems in the development of mental processes, educational psychology, psychopathology, and defectology. The physiology of higher nervous activity was not included; following the traditions of Soviet science, it has long since become independent of psychology and now constitutes a special division of physiology in its own right. This subdivision is not customary in American and British science, where the problems related to higher nervous activity are part of general psychology in its broader sense; the American editors have therefore included in this handbook special chapters devoted to the investigation of psychophysiological bases of behavior.

Attempts at acquainting the English-speaking reader with the investigations being carried out by Soviet psychologists have until now been of a relatively fragmentary nature. The present work, however, differs from these in that the authors of the chapters present the main branches of Soviet psychology as fully as possible; thus the reader will find a relatively complete account of what has been accomplished by Soviet psychological science within the past several decades.

A number of original fields have emerged in Soviet psychological science, distinguishing it from the study of psychology in other countries. The scientific-materialist approach to psychological phenomena impels us to regard mental processes as a historically established and highly organized activity of man; naturally enough, therefore, the present volume represents an attempt to clarify the nature of the *historical method* which underlies all Soviet psychological investigations.

Soviet psychology has never accepted the limits imposed by positivist descriptions of mental phenomena or behavior, aiming instead to fathom their *physiological mechanisms*. This volume therefore contains chapters which demonstrate how much psychological science benefits from studying the dynamics of the higher nervous processes underlying the behavior of animals and man.

In the section dealing with the problems of general psychology the reader will find chapters describing investigations into sensation, perception, memory, and thinking, subjects widely represented in Soviet psychological science.

One of the features disinguishing Soviet psychology is that its approach to basic problems proceeds from the conception of development, applying the results from a widely expanded series of special investigations on the *development of mental activity*. Founded as far back as the middle of the nineteenth century by the great Russian physiologist Sechenov, and given a new impetus by the outstanding Soviet psychologist Vygotskii, these traditions have borne rich fruit; the number of chapters devoted to the development of mental processes and to the formation of complex forms of cognitive activity reflects the unabated interest with which these branches of science are being pursued in the Soviet Union.

Great attention in Soviet psychological investigations has also been paid to the problems of *underdevelopment and disintegration of cognitive processes*, so that the reader will find surveys of work devoted to neuropsychology, psychopathology, and defectology.

The intensive growth of Soviet psychological science, which draws into its orbit an ever increasing number of new fields of knowledge, of course makes it impossible to cover uniformly in one volume all of its branches and to reflect all of its recent advances.

There is every reason to believe, however, that by covering, as fully as possible, the main branches of Soviet psychological science, this volume will serve its principal purpose: the dissemination of correct information on the development of psychological science in the Soviet Union, contributing thereby to a further improvement of mutual understanding among the psychologists of various countries.

Moscow

EDITORS' PREFACE

ALTHOUGH THE LAST DECADE has witnessed a dramatic increase in contacts between Western and Soviet scientists, ideological, linguistic, and cultural differences have combined to limit the extent and fruitfulness of scientific communication. This book was undertaken because both the American editors and their Soviet colleagues had experienced the waste engendered by ignorance. The book's structure can best be understood in the light of previous attempts to present Soviet psychological sciences to the American reader and the recent increase in exchange of scientists which made clear the inadequacies of the present situation.

When the idea of undertaking this book first began to take form, both editors were personally concerned with the problem of Soviet-American scientific communication. One of the editors, Irving Maltzman, was doing research on orienting responses and learning which led him into an area known to be of great interest to Soviet psychologists. Unfortunately, the publication of some of the primary material on this subject did not provide him with the details he needed to answer problems raised by his work. Where were the details published and how could they be obtained?

The answers to these and other questions were being sought by Michael Cole, who, following related interests, was spending a year at the Psychology Department of Moscow State University under the auspices of the Soviet-American cultural exchange program. Cole had information problems of his own; he had gone to Moscow hoping to work on the use of conditioned-reflex methods for the study of word-meaning in children. Somewhat to his dismay, this topic was considered more or less wrapped up by earlier research and was no longer the subject of concerted study. It was necessary to develop a new research program with the aid of his scientific adviser, A. R. Luria.

It was in this context that Professors Cole and Luria first began to explore ways of improving their respective colleagues' knowledge and understanding of each other's work.

Since that time, a great deal has occurred to improve matters: the journal *Soviet Psychiatry and Psychology,* now expanded into two separate periodicals, began to publish in the United States, Stevens' authoritative (if somewhat dated) *Handbook of Experimental Psychology* as well as several other important contemporary books have been translated in the Soviet Union, and several monographs by leading Soviet psychologists and physiologists have been published in English. Professor Razran continues to publish surveys of Soviet research, while Professor Brozek and his colleagues periodically review and summarize books published in Eastern Europe. Translation programs supported directly and indirectly by the Federal Government continue to grow. Another development, not to be overlooked, was the fact that the Eighteenth International Congress of Psychology, which was held in Moscow in the summer of 1966, provided the opportunity for numerous personal exchanges between Soviet psychologists and their colleagues from other countries. Undoubtedly some of these exchanges continued on an informal basis. Yet many inadequacies remain. Since it was the intention of this book to reduce these inadequacies in communication, it is worthwhile to list them as a partial explanation for the text that follows.

First, there is the problem of language. We do not mean by this problems of translation in the narrow sense, although these exist, but rather the problem of interpreting terms whose meaning has accrued over generations in a theoretical context that is strange to the uninitiated. Terms such as "excitation," "reflection," and "psychic" mislead us by their seeming familiarity; they have taken on special meanings which we cannot easily glean from a research article which assumes our familiarity with their meaning (just as Russians would be, and have been, misled by too literal translations of "habit," "reaction potential," and "cognitive map"). Too often this language problem has led us to reject out of hand research that is, in fact, quite congenial.

Second is the problem of research strategy; this amounts to a cultural difference which only now seems to be disappearing as each tradition accommodates to the other. We have in mind here the Soviet proclivity to conduct research in a manner deemed overly informal by their method-conscious American counterparts; reliance is often placed on individual subjects or small groups whose performance illustrates the conclusion the author is interested in. Control groups are not often included, with reference being made to earlier observations which confirm the significance of trends observed in the present case. This research model seems to parallel the strategies of classical physiology.

On the other hand, there is much that can be said for their approach to research. Its assiduous concern with qualitative detail may suggest the presence of variables which otherwise might be overlooked. It emphasizes the complexities of the processes involved and decreases the likelihood of overgeneralization and oversimplification.

The strategy of long-term and repeated experiments with a small number of subjects who reliably demonstrate a phenomenon, characteristic of at least the conditioning research, provides information not always obtainable in the large-group fifty-minute experiment. Running subjects to steady states is as much a characteristic of Soviet conditioning studies as it is of American operant conditioning studies.

Next is the related problem of the manner in which research is reported. Neither in their reports of individual experiments nor in their general review articles do Soviet researchers provide the detailed information about procedures and results which are the backbone of Western scientific communication. In either case this style of communication, intended primarily for their Soviet colleagues, is often confusing to the American reader; Ivanov-Smolenskii's well-known method of studying verbal conditioning is not well known outside the U.S.S.R., and many of the theoretical disputes (over the number of basic types of higher nervous activity or the proper Marxist interpretation of the role of language in the development of consciousness) seem little short of bizarre. It is perhaps instructive to imagine the plight of one of our Soviet colleagues trying to read an APA journal in which he is likely to encounter intricate arguments over drive reduction or the appropriateness of some verbal association norm, the content of which is never explained.

Another problem is comprehensiveness. As the discussion above indicates, it is hard to understand small parts of the picture without some knowledge of the context and history of the problems discussed. If the meaning of theoretical terms and the justification for certain experimental techniques are historically determined, the genesis of the problem area must be understood in order to comprehend fully the purpose and significance of a particular experimental investigation.

We have tried to overcome this problem by including background and historical material in the Introduction, notes, and the body of individual chapters, so that a more complete setting for a given research area is available. Historical and theoretical background information of this kind, providing as they do some form of rationale, should make the individual studies more understandable than they would otherwise be if read in isolation.

A last problem is timeliness. With the accelerating pace of scientific achievements, the delays of years and sometimes decades which have accompanied scientific communication in the past are no longer tolerable.

Almost inevitably, duplication of effort and wasted time will result from a few years' delay in communicating relevant facts and theories.

Our intention upon undertaking this handbook was to create a truly Hegelian synthesis of comprehensive coverage, detailed reporting of research designs and results and contemporaneousness. In order to achieve these goals Michael Cole, in the spring of 1965, made a special trip to Moscow, where he met with Professors Luria, Leont'ev, Smirnov, and many of the contributors to this volume. The list of chapters and their contents were gone over in some detail, with an eye to making the presentation understandable to professional, if uninitiated, readers. However, in the course of the following year, it became evident that the best of intentions cannot completely overcome the weight of long traditions. Many of the authors, in an effort to assist us in making the volume as comprehensive as possible, expanded on their previous work, using as a springboard articles they had written for the two-volume *Psychological Sciences in the U.S.S.R.* However, the degree of detail did not add very much to older work and the descriptions of new work were not as extensive as we had hoped for. And, true to tradition, the authors adhered to the *style* of their previous writing.

Several authors were able to find the time to write articles specifically for this volume.

In a few cases the press of other commitments delayed writing of chapters to the point where we feared that the material would be outdated if delayed any longer. Not wanting to exclude this material, we brought together material published in various sources which provides a representative picture of the work being considered. In each case our Soviet colleagues were helpful in providing us with material for these composite articles.

With respect to some of our aims which were the basis for undertaking the editing of this volume, our reach exceeded our grasp. In other respects the material obtained and presented here was highly gratifying and exceeded our expectations. Much of the Soviet research is marked by a high degree of ingenuity and an innovative character that outstrips its Western counterpart. This is apparent both in the experimental techniques and in the interpretations offered. Such innovativeness is apparent in areas not well known in the West, such as developmental psychology, and in areas thought to be known, such as conditioning. The concern with important variables of maximum generalizability outside of the laboratory, the utilization of novel experimental procedures and variations of standard procedures even in the case of classical conditioning, the disinclination to engage in parametric studies of unimportant variables lacking generality, the sustained investigation of a problem by an individual investigator, and the obvious dedication to the highest principles of scientific research that we saw in our personal encounters with Soviet investigators are all refreshing, stimulating, and important aspects of their work.

We hope, and expect, that the intellectual stimulation, surprise, and delight that we experienced in reading many of the sections in this volume will also be experienced by the reader.

The expert assistance of the translators of this volume—Rosa Glickman, Elka Schuman, David G. Nichols, and Lynn Solotaroff—is gratefully acknowledged. Any inaccuracies or inconsistencies in translation which remain in the final text are the responsibilities of the editors.

In giving credit to the many people who made this book possible we want especially to thank Professors Leont'ev, Luria, and Smirnov, who counseled us in the selection of material from their Soviet colleagues. Dr. Nina N. Korzh's assistance in coordinating the collection of materials and obtaining biographical information is also gratefully acknowledged.

Support from a Carnegie Corporation grant permitted Irving Maltzman to concentrate upon his editorial duties during the summer months. It is gratefully acknowledged for this and other reasons.

Lastly, we wish to thank the Soviet and American governments for making possible the international cooperation without which none of this work would have been possible.

September 1968

Michael Cole
Irving Maltzman

CONTENTS

A HANDBOOK OF Contemporary Soviet Psychology

EDITORS' INTRODUCTION

Historical Background

The men and women in the U.S.S.R who are engaged in experimental psychology work in two separate Soviet disciplines: psychology and a branch of physiology called psychophysiology or "higher nervous activity." The study of "higher nervous activity" is in many respects closer to American experimental psychology than is Soviet "psychology." Pavlov, who founded this branch of physiology and is the popular symbol of Russian psychology, was not a psychologist at all. Thus, we must keep these two branches of Soviet psychological science separate if we are adequately to reflect the historical tendencies of each.

As with so many other aspects of contemporary Soviet culture, an understanding of today's developments must be sought in a review of events preceding the advent of Soviet power. In the case of psychophysiology, the starting point is the 1863 publication of Sechenov's monograph *Reflexes of the Brain.* This brief work was written shortly after Sechenov returned from Germany, where he had studied with some of Europe's most renowned physiologists. Sechenov's central thesis was that psychic life (ideas, intuitions, etc.) is synonymous with reflex actions of the brain. (Thus he saw no need—in fact, he considered it harmful—to posit the existence of a psyche independent of brain matter.) It followed that the proper way to study such phenomena as the association of ideas was to study the relation between reflexes. So controversial was this thesis in the Russia of the 1860's that the book was banned for several years.

One other paper written by Sechenov is of particular interest, in that it marks the beginning of the division between psychophysiology and psychology. In *By Whom and How Shall Psychology Be Studied?* (1873) Sechenov maintained that psychology as studied by the consciousness-centered psychologists of the time was a hopeless enterprise. He advocated that physiologists using the objective reflex method should take over the field, a viewpoint still echoed in Soviet science today.

While Sechenov was propagandizing for a new physiological psychology, a new generation of Russian students was abroad absorbing another new brand of psychology—the "structuralism" of Wilhelm Wundt. These men sought to decompose thinking, sensation, and emotion into their basic "elements," using the method of trained introspection. Their dissatisfaction with the speculative psychology of the early nineteenth century was less a question of philosophy than of methodology. They substituted measuring instruments for armchairs, yet retained the old psychological categories. Adherents of this "psychological" approach to psychology were the predecessors of today's Soviet psychologists.

The program for an objective physiological psychology which Sechenov advocated was ahead of its time. It was not until forty years after the publication of *Reflexes of the Brain* that Pavlov began the experimental work that would give substance to Sechenov's ideas. (The American movement toward an objective psychology, which began at about the same time, was to find its first clear expression a little later in the work of Watson.) Pavlov often expressed his indebtedness to Sechenov and displayed also Sechenov's distaste for traditional, philosophically oriented psychology. Time and time again Pavlov blamed the backwardness of a science of the brain on the contemporary psychology, proposing to replace it by the study of "higher nervous activity." In describing his own early attempts to deal with conditioned reflexes (which he at first regarded as merely a nuisance in the study of digestive processes), his low opinion of psychology is clearly stated:

> Why had we formerly, like cowards, returned to the old subjective methods? The secret is simple: because the subjective method is the method of thinking without real causes, because psychological reasoning is indeterminate reasoning, recognizing phenomena, but not knowing whence they came and where they lead. . . . The psychological explanations were fantastic and without basis (Pavlov, 1927).

Thus, prior to the advent of Soviet power, the main divisions between psychology and psychophysiology (which together correspond to our discipline of psychology) were already clearly drawn. In this respect, there was little change in the decade following the October Revolution. But the period from 1917 to 1929 did mark a high point in wide-ranging experimentation and in new approaches to the study of both psychology and psychophysiology; and significant developments took place in established laboratories.

Psychophysiology benefited greatly from the accession to power of a materialist, science-oriented regime. Pavlov's laboratory, freed from the suspicious eyes of the Tsarist church, enlarged its staff tenfold after the Revolution. The authorities took special care to ensure that his laboratory was well equipped and his animals well fed (no small feat during the first post-October years). Another great Russian psychophysiologist, Bekhterev, also expanded his output during this period. Bekhterev, who had developed a general physiological-psychological theory based on the study of psychological phenomena such as the formation and modification of reflexes, which he termed "reflexology," was in fact the more influential of the two men during this period.

In psychology proper, the 1920's represented a period of unprecedented experimental and theoretical innovation. Every known school of psychological thought had its adherents: behaviorists, gestalt psychologists, reflexologists, reactologists. Even a Freudian circle existed at that time. In the general search for a materialist psychology consonant with Marxism, each school asserted its particular affinity with the ideas of Marx and Engels. If any one school of thought could be said to dominate during the period, it would be the system of "reactology" developed by Kornilov, Director of the Moscow Institute of Psychology. Reactology was an attempt to synthesize the variegated concepts then popular in psychology, with the addition of some Marxist philosophy. It reflected the view that psychology should be concerned with the study of simple reactions since, by measuring the speed, form, and duration of these reactions, one could measure mental energy. To demonstrate the philosophical advantages of reactology, Kornilov wrote a *Textbook of Psychology from the Standpoint of Dialectical Materialism,* which went through five editions between 1926 and 1931.

The advent of a new era in Soviet psychology was marked by the publication in 1929–1930 of Lenin's *Philosophical Notebooks.* This event stimulated the Party cell of the Moscow Institute of Psychology to re-examine the contemporary schools of psychology in order to establish the correct Party line for the discipline. Never again would the influence of the Party be as diffuse and indirect as it was in the 1920's.

No one seems to have been very certain as to exactly what type of psychology was implied by Marxist principles, but the Party decided that the schools of psychology popular until 1930 did not fill the bill. Consequently, the number of schools began to dwindle rapidly. One of the first to go was Kornilov's reactology, which was found to be vulgarly mechanistic, presenting man as a passive reactor instead of an active initiator, and hewing too closely to American behaviorist (and thus capitalist) psychology. (Kornilov shared with the behaviorists the view that only objectively definable and measurable aspects of behavior could be the subject matter of psychology.) The same type of argument was used to undermine the other contenders, so that by the middle 1930's several of the schools of Soviet psychology had disappeared.

The single most important event in the development of Soviet psychology during that era was the 1936 decree of the Party's Central Committee, on pedological perversions, which outlawed all forms of psychological testing, including IQ tests and those based on "projective" techniques, such as the Rorschach. Until 1936, the use of paper-and-pencil psychological tests had been standard practice in Soviet industry and education. Many of these were simply translations of such American tests as the Stanford-Binet. Under Stalin's guidance, the Party now decided that such tests were at least worthless, and almost certainly harmful, and the assumption that any paper-and-pencil test could determine a "fixed" number measuring a person's inherited capacities was called a bourgeois hoax. It was argued that this notion ran directly counter to the correct Marxist position that man is formed by his socioeconomic environment and that the new socialist environment would produce a "new Soviet man."

Although in part this argument was a simple reflection of Marxist-Leninist doctrine, the general objections to testing were not unlike those often heard in the United States. A sampling of the work of those who were involved in the Soviet testing movement in the 1920's yields a fair amount of evidence to back up the claim of the Central Committee that the testing was indeed worthless (Mintz, 1962). It is only in recent years that cautious experiments with the use of such tests have again begun in the U.S.S.R.

At about the same time that rival schools of psychology disappeared from the scene and the testing movement was terminated, the many psychological journals that had come into being during the 1920's were discontinued; psychologists who wanted to publish their work had to turn to educational journals for an outlet.

Students of the Soviet psychological scene are generally agreed that the discipline went into a decline during the period 1935–1950 (Bauer, 1952; Razran, 1958). Psychological textbooks devoted a great deal of space to discussions of the tasks of psychology in the light of Marxism-Leninism, and political and philosophical references often seemed to outweigh the psychological, while references to foreign authors were either absent or derogatory.

Yet recent evidence indicates that this picture of complete barrenness, based on the material that had reached print at the time, is overdrawn. The severe ideological restraints placed on Soviet psychology during the Stalinist period found their expression in part in the lack of publication outlets for the psychologists: since psychology was viewed as an arm of education and since the only way to publish, therefore, was through an educational journal, only work that fitted a strictly educational format found its way into print. In 1959–1960, however, a two-volume handbook of Soviet psychology was published, and the contents indicate—albeit indirectly—that meaningful research had not altogether ceased during Stalin's time. The handbook includes many references to work done during the 1930's and 1940's which was unpublished at the time or appeared only in the form of *zapiski* (notes) of the institution where the research was done. (It is this handbook which forms the backbone of the present volume.) Evidently, students of Kornilov, Bekhterev, and the other leading figures of the 1920's were busy in the 1930's even though they could not publish their findings; many monographs covering work then done remained unpublished as late as the 1950's.

During the war years, Soviet psychologists were reorganized in laboratories for the study of various military problems as well as the problem of rehabilitation following brain injury and other battle-related disabilities. This wartime work of many of the Soviet Union's leading psychologists is only now becoming known in the West.

The psychophysiologists went very much their own way during the 1930's and World War II. The Pavlovian laboratories undertook a wide variety of investigations of far-ranging import. Thus, the Pavlovian experimental station at Koltushi, outside Leningrad, was the scene of large projects on anthropoid behavior, directed by Voitonis. Pioneering work was begun in the use of electrodes for the study of brain functions, and new techniques were developed for the study of conditioning of the internal organs. Modifications of Pavlov's reflex theory, introducing the notion of feedback systems, were elaborated by Anokhin and others. In general, the amount of data collected by the psychophysiologists during the period prior to 1950 is staggering (see Razran, 1961).

The year 1950 marked another turning point in the development of Soviet psychology. It followed the hundredth anniversary of Pavlov's birth, an event which received a great deal of attention in the press and the academic world. With the flood of anniversary literature, Pavlov was elevated to the position of a demigod of Soviet biological science, and events soon showed that the extraordinary attention given to the physiologist's birthday was more than a token of grateful admiration. Politics was involved, with Stalin himself evidently the instigator.

In a recent essay, Tucker makes an interesting case for Stalin's direct involvement in the events which followed the Pavlovian jubilee (Tucker, 1963). These events included a Joint Session of the U.S.S.R. Academy of Sciences and the U.S.S.R. Academy of Medical Sciences on the teachings of Pavlov, and the subsequent forced Pavlovianization of Soviet psychology. Tucker argues that during the late 1940's, when faced with difficult domestic problems, the government, and Stalin in particular, reacted with plans to "transform" the source of the difficulty. Pavlov's conditioned reflex was made the model for the transformation of man in the same way that Michurin's genetic theory had been made the model for the transformation of nature. It was believed that, through an understanding of the laws of conditioning, the behavior of men could be directly controlled and thus transformed. The 1950 Joint Session was convened with the explicit purpose of forcing deviant physiologists back into the fold and effecting total Pavlovianization of psychology.

Evidence of Stalin's direct involvement comes from Bykov, one of the organizers of the 1950 Joint Session, who wrote: "The initiator of the events that have elevated the teachings of Pavlov in our country, the initiator of the creation of the most favorable conditions for the development of Soviet psychology [is] . . . Joseph Vissarionovich Stalin" (quoted in Tucker, 1963, p. 105). Unhappily for many of the participating physiologists and psychologists, their work was not recognized as being within the realm of the "creative developments" which the 1950 Joint Session required of workers in the medical sciences.

Before 1950, Pavlov was certainly the leading figure in Soviet physiology, and psychologists habitually referred to the study of "higher nervous activity" as the science of the "substratum of the psyche" (i.e., the physiological foundation of the mind). Nevertheless, Pavlovian theory was not a conspicuous part of their conceptual framework. Consequently, many of the Soviet Union's leading physiologists and psychologists came under attack: the psychologists for failing to use Pavlov "creatively," and the physiologists for deviating from Pavlov's teachings. During the 1950 meetings and the later sessions held by a special Scientific Council on Problems of the Physiological Theory of Academician I. P. Pavlov, individual scientists were called in to confess their errant ways. They were accused of modifying Pavlovian theory, the adoption of new methods, favorable references to foreign scientific work, and regression to "pre-Pavlovian idealism." In the case of Orbeli, then Director of the Institute of Evolutionary Physiology, the additional charge was made that he deviated from "progressive Michurinist" genetic theories.

The psychologists received their share of criticism too. They were accused mainly of ignoring Pavlov rather than of distorting his teachings. Many of them attending the 1950 Joint Session were at a loss as to just what they should do, and some went so far as to write a joint letter to Ivanov-Smolenskii, a leading figure at the Joint Session, inquiring, "What is the subject of psychology, and what are its tasks?"

In the light of this interference in the internal development of psychology and psychophysiology, it would seem logical to conclude that these sciences were in for a long drought. This was indeed the conclusion reached by many American psychologists when the proceedings of the 1950 Joint Session were published.

However, events have not borne out this gloomy prognostication. The fifteen years since 1950 have seen rapid, though uneven, growth in both psychology and psychophysiology. Setbacks have occurred, to be sure, but the overall trend has been unmistakably in the direction of more scientific output, higher quality of work, and wider theoretical horizons. What has accounted for this trend?

First, of course, there was the death of Stalin, which affected developments in psychology and psychophysiology, as it affected everything else in the Soviet Union. Because of Stalin's direct involvement, changes in certain scientific fields after his departure were rapid and far-reaching. The most striking general change was the decrease in dogmatism. By the middle of 1954, an article in *Pravda* (by Sobolev, a physicist) had made "caustic reference to the unmerited claims of certain Soviet scientists to monopoly of the truth, mentioning three names in this context: Lysenko, Bykov, and Ivanov-Smolenskii" (quoted in Tucker, 1963, p. 115).

A second point is that the events surrounding the 1950 Joint Session should not be equated with the genetics purge of 1948. There is a natural tendency to draw a parallel between Lysenko on the one hand and Bykov and Ivanov-Smolenskii, the chairman of the 1950 Joint Session, on the other. However, the analogy is a poor one. The political nature of the role which the latter two men played is unquestionable, but the opportunity to reassert the prestige of their viewpoint against what they believed to be a stagnant and misguided status quo was in line with their scientific convictions. The influence which they exerted on psychology and the physiology of higher nervous activity differed in outcome for each branch because of dissimilar conditions within them at the time of the 1950 Joint Session.

The first response of the psychologists to that situation was to present all of their ideas with a thick overlay of Pavlovian terminology while retaining their traditional psychological concepts. However, eventually the changes turned out to be more significant than the acquisition of a new vocabulary. It was remarked earlier that Soviet psychology in the 1930's and 1940's left much to be desired; it indulged in philosophizing about the qualities which man *ought* to have, with little attention devoted to an experimental analysis of the qualities man *does* have. There is thus little wonder that, when confronted with the demand to make their science more "Pavlovian," the psychologists first resorted to a mere change of terminology. But because Pavlov's influence was above all toward an empirical, experimental science, the new requirements meant also that many psychologists had to get out of their armchairs and into the laboratory. In this respect, then, the outcome of the Joint Session had a positive effect.

This appraisal does not imply that all the problems of Soviet psychology were soon to be solved. The areas of investigation shut off in the 1930's remained closed. Years of isolation from the world scientific community and neglect of experimental techniques had left their mark. Nevertheless, psychology had been pushed firmly onto a new path.

Unlike the psychologists, the Soviet psychophysiologists had a flourishing science in 1950. The Pavlovian school dominated the study of physiological problems related to psychology, although some scholars supported theories that differed greatly from Pavlov's and there were many shades of opinion even among his students. For all the scientists whose views were not exactly in line with traditional Pavlovian ideas, the Joint Session was of course a disaster. The attacks to which such men were subjected have already been described. In addition, great pressure was applied to get them to renounce their views publicly; work in their laboratories was disrupted and attempts were made to have their co-workers renounce them.

Fortunately, this concerted attack on "physiological deviationists" was never completely successful, and in a few years the influence of the Joint Session came to an end. A most important factor, as mentioned previously, was Stalin's death, which cut short the supremacy of Bykov and Ivanov-Smolenskii; another factor was the courage of the individual scientists who were attacked during the Joint Session. These men never stopped teaching and developing their ideas. They retained the loyalty of their co-workers to such an extent that, when the extreme pressure which followed the Joint Session was removed, they were able to take up where they had left off.[1]

Psychology, as was stated earlier, showed a great spurt of activity after the 1950 Joint Session. By 1955, the initial period of dislocation had been overcome and several new areas in psychology were undergoing rapid development. A new psychological journal, *Problems of Psychology,* appeared. In the inaugural article, Rubinshtein asserted the need to study the psyche as an autonomous force, but he also maintained that the study of psychology must be linked with the experimental study of "higher nervous activity." The need to stay within a broadly Marxist-Leninist, as well as a Pavlovian framework was not neglected.

The way in which Soviet psychologists accommodated themselves to this framework can be illustrated by two new and important areas of psychological research developed in the 1950's: verbal behavior and the reflex basis of perception (Luria, 1961; Sokolov, 1963). The original source for the very large number of studies on verbal behavior and language learning in that period was the idea, put forth by Pavlov a few years before he died, that language acts as a "second signal system." Pavlov held that because words are abstractions by their very nature, they act as "signals of signals." Thus, when Ivanov-Smolenskii set about to promote studies of the second signal system in 1950, the stage had been set. There followed a huge outpouring of work, which is still going on and which has attracted the interest of many American psychologists. It is this research which we have tried to represent in the present volume.

Future Developments

Future developments and relative emphases in Soviet psychology are presaged by the 23rd Congress of the Communist Party of the Soviet Union,

[1] Indicative of the support these men enjoyed is the fact that Anokhin now heads the Sechenov Institute of Physiology in Moscow, and Beritashvili heads the Institute of Physiology in Tbilisi (named in honor of Beritashvili!), although both were bitterly attacked in 1950.

which met in 1964. There was a re-emphasis of the Leninist principle of objective scientific examination of reality, and a condemnation of subjectivism and voluntarism. It is significant that the foundations of psychology were presented in general terms as resting upon scientific objectivity as formulated by Lenin, with no reference to Pavlovian principles as the framework within which the problems of psychology are to be studied. On the contrary, there was a broad appeal to utilize the best available principles stemming from recent achievement in the natural sciences, particularly cybernetics, and in the social sciences. From these statements it seems reasonable to predict that the use of Pavlovian principles will continue to decline in the established areas of psychology and higher nervous activity as well as in the newer, developing areas of research.

Considered to be most important and worthy of more intensive study than they have received in the past are these subjects: problems of consciousness and behavior and of the interrelations between conscious and subconscious states, and, more generally, problems of personality, social psychology, and educational and applied psychology broadly interpreted. Theory and research on human motivation, interests, and attitudes, on small-group behavior, and on forces determining cultural change are some of the issues for study in the area of personality and social psychology. Educational psychology must face the problem of developing methods for training the "new Soviet man," preventing school dropouts and juvenile delinquency, and generally improving methods of teaching. In conjunction with social and applied psychology, methods of job training, improvement of work skills, and the promotion of interest in work must be developed. Applied psychology faces many tasks: determining the conditions fostering the productivity of labor, job satisfaction, optimal work conditions, man-machine problems, and a variety of other problems familiar to applied psychology in the West. The dissemination of psychological knowledge to other professions is also important, for example, to medicine, law, and business administration and personnel selection. It is quite plain that, if the foregoing problem areas show the desired growth in theory and research, Soviet and Western psychology will become increasingly alike in research goals and methods.

The chapters included in this handbook are, we believe, a fairly representative sample of recent psychological and relevant physiological research in the U.S.S.R. They also reflect our personal interests, which are primarily in the area of learning. The relatively small number of chapters on learning and conditioning might otherwise be even smaller. Learning and conditioning, contrary to popular opinion, are not the primary interests of Soviet psychologists. A common misinterpretation of Soviet psychology is that it employs, almost exclusively, classical Pavlovian conditioning methods and that all phenomena are forced into a common theoretical framework which views behavior as the sum of atomistic, elementaristic reflexes. Psychology in the U.S.S.R. was never like this, was never restricted to Pavlovian conditioning, and certainly it is not today. Pavlov's theories are influential, but these—and the empirical data upon which they are based—are far more complex than suggested by the typical American textbook treatment. An examination of current Soviet research indicates that relatively little classical conditioning is being conducted, much less than in the United States. It has always been done primarily by physiologists, those investigators concerned with "higher nervous activity." But behavioral conditioning studies are on the decline even among these physiologists. Since they are trained as physiologists and their principal interest is the functioning of the brain and its relation to behavior, they are employing modern electrophysiological techniques for investigating brain activity. They are no longer restricted by the lack of adequate technology, as in Pavlov's time, to behavioral studies which could provide only a relatively gross basis for inferring brain activity.

Developmental Psychology

If one area might be singled out as receiving major emphasis in Soviet psychology, it would be developmental research. The emphasis on a developmental approach to problems may be traced back to the founder of modern Russian physiology and psychology, Sechenov, and in more recent times to the brilliant innovator Vygotskii. The paramount concern with developmental problems, and the adoption of a developmental approach to a variety of other problems, are apparent in the relatively large number of chapters we have included from this area. The chapters by Bozhovich on personality of schoolchildren and problems of education, Gal'perin on the development of thinking, El'konin on the psychological development of preschool-age children, Luria on speech development and its relation to the development of mental processes, Smirnov and Zinchenko on problems in the psychology of memory, Zaporozhets on sensory training, and Kasatkin on the origin of conditioned reflexes, are all primarily concerned with the review and analysis of developmental studies of various psychological processes. The basic concern with a developmental analysis of various processes is also apparent in Luria's chapter on the neuropsychological study of brain lesions and the restoration of damaged brain functions, Zemtsova's on perceptual activity in the blind, and by Shif's on mental retardation, Ladygina-Kots' on the psychology of primates, and A. N. Sokolov's on speech mechanisms and thinking.

El'konin traces the history of developmental psychology in the Soviet Union and describes its characteristic features, including the rejection by and large, of psychological tests. His chapter summarizes research on the development of a number of important functions. Theories and research on play in young children are examined; the role of play in psychological development and the changes in the nature of play and of its interrelations with other variables are discussed. The stress throughout this research, as well as research and theory in the developmental area generally, is on the role of different social activities and interrelationships with adults in the psychological development of the child. It is not the environment, but the *social* environment and the changing social relations interacting with the maturing intellectual processes of the child that are emphasized in the analysis of the developing child.

El'konin presents a detailed review of research concerned with the development of speech and the understanding of speech. The interrelationship between the earliest forms of movement and of visual orienting and exploratory behavior is noted in the research literature. The developing use of implements is traced, as well as the development of perception and the formation of images. Research concerned with the nature and origin of thinking is reviewed and Piaget's interpretation is questioned. Differences with Piaget's theory of egocentric speech are repeatedly remarked by El'konin and other contributors to this handbook. Such disagreements are traced to Vygotskii, who pointed out that egocentric speech is a function of social conditions. It is a form of thinking, planning for the solution of a task, and is a transition to internal speech. The greater the possibility of collaboration with a child or an adult, the less does egocentric speech predominate; with a familiar child egocentric speech is relatively uncommon. Egocentric speech is abbreviated in proportion to the development of a child's independence.

Gal'perin's chapter is concerned with a more circumscribed developmental area, the development of mental acts or thinking. He explores the hypothesis that mental acts pass through a series of stages and that at each stage a given activity undergoes a variety of changes and is therefore performed in a new manner. Gal'perin also considers the different kinds of orienting responses (OR) to a problem task. Each type of orientation is a result of training and uniquely determines the course of problem solving. It is apparent that the conception of characteristically different orienting responses to a problem is not used in the same fashion as the concept of OR defined by physiological responses or even by the behavioral search response, the "tactile component" of the OR discussed by E. N. Sokolov. Orientation is used here as an intellectual operation which plays a selective role in determining the general approach to problem solving. It is assumed that all mental activity is aided by the organism's orientation to external and internal events. The measurement of this process and its relationship to the OR defined in terms of physiological responses or investigatory behavior is an important task which remains to be thoroughly explored. One

The approach to personality, once again, emphasizes the *interaction* between environmental or life conditions, and the developing child. Vygotskii's profound influence is apparent. That the same life experiences may have very different effects upon the same child at different ages, or two children of the same age, depending upon the particular personality structure, its motives, needs, and degree of intellectual comprehension, is an important contribution of Vygotskii's thinking.

Clearly, the approach to personality is not that of the familiar stereotype of a mechanistic, atomistic, elementaristic concatenation of conditioned reflexes. In contrast, Bozhovich presents "the study of personality as an integrated structure in the context of its complex interactions with reality." In essence this is the Pavlovian approach of the study of the complete organism. Pavlov believed that we can correctly understand the physiological laws of an organ only after we understand the physiological function of the organ in the life activity of the whole organism taken in the context of its actual life conditions. He considered this the only possible approach for the "mastery of the subject of study."

The characteristics of the child mediate the influence of the environment. It is not enough to look at the objective environment. The main task is to find within the mediation the crucial link which defines the influence exerted on the child by his environment. Vygotskii said that the crucial link is the affective attitude of the child. Analyses of the mediating experience must include an analysis of the child's needs, the conditions giving rise to the needs, and the possibilities of satisfying them.

Bozhovich reviews studies concerned with the personality characteristics contributing to poor learning performance and behavior problems in school. It is generally concluded that the attitude of a schoolchild toward his studies depends primarily upon the extent to which his studies have become a means of fulfilling his need for a new social status. A pupil's poor behavior is often a reaction to someone's attitudes toward him or to the failures he encountered, or it may be his only means of asserting himself in his environment and maintaining self-respect. In her analysis of personality Bozhovich recognizes and emphasizes the role of conflict and affective arousal. But she rejects the classical Freudian approach.

> Turning to the Freudian interpretation of the content and origin of affective conflicts, it is apparent that our data can be attributed neither to primary biological inclinations or demands, nor to a failure to satisfy the primitive demands evoked in early childhood. No demand, including social demands, will be permitted into consciousness if it is in direct conflict with the child's other demands.
>
> We have only recently begun to study the affective life of children in our laboratory. In future investigations concerning the psychology of personality it is absolutely necessary to pay particular attention to both affective life and

to other unconscious psychological processes, to study their particular features, their origins, and their role both in the behavior of the child and in the formation of his personality.

An influence, not always apparent, which is related to theories of developmental psychology is explicit in Ladygina-Kots' discussion of primate behavior; this is the influence of dialectical materialism. Developmental studies of anthropoid behavior are related to the ideology of dialectical materialism, especially the concern with the development of the human traits of speech, work, and the higher mental processes. Soviet primate research is directed principally toward the study of the ape's skills and problem-solving abilities. In point of view, the studies oppose what are considered to be both mechanism and anthropomorphism. Comparative studies of the development of the ape and child are described and the qualitative differences between the two noted. An important finding with implications for theories of speech development is the report that sounds do not evoke orienting reflexes in young apes to the extent that they do in children. Comparative studies of vocal behavior, social behavior, and studies of imitation are summarized. All of these studies, especially the studies of problem-solving behavior, are characterized by detailed qualitative analyses of the behavior of the animals.

Soviet investigators in the area of primate problem solving reject the ahistorical approach of gestalt psychology represented by Köhler's research. His is an approach which tends to neglect the influence of past experience, the role of previously acquired associations in problem solving, and which emphasizes the visual field at the moment. Soviet investigators have attempted to provide a learning interpretation of primate problem solving based upon conditioning principles. Soviet investigators also emphasize that problem solving is not simply a chain of conditioned reflexes. The ape's skill in problem solving is derived from intellectual operations, the ability to perceive relations. But the ape's intellect is qualitatively different from human intellect, a conclusion Ladygina-Kots reaches after a detailed analysis of problem-solving behavior.

Certainly, the absorbing and detailed descriptions of Raphael in the course of his various adventures in problem solving will stand alongside those of Sultan as a minor classic in the area of primate problem solving.

The influence of dialectical materialism as well as that of Pavlov is expressed in the following passage from Ladygina-Kots' description of the Soviet orientation toward research on problem solving in primates: "It is often asserted that the great physiologist I. P. Pavlov wanted to reduce human behavior to the sum of its conditioned reflexes. However, more profound knowledge of his work shows that I. P. Pavlov rejected neither the ideal of 'gestalt' nor the idea of 'unity,' but for him 'gestalt' is a new quality which arises as the result of the interaction of definite elements of the phenomenon."

An area in developmental psychology which relatively recently has begun to attract considerable attention in the United States, conditioning in infants, has been a subject of study for many years in the U.S.S.R. Kasatkin reviews many of the Soviet studies in this area, which, again, have been influenced by the stress in Sechenov's writings on the study of the origin and development of reflexes as necessary for an adequate analysis of complex psychological processes. Kasatkin's review presents a variety of interesting experimental results. Analyses of the different stages through which a conditioned reflex evolves when it is developed in a young infant is characteristic of the concern of Soviet investigators for qualitative details. An interesting finding is that there are consistent differences in the extent to which various conditioned stimuli and unconditioned reflexes may yield conditioned reflexes.

Abnormal and Social Psychology

Another area of study in the U.S.S.R. which has received relatively extensive experimental study, in contrast to the lack of interest in the United States (although interest is now increasing), is psychological investigations of the handicapped. Zemtsova describes investigations of the characteristics of perceptual activity in the blind. The theory of compensation, based upon Pavlov's theory of higher nervous activity, is presented, and investigations of partial forms of compensation occurring in cases of total loss of vision are reviewed. Among the studies reported are those concerned with the development of blind children and the content and methods of their training and education.

Physiological investigations indicate that the structure and composition of the components of the orienting reflex are altered in blind individuals. Changes in the orienting reflex are most pronounced in response to auditory stimuli. Blind subjects show an augmented orienting reflex to auditory stimuli which is highly resistant to habituation in comparison with the response elicited in normal subjects. The interpretation of these results is that auditory stimuli have greater signal significance for the blind than for the sighted subject.

Processes of compensation in the blind are social in nature as well as physiological. The significance of the work engaging the blind person, his desire to keep and strengthen his community position, and his level of motivation all influence the extent to which he can compensate for his loss.

Research is reviewed on the formation of complex images in the blind, showing that images reflecting spatial and temporal relationships between objects can be formed. Also discussed is research on the use of auditory cues in the perception of obstacles from a distance, as well as a variety of studies of both complex and simple perception.

Shif, in her chapter on the development of children in schools for the mentally retarded, emphasizes the potential for improvement of the mentally retarded child under favorable environmental conditions. Soviet psychologists have systematically studied retarded children of different age levels and have traced the course of their development under the influence of special training techniques. Emphasis is upon comparative developmental research, comparisons of the unique development of the retarded child with the development of the normal child under the same problem conditions and with the same methods of investigation. Soviet research on the mentally retarded has a definite pedagogical direction: It is designed to yield information contributing to the formation of didactic principles for the training and education of the retarded child.

Shif reviews studies of perception, memory, and language and thought in retardates, always suggesting the intimate relationship between research and educational practice. Several types of perceptual studies are described. Tachistocopic experiments show that retardates have higher perceptual thresholds than normal children. They require considerably longer exposure times than normal children for the recognition of objects. Naturalistic studies indicate that the retardate's perception of objects in the street is relatively undifferentiated and limited. Normal children note many more differences in objects and greater detail. Size constancy is also affected in retardates; an object moved some distance from the retardate is judged to be smaller than that object when close. The fact that retardates have difficulty with orientation in space and with locomotion is a consequence not so much of deficiencies in their motor systems as of inadequate space perception and a lowered ability to orient toward and investigate relevant cues.

Soviet investigators find that the most favorable conditions for improving perception are created when, during the perception of the object, the process of analysis and synthesis is accompanied by various types of practical activities involving physical objects.

While the difference in perceptual ability between the normal and retardate is marked, the difference in memory is even more striking. Of course, inadequate perception and the failure to orient to appropriate cues will appear as a loss of memory when learning never actually occurred. Beyond this obvious source of memory failure, developmental studies trace the trends in object and word memory and the effects of different training methods. An important pedagogical finding is that, if material is presented in several ways, and if the retardate is questioned on the material in different ways, he then shows considerable improvement in his ability to reproduce the material as compared to the repetition of the materials in an unvarying manner. In schools for the retarded this method of "modified repetitions" is now replacing the previously employed drill with the monotonous repetition of content and form.

An interpretation of these findings is that the method of varied presentations maximizes the occurrence of orienting reflexes and does not produce as rapid a loss of attention as the repetition of learning materials presented in an unchanging manner. While the former method of presentation would better maintain orienting reflexes in normal children as well as retardates, and thereby facilitate learning and retention, its effect may be disproportionately greater with retardates, who suffer from a lack of adequate orienting reflexes.

Shif reports that the relationship between language and thought in retardates differs from that of normal children. Verbal behaviors acquired by retardates do not play the same role in effecting changes in their thinking as in the case of normal children. The retardate has difficulty in distinguishing verbally the wide variety of surface properties of objects, and in designating the material of which they are made. The identification of colors is also difficult. However, observations show that retarded children working in shops apply many descriptive terms. The poverty of the retardate's active vocabulary is due not so much to difficulties in acquiring or learning words as to the impoverished thought processes and the inadequate transformative role of words in the development of his thinking. Verbally acquired knowledge does not seem to have the same basic influence on the retardate's development as it does in the normal child. Training which depends primarily on verbal methods is therefore not possible with these children. This illustrates the principle that the development of complex forms of mental activity is best achieved when training is closely associated with various kinds of practical activities, such as work in shops or agriculture.

Related to research on the handicapped is the extensive research program on the neuropsychology of brain lesions. Luria briefly reviews the pre- and postrevolutionary history of psychiatric and neurological research and the intimate relationships between clinical psychology and neurology and psychiatry. Again, Vygotskii looms as a major historical figure in what would be considered clinical psychology. In addition to his contribution of a method for studying concept formation, which is applied in the analysis of the alteration of thinking in schizophrenia, aphasia, and mental retardation, Vygotskii's work stimulated a wide range of investigations in abnormal as well as normal psychology, and influenced the basic orientation toward the neuropsychology of abnormal behavior. Vygotskii's work combined with Pavlovian theory provides a rapprochement between psychology and physiology in the area of neuropsychology.

Luria emphasizes that functional cortical systems underlie psychological processes: there is no strict cortical localization of complex psychological activities. Compensation is possible because new functional cortical systems may be organized through retraining, following injury to cortical regions involved in a previous functional system. A given psychological activity may be mediated by any number of different functional cortical systems.

Luria provides an extensive review of studies of speech and motor disorders; much of the research on the effects of cortical lesions is the consequence of the efforts of Luria and his colleagues, efforts reported in two books recently published in the United States. Luria's chapter summarizes the methods of investigations and the kinds of results obtained from his research program.

Another relatively new area of psychological investigation in the U.S.S.R., microsociology, is described by Kerbikov. Although Moreno's theories are rejected on ideological grounds as idealistic, bourgeois, and downright mystical, his sociometric methods are being used in group research.

Small-group research can make a contribution to problems in engineering psychology, such as the selection and analysis of teams manning space ships and radar and communication systems. Small-group research also has a useful potential for the empirical investigation of interrelationships among members of collectives generally, a motive contributing to the current Soviet interest in group interactions. Soviet investigators do not believe that sociometric methods provide information on basic problems of motivation, the origins of the personality of the members of a collective, or the influence of the group on the personality of the individual. Adopting the point of view that sociometric methods are useful within limits, Kerbikov describes some of the recent Soviet research employing the technique.

A related field, social psychiatry, is also a relatively radical new development, radical because it deviates from classical Marxist ideology. If an ideal society has been formed, then neuroses, assuming that they are functional, should be eliminated. They obviously have not been eliminated in the U.S.S.R. The point made, therefore, is that remnants of bourgeois society still persists and result in a less than perfect family relationship. The fact that the family is recognized as the group of greatest importance in developing personality is also significant. The implication of social psychology for psychiatry is apparent: neuroses develop in a social context. They are the consequence of the influence of man on man. As Kerbikov indicates, the social factors leading to emotional disturbances seem to be much the same in the Soviet Union as in the West—personal and family relationships. It is also the case in the U.S.S.R. that juvenile delinquents tend to come from broken homes, have alcoholic parents, and so on.

In his chapter, Feigenberg presents a theoretical interpretation of schizophrenia and some novel experimental data in support of the hypothesis. The theoretical approach adopted by Feigenberg is closely related to the positions formulated by Anokhin, Beritashvili, Bernshtein, and Sokolov. He indicates, as does Sokolov, that the orienting reflex is a response to the amount of information in a signal. The less probable a signal, the more information it contains, the larger the OR. All organisms, to varying degrees, predict the occurrence of signals on the basis of the probability of occurrence of the signal in the past. Probability prognosis is a fundamental characteristic of the brain.

Feigenberg's research is concerned with the analysis of the schizophrenic's ability to make probability prognoses. On the basis of the experimental results he obtains, Feigenberg asserts that the basic defect in schizophrenia, which varies in severity with the type of schizophrenia, is a breakdown of the probability-prognosis mechanism. A defective OR is a manifestation of this loss in ability to utilize past experience for the organization of future activity. The nonobvious predictions following from this hypothesis, for example, the absence in schizophrenics of illusions found in normal subjects, appear to support the hypothesis. These interesting findings reported by Feigenberg are clearly in need of further corroboration.

Our own feeling on the matter is that research on the OR, in the Soviet Union as well as in the United States, has been overly concerned with the experimental variable of "novelty" of stimulation, the probability of stimuli, or the discrepancy between past and present stimuli. Another variable determining the OR is the significance of the stimuli, as indicated by Feigenberg and Sokolov. But this variable, essentially conditioned ORs, or the reinforcement history of stimuli, has been relatively neglected in research on the OR. We suspect that it is of considerably greater importance in differentiating schizophrenic types, and other kinds of deviant behavior, than probability prognosis.

Feigenberg's theoretical discussion is also of general interest in indicating the close relationship between emotion and the OR, particularly in relation to Cannon's emergency theory of emotions. In this respect he appears to follow rather closely the formulation of Beritashvili.

In his chapter on the experimental investigation of cognitive functioning in schizophrenia, Polyakov describes a number of experiments providing some striking results which are in accord with the conception of defective probability prognosis in schizophrenics. In terms more familiar to American psychologists, his research suggests that the habit-family hierarchies of normals and schizophrenics differ in that uncommon responses tend to be more dominant in the latter case.

Polyakov investigated the thought processes involved in generalization and comparison, auditory and visual perception, and problem solving. The nonobvious findings obtained are that, in situations in which the solution to a problem involves responding to a "latent attribute,"—making an uncommon but appropriate response—the schizophrenics were superior to the normal subjects. In an experiment in which the endings of phrases were embedded in noise, the schizophrenics tended to perceive the more probable phrase endings less accurately than normals, and the less probable endings more accurately.

Psychoanalysis for many years had essentially been ignored—much less practiced—in the Soviet Union. Recently, however, discussions of Freudian theory have occurred with increasing frequency. In his chapter on the unconscious, Bassin provides some background to the recent Soviet interest in Freudian theory, in particular the theory of the unconscious. Bassin's discussion is limited primarily to the Freudian theory of the unconscious, since it is considered to be the key concept in psychoanalytic theory. The theory is criticized on ideological, methodological, theoretical, and empirical grounds. Nevertheless, Bassin emphasizes that there is a great need to study the problem of the unconscious, or as he prefers to call it, noncognized activity. The problem is to provide an adequate account of such phenomena. Freudian theory has failed to do so. The problem of the unconscious, descriptively, is the problem of dissassociation, a dissociation between the objective effects of a stimulus and consciousness of stimulation. In other words, there are noncognized forms of complex cerebral activity as well as conscious forms which participate in the formation of behavior.

The existence of noncognized forms of higher nervous activity and the important role of these in the behavior of man was never denied in Pavlovian teaching. It was widely recognized that various types of complex stimuli may act on man as signals, eliciting complex kinds of behavior, without his being clearly aware of them. However, Freudians fail to recognize the multi-determined relations between noncognized higher nervous activity and the activity of consciousness. The Freudian notion of the unconscious is extremely limited in its generality, since it is restricted solely to dynamic relationships, the conflict between conscious and unconscious higher nervous activity. But even this relationship is oversimplified. The principal theoretical criticism of the Freudian conception is that it fails to offer a general theory of the unconscious.

Bassin concludes that the data forming the basis of Uznadze's theory of set provide the best available approach to the study of noncognized activity. Set is a concept which manifests the essence of unconscious activity. It is a function of previous experience, and it affects behavior in its most complex, meaningful, and substantially psychological aspects. Most importantly, set is accessible to objective experimental research. The concept of set plays the same role as the invisible "bridge" between certain forms of conscious experience and objective behavior represented by the Freudian conception of the unconscious.

Acceptance of the large body of experimental research on set does not entail acceptance of Uznadze's theory of set. Bassin elaborates the possibility of interpreting the phenomena of set in terms of Pavlovian principles. Aspects of noncognized activity may thus be reinterpreted in terms of Pavlovian principles.

Ideological grounds for acceptance or rejection of psychological theories are much less evident in contemporary Soviet psychology than in earlier days. A vestige of Marxist ideology, serving as a basis for criticism of a foreign theory, is present in Bassin's chapter. It is more explicitly discussed, and disputed, by Musatti, an Italian Marxist psychologist, in a debate on Freudianism with Bassin (Bassin, 1960a, b; Musatti, 1960). It is apparent that, despite ideological grounds for criticizing Freudianism, current Soviet theoreticians and psychologists are seriously concerned with problems that psychoanalytic theory has concerned itself with in the past.

General Experimental Psychology

The important practical and theoretical implications of the conception of functional cortical systems is strikingly evident in the chapter by Leont'ev. He notes that, while structure is biologically determined, function is socially determined. The psychological abilities of man are not the inviolate consequence of localization in the brain. They may be developed; and new functional organs or functional cortical systems may be developed which permit almost unlimited forms of compensation. Leont'ev demonstrates this capacity for compensation in a series of ingenious experiments which train individuals to improve their ability to discriminate tones, and in a special series of experiments on the facilitation of vibratory sensitivity.

Sechenov believed that the structure of sensory processes includes motor acts and their sensory feedback. There is an intimate cortical connection between sensory stimulation and the sensory feedback from the organs involved in vocalization. Basing his approach upon Sechenov's hypothesis, Leont'ev describes the methods he employed to train tone-deaf subjects to "intune" the sounds that they must discriminate. Marked improvement in discrimination thresholds are obtained as a consequence of such training. Further training methods yield transfer effects and the "interiorization" of the comparator process underlying the ability to discriminate sounds. Subjects can be trained to discriminate sounds that are beyond their singing range, so that vocal "intuning" is no longer possible. Leont'ev provides further support for the conception of functional systems of perception by demonstrating that analogous results may be obtained in a different sense modality. Employing vibratory sensitivity as the sensory system, he demonstrates that vocalizations "attuning" the voice to the frequency of vibrations facilitate vibratory-discrimination thresholds.

Leont'ev's review of research on the training of auditory discriminative ability provides striking evidence that human abilities are not strictly biologically determined. He demonstrates convincingly that in at least one area of sensory abilities the apparent limits are modifiable through training.

An area of study which is rather unique to the U.S.S.R. is described by

Natadze: the long-term investigation of set begun by Uznadze and continued by his students and colleagues in the institute bearing his name. Natadze traces the origin and development of Uznadze's conception of the psychology of set. The study of set as an empirical phenomenon began with the experimental investigation of perceptual illusions in various modalities. The principles governing the manifestation of set were established in a series of studies conducted during the 1920's. Many of these early studies were designed to refute the then-current interpretations of set in terms of peripheral mechanisms, motor impulses, or central mechanisms such as expectancy. An alternative interpretation is offered and supported by extensive experimental findings: set is an integral state of the organism, "a degree of mobilization of the individual as a whole, which expresses itself in a wide variety of perceptual modalities and therefore cannot be reduced to the peculiarities of motor impulses."

Research reviewed by Natadze demonstrates the generalization of a set established in one modality to a second modality. For example, a set established to kinesthetic cues transfers to the visual modality, and vice versa. Investigations of the conditions necessary for the formation of sets are presented, as well as animal research which demonstrates the establishment of perceptual sets manifested primarily as contrast illusions. Also described are studies of the psychopathology of set. In sum, an extensive body of interesting research is reviewed, research which until recently was largely unknown in the West. It is worth noting that this relatively large body of systematic research, conducted over many years, has been largely free of Pavlovian concepts and in fact is posed by some investigators as a body of findings which cannot be readily subsumed under the classical principles of conditions. Other Soviet scientists accept the experimental findings but not the interpretation of the investigation of the Uznadze institute.

In contrast to the research on set, Lomov, in describing the field of engineering psychology in the Soviet Union, describes an area of research that had much in common with comparable research in the United States and Great Britain. A reason for the similarity, in part, is that it is a relatively new branch of psychology and therefore has been more readily influenced by developments abroad. Research described by Lomov frequently makes use of information-theory measures in the analyses of reactions to signals; but there is also recognition of the limitations of this approach to the processing of signals. The influence of Sechenov is evident in research concerned with motor skills in that there is a basic concern with intellectual operations that regulate motor skills. Such skills are viewed not as simple sequences of conditioned reflexes but as complex behavior patterns under the control of higher mental processes. The characteristic Soviet concern with qualitative differences in performance is manifested in the classification and interpretation of different kinds of motor acts presented by Lomov.

Considerable emphasis upon developmental problems is evident in the chapter by Smirnov and Zinchenko on selected problems in the psychology of memory. They review studies of what they call involuntary and voluntary retention. The former does not involve mnemonic activity whereas voluntary retention explicitly involves mnemonic activity. Two types of involuntary retention are described in the context of studies employing preschool- and school-age children. One kind is a product of goal-directed activity and is more significant than the second kind, which is a product of various, frequently chance, orientations to background stimuli. The latter is what is commonly called incidental learning. Studies are reviewed on investigations of involuntary retention at the level of the second signal system, involving verbal materials, and of involuntary retention at the level of the first signal system. Variables investigated include instructions and motivation.

Of particular importance are the studies of voluntary retention. A qualitative approach is common, characterized by a concern with "dynamic" processes in memory, the kinds of inventions, distortions, and interpolations that occur during reproduction. Characteristics of the different mnemonic devices employed in memory are examined developmentally. In addition to the characteristically Soviet type of research on memory, interesting because it tends to differ so much from studies in the United States, some more recent experiments show an American influence in their use of information-theoretic measures and the study of memory span. The information-theoretic approach, however, is subjected to cogent criticism.

The developmental approach is emphasized by A. N. Sokolov in his review of studies of internal speech and thinking. Research in this area and its theoretical interpretation has been strongly influenced by Sechenov, Pavlov, and Vygotskii, and emphasizes the unity and reciprocity of thinking and speech. Thought is not only expressed in speech but is formed and carried out in it. Language not only gives names to objects—it permits the abstraction of their properties and relationships. Sokolov emphasizes that thought and speech are not identical, and he rejects the motor theory of consciousness. The theories of Sechenov, Pavlov, and Vygotskii are reviewed, and theoretical revisions and extensions by more recent investigators are described.

Sokolov reports on a diverse body of literature centering upon experimental studies of the relationship between silent speech recorded electromyographically and external speech and thinking. One type of study manipulates speech articulation, either impeding it mechanically or facilitating it. Generally, mechanical delay of articulation when teaching children reading or writing, and in aphasics, produces a variety of difficulties in perception, comprehension, and the recall of words. In normal adults interference with articulation does not have a negative effect, but may even facilitate thinking. These opposed effects are reminiscent of some of the apparently contradictory results obtained in studies of stimulus predifferentiation and labeling conducted in the United States.

Sokolov reviews conditioned-reflex methods of studying speech, including studies of generalization between the first and second signal systems, semantic generalization, and conditioning and generalization to phrases and sentences, as well as conditioning to numbers and generalization to arithmetic operations involving the numbers. Sokolov also reports on electromyographic studies of internal speech which have investigated the variables determining the occurrence of motor impulses from the speech mechanisms under such conditions as listening, solving problems, and conducting stereotyped activities. The general finding is that all forms of internal speech associated with the need to reason in a relatively complex manner are accompanied by heightened speech motor impulses. Repeated activity leads to a reduction in impulses. Motor impulses also decrease when the solution of a problem becomes stereotyped or when the operations for solving a problem are very simple. It would appear that conditions determining variations in speech motor impulses correspond to those responsible for variations in orienting reflexes.

A review is given on experiments which have examined individual differences in age, education, interest, and effects of physical handicaps in relation to internal speech and thinking. Considerable research on this problem has been conducted with deaf-mutes and aphasics, and the interesting findings with these groups are reported.

Studies of young children indicate that kinesthetic impulses arising during the articulation of words are a necessary condition for analyses of the sound structure of words in writing and reading, and serve to refine the composition and sequence of the sounds in a word. Data are also presented on the transition from internal to external speech and writing in schoolchildren, indicating that internal speech precedes the act of writing.

In their chapter, Teplov and Nebylitsyn recognize that the study of individual differences among people is one of psychology's most important tasks. Use of paper-and-pencil tasks for this purpose is rejected. Their reasons for objecting to the use of tests are clearly stated. It is not an opposition to tests per se or a matter of ideology or principle. Their primary objection is that most paper-and-pencil tests lack a foundation in sound, experimentally based theory. As they put it, if the physiological or psychological meaning of a test is not clear, no amount of correlational or factor analyses will make it clear. As a consequence of the lack of sound, experimentally based theory, the test approach has been relatively barren of fruitful new insights and principles. Tests have not yielded new directions in the study of individual psychological differences, even though individual tests may be of scientific interest. In contrast to the paper-and-pencil test approach, the aim of Teplov and his staff has been the experimental study of individual differences based upon the typological properties of higher nervous activity, the approach originally formulated by Pavlov. Late in his life Pavlov believed that the basic properties of the nervous system, such as strength, mobility, and equilibrium of excitation and inhibition, should serve as the foundation for his theory of animal types.

Teplov and Nebylitsyn critically discuss Pavlov's theory of types and conclude that the crucial problem is not the classification of different types, but the determination of the different parameters or properties of the nervous system as measured by various physiological and behavioral measures and of the relationships between these and various psychological activities.

The meanings of the original concepts of equilibrium and strength of the nervous system are analyzed, and it is noted that a number of ambiguities are present. Teplov and Nebylitsyn introduced a new property of the nervous system, dynamicness, which is measured by aspects of the orienting reflex. They report that speed of conditioning is related to components of the orienting reflex rather than to strength of the nervous system. Research demonstrating the relationship between measures of the orienting reflex and the speed of conditioning has also been reported in the West (Maltzman, 1967). Dynamicness is a parameter determining the speed of the organism's primary adaptation to conditions which exist. When the reaction must be maintained for a prolonged period at the normal level, strength of the nervous system is the important parameter. When there is a need to reverse the form of the activity, mobility of the nervous system becomes important.

Methodological problems in the measurement of properties of the nervous system are stressed by Teplov and Nebylitsyn. The importance of controlling the instructions given the subjects, personality variables, and experimental procedures and methods of measurement are all discussed in a critical manner. Some of the results from recent research by the group is described, and provide a wide range of interesting information.

The provocative results reported by Teplov and Nebylitsyn on the relationships between individual differences in properties of the nervous system and performance in conditioning and perceptual situations are clearly in need of replication and further study. The evidence already available indicates that the study of individual differences employing physiological measures may be an extremely fruitful approach to this important area of psychology.

Higher Nervous Activity

A simple way to characterize this area of research is that it is concerned with the relationships between brain activity and behavior. Conditioning studies have since their inception attempted to infer the nature of activity in the nervous system from the behavioral changes obtained in conditioning. As a consequence of technological advances, the activity of the brain no longer need be inferred from performance changes, but may be recorded directly.

One of the more interesting approaches to the problem of the relation between brain activity and behavior is represented by the work described by Livanov in his chapter on the application of electronic-computer techniques to the analysis of biolectric processes in the brain. He describes some of his results obtained with the "toposcopes," and the related procedures for recording and analyzing these results from as many as 100 points on the cerebral cortex. Whether or not an increase, decrease, or no change occurs in the bioelectric activity at each of the points is determined. Changes at each point are compared with every other point. By this procedure Livanov determines constellations of points, areas in the cortex, manifesting synchronous activity. Independent constellations may be present simultaneously in the cortex, showing a high degree of synchronous activity within the given area independently of other constellations of activity. Some points in the cortex that respond simultaneously with more than one synchronized system are also found. Although there is constant fluctuation within a constellation, these constellations persist over time, and the arrangement of constellations may appear in the same cortical areas in different subjects under the same experimental conditions. Livanov notes the different conditions affecting the development and persistence of constellations of synchronous activity, and some of his interesting work in classical conditioning of defensive reflexes in rabbits is described.

Livanov has also used his toposcope in the investigation of synchronous cortical activity in humans during problem solving, specifically, mental multiplication. There is a marked increase in the number of intercorrelated points, particularly in the frontal lobes, during problem solving. The topography of the bioelectric activity changes during the course of problem solving. Although the frontal lobes show the greatest amount of activity early in problem solving, once the problem is solved the region of the central gyrus shows the greatest activity. Administration of a tranquilizer results in the virtual elimination of activity in the frontal areas while leaving the other areas relatively unaffected. There is concomitant deterioration in problem-solving performance.

Slonim presents a Pavlovian approach to ethology. He contrasts the approach with that of European ethologists as well as with the relevant concepts of theorists such as Anokhin, who utilize cybernetics as a source of hypotheses. Slonim points out that some of the apparent differences among the various approaches to ethology are simply terminological in nature. The ecological-physiological approach described by Slonim does, however, differ from the usual ethology in certain important respects, because it is a combination of physiology, ecology, and behavioral analysis. The chapter summarizes three areas of research in ecological physiology conducted in natural settings: quantitative and qualitative characteristics of behavior, and the study of individual reflexes that are necessary for the understanding of members of a given species. Much of the research is novel and informative, providing a blend of physiology and ethology. One example is an obvious relationship: the relative eating time of different species is closely related to the caloric content of their diet. There is an inverse relationship between the duration of the eating period and the caloric content of the food consumed. Of interest to behavior theories is the observation that water deprivation may either increase or decrease motor activity in different species, depending upon ecological specialization.

Of general interest are the reported results of studies showing qualitative differences in the action potentials aroused in the same muscle groups in different species by the same kinds of stimuli. Results of this kind emphasize species-specific characteristics of components of the orienting reflex. Although an undifferentiated phase of arousal may be the same for all species, the phase peculiar to each species in terms of motor activity is particularly striking.

Slonim's chapter indicates that the physiological analysis of structure and function in many different species under naturalistic conditions provides valuable information which may broaden our understanding of adaptive behavior and serve as a useful antidote to oversimplified generalizations stemming from limited experimental laboratory conditions.

Pavlovian classical conditioning, of course, has been the most frequently used procedure for the study of animal learning in the Soviet Union. However, several influential investigators, such as Anokhin, Beritashvili, and Kupalov, have made extensive use of variations of instrumental conditioning. The general acceptance of instrumental conditioning as a procedure for studying higher nervous activity is reflected in the fact that Kupalov, one of the leading investigators employing the method, was for many years head of the conditioning laboratory in the Leningrad Institute of Experimental Medicine, first established by Pavlov. It is apparent in Kupalov's chapter that there is an easy theoretical transition from Pavlovian conditioning to the conditioned place reflex procedure. No fundamental differences are recognized in the learning principles involved. The shaping method described for establishing conditioned place reflexes is comparable to Skinnerian methods developed quite independently in the United States for shaping operant conditioning.

Research described by Kupalov indicates that the "law of strength" found to hold in Pavlovian conditioning holds also for the more complex behavioral changes studied by the conditioned place method. Intensity of the CS and the UCS, variations in amount of incentive and motivation—all influence conditioned place reflexes in a fashion similar to that found in Pavlovian conditioning.

The chapter on conditioned defensive reflexes by Skipin and his associates describes the development of a technique for the investigation of escape and avoidance conditioning. Development from simple negative classical conditioning through escape conditioning to a method in which the instrumental conditioned response is a movement of a nonshocked limb, whereas the unconditioned response movement of the shocked limb does not effect the shock, is described in some detail.

In the earliest method employed, stemming from Bekhterev's work, an exteroceptive stimulus, the CS, is accompanied by electric shock regardless of the occurrence of a conditioned response. Withholding the UCS results in extinction. Soviet investigators such as Skipin were dissatisfied with this method because it neglects the signal value of the CS. The biological significance of defensive reflexes, their adaptive value, could not be adequately explored with this method.

A second method was developed which permitted a transition from escape to avoidance behavior. The animal first learns to lift its leg when shocked and to maintain it at a certain height in order to avoid further shock. It later learns to lift the leg to a CS prior to the onset of shock and thereby avoids the UCS entirely. But this is a highly complex situation. An attempt was therefore made to obtain a simpler conditioning situation which would still permit the use of signal stimuli. When the shocked limb is lifted to a designated height the shock is terminated, but lowering the limb beyond this point reinstates the shock. The animal develops a conditioned defensive reflex to the electric shock, which comes to serve as a CS as well as a UCS.

The latter method evolved into a technique for heteroeffector classical defensive conditioning. Movements of the left front paw were recorded, and those of the right hind paw, which receives the shock, as well. Administration of shock results in movements of both paws. When the nonshocked left front paw is lifted to a certain height, shock is terminated. Eventually, the stimulated hind leg may not move at all while the unstimulated front paw is immediately lifted to the designated height at which the shock was administered.

Presentation of an exteroceptive stimulus for 10 seconds prior to the onset of shock, in just a few trials results in avoidance conditioning; the left front limb is raised to the designated height prior to the onset of shock. Despite the complete avoidance of shock, the avoidance response persists over many trials without extinguishing.

Employing the method of heteroeffector classical and avoidance conditioning, a number of studies are reported on such problems as the interactions between the CR and UCR during acquisition and extinction, varying intensities of the CS and the UCS, and the like. Utilization of this conditioning procedure precludes simple interpretations of conditioned responses as fractional components or anticipations of the UCR; the truism that the entire organism (by which we mean primarily the CNS) is involved in conditioning is all too often forgotten.

The experimental results obtained with this novel conditioning procedure are interesting in their own right. Interesting also, and novel for most Western psychologists, is the type of interpretation given the experimental results. Interpreting effects of varying the intensities of the UCS in terms of changes in the physiological strength of the CS is unlike the usual S-R theoretical interpretation; but it is testable at the neurophysiological level, and it is in accord with the behavioral data. What in Pavlov's day was gross physiological speculation about unobserved phenomena occurring in the brain is today much more closely rooted in neurophysiological data. Although still speculative, theoretical interpretations of behavioral results in terms of physiological events in the brain are much closer to the realm of verifiability than they were in Pavlov's lifetime. Such interpretations have the advantage, potentially, of relating and integrating behavioral and physiological data, a gain in generality not possible when investigations and theorizing are limited to only one of these areas of observation.

The only study of adult human conditioning represented in the present volume is Vinogradova's chapter on specific and nonspecific systems of reactions in the course of the formation of a conditioned connection in man. Most experiments on stimulus generalization of physiological responses have been complicated by the difficulty of differentiating the elicitation of an orienting reflex from the effects of generalization of the conditioned association. By first conditioning a defensive reflex which can be differentiated from an orienting reflex, Vinogradova is presumably able to demonstrate pure generalization gradients of conditioned defensive reflexes independently of the orienting reflex. An analogous experiment on semantic conditioning and semantic generalization of the orienting and defensive reflexes has been reported by Luria and Vinogradova.

The chapter describing the research of Asratyan and his associates is concerned with the examination of the locus of extinctive inhibition in the reflex arc, research of importance for behavioral theories of inhibition during extinction that have been formulated in the United States. The research described in this chapter is also important for its implications concerning the necessary conditions for learning and the relationship between classical and instrumental conditioning. More specific questions of concern to investigators in the United States are also examined in the research reviewed, including the conditions under which backward conditioning may occur, and the influence of the CS upon the UCR.

Bernshtein (recently deceased), Anokhin, Beritashvili, and, more lately,

Feigenberg and Sokolov, have been leading proponents of the view that the conception of the reflex arc, a basic conceptual scheme in nineteenth century physiology, including Pavlov's formulation, must be supplanted by the conception of the reflex loop. This attempted revision of classical physiological theory met with effective opposition during the 1950's following the establishment by the Academy of Sciences of an orthodox Pavlovianism as the basis for the formulation of physiological concepts. Despite the opposition, papers critical of the reflex-arc conception continued to be presented. It now appears that the revisionists are becoming the dominant group among physiologists and psychologists concerned with such problems, matters related to the general systematic orientation toward problems of higher nervous activity. Such revisions of course have been criticized, although these criticisms are not represented among the papers of the present volume. A leading critic of the revisionists, Asratyan, is represented only by his experimentally oriented work.

A distinctive feature of the reflex-loop conception in contrast to the reflex arc is the emphasis upon "feedback" principles in the former, an emphasis upon return afferentation or afferent signals stemming from activity which in turn serves as a basis for controlling and regulating activity and anticipating future environmental events. Probability forecasting, probability prognoses, images, acceptor of effect, and the neuronal model—all are conceptions of this kind.

It is interesting to note that the physiologists initially promulgating such notions, Anokhin, Bernshtein, and Beritashvili, were all involved in research on what would be considered instrumental behavior and instrumental conditioning rather than simple classical conditioning. Instrumental behavior, more obviously than classical conditioning, poses questions of goal-directed or purposive behavior, as evidenced by the formulations of Tolman and Hull in this country during the 1930's. Soviet theorists such as the men under discussion insist that conceptions such as the reflex loop and directed behavior also hold for classical conditioning. Here they tend to diverge from neobehaviorist theorists.

As Bernshtein points out, formulations in harmony with the revised conception of the reflex loop may be found outside the biological sciences, in cybernetics broadly interpreted. The behavioral and physiological properties of the organism in harmony with cybernetics are that the organism's behavior acting upon the environment is controlled and regulated, thereby providing for correction of the activity.

The theorizing of the revisionists, Bernshtein, Anokhin, Beritashvili, Sokolov, and Feigenberg, however, is confronted with a basic problem: the specification of the relationship among image, neuronal model, and similar concepts, assumed changes in the cortex, and performance. In their hands it becomes a physiological problem rather than a problem of behavior theory. It is a problem that Tolman could never adequately solve, which is why Guthrie was led to conclude that Tolman left his rats buried in thought.

As has been cogently pointed out, much of behavior theory is actually guesses at laws of behavior. It is becoming increasingly apparent that these guesses cannot be accurate or adequate if the bases for the guesses are restricted solely to behavior. But if the problem is to relate the "image" to overt behavior, research restricted to acute preparations of physiological measures without concomitant behavioral measures likewise may contribute little of importance to psychology.

No one more strikingly represents the divergence from the oversimplified conception of the Pavlovian stereotype than Beritashvili, perhaps the outstanding contemporary Soviet physiologist and psychological physiologist. Engaged in a great variety of physiological and behavioral studies, including conditioning studies, he was not a pupil of Pavlov but a student of Ukhtomski, a leading figure in the Leningrad school of physiology at the turn of the century. Ukhtomski in turn was the outstanding student of Sechenov, the father of modern Russian and Soviet physiology. Beritashvili's theorizing has clearly been influenced by Sechenov and, in part because of this, differs from the stereotyped conception of atomistic, elementaristic, reductionistic, conditioned-reflex-concatenation view of behavior.

Beritashvili believes that there are two kinds of learning, the learning of images or perceptual learning, and the learning of conditioned reflexes or motor skills. The learning of images occurs in a single trial and is relatively permanent. The learning of conditioned reflexes takes many trials and is relatively unstable:

> In perception the bonds between sensory neurons arise immediately on the first influence of an object and later on they are present, making possible the reproduction of images for a long time, sometimes almost the entire lifetime. These images actually do not extinguish with time, even when repeatedly reproduced without a new perception. Apparently the neural bonds between the sensory neurons are qualitatively different from the temporary bonds (in projection-area pyramidal cells) on which the development of a conditioned reflex depends. Bonds of the latter sort require numerous repetitions for their formation and strengthening; moreover, they rapidly extinguish if they are not practiced.

There is a qualitative difference between psychological, voluntary activity and conditioned reflexes. Voluntary activity in young children and higher organisms is image-directed behavior. In normal adults it is behavior directed or regulated by plans. Involuntary behavior, conditioned reflexes, is qualitatively different. In his chapter Beritashvili describes studies which he takes as support for the differentiation. He points out that orienting behavior and emotions can be evoked at the same time. Orienting behavior is based upon the excitation of sensory complexes in the neocortex while emotional changes are a function of the excitation of sensory complexes in the archipaleocortex. Because they are quite different processes but may be evoked under the same conditions, there has been a tendency, particularly in the United States, to theorize that the physiological changes represent emotional changes solely, ignoring the possibility that complex processes of thinking and perception, attention, and so on, may be manifested at the same time, and manifested in a similar fashion peripherally.

Beritashvili is a striking example of how much closer psychological physiologists of the Soviet Union may be to, say, Tolman, in terms of the kind of psychological theories they formulate, than to Hull, who used the classical conditioning situation for deriving principles of behavior. However, there is an obvious and fundamental difference between the theorizing of Beritashvili and Tolman. Beritashvili is an experimental physiologist, and he is concerned with determining the physiological and anatomical correlates of his psychological or behavioral concepts. He is in the tradition of Sechenov. Tolman eschewed physiology, developing instead a molar behaviorism. When Soviet psychologists are considered, where there is no explicit dependence upon physiological data and theories, then the purely psychological or behavioral theories are generally much closer to Tolman's type of cognitive psychology, or more current so-called cognitive theories, than they are to Pavlovian theory or neobehaviorist learning theories.

E. N. Sokolov, in his chapter, assumes that instrumental search or investigatory responses are basically the same as the physiological components of the OR. This assumption is in urgent need of careful quantitative study employing concomitant recordings of physiological measures of the OR and behavioral investigatory responses. Sokolov assumes not only that the principles holding for the physiological measures of the OR hold for the "tactile component" of the OR, search movements, but that these search movements are regulated by a hierarchy of hypotheses which correspond to a hierarchy of neuronal models. The occurrence of particular search movements depends upon the system of neural models used by the subject in recognizing an object. Sokolov assumes that the systems of neural models employed correspond to hypotheses and that they are equivalent to the neuronal model of the stimulus.

In his chapter "Cybernetics and the Integrative Activity of the Brain," Anokhin outlines the characteristics of a physiological model that he has found useful in analyzing behavioral acts and that has stimulated research on various integrative functions of the brain in relation to behavior.

The initial, and in many respects the most important, stage in the integrative activity of the brain leading to a behavioral act is the stage of *afferent synthesis.* It permits the thorough processing, comparison, and synthesis of the sensory information entering the central nervous system. It provides the necessary relevant information for the decisions occurring under the conditions leading to adaptive behavior. There are three parameters involved in every adaptive act: what to do, how to do it, and when to do it. Information necessary for each of these decisions is processed, selected, and compared in the phase of afferent synthesis.

There are two aspects to afferent synthesis: the specific mechanisms involved, and the nature of their interaction. There are four qualitatively different mechanisms constituting or carrying out the functions of afferent synthesis. The first is the role of the dominant motive. Primary and secondary drives have a selective role in processing information by energizing only relevant associations, only those associations related to the arousal or reduction of the need in question. In this manner motives eliminate surplus information. Anokhin describes the results of a variety of electrophysiological and biochemical studies conducted in his Institute which support the notion of the selectivity of drives. Such evidence is contrary to the notion of a generalized drive or arousal state which energizes all habits present at the moment. The dominant motive, in Anokhin's scheme, determines what the organism must do.

Environmental afferentation is a second process involved in afferent synthesis. The characteristic, constant stimuli from the environment in the conditioning chamber, for example, prepare the dog for the salivary response. Environmental afferentation establishes a "subliminal" neural model of the environment which, when integrated and activated, culminates in an appropriate act. Environmental afferentation is important to the organism because along with the dominant motivation it predisposes the organism toward adaptive acts determining how to do it.

Activating afferentation is important because it determines the third parameter of the adaptive act, when to do it, as illustrated by the role of the CS in the classical conditioning experiment. Activating afferentation, as the term implies, activates the "subliminal" neural model created by the environment and motivation into overt behavior.

Memory is a fourth component of afferent synthesis. Anokhin briefly discusses biochemical theories of memory and memory retrieval in this connection.

A second major problem in the analysis of afferent synthesis is the nature of its *dynamics.* How do the above processes of motivation, environmental afferentation, memory, and so on, interact? Their interaction (communication) from different elements in the brain is facilitated by the operation of the orienting reflex and centrifugal activation and inhibition. Ascending influence from the hypothalamus and the reticular formation on the cortex facilitates formation of connections relevant to the dominant motive, while the centrifugal influence on receptors produces increased sensitivity and discriminability.

The *predictor apparatus* or acceptor of effect is a second major process entering into the formation of adaptive behavior. Afferent synthesis leads to a decision, the selection of certain activities from among a great variety of alternatives. The *acceptor of effect* is the process which perceives information about the results of an action and integrates the results of an adaptive act. This process permits the correction and regulation of acts. Observations supporting the role of this hypothesized mechanism stem from a variety of experiments conducted in the Soviet Union and the West. One of the first experiments of this type, switching the kind of reward obtained by the animal, was conducted by Anokhin himself.

The third, fourth, and fifth processes contributing to the integrative action of the brain as it relates to adaptive behavior are intimately involved with the occurrence of reinforcement, the effects of the reinforcement, and the discrepancy between reinforcement received and reinforcement anticipated. Hypothesizing about these processes, which Anokhin deems essential for an adequate account of brain function and behavior, requires going beyond the classical notion of a closed reflex arc. It requires the use of notions stemming from cybernetics.

Whether or not one agrees with Anokhin's type of theorizing, there are many fruitful specific hypotheses and important experimental results that he presents which must be considered in their own right. For example, the results reported and the hypotheses entertained concerning the neurophysiological effects of drive, the role of the orienting reflex, the emotional consequences of a discrepancy between anticipated and obtained goals, are all pertinent to any theory of behavior.

Coming upon Soviet psychology and psychological physiology for the first time is a little like Darwin first visiting the Galápagos. Different forms of species have evolved, as a result of isolation and interbreeding, which are adaptable to their environment. There are some exciting and stimulating surprises, and some disappointments. The often-encountered inventiveness and freedom from conformity to oversimplified doctrines are refreshing and, to the uninitiated, quite revealing. All too often Soviet psychology has been characterized as a rigid adherence to Pavlovian conditioning. This is simply not the case; but Pavlovian conditioning research and theory is itself far more sophisticated and complicated than the stereotyped and grossly oversimplified picture presented in most American textbooks.

Because of isolation from the work in the U.S.S.R. and because of its intellectual and cultural environment, psychology and physiology in the United States evolved in a different fashion. Each has much to learn from the other. With closer contact and communication between the peoples of our countries, the psychologies of both should be enriched. To such peaceful cooperation in the pursuit of that most important common goal, knowledge of man, we dedicate this book.

References

Anan'ev, B. G., *et al.* (Eds.). *Psychological Sciences in the U.S.S.R.* (In English.) Washington, D.C.: U.S. Joint Publication Research Service, Vol. 1, 1961, Vol. 2, 1962.

Bassin, F. V. A critical analysis of Freudianism. *Soviet Rev.*, 1960, *1*, 3–14. (a)

Bassin, F. V. A rejoinder to Professor Musatti. *Soviet Rev.*, 1960, *1*, 27–44. (b)

Luria, A. R. *The role of speech in the regulation of normal and abnormal behavior.* London: Pergamon Press, 1961.

Luria, A. R., and Vinogradova, O. S. An objective investigation of the dynamics of semantic systems. *Brit. J. Psychol.*, 1959, *50*, 89–105.

Maltzman, I. Individual differences in "attention": The orienting reflex. In R. M. Gagne (Ed.), *Learning and individual differences.* Columbus, Ohio: Charles E. Merrill, 1967. Pp. 94–112.

Mintz, A. Introduction to contemporary Soviet psychology. In R. A. Bauer (Ed.), *Some views on Soviet psychology*. Washington, D.C.: Amer. Psychol. Assoc., 1962.

Musatti, C. L. An answer to F. V. Bassin's criticism of Freudianism. *Soviet Rev.*, 1960, *1*, 14–27.

Pavlov, I. P. *Conditioned reflexes.* London: Oxford Univer. Press, 1927.

Razran, G. Soviet psychology and psychophysiology. *Science,* 1958, *128,* 1187–1194.

Razran, G. The observable unconscious and the inferable conscious in current Soviet psychophysiology: Interoceptive conditioning, semantic conditioning and the orienting reflex. *Psychol. Rev.*, 1961, *68,* 81–147.

Sokolov, E. N. *Perception and the conditioned reflex.* London: Pergamon Press, 1963.

Tucker, R. C. Stalin and the uses of psychology. In *The Soviet political mind.* New York: Praeger, 1963.

The 23rd CPSU Congress and the goals of psychology. *Vop. Psikhol.*, 1966, *12*, 3–9.

PART I

DEVELOPMENTAL PSYCHOLOGY

1

The Psychology of Primates

N. N. Ladygina-Kots and *Y. N. Dembovskii*

EDITORS' INTRODUCTION

This chapter is a compilation of two sections from Y. N. Dembovskii's The Psychology of Apes, *written originally in Polish and published in the Soviet Union in 1963. The first section (constituting the first part of our chapter) was written especially for Dembovskii by N. N. Ladygina-Kots, who died in 1963, prior to its appearance.*

Ladygina-Kots began her studies of primate behavior in 1913, when she founded the zoo-psychological laboratory of the Darwin Museum in Moscow. In addition to her many monographs on the evolution of behavior, particularly in the lower primates, she published a two-volume description of her experiment in raising a chimpanzee in her home along with her own child (Ladygina-Kots, 1935). Unfortunately, this work, which is reminiscent of similar experiments by the Kelloggs (1933) and the Hayeses (1951), is very difficult to find in American (or Soviet!) libraries. Her contribution here, as its title indicates, is designed to give an overview, to approximately 1960, of Soviet research on primate behavior. For a review of contemporary Soviet efforts in the area of primate behavior, the article by Bowden (1966) is recommended.

The second part of our chapter is taken from Chapter 5 of Dembovskii's The Psychology of Apes. *It describes, in considerable detail, the unique experiments carried out by Vatsuro, a student of Pavlov's, on the chimpanzee Rafael. This work has attracted relatively little attention in the West, although it bears importantly on interpretations of Köhler's classic (1925) studies. For other accounts in English of Rafael's exploits, see Razran (1961) and Denisov (1958).*

An Overview of Soviet Studies in Anthropoid Psychology

Fundamental research on the behavior of apes has been connected with the problems of anthropogenesis, of the dialectical-materialist understanding of the development of the mind, and of the biological premises of specific human traits—work, speech, cognition. Therefore, research has been directed primarily towards the study of the ape's skills and reasoning ability and, to a lesser degree, to his inherent, instinctive forms of behavior, emotions and imitation.

Many of the experiments have compared the behavior of higher and lower apes or the behavior of anthropoids and children. In addition, observations have been made on the ontogenetic development of the human child and the young of the chimpanzee.

In the study of the animals' behavior, Soviet scientists have fought against both the mechanistic tendency and the tendency to anthropomorphize their behavior. This is in the tradition of Russian science represented by the founder of comparative psychology, the biologist-Darwinist Vagner (1913) and by the physiologist Pavlov (1949).

The conclusions of many Soviet scientists testify against the erroneous point of view of certain leading foreign scientists, who adhere to the Gestalt theoretical position (Köhler, 1925) concerning the basis of the ape's intellectual processes. Soviet scientists have also revealed the error of the views of those foreign researchers who have minimized the qualitative difference in the intellect of the higher apes and man (Yerkes, 1925, for example).

The Development of Behavior in the Ontogenesis of the Ape and Man

Tikh, working at the Sukhumi primate station, investigated the ontogenetic development of basic types of innate behavior in the young of the ape and in the human child (1949a, b, 1957). She studied the development of appetitive, defensive, orienting, sexual, parental, and gregarious behavior in the lower apes. She was especially interested in the grasp and clasp reactions (unconditioned reflexes) specific to the ape. In specifying the moment at which these reactions appear in the ape and the stimuli which evoke them, Tikh was able to distinguish them from the same behavior in the human child.

While the young ape prompts his mother to breast-feed him by scratching at her body with his hands, the human child in the same situation emits a characteristic "hunger" cry. The defensive reaction of the young ape is to clutch and grasp at his mother's fur. In the human child this reaction appears only in a rudimentary form; it has clearly lost its adaptive significance. Tikh makes a strict distinction between clasping and grasping. In the latter there is a functional differentiation of the fingers which does not occur in the former. Forms of locomotor activity develop in distinctly different ways. Beginning with a single crawling stage in both child and ape, the latter turns to movement on all fours, the child to walking upright. Parental and sexual behavior appear in both ape and human child before sexual maturity.

Tikh examines in great detail the development of the orienting reflex, which is very prominent in the ape. Acts of manipulation are characterized by significantly greater analysis but considerably weaker synthetic activity. In contrast to this, in the human child practical synthesis appears early, attaining greater complexity in the child's growth.

The difference between the developing young of the ape and children is that, for the ape, sounds do not evoke the orienting reflex. Children, on the contrary, are greatly diverted by sounds, including the sound of their own voices. The ape's ability to imitate sounds and movements is very undeveloped compared to that of man. Tikh concludes that there are certain ontogenetic similarities in the development of the ape and man. While the primeval forms of activity (feeding, defense, or orienting) are retained in man, new forms of activity such as imitation have developed in the process of anthropogenesis. Such new forms of activity sharply distinguish the behavior of these two comparable primates.

Gregarious Relationships and Interaction in Apes

Tikh studied thoroughly the social behavior of adult apes (*Papio hamadryas*) at the Sukhumi primate station, where they lived in spacious enclosures (1949a). Her results, similar to those of Voitonis, have led to basic corrections of Zuckerman's (1932) conclusions. The latter observed apes primarily in the cramped conditions of the London Zoo. Tikh refutes his conclusions regarding the decisive significance of sexual factors in the behavior of the ape community.

She advances four basic conditions of baboon society:

(1) The need for common defense from enemies.

(2) Sexual needs.

(3) The need for mutual warmth, related to the peculiarities of thermoregulation in the ape.

(4) The duration of the mother-child association resulting from the prolonged period of dependence in the young.

With these basic factors in mind, the author emphasizes the significance of the selective relationship which apes have among themselves, the presence of "grouping." This is the basis for both "friendly" and hostile relationships.

Tikh has conducted extremely interesting experiments on the sounds which the ape utters in order to satisfy certain needs. Analyzing organic sounds such as groans, she ascertained that apes could be taught to use these sounds as a signal of their need for certain kinds of food. For instance, she was able to reinforce the sound *kkh* at the presentation of nuts, *kkh-kkh* for biscuits, *kkh-kkh-kkh* for sugar. Pankratova's experiments with pavian anubis apes in the laboratory of Voronin (1957) indicated that the troupe sounds *hm-hm* and *tse'tse* are usually uttered when establishing contact among themselves and when searching. They may also be conditioned as signals expressing a need for food.

Tikh did not analyze her observations of "imitative" signal movements, although she feels that the apes' expressive gestures are the biological antecedents of speech development. The later experiments of Ulanova (1950), conducted in Protopopov's laboratory (1950), indicated that it is possible to analyze the ape's signal gestures.

Ulanova (1950) conducted experiments to study the ability of the macaque to give conditioned signs indicating the need for various kinds of solid and liquid food (nuts, strawberries, apples, bread, radishes, milk, coffee, tea). There was a visual-kinesthetic order to these signs. The experimenter taught the animal to compose its fingers in certain ways. In the beginning the animal was trained to stretch his hand to the experimenter at the sight of the food, but he was not allowed to take the food until he had made the appropriate sign (Ulanova, 1950, p. 132).

For example, the signal for nuts was the formation of an *O* with the thumb and index finger; for strawberries, the sign *C;* for bread, *A;* for apples, *V;* for radishes, *F.* To obtain tea or coffee the ape had to clench his right hand and grasp it with his left. The ape was able to correctlv reproduce the sign for bread after 152 trials; for radishes, after 198; for apples, after 448; for strawberries, after 576; for water, after 209.

It was especially difficult for the ape to make the sign for liquid food, which required a movement of both hands. He reproduced the sign for apples very accurately. Ulanova concludes that the speed with which the animal learns the conditioned sign depends on the desirability of the particular food. It was easiest to form the sign for bread and apples. The animal used these signs independently, while the signs for other kinds of food were neither firmly nor accurately established.

Complex Learning and Problem Solving in the Ape

We will now turn to the problem of the formation of skills in monkeys and apes. For example, we studied adaptive motor skills in the macaque and rhesus, using the "problem box." The box contained a reward, but could be locked by various mechanisms: hooks, latches, levers, bolts. The process of skill formation began with disorderly attempts, the rejection of unsuccessful movements, and the retention of those movements which led to opening the mechanism and the reward. It was definitely observed that the ape increasingly relied on his successful attempts and with each trial the duration of the operation was shortened. But each acceleration of the solution was observed primarily when single-stage mechanisms were involved. When the task involved a series of operations, success did not follow so noticeably. The animal long retained unnecessary movements. As a result the speed of opening did not decrease systematically.

It should be especially emphasized that in learning to open various mechanisms kinesthetic perception dominated visual perception. The ape was not always able to determine the nature of the mechanism visually—which to unlock, which to lock; frequently only motor attempts led to successful resolution of the problem. Frequently the macaque would open the mechanism, then close it, and only after unsuccessful attempts to open the door of the box would he again begin to open it. It was especially difficult for the ape to open bolts which had mobile secondary mechanisms (chains, hanging locks). Persistent attempts to open these parts prolonged the entire operation.

This kind of skill formation in the ape in all probability indicates the inability to grasp the significance of essential and inessential parts of the mechanisms, the inability to understand the effect of his movements on the solution of the task. It was clear that these solutions were based on visual-kinesthetic temporal associations involving repeated trials, that is, associations of a space-time nature.

Protopopov and his colleagues at the Animal Behavior Laboratory in the Kharkov Institute studied skill formation in monkeys (1950a). Protopopov concluded from his research that the ape's first attempts to solve a problem are not chaotic (as Thorndike, in particular, argued). They are instinctive and, often, inappropriate but tentative ways of solving a problem, which gradually change by means of individually acquired appropriate responses.

Further, Protopopov argues that the formation of skills in the monkey does not depend on accidentally successful movements, but on actively directed movements. The intensity of the stimulus also influences the formation of skills in the ape. In an experiment involving sticks, the ape began by trying in every way possible to reach the fruit with his hand, but he was unable independently to apply the stick in order to reach the reward. Only when the task was simplified, when the free end of the stick was attached to the reward, was the ape able to use the stick to draw the reward to himself. (An analogy is the association of fruit on the twig of a tree.)

Later, after several attempts, the association of stick with the fruit was so firmly established that no matter where the stick was placed (in a distant but accessible place) the animal used it to reach the fruit. Moreover, the ape even searched for the stick when it was removed from his field of vision: hidden in a cabinet or placed on the cage's ledge or in other places in the cage.

Protopopov concluded that the ape never makes appropriate responses without preliminary attempts. These attempts are both of an instinctive and of an individually acquired nature, that is, they consist of phylogenetic and ontogenetic experiences which are difficult to distinguish from each other. He explains the sudden solution of a problem in certain cases either by the similarity of the situation to the animal's natural environment or by the traces of past experiences.

Protopopov's colleague, Khil'chenko (1950a, b, 1953) working with rhesus monkeys, came to analogous conclusions. Comparing the process of problem solving between apes and monkeys, Khil'chenko concludes that "there are no differences in principle in the formation of ontogenetic experiences in monkeys and apes; i.e., there is no justification for postulating a great difference between monkeys and apes in this respect, neither is there reason to liken the behavior of the apes to human behavior" (1950, p. 120).

Another of Protopopov's colleagues, Rushkevich (1950) studied the baboon under the following conditions. The reward was arranged on the experimental table and hidden by a screen which moved about. The animal was required to get the fruit with a stick by using a turning movement. The long training period involved shifting the reward by turning from right to left. As a result, the apes were unable to shift immediately, when it became necessary, to a left to right movement. It appeared that the kinesthetic associations which they had acquired were very strong compared with the visual. They mastered the new movement only after prolonged training.

The basic conclusion of this work is the following: The baboon has little ability to manipulate tools (sticks), and when he does use them, he does so clumsily and awkwardly; he is barely able to make subtle and differentiated movements with his hand when it is equipped with a stick; he learns to make simple turning motions with the stick only with difficulty and is incapable of modifying the skill in an essentially new situation; in each new situation he behaves as before, although such movements may be senseless and incongruous in the new situation. The baboon, acquiring a skill by "transfer of experience" reveals surprising sluggishness and "stupidity" (Rushkevich, 1950, p. 121).

This conclusion is documented in another series of experiments by the same author, who set the animal the task of finding a roundabout way to remove the reward from a four-cornered box, one wall of which was open. The baboon easily withdrew the reward with his finger through the open wall of the box, turning it to the right, to the left, and forward. However, when it became necessary to remove the food with a tool (stick), the ape was unable to do it.

The results of the comparisons given above show clearly that it is extremely difficult for the lower ape to use auxiliary objects. The difficulty is not so much the technical inability to use a stick. The primary obstacle is the inability to establish a direct connection between himself (or, more accurately, his hands) and the reward when getting the reward involves some kind of auxiliary object.

The experiments of Levykina (1959, p. 180) with mandrill baboons established that the ape was unable to use a stick to get gelatin which was placed behind the bars of the cage when the stick lay parallel to the grating. The animal was limited by the fact that he tried to draw to himself the plate on which the reward lay by pulling the stick.

Then the task was somewhat simplified. The stick was placed perpendicular to the grating alongside the reward. The ape was again unable to get the gelatin with the stick, although he took the latter in his hands, sniffed it, examined it, and tasted the end which lay near the reward. Only when the experiment was still further simplified, when one end of the stick was submerged in the reward, did the ape pull the stick out of the gelatin and lick it.

The conditions of the experiment were made complicated again. A dry stick was placed parallel to the stick next to the gelatin. The baboon pulled the stick out and licked it; it did not occur to him to dip it into the gelatin again. Moreover, he took the dry stick and licked it, but did not try to use it to get the reward.

Levykina emphasizes that the ape's improvement in solving this task consisted only in that he learned to distinguish between two sticks: the one submerged in the gelatin and the dry one. The pavian learned to pull out the stick in contact with the gelatin, but never attempted to plunge either stick into the gelatin, that is, to use the stick as a tool.

Studying the ability of the young anthropoid ape, the chimpanzee, to use a stick as a tool to obtain a reward, Khil'chenko observed that he used it correctly only after 26 days (1953). In connection with the above, the experiments conducted by Novoselova with chimpanzees should be mentioned (1959). Her experiments proved that even in this relatively highly organized ape (in contrast with lower apes) the use of a stick is an individually adaptive action and not an innate form of behavior. The process of learning to use a stick to reach a fruit, which is beyond the hand's reach, proceeds gradually. It begins with the use of the whole arm as a lever and proceeds to specialized movements of the hand as an organ, not only to hold the stick but to direct its movements as a specific tool.

Roginskii's adult chimpanzees (8 to 16 years of age) had experience in manipulating sticks and therefore immediately used a stick to reach a distant reward. Of the lower apes, only the chacma baboon was able to use a stick correctly from the first (Roginskii, 1945). Roginskii, however, writes that there is no gap between the chimpanzee and the lower ape of the kind that Köhler describes. There are unquestionable differences in the abilities of apes and monkeys to solve complex problems, but they are differences of degree rather than of essence and have a quantitative rather than a qualitative character.

Roginskii concludes that in solving tasks involving the use of sticks, skills and intellect form a unity which is difficult to analyze into components. He writes that chimpanzees acquire skills more quickly than other animals; they are extremely flexible and easily adapt to new conditions. A chimpanzee can solve the same problem in different ways. When the task changes he immediately changes his techniques. The ape's skills are derived from intellectual operations the essence of which is the ability to perceive connections and correlations between objects.

Roginskii opposes Köhler's position that the chimpanzee is "the slave of his visual field" and that his intellect is similar to the human intellect. We feel that Roginskii's concept of the ape's intellect requires more precise definition. In our view, the only evidence for the existence of intellect in the ape would be *new* adaptive associations in situations *new* for the animal.

Of course, intellectual solutions of this or that task depend upon individual experience acquired earlier. They depend not upon stable skills, but upon the ability which permits the animal to reconstruct his behavior anew in accordance with new situations. Only when the animal "guesses" how to use earlier acquired methods and actions in a new combination may we assert that the solution rests on newly formed temporary associations and is, in fact, an intellectual solution.

Problem Solving and the Ape's Use of Tools

We turn now to a review of other research by Soviet scientists on the ape's intellect. These researches are primarily an analysis of the ape's ability to use auxiliary objects as tools to obtain a reward.

We conducted a five-year experiment to study tool-using activity of the chimpanzee. We used the following methodology (Ladygina-Kots, 1959).

A reward wrapped in paper was placed in a narrow metal tube (20–40 cm. long and 4.5 cm. wide). It was possible to get the reward by pushing it out of the tube with a straight stick. We asked the following questions:

1. Is the chimpanzee capable of using the stick immediately to get the reward?

2. Can the chimpanzee recognize and choose a suitable object from among unsuitable ones in order to get the reward?

3. Can the chimpanzee independently modify the unsuitable object (a branch, a twisted wire, etc.) in order to render it suitable for obtaining the reward?

4. Can he put two objects together in order to get the reward (put two short sticks together to make one long one)?

To answer the first question, the ape was given a straight stick as long as the tube. (The reward was placed in the tube in the ape's presence and pushed inside with the stick.) But the ape, taking the pipe in his hands, did not imitate the experimenter. Instead, he put first the index finger of one hand and then of both hands into the opening of the tube. Only the failure of this method induced him to use the stick, which he immediately used correctly. He pushed the reward out with the stick although he had not had similar earlier experience.

In further trials the ape was given completely different objects in no way similar to the stick (fork, a metal pestle, a stem with a flower at the top, a narrow iron bar, etc.). The chimpanzee immediately and successfully used these objects as tools.

Whenever the ape was given several objects (both suitable and unsuitable for obtaining the reward and differing in form, length, width, thickness, and density), he differentiated perfectly between the various cues and chose the one most suitable for the task. When the chimpanzee was given several objects with different characteristics—for example, when one object was suitable in length but not in form (a curved stick) and another was of the right shape (a straight stick) but the wrong length (short)—the choice was based on the length and not the shape of the object.

When the choice was between a thick but soft cord and a firm, thin wire, the chimpanzee made errors: that is, he chose the cord in the beginning, but immediately discarded it and chose the wire. When the ape was given five objects identical in form and size but varying in rigidity (a piece of soft cord, elastic wire, a small stick, the stem of a flexible plant), he chose the one most suitable for obtaining the reward—the small stick.

In the third series of experiments the chimpanzee was given objects to be used as tools which required judgment and analysis of parts (e.g., a switch from a piece of wicker basket, a piece of wire from a wire triangle or some other complex wire figure). The chimpanzee quickly noted the appropriate element, separated it, tore it away from the complex, and successfully used it to obtain the reward. Moreover, he was able to tear thin splinters from wide planks or boards and use them as tools to obtain the reward.

In the fourth series the chimpanzee had to modify unsuitable objects in order to use them to obtain the reward. He was given a branch with leaves, or a piece of wire bent to shape various letters of the alphabet. The chimpanzee turned them all into tools with which he was able to obtain the reward: he tore from the branch the side shoots which prevented its entrance into the opening of the tube; he straightened the wire and was able to push the straight end into the tube.

The chimpanzee was given a stick with soft wire cross-beams, or expandable planks fastened only in the center. Instead of pressing the wire to the shaft of the stick or pushing together the ends of planks in order to have a narrow instrument, the chimpanzee fell back on habit. He was able to apply only the methods which he had previously mastered to break objects down to form usable instruments. With great difficulty he tore off the side extensions of wire or broke the protruding ends of the planks and used the resulting smooth straight tools to obtain the reward.

In the fifth series of experiments (over 100 in all) the ape was given short bamboo sticks to put together, and simple short sticks to tie together. The chimpanzee was able to join the sticks only in isolated cases. He made no attempt at all to bind them, although in play he revealed the ability to join and bind objects. Moreover, he frequently took apart sticks made of two or three joined pieces and pushed them into the tube—without, of course, pushing the reward out.

How does one explain these interesting phenomena? On the one hand, the ape is extremely successful in solving problems involving complicated differentiation in a complex of elements and of working them over in order to render them suitable as tools. On the other hand, he is unable to join or put together elements when it is necessary to make a longer tool.

We explain this in three ways: biological, physiological, and psychological.

The biological reason: in the natural conditions of his life the chimpanzee daily engages in destructive activities, such as breaking up twigs and branches to build his night nest. This requires independently judging whether or not the bifurcation of a tree is suitable for his nest, as well as judging the thickness of the branches which lie under it. However, piling up broken parts of the tree top or plaiting their thinner peripheral ends, the ape never has occasion to bind or put the ends of the branches together. And he does not do this in captivity either.

The physiological reason: the chimpanzee forms a conditioned reflex to using single, firm objects to push the reward out of the tube and to removing all extraneous extensions on the object. He perceives any component tool as a negative cue indicating that the tool is unsuitable to the task. Therefore he stubbornly resists joining such objects. In fact he will sometimes even refuse to use an already joined tool.

The psychological reason: As a result of repeated use of a straight, smooth stick, the chimpanzee retains a generalized visual model of the suitable tool with specific characteristics—length (corresponding to the tube which contains the reward), thickness (corresponding to the diameter of the tube's opening), and form.

This generalized visual model inhibits the act of putting the parts of the stick together. In all of his previously successful attempts any extraneous element delayed the process of reaching the reward. The chimpanzee did not grasp the significance of his play, during which he joined short sticks to form a long tool or take apart an already joined one. He was unable to comprehend this cause-effect relationship. This is the essence of the qualitative difference between the chimpanzee's intellect and human intellect.

But it would be incorrect to deny in general the presence of intellect, or reasoning ability, in the chimpanzee. It becomes apparent, for instance, when the chimpanzee establishes the necessary connection between the tool and the tube which contains the reward and uses any firm, smooth, long, narrow object. The chimpanzee's intellect manifests itself in the choice of the correct object (tool) from among a series of unsuitable objects (according to length, thickness, density, form). Only the presence of intellect helps the chimpanzee to transform the unsuitable object by means of his hands and teeth into one that is correct for the task of dismembering the parts of a complex of objects or even of a whole object (splinters from the board). We repeat, however, that the chimpanzee's intellect differs qualitatively from that of the human being.

Comparison of apes and monkeys indicates that the former's intellect is higher than the latter's. For example, lower apes use a tool to obtain a distant reward only in exceptional cases (Roginskii, 1945). They are unable to cope with the experiments involving a reward-containing tube (Levykina, 1959). Only Klüver's capuchin was able to obtain the reward from the tube with a stick (1961). Higher apes, even young ones (6 to 8 years old) were able to use sticks to obtain a reward (Levykina). They were able to manipulate not only straight, clean sticks, but gnarled ones and twigs as well. They were able to tear off the hindering protuberances in order to insert the object into the tube. All these, as well as other observations indicate the differences in the intellect of apes and monkeys (but only of degree, not of essence).

Reasoning and Problem Solving in the Ape

Several Ukrainian psychologists from Protopopov's laboratory studied the primate's reaction to relative cues. They showed that the ape is capable of abstraction and generalization. Protopopov concludes that monkeys, as well as dogs, perceive elements of a situation using both absolute and relative cues (1950). The experimental animal's ability to grasp relationships and to generalize from them indicates his ability to think abstractly. This process is the biological antecedent of specifically human reasoning or, as Pavlov put it, "abstraction of reality."

Biryukovich's experiments (1950) indicated that apes and monkeys (baboons and rhesus) are capable of correctly responding to the intensity of color in objects (dark-light). In Khil'chenko's experiments (1950a), baboons were able to distinguish size of squares attached to boxes. The smaller box was 100 square cm., the larger, 225 square cm. The space between the boxes was 5 cm. The reward was always placed in the smaller box. The position of the boxes was changed in order to avoid having the ape make his choice according to topographical cues, that is, the position of the box. After the ape had acquired the habit of choosing the box with the smaller square, the squares were replaced by circles and then by triangles (25/40 square cm.). Regardless of the changed shape, the animals continued to choose the box with the smaller figure.

Then the apes were given two cube-shaped boxes of different sizes, followed by different sized prisms and pyramids. The ape's choice of the smaller figure persisted despite the changes in form. This indicates that the lower apes were able to generalize on the basis of relative cues, that is, they mastered the ability of elementary abstraction. But Protopopov emphasizes that in apes "the relative cue is not entirely abstract in the sense that the word is abstract for man. It can only be discerned in clearly presented concrete objects." This is abstraction *in concreto,* when the "cue is not separate from the object, but shades off from it. . . . True abstraction manifests itself in the total separation of the cue from the actual object. This is possible only when the cue can be expressed in words. Thus, man is capable of true and total abstraction" (Protopopov, 1950, p. 163).

Markova (1961) established the presence of elementary abstraction in her experiments with monkeys. The experiments were conducted by the method of allowing the ape free choice of objects which he could compare. Choices of any objects were at all times encouraged by the experimenter. When three rhesus monkeys (two males and one female) had to compare two figures (selected from a set containing a ball, a cube, and a pyramid), some showed a preference for the ball, others for the cube, and still others for the pyramid.

The monkeys retained their preferences even when the following substitutions were made: first, the dimensional figures were replaced by flat ones of the same shape—glued or drawn on a black ground. Then the latter were replaced by figures outlined in black, and finally by figures drawn with dotted lines. The animals who preferred the ball, when given a choice of a ball, a cube, and a pyramid, chose a circle when given the choice of a circle, a square, and a triangle. Animals who in the original choice had preferred the cube to the ball and pyramid chose the square from among the flat figures.

The flat figures were then replaced by objects cut from paper and pasted on cardboard or simply drawn on cardboard. The apes retained the same principle of choice. It is interesting to note that they tried to grasp not the card itself with the pasted or drawn figure, but the center part of the pictured figure. The earlier principle of preference was retained whether the figure was outlined in black, contoured or outlined in dotted lines.

The percentage of the preferred choice usually changed each time the nature of the compared figures were changed. The results are indicated clearly in Table 1–1.

Table 1–1

Compared objects	Preferred choice
Dimensional	92%
Flat	84
Flat, against a background	82
Continuous outlined form	82
Outlined in dotted lines	72

It is understandable that, the less the degree to which the compared figures resembled the concrete object, the less often was the preference realized. This indicates that weak perception of the concrete object, that is, transfer to an abstraction of the essential cues of the object, hinders the choice of the preferred cues.

Markova's experiments also indicate that lower apes are capable of distinguishing circularity, four-sidedness, and triangularity. Thus, Soviet scientists have concluded that the monkey is capable of differentiating the characteristics of objects (color, form, size) and shows preference for certain characteristics of objects. He is capable of conceptualization, generalization, abstraction, and elementary reasoning. His intellect, however, differs qualitatively from man's intellect. The monkey's abstraction is only elementary, not a complete, abstraction. The latter is a characteristic only of man.

A Case History in the Study of the Higher Nervous Activity of Anthropoids: Rafael

Köhler's experiments with chimpanzees (1925) represented an important step in the study of anthropoid psychology. His results, which were immediately verified by other experimenters, are widely cited in the scientific literature. It is difficult, however, to agree with Köhler's idealistic interpretation of his results. He was one of the original proponents of the gestalt principle. For Köhler, "gestalt" is a basic law of nature which dictates that we conceive of all the phenomena of reality as total configurations: physical and chemical phenomena, laws of nature and mathematical formulas. According to Köhler, the chimpanzee's behavior is determined by the presence of a configuration and is to be understood as the animal's perception of the whole situation. In every case conditions were created for the chimpanzee in which the animal could visually comprehend that which was necessary for the solution of the task. Theoretically, the direct path to the food reward was blocked, and the chimpanzee had to reach it in a roundabout way. The nature of the animal's behavior was always determined by the geometric structure of his field of vision as a whole. Thus, by narrowing the task, Köhler reduced the chimpanzee's behavior to its perceptual basis alone and, simultaneously, to the immediate stimulus. In his opinion the chimpanzee is the "slave of his field of vision."

In 1948 there appeared extensive work by Pavlov's colleague Vatsuro (1948), in which the latter examined the chimpanzee's behavior viewed as the complex interweaving of conditioned and unconditioned reflexes, and interpreted this behavior from a materialistic point of view. The division of the animal's behavior into a series of reflexes often leads to very intricate formulations, but ultimately they are found to fit precisely to the principles worked out in the course of many years by the Pavlovian school. This work constitutes an attempt to translate the complex relations of the animal's behavior into physiological terms.

From the point of view of a dialectical materialist such as Vatsuro, unity (or gestalt) is a new quality accessible to concrete research. Analyzing the separate processes, the dialectician understands unity not as their sum, but as reciprocity in the broadest sense of the word. The very fact of reciprocity and interdependency leads to the recognition of the causes of reciprocity, which will become the causal factor underlying unity.

Vatsuro set himself the task of explaining the animal's behavior in the experimental setting on the basis of the theory of conditioned reflexes. It is often asserted that the great physiologist Pavlov wanted to reduce human behavior to the sum of its conditioned reflexes. However, more profound knowledge of his work shows that Pavlov rejected neither the idea of gestalt nor the idea of unity; but for him gestalt is a new quality which arises as the result of the interaction of definite elements of the phenomenon. In 1932, Pavlov wrote, "The theory of reflex behavior rests on three basic principles of precise scientific research: first, the principle of determinism, i.e., there is a stimulus, cause, a reason for any given behavior or effect; second, the principle of analysis and synthesis, i.e., the primary division of the whole into its parts, its units, and then once again the gradual reconstitution of the whole from its elements; and third, the principle of structure, i.e., the distribution of force acting in space, the timing of dynamics to structure" (Pavlov, 1949). It is worth emphasizing again that the "reconstitution of the whole from its elements" must not be understood as simple summation, but as true reproduction of the whole as the result of interaction. Vatsuro accepts the following premises, which correspond to those of the theory of conditioned reflexes:

1. The behavior of the animal is integrated activity, the expression of both the analytical and integrative functions of the central nervous system.

2. The behavior of the animal is the result of the complex interaction of conditioned and unconditioned reflexes which lead to the formation of unified structures. They are qualitatively different from the elementary processes which gave rise to them.

3. The individual act of behavior represents a reaction provoked by the given stimulus but dependent upon the available qualitative-functional background of the central nervous system and traces of past stimuli as well as upon those conditioned reflex connections which the animal acquires in the process of his individual experience.

4. The conditioned reflex is not a strictly isolated reaction but rather the expression of the brain's synthesizing activity acting as a single organic unit.[1]

An experimental methodology has been worked out from this point of view. As has been affirmed in the numerous works of the Pavlovian school, it is possible to obtain conditioned reflexes to a sequential complex stimulus consisting of separate stimulus elements. A complex stimulus differs from any other complex, even one which consists of the same elements applied in a different order. Each object in the external world has a number of physical qualities, for example, color, form, weight, and elasticity, which interact with the various analyzers of the organism. In other words, the object is a complex of separate stimuli which act simultaneously on our senses. If a temporary connection is established between the object and some kind of unconditioned function of the organism, the object acts first of all by means of those of its qualities which most forcefully correspond to the perceptual abilities of the given animal. This makes possible the comparison of the relative importance of various analyzers.

All of Vatsuro's experiments were conducted on a male chimpanzee named Rafael. This chimpanzee came to the laboratory in 1933, and in the course of 9 years various experiments were conducted on him. Vatsuro began experimenting with him in 1937, after Pavlov's death. The animal lived in a three-room apartment consisting of a sleeping room, a dining room, and a large glass-enclosed pen. During the summers he regularly spent many hours in the open air. Despite the painstaking care and strict regimen, Rafael had pneumonia twice, dysentery once, and several colds. When the experiments began Rafael was 12 years old and weighed 64 kg.; that is, he was a full-grown male. This had its difficult aspects. He had a stormy temperament and tremendous physical strength which more than once terrorized the experimenters. However, Vatsuro emphasizes the "nobility"

---

1. *Editors' note:* It hardly seems necessary to call attention to the striking difference between these "premises," particularly the last, which form the basis for an analysis of complex behavior in terms of conditioning, and the formulations of such learning theorists as Hull and Osgood. The understanding of conditioning by Soviet Pavlovians and American learning theorists has been of a radically different sort. This difference is evident in the present as well as in other chapters in this volume.

of Rafael's character. For instance, Rafael never attacked the attendants without warning. When preparing to commit an aggressive act he would assume an upright position, walk in circles lightly knocking on the wall with the back of his hand. When he first approached an opponent, Rafael would only tap him lightly with his hand as if to "challenge" him symbolically. Then he would literally throw himself on the opponent, dragging him by the feet and grabbing him with his strong teeth. Such attacks were not without their dangers. Therefore, it became necessary to find some means of defense. At first a stick was used, but this was more dangerous for his trainer than for the chimpanzee, for Rafael would rapidly disarm the opponent, and in his hands the stick became a threatening weapon. Finally a stick with many nails protruding from it was used. This was directed at the chimpanzee when he behaved aggressively and was enough to suppress his attempts at attack.

Because of his growth it became necessary to change the conditions of Rafael's enclosure: he learned to break the glass with his hand and escape. Large iron cells were constructed. He was led from cell to cell in a closed vehicle. From time to time the animal was taken to a forest and set free. When Rafael won his own freedom by breaking the windows and running away he would become very disobedient. It was necessary to devise a very cunning method in order to capture him. The hunters of the neighborhood were asked to set off a cannonade of blank cartridges around the chimpanzee. Then Rafael would fall into a panic, throw himself on his trainer, and allow himself to be led back without opposition. It is interesting that on those occasions when he was set free he showed not the slightest desire to run away. He always stayed very close to the trainer and would become anxious when the latter walked away.

After a time Rafael changed in his behavior toward the bed which was situated in his bedroom. Instead of lying down on the mattress and covering himself with the blanket, he tore the mattress apart and made a primitive nest of its contents. Therefore it was necessary to relinquish this "anthropomorphic" device and simply give him fresh hay or straw. Every day before he went to sleep Rafael shoveled the hay around so that he surrounded his body with a bolster, paying no attention to the litter inside the nest. His body lay on the bare boards and only his head and feet rested on the hay.

Rafael was fed three times a day. He was given fresh and canned fruit, bread and cocoa made with milk and sugar. He had an immense appetite which corresponded to his powerful build and great physical activity. In the course of a day Rafael ate about 4.5 kg. of various food products and drank three liters of cocoa.

The chimpanzee was prone to respiratory infections. The apartment in which he was kept had an automatically regulated temperature of 25–30 degrees centigrade; the humidity of the air was maintained by means of a fountain. The deficiency of ultraviolet light was corrected by the periodic use of a quartz lamp. Rafael took very well to all kinds of physiotherapy and willingly submitted to the doctor's examinations, but he did not like medicine. He was delighted with hot water bottles, compresses, radiant heat, and, especially, warm baths. The sight of an attendant with rolled-up shirt sleeves or the sound of water running in the bath filled him with ecstasy. However, there was yet another reason for this reaction. While bathing he regularly consumed the soap suds with great relish.

In order to protect the animal from infection the attending personnel were examined daily by a doctor. Outsiders, as a rule, were not allowed into the laboratory. All these precautions preserved the animal's health under the conditions of Leningrad's climate for a period of 9 years.

The first series of experiments was devoted to a study of the speed of formation of conditioned visual and kinesthetic associations. A box measuring 35 by 35 by 40 cm. with doors facing the animal was placed within arm's reach in front of his cage. In front of the box on the floor lay two sticks which, in the first experiments, differed only in color (one black and one white), and in subsequent experiments, only in weight. In a series of visual problems the "correct" stick was the black one. The animal had to put the stick into an opening in the roof of the box and open the door, in return for which a food reward was made available. When the sticks differed only in color it was very difficult for the chimpanzee to acquire the skill. For a long time the animal executed the task at almost a chance level. The position of the sticks seemed much more important than their colors. He mastered the task only after 161 trials, but from that time on, Rafael never made an error. In the following sessions the sticks differed only in weight: one weighed 1,600 gm., the other 900 gm. They were the same size and of the same dark yellow color. In this case the habit was acquired much more easily. It was clear that he was making the discrimination after only 16 attempts, and after 5 days there were no more errors.

After the chimpanzee learned to make these discriminations without error, it was difficult to tell which was more important for him. Therefore, a third series of experiments was conducted in which the two discriminative attributes were in conflict. In this case the positive visual cue of color (black) was united with the negative kinesthetic cue (heavy) (in the previous series the "correct" stick was the light one). At first Rafael chose the black, heavy stick (visual choice), held it in the air for a moment, then laid it on the ground, again picked it up and once more laid it on the ground without trying to open the box; then he picked up the white, light stick and placed it in the opening of the box, thus obtaining the reward. The next time the chimpanzee picked up both sticks, held them in the air for a moment (comparing their weights), and then placed the white stick in the opening.

Apparently the mechanism of the whole process corresponds to the mechanisms of the so-called ultraparadoxical phase in the formation of the conditioned reflex when the positive stimulus acquires negative aspects, and vice versa. In this experiment, two contradictory conditioned signals were united in the black stick—the positive color black and the negative heavy weight. The inhibiting action of the greater weight was dominant and therefore inhibited the positive influence of the black color. As a result of positive induction the contradictory white color acquired the sign of the positive stimulus. This corresponds precisely with the consistent results of experiments with dogs and obeys the laws of conditioned reflexes. The inference that kinesthetic signs of the object (in this case, weight) are more meaningful for the animal than visual cues was quite important for us.

Vatsuro studied the interaction of the separate components of a complex stimulus using the same technique. Now two sticks which differed in several ways were given to the animal. They were two metal pipes of the same size. One contained water heated to a temperature of 17 degrees centigrade, and the other to 50 degrees. The warm stick was blue; the cold was red. The warm stick was heavy and was consistently placed to the left of the red stick.[2] In other words, Rafael had to distinguish the red stick (light, cold, right) from the blue stick (heavy, warm, left). The first stick was negative; the second was positive (led to the reward). A further complication resulted from the fact that, for 2 to 3 months preceding this experiment, greater weight and high temperature had been used in other experiments as negative cues. Rafael began to show little interest in food so a live cat was used as a reward instead. The cat was placed in the box and allowed to run out whenever the roof was opened. This was a powerful stimulus for the chimpanzee.

In the following sessions Rafael picked up the blue stick, but immediately put it down and put the red stick in the opening of the box. In further experiments the chimpanzee always chose the red stick first (negative). Only after 71 attempts did the animal react positively to the blue stick. There is no doubt that in the course of acquiring the habit the animal was "guided" not by visual perception but by direct contact with the stick. The correct choice followed only after this direct contact was made. Thus, the choice was based on conditioned-reflex associations, which in turn were based on kinesthetic and warmth cues. Only later did the animal learn to distinguish the sticks visually as well.

In order to study the weight factor, all other factors were excluded; with this in mind the animal was given two blue sticks of the same temperature. One weighed 5,350 gm., the other 3,650 gm. The relative positions of the sticks were changed. Now, on the basis of weight alone, the animal made

2. *Editors' note:* This procedure seems to introduce the possibility of position being used as the critical cue. The description is not full enough to permit an exact evaluation of this possibility.

a completely clear distinction. That is, in this case the conditioned-reflex associations not only were retained but were significantly strengthened.

Analogous experiments were conducted in order to analyze the influence of visual cues. This influence turned out to be rather significant, although the number of errors indicates that the visual associations were weaker than the kinesthetic.

Finally, the influence of temperature was studied. The influence of temperature analyzers was not significant. The number of correct reactions was no higher than 60 per cent, indicating that they were the results of chance choices.

In a series of experiments, the method of conflicting cues was used, which required the participation of different analyzers—for example, combining positive and negative cues in one stick: blue color with low temperature. It is interesting to note that, when weight was reinforced, the kinesthetic factor dominated: Rafael consistently chose the heavy (positive cue) red (negative cue) stick. However, when the kinesthetic factor was eliminated and two sticks of the same weight were used, he always chose the blue stick (positive cue). Consequently, when the kinesthetic factor was operative, the visual factor was inhibited. This inhibition had a certain degree of positive significance. Despite the actual reinforcement of the negative cue (red color combined with the greater weight), the significance of blue was not eliminated.

Vatsuro devoted a series of experiments to the study of the so-called "aha-reaction." By this we mean the sudden solution of a task, the animal seemingly "hitting upon" the solution. The following behavior is characteristic: after a series of unsuccessful attempts the animal stops all movement and then he may suddenly arrive at the solution after a short rest. This behavior is in complete contrast to trial-and-error learning, where the solution has a chance character. Vatsuro agrees with this interpretation when it applies to human behavior but is more cautious about its application to animals. The insightful solution passes through three phases: (1) the phase of chaotic activity; (2) the phase of external calm; and (3) the phase of adequate response. A physiological interpretation of these phenomena is entirely possible. In the first phase, under the influence of the animal's orienting reflex the kinesthetic analyzer is aroused. This is followed by chaotic manipulations. Since these manipulations have nothing to do with the solution, they are not reinforced. As a result the reaction is extinguished and inhibition sets in. Secondary arousal of the kinesthetic analyzer now occurs under the influence of remote impulses, most likely of a visual nature, since the animal makes no attempt at solution in the second phase. The third phase is based on the animal's utilization of remote conditioned-reflex associations. In all cases of the "aha" type of solution we are dealing not with some kind of completely new reaction but always with the reproduction of already existing and earlier acquired connections and associations.

A rather complicated method was devised to analyze this problem. Two boxes, one on top of the other, were placed before the chimpanzee. A metal handle which could be turned easily was placed in the wall of the lower box. Some kind of bait was placed in the upper box. In the first stage of the experiment Rafael had to turn the handle twice counterclockwise. At the end of the second turn a bell rang, and in 2 to 3 seconds the door opened and the animal received the reward. After 12 attempts Rafael began to turn the handle in the necessary direction, using his left hand most of the time. After 28 attempts so well established was the association of his handle-turning response that the animal tried to open the door by himself without waiting for the bell. However, the reward was not given to him before the bell. The fact that the bell alone had not become a signal for the reward was established by 46 trials on which the bell was sounded immediately after the food was placed in the box, without waiting for Rafael to turn the handle. However, Rafael did not try to open the door directly, but turned the handle instead. The same thing occurred after 223 trials.

A small alteration was made in the organization of the experiment: the boxes were placed a short distance apart: the food was placed in one and the handle in the wall of the other. After 285 trials Rafael discovered that the bell was a signal. When the bell rang he stood up, went to the box with the handle, turned it twice, and then turned to the box which contained the food. However, even after this the bell was a weak and unreliable signal. Hence the kinesthetic analyzer has greater significance than the auditory analyzer because the connection between turning the handle and food was formed much earlier and with greater ease than the connection between the bell and the reward. Apparently the stimulus of the kinesthetic analyzer evoked negative induction which greatly hampered the establishment of conditioned reflexes from other analyzers. Constant inhibition of the kinesthetic associations (the animal was not reinforced for running to the reward box without a previous bell), on the contrary, facilitated the rise of other conditioned associations.

In order to prove the validity of this interpretation, it was necessary to evoke special and profound inhibition of the kinesthetic analyzer. One of a series of such experiments will be described. After the food was put in the box Rafael turned the handle twice and, without waiting for the bell, went for the reward. Since he found no reward (inhibition of kinesthetic association) he returned to the handle, turned it several times and again looked for the reward, trying to open the box in order to get it. Once again he went to the handle and from there again to the box with the food. Finally, the chimpanzee fell into a rage, stamped his feet, and turned away from that box. Ten to fifteen seconds later the bell sounded. Rafael immediately approached the food box and received the reward. This behavior was unsystematically repeated several times.

In the following experiments a button which rang a bell was placed on the floor. Rafael quickly learned to press the button—not to receive a reward, but simply as play. After he mastered this skill the previous experiment was repeated. In 11 trials Rafael, after the box was loaded with food, would approach the box with the handle, turn it once and go for the food; when he received none, he would return, turn the handle several times and again turn to the reward. Again he returned to the handle, turned it 8 times, from time to time glancing at the button and again attempting to get the reward. Finally he returned to the handle, turned it, sat beside the button, and began to spit on the floor. After 3 to 4 seconds, he suddenly rose and pressed the button. The door opened and Rafael hurried to the reward.

The described phenomenon fits the "aha response" precisely. In this case the animal's sudden solution of the problem was based on already existing conditioned-reflex associations (press the button—bell). Secondly, the solution occurred after repeated inhibition of the kinesthetic factor (turning the handle without producing the bell did not lead to the reward). This was accompanied by a transition from stormy activity to almost complete calm. The chimpanzee was never observed to turn on the bell without previous severe inhibition of the kinesthetic response.

Generally speaking, the greatest error in Köhler's view is his antihistoricity: he takes no account of the fact that the chimpanzee has his own past during which he has acquired many habits, and that he turns to them in the experimental situation.

When the animal reaches for a fruit with the aid of a stick, this is by no means a new situation for him. Under natural conditions the chimpanzee manipulates branches and twigs. In captivity he does the same with the stick. The animal uses the stick to thrust into the opening of the case, to catch ants, to drink wine mixed with water out of a tub, to dig in the ground, to kill insects, and so on. It is not surprising that, when the animal cannot reach the fruit with his hand, he uses the stick as an extension of his hand. The point is not that behavior is determined by the unity of the visual field as Köhler thinks, but by the presence of existing temporary associations which were acquired earlier. In the absence of a stick the chimpanzee tries to pull the fruit to him with any object at hand: an old shoe, a torn hat, or a stone. From the point of view of the theory of conditioned reflexes, the animal's behavior is completely natural.

Vatsuro also explains the animal's preparation of tools by a hypothesis completely different from Köhler's. Köhler does not doubt the fact of the chimpanzee's use of tools, but he maintains that the ape *always* manipulates sticks, twigs, or straw in order to insert them into all possible cracks and openings. The chimpanzee Sultan was to a certain extent already prepared to solve the tasks set before him. It was nothing new for him to place one bamboo stick in the opening of another. It is likely that he would do the same thing, while playing, without any kind of enticement.

In his experiments, Vatsuro gave Rafael two components with which to construct a stick. It was possible to note the very moment at which the animal grasped the essence of the solution to the task. Rafael tries to get the fruit first with one stick and then with the other, falls into a rage and throws both sticks in the air. Later he once again shows interest in the sticks, stubbornly attempting to get the reward, but as before, without success. On the following day he again tries both sticks, becomes angry. Then he sits down and examines one of the sticks, picking at its specks and uneven spots with his fingers. Suddenly he notices the opening at the end of one stick and scratches at it with his nails. He places the stick vertically with the opening upwards and sticks a few pieces of yesterday's food in the opening. Then he places the thinner stick in the opening of the thicker one, but does not use the lengthened stick to get the fruit. Instead he breaks it apart; then he again puts the two sticks together, repeating this operation several times. After a fairly long time he used the stick to get the fruit. Despite this, Rafael continued to take the stick apart and put it together again for the sake of play. On the following day after various attempts he finally joined both sticks and used it to get the food. However, a bit later the chimpanzee would again attempt to reach the food with just one stick. He joined them only when this did not work.

After a 10-day interval the experiments were repeated under slightly different conditions. In this case the thicker stick had three side openings, in addition to the one on the end. Rafael immediately began to manipulate both sticks separately. Then he sat beside the cage which separated him from the fruit and began to examine both sticks attentively. Holding the thick stick in an inclined position, he placed the thinner one in the center side opening of the thicker stick. The result was a stick in the shape of the letter *T*, that is, a "tool" which was no longer than its components and which was, in addition, extremely awkward to use since it got caught in the bars of the cage. Despite this, Rafael stubbornly attempted to use it to draw the fruit to him. Only after repeated failures did he refuse to make further attempts and, overcoming the difficulty, pulled the sticks back into the cage. Then the chimpanzee separated the sticks and began to put the thin stick in the various openings of the thicker one. He once again put one stick in the side opening of the other and he once again tried to reach the fruit without success. After many incorrect combinations and separations of the sticks he finally joined them correctly, but did not try to reach the fruit. He continued to join and separate them in various combinations.

An analysis of these facts permits us to choose the moments which were important for an understanding of the mechanism of the solution: (1) the correct solution did not occur immediately; (2) repetition of the experiment did not evoke immediate reproduction of the previous solution; (3) Rafael joined the sticks even in the absence of the reward; (4) originally the sticks were joined without effectively lengthening the tool as a whole; (5) in the process of repeating the experiments, the animal, as a rule, repeated all the previous errors. All this does not indicate an intellectual solution of the task. The manipulation of the sticks cannot be considered a part of the whole process of food acquisition since it has its own stimulation. It may occur with the same success both with and without a reward. There is no doubt that the aim of manipulating the sticks is not to lengthen the stick. The ape's frequent errors even after the solution of the task indicate the absence of his comprehension of the situation.

At the same time all of Rafael's behavior indicates the arousal of temporary conditioned associations. It is necessary to reckon seriously with the fact that the intensity of the chimpanzee's aspirations towards the goal in the course of the experiment wavers within broad boundaries—from maximal aspiration to almost complete inhibition. The ape's entire life is bound up with clearly expressed orienting reflexes which depend on ecological conditions. Inhibition of an arbitrary reaction evokes a sudden and significant strengthening of the orienting reflex. This explains the so-called curiosity of the ape and his interest in the trivial details of situations. By evoking the champanzee's desire for food, making the food inaccessible to the length of his hand, and at the same time inhibiting this desire with deterrent conditions (a stick too short for the task), we evoke the inhibition of the earlier orienting reflex. As a result, the objects closest at hand, especially those which the chimpanzee actually holds in his hands, become the object of increased attention. Rafael notices the side openings in the thicker stick and puts into them anything he has in his hand, including the end of the thinner stick. When this reaction is repeated time after time without producing any results, inhibition naturally sets in. Then the sight of food lying on the floor once again becomes a strong stimulus which evokes aspirations for the food. Now the act of placing one stick in the other serves as a means of acquiring the food. The effect, obviously, depends on how the sticks were put together. This, of course, could be a matter of accident. In Köhler's experiments there was only one possible way to put the sticks together, and, consequently, the imaginary single-mindedness of the chimpanzee's behavior followed.

Vatsuro did not directly observe the construction of a pyramid with boxes or pole vaulting. In the course of the four years preceding Vatsuro's research, Rafael was used repeatedly in various biological experiments in which he worked with boxes and pole vaulting. These experiments corroborated the phenomena which were described by Köhler. In all observations involving the construction of a pyramid of blocks, the significant motor skill manifested itself as a generalized tendency to "place upon." For example, in the experiments of 1934, after unsuccessful attempts to obtain the reward from a height of two boxes, Rafael grabbed a third box and put it on his head! Similar facts speak clearly of the decisive role of kinesthetic associations.

Vatsuro (1948) devoted several experiments to the detour (*Umweg*) problem. A wide board is placed on the floor in front of the cage. The food is placed behind a 5-cm.-high horizontal plank which is placed parallel to the cage behind the board. Rafael was given a long stick. The animal immediately used it to pull the food to himself, but the food was blocked by the plank. Then the chimpanzee by means of forceful movements behaves in such a way that the food slides along the plank to the edge and rolls around it. Then it was a simple matter to obtain the food with the stick.

The conditions of the experiment were gradually complicated by constructing a labyrinth of planks with openings. (See Figure 1–1.) In system *a* the ape was easily able to knock the food out of the labyrinth and draw it to himself with the stick. In system *b,* in addition to the opening on the side op-

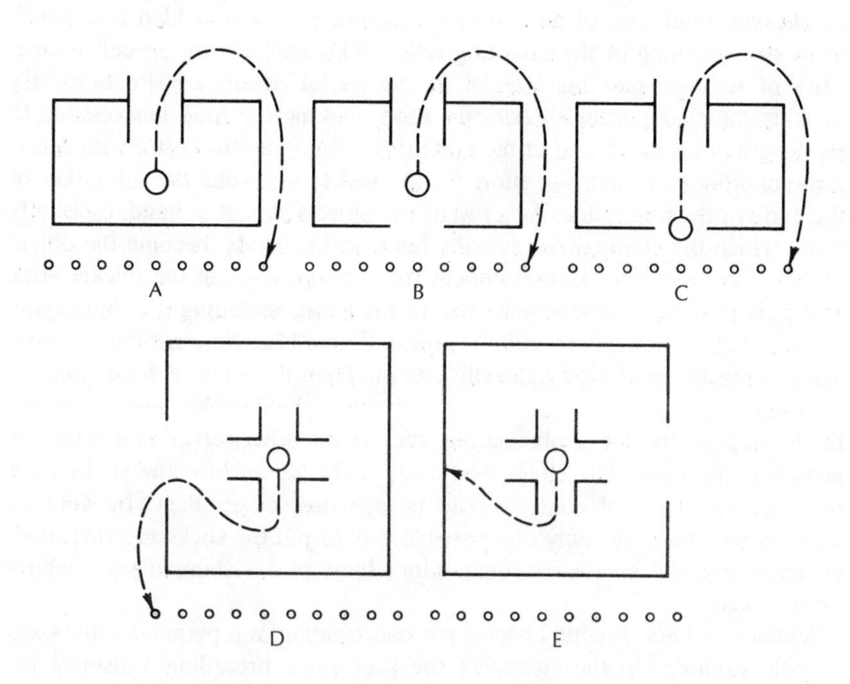

Figure 1–1. Plan of mazes used in Vatsuro's experiments.

posite the ape, we see a second opening closer to the animal. Despite the fact that now the solution of the problem consists simply in drawing the food to himself, Rafael behaves as he did before, pushing the food out of the labyrinth and only then pulling it in. In system *c* the food is so close to the animal that only minimal movement of the stick is necessary to obtain it. But Rafael stubbornly pushes it away and only then draws it to himself. It is clear that adequate behavior, that is, behavior corresponding to the given conditions, develops slowly and gradually. The ultimate condition for obtaining the reward was pushing it out through the opening in the labyrinth. This evoked the firm association "food—opening." But the kinesthetic association consistently interfered with the visual association. These relationships arose during the subsequent trials when the associations were firmly established. But the changed conditions of the task (altering the scheme of the labyrinth) did not change the animal's behavior. In two subsequent cases, *d* and *e*, Rafael at first responded correctly (in task *d*), then once again repeated the previous movements which made no sense (in labyrinth *e*). The animal's behavior does not lend itself to interpretations in terms of "scrutinizing" the situation, but it is comprehensible from a physiological point of view since it indicates the predominance (already well known to us) of the kinesthetic analyzer, which in this case impairs visual discrimination.

In earlier experiments Rafael learned to construct a pyramid, using five different shapes which could be united with the aid of pins and which fit into the opening only in a definite sequence. The ape mastered this task and never erred in his choice of the corresponding parts of the pyramid. At first glance the kinesthetic factor plays no role in this behavior. On each trial the respective positions of the scattered parts were different in order to avoid automatic movements and to make his movements a function of the changing visual situation. In order to clarify the role of the kinesthetic factor in the animal's behavior, five parts of the pyramid at one third the size of the others were prepared. On the first trial the ape's movements were helpless and chaotic, but in the end Rafael suddenly solved the problem; in the second trial his behavior was already more goal-directed, and the animal soon learned to build the pyramid without error. Characteristically, from the very beginning Rafael immediately picked up the necessary part of the pyramid, but turned it over in his hands several times and threw it away.

This indicates that kinesthetic and visual factors were associated together in one complex whole. When the parts of the pyramid were smaller only by half, the visual factor changed to an insignificant degree, but the kinesthetic altered very noticeably. The latter inhibited the influence of the visual factor. This indicates that positive and negative visual associations are formed on the basis of earlier existing kinesthetic associations. In this way visual associations create conditioned reflexes of a higher order, becoming cues which are reinforced by means of kinesthetic stimuli. This is shown by the arousal of the motor habit. In the beginning a definite type of movement is established which becomes more precise with time. Rafael takes one part of the pyramid and simply places it on another. Later, besides the motions of lifting and releasing, rotary motions appear which permit the pins to fit into the corresponding openings. Gradually the quantity of incorrect choices decreases: in the beginning the animal discards the incorrect figure only when he is unable to unite it with another (kinesthetic criterion), then he discards the inappropriate part immediately after picking it up (visual criterion). Finally, he makes the correct choice solely on the basis of visual cues. In this complicated system of associations the visual factor is the first signal stimulus. It is as if it is reinforced by the kinesthetic stimulus and the latter is ultimately associated with the unconditioned reinforcement (food reward). Once again, the enormous role of kinesthetic factors in the life of the chimpanzee is confirmed.

Experiments with extinguishing fire led to the same conclusion. A tall box with a hole in the side wall was placed in the cage. Directly under the opening a tin box filled with alcohol was placed on a small platform. Fruit was placed in the opening and the alcohol was set on fire in order to prevent the chimpanzee from reaching the reward with his hand. After many trials Rafael learned to put out the fire. He was able to pick up the tin container, go to the water tank, open the faucet, pour water in the container, and thus extinguish the fire. After this habit was established certain complications were introduced. The ape was given a container with a hole in the bottom and a long wooden stopper. Rafael long and stubbornly tried to fill the container with water, but since he was unable to use the stopper, the water leaked out through the opening. Then he was given a metal ball which, if placed in the container, rolled to the opening and covered it.

The first solution may be considered accidental. Rafael, playing, put the ball in his mouth, looked at the inaccessible reward, opened the faucet, took some water in his mouth, and spit it into the container. The ball fell into the container with the water and closed the opening. Now he was able to extinguish the fire and obtain the fruit. Since the chimpanzee's actions evoked the unconditioned reinforcement, he repeatedly put the ball in his mouth, filled his mouth with water, and spit them both into the container. If the ball fell into the container first, the chimpanzee even in this case behaved stereotypically: removed the ball from the container, put it in his mouth, filled his mouth with water, and then spit them into the cup together and extinguished the fire. As in the previous cases, the animal's behavior seems unintelligent. However, it has great meaning if interpreted from a physiological point of view, that is, if one takes into account the stimulus and the reaction, acknowledging the dominant significance of the kinesthetic analyzer which was the basis for a firmly established habit.

Even more interesting was the ape's behavior in a different situation which could be solved in several ways, which the animal already knew. Rafael was able to open the apparatus in two ways. The apparatus looked like a box with doors. The doors opened when a metal handle remote from the box was pulled out, but closed as soon as the handle was released. The chimpanzee was unable to reach the fruit with his hand since the handle was too far away. The problem could be solved in two ways: either by pushing a cord through the opening in the handle or by driving into the floor a nail to which the stretched-out handle clung. Rafael had learned both means separately. He was given a cord, a nail, and a hammer. He picked up all three objects and prepared to drive the nail in at the necessary point, but the cord in his hand hindered him. Then he threw the nail away and began to push the string through the opening in the handle, still holding the hammer. Then he placed the nail in a crack in the floor and began to wind the string around it. Finally the animal fell into a rage and ceased working completely. These chaotic actions can be interpreted as a battle between different mutually exclusive tendencies. In the course of the battle first one triumphs, then the other. Such a state is possible when the strength of both habits is approximately the same.

We observe a different phenomenon when the strength of the habits is not the same or some are older and others are more recent. In such a situation the existing associations reproduce themselves by turn, according to the degree of remoteness. Here is an example. Rafael was able to extinguish a flame not only with water which he poured into the container from the tank, but in the absence of water as well. In the absence of water he would urinate into the container and pour the urine on the fire. Moreover, he could scoop the water from various open tanks with the container. In one experiment, the chimpanzee was placed on one of two rafts floating in the lake. The other raft carried a water tank with a faucet. Rafael was on the neighboring raft, which had a box containing a mug. The box opened with the aid of a special block which had to be placed in a special opening. The chimpanzee was able to do this. Finally, on one side lay both a long bamboo pole and the previously described apparatus with the fire. When the experimenter placed a reward in that apparatus, Rafael would open the box correctly, obtain the mug, join the two rafts using the pole, go over to the neighboring raft, and pour water into the mug, ceaselessly turning the faucet. Then he urinated into the mug, returned to the first raft, and extinguished the fire. The third time the animal again tried to pour water into the mug from the tank, then tried to urinate once again. Finally, he scooped water from the lake and extinguished the fire with it.

These various experiments clearly indicate that, at least in the beginning phases of the establishment of habits, the kinesthetic components and kinesthetic associations are heavily dominant. The significance of objects is conditioned not to the activating structure of the situation, as Köhler thinks, but by the ape's active familiarity with the objects acquired in the course of manipulating them. Such a formulation permits us to substitute for Köhler's idealistic interpretation a strictly materialistic explanation.

At the end of his book Vatsuro discusses the question of intellect. This is a difficult problem because of the absence of a complete physiological theory based on the study of conditioned reflexes. Pavlov saw the specific characteristic of human thought processes in the existence of "a second signal system," that is, speech. "If our senses and concepts of the surrounding world are the first signals of reality for us, concrete signals, then speech which is above all a kinesthetic stimulus going from the speech organs to the cortex is the second signal, the signal of signals. It is the abstraction of reality which allows us to generalize. This is the basis of our extra, *specifically human, higher reason*" (1949). Pavlov did not deny that animals have the ability to reason, but he felt that reason in animals is particularly concrete. It is impossible to understand the genesis of human intellect without knowing the origins of its rudiments in animals. " 'Rational' behavior," writes Rubinshtein, "must be adequate to the situation, utilizing the correlation between objects expediently; this expedient behavior must be a new act for the given individual and must be achieved not blindly, accidentally, but as the result of cognitive discernment of objective conditions essential for action" (1946). In short, rational behavior is associated with the utilization and reworking of past experiences.

In conclusion, let us sum up the results of Soviet research on the behavior of those apes closest to man. Apes accurately perceive the various cues of objects (color, form, size); they retain the traces of their perceptions, which are imprinted as visual models, as concepts of the objects; they are capable of generalized concepts. Apes can work out complex visual-motor skills. They have elementary, concrete, figurative reasoning (intellect) and are capable of elementary abstraction as well as generalization. In their possession of these characteristics they approach the human mind. However, their intellect differs qualitatively from man's. The latter has language, communicates by means of words which act as signals of the signals, as a system of codes. The ape's sounds, which are extremely varied, express only his emotional state and do not have a directive function. Apes have only the primary signal system of reality. This is true of all other animals.

As the experimental results show, apes are capable of complex forms of activity such as construction and even tool-using. Although they can build a figure of several parts by imitation of a model, they never attempt to construct something according to a mental image as do children. They can imitate man's use of a pencil by drawing various lines on paper, but they never attempt to reproduce even the simplest object from their environment.

Tool-using behavior in the ape has certain special characteristics. He uses auxiliary objects as tools, but they have no specific significance for him and he destroys them as soon as they fill the immediate need. Higher apes are able to alter an unsuitable object in order to make it fit a specific task; they can even construct a tool from several parts, but unification of parts was done unintentionally, accidentally, during play. The associations which the ape establishes are space-time relationships and not cause-effect relationships. This was revealed when the experimental conditions were altered and the apes immediately lost the correct path to the solution of the problem.[3]

References

Biryukovich, P. V. The formation of a conditioned response to relative cues in lower apes. In V. P. Protopopov (Ed.), *Investigations of higher nervous activity in the natural experiment.* Kiev: Gosmedizdat, 1950.

Bowden, D. Primate behavioral research in the USSR: The Sukhumi medico-biological station. *Folia Primat.,* 1966, *4,* 346–360.

Denisov, P. K. The analytic and synthetic function of the cerebral hemispheres in the chimpanzee. *J. higher nerv. Activity,* 1948, *8,* 845–854. (Published in English by Pergamon Press, London, 1958).

Hayes, C. *The ape in our house.* New York: Harper, 1951.

Kellogg, W. N., and Kellogg, L. A. *The ape and the child.* New York: McGraw-Hill, 1933.

Khil'chenko, A. E. The formation of responses to relative stimuli (size relations) in lower apes. In V. P. Protopopov (Ed.), *Investigations of higher nervous activity in the natural experiment.* Kiev: Gosmedizdat, 1950 (a).

Khil'chenko, A. E. The formation of elementary and complex habits in lower apes. In V. P. Protopopov (Ed.), *Investigations of higher nervous activity in the natural experiment.* Kiev: Gosmedizdat, 1950 (b).

Khil'chenko, A. E. Investigation of the higher nervous activity of anthropoids (chimpanzees). In *Problems of physiology.* Kiev: Izd. Akad. Nauk SSSR, 1953, No. 4.

Klüver, H. *Behavior mechanisms in monkeys.* Chicago, 1961.

Köhler, W. *The mentality of apes.* New York: Harcourt, Brace, 1925.

Ladygina-Kots, N. N. *The young of the chimpanzees and the human child: Their instincts, emotions, games, habits and expressive movements.* Moscow: Izd. Gos. Darvinskogo Muzea, 1935.

Ladygina-Kots, N. N. The development of the mind in the process of the evolution of organisms. *Sovet. Nauka,* 1958.

3. *Editors' note:* Tool-using behavior of apes in their natural habitat has more recently been extensively observed and documented in detail by Jane Van Lawick-Goodall.

Ladygina-Kots, N. N. *Activity involving the use of tools and construction in higher apes (chimpanzees)*. Izd. Akad. Nauk SSSR, 1959.

Levykina, N. F. Features of the activity of lower apes involving objects. In *Proceedings of the First Congress of the Psychological Society*. Vol. 2. Moscow, 1959.

Markova, A. Y. The process of elementary abstraction in lower apes. *Vop. Psikhol.*, 1961, No. 6.

Novoselova, S. L. Formation of the habit of using a stick in chimpanzees. *Sovet. Antropol.*, 1959, No. 4.

Pavlov, I. P. *Pavlovian Wednesdays*. Vols. 1–3. Moscow: Izd. Akad. Nauk SSSR, 1949.

Protopopov, V. P. The formation of motor habits in animals using the obstruction method. In V. P. Protopopov (Ed.), *Investigations of higher nervous activity in the natural experiment*. Kiev: Gosmedizdat, 1950. (a)

Protopopov, V. P. The processes of abstraction and generalization in animals and man. In V. P. Protopopov (Ed.), *Investigations of higher nervous activity in the natural experiment*. Kiev: Gosmedizat, 1950. (b)

Razran, G. Raphael's "idealless" behavior. *J. comp. physiol. Psychol.*, 1961, *54*, 366–367.

Roginskii, G. A. *The mind of the anthropoid ape*. Leningrad, 1945.

Rubinshtein, S. L. *Fundamentals of general psychology*. Moscow, 1946.

Rushkevich, E. A. The motor habits of the lower apes. In V. P. Protopopov (Ed.), *Investigations of higher nervous activity in the natural experiment*. Kiev: Gosmedizdat, 1950.

Tikh, N. A. The ontogeny of behavior in apes. Formation of the grasping and clasping reflexes. *Trudy Suk. Biol. Stan. Akad. Med. Nauk SSSR*, 1949. (a)

Tikh, N. A. Vocal conditioned reflexes in apes. *Novosti Med.* 1949, *4*. (b)

Tikh, N. A. The ontogenesis of the behavior of apes in the light of the problems of anthropogenesis. In *Materials of a Conference on Psychology (1–6 July 1955)*. Izd. Akad. Pedag. Nauk RSFSR, 1957.

Ulanova, L. I. The formation of conditioned signs, indicating a need for food in apes. In V. P. Protopopov (Ed.), *Investigations of higher nervous activity in the natural experiment*. Kiev: Gosmedizdat, 1950.

Vagner, V. A. Biological foundations of comparative psychology. *St. in Psychobiol.*, 1913.

Vatsuro, E. G. *Investigations of the higher nervous activity of anthropoids (chimpanzees)*. Leningrad: Akad. Med. Nauk SSSR, 1948.

Voronin, L. G. *The comparative physiology of higher nervous activity*. Izd. Moskov. Gos. Univer., 1957.

Yerkes, R. M. *Almost human*. New York: 1925.

Zuckerman, S. *The social life of monkeys and apes*. New York: Harcourt, Brace, 1932.

2

The Origin and Development of Conditioned Reflexes in Early Childhood

N. I. Kasatkin

EDITORS' INTRODUCTION

The use of conditioned-reflex methodology in the study of developmental psychology has a very long history in Russian science. Prior to the Revolution, Krasnogorskii studied salivary conditioning in children. In the mid-1920's, as part of Bekhterev's general program for the development of a general, objective psychological system, "reflexological" studies of newborn infants were begun by Figurin and Denisova. The published accounts of these early studies of the ontogeny of conditioned reflexes are now bibliographic rarities which are difficult to obtain even in the U.S.S.R. The best summary of this research in English may be found in Razran's monograph (1933). For a brief account of very recent Soviet efforts in this area, Brackbill's (1962) account is quite good.

N. I. Kasatkin is an intellectual descendant of Bekhterev. He is presently Director of the Laboratory for the Study of the Higher Nervous Activity of Children, Sechenov Institute of Evolutionary Physiology, in Leningrad.

The Origin of the First Conditioned Reflexes[1]

How do the first conditioned reflexes arise? At what age do they first appear? Answers to these questions are contradictory, encompassing a wide age range. Thus, some authors believe that conditioned associations occur in the fetus during the last months of pregnancy, while others deny their presence even in the child's first half-year of life. The former view was held by Watson (1934), who felt that "the acquisition of habits, without question, begins in the mother's uterus (there is no basis to assume that conditioned reflexes do not arise there)." However, as its author acknowledges, this opinion was purely speculative. Actual attempts to form conditioned reflexes in the fetus during the last 2 months of pregnancy failed to yield convincing results (Sontag and Wallace, 1934; Spelt, 1948). Similarly, the opposing opinion that conditioned reflexes do not exist in the first 6 months of life (Krasnogorskii, 1954) has proved incorrect. It has been shown experimentally that conditioned reflexes are formed in the course of the first or second month of the child's life. Subsequently, Krasnogorskii (1958) changed his point of view and asserted that the cortical cells of the newborn infant are sufficiently mature to allow the formation of conditioned reflexes in the first days after birth.

The results of experimental studies devoted to this question are both numerous and contradictory. Golubeva (1959) discovered that conditioned reflexes appear extraordinarily early in premature children. She showed that the conditioned sucking reflex can be developed in the third to tenth day of life if the conditioned stimulus is tactile stimulation of the skin of the cheek. She asserts that this reflex was developed even in a fetus of 20 to 30 days which was born weighing 790 grams. However, this interesting fact indicates no more than the expansion of the reflexogenous zone and the wider irradiation of excitation by a tactile stimulus. The early appearance of conditioned reflexes in the behavior of newborns who were fed at intervals of 3.3 or 4 hours was claimed by Bystroletova (1954). Most of the children, beginning at 3 to 5 days, manifested general agitation, sucking motions, and cries for several minutes before feeding. At 7 to 8 days this general agitation became more distinct. The reaction at 3 to 5 days was interpreted as the conditioned reflex at the time of feeding. However, there is another possible explanation. Before the feeding the hunger center is stimulated by "hungry" blood. Accordingly, motor activity, sucking motions, and cries are increased because of irradiation of arousal. If the child is fed at equal time intervals, arousal

1. *Editors' note:* The terms "response" and "reflex" are used almost interchangeably by both Soviet and American investigators of conditioning, and are so used in the discussion which follows.

of the hunger center occurs periodically, settles into a definite rhythm, and begins to regulate itself. Thus there is no basis for interpreting changes in agitation as evidence of conditioning.

Marquis (1931) studied conditioned reflexes in newborn children at an earlier age than did the previously mentioned workers. He began the development of a reflex to sound from the second day of life and found that a conditioned food reflex is formed by the fifth day. However, the criterion of cessation of motor activities and crying under the influence of sound which Marquis used is not promising. It is possible that the influence of sound in this experiment coincided with the increase of eating activity, and that the reduction of crying and movement encouraged the appearance of more distinct sucking movements.

More convincing facts were obtained in the study of food leucocytosis in newborn children (Krachkovskaya, 1959). The number of leucocytes increased during the hour after feeding in the majority of the children, beginning on the sixth day of life. This phenomenon may be viewed as an unconditioned response of the blood to the reception of food. Beginning with the eighth day, the number of leucocytes increased 15 minutes before feeding as well. This white-blood-cell reaction indicates the formation of a conditioned reflex to the time of feeding. This finding was checked by a change in the feeding routine: instead of 3-hour intervals, the feedings took place at 4-hour intervals. For a short time, the increase in the number of leucocytes occurred according to the old schedule. But since the conditioned reflex was not reinforced, 2 to 3 days after the change in routine it was extinguished and, instead, a response developed to the new feeding time. These facts indicate the rapidity with which the conditioned leucocytic reflex changed in response to the time of feeding, the rapidity of its extinction and, with the same rapidity (after 8 to 15 combinations), its adaptation to the new feeding time.

There has been an attempt to form a conditioned eyeblink reflex to a flash of light (Wenger, 1943). Several seconds before the light was turned on, the sole of the child's foot was scratched. The first signs of unstable conditioned reflexes appeared 4 to 8 days after birth, after 124 to 283 trials: for example, the child began to blink at the onset of the tactile stimulus—before the light was turned on. However, the reflex was sometimes very shaky, for no apparent reason, at 9 days after birth. In other cases, despite the cessation of the reinforcing light, the number of positive responses suddenly increased significantly. The control observations on newborns in whom the conditioned reflex had not been developed yielded very ambiguous results.

Generalizing from the experimental data, it might be said that, following the child's transition from intrauterine life, numerous new stimuli coincide with innate forms of nervous activity. Under the influence of these stimuli, very soon, possibly in the first days of life, the signs of extremely unstable conditioned associations appear. Another assumption is also possible: formation of conditioned reflexes begins first of all in the interoceptors on the basis of the food reflex, biologically the most important, because the first conditioned reflexes guarantee the child's more reliable adaptation to different conditions of existence and, primarily, to new means of feeding.

The Sequence of the Formation of Conditioned Reflexes

Progressive morphological changes occur in the cerebral cortex during the first months of life. They are perfected at different rates in different parts of the brain. Similarly, the child's receptors do not become ready for activity simultaneously. Some of them, for example, the vestibular, are already functional in the uterine period. Others, the visual, for example, pass through a long process of formation after birth. Therefore, different analyzers in both the central (cortical) and in the peripheral (receptor) areas are at varying levels of functional readiness in each period of development. Consequently, conditioned reflexes also pass through a definite sequence related to the various analyzers.

It is known that the receptors in the nonauditory part of the inner ear begin to function in the uterine period. Stimulation of the vestibular apparatus in newborns leads to many reflexes: the grasping reflex, righting reflexes, nystagmus, and others.

Natural *conditioned vestibular reflexes* have been found to form around the fifteenth day of life (Bekhterev and Shchelovanov, 1925), between 21 and 27 days (Denisova and Figurin, 1925) and from 10 to 18 days of life (Kol'tsova, 1958). The child's typical feeding position at the mother's breast is the conditioned stimulus. In previously swaddled children, the conditioned stimuli are tactile, proprioceptive, and vestibular. The conditioned reflex is manifested in searching movements of the head, sucking movements, and opening of the mouth. On the ninth day of life some children who are upset and crying become calm as soon as they are placed in the feeding position. On the tenth day 26 per cent of the children, in addition to becoming calm, begin sucking motions. On the eleventh day the percentage rises to 66 per cent (Kol'tsova, 1958). The important fact in these observations is that sucking movements and reduction of crying were originally evoked by other tactile-kinesthetic and, apparently, vestibular stimuli associated with changes of body position. Only at 16 to 18 days of life was there a precise conditioned reflex in response to a definite feeding position.

Thus, according to these authors the first natural conditioned reflex appears between the tenth and twenty-seventh days of life in response to the complex of tactile, proprioceptive, and labyrinthine stimuli which accompany feeding.

Further experimental research established the dominant role of the labyrinths in the formation of this conditioned reflex. Nemanova (1935) used rocking the child in the cradle to stimulate the vestibular apparatus. Simultaneously, air was blown onto the child's face in order to evoke blinking. While formation of this conditioned reflex begins within 10 to 13 days after birth, it first appears in weak and unstable form within 2 to 3 days after birth. The conditioned reflex gradually becomes clearer, and in the second month it becomes stable. If conditioning is started later—in the second month—the conditioned reflex is obtained in the first day and immediately becomes clearly expressed. By reinforcing rocking in the cradle with milk, the conditioned reflex can be observed on days 21–24 as rhythmic sucking movements. In the beginning the reflex is not consistent; it becomes stable only in the second month. Thus, in the second to fourth weeks of life it is possible to form an unstable feeding and defensive vestibular conditioned reflex. In the second month this reflex becomes stable and well expressed.

Stimulation of the proprioceptors (muscle receptors, joints, and ligaments) can be considered a component in the complex stimulus involved in the formation of natural conditioned reflexes in infants. Experiments have shown that repeated straightening of the half-bent foot is a conditioned stimulus for defensive or feeding reflexes. If conditioning of this reflex is begun after 7 days of age, it will first appear after 16 to 24 days. Characterized at first by extreme weakness and instability, conditioned proprioceptive reflexes achieve relative stability only 3 to 4 months after birth (Kasatkin, 1949).

Like the proprioceptive component, the tactile is part of the complex stimulus of early natural conditioned reflexes. However, artificial conditioned reflexes formed in response to tactile stroking stimuli are developed later than those to stimulation directed to other analyzers. It is possible that the exact nature of the conditioned stimulus applied locally to the skin of the chest, thigh, shin, or sole of the foot is very significant. If conditioning of the skin-tactile reflex is started on the tenth day or later, conditioning is complete sometime during the second month but remains unstable. It achieves stability and clarity only in the third month of life.

Various odoriferous substances may be used as conditioned stimuli if they are brought to the nose unnoticed on cotton or mixed with an air current wafted past the nose. At the age of 2 to 4 months the *conditioned olfactory reflex* is formed rapidly—after twelve to seventeen trials. If conditioning begins earlier, at 12 to 16 days, it develops in response to odors which stimulate the trigeminal nerve in the fourth week, but conditioned reflexes involving the olfactory nerve occur somewhat later, in the second month (Kasatkin, 1948).

The taste receptors receive adequate stimulation from the moment of birth and possibly even earlier (Windle, 1941) but study of motor feeding conditioned reflexes is made more difficult by the distribution of receptors in the mouth cavity. On the other hand, defensive *conditioned taste reflexes* are easy to work with (Nemanova, 1941). Thus, if work with this reflex is begun during the first month of life, the first sign of it appears at the end of that month; in the beginning of the second month the reflex is quite distinct although sometimes it does not become stable until the end of the month. A conditioned reflex to a water stimulus can be developed in 3-month-old babies after one trial.

Conditioned auditory reflexes formed on the basis of food, defense, and orienting unconditioned reflexes (crying and inhibition of movement) permit a more detailed examination of reflex formation.

When development of the conditioned *feeding* reflex (sucking movements prior to onset of the reinforcement) is begun around the eleventh day of life, a clear conditioned reflex appears in the course of the third or fourth 10-day period. In the beginning it occurs only once or twice in a session. Then it appears more frequently, and after two to six sessions it appears at least 50 per cent of the time. Finally, it appears on 70 to 100 per cent of the stimulus presentations. It remains at this level for 2 to 4 months of life. Thus, a striking and stable conditioned auditory reflex is formed in all children in the second month of life, regardless of the age at which it was started (Kasatkin, 1935; Kasatkin and Levikova, 1935a).

Research on the conditioned *defensive* (blinking) reflex was conducted on children 7 days old and older (Denisova and Figurin, 1935; Kasatkin, 1955; Kantrow, 1937). Six to seven trials were conducted each day. A momentary blink was noted in a 9-day-old child after one conditioned-stimulus–unconditioned-stimulus combination; on the tenth day the conditioned reflex appeared after two trials; and on the eleventh, fourteenth, nineteenth, twenty-first, twenty-third, and twenty-fourth days it again appeared after one trial. At the end of the month—on the twenty-sixth and twenty-eighth days—the conditioned blink occurred on three trials and, finally, on the twenty-ninth day—on five out of the six trials. After a few vacillations the conditioned reflex appeared six times in seven trials on the thirty-third day of life. After this it remained extremely stable. A clearly manifested conditioned reflex formed very early in this child, soon after the first signs of conditioning appeared. This example is typical of children with whom work on the conditioned reflex was started in the first month of life. As a rule, the conditioned reflex first manifests itself once or twice in several trials. Beginning with the twenty-sixth to thirty-first day it appears in every session and, simultaneously, the number of positive responses per day increases. In the first half of the second month the new conditioned reflex occurs in an absolute majority of trials—in 70 to 90 and even 100 per cent. The age at which both the defensive and feeding reflexes are formed does not depend on the age at which the experiment was begun (see Table 2–1).

Table 2–1

Conditioned reflex	Age in days		Development of stable conditioned reflex	
	Start of experiment	Appearance of stable conditioned reflex	Sessions	Trials
Auditory-defensive	10	31	20	219
	30	30	1	8
Auditory-feeding	11	29	14	105
	30	33	2	21

When a light is suddenly flashed into the eyes the same defensive reflex develops as when the air current is passed in front of the face—blinking and closing the eyelids. Shriftzetser (1935) conducted a study on the formation of a reflex in response to this stimulus and found the results to be the same as in the aforementioned examples. There were no differences in either the age at which the first conditioned reflex appeared or its further consolidation. Possibly, this is because both reflexes have a common efferent path, but different afferent paths.

A conditioned reflex was formed on the basis of the newborn child's orienting reflex—turning the eyes and head to the source of light (Kasatkin, Mirzoyants, and Khokhitva, 1953).

In studies with infants beginning at about 2 months of age it was established that an unstable auditory reflex can be first formed around 2½ months after birth. At 5 months of age the reflex becomes stable and clear. At a later age the reflex is formed very rapidly after a few trials.

Conditioned visual reflexes have been studied primarily with the use of food reinforcement. An air puff was used as the unconditioned reinforcement in only one study. In that case the conditioned signal was the reduction of light intensity. When the conditioned stimulus (a light passed through a colored filter) is reinforced with milk, the first conditioned reflex appears in the majority of children at the beginning of the second month of life. At the end of this month it is stable regardless of the age at which its development was begun (Kasatkin and Levikova, 1935a, b; Zonova, 1964).

In addition to the above-mentioned research on newborns, *conditioned polyuria reflex* in children in the first half-year of life has been studied. Zamkova and Chernousova (1952) studied four children ranging in age from 4 months and 10 days to 7 months and 7 days. They were fed artificially on yogurt from a bottle and semolina cereal from a spoon. After they drank the yogurt, marked polyuria was observed, manifested by an increase in frequency of urination and by the development of mild diuresis. The cereal did not evoke changes in urination. If the child ate the same amount of cereal by sucking it from the nipple from which he usually drank the yogurt, the diuresis increased markedly. Control experiments established the conditioned-reflex character of the increase in diuresis. The conditioned stimulus was the sucking movements which arose when the child drank yogurt from the bottle, that is, the method of feeding. Thus, it appears that cortical control of kidney function is established by the fourth month of life.

Malakhovskaya (1954, 1964) studied the formation of the conditioned reflex based on an unconditioned reflex which has not yet completed its development. She used the Babinsky reflex (flexion of the toes to stroking of the sole of the foot) as the unconditioned reflex. The *conditioned* Babinsky reflex could be developed only in the second month. Moreover, the presence of a conditioned reflex changed the course of the maturing unconditioned reflex.

So far, only one study of *motor conditioned reflexes involving the so-called voluntary movements* has applied new methods for developing a motor reflex in children from two weeks to eight months of age (Vakhrameeva 1958, 1964). The conditioned stimulus was a weak air puff to the eyes, which was paired with passive bending of the arm at the elbow. When the bend in the arm approached a 180-degree angle, the air stream stopped. With the combination of the air stream in the eyes and passive arm bending, the unconditioned stimulus of the blinking reflex turned into a conditioned signal for the arm movement.

The conditioned reflex was formed in one child on the nineteenth day of life; in two children an unstable reflex appeared in the sixth week; and in all the children the reflex could be formed after 1.5 to 2 months of age. These reflexes were notable for their oscillation, which was manifested in periodic reduction or disappearance. Conditioned reflexes were formed much more rapidly and with great stability in children after 4 months of age. Thus, conditioned voluntary movements can be developed at 1½ to 2 months of age, and in some cases at the end of the third week of life.

In comparing conditioned reflexes according to the analyzers which they involve, one cannot help but note that the vestibular and auditory conditioned reflexes appear at an earlier age than the visual conditioned reflexes. This fact was corroborated in special studies of children from 7 to 11 days of age and older. All began training to develop *several conditioned reflexes*. The results indicated that auditory reflexes were developed much earlier than proprioceptive reflexes (Kasatkin, 1951). When training of four conditioned reflexes was begun simultaneously (vestibular, auditory, visual, and tactile) the majority of the children manifested the vestibular reflex first, but some the auditory. Then came the visual and finally, in all the children, the tactile (Nemanova, 1940; Nemanova and Levikova, 1940). The sequence of the formation of various conditioned reflexes depended on the child's age, the functional readiness of the sensory organ, and possibly, the nature of the conditioned stimulus. If the several conditioned reflexes were started later (in the third to fourth months of life), they usually formed simultaneously.

Conditioned reflexes in premature babies are of special interest. The premature child has to contend with new conditions of existence prematurely. Therefore, it can be assumed that the new environment has a stimulating effect on the formation of neural processes. Experiments have supported this assumption, for the conditioned auditory blink reflex was formed in the first half of the second month of postnatal life in babies born 1 to 2 months prematurely with a birth weight of 1,610 to 2,100 gr. The formation process was exactly the same as in full-term babies. In all of these premature babies the conditioned reflex was formed at approximately the same age (Kasatkin, 1936, 1951). In subsequent studies, these data were confirmed and expanded (Volokhov et al., 1955). In particular, it was shown that the conditioned reflex forms later in the more premature children: in babies born 2 to 2½ months prematurely, the reflex formed in the middle of the second month. Babies born 3 or more months prematurely did not form the conditioned reflex until the middle or the end of the third month of postnatal life. Therefore in the more premature babies the auditory conditioned reflex still forms in a period between the moment of actual birth and the time of the normal termination of pregnancy.

Differentiated Conditioned Reflexes

The process of differentiating between external and internal stimuli is closely linked with the formation of positive conditioned reflexes and accompanies it at all stages of ontogenesis. The formation of differentiations which differ in difficulty characterizes the functional ability of the child's analyzers at various age levels.

Many studies have found that stimulation of one pair of semicircular canals can be distinguished from stimulation of the other pair at a very early age, usually at the end of the second or the third month of life. For example, if the conditioned blinking or sucking reflex was developed in response to up-down rocking, differentiation can be developed between that and side-to-side rocking (Nemanova, 1935).

As for *taste* stimuli, in the first half of the second month the child distinguishes plain water from sweet (5 per cent sugar solution). At 3 months he differentiates even lower concentrations of such tastes as sweet:

sugar, 2 per cent solution; salt, 0.4 per cent solution; and sour, 20 drops of lemon juice in 100 milliliters of water. In the course of the fourth month a child can form a conditioned blink reflex to the taste of sour water and can develop a sensitive differentiation to the taste of sweet and salty water. Only limited data are available for differentiation of tactile stimuli. It has been established that, at 3 months, differentiation of the location of tactile stimulation is quickly developed when the stimulated points are distributed at significant distances from each other.

Differentiation of *smells* has been noted at an early age. At the end of 2 months of life two odors presented on separate trials could be differentiated although the differentiation was still unstable during the third month and became stable only during the fourth month (Kasatkin, 1948). Sixty- to sixty-six-day-old children can differentiate between the odors of turpentine and almond, as well as camphor and cologne. At 3 months the child is capable of distinguishing one odor from among six others (Nemanova, 1939). Thus, olfactory, feeding, and defensive conditioned reflexes are possible, if unstable, at the end of the second or during the third month of life, while they are stable and rapidly developed in the fourth month.

In order to study the auditory analyzer in newborns ranging in age from 1½ hours to 18 days, Bronshtein and Petrova (1952) used the orienting reflex. The basic change in the sucking movements to sound indicating the presence of an orienting reflex was delayed sucking. The response gradually extinguished. A new sound again evoked the response. This phenomenon was used to determine the limits of sound analysis. The majority of newborns reacted to pitch changes beyond an octave, while a minority reacted only to changes within the octave. On the third day of life babies also differentiated changes in the position of a sound—on the right or the left.

Using the method of conditioned reflexes with older children, we established that they are capable of differentiating sounds differing only in pitch beginning with the third month of life. They can differentiate a tone which differs from the standard tone by 11½ musical tones (or a tone of 640 cps from one of 172 cps). They can form an unstable differentiation between four tones (Figurin and Denisova, 1949). In the late fourth or early fifth month, children differentiate a difference of 5½ tones (640 cps from 344 cps). In the sixth month differentiation improves significantly and the child distinguishes the difference between 810 and 890 cps or 710 cps. In the seventh month the child can distinguish a tone which differs from the standard by ⅔ of a musical tone (or 40 cps) if the test stimulus is above the standard and by 1 musical tone (or 60 cps) if the test stimulus is lower than the standard (Nechaeva, 1954). These facts provide some idea of the differentiation of pitch in the first half-year of life. But these differentiations are not necessarily the limits and it is possible that the child at that age can distinguish even more subtle tones. The data reflect the tendency towards functional perfection of the auditory analyzer early in life.

Studies of the visual analyzer established that the child of 3 to 4 months can discriminate yellow or red from green. However, in the third month the discrimination between green and the two other colors was obtained only on certain trials. The majority of the children developed stable differentiation in the fourth month of life. Zonova (1964), who used colored stimuli of equal intensity in her studies, discovered that during the first month of life it is considerably easier for children to distinguish between red and green, and especially between red and blue, stimuli than between neighbors on the color spectrum such as red and yellow.

General Laws of the Formation and Differentiation of the Conditioned Reflex

Healthy babies develop the first conditioned reflexes at a very early age. All reflexes pass through the same general stages of development. It is sometimes impossible to establish the conditioned reflex nature of a reaction in the first days and weeks of life since the blinking, sucking, and orienting movements arise spontaneously and independently of external influences. This does not exclude the possible accidental coincidence of unsignaled spontaneous responses and the conditioned signal. However, careful experimentation makes it fairly certain that conditioning does occur during the first 2 to 3 months of life.

It can also be assumed that morphological maturity of both the brain substrata and more general physiological processes is necessary for the formation of the first conditioned reflexes. These processes, which are prerequisites for the development of conditioned reflexes, are, apparently, the periodic cyclical processes associated with hunger and satiation, sleep and wakefulness. They are already present in the child's first days of life.

With a few exceptions, conditioned reflexes are weak and unstable up to the fourth or fifth week of life. As a rule, the conditioned reflex occurs one to three times in a session, not on every trial. If conditioning is begun in the second month it also appears only from time to time within a session, but becomes stronger much more rapidly. The conditioned stimulus is weakly associated with the unconditioned reflex up to the fourth week. The connection which thus develops is easily disturbed despite the reinforcement. Apparently, this primitive form of associative activity is typical of the cerebral cortex in early childhood. The younger the child at the beginning of the experiment, the more combinations are necessary in order to produce a strong and clear conditioned reflex. A firm and well-expressed conditioned reflex is sometimes formed in the fourth week and almost always in the second month. In some cases, however, it is still unstable in the second and third months. The age at which the conditioned reflex is formed as well as its subsequent strengthening depends on the particular analyzer involved. Varying periods (from several trials in the course of one day to many days) are necessary both for the development of an early conditioned reflex and its subsequent extinction. During this time not only the receptors affected by the conditioned stimulus are perfected but the maturation of the associated unconditioned reflex is also taking place.

Several stages are discernible in the formation of the first and earliest conditioned reflexes:

1. *The stage of initial nonspecific responses.* Any stimulus applied as a conditioned signal evokes more or less complex local responses and, at times, the orienting response.

2. *The stage of inhibition or distinct orienting responses.* The influence of the conditioned stimulus is expressed in the delay of general activity, in the decrease or complete cessation of movement and voice sounds, and the like. Almost simultaneously, the conditioned signal begins to evoke vague, conditioned reactions, sometimes once or twice in a session. These may be the result of accidental coincidence of the signal with spontaneous responses or the sign of developing conditioned reflexes.

3. *The stage of unstable conditioned reflexes.* The conditioned reflex appears only rarely—one to three times in a session and usually in a weak form. However, it is definitely there. Sessions in which the conditioned reflex occurs become more frequent. As a rule, the conditioned reflex remains in this form until the fourth week of life.

4. *The stage of stable conditioned reflexes.* The conditioned reflex occurs in a vivid, stable form. It is manifested on not less than half, and often in all, of the presentations of the conditioned stimulus. The rapidity with which the conditioned reflex occurs in this stage depends primarily on the age of the child at the beginning of the experiment. The younger the child, the more prolonged is the course of learning.

In addition to the formation of temporary associations, the analysis of internal and external stimuli occurs in the brain cortex. The elaboration of discriminations of varying degrees of difficulty determines the capacity of the child's analyzers.

Discrimination in very young children begins immedately after the appearance of positive conditioned reflexes. In the second month stimuli can be discriminated by means of the conditioned-reflex technique. As a rule, conditioning is very stable. This function quickly becomes perfected in the third month. In the third and fourth months it is possible to work out more stable and subtle discrimination with all the analyzers. Discrimination begins either with generalization of the stimuli or "from the beginning," if the unreinforced stimulus is significantly different from the positive one. Sometimes discrimination appears to develop immediately, but after several trials is replaced by generalization. Only then does it gradually begin to really develop.

If both stimuli were generalized in the beginning, in the course of a short period both the positive and the negative stimuli will evoke the same response. In a short time the response to the unreinforced signal becomes weaker; in certain cases it disappears entirely. In the beginning, discrimination occurs on certain trials with the unreinforced stimulus. Finally, differentiation becomes stable and appears on consecutive trials. As it develops, deviations from the typical process can be seen in the form of a sudden increase of discrimination: generalization of stimuli is immediately replaced by discrimination. This is retained in all of the following trials. Sometimes the negative stimulus of the conditioned food reflex evokes a negative response in the form of increased crying. This also occurs during the extinction of this reflex.

The development of unmistakable conditioned reflexes involving the external analyzers indicates the participation of the cortex in their formation. When the child's cortex reaches the necessary level of development it begins to fulfill specific functions in the formation of various positive and inhibitory temporary associations.

References

Bekhterev, V. M., and Shchelovanov, N. M. Foundations of genetic reflexology. In *New developments in reflexology and the physiology of the nervous system.* Vol. 1. Leningrad-Moscow: Gosizdat, 1925.

Brackbill, Y. Research and clinical work with children. In R. A. Bauer (Ed.), *Some views on Soviet psychology*. Washington: Amer. Psychol. Assoc., 1962.

Bronshtein, A. I., and Petrova, E. P. Studies of the auditory analyzer in newborns and infants. *Zh. vyssh. nerv. Deyat.*, 1952, *2,* No. 3.

Bystroletova, G. N. The formation of the conditioned reflex associated with the daily rhythm of feeding in newborns. *Zh. vyssh. nerv. Deyat.*, 1954, *4,* No. 5.

Denisova, M., and Figurin, N. L. The first combinative reflexes in infants. In *Problems of genetic reflexology*. Leningrad-Moscow: Gosmedizdat, 1925.

Denisova, M., and Figurin, N. L. Early conditioned reflexes in infants. *Sovet. Pediat.*, 1935, *6.*

Figurin, N. L., and Denisova, M. P. *Stages in behavioral development in children from birth to the first year*. Moscow: Medgiz, 1949.

Golubeva, E. L. Conditioned appetitive reflexes in premature babies. *Akusherstvo i Ginekol.*, 1959, *1,* 58.

Kantrow, R. W. An investigation of conditioned feeding responses and concomitant adaptive behavior in young infants. *Univer. Iowa Stud. Child Welf.*, 1937, *13,* No. 3, 1–64.

Kasatkin, N. I. The development of auditory and visual conditioned reflexes and their differentiation in babies. *Sovet. Pedag.*, 1935, No. 8.

Kasatkin, N. I. Auditory conditioned reflexes in premature babies. *Byull. VIEM,* 1936, 23–24.

Kasatkin, N. I. *Early conditioned reflexes in the ontogenesis of man.* Moscow: Izd. Akad. Med. Nauk SSSR, 1948.

Kasatkin, N. I. Proprioceptive conditioned reflexes in infants. *Byull. Biol. Med.,* 1949, *2.*

Kasatkin, N. I. *The development of higher nervous activity in young children.* Moscow: Medgiz, 1951.

Kasatkin, N. I. Early ontogenesis of the human conditioned reflex. In *Proceedings of the Nineteenth International Congress of Physiology.* Moscow: Akad. Nauk SSSR, 1953. P. 65.

Kasatkin, N. I. The functional nature of the auditory analyzer in the child. In *Eighth All-Union Congress of Physiologists, Biochemists, and Pharmacologists.* 1955. P. 285. (Abstract.)

Kasatkin, N. I., and Levikova, A. M. On the development of early conditioned reflex differentiation of auditory stimuli in infants. *J. exp. Psychol.,* 1935, *18,* 1–19. (a)

Kasatkin, N. I., and Levikova, A. M. The formation of visual conditioned reflexes and their differentiation in infants. *J. gen. Psychol.* 1935, *12,* 416–435. (b)

Kasatkin, N. I., Mirzoyants, N. S., and Khokhitva, A. P. The orienting reflex during the first year of life. *Zh. vyssh. nerv. Deyat.,* 1953, *3,* No. 2, 192.

Kol'tsova, M. M. The rise and development of the second signal system in the child. *Trudy Inst. Fiziol. im. Pavlova. Vol. 4,* 1949, Vol. 49.

Kol'tsova, M. M. *The formation of higher nervous activity in the child.* Moscow: Medgiz, 1958.

Krachkovskaya, M. V. Reflex changes in the number of leucocytes associated with feeding in newborns. *Zh. vyssh. nerv. Deyat.,* 1959, *9,* No. 2.

Krasnogorskii, N. I. *Studies of higher nervous activity in man and animals.* Moscow: Medgiz, 1954.

Krasnogorskii, N. I. *Higher nervous activity in the child.* Leningrad: Medgiz, 1958.

Malakhovskaya, D. B. The interrelations between the unconditioned and conditioned Babinsky reflex in children. In *Proceedings of the First Scientific Conference on Developmental Morphology and Physiology.* Moscow: Izd. Akad. Pedag. Nauk RSFSR, 1954.

Malakhovskaya, D. B. The characteristics of the conditioned reflex based on the developing clutching reflex in very young children. In *From the simple to the complex.* Moscow-Leningrad: Nauka, 1964.

Marquis, D. P. Can conditioned responses be established in newborn infants? *J. genet. Psychol.,* 1931, *39,* 479–492.

Mirzoyants, S. The conditioned orienting reflex and its discrimination in the child. *Zh. vyssh. nerv. Deyat.,* 1954, *4.*

Nechaeva, T. P. The functional characteristics of the auditory analyzer in young children. *Zh. vyssh. nerv. Deyat.,* 1954, *4,* No. 5, 619.

Nemanova, T. P. The earliest positive and negative conditioned reflexes in response to vestibular stimulation in the infant. *Vop. Pediat.*, 1935, *7*. No. 4.

Nemanova, T. P. Conditioned reflexes to olfactory stimuli in infants. *Fiziol. Zh. SSSR*, 1939, *27*, No. 6.

Nemanova, T. P. The sequence of the appearance of conditioned reflexes in the sensory organs during the first months of life. Communication 1. *Vop. Ped. Okhr. Mat. Det.*, 1940, *12*, Nos. 2–3.

Nemanova, T. P. Conditioned reflexes to taste stimuli in the first months of life. *Fiziol. Zh. SSSR*, 1941, *30*, No. 4.

Nemanova, T. P., and Levikova, A. M. The sequence of the appearance of conditioned reflexes in the sensory organs during the first months of life. Communication 2. *Vop. Ped. Okhr. Mat. Det.*, 1940, *12*, No. 5.

Orbeli, L. A. Landmarks in the study of higher nervous activity in the child. In *Seventh All-Union Congress of Physiologists, Biochemists, and Pharmacologists*. 1955. P. 460 (Abstract).

Pavlov, I. P. *Collected works*. Izd. Akad. Nauk SSSR, 1951.

Razran, G. H. S. Conditioned responses in children. *Arch. Psychol.*, 1933, Whole No. 148.

Shriftzetser, M. O. The defensive reflex to strong light as the development of the earliest conditioned reflex in infants. *Vop. Ped.*, 1935, *7*, No. 6.

Sontag, L. W., and Wallace, R. F. Preliminary report of foetal activity. *Amer. J. Dis. Child*, 1934, *48*.

Spelt, D. K. The conditioning of the human foetus *in utero*. *J. exp. Psychol.*, 1948, *38*, 338–346.

Vakhrameeva, I. A. The development of conditioned motor reflexes of so-called voluntary movements in the first months of life. *Dokl. Akad. Nauk SSSR*, 1958, *123*, No. 5.

Vakhrameeva, I. A. The formation and course of bilateral conditioned motor reflexes in young children. In *From the simple to the complex*. Moscow-Leningrad: Nauka, 1964.

Volokhov, A. A. Interrelations of conditioned and unconditioned reflexes in ontogenesis. In *Eighth All-Union Congress of Physiologists, Biochemists, and Pharmacologists*, 1955. P. 141 (Abstract).

Watson, J. B. *Psychology as a science of behavior*. (Translation from the English.) Gosizdat Ukrainy, 1934.

Wenger, M. A. Conditioned responses in human infants. In H. F. Wright and J. S. Kounin (Eds.), *Child behavior and development*. New York-London: 1943. Pp. 67–86.

Windle, W. F. *Physiology of the fetus: Origin and extent of the function in prenatal life*. Philadelphia: Saunders, 1941.

Zamkova, M. A., and Chernousova, A. P. Conditioned-reflex polyuria in the first half-year of life. *Byull. eksper. Biol. Med.*, 1952, *10*, 23.

Zonova, A. V. Color vision in children in the first months of life. In *From the simple to the complex*. Moscow-Leningrad: Nauka, 1964.

3

Some of the Psychological Problems of Sensory Training in Early Childhood and the Preschool Period

A. V. Zaporozhets

EDITORS' INTRODUCTION

A. V. Zaporozhets is Director of the Institute of Preschool Education of the Academy of Pedagogical Sciences in Moscow. He is one of the many students of Vygotskii who went on to become a leading Soviet psychologist. His studies of the development of sensory and cognitive functions began in the 1930's in Kharkov (where Leont'ev was then working). During the war he worked on the problem of restoring damaged or destroyed functions (cf. Leont'ev and Zaporozhets, 1960). Following the war he moved to Moscow, where he resumed the developmental research which has been his concern ever since.

In collaboration with El'konin he has published two books on developmental psychology, which are as yet available only in Russian (Zaporozhets and El'konin, 1964; Zaporozhets and El'konin, 1965).

The bulk of this chapter is taken from a recent book edited by Zaporozhets and Usova (1963). Specific extended examples from the work of Zaporozhets' collaborators, Ruzskaya and Venger, are cited in the chapter. The cooperation of all three contributors is gratefully acknowledged.

SENSORY TRAINING, which is aimed at developing processes through which the child senses, perceives, and forms graphic ideas, is one of the most important units of the entire Soviet system of preschool education. It is particularly important now at a time when we are establishing a unified system of preschool education which, in addition to the preschool level, will also cover the earliest stages of child development—infancy and the prekindergarten period.

Krupskaya,[1] as we know, emphasized the enormous role which impressions formed in the earliest years of childhood play in the individual's cultural development. She commented on the need "to strengthen and develop the child's senses of sight, hearing, touch, and the like from early childhood, since it is through these organs that the individual acquires knowledge of the external world" (Krupskaya, no date).

Soviet theories of preschool education and child psychology, proceeding from the philosophical tenets of dialectical materialism, maintain that the growth of sensation and perception is a necessary prerequisite for developing more complex intellectual processes in the child.

Because the development of sensory processes figures so largely in shaping intellectual abilities, it is intrinsically vital in furthering the child's ability to handle practical activities. In the middle of the nineteenth century Sechenov pointed out that any purposeful act "is regulated by the senses"; or, in the language of contemporary psychology, is accomplished through intricate systems of "return afferentation" (Anokhin) by means of the mechanisms of "sensory correction" (Bernshtein).

One sometimes hears it argued, quite unsoundly, that since the role that sensation plays in learning and work these days has inevitably declined owing to increased technology, it would be pointless to devote serious concern to sensory training. However, as Anan'ev (1960) rightly noted: "Both from the standpoint of learning and of work, it is erroneous to formulate the issue this way. The greatest advances in science and technology assume the participation of a person who is not only capable of thinking, but also of *feeling*." These achievements demand that a worker have a highly developed capacity for sense perception.

In discussing the place that sense perception occupies in the entire course of a child's cultural development, we should keep in mind that sensory processes are not only important in acquiring and mastering specific areas of knowledge and practical skills, but in developing one's abilities as a whole. When one considers that the majority of these abilities are clearly rooted in sensation (tonal hearing, for example, being the sensory basis for

---

1. *Editors' note:* Lenin's wife and a prominent Soviet educator.

musical skills, visual perception of form, and color the basis for graphic skills, a keen kinesthetic sense the foundation for various motor skills, etc.), and that sensory processes undergo intensive development during infancy and the preschool period, it is evident that training in sense perception is significantly related to the child's subsequent development. It helps to prepare him for creative, socially beneficial work in adult life.

However, despite the undeniable value that such training has for preschool children, as demonstrated both by an analysis of the kindergarten programs and by special research studies, we have not devoted enough concern to this area of educational work. Our educational programs do not have a precise set of requirements for developing sensory processes at various stages during the preschool period; nor do they stipulate ways to select sensory tasks that would allow for the proper order and continuity of training. In a number of instances outdated methods are used which are quite ineffective in teaching. This makes our training programs less productive and has a negative effect on the child's ability to learn, to develop various intellectual, artistic, and practical skills.

The cause of this unsatisfactory state of affairs, apparently, is not that teachers and methodologists have failed to put forth the necessary effort, so much as a failure to work out in detail theories of preschool education which would provide the scientific principles we need to structure programs and methods of sensory training for use in the Soviet kindergarten.

The bourgeois educational systems of Froebel, Montessori, Decroly, and others have been subjected to a sound critique by a number of Soviet educators who introduced many worthwhile proposals intended to restructure sensory training according to the aims and principles of Soviet preschool education. However, for a number of reasons this work was not completed; hence, it did not lead to the creation of a complete system of sensory training which could have met the needs of our time: to develop a new type of individual, a member of a communist society who must achieve an incomparably higher level of general development (including, of course, intellectual development) than people in the societies that the above-mentioned educational theories had in view.

Hence, under the supervision of Usova, the Laboratory of Experimental Didactics, Institute of Preschool Education, Academy of Pedagogical Sciences, R.S.F.S.R., undertook to work out the theoretical and experimental issues that are related to a program of sensory training which can be used in the Soviet kindergarten. Inasmuch as the new educational system must be based on principles developed by modern psychology, this work was coordinated with research studies carried out by the Laboratory on the Physiology of Growth at our Institute, as well as with research by the Laboratory on the Psychology of Preschool Children in the Institute of Psychology, the Academy of Pedagogical Sciences.

While Froebel's system was based on the idealist metaphysical conceptions of German psychology, and Montessori's on the dualist theory of the psychophysiology of the sense organs proposed by Fechner and Wundt, the Soviet system of sensory training is rooted in the findings on sensation and perception acquired by Soviet materialistic psychology. The research studies that Soviet psychology has conducted proceed from the Marxist-Leninist theory of knowledge, while the interpretation of the physiological mechanisms of sensory processes is one that makes use of Pavlov's theory of reflex activity. Of the most important positions which constitute the psychological basis for the Soviet system of sensory training, we select for examination here those which radically distinguish it from bourgeois educational systems.

Assumptions of a Theory of Sensory Training

The first of these positions concerns our conception of the impetus for the development in the child of a capacity for sensation and perception and the part that training plays in this. Froebel, Montessori, and Decroly (despite their differences) operated from the mistaken psychological premise that the basic sensory abilities exist, as it were, in ready form at birth; they thus reduce sensory training to ways in which these abilities can be given practice. Soviet preschool educational theory, drawing on current findings in psychology, regards sensory development as the development of new processes and abilities that the child does not have at birth but which he acquires under the influence of an active program of instruction. The pedagogical treatment of this problem is based, then, on ideas advanced by Soviet psychologists (Vygotskii, Rubinshtein, Leont'ev, and others) with regard to the function of common sensory experience in the psychological development of the human being.

Though Soviet investigators indicate how important it is for the child to acquire common sense experience, they do not deny that part of this development has to do with the maturation of the analyzing systems which adapt the child to his environment. However, this process of maturation and adaptation merely furnishes prerequisites that the child needs to move on to a new and higher level of growth; maturation does not provide the impetus for the child's developing distinctly human sensory process.

Organically, the child is equipped with some of the prerequisites for sensory development (inherent anatomical and physiological features peculiar to one or another type of analyzing system), but to develop the distinctly human sensory abilities he will need later in life, to do work that is materially productive, or to pursue some scientific or artistic interest, his training cannot be confined to the mere exercise of his sense organs. His ability to handle sense data must be molded through training based upon a specific scheme of instruction.

This view of sensory development allows for a different approach to the problem, even for a thorough reappraisal of traditional programs of sensory training. As a rule these programs were uneven; they tended to exclude activities that would develop such abilities as musical and phonemic hearing. However, even with the limits that were natural to formal educational approaches in this area (work on developing the child's perception of size, shape, color, etc.), these programs merely provided endless training in the most elementary sensory functions: the ability to recognize and distinguish objects by one or another group of features. Yet, as current experimental studies in psychology and physiology have shown (in particular, some extremely interesting research Venger carried out in our laboratory in which babies of 3 to 4 months orient differentially to objects), infants in their first six months of life are capable of an elementary type of perception, such as the ability to distinguish objects in terms of shape, size, etc. Hence, any system which trains children between 3 and 7 years of age in similar types of differentiation can hardly be conducive to furthering the child's sensory development.

As distinct from the latter type of program for sensory training, ours needs to be expanded considerably so that it will cover not only distinctively human sensory skills such as the ability to perceive pitch and speech sounds, but will also provide a completely different approach to determining the nature of material that should be used in this training. Our programs should not be restricted to techniques for acquainting the child with perceptible qualities of objects, or to monotonous training in the ability to distinguish and recognize such qualities. It must also have some provision for equipping the child with the necessary means for generalizing from his examination of things (techniques of listening, inspecting, probing, etc.). It should enable the child to compare the features he observes in objects with conventional systems of standards that have been worked out for sense data—for example, the musical scale, the accepted scale of pitch relationships; the "network of phonemes" in the child's native language; a system of geometrical forms. These are systems of "sensory" qualities which have been developed after centuries of experience in productive, scientific, and artistic work; they represent attempts to extract from the endless variety of data in perceptible reality that which is most fundamental, most vital for realizing certain practical ends in life and for acquiring knowledge of the world. Along with these standards, a distinct language has been developed with which to designate these qualities.

In childhood the individual acquires a knowledge of systems such as these and learns to use them as measures or standards by which to analyze the surrounding world and to order his own sense impressions. This is a process which begins even before a child enters school. However, since the existing programs of sensory training generally fail to provide any sequence of training in methods by which to use conventional standards of sense data, by and large the process is allowed to develop spontaneously, without supervision. As a result it proves to be fairly ineffective, as witness, for example, the data published by Kislyuk and Pen'evskaya (1963).

Research such as Sakulina's (1963) and Korzakova's (1963) studies on developing children's perception of form through drawing, El'konin's and Zhurova's (1963) studies on the growth of phonemic hearing in preparing preschool children to read, Vetlugina's (1963) work in developing children's abilities to distinguish pitch and rhythm through musical activities, as well as other studies, indicate that with guided, systematic instruction in the use of measures or standards of perceptible qualities, these and other types of perception can be developed to a considerably higher degree than would otherwise be possible.

Thus, as part of the training Sakulina (1963) gives children in drawing, she introduces ways to acquaint them with elementary geometrical forms (circles, squares, triangles, etc.), and with certain features by which they can differentiate these figures (the fact that some are drawn with a curved or broken line, etc.). In this way she provides children with methods of analysis that will enable them to draw inferences about figures—methods they will put to extensive use later on when they observe and attempt to reproduce highly complex and diverse types of objects in the world about them. Similarly El'konin and Zhurova (1963), in training 5-to-6-year-old children to distinguish sounds in their native language by clarifying their phonemic nature (pointing out to the child that, for example, by changing the *e* sound in the word *kēt* to *o,* one gets a completely different word—*kot*), managed to improve these preschool children's phonemic hearing. Through this training they reached a point where they could begin to master reading, writing, and the more complex types of oral speech. Finally, Vetlugina's (1963) work demonstrates that if one trains preschool children to discriminate tones according to conventional parameters (duration, pitch, etc.), and then acquaints them with the corresponding musical notation for these tones, their capacity for musical hearing can be greatly enriched.

However, in discussing the importance of the child's acquisition of common sensory data, of providing him with a genuine program of training that will not be restricted to mere exercise of his sense organs, it should be stressed that, although such training at the preschool level is, of necessity, empirical, using teaching objects of which the child has an immediate grasp, it ought to do more than teach him the individual elements which comprise systems of sense data. In addition, it should familiarize him with some of the simplest relationships that hold between these elements. The data of educational and psychological research indicate that the preschool-age child can learn methods of relating sounds according to pitch (one sound is lower, another higher), and can grasp a distinct change of pitch within musical phrases (in one instance tones become higher, in another, lower).

A child can also master the idea that some figures are drawn with broken lines (triangles, rectangles) and that these differ from each other by virtue of the number of angles (or sides) they possess; one figure can be converted into another by removing or including a corresponding element.

As research by Boguslavskaya (1963), Zinchenko (1961a, b, 1962), Ruzskaya (1954), and others indicates, if training is organized along certain lines, the preschool-age child is capable not only of becoming quite precise in his ability to ascertain and reproduce relationships between the elements of a system, but does so at a fairly high level of generalization. For example, in Sakulina's (1963) experiments, once children had been taught to distinguish a triangle from a rectangle according to the number of angles in each, they were able to apply this principle to polygons that were totally new and unfamiliar to them. And they could define these correctly as pentagons, hexagons, and so forth.

Thus, as distinct from the older programs for sensory training, ours is systematic not only in that it carefully selects teaching materials but in that it also acquaints children (on a practical, operative level, not on the level of theory) with the principles by which conventional systems of standards for sense data have been constructed. It is a program that is designed to make children aware of the peculiar interrelationships that hold between elements of a given system.

In general outline, these are the psychological views we hold with regard to the function ordinary sense experience has in developing children's capacity for sensation and perception. We can now define more precisely what the principal points of difference are between our system and the formal didactic systems (of Montessori and others) and between the "substantive" or "pragmatic" systems, as they are otherwise termed—those proposed by Decroly and others. In the former type the focus was mainly on training children how to distinguish and recognize artificial "abstract" forms which had been selected for teaching purposes. Under these systems, however, children were not taught how to use such forms as standards they might apply when trying to isolate and reproduce qualities they perceived in reality.

By way of reaction to this formal didactic method, the adherents of the "substantive" systems of sensory training tried to acquaint children with the diversity of forms, colors, and sounds to be found in the world. But on the whole they failed to equip the child with a means of becoming oriented to his surroundings. Consequently, both these systems were completely unsatisfactory, for they did not provide tasks that would consistently develop methods by which a child could orient himself to the world of perceptible phenomena.

As we pointed out, the Soviet program of sensory training provides ways in which the child will successively master a system of conventional standards of sense data. He is taught how to use these effectively to analyze and synthesize the qualities he perceives in surrounding objects. This use of standards requires that, in addition to a knowledge of sensory patterns (graphic ideas about the basic colors, elementary forms, etc.) a child be able to compare these with qualities in real objects; that he also be able to detect other relationships between the parts of objects.

For example, Boguslavskaya's experiments (1963) indicate that what a child learns about a triangle (as a figure having three angles) from teaching materials that use equilateral triangles, will prove valuable in orienting him to his surroundings only if he is specifically taught how to compare other variants of this figure with the pattern he has learned. Thus, even 4-to-5-year-old children can be taught how to make a visual comparison of triangles in terms of their general proportions, the type of angle at the apex, and the like. When new figures were shown to children in these experiments, they said that these were also triangles, only that one was "tall and kind of pointed" while another was "tiny and wide."

More complex skills, however, are needed to analyze combined forms which have compound structures—the typical composition of most objects in the world around us. After all, objects that form regular squares or circles are to be found more rarely than Montessori assumed. In the majority of cases the forms of objects a child sees about him in his life at home, in the animal and plant figures he perceives, represent an intricate combination of a number of simple geometrical elements. The child has yet to learn to break such combined forms down into their elements and, on the basis of his analysis, try to recreate the forms (through drawing, modeling, design work, etc.).

An experiment designed to develop skills of this type in preschool-age children (that is, the ability to analyze the spatial characteristics of compound objects) is to be found in research by Sakulina (1963).

She taught children to recognize the general form which characterizes an object as a whole. What she did was to teach them how to distinguish the basic form of an object (of the major part, the largest area of the figure) and the form of its details. It is only by acquiring skills such as these that a child can effectively use his store of sensory patterns to analyze and synthesize the reality he perceives. A program of sensory training ought certainly to provide ways in which these skills can be developed.

Perceptual Orienting: Experiments on Modeling Haptic, Visual, and Auditory Dimensions

These being our findings with respect to the "operative" nature of sensory processes, we can now take up a second fundamental position maintained by Soviet psychology, a viewpoint which must be taken into account in structuring a system of sensory training. In brief, this view holds that, as distinct from the receptor theory of sensory impressions which prevailed in psychological and educational theory for many years, current physiological and psychological research indicate that sensation and perception (expressed physiologically as reflex-type actions) display unique orienting functions. An analysis of experimental data indicated that the process of perception includes not only receptor and central components, but effector components as well. The sensory model itself can be interpreted, according to Anan'ev (1960) "as a reflex effect of the function of the analyzer." This can be seen most graphically in certain forms of perception such as touch and sight. A person cannot recognize the form, size, and other spatial characteristics of objects without certain hand and eye movements which consecutively examine the various parts of an object. In the course of these movements, the hands or the eyes reproduce, as it were, the features peculiar to the object itself.

As Leont'ev describes it (1965), what happens is that the movements of the receptor apparatus "assimilate" specific features of the object perceived; this produces a mold or copy of the object, the creation of a unique model of it. The more precise and detailed this model is in the way it reflects specific features of the object, the more adequate is one's perception of that object. Hence too, the more capable one will be of differentiating it from other objects.

This point in particular was established in research by Zinchenko (1961b) and Ruzskaya (1954), who in certain cases had preschool-age children familiarize themselves with a figure by means of touch, in others, by examining the figure visually. The purpose of this experiment was to see if the children would be able to spot the object later from among a group of other objects. The following is taken from an account of this experiment.

> As material for the experiment we used two plane objects of irregular shape, selecting these from the set of standard figures which are generally used in experiments on touch, objects we ourselves had made use of earlier (Zinchenko and Ruzskaya, 1960, No. 3). The two objects we used differed from the latter set merely by virtue of being three to four times larger.
>
> The figures were used separately and were mounted on a table by means of a special base. Since the base contained clamps which held the figure secure, it remained stationary throughout the experiment. A soft fabric screen, which was fastened to the table by means of a frame, was placed between the subject and the figure. This screen contained openings for the child's hands. During the experiment the subject's hands were placed on the side of the screen where the figure had been set up on the table for him to probe.
>
> In order to record the child's hand movements, we used a moving picture camera, which operated according to a system of frame exposures. By

means of a special electric motor the exposure could be done at the rate of one frame per second in some cases; in others, 12 frames per second. The time interval between frames needed for a precise reading was maintained throughout. The distance between the camera and the figure (and thus between the camera and the surface on which the child's hands moved) was approximately 150 cm. We used a frame projector to read the film. About 10,000 frames were read.

Preschool children of four age groups were the subjects in the experiment: 3–4, 4–5, 5–6, and 6–7 year olds. Altogether 24 children participated.

In accordance with the tasks we had set ourselves, two series of experiments were carried out. The conditions of the first experiment were such that the child had to perform a perceptual act, the main task of which was to examine the object. In the experimental set-up the child was told that there was a figure located behind the screen which he was to get a good feel of so that he would be able to find it later among a group of other objects. At a signal from the experimenter the child began to probe the figure (the same signal to start the camera). Each child was given two test figures, one at a time, which he was to probe in order to familiarize himself with it. A 60 second exposure was made of the child's probing of each figure.

Under the conditions of the second series of experiments the children had an opportunity to perform an act of identification. The task was to learn something about a figure and then try to recognize it. The experiment was set up as follows. A child was shown a figure for 10 seconds, during which he was to familiarize himself with it visually. After that, either that or another figure was attached to the stand behind the screen and the child was asked to probe it well and "guess" whether or not it was the same figure he had seen. At a signal from the experimenter both the child's probing of the test object and the exposure were begun. As soon as the child "guessed" (either did or did not recognize the figure) the trial was terminated, and with it, the exposure. The duration of the exposure in this series depended upon how rapidly a child managed to answer.

An analysis of the materials in the experiments indicated that there are significant differences in the kind of probing movement preschool-age children perform with their hands, depending upon the tasks they are given (perceptual, cognitive, or identifying), and upon the age of the child.

First let us consider the external features of the probing movements made by children of the various preschool age groups when faced with perceptual, cognitive, or identifying tasks.

With the perceptual, cognitive, and identifying tasks of the first series of experiments, a distinct development in the motor behavior of the hands was observed (from the youngest to oldest groups). In addition to changes in the general mobility of the hands, changes were noted, too, in the means of probing used by children of the different age groups.

Thus, the hand movements of the 3-year-olds hardly resembled probing movements. They were more like "grasping" or "touching" movements. The child simply "played" with the figure: placing his palm on the edge (the contour), he would clap the middle of the figure with his fingers, his palm remaining still. He would keep this up for practically the entire 60-second period. (See Figure 3–1.)

The hand movements of the 4–5-year-olds differed somewhat from those of the 3-year-olds, though there were many points of similarity. We noted the same grasping of the figure by the phalanges of the four fingers (index, middle, ring, and little fingers), the palm remaining on the contour of the figure. But the 4–5-year-olds maintained this position for only a relatively

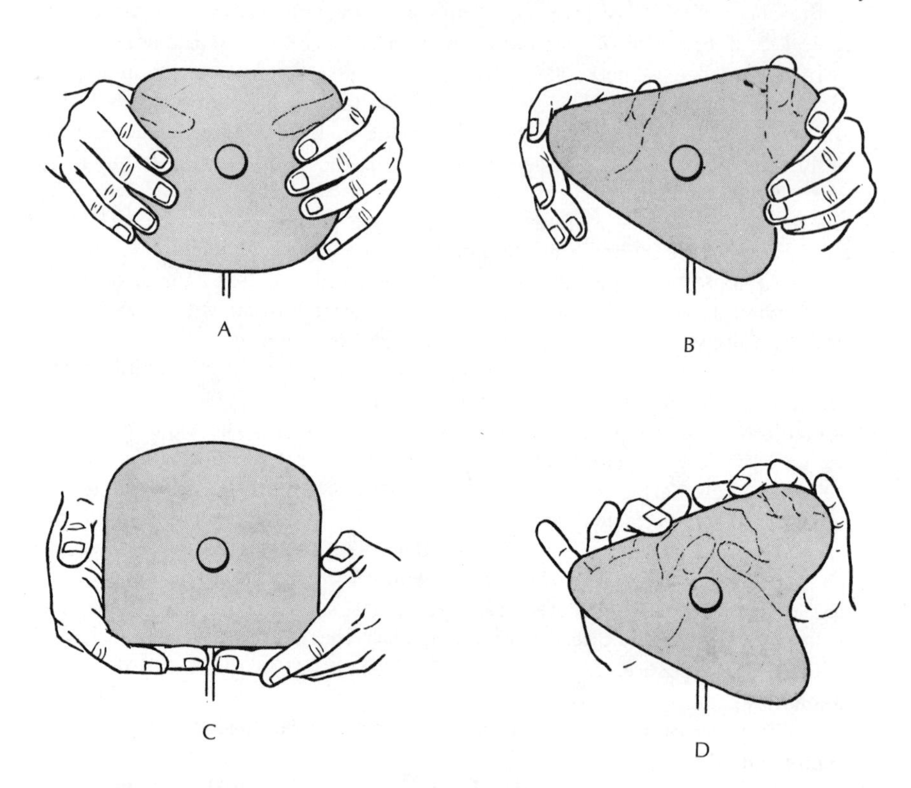

Figure 3–1. Position of the hands when the child feels the test figure, for children of the following ages: (*A*) 3 years 4 months; (*B*) 5 years 6 months; (*C*) 6 years 5 months; (*D*) 6 years 7 months.

short time. In the probing of the figure and its contour which followed, the palm and the bends in the middle of the fingers, as well as the area between palm and fingers, were active. The tips of the fingers touched the contour of the figure rarely—accidentally. As a rule, only one hand was active in carrying out the movements.

The 5–6-year-olds probed the figure with both hands simultaneously. Left and right hands would come together simultaneously or at once diverge from each other. It was noted that children of this age did a more thorough examination of the figure, though no extensive probing of the contour was observed. The children merely did a careful examination of one characteristic feature of the figure (a recess or a protuberance in it).

Children in the 6–7-year-old group traced the contour of the figure—mostly with their fingertips.

The methods of solution children of the different age groups used corresponded exactly with their degree of success in solving the task. In an overwhelming majority of cases the 3-year-olds could not locate the figure among others after their probing, while the 6–7-year-olds managed to do this with no trouble each time.

On the whole, one notes with haptic perception of a form under conditions that call for a perceptual task, the nature of the probing movements by children of the various age groups is as follows: there is increased mobility of the hands (by age 5); with the switch to the palm (which up to age 5 appears to be the chief organ of touch) the fingertips are put to use as well; probing is then carried out bimanually, the object of inspection becoming the entire contour of the figure, not just separate parts of it (by age 6, that is).

These findings would seem to confirm that it is only by age 5 that a system of strictly perceptual, cognitive functions begins to develop, the characteristic feature being extensive movements that are carried out consecutively by the receptor apparatus. The result is that a cognitive perceptual task is performed with more or less adequate means, even though these are as yet not fully developed. It may be assumed that up to age 5 children use other means to perform a cognitive task—that is, practical operations by which they manipulate an object. In our view, the results and hypotheses we have arrived at here could be made use of in working out some of the problems connected with sensory training for younger preschool children.

In the experiments of the second series, when the subjects were faced with the task of recognizing a figure, their perception of its form was rapid—considerably more rapid than it had been when they set out to acquaint themselves with the figure. The rate of probing movements, though, was markedly slower. In the second series a child would immediately grasp the entire figure, looking for and specifically noting features by which he might recognize it. (See Figure 3–2.) Hand movements were kept to a minimum.

It should be noted that the difference between the types of probing movements used in the task of recognition and those used for perception, was most pronounced among the older preschool groups (5–7-year-olds). Even when confronted with the task of identifying the object, the 3–5-year-olds exhibited the same "grasping" playful quality of movement they had when they tried to familiarize themselves with the figure. The result was that in both series of experiments, the children were unable to solve the problem correctly. Only the children in the younger preschool group who had been taught specifically how to carry out a detailed, perceptual examination of the object's form (by tracing its contour), showed any inclination to take hold of the figure even for a minute to try to identify it, not simply play with it.

One can assume that not only are identifying operations performed more rapidly and in less detail than perceptual functions, but they are themselves a product of the latter. To be sure, it would require further research and evi-

Figure 3–2. Position of the hands in the attempt to recognize the test figure: (*A*) 5-year-olds; (*B*) 6-year-olds.

dence to establish this point. But even in these experiments it is sufficiently clear that, when faced with the job of having to familiarize himself with a test object, a child performs certain identifying and perceptual operations which differ both with respect to the rapidity and range of movements he carries out in each instance.

However, not only touch and sight, but other types of perception are carried out by means of special orienting functions which model the features of a given object. This was demonstrated in research by Leont'ev and his associates (Leont'ev, 1965; Leont'ev and Ovchinnikova, 1958; Leont'ev and Gippenreiter, 1959; Gippenreiter, 1957, 1958) with regard to auditory perception of musical tones, and by Endovitskaya (1959) and Repina (1961), who did similar research with preschool age children as subjects. They found that the ability to determine the pitch of tones is closely related to a subject's capacity to reproduce the tones by means of vocalization (which a person can do, of course, without hearing tones). El'konin and Zhurova (1963) observed similar phenomena with respect to the development of phonemic hearing in children. They established that it is a considerable help to the child in analyzing the sound characteristics of a word if he models the features of certain verbal sounds by intoning them.

Recent research indicates that from infancy on a child's sensory functions undergo a lengthy course of development, so that by age 7 these are much improved. Earlier in this account we noted that even during the first half year of life a child is able to distinguish objects according to shape, color, and certain other features. However, since this ability to differentiate does not appear to result from any organized attempt to examine the principal qualities of objects, it cannot serve to orient the child adequately to even the simplest practical operations he may wish to perform with objects. This is most apparent in studying the development of the grasping movements infants make; it is only gradually, during the second half year of life, that these movements are sufficiently appropriate for the child to operate in terms of the position, shape, and size of objects. The development and refinement of exploratory modeling functions by the sense organs (essential for detailed, precise models of perception) is a gradual process which continues through the entire preschool period.

Ginevskaya (1948) asked preschool-age children to familiarize themselves with objects on a table by means of touch, since their eyes were covered. It was found that the probing movements children make with their hands vary according to the age of the child. In the case of the younger children in the preschool groups (3–4-year-olds), these movements were quite primitive, and were indistinguishable from mere manipulation of the objects. The children tried to knock, roll, or move the objects and by means of these practical or playful actions, familiarize themselves with the objects. At a somewhat later stage of development (4–5 years) a child tries to find out what an object is by squeezing it tightly in his fist. However, in doing so, his hand remains still; he does not carry out any searching or probing movements. Finally, the older preschool children (6–7-year-olds) were observed to make extensive use of more refined methods of examination. Along with the touch methods described above, these children make sensitive probing movements with their hands. By means of these they trace the contour of an object, get a sense of how flexible it is and what its general texture is. As a result, they build up a richer store of models which correspond more precisely to the specific features in the objects they have perceived.

Similar findings were obtained by Boguslavskaya (1963), who investigated how preschool-age children of various age groups try to learn something about a figure visually in order to be able to recognize it later among a number of other objects. Although the younger children merely took a quick look at the object (being more anxious to take hold of it and manipulate it), the older groups usually inspected the object at length before they attempted any practical manipulations with it. Owing to this, they were more effective in dealing with sensory tasks.

In their research studies Boguslavskaya and Ginevskaya merely observed the orienting movements children performed with their hands and eyes, but did not record them. Hence, their findings allow only for a general description of the growth of such movements at the preschool level. The same process was studied in greater detail in the above-mentioned research by Zinchenko and Ruzskaya, who used a moving picture camera to record the children's movements.

Data obtained in a later study of children of different age groups allows us to compare the development of children's hand movements in experiments involving touch perception with the development of eye movements in experiments which permitted subjects to carry out a visual examination of a figure. The following observations are excerpted from Zinchenko and Ruzskaya's report (1962, No. 3, pp. 87–90).

> The hand and eye movements of the 3–4-year-old children had a number of features in common. (See Figures 3–3 and 3–4.) Their hand and eye movements did not single out the contour of the figure or move along its surface. These children made relatively few movements with their hands and eyes, fixing on certain parts of the figure for lengthy periods of time.

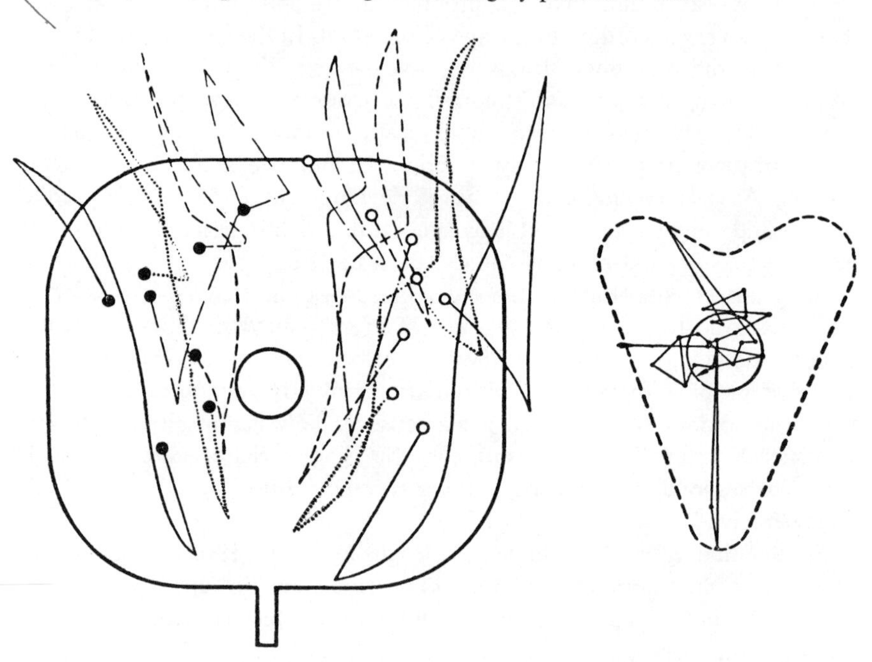

Figure 3–3. (*left*) Trajectory of the finger movements of the 3–4-year-old children. The black circles indicate fixation of the fingers of the right hand; the light circles, those of the left hand. The lines depict the trajectory of finger movements: solid line—little finger; dot-dash combination—index finger; dashed—middle finger; dotted—the ring finger.

Figure 3–4. (*right*) Trajectory of the eye movements of the 3–4-year-old children.

> At this stage of development children do not use any methods by which they can examine the contour of an object. They are more oriented to the size of an object, its surface, or texture rather than to its configuration.
>
> The motor behavior of the 4–5-year-old children was characterized by an increased number of hand and eye movements, many of which ranged quite far—as though measuring the surface of the figure. As with the younger group, their hand and eye movements focused primarily on the inner part of

the figure, no hand movements being made along the contour. However, some difference was noted in the way children attempted to learn about a figure visually, as distinct from touch methods.

The eye movements would fix closely on the most typical features of the contour of the figure. At this stage children are not oriented merely to the size of a figure but to certain qualities having to do with the form as well. This may be regarded as the beginning of an attempt on their part to single out enough sense data visually to deal with the task of recognizing the figure. Thus, with respect to this parameter, too, sight outstrips touch. Hence, the marked decrease in errors by the 4–5-year-old children in attempting to recognize a figure visually as compared with the results of the younger children.

With the 5–6-year-olds no fundamental changes were noted in the motor behavior of the eyes as compared with that of the 4–5-year-old groups. It cannot be said of children of this age that they tend to single out the contour as the part of the figure which could give them most information. Nonetheless a considerable part of the contour does become an object of inspection for them, as can be seen from the way they probe the figure. And while the children use their hands to distinguish certain features of the contour, these are not always the most typical. Hence in their attempts to learn about a figure either by sight or touch these children fail to explore most of the contour; still, their eyes, more often than their hands, tend to focus on the contour, with the result that when they try to identify the figure at sight in the control experiments they are almost always correct.

As for the 6–7-year-olds, the majority of their hand and eye movements "moved" along the contour of the figure. (See Figures 3–5 and 3–6.) There

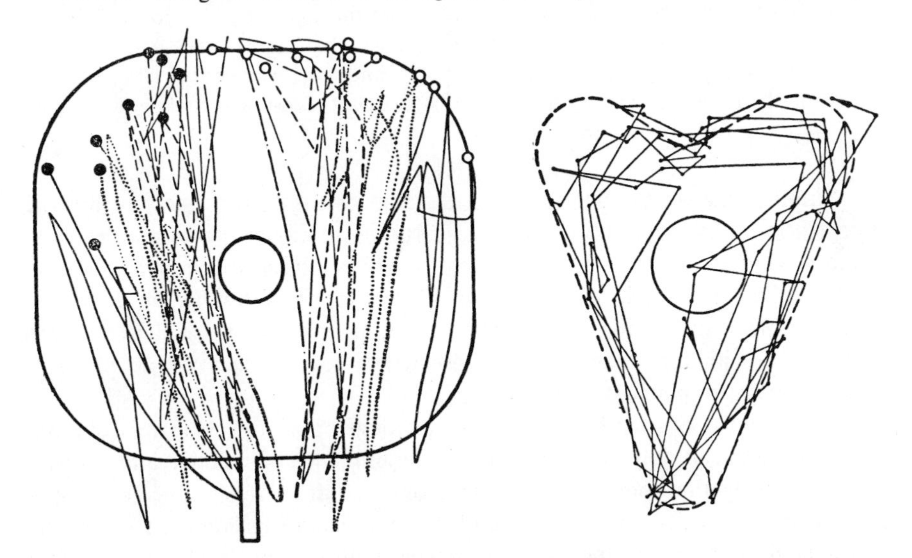

Figure 3–5. (*left*) Trajectory of the finger movements of the 6–7-year-old children. Lines refer to same fingers as those in Figure 3–3.

Figure 3–6. (*right*) Trajectory of eye movements of the 6–7-year-old children.

was a considerable drop in the number of movements they made along the edge. Both their hand and eye movements tended to fix on any one spot for only brief moments at a time. However, the eye movements with which they traced the contour of the object differed somewhat from the hand movements, being freer and far more detailed than the latter. Their eyes would glance from one side of the figure to another, and then back again. Also, the children made a visual comparison of individual parts of the contour, trying to determine their relationship to each other.

Thus the development of both sensory modalities meant that the child could acquire enough sense data to handle the task, and that he could do a better job of examining the object. With respect to a number of parameters we considered (productivity of knowledge, ability to select the object, sensory training, methods used to examine a form) touch lagged considerably behind sight. In order to clarify the interrelationship between the two types of perception (touch and sight) one would have to isolate the functions performed by the hands as sense organs (that is, whether they are used to manipulate objects to perform some action, or to get information). The development of each of these functions should then be studied individually.

In this experiment we have tried to demonstrate that the cognitive functions which the hands perform originate and develop under the control of vision. (We will not take up the question of the development of touch in blind persons in this account.) However, the question remains: what does the hand contribute to sight, not as an organ of touch, but as one which manipulates and performs practical operations with objects? Apparently, some important qualities of visual perception, such as objectivity and a sense of the spatial dimensions of an object, are acquired through the aid of touch. At the same time, one should not minimize the role which sight plays in developing a child's capacity to manipulate objects and perform practical operations with them. At a very early stage in life it is the eye which begins to deal afferently with manual operations.

Similar data on the way children develop orienting functions during the preschool period were obtained in research on tonal and phonemic hearing, and in studies on motor and kinesthetic perception. As Neverovich (1954, 1957) has indicated, improvement of the latter is bound up with the development of unique testing and orienting movements which children carry out with their hands. It is these which reveal the internal, proprioceptive pattern of an external act.

The child's sensory functions will not develop in this way in isolation. Such growth can only take place under the influence of practice and instruction in using the common sense data one acquires. If sensory training is allowed to take its own course, and no organization is imposed on it, the results are not too productive. The process will be considerably more effective if the child is specifically taught methods he can use to examine objects, and suitable standards to apply to the sense data he acquires.

Thus, data which have been collected by Sakulina, Korzakova, El'konin, Vetlugina, and others indicate that in order to improve a child's visual perception of the spatial characteristics of objects, or his grasp of sounds in music and speech, it will not do merely to familiarize him with a number of geometrical forms (or sounds) which differ in some distinct way. The child must be taught how to make use of measures or standards of sense data by means of activities that orient him to explore an object. In this way he will be able to depict the qualities he perceives in an object in his own reproduction of it.

In order, then, for a child to get an accurate perception of the form of an object which he either sees or experiences through touch, he must be taught how to follow the contour of that object with his hands or eyes. If he is to learn to distinguish a sound in a word, he must be taught how to intone the sound, differentiating it from other sounds in the word and emphasizing its phonetic features. Formal didactic systems were not sufficiently concerned with developing sensory functions of this kind in the child; yet any solid, organized program should make these functions a subject of particular concern, and provide the child with systematic guidance. The psychological findings we have noted are of primary importance in developing methods to be used in sensory training.

Let us consider now an experiment Ruzskaya (1954) used to study the development of preschool-age children's perception of form. In these experiments a table on which there were two response keys and a toy garage with a car in it were placed in front of the child. A small screen was pasted to the top of the garage, and on this geometrical figures were shown to the child by means of a special device. When certain of the figures appeared (triangles) the child was supposed to depress the left key, with others (rectangles), the right key. The correct response was reinforced by having the toy car come out of the garage.

In training sessions the children obtained practice in distinguishing the forms of a pair of figures which were shown to them many times. When they had demonstrated they could differentiate between the forms, the experimental trials were begun. In these, the same setup as that described above was used, and the children were shown different variants of the figures in a variety of positions. All the preschool children made a great many errors trying to select the necessary key, but the number of errors was particularly high for the 3- and 4-year-olds.

In experiments which followed, Ruzskaya made a special point of having the child develop better ways of familiarizing himself with the objects. He was given a pair of figures (a triangle and a rectangle) which had been cut out of pasteboard. With these as models (standards), the child was taught how to trace the contour of each figure successively with his finger and was told to watch and follow the movements of his hands. He was instructed to focus on the changes in direction his movements took at the angles and to count these out loud each time they came up (one, two, three). During the course of instruction the difference in the number of angles and sides in the figures was explained to the child. Gradually he learned methods by which he could distinguish any variant of a figure, regardless of how it was arranged. After the training period a sudden improvement was noted in the children's ability to distinguish the figures shown on the screen. The majority of the children—even the 3–4-year-olds—began to solve the problem correctly, making mistakes only with the most complex types of figures.

While the children in Ruzskaya's study were taught how to make direct use of certain hand and eye movements which are needed to form a copy of an object—a model of a figure one perceives—and were also taught how to compare this with a standard, in certain other studies a different course of sensory training was tried. In this method sensory knowledge was mediated in the following way. A child was taught how to model qualities in an object he perceived by first using other objects. These, in turn, helped to improve the children's ability to model objects directly—to copy objects by means of the movements of the sense organs involved in perception.

Boguslavskaya's research (1963) was concerned with the way in which preschool-age children develop visual perception of pictures, both of concrete objects, such as a shovel, vase, apple, and so on, and of abstract geometrical figures. It turned out that not only the younger children (3–5-year-olds), but a good number of the older ones (5–7-year-olds), limited their inspection to a brief glance at the objects. Thus the image they formed of it was quite incomplete and fragmentary. And while children can learn enough about an object through such a cursory examination to recognize it by one or two typical features, they do not learn enough to reproduce it in a drawing or a design. For in order to depict a thing, one must get a better perception of it, a more complete and detailed sensory image. In subsequent experiments Boguslavskaya taught the children how to model the form of the objects they perceived by having them lay out the figures with matches, strips of paper, and so on. Thus their activity was organized in a specific way, and it was explained to them that this was to help them become better acquainted with the object so that they could do a more exact drawing of it later on. Under these conditions, the models the children made were not ends in themselves, not the final product of their activity (as is usually true in drawing or design work), but a means of solving certain subsequent cognitive and practical problems. After the practice sessions the children all performed far more effectively, as evidenced by the considerably greater accuracy of their drawings (and this, despite the fact that with this procedure they had had no training in drawing).

A special instance of sensory training that used intermediary modeling as an aid was one in which children were taught how to model the qualities and relationships of certain objects by first using other objects which they had perceived through different analyzers. This was a type of training used to develop children's ability to grasp tones.

This research by Endovitskaya (1959) and Repina (1961) revealed that it is very difficult for preschool-age children to distinguish the pitch of pure tones (those produced by a sound generator). Their thresholds of discrimination in these experiments were extremely high.

In the developmental experiments objects were introduced whose spatial characteristics and relationships seemed to "model" those of pitch relationships. Thus, Repina staged a dramatic scene for the children using a big toy bear (the father bear) who uttered very deep sounds, a mother bear who was smaller and spoke in higher tones, and a tiny baby bear, the son, who spoke in even higher tones. After the experimenter and the children had acted out scenes in the life of these characters, the bears were hidden in various places and the children tried to tell from their voices where the animals could be found. It appeared that after their training even the younger children (the 2–4-year-olds) had no trouble discerning the pitch of the voices the toy animals used; they were also able to distinguish better any tone they heard for the first time—tones that were completely unrelated to the objects they had come to know in the experiment.

Endovitskaya used a more complicated model of pitch relationships but one that would have wider application. She gave the child a rectangular-shaped carriage with four equal square sections in it, and a doll which the child was to have jump from one square to another, depending upon the tones he heard. If the difference in pitch between tones was slight, the doll was to jump from the first to the second square; if the difference was greater, to the third square, and so forth. In the begining the child practiced how to carry out these steps with the experimenter; after that he performed them himself. The training the children received in modeling pitch relationships considerably improved their ability to distinguish the pitch of tones.

The third position we maintain with regard to the psychology of sensory training has to do with the conditions that are necessary for the development of sensory processes. In essence, this is that sensory functions can only develop in a varied context of activity, through practical activities that the child performs with objects that come up in his daily life during early childhood and the preschool period: drawing, clay modeling, constructing designs, studying music, conversing with others, performing physical exercises, learning skills through play, and the like.

In infancy and the preschool period a child acquires a certain amount of sense data through play when he tries to manipulate objects for some practical purpose (to get hold of an object and move it, or to place one object inside another, etc.). However, even at this stage of the child's development, with the proper instruction sensory functions can be separated from the purely practical, and the child can learn to use these to orient himself towards the latter—to anticipate what he must do. The following account of experiments with very young children (Venger, 1965) should serve to illustrate this point.

These experiments dealt with the way young children learn to perceive form by mastering certain practical activities. A method was used which required that children pull objects through an opening of a certain shape; we investigated how they learn to judge the shape of objects in trying to use them for some objective purpose. This method embodies a fundamental phase of any purposeful activity which requires that one take into account the form of objects; the children had to select and place two objects in a reciprocal relationship on the basis of certain spatial characteristics the objects had in common.

This type of task had been used as a teaching method in Montessori's system (1915). Some of the results on the way children of preschool age performed the task can be found in papers by Boguslavskaya (1961) and Shuleshko (1960). The data on performances by infants and prekindergarten children have been described by Efrussa (1931). All these writers noted that children used one of two types of solutions for the tasks: a trial-and-error method of solution through practice or one the child had worked out "in his mind." The latter type of solution was the better of the two and was used by children who were somewhat further along in their development. However, with regard to both types of solution none of the studies tried to determine what type of task a child solves by means of perception.

In our experiments we used eight types of grilles which differed in terms of the shape and arrangement of the openings they contained. (See Figure 3–7.)

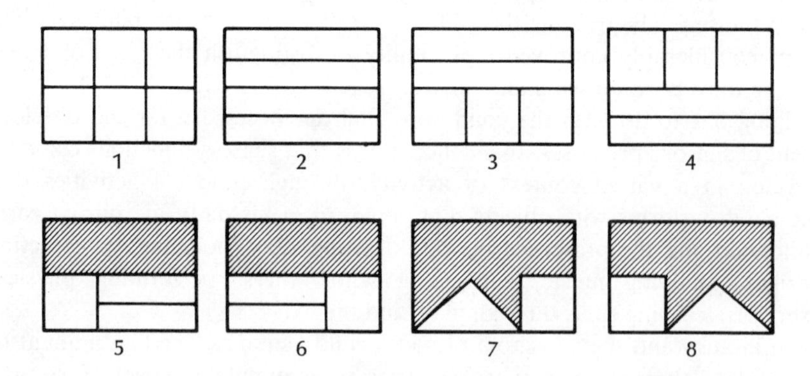

Figure 3–7.

The openings were of the following shape and dimension: (1) a square 12 by 12 cm.; (2) a rectangle 6 by 24 cm.; (3) an equilateral triangle, the sides of which were 17 cm. long.

As the experimental objects we used: (1) a cube whose side measured 10 cm.; (2) a prism with a square section, the length of the side of the base being 16 cm., the height 3 cm.; (3) a prism with a triangular section, the length of the side of the base being 16 cm., the height 8 cm. (See Figure 3–8.) Accordingly, the side of the object facing the child had either a square, rectangular, or triangular shape.

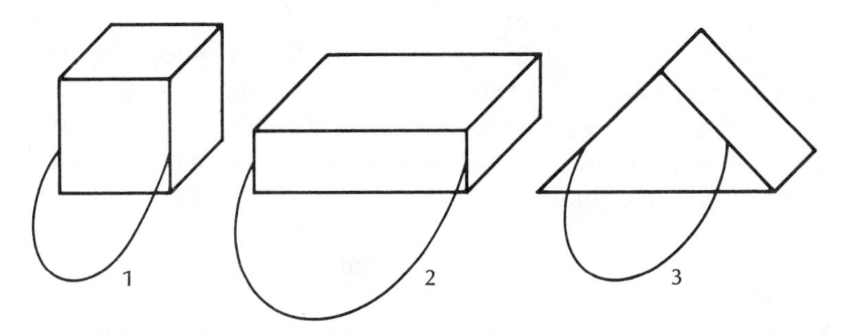

Figure 3–8.

In each series of experiments no more than two types of objects and two corresponding types of openings in the grilles were used. Thus the subject operated merely with two radically different forms. This considerably lessened the difficulty of organizing the child's activity. Each of the objects could only be pulled through an opening that corresponded to the shape of the side of the object facing the subject, but not through openings having any other shape. Hence, this eliminated the possibility of inadequate solutions; either a task was solved correctly or not at all. When the child failed to solve the task he had to repeat his performance until he had achieved positive results—regardless of whether he was able to distinguish the correct solution from the incorrect, a factor that had figured so largely in other research studies.

The objects were made out of pasteboard. These were painted blue and covered with a clear, polyethylene film. By means of cords that were sewed on to the objects, the child could easily hold them in place and slide them through the openings. When the child held the object by the cord, the side facing him had the same position as did the opening in the grille which corresponded to it in shape. This eliminated the need for the subjects to combine two tasks as they had done in earlier studies: to select and link up an object with a "counter-object," and to line the two up so that they were in identical positions.

During the experiment the child was seated at a little table where the grille to be used had been set up in a vertical position. The experimenter pointed out the pair of objects behind the grille and asked the child to "get hold of the block through the little window and play with it." If the child did not begin on the task at once, the objects were given to him for a few seconds to play with. Then they were picked up, and, as the child looked on, were placed behind the grille, the experimenter once again asking that the child "get hold of the block." Depending upon the conditions in each series of experiments both or only one of the objects could be pulled through the grille. Once the child had performed the task he was asked to "give the block to the man." Then he was shown the next pair of objects. In another variant of the experiment the objects were handed to the child one by one and he was asked to "give the block to the man through the little window." (This variant was used only with the 3-year-old children.) We should emphasize that all of the children took a distinctly positive attitude toward the experiments, regarding them as a kind of interesting game, and enjoyed participating.

The experiments were carried out in Children's Home No. 12 in the October Region of Moscow. Twenty-seven children ranging in age from 7.5 months to 3 years acted as subjects.

Our purpose in conducting these experiments with children in their first and second year of life was to determine whether in performing the task of pulling objects through openings a child this age is capable of: (1) judging the shape of objects and of selecting only those which can pass through the openings in the grille; (2) judging the shape of an opening so that he will only pull through objects which fit that opening; (3) simultaneously judging both the form of an object and that of an opening at a given stage of development so that he will pull each object through the right opening. Furthermore, it was important to determine whether, through repeated attempts to perform the operation, a child could learn to judge the form of objects if it appeared that he was not capable of this from the start.

In conjunction with the third task, three series of experiments were carried out. In the first series grille No. 1 (see Figure 3–7), in which all the openings were square, was set up before the child. Behind the grille were a pair of experimental objects (Nos. 1 and 2, a square and a rectangle—see Figure 3–8). (The description of shape refers to the surface facing the child.) In order to keep the child from becoming fixated on one side, we alternated the position of the objects each time they were presented. Two groups of children participated in the experiment, one consisting of six children aged 7.5 months to 1 year, the other, seven children aged 1 year and 1 month to 1 year and 8 months.

At the beginning of the experiment all the subjects pulled and grabbed at the figures they were shown. However, after a certain number of attempts with both objects—some of these successful, others not—the children gave up trying to pull the rectangular figure through the square openings. It took children who were less than a year old 5–29 presentations of the objects to learn how to select the "positive" of the two figures (the square); children in their second year of life required 1–4 presentations.

In the second series of experiments grilles Nos. 5 and 6 were shown alternately to the children; hence, the square opening was replaced each time by the rectangular. A pair of identical objects (squares) was placed behind the grille. The experiments were carried out with 7 children ranging in age from 1 year to 1 year and 4 months of age.

It appeared that it was immeasurably harder for the children to judge the form of the opening in the grille than that of the object—the task that had come up in the previous series. Of the 7 subjects, 4 were simply unable to do this; the other 3 children learned how to select objects which could be pulled through the square opening, but they needed a good number of practice trials for this (20, 24, and 50).

The third series of experiments used one variant for those children who had participated in the first series and another for those who had been subjects in the second series.

The first variant: Four subjects, children in their second year of life, who had been the quickest to learn how to judge the form of the experimental object when given the task of having to pull this through an opening in grille No. 1 (the grille with square openings), were asked to do this with the same objects and grille No. 2 (which had only rectangular openings). All of the children paid no attention whatever to the fact that the grille had been changed and stubbornly tried to pull the square object through. Thus it turned out that what they had accomplished in experiments in the first series—selecting an object having a certain form—in no way implied an ability to discern any correspondence in form between that of the object and the opening in the grille.

After the grille had been switched a number of times the children refused to try to deal with the objects. None of them learned how to judge the form of the object and that of the opening simultaneously.

The second variant: Three children in their second year of life, who had learned to judge the form of the opening in trying to pull square objects through the grille, were asked to use the same grilles (Nos. 5 and 6) and a pair of rectangular objects. All the children persisted in trying to pull these objects through the square openings. Consequently, in this case, too, the children had not caught on to the idea that the forms of the objects corresponded to those of certain openings. Their selecting an opening with a distinct form as the positive one in the second series was in no way linked to an ability to gauge the form of the objects.

To sum up the result of experiments with children up to age 3, it can be said that at this age children as a rule do not discern any correspondence in form between the object and the opening in the grille. The efforts they make tend to be disorganized. Success or failure only leads to a gradual inhibition of inadequate attempts until they can finally distinguish a difference between a "positive" and a "negative" object (or a "positive" and a "negative" opening).

We began our experiments with children in their third year of life by immediately giving them tasks which required that they be able to judge simultaneously the form of the objects and that of the openings. Seven children, ranging in age from 2 years and 3 months to 3 years, took part in the experiments. Four series of experiments were carried out with each of them.

In the first series grilles Nos. 3 and 4 were alternately set up in front of the subject. Thus the square and rectangular openings constantly changed position: in one presentation they would be at the bottom of the grille, in the next, at the top. With each type of grille a child was shown several pairs (2–6) of experimental objects (squares and rectangles) in turn, which he was to try to pull through the openings in the grilles. In some cases a pair consisted of identical objects, in others not. In the latter case the way in which the pair was arranged was alternated each time so that a given form would appear first on the right, then on the left.

The experiments continued until the child reached a point where he was able to pull both objects into the appropriate openings regardless of the order in which the objects were presented. Then the child was asked to perform the reverse operation with the same object and the same types of grilles—that is, they were told to "give the block to the man through the little window." During this activity the objects were arranged in the necessary position and handed to the subject one at a time.

A common feature of all the experiments in this series was that none of the subjects reached a point where he could pull both objects through "on the spot" without making errors. But the end result was that all the children learned how to perform the necessary operation with each object. In other respects the course of these experiments varied in terms of the amount of practice trials each subject needed (a range of 5–68) and the manner in which each of the children performed the operations.

In the course of practice not only did the proportion of correct and incorrect responses change, but the children's reactions took on a different quality, especially when they made faulty attempts to deal with the task. At the start of the experiment all the children except Nadya A. and Korina K. persisted in these incorrect attempts. A child would try with all his might to drag an object through an opening in which it did not fit, and would only switch to another opening after considerable time. Often it was only after the experimenter pointed out to him that he should try another opening that he would do so. Throughout the balance of the experiment these faulty attempts were less prolonged and persistent; usually toward the end of the experiment a child had merely to touch the edge of the wrong opening with the object and he would shift over to another opening. The child's attempt to drag the objects toward him had obviously become a test, an effort on his part to see if the object fit the opening; the operation thus assumed a new function—that of orienting the child to the material. Usually once the operation took on this new quality, the child was able to perform the task correctly. Apparently what we observed here was that process whereby attempts to perform a given act generate specific orienting functions, a fact that had been noted earlier by Podd'yakov (1960).

As for Nadya A. and Korina K., in all probability the faulty attempts these little girls made at the start of the experiment were actually "tests." An important fact to be noted is that no "test" trials of this nature were observed among children before the age of three.

In the second series the children were given the same objects they had used in the first series, as well as grilles Nos. 5 and 6, in which the square and rectangular openings were not situated one above the other but were lined up horizontally. The objects were handed to a subject one by one and he was told to "give them back to the man through the little window." During the course of the experiment each child had to push a total of four objects through corresponding openings.

While in the first series the children had had a chance to grasp the idea that certain objects fit certain openings, in the second series they had no opportunity to do any additional testing; for the only change here was in the arrangement of the openings in the grilles.

Contrary to our expectations, two subjects, Vova K. and Sasha O., resorted to practical trial and error methods again in the second series of experiments. Hence, though they had performed the task correctly in the first series, they had not discerned a correspondence of form between objects and openings but had operated merely on the basis of a more elementary type of orientation. It may be assumed that they had become oriented to a general difference in the form of the objects and the various types of grilles, as well as to the direction of their own movements in fitting objects through the openings (that is, movements made upwards or downwards).

The other five subjects were able to handle the task immediately and were not confused by the fact that the openings were arranged in a way that was unfamiliar to them. This means that in the first series these children had been able to learn the correspondence between the forms of certain objects and openings.

In the third series of experiments the same children were shown a new pair of objects (a square and a triangle) and grilles Nos. 7 and 8 (which had square and triangular-shaped openings). As in the previous series, the objects were handed to the subject one by one and he was asked to "give them back to the man through the little window." Each object was presented one time only with each type of grille.

Six of the children in the group managed to do the assignment by using orienting movements they had developed through practice. Thus the change in the form of objects and openings meant they had to devise a new solution to this task, and the means they used to solve it did not differ essentially from those they had worked out in the first series of experiments. However, one subject—Korina K.—was able to carry out the assignment in the third series from the outset. This indicated she had made the transition we were anticipating—that is, she had moved on from her attempts to test out a solution in practice to a way of performing the operation "in her mind." And, as the child's behavior indicated, this implied that visually she had been able to grasp the idea of a correspondence in form between objects and openings. The child would grasp an object, and as she was carrying it over to the grille would glance back and forth from the object to each opening, and from one opening to another. Immediately thereafter she would push the object through the right opening with no hesitation whatever. Thus practical trial and error methods had given way to a unique visual method of testing, a way of determining visually whether the object fit the opening.

The method used in experiments in the fourth series was identical to that used in the third except that we had set up a removable, clear polyethylene film a slight distance in front of the grille. As each object was handed to the child he was told, "Take the block and show me which window it can get through. Then I'll lift up the film and you'll hand me the block through that little window."

Four subjects—Vova K., Sasha O., Vova F., and Vitya F.—were completely helpless under these circumstances. They would pull an object over to any opening at random, and after the film was removed would try to shove the object through an opening. In some cases the children tried to push the object through the film. Korina K., however, as in the previous series, would glance back and forth a number of times from the object to the openings and then carry each object over to the right opening, making no mistakes. But the most interesting result was that obtained in experiments with Natasha S. and Nadya A. The introduction of the film proved to be the turning point for these little girls. They shifted from practical trial and error methods they had used in the third series to visual methods to link up objects and openings. They would move an object over to one of the openings, and if the latter did not appear to match its form, would slide the object along the film to a second opening. In some cases, after they had placed an object in front of the proper opening, they would shift it over to another opening, and then back again to the former location. As a result, these children always managed to place the object in front of the right opening, and when the film was removed would push it through as required.

Conditions Necessary for Training Perceptual Analysis

Our experiments showed that when a child uses practical trial and error methods to solve a task which requires that he take into account the form of objects, he is not, in fact, performing the act of perception specifically needed for the task. Initially he learns through practice how to place one or another of the objects; only later does he notice that an object has specific features which distinguish it from others. Apparently, though, the features he singles out for attention are not always the ones which are most important in terms of the task at hand. In other words, he uses perception here to make a choice that will give him a general orientation to his surroundings.

The second method of dealing with a practical problem—solving it "in one's mind"—is an altogether different thing. Here the child uses perception to link up the specific features that will help him perform the task; he perceives the need to single out precisely those qualities in the objects which will objectively determine whether he can operate with them as he must in a given situation. In our experiments the qualities that mattered were the contour and size of the objects and the "counter-objects"; preferably, the qualities of both taken into account together.

Activities that are more complicated, those a child begins to master at a somewhat later stage in life, prove to be particularly valuable in developing perception. It is with activities such as these that a child first encounters a task that will properly provide for the conditions under which he can acquire the skills and qualities of sense perception peculiar to man: a capacity for musical and phonemic hearing, the ability to make a visual analysis of a complex form or of the color objects as reproduced, proprioceptive means of anticipating a scheme of action that will be suitable for certain movements, etc. The formal educational exercises (of the type that Montessori used) could never, in and of themselves, develop these sensory qualities in the child. Under the best of circumstances these are suitable only as auxiliary means in teaching, to further develop skills which, as we have noted, take shape through activities that are more complicated in nature.

It is only with the shift to activities involving building or drawing that a child is faced with the job of having to do a detailed visual examinaton of the form, size and spatial arrangement of an object. The inclusion of musical activities in a program requires that he also develop more advanced techniques by which to analyze pitch relationships. In distinctly human activities such as these, one needs to become oriented not only to various characteristics in the material; one must also develop the ability to reproduce the external image of an object with all its characteristic features. The object thus functions as a model which the child actively attempts to reproduce in one or another type of material.

However, if these activities are to have the proper impact on a child's sensory development, they must be organized in a specific way and the child be given systematic guidance from his teacher. As Luria's research (1948) indicates it is not every type of activity with building materials that will aid a child's perception of space, nor, as Sakulina has shown (1963), does every type of drawing activity improve a child's visual analysis of the form of objects. Vetlugina (1963) also arrived at similar conclusions with respect to musical activities in studying how children develop an ability to distinguish pitch and rhythm.

What is most important is that training be so organized as to present the child with the task of having to produce something which resembles the sample object he has been shown. In addition, one must organize not only the performance but the orienting aspect of the child's activity. That is, he must be taught methods by which to examine those qualities in the test model which he will have to reproduce in his own work; he should also learn ways in which he can analyze his own product and compare it with the test model. By means of such instruction the child will acquire and put to use standards of sense data that will apply to an analysis both of a test object and of his own creation.

As the above-mentioned research by Luria confirms, preschool-age children are not able to use purely visual means to break a test object down into its component parts. They generally try to deal with such a problem through practical means, by testing various combinations, until they achieve the desired result. In an attempt to get children to make the transition from this primitive level of dealing with a problem to a higher level of operating, Sokhina modified the task in such a way that what was of primary importance was not the practical result but the child's preliminary orientation toward the means by which he could achieve his end. This being the purpose, the test model and figures similar to the elements which composed it (plane figures of various shapes) were placed under glass. Before attempting to reproduce the test model the child had to point out which of these figures he would have to use. Then the experimenter took out the figures the child had indicated and the child set to work to apply these to the job of reconstructing the figure; during this process it became clear to him whether or not he had been right in the preliminary visual analysis he had made of the parts. When, after a number of unsuccessful attempts, the child discovered that the task at hand was difficult and that he had been wrong in his choice of figures, he was given some patterns cut out of plain white paper which corresponded exactly to the test figure and its constituent elements. The child then placed these copies of the elements over the copy of the test figure. In this way he was taught how to distinguish the parts out of which the latter could be constructed. In this case the patterns of the elements represented standards of the forms the child would have to use in order to analyze the complex structure of the test figure; fitting the sample elements on to the copy of the test figure served as a means whereby the child could make such an analysis.

The result of this instruction was that all the children 4–7 years of age considerably improved their ability to analyze a complex form visually. In the majority of cases, they could indicate correctly, with no preliminary work on models, which of the geometrical elements would function to construct a figure, and they were able to judge approximately how these elements had to be arranged.

We should note that certain additional devices proved necessary in order to achieve similar results in teaching young children (4–5-year-olds). These were aimed at getting the children to regard the work they did with the pattern models not as a solution to a practical task but as a means of analyzing the form of the test figure so that they would be able to build it later on. This was done by making the basic construction task more attractive (by having the children put together a handsome design from a figure that had been cut out of brightly colored pasteboard), while at the same time making the preliminary operations less appealing (having the children operate with patterns that had been cut out of plain, soft white paper).

The experiments showed that beginning at about the age of 4 children can quite easily learn this simple method of modeling a test figure they see. The effect of such training is that children are later considerably more accurate in their ability to break a figure down into its elements by means of visual analysis.

A Theory of Perceptual and Cognitive Development

Thus, as with research carried out by El'konin, Endovitskaya, Podd'yakov, and others, this study testifies to the effective way in which modeling influences a child's sensory development, and indicates the considerable opportunities that similar types of modeling activities offer in teaching.

However, what remains is for us to clarify the nature of the effects we have observed in the present instance. Is modeling merely an external auxiliary means that facilitates the course of these or other sensory processes, without altering their essential nature, or does it result in a fundamental reorganization of perception, a transition to a new and higher stage of development?

On the basis of the facts at our disposal and of certain general theoretical views we hold with regard to perception, we assume that the latter is true. I have in mind by way of theory the idea of interiorization which was introduced into Soviet psychology by Vygotskii (1960) and subsequently developed further by Leont'ev (1965). Recently Gal'perin (1959, 1966) devoted intensive study to further elaborating and systematizing this theory.[2]

According to this theory, which I feel is of cardinal importance in general psychology, the development of mental processes begins with certain external operations that an individual performs with objects. Subsequently, given certain conditions, this process acquires an orienting, cognitive function which, once it has undergone a series of changes and becomes contracted, is ultimately converted into an internal operation, one that takes place on the plane of ideas. A similar type of interiorization is to be noted in the development of sensory processes in children when modeling is introduced as an element that helps to mediate perception.

Thus, in Endovitskaya's research (1959), which dealt with the problem of developing musical hearing in preschool-age children, it was found that initially a child needs some external, material prop to help him discriminate sounds according to pitch—for example, a network of boxes drawn on paper, into which dolls are moved, their movements modeling the pitch relationships of the acoustic signals that the child perceives.

However, after a child has had some practice with this, his need for external props diminishes and he begins to distinguish the tones without the network of boxes. Apparently, the explanation is that the child has interiorized the procedure and has begun to use an internal model he has formed, one which represents a scale of a number of tones. It is with this that he compares the tones he hears.

Similar changes in development were noted by others in studying children's visual perception of the spatial characteristics of objects.

It is interesting to note that in the kind of interiorization which takes place with sensory processes there is a complex interaction of natural and intermediate types of modeling, with the result that under the influence of the latter the former are reorganized. Thus, initially it is extremely important that a child draw an object, or model it in some graphic way in order to get a precise grasp of the form, position, and other spatial characteristics of that object. Once he has followed the course his drawing takes with his eyes, he is better able to inspect an object visually. Through the aid of certain means that are natural to visual perception the child learns to draw and reproduce a copy of an object in a more detailed and precise manner. Consequently, the general nature and productivity of his sensory processes are substantially changed by this activity.

Hence, the data available to us allow us to assume that the types of intermediate modeling we have described are not merely external, auxiliary measures; owing to their influence (under certain conditions at least), there is a fundamental restructuring of the sensory processes which marks their

2. *Editors' note:* See Chapter 7 of this volume, by P. Y. Gal'perin.

true development, a fact that is of particular interest from the standpoint of preschool educational theory.

But the problem is not limited merely to this. Because a highly developed capacity for sensation and perception is needed in the most diverse types of creative work, the development of the child's sensory processes is of value in itself. Nonetheless it is a process which should not be treated in isolation but in conjunction with the course of the child's intellectual development as a whole.

What relationship, then, does the development of perception have to that of thought? To what degree does sensory training serve as preparation for the development of the child's thought processes?

This is a complex issue which has been dealt with specifically by Shchedrovitsky and others at the Institute of Preschool Education, and in this chapter we can only consider it in the most general way.

As we know, this problem has led to some heated debates among specialists in preschool education and child psychology. On the one hand, those who hold a rather crude view of the senses believe that the accumulation and association of a variety of sense experiences will result in the formation of ideas, judgments, inferences, and so on. On the other hand, those who take an extremely idealistic position maintain that the genesis of thought is in no way linked to the sense experiences one acquires, that it comes about as certain innate intellectual abilities begin to mature.

At first glance it would seem one could arrive at a satisfactory explanation for the transition from sensory to intellectual processes merely by reference to the generalizing function of language. Yet, as Vygotskii pointed out, a word can be made to serve an extremely wide range of purposes, and a child must undergo enormous development before words can become something other than mere indications of things to him, and he is able to understand that they embody ideas.

The solution to this complex and entangled issue can only be arrived at, apparently, through concrete application of the general Marxist view concerning sense experience as the source of human knowledge and the dialectics involved in the transition from sensation to thinking.

During the development of a child's activity, as its content and structure become more complex, the changes that occur in its orienting function prepare for the conversion of the latter into intellectual, conceptual processes. What is of decisive importance here is the change in content, primarily the transition from one's reproducing perceptible qualities in objects to reproducing internal qualities which are not subject to view but are implied.

On the basis of experimental facts one can demonstrate that, given a distinct scheme of training in which a child systematically learns certain methods of orientation, he begins to gather and develop types of modeling experience which at a later date will enable him to reproduce certain latent relationships within objects. It is in this way that operations of a strictly intellectual, conceptual nature take shape.

The one striking fact which emerges from the research discussed here is that at the orienting stage of development and training the child confronts, as it were, two spheres of reality: the world as depicted and that which depicts the world as modeled, and that which actively models. Gradually the child learns to relate these spheres of reality in a certain way: to regard and use the one as a copy or substitute for the other.

While both these spheres and the activities related to them take place on one plane, they are of a material nature and can be compared graphically. For example, in the experiments conducted by Sokhina, a child could actually place a paper model on the real test figure and with his own eyes become convinced that the form and dimensions of the two coincided. However, since a specific functional dependence had already been established here, it took only one step to "break away" from the use of the model on the test figure, to induce the child to operate with models in the absence of objects—that is, merely by keeping these in mind, as Gal'perin puts it, by assuming the existence of the real objects.

What we have outlined here are the general psychophysiological principles on which to organize sensory training so as to provide a basis in sense perception for some of the simplest, most basic conceptual operations. In particular, this system would develop skills with elementary forms by having the child model objects in the environment; as a result he would later develop more complex types of symbolic behavior, those which are essential to his mastery of mathematics, physics, biology, and the other areas of the scientific knowledge that man has acquired.

References

Anan'ev, B. G. *Psychology of sensory cognition.* Moscow: Izd. Akad. Pedag. Nauk RSFSR, 1960.

Anokhin, P. K. (ed.) In *Problems of higher nervous activity.* Moscow, 1949.

Bernshtein, N. A. *On the structure of movements.* Moscow, 1947.

Boguslavskaya, Z. M. Development of means of visual shape investigation in preschool children. *Abstracts of the Second Conference of the Association of Psychologists.* Moscow: Izd. Akad. Pedag. Nauk RSFSR, 1963, No. 2.

Efrussa, P. O. *The psychology of early childhood.* Moscow-Leningrad: OGIZ Gos. Uch.-Pedag. Izd., 1931.

El'konin, D. B. An experimental analysis of the initial stage of reading instruction. In *Problems related to the psychology of educational activities of junior school children.* Moscow: Izd. Akad. Pedag. Nauk RSFSR, 1962.

El'konin, D. B., and Zhurova, L. E. A contribution to the problem concerning the development of phonemic perception in preschool children. In *Sensory training of preschool children.* Moscow: Izd. Akad. Pedag. Nauk RSFSR, 1963.

Endovitskaya, T. V. On discriminative pitch sensitivity of preschool children. *Dokl. Akad. Pedag. Nauk RSFSR,* 1959, No. 5.

Gal'perin, P. Y. Development of investigations on the formation of mental operations. In *Psychological science in the U.S.S.R.* Vol. 1. Moscow: Izd. Akad. Pedag. Nauk RSFSR, 1959.

Gal'perin, P. Y. The psychology of thinking and the doctrine of stage-by-stage formation of mental operations. In *Study of thinking in Soviet psychology.* Moscow: Izd. Nauka, 1966.

Ginevskaya, T. O. The development of hand movements during tactile exploration in preschool children. *Izv. Akad. Pedag. Nauk RSFSR,* 1948, No. 14.

Gippenreiter, Y. B. An analysis of the systemic structure of auditory perception. Communications 1, 2. *Dokl. Akad. Pedag. Nauk RSFSR,* 1957, No. 4, 1958, No. 1.

Kislyuk, G. A., and Pen'evskaya, L. A. Study of the extant level of development of shape perception in preschool children. In *Sensory training of preschool children.* Moscow: Izd. Akad. Pedag. Nauk RSFSR, 1963.

Korzakova, Y. I. The shape of an object as mastered and reproduced through modeling by preschool children. In *Sensory training of preschool children.* Moscow: Izd. Akad. Pedag. Nauk RSFSR, 1963.

Krupskaya, N. K. On the problem of the socialist school. In *Pedagogical works.* Vol. 2. Moscow: Izd. Akad. Pedag. Nauk RSFSR.

Leont'ev, A. N. *Problems in the development of the mind.* (2nd ed.) Moscow: Izd. Mysl', 1965.

Leont'ev, A. N., and Gippenreiter, Y. B. An analysis of the systemic structure of auditory perception. Communication 8. *Dokl. Akad. Pedag. Nauk RSFSR,* 1959, No. 2.

Leont'ev, A. N., and Ovchinnikova, O. V. An analysis of the systemic structure of auditory perception. Communication 5. *Dokl. Akad. Pedag. Nauk RSFSR,* 1958, No. 3.

Leont'ev, A. N., and Zaporozhets, A. V. *Rehabilitation of hand function.* New York: Pergamon Press, 1960.

Luria, A. R. The development of constructive activity in the preschool child. In *Problems in preschool child psychology.* Izd. Akad. Pedag. Nauk RSFSR, 1948.

Montessori, M. *The method of scientific education as applied to children's upbringing in orphanages.* Moscow, 1915.

Neverovich, Y. Z. The role of orienting-investigatory activity in habit formation in children. In *Papers presented at a conference on problems of psychology.* Moscow, 1954.

Neverovich, Y. Z. The role of orientation in the formation of complex motor systems in children. *Abstracts of Papers presented at a conference on Problems Related to the Orienting Reflex.* Moscow, 1957. (Abstract.)

Ovchinnikova, O. V. An analysis of the systemic structure of auditory perception. Communications 3, 6, 7, 9. *Dokl. Akad. Pedag. Nauk RSFSR,* 1958, No. 1, 1959, No. 1, 2, 1960, No. 3.

Podd'yakov, N. N. Features of the orienting activity of preschool children during the formation and automatizing of practical acts. *Vop. Psikhol.,* 1960, No. 2.

Podd'yakov, N. N. Formation in preschool children of the ability to visualize clearly the displacement of objects in space. In *Sensory training of preschool children.* Moscow: Izd. Akad. Pedag. Nauk RSFSR, 1963.

Repina, T. A. On some techniques of studying pitch sensitivity in preschool children. Communications 1–3. *Dokl. Akad. Pedag. Nauk RSFSR,* 1961, Nos. 4–6.

Rubinshtein, S. L. *Foundations of general psychology.* Moscow, 1946.

Ruzskaya, A. G. The role of direct experience and words in the formation of generalizations in preschool children. Candidate's dissertation, Moscow, 1954.

Sakulina, N. P. The significance of drawing in the sensory training of the preschool child. In *Sensory training of preschool children.* Moscow: Izd. Akad. Pedag. Nauk RSFSR, 1963.

Shuleshko, E. E. Features of the orienting-investigative activity of children during the visual evaluation of the forms of flat geometric figures. *Dokl. Akad. Pedag. Nauk RSFSR,* 1960, No. 2.

Venger, L. A. Object-shape discrimination by young children. *Dokl. Akad. Pedag. Nauk RSFSR,* 1962, No. 2.

Venger, L. A. On the modes of visual perception of object shape in early and preschool age. In *The development of cognitive and volitional processes in preschool children.* Moscow: Izd. Prosveshchenie, 1965.

Vetlugina, N. A. The development of perception of pitch and rhythm relationships in the process of singing instruction offered to preschool children. In *Sensory training of preschool children.* Moscow: Izd. Akad. Pedag. Nauk RSFSR, 1963.

Vygotskii, L. S. *The development of higher mental functions.* Moscow: Izd. Akad. Pedag. Nauk RSFSR, 1960.

Zaporozhets, A. V., and El'konin, D. B. *Psychology of the preschool child: Development of cognitive processes.* Moscow: Izd. Akad. Pedag. Nauk, 1964.

Zaporozhets, A. V., and El'konin, D. B. *The psychology and personality of preschool children.* Moscow: Izd. Akad. Pedag. Nauk, 1965.

Zaporozhets, A. V., and Usova, A. P. *Sensory training of preschool children.* Moscow: Izd. Akad. Pedag. Nauk, 1963.

Zhurova, L. E. The development of auditory analysis of words in preschool children. *Vop. Psikhol.,* 1963, No. 3.

Zinchenko, V. P. A comparative analysis of touch and vision. Communications 1–11 (Communications 1, 3, 4, 5, 7, 8, 9, 10, 11, done jointly with A. G. Ruzskaya). *Dokl. Akad. Pedag. Nauk RSFSR,* 1959, No. 5, 1960, Nos. 2, 3, 5, 6, 1961, Nos. 4, 6 (a), 1962, Nos. 1, 2, 3.

Zinchenko, V. P. Perception and action. *Dokl. Akad. Pedag. Nauk RSFSR,* 1961, No. 5. (b).

4

Speech Development and the Formation of Mental Processes

A. R. Luria

EDITORS' INTRODUCTION

A. R. Luria is perhaps the best known of the psychologists represented in this volume; more than twenty of his articles and books have been published in English since the mid-1920's. In 1929, he attended the International Congress of Psychology in New Haven, where he gave a joint paper with his colleague and friend L. Vygotskii. During the 1920's, Luria worked at the Institute of Psychology and other institutions in Moscow. He had come to Moscow from Kazan at the invitation of Kornilov, then head of the Institute. At that time Luria's work was centered on the function of speech; special concerns were the role of speech in controlling affective processes (his book The Nature of Human Conflict *is well known in the West) and the development of mental processes. It is this latter work which forms the basis for this chapter.*

Although Luria is perhaps best known in the West for this work on speech processes, most of his career has been spent on research in the area of neuropsychology, which forms the content of his other contribution to this volume. It was his interest in speech, or more specifically, the pathology of speech, which led Luria into neuropsychology. While struggling with the problem of the relation between language and thought, both Luria and Vygotskii became interested in various types of speech pathology, among them aphasia. The study of aphasia led Luria to the study of the brain correlates of aphasia and thence to the study of brain processes in general.

Events in the early 1950's resulted in a prolonged "vacation" from neuropsychological research; because of the controversy then raging over the role of psychology in Soviet science, Luria the psychologist was required to leave his position at the Institute of Neurosurgery for work at the Institute of Defectology. Ironically, by the time this latter work had become known to the English-speaking psychological public (e.g., Luria, 1960), Luria was back working as a neuropsychologist.

At the present time, Luria is Professor of Psychology at Moscow University and the chief of the diagnostic research section at the Burdenko Institute of Neurosurgery.

THE PROBLEM OF SPEECH and its role in the formation of mental processes occupies a special place in Soviet psychology. Soviet psychologists proceed from the position that even the most complex manifestations of mental life are formed in the process of active reflection of reality. Complex mental processes are formed during the child's association with adults. They are complex functional systems formed with the intimate participation of language. That is why the study of how social relations are developed in the child, how he masters language, how, with the aid of speech, he masters the experience of prior generations, and finally how speech aids the formation of higher, conscious mental activity—constitutes a fundamental part of psychology.

Historical Background

Studies of Associative Behavior

In the first decade of Soviet psychology the psychological analysis of speech processes was not based on a recognition of the significant role which speech plays in the formation of mental processes, but was devoted only to an analysis of special problems of speech in the child. The *content* of the child's speech processes was subjected to careful analysis, attempting in this manner to characterize the basic features of the child's thinking. In addition, there were investigations which examined the basic *forms* of children's speech, describing the relations which characterize the basic developmental stages of conscious processes.

The content-oriented group attempted on the basis of day-to-day mass inquiries to determine the development of a child's vocabulary in relation both to the age of the child and to the environmental conditions under which the child developed (Rybnikov, 1930). This same group attempted to sketch the boundaries of the child's "circle of ideas" or "the content of his knowledge." On the whole, this research did not go beyond statistical summaries and consequently did not achieve independent scientific significance.

A second group of investigators attempted to describe the basic forms of connections being established with the aid of speech and to study certain dynamic features of the course of speech responses. To this group belongs the early work of Ivanov-Smolenskii (1922). He studied the character of speech-associated responses at different stages of development, attempting to describe the relationship between basic forms of connections developed in the child during a conditioning experiment. This work approached the analysis of the basic forms of speech connections from a reflex-chain position. It was one of the first Soviet works on the physiological analysis of speech reactions; it was natural that it had a considerable effect on the further development of this field.

The well-known investigations of Kornilov (1922) also belong to Soviet psychology's early period. He investigated a series of reactions graded in complexity from simple motor reflexes to associative speech responses. By measuring the latent period and amplitude of the motor response, Kornilov attempted to determine those energy losses which characterize the transition to more complex reactive processes. This was the first work in Soviet psychology where the investigator viewed speech responses as behavior acts and used precise experimental methods for their study. Thus Kornilov's work was quite significant. Although the attempt to measure the energy lost in associative processes was based on a clearly false, mechanistic premise, it had a great effect upon the development of a natural-science approach to the study of certain aspects of human behavior.

Intensive research on children's speech responses, conducted under the supervision of Luria and reported in the form of two books, began in the 1920's. In the first of these, Luria (1928) presented a detailed study of the basic formative stages of speech responses and described the evolution of certain basic mechanisms which underlie these stages. The author showed that the initial form of speech connections typical of a younger age group is not an association of the two object meanings, as was previously believed, but an elementary predicative judgment ($S \rightarrow R$) in which a given object word is connected with a word signifying action or quality. "Associative-type" connections, in the narrow sense of the word (like "table—stool," "home—roof"), are, in the author's opinion, artificial structures which originate much later and relate chiefly to school age, when such connections originate under the influence of classroom teaching. Based on an analysis of the latency of speech responses, this research showed that reaction time permits one to trace the gradual strengthening of speech responses through its basic stages. At preschool age speech responses are not automatized, resulting in highly variable reaction times. Only by school age (about 7 years) do these associations acquire a relatively smooth and highly automatic character. We know that "predicative" responses which are in essence elementary judgments (but not the associative connections of two object meanings) have occurred swiftly and automatically since an early preschool age. This observation is supported by the latency evidence; the latencies of these responses manifest very little variance. "Associative" reactions representing the connection of two substantives usually manifest significantly longer latencies with considerably greater variance, indicating less automaticity of this type of speech reactions.

This series of investigations, which led to a description of the basic forms of associative connections typical for successive stages of mental development, was important not only because it was one of the first attempts to trace systematically the development of verbal connections in childhood, but also because it correctly noted that the forms of connections established in the living speech of the child are basic for this development. Moreover, these everyday connections (and not artificial associations of two object values) are the fundamental, earliest, and strongest form of speech connections.

In the second book (Luria, 1930), an attempt was made to study experimentally the features of speech reactions of children growing up under various conditions. In contrast to the numerous investigations of how the child's vocabulary differs according to the conditions in which he develops, this work sought to distinguish the unifying influences (those causing stereotyped, unitary responses) from the separating influences (those causing individual, diverse speech connections) arising in this or that environment.

Concretely, this investigation consisted of studies comparing the diversity in those associative (verbal) reactions which were exhibited by a significant number of children growing under different fixed conditions (rural or city, stable or changing environment). The child was read a word and asked to say the first word that came to mind. If the number of diverse verbal responses given to a specific word stimulus was small and if a significant number of the children investigated responded to a given word in one and the same way, it was possible to assert that the environment in which the children lived acted on the entire group in a cohesive, unifying manner. On the other hand, if the majority of children in a given group responded to this or that word with diverse speech responses, it was possible to conclude that the cohesive, unifying influence in the environment was minimal and that environmental conditions acted rather in a separating, individualizing manner.

As the data showed, the uniformity of speech responses among rural children was considerably greater than among city children. Diversity of speech reactions was also very great among abandoned children whose environment was marked by significant variability.

The investigation of the psychophysiology of *affective processes* through verbal associations was another important subject studied by Soviet psychologists in the 1920's. In the beginning of this century, Jung, Wertheimer, Lippman, and others made the first attempts, by analyzing verbal associations, to conduct objective investigations of affective processes. These authors used the so-called association experiment, first developed by Jung and his associates.

Although Jung's method had a number of unquestionable advantages over other, earlier methods of investigating emotions, it suffered from substantial shortcomings. These included the fact that the method lacked sufficiently objective indicators to permit differentiation of an authentically affective disturbance of the associative processes from a delayed verbal response caused by a distraction or intellectual difficulties. In order to eliminate this defect, Jung's associates (Nunberg and others) suggested that the associative experiment be accompanied by a recording of pneumo- or plethysmograms, and sometimes even galvanic skin reactions. However, even this suggestion did not eliminate the difficulties indicated above; disturbances of respiration, pulse, or galvanic skin reaction could be caused either by the affective character of the stimulus, by an orienting reflex to some distracting stimulus, or by some kind of intellectual difficulty.[1]

In order to eliminate these difficulties and to make the investigation of affective processes accompanying speech reactions more objective, Luria (1930, 1932) introduced the so-called combined motor method. It consisted of asking the subject, to whom a specific word stimulus was given, to respond not only to the word stimulus by the first word entering his mind but also to squeeze a pneumatic bulb. It was assumed that this motor reaction was conditionally connected with the verbal response, and would thus reflect the dynamics of the speech response. The nature of the motor response curve, recorded on a kymograph, would reflect, in different ways, simple intellectual inhibition, the delay of a verbal response which the subject does not want to emit and, finally, the affective disorganization of associative processes which can occur in severe affective conditions.

The basic idea of the combined motor method is that recording responses which are conditionally associated with verbal processes in a single functional system provides the best objective indication of hidden affective

1. *Editors' note:* This problem is still prevalent. Many Western investigators take every indication of peripheral autonomic activity such as the GSR as an indication of emotion. Yet, as Luria points out, such activity may be a consequence of any one of a variety of quite different processes. Peripheral autonomic activity is not an unequivocal indication of anxiety, much less equivalent to anxiety.

processes. This idea was confirmed in a series of investigations[2] conducted by Luria and his associates (Leont'ev, Lebedinskii, and others). These included studies of associative responses in students during examination time, in criminals, in persons intentionally hiding the content of an experience familiar to them, and in neurotics (Luria, 1930, 1932). A number of investigations were conducted to determine the possibility of discovering the objective symptoms of affective experiences which were suggested to the subject in a hypnotic state and which (remaining in the unconscious) continued to have an influence on the behavior of the subject. Artificial conflicts were produced in subjects so that the normal flow of their verbal associations was disturbed and a change in the nature of their combined motor responses was produced. Finally, a whole series of investigations were conducted wherein the features of the combined verbal motor responses of the child were subjected to special analysis (Luria, 1932).

All of these investigations convincingly indicated that the combined motor method actually can use a motor reaction conditionally associated with a speech process in order to arrive at an objective analysis of the dynamics of the flow of verbal responses. It is our contention that the combined motor method provides a better approach to the investigation of the affective processes than any other previously used method of psychological experimentation.

The Earliest Forms of Speech

Early Soviet speech research failed to go beyond the study of special problems of speech activity (the development of the child's vocabulary, the structure of verbal associations, or speech reflection of affective processes). Consequently, the second decade of its development marked an important turning point, for it was during this period that the problem of speech was introduced into a considerably wider channel of thinking. The study of speech, its development, and its role in the formation of mental processes became the principal theme of Soviet psychology.

Historical Background

Substantial shifts in the study of speech processes also occurred in the foreign psychology of this period. At the beginning of the century, the Würzburg School most clearly formulated the idea that thought and language are independent; it also expressed the most extreme idealistic viewpoints on consciousness as a system of direct experiences. But in the 1920's the situation changed significantly.

At this time Piaget's first works appeared. Piaget pointed out the close

---

2. *Editors' note:* See Luria, 1961, for a detailed description of this method and the type of experiment conducted with it.

interrelation of the child's thinking and speech and attempted to show the principal stages of language evolution and its role in the formation of consciousness. Coming under the obvious influence of Freudian ideas, Piaget expressed the notion of the primarily autistic, direct nature of the child's thinking. At the same time, he assumed that, in intercourse with one's associates (adults and children) and with a mastery of the language, there occurs a gradual "socialization" of the child's thinking. The apparent supremacy of "egocentric speech"—social in form, but deeply individual and autistic in content—which Piaget attempted to demonstrate by studying 4- and 5-year-old children, only reflected, in his opinion, the transition from a biological to a socialized form of activity.

To this same period belongs the publication of the well-known works of Cassirer (1953), who attempted to show the role of the word in the formation of consciousness. In his well-known investigation of "the philosophy of symbolic forms," he supported the viewpoint that the word appears in that form in which basic abstract types of spiritual activity manifest themselves. The word translates a concrete human activity to the level of "categorical consciousness" and "categorical behavior." Cassirer's viewpoints, upon which the psychopathological investigations of the well-known German neuropathologist Goldstein were based, received wide propagation in Western European psychology and helped to increase the attention devoted to the study of the role of language in the formation of human consciousness.

It is apparent, however, that these investigations proceeded from theoretical positions deeply alien to materialistic science. Piaget attempted in his early works to defend the position that the child is initially a biological creature all of whose behavior is determined by deep instincts and is only later pushed aside by social activity. Cassirer, on the other hand, held that abstraction is a primitive category of the mind which is only embodied in the word and through the latter's mediation raises consciousness to a higher, truly human level. The role of speech in the formation of consciousness and thinking was posed as a basic problem of psychology, but was solved by means deeply alien to the materialistic approach to the development of complex mental processes.

A significant contribution in the materialistic solution of these problems was made by Soviet psychologists, especially by Vygotskii. As early as the end of the 1920's Vygotskii expressed the idea, which he often repeated (1934, 1956), that the child is, from the very beginning, a social being. Association with his family is from the very beginning a basic form of the child's vital activity. The relation of the child to things is conditioned at an early age by his association with adults, and the overall formation of his mental activity occurs in the process of this association, the means of which change but which always remains the basic driving force in development.

Sharply distinguishing human mental development from the development of animal behavior, Vygotskii noted that in the animal world the formation of new connections always occurs in the process of *individual* experience. Each animal must acquire all connections anew, thus exhausting the mechanisms described by Pavlov for the formation of new conditioned-reflex connections on the basis of congenital, inherited experience. In man, *mental development includes mastery of the total of human experience,* which is transmitted through concrete activity and above all through language. Development through mastery of the total of human experience is not limited to a simple mastery of new knowledge, of new *contents* of consciousness. The process of mastering human experience is transmitted by speech and leads to the formation of *new methods of activity,* a new interrelationship between "mental functions," new functional systems and, in the final analysis, to the origin of those "higher psychological functions" (for example, voluntary attention, active memory, voluntary action) which are described by idealistic psychology as the appearance of primitive forms of existence of the mind, but whose formation lacks a scientific explanation.

Social Factors Influencing Speech and Thinking

From the very beginning of his development, the child lives and acts in close association with an adult. In the intrauterine period the child is connected with the mother physically, and after birth (during the period of breast feeding) he remains connected with her biologically. He continues to be connected psychologically with the mother as well as with other adults during later development. The child is by no means secluded within itself, an "autistic" being. Foreign investigators frequently ask themselves the questions: "How is the autistic consciousness of the child, primarily secluded, gradually 'socialized'?" "How is the small autist and 'egocentric' converted into a social being?" Since, as we have indicated, the child is always in contact with others, this problem can be posed in a more complex, but at the same time more interesting form; the task is to trace how the forms of association connecting the child with surrounding adults are changed; how the elementary, direct forms of association which initially have an emotional-active character gradually become conditioned by speech; how this verbal behavior becomes separated from overall behavior into a special activity depending on a system of language; and how on the basis of these complex forms of verbal associations new forms of mental activity, which are social in their origin and speech-conditioned in their structure, begin.

These problems—the problem of the stages of speech development as a complex form of activity and the problem of the role of speech in the formation of complex mental processes or functional systems (regarded improperly by idealistic psychology as primitive "properties" of the mind) —are central for Soviet psychological research.

In the beginning of the child's second year there occurs a rapid development of speech which precedes the important period of formation of the ability to understand another's speech and which in the 17-to-19-month-old takes a considerable leap forward. However, the basic features characterizing these stages and the basic factors leading to the rapid development of the child's speech in the middle of the second year have been rather insufficiently studied.

In the old psychological literature it was noted that the first stages in the development of the child's ability to understand another person's speech in no way led to a simple accumulation of vocabulary. Rather, this ability involved a process of *gradual discrimination of verbal signals from all the remaining components of the situation acting on the child.* In the works of Rozengart-Pupko (1948), Kaverina (1950), and especially Kol'tsova (1958) it was demonstrated that the earliest stage of understanding a word is not the original grasping of a word's meaning, which takes place in the child of preschool and even later nursery age. The adult's word does not immediately become that "signal of signals" which it will become in the later stages of development.

As the investigators mentioned above have shown, during the first six months of life the child begins to react to the words of the adult just as he has already begun to experience direct emotional-active associations with adults (which are reflected in fixation of the eyes on the face of the adult, in a responsive smile to the smile of the adult, attempts to reach the adult, and the like). Certain words, beginning in the fifth and sixth months, produce an orienting response in the form of turning of the head and the eyes, a smile, and later even the execution of very simple actions (turning his attention to the object indicated, reproduction of certain movements, and so forth) in response to words addressed to the child. However, it would be erroneous to think that the word acts as a ready, clearly isolated signal or even that the lexical side of the word is a dominant part of any complex stimulus.

Kol'tsova (1958) and others have shown in detail that the adult's word at this stage produces the desired reaction only if the word has a specific intonation, is accompanied by specific gestures, and is uttered by a specific person and in a specific situation. Kol'tsova's observations indicated that in the earliest stage a word addressed to the child can elicit the necessary conditioned response only in the presence of all of the conditions designated above. If the child in a sitting position can be stimulated to make the necessary movement by the words "Give me your hand," accompanied by appropriate gestures, it would still not be possible to elicit these movements if the position of its body is changed. Only after a certain time does the position of the child's body cease to have a decisive effect on the word's ability to stimulate the necessary movements. In order to obtain these responses, it is necessary, as before, that the words addressed to the child be accompanied by appropriate gestures, be given with a specific intonation and in a specific circumstance. Only somewhat later do these factors gradually cease to play a decisive role; the verbal complex begins to acquire its relative independence from the particular situation, then from the accompanying gesture, and finally from the intonation with which the given word is uttered.

This indicates that the word addressed to the child is in no way a symbolic signal in the beginning. The second half of the child's first year involves separating the significant word from the entire complex of actions influencing him. The word, once divorced from the particular circumstances, gestures, and intonations, gradually becomes that "signal of signals" which preserves its independence irrespective of the conditions in which it occurs.

It seems clear that the first stage in the formation of a word as an independent signal which evokes a specific response is the separation of the verbal signal from the entire complex of stimuli acting on the child. The second stage is the formation of a clear system of generalized relations which are represented in the word. This second stage was traced by Kol'tsova (1958). Kol'tsova's experiments indicated that, although a conditioned response is formed to a word which represents only a complicated vocal complex for a 7-to-8-month-old child, it is possible to see how this relation initially acquires a generalized character. However, the word, still very generalized in its meaning, also remains very unstable. If only three conditioned connections have been worked out for this word (for example, "book"), then extinction of one of these connections easily leads in the child to loss of the signal meaning of the whole verbal complex. Only if a given word has a significant number of conditioned connections (20–30) does the verbal complex acquire a stable and generalized character. Then the word begins to relate only to a specific group of objects, is easily differentiated from extraneous relations, and in this manner acquires a clear objective meaning.

The ability to form relatively clear objective meanings for words is the child's most important achievement in the first months of his second year. However, observations indicate that this achievement is still far from consolidated and that those words which apparently are already mastered by the child still do not have sufficient stability or clarity of semantic meaning.

One is easily convinced by simple experiments of the superficial instability of word meanings which continue to be manifested in the 16-to-20-month-old child. Luria (1961) conducted a study in which a child was alternately shown a small cup and a block standing in front of him, each time uttering the word for block, which was well known to the child. If the object being named was placed two or three times on the right side, it was incorrectly named when later placed on the left. This becomes especially clear if a delay as short as 5–10 seconds is put between the word named and the child's pointing motion. Such "alienation of the meaning of the word," pointing to an instability of verbal signs (observed in the adult only in certain forms of pathology), arises as the result of inertness in the nervous processes peculiar to this age. Only after considerable reinforcement of the verbal connections does the stability of verbal designations increase.

This is not the most characteristic feature of speech development in this stage, however. At first glance one might think that by the beginning of the second year of life the child masters many of the words in his "passive vocabulary," which have just as clear a meaning as adult words, and that this vocabulary creates a sufficient basis for the simplest forms of speech intercourse. This impression is, however, very erroneous. True, at this age intonation and gesture cease to be important components of the speech being perceived, and we no longer note cases in which the child, clearly reacting to intonation, at the same time turns his head to the window upon hearing the phrase *"Où est la fenêtre"* or *"Wo ist das Fenster?"* When the 2-year-old child clearly points to the appropriate object while naming it, it does not quite mean that the representation of the object by the word has been adequately formed yet.

Generalization and Discrimination of "Meaning"

Experiments conducted by Rozengart-Pupko (1948) and others demonstrate this phenomenon quite adequately. Ordinary observations indicate that the child at around one year of age strongly connects the word *golovka* (little head) with *golova* (head), the word *utka* (duck) with a type of bird, and so forth. However, if a doll with a torn-off head is presented to a child who is asked the question, "Where is the head?" the child without any hesitation points to the top of the headless body, repeating the habitual gesture. If the child is asked, "Where is Papa?" (to which he usually responds by pointing to a portrait on the wall) he will continue to reproduce the same gesture even if that portrait is absent.

Of greatest interest are the experiments of Rozengart-Pupko (1948) in which she succeeded better than anyone else in analyzing the actual content of those words which have strong objective meaning for the child. While she was suggesting various words to the child, she offered a number of objects from which the object being named was always absent, but which had some attribute in common with the missing object. These experiments indicated that the 2-to-3-year-old child is confused by the situation; not finding the required object, he might go look for it in another room. A younger child, just turning 2, would confidently pick an object having any kind of aspect in common with the object named. Thus, to the words

"Give Ko-Ko" (a hen) the child might give a plastic ball with a protruding edge (bill); to the words "Give the mouse" it might give a plush glove, etc. These experiments convincingly show that, in initial stages, the word reflects not the object as a whole, but only some major attribute of the object, and this results in that apparent "diffuseness," or generalization, of early verbal meanings to which many authors have referred.

This diffuseness of the primary meaning of words has been noted by many Soviet authors. Konnikova (unpublished) and others have adduced numerous examples of how the child's earliest words, known in the literature as "autonomous speech," designate not the object, but any significant attribute of the object. Thus, Bozhovich (unpublished observation) pointed out that the child who designates a cat by the sound *kkh,* also uses the vocal complex to designate fur (by its softness), a pin (which also scratches), a sharp stone, and so on. These observations confirm the fact that the primary word is connected not with the entire complex of signs entering into the composition of the object, but only with individual and broadly generalized attributes.

Soviet investigators were able, in addition to describing this original "meaning" of the word, to show experimentally how the objective meaning of the word can be changed. Shvachkin (1954) presented wooden toys painted different colors (for example, a red-and-green iron, a red-and-green boat, etc.), to a 16-to-20-month-old child. He named these objects by using words still unknown to the child. Having established a connection between the name and the object (for example, red iron or green boat), he then asked the child to give him the object named, allowing the child to select it from a number of objects differing in color and form. The children easily selected the objects of a specific color, transferring the meaning of the word with which they trained from the red iron to the red boat or from the green boat to the green iron. This fact indicated that the signaling attribute was only the color of the object and that, consequently, the word had a more primitive meaning for the child than the adult. However, when the experimenter later permitted the child to play with the object, thereby training him and in practice isolating the signs essential to the object (in the experiment the child pressed with the iron, and pushed the boat in the water), the situation was substantially altered. The word took on a new meaning and became the name of an *object.* On a test session the child selected another object, of the same type but different in color, in response to the named word.

All of these experiments, which have subsequently been repeated by other investigators, have great theoretical significance. They show that the formation of the simplest function of the word—the function of designating the object (or "object attribution")—is by no means a simple act "of connecting the vocalization of the word with an image of the object." It is rather a very complex and lengthy process of isolating an adequate signaling attribute to which the verbal symbol is then connected. This lengthy process can be broken down into a number of stages, during which the child's elementary orienting responses initially play a leading role. Later, visual cues are more important. Finally, the process is regulated by those practical manipulations with the object which are carried out with adult instruction and which synthesize the complex of object signs and thus complete the formation of the nominative function of the word. There is every reason to believe that this complex process characterizes not only the basic steps of understanding another person's speech but also the basic stages in the formation of the child's own speech.

Concept Formation and Semantic Systems

Linguists distinguish two aspects in the semantic content of each word. One of these is the designating, nominative function of the word, discussed above. The other is the system of generalizations which every word represents, the system of associations and relations which are reflected in them.

The fact that every word generalizes means that the system of generalizations which characterizes a word is determined not only by the linguistic structure of the word, but also by its usage, which varies with different stages of development, with different tasks and with different people. For example, the word *chernil'nitsa* (inkwell) not only designates an object well known to everyone but also introduces that object into a complex system of associations and relations. The root *chern* (black) places it in the category of colors and is included in the same series with the concept of red, white, blue. The suffix *il* relates this object to objects possessing the quality of instrumentality (ink, whitewash, etc.). The suffix *-nits* relates it to objects serving as receptacles (sugar bowl, ashtray, etc.). The inflexion *-a* is a conditional grammatical category in the nominative feminine gender. If the case ending is changed, the word is related to a category of words standing in different relations to one another. Thus, each word actually classifies the content being designated by it, transmitting a total human experience to the listener or the speaker and abstracting complex systems of ties and relationships from the real world.

The external form of the word itself is a powerful means of systematizing experience. But that system of generalizations which is called by many authors the "internal form of the word" and whose variability is especially great, is no less significant.

The word *fabrika* (factory), while remaining externally invariable, can evoke an absolutely dissimilar complex of connections in different people of different ages and in different situations. In the young child who sees the smokestack of the factory or the father who "comes from the factory," this word can stimulate a series of unclear emotional experiences and it can be the signal to reproduce a series of impressions which the child experienced when it heard this word for the first time. In schoolchildren it is associated with complex and distinct images to which a whole complex of obvious associations belong. For economists, *fabrika* represents a system of complex and abstract and economic relations having nothing in common with the clear associations of the schoolchild.

Having rejected the investigation of meaning by asking subjects to define concepts (a method which assumes adequate development of a system of verbal equivalence), Vygotskii and his pupil Sakharov developed a method which permitted them to study more closely the role which the word plays in the analysis of objective associations and relations.

Beginning with the methods developed by Ach for an analysis of concept formation, Vygotskii substantially changed the procedure. The basic technique was to present to the subject blocks which differed from each other in volume, shape, height, and color. The problem was to sort the blocks into four categories. Associated with each category was an artificial word, printed on the bottom of each block. The basic experiment proceeded by having the subject select the blocks that, he believed, belonged in each of the four groups. An incorrect block was then chosen by the experimenter, who turned the block over, revealing the label. The subject sorted the blocks again and the process was repeated until the correct classification was made.[3] Although the artificial character of the concepts had its disadvantages, it had the advantage of forcing the person being tested to abstract and to establish new associations and interrelations. The presence of the word as a means of learning verbal meaning ensured that concept formation proceeded in continuous association with the actual change of verbal designations.

In the earliest stages of development, grouping geometric figures into one whole designated by a single word is very difficult. In response to this task the child simply selects all figures which fall within his gaze, uniting into one conglomerate set all those blocks which he sees. The word still does not play the role of a unifying sign, and grouping does not continue beyond the limit of this random, syncretic approach to objects, which has been well described in the works of Piaget. Such syncretism without preliminary orientation to attributes and without preliminary analysis constitutes the earliest stage of thinking, in which the word does not play a substantial role but is subordinated to the influence of immediate impressions, according to Vygotskii.

After this first syncretic stage there follows a second stage which has a

3. *Editors' note:* For a complete description of this experimental technique see Vygotskii, 1962.

distinct and internally regular structure. Attempting to select all objects which are designated by one artificial word, the child makes a preliminary analysis of the group of objects placed before him and singles out certain attributes. However, this signal attribute is far from obligatory and may change from trial to trial. Thus, referring to the designation "RAS" from a large red cube, the child associates it with a red pyramid (color association), a small green cube (form association), and a large blue cylinder (size association). The conditional designation in no way resembles the original concept at this stage; rather, it resembles a family name.

Only in the next stage, which is formed under the influence of systematic training, is there substantial change. The word, changing its structure, is given a new, important meaning in the execution of the task. In this stage which, according to Vygotskii, is attained only during adolescence, the word becomes freed from the influence of direct impressions. It abstracts now one, now another attribute and synthesizes them into a complex of attributes. The process of classification acquires a complex character mediated by the word. The selection of each figure is determined not by direct impression, but by a stably preserved system of attributes abstracted with the aid of the word and shared by the objects selected in the required group. Generalizations underlying the word lose their concrete character. A system of abstract meanings becomes the guiding criterion for further intellectual operations. The word becomes the basic instrument of thinking, and thinking acquires a mediated character.

The first and most important accomplishment of this research was the elimination of the gap between thinking and speech which dominated many schools of foreign psychology. Vygotskii took as his basic task the tracing of the unity of thinking and speech and the description of the stages in the formation of thinking together with their dependence on the formation of word meanings. This contrasts with the Würzburg position that speech and thought are separate. The formula "The thought is expressed in the word," which assumes the presence of a complete thought only cloaked in words, was replaced by the materialistic formula "The thought is carried out in the word." The experimental proof that the meanings of words *develop* was the second accomplishment.

Vygotskii's work was critically important because it made the sequential development of speech and thinking from 7 to 15 years of age the subject of special psychological investigation. The problem became to study not only the expansion of content but also the structural changes in verbal thinking.

Vygotskii also believed that the change in semantic structure which he established in his experiments was accompanied by *a change in the interrelationship among those psychological processes* which comprise the intellectual operation.

In analyzing these facts it is apparent that each stage in the development of generalizations is characterized by a change in the relationship among the basic mental functions taking part in them. In other words, *each new degree of generalization is accomplished by a new functional system*. In the syncretic unification which characterizes the first stage in the development of a generalization, a leading role is played by the direct impression and only a minimal role by the word. This form of generalization, which Vygotskii designated as complex or situational, is formed primarily by visual connections of previous experience and is in essence a reproduction of the actual relations with which the child has dealt previously. The effective memory fills the semantic structure with concrete speech content and determines the nature of the operations accessible to the child. Finally, the higher form of generalization, which conceptual thinking represents, is a psychological process carried out primarily by complex and specific connections which abstract the necessary attributes and unite the objects of the external world on the basis of this complex mediated operation. According to Vygotskii, the development of thinking is not the mastery of certain logical operations; it acquires its own complex psychological content. At the same time, the semantic development of speech becomes a *systemic development*. The study of changes in the forms of thinking becomes the study *of semantic and systemic structure and consciousness*.

These functional features of concepts, described in detail by Vygotskii in his basic work, prove to be very different when one compares formation of everyday and scientific concepts. As Shif showed (1935), the everyday concepts are mastered by the child in the process of his personal practical experience. The words designating these concepts are expressed by an acquired system of links and are correctly used. But for a very long time they are not included in a system of complex common relations; they do not obtain verbal equivalents, and they are not used voluntarily or consciously. In contrast, words designated as "scientific concepts" have an entirely different origin and an entirely different history. They are acquired in the process of school training and are mastered from the beginning in the form of verbal formulations which only later obtain practical content. From the very beginning they are used consciously and voluntarily; they are included in a specific system of hierarchical relations, and because they are sometimes based on an inadequately defined body of factual knowledge, they frequently display a tendency to break away from this factual experience and to revert to a system of empty verbal formulations.

The description of various means of developing everyday and scientific concepts, first given by Shif and then broadly developed and introduced into a complete system of theoretical views by Vygotskii (1956, Ch. VI), signified the transition to a new group of psychological problems: an analysis of internal regularities in the acquisition of *knowledge* and the basic mechanism of the structure of conscious cognitive processes. Having stated the important psychological position that *"consciousness comes through the gateway of scientific concepts"* (1956, p. 247), Vygotskii proceeded to a new and most important branch of psychology—the basic regularities of conscious forms of human thinking.

The characteristic feature of the adult's verbal meanings is that *the word preserves in itself all systems of connections inherent in it,* beginning with the very elementary and visual and ending with the very complex and abstract. Depending on the task, any one of the systems of connections can become dominant. Without this ability, flexible thinking is impossible. The person who uses abstract relations for the solution of more concrete everyday problems always risks finding himself in the position of a schizophrenic patient whose behavior loses its sensible and adaptive character because his second signal system is damaged.

However, while it cannot be disputed that the word always preserves the entire *system of earlier connections,* the investigation of exactly what concrete relations are included in these systems of connections, of which connections are dominant and which subordinate, and finally of how various conditions can change the usual relations among these systems of connections continues to present significant difficulties. Both the method for determining verbal meanings and the Vygotskii method of classifications pertain to the study of *actual connections* and are not suitable for establishing the system of *potential connections,* which are concealed by the word. In order to obtain direct indices of these potential connections it is necessary to use certain psychophysiological methods involving involuntary responses.

Semantic Conditioning and Generalization

Shvarts (1948) found that if a normal adult subject is presented several paired presentations of a neutral word, *doktor* (doctor), with an unconditioned stimulus, an appropriate conditioned vascular or photochemical reflex was produced. Furthermore, this conditioned reflex could also be obtained for the semantic equivalents of *doktor,* the words *vrach* (doctor), *lekar* (doctor), etc., while words similar in sound to the term, such as *diktor* (announcer), did not produce any conditioned reaction. Shvarts also found that if a subject is given a small dose of chloral hydrate, causing an inhibited condition of the cortex, the semantic equivalents *lekar* and *vrach* ceased to produce vascular or photochemical reactions. However, in contrast to the control experiment, such a reaction began to appear to the word *diktor.*

Shvarts' experiment showed convincingly that an *entire complex of relations is hidden behind each word* but that in the normal state more-elementary and less-substantial vocal connections are suppressed by semantic connections. In an inhibitory state of the cortex, semantic connections may be weakened and previously inhibited vocal connections may emerge. It is easy to see that this conditioned-reflex investigation using pharmacological agents provides great possibilities for investigating the *real* interrelations of connections underlying the word and their changes in different states of the cerebral cortex.[4]

Thus, this series of experiments permitted the detection of three distinct systems of meanings, each occupying a different place in the cortical activity of the subject: one of these produced not only a motor but also a vascular reaction, evidently representing the basic, actual nucleus of the connections; the second system, which did not cause a voluntary motor reaction, continued, however, to produce vascular reactions which were signs of potential connections not being manifested openly; and, finally, the third system did not cause either of these reactions, referring, thus, to a system of connections, well differentiated from the conditioned words in the consciousness of the normal person. However, as these experiments showed, a group of connections which under normal conditions are clearly differentiated from the basic system can be activated and begin to produce inappropriate reactions. There is no doubt that this entire series of experiments (in summary form published by Luria and Vinogradova, 1959), uncovers new and extremely important prospects for the objective investigation of verbal meanings and the systems of connections underlying them.

Connected Discourse

We have dwelt on the contribution which Soviet psychology has made to the analysis of semantic structure and the development of verbal meanings. However, this topic, important as it may be, does not exhaust the psychological analysis of speech. The word and the connections underlying it are the cellular fabric of the second signal system; however, the unit of speech is not so much the individual word as the *connected utterance.* The sentence and a significant part of that which is conveyed to us by speech is based on the possibility of connecting individual elements into a word combination, or a *syntagma.* There is every reason to believe that, if the first stage of the origin of language should be considered the appearance of the first word, then the second, very important stage is connected with the formation of the first syntagma, which reflects the connection between the object and the action or between two objects and two events.

As we mentioned earlier, at the end of the first year of life the child, while gradually enriching his passive vocabulary, masters certain series of words which produce a corresponding orienting or active response. It is

4. *Editors' note:* Recent studies have shown that alcohol produces a similar shift from semantic to phonetographic generalization.

important to remember that these words are always in the form of the simplest connected utterances. The sentences "Make a boat," "Raise your hands," and the like are typical instructions which may be addressed to the child at the end of the first and the beginning of the second year. Does this mean, however, that a child this old actually perceives the phrase as a synthetic stimulus?

The observations of Kaverina (1950), Rozengart-Pupko (1948), Kol'tsova (1958), and a number of other investigators indicate a negative reply to this proposition. In the early stages, when the leading role is played by intonation, a young child actually reacts to a phrase as a single complex. In later stages the child reacts to that basic word to which the conditioned connection was formed. Consequently, the child to whom the phrase "Put the ball on the table" is spoken obeys the instruction and performs this same act even in response to the changed phrases "Put the wheel on the table" or "Put the ball on the bed." The young child, who does not carry out a preliminary analysis and synthesis of instructions, may be able to react to the phrases "Come here" and "Where is Daddy?" but cannot combine these phrases into a new structure "Come to Daddy."

Most important is the fact that in the initial stages of development connected discourse is understood by the child only within the limits of a specific, concrete situation. The meaning of speech is determined not so much by the relation between the words themselves as by the connection with a specific situation originating in the perception of some object which is recalled by a sentence. For instance, a 10-to-12-month-old child can execute the instruction "Close the pencil case" only if the cover of the pencil case comes within his field of vision. He cannot execute this instruction if he first has to turn in the direction of the pencil case (Kaverina, 1950). A 15-month-old child easily executes a spoken instruction ("Put the ring on the stick") if the ring is in his hand, but he cannot execute the command "Take the ring off the stick," which contradicts the act for which he has been prepared by his initial action.

The speech perceived by the child is not an independent system of signals; it can act only within the limits of its concrete context. To use Buhler's expression, it is perceived "sympractically." If the subject exists in the sentence presented to the child, then the predicate exists in the visual situation directly perceived by him.

Related data were obtained in older children by Sokhin (1951), using more complex word combinations. He showed that the 2-to-2½-year old child, who easily perceives sentences in which the relation between two objects is established by a preposition, is guided not by the logic of the relations of the words implied by the syntagma but by the logic of the immediate object relations required for the execution of the appropriate instruction. Similar facts have been described by Morozova (1948), who showed that the execution of a verbal instruction by the preschool child is determined not so much by its grammatical structure as by how much the phrase addressed to him corresponds to his own motives and also the degree to which the instruction contains signals that reinforce existing connections in the child's repertoire. This intimate connection between speech and the immediately perceived situation, this "sympractical" character of the action of speech, persists for a very prolonged period.

Only during the preschool age (4–7) does this situational, sympractic comprehension of connected speech begin to recede into the background. Gradual separation of the child's speech from practical action becomes the essential factor in the formation of the *child's speech structure*. If the word is learned only in the practical situations in which it is used, there are no objective conditions created in the child to force the word (or the entire expression) to acquire a differentiated character. *Tpru!* can designate either "horse," or "they're off," or "stop"; the meaning is determined by the situation, gesture, intonation of the utterance, and so forth. The objective necessity for *morphological differentiation* of the word occurs only when the word is separated from the sympractic context. This differentiation, marking the end of the period of autonomous speech, is first manifested in the appearance of suffixes. When a suffix is joined to the word *tpru,* the new word, *tprun'ka,* has a narrower meaning and it begins to designate a "horse." For the designation of the action, "stop," it becomes necessary to form new, special words. The formation of grammatical structure powerfully stimulates the separation of speech from its immediate, practical context (Luria and Yudovich, 1956).

The subsequent development of speech manifests a greater separation of speech from sympractical context, greater elaboration of the connective character of speech, and a more complex and differentiated "contextual" structure. Understanding speech depends more on the perception of the structure of what is spoken, and the intonational-gestural aspect begins to play only an auxiliary role. Isolation of speech as a special activity, based on an extensive grammatical system, is characteristic of the development of speech comprehension. The same process characterizes the development of the *child's active speech.*

The psychological literature describes how, in the very early stages of development, the child's words are "single-word sentences" which can be understood only in the immediate situation in which this word is pronounced. In addition, the subject may be contained in the word while the predicate is contained in the accompanying action of the child.

The direct connection between the child's actions and his speech in its early form has been described by several Soviet psychologists (the work of Kaverina, 1950, and Lyublinskaya, 1956a, b, is representative). This relation between action and speech appears with special clarity in children whose speech development is retarded (Luria and Yudovich, 1956). In this case, two twins with retarded speech were studied. The special conditions created by the twins' very close relationship led them to develop an autonomous language which they used to deal with concrete situations. This language was intelligible in the absence of any discernible semantic system on account of the concrete situation in which it was included. The "twin situation" served as an additional factor inhibiting the development of speech and created a situation where 80 per cent of the twins' expressions (they were 5 years old at this time) were grammatically amorphous and unintelligible outside of the concrete situation. Most interesting, however, was the result of separating the twins and housing them in different groups in nursery school. Their separation eliminated the "twin situation" and three months later there was evidence of a developing verbal speech in which only 44 per cent of the expressions in one twin (the one receiving special speech training) and 60 per cent of the expressions in the other (the control twin) remained completely unintelligible outside of the situation. It was also found that an overwhelming number of their sentences (80–85 percent) had already acquired a grammatically formed character. A short time thereafter the number of amorphous expressions which could be understood only in sympractic situations was reduced to zero.

The Written Speech of the Child

Investigations of detailed, contextual forms of speech lead us directly to an analysis of the development of the *written speech of the child*. Careful analysis by Vygotskii (1956) and El'konin (1954) indicated that written speech represents an entirely new psychological phenomenon, different from oral speech in its origin and in its structural and functional features.

Oral speech forms during immediately practical intercourse and its component elements long remain insufficiently conscious, unseparated by the child from general speech activity (Morozova, 1948; Karpova, 1955). Written speech follows exactly the opposite course. It is always the product of special training, which presupposes the separation of individual words from the flow of living speech and individual sounds from the living word. It also involves abstraction from individual phonations of sounds and the conversion of sounds into stable phonemes. This process of analysis, described in the Soviet literature by Luria (1950), Nazarova (1952), and others is a necessary technical premise for the act of writing, which from the very beginning requires conscious effort.

Oral speech always originates in close connection with immediate experience, as, for example, in sympractical and situational activity. It relies on intonation and gesture and usually becomes intelligible only if the general setting of the conversation is considered. It permits extensive abbreviation. For a prolonged period it continues to bear traces of the period when the subject was contained in speech and the predicate in a gesture, a tone, or in the immediate situation. Written speech, on the other hand, is deprived of this sympractical context, and therefore it must be more detailed, contextual, or, to use Buhler's term, synsemantic. Written speech like a work of art, to paraphrase Leonardo da Vinci, should contain within itself all means of expressiveness and in no way depend on the concrete environment.

It is easy to see that from the very beginning conscious, voluntary written speech, which differs from oral speech in its motivation and grammatical structure, should have an entirely different psychological structure and should serve entirely different functional systems. This difference is reflected in a different relation of written speech to the processes of learning and inner speech. It can scarcely be doubted that both oral and written speech are a most important means of communication. However, of foremost importance in written speech is another function. Written speech is bound up with the inhibition of immediate sympractical speech connections. It assumes a much slower, repeated mediating process of analysis and synthesis, which makes it possible not only to develop the required thought, but even to revert to its earlier stages, thus transforming the sequential chains of connections into a simultaneous, self-reviewing structure. Written speech thus represents a new and powerful instrument of thought.

The significance of written speech for the formation of mental processes was subjected to an exhaustive analysis in the investigations of El'konin (1954) and others, who traced not only those conditions of the child's psychic development which are necessary for the formation of written speech, but also those functions which written speech fulfills at different stages of its development and those forms which it adopts.

The functional and structural features of written speech have still another important feature; they inevitably lead to a significant development of *inner speech*. Because it delays the direct appearance of speech connections, inhibits them, and increases requirements for the preliminary, internal preparation for the speech act, written speech produces a rich development of inner speech which could not take place in the earliest phases of development.

Even in his early works on the social basis for the child's so-called egocentric speech, Vygotskii (1956) noted various changes in speech depending on the extent of the child's development. Vygotskii's observations indicated how egocentric speech, which is unusually loud and detailed, gradually reduces until it becomes abrupt, incomplete whispered speech, and then completely vanishes. Vygotskii, in contrast to Piaget, suggests that this sequence represents not "the dying off of egocentric speech" but a much more important process: transition from extended (or developed) speech to a "folded" speech. This process represents formation of inner speech arising in the second half of the preschool age (5–6), and is gradually enriched later on, especially beginning with the development of written speech.

Vygotskii has suggested that the process of abbreviation and "interiorization" of speech (its transition to inner speech) leads to important functional and structural changes in those features which characterize inner (oral or written) speech.

While external speech always remains, above all, a means of intercourse with others, inner speech, because it is "speech for oneself," completely loses this function. As Vygotskii indicated, because inner speech is "conversation with oneself" it means that the subject is well known and therefore its basic function is not to be a developed and comprehensible utterance for another person, but a fixation of those elements of the utterance which should be developed in further speech. Therefore, inner speech cannot be considered "talking to oneself." It is rather the important link between unfolded speech and thought and between the general thought and the developed utterance.

However, these functional features of inner speech, which are so distinctly different from external speech, do not exhaust its characteristics. The structural features which distinguish inner speech are just as important. Because it is "speech for oneself," serving above all to fix and regulate intellectual processes, and because it has a largely predicative character, inner speech necessarily ceases to be detailed and grammatical. It contracts, acquires a folded, grammatical structure, always preserving, however, the possibility of developing into a complete, differentiated and complex utterance.

The Role of Speech in the Development of Higher Psychological Functions

Soviet psychology holds that higher forms of reflection, which are expressed in active, voluntary, and conscious forms of activity, are the result of the work of the brain as manifested *in social conditions,* and are not inherent properties of the mind. Soviet psychology conceives of mind as the product of social life and treats it as a form of *activity* which was earlier shared by two people (that is, originated in communication), and which only later, as a result of mental development, *became a form of behavior within one person.* In the first stage of development some action may be carried out by the child on command of an adult. Later, having mastered this social stimulation and transformed it into a mode of behavior, the child begins to carry out this action according to his own command. In the first stages of development the attention of the child is organized by the adult with the aid of a gesture or by naming an object. As a consequence, the child develops the ability independently to organize his attention by a similar method, which then becomes voluntary. Complex forms of conscious activity ("higher psychological functions") are least of all initial "properties" of mental life or inherent qualities of the brain. They are functional systems formed by the social experience of the child. An essential role in this formation is played by speech, which is the basic means of communication and which serves as the basis for the second signal system. The second signal system represents "the new principle of nervous activity" and serves as the "higher regulator of behavior."

The first investigations devoted to the role which speech plays in the formation of mental processes belong to the early period of Soviet psychology. At the end of the 1920's Vygotskii, studying the "egocentric" speech of the child, turned his attention to the fact that such speech appeared with special clarity when any sort of difficulty arose. Artificially producing such a difficulty while the child is carrying out some kind of task (e.g., the child is asked to draw on a piece of paper; then a pin which supports the paper is removed or one of the colored crayons is inconspicuously taken away) always evoked an outburst of "egocentric" speech from the child. Further observations indicated, however, that this was not really "egocentric" speech. Although it remained speech addressed to another, at the same time it acquired new functions. With the aid of such speech the child was able to orient to the situation, creating as it were a "copy" of this situation. Then, mobilizing the connections of past experiences, the child attempted to find an escape from the problem which had been created. Speech analysis of the situation assisted the further organization of action, indicating that his speech helped to regulate his activity.

The data obtained by Vygotskii coincided with the observations described about the same time by Buhler (1930) and Getzer. They established that in the initial stages of development the child may draw some sort of picture and only later give the drawing a name. In later stages the relation of action to speech is reversed. The child initially formulates an idea in speech and then translates this idea into action. This indicates that the speech of the child, which began as a means of intercourse, becomes a means of orientation to the activity; it begins to mobilize previous experience and regulate activity. Only at an older age does this external speech of the child which directs his action gradually "fold up" and, passing through a stage of whispered speech, become converted into inner speech, which continues to play the role of the regulator of activity even though to a less detectable extent.

However, there is a substantial obstacle to attributing the development of higher forms of behavior solely to speech organization. The development of the child's speech proceeds on a parallel with his general maturation. Thus it is possible to interpret the development of mental activity as a result of the general development of the child, rather than as the result of the increased participation of speech processes in the organization of activity. Therefore, an experiment became necessary in which participation of speech and general development of the child as related to maturation would be maximally separated, and the role of speech in the formation of mental processes could be studied in as pure a form as possible.

Such an experiment was conducted in 1935–1936 by Luria and Yudovich. The results were published many years later (1956). The authors studied a pair of identical twins in whom, owing to a number of genotypical factors, late development of speech was observed. This condition was aggravated by the "twin situation." Because they lived in a common situation and spent most of their time talking to each other, the twins understood each other with "half words" and did not need to develop full-valued speech. In both children, who were 5 years old at the time, almost all speech consisted of amorphous exclamations and individual, phonetically perverted words whose meaning could be understood by an outsider only with a knowledge of the corresponding circumstances.

Most important, however, was the fact that all the behavior of these bright children was extremely primitive. They did not participate in the common role and object play. They could not sculpt, draw, or build structures from blocks and were limited to games which involved manipulation of the materials only as adjuncts to the ongoing activity.

The experiment conducted with these children consisted of separating them and housing them in different groups in nursery school. One of them received additional speech training. The elimination of the "twin situation" created the objective situation necessary for developing the speech forms of normal intercourse, and after three months both twins developed relatively full-valued and extroverted speech.

However, the most important result of this experiment consisted of the fact that, with the development of speech, all the activity of these children was reorganized: role and object play appeared; disorderly drawing with a pencil on paper was replaced by meaningful content-centered drawing; disorderly rolling of clay was replaced by modeling; constructive activity, which had been absent earlier, appeared; and typical forms of intelligent and intellectual behavior were observed. The short time required to develop full-valued speech in these children eliminates maturation as an explanation and permits one to attribute the shifts in the structure of their activity to the development of new modes of speech.

Effects of Verbal Labels on Discrimination

Foreign researchers (Gelb, Goldstein, and others) have repeatedly shown what great changes the word introduces into the course of *receptor processes.*[5] Naming this or that color or figure by a specific word, we impart

5. *Editors' note:* Many of these studies are similar to investigations in the United States in the area of acquired distinctiveness of cues and stimulus predifferentiation. In both Soviet and Western studies it is not always clear whether the critical variable is the differential speech or verbal label or the facilitation of appropriate orienting reflexes. In cases of "voluntary attention" the prior speech activity is necessary for appropriate orienting.

to the process of their reception a certain constant abstracting and generalizing element and thus guarantee constancy of their perception.

Having studied the nature of object perception in the 1½-to-2-year-old children, Rozengart-Pupko (1948) showed that a distinctive feature of perception at this age is that one or another isolated attribute acquires signal significance and thus comes to dominate perception. Thus, when shown a plush bear and asked to choose the "same thing" from among several objects, the child might not select a bear made of another type of material or painted in a different color, but a plush glove or ball instead. The situation was radically changed when the word designating the object was introduced and the experimenter asked the child to give him the specific object: "Give me the bear," "Give me the cup," "Give me the duck," and so on. In these cases the object constantly appeared as the dominant attribute of the things being perceived. To the request "Give me the bear," the child easily selected the wooden or plaster bear, abstracting "bearness" from the attributes of color, form, size, or material.

The experiments just described show the role of words in the analysis of the object and in increasing the constancy of perception. By contrast, the investigations of Lyublinskaya (1956a, b) and her associates make it possible to evaluate the essential importance of words for differentiating the elementary attributes of objects or for forming elementary discriminations. In these experiments, children in the age group from 13 months to 31 months were required to discriminate between color and size in order to find candy hidden under a cup painted a specific color or having a specific size. Experiments by Lyublinskaya's associates, Shipilova and Surina, had shown earlier that, if formation of such a discrimination is accompanied by verbal labeling of the critical attribute, it proceeds 1½ to 3 times faster than nonlabeled discrimination. A discrimination formed in this way is also much stronger, is preserved several hours and even days after the learning session, and is easily transferred to new material.

Similar results were obtained in preschool-age children in experiments which involved discrimination of various designs on the wings of otherwise similar butterflies. Here the designation of these patterns by a word enabled the child to analyze the images presented to him, to break up the critical attributes and as a result of this, to form a more rapid, permanent, and easily transferable discrimination. The phenomena described by Lyublinskaya were further developed by Ruzskaya (1954) in studies on the role which speech plays in the formation of discriminations and generalizations involving geometric figures. As her experiments showed, at different preschool ages, children's speech fulfills different roles, exerting a sharply varying influence on the process of comparison, discrimination, and generalization of figures. In the 3-year-old child, the naming of geometric figures frequently could not improve their discrimination and generalization. At this age, the word was likely to isolate random, unimportant attributes and sometimes even hindered correct generalization of the figures. In older preschool children such labeling greatly accelerated and improved the formation of the appropriate discrimination. Ruzskaya's investigation establishes the point that it is necessary to organize a preliminary orientation which is comprehensible to the child in order to guarantee the adequate, directive influence of a verbal system upon visual discrimination. The apparent discrepancy between these data and the results obtained by Lyublinskaya is explained by the greater complexity of the task presented here.

The role of words in distinguishing critical attributes and increasing the subtlety of discriminations is maintained even in older subjects, including adults, and is, consequently, a general law in the formation of a finer discrimination. This fact has been established by the investigations of Samsonova (1955), conducted with adults, and of Khomskaya (1956), conducted with school children. In the first of these investigations the instruction to characterize verbally small differences in shades of meaning led to the elaboration of finer and firmer discriminations. In the second, children who had to react silently to a subtle color or sound difference achieved coarser and less stable discriminations than children who accompanied each reaction with the words "dark" and "light" or even by the words "necessary" and "not necessary." In all of these cases speech, distinguishing the signal attribute and fixing it, proved a powerful means of making sensory analysis more precise and stable.

An essential aspect of the role of speech (the participation of the second signal system) is the fact that it not only distinguishes and fixates critical attributes, but even changes their relative power. This very important fact has been established in the investigations of Martsinovskaya (1958), on preschool-age children, and of Vinogradova and Sokolov (1955), who used both school children and adults as subjects.

In her investigations of the role of words in changing the relative effect of components in a complex stimulus, Martsinovskaya showed preschool children two figures, a red circle on a gray background and a green circle on a yellow background. The child was asked to point to the first figure with his right hand and to the second with his left. Test trials showed that in both cases the dominant component of the complex was the color of the circle, because the child continued to react with the right hand to the red circle on a yellow background and with the left hand to the green circle on the gray background. If the experimenter reinforced the weak component of the complex by asking the child to react with the right hand to the yellow and the left hand to the gray background, the resultant changes were different for younger and older children. For the younger children (3 to 4 years old) this speech reinforcement of the weak component did not lead to any noticeable changes, and the children continued to react to the color of the circle. However, the verbal instructions sharply changed the character of the reaction for most 5-to-6-year-olds: the dominant component of the complex became the figure.

The effect of verbal reinforcement of the weak component could be increased by making the verbal label meaningful; that is, by including it in a firmer and broader system of relations. This was successfully done by Abramyan (unpublished). Three-year-old children who went through tests similar to Martsinovskaya's (except that drawings of airplanes replaced the circles) were asked to react with the right hand to the yellow background ("because the airplane can fly in good weather, when the sun is shining") and with the left hand to the gray background ("because in bad, gray weather the airplane cannot fly"). In this case the attribute reinforced by speech became dominant and, even when the airplane was a different color, even the youngest children began to react to this physically weak but verbally established critical attribute.

Additional data concerning changes in the relative strength of stimuli caused by a word were obtained by Vinogradova and Sokolov (1955). Especially important in this work was their use of involuntary vascular reactions.

A series of tones of different intensities was presented to the subject, whose vascular responses were measured with a finger plethysmograph. Each tone produced a contraction of the blood vessels, which is the vascular component of the orienting response. Within certain limits, the amplitude of these vascular reactions increased in proportion to the intensity of the tone; with prolonged repetition the vascular orienting response to the tones was extinguished. The situation changed, however, when the subject was instructed to react by moving his right hand to weak sounds. This instruction, because it imparted signal significance to a particular tone, produced steady and nonextinguishing orienting vascular responses to weak tones. Extraneous sounds, exceeding the signal tone by many times in intensity (e.g., the sound of metal thrown against the window), produced no vascular changes.

All of these facts convincingly indicate that significant changes in perception can be wrought by words which impart meaning to the stimulus.

Complex Functional Systems Mediated by Speech: Voluntary Attention

A considerable number of investigations have been devoted to the analysis of processes involving complex functional systems mediated by speech. Since we cannot cover the full range of studies on complex functional systems in a review which is of necessity selective and historical in nature, we will describe only a few examples which establish the logic of the argument underlying these investigations.

It is well known that the orienting reflex originates in response to strong or novel stimuli. It is also well known that these stimuli always come from the external or internal environment of the organism. However, in the human (in contrast to animals) these stimuli can also come from the social environment, from those persons with whom the child is associated. If the mother shows the child an object, saying "This is a cup," this object is the one distinguished from all other objects and as a signal becomes a strong component of the complex of stimuli acting on the child. We say that the cup begins to attract the child's attention, which at this time remains "involuntary" in its form but social in its content.

However, when the growing child, whose behavior develops in intimate interaction with adults, begins to *point* to the object proper, to change its position in space, to note its additional important attributes, or simply to call it by a specific word, he produces changes which begin to act on him as a type of "feedback." Subsequently, these changes initiated by the child begin to attract his attention. In this case we have a new structure in the organization of attention, which remains reflexive in its nature but acquires the quality of a mediated act and becomes, in the original scientific sense of the phrase, *voluntary attention.* By "voluntary attention" we should understand a reflex act, social in origin and mediated in its structure, in the presence of which the subject *begins to guide himself by the very changes which he has produced in the environment; and in this way he masters his own behavior.*

This course of thinking enters into earlier works by Vygotskii and Leont'ev devoted to the genesis of voluntary attention. In the first of these works, which was written toward the end of the 1920's in an attempt to show that "the root of voluntary attention should not be sought within but outside of the child's personality" (Vygotskii, 1956), Leont'ev (1931), working under the direction of Vygotskii, attempted to fathom how the attention of the child is organized and how it can be converted into voluntary, actively mediated attention. This process is illustrated by a game in which the child responded to questions by naming colors, but was forbidden to repeat the name of any color. It was natural that the child, attempting to carry out this task directly, could not remember the colors named earlier and inevitably failed in the game. Attempts to strengthen his voluntary attention by direct instruction ("Pay attention!") did not lead to the desired result. However, when the child was given several cards, each of a different color, and allowed to draw out a card as each color was named, all further activity acquired a mediated character. Abandoning the attempt at a direct solution of the problem, the child began to mediate his further activity by using the cards before him, which now acted as an inhibiting signal, and by this means he successfully coped with the task. The changes he made on the external environment led to the creation of new, reverse afferent pathways influencing him and causing the appearance of a new functional system: a system of voluntary attention. In the young preschool child such mediated activity was still not sufficiently stable, and the external changes created by the child were more likely to distract him than to become signals directing his activity. In young school children, steady, external, mediated attention proved possible, greatly improving performance. In older school children external mediation was replaced by inner mediation. The subject began to rehearse the colors which they had already named, thereby forming a system of inner speech signals which was sufficient for him to cope effectively with the task. Attention which initially had an immediate character acquired first an externally mediated structure and then, with the aid of speech, became a complex, organized functional system.

In another series of experiments (Vygotskii, 1956), the child was required to find nuts hidden in one of two cups. Both cups, the empty one and the one with the nuts hidden in it, were covered with white cardboard covers on which were pasted small pieces of light and dark gray paper. Three-year-old children attempted to solve this problem directly (i.e., disregarding the colors); because they did not attend to the attributes distinguishing each of the cups, they naturally failed. It was necessary for the experimenter *to point a finger* at the dark gray paper, thereby converting it into a positive signal, for the course of the experiment to change. An indicative gesture changed the nature of the child's orientation, transforming the task into an externally mediated operation. The child, now oriented to the "black paper," which was physically a weak stimulus but which had acquired an expressed signal meaning, was always able to solve the problem.

The most important aspect of these results was the fact that for school age children this externally mediated operation easily converted itself into an operation mediated by speech. When, in a later series of experiments, a child was asked to find nuts in a group of cups, some of which had red and others blue covers, the child in the beginning responded randomly and found the nuts under the red cover. He then immediately reached the conclusion that "The nuts are under the red cover," making no further move toward the blue cover, to which his speech system attached a conditioned inhibiting meaning. If, on subsequent trials, this critical attribute was extinguished and small light and dark gray marks were made the basis for solution, this time glued to various colored covers, it was only a matter of distinguishing these signs with the aid of the indicative measure. This made them strong components of the complex so that the structure of the operation was again altered and the child began to mediate subsequent activity, responding to the signals which are weak in the physical sense but strong in functional meaning.

The Role of Speech in Imagination and Thinking

Investigations of the role of speech in the formation of imagination and thinking constitute a major chapter in Soviet psychology. Also of great importance are studies of the role of speech in the formation of new associations (conditioned responses), which is one of the most important problems of the psychology and the physiology of human higher nervous activity. Investigations devoted to this problem are also of interest because they have developed with special rapidity in recent years and constitute a field at the boundary between psychology and the physiology of the cerebral cortex. Pavlov has stated that the word represents a new principle of nervous activity—the principle of abstraction—and, at the same time, the generalization of innumerable signals. The word is a "signal of signals" which constitutes the foundation of the *second signal* system. Close interaction between the first and second signal systems is a distinctive feature of human higher nervous activity.

In a series of investigations, Ivanov-Smolenskii (1951) has shown that the second signal system, which stores systematized previous experience, produces a special type of connection (association) that is formed in an abrupt, rather than a gradual, fashion and that it is precisely this type of connection which underlies human intellectual behavior.

Temporary connections (conditioned reflexes) are formed in animals as a result of combining a neutral stimulus with an unconditioned (reinforcing) stimulus. With repeated presentations of this combination the newly formed temporary connection is strengthened. If reinforcement is eliminated, the connection is extinguished. The formation of a temporary connection passes through a number of stages beginning with the stage of elementary generalization and ending with the stage of concentration of nervous processes which imparts a clear-cut character to the fully formed connection. Alteration of the elaborated system of connections takes place by means of new reinforcement of both the positive and the inhibited stimulus. Transfer of the system to new conditions and especially the formation of a connection to any abstract attribute (e.g., to the next stimulus in the series) is difficult if not impossible for an animal.

Are these laws completely transferable to human learning or do substantial changes occur, in which the "new principle of nervous activity," as represented by the word, appears? Recent investigations (Luria, 1956) have shown that all of the laws characterizing the formation of new temporary connections in animals undergo some change when applied to humans, for whom the formation of new connections occurs in close connection with the verbal system. In animals the formation of new temporary connections occurs when a nondifferentiated neutral stimulus is combined with unconditioned reinforcement. Human conditioning can occur without unconditioned reinforcement and, as Ivanov-Smolenskii has shown, it is usually of a conditioned-conditioned, not a conditioned-unconditioned, nature.[6]

In animals the elaboration of a new system of connections requires many trials and, as a rule, passes through a phase of elementary generalization and only subsequent specialization. This contrasts with the human, who formulates the association in a speech system. Human conditioning can pass over these elementary phases and immediately acquire a specialized character. A person who formulates a rule such as "push with the right hand in response to blue signals and with the left hand in response to red signals" will from the beginning refrain from pushing in response to orange, light blue, or green signals which are visually similar to those to which he must respond.

Preservation of a system of connections in animals requires constant reinforcement. This rule proves not to be obligatory for people. After removal of the reinforcement, the system of connections is maintained by the rule which was formulated. The system is preserved because it is supported by the correspondence of the external response to this internal rule. Transfer of the reinforced system to a system of "self-regulation" is one of the distinctive features of human higher nervous activity.

As we indicated above, the alteration of an elaborated system of connections is difficult for the animal and requires new, prolonged training accompanied by constant reinforcement of each altered link. In the human a single presentation of one of the members of the elaborated system with new reinforcement, opposite in its meaning, immediately produces a general verbal formulation: "Aha, now it is necessary to do the opposite!" The new system becomes strong in a single trial. It is not even necessary to reinforce the second member of the pair of stimuli. An important trait characterizing formation of new connections in humans is the fact that these connections are never defined solely by visual, direct stimuli. For the human adult, who has a verbal system and easily abstracts the required attributes, going beyond the limits of direct, visual signals, proceeds, in principle, with no greater difficulty than the formation of a system of reactions to concrete stimuli. Recently, Luria and Polyakova (unpublished) succeeded in showing that responding to a constantly changing location (to the abstract sign of "the next element"), which is impossible for animals, is easily learned by

6. *Editors' note:* The regulatory role of speech, corticofugal influences, in human classical conditioning has not been sufficiently recognized by Western investigators. In part this has been due to the almost exclusive use of noxious UCSs so that, for example, rapid extinction of the conditioned GSR produced by instructions that the UCS will no longer occur is ascribed to a reduction in anxiety. But the same effect could be obtained in conditioning with an innocuous UCS. In both cases the role of speech mediating the autonomic changes is undoubtedly far more important than anxiety reduction.

the 3-year-old child who can speak, but was impossible for the 1½-to-2-year-old child whose speech system was still insufficiently developed.

The use of a verbal system in the formation of new temporary connections is typical for the mental activity of the human adult and the school child. However, it is still not quite characteristic for preschool-age children and especially children of young preschool age. Experiments by Paramonova (1955) with 3-to-6-year-old children indicate the extent to which the formation of new connections in the preschool child differs from the same process in children 5 to 6 years of age and differs even more in school age children. In schoolchildren the elaboration of new temporary connections (the formation of motor responses to light signals by the method of speech or other reinforcement) proceeds as we described above for adults. Such a subject typically forms a generalized speech connection after the first two reinforcements: "Aha, press the button for a red light, but for a green light, don't!"—and thereby strongly reinforces this reaction. In contrast the 3-year-old child forms a new system quite differently.

Most often, Paramonova observed, speech reinforcement of a signal by the word "push" rapidly forms the desired connection in the 3-year-old. This connection is generalized so that the child begins to push the button in response to all signals presented to him (sometimes even emitting a motor reaction independently of the signal). If an attempt is made to produce selective inhibition by saying "Do not push" in the presence of a second green signal, the inhibition is also generalized and consequently the child stops pressing both in response to inhibitory signals and in response to positive signals. The system of selective generalization (or, using Ivanov-Smolenskii's term, "selective irradiation"), which words usually produce, does not develop in this case. A system of selective positive reactions to red signals and inhibitory reactions to green signals forms only gradually, passing through a stage of generalized reactions to gradual concentration. The system requires constant reinforcement and rapidly disappears after removal of this reinforcement. It is different in this respect from the systemic elaboration of a new connection which is characteristic of older children and adults. Essential is the fact that the speech formulation of the connection being elaborated does not precede the formation of a strong motor response but significantly lags behind it. The child who firmly reacts by pressing the button in response to each green signal but refrains from responding to red may, for a long time, answer the question, "What did you see?" with the name of either color. Asked what he did, he may reply, "I had dinner," and if the question is clarified by the appropriate explanation ("When did you press?") he still might respond, "Today." Lack of a strong connection between direct signals and the child's speech proves to be characteristic (within the limits of our laboratory conditions) for children of 2½ to 3 years of age. Only in the 3½-to-4-year-old, whose speech is more developed, do we note a qualitative change as a result of which the child's speech begins to affect the formation of new connections. Speech now serves as a means of orienting to stimuli, and the entire process for forming of temporary connections is thus altered.

Experiments with normal preschool-age children make it possible to observe the development of the role of speech in the formation of temporary connections (we might term this process the formation of an interaction between the two signal systems). Similarly, observations on mentally retarded children and on patients with pathological conditions of the cerebral cortex make it possible to see how this participation of speech in complex forms of mental activity is delayed or disturbed.

Investigations by Mescheryakov (1955, 1956), Martsinovskaya (1958), and others provide evidence concerning the effects on inadequately developed speech on the formation of complex reflex systems. Children with pronounced forms of mental retardation could form new temporary connections with relative ease in only the simplest conditions (e.g., each red signal presented to the child was accompanied by the order "Press!" and each green signal by the order "Do not press!"). In children with the severest forms of mental retardation (imbeciles) this procedure produces only a slow, gradual elaboration of the desired system of responses. This response system is not mediated by speech; it is unconscious. It begins as primary generalization and requires constant, uninterrupted reinforcement of each reaction. In children with less pronounced forms of mental retardation the elaboration of temporary connections under the simplest conditions can proceed quite normally, accompanied by verbal formulation of the necessary rule and an adequate verbal report.

However, it is sometimes sufficient to slightly complicate the experiment in order to indicate the retardate's limited use of speech in the formation of new connections and to see how easily the speech of the mentally retarded child begins to lag behind the problems presented to him. In some cases speech even ceases to play any role in this complex process.

A very simple experiment illustrating this effect involves the elaboration of a second, new system of connections. The subject is a severely mentally retarded child who has already formed a system of positive reactions to red signals and inhibitory reactions to green signals. This subject is presented trials which involve positively reinforcing a yellow and inhibiting a white signal. An alternative procedure is to reverse the reinforcement contingencies with the red and green signals. It is soon obvious that the newly formed response system is not mediated by speech. The system of speech connections ("It is necessary to press the button for red; for the green do nothing") was inert, so that the child could not immediately switch over to a system of new speech formulations. Therefore, the elaboration of the second system of connections frequently occurs more slowly than the elaboration of the first system. If a whole series of problems is presented, the process entirely loses the characteristics of conscious and systemic elaboration mediated by speech which characterized it in the first case. Even after he has elaborated a new (or reversed) connection, the child may state that he "pressed the button when it was red and did not press the button when there was a green light," even though both of these lights had long ceased to figure in the experiment or occurred in the opposite fashion.

If we further complicate the task by requiring the child to work out a system of differential responses which require preliminary analysis of the critical attribute, then the disturbance of the role of speech in the mentally retarded child manifests itself quite clearly. In Martsinovskaya's experiment (1958) the shorter of two stimuli, similar in color, is positively reinforced and the longer of two stimuli, similar in color, is negatively reinforced.

In order to be able to respond correctly, the subject must analyze the stimuli, separating out the signal attributes (duration, or sequence of the stimuli). This process assumes the existence of a preliminary orientation to the stimuli which is always accomplished with the aid of speech in a normal subject. In the mentally retarded child the underdeveloped and inert speech system does not analyze the system of stimuli being received. It does not separate out the required signal attributes, and the child immediately reacts to the stimuli being received and the reinforcement which is given in the form of the speech command "Push it!" or "Do not push it!" Speech is not converted into a system appropriate for selecting information but is immediately generalized, leading in some cases to a generalized motor reaction to all signals and in other cases only to generalized cessation of all further motor reactions. In these cases the process of formation of a new connection does not involve that mediated speech system whose conscious and systemic character we described above. The process is more similar to the gradual development of conditioned reflexes which is characteristic of animals.

These facts are of paramount significance for psychology. They show that the participation of a verbal system in the elaboration of new connections is typical for the higher nervous activity of man and that all development of higher mental processes takes place by means of formation of complex functional systems with the aid of speech.

Development of the Regulatory Role of Speech

Investigation of how the regulating role of speech is formed in the behavior of the child should begin with an analysis of how the child behaves when given a speech instruction from an adult. It is well known that in the latter months of the first year of life it is possible to elicit specific movements by a speech command and that to the call "Make a boat!" or "Give the hand!" the child responds with appropriate movements.

However, closer examination shows that the initiating function of the adult's speech is still very limited in this first stage of development. As the observations of Kaverina (1950), Rozengart-Pupko (1948), and others show, speech addressed to the child can cause the desired movement only if the instruction is accompanied by direct emotional-active contact or, at least, if it does not occur in conflict with any focus of excitation dominating the child. If a child who is engaged in putting a ring on a rod is asked to "Take off the ring," he will instead continue the action of putting the ring on the rod, which he began earlier and which has become dominant (Polyakova and Krylov, unpublished).

If the 15-to-18-month-old child has begun to turn over a small cup, the instruction "Set the small cup upright" leads him to energetically turn the cup over although under other circumstances he is perfectly capable of fulfilling this instruction. If the 18-to-20-month-old child, chasing a ball, is instructed to "take the *doll,*" just as he is about to catch the ball, he merely chases the ball all the more actively. In all of these cases a speech instruction which is a sufficiently strong stimulus to set an action into operation proves to be weak in inhibiting a dominance established earlier. Instead it acts as a supplementary stimulus which only strengthens the dominance.

The child's difficulty in subordinating his actions to the regulating influence of speech can be more clearly understood if we assume that the child is in a state where speech will play an initiating but not an inhibiting role and in which the child's motor system will come under the constant excitatory influence of kinesthetic signals.

If, as was shown by Yakovleva (1958), a rubber balloon is placed in the hand of a 2-year-old child and from time to time it is suggested that he squeeze it, he will easily execute the instruction, continuing, however, to produce the squeezes independently of the speech instruction. Putting those motor reactions into operation with the aid of speech does not present any difficulty, but stopping them with inhibiting speech instructions does. If we say "Don't squeeze any more!" or "Stop squeezing!" the child only strengthens these absolutely involuntary responses. The inhibiting speech instruction causes nonspecific excitation just as in the experiments we described above, reinforcing the dominant action.

These observations indicate how unstable the initiating and even the inhibiting action of the speech instruction can be for the 1½-to-2-year-old child. However, the directing and regulating influence of a speech instruction, which short-circuits a specific system of preliminary connections and attempts to subordinate them to the subsequent behavior of the child, proves to be still less stable at this same age.

When we give a 2-to-2½-year-old child who holds a rubber balloon in his hands the conditional instruction, "When the light is red, you squeeze the ball," we find that such an instruction, which requires a preliminary synthesis of individual elements and an appropriately delayed inhibition of the motor reaction, does not produce the necessary organized action. Instead, the child is likely to react to each fragment of instruction addressed to him:

hearing the fragment "when a light appears," he begins immediately to look for a light; hearing "you squeeze the ball," he immediately begins to squeeze the ball. Frequently, the fragment of the instruction indicated immediate squeezing which was then supported by the influence of the constant kinesthetic stimuli from the ball. Consequently the child keeps on squeezing. At the same time, when the light signal occurs, it causes an orienting reaction which acts as an external inhibitor and he stops the continuous squeezing.

It is characteristic that all attempts to terminate squeezing with the aid of an additional inhibiting instruction failed. The commands "Stop!" and "Don't squeeze any more!" acted nonspecifically, causing only an intensification of motor reactions begun earlier. It is natural that the speech of the child, still not developed to any extent, cannot act as a factor regulating the execution of the instruction.

As a careful analysis has shown, the impossibility of inhibiting motor reactions in the 2-to-2½-year-old child once these reactions have been elicited was dependent on the fact that the experimenter's instruction only set into operation motor reactions which were supported by constant kinesthetic impulses from the ball in the child's hand, while there were no impulses to stop the action. In order to obtain inhibition of the elicited movement, it would be necessary to provide a special inhibiting impulse which would stop the cycle of involuntary reactions. This impulse would be another command which would initiate a new action, thereby automatically stopping previous motor reactions. In this case inhibition of the initiated movement could originate as a result of a clash of two excitations.

This method was used by Yakovleva (1958). The child was instructed to press the balloon in response to light and then immediately to place his hand on his knee, thereby achieving the cessation of the first act. However, the double action caused by this instruction can be gradually removed by suggesting to the child first to press the ball and place his hand on the edge of the table, then to press on the ball and place his hand on the table next to the ball. Using this approximation technique, the child is eventually able to continue to hold his hand on the ball after pressing, no longer performing the additional motion which is now inhibited by the implicit execution of the second part of the instruction.

The formation of voluntary motor inhibition at this early stage of development can also be obtained by presenting an inhibiting signal which emanates from the child's motor response to the starting signal. This inhibitory feedback signal serves as a distinctive "acceptor of action" (Anokhin, 1955). It is well known that the kinesthetic analyzer (the muscle-sensing apparatus) matures relatively late and that the flow of nervous processes within this analyzer continues for a very long time to be characterized by a certain diffuseness. Therefore, natural kinesthetic impulses traveling from the child's motor apparatus to his cortex are long inadequate for regulating the flow of his movements. To obtain a sufficiently effective "reverse afferentation" it is necessary to convert the kinesthetic signal into an *exteroceptive signal* and to make this exteroceptive signal, which originates from the natural movement of the child and which serves as the signal for stopping the action, sufficiently clear. It is sufficient to make the movement of the child cause any external signal. For example, the response may turn off a light or ring a bell, signaling that the desired action has been completed. By causing the signals through his own movements and by submitting them to his influence, the child can voluntarily master his own movement. While remaining completely reflexive in nature, his movement is composed of two reflexes, the second of which (by virtue of the meaning assigned to it by speech) is an inhibitory reflex to the stimulus caused by the child himself.

A study by Tikhomirov (1958) provided new methods for forming voluntary action in the child. Convinced by experiments with 3-to-3½-year-olds that these children could completely organize their own movement after this movement had once been controlled by an exteroceptive signal which it produces, Tikhomirov substituted the child's own speech (or, more precisely, vocal) reaction for this exteroceptive signal. He asked the child to say the word *raz!* (one!) or more simply—to give a vocal response *tu!* whenever he squeezed the ball. The speech (vocal) response has a more perfectly concentrated and active neurodynamic structure than the motor response of the hand. Moreover, it is not under the influence of constant kinesthetic stimuli originating from the ball, and consequently it is not only more easily subjected to instructions but also acquires a strictly coordinated signal character. Most important, it is able to render a regulating influence on the motor responses occurring simultaneously with it. It was sufficient to provide the child with a combination of the motor reaction and his own speech response to make it possible for the motor reactions to acquire an organized character. Unnecessary intersignal movements disappeared and motor responses began to come under the control of manifest external signals. The elimination of supplementary speech (vocal) responses eliminated this regulative role of speech and again returned the child to the state of nonorganized motor responding.

The same effect was produced when speech responses were elicited in conjunction with more complex actions. The 3-to-3½-year-old child, by accompanying his reactions to the conditioned signals with the words *raz-dva!* (one-two!) or *tu-tu!*, responded to each external signal with two squeezes. This would be entirely impossible for him without the participation of these additional regulating speech responses. It would be erroneous, however, to think that in this case we have complete speech regulation of the motor act in a 3-year-old child.

As Tikhomirov's subsequent experiments showed, the regulating role was not played by a system of complex semantic connections but by an *impulsive action of the word as an additional signal* stimulating and intensifying the motor reaction. If a child, who has just fulfilled the task to squeeze twice, using his own vocal reactions, *raz-dva!* (one-two!), or *tu-tu!*, receives another instruction ("Squeeze twice each time"), the new conditions fundamentally disturb the functional system. He is deprived of the double impulse which the *tu-tu!* reaction had. The new instruction has a stimulating impulse pattern similar to a single but extended impulse, causing this complex speech reaction to cease producing the necessary double movements and to become a single prolonged squeeze that clearly corresponds not to the instruction's semantic meaning but to its impulse characteristics.

This same effect occurred accidentally in another experiment on the formation of a system of discriminated responses (squeezing in response to a red signal and refraining from squeezing in response to a green signal). The squeeze to the red signal was combined with the speech response "Do!" (or "Squeeze!") to obtain the organized motor reaction. However, in an attempt to reinforce the inhibition of squeezing in response to the green signal by the words "Don't do!" uttered by the child himself, we obtained not an inhibition of the negative response but a complete disinhibition of the entire motor reaction. The child yielded to the influence of the initiating impulse originating from the speech reaction, which was inhibitory in its meaning but positive in its impulse characteristic, and responded positively to both stimuli.

All this indicates that the first stage during which the speech of the child itself plays a regulating role in the organization of motor reactions is a stage in which the regulating role is accomplished by the nonspecific impulse influence of speech and not through the action of a complex system of semantic connections.

Only at 4½ to 5 years is organization controlled by the selective, semantic side of the speech system. What is particularly noteworthy in this case is that the regulating role is accomplished not by external speech accompanying the child's motor reactions, but by its shortened traces, which constitute the basic content of the child's inner speech.

Future research should outline those stages through which this process moves and should describe more closely the complex stages in the formation of the completed mechanism of speech regulation of voluntary actions.

References

Anokhin, P. K. Features of the afferent apparatus of the conditioned reflex and their significance for psychology. *Vop. Psikhol.*, 1955, No. 6.

Buhler, K. *The mental development of the child.* New York: Harcourt, Brace, 1930.

Cassirer, E. *The philosophy of symbolic forms.* New Haven: Yale Univer. Press, 1953.

El'konin, D. B. Features of the interaction of the first and second signal systems in children of preschool age. *Izv. Akad. Pedag. Nauk RSFSR,* 1954, No. 64.

Ivanov-Smolenskii, A. G. Biogenesis of speech reflexes. *Psikhiat. Neurol.,* 1922.

Ivanov-Smolenskii, A. G. The joint operation of the first and second signal systems in the brain. *Zh. vyssh. nerv. Deyat.,* 1951, No. 1.

Karpova, S. N. Realization of the verbal component of speech by a preschool child. *Vop. Psikhol.,* 1955, No. 4.

Kaverina, E. K. *Speech development in children in the first two years of life.* Moscow: Medgiz, 1950.

Khomskaya, E. D. Pathology of the interactions of both signal systems in mentally retarded children. In *Problems of higher nervous activity in the normal and abnormal child.* Vol. 1. Moscow: Izd. Akad. Pedag. Nauk RSFSR, 1956.

Kol'tsova, M. M. *Formation of higher nervous activity of the child.* Moscow: Medgiz, 1958.

Kornilov, K. N. *Study of human reactions.* Moscow: Gosizdat, 1922.

Leont'ev, A. N. *The development of memory.* Moscow: Izd. Akad. Komm. Vospit., 1931.

Luria, A. R. *Speech and intellect in child development.* Moscow: Izd. Akad. Komm. Vospit., 1928.

Luria, A. R. *The speech and intellect of urban, rural, and neglected children.* Moscow, 1930.

Luria, A. R. *The nature of human conflicts.* New York: Liveright, 1932.

Luria, A. R. *Essays on the psychophysiology of Handwriting.* Moscow: Izd. Akad. Pedag. Nauk RSFSR, 1950.

Luria, A. R. The role of the word in the formation of temporary connections in normal and abnormal development. Moscow: Izd. Akad. Pedag. Nauk RSFSR, 1956. (Also issued in English edition: Luria, 1961.)

Luria, A. R. Verbal regulation of behavior. In M. A. B. Brazier (Ed.), *The central nervous system and behavior: Transactions of the third conference.* New York: Josiah Macy, Jr., Foundation, 1960.

Luria, A. R. *The role of speech in the regulation of normal and abnormal behavior.* J. Tizard. (Ed.) New York: Pergamon Press, 1961. (English edition of Luria, 1956.)

Luria, A. R., and Vinogradova, O. S. An objective investigation of the dynamics of semantic systems. *Brit. J. Psych.,* 1959, *50,* 89–105.

Luria, A. R., and Yudovich, F. A. *Speech and the development of the mental processes of the child.* Moscow: Izd. Akad. Pedag. Nauk RSFSR, 1956. (Also published in English edition by Staples Press, London, 1959.)

Lyublinskaya, A. A. Certain features of the interrelationship of the word and visual material in the formation of ideas in the preschool child. *Vop. Psikhol.,* 1956, No. 1. (a)

Lyublinskaya, A. A. *Essays on the mental development of the child.* Moscow: Izd. Akad. Pedag. Nauk RSFSR, 1956. (b)

Martsinovskaya, E. N. Disturbance of the regulating role of speech in mentally retarded children. In *Problems of higher nervous activity in the normal and abnormal child.* Vol. 2. Moscow: Izd. Akad. Pedag. Nauk RSFSR, 1958.

Meshcheryakov, A. I. On the participation of past experience in the elaboration of temporary associations in the human being. *Vop. Psikhol.,* 1955, No. 3.

Meshcheryakov, A. I. Participation of the second signal system in the analysis and synthesis of chain stimuli. In *Problems of higher nervous activity in the normal and abnormal child.* Vol. 1. Moscow: Izd. Akad. Pedag. Nauk RSFSR, 1956.

Morozova, N. G. Development of the attitudes of preschool children to a verbal task. *Izv. Akad. Pedag. Nauk RSFSR,* 1948, No. 14.

Nazarova, L. K. Role of speech kinesthesis in writing. *Sovet. Pedag.,* 1952, No. 6.

Paramonova, N. P. The development of the physiological mechanism of voluntary movements. *Vop. Psikhol.,* 1955, No. 3.

Rozengart-Pupko, G. L. *Speech and the development of perception at an early age.* Moscow: Medgiz, 1948.

Ruzskaya, A. G. The role of immediate experience and words in the formation of generalizations in preschool children. (Candidate's dissertation, Moscow 1954.)

Rybnikov, N. A. Problems in studying the language of children. In *Problems of contemporary psychology.* Vol. 5. Moscow: Gosizdat, 1930.

Samsonova, V. G. Differentiation limits in verbal and motor reflex reactions. *Trudy Inst. Vyssh. Nerv. Deyat. Akad. Nauk SSSR,* 1955, *1.*

Shif, Z. I. *The development of everyday and scientific concepts.* Moscow: Uchpedgiz, 1935.

Shvachkin, N. K. Experimental study of the child's early generalizations. *Izv. Akad. Pedag. Nauk RSFSR,* 1954, No. 54.

Shvarts, L. A. The word as a conditioned stimulus. *Byull. eksper. Biol. Med.,* 1948, *25.*

Sokhin, F. A. Certain problems in mastering the grammatical structure of a language in the light of I. P. Pavlov's physiological studies. *Sovet. Pedag.,* 1951, No. 7.

Tikhomirov, O. K. Formation of voluntary movements in preschool-age children. In *Problems of higher nervous activity in the normal and abnormal child.* Vol. 2. Moscow: Izd. Akad. Pedag. Nauk RSFSR, 1958.

Vinogradova, O. S., and Sokolov, E. N. Dependence of the orienting reflex on the strength of the stimulus. *Vop. Psikhol.,* 1955, No. 2.

Vygotskii, L. S. *Thought and speech.* Moscow: Izd. Sotsekgiz, 1934. (Also available in English edition: L. S. Vygotskii. *Thought and language.* Edited and translated by Eugenia Hanfmann and Gertrude Vakar. Cambridge: M.I.T. Press, 1962.)

Vygotskii, L. S. *Collected psychological investigations.* Moscow: Izd. Akad. Pedag. Nauk RSFSR, 1956.

Yakovleva, S. V. Certain features of the process of formation of voluntary behavior in preschool-age children. In *Problems of higher nervous activity in the normal and abnormal child.* Vol. 2. Moscow: Izd. Akad. Pedag. Nauk RSFSR, 1958.

5

Some Results of the Study of the Psychological Development of Preschool-Age Children

D. B. El'konin

EDITORS' INTRODUCTION

The classical problems of developmental psychology constitute one of the main battlegrounds on which the theoretical and ideological engagements of Soviet psychology have been fought. In the 1920's, several psychological schools—the Freudians, Bekhterev and his co-workers, and Vygotskii—claimed developmental psychology as their own domain. As El'konin makes clear, the laws governing cognitive development are considered an important link in constructing a Marxist theory of the relation between society and the individual. This background also helps to account for the polemical nature of many of the theoretical statements.[1]

Unfortunately, El'konin's review does not reflect the very recent increased interest on the part of Soviet researchers in Western developmental research. Most influential in this regard have been two books: Flavell's (1963) summary of Piaget's research and Bruner's The Process of Education. *El'konin has himself moved*

1. *Editors' note:* His long discussion of the 1936 decree of the Central Committee on "pedological perversion" shows his continuing concern with this issue. "Testing" is still an epithet to be tossed at an intellectual enemy, although the strict dogmatism of the 1930's is a thing of the past.

from an interest in early development to a study of learning in an experimental school. (El'konin and Davydov, 1962). He has been a leading researcher at the Institute of Psychology in Moscow for many years.

Historical Introduction

By decree of the Soviet of People's Commissars on November 12, 1917, preschool education was incorporated into the public-education system. This decree implemented the great idea of the founders of scientific communism that workers' children should have access to communal education from an early age.

The vigorous growth of the system of communal education for children of nursery and kindergarten age reflected a special interest in the psychology of young children. In the immediate post-Revolutionary period, psychologists had not yet developed their own methods or collected their own data and were limited to generalizations of facts derived from Western European, American, and pre-Revolutionary Russian psychology. During this period, the construction of a child psychology based on the principles of Marxism-Leninism was considerably impeded by the influence of the pseudoscientific ideas of "pedology." [2]

The central problem of child psychology—the problem of development—had to be extricated from the incorrect methodology of the "two-factor" theory of bourgeois science. The "two-factor" theory fluctuated between "biologization," in which biological and hereditary factors were considered the primary elements in development, and "sociogeneticism," in which the influence of environmental conditions was regarded as primary. The leftist phrases of the so-called "sociogeneticists" in their campaign against the "biologizers" dovetailed with fatalistic bourgeois theories of the determination of development by unalterable environmental factors. In the process the infant was left a passive being, deprived of any life and activity of its own, and the crucial role of training and education in the development of children was ignored. Pedology (test research, which purported to measure the "intelligence quotient" of children) contributed to a false solution of the basic question of the laws governing the development of the infant mind. These pseudoscientific methods of child research afforded the opportunity for various sorts of interpretations in the spirit of the two-factor theory.

The pseudoscientific test studies were extended to children of infant and

2. *Editors' note:* "Pedology" is a Russian neologism used to refer to Western-style educational psychology, which at the time was characterized by the extensive use of mental tests and complex statistical paraphernalia.

preschool age in the form of various "intelligence scales" and tests of speech, locomotion, and other aspects of infant development. Divorcing the study of the development of the infant's psychological processes from the solution of the basic problems of general psychology had a deleterious effect both on the development of general psychology and on the development of child psychology. As a result of the monopoly of pedology, psychology was deprived of an outlet into pedagogical practice and of the use of genetic analysis of developmental processes. In child psychology the basic problems of infant development—namely, the development of psychological processes and of consciousness—were ignored.

The beginning of a new stage in the development of child psychology in general and of the psychology of the infant and preschool-age groups in particular was related to the decree of the Central Committee of the Communist Party, "On pedological distortions in the system of People's Commissariats of Education," dated July 4, 1936. This decree quite clearly exposed the reactionary essence of the fundamental pedological "law" concerning the fatalistic determination of the destiny of children by biological and social factors, by the influence of heredity and of some sort of "immutable environment." The decree showed that this "law" is in blatant contradiction to Marxism and to the practice of socialist construction and communist education and training. At the same time, it exposed the fundamental fallaciousness of the basic methods of pedological research, of the various test-type measurements which pretended to have a scientific foundation but were in reality only pseudo-objective and represented a "deliberate mockery of the pupils, contradicting the tasks of the Soviet school and flying in the face of common sense."

Infant psychology became a leading branch of psychology. Enriched by Marxist-Leninist methodology, which had at this point become the basic methodology of psychology, infant psychology occupied an important place in the solution of the tasks facing psychology as a whole.

It would be wrong to ignore entirely the studies of infant and preschool-age groups that were done in the period of the supremacy of pedology. A number of scholars and scientists accumulated factual materials on the development of the infant which in no way derived from the pseudoscientific conceptions and methods of pedology and represented a genuine contribution to the study of infant development.

Leningrad Psychologists

In the 1920's a special developmental clinic was organized at the Leningrad Institute for the Study of the Brain. Bekhterev was its initiator and it was here that Shchelovanov and his colleagues began their complex study of the process of infant development. This was the first institution in the world in which such systematic studies were conducted. The first work to come out of this clinic on the development of normal children had a reflexological bias.[3] After systematic, day-by-day observations, Figurin and Denisova published very important work (1929a, b) which was the first in the world literature to establish the stages of infant development in the first year of life. It should be stressed that this work is on a considerably higher level than analogous works by the American investigator Gesell, who made a study of infant development in early childhood by the successive-stages method.

The authors of this excellent work were the first to draw attention to the role of orienting reactions ("concentration reactions," in their terminology) in the development of the infant in the first year of life; they discovered the phenomenon of the "animation complex," arising as a reaction to adult speech at the end of the first and the beginning of the second month. They traced the phases of development of the infant's receptor and motor activity, the development of grasping movements with objects, the development of vocal reactions, and the infant's first words.

They also showed the role of orienting activity in the development of the ability to manipulate objects and games. It should be noted that these investigations indicated the utility of training in the first days of the infant's life and showed the possibility of a campaign against "hospitalism," which has a deleterious effect on the development of young infants. Although these studies were published in a pedological framework, they had nothing in common with the use of the pseudoscientific pedological methods or with the pseudoscientific methodology of the fundamental "law" of pedology. The facts they gathered have passed into the common fund of our knowledge concerning the development of infants at an early age, and Soviet science is rightly proud of them.

Subsequently this fine institution was transferred to the public-health agencies and was divided into two sections: one, headed by Shchelovanov, was transferred to Moscow, while the other, headed by Figurin, remained in Leningrad as an integral part of the Pediatric Medical Institute. Prior to the decree of the Central Committee, several important works were published as a result of studies carried out in these institutions, a system of institutions for training young children was established, and on the basis of meticulous studies of the development of young children, Shchelovanov and Aksarina (1925) wrote a textbook for the pedagogical personnel of these institutions. Rybnikov (1926a, b) collated and systematized data on the development of speech in children. The rich factual material collected in his books, although of a purely descriptive nature, continues to be of interest to the contemporary investigator.

---

3. *Editors' note:* "Reflexology" refers to the theoretical position of Bekhterev. El'konin was himself a student in Bekhterev's institute.

Moscow Psychologists

The talented psychologist Basov, who in the first years of the development of Soviet psychology opposed the prevailing mechanistic tendencies, worked with a team of co-workers on the problem of development in the preschool child. Fighting against subjectivism in the interpretation of the facts of infant behavior, Basov developed a method for objective observation of children. During this period Vygotskii, one of the Soviet Union's most able psychologists, was in the vanguard of the fight against mechanism and behaviorism and produced many valuable works. In the last years of Vygotskii's life (he died in 1934), in his work on the development of the infant's psychological processes, he was drawn into the stream of pedology. In spite of this, Vygotskii produced a number of studies of the utmost value for child psychology. His research on the development of thinking and speech and on the problem of instruction and development (1934, 1956 a, b) is of special note. Vygotskii was the first to present a critique of Piaget, who considered egocentrism the central characteristic of preschool children. On the basis of experimental and theoretical research, Vygotskii established the social nature and origin of so-called egocentric speech. As opposed to Piaget, who asserted the initial solipsism and autism of the infant and claimed that they are only gradually supplanted by the social thought of the adult, Vygotskii held that the initially (by its very nature) social liaison of the infant with the surrounding reality is the basis for the gradual development of his individual consciousness.

In his critique of the theory of egocentrism, Vygotskii advanced a number of propositions about the role of practice and activity in the development of the infant consciousness. He wrote:

> Activity, practice—these are the new concepts which permit us to view the multiple functions of egocentric speech from a new vantage point, and to note an entirely new aspect in the development of the child's thought, which, like the dark side of the moon, usually remains outside the observer's field of vision.
>
> Piaget asserts that things do not work on the mind of the child. But we have seen that, in a real-life situation, where the egocentric speech of the child is linked with his practical activity, where it is linked with the thinking of the child, things really do work on the mind of the child. Things mean reality, but reality not passively reflected in the perceptions of the child, not cognized by him from an abstract point of view, but rather reality with which he tangles in the process of practical activity (1956a, p. 92).

Vygotskii was the first in Soviet child psychology to direct attention to the problem of instruction and development and to emphasize the leading role of instruction in the development of the child. Thus, he wrote: ". . . only that instruction is good which keeps ahead of development." He also applied this proposition to schoolteaching (1956b). Considering the relationships between instruction and development to be variable, Vygotskii showed that with the transition to preschool age there also arises the possibility of a transition to a new type of instruction, different both from the instruction given in early childhood and from school instruction.

While defining certain specific features of instruction at the preschool age and posing the question of the possibility of teaching reading and writing at this age, he warned at the same time against a mechanical transfer of the program and methods of schoolteaching into the preschool age, against the conversion of "schools for the little ones" into "little schools."

In his characterization of the preschool period of development, Vygotskii started from this important principle:

> It would be a hopeless effort to attempt to characterize the features of the mind of the preschool-age child, starting not from the integral whole but from the individual parts, attempting to characterize attention, memory, and thought separately. As research shows and as experience teaches us, the most essential thing in the development of the child and his mind is not only the fact that the individual functions of the child's mind grow and develop in transition from one age to another, but also that as the personality of the child grows and develops his mind grows and develops as an integral whole (1956b, p. 430).

Vygotskii's grasp of the most important features in the development of the preschool-age child was valid. However, he had an erroneous conception of the origin of various individual aspects of the child's development, which he considered to be the result of a change in the structure of consciousness. On the contrary, the change in the structure of the mind, which occurs during preschool age, is the consequence of the new relations which are coming into being, of a new type of activity on the part of the preschool-age child. The development of memory at this age, which he considered to be the center of consciousness, is itself determined by new relations, by the new activities and new tasks with which the child is faced in this period of his development.

It must be noted that, during the last years of his life (when he had been drawn into the current of pseudoscientific pedology), Vygotskii was distinguished from the pedologists by his psychological orientation; for him the problem of the concrete psychological characteristics of consciousness and of its development remained the central problem, on which he worked to the last days of his life.

Even before 1936, some psychologists who had not been drawn into the orbit of pedology had been working on the question of the relation between the development of consciousness and activity, of thought and practice.

Rubinshtein advanced the thesis of the formation of human psychological life in the process of activity; in *Fundamentals of Psychology* (1935), he made the first theoretical attempt to explain the motive forces of psychological development without recourse to the two-factor theory, to the false notion of the determining influence "of heredity and an immutable environment" on the course of development. He wrote: "The internal contradictions between conscious relations reflected in self-awareness and real relations objectively determining consciousness and behavior are the motive forces of psychological development" (p. 147). This question then arises: How do the child's relations with the reality "of concrete forms of activity (play, study and later production work), by means of which the child and later the adolescent is actively integrated into the world about him," (p. 148) determine his mental development?

In his subsequent works, Rubinshtein elaborated on the development of the mental life of the child. He wrote (Rubinshtein, 1946) that the "motive forces" of the development of personality reside in this activity of the personality—in the internal contradictions between the forms of an ever more conscious activity of the child at the level of development which he has already attained and that new content which he is in process of mastering. He also examined critically the theory of the formal developmental levels of individual mental processes and showed that they do not directly depend on age, as such, but rather on the concrete content which the child masters in the course of development. Therefore, children of the same age—or any one child—may reveal various levels of development of individual mental processes as a function of the concrete content of the task to be resolved and the concrete activity involved.

Kharkov Psychologists

At about the time Rubinshtein was doing his work, another group of psychologists, under the direction of Leont'ev in Kharkov, was carrying out an experimental project aimed at explaining the role of practical "object" activity in the development of generalization and of other aspects of mental development. This work, begun in the 1930's, sought to extend Vygotskii's research on the development of children's thought, more specifically, the development of generalization. These projects were also directed against Vygotskii's tendency to overestimate the role of speech and communication in this development. They were concerned with the internal mechanisms of the development of generalization and with the significance of the practical "object" activity of the child in this process. The first studies, by Asnin (1941), showed that generalization arises in the process of the solution of a number of practical tasks—in activity which is conventionally called "transfer." "Generalization," wrote Asnin, "is formed in the process of transferring a method of action from one task to another, similar task" (1941, p. 126).

Lukov's work (1937) showed that the infant's recognition of speech is a direct function of his mastery of action with objects. The development of the child's recognition of speech is determined, not by the growth of introspection, but by a change in his relation to objective reality. This change is what leads to mastery of the world of objects. But since the objects the child meets are not objects of his passive contemplation, but rather objects of his activity, the child, in dealing with the object, masters together with that object his own activity, i.e., he acquires a knowledge and experience of activity. This experience, reflected in speech, is a system of possible actions with respect to the object named. Gal'perin (1937) showed conclusively that there is a fundamental difference between the instrumental operations accomplished by a human being (including children of preschool age) and the use of auxiliary instruments by animals. This research also showed the genetic roots of thought and the dependence of its development on practical activity. "Thought represents an individual form of the activity of a subject, a form which arises at a certain definite level of development of his practical activity (out of that activity, on the basis of that activity, as a proliferation of that activity). Thought takes over from practical activity its experience, its content, its techniques, the direction of its movement, and thus represents in the initial stages nothing other than the mental reproduction of that practical activity" (Gal'perin, 1954, pp. 85–86).

These investigations, like a number of others devoted to the problem of the assimilation of concepts, were originally summed up by Leont'ev (1935). In this article Leont'ev wrote: "In considering the development of a word's meaning, we must first accept the notion of an alteration in the child's generic type of activity, which then determines alterations in the corresponding stages of consciousness and speech. . . . This alteration of a generalization which reflects reality is a concrete form of an alteration of consciousness, an alteration which occurs as a result of the alteration of the activity of the subject in relation to reality."

Overcoming the pseudoscientific two-factor theory required the elaboration of new principles of experimentation. Asnin made the first efforts to define new principles of experimental research on the processes of mental development. He took as a point of departure (in work conducted under the direction of Leont'ev) the principle that "in reality, intellectual action does not represent the manifestation of a ready-made faculty, but rather arises and is formed in the process of activity, in the process of completing tasks. In accord with this, the real criteria of (experimental) reliability must be sought in the experiment itself, in the content of the activity which is accomplished by the test subject in the process of fulfilling a task, not in external conditions of research" (1941, p. 36). Asnin showed experimentally that completely favorable external conditions of an experiment do not guarantee the reliability of the data obtained. Not only is the presence of the experimenter during the experiment an external condition of the experiment, but the relations between the subject and the experimenter, which are of vital importance for the results, are developed in the course of the experiment itself. In addition, the attitude of the child toward the task—the motives for his actions—is formed in the course of the experiment itself and determines the character of his activity. Asnin concluded that "the same assignment will be fulfilled by the child differently and with varying degrees of success as a function of the role of the particular task in the activity, the goals of the activity, and the relationship that is established between the participants in the experiment. The consideration of these elements in research is of crucial significance for the determination of the reliability of the results of a psychological experiment" (1941, p. 137).[4]

The concrete studies of the processes of child development which were carried out under Leont'ev's direction were summarized by him in a special article (1945). He formulated the question of motivation as follows:

> And so, a change in the child's position within the system of social relationships is the first thing which must be noted in any effort to obtain a solution to the problem of the motive forces behind the development of mental life. However, by itself, this position does not, of course, determine development; it only characterizes the stage already achieved. What does directly determine the development of the child's mental life is his life itself, the development of the real processes of this life, in other words, the development of the child's activity, both external, practical activity and internal, reflective activity. And development of activity depends, in turn, on the conditions of life at the given moment.
>
> Thus, in the study of the development of the child's mental life, the starting point should be an analysis of the development of his activity in given concrete circumstances. Only with such an approach can one explain the role both of the external conditions of the child's life and of the rudimentary faculties which he possesses. Only by such an approach, starting from an analysis of the developing activity of the child, can one also properly understand the leading role of training, which influences the child's activity and his attitude to reality (e.g., which determines his mental life, his consciousness) (1945, p. 35).

4. *Editors' note:* This sensitivity to the effects of the experimenter upon the subjects' behavior and the interaction between subject and experimenter with a resultant change in behavior of the subject during the course of a study is a laudable characteristic of a great deal of the Soviet research. Western psychologists could profit from this keen appreciation of the qualitative aspects of the experimental situation in relation to the subjects' behavior. Studies of the effects of experimenters' biases are only one aspect of the more general problem of the effects of the interaction between experimenter and subject.

After the 1936 decree "On pedological distortions in the system of People's Commissariats of Education," the study of the process of the mental development of children of preschool age proceeded along the following lines:

1. Study of the features of higher nervous activity.
2. Study of the basic types of activity of preschool-age children: play and work—their influence on the processes of mental development.
3. Study of the development of speech and its role in mental development.
4. Study of individual aspects of development: movements, perception, memory and thought.
5. Study of the formation of personality in the preschool child.

Children's Activity: Play and Work

The fundamental role of activity in the mental development of children, advanced in Soviet child psychology, has restored interest in play and games, an interest which had been lost during the period when pedology was dominant. Play—specifically, topical dramatic play—has been recognized as the preschooler's most important activity, and a systematic investigation of it has begun. In contrast to the theories which consider play either a manifestation of instincts or a special childhood world in which the child lives in retreat from reality, Soviet psychologists have viewed topical dramatic play as a form of activity arising out of the child's life in society and representing a special type of liaison between the child and society.

Development of Instrumental Activity

Figurin and Denisova (1929a, b) have shown that one of the earliest forms of play occurs after the formation of the act of grasping, when the development of movements passes over into a new phase, consisting of the appearance and intensive development of repeated and chain movements. They also made a special study of the influence of the novelty of an object on the stimulation of action (play) with it. The authors have shown that a dominant interest in novelty, which is typical of man, is revealed as early as the fifth month of life. Abramovich (1946) has also studied some of the conditions under which novelty affects the child during the first year of his life. Presenting children with objects of varying degrees of novelty and complexity, he found that objects which are bright and vivid but too familiar do not attract a child, just as objects which are entirely unfamiliar and complex in form do not attract him. A child is most attracted by "half-familiar" objects; entirely unfamiliar objects can attract only when they appear together with an adult who is familiar to the child.

In these studies it was shown that novelty in conjunction with an active orienting reaction not only stimulates the grasping of the object, but (and this is the key point) stimulates the manipulative movements of the child; manipulative play during the first year of life is an activity excited by external objects, their "novelty," and reinforced by the effect of the ever new qualities of the object which are brought to light in the course of its manipulation. The facts contained in these studies contradict the theory of "functional satisfaction," advanced by Buhler, at the basis of which lie incorrect notions about the child as a being turned not toward the external world but toward a world of internal, organic sensations.

The emergence of the prerequisites for topical dramatic play in the course of the development of actions with objects has been studied in detail by Fradkina (1946). Careful, systematic observations and special experimental tests carried out on children aged from 1 to 3 years showed that the basic stages in the development of "object" actions are threefold: the creation of play situations; the emergence of a role; and the alteration of the structure of action. In the very beginning, the child repeats an action only on those objects which had originally been used with the given action. Subsequently there emerges the possibility of transferring actions to other, nonidentical objects as well. A new form of assimilation arises when the child reproduces adults' actions with objects, when these actions have not been directly demonstrated to him but only observed by him.

The nature of this sort of assimilation is not well understood; it can only be assumed that it arises on the basis of the child's considerably improved orientation, which permits the formation of an image of the actions of another human being. The new method of assimilation considerably widens the scope of actions which can be assimilated. At the same time there arise new possibilities for transfer of actions: (1) transfer of actions from one object to another; (2) transfer of actions to new circumstances. As a result of transfer of actions and their connections with new objects, the actions become more generalized. The generalized character of an "object" action is a paramount prerequisite for the appearance of play actions.

Neverovich (1948) studied the mastery of "object" movements in early childhood. Suggesting to children that they reproduce "object" actions in various circumstances, Neverovich showed that in early childhood actions cease being tied to specific objects. This finding is in accord with data obtained by Fradkina. The separation of action and object is the prerequisite for a word replacing an object not available for the execution of an action. Simultaneously, according to Fradkina, one begins to see one sort of object used as a substitute for others. It has been established that children always begin by acting with objects in a definite play fashion and only later call them by new play names corresponding to the actions.

Make-believe conditions, which are a prerequisite for dramatic play, begin to emerge.

The condition for the appearance of a role is that the child begin to identify his action with the actions of adults. In early childhood the child begins by acting like a grownup, identifies his actions with the actions of adults, and only then begins to call himself by their names. Roles in children up to 3 years of age are characteristically not generalized but rather are the roles of specific adults.

Toward the end of early childhood the structure of actions changes from single acts into a chain which reproduces the essentials of real actions. Thus, according to Fradkina, under the direction of adults a number of prerequisites for the transition to dramatic play arise during the child's "object" activity: (1) generalization of "object" actions; (2) the use of certain objects as substitutes for others; (3) the reproduction of a chain of adult actions. However, these prerequisites do not by themselves guarantee the transition to topical play. The problem of the conditions for the transition from "object" play to topical dramatic play has not yet been sufficiently studied.

Aksarina (1944), studying the conditions contributing to the development of play in older preschool children, showed the significance of three conditions: (1) the presence of varied impressions of surrounding reality; (2) the presence of playthings and educational aids; (3) frequent association between the child and adults. Of crucial significance, in the opinion of this investigator, is the educative influence of the adults.

Development of Role Playing

El'konin (1957) hypothesized that a change in the relationship between the child and adults is essential for the emergence of dramatic play. If the conditions of training are what they should be, this change occurs toward the end of early childhood. Because of the mastery of "object" actions, there is a decrease in the joint activity of the child with adults which is characteristic for early childhood, and a growth of independence. A certain emancipation of the child from grownups occurs. At the same time, because of the child's increased capacities a tendency to participate in the activity of adults emerges which the child cannot fulfill. From these contradictory tendencies a new type of relationship between the child and adults is engendered, namely, dramatic play, in which the child takes upon himself the role of an adult and reproduces adult activity, and adult relations to things and to other people, in special "object" play conditions created by the child himself.

Slavina (1948) has shown that even in the very earliest stages of dramatic play, when games consist of manipulative, monotonously recurrent actions with objects, role playing substantially alters the very sense of these manipulations. It was shown that play activity is social in its meaning, expressing a relation and attitude to other human beings via an action with objects.

Topical play is specially sensitive in the sphere of human activity and relations. Presenting preschoolers with situations in which either objects (their qualities, destination, etc.) or individuals (their activities and relations with other human beings) were brought into the foreground, Koroleva (1957) showed that in the first type of situation dramatic play did not appear in the child even when it was deliberately stimulated by specially selected toys. In the second situation dramatic play emerged readily and continued for a long time, constantly being enriched in its content. In the light of these experimental facts play is conceived (in contrast with the theories of Western European psychologists such as Koffka, Lewin, and Piaget) as an activity which is social by its very nature, not as a means of retreat from reality into the infant's "special world."

As numerous observations have shown, certain subjects of juvenile games predominate among both younger and older preschoolers. However, a certain definite developmental pattern can be observed. According to Usova (1947), and others, the subjects of juvenile games develop from games whose content is taken from the home to games with industrial themes and, finally, to games with sociopolitical overtones. A basic influence on this development is exerted by the familiarity of the child with the world around him, by the expansion of his horizon.

According to Usova's data (1947), 3-year-olds form brief (about 5 minutes) small groups (2 to 3 children). The groups are very fluid. At the age of 4 to 5 years the group embraces from 2 to 5 children and the amount of time spent playing together increases to 40–50 minutes, although in 50 per cent of the cases such a grouping is only maintained for about 15 minutes. In older preschoolers (6 to 7 years of age), the groups become larger and more protracted. Educational work exercises a great influence on the organization of groups for games. One year of training sufficed among a younger group to lengthen collective play and to increase considerably the number of children included in a group.

Zalogina (1945) was the first to call attention to the fact that in collective play or games there exists, over and above the plane of the relations between the children dictated by the roles assumed, the further plane of the real relationships between the children. These real relationships within the group of playing children emerge as an organizing, supporting, and controlling feature of the execution of the roles by each of the players. The group of playing children emerges as a real collective, in which the children enter into real relations with one another and get real practice in group relationships.

Studies have shown that the adult relationships reproduced in the game, the so-called make-believe relationships, may be on a higher level than those real relationships into which the children enter either in the process of the game itself or in other forms of collective activity. An interaction occurs between the real and the make-believe relationships. On the one hand, the real relations exert an organizing and controlling influence on the make-believe relationships; on the other hand, in the make-believe relationships the children are practicing acquiring and mastering new forms of social relations which are transferred to real relationships. Cherkov (1949) has convincingly demonstrated that play leads to an active mastery of the standards of social behavior, which are transferred into all spheres of the child's life.

Studies by Leont'ev (1944), Fradkina (1946), Slavina (1948), El'konin (1948), and others have established that in fully developed dramatic play there are three interconnected elements: (1) the role of an adult which the child assumes; (2) play actions, by means of which he reproduces the activity and relations of adults; (3) "object" play (make-believe) conditions with which and in which the child acts. The central unit of every dramatic game is the adult role assumed by the child. El'konin (1948) showed that one of the essential conditions required before the child assumes any sort of role is an analysis of the activity and relationships between adults. This precondition, however, is not sufficient. An equally important condition is a positive emotional attitude toward the grownups who are performing these activities. The features of this sort of emotional attitude have not been sufficiently studied.

In an unpublished work Vygotskii expressed the belief that each role assumed by a child in play contains certain definite rules embracing both conduct as a whole and the methods, character, and logic of actions. The presence of such internal rules in role playing has been experimentally demonstrated by El'konin (unpublished research), who created situations in which the rules that follow from a certain role and actions that are attractive to the child are in conflict. This experiment showed that obedience to the rule connected with the role and a refusal to give way to momentary desires are a constant element of almost every role. It was shown that it is the process of subordination to the rule that provides the specific satisfaction experienced by the child during the game. The constant abstention from momentary, immediate desires in favor of subordination to the rules connected with the execution of the assumed role is the source for new motives of activity and for volitional forms of behavior associated with these new motives. An experimental comparison of obedience to a rule isolated from a role and obedience to a rule inherent in a role showed that role playing considerably increases (in younger and medium preschoolers) the obedience to the rule. In the research of Manuilenko (1948) there are materials which show that the group also exerts a great influence on the obedience to the rules included in the roles. In a group of children at play the obedience to a rule is considerably more effective than outside of such a group.

Some Western European investigators (e.g., Koffka and Lewin) believe that the adult roles assumed by a child in a game or at play transport the child into a new, imaginary world, a world of symbolism and arbitrariness with its own special laws of complete freedom. In experiments carried out by El'konin (1948) it was shown that the logic of the actions performed by a child in a game or at play exactly reproduces the logic of the real actions of adults and that the introduction of even the smallest amount of arbitrariness is rejected by the players. Only the very oldest preschoolers accept an arbitrary fulfillment of the roles they have assumed. They may even consider extremely arbitrary performance of roles as a game all its own. These experiments have shown that play is by no means a special sphere in the child's life in which the laws of an unreal world prevail but rather that its laws and rules are no less strict and firm than those obtaining in reality. Symbolism and arbitrariness are not characteristic of dramatic play at the preschool age and are not a condition for its emergence but rather emerge themselves at the end of the preschool age in the course of the development of play. They mark the beginning of the disintegration of the preschool forms of dramatic play and the transition to new forms characteristic for the subsequent developmental period.

One of the characteristic features of dramatic play is the child's creation of special make-believe conditions: certain objects (real) replace others (make-believe). At first glance it seems that in such play "anything can be anything else," that the child acts entirely freely and the objects brought into his play represent arbitrary symbols. Observations have shown that the objects used to replace the other objects bear definite relationships with them. The choice of a replacement object is strictly determined by the possibility of performing with the object in question the activity required by the game, that is, by the possibility of transmitting the sense of the adult activity being reproduced via activity with this object.

Influence of Play on Other Processes

El'konin (1954) contended that the mechanisms for interrelating the first and second signal systems, which are in evolution during preschool age, underlie make-believe renaming.

Lukov (1937) investigated the question of renaming the objects in a game or at play. He found that the relation between the word and the object (the method of action with it) does not remain constant throughout preschool age. As a rule, the previous, preplay use of objects renders renaming more difficult, and this difficulty is all the greater, the more clearly comprehended the function of the object has been; whereas it is less in the case of objects lacking a clearly defined function.

Zaporozhets (1954b), who studied the development of the motor functions in the preschool age group, has shown that play represents the first form of activity which presupposes a conscious reproduction and perfection of new movements. On the basis of his experiments, it was convincingly demonstrated that the development of the motor sphere of the preschooler occurs to a considerable extent within the context of his play activity. Endovitskaya (1947) has shown experimentally that when elementary sensory acts are included in a play situation visual acuity is significantly increased. Consequently, dramatic play contributes to the development of even elementary sensory functions. Istomina (1948) has given evidence that in the context of dramatic play children remember a greater number of words than in an ordinary laboratory experiment on recall. Manuilenko (1948) compared the degree of control of behavior among preschool children during dramatic play and in the context of a direct assignment by an adult and found that control of conduct arises sooner in play.

Of course, it must not be assumed that dramatic play exerts its influence on each individual mental process—on the development of movements, perception, memory, and speech as separate processes. Such influence is possible only when these processes are directly built into the play activity. Play exerts a generic influence on the development of all mental processes, primarily because the psychological mechanism of voluntary behavior is formed in it. During play the child learns to determine his own conduct in accordance with an image, a rule, a standard of conduct. Consequently, a fundamentally new form of conduct—and through it the perfection of individual psychological processes—occurs during play.

The Development of Speech

Soviet child psychology has devoted a great deal of attention to the emergence and development of speech. This research has followed several lines: (1) initial stages of the emergence of speech; (2) development of the various forms and functions of speech; (3) assimilation of the grammatical structure of the native language; (4) development of the auditory aspect of speech.

Infancy

Krasnogorskii (1952), Kol'tsova (1951), and Barabashova (1956a, b) investigated the physiological mechanisms of the emergence of speech. The word initially emerges as a first signal system stimulus and only gradually acquires the properties of a special stimulus. The mechanism of the temporary connection[5] underlies the connection of a word with the object which it designates, according to these studies. Barabashova's data indicate

5. *Editors' note:* The Pavlovian term for a conditioned reflex.

that a dominant role in the establishment of a temporary connection between the word and the object is played by the orienting reflex. The strongest reflex at the end of the first year of life is orientation to visual stimuli; consequently, the association between word and object is most easily established on the basis of the visual orienting reflex. These facts coincide with earlier data of Rozengart-Pupko (1948), who showed that the understanding of words first originates on the basis of visual perception. According to Fradkina's data (1955), the understanding of speech by linguistic means per se emerges only toward the end of the first year of life. Prior to this (at 7 to 8 months of age) the formation of a temporary connection to a word is not distinguished in any way from the formation of a connection to other auditory stimuli; afterward (10 to 11 months of age) the formation of a conditioned reflex[6] to a word requires only one fourth of the reinforcement that is necessary for the formation of such a reflex to other auditory stimuli.

In almost all these experiments it is noted that initially the word emerges as a complex stimulus in which a strong component is the accented syllable or an intonational nuance. Only gradually does differentiation of a word emerge according to its phonetic characteristics. Barabashova (1956a, b), defined a number of specific features in the differentiation of words in her research on conditioned connections to verbal stimuli. Among these were: (1) The motor component of the orienting reaction, on the basis of which the connection is formed, is altered; the orienting reaction is directed not to an object but to an adult. (2) Conditioned connections are formed with the same speed no matter what the reinforcement procedure; the physiological mechanism of their formation is the same as in the case of the formation of conditioned connections between two indifferent stimuli, and the connections are bidirectional. (3) The external expressions of conditioned connections to verbal stimuli are unstable, but the underlying bond is more solid than for nonverbal stimuli. The response to a verbal stimulus is retained after the orienting reaction to the object has been extinguished. The great stability of the connections between name-words and objects indicates the special significance of the word as a stimulus. It is difficult to alter such a connection once it has been established.

As a number of investigations have shown, the understanding of words in the early stages of development is built not on the perception of their phonetic composition but rather by catching the general rhythmic-melodic structure of the word or phrase. Shvachkin (1948) called this stage in understanding the period of prephonemic speech development. The succeeding period, in which the perception of the phonemes acquires ever greater

6. *Editors' note:* The words "response, "reaction," and "reflex" are used interchangeably in this volume in accordance with contemporary usage.

significance, he called the period of phonemic speech. Shvachkin made a detailed investigation of the infant's perception of speech in the phonemic period. By teaching children to understand words differing from one another by a single phoneme, he established the general course of phonemic development in children aged from 11 months to 1 year 10 months. According to his data, phonemic development passes through the following six stages: (1) differentiation of vowels, (2) differentiation of the presence of consonants, (3) differentiation of sonorants and articulated plosives, (4) differentiation of hard and soft consonants, (5) differentiation of sonorants, (6) differentiation of plosives (each of the stages itself consisting of consecutive stages). Toward the end of the second year of life, the infant makes use of a differentiated perception of all the phonemes of the Russian language in his understanding of speech. Shvachkin stresses the significance of hearing in distinguishing the finest acoustic nuances in both the earliest stages of the development of phonetic perception, and in the final ones. This is specially important in the differentiation of consonants whose articulations have a close resemblance (e.g., in the articulation of voiced and unvoiced consonants). In differentiating between them, the child must orient not to the similarity in articulation but to the very fine differences in auditory cues.

Intensive development of the child's active vocabulary and mastery of pronunciation occur simultaneously with the development of auditory speech perception. The assimilation of the auditory concomitants of language and its use in the child's active speech have been most fully studied by Gvozdev (1948). He showed that, in place of required, but unassimilated, sounds, those sounds already present in the child's speech that are closest in articulation to the missing ones often appear. The system of substitution is based, in the main, on the articulational affinity of the sounds, in the first instance on their grouping in terms of place of formation, more rarely in terms of method of formation. Gvozdev established that the assimilation of a new sound does not, in the majority of instances, occur all at once; it is rather a gradual process via intermediate sounds, primarily those which are transitional between the new sound and the substitute. This research indicates the exceptionally early appearance of auditory checking on the pronunciation of newly assimilated sounds. Among the factors determining the assimilation of the auditory side of speech, Gvozdev specially underscores the role of the motor sphere, the elaboration of the required articulations.

In the foreign literature, the question of the period of so-called autonomous speech has been widely treated (Ament, Preyer, Stern, and others). Well-known instances are those in which the very same word (most often in the phonetic sense representing a fragment of some word from the language of adults) is transferred from one object to others and thus begins to have many meanings. A study by Konnikova (1947) was concerned with the psychological nature of these multimeaning words. On the basis of many observations and special experiments, the author showed that speech during this period is not "autonomous" but rather represents a natural transitional stage from nonlinguistic to linguistic forms of communication. The possession of many meanings by a word is a characteristic feature, not only of those words which relate to various objects, but also of those which are stably associated with one object. At this period, words having a single meaning in their external manifestations possess many meanings in their internal structure. Konnikova convincingly showed that the multiple meanings of words at this period are a function of the character of the activity of the child and his relations with adults. These words are, in terms of their origin, interlaced with and welded to actions in affective situations with adults or performed with the aid of adults. Consequently they reflect not a certain specific object, but rather the entire situation of the action as a whole. The generalizations underlying these words are situational, affective generalizations. Thus the possibilities for using these words for communication are exceptionally limited. The disintegration of these generalizations is most intimately linked with the transition to "object" activity. Konnikova's research is fundamentally important, since it is the first to consider the development of speech, specifically the development of the meanings of children's words, as a function of the character of the relations between the child and adults, of the character and content of the child's activity.

Gvozdev (1949) divides early childhood (up to 3 years of age) into two periods, in terms of the assimilation of language. The first (from 1 year 3 months to 1 year 10 months) is characterized as the period of sentences consisting of amorphous word-roots which are used in a single constant form in all instances in which they are employed. This period clearly breaks down into two parts: (1) the phase of the one-word sentence and (2) the phase of sentences of several words (though in the main two-word sentences). The second period (from 1 year 10 months to 3 years) is characterized as the period of assimilation of the grammatical structure of the sentence, connected with the formation of grammatical categories and their external expression. It is distinguished by the rapid growth of various types of simple and complex sentences. Because the child's activity is carried out in the majority of instances either together with adults or with their aid, communication bears a situational character, assuming a dialogue form.

Preschool

The transition to the preschool age is characterized by a change in the manner of life of the child, by the emergence of new relations with adults and of new types of activity, all of which necessarily leads to a differentiation of the forms and functions of speech. Because of the growing independence of the child and the need for communication with adults, there arise new communication tasks, consisting of the transmission by the child to adults of his experiences and impressions and of plans that have arisen apart from direct communication with the adults. A new form of speech, the report or narration, is developed. The new demands of communication and activity which lead to the emergence and development of new forms and functions of speech inevitably give rise to an intensive mastery of language.

Leushina (1941), in her study of the features of coherent speech in preschool age groups, set the children various tasks in various communication contexts. On the basis of a large amount of experimental material, she showed that speech in the same children may be now more situational, now more contextual, as a function of the tasks and context of the communication. At the same time it was demonstrated that there is a noticeable decrease in the indices of situationality during the preschool period and a growth of contextuality even in cases of tasks and contexts stimulating situational forms of speech.

Thus it has been shown that the preschool period is a period of "contextual" speech. The bases for this development are the new relations between the child and adults, the new types of activity of the child, and, in connection with this, the new communication tasks. The mastery of vocabulary and grammatical structure becomes a necessity. In connection with the emergence in the preschool period of the new types of independent activity by the child (play, drawing, modeling, building, and the like), new functions of speech also emerge.

In the 1920's, Piaget began to publish his work devoted to the problem of the development of speech in children (Piaget, 1926). He was the first to describe the new form of speech as "egocentric." In contradistinction to "socialized" speech, which fulfills the function of communication, egocentric speech, Piaget stated, does not fulfill this function but constitutes talking to oneself. According to Piaget's data, egocentric utterances occupy an important place in children of younger preschool age and gradually decrease with age, being supplanted by socialized speech. The problem of egocentric speech occupies a central place in Piaget's conception of child development. Egocentric speech is for Piaget a symptom of egocentric consciousness, growing out of a primordial autism of the infant. Vygotskii (1934) was the first Soviet child psychologist to subject Piaget's theory of egocentrism to a sharp theoretical and experimental critique. In experimental research, the essence of which consisted in elucidating the manner in which a decrease or increase in the social elements of a situation will influence the egocentric speech of a child, it was convincingly demonstrated that every complication and hindrance of communication led, not to an increase, but to a *decrease* in the egocentrism of speech. These results led Vygotskii to assert that egocentric speech is by its nature social speech, a special form of speech to oneself. In connection with the fact that egocentric utterances increase sharply upon introduction of complications into the course of activity, Vygotskii advanced the contention that egocentric speech is a means of thought, that is, a reflection of a plan for solution of a task. On this basis he came to the conclusion that egocentric speech does not disappear, but rather is converted into internal speech.

Of interest are facts obtained in research by Syrkina (1934). She showed the dependence of egocentrism on both the character and content of activity and on the character of communication with those around the speaker. She measured the amount of egocentrism in communication with a strange adult (the experimenter), with strange children, and with familiar children in cases of freehand drawing and in the resolution of an intellectual task. The greatest amount of egocentrism is obtained in communication with an unknown adult, less with unfamiliar children, and least with familiar children. In the case where the objective conditions for communication are the same, the egocentrism of speech depends substantially upon the possibilities of real collaboration; the higher the possibility of real collaboration, the lower is the coefficient of egocentrism in juvenile speech. Since the forms of collaboration depend substantially upon the content and character of the activity, it is natural that the functions of egocentric speech should also prove to be different in different kinds of activity, reflecting the possible forms of real collaboration. The facts obtained in this research led El'konin (1958) to say that egocentric speech grows out of social speech and the real collaboration of children with adults. Egocentric speech is not only social in its origin but is also socially directed—a unique spoken equivalent of a practical collaboration in any activity; upon the appearance of difficulties it reflects the possible content of collaboration and aid; it objectively fulfills a regulatory function with respect to the activity. Egocentric speech is abbreviated not in proportion to the development of collaboration, as Piaget thought, but rather in proportion to the development of the child's independence.

There is every reason to suppose that at the root of the development of this speech function lie alterations in the interrelations of the first and second signal systems which occur throughout the preschool age. Many studies have been devoted to the question of the interrelations of the first and second signal systems. Kapustnik's (1930) research first established the fact that, when a conditioned reflex to an external stimulus is formed in a child, the verbal symbol of this stimulus is included in the connection; and, when a conditioned reflex is formed to a word, the immediate stimulus signified by that word also becomes part of the connection. Ivanov-Smolenskii called this phenomenon selective generalization or irradiation. In the further studies by Senkevich (1952), Smolenskaya (1934), Traugott (1934), Khozak (1934), and others, it was established that various types of inhibitory (differential) conditioned and complex stimuli are transmitted from one signal system to the other. However, as further studies showed, the interaction of the signal systems on the basis of selective irradiation is only one form of interaction. This form of interaction, as El'konin's (1954) data have shown, takes place even in the youngest preschoolers. The same research showed that, in the second half of the preschool-age period, there arise new interrelations of an inductive type between the signal systems. Pavlov pointed out that in the normal state the second signal system takes "under its wing" the activity of the first signal system. This means that the second signal system, being more mobile, can exert a regulatory action on the first signal system, and emerges as a regulator of activity with respect to directly perceived stimuli.

Numerous studies by Luria (1948), Luria and Yudovich (1956), and their collaborators have been devoted to the question of the interrelation of the two signal systems in the formation of motor reactions.[7] In connection with research on the formation of motor habits and voluntary movements in preschool-age groups, the question of the interrelation of the signal systems and of the regulatory role of the second signal system was studied by Zaporozhets (1954a, b) and his collaborators. In these studies it was shown that the capacity for establishing a complex system of actions according to a verbal instruction grows steadily during preschool age. The developmental capacities for the execution of a complex action according to a verbal instruction are directly related to the alteration of the character of orientation in the context of the imminent action. Teaching children to orient by various methods, it is possible to raise the execution of actions elicited by a verbal instruction to a higher level. At the same time it was demonstrated that even in preschool years the formation of comparatively abstract forms of orientation is possible. The child may be brought to an understanding of verbal instructions only if this understanding is organized in such a way that he can orient actively in the context of an imminent action. Zaporozhets emphasizes, on the basis of experimental facts, the crucial significance of the organization of orienting activity for the restructuring of the interaction of the signal systems.

An intensive development of coherent speech at the preschool age is impossible without the assimilation of the grammatical structure of the child's native language. Of primary importance in this field is the fundamental work of Gvozdev (1949) mentioned earlier. This research represents a systematic description of the process of communication with adults,

---

7. *Editors' note:* For details on these studies, see Chapter 4 of this volume, by A. R. Luria.

embracing all its aspects: syntax, morphology, and processes of word formation and word inflection. It was carried out with unusual meticulousness by a highly qualified linguist. Mainly linguistic in its content, it does not provide an answer to the question of the psychological and physiological mechanisms of the process of the assimilation of language. However, revealing as it does the logic of the process of assimilation, such research is an essential condition for a subsequent psychological analysis of this process. Gvozdev generalizes the material collected by him and relegates the preschool age to the third period of assimilation, the period when the morphological system of the Russian language, characterized by the assimilation of the types of declensions and conjugations, is mastered. In this period, the individual types of declension and conjugation of morphological elements, become discriminated. At the same time all the singular forms are, to a great extent, assimilated. Characterizing the results of the assimilation of Russian grammatical structure which the child achieves in this period, Gvozdev writes:

> The level of mastery of the native language attained by school age is very high. At this time the child has already mastered the entire complex system of grammar, including the most subtle laws of syntax and morphological order found in the Russian language, and likewise a firm and faultless utilization of a plethora of special idiosyncratic forms, to such a degree that the language he has assimilated becomes for him a genuinely native language. In this language the child obtains a perfect instrument of communication and thought (1949, p. 68).

Buhler once contended that underlying assimilation of the grammatical structure of a language is the child's discovery of the inflectional nature of the language. After this discovery and understanding of the basic principle of inflected languages, that various objectively existing relations can be expressed in speech by way of changes of the morphological parts of words, the assimilation of grammatical structure does not present any difficulties; and it is precisely for this reason that the child assimilates a language comparatively easily and rapidly. Such an explanation cannot be accepted by Soviet psychologists and has more than once been subjected to criticism.

Independent word formation, frequently encountered in the speech of the Russian child, is an index of the child's assimilation of suffixes. Bogoyavlenskii (1957) subjected this question to an experimental test. After a preliminary explanation of the meaning of several unfamiliar words, he presented them in a story as new forms with the suffixes *-enok, -ishche, -nik, -shchik*. It was discovered that the children understood word formations with the suffixes *-enok, ishche;* understood less well those with suffix *-nik;* and with greatest difficulty those with suffix *-shchik*. The author explains the comparative difficulty of understanding words with suffixes

-nik and *-shchik* by the fact that in the case of word-constructs with these suffixes there is a change in the basic lexical meaning of the words, whereas in the case of constructs with diminutive augmentative suffixes (*-enok, -ishche*) it remains unchanged. In another series of experiments, Bogoyavlenskii asked the children to pronounce the diminutives of words deliberately chosen for their unfamiliarity. The majority of the children easily coped with this assignment.

Sokhin (1956) undertook a purely theoretical attempt to explain the mechanisms lying behind the assimilation of grammatical forms in the light of Pavlovian theory. Analyzing, on the basis of Gvozdev's materials, the mastery of the instrumental case and the alteration of the verb according to gender in the past tense, Sokhin notes three stages. In the first, a stereotype is established and generalized. On the basis of the stereotype there arises a conventionalized use of the same forms: the instrumental case always with the ending *-om* (proper only to the masculine case); and the verb always in the feminine form, with the ending *-a*. In the second stage, because of the need to communicate, this generalized relationship becomes unsettled; new forms of expression of the same grammatical relations appear. A new stereotype arises, which subordinates to itself the first; for instance, the *-oi* endings (proper only to the feminine case) begin to dominate in the instrumental case, and the endings of the masculine gender in the conjugation of verbs. At the third stage there occurs a differentiation of the generalized relationships; the functions of these two stereotypes are delimited (there occurs a differentiation of the endings of the instrumental case as a function of gender). According to Sokhin, the mastery of the grammatical structure of a language occurs on the basis of a complex of dynamic stereotypes and their generalization and subsequent differentiation. Sokhin's conclusions raised a number of questions for further research. For instance, it remains unclear how the original orientation to a specific morphological element of a word arises.

In another study, Sokhin (1955) investigated the formation of the child's understanding of the preposition as a grammatical form expressing relations between objects. The method of investigation consisted in a study of the understanding of the preposition as a function of the concrete, sensory features of the relationships which the preposition expressed. An instruction was presented in which a change was made in the objects which were supposed to be put into relations expressed by the preposition *na* (on). In this research it was established that, at the first stage, the understanding of grammatically constructed utterances is determined substantially by nongrammatical elements and relies directly on object relationships. The preposition is not yet isolated in the sentence as an independent grammatical element. At the following stage the grammatical element is isolated and becomes a signal of objective relationships, but it is not yet tied in with a concretely objectified form of these relationships. At the last stage there occurs an abstraction from the concrete objective relations, and the grammatical element becomes a grammatical form expressing objective relationships independently of the concrete context. There is every reason to suppose that this is the path followed not only for the formation of the meanings of prepositions, but also for case endings, suffixes, prefixes, and the like.

Serebrennikova (1953), who made a study of the 3-year-old's mastery of the noun declension system, stresses that the breakthrough in the development of speech, consisting in the transition to grammatical formation of words, occurs as a result of the perfection of phonemic hearing and articulation. The development of phonemic hearing gives the child these capacities: (1) to isolate the less-accented syllables in a word, the result of which is a development of the word; (2) to isolate the word in the general stream of adult speech, the result of which is the growth of the child's vocabulary; (3) to isolate within words the morphological elements (signifying relations between objects), on the basis of which a mastery of the grammatical forms occurs.

Facilitating the Acquisition of Grammar by Inducing Appropriate Orienting Reactions

How a young child masters language is one of the urgent questions in child psychology and education concerned with this age. Of vital importance in this process is the orientation to the acoustic pattern of language. Popova's (1956) investigation dealt with the question of whether such orientation can be formed in children aged from 1 year 10 months to 3 years 6 months. Agreement between masculine and feminine nouns and the past tense of verbs, very common and difficult in Russian, served as material for the study. In the first part of the investigation the usual characteristics of this process were elucidated. For this purpose, masculine and feminine nouns were included in a game in the course of which the child had to form sentences consisting of two words (a noun, and a verb in the past tense agreeing with the noun in gender). It was established in this part of the study that the formation of such agreement is very slow, passing through four stages: in the first stage, the predominant form of agreement is agreement characteristic of feminine nouns; in the second stage, agreement in the masculine gender begins to predominate; in the third stage, there is a confusion of these forms; and finally, at the fourth stage, correct agreement is formed.

An analysis of findings obtained in this part of the study permitted the conclusion that the formation of correct agreement is based on the child's orienting in relation to the sound of the word (in this case the word ending) in its original form. In the second part of the experiment an attempt was undertaken to teach children to make proper agreement. A group of children which had not established agreement was specially selected for this purpose. They were shown pictures depicting objects on a table and told a story about the picture in which nouns and past-tense verbs agreed in gender. The children quickly memorized these little stories, then repeated them to the experimenter. In the course of retelling the stories a correct use of agreement was encouraged (verbally), whereas an erroneous one was corrected. When agreement was correct, the experimenter specially emphasized the endings of noun and verb. Instruction continued until correct agreement was achieved for all the words presented in the experiment. After this the children had to learn correct agreement for other words as well. Instruction by this method has shown, first, that some children failed to develop correct agreement; second, that establishment of agreement passes through the same stages as it does in a child's normal speech practice; third, that a great number of repetitions of word combinations by the experimenter and the subject himself is necessary to establish agreement. Thirteen children were subjected to instruction of this kind; eight needed over 200 repetitions and five needed over 300. It turned out that this simple accumulation of experience in social intercourse without specially organizing the child's activity in relation to linguistic material, in the course of which establishment of orientation with reference to the word's sound form would take place, does not lead to a sufficiently rapid mastering of word agreement.

In the third stage a new method of instruction was used. This was done in the form of a game in which the children had to bring small animal figures, with names consisting of masculine and feminine nouns, into a toy house. Whenever the child responded to the experimenter's question with correct noun-verb agreement, the doors of the toy house opened and the animal was let in; if not, the doors did not open. The experimenter pointed out the error, and unless the child corrected it immediately, the experimenter mentioned the error again and passed on to the next animal. This method was found to be very effective. All the children without exception, even those who scored lowest at the beginning of instruction, were able to form correct agreement. The process was relatively quick. Of twenty children, twelve needed less than 50 repetitions; three, from 50 to 100; five, over 100. None needed more than 200 repetitions. The conditions created by this method of instruction result in a shortening of the ordinary stages of agreement formation or even in the omission of some of these stages. The data from the last series of experiments indicate that orientation with respect to the formal attributes of words emerges very early in children, and that by creating certain conditions it becomes possible to form such orientation in full even in very young children.[8]

8. *Editors' note:* This experiment also has interesting theoretical implications which suggest the necessity of distinguishing between the processes of discrimination, the establishment of appropriate perceptual orienting responses, and differentiation, the establishment of appropriate instrumental responses. It is apparent that the efficacy of

Zakharova (1955) investigated mastery by preschool-age children of the categories of noun cases. In this research it was established that throughout the preschool age there is a considerable increase in the number of relations expressed by each case. The assimilation of the case forms occurs in a definite sequence: nouns of feminine gender ending in *-a* and of masculine gender ending in the hard sign are assimilated first; somewhat later, the masculine and feminine gender ending in the soft sign are assimilated; still later and with great difficulty the same thing occurs with the neuter gender. Assimilation of noun declension of the neuter gender clearly reveals the dependence on accent or lack of accent on the ending: the declension of nouns with an accented ending is assimilated more rapidly than that of nouns with an unaccented ending. Even in junior preschool-age children there are instances of "dual" declension of the very same word as a function of how it is pronounced in the nominative case.

On the basis of her research, Levina (1940) noted five basic stages in the development of linguistic awareness. In the first stage there is a complete absence of any differentiation of sounds, of any understanding of speech, or of any active speech by the child. This is the pre-phonemic stage of speech development. In the second stage only markedly different phonemes may be distinguished. The child's pronunciation is incorrect and distorted. He does not distinguish proper and improper pronunciation by other people or himself, and reacts in the same way both to a properly pronounced word and to words pronounced as he himself pronounces them. At the third stage decisive shifts occur. The child begins to hear the sounds of the language in accord with their phonetic marks. He likewise recognizes improperly pronounced words and is capable of making a distinction between a correct and an incorrect pronunciation. At this stage the previous babbling background and the new linguistic background that is just in the process of formation coexist. Speech still remains incorrect but an accommodation to a new perception is beginning, an accommodation expressed in the appearance of intermediate sounds between the pronunciation of the child and the pronunciation of adults. At the fourth stage, new forms of sound perception gain the ascendancy. However, the previous form is still not entirely supplanted. The child at this stage still recognizes improperly pronounced words. The act of speech is attaining almost complete correctness. Finally, at the fifth stage the process of phonemic development is completed. The child hears and speaks properly. He ceases to accept improperly pro-

operant conditioning in modifying behavior in many cases is not due to the learning of operant responses, which in fact are already learned prior to entering the experimental situation, but the shaping of appropriate orienting reflexes. It is no longer necessary to make inferences about hypothetical perceptual responses inferred from the very same behavior they are assumed to explain or to resort to grossly irrelevant analogues of observing responses. It is possible to obtain concurrent measures of orienting responses that are distinguishable from instrumental responses, as various contributors to this volume amply demonstrate.

nounced words. He is acquiring subtle and differentiated aural images of words and individual sounds. Gvozdev's work (1948), pointing out that from the age of 2 or 3 years children begin to recognize the peculiarities of their own pronunciation and even to defend an improper pronunciation, may be cited as relevant at this point.

At preschool age the child is going through, in the main, the last two of Levina's stages. A new, higher stage of phonetic development occurs in connection with the mastery of reading and writing, which require the capacity to analyze the aural composition of words. The possibility of facilitating aural analysis of words by children of preschool age was experimentally studied by El'konin (1958). As a result of this work on the development of speech at preschool age, theories of spontaneous development of the speech of the child were contradicted. The factual and theoretical inconsistency of the conceptions which attempt to explain the process of the development of speech by "intuitive discoveries" of the nominative function of the word and of the inflectional nature of language, particularly by "linguistic feel," "instinct," or the like, were also demonstrated. It was shown that underlying the development of the child's speech is his assimilation of language in direct communication with adults. Assimilation is a process which has its own logic and is determined by the conditions of life and activity of the child.

A number of experiments have been devoted to the role of speech in the development of various spheres of the psychological life of the child. Rozengart-Pupko (1948) and Lyublinskaya (1948, 1954) clarified the role of speech in the development of perception, in formation of representations, and in the whole of the cognitive activity of very young and preschool-age children. In these experiments it was shown that the mastery of the word and its utilization substantially altered the perception of an object, its individual aspects and relationships. The introduction of the word as designating certain definite properties of objects is of crucial significance for the formation of representations. The assimilation of words gradually restructures the immediate sensory cognition of reality. This is natural since it is by means of the word that the process of cognition is converted from an immediate process into one directed by adults.[9]

The Development of Motor and Cognitive Functions

The Development of Motor Skills

In the general course of the child's development, an important place is occupied by the development of the motor sphere, of movement and motor habits. Thanks to the development of the motor sphere, there is an increase

9. *Editors' note:* For a fuller description of this work, see Chapter 4 of this volume.

in the contact of the infant with the surrounding world. In Soviet child psychology, immediate practical activity is held to be of great significance for mental development; therefore it is natural that a good deal of attention should have been devoted to the study of the development of movements and motor habits.

In the works of Shchelovanov, Figurin, and Denisova, already mentioned, the development of movement in the first year of life was studied. Of fundamental importance is their description of the relationship between the development of the earliest forms of movement and the development of early forms of orienting-exploratory activity, especially the visual orienting reaction. Shchelovanov and Aksarina (1955) pointed out that the development of movements of the hand under the control of and on the basis of vision, fundamentally distinguishes the development of the child's very early movements from motor development in animals. Gal'perin (1937) was the first to emphasize the fundamental difference between tools as used by man and auxiliary instruments used by animals and to trace the development of the use of implements by children. He places the beginning of the mastery of implements in early childhood. However, the use of only a few household tools and appliances is mastered in early childhood. Decisive advances in the mastery of implements occur at the preschool age.

According to Gal'perin's data, the mastery of implements passes through four stages. At the first stage the children constantly repeat, with small variations, ineffective actions of a particular type. Gradually, more and more successful techniques appear; but they are not singled out by the child from the common mass, nor are they fixed in his mind. At the second stage, there appear sections of activity when during the course of a comparatively protracted period, the child repeatedly performs the same operation. Some convenient position of the tool, which he has come upon by chance, is held on to, and the child's effort is directed toward making use of it. At the third stage, the child makes active efforts deliberately to create the favorable position. Typical are the isolation of individual techniques that have proven successful in past experience and persistent efforts to reproduce them. Finally, at the fourth stage, the child takes into account the properties and connections of things and begins to master the habit of executing the appropriate movements.

It is entirely natural that the mastery of various tools as a function of their complexity may be found in one and the same child at different levels. As is shown in the unpublished research of Neverovich, devoted to an analysis of the formation of striking movements with the hammer, children of preschool age rarely reach the highest stage of mastery and usually remain at the second stage. In this research it was demonstrated that the difficulties of mastery are complicated by the fact that the child, imitating an adult and trying for the first time to reproduce an operation with the implement, devotes his main attention not to his own movement, by means of which the operation is being executed, but rather to its result. If this set of the child towards the result can be removed, the effectiveness of the implemental operation is considerably increased.

Considerable work has been carried out on the study of the psychological features of the formation of movements and motor habits by Zaporozhets (1948, 1954a, b) and his collaborators.[10] It was shown that the basic function of movements changes substantially. For example, in the context of play or competition, the indices of jumping were considerably improved in comparison with what they were in the context of a simple assignment. Detailed analysis has shown that behind the purely quantitative alterations there lies a profound qualitative restructuring of the movements. The principal alteration consists in the fact that the movement begins to disintegrate into two interconnected phases, preparation and execution. The isolation of the preparation phase leads to a new type of organization of the motor act: the imminent movement is correlated with the task it is supposed to complete. Precisely this different organization of movements, this qualitatively new regulation of them, is what leads to the quantitative alterations.

Further studies have sought to discover the psychological content of the preparatory phase for the fulfillment of an action. On the basis of the reflex theory of Sechenov and Pavlov, Zaporozhets asserted that orienting-exploratory activities play a crucial role in the formation of motor habits and voluntary movements. Orienting behavior represents the content of the preparatory phase. In the elaboration of motor habits by various means (by means of independent trials, imitation, with the aid of verbal instruction) it was discovered that, aside from the instrumental directive movements serving directly the attainment of a result, the child performs a number of actions which, by their character and role in the subsequent behavior, are substantially distinct from the directive movements. While not leading directly to the attainment of the final result, this activity makes it possible to more accurately orient to the situation and assures the execution of the instrumental movement in accord with the conditions of the task. Such activity was called orienting-exploratory. Further experiments sought to form the various motor habits with abbreviated orienting-exploratory activity or without preliminary orientation. These experiments showed that the level of intensity and uniqueness of the orienting activity influences the speed of habit formation, the character of the motor behavior of the child, and the subsequent functioning of the habit. Experimental data indicate that, as a result of orienting-exploratory activity, the child forms new connections and activates old connections corresponding to the conditions of the task.

10. *Editors' note:* See Chapter 3 of this volume, by A. V. Zaporozhets.

In another series of experiments it was shown that the orienting-exploratory activity itself does not remain constant. In the earlier stages motor-tactile orientation is of crucial significance in the formation of motor habits; subsequently the eye, which used to follow the hand, accumulates its experience and obtains the capacity to fulfill orienting-exploratory movements on its own. In the later stages there emerges the possibility of verbal regulation of the formation of the motor habits. Underlying this capacity is orienting-exploratory activity, which occurs without any direct perception of the conditions by way of a mental orientation within the situation. At this highest stage the orienting-exploratory activity is converted into mental activity. These data obtained by Zaporozhets are of fundamental importance. In the first place, they show the possible origin of mental activity in orienting-exploratory activity; secondly, they reveal the psychological content of the preparatory stage of the formation of motor habits and of the regulation of voluntary movements. The experimental facts obtained in these studies are also important because they reveal a basis for the qualitative alterations of the motor behavior of preschool-age children. It is this behavior which, in the strict sense of the word, becomes voluntary, that is, psychologically regulated in accord with the conditions of an imminent action.

The Development of Perceptual Skills

The early age periods, including the preschool, are periods of the dominance of the direct sensory cognition of reality. Naturally, attention has also been devoted in Soviet child psychology to the study of the development of perception. The accumulation of sense experience begins at a very early age. According to the data of Shchelovanov, Figurin, Denisova, and others, the development of perception is dependent upon orienting reactions appearing in a certain definite order beginning with the first weeks of life, in the form of an optimal setting of the organs to the stimulus with complete or partial inhibition of movements. It is precisely on this basis, beginning with the first month of life, that the first conditioned reflexes from all analyzers are formed.[11]

In the initial period of development, according to Rozengart-Pupko (1948), visual perception is of predominant significance. Since the satisfaction of the basic needs of the child is accomplished by adults, the first visual reactions are directed to the adults who are looking after the child. On the basis of visual perception of the face of the speaking adult the first reactions of animation arise, and the first following movements arise. Objects begin to attract the child only when they are objects involved in the activity of adults. The development of visual perception is from the very beginning bound up

11. *Editors' note:* For more detail, see Chapter 2 of this volume, by N. I. Kasatkin.

with the movement of the eyes: initially direction of the gaze to an object arises, later a following of the object, and finally an examination of the object by way of movements of the eye along and around the object. It may be assumed that the "movements of the eyes along and around the object" are the basis for the formation of the visual image of the object. Of great significance for the development of perception is the inclusion of the word in the process of communication of the adult with the child. As the investigations of Rozengart-Pupko (1948) and Shvachkin (1954) have shown, the initial generalizations arise in connection with the use by the adults of words in communication with the child. The understanding of the first words which name objects (Barabashova, 1956a, b) arises on the basis of the visual analyzers (the difference in the significance of the analyzers for the establishment of a connection between the name-word and the object is eliminated by the age of 3).

Development of the movements of the hand likewise occurs under the control of the visual analyzer. However, even in the first year of life, the development of manipulative and "object" actions[12] with objects begins to be subjected to the activity of perception. Dunaevskii (1956) has shown that the child reacts to stimuli, at least to some of them, not only by directing the analyzer to the source of the situation, but also by hand actions. The orienting reflex which Pavlov characterized as a "what's that?" reflex is supplemented by the "what is this for?" orienting reflex. The combination of visual perception with manipulation leads to the formation of connections between the visually and tactual-kinesthetically perceived qualities of objects, which underlie the perception of shape, size, volume, and remoteness of the object. The visual analyzer accumulates these connections, as a result of which it becomes possible to get along with only visual perception of all these qualities. This provides great advantages, both in terms of the speed of analysis of what is perceived and in terms of the possibility of simultaneous grasping of a great number of individual components, on the basis of which the formation of an image of the object becomes possible.

Ginevskaya (1948) has shown that an important feature of the perception of young preschoolers is represented by the undifferentiated nature and incompleteness of the images which arise in the process of familiarization with objects by means of touch. Younger children orient to some one property, most frequently a functional one; medium preschoolers try to extrapolate characteristic properties of the external appearance of the object but do not undertake planned attempts to feel it out; only older children (6 years of age) are not satisfied with first impressions in recognition, do not orient to individual properties, but rather undertake planned attempts to feel

12. *Editors' note:* The term "object actions" refers to acts directed at concrete, palpable objects, rather than the instrumental use of these objects for other goals or thought about the objects.

the object and look for properties essential for the formation of an image. In this way perception by touch becomes an independent activity which fulfills the task of creating an image of the object.

The features of the formation of an image of objects in younger preschoolers are determined by two criteria: the task of practical mastery of an object may not require a detailed differentiated image; the process of perception is not differentiated from practical activity with the object. Nekhlyudova (1924) studied the subordination of visual perception to the task of searching for an identical object according to a model. She showed that at the preschool age there arises the necessity of a more detailed familiarization with a model. Younger children do not try to concretize an image and use the most generic notions of an object generalized in a word; older children make use of a more or less articulated image created on the basis of a more detailed analysis. Accordingly, the very process of searching is itself substantially reorganized; in younger preschoolers the search for an identical object bears a chaotic character and requires reliance on external actions (for example, on movements of the hand); the older preschoolers require this considerably less, and the search acquires traits of an organized process. Yakobson (1957) showed that the capacity of the eye to follow the contours of an object is likewise formed gradually. Initially, this sort of following is impossible and requires the support of the hand in tracing the contours, and only gradually does it become an independent act. Yakobson expressed the opinion that the visual capacity to trace the contours of an object underlies the abstraction of form and is one of the conditions of the formation of the capacity to reproduce the outline of shapes.

Luria (1948) has shown that the formation of individual perceptual operations depends substantially on the conditions of activity. In his experiments the formation of analyzing operations occurred more successfully when the image was given in an indistinct form and the child was required to articulate those elements out of which the image was supposed to be reproduced.

In the studies of Kolodnaya (1954) and Kozyreva (1949), the perception and differentiation of right and left occurred on the basis of a more actively operating right hand. The perception of spatial relations between objects is connected with practical orientation among them and with the degree of differentiation of these relations in the speech communication of adults with children. Mukhin (1941), Shabalin (1939), and others have investigated the perception of shapes and colors by children of preschool age. This research has shown that children may distinguish objects according to both shape and color as a function of the task which confronts the child and of the conditions of the activity. For the perception of relative or absolute color qualities of an object, the character of the relationships between the color and the object are of basic importance. The most favorable conditions for the perception of color in its absolute qualities are present in those instances when the color emerges as a characteristic trait of the object. Research, using the process of touching, showed the importance of movement in relation to the object, without which the appropriate image is not formed. Istomina (1956) made a study of the perception and naming of colors in preschool-age children and found that the formation of connections between the word and the color is a later formation than the proper discrimination of colors: the sensory differentiation of colors precedes differential response to color.

The question of the development of the elementary sensory functions at preschool age has not been studied sufficiently. The data obtained by Arkin (1931) and Endovitskaya (1955) demonstrate that substantial advances occur in the development of visual acuity, exactness of distinction of color tone, and tonal hearing during the entire preschool period. Endovitskaya has demonstrated that development occurs under the following two conditions: when external stimuli are important for the execution of an act, and when in the course of the activity there appears a need, not only to act in accord with perceived stimuli, but to designate these stimuli verbally.

Several investigations were devoted to the study of more complex kinds of perception. Ovsepyan (1939) made a study of children's perception and comprehension of the content of pictures and demonstrated that the fullness of perception of a picture's content depends on the degree of comprehension of the content of the picture as a whole. When, because of the complexity of the material depicted, the child did not comprehend its content, he listed only individual objects in his narration; in cases of a more accessible content, the child not only listed the objects, but also narrated actions and relations. All the research carried out in Soviet psychology demonstrates that, at the preschool age, perception is converted into an activity subordinated to the task of forming an adequate image of the object.

The Development of Thought

The problems of the development of thinking at junior ages, specifically at preschool age, have interested Soviet psychologists, not only with the aim of discovering the features of the development of thinking at these ages, but also because such research casts light on the nature and origin of thinking in general.

The research of Gal'perin (1954) has brought to light the origin of the earliest manifestations of thinking. By setting children a series of practical tasks, the solution of which required the application of the simplest instrument or tool, Gal'perin established the basic stages in the mastery of implemental operations. He demonstrated that the emergence of intellectual operations in the child is bound up with the developing use of implements in practical activities. At the same time it was shown that intellectual operations are initially isolated from practical activity and then begin to serve the latter.[13]

Zaporozhets (1954a, b) and Lukov (1937) subjected to an experimental critique the ideas of syncretism, insensitivity to conflict, and contradiction of juvenile thought established in the research of Piaget. By suggesting to children that they make statements about the way various objects float on water and then giving the children an opportunity to check on these statements, it was demonstrated that even in a 3-year-old child there arises a unique nexus of judgments as a result of practical experience, although the judgment is not voluntarily established and is still not substantiated. Under the influence of the perception of a series of analogous facts, the child begins to assume that subsequent events will occur in a similar way. Subsequently, in the second half of the preschool age, active efforts to coordinate his judgments and to find a basis for their coordination appear. Thanks to the isolation of this substantiation, judgment acquires a convoluted character. To substantiate his judgments, the child appeals to his practical activity. This research shows the aspiration of children to penetrate more and more deeply into the causal nexus between objects in the substantiation of their judgments. Subsequently, the child's capacity for establishing causal dependencies between physical phenomena as exemplified by floating objects was studied in the work of Venger (1958). On the basis of an explanation by children of floating objects, he shows that even 4-year-olds look for reasons for the floating. Which properties of the objects the children connect with floating depend on which of these properties can be isolated by the children. After teaching the children the characteristics of the material out of which various things are made, Venger demonstrated that, as soon as the children learn how to distinguish the objects according to material, they begin to explain floating by features of the material and to give appropriate reasons. Venger demonstrated that children's causal explanations at this age are limited by the properties of objects accessible for isolation.

Lyublinskaya (1954) showed that it was in the resolution of practical tasks and the overcoming of difficulties that the formulation of the question of the causes of the difficulties appears. The emergence of such questions exerts a vital influence on the very process of solving a practical task, imparting to all the actions a bias toward searches for the proper solution.

The features of visual-graphic thinking were studied by Khomenko (1941), Kontsevaya (1941), and Titarenko (1941), who investigated the way in which children of preschool age understand various genres of literary production (fables, fairy tales). It was shown that the transition to visual-graphic thinking is most intimately related to the emergence of new

13. *Editors' note:* For a further development of Gal'perin's views, see Chapter 7 of this volume.

types of activity requiring reliance on representations of the object. These new conditions of activity are most clearly evident in dramatic play, which requires operating with images of objects and by that very fact forms thinking activity which relies on images. Research on children's understanding of literary productions has shown that it relies on images and represents a unique activity of empathy and cooperation with the hero of the literary work.

The question of the transition to rational forms of thought has been clarified by Minskaya (1954). Her investigation dealt with the transition from object manipulation to reasoning and thinking in children of preschool age. Children of preschool age (from 3 to 7 years old) were given problems which required a reasoning out of very elementary mechanical connections and relationships using levers of various kinds. The goal was an attractive prize placed beyond arm's reach on one arm of the lever. The system had to be set in motion in such a way as to reach this target. The problems were presented in three different ways: (1) in an object-manipulative form where the entire system was in front of the child and he had to solve the problem in a practical way, by manipulating the levers; (2) in the form of a graphic image, where the child was shown a drawing depicting a system of levers and a child looking at it (the subject had to tell how the child in the picture would have to act in order to reach his goal); (3) in verbal form: a problem story describing a situation similar to that in which the child found himself when presented with the problem in the palpable form (the child had to state how the problem could be solved by the main character in the tale). There were six problems in each of the three varieties. The investigation consisted of three series of experiments performed on various groups of children of the above age.

The task of the first test series was to analyze the problem solving according to the three forms of presentation. The data obtained are tabulated in Table 5–1, which represents the ratio of correct solutions to the total number of problems, in per cent. An analysis of problem solving by the children showed a relationship between successful solution and the character of the children's orientation under the conditions posed by the problem.

Table 5–1 *Per Cent Correct Solutions as a Function of Problem Type*

	Type of Problem Presentation		
Age	Object-manipulative	Pictorial	Verbal
3–4 yr.	55.0	17.5	0
4–5	85.0	53.8	0
5–6	87.5	56.4	15.0
6–7	96.3	72.0	22.0

The higher the type of orientation, the closer it approaches a purely visual analysis which traces the relationships between the chief elements of a situation. The more complete the orientation, the more effective is problem solving.

The second experiment was aimed at elucidating the effect of instructions about solving problems presented in an object-manipulative form on the later solution of similar problems presented in pictorial or verbal form. The way in which children solve problems in pictorial and verbal forms was first established before any attempt at solving similar problems in an object-manipulative form was investigated. The correct solutions obtained in this experiment were even fewer than they were in the first series. Special instructions in object-manipulative problem solving were then given in the second part of the second experiment. The experimenter demonstrated and explained the method of problem solving to the child. In the course of solution of the first problem the experimenter prompted the child to divide the system into its main elements (axis, points of application of force, points of target location). Having solved the problem, the child explained orally the method of solution to the experimenter, pointing out the relations between the spatial interrelationships of the elements in the situation and the methods of solution. In the course of problem solving a comparative analysis of spatial relationships was made. Instruction accompanied the first three problems, the next three serving as control and at the same time as additional practice. The experimenter pressed for problems to be fully solved by the child in the object-manipulative form, whereupon, if successful, the children were given similar problems in pictorial and verbal forms. The efficacy of solution was the basis for assessing the effect of instruction in object-manipulative problem solving on the problem solving of the other two types. The data obtained from this experiment showed that the effectiveness of problem solving increases when preliminary instruction is given on the object-manipulative form. This is not always the case, however; although the experience gained in the process of object-manipulative problem solving is a necessary condition for a transition to thinking based on graphic images and verbal processes, not every practical experience ensures such a transition. Not every child develops this orientation in relation to the conditions of a problem. It was then assumed that, if children's orientation is so organized as to correspond to the essential conditions pertaining to objects and if the orientation's main content becomes a search for relationships among the chief components of the device, transition to graphic-image and verbal thinking would be facilitated.

It was this question that the third experiment was aimed at: to direct orienting-investigatory activity particularly to all three main components of the device. For this purpose the conditions of the problem were made more complex. The loci of all three lever components were varied from experiment to experiment, in some being concealed from the subject; by manipulating the lever, the subject was to locate the site of the axis and determine the relationships between the main elements of the lever. Thus, conditions were created for organizing the children's orienting-investigatory activity and for actualizing personal contact with the experimenter in the course of problem solving. The children were specifically instructed in tracing with a finger the direction of strings whereby levers were set in motion, in finding hidden axes, and so on. Following such instruction, control problems were presented as in the second test series. This training resulted in a decisive shift. Children from 3 to 4 years of age solved 83.3 per cent of the problems presented in pictorial form, while 60 per cent of the problems presented verbally were solved. For children aged 4 to 5, the corresponding figures are 90 and 86.7 per cent. Children aged 5, 6, and 7 solved all the problems.

Zakharov (1954) showed that the organization of the orienting-exploratory activity of children in relation to objects, directed to the isolation of those of their attributes which enter into a generalization, is of predominant significance for the process of generalization.

A comparison of the formation of mental actions on the functional plane and formation of rational, verbal thinking at the preschool age shows that the preschool age is a period in which a differentiation of intellectual operations from practical activity and a primary emergence of verbal forms of thinking and of mental actions are occurring.

Development of Personality

Although the question of the development of the personality of the child has been elaborated less fully than the questions previously treated, the accumulation of factual material of this type nevertheless provides a basis for a few generalizations. Vygotskii was the first Soviet child psychologist to put forth a general theory of preschool development (1956b). In accord with his generic conception of consciousness and its development, he believed that "the most essential thing in the development of the child and his consciousness is not only the fact that individual functions of consciousness of the child grow upon transition from one age to another, but . . . that the personality of the child . . . the consciousness of the child as a whole grows and develops. This development and growth of consciousness makes itself felt in the first instance in the fact that there are changes in the relationships between individual functions" (p. 25). Vygotskii believed that in the preschool age there is an entirely new system of functions being formed. The key role is played by memory. Consequently, the cardinal characteristic of the preschool age is the accumulation and processing of immediate experience by the child. Such a new system of structuring consciousness leads to a number of consequences. First, there is a radical change in the thinking of the child, which causes the transition to thinking in images and representations[14] that signifies the first stage of abstract thinking. The second consequence is the restructuring of the character of interests and needs. The first affective generalizations, substitutions, and changes of interests arise. The third consequence is the transition to entirely new types of activity, which may be called creative, in which the child proceeds from plan to action. Finally, at the preschool age internal ethical standards emerge for the first time; ethical rules are developed; the first general representations concerning the world, nature, and self are also developed; and there arises the first rough draft of a child's outlook and philosophy.

The factual changes pointed out by Vygotskii really do occur at the preschool age. However, subsequent research has demonstrated that they cannot be related to the dominant position of memory and that it is not at all a new structure of consciousness which determines the development of the activity of the child and his relations with adults; but, on the contrary, it is the emergence of a new type of relation of the child with adults and of new types of activity, which determine the changes of consciousness as a whole and of its individual functions. Vygotskii gets much nearer to the nub of the question when he characterizes the type of teaching, that is, the type of relations with adults, which emerges in preschool age. Unfortunately, he did not succeed in developing fully his ideas concerning the special relations between child and adults that arise in the preschool age.

Leont'ev (1945, 1948) was the first after Vygotskii to propose a general theory of preschool personality development. Preschool childhood, according to Leont'ev, is a period of an initial development of the personality "mechanisms" of behavior. The development of personality consists in a subordination of motives which appears at the beginning of the preschool age and develops over its whole course. Leont'ev considers these changes in the structuring of activity crucial and relates them to all those concrete alterations which are observed in the preschool age, especially emphasizing the development of the voluntary nature of certain psychological processes.

Matyushina (1945) studied the question of the conflict of motives during the preschool period. As a function of the character of the task facing the child, the subordination of motives may emerge in various forms: the same motives may turn out to be either more or less effective in the subordination of immediate impulses. Golubeva (1955), when she set children tasks which required the overcoming of difficulties and were connected with an experience of success or failure, discovered that motives of a social nature (an act for the success of the whole collective of children) begin to emerge even in

14. *Editors' note:* The word "representation" is used here to signify a class of internal mechanisms which code the individual's experiences. Symbols are one type of representation, but a unique motor pattern could also be an example.

the medium age group and acquire great significance in the older age group. The motives of success and failure in younger children do not exert any sort of influence on the overcoming of difficulties. In the medium preschool-age group, failure does not stimulate any manifestation of perseverance, while success does stimulate it. In the older preschool children, both success and failure acquire motivating significance. In some of these children there appears an interest in the process of overcoming difficulties. A new point in the behavior of older preschoolers is the consciousness of the fact that a retreat in the face of difficulties casts them in a bad light; therefore the majority of children of this age stubbornly refuse to "give in" even after they have ceased the activity in question.

A study by Neverovich (1955) has shown the nature of the force of various motives in children's execution of a work assignment. Motives which are social in their content acquire great force even in the smallest children, provided that the connection between the content of the work to be carried out and these motives is clear to the children. At the same time it was established that these motives are assimilated by children in work activity.

Closely related to the appearance of the system of motives and their subordination stands the emergence of primary moral evaluations. Their development at the preschool age is manifested in the relation and attitude of the child to the heroes of literary works. Zaporozhets (1948), summing up the work of his collaborators devoted to the analysis of the preschool child's perception of literary works, shows that the transition from a simple unmotivated evaluation, fused with an immediate emotional attitude, to a motivated moral evaluation is bound up with the development of internal empathy and cooperation in thought with the heroes of the literary works. The question of the extent to which children can subordinate their own conduct to ethical norms has been treated by Ibragimova (1952). It was shown here that the rudiments of a sense of duty are engendered even in the youngest preschoolers under the influence of an evaluation by adults of an act done by the child.

According to Ibragimova's data a moral sense of duty emerges in the child first in relation to children of his own age, then in relation to adults, and later in relation to babies or younger children. All these manifestations of a sense of duty are represented fairly broadly in the medium preschool-age group. The basic condition for the emergence of moral feelings over the course of the entire preschool age period is the moral evaluation of actions and deeds on the part of adults. Intimately linked with the appearance of new motives for activity at preschool age, their subordination, and the formation of ethical feelings and instances, is a radical restructuring of the entire conduct of the child.

Manuilenko (1948) has investigated the problem of the development of voluntary behavior. Her data show that behavior mediated by representations first appears at the preschool level. The vital point is not the content of the image which is mediating the child's behavior, that is, the question whether it is given in the form of a generalized rule or in the form of an image of the conduct of a concrete person. The important thing is that the image of behavior for the first time emerges as its regulator; for the first time behavior begins to be compared with an image, and the latter begins to emerge as a model. It is precisely at this point that a qualitative alteration of all behavior occurs; from being unmediated it becomes mediated by standards and rules of conduct. The question as to how one ought to behave and the necessity to create a preliminary image of behavior arises for the first time. At the senior preschool age, as the data of Manuilenko have shown, the direction of his conduct becomes the object of the child's consciousness.

In the research of Ibragimova and Golubeva there are references to the formation of self-evaluation in preschool children. It has been found that older preschoolers are able to evaluate not only their comrades but themselves as well in those cases in which the evaluated qualities have sufficiently obvious indices. The emergence of self-evaluation and the discovery of his own experiences represents a cardinal result of the child's development during preschool age.

Thus, the research devoted to the formation of individual aspects of personality shows that the preschool age is truly a cardinal period of the development of the personality.

References

Abramovich, R. Y. Development of infant behavior with objects in the first year of life. Candidate's dissertation, Leningrad, 1946.

Aksarina, N. M. Peculiarities of development of children of preschool age and their training in crèches and children's homes. Candidate's dissertation, Moscow, 1944.

Arkin, E. A. *The Child from the ages of one to four.* Uchpedgiz, 1931.

Asnin, V. I. Development of visual-actional thought in the infant. (In Ukrainian.) In *Trudy Ukr. Con. Psikhol. Pedag.* Vol. 2. Kiev, 1941.

Barabashova, Z. I. Role of various analyzers in formation of conditioned connections to verbal stimuli in children at an early age. *Izv. Akad. Pedag. Nauk RSFSR,* 1956, No. 75. (a)

Barabashova, Z. I. Description of conditioned connections to verbal stimuli in children at an early age. *Izv. Akad. Pedag. Nauk RSFSR,* 1956, No. 75. (b)

Bogoyavlenskii, D. N. *The psychology of the mastery of orthography*. Moscow: Izd. Akad. Pedag. Nauk RSFSR, 1957.

Bruner, J. S. *The process of education*. Cambridge: Harvard Univer. Press, 1960.

Cherkov, A. V. Psychological analysis of the child's mastery of the standards of social behavior on the basis of play and games. Moscow, Candidate's dissertation, 1949.

Dunaevskii, F. P. An attempt to study the higher nervous activity of children in the first years of life. *Izv. Akad. Pedag. Nauk RSFSR,* 1956, No. 75.

El'konin, D. B. Psychological problems of preschool play and games. In *Problems in the psychology of the preschool child*. Moscow: Izd. Akad. Pedag. Nauk RSFSR, 1948.

El'konin, D. B. Features of the interaction of the first and second signal systems in children of preschool age. *Izv. Akad. Pedag. Nauk RSFSR,* 1954, No. 64.

El'konin, D. B. *Creative character games of preschool children*. Moscow: Izd. Akad. Pedag. Nauk RSFSR, 1957.

El'konin, D. B. *Development of speech at the preschool age*. Moscow: Izd. Akad. Pedag. Nauk RSFSR, 1958.

El'konin, D. B., and Davydov, V. V. *The psychology of learning in the elementary school*. Moscow: Izd. Akad. Pedag. Nauk RSFSR, 1962.

Endovitskaya, T. V. Dynamics of the elementary sensory functions at preschool age. Candidate's dissertation, Moscow, 1947.

Endovitskaya, T. V. On the problem of the development of visual sensations in children of preschool age. *Izv. Akad. Pedag. Nauk RSFSR,* 1955, No. 64.

Faddeeva, V. K. Features of the interaction of the first and second signal systems in the formation of a conditioned reaction to a complex stimulus in children. *Zh. vyssh. nerv. Deyat.,* 1956, *1,* No. 3.

Figurin, N. L., and Denisova, M. Stages of child development from birth to one year. In *Problems of genetic reflexology*. Leningrad, 1929. (a)

Figurin, N. L., and Denisova, M. The experimental investigation of reactions to novelty. In *Problems of genetic reflexology*. Leningrad, 1929. (b)

Flavell, J. H. *The developmental psychology of Jean Piaget*. New York: Van Nostrand, 1963.

Fradkina, F. I. The psychology of play in early childhood (the genetic roots of preschool play). Candidate's dissertation, Moscow, 1946.

Fradkina, F. I. The origin of speech in the child. *Uch. Zap. LGPI im. Gertsena,* 1955, *12*.

Gal'perin, P. Y. Psychological differences between human tools and auxiliary resources employed by animals and their significance. Candidate's dissertation, Kharkov, 1937.

Gal'perin, P. Y. Experience in the study of the formation of mental activities. In *Reports of a Conference on Problems of Psychology (3–8 July 1953)*. Izd. Akad. Pedag. Nauk RSFSR, 1954.

Ginevskaya, T. O. Development of hand movements in touching. *Izv. Akad. Pedag. Nauk RSFSR,* 1948, No. 14.

Golubeva, A. N. Psychological features of the manifestation of perseverance in preschool-age children. Candidate's dissertation, Moscow, 1955.

Gvozdev, A. N. *Mastery by the infant of the auditory aspect of the Russian language.* Moscow: Izd. Akad. Pedag. Nauk RSFSR, 1948.

Gvozdev, A. N. *Formation in the infant of the grammatical structure of the Russian language. Parts I and II.* Moscow: Izd. Akad. Pedag. Nauk RSFSR, 1949.

Ibragimova, R. N. First beginnings of a feeling of duty in preschool-age children. Candidate's dissertation, Moscow, 1952.

Istomina, Z. M. Development of voluntary memory at preschool age. *Izv. Akad. Pedag. Nauk RSFSR,* 1948, No. 14.

Istomina, Z. M. Influence of the verbal image and of visual material on the development of speech in the preschool child. *Izv. Akad. Pedag. Nauk RSFSR,* 1956, No. 81.

Kapustnik, O. P. Interrelation between direct stimuli and their symbols. In *Basic mechanisms of the conditioned-reflex activity of the infant.* Leningrad, 1930.

Khomenko, K. E. Young children's understanding of artistic images. (In Ukrainian.) *Uch. Zap. Kharkov. GPI,* 1941, *6.*

Khozak, L. E. Attempts to modify a child's speech by experimental organization of his activity. In *Approaches to the study of the higher forms of the neurodynamics of the child.* 1934.

Kolodnaya, A. Y. Development of a differentiation of the directions "right" and "left" in preschool-age children. *Izv. Akad. Pedag. Nauk RSFSR,* 1954, No. 53.

Kol'tsova, M. M. The comparative role of the various analyzers in the development of the generalizing activity of the word in the infant. *Vop. Psikhol.,* 1951, No. 4.

Konnikova, T. E. Initial stage in the development of speech. Candidate's dissertation, Leningrad, 1947.

Kontsevaya, O. M. Understanding of fairy tales by children. (In Ukrainian.) In *Trudy Resp. Konf. Pedag. Psikhol.* Vol. 2. Kiev, 1941.

Koroleva, N. V. The role of play in the formation of a positive attitude to labor in older preschool-age children. In *Psychological problems of play and instruction at preschool age.* Moscow: Izd. Akad. Pedag. Nauk RSFSR, 1957.

Kozyreva, A. E. *On the problem of the initial development of the perception of space in children.* Leningrad: Izd. Leningrad. Gos. Univer., 1949.

Krasnogorskii, N. I. On the physiology of the development of childhood speech. *Zh. vyssh. nerv. Deyat.,* 1952, No. 4.

Leont'ev, A. N. The mastery of scientific concepts as a problem for educational psychology. Unpublished manuscript, 1935.

Leont'ev, A. N. Psychological bases of preschool play and games. *Sovet. Pedag.,* 1944, Nos. 8–9.

Leont'ev, A. N. Toward a theory of the development of the infant mind. *Sovet. Pedag.,* 1945, No. 4.

Leont'ev, A. N. Mental development of the infant during the preschool age. In *Problems of the psychology of the preschool-age child.* Moscow: Izd. Akad. Pedag. Nauk RSFSR, 1948.

Leushina, A. M. Development of coherent speech in the preschool child. *Uch. Zap. LGPI im. Gertsena,* 1941, *35.*

Levina, E. *Reading and writing deficiencies in children.* Moscow: Uchpedgiz, 1940.

Lukov, G. D. On the recognition by the infant of speech in the process of play. Candidate's dissertation, Leningrad, 1937.

Luria, A. R. Development of constructive activity of the preschool child. In *Problems of the psychology of the preschool-age child.* Moscow: Izd. Akad. Pedag. Nauk RSFSR, 1948.

Luria, A. R., and Yudovich, F. Y. *Speech and the development of the psychological processes in the infant.* Moscow: Izd. Akad. Pedag. Nauk RSFSR, 1956.

Lyublinskaya, A. A. Mastery of spatial relationships in the preschool child. In *Problems of psychology.* Leningrad: Izd. Leningrad. Gos. Univer., 1948.

Lyublinskaya, A. A. The role of speech in the development of visual perception in children. In *Problems of child and general psychology.* Moscow: Izd. Akad. Pedag. Nauk RSFSR, 1954.

Manuilenko, Z. M. Development of voluntary behavior in children of preschool age. *Izv. Akad. Pedag. Nauk RSFSR,* 1948, No. 14.

Matyushina, N. M. The conflict of motives in children of preschool age. Candidate's dissertation, Moscow, 1945.

Minskaya, G. I. Transition from visual-actional to ratiocinative thinking in children of preschool age. Candidate's dissertation, Moscow, 1954.

Mukhin, S. V. Perception of the color and shape of objects by preschool-age children. *Uch. Zap. MGPI im. Lenina,* 1941, No. 27.

Nekhlyudova, A. I. On the problem of the development of the processes of perception in children of preschool age. In *Experiments in the objective study of childhood.* Leningrad, 1924.

Neverovich, Y. Z. Mastery of movements of objects at pre-preschool and preschool ages. *Izv. Akad. Pedag. Nauk RSFSR,* 1948, No. 14.

Neverovich, Y. Z. Motives of work activity of the preschool-age child. *Izv. Akad. Pedag. Nauk RSFSR,* 1955, No. 64.

Ovsepyan, G. T. The development of observation in children. *Uch. Zap. LGPI. im. Gertsena,* 1939, *18.*

Piaget, J. *The language and thought of the child.* New York: Harcourt, Brace, 1926.

Popova, M. I. On the problem of the mastery of the grammatical elements of language by children of pre-preschool age. Candidate's dissertation, 1956.

Rosenfel'd, F. S. Features of tactile perceptions in the preschool child. *Izv. Akad. Pedag. Nauk RSFSR,* 1948, No. 17.

Rozengart-Pupko, G. L. *Speech and the development of perceptions in early childhood.* Moscow: Izd. Akad. Med. Nauk, 1948.

Rubinshtein, S. L. *Fundamentals of psychology.* Moscow, 1935.

Rubinshtein, S. L. *Fundamentals of general psychology.* Moscow, 1946.

Rybnikov, N. A. *Vocabulary of the Russian child.* Moscow-Leningrad, 1926. (a)

Rybnikov, N. A. *Language of the child.* (2nd ed.) Moscow, 1926. (b)

Senkevich, Z. L. On the interaction of the first and second signal systems in the elaboration of conditioned inhibition and conditioned disinhibition to the very same stimulus. *Zh. vyssh. nerv. Deyat.,* 1952, *2,* No. 5

Serebrennikova, N. P. On the problem of the mastery by pre-preschool children of the elements of the grammatical structure of the language. Candidate's dissertation, Leningrad, 1953.

Shabalin, S. N. Perception of shape by the preschool child. *Uch. Zap. LGPI im. Gertsena,* 1939, No. 18.

Shchelovanov, N. M., and Aksarina, N. M. *Training of young children in institutions for children.* 1925. (3rd ed., 1955.)

Shvachkin, N. K. Development of phonemic perception of speech in early childhood. *Izv. Akad. Pedag. Nauk RSFSR,* 1948, No. 13.

Shvachkin, N. K. Experimental study of early generalizations of the infant. *Izv. Akad. Pedag. Nauk RSFSR,* 1954, No. 54.

Slavina, L. S. Development of the motives of play activity of the child. *Izv. Akad. Pedag. Nauk RSFSR,* 1948, No. 14.

Smolenskaya, E. P. On verbal symbols of the conditioned and differential stimulus. In *Approach to the study of the higher forms of the neurodynamics of the child.* 1934.

Sokhin, F. A. Initial stages of the mastery by the child of the grammatical structure of the language. Candidate's dissertation, Moscow, 1955.

Sokhin, F. A. Some problems in the mastery of the grammatical structure of language in the light of the physiological theory of Pavlov. *Sovet. Pedag.,* 1956, No. 7.

Syrkina, V. E. The problem of egocentric speech in the researches of Piaget. Work submitted for diploma, LGPI im. Gertsena, 1934.

Titarenko, T. I. The child's understanding of a tale. In *Trudy Resp. Konf. Pedag. Psikhol.* Vol. 2. Kiev, 1941.

Traugott, N. N. Interrelation of direct and symbolic projection in the process of the formation of conditioned inhibition. In *Approach to the study of the higher forms of the neurodynamics of the child.* 1934.

Usova, A. P. On the problem of creative games and play of children at the preschool age and the rules of managing them. *Uch. Zap. LGPI im. Gertsena,* 1947, No. 56.

Venger, A. A. Development of the concept of causality in children of preschool age. Candidate's dissertation, Moscow, 1958.

Vygotskii, L. S. The problem of development in structural psychology. In *Fundamentals of mental development.* 1934.

Vygotskii, L. S. Thought and speech. In *Selected psychological researches.* Moscow: Izd. Akad. Pedag. Nauk RSFSR, 1956. (a)

Vygotskii, L. S. Instruction and development at preschool age, In *Selected psychological researches.* Moscow: Izd. Akad. Pedag. Nauk RSFSR, 1956. (b)

Yakobson, S. G. Correlation of sight and touch in the perception of shape by children of preschool age. *Vop. Psikhol.,* 1957, No. 3.

Zakharov, A. N. Conditions for the formation of generalization in children of preschool age. Candidate's dissertation, Moscow, 1954.

Zakharova, A. V. On the problem of the development of the grammatical structure of speech in children of preschool age. Candidate's dissertation, Moscow, 1955.

Zalogina, V. P. Training of an amicable children's collective in a creative game. In *Creative games in kindergarten.* Moscow: Uchpedgiz, 1945.

Zaporozhets, A. V. Modification of the motor activity of the preschool child as a function of the motives and conditions of its exercise. *Izv Akad. Pedag. Nauk RSFSR,* 1948, No. 14.

Zaporozhets, A. V. Modification of the interrelations of the two signal systems in the process of the development of the preschool child. In *Reports at a Conference on Psychology (3–8 July 1953).* Moscow: Izd. Akad. Pedag. Nauk RSFSR, 1954. (a)

Zaporozhets, A. V. Development of voluntary movements. In *Reports at the Fourteenth International Congress on Psychology.* Moscow: Izd. Akad. Pedag. Nauk RSFSR, 1954. (b)

6

The Personality of Schoolchildren and Problems of Education

L. I. Bozhovich

EDITORS' INTRODUCTION

L. I. Bozhovich is Director of the Laboratory of the Psychology of the Upbringing of the Schoolchild at the Institute of Psychology in Moscow.

"Upbringing" is a very general Russian concept which has often been rendered in English translations as "training." As used by Soviet psychologists, upbringing refers to all aspects of the child's development; this includes not only fostering his intellectual development through improved curricula and teaching methods, but development of his moral character, personality, and social behavior as well.

In this chapter, Bozhovich is primarily concerned with the relation between the child's personality and his education. Her contention that there is a need to develop experimental techniques (as opposed to the heretofore ubiquitous observational—or "natural experiment"—approach) reflects an important trend in Soviet psychology. Boarding schools are more common in the U.S.S.R. than in the United States, and the resulting increased contact between the psychologist-educator and the child has fostered quasi-experimental studies of the schoolchild "in vivo" (Bozhovich, 1960; El'konin and Davydov, 1962).

Bozhovich is among the group of psychologists (which includes Leont'ev, Luria, Shif, and others represented in this volume) who were associated with Vygotskii. The point of view developed here can be considered an extension of Vygotskii's basic concepts into the area of personality development.

The Life Conditions of the Schoolchild and the Formation of His Personality

Interaction of Status and Experience in Social Movement

The study of personality in the U.S.S.R. is a branch of psychology in which relatively little work has been done. This is primarily because of the methodological difficulties which arise from attempts to study man's personality within the complex conditions in which it operates and develops. During the past fifteen to twenty years, however, the number of studies in this field has increased considerably in the U.S.S.R. As a result of this increased activity, a number of facts and principles have accumulated which, although they do not place this branch of psychology on the same level of development with others, still make it possible to note considerable progress.

One of the characteristic features of this research was the attempt to discover regular relations between a child's life conditions and the characteristic features of his personality. It investigated the question of how certain traits form in children and what conditions at home and school influence their formation. In particular, it asked: What are the guiding and determining factors in these conditions, and how can the life of a child be organized so that the formation of his personality proceeds according to the aims of education?

Another goal of these studies was to understand personality as an integrated structure, while still considering its complex relations with reality. Researchers had to study not single or isolated manifestations of personality, but rather the sum of its vital manifestations. This approach—that is, to study personality as an integrated structure—was most useful for pedagogical practice. A pedagogical bias also characterized these studies, and, consistent with this bias, the method adopted was to study the child in the classroom to determine the influence and factors within this context that affected the formation of the child's personality.

Another characteristic feature of these studies was that researchers were not satisfied passively to record the changing features in a child's personality. Instead they attempted actively to mold these features by finding optimal conditions and methods of action. Accordingly, one of the basic methods of research was the psychopedagogical experiment, that is, the study of a child's personality in a classroom setting.

Investigations of this type are undoubtedly of pedagogical importance: they reveal connections between the various features of a child and the external factors which act upon him. For example, investigations conducted under our direction by Shestokova (unpublished) established that the most important influence on the interactions of first-grade children with one another, on their relations to the environment, and on their grades came not from their parents but from their teacher, who was the center of the school situation for children of this age. For many of these children the authority of the teacher remained dominant even in the family situation. However, the situation was different among older students, with whom the influence of friends gradually increased in importance. Shestokova's study established that, if the teacher was not successful in forming a friendly children's collective (this applies to third- or fourth-grade students) on which he could base his teaching, then he was likely to lose control of the class. The children stopped listening to him and would listen only under threat of punishment.

Increasing influence of peers

Another investigation, by Makhlakh (1963), established that there were important conditions, especially the social opinion of the collective, under which it was possible to train positive behavior traits in children.

Although investigations of this type are useful, they suffer from certain general inadequacies. The most important of these is the fact that while they establish a connection between certain external conditions and psychological consequences, they do not reveal the internal structure of the psychological phenomena which are evoked, nor do they explain the process by which they are formed. For example, Kovalev (1950) succeeded in observing the conditions under which certain children exhibited negative traits (e.g., shyness or rudeness) and also succeeded in retraining these children. However, this type of investigation does not provide us with a deeper understanding of the psychological nature of the foregoing negative character traits, nor does it provide us with an understanding of how they are formed.

In our investigations on the influence of life conditions in the formation of a child's personality, we tried to overcome this inadequacy by beginning with the basic tenet that these life conditions per se do not directly and immediately determine a child's personality. It is a common observation that different traits can develop from the same set of external conditions. Therefore we believe that the most important factor is the child's interaction with these external conditions.

Vygotskii (1934) was the first Soviet psychologist to state this principle. He stated that a correct understanding of the effects of environment on the development of the child comes only from a relative, rather than absolute, approach to environment. According to Vygotskii, environment alone does not account for development, because an "element of the environment" affects children of different stages of development in different ways. For example, a child of six months and the same child three years later can experience identical statements made by the people around him and yet be affected differently by these statements because his ability to comprehend has changed with age.

In studying the objective content of a child's relations with his immediate environment and the influences of the environment on the child, it is necessary to remember that the extant, already formed psychological characteristics of the child mediate the influence of the environment. Thus, it is not enough to look at the objective content of the environment; the main task is to find the crucial link which defines the influence exerted on the child by his environment.

Vygotskii believed that this crucial link is the way in which the child "experiences" the "element" of the external environment which is acting upon him. He came to the conclusion that, in order to understand how a certain circumstance or event influences a child and what role it plays in his psychic development, it is necessary to analyze how the child "is affectively related" to this circumstance, in other words, how he "experiences" it. The "experience" constitutes the "prism" through which the environment is refracted, and it is this mediation that influences the psychic development of the child.

It is correct but not sufficient to say that the formal knowledge which a child possesses does not influence the development of his thought if he is not really interested in the knowledge which he is assimilating. To fully understand the process, one must try to discover why the child has acquired this attitude toward knowledge and not another.

Vygotskii believed that a child's ability to understand the circumstances or events acting upon him, or the level of development of his generalizations, determined the character of an "affective attitude." For example, a small child and a teen-ager will experience a mother's severe illness in completely different ways because each interprets this event differently. The little child may even welcome this event if one of its consequences is that adults pay less attention to him, thus leaving him free to do as he pleases. Thus, though this event may leave the small child unaffected, it may cause the teen-ager much distress and may even result in a change of character.

However, it is also observed that a child of a certain level of understanding may experience and react to the same factor within his environment in different ways at different times. For example, a child can fully understand the rational nature and even the necessity of a requirement imposed upon him, but still refuse to submit to this requirement because it conflicts with other needs present at the particular moment.

Vygotskii's principle, that an "experience" is determined by the degree of understanding, also conflicts with the fact that explanations in themselves are not capable of changing the affective aspect of the child's attitude toward reality, that is, they are unable to cause a change in his "experience." Moreover, pedagogical facts indicate the opposite: understanding depends upon the affective attitude of the child towards the circumstances acting upon him.

Some psychologists have expressed the idea that man's experiences (his feelings, strivings, emotions, etc.) are a reflection of the degree to which his needs are met. From this point of view, negative experiences indicate unfulfillment of a subject's needs and consequently the presence of some sort of disharmony between the subject and his environment, and positive experiences reflect a state of adaptation and harmony. Taking this idea a step further, it may be said that the function of experience is to orient the subject within his environment and consequently motivate him.

Other psychologists have stated that cognitive processes as well as personality traits form as a function of the development of a person's needs. Here it must be remembered that man is a social being whose needs include not only primary physiological drives which must be satisfied, but also social needs and personal demands that he inflicts upon himself. From this it follows that Vygotskii correctly termed experience a "prism" which refracts the influence of the environment and at the same time guides the course of the child's psychological development. His only mistake was in identifying the critical variable as understanding.

An analysis of experience must include an analysis of the child's needs, of the conditions which gave rise to these needs, and of the possibilities for satisfying them. From this point of view Vygotskii's main factor—the level of development of generalization—is only one of the components involved.

With this point of view in mind, let us return to Vygotskii's example of the young child and the teen-ager. His interpretation is in part correct; perhaps the young child, because of his restricted understanding, is not deeply affected by his mother's illness, and perhaps the teen-ager is profoundly affected. This may not, however, be the case. In order to predict exactly what influence the mother's illness will have on the formation of the child's personality, it is necessary to examine the child's relation to his mother and those of his needs that are not satisfied because of the mother's illness. A different interpretation might be that the teen-ager, in spite of his complete understanding of the event, experiences neither feelings of pain nor a fear of loss if he conceives of his mother as a hindrance to his freedom, and as a person who interferes in the realization of his strivings and goals. The little child, on the other hand, who can understand neither the terrible threat of the illness nor the mother's suffering might suffer greatly from the event, perhaps from feelings of loneliness or rejection, which in turn can affect the formation of his character.

One might also object that, with Vygotskii's analysis, one cannot reliably predict exactly what influence the mother's illness has on one or another of her children. Prediction may be possible in principle, but it is difficult to carry out in practice because it involves an analysis of complicated internal and external conditions. Slavina (unpublished) studied children with affective disturbances and aggressive behavior in our laboratory and found it sometimes possible not only to untangle the complex web of the child's unfulfilled needs but also to overcome the child's negative experiences and negative behavior by using proper pedagogical measures.

Thus, the development of any mental property, including the development of generalizations, can be understood only from an analysis of the child's mutual relations with his surrounding environment which give rise to the need for these properties. "Experiences" must also be explained in terms of the relation between the event or circumstance acting upon a child and his personal needs.

Thus, it is necessary to obtain, in these studies in children's personality, an objective characterization of the child's interaction with reality. This will permit us to understand how this reality is "experienced" as well as the influence it has on the formation of the child's personality.

The first investigations along this line in our laboratory consisted of the study of individual unsuccessful and undisciplined schoolchildren. We have attempted to analyze the psychological features which directly contributed to the poor performance and poor behavior of these students, and in this process, attempted to discover those conditions in the child's life which would allow us to understand the origin of the difficulty.

At first, the practical purpose of this work, conducted with the cooperation of teachers, was to help pedagogues and instructors develop a proper attitude toward the study of children and toward the requirements imposed by the school on the children's behavior. However, this end gradually became a means: a change in an attitude became a method for studying this attitude itself and the rules governing its formation. In other words, the fundamental method of investigation became the *active transforming experiment,* which was carried out under actual pedagogical conditions.

During the study of schoolchildren who were experiencing difficulties, of some sort, it was discovered that the vast majority of these children do not progress at all. Their progress does not equal their potential because these children have acquired unfavorable attitudes toward studying and toward school. Some children expressed a clear dislike for studying and for everything associated with studies; others were completely indifferent to their academic achievements, and a third group lacked confidence in their ability.

An analysis of the conditions producing these attitudes revealed that they depended primarily on two factors: the extent to which school work determined the position of the pupil among those around him and affected his relations with these people, and the extent to which a pupil is capable of responding to the requirements imposed on him by his studies. For example, if a child's status at school and at home is determined by his study progress, and if this child is unable to achieve a good rate of progress, he reacts strongly to these circumstances and develops a negative attitude toward studies and sometimes even toward the school (Bozhovich, 1951, pp. 18–23). If, however, a child occupies a favorable position at home because of his other qualities, and his academic progress is not considered important, we observed that this child does not even attempt to study better and is quite satisfied to be an average or even a weak student (Bozhovich, 1951, pp. 9–10). A number of facts which support this observation can be found in a study by Slavina (1951) on the role of the family in the formation of a child's attitude toward studies and toward school in general. This study describes a case in which two siblings lived under the same external conditions but developed different attitudes toward their studies because of the parents' different attitudes toward each child's academic progress. The same study describes a case in which a child with a very low level of intellectual development and no intellectual interests at all still made a great effort and studied quite well, only because he knew his education would be his only means of supporting his mother and younger brother (he was fatherless). The study also showed that the children who did poorly at school, but who could compensate for this at home by doing housework, for example, or caring for younger children, frequently became completely unconcerned about their progress in studying and were quite satisfied with their status as poor students.

These facts can be understood more easily if we consider that enrollment in school represents a turning point in the life of a child: the child's new role as a pupil gives him new rights and responsibilities. For the first time he becomes engaged in a serious and socially significant activity in which his status and his relations with the people around him depend upon the extent to which he is able to fulfill these responsibilities.

Some of our data (Bozhovich, 1948) indicate that by the end of the preschool period the vast majority of children begin to get bored with their preschool mode of life and dream of becoming good students and of fulfilling all the responsibilities imposed upon a schoolchild. In other words, at the end of the preschool period, children begin to strive to achieve a new social status and to perform a new socially significant type of activity.

In the light of these data, it becomes clear that the attitude of a schoolchild toward his studies depends primarily on the extent to which his studies have become a means of fulfilling his need for a new social status. If a child, after first entering school, does not immediately feel a change in his status, and if progress in his studies does not change his relations with his parents, then he might fail to attach any value or significance to the status of "schoolchild." At the same time, the responsibilities of this status lose their attraction and the difficult aspect of studies becomes a dominant factor. In such cases, many children begin to develop an indifferent and sometimes even negative attitude toward their studies. The specific nature of such an attitude depends on several factors: the child's general development and the development or lack of development of his intellectual interests; the difficulty which he encounters in his studies; and, most important, the child's ability to satisfy his need for a new mode of life with some other activity.

Furthermore, we can now better understand the emotions associated in some children with studies and school. It must be pointed out that school, and the personal relations children experience there, constitutes the main content of the life and activity of children at this age. Therefore, difficulty in winning a definite status within this context can induce a conflict in the child.

Research conducted on undisciplined schoolchildren validated these observations. These data showed that a pupil's poor behavior was very often a reaction to someone's attitude toward him or to the failures he encountered, or it was his only means of asserting himself in this environment and maintaining his self-respect. We frequently observed that children who were unable to attain a desired status at school through their academic ability "asserted" themselves by playing the role of "incorrigibles," "clowns," etc.

We frequently encountered undisciplined schoolchildren who committed breaches of discipline because they had lost the previously acquired status of a good or outstanding student. An example of this, in research conducted by Dragunova (1960), is the case of a teen-age girl who exhibited such socially negative traits as stubbornness and negativism, a malicious attitude toward those around her, conceit, and a complete refusal to submit to rules of conduct in school. An analysis of the life of this girl showed that during her early schooldays she had ranked as a good pupil in her class, not so much because of her own merit as because of the teacher's erroneous impression of her. In the fifth grade, however, she lost this good standing, and the entire set of traits described above proved to be a reaction to this loss.

It was also observed that each child, as a function of his age and his individual characteristics, occupied a certain position among his peers, and that in accord with this position he had to fulfill certain related demands. Fulfillment of these demands led to peer approval, while nonfulfillment led to censure and to the loss of the child's position in the group.

In addition, these investigations showed that no matter what position we put the child in and no matter what demands we made on him, if he did not himself experience a need to preserve a given position he would not strive to fulfill our demands and they would not become a real factor in his development. The need to occupy a certain position and to fulfill certain demands depended on how external conditions present at a given time stood in relation to already formed psychological traits.

The effect of a discrepancy between the requirements imposed on a child and his own needs was shown especially clearly in our research on first-graders who were not yet ready to go to school (Bozhovich, 1948, p. 12). In such cases, the position which the child assumed after entering school corresponded neither to his attitude toward it nor to the behavior, needs, and urges conditioned during his previous history of development. Though objectively a schoolchild, such a child inwardly remains a preschooler: he does not acknowledge studying as a serious and socially significant matter and continues to view his studies as a game, ignoring the demands of the teacher and flippantly, without ascribing any special importance to this fact, violating the rules of school conduct. In such cases, the demands which life imposed on the child, since they clashed both with his potential and with his needs, were unable to elicit the required behavior and consequently could not influence his further mental development.

A similar contradiction, but one which occurred in different children and in a different context, was observed in a boarding school, where our attention was attracted by the fact that certain children started to exhibit a tendency to do things in an underhanded way and to behave differently in front of their instructors than in their absence. After analyzing this behavior, we became convinced that the reason for it was that these children, having lived under very unfavorable conditions prior to entering boarding school, were extremely fond of the school and were afraid of being expelled. Upon entering the school they, and the other children, were immediately subjected to stringent requirements concerning discipline, neatness, diligence, and the like; however, the children discussed above were unable to fulfill these requirements immediately since their previous family training had not properly prepared them. Thus, as a reaction to the resulting situation they started to develop the above-mentioned character traits. These traits, although they violated the requirements imposed upon the children, nevertheless fulfilled their need to retain a position at the boarding school.

All of the above statements illustrate the fact that in order to understand how certain traits are formed in the child one must distinguish between the child's objective situation and his "internal position," that is, his reactions, resulting from his past development, to his surroundings and especially to his status and the requirements attendant on that status. An analysis of the objective status of a child makes it possible to understand the requirements which the environment imposes upon him, while a study of his internal position makes it possible to understand his needs. Our research showed that when it was possible to understand the "internal position" of the child, not only did his attitude with respect to individual phenomena become clear, but also his attitudes toward reality, and the specific behaviors which reflected these attitudes. At the same time, our attempts to reconstruct a child's attitudes toward objective phenomena of importance to him disclosed that it was impossible to achieve this goal without changing his entire internal position.

We have also shown the important role played by the relation between the child's needs and the possibilities of satisfying these needs, for example, his need to maintain a given place in his relations with other people. This indicates the tremendous role in the psychic development of a child played by any conflict between present needs and previously formed potentials. This is quite understandable, since no conflict between external requirements and the potential of the child can serve as a source for the formation of new factors until his external conflict becomes internalized, that is, until it becomes a reflection of the child's needs. To ignore this principle is to ignore the fact that the psychological characteristics of personality, once formed, determine the nature of the influence of the environment on the child.

Our conclusions concerning the role of the child's objective status and internal position in the formation of his personality find support in studies conducted by other psychologists, although a sufficiently clear distinction between the external situation of a child and his internal position has often been suggested.

Vygotskii, in order to understand the specific conditions underlying development, turned to an analysis of the child's status within his system of important relations and to an analysis of the experiences connected with this status. In his 1934 lectures, mentioned above, the author tells of a case which clearly exemplified the interdependence between the child's status in the family, his experience of this situation, and the significance of these factors on the formation of his personality. This case concerned three fatherless children being raised by a mother who periodically suffered from serious psychic disturbances. The difficult living situation affected the development of these children in completely different ways: the youngest child was retarded in his psychic development and was timid, passive, and shy; the older child, on the other hand, had traits of an early maturity and was active, sober-minded, thoughtful and, according to his neighbors, reliable.

Vygotskii then asked why such a great difference in the character and development of these children should occur and concluded that each child, depending on his age and level of understanding, experienced the phenomena of life around him in a unique way and consequently assumed a unique attitude toward these events.

Moreover, after Vygotskii made this statement and further analyzed the detailed situation in which each child developed, he stated that the youngest child could only respond to this situation by developing defensive neurotic symptoms. His difficult conditions and his helplessness, because of his youth, left him in a position where he had to passively accept the negative effects of his environment. In contrast, the oldest boy, who was already ten years old when his mother became sick, was placed in the position of senior member of the family, and was responsible for the entire family. Indeed, during his mother's fits of illness he took care of the younger children and organized the daily life of the family. According to Vygotskii, the fact that the child had to fulfill a special role determined the type of development which was characteristic for this particular child. Thus, although Vygotskii did consider the child's understanding and experience of this situation the main factors in his development, he nevertheless analyzed the child's actual *status,* which conditioned his experiences, and his attitudes toward reality, in order to understand the causes of the child's behavior and development.

It should be noted that many Soviet psychologists, without explicitly suggesting the concept of "status," have used this concept as a basis for an analysis of the child's development. A study by Kovalev and Myasishchev, devoted to a study of character (1957), gives an example of how two young girls (zygotic twins) developed differently because each of the girls was assigned a different role by the family: one of the girls was considered the elder and was called the elder sister from early childhood. She was entrusted with the supervision of her "younger" sister and was responsible for her behavior, and later she was the first one to perform various errands, such as going to the store and sweeping the floor. "Consequently," the authors of the study conclude, "a difference in the attitudes adopted by the parents toward children also determines differences in their characters even when the children live and are educated under the same conditions and have the same natural inclinations . . ." (1957, p. 192).

Although these authors were able to get along without the concept of "status," it is quite clear that no kind of attitude assumed by the parent is capable of determining anything in the child's personality, if it causes no change in the child's mode of life, in his personal demands, or in his behavior.

Shnirman, in his study of collectives (1956), also came to the conclusion that "the influence of the collective on the personality of the child depends not only on the characteristics of the collective itself but also on the position which the child occupies in the group as a result of his own individual peculiarities."

Thus it can be concluded that the formation of a child's personality is determined, first, by the place which the child occupies in his system of human relations, and, second, by the relation between the requirements imposed upon him by life and those psychological characteristics which he possesses at the particular moment. It is precisely this relation which engenders those needs and desires and goals which, by refracting and mediating the influence of the environment, become the motivational force in the further development of a child's mental properties.

These principles are valid not only for an understanding of individual characteristics of a child's personality, but also for an understanding of the psychological structure typical of children in various groups.

The Development of Social Motivation in School

Other studies conducted in our laboratory, on the motivation of study behavior, also testify to the great importance of the child's family position for an understanding of his attitudes toward reality.

We were concerned with the role of these motives, their origin and development, and their change during a child's life. We therefore adopted a genetic approach in our research by analyzing the process of the formation and development of study motives in individual children, and, mainly, by determining the specific features of these motives in children at various stages of their development. We were interested, first, in the change, occurring with age, in the content of study motives; second, in the role which different motives play in the life and study activity of a child; third, in the manner in which the significance of each of these motives changes; and finally, in the kind of system formed by a child's study motives at various stages of his development. At the same time, the main purpose of our research was to determine the laws governing the appearance, in a given child or at given ages, of certain study motives and not others, as well as an understanding of the laws governing the changes of these motives according to age.

In order to solve these problems, we had to examine study motives in close association both with the overall personality of the child, as well as with the nature of his mode of life and the place which studies occupied in the child's life.

We used various methods in this research because we were striving for a maximum degree of objectivity. At the same time, we observed one basic methodological principle; that is, we made sure that every fact in our research was treated twice—once from the child's viewpoint and once according to an objective index. For example, when talking with children we always posed questions of two different types; some questions demanded direct answers from the child concerning his motives, while others sought the same information in a more indirect manner. The latter type of question revealed a child's study motives, though the child was not directly questioned about his studies (Bozhovich, 1951, pp. 31–32). As a result of the comparisons we obtained from this type of questioning, we could ascertain not only the factors which characteristically motivated a child to study, but also the relation between these actual motivating factors and those motives which the child could express.

This research was conducted on schoolchildren from the first to the tenth grades, as well as on older preschool children.

After examining the early data obtained from this research, we were able to establish the fact that the study activity of schoolchildren is always stimulated by a system of motives which are linked by a complex and sometimes even contradictory relation. During the course of subsequent research, it was found that this applies not only to study activity but also to any of the child's other activities (work, social activity, etc.).

A further analysis of study motives showed that they differed from each other not only with respect to their content, which constituted the principal basis for their classification, but also with respect to the function performed and to their origin.

From the standpoint of function and motive power, we have to distinguish between motives which immediately elicit study activity and motives which merely guide or orient this activity in a certain direction and impart to it a certain "personality" implication. Using Leont'ev's terminology, we designated the former as "directly stimulating motives" and the latter as motives "imparting a meaning."

We found that a combination of these motives is necessary for normal development of the child's study activity as well as for the proper development of the child's personality during this activity. An absence of motives "imparting a meaning" indicates that the child's study activity is not an important factor in his life and that it lies outside his vital relations and purposes and, consequently, is devoid of any deep personal meaning for the child.

However, the presence of motives imparting meaning alone cannot elicit normal everyday study behavior. Suppose a pupil is anxious to get an education, realizing that this education will enable further valuable creative activity or might secure him a definite social position. These are long-range goals and thus do not motivate a child, especially in the junior and medium grades, to sit down and do his homework for the next day at the proper time. Additional incentives which are more closely and directly associated with a child's daily life and daily study activity are necessary in this case. One such incentive is an evaluation of the child's knowledge in the form of a grade which secures a definite status within the class and a definite attitude toward the student on the part of his classmates.

Consequently, whereas motives "imparting meaning" crystallize a child's long-range aspirations, "directly stimulating motives" crystallize his immediate needs. Therefore, the development of both types of study motives and a deep internal connection between these motives are important factors in the correct organization of study activities and in the healthy formation of personality.

Our research has established the fact that motives which directly influence study activity can fulfill an educational role only when they apply to the content of studies or inculcate social approval of these studies. If, on the other hand, the motivation for learning is in the form of awards or threats of punishment, then, though these motives may in some cases have a great effect, the outcome is nevertheless likely to be a mere formal assimilation of knowledge and is also likely to contribute to the development of undesirable personality traits.

Thus, a study of the influence of grades on study activity has shown how the function of a grade changes and how its negative influence on the child arises when a grade loses its internal connection with the content of studies (Bozhovich, Morozova, and Slavina, 1951b). This work established two main functions of a grade: (1) it reflects the level of knowledge of a pupil and thereby constitutes an index of his progress, and (2) it represents an evaluation of the quality of the work and a personal evaluation of the child as a schoolchild, and thus expresses a public opinion about the child. These aspects are mutually interdependent, although they are not always interrelated in the opinion of the children.

In some cases, when a grade is not properly used (e.g., when it is given for mechanically learned or memorized lessons, or when the grade is given to reward good behavior in class rather than the knowledge obtained, or when the class opinion overvalues good grades), it becomes a fetish with students and is considered a means of gaining a certain social status rather than a method of evaluating what they have learned. The results of this overemphasis on grades are that negative traits such as competition and feelings of ambition become more important to children than sheer interest in knowledge. These data demonstrate clearly the necessity of establishing a proper motivation for study, especially in view of the close relation between a child's study motives and the subsequent formation of his personality.

An even more substantial difference between study motives comes from an analysis of their origins. In this case, also, two types of motives can be identified which, though closely related, have different origins and different developments.

One type of motive is directly associated with the child's actual study activity—its content and method of execution. Many schoolchildren, for example, study in order to learn new and interesting facts. They experience direct pleasure from reading, writing, and counting; they like to overcome difficulties and to work through to the solution of a given problem. The other type of motive goes beyond the intrinsic satisfaction of studying and is related to external social values.

Morozov (1955) conducted research in our laboratory with the first type of motive (study interests) in junior schoolchildren. He showed that children who are thus motivated are interested not only in the knowledge which they obtain in school but also in the actual process of assimilating knowledge. Morozov found that these students, when confronted with a selection of easy or difficult study assignments, generally preferred the more difficult and complex ones. This was typical not only for good students but also for average and even some poor students. (See Tables 6–1 and 6–2.)

Table 6–1 *Types of Study Assignments Preferred by Third- and Fourth-grade Students*

Type of assignment	Grade: Third	Grade: Fourth
Dictation	17%	7%
Exposition	23	26
Essay	60	67

Table 6–2 *Choice of Arithmetical Problems Varying in Difficulty as a Function of the Student's Success (Grades 1–4)*

	Successful students			Unsuccessful students
	Excellent	Good	Passing	
Percentage of students choosing the difficult task	90	84	73	50

This intrinsic motivation undergoes a change and develops with age. However, it is possible to understand its content and development only if we understand the formal development of the study process itself.

Research by many authors, including Morozov, has shown that the child's first academic interests involve mainly the individual facts and events in the study material. However, as the child accumulates the facts and ideas contained in a subject, he comes to develop an interest not only in facts per se, but also in the causal relations between these facts and events. For example, as the child assimilates the fundamentals of the sciences, he develops a need to learn about the surrounding reality and about the laws governing this reality. Then, as his knowledge of the subject increases, he becomes interested in all that science has discovered about this particular aspect of his environment; moreover, he becomes interested in the process used to make these discoveries. Consequently, one can understand the child's changing study interests only by analyzing how the child assimilates the fundamentals of the sciences, for example. Similarly, it is possible to understand the child's satisfaction in solving a difficult problem or the pleasure of experiencing an intellectual effort (also examples of intrinsic motivation) by analyzing the actual process of the child's study behavior.

However, we can understand the child's intrinsic motivation or social motivation only by studying his general attitudes and relations with people instead of just his study activity. The inherent satisfaction of learning is not enough to motivate a child to study. Studying is a socially significant activity which will secure for the child society's approval and which will, to a large extent, determine his future. We have termed these motives "broad social motives of study" since they transcend the narrow limits of actual study and are associated with the child's general attitudes toward reality.

These motives vary greatly in content. They may include a desire for teacher approval, for peer approval, or for parental approval. Or the child may be motivated to work for good grades so that he can get into a higher educational institution. At the same time, every child, at every developmental stage, is always motivated by some basic need ("primary motive") which crystallizes his most vital needs and determines the nature of all other motives related to his study activity.

A genetic analysis of the primary motive for study in children of different ages has disclosed a definite developmental trend. At first the primary study motive is a desire to participate in a socially significant activity, which leads the child into a world of new relations and secures a new social status for him. All factors which emphasize the social significance of study and its serious compulsory nature motivate the child of this stage to study. Students in the lower grades attach special value to the teacher's requirements and praise, to the parental attention and respect given their study endeavors, and to the evaluation of their progress offered by those around them.

In older children, this primary study motive changes with changes in their lives and in their relations with people around them. Having become a pupil, a child enters into a special new school life which becomes the center of his life. At this stage, he is striving to win a definite place in the school and in the school collective, and to establish himself as a good pupil. Thus, at this age, the opinion of the class, as well as grades which reflect this opinion, become strong motivational forces.

Finally, when a pupil reaches the higher grades, he is primarily motivated by thoughts of his future—what he will do after school, what position he will hold within the society. School matters and school relations are now consciously reinterpreted with these questions in mind. The student is now especially motivated by the grades he obtains, which reflect his knowledge and thus figure highly in his future profession. He begins to manifest a special interest in the subjects which pertain to his chosen field of interest.

Table 6–3 demonstrates the developmental trend of this primary motive. There is no doubt that these data concerning the broad social motives for study activity apply to the laws governing the formation not only of study motives, but also of motives stimulating any of the child's other kinds of activity.

Table 6–3 *Distribution of Students of Different Classes by Leading Motive in Study Activities (%)*

	Grades in school								
Motive	1–2	3	4	5	6	7	8	9	10
Striving related to schoolwork	80	63	26	16	21	25	18	16	12
Competition for position in group	20	37	67	74	46	45	37	24	14
Future position	0	0	3	7	23	22	20	45	69
Other	0	0	4	3	10	8	25	15	5

The Role of a Knowledge of Moral Principles in the Formation of the Personality of Schoolchildren

Many psychological studies of personality center on an investigation of the role of the schoolchild's moral concepts in the development of personality. The concern is with the great importance of inculcating the proper forms of social behavior and certain moral qualities.

Thus, it seems that Sechenov was right to emphasize the ever increasing role of consciousness in man's behavior. He pointed out that for older children "not only sensual motives but also thought and moral feelings determine behavior. Behavior itself is mediated by the defining thought and thus becomes an act" (1947, p. 268).

Our observations in schools also demonstrated the great importance of cultivating, through education, social forms of behavior in children and especially in children of middle and senior school age.

At the same time, however, the relation between the knowledge of standards of moral behavior and the formation of moral acts is by no means simple and unequivocal. Moreover, one can overemphasize a mere knowledge of these standards (by talking about them, explaining them, and drumming them in) to the exclusion of actually putting them into practice. This can result in a type of formalism in which a child can know moral standards and rules, and yet not follow them in his personal behavior.

A number of studies have demonstrated the fact that some schoolchildren, even older schoolchildren, are unable to properly grasp the content of moral concepts even though they have reached a relatively well-developed stage in their moral behavior. Krasnobaev (1956), for example, collected material on this subject by talking with senior schoolchildren and having them write compositions. He concluded that the content of ethical concepts in these children often failed to correspond to the developmental potential of the students, to their general intellectual development and to their experience in the field of moral behavior.

The same results were obtained in an earlier study by Selivanov

(1949) on the degree to which seventh- and eighth-grade children understand moral-volitional properties of personality. Only about half of these teen-agers (49.8 per cent) were able to grasp the content of these concepts. About one fourth (25.4 per cent) were unable to verbalize their thoughts on these concepts, while the remaining students (24.8 per cent) gave an incorrect definition of them.

An extensive study on the characteristics of moral concepts in schoolchildren was conducted by Krutetskii (1953). He worked with students in the fifth to tenth grades and studied the nature and extent of their understanding of ten concepts of moral qualities. Again, the data indicated that students, even those in higher grades, did not fully grasp these concepts.

These data suggest that the absence of sufficiently generalized and well-formed moral concepts in students accounts for the inconsistency between their understanding and their behavior and hinders a proper orientation toward moral behavior.

This assumption is confirmed by a number of studies. For example, the research of Rubtsova (1956) has shown that the youngest and middle school-age groups of children often incorrectly evaluate certain acts because their knowledge of the moral essence of these acts is not sufficiently generalized. Accordingly, some schoolchildren, when given a story to read, considered a child in this story cowardly because he had experienced a feeling of fear while performing a brave act. In the opinion of these children, bravery meant the absence of fear, not the overcoming of fear ("since he was afraid, he was not brave"). The absence of a sufficiently generalized knowledge of moral qualities leads to situational and subjective moral evaluations. According to the data obtained by Rubtsova, children belonging to the youngest school-age group evaluate the hero of a story in different ways, depending on what aspect of his behavior has made the greatest impression upon them, and also depending upon the type of situation in which the hero's qualities were manifested.

In the study just mentioned, children of the younger school age were asked to characterize the hero of a story in which a little Dutch boy closes a hole in the dike with his finger, sits this way all night, and thus saves the people. All the students positively evaluated the little boy and noted his high moral character. In a variation of the story, the difficulty of completing the act was increased, but the result was less significant because no matter what the child did danger was averted. It turned out that in this variation most of the children did not give such a high moral evaluation of the child's act because he "didn't save anyone."

Data on the subjectiveness and situation-bound nature of the schoolchildren's moral evaluations were also obtained in our laboratory by Dragunova. In this investigation it was established that the same act is evaluated differently by children as a function of the consequences of the act. Thus, the students negatively evaluated a child who wanted to help his mother wash the dishes but who, because of his ineptitude, broke a dish.

Maliovanov (1951) studied the relation between level of moral knowledge and daily behavior in a special group of teen-agers. This group was chosen because of a characteristic inability, as a result of an insufficient realization and generalization of moral concepts, to discern and understand the connection between their daily actions and the high requirements of communist morality. While wanting, for example, to perform heroic deeds, these schoolchildren did not always consider it necessary to perform their daily duties, that is, to study diligently and to exhibit disciplined behavior in school and at home. This type of behavior undoubtedly indicates that, though these students have fairly well-developed moral feelings and generally healthy personalities, they nevertheless do not fully understand moral principles.

In this investigation it was experimentally demonstrated that the behavior of adolescents is highly changeable and that it is possible to find a connection between their daily behavior and the high principles which they always desire but rarely manifest.

Thus a series of psychological investigations has established the fact that there is a strong relation between the level of a student's moral knowledge and his use of this knowledge to guide him in practical life.

The question then arises as to why a number of schoolchildren exhibit a level of understanding of moral concepts which is not sufficiently high for their age. Almost all researchers who have studied this problem believe that the main reason lies in the fact that these concepts are assimilated by schoolchildren empirically, without any general theory and without the special and consistent guidance of the teacher. This is precisely the reason for the elementary, fragmentary, and unsystematic nature of these concepts.

Krasnobaev (1956) found that increasing a schoolchild's understanding of moral ideas and concepts had an effect on the stability and nature of his behavior. This indicates that the school also has the necessary function of introducing special training in the field of morality. Makarenko, on the basis of much experience in schools, believed that even older children should be taught morals. But in our country, communist morality is learned incidentally, unless one considers the elements of moral education learned from a study of literature and history.

The Importance of Moral Habits in the Formation of the Schoolchild's Personality

The absence of a complete knowledge of the principles of communist morality, however, is not the main cause for a gap between a child's words and deeds. An insufficient realization and generalization of moral concepts can confuse a child during his evaluations of the behavior of those around him and of his own shortcomings. However, the absence of a corresponding level of moral knowledge cannot explain those cases in which children behave badly even with sufficient knowledge of standards and rules of behavior.

In a study by Maliovanov (1953), such behavior was displayed by a group of adolescents that he selected. These students, though only a small sample, had the following characteristics: (1) knowledge of moral standards; (2) an ability to determine the moral requirements imposed upon their behavior; (3) an ability to identify the basic attribute of moral concepts; (4) the capacity to evaluate a moral act correctly and to pinpoint the behavior necessary in different situations. Yet these adolescents did not, and did not want to, behave according to these principles. They could and did make these demands on their friends but did not feel it necessary to impose these demands upon themselves.

However, such cases are not representative of all schoolchildren. More typical are the students who know moral norms and behave badly not because they consciously want to but because good behavior, in their own words, "somehow does not come off." These children honestly try to behave according to the rules they know; however, they belong to the group of poorly disciplined students. They do not know how to work in a systematic way, act in an organized manner or submit to the requirements or demands made by adults. According to our data this description is characteristic of the majority of undisciplined students, particularly in middle and upper school-age groups.

It becomes clear that the reason for the inconsistency between words and deeds in all of the cases mentioned above does not lie in the nature of the moral knowledge possessed by the students, but rather in the absence or incorrect formation of other factors, especially in the absence of stable moral habits.

On the basis of his experience in character training and retraining, Makarenko wrote: "I acknowledge the possibility of a situation in which a schoolchild will exhibit proper Soviet patriotic notions, but will not be trained in correct Soviet habits." "This is particularly important," he says, "when we speak about the cultivation of qualities such as patience and an ability to overcome prolonged difficulties. No matter how many correct notions as to what should be done or must be done that you can create, if you do not cultivate the habit of overcoming prolonged difficulties, I am entitled to say that you have not cultivated anything. In a word, I demand that the life of a child should be organized as an experience which cultivates a definite group of habits" (1951, pp. 279–280).

We can say without exaggerating that, even among the pre-eminent educators of the past, there is not a single one who did not attribute tremendous importance to the formation of habits. It is true that not all of these educators believed that habits were positive aspects of human behavior. Some of them believed that habits create routine behavior and detract from flexibility, but this attitude was the result of a limited conception of habits as mechanical and sluggish actions which resist conscious regulation or control.

Most Soviet psychologists also note the tremendous importance of habits in the formation of the moral aspect of personality. For example, Rubinshtein asserts that a person's world outlook and morals assume the form of habits —namely, customary manifestations of moral behavior. Thus transformed into habits, they become "second nature" to individuals (1946, p. 667).

Among Russian educators, Uchenskii was one who put special emphasis on habits in the formation of proper forms of behavior, but also looked upon them as the most important component of character: "Conviction itself becomes an element of character only when it becomes habitual. Thus a habit is that process by means of which a conviction becomes a propensity and a thought is put into action."

In spite of this acknowledged importance of habitual forms of moral behavior in the development of a child's personality, very few psychological studies of this problem have been made. There is little experimental data available on the nature and development of moral habits and customs or on their place in the complex set of human character traits. There are not even the facts and observations which are available in other branches of the psychology of personality in schoolchildren.

Shnirman was one of the first Soviet psychologists who attempted to analyze the process and the conditions necessary for the cultivation of moral habits in schoolchildren. He presented factual material on the different ways in which the habit of doing independent work can be formed. The data collected in this investigation showed that the formation of habitual behavior cannot be reduced simply to strengthening actions through repetition. It is, rather, a complex process involving the development of forms of behavior and entails the destruction of some earlier connections and the formation of new ones. It also showed that it is impossible to understand the development of the habit of independent work without taking into consideration the schoolchild's entire personality and whether or not the formation of such a habit is consistent with his personality.

In our laboratory we have also studied—first, through observations and, later, experiments—problems concerning the consolidation of habits and problems of the role played by habits in the formation of personality qualities. This cycle of studies, which is still in progress, was initiated by Slavina (1956), who investigated the role of habitual forms of behavior while attempting to train first-graders to fulfill their study duties diligently and responsibly.

The task undertaken in this research was to validate, through psychopedagogical experimentation, certain psychological principles established in previous research carried out in the laboratory. In work with backward and undisciplined schoolchildren it was found that positive qualities can be inculcated in these schoolchildren only by having the children systematically and persistently repeat the desired behavior. It was observed that, during the process of such an "exercise," it was the function of the class to react to any deviation from the prescribed behaviors with the aim of eliciting only the desired behavior. Only when the preceding conditions are maintained for a relatively long period of time is it possible to teach the desired forms of behavior so that they will not extinguish at a later date. As a result of these observations the hypothesis advanced was that qualities or properties of the personality are basically forms of the child's behavior which have become consolidated and habitual.

At the same time, the appearance of this consolidated or habitual behavior takes place only when the behavior satisfies definite motives, particularly when it is behavior that the child wants to develop. If, on the other hand, the particular form of behavior is more of a compulsion, then, although the child does acquire the habit of acting according to the demands of those around him, he does not develop the need to behave this way when this external requirement is absent. Thus, behavior which develops as a result of compulsion does not fulfill the main requirement which Makarenko suggested for checking proper moral training: that is, the child should behave correctly not only in the presence of other people, but also when he is alone. The structure of the child's stable behaviors, and consequently the nature of his personality, includes not only a firmly established and habitual system of actions but also a firmly established system of attitudes toward reality. For this reason, conditions necessary for training stable forms of behavior include a correct organization not only of the child's behavior but also of those motives according to which this behavior is realized.

The purpose of Slavina's research was to verify these principles. This author attempted to clarify the role assumed by a system of habitual forms of behavior in the formation of responsible attitudes toward study obligations, as well as the type of conditions which must be observed in order to consolidate these forms of behavior.

She was able to ascertain the children's real motivation by presenting a task in which they not only had to learn to write or count (or whatever the task demanded), but also had to learn how to work diligently and neatly. All students who came to school with no homework or poorly done homework had to remain after class and do the assignment as well as they were able to. In addition, a system of control was set up by the children themselves, by which they were supposed to check not only the study progress of every student but also his progress in mastering corresponding forms of behavior. This control fixed the attention of the entire children's collective upon the educational task entrusted to the collective, and contributed to the organization of a public opinion regarding this work.

This psychopedagogical experiment was conducted in several first-grade classes with the active participation of teachers, who carried out educational work and general training [1] with the students according to the method indicated above.

The results of this research confirmed the enormous importance of developing stable forms of behavior in the formation of moral-psychological qualities of a child's personality. If it was possible to ensure a steady and systematic fulfillment of the requirements imposed upon the students and if at the same time the fulfillment of these requirements was willingly undertaken, all students developed the habit of always preparing their lessons neatly and conscientiously and of attending to the assignments given by the teacher in class. A very reliable indicator of this fact is the gradual decrease, covering a period beginning with the first day of school and extending over the first twenty-five days, in the number of children who came to school with lessons unprepared.

The results of this research also indicate that, in addition to the habit of always fulfilling their study obligations at a high level, the children were careful to start their homework at the proper time; they tried to do their homework as well as possible; they were ashamed to bring to school lessons which had not been done at all or had been poorly done; they were proud to realize that they had learned how to "work hard"; and so on.

However, success was not achieved in all classes. In one class, where the teacher forced the children to remain after class as a form of punishment, the children developed neither the necessary habit nor a proper attitude toward their work.

These data also indicate that the formation of stable forms of behavior and the appearance of corresponding personality traits can successfully take place only if training in definite forms of behavior is carried out against a background of positive motivation, and not by means of coercion.

A further study of moral habits in our laboratory was directed at finding those general forms of habitual behavior which underlie a responsible fulfillment of various types of activity. Approximately thirty children in the first and fifth grades needed supplementary lessons at the start of experimental work. After a three-month period only one or two first-grade children needed supplementary lessons while in the fifth grade, where keeping the children after their usual lessons was a form of punishment, twenty-four children needed supplementary lessons (see Figure 6–1). One of the tasks

1. *Editors' note:* The Russian word *vospitatel'nii* has been translated here as "general training," the term deemed most appropriate in this context. No exact translation is possible, but the general notion of "upbringing" is often used in the translation of this word.

undertaken in this connection was to combine the methods used for carrying out a specific type of activity with methods used for the responsible performance of any kind of activity. This research was intended to bring us closer to an understanding of how the factors leading to responsible performance of a certain type of work can determine the behavior of a schoolchild in a wide variety of different situations.

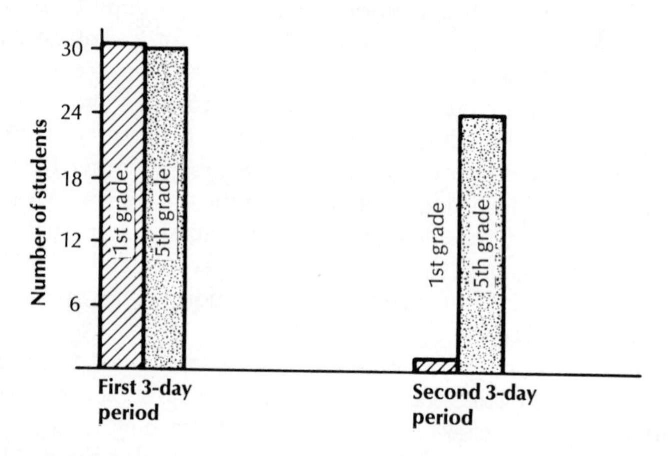

Figure 6–1. The number of children studying after school during a three-day period as measured at the beginning of supplementary work and two months later.

Slavina (1961) sought a solution to this problem in a study in which young schoolchildren were given the task of responsibly completing a Pioneer assignment. This assignment was selected as a subject of research because its concrete content varied from time to time: collecting scrap metal, making a report, helping a comrade in his studies, and so on. Thus the fulfillment of this assignment assumes, as a necessary condition, the extrapolation of generic behavior characterizing the responsible fulfillment of any kind of assignment received by a Pioneer youngster.

This investigation began with observations of those students who always carried out their chores in contrast to those who, although they gladly accepted new tasks, did not usually fulfill them. It turned out that the students who responsibly completed their work were active from the moment they were given the task. They asked questions concerning the content of the task, the period in which it had to be carried out, and the sequence of events that would be needed to fulfill the task.

As a result of these observations, the hypothesis was formed that the children who responsibly carried out their chores mastered certain methods or means of behavior which constituted the most important component of responsible behavior. The most important of these means were: (1) the ability to immediately think about the given task and understand it; (2) the ability to begin immediately to fulfill the task either by a practical act or, if this were not possible, then in the form of thought activity, such as a plan.

For the experiment we chose students who gladly, guided by social motives, agreed to undertake a given chore. The chosen students were divided into two groups: an experimental group in which the students were not only given a chore but also corresponding means of behavior, and a control group for whom the presentation of the task was not accompanied by any recommendations.

Any differences in the way in which the two groups fulfilled the tasks we hoped to attribute to the differences in the means of behavior used by students in the different groups. The chore consisted of preparing a collection of multicolored blocks to be used in teaching nursery-school children. Thus, this chore was socially motivated and consisted in the preparation of a series of separate objects which permitted us to record the results quantitatively, giving us an objective measure with which to compare the control and experimental groups.

In order to ensure that our subjects were socially motivated and had volunteered for this reason, we devised the following selection process: the child was brought to a specially designed experimental room with two tables, one of which contained the materials needed to make blocks for the nursery children and the other of which contained all sorts of toys. The child was first taught how to prepare the experimental blocks and was also made aware of the toys on the other table. Then the child was asked what he wanted to do: he could either continue to make blocks or he could begin to play with the toys. This condition was necessary to exclude from the experiment those children who had an immediate interest in preparing the blocks. Otherwise it would be impossible to tell whether the children completed the experimental task because of the social motive or because of some immediate interest.

The last part of the methodology was decisive. Those children who chose to play were left in the experimental room and began to play. In five minutes, sure that the children were distracted by the toys, the experimenter unexpectedly entered the room, interrupted their play, and told them that the little children in the nursery school had too few toys, that they were bored, that they were crying, and that the director of the nursery school had asked the schoolchildren to make multicolored blocks with which the little children could play. These blocks would help the little children to learn how to count and how to distinguish colors. Then the experimenter added, "Of course I didn't promise her anything. I said I would simply relate the message to the children and that those who wanted to could help and those who didn't want to wouldn't be made to help." Then the students were again asked to choose between the toys and preparing the blocks. Those students who chose to prepare the blocks (as opposed to the first time when they chose the toy) became our subjects. The rest of the students were excluded from the experiment.

We hypothesized that the decision to make the blocks for the nursery-school children instead of playing with the attractive toys was a sufficient indication that the child was socially motivated to fulfill the experimental chore. After the selection of subjects the main series of experiments was begun.

As we have already said the selected children were divided into two groups, a control group and an experimental group. In both groups the task was given individually and its fulfillment was postponed; that is, the child was given the task to do at home with a time period of three days. The only recommendations made to the experimental group were to repeat the task (thus forcing the child to think about its content and to relate it to himself) and to plan his work carefully ahead of time. It was assumed that our recommendations would provide for a more successful completion of the task.

The main results of this study were the following: (1) The proportion of completed tasks in the experimental group was higher than the control group (82 per cent vs. 61 per cent). This indicates the utility of the methods recommended to the experimental group. (2) Completion of the chore in the experimental group hardly changed from one grade to another (81 per cent in the first grade, 84 per cent in the third grade). In the control group, however, this change was significant (51 per cent in the first grade, 69 per cent in the third grade). This indicated that the younger the child, the more significant is the means of organizing his behavior. Evidently, the older children have in some way mastered these methods. (3) A decrease in the number of completed tasks from the first chore to the fifth (in all there were five chores) was less in the experimental group than in the control. For example, for the first grade this difference was 26 per cent for the experimental group and 52 per cent for the control group. This means that certain methods of behavior enable the children to fulfill the chores even in the face of weaker primary motive strength.

These data establish the proper means for giving children Pioneer-type chores under ordinary school conditions. In further observations it was found that in those Pioneer groups in which these methodological principles were used the number of unfulfilled chores was significantly reduced.

Studies conducted by Yakobson (1961) and Prokina (1961) are also concerned with the problem of the consolidation of habitual forms of behavior. The first of these studies involved an experimental investigation of those conditions in which a pupil learns to work without being distracted. Subjects were several lower-grade pupils, who were making good progress and who displayed ability and an interest in knowledge, but who did not know how to organize their work. During the course of preparing a written lesson these children became distracted, on the average, over twenty times. In most cases these distractions lasted a long time and were spent in some other kind of activity, such as play or reading. These interruptions occurred at various points of the child's studying; for example, copying was broken off in the middle of a sentence, a word, or even a letter. The duration of continuous work varied from ten seconds to three minutes, and on the average was equal to thirty to fifty seconds.

The experiment with these children was carried out while they did their homework and involved the following problems: (1) to find conditions under which the schoolchild could work without being distracted by varying the conditions of their activity; (2) to trace the consolidation of the forms of activity in the context of various motivations; (3) to verify whether or not the subject could utilize a method of organizing his activity which he had assimilated during the performance of a different activity; and (4) if such transfer cannot take place, then to undertake a search for those conditions which would produce more generalization.

It was found that, although constant reminders not to be distracted do result in an acceleration of work (since the child returns more rapidly to his work), this method does not reduce the number of distractions, does not change the structure of the child's activity, and does not speed up the preparation of the lessons from one time to the next. In other words, an activity which is organized by means of external stimulation, as a rule, is not assimilated, no matter how long we use this method. A variation of this method, however, yielded different results. The experimenter got the child to agree in advance that he would try to work without any distractions, and that every time that he became distracted the experimenter would start a stopwatch which would show the child both that he had been distracted and the amount of time which was consumed by this distraction. In this case the child reacted quite differently: namely, there was a sharp decrease in the number of distractions. When distractions did take place, their duration was greatly reduced and they did not interrupt an action which had been started. In a sense, the distractions themselves become more organized.

The foregoing experiment confirmed once more that the assimilation of a definite form of behavior requires a constant motive which is very significant to the child and helps him master this form of behavior. At the same time, it was shown that this means (in this case, the starting of a stopwatch which recorded the distraction of the child) should not be externally applied, but should be utilized by the child so that he may reach the goal he has established for himself.

Prokina (1961) studied another form of organized behavior—namely, entering the classroom. A first-grade class, characterized by a high degree of disorganization, was selected for this purpose. The investigator's task was to organize a certain form of behavior and to consolidate this behavior by means of systematic practice. The behavior of the children was broken down into several successive time segments (hearing the sound of a bell, the children had to line up wherever they were, come to attention, enter the classroom quietly, and sit down quietly at their desks), and the performance of these actions was made a condition for winning a contest. Thus the children were given a general motive for the behavior of learning how to line up quickly and efficiently, and public opinion was organized around their activity. However, in spite of the apparent fulfillment of all necessary conditions, it was not only not possible to "consolidate" the necessary form of behavior, but also there was no success in achieving a stable reproduction of this form of behavior. A change, however, could be achieved by using an hourglass, to which the children oriented the process of lining up. Thus, in order to develop skill at lining up in an organized manner, the following factors were necessary: (1) creation of a firm social motive, (2) breaking the behavior down into individual segments, and (3) using an hourglass, which served as a visual or graphic gauge of the time consumed in lining up and thereby became a means for mastering a tempo of behavior. The behavior organized in this manner was preserved even after the use of competition and an hourglass was stopped.

Prokina verified these results in the organization of more complex activities which demanded a significantly greater amount of time. These tasks involved having the children of a boarding school fulfill the so-called morning regime, which included washing themselves, washing the dishes, and dressing. This work had a practical value because the boarding school pupils who were chosen for the experiment wasted forty to fifty minutes in the morning in fulfilling these chores and as a result were late to breakfast and even to their school lessons. The experimental results indicated that this time could be shortened to a third of normal.

This study not only indicated again the effectiveness of the conditions noted by Prokina in the first experiment but also specified more clearly the significance of each of the conditions in the formation of the corresponding behavior. The analysis of these conditions, as well as their place and function in the formation of organized behavior, permitted us to understand several components of the qualities which we were studying.

Although the research described above does not yet give a sufficiently clear idea of the structure of moral habits, it does nevertheless disclose the complex structure of these habits and it clarifies certain conditions which are significant in their formation. As a result of these studies, it was possible to undertake a psychological analysis of personality traits of the child and of his appearance on the basis of a consolidation of stable forms of behavior.

At the present time we can make the following rather general conclusions:

1. The basis for the formation of any trait is made up of certain forms of behavior which are mastered by the student by means of systematic practice.

2. This mastery occurs only under certain conditions, the most important of which is the presence of the proper motivation for the given activity. In other words, during this practice the child masters only those components of activity (or behavior) which correspond to his needs. Apparently it can be said that the structure of a personality trait is composed of both a definite motive and a definite form of behavior.

Certain Problems of Education in the Light of a Psychological Study of the Personality of Schoolchildren

The results of the research studies described above are significant not only for a deeper and more accurate understanding of the psychological principles governing the formation of a child's personality, but also for solving a number of pedagogical problems and, most important, for devising methods of moral education.

We have already stated that research devoted to an analysis of moral ideas and concepts, even after having shown the relationship between the behavior of a child and the level of his moral knowledge, could still not explain those cases in which a child who had a sufficient knowledge of standards and rules of behavior still did not attempt to behave accordingly.

As a result of research conducted on the problem of the appearance of stable forms of behavior, it was definitely established that, in order for a child to be guided by standards of behavior, he should have practice in social behavior, during which the appropriate feelings and habits are formed and consolidated. Moral knowledge can become effective only when it is sown on prepared "soil," that is, only when this knowledge is based on an experience of social behavior which has been assimilated and generalized by the child.

From this standpoint, which differs sharply from the intellectual interpretation of personality formation, the main content of the educational process involves the organization of the life and activity of the child in a collective. This organization should create the necessary conditions for the manifestation and consolidation of socially desirable personality traits. Verbal instruction (persuasion, explanation, etc.), must take place as the child accumulates moral experiences.

These conclusions require a consistent application of Makarenko's idea that no valuable properties of a child's personality can be cultivated without "special exercises in a collective" (1950, p. 653). "No science is more dialectic in its nature than pedagogy," he wrote, "and the elaboration of necessary behavior is primarily a question of experiences, skill, and prolonged exercise in those qualities which we need. Our Soviet collective, equipped with such trapezes and horizontal bars as we need right now, must serve as the gymnasium for such exercises." He expresses the same idea when he talks about the importance of acquiring a "tradition of behavior." "Sometimes," he writes, "we abuse the word 'conscious.' Our behavior must be conscious behavior, but this does not at all mean that we should always appeal to consciousness when we are concerned with problems of behavior. This would constitute an excessively unprofitable burden on consciousness. A broad ethical standard becomes effective only when its 'conscious' part is changed into general experience, tradition and habit" (1951, p. 411).

In all our research, one common idea is developed and confirmed experimentally: that the moral foundation of the child's personality is the result of an assimilation of originally external forms of social behavior, which occurred during the course of the child's actual relations in a collective. Such an understanding of the basic content of the moral development of personality suggests, to a certain extent, the content and program of a moral education, for example, education in the forms of social behavior.

Unfortunately, up to the present time this position has not been given its deserved attention. It is considered necessary to observe the entire set of demands made on the child by the whole pedagogical and children's collective in the school. This approach seems correct because it is this set of demands which plays a decisive role in the formation of necessary motives for behavior. At the same time it is not realized that, before a child can fulfill the pedagogical demands made of him, he must be taught those behaviors he is expected to exhibit. A teacher would not think of demanding that the child correctly solve a problem or correctly write some words, if he had not been taught them. However, these same teachers demand accurateness and conscientiousness from the students, not having taught them these qualities. Moreover, the children who do not submit themselves to the teachers' demands are censured and punished, while the teachers fail to realize that punishment under such conditions may evoke only a negative reaction to the demands being made.

According to our data, the principle that the child's personality is formed while he acts must be supplemented by the principle that a particular activity can elicit various psychological qualities, depending upon the needs and motives which stimulate this activity. This is because the child does not assimilate the entire content of his activity or all of the methods of interacting with the people around him, but only those aspects that correspond to his needs.

This principle is of crucial importance in developing a method of moral education, since the classroom is thus in accordance with this principle, responsible not only for the organization of certain methods of behaviors, but also for the organization of those needs which insure the assimilation of these methods. In other words, it is necessary, while inculcating a particular quality in a child, to elicit the behavior or activity during which the quality is formed.

Let us consider from this standpoint, for example, the conditions under which the knowledge assimilated by schoolchildren becomes a conviction (Bozhovich, 1949). According to experimental data the most important condition for such assimilation is the child's need to acquire bits of knowledge which are supposed to be assimilated. This need may be of various sorts: it may be the need to utilize in practice the knowledge acquired during a lesson, or it may be a need for a theoretical understanding of reality. In both cases, however, the child's desire to acquire certain pieces of knowledge is exactly what the teacher is striving to achieve.

The same principle stands out just as clearly during the cultivation of a child's personality in a collective. It is known that a basic condition for an effective education is the organization of spontaneous activity in a children's collective. However, the spontaneous activity of a collective is such that social aims and problems become the aims and problems of both the children's collective as a whole and of each child forming a part of this collective.

A very interesting analysis of a pedagogical experiment aimed at the education of a Pioneer collective group is given in a study by Konnikova (1957), who rightly points out that "the intensity of the educational effect exerted by the collective activity of children is greatly increased when this activity is done of their own accord. This happens when schoolchildren need to achieve a goal which they have set themselves."

This principle is in full agreement with Makarenko's principle of the development of a children's collective. He broke down the progress of a children's collective into successive stages based upon the children's attitude assumed toward given requirements. During the first stage, these requirements remain external to the collective; during the second stage, these requirements are "adopted" by the leading or active group of the collective, which imposes these requirements upon the rest of the collective; during the third stage, the demands made by the instructors are already adopted by the entire children's collective, which itself imposes them upon "individual deviates." Finally, during the fourth stage, the demands made by the instructors become the personal demands of each child within the collective who now imposes these requirements upon himself without the support of the collective or of any sort of external checking.

The methods of moral education cannot be limited to an indication of the principles to be adopted; the methods for carrying out these principles must be pointed out. It is not enough, therefore, to formulate the problem of a "transfer" whereby the requirements imposed upon the child become his own personal requirements; it is also necessary to point out methods for solving this task. Unfortunately, these methods have so far been studied very little. However, certain ways of solving this problem can be tentatively outlined.

One of the most direct methods for solving this problem is to organize the child's activity in such a way that the requirement in question becomes an inherent part of an already significant goal of the child.

Leont'ev experimentally validated this approach. Subjects were the children in an aircraft-model construction group, who enjoyed building airplane models but had no desire, in spite of the demands made by the leader of the group, to study the physics of airplane flights. Instead of being told simply to build aircraft models, they were instructed to build these models so that they could "fly" over a certain distance. In thus attemping to improve their models, the members of the group were confronted with the fact that they did not have the necessary theoretical knowledge. It was found that the same children who had previously refused to study theoretical problems, now enthusiastically began to study these problems (1947, pp. 35–36).

Other educators have used other methods based on the same principle. For example, Konnikova (1957) cultivated a sense of discipline in the students of a poorly disciplined class by having them organize some kind of interesting activity which could be carried out only with the strict discipline of those participating in the activity. Under these conditions, discipline became a means which had to be mastered in order to achieve the desired goal.

Closely related to this method, in terms of its effect, is a system of competition as an effective means of developing necessary motives for behavior. Here, the achievement of pedagogically significant goals becomes the condition for the personal success of a pupil or for the success of the collective of which the pupil is a member. This is why it is possible through competition to stimulate the activity and independent action of children, even in regard to something which is entirely devoid of interest for them.

But for this very reason this method may also lead to undesirable consequences. First of all, it may evoke unhealthy competition among children and even harmful feelings concerning each other's success. Secondly, the behavior which motivates honesty may not be mastered and may disappear as soon as the competition is stopped. However, Makhlakh and Prokina in studies done in our laboratory developed conditions in which the negative consequences of competition were averted so that the competition could be used for educational purposes. Among such conditions were the following: (1) the presence of a socially significant purpose which was favored by the whole group; (2) organization of competitions between groups rather than between children; (3) evaluation of the progress of each collective without indicating its place among the other collectives; and (4) organization of cooperative activity among children by eliminating breaks caused by more backward students.

Finally, we should also consider the role of play and games in the process of education. The introduction of play into educational work represents a means of stimulating the spontaneous activity of children. The importance of play is stressed by past and present outstanding educators. In the field of Soviet pedagogy, Krupskaya and Makarenko have devoted a great deal of attention to play. Psychological research in this field enables a better understanding of this "mechanism."

Vygotskii's analysis of play showed that the indispensable elements in every type of play or game were the "game rules" which are followed by every child who engages in play. He showed that whenever there is "an imaginative situation, there are also rules of play. In addition, fulfillment of these rules is a basic purpose of the game and their attainment gives the child a feeling of accomplishment in the game." A specific characteristic of these rules, in contrast to adult rules, is the fact that the child himself can participate in the formation of these rules. In other words, game rules are developed by the child for his own use and correspond to his personal needs. "A significant characteristic of play," Vygotskii has said, "is a rule which has become an affect." Hence, it follows that a game rule is an "internal rule" for the child, and not a rule which he is forced to obey (Vygotskii, 1956).

If we analyze the nature of game rules it becomes apparent that the rules of behavior devised by the child are based on the ideal qualities of the person with whom he identifies. Having assumed this person's role, the child also voluntarily fulfills the requirements which society imposes upon the behavior of this person. A game includes within itself a "mechanism," with the aid of which external requirements become the internal requirements of the child. And in the process, the child usually strives to reproduce the best qualities of the person whom he is trying to represent. In a study of role playing, Makhlakh (1961) noted the fact that children, even when assuming a negative role, tried to express positive qualities in this role.

On the basis of these facts, we can understand the tremendous educational possibilities offered by play or games. The point is not only that, while playing, children do everything more gaily and with greater interest, but also that, with the "mechanism" of play, children will comply with requirements not because they are orders given by an adult, but because they fulfill their own needs.

Let us now consider two methods of using play for educational purposes. The first of these methods consists of placing the children in a play situation in which they accept the requirements imposed upon them in this imaginary situation. This method was described by Fradkina, who studied the work done by a teacher named Barkova. In her work with sixth-grade students, Barkova took advantage of the dream of these youngsters to become sailors, and developed a game involving a ship called "The Sea Hawk." The students in her class considered themselves "the crew of the ship," and regarded their school duties as duties which they, as sailors, had to fulfill in a model fashion. These duties included always being well disciplined and always efficiently mastering all knowledge. Thus, the ship game became a means for solving important educational problems. Giving the child a role to play made it easier for him to accept and fulfill difficult and uninteresting requirements.

Another teacher, Gel'fan, used a different method—play as a means of enabling the child to first set himself the task of acquiring a certain quality or a certain form of behavior and then of mastering this quality of behavior. For example, this teacher proposed games with certain slogans ("Be ready on time" or "Don't fall asleep while working" or "Do it yourself and help somebody else"). The children carried out their slogan and noted every correct act they made by moving a small flag along a path which led to an interesting picture, such as a plane, an automobile, or a steamship. When the child reached the end of this path, he won the right to "take a ride" in a plane, an automobile, or a steamship. The content of the game changed according to the age of the participants, their number, the place where the game was performed, and so forth, but the pattern of the game was always the same. This type of game was tested under various conditions with good results.

The basic mechanism of these games is a "transfer" in which the child internalizes the requirements imposed upon him so that they become personal needs. However, a very important fact is that the game clarifies for the child a method of behavior and the problem in terms of mastering this method.

The above-mentioned methods of play for educational purposes do not constitute a full picture of its possible uses. But regardless of the form that play takes, a very important factor in all of these cases is that the game should not be regarded as a supplement to the child's "serious" activity. The game must constitute this "serious" activity.

Affective Conflict and the Freudian Unconscious

In conclusion, we would like to note a number of problems for future studies. First of all, the effects of the child's "unconscious" on his behavior should be taken into account.[2] The efforts of Soviet psychologists to overlook Freud's "unconscious" and, in general, "depth psychology" are quite understandable, as are our efforts to show that man is by no means a puppet dancing at the will of dark forces, but rather the master of his behavior and capable of controlling his acts through consciously formulated tasks and consciously adopted solutions.

2. *Editors' note:* The assessment of Freudian psychology by Soviet theoreticians is treated more fully by F. V. Bassin in Chapter 14 of this volume.

However, during this struggle against the supremacy of the "unconscious," consciousness was considered a demiurge of the personality. It was believed that it is sufficient merely to convince a child and to cultivate his consciousness in order to educate him or train his entire personality. We cannot agree with this interpretation of the exaggerated importance of consciousness. In our research, we are constantly confronted with factors, lying outside the consciousness of a child, which must be considered by both psychologists and educators. In the study of the nature of a child's motivation to study, we found that the child's social needs are the major incentives for study and, furthermore, that generally the child is not consciously aware of this motivation.

The role of the unconscious is particularly important in the affective life of the child. Children often give affective reactions which are unexpected to the people around them and to themselves. With this in mind, our laboratory has undertaken the study of the child's affective life and its significance in the formation of personality. Neimark is conducting research on experimental methods for the study of affective experiences and their function. Slavina is studying the affective behavior of individual children to discover the conditions in which affective experiences are elicited in children of different ages and to find means for dealing with them.

In these investigations it has been found that it is essential to understand the internal motivational tendencies of the personality in order to elicit affective experiences. Affect is elicited when the child is not able to find a way out of an internal conflict, that is, when he is not able to satisfy one of his demands without threatening the loss of another. This is why the most critical affective states are found when an adult tries to force a child to understand something the child does not want to understand so that he can avoid confronting the inconsistencies of his internal tendencies.

In this way we discovered that the mechanisms for evoking affective reactions are very similar to those which Breuer discovered and which became the fundamental explanatory principle in Freud's teaching. However, we have obtained data which permit a non-Freudian interpretation of the origin and content of children's affective conflicts.

Careful study of the life history of the children who manifest negative forms of behavior (that is, children who are touchy, secretive, rude, aggressive, etc.) showed that these children had experienced a failure to achieve the level of the demands made on them by themselves and by others. Most often this type of affective experience is related to a lack of success in studies and sometimes in work, if work occupies a significant place in the child's life and in his relationships with others.

Further study of these affective conditions revealed that the children who display these negative behaviors often have goals which are inconsistent with their abilities. That is, they possess a sufficiently high self-esteem to strive for a definite position in the group, but do not have the abilities which would guarantee them the desired position. All the children studied also manifested what appeared at first glance to be "imperviousness to experience." They did not want to admit their inadequacies and attributed them instead to other people or to objective conditions.

As mentioned above, Neimark (1961) tried to find the factors which produce acute affective conditions. In this investigation the author was able to experimentally isolate a form of acute affective experience which was conditionally termed "the affect of inadequacy." As the experimental data indicated, underlying the "affect of inadequacy" was a gap between the student's abilities and his goals. When the child's goals are on a level with those of his peers, the "affect of inadequacy" as a rule is not evoked (although the child even here reacts emotionally to lack of success). But if, underlying the child's goals, there is a demand for a particular level of self-esteem, evoked as a result of an earlier experience, he will as a rule exhibit "the affect of inadequacy." In other words, he affectively rejects any reality which does not reinforce his self-esteem and instead threatens to destroy his emotional feelings of well-being.

Turning to the Freudian interpretation of the content and origin of affective conflicts, it is apparent that our data can be attributed neither to primary biological inclinations or demands, nor to a failure to satisfy the primitive demands evoked in early childhood. No demand, including social demands, will be permitted into consciousness if it is in direct conflict with the child's other demands.

Conclusion

We have only recently begun to study the affective life of children in our laboratory. In future investigations concerning the psychology of personality it is absolutely necessary to pay particular attention to both affective life and to other unconscious psychological processes, to study their particular features, their origins, and their role both in the behavior of the child and in the formation of his personality.

A second problem which requires significantly more attention is the problem of methodology. We have already described the major approach to the study of the personality of the child in Soviet psychology: that is, the study of personality as an integrated structure in the context of its complex interactions with reality. In essence, this is the Pavlovian approach of the study of the complete organism. Pavlov believed that we can correctly understand the physiological laws of an organ only after we understand the physiological function of the organ in the life activity of the whole organism taken in the context of its actual life conditions. He considered this the only possible approach for the "mastery of the subject of study."

The same approach should be used in the study of the personality of the child. Directed at the study of individual aspects of the child's personality such a study must always be concerned with the problem of the function which a given psychological "formation" performs in the complex system of the child's interaction with reality. This means that research in the field of the psychology of personality must not be limited to the study of one or another psychological characteristic; this research must be concerned with the manner in which these characteristics, which form the influence of the conditions found in the life and education of the child, determine his behavior and activity.

This integrated approach is already being followed by Soviet psychologists in several studies of individual mental processes. Dobrynin and his associates (1954) have shown the dependence of various cognitive processes upon the "significance" of the object toward which the child's cognitive activity is directed.

This same dependence of individual mental processes on their relation to the personality is reflected in the work of Myasishchev (1949) and Smirnov (1948) and also in the studies currently in progress in our laboratory. Slavina (1954) found that certain children, when confronted with the necessity of solving a given problem, exhibited an exceptional intellectual passivity. These children were unable to perform even the most elementary intellectual operations and did not make any kind of intellectual effort. The investigator would have arrived at an erroneous interpretation of the character and level of the child's intellectual development if he had considered only the intellectual process present in this case, and not the child's personality as a whole and his view of the assigned study problem. However, a study of the intellectual activity of these children in the proper context of their general attitudes toward studying and their attitude to this particular problem would have led the author of this study to a completely different conclusion. It would have made it possible to understand the child's "intellectual passivity" and to reconstruct the child's intellectual activity by removing any obstacles.

Thus, the foundation of research on the study of personality in schoolchildren has been established in Soviet psychology. Not only does this foundation permit a proper study of the psychology of personality, but it also makes it possible to apply the conclusions thus obtained to educational theory and practice. An adequate experimental method for objective studies of personality has not yet been found. The present methods used, such as observation, talks, compositions, diaries, and natural psychopedagogical experiments, are predominantly descriptive in nature, and are not capable of fully disclosing the causal nexus and relations in the formation of the personality of the child. Some psychologists have expressed the thought that the integrated approach to the study of personality would seem to exclude a strict experiment of any sort, especially if such an experiment is set up under laboratory conditions. "It is quite obvious," writes Kovalev, "that laboratory experiments cannot be used as a means for studying significant characteristics of a school child" (1949, p. 25). Levitov, Shnirman, and others who advocate the study of the integral personality have also spoken out against laboratory experiments.

In contrast, we believe that further thorough investigation of the personality of the child requires the use of adequate experimental methods.[3] No research can be done without an analytical approach to the phenomena being studied. However, in breaking personality down into separate phenomena, we must at the same time know how to preserve all of their complex interrelationships within the integrated personality of the child.

References

Bozhovich, L. I. Psychological problems concerning the child's preparation for school learning. In A. N. Leont'ev and A. V. Zaporozhets (Eds.), *Problems in the psychology of schoolchildren.* Moscow-Leningrad: Uchpedgiz, 1948.

Bozhovich, L. I. The problem of formalism in school knowledge. *Sovet Pedag.,* 1949, No. 1.

Bozhovich, L. I. Attitude toward learning as a psychological problem. *Izv. Akad. Pedag. Nauk RSFSR,* 1951, *36.*

Bozhovich, L. I. *Psychological studies of boardingschool children.* Moscow: Izd. Akad. Pedag. Nauk, 1960.

Bozhovich, L. I., and Blagonadezhnoi, L. V. (Eds.). *Problems in the psychology of schoolchildren.* Moscow, 1961.

Bozhovich, L. I., Morozova, N. G., and Slavina, L. S. The development of study motives in Soviet schoolchildren. *Izv. Akad. Pedag. Nauk RSFSR,* 1951, *36.* (a)

Bozhovich, L. I., Morozova, N. G., and Slavina, L. S. Grades as a motive for study behavior in schoolchildren. *Izv. Akad. Pedag. Nauk RSFSR,* 1951, *36.* (b)

Dobrynin, N. F. Problems of the activity of personality and consciousness. *Uch. Zap. Moskov. Gorod. Pedag. Inst.,* 1954, *36,* No. 2.

3. *Editors' note:* The stress placed by Bozhovich on the development of habits of moral behavior and of working for the good of the group is a reflection of the general Soviet attitude which is expressed in the communication media and in the attitude of the citizens. We found far more explicit stress placed on the importance of morality and high ideals in youth in the Soviet Union than in countries in the West with which we are familiar. Whether moral *behavior* of the Soviet youth is different than that of Western youth is an interesting and important empirical problem.

Dragunova, T. V. Description of the case of Vala G. In L. I. Bozhovich (Ed.), *Psychological studies of boardingschool children*. Moscow: Izd. Akad. Pedag. Nauk, 1960.

El'konin, D. B., and Davydov, V. V. *The psychology of learning in the elementary school*. Moscow: Izd. Akad. Pedag. Nauk RSFSR, 1962.

Fradkina, F. I. The role of play in the formation of study interests. *Izv. Akad. Pedag. Nauk RSFSR*, 1955, No. 73.

Konnikova, T. E. *Organization of a student collective in school*. Izd. Akad. Pedag. Nauk RSFSR, 1957.

Kovalev, A. G. *On the work of the class leader in the study of the schoolchild's personality*. Simferopol: Krimizdat, 1949.

Kovalev, A. G. World outlook as a factor in character formation. *Izv. Kri. Pedag. Inst*. Vol. 15, "Psychology," 1950.

Kovalev, A. G., and Myasishchev, V. N. *Psychological characteristics of man: Character. 1*, Leningrad, 1957.

Krasnobaev, I. M. Formation of ethical concepts in senior schoolchildren. In *Reports presented at a Conference on the Psychology of Personality*. Izd. Akad. Pedag. Nauk RSFSR, 1956.

Krutetskii, V. A. Characteristics of certain moral concepts in senior schoolchildren. Candidate's dissertation, Moscow, 1953.

Leont'ev, A. N. Urgent problems in the development of the mental life of the child. *Izv. Akad. Pedag. Nauk RSFSR*, 1945, No. 14.

Leont'ev, A. N. Psychological problems of the consciousness of learning. *Izv. Akad. Pedag. Nauk RSFSR*, 1947, No. 7.

Leont'ev, A. N. *Problems of the development of mental life*. Izd. Akad. Pedag. Nauk RSFSR, 1959.

Levitov, N. D. The influence of personal example on the character formation of students. *Uch. Zap. Inst. Psikhol.*, Moscow, 1941.

Makarenko, A. S. *Works*. Vol. 1. Moscow, 1950.

Makarenko, A. S. *Works*. Vol. 5. Moscow, 1951.

Makhlakh, E. S. Psychological features of concrete play in school-age children. In L. I. Bozhovich and L. V. Blagonadezhnoi (Eds.), *Problems in the psychology of shoolchildren*. Moscow, 1961.

Makhlakh, E. S. Psychological conditions for the formation of certain socially valued qualities in the personality of schoolchildren. In *Speeches at the Second Congress of the Society of Psychologists*. No. 5 Moscow, 1963. (Abstract)

Maliovanov, A. L. The role of moral persuasion in the formation of moral behavior in Soviet adolescents. Candidate's dissertation, Moscow, 1953.

Morozov, M. F. The appearance and development of study interests in junior schoolchildren. *Izv. Akad. Pedag. Nauk RSFSR*, 1955, No. 73.

Myasishchev, V. N. Mental functions and relations. *Uch. Zap. LGU*, 1949.

Neimark, M. S. Emotional reactions of schoolchildren to difficulties encountered in their work. In L. I. Bozhovich and L. V. Blagonadezhnoi (Eds.), *Problems in the psychology of schoolchildren.* Moscow, 1961.

Prokina, N. F. Conditions for the formation of organized behavior in boarding schoolchildren in their daily routine. In L. I. Bozhovich and L. V. Blagonadezhnoi (Eds.), *Problems in the psychology of schoolchildren.* Moscow, 1961.

Rubinshtein, S. L. *Fundamentals of general psychology.* Moscow: Uchpedgiz, 1946.

Rubtsova, T. V. Characteristics of the formation of moral qualities in the personality of schoolchildren of different ages. *Vop. Psikhol.,* 1956, No. 4.

Sechenov, I. M. *Selected philosophical and psychological works.* Moscow, 1947.

Selivanov, V. I. *Volitional training in schoolchildren.* Moscow, 1949.

Serebryakova, E. A. Self-confidence and conditions of its formation in schoolchildren. Candidate's dissertation, Moscow, 1955.

Shnirman, A. L. The collective as a vital condition for the formation of the personality of schoolchildren. In *Reports presented at a Conference on the Psychology of Personality.* Izd. Akad. Pedag. Nauk RSFSR, 1956.

Slavina, L. S. The role of the family in the formation of a child's attitude toward school studies. *Izv. Akad. Pedag. Nauk RSFSR,* 1951, No. 36.

Slavina, L. S. On certain peculiarities of the mental work of backward students. *Sovet. Pedag.,* 1954, No. 1.

Slavina, L. S. The formation of first-grade pupils' fulfillment of studies. *Vop. Psikhol.,* 1956, No. 4.

Slavina, L. S. The role of motive and means of behavior in the schoolchild's fulfillment of social tasks. In L. I. Bozhovich and L. V. Blagonadezhnoi (Eds.), *Problems in the psychology of schoolchildren.* Moscow, 1961.

Smirnov, A. A. *Psychology of memory.* Moscow-Leningrad, 1948.

Smirnov, A. A. Problems in the psychology of the personality of Soviet schoolchildren. *Sovet. Pedag.,* 1950, No. 2.

Vygotskii, L. S. *Thought and speech.* Sotsekgiz, 1934.

Vygotskii, L. S. *Collected psychological investigations.* Moscow: Izd. Akad. Pedag. Nauk, 1956.

Yakobson, S. G. A study of the schoolchild's organization of schoolwork. In L. I. Bozhovich and L. V. Blagonadezhnoi (Eds.), *Problems in the psychology of schoolchildren.* Moscow, 1961.

7

Stages in the Development of Mental Acts

P. Y. Gal'perin

EDITORS' INTRODUCTION

P. Y. Gal'perin began his professional career in 1928 as a neuropsychologist. In the late 1930's, he began to develop the general theory of cognitive development which is summarized in this chapter. After World War II, Gal'perin became a lecturer at the Department of Psychology of Moscow State University, where he is still working.

Although he is not so prolific as some of his colleagues, Gal'perin's theorizing has been influential in Soviet psychology, as the references to his work by various authors in this volume indicate. His work is attractive to Soviet psychologists because he has presented an outline of the sequence of ontogenetic changes which must occur for the development of conceptual behavior.

In recent years, his theory has been used as a basis for the development of programmed-learning materials. His colleague and student N. F. Talyzina is the head of the newly formed Department of Programmed Learning at Moscow State University. Since a great deal of emphasis is being placed on this new discipline by Soviet planners, Gal'perin's ideas will undoubtedly receive even wider attention in coming years.

OUR BASIC HYPOTHESIS is that the formation of mental acts passes through a series of stages. At each stage a given activity is carried out in a new form and undergoes changes in several directions. In order to analyze the numerous and interwoven changes which take place, we have classified them according to four properties (or parameters) of activity. Each of these distinct properties is characterized by an index, and it can thus be considered a separate parameter. The subject's activity, in turn, can be characterized by the four basic parameters.

The basic parameters of activity are: (1) the *level* at which it is fulfilled; (2) the amount of *generalization;* (3) the *completeness* of the operations accomplished; and (4) the degree of its *mastery*.

We distinguish five levels of an act: (1) familiarization with the task and its conditions; (2) an act based on material objects, or their material representations or signs; (3) an act based on audible speech without direct support from objects; (4) an act involving external speech to oneself (with output only of the result of each operation); and (5) an act using internal speech. These levels indicate the basic transformation of an act as it becomes mental.

The other three parameters indicate the quality of an act at each level: the level is higher, as (1) generalization, (2) abbreviation, and (3) mastery of the act are higher.

The Level at which a Mental Act Is Fulfilled

We shall concentrate on the question of the changes in the level of activity since this process constitutes the basis of the formation of mental operations by stages. Changes in activity connected with the remaining parameters will be noted only in connection with these levels.

Any learning of a new act, even if by "blind trial and error," assumes some familiarity with the task and begins with that assumption. However, since at that point there is still little practical familiarity with the task, one's idea of it will be no more than preliminary. As we have just noted earlier, this is the stage of the preliminary notion of the task. Investigations have demonstrated that making use of trial and error as a preliminary method of familiarization is very awkward (Gal'perin and Talyzina, 1957). Besides, it is not necessary since the task can be presented in a form such as a memorandum or outline drawing. Such "materialized" presentation makes the task much simpler. The act becomes easier to accomplish at a much earlier age, and the process of formation proceeds in a more organized fashion.

To master an act means not simply to remember it, but *independently to repeat it with new material and to obtain a new product from this material.* It does not mean to remember how an act was executed by someone else, but to execute it by oneself. Therefore, a model of activity and its results are not in themselves enough. It is also necessary to have a reference point in the new material which will permit correct execution of the whole task by going from one point to another. Such a reference point assumes analysis of the task and its objective conditions. The model of the end product of the act is divided into its component parts according to the order in which they should be executed. This division takes into account, first of all, the objective composition of the task and the ways to fulfill it. In the second place, it is critically important to take into account the subject's ability independently to fulfill each operation. Hence, the act is broken down into operations which are scaled to the subject, adapted to his personal knowledge, his abilities, and his habits. Then, when this reference point is transferred to new material, it will permit the subject to carry out the new act by means of separate operations.

Such a plan for a new act is the *orienting basis of an action.* Its formation is the critical event in the first stage of the formation of an action. The orienting basis is the most important aspect of the psychological mechanism of an action. It defines the outline of each operation and guarantees control of the action in the process of execution. The orienting basis of an action may be formed in different ways with varying degrees of success.

Types of Task Orientation

On the basis of our observations of physical, grammatical, and arithmetical tasks, we have postulated three basic ("pure") types of orientation to a task. *Each of these uniquely determines* the course and the result of training.

An obligatory part of the orienting basis of the first (trial-and-error) type consists in the formation of some kind of notion concerning what is to be attained and in what kind of circumstances it must be attained. This is a very nebulous "notion," and in many cases it is incomplete, not formed at all, or formed in such a way that the subject is unable to fulfill the task in its entirety and in the correct order. The subject blindly seeks the necessary conditions. If the task is arranged so that accidental solutions are possible, the subject gradually distinguishes and organizes the "correct" operation. Therefore, the formation of the action proceeds slowly by trial and error. The subject orients to the act according to the summary impression received from the conditions and sequence of the operations themselves, accompanied by the final "success." As a result, the accomplishment of an individual task may be accurate, but the act remains very unstable if there is a change in the conditions. Hence, successful solutions never reach 100 per cent, transfer to new tasks is insignificant, and the act is extremely limited with respect to the conditions and forms of its execution.

The orienting basis of the second type contains all the directions necessary to execute the new task. When these instructions are strictly observed, the learning proceeds, in principle, without errors and considerably faster than when the first type of orientation (trial and error) is used. The problem is broken into parts, and the act is also broken into separate operations. This increases the subject's ability to analyze new tasks. Consequently, the subject is able to reliably solve the problem, the responses are stable in the face of changed conditions, and there is significant transfer to new tasks. Transfer is conditioned by the similarity of elements in the previous and the new tasks as well as by the spontaneous transfer of methods of analysis.

Orientation of the third type is distinguished by the primacy of the kind of analysis of new models which permits isolation of their structure and the characteristics leading to correct recognition or repetition. First, the subject learns general methods of analysis at the same time that he learns acts connected with concrete phenomena. Thus, instruction with the third type of orientation is significantly more complex than the previous types. For the first few examples, this procedure requires the same or only slightly more time than is required with orientation of the second type. Subsequently, when the analysis is sufficiently assimilated, the subject can produce it independently with any phenomenon in the given area and correctly execute new tasks from the very beginning. If the instructions encompass a sufficiently large number of tasks, the tempo of instruction increases sharply after the first few tasks. In general, such instruction subsequently takes much less time than instruction of the second type, let alone of the first type.

Errors are insignificant in instruction with the third type of orientation. They occur primarily at the beginning of training and relate almost entirely to instruction in the analysis of the conditions for the new tasks. The newly formed act is very stable under changed conditions. Within the limits of a given field there is almost unlimited transfer. When the training is completed, each new task of the same type is correctly executed immediately. Further training only increases the degree of mastery, fluency, and confidence. From our description of these three basic learning processes, it is obvious that the types of learning described in the literature ("trial and error" or "immediate, errorless, insightful" learning) coincide with the learning processes of the first and second types. The important distinction between these processes is in type of orientation. Learning with orientation of the third type, as far as I know, has not been previously described.

The type of orientation to a task is noted at the first stage of the formation of a new act, that is, before the pupil has really begun to execute the task. Thus, the fate of a future act (specifically, mental act) is determined to a great extent at the very outset, when it seems that learning has not even begun.

Of course, there is no reason to think that this first encounter irreversibly determines the future of learning. Subsequent practice may correct a great deal, may provoke a reinterpretation of the act, and may change the type of orientation. However, it must be borne in mind that this will be *relearning,* which is always more difficult than initial learning. Relearning is hampered because for the most part we see only the poor results of our act and not the cause of the difficulty. Thus, practice may not have the desired effect if it leads to reinforcement of spontaneously developed, incorrect orientation.

No matter how persistent the orientation basis of an act is, it is never more than a system of instruction as to how to execute the new task. It is not the act itself; and without performing the activity it is impossible for the subject to learn.

We know that, at an early (preschool) age, learning a new act is dependent on the use of objects; that is, it begins in the *material form* of the act. Should we therefore begin the formation of a new mental act in the same way with older children? At first glance, this idea seems questionable, because it seems natural to think that accumulated experience eliminates the necessity of "beginning at the beginning" each time.

However, our investigations (Gal'perin and Talyzina, 1957) have shown that for fourth- to eleventh-grade schoolchildren a new act (and we emphasize new *act,* not just new *knowledge*) is successfully shaped only if we begin with its external form. But this external form is not the same as it was for the young children. Rather, it is now any form of schema: diagrams, outlines, drawings, models, or simply written notes. *All such representations accurately reproduce the characteristics and relationships of concrete things which are important for the act and permit the subject to accomplish the act by using these substitutes.* In all these cases we are speaking of an objective, materialized representation of thought properties and the relationship between things. The objective schema is a materialization of these properties and relationships. Therefore, we use the term *materialized* for an activity involving such schemata, reserving the term *material* for activity which actually manipulates objects.

The materialized form of an action is functionally equivalent to material activity and retains its basic virtues. However, in many cases the materialized form is much more convenient and accessible. When the object of activity transcends the limits of direct perception, the materialized form generally offers the only possibility for execution of the action since it is impossible to work with the objects. Thus, materialization expands the ability to retain the most important conditions for systematic formation of new mental activity, beginning with its psychologically primary (external material) form.

This capacity must be exploited in every way possible. True, it is not always necessary or possible to learn a new action of a higher order according to the original process, but in order to master the action, it is always necessary to proceed from its psychologically initial, materialized form. This is an obligatory precondition to full-valued mental activity. In essence, the requirement is simple: to take into account not only the objective sequence of knowledge, but also the psychological sequence of stages of mastery beginning with the material level and ending in mental activity.

At the present time we do not have any experimental data which indicate the possibility of forming a mental act directly in the mind. We do not deny such a possibility, but our analysis of the process leads us to believe that each new mental act must be formed from the beginning as something external, material, or materialized.

Apparent deviations from this rule arise from several misconceptions. First, the stages in the formation of mental action are not taken into account by the teacher, who is only interested in the end results of what he wants to teach, the scientific concept of the act. Consequently, he is likely to give too little attention to the basic processes involved. Secondly, materialized action (e.g., calculation on paper) is usually viewed as mental action, since the execution of the action "on paper" is not viewed in terms of what it represents to the pupil, but for what it means to the teacher (the expression or verification of a mental act).

A significant role in this apparent deviation from the normal sequence is played by the still inadequate distinction between new knowledge and new mental acts. In this connection, we have experimentally demonstrated (Talyzina, 1957) that new knowledge, when it does not require a new mental act, may be assimilated directly at the level of existing mental acts, that is, directly "in the mind." Another source of the idea that it is possible to assimilate a new action directly in the mind is an inadequate distinction between "understanding" the new act and mastering it. "Understanding" means the ability to trace mentally the relationships in the model or the conditions of the task. This kind of orientation always occurs with the aid of existing mental acts, which are directly mental and in this sense "in the mind." But mastery of a new act is something beyond mere understanding. Mastery cannot be successful without the use of this "understanding" to execute the act with new material, if not concretely, at least "on paper" (i.e., in its materialized form).

What can higher mental development change in this sequence of mastering an act? It makes it possible to discern immediately the fundamental relations and use them in an abstract form. These relations constitute an important part of the orienting basis of the act, but the problem is to use this basis in order to master the act itself. Such mastery occurs only in the course of the act, and it is clear that initially it is most convenient to carry out the act in its materialized form.

As far as we know, only the materialized form of an act can guarantee systematic control of the formation of a full-valued act. Therefore, the first task in learning a new act is to find the initial material or materialized form of the given act and to establish its contents precisely. This is by no means easy. The initial material forms of an action may bear little or no external similarity to their conceptual forms. The psychologist must search for these initial forms of an act, which is not only very difficult but may actually fall outside his usual field of competence.

Once the initial form of a new act is established, we meet with new difficulties. Not only the material but even the more abstractly presented, materialized objects have many properties which are not essential to the given act. In order to distinguish the necessary from the unnecessary properties these abstract objects must also be the subject of instruction, as a result of which the act itself comes gradually to change the model of the act and, consequently, the act becomes developed and generalized.

To develop the act means to point out the composition and sequences of all of its component operations and their correspondence to the changes in the material. As has already been noted, this requires breaking the action down into operations of a magnitude which the pupil can independently trace and subsequently execute. For example, in the explanation of addition, we first form individual items from the objects, then we put them together into one general group, and, finally, we count the items one at a time. The analysis of the development of an action is the first requirement for demonstrating and elucidating its objective logic.

The Generalization of Mental Acts

The second requirement is generalization. To generalize an act means to distinguish from among the many diverse properties of an object those properties which are necessary for the fulfillment of the act. Investigations (Patina, 1957) have convincingly shown that generalization is most successful when it occurs as early and as extensively as possible with the most diversified material possible (i.e., when all the cues except the distinguishing ones are extremely varied). Under such conditions the child does not form associations between the action and its nonessential properties.

Only as the result of the simultaneous development and generalization of an act does its true content become clear to the pupil. Thereafter, it should be mastered to the point of correct and fluent (but not automatic) execution. When this is achieved, the reverse process—sequential abbreviation of the act—can begin. Constantly repeated operations whose results are known beforehand are no longer executed. The pupil begins with the results and moves directly to the next operation. For example, addition actually means combining several items into one group. Not even a great mathematician can do addition without assuming this combination. The mathematician assumes the results of combination without even thinking, but children at the very outset of training actually do it, since for them, without actual combination there is no addition. However, they learn quickly that the results of the operation are always one and the same: the formation of a general group that one may then simply assume. Therefore, physical addition (combination) is the first thing excluded from arithmetical "addition."

The Abbreviation of Mental Acts

Frequently, abbreviation occurs "by itself" and in an uncontrolled manner. This is often undesirable, because the student does not realize why it is possible to pass to the next operation without executing the previous, objectively necessary operation. In practical terms abbreviation always reinforces itself, since the action can be performed more quickly and, "in any case," the result is correct. For the most part, spontaneous abbreviation occurs without understanding of the underlying principle and is thus limited to specific cases. Thus, in each new situation it is necessary to guess all over again. The way in which the abbreviation occurred as well as the abbreviated contents are easily forgotten. The return to the developed action becomes impossible, and the pupil can only execute the abbreviated action mechanically, illogically, and without comprehension. On the other hand, conscious execution of abbreviation means to distinguish its objective basis to form a notion (if not a concept) of a "new reality" which is retained side by side with the objective contents of the action and which permits the pupil to form an orienting movement based on the objective associations.

Belov (1956) showed the great importance of consciously developing simple abbreviations. Having mastered the principle of abbreviation in model form, the child easily transfers it to a far more complex and conceptually important level. If conscious abbreviation is not established early, its development later, in more complex situations, is excessively difficult. Abbreviation in easy situations often occurs spontaneously in accordance with the obvious logic of the things themselves. But we emphasize that only *conscious* mastery of the abbreviation process can guarantee extensive transfer and the development of new action, a necessity in very difficult conditions. Only conscious development of abbreviation guarantees understanding of the connections between the operations he executes.

This connection not only permits the pupil to recover the full content of a mental act when he needs to, but also enables the student to keep the abbreviated contents "in mind" during the execution of the action. We do not really know what it means "to have something in mind," but that such a process exists is an indisputable fact of the greatest significance. To deny it because of our lack of understanding would be childish rigorism. Furthermore, it is important to emphasize that, although abbreviated operations are not actually executed, they nonetheless participate in actions in a very tangible manner. This becomes apparent when compared with action which is executed without any real understanding ("according to a formula").

The presence of a "presumed," but unmanifest, content of an act indicates that the act is not only not limited by its actual operations, but that even the orienting, really psychological part of an act is not limited by the process of its externally manifested orientation. The psychological mechanism includes the entire system of previous forms and variations of the given act which are no longer directly executed, but which one "has in mind." This guarantees that the act will retain its objective logic even in its abbreviated form which *appears* to be illogical.

The abbreviation of an operation and its transfer to the position of a "provisionally performed" operation does not mean the transition of this operation to the mental plane. On the mental plane the abbreviated operations are only presumed, not executed. The general rule is that the act as a whole remains at that level which involves elements absolutely necessary for execution of the act. As long as the execution demands the slightest material support, the act will linger at the material (or materialized) level. When written calculation or analysis is necessary, not for purposes of consolidation or communication but to enable completion of the act, the action is not yet a mental one.

Once the act has attained the highest material or materialized level (the greatest generalization, abbreviation, and mastery), it is necessary to tear the action away from its previous material support. How is this done and in what form should it be transferred?

Such a transfer may occur "by itself." However, this is very rare: most acts without direct material support must be specially taught. Systematic training of the older preschool children takes the following form. For example, in the teaching of addition, the child is presented with two small groups of objects, asked to count them and then, turning away (either by closing the eyes or by covering the objects), is asked to count how many of each there were. If the child makes errors, he repeats the process with new quantities until he begins to execute the task in response to spoken numbers without preliminary physical demonstration with the objects. The child's behavior and his answers to questions indicate that, in the beginning, when working without objects, the child tries to visualize them and to count objects in his imagination as he earlier counted the material objects. It seems that we are dealing here with transfer of an act to the plane of visual imagery, which amounts to a direct transition to the mental plane.

In the beginning this was our view, too. But more careful examination of this transfer and its conditions convinced us that the process is by no means so direct. Only in a very few children are the representations clear and stable enough to serve as the hoped-for object of mental action and even then they are suitable only for small numbers. If the number of objects is greater than five, they must find better representations. Otherwise, the "attachment" to the representations begins seriously to limit the child's capabilities. Actually, for the majority of children, these representations turn out to be a short episode. The images are themselves an auxiliary means for the execution of verbal operations, to which the children quickly transfer. Characteristically, this process is viewed in the reverse order not only by the child, but by the experimenter. It is usually speech that appears to be the auxiliary means.

Investigations have shown that, in the presentation of even the simplest mathematical problems, good results can be achieved only with preliminary and sufficiently verbal development at the stage of a material act. An act accompanied by audible speech is retained much longer than a so-called ideational act (which is usually executed with the aid of that very same audible speech). Without audible speech the young child cannot act. Even restricting the child to a whisper or to voiceless lip movements significantly hinders and even precludes the act. The effects of these procedures clearly differentiate stages in the progress toward an act "to oneself." This all seems to indicate that the chief content of the new stage which follows the stage of material action is "action in audible speech" (without the immediate support of objects).

This new plane cannot yet be called mental, for in fact the child is still unable to act in his mind. The formation of such an ability occurs in the following stage. To adult thought, accustomed to things and processes which are manifested either materially or mentally, the clear significance of audible speech seems strange. It is stranger still because we are accustomed to thinking by means of speech and not about it or of what it communicates, that is, of objects and material processes. Nevertheless, the existence and special role of an independent plane of audible speech follows from the existence of language, which embodies objectively existing social consciousness. The psychological significance of this special plane is emphasized by cases in which it seems to be missing. This occurs primarily in children for whom action through representation becomes a stable form for behavior. They execute an action silently, but are completely incapable of executing it aloud. One might think that they have spontaneously transferred from action with objects to action in the mind. But this mental action is highly imperfect (Golomshtok, 1957). It is limited to very small quantities, and in most cases the action is incorrectly executed. Solutions are characteristically only approximate ones, vacillations around the correct answer, and the operation is always insecure and unstable (the child may suddenly give a second answer, accidentally substituting an incorrect answer for the correct one). These children consistently showed a very strong tendency to turn to the objects and often attempted to compensate for their absence with some kind of movement. In a word, their mental action was always very incomplete. To correct this situation we had to return to the stage of the objective act and, using it as a foundation, work out its verbal accompaniment. Only then was it possible for the child to free himself from the objects, cautiously formulating the act in audible speech.

Even in those cases in which there is an act in terms of concepts without the stage of audible speech, the act is very limited and still dependent on some kind of spontaneous verbal process. It is very unlikely that speech can be completely absent. Furthermore, it seems that children who appeared to skip the stage of audible speech were poor verbalizers at the level of work with material objects. Teachers and educators do not usually insist on verbalization of an action, because they consider it an encumbrance in class work. Children for whom speech is an additional difficulty naturally avoid it. The negative consequences of this omission are easily overlooked, since even poor speech may be sufficient for the initial uncomplicated tasks.

Even in those cases where, initially, it seems that verbal analysis is unnecessary, its necessity becomes apparent with further inspection. In fact, certain acts are successfully transferred to the mental plane without special verbal analysis. These are acts whose verbal formulations were very simple and consistent from the very beginning. The direct transfer of such acts to the internal plane, without special development of the stage of "audible speech without objects," occurred more slowly and with more difficulty in our experiments than when instruction did not skip that stage (Gal'perin and Talyzina, 1957). Therefore, it is very likely that in cases of direct transfer the verbal formula of an action occurred simultaneously with the formation of the material action and, consequently, did not require a separate stage.

To this must be added certain general considerations and experimental data which indicate that ideas cannot be considered as a separate mental plane of an act isolated from the plane of perception or from the support of speech or language, which embody an objective system of social ideas. Without the aid of speech, sensory models of past experience emerge in perception either as dreams or hallucinations, that is, as analogues of perception. It is not an exaggeration to say that, without the aid of speech, sensory phenomena can neither be voluntarily reproduced nor distinguished by the subject from the plane of perception. Freedom from the direct support of objects demands a new kind of external support, namely, one which can be transferred to the mental plane. Only speech fits this description. It follows, then, that speech itself must become the full-valued representation of the act and the conditions of its occurrence.

Consider the following facts: a high degree of generalization is achieved even at the level of material action; actions, signified by words and distinguished from objects, all convert to the abstract; the abstract is very inconvenient (strictly speaking, impossible) to represent, but easy and convenient to use in terms of verbal designations; children (unless retarded) very quickly begin to talk about an action without making an effort to picture it. Taking all these facts into consideration, inevitably we come to the conclusion that the plane of audible speech (without reliance on objects or their material images) is the third stage of a mental action. Once again we emphasize that an action in audible speech is not material or materialized, nor is it yet a mental action, since the pupil is not yet able to perform it silently "in his mind."

As has been stated, the audible-speech stage is not always discernible as an independent period of instruction and may be combined in time with the stage of material action. But the point is not one of external separation or union of stages. The important thing is the work which must be executed and the results which must be achieved. The task is to give the child's speech a new function and then to use this new function to expand the potentialities of an action (e.g., the potential for fulfilling an action without material objects or their materialized substitutes).

The Role of Audible Speech in Forming Mental Acts

In the first and second stages, speech is primarily an indicator of the phenomena which reveal themselves spontaneously in perception. The pupil's basic task is to note these phenomena and master them. Then speech becomes the vehicle for the entire process, that is, both the objects of the action and the action itself. In the early stages, verbal precision was not so important since that which had to be communicated was before one's very eyes. In the third stage, however, language emerges as a special, unique reality upon which the action relies. This reality has its own firm laws, whose basic requirement is communication.

The demands and conditions of this new reality now become the primary objective of the student's behavior. He must execute the action verbally so that it is comprehensible not only to himself but to others as well. The primary objective of his consciousness is no longer the material content of the action, but its verbal expression. Social understanding of the action becomes the direct objective of his mastery.

The formation of this new linguistic form of action occurs in the following way: the experimenter requires the performance of an action aloud and in a form which correctly represents its objective content. Verbal acts begin to function to control first another person and later the child himself. He begins to relate to his speech act as the teacher relates to it and for the first time forms a personal awareness of this action.

Verbal acts follow the laws of language and are simultaneously a reflection of material acts. To this end the material (materialized) act unfolds anew and, step by step, is transferred to the verbal plane. Definite terms and turns of speech are related to definite elements and operations of the course of the material act. This is a rather complicated process during which speech changes from an accompaniment of material action to an independent plane of action; a new context for the action is created and the child learns to use this new tool.

Because of the control and the instructions of the experimenter, the child is obliged to orient himself not only to the material content of the act but to its verbal expression. He must distinguish and compare these two aspects of the situation. This necessity gives rise to two typical deviations from correct execution. First, the verbal formula may become fixated prematurely. Since the subject's orientation always relies on more consistent, stable cues, constancy of the verbal formula leads to orientation to form without sufficient account of the material content. "Verbal," "formal" knowledge is the result. The second deviation occurs if the student is occupied only with the objective content of the action and does not work out its representation in speech. The end product is the ability to solve problems without the ability to reason about them. This restricts the potentials of an action to the framework of those tasks whose contents can be observed on the visual plane.

This second deviation points up the fact that the goal of training in verbal action is not only to eliminate the need for manipulating objects. Manipulation is not as burdensome as it appears at first glance. Various devices which are quite convenient and have existed for a long time (e.g., the abacus, counting beads, strings with small knots, etc.) sufficiently reduce the unwieldiness of objects. The great virtue of verbal action is not that it breaks away from direct contact with objects, but that, of necessity, it leads to the formation of a new object of action, namely, abstraction. Abstractions simplify an act to an extraordinary degree, liberating it from changes in the material. By creating an unchanging object, abstractions provide for high stereotypy of action and consequently for rapid automatization. Finally, abstractions are the most important condition (but only a condition!) for the formation of concepts, which eliminate the restrictions that inevitably accompany sensory material.

The experiments of Davydov (1957) and Nepomnyashchaya (1956) on early arithmetical concepts established that neither generalization by itself nor generalization with abstraction is adequate for the formation of a concept. While they both permit a transition from concrete things to abstract elements, the latter remain in a set which does not reveal their simple essence (in this case, volume, number). The name "number" is only an indicator of all the elements of a set taken separately. Moreover, the formation of a concept means the appearance of that kind of new characteristic as the new mode of mental action, which will greatly expand its potential.

Furthermore, formation of this new mode demands a new return to the material objects (or their materialized representations) and repeated activity with them as abstract entities. Repeated practice is necessary to effect new abbreviations of the action and spontaneous transfer from these entities to the general result of the action. When the process is spontaneous such abbreviation does not always occur and, equally important, is not always in the fullest and best form. The result is that the transfer of action to the audible-speech plane is not always accompanied by the formation of concepts.

However, the substitution of abstract objects for sensory material has such great advantages that the energy spent on translating action to the verbal plane is justified. To the extent that earlier generalization of the objects and operations of an act occurred, the transfer to the verbal plane means a break with the direct presence of things and the inevitable formation of abstractions. With generalization from the concrete content of objects, the characteristics and properties essential for the act are discerned when such generalization occurs. When the act is transferred to the verbal plane, only the traits and characteristics of objects which are reinforced by separate words are selected as the meanings of the words. It is in the *absence* of the things themselves that they acquire abstract meaning.

Abstractions are achieved only as a result of speech and are retained only in speech. They exist solely in the meanings of words. The child is able to deal with abstract material only because of the audiomotor basis of these word meanings. In the beginning the child is unable to think of abstract content but then he subsequently comes to express abstraction in speech. The illusion of such a capacity appears, as we shall see, only in the next stages of the formation of mental action. Because words have a material basis and in this sense are material things (not *only* material, but *also* material), the child can act with them as he does with any material object. Speech is the only thing in our environment which can restore the pure, abstract content of an action in consciousness, and can check, correct, or change this content in a word. A word is the only means of voluntary activity in this abstract form.

We must emphasize that transferring an act to the verbal plane means not only expressing the act in speech, but above all verbally executing a material act; that is, it not only means communicating about the action, but it is an act in a new, verbal form. Speech is a form of material act, not simply communication about a material action.

Like every new form, an act in audible speech is at first formulated in extended ("unfolded") form, and then passes through a series of changes in the basic parameters. First, the generalization of the verbal form itself must be made secure. Speech changes, adapting itself to the given circumstances of the task and to the possibility of expressing the action both in "one's own words" and strictly according to a formula. Then the action must undergo several sequential abbreviations. These abbreviations usually occur more easily than they did on the previous level; frequently, this occurs spontaneously. However, even these abbreviations must be consciously "worked out" (i.e., discovered by virtue of their objective bases and then adequately mastered). Only then can they become the foundation for the transfer of an act to the mental plane—the plane of individual cognition, distinct from the plane of the things but simultaneously correlated with it.

The transfer to action "in the mind" and the conditions which must be met in order to ensure this transfer are so varied that we must distinguish two subsequent stages, which occur one after the other, without a sharp break between them.

Externalized Speech and the Formation of Mental Acts

The first of these (the fourth in the total sequence of stages) begins with the transfer of the audible-verbal action to the internal plane and ends with the soundless utterance of the action entirely in the mind. This would seem to be simply "speech minus sound." In fact, it requires a significant reconstruction of speech. "In the mind" the audible form of speech becomes a representation, the audible image of the word. This image is more stable than visual representation because it retains the verbal articulation and kinesthetic pattern on which it is based. But the articulation must change; now it produces only the image of audible speech, not audible speech itself.

As always, the changed conditions of the act require a new familiarization with the external requirements so that the development of the audible-speech plane can be repeated at the mental level. Hence, the first form of mental act is clearly developed as *external speech to oneself*. Insofar as the articulation mechanism of this speech is somewhat different from audible speech, it requires mastery anew. This clearly occurs in children, and in adults, when they first learn to read to themselves. But the auditory form of this speech to oneself and its material contents are in no way different from its audible-speech form. Hence, as soon as external speech to oneself is sufficiently mastered, all the achievements of the previous period (generalization and abbreviation) are spontaneously transferred to the new level and speech to oneself quickly passes to its highest form, that of internal speech.

At first we control action in external speech to oneself by forcing the student to execute it only in separate operations. Naturally, during this period the action cannot be abbreviated. But when the pupil begins to execute all the operations without error and so quickly that he can give the correct answer as soon as he receives the proper information, we remove our control of each step and pass to control of the final result. The final and fifth stage of formation of a mental operation begins at that moment.

Retention of the total verbal formula is absolutely necessary in audible speech (directed to another) or in external speech to oneself (directed to oneself as well as to another). Later, when these forms have been mastered, this is no longer necessary. At this point the verbal formula itself is quickly abbreviated. Only the general formula containing an indication of the original data, the action taken with respect to these data, and the result remain. Only an insignificant fragment of all the intermediate operations of the material action is retained in consciousness. Enough remains in consciousness for the purpose of identifying words when they are reproduced. External speech (although it is produced to oneself) begins to turn into real internal speech.

Investigation of speech in the last stage of the formation of mental activity (Gal'perin, 1957b) leads to the conclusion that speech fragments which seem strange to the observer are nothing more than particles of external speech to oneself in the process of becoming internal speech or in the process of reverse movement from essentially internal speech to external. These fragments characteristically appear when it is necessary to arrest the automatic flow of thought and once again to discern some part of the objective content of the action in order to adapt it to the individual conditions of the task.

Inner speech in the true sense of the word is not characterized by the fragmentary verbal component, but by the automatic flow of abbreviated forms. This flow is not so much complete and exact as simply aroused. It is reflected in consciousness only by the undefined "feeling" about the direction in which the process is moving, and by its "correctness" (agreement or disagreement with a model). If internal speech is formed consciously to some degree, this abbreviated content appears in the form of the phenomenon of "having in mind." If it is formed in an uncontrolled manner, the action in internal speech becomes an "imageless thought." The "feeling," which is evidence of the abbreviated content of verbal activity, serves as a control over the developing dynamic stereotoype, as Pavlov correctly and perceptively noted.[1] But true internal speech is internalized to such an extent that only the most subtle introspection can capture even a fleeting shadow of it. Only the consistent logic of the formation of a mental action permits elucidation of the process of its formation, its specific function, and its characteristic form "in consciousness."

Introspection and Thought

In the last stage of the formation of a mental act in inner speech, the material audiomotor component departs from consciousness. Consequently the two parts of an action, operative and control, merge and are transformed into different but indivisible sides of the same phenomenon: one is

1. *Editors' note:* "Dynamic stereotype" is a Pavlovian term which originated in classical conditioning experiments when a response was conditioned to a particular sequence of stimuli.

the objective content of the action (nonpsychological) and the other is the act of thought about this objective content (essentially psychological but without content). In introspection, thought exists only in this form; when the act has not yet reached the plane of internal speech, it presents itself as action, not as thought. The problem is that the process which in reality links these various stages is beyond the bounds of introspection. If the investigation of thought (the final form of mental activity) is limited to introspection, the misunderstandings concerning its nature which have occurred repeatedly in the history of philosophy and psychology are inevitable. Three such misunderstandings warrant a short discussion.

The first misunderstanding is that when thought is examined "empirically" as a phenomenon of internal experience, hence as something tangible and ready-made, we will find nothing in it except the consciousness or feeling of its ideational activity. Thought is so empty of content that the representatives of classical associationism could properly demand: "Either show the content of this activity or acknowledge that it coincides with the fact of cognition of certain material content and the appearance of this content in consciousness" (James Mill).

The second misunderstanding consists in the fact that, in relation to thought as subjectively revealed in such empty form, verbal expression seems to be something external and optional, a sort of conventional verbal shell. This is not surprising, since subsequent verbal communication is no longer the same speech whose abbreviation is the idea we observe, but a different speech whose aid we invoke in order to communicate about a thought as an external object. When we try to renew the speech which served as a basis for the formation of the thought, speech emerges not as thought but as verbal meanings of the material content of the action. Thought as a psychological phenomenon disappears and we are left with linguistic reality. The genetic link between speech and thought can be discovered only in the process of the formation of a mental action. Outside of the actual process of the transformation of speech into thought, their similarities only hinder comprehension of their actual bond.

The third misunderstanding is that the material content of an action (e.g., the mathematical content of arithmetic calculations) is believed to be an action in the true sense of the word, independent of whoever executes it. But the mechanisms of its execution are attributed to separate processes (abilities and habits) which are linked with the action but are said to be different from it. Abilities and habits are viewed not as characteristics of the subject's action, but as special, truly psychological processes. Between habits and abilities on the one hand, and the act viewed as an objective process on the other, there is a sharp demarcation. Psychologically, this position destroys abilities and habits, which represent the psychological content of an act, and bars the path to objective study of psychological phenomena, since it is precisely the act of the subject in conjunction with his orientation and performance which is the key to their study.

All of these misunderstandings are explained by the uncontrolled and, consequently, irreversible transformation of verbal forms of material action into internal speech. When the results of this transformation are regarded as primary data (as they appear in introspection) we encounter the well-known pseudoproblems of "pure thought" and its expression in speech, the individuality of psychic phenomena as compared to the material, the relationship among psychic phenomena, and so forth. This follows from the notion of psychological reality as only that which is found in introspection, that is, the subjective-idealistic comprehension of the subject of psychology, the conviction that only the "phenomena of cognition" are the true and full content of psychic phenomena. But introspection cannot reveal the true content of all that underlies mental action. Only objective genetic investigation can establish this content and provide understanding of why a mental act is open to introspection in one form or another. Only by tracing the process of formation of a mental act can one reveal this hidden psychological process and link it with the phenomena of cognition and behavior.

Explanation of the true content of a mental act—not only the practical ability to execute material action in the mind, but the lawful transformation of material action to thought about the action—is the first step toward a solution of the problem that was posed initially, the problem of the concrete content of mental activity.

The Formation of Images

The second step in understanding the content of mental processes is to clarify the psychological mechanism of images. The change from mental acts to images is a difficult task, because images are, in a sense, directly opposed to actions; an act is a process, while an image is a static entity in which the object and the act meet. Images are formed on the basis of those very acts which are then reflected in these images. The question then amounts to asking how an image is formed as a product of an act with objects.

The process of forming sensory and abstract images, of concepts, was studied experimentally using classroom concepts and generalized perceptual images (Gal'perin and Talyzina, 1957; Gal'perin, 1957b). The basic traits of this process stand out clearly in the formation of concepts, which arise initially as images. For this purpose, we studied the learning of geometric concepts.

The main vehicle of concept formation for children in our society is classroom training. In such teaching, the content of a new concept is usually directly communicated. Nonetheless, the concept as an integral image does not arise immediately. It is well known that mastery and automatization of a process using a concept lead to the point where the concept seems to be directly perceived in material. Familiarizing himself with the material, the student "sees" that "this is vertical" or "perpendicular," or, on the contrary, "does not see" it. But the process of forming such a "perception" and its mechanism has not hitherto been studied.

Because we wanted to study the formation of concepts from their beginning in acts on the basis of which, according to our assumptions, concepts are formed, it was especially important that we clarify the following questions: (1) What is the basic task which leads to the formation of a concept as an image? (2) What is the concrete content of an act in its application to a concept (naming these acts does not reveal their true content)? (3) What alterations of these acts are necessary in order that the separate signs of the concept shall be converted into an image in which its entire content can immediately be discovered? Previous observations indicated that all this occurs, but did not reveal the conditions and laws of the process.

We analyzed the psychological situation at the beginning of the training of a new concept and tried to clarify the process which underlies each application of the concept. We concluded that the first necessary act in the utilization of a new concept is to recognize the concrete phenomena which are relevant to it, the so-called "underpinnings of concepts." We believe that this recognition underlies the formation of many classroom concepts. The act of recognition must also be formed, so we analyzed its step-by-step development. Using the results of this analysis, we were able to control the entire process and were also able to control both the changes in the act itself and the phenomena to which it gave rise. The general outline of our experiments was as follows.

First, we explained to the subject, in detail, the conditions which constitute the phenomenon (concept), its characteristic cues, how and in what order it was necessary to look for these cues in the material, and how to evaluate the results of this research. The properties and examples or signs of the concept (phenomenon) were briefly written in a column and numbered on a card. This was the "materialization" of these properties and signs, the most important condition for correct organization of the new act in its early stages.

Using this "educational card," the subject analyzed the material aloud step by step, established the presence or absence of each sign and then drew a general conclusion: the given phenomenon does or does not fit the concept in question. This was the stage of materialized action, which permitted the subject to strictly maintain the outlined organization, accurately control its execution, and quickly master it.

Several kinds of tasks of varying difficulty were presented in the material. The order of their presentation was outlined beforehand and represented the best possible differentiation of the essential traits. Therefore, the object of the action and the action itself were quickly generalized. This further helped the discrimination of the constant components. The contents of the "educational card" were quickly memorized (without overlearning) and soon the subject no longer had to look at it. Then the card was taken away and the subject was asked to continue, using the same order, and to name the contents of each line aloud. This was action on the plane of "audible speech without objects."

When this action was quickly and correctly executed, the method was changed again. The teacher simply said the number of the sign as it appeared on the card. The subject had to remember it silently, silently apply it to the material, and say aloud whether or not it was applicable. Finally, a general conclusion was made on the basis of the results of the separate operations. This procedure eliminated both a premature curtailing of the action and its distortion when it was transferred to the mental plane. It permitted the student to retain control of the act, operation by operation, even when he executed it to himself.

Once this form of the act was quickly and correctly executed, the method was once again changed: we warned the subject to execute the act entirely by himself without any instructions from the teacher and to inform the teacher only of the final result. In this way we eliminated the division of the act into separate operations, thus pointing the way to unified and abbreviated execution of the task to be followed by automatization. This occurred quickly, and the mental act passed to the concluding stage.

Then the process of recognition acquired the following form: having acquainted himself with the material, the subject encountered some aspect of it and, without analyzing it, immediately recognized the presence or absence of a sought-for phenomenon (a concrete number, perpendicular, vertical, definite structure, etc.). Initially the concept spontaneously appeared before him in its concrete incarnation, as it were. Only afterward would the subject methodically analyze the object in order to verify its nature for himself or for the teacher.

How did this "spontaneous perception" occur? At the end of instruction, the act—now generalized, transferred to the ideational plane, abbreviated to a "formula," and automatized—became a mechanism which went to work as soon as the subject encountered an aspect of the material which had become a "rote stimulus" as a result of training. This mechanism worked until the subject began the analysis. It worked automatically and unconsciously so that the subject was aware only of the final product, which appeared immediately. The characteristic signs of the concept appeared simultaneously as characteristics of the actual object and therefore as a single unit.

An analogous stage-by-stage formation of mental operations and concepts can be illustrated in the field of elementary arithmetic. The description is given without taking into account methodological requirements *per se*.

To begin with, the instruction in arithmetic starts with a demonstration of the significance of measurement in various walks of life, and with a suggestion that the child measure different objects. For this purpose a measure is necessary—and so we explain the basis for its selection. Next, we carefully differentiate the notion of its quality—its parameter—and its dimensions, emphasizing that any measure may contain smaller measures, so that the one chosen by us may itself be part of a still larger measure.

Problem

I. We introduce the concept of a unit (as "that which is equal to its measure") and the numbers 2, 0, 3 (according to the intuitive rule $n + 1$); after these numbers have been learned, we turn to mastering the concept of this rule itself. We construct Figure 7–1. We call this diagram "stairs" and, with

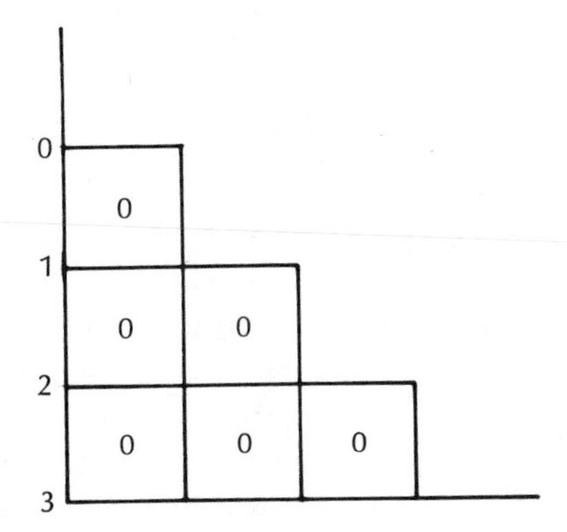

Figure 7–1.

its help, demonstrate that each number (strictly speaking, its set) is larger by one element than the number which precedes it, and by one element smaller than the number which follows it. For the sake of simplicity this rule is divided in two parts: (1) each following number—larger by 1; (2) each preceding number—smaller by 1.

Both the "stairs" and the rules are recorded on a card: the former on the left, the latter on the right; together they form the "orienting base for action." Making use of such a card, the child (S) on instructions from the experimenter (E) constructs various "numbers" (sets): E points to a pile of objects whose number far exceeds the arithmetical knowledge of S and asks S without counting this group (this is n), to name the following "number." S consults the card, selects from the two rules the one that is appropriate for this case (the "following") and, following the rule, adds another element to this group; or, if the instruction is to name the preceding "number," subtracts one element from the group. This is materialized action.

Shortly thereafter *S* ceases to consult the card, which is at first turned over and then removed altogether. Having received his instruction, *S* begins to reason aloud: "The next number? Well, then we have to add one piece," etc. This is a vocalized form of action. When this action begins to occur rapidly and without error, *E* instructs *S* to "solve the problems silently," reporting only the result. This stage represents action at the intellectual level.

Next we pass to the study of numbers higher than "3." *S* constructs each of them on his own, according to the rule $n + 1$. *E* supplies their names and notation, whereupon the numbers are studied by means of various additions and subtractions within the boundaries of the particular number.

Problem

II. The natural numbers from 11 to 20 are expressed directly by means of numerals belonging to two adjacent categories: this is done by dividing a sheet of paper with a vertical line with the agreement that the right side be reserved for "small units" (in order to distinguish the name of this category from the name of the entire class of units), and the left side for whole tens. Thus one category of ten numerals will be symbolized by the numeral "1," with the difference that this time it will be placed in another category, to the left of the center line. This is a new, large measure containing 10 small measures or small units: as soon as 10 small measures or units are accumulated, they are united into one large unit (a rubber band is put around 10 matches), the numeral "1" being placed to the left of the line to represent it.

Next comes the mastering of numbering: *E* names a number belonging to the second ten, and *S* lays it out (with the help of ready-made numerals), or, conversely, *E* lays out some number from the second ten, and *S* reads it. Then it is explained how numbers greater than 20 should be read, how they differ from the names of numbers belonging to the second ten; this is followed by the notation and reading of all numbers, including 99. This, of course, presents no great difficulty.

Having mastered the numbering, the next step is the addition and subtraction within the framework of 99. The operations are carried out on the same sheet of paper, "by column": underneath the first number the second one is laid out, on the side to the left—the sign of operation; beneath the second number a line is placed in the form of a piece of wire, and below that is put down whatever "comes out" in each category, from right to left. The word "category" is introduced unobtrusively, in passing; it is used persistently while demonstrating that only those operations are repeated in each category that are already familiar from the program related to the first category of ten numerals.

The novel elements are addition and subtraction transcending the number 10. We demonstrate and explain in detail the rule "before and after 10" as follows: to add up to ten, then to carry over this ten into the next (on the left) category, the rest of the "small units" remaining in the previous category; or to subtract at first all the "small units," and should they not suffice—one ten is to be borrowed; the number of tens will become less by one, the remainder of the "small units" to be recorded in their category. All kinds of additions and subtractions up to 99 follow, accompanied at first by a complete laying out and voicing of all the components—the stage of materialized action; then this is done with voicing only and without recording the result; next—without recording the second number; and finally, without recording the first number—vocalized throughout. In transition to the mental plane the problems to be solved are again recorded, but the operations are carried out mentally, only the results of operations in each category and the end result being voiced.

After the operations of addition and subtraction across the boundaries of categories have been mastered, the categories have to be expanded: 10 within the second category yields a still larger measure—a new unit; it is placed in a new, third category which is separated by a vertical line to the left of the tens. Then it is demonstrated that this new measure is equal to 10 tens or 100 "small units" and is therefore called a "hundred"; in the form of categories it is represented as "1/0/0" and written as "100."

By this method the next stage to be mastered is numbering up to 999, followed by addition and subtraction of three-digit numbers in the form of a column and with a record by categories on a card. As with 100, so later the number 1,000 is introduced; and the children are shown that in this way it is possible to increase numbers (to the left) to infinity. To facilitate their understanding it is done as follows: here is the class of single units, and here we have the beginning of the class of thousands. Each class will contain single units, tens, and hundreds. But in the first class this will be ones, tens, and hundreds of "small units"; in the second class—ones, tens, and hundreds of thousands (we draw dividing lines: gray between categories; red between classes); in the third class we now have millions—ones, tens, and hundreds of millions; and in the fourth class, billions—singles, tens, and hundreds of billions. The table now looks like the following:

Billions			Millions			Thousands			Single Units		
100	10	1	100	10	1	100	10	1	100	10	1

The table, the size of a sheet of paper placed horizontally, is prepared beforehand, and each pupil is given one. He also has small ready-made numerals. Again, first to be learned is the numbering, followed by addition and subtraction; but this time it is done within the framework of hundreds of billions.

When the children begin to orient themselves with ease in regard to classes, we remove the designation of categories but still retain the lines separating them; the children continue to name categories. Some time later those lines too are removed—the previous grid is replaced by a new one containing only the divisions between classes, their names, and blank spaces which formerly contained the designations of categories. When under these conditions the operation becomes faultless and rapid, the legend (and only the legend) for classes is removed. Each change of this kind produces at first a slowing down of an operation, and a more distinct vocalization; but as learning progresses both orientation and performance are reduced in time, the operation occurring with ever increasing smoothness and rapidity.

After the operations on the basis of such a "blind" grid have been mastered to a sufficient degree, the grid is replaced by another which retains only the divisions between classes. When this grid is mastered too, the sheet is turned over, its blank side on top, and the children start laying out numbers, accompanied by vocalization and distinct, but empty, spaces between classes. Soon afterward the sheet is removed, so that the numbers are either laid out directly on the table or are recorded directly in the notebook. The numbers and operation, however, still have to be vocalized. Then this, too, is abolished, the operation being performed mentally; only its results are reported and recorded.

Thus, the grid of the decimal system is at first explained in detail and represented pictorially. This is the stage of formation of the orienting basis for action.

With the aid of such a grid on a card, *S*'s performance—the writing down or reading aloud of numbers, addition and subtraction—is also materialized. This is the stage of materialized action.

Then parts of this grid are gradually removed: designations of categories, their dividing lines, designations of classes, their dividing lines. *S* reproduces them, however, orally (as an operation progresses), at first in detail, subsequently—in a more and more abbreviated form. This is the audible stage.

Subsequently the operation is carried out mentally, but at first in parts. *S* reports the result of each partial operation. This is the stage of "externalized speech to oneself."

The final stage begins at the moment when control over individual parts of operation is removed and the action is controlled only in respect to the final result. Mental action grows shorter and becomes automatized. This is the fifth and final stage of development of mental action.

References

Belov, N. D. Conditions for the full-valued abbreviation of acts. Diploma experiment, Moscow State Univer., Psychol. Dept., 1956.

Davydov, V. V. The formation of initial concepts of quantity in children. *Vop. Psikhol.,* 1957, No. 2.

Gal'perin, P. Y. The problem of internal speech. In *Materials of the Conference on Psychology (June 1955).* Moscow: Izd. Akad. Pedag. Nauk RSFSR, 1957. (a)

Gal'perin, P. Y. The mental act as the basis for the formation of ideas and images. *Vop. Psikhol.,* 1957, No. 6. (b)

Gal'perin, P. Y., and Talyzina, N. F. The formation of initial geometric concepts on the basis of organized activity of the student. *Vop. Psikhol.,* 1957, No. 1. (Reprinted in N. O'Connor [Ed.], *Recent Soviet Psychology.* London: Pergamon Press, 1961.)

Golomshtok, I. E. The form of arithmetic acts and its connection with the student's success. *Dokl. Akad. Pedag. Nauk RSFSR,* 1957, No. 3.

Nepomnyashchaya, N. I. The problem of the psychological mechanisms of the formation of a mental act. *Vestnik MGU,* 1956, No. 2.

Patina, N. S. The formation of the motor habit of writing as a function of the type of orientation to the task. *Vop. Psikhol.,* 1957, No. 4.

Talyzina, N. F. The problem of mastering initial geometric concepts. In *Materials of the Conference on Psychology (June 1955).* Moscow: Izd. Akad. Pedag. Nauk RSFSR, 1957.

PART **II**

ABNORMAL AND SOCIAL PSYCHOLOGY

8

The Neuropsychological Study of Brain Lesions and Restoration of Damaged Brain Functions

A. R. Luria

EDITORS' INTRODUCTION

The research summarized in this chapter defines the boundaries of Luria's major area of interest, neuropsychology. From the time when he first became interested in speech pathologies in the 1920's, Luria's primary concern has been the understanding of brain functions peculiar to man. In recent years, several of Luria's books on this topic have been published (Luria, 1963b, 1966a, 1966b), although some of the research was completed more than twenty years ago while Luria was serving in the army.

Luria's fundamental assumption is that there is no strict cortical localization of psychological activities. The cortex is organized into functional systems, and these systems, developed as a consequence of interactions with the environment, are the bases of psychological activities. Damage to a cortical area participating in a functional system need not produce permanent loss of a psychological function or activity, since the latter is not a consequence of localized cortical activity. A new functional cortical system may be organized, as a result of training, which would successfully mediate the psychological activity.

A recent review of Luria's work by Bowden (1966) provides a helpful summary to the key notion, the functional cortical system, around which Luria organizes his theory of the organization of the human brain. Bowden notes that there are four major postulates to which Luria has adhered throughout most of his career. The first is that the cerebral component of any functional cortical system results from the interaction of a constellation of cerebral areas. Thus, a functional system is localizable in the sense that damage to any one of the areas involved destroys the functional system. Defects will appear in the psychological activities dependent upon this functional cortical system. Second, a given psychological activity, for example reading, may be performed in different ways, that is, by different functional cortical systems. Thus a psychological activity is not localizable in the sense that if damage to a structure destroys a functional cortical system upon which reading is based another functional system cannot be developed which would carry out that same activity of reading. Third, the most important adaptive functions that man possesses, such as abstraction, computation, and speech itself, depend upon functional cortical systems which are acquired rather than innate. The fourth major assumption is that the most important determinant of functional cortical systems in man is the organization of the social environment.

For the interested reader, the chapter which follows can serve as an introduction to Soviet neuropsychology. Thanks to Luria's prodigious output and numerous translations, the material for further study is readily available.

The repeated use of mentalistic-sounding terms in this and other chapters should not mislead the reader into believing that Soviet psychologists are mentalistic- or consciousness-centered psychologists. They do not accept a "mind stuff" separate and distinct from behavior. But they are much less concerned about niceties of operational definitions and unambiguous terminology than Western psychologists. They believe that it is more important to consider the qualitative complexities of behavior adequately than to promote a false impression of conceptual rigor.

Pre-Revolutionary Background

At the time of the Great October Revolution, Russian medical psychology already had solid, long-standing scientific traditions. As early as the 1860's the founder of Russian physiology and materialist psychology, Sechenov, had begun his work on a reflex type of interpretation of mental phenomena. He saw a great opportunity to found a medical psychology which would provide a scientific analysis of intellectual mechanisms. He also sought the recognition of therapeutic techniques for mental illness.

Sechenov's materialist principles and analysis of the major facts of the pathological modifications of mental life were applied only in physiological experiments on animal subjects or in individual observations of pathological states in man, but in the 1890's various psychiatric and neurological institutions began to appear all over Russia. Psychological laboratories at these institutes sought to introduce experimental methods into the clinical treatment of nervous and mental diseases; the first such laboratories were founded by Bekhterev at the Kazan Psychiatric Clinic and by Korsakov at the Moscow Psychiatric Clinic. Some time later more laboratories appeared, and Rossolimo began psychological studies at the Clinic of Nervous Diseases at Moscow University. Publication of a journal, *Survey of Psychiatry, Criminal Anthropology and Experimental Psychology* (later changed to the *Newsletter of Psychiatry, Neurology and Criminal Psychology*), was begun. The experiments published in these journals concerned the modifications of reaction time, associative processes, attention, memory, and emotional states as a result of various mental illnesses. This work represented a significant contribution by physicians and psychologists who collaborated on a new, objective approach to pathological changes of the mind.

The work of this early period (prior to 1910) on the application of psychological methods to clinical practice was restricted to isolated experimental studies, some of which led to the discovery of new and important facts. But even in the first years of the twentieth century this experimental research was beginning to develop certain definite trends whose significance far transcended the bounds of any one area of experimental psychology.

Rossolimo (1928)[1] and Bernshtein (1922) made the first attempts to introduce systematic psychological experimentation into clinical diagnosis. Rossolimo developed a battery of psychological experiments which he believed would objectively establish the state of mental functions which had been modified by various pathological conditions of the brain. He believed that these experiments expressed the generic functional disturbances characteristic of different brain lesions and yielded a "profile of modification in the dynamic of mental life." Rossolimo encountered great difficulty in his effort to create "psychological profiles" characteristic of various pathological states. Since a scientific theory of the structure of mental processes had not yet been developed, he had to base his conclusions on the idealist "empirical psychology" then current, to which he added a number of supplementary ideas. The successful solution of his task was hindered by an oversimplified experimental and quantitative approach.

There is no doubt, however, that the very attempt to involve psychology in the solution of clinical problems and the attempt to introduce experimen-

1. *Editors' note:* This work was published in summary form many years after it was initiated.

tal techniques into neurological clinical work indicated progress. It should also be noted that the very idea of aiding the diagnosis of particular pathological states by comparing the "profiles" of various mental functions as a function of different disturbances of the brain's activity was of considerable interest in those days.

Whereas the Rossolimo system developed within the confines of a clinic, Bernshtein's (1922) "clinical techniques for the psychological examination of the mentally ill" grew out of psychiatric examinations. A leading psychiatrist himself, Bernshtein felt an acute need to introduce the exact methods of experimental psychology into the clinical examination of mental illness. The techniques which he developed diagnosed the character of the deficits in perception, assimilation, comprehension, attention, memory, and associative processes in a way that was relatively accurate and open to comparative analysis. Renouncing a formal and pseudo-quantitative approach Bernshtein concentrated instead on a qualitative analysis of those disturbances of the brain's activity characteristic of various mental illnesses and introduced many new and important postulates into clinical psychology. There is no doubt that the many experimental techniques he introduced, as well as a number of the psychological facts he discovered, are still of interest today.

Bekhterev's early work (summarized in Bekhterev, 1933) concentrated on the application of objective techniques, such as those based on reaction time, span of attention, and scope of associative processes, to the study of those aspects of psychological activity that were altered by pathological conditions. He carried out the first systematic studies of conditioned reflexes in a patient. This work yielded basic facts about the disturbance of associative processes, ideo-motor reflexes, and memory. Bekhterev also made the first attempts to apply the psychogalvanic reflex techniques to the study of pathological states. The wide-scale introduction of experimental psychology into clinical practice is connected not only with the name of Bekhterev himself but also with a number of his pupils and followers: Myasishchev (1938, 1939), Golant (1935), and others. This school was important in uniting experimental psychology and clinical medicine despite a number of mechanistic oversimplifications inherent in "reflexology."

Pavlov played a leading role in the further development of the study of pathologically modified psychological activity. In the pre-Revolutionary period his research was entirely devoted to the study of the higher nervous activity of animals. However, it later developed into a series of experimental investigations on the higher nervous activity of normal and abnormal humans. This reflex approach to mental activity originated with Sechenov. It became an exact, scientific branch of physiology through the efforts of Pavlov, and it represents the basis upon which Soviet medical psychology developed.

Early Soviet Research

The first application of experimental psychology to the objective study of pathological brain conditions after the October Revolution was in the work of Ivanov-Smolenskii, a student of the Bekhterev school. Calling his research "biogenesis of verbal reflexes," Ivanov-Smolenskii correctly concluded that there are objective indicators in the study of verbal associations (and especially of spoken answers to verbal stimuli) which are altered by pathological brain conditions.

Ivanov-Smolenskii also suggested the use of the traditional "psychic reaction" method in physiological and physiopathological research.[2] He changed the technique and replaced the usual study of psychic reaction (which uses only a spoken instruction) with another method—namely, the elaboration of a motor reaction with the aid of "spoken reinforcement" (Ivanov-Smolenskii, 1950).

A second group of investigators who were attempting to bring psychological experimentation into closer liaison with clinical medicine worked at the Moscow Institute of Psychology, then headed by Kornilov. The contribution of their projects to clinical psychology was connected with the "combined motor method" introduced by Luria and his colleagues and applied to objective research into pathologically modified human activity.

These investigators began their study of functional disturbances of behavior by using a traditional analysis of the associative processes. However, they noted that a far better approach would be to study these associative responses in conjunction with the motor responses of the hand. The motor responses give an objective evaluation of those disturbances in excitation and inhibition that are characteristic of disturbed associative processes in pathological states, which in turn cause a disturbance of organized, balanced forms of activity. The use of this "combined motor method" [3] (Luria, 1960a, b; Luria and Leont'ev, 1926; Luria and Lebedinskii, 1929) provided information on the dynamics of the affective processes, on the objective mechanisms of the affective complexes, and on the consequences of acute conflicts and neurotic states. The "combined motor method" later permitted us to study important mechanisms involved in the regulation of human behavior and to develop techniques with the aid of which it has been possible to restore organization to disorganized behavior.

Another group of projects, connected with the names of Kravkov (1950) and Kekche'ev (1947), provided an exact analysis of sensory processes.

---

2. *Editors' note:* The Ivanov-Smolenskii technique amounted to asking the subject to respond in the presence of a given stimulus, but not in the presence of other stimuli.

3. *Editors' note:* Described at greater length by Luria in Chapter 4 of this volume.

These studies, which started as psychophysiological research, not only created a new Soviet school of psychophysiology, but also enabled the clinician to assess, with more accurate methods than before, the alterations in sensations associated with various forms of the pathology.

Whereas the research described thus far consisted of introducing the techniques of general psychology and psychophysiology into clinical practice, the research of the next era grew out of clinical work itself and was based on newly developing concepts in Soviet psychology. This research gives a true picture of Soviet clinical psychology, which has become integrated with neurology and psychiatry and has also been the starting point for many studies which introduced psychological methods into the diagnosis and treatment of behavior disturbances in cases of pathological brain states.

There is no doubt that the accomplishments of this era are closely linked with the work of Vygotskii, who introduced many new techniques, the development of which has occupied the time since his death.[4] Prior to Vygotskii, psychology was mainly a science concerned with the study of isolated psychological functions. Vygotskii's work (only a portion of which was published during his lifetime) changed the situation substantially. By showing that the higher mental processes (active attention, voluntary recall, and abstract thinking) develop as a result of the child's interaction with adults and his experimentation with objects and with speech, Vygotskii brought the problem of *instruments* which organize psychological processes into the foreground of psychological research. Primary among these is the role played by speech in the organization of all human behavior.

Vygotskii proposed a special method for the study of higher mental processes, which he called the "method of dual stimulation." Using this method, he carried out a series of studies on the basic mental processes (active attention, voluntary recall, etc.). His findings showed that the meaning of a word, which is the basic instrument of abstraction and generalization, changes during the course of the child's development and plays a different role both in the reflection of reality and in the mediation of mental activity at various stages of development. With this approach, he could study objectively both the formation of higher mental functions in ontogenesis and their disintegration in pathological brain states. Because of Vygotskii, Leont'ev, and their collaborators, processes which formerly had been at best merely described were now viewed as the products of complex development, during which a child's interactions with those about him are gradually assimilated to constitute his own mental activity. This viewpoint led to the scientific study of higher psychological functions such as active attention, voluntary memory, and volitional behavior. In turn, as a result of this work, the study of the *structuring of mental activity* during its development and disintegration (the

4. *Editors' note:* In 1934, of tuberculosis.

genesis and pathology of the higher psychological functions) became a subject for psychological research. An experimental approach was now used in the analysis of how the forms of reality are experienced at successive stages of development, how these forms are disturbed in pathological states of the brain, how relationships among basic psychological processes (perception, recall, and abstract, generalizing speech) change at the various stages of ontogenesis, and how they change in the various forms of pathological alterations of mental activity.

Vygotskii's theoretical position emphasized the uniqueness of man's mental life (a view close to Pavlov's basic idea of the interaction of the two signal systems). This position made the objective study of consciousness feasible and placed it in the center of Soviet clinical and general psychology.

Vygotskii attributed fundamental importance to the investigation of the pathological development of speech and thought. He proposed a method for the experimental investigation of concept formation (the so-called Vygotskii-Sakharov method), and, applying it to the study of thought alteration in schizophrenia, was the first to demonstrate the thought structures characteristic of this illness. These studies showed that the special (according to all data, inhibited) state of the cerebral cortex, which is characteristic of schizophrenia, inevitably disrupts the system of connections underlying words and thereby causes a disintegration of the system of concepts. This system is replaced by thinking in terms of complexes. Vygotskii saw the basic symptom of schizophrenia as this unique alteration of the semantic structuring of the word. His approach, using objective experimental psychological techniques (Zeigarnik, 1934; Bassin, 1938; and others), led to the study of semantic disorganization in schizophrenia and also to an analysis of those affective alterations which characterize the mind of the schizophrenic.[5]

It is to Vygotskii that efforts at a meticulous analysis of the alterations of speech and categorical thinking which occur in aphasia should be credited. Studies undertaken by Vygotskii, or on his initiative, made it possible to show that speech disturbances occurring from focal brain lesions lead not only to substantial alterations in abstraction and generalization but also to changes in the relations among the basic psychological processes, imparting a considerably more concrete character to reflections of reality. These studies (Vygotskii, 1928, 1933, 1956), carried out almost simultaneously with the famous work of Goldstein, showed convincingly that conceptual thinking is disturbed in aphasia and that forms of communication acquire a more stimulus-bound, situational character.

Of special importance is the work concerned with disturbances of phonemic hearing in aphasia. These studies, often mentioned in Vygotskii's

---

5. *Editors' note:* See the most recent American publication (Vygotskii, 1962) for a description of the basic techniques and theory.

talks and published by Luria in 1948, showed that there are forms of brain damage, in many respects opposite in effect to those causing aphasia, which are characterized by the fact that speech processes are *not* affected, but, rather, become the basic instrument of compensation for the behavior which was affected by the brain damage. The first experiments on this special type of mental disturbance were those which demonstrated how the defective behavior of the parkinsonism sufferer acquires organization with the aid of speech. With this form of brain damage the retention of the higher mental functions acts as the instrument of compensation for primary defects. These experiments showed that voluntary movements destroyed by parkinsonism as a result of the pathologically altered tonus can, to a certain extent, be compensated for by bringing them into the system of cortical afferentations and by imparting to them a special meaning with the aid of spoken connections. These experiments on the restoration of voluntary movements in parkinsonism patients, done as early as 1926 on Vygotskii's initiative, were the means of approaching the psychological structure of the volitional act as complex mediated activity. A number of Vygotskii's experiments, devoted to the problem of hysteria and the deciphering of "hypoboulic (subvolitional) mechanisms," have not been published either in his or his students' works. In this series of studies, Vygotskii attempted to show that in the normal mind the crucial role is played not by unconscious (hypoboulic) mechanisms but rather by socially conditioned, "superficial," conscious mechanisms, which should be the basis of a genuine, scientifically grounded psychotherapy.

Vygotskii demonstrated that certain regions of the cerebral cortex, especially those connected with speech, are important not only for the individual, partial forms of mental activity (auditory, visual, and tactile analysis and synthesis), but also for the structuring of complex forms of the higher mental processes as a whole. However—and herein lies the central postulate which Vygotskii contributed to the solution of this problem—the *functional significance of a given region of the cerebral cortex for an entire system of mental processes varies for different stages of development.* In the adult, for whom the functional systems are already developed and in whom the leading mediating and regulatory role is always played by complex forms of activity (especially those connected with speech), destruction of a given center always influences the normal operation of a lower center dependent on it. The situation is different in the early stages of development, when destruction of a specific cerebral center which serves as a foundation for the further development of more complex structures influences the systematic underdevelopment of *higher* centers which are only genetically dependent on the affected region. This inversion of a focal lesion's systematic influence during development and deterioration was demonstrated by Vygotskii in a number of concrete instances.

In addition to his contributions to the general theory of neural and mental illness, Vygotskii also contributed to the theory of the mental development of the defective child. An oversimplified approach had long prevailed in studies on the defective child (the mentally retarded, the deaf-mute, the blind, the child with speech defects). Researchers believed that defects in the development and behavior of defective children were the direct result of various brain defects. Therefore the defects in mental activity encountered in deaf-mutes or children hard of hearing were believed to be the results of secondary brain lesions which were the immediate causes of this defect.

Vygotskii, however, believed that these defects were not the simple result of brain lesions, but rather a *secondary result* of the child's abnormal development. If one or another prerequisite to this development is damaged, then the entire development of the child acquires an abnormal character and, therefore, comparatively small defects (for instance, a slight impairment of hearing) may have far-reaching consequences. This point of view, based on a great many observations and later developed by a number of Vygotskii's pupils (Boskis, Levina, Pevzner, and others), created a new, dynamic approach to the development of the defective child and became the theoretical basis of Soviet defectology.

Vygotskii's work spurred the development of Soviet psychology and initiated a broad spectrum of studies in which psychology was used for the solution of urgent problems in neurological and psychiatric clinical work. The distinguishing feature of these studies was that all of them transcended the bounds of specific projects which studied this or that isolated process (association, memory, etc.) in pathological states of the brain. This movement changed former efforts to limit psychological experimentation in clinical work to the formal application of a battery of tests. The basic task of all these projects was to provide a description of the entire pathological syndrome based on meticulous psychological research, thus improving the structural analysis of the alterations which occurred as a result of pathological cerebral activity. In short, this branch of psychology was faced with the task of utilizing the techniques of experimental psychology to characterize the syndrome, to identify both the primary lesion directly connected with the basic defect and the secondary, systematic disorders resulting from this primary lesion but obscured by the superficial clinical picture. If, for example, the symptom of an illness is a writing disorder, it would be entirely unscientific to assume that the patient's "writing center" is damaged and to simply note this fact clinically. Skillfully conducted psychological experiments have revealed basic defects underlying certain disorders which were entirely different from the assumed causes. For example, it was found that, in some cases, a disturbance of phonemic hearing underlies the disturbance of writing; in others, a disintegration of the articulative analysis of sounds underlies a disturbance of spatial analysis and synthesis of written letters or inertia of motor acts; and so forth. This preliminary work delimiting and giving a better qualitative description of each defect, has permitted an approach to real explanation and in the final analysis has opened the way to physiopathological analysis.

In the first decade following the death of Vygotskii, Soviet psychopathologists were occupied mainly with the psychological analysis and characterization of defects which arise in pathological brain conditions. In the second decade, their work involved another extremely vital task—the transition from a psychological clarification of the syndrome to its physiopathological explanation. Thus, from the refining of research methods, they progressed to the task of achieving a rapprochement between psychological and physiological analysis, which was based on Pavlov's theory of higher nervous activity. Without Pavlov's theory this field would never have come to its logical goal nor ever have acquired that explanatory power which is provided by a scientific physiopathology of the higher nervous activity.

The Study of Aphasia

Considerable attention in Soviet medical psychology has been devoted to the psychological analysis of speech disorders and the various syndromes of aphasia.

The basic clinical forms of aphasia have been described in the literature here and abroad. But we feel that Soviet researchers have a better approach to their qualitative analysis. Soviet researchers abandoned the naive symptomatological approach which considered phenomena such as disturbance of memory for the spoken word, paraphasia, and agrammatism as direct manifestations of focal disorders which had allegedly damaged specialized "centers" of various complex psychological processes. They began to consider these symptoms the secondary results of specific lesions, directly connected with the functions of various areas of the cerebral cortex. They believed that the complex and varied disorders of speech activity are a result of the *lesion* of a particular physiological condition essential for the execution of the speech act (for instance, auditory analysis and synthesis, synthetic unification of stimulations into one simultaneous whole, etc.). Many Soviet psychologists therefore attempted meticulous structural analyses of speech disorders so that they would be able to understand the varied and complex symptoms of speech disorders as the systemic result of a particular lesion in the cortex. The strategy of linking these speech disturbances with a careful analysis of the alterations in the functioning of the affected sections of the cerebral cortex provided a more accurate understanding of the many syndromes observed in various forms of aphasia.

Thus, Levina (1951) and Boskis (1953) showed that a disturbance of phonic hearing underlies the underdevelopment of speech and writing in the alalic child. In an analysis of neurosurgical data, Luria (1947) described the consequences of disturbed phonemic hearing caused by the destruction of the systems in the left lateral cortical region. The analysis of syndromes arising from a lesion of the left lateral region, described in these studies and in Bein's monograph (1950), permitted us to relate the presence of such lesions to disturbance of a word's auditory structure, alienation of the meaning of words, disturbance of writing and reading, defects of the lexical and grammatical aspect of speech, and particular disturbances of thought. This material made it possible to advance the study of the sensory disorders of speech and to overcome those difficulties which had been encountered by the researchers who had attempted to explain the phenomena of sensory aphasia either as due to particular auditory disorders or as generic alterations of thought not connected with speech. Soviet investigations carried out in recent years show the way in which auditory analysis and synthesis is damaged by lesions of the left lateral region (cf. Babenkova, 1954), making it possible to relate these studies to a physiological analysis of the function of the auditory analyzer.

Other forms of aphasia have been as fully analyzed, resulting in a discovery of other aspects of speech activity. Luria (1947), among others, analyzed the way in which the semantic and logicogrammatical aspects of speech are damaged and the physiological mechanisms (in the form of destruction of simultaneous syntheses) that underly these disturbances. A description of the syndrome arising from parieto-occipital lesions (which invariably occasion a disorder of spatial syntheses, understanding of complex speech structures, and counting [Kolodnaya, 1953]) led to efforts to use a psychological approach in the analysis of one of the most complex syndromes arising from cortical lesions. New facts were obtained in the analysis of motor aphasias, among which two divergent forms were distinguished: a disturbance of articulative analysis and synthesis of words on the one hand, and a disturbance of the sequential system of auditory syntheses on the other (Luria, 1947). Finally, detailed study of those forms of speech disorders which occur in diseases of the posterior lobe of the left hemisphere enabled us to describe the peculiar form, "dynamic aphasia." As a result of central destruction, a profound defect of active, extended speech occurred, manifesting itself in persistent, repetitive speech. Special research provided a detailed description of this syndrome and established its intimate connection with the disturbance of internal speech (Luria, 1964).

In the research just described, efforts were made to subject speech disorders to a psychophysiological analysis in order to clarify the relation between disturbances of a complex speech process and lesions in the cortical sections of the various analyzers. This basic task was also the theme of Luria's monograph *Traumatic Aphasia* (1947), in which the author considered the various forms of speech disorders to be the result of focal lesions in the various analyzers.

Summary data on this problem, published by Luria (1962, 1963a), resulted in a new classification of aphasia, based on clinical analyses of the speech disturbances which result from focal brain lesions (Luria, 1964).

General Studies of Speech and Motor Disorders

A different method of analyzing speech disorders was developed by Kogan (1957), Chlenov (1934), and others. In contradistinction to the research discussed earlier, this important series of projects focussed on the phenomena common to all forms of aphasia rather than on a differential study of the various forms of aphasia. These authors noted that the various connections elicited by words were oversimplified in aphasia. The meanings of words are bound to the particular habitual contexts in which they occur, resulting in a limited use and understanding of words.

Luria also studied the nature of defective visual perception in bilateral lesions of the occipito-parietal area (1959). He showed that it is impossible in such cases to perceive isolated groups of elements and simultaneously synthesize them into a whole. These data are similar to the phenomena described by foreign scientists as "amorphosynthesis" (Denny-Brown, 1951) or disturbances of visual attention (Patterson and Zangwill, 1945). An analysis of the eye movements of these patients showed that those who could perceive only one element at a time could not systematically transfer their gaze from one point to another. Their visual perception suffered considerably as a result of defectively organized eye movements (Luria, Pravdina-Vinarskaya, and Yarbus, 1963).

Finally, the data were analyzed for deficiencies in visual perception which arise from frontal lobe lesions. As was shown in research conducted in the 1930's but published only recently, massive destruction of the frontal lobes leads not only to disturbances of active visual behavior, but to gross disturbance of visual perception as well: the patient is unable to analyze the information contained in a complex visual object (e.g., a picture) and his perception thus becomes passive and fragmentary (Luria, 1963a, b). Further study revealed certain physiological mechanisms which underlie this defect. Patients with frontal-lobe damage were able to follow a moving object, but found it exceedingly difficult to transfer their gaze from one isolated point to another (Luria and Khomskaya, 1962). Disturbance of active searching ability in the frontal-lobe patient produces gross disorganization of the active searching movements of the eyes. This can be verified by recording eye movements while pictures are being examined. It was shown that eye movements in such cases were no longer organized. Changing the patient's task did not evoke corresponding changes in his eye movements (Luria, Karpov, and Yarbus, in press).

Soviet psychopathology has devoted a great deal of energy to a study of disturbances in motor processes resulting from brain lesions. The successes of neurosurgery have permitted an analysis of motor disorders and the description of their constituent components. Two different syndromes can be singled out from an analysis of the alterations in motor processes which occur in lesions of the parietal and premotor areas. Observations of patients and a number of special investigations have shown that in parietal lesions the innervational pattern of the motor act results in disturbance of spatial analysis and synthesis or in disturbance of kinesthetic analysis and damage to the correctness and accuracy of movement. However, the disturbance of movements acquires an entirely different character in lesions of the premotor area. In such cases, the accuracy of individual movements remains intact, but there is a drastic disturbance in the process of switching from one movement to another; the deinnervation of the previous motor act, which is essential to switching, is hindered, the smoothness and automatic nature of movements is disturbed, and the "kinetic melody," which characterizes each motor act, disintegrates (Luria, 1962, 1963a, b).

This description of motor disorders caused by postcentral and premotor lesions, as well as the descriptions of the early symptoms of these disorders (Luria, 1947, 1957b), has permitted us to offer a more precise theory of the disturbance of movements in man. This has been further clarified by correlating the clinical analysis of motor disorders with the disturbances of the motor processes obtained in physiological experiments involving deafferentation of the extremities in animals (Orbeli, 1935; Anokhin, 1955).

Whereas the research just described was devoted to an analysis of the motor disturbances arising from organic focal brain lesions, another important series of studies (Bernshtein, 1947; Leont'ev and Zaporozhets, 1945) was devoted to a detailed analysis of the structured levels of movements and their disturbance when afferent impulses are altered in various ways. These studies showed that a thorough psychophysiological analysis of the structure of the motor act and the system of afferent impulses which regulates it is the only source of a reliable qualititative analysis of motor disorders. This type of analysis also provides a scientific basis in terms of the central regulation of the motor acts for the restoration of movements following their pathological alteration in various disturbances of the peripheral motor apparatus.

Lesions of the Frontal Lobes

A number of Soviet psychologists studied the complex disturbances of purposive activity and thought caused by focal brain lesions. Of interest in this respect is the research on those disturbances of mental activity caused by frontal-lobe lesions. Disturbance of the complex forms of purposive activity has long been connected with damage to the frontal lobes. Bekhterev considered the frontal area one of the cardinal "psychoregulatory" apparatuses. Pavlov pointed out that, even in lower animals, frontal lesions do not lead to a disappearance of various individual types of analysis and synthesis, but rather cause a profound alteration of the entire activity of the animal, making it a "hopeless invalid." He accounts for this by ascribing a direct role in the central control of motor analysis to the frontal area, due to which the frontal lobes play a substantial and vital role in the regulation of behavior. Anokhin and his colleagues, who contributed a great deal to the experimental study of the behavior of animals deprived of frontal lobes, came to the same conclusion (Anokhin, 1955; Kolodnaya, 1953).

Shumilina's (1949) research has shown that extirpation of the frontal lobes in the dog results in the extinction of complex forms of motor choice reactions. They are replaced by perseverative movements which have no adaptive function. In the last twenty years important data regarding the role of the lobes has emerged from Luria's laboratory (1962, 1963a).

Our research has indicated that the ability to listen to and follow oral instructions is developed in the first three to four years of the child's life. The two-year-old child is not yet able to follow the adult's instructions and every motor impulse irradiates, leading to uncontrolled motor reactions. Therefore, the adult's instructions at this point in the child's development may set a reaction in motion, but cannot stop it. Further, spoken instructions cannot build a preliminary program of desired activity (Luria, 1959, 1960b, 1961). Only in the fourth year does the system of spoken signals become so firm and at the same time so flexible that it has some regulatory influence on the child's motor reactions. This process of the formation of the regulatory role of speech is delayed only in cases of abnormal development. When spoken instructions play no firm regulatory role in the activity of the seven-to-nine-year-old child one has a reliable indication of massive pathology (Luria, 1961).

Further research has demonstrated that these complex forms of the regulation of voluntary activity suffer considerably in lesions of the frontal lobes. Meshcheryakov's research (1953) indicated that patients with massive destruction of the frontal lobes are unable to carry out even the simplest acts according to spoken instructions. They can remember the command and repeat it (echolalia), but the command loses its significance as a signal and no longer elicits the necessary motor reaction. To an even greater degree, these patients are unable to produce motor reactions to a conditioned signal whose significance was previously determined by spoken instructions. This deficiency was carefully examined by studying the course of choice situations in these patients. Ivanova's research (1953) showed that patients with massive destruction of the frontal lobes were unable to make choices (e.g., to squeeze the balloon with the right hand in response to one signal, with the left hand in response to another signal). This complex set of movements is replaced by inert repetition of the same reaction or by stereotypic alternation of the right and left hands which loses its connection with the conditioned stimuli.

This pathology expresses itself even more clearly when the patient is required to differentiate between effectors (e.g., when required to respond to one sound by squeezing lightly and to another by squeezing firmly), or to carry out conflicting reactions (e.g., when required to squeeze lightly in response to a loud sound and to squeeze firmly in response to a weak sound). These unpublished experiments, conducted by Khomskaya and Marushevskii, indicated that the patient with a lesion in the frontal lobes has great difficulty in reacting to the conditioned significance of a signal presented by means of spoken instructions. His movements quickly become echopraxic and the movement is a passive repetition of one of the characteristics of the signal. The work of Luria, Pribram, and Khomskaya (1964) yielded analogous results. In all these cases the patient's own spoken instructions had either a very weak influence over his motor processes or none at all. Filippycheva (1952) conducted several experiments in an effort to analyze these phenomena physiologically and to reveal the pathological inertia in the motor system which underlies the observed defects. She showed that lesions disturb the flexibility of the neural processes in the motor area as well as destroy the signal function of speech. Livanov and his collaborators [6] demonstrated that each kind of psychological stress evokes its own peculiar changes in electrophysiological activity and that this appears primarily in the frontal lobes.

No less interesting is research which indicates that the effect of destruction of the frontal lobes is not limited to disturbances in the regulation of voluntary behavior. It also leads to gross defects in the complex forms of regulation of autonomic processes.

The research of Sokolov (1959) and Vinogradova (1956) established that each presentation of a new neutral stimulus evokes a series of autonomic components of the orienting reflex—contraction of peripheral blood vessels and dilation of the vessels in the head. This reaction extinguishes with repetition of these signals unless the stimulus is given signal significance by spoken instructions (e.g., count the signals and react to them with a responsive movement) in which case the reaction remains quite stable.[7]

Khomskaya and her collaborators (1960, 1961, 1964) showed that the regulatory influence of spoken instructions on the autonomic components of the orienting reflex is retained in patients with focal destruction of the posterior sections of the brain (parietal, temporal, occipital). However, this influence is very unstable in patients with destruction of the posterior lobes and may disappear completely when there is destruction of the pre-

---

6. *Editors' note:* See Chapter 25 of this volume, by M. N. Livanov.

7. *Editors' note:* See Chapters 23 and 24 of this volume, by E. N. Sokolov and O. S. Vinogradova.

frontal and medial sections of the cortex. Analogous defects in the regulatory activity of the cerebral cortex were found by Khomskaya (1964) in patients with frontal-lobe destruction (unpublished data). These experiments indicate the significance of the frontal lobes in regulating not only motor processes but autonomic and electrophysiological reactions as well.

This research has demonstrated that defects caused by destruction of the frontal lobes are not limited to the regulation of relatively simple motor and autonomic reactions: they lead to significant disturbances in complex programs of human physical activity as well. Twenty years ago Luria (1948) described the significant disturbances in the order and structure of activity caused by destruction of the frontal lobes. Later, Filippycheva (1952) and Spirin (1951) also studied the disturbance of complex forms of activity in massive lesions of the frontal lobes. However, only recently have the disturbances of complex behavior which occur with destruction of the frontal lobes been studied in sufficient detail.

The research of Luria, Pribram, and Khomskaya (1964) has shown that, for patients with a frontal lobe lesion, complex programs of activity become impossible. This leads to significant simplification and, at times, to the disintegration of these programs. Tikhomirov (1961) analyzed the simplification and disintegration of complex programs of activity and showed how the active search for the necessary program, which is the basis of complex, heuristic thought, is disturbed by the destruction of the frontal lobes.

These investigations permit a more detailed understanding of the disturbance of intellectual activity which is produced by destruction of the frontal lobes. At the same time we are able to enrich our understanding of the role of the frontal lobes in the organization of the most complex forms of cognitive activity.

In recent decades there has been a tendency to view disturbances in complex cognitive behavior, resulting from destruction of the frontal lobes, as a disturbance of categorical behavior (Goldstein, 1948; Halstead, 1947). However, these experiments have not provided a framework for careful examination of the changes in the structure of mental activity which result from destruction of the frontal lobes nor do they permit us to proceed to an analysis of the underlying neurophysiological changes. Therefore, experiments which involve neurophysiological analysis of defects in intellectual processes are very important.

At the end of the 1940's research was devoted to the analysis of how construction tasks are affected in patients with massive frontal-lobe lesions. Gadzhev (1951) presented frontal lobe patients with the task of constructing a large cube from separate parts and found that the orienting basis of intellectual activity is substantially disturbed. In addition, the "strategy" of activity suffers significantly. This does not occur in patients with focal destruction of the posterior lobes of the brain. Recently, Tsvetkova conducted experiments with frontal-lobe patients on the problem of constructing a figure from separate blocks (Luria and Tsvetkova, 1964). This research confirmed the hypothesis that the most basic characteristics of the behavior of these patients are the disturbance of preliminary orientation in complex tasks, disintegration of the "orienting basis of decision," and the substitution of the genuinely intellectual structure of activity by fragmentary attempts. A further study of the patients' analyses of a literary text produced analogous data, as did a study of the way in which they attempt to solve arithmetic problems (Luria and Tsvetkova, 1964).

The Analysis of Individual Cortical Areas and the Restoration of Brain Functions

One of the most important achievements of Soviet psychology in recent years is the elaboration of basic techniques for a neuropsychological analysis of the important forms of mental activity and the application of precise psychological methods to the analysis of the role played by separate areas of the cortex in mental processes. Soviet clinical psychology has conducted many investigations of those alterations in mental activity which occur as a result of cerebral lesions. As a result, it has made a substantial contribution to a more precise diagnosis of these lesions and a more accurate recognition of the mechanisms which underlie them. However, our exposition of what has been done by Soviet psychology to aid clinical practice would be far from complete if we did not consider the Soviet psychologists' contribution to a study of the restoration of functions damaged as a result of lesion in the brain or the peripheral nervous system.

The restoration of functions damaged by injury, tumor, or hemorrhage is one of the cardinal tasks of practical medicine. It would be wrong, however, to conceive of this task narrowly and not to take into account the role of a system of psychologically based exercises and periods of active restructuring of the functional systems used along with preventative and medical measures. The restoration of damaged functions is at one and the same time a matter of medical treatment and a matter of psychologically based education.

Medicine well knew that the functions of the damaged sections of the brain could not be directly restored and that the functions of the damaged peripheral nervous system can be restored only exceptionally slowly as a result of the regeneration of the central segments of the nerve which very gradually reaches the periphery. Therefore it has paid special attention to restoration of functions by the "vicarious method" (transferring them to other organs, most often symmetrical ones) and by the disinhibition of functions where the damage to segments of the nerve fiber led to their temporary inhibition.

Soviet psychologists who worked on the problem of restoring functions did not restrict their attention to these two methods. They also studied the elaboration of a third method: restoring damaged functions by way of their *functional* restructuring. Perhaps the most important projects conducted by Soviet psychologists were those on the question of the mechanisms for restoring functions in cases of lesions of the peripheral nerves or the motor-support apparatus. These projects, conducted under the direction of Leont'ev and Zaporozhets (1945), with the participation of Gellershtein (1943), substantially advanced our knowledge concerning the mechanisms for the restoration of motor functions. There is no doubt that their success was prepared by the previous works of Soviet physiologists.

Even in the early studies done by Orbeli (1935) and Anokhin (summarized in 1955), it had been shown that a decisive role in the structuring of movements is played by the system of afferent impulses, which regulate the regular flow of the motor act. From this viewpoint, Soviet psychologists tried to apply the idea of restructuring afferentation for the compensation of those defects in the motor processes which arose as a result of injury to the peripheral nerves. Having established that these injuries are accompanied by a profound disturbance of proprioceptive afferentation and that in this way the disturbance of the movement is to a greater extent the result of a disturbance of sensitivity than it is the result of an immediate paresis, Leont'ev and his colleagues set themselves the goal of altering the system of afferentations by substituting intact exteroceptive afferentations for the damaged proprioceptive ones, thereby securing a successful compensation of motor defects. The results of these projects showed that a patient with deafferentation of the arm may be able to raise the arm only to a negligible height upon direct instruction or command, but that by interpolating a system of visual afferentations (e.g., suggesting to him that he raise the arm to a certain definite point) or by making the transition to object activity (e.g., suggesting to the patient that he reach up to an object hung at a great height or catch a ball or the like), the limits of the damaged extremity's movements can be considerably expanded. The incorporation of a movement into a system of new afferentations and the restructuring of movements by relating them to objects has proved an important principle for the restorative therapy of the motor-support apparatus. A system of work therapy, founded on these principles, which employs a rational alteration of the afferentations of the damaged movements and a well thought out organization of the motives for the action to be performed, played a vital role in the therapeutic measures used during World War II.

The work done by Soviet clinicians and psychologists on the restoration of damaged functions was not limited to lesions of the peripheral nerves and motor-support apparatus. Of almost greater scope were studies devoted to the restoration of functions damaged as a result of injuries to the cerebral cortex.

It is well known that brain cells damaged by injury or other pathological processes cannot be restored. Only in those cases in which cells have been temporarily put out of operation due to diaschisis or excessive inhibition occasioned by a trauma can a restoration of their original function be expected. In other cases the only possibility which might lead to the restoration of the damaged function is the method of restructuring the functional systems.

Experience has shown that every injury to the brain is accompanied by an effect far wider than that occasioned by the immediate lesion of one or another group of cells. One explanation for this wider effect is that a certain definite zone of the cerebral cortex located near or sometimes even far from the damaged one goes into a state of excessive inhibition and temporarily ceases to function. Soviet pharmacologists, physiologists, and clinicians have demonstrated that a vital aspect in such lesions is the disturbance of synaptic conductivity and that this damaged conductivity may be restored by drugs of the anticholinesterase group. The use of these substances to restore functions damaged as a result of the functional destruction of conductivity accompanying a brain injury led to a series of projects devoted to the restoration of functions after a war injury to the brain. As research conducted by a number of Soviet authors proved, the efforts to restore damaged functions with the aid of this sort of pharmacological intervention proved exceptionally productive and a number of published works convincingly demonstrated the important successes which could be achieved by bringing about a disinhibition of temporarily inhibited functions in this way.

However, the restoration of damaged functions by way of their disinhibition was only one small portion of the work carried out by Soviet psychologists during World War II and in the postwar years. A considerably greater place was occupied by work on the restoration of damaged functions of the brain by restructuring their function. It was these studies which contributed to a theory of the disturbance and restoration of mental processes due to focal brain lesions.

Soviet psychology had access to the important and detailed experience from special pedagogy. Teaching deaf-mutes, blind children, and children with hearing and speech defects (the theoretical foundation for which was greatly advanced by Vygotskii) served as a model which could be successfully utilized for the restoration of speech, writing, and reading that had been damaged as a result of focal lesions. The restoration of damaged functions by way of their restructuring was carried out in a number of projects involving whole teams of Soviet psychologists in a number of special rehabilitation hospitals. The results of these projects were published in a book by Luria (1947) and in a research anthology under the editorship of Zankov that summarized the work of the team which he had led (1948).

The basic principle of these projects was the concept of restructuring functional systems by first qualitatively analyzing the defect to discover both primary (and most often irrevocable) lesions occasioned directly by the influence of the injury and the systemic secondary alterations which could be overcome by utilizing the functional restructuring of the system with the use of other intact links. If the complex processes (speech, writing, reading, counting) damaged by a lesion in one or another area of the brain were homogeneous functions, localized in certain narrowly limited sections of the cerebral cortex (known in the old neurological literature as "centers of speech," "centers of writing," "centers of counting," and the like), no restoration of these damaged functions would be possible.

However, research showed that every "function" which is damaged in cases of cerebral lesions is in actual fact a complex *functional system,* based on the joint operation of many sections of the cortex, each of which is a part of the cortical representation of one or another analyzer and plays its own special role in the execution of given activity. Therefore, in any lesion involving this section, all of the processes which rely on the participation of the given cortical zone suffer. For example, in cases involving a lesion in the auditory analyzer, there is a deficit both in understanding speech and in writing which requires a special analysis of the composition of the words to be written, and identification of the objects based on the reproduction of sound complexes comprising the words. On the other hand, because of the systemic structure of the functions, destruction of the most varied sections of the cerebral cortex entering into the composition of the auditory, visual, and motor analyzers may lead to disruption of one and the same functional system (voluntary action, speech, writing). But each lesion can always be distinguished by unique peculiarities, and, most important, can be compensated for by interpolating new, intact sections of the cerebral cortex into the execution of the damaged act. The basic techniques for such a restoration of functional systems were worked out by Soviet psychologists during World War II. In no sense were they a direct transfer into the clinic of the techniques which had been worked out in the instruction of deaf-mutes and the hard-of-hearing. Naturally, the concrete forms for restoration of the damaged functions through the restructuring of functional systems were profoundly different when one compared instances in which speech, writing, or reading had been damaged, as a result of primary damage to auditory analysis and synthesis, with instances in which the disturbance was due to damage to the kinesthetic base of articulation or disturbance of visual-spatial synthesis. However, the basic principle of restoration of the functions through a restructuring of the functional system and especially through an incorporation of the system of semantic connections (connections formed on the basis of the second signal system) remained identical for all these lesions, regardless of their concrete forms.

Precisely because of the usefulness of this principle in applications to the most varied disturbances, the scope of the work on restoration of damaged brain functions proved to be very broad. Soviet psychologists published a number of special works on the restoration of speech, writing, and reading, on the restoration of the processes of counting and spatial operations, and on the compensation for praxic and gnosic defects, and attempted the solution of a number of problems connected with the restoration of thought dynamics damaged by various lesions of the cerebral cortex (Luria, 1947; Zankov, 1948).

A theory of programmed restoration of training for patients with brain destruction was based on neuropsychological research in focal brain lesions and on the general concept of the formation of intellectual activity originating with Vygotskii (1928). It proceeds from the fact that, in order to restore functions which are destroyed in focal brain lesions, there must be a system of programs which differ according to the area of the brain which is affected. For example, in parietal and parieto-occipital lesions, which produce disturbances of spatial (simultaneous) synthesis (Luria, 1948), the program must involve methods which provide the patient with a consecutive series of external means with which to form a concept of space. The restoration of this concept can lead to compensation for the observed defects (Luria and Tsvetkova, 1964). In destruction of the frontal lobes, when the separate operations necessary to carry out a particular activity are retained, but goal-oriented behavior and its control are disturbed, programs of rehabilitation training must include a series of consecutively applied methods of behavioral organization. These programs involve breaking down the patient's activity into a series of consecutive stages, each of which is dictated by external indicators and which only gradually become abbreviated.

As this research has shown, by using construction activity, analysis of texts, and solutions of arithmetical problems (Luria and Tsvetkova, 1964), these programs for behavioral organization may lead to important results for the rehabilitation of patients with frontal-lobe lesions.

There is no doubt that all these projects contributed a great deal both to the theory of the structuring of mental activity and to the practice of its restoration and also provided material which was vital for the study of the physiology of man's higher nervous activity.

References

Anokhin, P. K. Features of the afferent apparatus of the conditioned reflex and their significance for psychology. *Vop. Psikhol.*, 1955, No. 6.

Babenkova, S. V. Features of the interaction of the signal systems in the process of the restoration of speech in various forms of aphasia. (From a study of the function of the auditory analyzer.) *Tez. Dokl. VII Sessii Inst. Nevrol.*, 1954.

Bassin, F. V. Loss of word meanings in cases of schizophrenia. Candidate's dissertation, Ukr. Inst. Psikhonevrol. Kharkov, 1938.

Bein, E. S. Psychological analysis of sensory aphasia. Candidate's dissertation, Akad. Med. Nauk SSSR, Moscow, 1950.

Bekhterev, V. M. *General principles of human reflexology.* (Translated from 4th Russian edition, 1928.) London: Jarrolds, 1933.

Bernshtein, N. A. *Clinical techniques of psychological examination of the mentally ill.* Moscow: Gosizdat, 1922.

Bernshtein, N. A. *The structure of movements.* Moscow: Medgiz, 1947.

Boskis, R. M. Problems of teaching and training deaf children. *Izv. Akad. Pedag. Nauk RSFSR,* 1953, No. 48.

Bowden, D. The functional system: Keystone to Luria's neuropsychology. Paper delivered at the Symposium on Historical and Systematic Aspects of Russian and Soviet Psychology, Amer. Psychol. Assoc. New York, September, 1966.

Chlenov, L. G. The body image and its disturbances. In *New developments in the theory of apraxia, agnosia, and aphasia.* Moscow, 1934.

Denny-Brown, D. The frontal lobes and their functions. In H. Feeling (Ed.), *Modern trends in neurology.* London: Butterworth, 1951.

Filippycheva, N. A. Inertia of the higher cortical processes in cases of local brain lesions. Candidate's dissertation, Akad. Med. Nauk SSSR, Moscow, 1952.

Gadzhev, S. G. Analysis of the processes of intellectual activity in patients with frontal-lobe lesions. Candidate's dissertation, Inst. Psikhol., Moscow, 1951.

Gellershtein, S. G. *Restorative work therapy.* Moscow: Medgiz, 1943.

Golant, R. Ya. *On disorders of memory.* Moscow-Leningrad: Medgiz, 1935.

Goldstein, K. *Language and language disorders.* New York: Grune & Stratton, 1948.

Halstead, W. C. *Brain and intelligence.* Chicago, 1947.

Ivanov-Smolenskii, A. G. *Pathological physiology of higher nervous activity.* Moscow, 1950. (Also available in English edition: *Essays on the pathophysiology of the higher nervous activity.* Moscow: Foreign Languages Publishing House, 1954.)

Ivanova, M. P. Disturbance of the interrelation between the two signal systems caused by a brain lesion as expressed in the formation of complex motor responses. Candidate's dissertation, Moskov. Gos. Univer., 1953.

Kekche'ev, K. K. Problems of psychophysiology. *Izv. Akad. Pedag. Nauk RSFSR,* 1947, No. 8.

Khomskaya, E. D. The influence of verbal instructions on the vascular and GSR components of the orienting response in various brain lesions. *Dokl. Akad. Pedag. Nauk,* 1960, No. 6.

Khomskaya, E. D. Verbal regulation of the vegetative components of the orienting reflex in focal brain lesions. *Cortex,* 1964, *1,* No. 2.

Khomskaya, E. D., Konavonav, V. V., and Luria, A. R. The participation of the speech system in the regulation of autonomic components of the orienting response in focal brain lesions. *Vop. Neurofiziol.,* 1961, No. 7.

Kogan, V. M. A study of the gnostic nature of speech on the basis of a dynamic analysis of aphasia. In *Proceedings of the Conference on Psychology.* Moscow: Izd. Akad. Pedag. Nauk RSFSR, 1957.

Kolodnaya, A. Y. Disturbance in the differentiation of right and left and the role of the cutaneous analyzer in its restoration. *Izv. Akad. Pedag. Nauk RSFSR,* 1953, No. 53.

Kravkov, S. V. *The eye and its work.* Moscow: Izd. Akad. Nauk Med. SSSR, 1950.

Lebedinskii, M. S. *Aphasia, apraxia, and agnosia.* Kharkov, 1941.

Leont'ev, A. N., and Zaporozhets, A. V. *Restoration of manual movements after war injury.* Moscow: Izd. Sovet. Nauka, 1945.

Levina, R. *A study of nonspeaking children (alalics).* Moscow, 1951.

Luria, A. R. *Traumatic aphasia.* Moscow: Izd. Akad. Med. Nauk SSSR, 1947. (Also published in English edition by Mouton, The Hague, 1965.)

Luria, A. R. *Restoration of functions after brain injuries.* Izd. Akad. Med. Nauk SSSR, 1948. (Also published in English edition by Pergamon Press, London, 1963.)

Luria, A. R. The combined motor method in the investigation of affective reactions. *Problems of contemporary psychology.* Moscow: *Trudy Inst. Psikhol.,* 1957, No. 2. (a)

Luria, A. R. The motor analyzer and cerebral organization of movement. *Vop. Psikhol.,* 1957, No. 2. (b)

Luria, A. R. Disorders of simultaneous perception in a case of bilateral occipito-parietal brain injury. *Brain,* 1959, *82,* Nos. 1–3.

Luria, A. R. *The nature of human conflicts.* (Translated and edited by W. H. Gantt.) New York: Grove Press, 1960. (Reprint of the 1932 edition by Liveright.) (a)

Luria, A. R. Verbal regulation of behavior. In M. Brazier (Ed.), *The central nervous system and behavior.* Vol. 3. New York: Josiah Macy, Jr., Foundation, 1960. (b)

Luria, A. R. *The role of speech in the regulation of normal and abnormal behavior.* London: Pergamon Press, 1961.

Luria, A. R. *Higher cortical functions in man.* Moscow: Izd. Moskov. Univer., 1962. (Also published in English edition by Basic Books, New York, 1966.)

Luria, A. R. *The human brain and mental processes.* Moscow: Izd. Akad. Pedag. Nauk, 1963. (Also published in English edition by Harper, New York, 1965.) (a)

Luria, A. R. *Restoration of function after brain injury.* New York: Macmillan, 1963. (b)

Luria, A. R. Factors and forms of aphasia. In *CIBA Foundation Symposium on Disorders of Language.* London, 1964.

Luria, A. R. *Higher cortical functions in man.* New York: Basic Books, 1966. (a)

Luria, A. R. *The brain and psychological processes.* New York: Harper, 1966. (b)

Luria, A. R., Karpov, B. A., and Yarbus, A. L. Disturbances of complex visual perception with lesions of the frontal lobes. *Brain* (in press).

Luria, A. R., and Khomskaya, E. D. An objective study of ocular movements and their control. *Psychol. Beiträge,* 1962, *6,* Nos. 3–4.

Luria, A. R., and Lebedinskii, M. S. Combined motor method in the examination of neural patients. *Trudy klin. nerv. Biol. Moskov. Gos. Univer.,* Moscow, 1929.

Luria, A. R., and Leont'ev, A. N. Investigation of the objective symptoms of afferent reactions. In *Contemporary problems of psychology.* Moscow, 1926.

Luria, A. R., Pravdina-Vinarskaya, E. M., and Yarbus, A. Z. Disorders of ocular movements in a case of sionulbar-agnosia. *Brain,* 1963, *86,* No. 2.

Luria, A. R., Pribram, K. H., and Khomskaya, E. D. An experimental analysis of the behavioral disturbances produced by a left frontal arachnoidal endothelioma (menineona). *Neuropsychologia,* 1964, No. 2.

Luria, A. R., and Tsvetkova, L. S. The programming activity in local brain lesions. *Neuropsychologia,* 1964, No. 2.

Meshcheryakov, A. I. Disturbances of the interaction of the two signal systems in the formation of simple motor reactions in cases of focal brain lesions. Candidate's dissertation, Inst. Psikhol., Moscow, 1953.

Myasishchev, V. N. The psychophysiological experiment in neural and mental clinics and clinical diagnosis. In *The psychological experiment in the nervous and mental clinics and clinical diagnosis.* Leningrad, 1938.

Myasishchev, V. N. The psychological significance of electrocutaneous indices. *Trudy Inst. Mozga,* 1939, No. 9.

Orbeli, L. A. *Lectures on the physiology of the nervous system.* Moscow-Leningrad, 1935.

Patterson, A., and Zangwill, O. L. Disorders of visual space perception associated with lesions of the right hemisphere. *Brain,* 1945, *68.*

Rossolimo, G. I. *The experimental investigation of psychomechanics.* Moscow: Moskov. Gos. Univer., 1928.

Sokolov, E. N. (Ed.) *The orienting reflex and problems of higher nervous activity.* Moscow: Izd. Akad. Pedag. Nauk RSFSR, 1959.

Spirin, B. G. Disturbance of the mobility of the neural processes after an operation on the brain. Candidate's dissertation, Akad. Med. Nauk SSSR, Moscow, 1951.

Tikhomirov, O. K. Investigation of optimal hypothesis testing in normal and pathological subjects. *Dokl. Akad. Pedag. Nauk RSFSR,* 1961, Nos 4–6.

Vinogradova, O. S. Certain features of the orienting responses to second signal system stimuli in normal and in mentally retarded school children. *Vop. Psikhol.,* 1956, No. 2.

Vygotskii, L. S. Defect and overcompensation. In *Mental-retardation, blindness and deafness and dumbness.* Moscow, 1928.

Vygotskii, L. S. The psychology of schizophrenia. In *Contemporary problems of schizophrenia.* Moscow: Medgiz, 1933.

Vygotskii, L. S. The problem of mental retardation. In *Selected psychological investigations.* Moscow: Izd. Akad. Pedag. Nauk RSFSR, 1956.

Vygotskii, L. S. *Thought and language.* (Translated by E. Hanfmann and G. Vakar.) Cambridge: M.I.T. Press, 1962.

Zankov, L. V. (Ed.) Speech disorders in cases of cranial trauma and their restoration. *Izv. Akad. Pedag. Nauk RSFSR,* 1948, No. 15.

Zeigarnik, B. V. The problem of understanding figurative words or phrases in cases of pathological alterations of thinking. In *New developments in the study of apraxia, agnosia, and aphasia.* Moscow: Ogiz, 1934.

9

Characteristics of Perceptual Activity in the Blind

M. I. Zemtsova

EDITORS' INTRODUCTION

M. I. Zemtsova began her research on teaching the blind in 1933. For the last fifteen years she has been the Director of the Laboratory of the Psychology of Blind Children at the Institute of Defectology in Moscow. "Defectology," a broadly used term in the Russian psychological lexicon, refers to any behavioral or physiological deficit. Two distinguishing characteristics of Soviet research in this area are (1) an emphasis on comparative psychophysiological analysis of the various analyzers and (2) acceptance of the principle that behavior defects should be studied in the context of the work which the defective individual can or must accomplish, so that maximum adaptability of the individual will result.

NO ONE WOULD CLAIM that loss of vision, which has such important significance for the life and activity of man, is without consequence for his development and perceptual activity. However, there are many facts to indicate that in the absence of vision man can still achieve a high degree of perfection in even the most varied and complex forms of activity. The problem to be considered here is how the means used to overcome the difficulties arising in connection with blindness are to be developed.

The basic principles of a theory of compensation based on Pavlov's theory of higher nervous activity and on recent advances in physiology may be summarized as follows:

1. The processes of compensation are based on the reflex principle and are subordinate to the general laws of higher nervous activity in a normal organism.

2. The afferent signals coming from the surrounding environment (and the associations which have been retained) have a great effect on the changes which occur as a result of various lesions within the organism. Man's activity is controlled by systems of afferent signals which stimulate and regulate his acts.

3. The analyzers, through which reality is perceived, do not function in an isolated fashion, but become connected through conditioned-reflex principles. Complex intra- and interanalyzer systems of connections, formed as a function of the content and conditions of the activity as well as the structure of the disturbed functions, support the processes of analysis and synthesis during the perception of reality.

4. The formation of dynamic systems of neural connections occurs most successfully during organized, purposive training. Definite stages in the development of the processes of analysis and synthesis are revealed during the course of this training. The cerebral cortex plays a leading role in any form of compensation, although subcortical structures (such as the reticular formation) also have a function.

The major concern of this study was with the partial forms of compensation which occur in cases of a total loss of vision. Other problems considered were the peculiarities of higher nervous activity and cognitive activity in the blind, how they compensate for the loss of vision, the placement of blind persons in practical professions, and the development of blind children—the content and methods of their training and education.

Many Soviet authors have demonstrated that the loss of visual perception is connected with serious neurodynamic changes. These changes are conditioned by the restructuring of the central nervous system resulting from the limited afferentation of cortical activity and the lack of direct sensory perceptions of reality.

The inability to see the surrounding environment makes it difficult to perceive the dynamic changes of reality and to orient in space. The consequence of this is a greater use of the intact analyzers (auditory, motor, tactile, olfactory, and others) used in the process of orienting activities. Thus the structure and composition of the components of the orienting reaction are altered in cases of a loss of vision.

Studies in which electrophysiological techniques were used showed changes in the course of the orienting reaction, especially in response to auditory stimuli (Asakhov, Zimkina, and Stepanov, 1955; Zimkina, 1957). Unlike those with vision, the blind manifest an intensified orienting reaction to auditory stimuli and for a protracted period of time this reaction does not fade. This occurs because sounds have a different signal significance for the blind than for those who can see. For the blind, sounds are important for orienting in space, for walking, and for cognitive activity. Because blind and normal people have different means of perceiving reality, the functional structures of their orienting reactions are also different. The loss of vision causes a restructuring of the interanalyzer connections and an alteration of the signal significance of many stimuli.

The results of the research done by Zimkina and her co-workers show that, during blind persons' orienting reactions to sounds, there occur powerful subcortical impulses which change the cortex and raise its tonus (Zimkina, 1957; Asakhov, Zimkina, and Stepanov, 1955). The investigators considered this one means of compensatory restructuring of the nervous system in the blind.

The structures developed in the orienting reaction are not strictly fixed; rather, they change as a function of the degree to which the conditions of orientation have become habitual for the blind. Under certain conditions, the orienting reactions to auditory stimuli in the blind are not intensified and, as with those who have vision, quickly fade (Novikova and Zemtsova, 1956; Paramonova and Sokolov, 1956).

The author collaborated on a study of the electrical activity of the brain in forty adult blind people, among whom were three who had been blind from birth (Zemtsova, 1956; Novikova and Zemtsova, 1956). Twelve of these subjects were studied intensively. The results of the investigation showed that the change of electrical activity in the cortex of the blind was significantly greater than that of those with vision. Their electroencephalogram was characterized by a different rhythm than in that of the seeing. Of the forty blind persons studied, the alpha rhythm was absent in the occipital and other areas of the cortex in thirty-seven cases. During the absence of the alpha rhythm (that is, fluctuations of electrical potentials at a frequency of 8 to 13 per second), a beta rhythm (fluctuations of 18 to 20 per second) was sometimes recorded for the blind subjects. In a significant number of cases the curve manifested a sharply flattened character. Fluctuations in the blind are characterized by a high frequency and a low amplitude of the bioelectrical potentials. However, in three of the forty blind a pronounced alpha rhythm was observed in the occipital and other regions of the cortex. The alpha rhythm in the blind, as opposed to that in the seeing, appeared more often in the central and frontal regions of the cortex. Little difference was discovered in the electroencephalograms of those blind from birth and those who had long ago become blind.

The presence of an alpha rhythm in only some of our blind subjects and not in others is proof of the fact that the neurodynamic changes which arise in the blind as a consequence of the absence of afferent impulses from the retina of the eye have a functional character. It was found that the application of different afferent stimuli (auditory, kinesthetic) produced changes in the electrical activity of the occipital area. This indicates preservation of intercentral connections and the input of impulses to the occipital area in the absence of any visual afferent stimulation from the retina.

Investigations indicated that the focus of the brain's electrical activity in a blind person is localized in the central region of the cortex, where alpha-like rhythms are observed in those with vision. The results provided a basis for the assumption that the electrical activity of the cortex of a blind person changes without impulses coming from the retina. This change is more apparent in the occipital region, where the most pronounced alpha rhythm is observed in those with vision, while none is observed with the blind. The results of the study showed that the neurodynamic changes embrace the entire cortex.[1]

Because of the absence of afferent input from the retina, the incoming sensory impulses (auditory, motor, etc.) have different excitatory and inhibitory influences on the electrical activity of the brain in the blind. This is explained, apparently, by the alpha rhythm in the frontal and central areas in the blind. Other results indicated that the loss of vision produced no special pathological phenomena in cortical activity. Slow waves (delta rhythm) were not observed on electroencephalograms of blind persons.

From these results, we see that the loss of vision causes neurodynamic changes which have the character of functional compensatory restructuring. These conclusions were confirmed in investigations concerning the electrical activity of the brain conducted at the Institute of Defectology by Novikova (Novikova and Zemtsova, 1956), who for several years studied 250 blind or partially blind schoolchildren.

Brain potentials were recorded on a 15-channel electroencephalograph. A linear correlation was established between the degree of acuteness of the remaining vision and the degree to which the alpha rhythm was expressed. It was established that the alpha-like rhythm represented a rolandic rhythm, which is recorded in the central region of the cortex significantly more often in the blind than in those who can see. In addition, the rhythm is more pronounced in the left hemisphere. These facts indicate that the rolandic rhythm is connected with compensating processes in the motor analyzer which develop when there is a loss or a significant disturbance of vision. Studies showed that upon loss of sight there was a restructuring of the activity of auditory, tactile, motor, and other receptors. In the absence of visual perception, the cortex is regulated by means of increased afferent input from

---

1. *Editors' note:* The fact that alpha rhythms are absent in the occipital areas of many blind subjects is pertinent to the still not entirely resolved controversy, about whether or not alpha rhythms are some form of mechanical artifact or whether they, in fact, reflect basic processes occurring at the cellular level. Zemtsova's results support the latter position. Her results further emphasize the importance of environmental stimulation for the development of normal brain functioning.

various receptors and by means of the formation of complex systems of dynamic connections (depending upon conditions) which play an important role in compensation. During micro-orientation, in some cases, additional afferent stimulation is obtained from varied organs and systems which are little used under the usual conditions of a functioning sense of sight (from the fingers, tongue, lips, and other organs).

Afferent input to the cortex of the blind is enriched not only by means of various sources of peripheral stimulation, but also by means of the vestigial reactions of the central nervous system. In persons who previously had the use of their sense of sight, vestiges of visual impressions are brought into systemic connections which enrich the representation of the surrounding environment. The vestiges of visual impressions gradually fade in proportion to the development of the various forms of compensation.

The fading of visual images denotes the restructuring of dynamic systems of connections and the formation of new systems, but this fading does not take place immediately. There is a certain inertia of neural processes; the former visual images sometimes come to the surface again in cases where a blind person experiences difficulties in getting oriented. The more the dynamic systems of associations have been connected with the visual component, the more difficult it is to extinguish the visual images. However, the retention of visual impressions depends on the content of the activity of the persons who have gone blind.

As mentioned above, the changes in neurodynamic connections which occur with a loss of sight are of a functional character and in principle have little effect on the development of other senses. The comparative developmental studies of auditory, cutaneous, and motor sensitivity in blind and normal children demonstrate this fact. Our study of audiometric measures of hearing, done with twenty-five blind and twenty-five normal children of 8 to 16 years of age, revealed that sensitivity to tones gradually increases with age to a certain level in blind as well as in normal children. No substantial deviations in the development of hearing in blind children were observed (Zemtsova, 1956).

Kekcheev and others have shown that kinesthetic sensitivity in blind and in normal children also develops according to the same principle (Kekcheev, 1946; Kekcheev and Belova, 1936). Kinesthetic sensitivity increases with age in blind as well as in normal children; however, blind children develop a greater sensitivity than normal children. Zemtsova offered the explanation that both at home and at work the blind person employs his kinesthetic sense to a greater extent because of the absence of visual perception, and consequently this sense becomes more highly developed. However, normal people, depending upon their particular activities, utilize various other sensory capacities (auditory, cutaneous, motor, and others) to a greater extent. Thus the fact is established that qualitative or pathological changes are not apparent in the sensory capacities of the blind.

Our studies showed that work activity plays an enormous role in the development of tactile and kinesthetic senses of the blind. The blind person's work activity enables him to develop an ability to evaluate kinesthetically the shape, size, and weight of objects and their proportional relationships, distances, directions, and so forth. This experience enables the blind person to orient himself correctly when perceiving classroom material, working, walking, and so forth. Studies of the movements of the blind in different planes (Zemtsova, 1956; Kekcheev and Kostina, 1936) have shown that, with certain conditions, the blind orient themselves in space very exactly and carry out delicately coordinated movements of the hands during even the most diversified work operations.

Many blind persons, given relatively constant working conditions, work just as well and are just as productive as normal workers. The participation of the blind in physical culture and sports is of great significance for training the art of movement and orientation in space.

The study of the processes of compensation in man has shown that these processes are very complex and represent a synthesis of biological and social phenomena. Therefore, they cannot be understood if attention is directed only to the physiological aspect of compensation. The very concept of compensation as a method of adaptation to exterior conditions demands the introduction of a series of amendments, when applied to man.

Man's compensations are determined by the content and conditions of the activity in which it takes place, by the individual's social relationships, etc. The specific aspects of compensation in man can be discovered only by a study of the psychological factors involved. A series of psychological studies has shown that the social relationships between people formed during the work process have an important significance in the formation of compensations (Myasishchev, 1957; Kogan, 1952). The social motives of activity, the social significance of the work done, the desire of the individual to keep and strengthen his position in the community—all are factors which have a great significance for how the individual behaves and how he compensates in the event of a functional inability to satisfy the above needs.

Krogius (1926) contributed much to the study of the psychological characteristics of the blind. The results of his twelve-year study of the perceptual activity and mental development of the blind showed that the blind can correctly interpret and evaluate surrounding objects and phenomena (and orient themselves to them) because of the extent to which their auditory, tactile, and other senses had been developed.

The most serious consequence of blindness is the resulting difficulty in perceiving the spatial properties of objects and the relationships between them. Krogius found that his blind subjects made more errors in evaluating the lengths of lines, the curves of arcs, the degree of an angle, and the positions of figures than the normal subjects. In the absence of sight, graphic representation suffers significantly. However, Krogius noted that the content of thoughts concerning the relationships of objects is similar in both blind and normal persons. As a function of intellectual growth, mediating thought processes come to play a more active role in compensation than do sensory impressions. This is true of both normal and blind persons.

Krogius also found that persons who have become blind have a great ability to remember visual representations and to relate objects to one another because of their recollections. He found that the blind have a great advantage over the normal in their ability to recall. They are markedly better than normal persons at remembering and reproducing words and numbers, memorizing poems, and retaining acquired knowledge for long periods of time.

Though not detracting from the significance of Krogius' work, one cannot, however, agree with some of his statements. In discussing how the blind differentiate obstacles, he correctly eliminated the ability to perceive qualitative specifics as a factor, but concluded that temperature stimuli were major variables. Sverlov's studies showed that the perception of obstacles is based on the formation of a complex system, the most important components of which were the auditory analyzer and auditory attention (Sverlov, 1949, 1955).

The Nature of Images in the Blind

Several authors have raised the question as to whether consciousness in the blind is abstractly schematic or is based on visual images. Shemyakin's research on topographic representations in the blind is of great interest in this regard. In experiments with both blind and normal subjects he showed conclusively that the blind as well as the seeing can mentally reproduce the correct shape of an object or a phenomenon. In these experiments the blind were fairly well able to reproduce the map of a locality, which represented the spatial positions of composite points and their relationships to one another and to the subject. His blind subjects were correctly able to indicate the direction of points in Moscow located on all sides of them with approximately the same accuracy as those with sight. The images which arose in the blind were not generic or schematized, but were characterized by a unique "motor visualization." The nature of images in the blind and the seeing was different, but their content was similar in that both groups of subjects reflected an objective, existing reality: for example, in the case above, the topographic map of a locality. Shemyakin noted that in topographic representations the chief factor is motor, not visual, images. It was possible, even without visual representations, to reproduce mentally the correct topography of a locality. However, this process of reproduction was carried out differently by the blind and the seeing. In determining the position and direction of objects, the seeing made great use of a turning gesture, which helped them represent the spatial relationships of objects. They relied on their recollection of complex visual images with all the factors present in actual viewing conditions and orientation in space. Normal subjects determined direction from a given point by mentally turning their bodies and gesturing with their hands, while the blind did not employ such techniques. Instead, they determined the position and direction of an object by relying on the movement of their fingers.

Shemyakin noted that the speed of visual survey does not necessarily determine an accurate or reliable estimate of direction because the motor component is the significant factor in this estimate (Shemyakin, 1940, 1941, 1954). He concluded that the blind have fairly distinct topographic representations and consequently, these representations can be formed without visual images.

Sokolyanskii (1954) and Yarmolenko (1947, 1948, 1954, 1957) demonstrated the possibility of forming complex images which reflect the environment in the absence of vision. Their studies were remarkable because they revealed that it is possible for even those without sight and hearing to form images which reflect spatial and temporal relationships between objects.

The question of how the blind can perceive odorless and soundless objects from a distance has interested researchers from ancient times on. Sverlov has recently done much experimental work on this question and found that the ability to sense obstacles is not peculiar to the blind; under certain conditions, it also occurs in the normal (Sverlov, 1949). However, because the blind must constantly use this ability, they acquire a greater proficiency at it. This ability develops markedly faster when it is trained under specific conditions, Sverlov showed that many cues, including auditory, kinetic, tactile, temperature, and other cues, function in the perception of obstacles from a distance (Sverlov, 1949, 1951, 1955). Auditory stimuli have a leading role in this, as does auditory attention. The blind person in the process of orientation perceives very small changes in the frequency, intensity, or tone of a sound. He can differentiate sounds according to tone, timbre, loudness, and direction—a significant fact in the study of the orientation of the blind.[2]

Under certain conditions, however, this major effect of auditory perception on the blind person's ability to orient himself and perceive obstacles from a distance is lost, and the person thus orients himself by means of the afferent input of other receptors. The question has more than once been raised by Soviet and foreign investigators as to how and to what degree touch can replace vision in the perception of objects. The work of the blind

2. *Editors' note:* Research by Dallenbach and his associates on "facial vision" led them to conclude that the perception of obstacles by the blind is based primarily on changes in pitch.

in technical modeling, relief drawing, and sketching clearly shows that the spatial representations of the blind and the seeing are equivalent in content

The interaction of visual and motor analyzers has great significance on the perception of objects. This was shown by Arana's studies with normal subjects and Kulagin's studies with the blind. According to these studies, the origin of illusions of heaviness is based on the development of systematic interanalyzer connections during the perception of the weight and volume of objects (Kulagin, 1957). Kulagin studied the illusions of seventeen blind children of various ages. He presented two plywood parallelopipeds of equal weights (145 gm.), but different volumes (the volume of one was 450 cubic centimeters, the other, 180 cubic centimeters). Though the weights were equal, both blind and normal subjects thought the 180-cubic-centimeter parallelopiped was heavier. This illusion of heaviness is evidence of the fact that, during the course of their actual experiences, the blind have formed concepts of the relation between the weight and volume of objects. Normal persons perceive weight with the aid of a kinetic sense and volume with the aid of vision, whereas the blind person perceives both weight and volume kinesthetically. The blind as well as the seeing react not to separate, isolated stimuli, but rather to the relationships between stimuli which have been formed and reinforced in their experience. Thus the object of greater volume seems lighter than the object of lesser volume. The signal significance of volume is of vital importance in stereognosis (the tactile recognition of three-dimensional objects).

Sverlov's studies (1957) on this question are of great interest. He presented (to subjects blind from birth and subjects who later became blind) sculptured portraits which the subjects were to recognize. The results showed that graphic perceptions are not absent in experimental subjects who had been blind from birth and had never had the use of sight. As a result of tactile perception of the sculpture, the blind children and adults exhibited vividly pronounced emotions (a smile, an exclamation, delight, etc.). Sverlov noted that the blind certainly could not, with the aid of touch, evaluate the subtleties of the exposition (such as the play of light and dark), but that they were better able to evaluate the shape and characteristic details (Sverlov, 1957). The blind person's image may be more meager than in the normal person's, but it does reflect reality. This image becomes richer, fuller, and more exact when a verbal description of the sculptured work precedes the tactile inspection of it. Thus, in spite of his limitations, the blind person's thought and speech enable him to re-create the forms of objects and phenomena never directly perceived. This factor is of great importance in the formation of spatial representations. All of this is a powerful means of compensating and overcoming the consequences of blindness, especially in children whose sense experience is limited.

Teaching Imagery to the Blind

It is known that the limitation of sense experience has a significant influence on the formation of graphic cognition and on spatial representations in blind children, which leads to a discrepancy between the development of verbal systems of communication on the one hand, and visual sense experience on the other. However, if the correct techniques and methods of training are used, it is possible to overcome the problems of the sensory cognition of reality in blind children and to secure the conditions for their normal development.

The difficulty which blind children have in learning the spatial properties of objects (shapes, sizes, directions, positions, and so forth) has an effect on their general learning ability and especially on their ability to learn geometric material. Their mistakes in estimating length measurements can be attributed not so much to the fact that they cannot see these measurements as to the fact that verbal explanations and training techniques do not contribute to the formation of proper concepts of specific units of measurement. A teacher can give them the name of measures; they can get some idea of them through touch, but they do not have the common, daily practice of employing these measurements. Thus, the connections they form, for example, between the tactile-motor image reflecting linear extension and the word designating the numerical expression of this measurement is not reinforced by the process of practical activity; the necessary correlations of image, word, and action are not achieved. The formation of representations of measures depends upon how often the students, in their experience, make practical use of the measurements of, in this example, different distances between objects.

However, given certain conditions and the correct methods of training, blind children can form accurate representations of measures of space and can master these measures in practice. With the mastery of knowledge and practical skills, their spatial representations are enriched. They learn to separate and to synthesize the symbols which are characteristic of the spatial properties of objects and relationships among them. The presence of concrete images allows them to form accurate connections between their images and verbal definitions. This is manifested by the objects that blind children can model and their verbal definitions of these objects. Those who have not mastered the skills of modeling are still able to recognize these objects—proof that they have made the proper connections.

The already present graphic images on which they can rely during the process of recognizing objects have a great effect on the perception of objects by blind children. The visual representations of shapes, lengths, positions, and directions also help the blind in recognizing objects. However, when younger children are blinded, visual representations are not yet sufficiently consistent and can extinguish if they are not reinforced. As a result images can become unclear and diffused. This is distinctly observable when children who have become blind since birth are asked to write on a flat surface.

Our studies have shown that in writing these usual "flat" letters, blind children rely on visual representations. As they produce a movement with a pencil on paper, they mentally break down the graphic outline of the letter into its component parts and then combine them into an integral composition. Because the process of writing is performed without visual control, the outline of the letter is inexact. Some children arbitrarily change the place of the letters in space; they arrange them in the most diverse positions; they mix them up and turn them around, sometimes to an angle of 180 degrees; that is, they do mirror-writing (not infrequently, this is observed even in first-grade children with sight). Sometimes one letter is replaced by another because of the resemblance of some component elements. The students mix up the spatial positions of the graphic elements composing the letters; they forget the proper forms; they confuse similar letters. They are also poor at differentiating the size, proportion, shape, and positions of the elements of letters.

The graphic image does not fade immediately, but changes gradually. The separate elements of the visual image do not fade at the same rate; the representation of the shape and composition of the letter is maintained for a long time, although individual elements may drop out of the general composition.

Adult blind persons do not lose the habit of writing letters in flat script. This is explained by the fact that, while they were able to see, they were in perfect possession of the habits of graphic linear writing and used them without special effort and without visual self-checking. As a result of much practice in writing, a stable connection between the visual and other analyzers had been formed. This permits them to retain the image of the letter sometimes throughout their lifetime and to use the habits of graphic linear writing. We encountered blind people who, after fifty to sixty years without vision, still retained the ability to write in ordinary script.

At the present time, training the blind in graphics has great significance, especially since Semevskii (1952), a teacher at the Moscow School for the Blind, developed a special mastic instrument for relief drawing and thus found a simple means for the preparation of relief drawings. The urgency of training the blind in graphics is growing in connection with the introduction of vocational education in our country and with the transfer of the schools for the blind to intermediate education. The use of graphic instruments is important in preparing students for practical activity. Therefore, it is no accident that this problem of training has been widely attacked by specialists occupied in the professional labor-training of the blind.

Roganov (1940, 1946) has made a great contribution to this problem. He developed a system of training the blind in relief graphics with an album of technical drawings. His trainees could easily read complex technical drafts and plans for the construction of machines, appliances, and instruments.

Many problems developed along with this practice of training the blind in relief drawing. First, there was the question of whether it was possible for one without sight to draft the image of an object in a relief drawing: how can a likeness of a three-dimensional object be transmitted in two-dimensional space in such a way that the blind person can reconstruct the object according to this image by the use of tactile perception? Can the blind person, using graphic means, re-create the objective image of an object by means of verbal description? Is it possible for a blind person to perceive a stereometric, three-dimensional drawing and re-create a complex object according to this drawing?

In order to answer these questions, we conducted some experiments on training the blind in relief drawing. We found that, with training, the blind can correctly correlate the image of an object with the image of the drawing and can note similarities between the object and its depiction in the drawing. Those who once had sight were more easily able to re-create the image of an object from a relief drawing of it.

It was observed that some blind persons, who had earlier learned to draw, struck a pose (position of the head, focusing of the eyes) typical of those who can see; that is, they reproduced the connections between the kinetic sensation of the hand and the kinesthesis from the eye muscles which normally develop in individuals. This "visual image" arises without any influence from the retina.

In a study done with Novikova (Novikova and Zemtsova, 1956), we found it possible to reproduce the visual-kinetic connections in the blind by recording the motion of the eyes and hands during the execution of relief drawings. The electrographic method permits an objective analysis of the complex processes of interaction between the visual and motor analyzers during the perception and the reproduction of the drawing. The results of our studies showed that, while the subjects made two-dimensional drawings of various objects and read the relief drawings, the movement of their eyes occurred simultaneously with the movement of their hands. This was seen quite clearly on the electromyogram and the oculogram of the blind. With more complex tasks, impulses from the muscles of the eyes increased. This is evidence of the presence of visual-kinetic connections (which form the basis of the visual image) obtained in the experience of those who had become blind as differentiated from those who had been born blind.

Visual-kinetic connections are more vividly revealed in the relief drawing of the blind. High-amplitude oscillations from the eye muscles and the hand simultaneously are recorded during the drawing. As soon as the process of drawing ceases, the activity curve resumes its initial form. With the cessation of the kinesthetic impulses from the muscles of the hand, the kinesthetic impulses from the muscles of the eye also disappear. The disappearance of impulses from the muscles of the hand and the eye during the tactile perception of the drawing and during the drawing itself do not occur at the same time. The kinesthetic impulses from the muscles of the hand disappear first, followed by the impulses from the muscles of the eye. The blind person seemingly continues to mentally survey the picture. The tactile investigation of natural objects is very important in re-creating images in drawings.

The blind have difficulty in translating a volumetric object into a flat likeness. The methods of depicting a volumetric, three-dimensional body as a flat, two-dimensional drawing are different for the blind and normal persons. This process is facilitated with the normal person by the presence of a full visual image of the object and of the picture and because of his experience (from childhood on) in relating volumetric objects to their flat representations on paper and in copying the depictive means of the adults around him.

The possibility of perceiving three-dimensional drawings has been proven by the long, experimental experience of training the blind in drawing and sketching and by experimental research. Volkov (1950) and others have shown that the laws of linear perspective do not depend on laws of visual perception. The theory of linear perspective is based on projectional geometry. Although the seeing person visually perceives the perspective changes of shape, his understanding of the sense of depiction is of prime significance.

The cerebral cortex fulfills the regulating role in visual perception by exerting an influence on the visual receptors. The impressions of objects make a comparatively reduced picture on the retina of the eye, but because of the regulation of the nerve cells of the occipital region of the cortex, we see the objects as they exist in reality. It is possible, with the aid of training, to achieve a reverse perception of objects. If the cortical nerve cells of the occipital region are damaged, the recognition of well-known objects becomes impossible and psychological blindness occurs.

The experimental studies done by Muratov (1957) on the blind person's ability to perceive depth with the aid of an audio-optical instrument showed that the blind can quite correctly estimate the perspective foreshortening of an object receding in depth using sounds converted from light signals. The dimensions of the object receding in depth to a certain distance are perceived as more reduced than the dimensions of the same object placed close. Consequently, the perception of perspective can be secured not only through visual analyzers, but also through auditory and other analyzers.

It was commonly believed that the perception of perspective depends exclusively on vision, and therefore is completely inaccessible for the blind. Accordingly, it was thought useless to teach the blind the perception of three-dimensional pictures. However, experiences in the teaching of drawing to the blind have shown that even those born blind can learn to understand perspective drawings. Kulagin's experiments (1960) showed that blind children, with special training and with the use of nonuniform point filling, can develop a tactile perception of perspective changes of the dimensions of geometric figures in relief pictures shown under different angles of rotation.

The verbal delineation of objects is also of great importance in the formation of an image. However, it can give an incomplete, sometimes distorted representation unless reinforced by the sense perception of an object. The work of Semevskii, who trained blind children in relief-projectional drawing, merits special attention (Semevskii, 1952). With training, his students exactly reproduced the image of the object in a relief, two-dimensional drawing and re-created it with modeling plastic in a three-dimensional model. Conversely, they easily re-created, according to a three-dimensional model, the images of the picture and transferred them to a two-dimensional projection. The transition from the model to the picture and from the picture to the model manifests their ability to analyze the image of the object and the image of the picture and their ability to use drawing techniques. The students correctly contrasted the lines of the object pictured and the lines of the contour of the two-dimensional drawing. Everything that was superfluous or fortuitous was screened in the relief drawing; only the most essential and typical symbols, which characterized the shape and structure of the object, were transferred.

The use of drawing has tremendous significance as a means of forming children's graphic perception and developing their spatial thinking. Drawing, modeling, and various kinds of practical work in schools for the blind equip the children with a means of perceiving reality. Having mastered the means of reading and of making drawings, blind children can more fully and more diversely express their representations and knowledge during the process of learning the fundamentals of the sciences. This permits the teacher to evaluate not only their verbal knowledge, but also their objective representations of reality.

Training in the making and reading of drawings enables the development, in blind children, of a graphic perception of reality and the formation of objective, spatial representations. It helps in noting and sorting out the essential symbols, in synthesizing them, in abstracting them from the accidental ones, and in properly transmitting the image of the subject in the drawing. The formation of graphic perception in the blind is accomplished on the basis of analysis and synthesis, processes which depend on the didactic techniques of teaching.

The processes of analysis and synthesis, as our studies have shown, are facilitated when students are faced with a problem which gives direction to their intellectual activity and when the objects are studied directly in the common experiences of the children. As students model objects, they more delicately perceive their shape, structure, size, and so forth. Through modeling it is easy to discover the problems in the blind child's representations. This method forces him each time to resort to a more subtle analysis of the volumetric form of the object.

Cutting out paper silhouettes of objects also has a great significance in the correct understanding of a drawing. It helps the students to better comprehend a two-dimensional shape and leads them to an understanding of projections. During this process, the students seemingly outline the linear contours of the objects.

The processes of forming an image are facilitated if the object being perceived has a practical, everyday significance for the blind person and if it interests him. Objects which the children use in practical play or work activities are more clearly and easily recognized. Direct perception is always accomplished by using the acquired knowledge and past experience of the children. Also of great importance in this process are the social contacts which permit the children to use the experiences of others, as well as their own.

The explanations of the teacher provide diverse concrete symbols of the object and help the students to extract the chief characteristics. In such explanations, the students' attention turns to the structural and spatial properties of the objects. In blind children the correct connection between word and image does not always occur. This often happens when the teacher does not attend to the development of graphic thinking in blind children and is satisfied with their verbal knowledge. A disparity between concrete representations and abstract concepts sometimes occurs not only in young children of early school age, but even in children of the senior classes in schools for the blind.

The impoverishment of graphic thinking and the limited opportunities for observation make generalization difficult for blind children. For normal children, the graphic, visual image of the object is a crucial element in its classification within a definite group. Blind children, however, classify little-known objects into certain groups mainly on the basis of social representations. The correlation between verbal designations of objects and their images is disturbed in these children, but with normal school-children, this disturbance is less pronounced. As a function of years of schooling, graphic thinking is more enriched in the seeing than in the blind.

As a result of their impoverished graphic thinking, blind children develop other methods of generalization, which are based, in a number of cases, only on vocal connections. Generalization is accomplished on the basis of the formation of a group of representative symbols and verbal connections with a former image. The graphic-vocal method of generalization is also encountered in seeing children of junior school age. This is explained by the limited store of representations of surrounding objects. If the objects are familiar to children through their experiences, they rely on graphic images during the formation of concepts. Kostyuchek's studies (1956) clearly showed that there are no observable disruptions in the correlations between verbal designations and the images of objects in concepts that are well known to blind children from their daily lives and work experience.

Oral and written speech play an enormous role in the processes of compensation and in the cognitive activities of blind children. Through language, the blind child consolidates his knowledge and communicates with those around him. This communication enriches his intellectual development and increases his conscious reflection of the surrounding world. The correlation of the sensory and the verbal does not remain unchanged. Complex interactions of graphic images and words develop in the process of schooling, depending on the extent of accomplishments and practical experiences. The size of the child's vocabulary grows and his understanding of word meanings increases. The role of the image qualitatively changes in the different stages of schooling.

Creative Imagination in the Blind

Creative imagination, one form of reflecting reality, has an important role in the processes of perception in the blind. The role of creative imagination is enhanced in the absence of a visual perception of reality. It helps to fill the gaps in the sensory images present in the blind. However, if no preliminary work has been done to familiarize blind children in some tangible way with the objects and phenomena confronting them, then the creative image can incorrectly reflect surrounding phenomena.

It is especially difficult for blind children to re-create images of the dynamic phenomena of nature from descriptions of landscapes and the like. In such cases it is typical of students to relate, in their accounts and stories, the logical aspect of the text rather than the concrete images. Sometimes the students use words and figurative expressions without relying on concrete and graphic images. It should be noted that normal children also have more difficulty in re-creating an image from descriptions of nature than they do in re-creating the meaning of the text.

Blind children very often introduce new elements into their tales, stories, and accounts, drawing on communications they have had or some emotionally embellished recollections of happenings in their personal lives. If they have observed the objects and phenomena being discussed in various works of literature in their daily lives or in special classes, they can re-create these images from immediate sensory connections. These images are considerably livelier, richer, and fuller. Such images are retained longer and are enriched and restructured with more knowledge and experiences.

There are various means of re-creating an image. In some cases the blind rely on direct sensory capacities (auditory, tactile, and kinetic stimulation). External stimuli evoke auditory, tactile-motor, and other representations contained in the experience of the blind person. Thus, the blind woman, Sh., perceiving by radio the auditory melodies of spoken letters, creates, under their influence, complex musical images. The blind man, G., under the influence of the same auditory melodies, re-creates the visual images of graphic signs of the Morse alphabet which he first encountered in a physics course he took while he could still see. The blind man, N., under the influence of these same auditory signals, re-created visual images of printed letters, and so forth. Thus, various associative connections between different components in various individuals are elicited by the same stimuli, depending on their particular experiences.

The re-creation of images in adult blind persons can occur with a limited reliance on immediate sensory elements. Skorokhodova's book *How I Perceive the World* (1956) is of great interest.[3] In one of her essays, "How I Picture What Is Occurring on the Stage," she notes that a direct graphic image as well as a verbal description of what is happening on stage make strong impressions on her. In describing the national dance of a Cossack, she notes:

> He seemed to be of medium size (although I was not told what size he was) with a laughing face and quick, sure movements. I could not visualize the upper part of the costume, but there seemed to be wide sleeves which billowed out during the dance; I visualized the lower part of the costume as wide bell-bottom trousers. As a result of sensing the sounds of the music (a piano) and the pounding of feet I could visualize how fast and with what enthusiasm the Cossack was dancing. His "fire" dance infected me; I was so electrified that I was ready to swear that I saw the dancer, that I was feeling his blouse with the billowing sleeves and his face inflamed with the dance which seemed to smile, showing strong, well-formed teeth. The image of the dancing artist arose in my imagination only because I sensed the vibrations of the gay music and the feel of the brisk footfalls (Skorokhodova, 1956, p. 246).

To show what perfection and creativity a blind person can exhibit, we conducted a series of individual experiments on the study of design thinking in blind engineers and technicians. With this goal in mind, we suggested

3. *Editors' note:* Skorokhodova is a deaf, blind person who is as famous in the U.S.S.R. as Helen Keller was in the United States.

that they develop the design of some original project, in an area familiar to them, and dictate it to a draftsman so that the latter could execute a sketch from their plan. The preliminary plan of the project and the dictation to the draftsman is a complex intellectual task which assumes a highly developed spatial imagination in the blind. The process of dictating the project meant that the blind, using their knowledge of the rules of projection drawing, transmitted, through words, a system of successive judgments and calculations reflecting the structural solution of the problem. In the dictation they operated with a complex system of conceptions, relying on graphic-spatial images of parts, assemblies, operating mechanisms, and the like. Drawing on their previous experience, they isolated individual fragments of complex images and established connections and relationships among them based on mathematical calculations. They clearly represented the relative positions of the operating mechanisms to themselves, mentally changed the positions of the parts in space, re-formed the separate assemblies, and united them into complex mechanisms.

Sometimes their speech was accompanied by descriptive movements, encircling the contour of the details with their finger on the table and in the air, making graphic "models" with bent paper, and so forth. This helped them to represent more distinctly the operating mechanisms and the relative position of the parts. They asked the draftsman several control questions to check themselves and to ascertain how closely their design solution had correlated with the technical requirements.

In the process of dictation the blind constructed new images, which were rearranged with new functions in the design solution—details, dimensions, the choice of the principles of connection, the interlocking of parts, and the like were varied.

With the use of words, the blind embodied their creative thoughts in a sketch technically executed by another person. Gradually, in the process of realizing the initial creative idea, their words are supplemented with specific actions (drawing with the finger on the table, in the air, and the like). This evokes associative connections which are present from their experience and serves as an impetus for further thinking.

The richer the knowledge and practical experience of the blind in a particular area, the wider are the possibilities for the creation and enrichment of the image of the design. We see that creative imagination is a powerful means of reconstructing complex visual-kinetic, audiovisual, and other images. However, it is necessary to take into account the fact that imagination represents a certain departure and withdrawal from reality. Therefore, not all that is in the imagination of man correctly reflects objective phenomena. In the absence of visual perception, without a visual basis and limit for the imagination, there is the danger of retreating into complete abstraction. In this event, the images may be created without relying on the concrete diversity of reality. The reality reflected in this case may be incomplete, sometimes even incorrect and distorted.

The images in the blind can be fantastic, even though these images always reflect objective reality to a certain degree. In order to avoid the distortion of images it is necessary for the blind person to create conditions so that their images have meaning within their practical activity. In this regard, the tasks of technical modeling, relief sketching, relief drawing, cut-outs, and other forms of practical work in schools for the blind are of great significance. In reconstructing an image, the preliminary verbal sketch plays an important role. On the basis of the perception and reconstruction of former representations and verbal sketches of objects and phenomena, children create new images which do reflect reality. Relying on previous experience and verbal description, they can represent a locality in which they have never been and create a distinct representation of operating machines, and the exterior form and structure of animals and plants which they have never seen.

Thus, the blind inventor, T., tells that when technical literature is read to him, he, according to the description of the construction of the mechanisms, distinctly imagines the interaction of the parts, the system of transmission, and the complex dynamic processes. During this process he sometimes forms ideas for a new design of a particular assembly or whole mechanism, a change in the interaction of the parts, and the like. In the description of technical details, his mind seemingly "races" ahead, relying on the knowledge of general laws and the technical principles of mechanical action. On the basis of a few initial data, he can distinctly imagine the whole complex, dynamic system of transmissions, the interactions of the parts, the possible links, and the terminal result of the action of the mechanisms as a whole.

Imaginative reconstruction has great significance for the student's mastery of the fundamentals of the sciences of physics, mathematics, geography, chemistry, biology, and drafting. It has especially great significance in the mastery of skills in machine control, electrical technology, radio technology, and the like. With the introduction in many schools of machine operations, electrical technology, radio technology, and construction assembly, imaginative reconstruction plays an exceptional role, since the above-mentioned disciplines make greater demands on the intellectual activity of the blind and on their ability to form complex generalizations which characterize the spatial properties and the spatial relationships between the objects. Spatial thinking in the blind plays an enormous role in the operation of mechanisms, in the making of measurements, and in the elimination of various sorts of malfunctioning. It acquires special significance in the solution of technical questions, in the use of the different types of appliances and measuring instruments, in the study of the organization of machines, engines and instruments, and in the reading of relief drawings.

Thus, we can see from the foregoing that the gaps of sense experiences in the blind can be closed only by properly developing the students' abilities in fields which are directed toward developing their activity and independence. The period of training in a school for the blind should devote a great deal of attention not only to equipping the students with the knowledge, skill, and habits necessary in their practical activity, but also to developing their thinking, speaking, and creative imaginations.

Image thinking and sense perception in the blind are enriched also by the use of special technical means of compensation. Special typhlo-instruments developed by various researchers provide these means (Germanov, 1957; Verbuk, 1957a; Muratov, 1957; Fishlev, 1959). These instruments permit the replacement of visual perception of optical symbols with an auditory perception of objects, thereby enriching the representations of surrounding reality by the blind.

The instruments developed by the Sverdlovsk Typhlo-Technical Laboratory of the Institute of Defectology permit the blind person to perceive many objects and phenomena by means of auditory signals.

Investigations using a computer to code visual signs showed that the blind were better able to perceive auditory and tactile signals than vibrations. Thus, when using phonic signals, it was found that, in the beginning stages of learning, auditory stimuli were correctly perceived 67.5 per cent of the time, tactile stimuli 56 per cent, and vibrations 50 per cent. This is interpreted to mean that the blind are better able to use a conditional code made up of auditory or tactile stimuli than normal, seeing subjects (Verbuk, 1957a; Fishlev, 1959). Table 9–1 indicates the percentage of correctly decoded conditional signals for blind and normal subjects.

Table 9–1

	Phonic	Tactile	Vibration
Normal vision	55.5%	42.3%	38.5%
Blind	79.5	71	62

The data obtained using this "typographical" instrument permit us to use these more effective methods for coding visual stimuli and guarantee that the blind can reliably receive information from written characters.

Foreign authors have also developed technological methods to compensate for blindness. Their work was reported at the international congress on the technological problems of blindness (1963).

The experimental training of a group of blind persons carried out by the Sverdlovsk Typhlo-Technical Laboratory on a phonetic device (Villey, 1931) showed that the blind, after a period of training in using auditory signals, can read any ordinary text with a speed of 300 to 400 signs a minute.

Sokolyanskii and Kulagin (1956) got positive results in training the blind to read ordinary script with the aid of a tactile device. In this case the usual flat-printed script is transformed, with the aid of the photo effect, into unique signals which are perceived by the blind through touch (Belyaev, 1958). However, these devices are still in the experimental stages. The efforts made thus far at broadening the perceptual potentials of the blind with the aid of technical means are still insufficient. Sokolyanskii and Kulagin are presently making further efforts at perfecting these devices.

The technical means of compensation are of great significance for the placement of the blind. Special test instruments and appliances permitting the blind, with the aid of touch and hearing, to determine readings with an exactness of up to 0.002 mm. (sliding calipers, inside calipers, micrometers, measuring rules, and electronic measuring devices) have been developed by several Soviet authors.

Socially useful labor is the most powerful method of compensating for and overcoming the limitations of blindness. Therefore, it is no accident that a large group of teachers, psychologists, engineers, and other specialists is devoting great attention to studies of the professions available for the blind and the prospects of their efficient placement. The introduction of intermediate education and vocational training in our country is of great importance not only for preparing students for practical life, but also for developing their cognitive potentials and for forming their personalities in general.

The study of the processes of compensation and the peculiarities of the mental activities of the blind is valuable to the effort to raise the quality of training, education, placement, and health safeguards of the blind. Relying on methods of compensation, it is possible, with the aid of scientifically based methods and the creation of the necessary conditions, to overcome the difficulties caused by blindness, to attain an all-around intellectual and physical development, and to secure their preparation for an active life.

References

Asakhov, B. D., Zimkina, A. M., and Stepanov, A. I. The peculiarities of the orienting reaction to audio stimulation in the blind. *Fiziol. Zh. SSSR,* 1955, *90,* No. 3.

Belyaev, I. G. The role of vision in the development of the functions of the motor analyzer. In *Peculiarities of the cognitive activity of the blind.* Izd. Akad. Pedag. Nauk RSFSR, 1958.

Bogolepov, N. K. *The effect of vascular lesions in the brain on motor functions.* Moscow: Medgiz, 1953.

Fishlev, Y. R. Substituting for visual functions in the education of blind children by use of photoelectric equipment. Candidate's dissertation, Sverdlovsk, 1959.

Germanov, M. M. The transformation of typographical symbols into forms perceptible to the blind. *Izv. Akad. Pedag. Nauk RSFSR,* 1957, No. 90.

Kekcheev, K. K. *The significance of interoception and proprioception for the clinic.* Moscow: Medgiz, 1946.

Kekcheev, K. K., and Belova, T. I. Developmental alterations of sensory proprioception. *Fiziol. Zh. SSSR,* 1936, *21,* No. 1.

Kekcheev, K. K., and Kostina, E. I. The physiological study of the orientation of the blind. *Fiziol. Zh. SSSR,* 1936, *21,* No. 5.

Kogan, V. M. Principles of placement and rehabilitation of invalids. In *Placement and rehabilitation for invalids.* Moscow: Izd. Tsen. Nauch.-Issled. Inst. Eksper. Trud. Organiz. Trud. Invalid., 1952.

Kostyuchek, N. S. Vocabulary of pupils in the first and second grades in schools for the blind. In *Teaching and training work in special schools.* Issue 2. Moscow: Uchpedgiz, 1955.

Kostyuchek, N. S. Study of blind and normal children of early school age. In *Teaching and training work in special schools.* Issue 2. Moscow: Uchpedgiz, 1956.

Kostyuchek, N. S. Representations, speech, and thought in students of the first through fourth grades in schools for the blind. *Izv. Akad. Pedag. Nauk RSFSR,* 1957, No. 96. (a)

Kostyuchek, N. S. Peculiarities of the perception of blind children of early school age. *Izv. Akad. Pedag. Nauk RSFSR,* 1957, No. 90. (b)

Krogius, A. A. *Psychology of the blind and its significance for general psychology and pedagogy.* Saratov: Author, 1926.

Kulagin, Y. A. Manifestations of the neural mechanism in tactile perception in the blind. *Izv. Akad. Pedag. Nauk RSFSR,* 1957, No. 90.

Kulagin, Y. A. The development of tactile perception of relief illustrations by students in schools for the blind. *Dokl. Akad. Pedag. Nauk RSFSR,* 1960, No. 1.

Kuzin, N. S. Accuracy of the work of the blind at the lathe in shaping rotating bodies. In M. I. Zemtsova (Ed.), *Preparation of students in schools for the blind in production activity.* Izd. Akad. Pedag. Nauk RSFSR, 1958. (a)

Kuzin, N. S. Teaching of machine operations to the blind in connection with general education in middle schools. In M. I. Zemtsova (Ed.), *Preparation of students in schools for the blind in production activity.* Izd. Akad. Pedag. Nauk RSFSR, 1958. (b)

Muratov, R. S. Compensation for blindness by means of special instruments for the blind. *Izv. Akad. Pedag, Nauk RSFSR,* 1957, No. 90.

Myasishchev, V. N. The problem of personality and relationships in the individual. In *Materials of a Conference on Psychology*. Izd. Akad. Pedag. Nauk RSFSR, 1957.

Novikova, L. A., and Zemtsova, M. I. Study of the functional condition of the brain in the blind by the method of electroencephalography. In *Reports at a Conference on Defectology (3–6 January 1956)*. Izd. Akad. Pedag. Nauk RSFSR, 1956. (Abstract)

Paramonova, N. P., and Sokolov, E. N. The reactivity of the auditory analyzer in the blind as investigated by the method of complex recording. In *Reports at a Conference on Defectology (3–6 January 1956)*. Izd. Akad. Pedag. Nauk RSFSR, 1956 (Abstract)

Pesin, I. B. Noncurricular activities in radio technology in schools for the blind. In *Teaching and training work in special schools*. Issue 4. Moscow, 1955.

Potapov, V. S. An experiment at setting up a production schedule for blind students. In *Collection of works dealing with the placement of invalids*. Leningrad, 1933.

Roganov, G. N. *Methods of instructing the blind in reading sketches for machine construction, kinematic schemes, and technical designs*. Moscow: Uchpedgiz, 1940.

Roganov, G. N. *Organizing labor among the blind and instructing them in work on the metal-cutting lathe*. Moscow: Uchpedgiz, 1946.

Semevskii, N. A. *The teaching of drawing in schools for the blind*. Moscow: Uchpedgiz, 1952.

Shemyakin, F. N. Toward the psychology of spatial representations. *Uch. Zap. Inst. Psikhol.*, 1940, *1*.

Shemyakin, F. N. The question of topographic representations in the blind. *Sovet. Nevropsikhol*, 1941, *6*.

Shemyakin, F. N. Investigation of topographic representations. *Izv. Akad. Pedag. Nauk RSFSR*, 1954, No. 53.

Skorokhodova, O. I. *How I perceive and picture the world around me*. Moscow: Izd. Akad. Pedag. Nauk RSFSR, 1954.

Sokolyanskii, I. A. Some observations on deaf-mutes. Preface to O. I. Skorokhodova, *How I perceive and picture the world around me*. Moscow: Izd. Akad. Pedag. Nauk RSFSR, 1954.

Sokolyanskii, I. A., and Kulagin, Y. A. Reading of flat-bed printing by the blind. *Vop. Psikhol*, 1956, No. 5.

Sverlov, V. S. *Obstacle perception and its role in the orientation of the blind*. Moscow: Uchpedgiz, 1949.

Sverlov, V. S. *Spatial orientation of the blind*. Moscow: Uchpedgiz, 1951.

Sverlov, V. S. Orientation of the blind. Candidate's dissertation, Moscow, 1955.

Sverlov, V. S. Perception of sculpture among the blind. *Izv. Akad. Pedag. Nauk RSFSR*, 1957, No. 90.

Verbuk, M. A. New possibilities for increasing palpability in schools for the blind. In *Teaching and training work in special schools*. Issue 1. Moscow: Uchpedgiz, 1957. (a)

Verbuk, M. A. How the blind can read a printed text by means of prearranged phonic signals. *Izv. Akad. Pedag. Nauk RSFSR,* 1957, No. 90. (b)

Villey, P. *Psychology of the blind.* (Russian edition.) Moscow-Leningrad: Uchpedgiz, 1931.

Volkov, N. N. *Perception of object and picture.* Moscow: Izd. Akad. Pedag. Nauk RSFSR, 1950.

Yarmolenko, A. V. *The influence of conditions of perception and earlier experience on the formation of tactile representations.* Leningrad, 1947.

Yarmolenko, A. V. The formation of spatial representations with a limited sensory basis. In *Problems of psychology.* Leningrad: Izd. LGU, 1948.

Yarmolenko, A. V. Interdependence of the first and second signal systems upon loss of hearing and sight. *Uch. Zap. LGU,* 1954, No. 147.

Yarmolenko, A. V. The role of motor sensations in sensory cognition upon loss of hearing and sight. In *Materials of a Conference on Psychology.* Moscow: Izd. Akad. Pedag. Nauk RSFSR, 1957.

Zemtsova, M. I. *How the blind compensate in cognitive and work activity.* Izd. Akad. Pedag. Nauk RSFSR, 1956.

Zimkina, A. M. On the orienting reaction. In *Materials of a Conference on Psychology.* Izd. Akad. Pedag. Nauk RSFSR, 1957.

10

Development of Children in Schools for the Mentally Retarded

Z. I. Shif

EDITORS' INTRODUCTION

Z. I. Shif began her research at Moscow's Institute of Defectology in 1934. A student of Vygotskii, Shif has long been interested in the comparative development of normal and defective children. Although her research has been carried out in an applied setting with all of its pressing demands, the resulting findings have broad implications for the understanding of cognitive development.

The close collaboration between Shif, Zemtsova, and Solov'ev (whose work is discussed at length by Shif) has made their Institute one of the world's outstanding research facilities for the study of defective children.

THE STUDY OF retarded children became a branch of the psychological sciences in Russia only after the Great October Revolution. Until then it had been primarily the concern of the medical sciences. The training and study of retarded children became the undertaking of the Ministry of Education. A network of state boarding and day schools was established in which such children received work training in addition to education.

At the end of the 1930's the scientific supervision of pedagogical work in this area was entrusted to the Experimental Defectological Institute. A planned and systematic study of the psychological characteristics of the retarded child was undertaken there under the guidance of Vygotskii. As far as we know the first experimental-psychological laboratory in the world for the study of retarded children was organized at this institute, which later became the Scientific Research Institute of Defectology of the Academy of Pedagogical Sciences, R.S.F.S.R., in which the study of retarded children continues to this day.

From the very beginning, Soviet psychologists have been concerned not only with the peculiarities of these children, but with their development under conditions of special corrective training. Psychological research centering around the mentally retarded (that is, children with psychological disturbances resulting from intrauterine or early-childhood brain illnesses) has revealed not only their defects but also their positive abilities. Russian physiology has proved that the human cortex is flexible, and that in cases of brain damage the cortex, under favorable conditions, can reorganize its functions. This is scientific confirmation of the clinical and psychological studies with mentally retarded children.

Foreign psychologists have studied the symptoms and levels of the mentally retarded, but have taken into account neither environment nor the possibility of development. These psychologists have equated school age and adolescent oligophrenics (mental deficients) with normal children of preschool age. They emphasize a "ceiling" for the mentally retarded child, that is, the limited possibilities for his development. Soviet experience in the training and education of the mentally retarded, as well as the results of psychological research, indicates, on the contrary, that the possibilities for development are significant. Soviet psychologists have systematically studied retarded children of younger, middle, and older school age. These studies have traced the course of their development under the influence of training. We defend the position that the basic laws of psychological development in normal children are equally valid for the mentally retarded child, although the latter develops in his own way. Thus, the problems and methods involved in studying the mentally retarded child are very similar to the methods of child psychology in general.

The psychology of mentally retarded children in the Soviet Union was conceived of as a comparative method for the study of normal and retarded children, since the unique development of the mentally retarded can be understood only by comparison with typical development. Comparative experimental research turned out to be even more essential in the study of problems which are significant in the mentally retarded child, but are frequently ignored or little studied in general child psychology. Among these many problems are the perception of the environment and spatial relations, modifications in memory such as concept changes in forgetting, and the modifications caused by repeated learning trials.

The experimental methods used involved the laboratory experiment, variations on the natural experiment, and the training experiment. In addition, the products of the children's activities were studied (e.g., compositions, sketches, and artifacts). The method of systematic observation was also extensively used.

Above all, the cognitive activity of these children was studied. It was shown that the primary characteristic of oligophrenic children is an inadequacy which effects their mind in many different ways; however, not all aspects of the mind are affected to the same extent. These inadequacies manifest themselves in many different ways as the nature of mental activity increases in complexity.

Psychological research on the mentally retarded has a definite pedagogical direction, yielding material which contributes to the formation of didactic principles, methodological tools of training, and education. The results of this research are summarized in this chapter.

Perceptual Deficits

Comparative studies on the perception of normal children and oligophrenics, conducted under the guidance of Solov'ev (1953b), convincingly demonstrate the incorrect nature of the viewpoint alleging that the oligophrenic child merely exhibits a defect in thought while his perception is preserved fully intact.

It is known that the rapidity of visual perception offers man vast possibilities for accurate orientation, for taking into account the peculiarities of his environment, and for adapting himself to its changes.

In comparative experimental investigations of the normal and the mentally retarded, the criterion used to measure the rapidity of perception was the length of time during which the image of an object, presented tachistoscopically, had to be shown in order for correct recognition to be achieved (Veresotskaya, 1940b). It was found that a short exposure, sufficient to allow normal first-grade students to recognize a contour image, caused a different recognition reaction among first-grade students from an auxiliary school.[1] This period of time was not sufficiently long to allow recognition; they were only able to perceive lines and spots. A 22-millisecond exposure was sufficient to allow normal children to correctly identify 57 per cent of the objects presented to them, while at the same exposure speed, the mentally retarded children could not identify a single object. Increasing exposure time to a value of 42 milliseconds allowed normal children to recognize 95 per cent of the objects presented, while the mentally retarded children still could only recognize 55 per cent. In the remaining cases false recognition took place since oligophrenics grasped the outlines

---

1. *Editors' note:* This refers to a school for children suffering from some abnormality (blindness, mental retardation, etc.). In the present context, a school for mentally retarded children is indicated.

of the objects only very sketchily, and were unable to achieve a dissected perception of their form or discern their characteristics.

With these results in mind, it was assumed that in the given context a pathological decrease in the mobility of cortical processes takes place in oligophrenics. A *slowdown* in perceptual processes appears to be a definite characteristic of these children, but this slowdown is not a permanent feature. Under favorable conditions a slight increase in the rapidity of object perception is observed in third-grade oligophrenic pupils, but their lag behind normals still continues to be quite significant, and is constantly observed in various forms of their activity.

Sluggishness is observed not only during the perception of individual objects, but even during the perception of combinations of objects. This results in the *narrow and limited* nature of oligophrenic perception constantly noted by educators. In one experimental study (Nudel'man, 1953), junior-grade auxiliary-school pupils had to enumerate the objects located in a section of the street visible from the school window. These pupils noted a much smaller number of objects than did normals, pointed out only the nearest and largest objects, and omitted the small ones. This was especially true in those cases where color was not an aid in identification. In summary: the perception of things located in the street was undifferentiated, limited, and meager.

The fact that these children can identify fewer of the parts and properties of objects than can their normal counterparts attests to the *undifferentiated* nature of their perception. This is also confirmed by the inability of oligophrenics to distinguish parts of an object having identical properties, and their ready identification of objects and properties of objects which are similar, but not identical (Zvereva and Lipkina, 1953; Shif, 1940; Petrova, 1956).

Certain peculiarities of spatial recognition have also been studied, as has the perception of spatial relations. One such study (Bein, 1940) has shown that an object moved back a distance of 3, 6, or 9 m. is perceived as being smaller in size than it actually is. Size constancy increases somewhat in the senior grades.

It is also known that perception and recognition are made somewhat more difficult when an object's usual position in space is altered. Tachistoscopic tests in which the images of objects were turned at an angle of 180 or 90 degrees disclosed certain difficulties in perception and recognition even in normal children. The differences observed between oligophrenics and normals were found to be especially noteworthy. An object shown upside down was as a rule not recognized at all by oligophrenics or was recognized as another object in its normal position. In addition to the difficulty experienced in distinguishing the spatial arrangement of objects, these tests also showed that the active perceptual adaptation necessary for the recognition of changes in spatial layout presented considerable difficulties for the oligophrenic. The difficulty experienced in an active reorganization of perception was also observed during tachistoscopic tests involving recognition with a gradual increase in time of object exposure. The inaccurate or sketchy manner in which an object was first identified was not overcome by the subsequent opportunity to perceive its outlines or by the correlation of its component parts during a longer period of time.

The difficulty of active perceptual reorganization, its changes and adaptation to changing conditions, and its inertness are manifested in the slow and idiosyncratic development of keen observation by the oligophrenic (Zankov, 1951). The organization of his observations requires constant attention and guidance on the part of the instructor.

Deficiencies in the perception of spatial relations are clearly observed during the examination of pictures by oligophrenics. Although perspective foreshortening is comprehended more easily than other spatial relations, a toy automobile sketched in the foreground of a picture was nevertheless frequently perceived as a real automobile, while a real automobile shown a long distance away in the same picture was often perceived as a toy. The *superimposition* of one set of objects on another set, which always caused an impression of depth in the normal child, caused a sharp disorientation among oligophrenics, resulted in an absurd breakdown between the superimposing and the superimposed objects, and in a meaningless synthesis of their parts (Veresotskaya, 1940b).

When oligophrenics perceive and examine pictures they may have difficulty in understanding those relations which bind the people and the objects shown into a single and topical whole. Solov'ev's work (1953b) showed that a lack of specificity in the recognition of items (caused by a weakness in the processes of analysis and synthesis involved in perception) is the reason why these items are combined by means of oversimplified bonds. This makes it more difficult for oligophrenics to understand the content of a picture. It was established that in the perception of pictures they are poor at differentiating the expressive movements which are characteristic of certain human experiences. For example, they are not always able to distinguish the portrayal of a pantomime from the portrayal of purposeful actions. It was also found that they have difficulty in distinguishing facial mimicry (Evlakhova, 1957). This deficiency considerably reduces their ability to understand the contents of a picture they are inspecting.

By the time oligophrenics reach the third or fourth grade they show a better perception of the items presented in pictures and of the semantic and spatial relations between these items. Senior-grade students are capable of understanding pictures describing a topic which they can grasp much more fully and intelligently (Stadnenko, 1958; Vasilevskaya, 1960a).

Thus, the slow, narrow, and undifferentiated perception, the weakness of analysis and synthesis during the perception of objects and their relations, as well as the difficulty experienced during the active readjustment of perception (all characteristics of oligophrenic perceptual processes), result in the fact that their survey of segments of surrounding reality is considerably more oversimplified and less truly comprehended than is the case with normals. The same phenomenon applies to the perception of pictures.

The fact that the entire mental activity of oligophrenics takes place on a significantly impoverished and modified sensory basis is clearly expressed in peculiar features of their activity.

For example, in the study of oligophrenic orientation in space, difficulties in locomotion were noted which can be explained not so much as resulting from the deficiencies of the motor system described in detail in the literature, but rather as a result of defects in their spatial perception and a defective surveying ability. Teachers have noted such examples of poor orientation as frequent search for the door of the classroom or their place in the class by recently enrolled children. It is difficult for these children to master the skill of going to school and coming home from school without an escort if the road is new to them and not extremely simple.

Observations and special research, specifically a research study concerned with color discrimination (Shif, 1940), have shown that the development of perceptual processes in oligophrenic children of the senior grades takes place not as a result of training in these processes per se, but rather as a result of the development of graphic thought processes, and specifically, as a result of graphic comparison.

It was established that frequent presentation of an object does not help much to make the perception of this object more differentiated. In order to overcome this identification of similar figures as being the same, the following system of exercises was developed. The discrimination was begun with the least similar figures, and then figures that were more and more similar were shown. This research work has shown how processes involving a graphic comparison and comprehension contribute to the improvement of perception and practical actions (Petrova, 1958a).

A number of studies indicate that perception reaches a greater degree of accuracy and that the practical activity associated with this perception is raised to a higher level if the perception and the activity are controlled by a concrete, guiding verbal instruction. If this instruction is very general and contains a large number of links, its effects are insignificant. According to the available data, the most favorable conditions for improving perception are created when, during the perception of the object, the process of analysis and synthesis is accompanied by various types of practical activity involving the children and the objects by which these processes are firmly established as a result of this activity. Thought and speech development play a considerable role in perceptual development. Certain complex forms of analysis, synthesis, comparison, and generalization (provided they are correctly organized) gradually become accessible to these children. The weakness observed in these processes is very significant in junior grade auxiliary-school pupils, but with a properly organized instruction program these processes are developed and in turn contribute to the development of perceptual and practical activity.

Memory Deficits

The peculiar features surrounding the oligophrenic's recall and use of school material has been studied by Zankov and his associates. In several older studies it was shown that the memory of oligophrenic children is particularly poor. Many authors believed that the amount of information available to oligophrenics was acquired in a non-mediated fashion, and that it was based on a well-preserved rote memory. The main cause of their defective memory was considered to lie merely in the extreme weakness of their meaningful recall.

Soviet psychologists have since shown that such a viewpoint is inconsistent *since it does not take into account developmental trends* of object and word memory seen in the children. A comparative study on the development of recall in normals and oligophrenics of various ages was undertaken by Zankov (1935). It has disclosed that rote memory for graphic and verbal materials is far lower in children studying in the junior grades of an auxiliary school than it is in normals of the same age. In addition, it was established that junior-age mentally retarded children did not know how to make independent use of the techniques of meaningful recall. Zankov has further shown that the oligophrenic children, *upon reaching the medium and especially the senior school-age group, make very great progress in meaningful recall and make very insignificant progress in rote memory.* The achievement of meaningful recall in the mentally retarded child and the difficulties involved in this connection were extensively considered during a study on the memorization and reproduction of pairs of objects and pairs of words (Zankov, 1935; Leont'ev, 1959).

It has been established that mentally retarded children require special instruction in the identification and utilization of associations with which to unite the material. The associations established by oligophrenics on their own are frequently superficial and do not result in a high-grade recall of material nor in a distinction between this material and similar material recalled by equally superficial associations. By following very careful and thorough instructions in techniques for achieving meaningful recall, oligophrenic children can learn how to make use of such a method of recall.

The establishment of a basic trend in the development of memory in mentally retarded children was of vital importance in understanding the peculiar features of memory in such children, and for the correct organization of their instruction. Let us clarify the latter point. From an erroneous assertion concerning the effectiveness of mechanical recall and the inaccessibility of meaningful recall for these children, it was believed necessary to train their rote memory, and thus it was considered pointless to become concerned with the development of complex memory processes in these children. Soviet schools for the retarded have, as a result of the findings of psychological research, overcome this misconception and have directed their efforts to the development of an ability to recall in a meaningful manner. Consequently they are making considerable progress in this respect. Research in child psychology has demonstrated that the effectiveness of voluntary retention considerably outstrips the development of involuntary retention from the end of the junior-grade school-age period. It has also clarified the dependence of both types of retention upon the activity context in which learning takes place (Smirnov, 1959).[2]

It has been found that the voluntary memorizing of mentally retarded school children is not significantly more productive than is their involuntary memory (Pinskii, 1954). Thus, groups of fifth- and seventh-grade auxiliary school pupils, after being warned before the reading of a story that they would have to tell the story in their own words, read the story twice, and were able to reproduce only 46.6 per cent of its composite semantic units. Other groups of pupils belonging to the same age group were not warned about the impending narration. When unexpectedly confronted with the necessity of a verbal account, these children were able to reproduce 40 per cent of the same semantic units, that is, almost as many of the required units as those pupils who had to give a verbal account after premeditated (voluntary) memorizing. The difference between the auxiliary school pupils and comparable normal school students amounted to a 30 per cent difference in favor of premeditated recall. These studies also demonstrate considerably less success in unpremeditated (involuntary) memorizing in school-age defectives as compared to normals. It has been shown that the main factor in the underdevelopment of both types of recall is the reduced level at which the oligophrenic fulfills the activity on which retention is based. These defects are manifested most strongly in the case of involuntary retention.

Zankov (1939) and Dul'nev (1940) have shown that the presence of a definite intention does not affect the course of reproduction in defectives

---

2. *Editors' note:* The term translated here as "retention" or "memorizing" (*zapomenanie*) has been variously translated as "remembering," "memorizing," "recall," and so on. "Retention" and "memorizing" are used here as the best general terms for the general process by which material is stored for use at some later time, regardless of the technique used to measure storage. The general topic of memory is discussed in Chapter 17 of this volume, by A. A. Smirnov and P. I. Zinchenko.

to the same extent that it does in normals. Thus, while intending to recall and reproduce the material in a definite sequence, or to recall and reproduce word for word, even senior-grade oligophrenic pupils, upon first familiarization, manage to reproduce this material in the same incomplete and inaccurate fashion as in those cases where they do not have this intention. An intention is carried out only after a repeated perception of the material, and after sufficient comprehension of it. The oligophrenic's weak or poor fulfillment of an intention, in addition to showing a basic difficulty in understanding the material, also constitutes a manifestation of an inability to subordinate his activity to a definite *totality* of requirements imposed upon him.

A considerable number of research studies have been devoted to certain peculiarities of recall in the oligophrenic. Recall "in pairs" has shown the manner in which the meaningful character of their recall develops. The children are required to make up a sentence in which they combine the words which are to be recalled. For example, in order to memorize the words "doll-ball," perhaps the sentence, "I play with the doll and the ball," was constructed. The words "soap-towel" were also united in a sentence: "I wash my hands with soap and dry them with a towel." When they were asked to reproduce these words, the children produced the whole sentence, and had considerable difficulty in extracting those words that they were required to recall (Zankov, 1939). These words were found to be "welded" to the context of their memorization. These children had difficulties in analyzing, that is, in liberating, words from those associations which had helped in their memorization. Several studies focussing on the peculiarities of text reproduction by fifth-, sixth-, and seventh-grade auxiliary-school students have shown that, in the memorization of a story, oligophrenics establish fewer connections between the parts of the story than do normal children (Dul'nev, 1940; Pinskii, 1954). It was also found that these connections are less essential and more superficial. For this reason, in terms of fullness of reproduction, it was found that sixth-grade pupils of the auxiliary school lagged far behind third-grade pupils in a regular school. (The number of thoughts reproduced by the former from the story presented to them was almost three times smaller than the number of thoughts reproduced by the latter.) Furthermore, only scattered portions of the story were reproduced—individual sections which were not closely connected and not among the most significant presented. In isolated cases, the few things which the children were able to memorize were reproduced in a rote manner and the coherence of the reproduced material suffered from the fragmentary nature of the reproduction. In other cases, the children presented the content in their own words, using very general expressions. This case resulted in a loss of reproductive concreteness. Both of these characteristic features of reproduction are associated with the characteristic speech shown by oligophrenic children. They assimilate with great difficulty and in an extremely insufficient manner the rich and extensive system of word meanings and expressions, and seldom acquire the skill of consistent narration.

Also worthy of attention are the numerous distortions of material which appear during the course of its reproduction. These distortions frequently consist of forced similarities between the presented material and material familiar to the children. During the reproduction of the material, a great deal of extraneous information was introduced, information which sometimes was only remotely related to the material which had been read. The introduction of this extraneous material is an indication of an insufficient distinction, in regard to content, between knowledge which has been recently assimilated and previous knowledge. It must be added that mistakes made by junior-grade oligophrenic students in the process of reproduction are not easily corrected even when the children realize these mistakes (Pinskii, 1952). The children experience great difficulty in modifying a reproduction which has once been performed. Therefore, the elimination of mistakes arising during reproduction requires considerable help on the part of the instructor and considerable effort on the part of the children. Recent research has indicated that it is necessary to help the retarded child carefully to interpret the material before asking him to learn and reproduce it. The first reproduction should be as well interpreted, complete, and exact as possible in order to ensure that the correct material is retained in memory. An incomplete initial reproduction not only deprives the child of the motivation to correct himself, but by virtue of the slow progress of his thinking actually retards him. In the senior grades, this characteristic is somewhat less apparent. Fullness and accuracy of reproduction by oligophrenics depend to a great extent upon the type of material that they have to reproduce. It also depends upon the nature of the connections which unite this material into a whole. One study sought to investigate the effect of different connections (sequential or causal) on the reproduction of material. Fifth- to seventh-grade pupils, in reproducing sequentially related material (e.g., a sequence of figures, words, or historical events), rely, if they are not given help, primarily upon certain external chance factors which unite the objects to be recalled. If certain links of the chain are similar and their differentiation presents a considerable difficulty, these links are confused and rearranged, resulting in a distortion of the correct sequence during reproduction. However, if the process of instruction is organized in such a way that the significant connections uniting the members of a series are explained to the children in a readily accessible form, and if these connections are consolidated in the proper manner, then the reproduction of a sequence becomes considerably more accurate. Seventh-grade students have exhibited definite progress vis-à-vis fifth-graders in the reproduction of material which is united by sequence relations.

Petrova (1958b) has shown that material containing causal relations which oligophrenics can understand, presented in the form of causal conjunctions, allows the children to rely upon these relations and use them successfully during reproduction.

As a result, such reproduction is more complete and accurate than the reproduction of a similar text in which the causal connections are understood, but not expressed in the texts. Here, too, a developmental increase in success of reproduction can be seen from the fifth to the seventh grades.

Starting from the fact that the memory of oligophrenics grows chiefly by drawing upon meaningful recall, Zankov (1949) has undertaken a number of studies devoted to the clarification of the importance of varying forms of repetition as a means of increasing the successful rate of reproduction. Psychological and educational research conducted in this connection (Shif, 1941; Zamskii, 1954) has shown that if a set of material was presented to mentally retarded children from several points of view, was consciously comprehended in many different aspects, and if during questioning the form of the questions was varied, then the mentally retarded children were able to reproduce the material better and were able to break it down more easily than in those cases where the material was repeated many times without modification, and thus assumed the form of learning by rote. This confirmed again that the development of memorization and reproduction in the mentally retarded draws upon semantic memory.

This particular group of studies has contributed to definite improvements in the development of a methodology for the consolidation of knowledge in the fields of natural science, geography, and history in auxiliary schools, where at the present time the "method of modified repetitions" is used during instruction instead of the previously employed monotonous method of repeating a single content and form.

The problems of how oligophrenics retain the knowledge they have acquired has attracted a great deal of attention on the part of psychologists. Educators and psychologists working in auxiliary schools are constantly noting the characteristic manner in which oligophrenics rapidly forget and are unable to call to mind the knowledge they have acquired. Solov'ev (1941) undertook a comparative study of the processes by which visual images are preserved and forgotten both in normals and defectives. It was shown that oligophrenic visual representation is considerably poorer and less differentiated than in normals of comparable age. Since oligophrenics are unable to notice the characteristic features of an object during the course of its perception, they naturally do not preserve those features in memory. In their drawings, the objects depicted have no details and are presented in an oversimplified spatial arrangement. In the mentally retarded, changes in these representations take place in a very clear form, and are expressed in the loss of the characteristic features present in the objects; by contrast normal children, whose representations are richer and closer to the original, preserve and even stress for a certain time those characteristic features. Only after a considerable period of time does a certain loss of their specificity take place, a loss which never reaches the same degree as that observed in the mentally retarded.

The absence of emphasis on the characteristic features of objects in oligophrenic memory is explained by Solov'ev as due to the fact that during the recall process the same intensive mental work characteristic of normals is not exhibited. Of particularly great importance in understanding the characteristic features of the oligophrenic mind is the change in the memory for similar objects which is observed in these people. This change is expressed in a drastic assimilation of these objects, and sometimes in their complete identification with each other. Solov'ev (1940) has been able to prove in a convincing manner that the processes of assimilation follow a much more rapid and clear-cut course in the mentally retarded child than in the normal school child. These authors have discovered three types of assimilation: (1) mutual assimilation of new impressions with old impressions which are similar; (2) mutual assimilation of similar representations (memories); and (3) sometimes, assimilation of old representations to new ones. It has been proven that assimilations of the three above-mentioned types take place not only in the field of visual representations, but also in the forgetting of verbal material. This fact is of basic importance since it shows that the hyperassimilation characteristic of oligophrenics manifests itself in various aspects of their activity.

A rapid and considerable capacity for assimilating previously acquired knowledge is a characteristic feature of mentally retarded children. A consequence of this assimilation is an oversimplification of all relations found in the consciousness of an oligophrenic.

The clarification of what might be considered the characteristic features of recall and forgetting in oligophrenics has contributed to an understanding of the peculiar nature of development of the children. The difference between their memory and the memory of normal children was found to be much more significant than the difference between these groups in the field of perception. By virtue of their rapid forgetting and extensive assimilation, oligophrenics experience a very great difficulty in the actualization of knowledge they have acquired for the solution of even relatively simple practical or intellectual problems. Their weak and unstable representations do not contribute sufficiently to the solution of a task which is in progress, and do not insure correct solution. The establishment of laws governing forgetting proved to be extremely important for conducting proper pedagogical work with oligophrenic children.

Solov'ev (1941) and Nudel'man (1941) have shown that in the senior grades it is possible to achieve a certain counteraction to the characteristic assimilation during the process of forgetting. If students of an auxiliary school are taught how to analyze, compare, and distinguish objects having various degrees of similarity, if this activity is accompanied by verbal explanations, and if knowledge imparted in verbal form is combined with an analytical perception of corresponding objects, then the children are less inclined to assimilate.

Thus, the development of memory in the mentally retarded is associated with an improvement of meaningful recall. The retention of pieces of acquired knowledge and measures aimed at combating their assimilation can be achieved to a certain extent by making use of analysis, and by developing graphic and verbal thought and speech in the children.

Speech Deficits

All authors have noted that speech appears in oligophrenics at a much later date than it does in normal children, develops much more slowly, and is characterized by a number of peculiar features. It is thus natural that the speech of oligophrenics differs to a very great degree from the speech of normals by the beginning of the school-age period.

Oligophrenics are also characterized by considerable defects in pronunciation. These are due mainly to poorly differentiated auditory perception. Defects in pronunciation give rise to corresponding mistakes in writing. In order to overcome these defects in pronunciation and writing, it is often necessary to conduct extensive work aimed at developing the processes of analysis and synthesis in the field of auditory speech perception. Frequently it is also necessary to perform special work aimed at correcting and developing their articulation.

There are also indications pointing to a retarded rate of oral and written speech in oligophrenics. This is associated by a number of authors with peculiar features in their motor system. The oligophrenic lack of expression in oral speech is also stressed, as well as the poor nature of its tonal structure (Feofanov, 1948).

A study of the motivation underlying oral and written speech has shown that oligophrenics usually exhibit a weak and underdeveloped inclination to engage in dialogue, present an extensive narration of what they have seen or read, or clarify those things which they do not understand or which require correction. A lack of coherence and comprehension in both oral and written speech is also noted by all authors. Peculiarities in the understanding of business and literary texts by students belonging to various auxiliary-school grades have also been described and studied in detail. The progress which these students make as a result of instruction has also been demonstrated (Vasilevskaya, 1960a, b).

The lag in various aspects of speech development limits the oligophrenic's contact with those around him and thus inhibits to a considerable extent the growth of his cognitive faculties and his acquisition of information transmitted by words.

Certain features of the oligophrenics' vocabulary have been described in greater detail than other problems concerned with their speech. Their characteristic vocabulary has been studied from many different approaches. For example, a study has been made of the manner in which students belonging to various grades of an auxiliary school understood the meaning of words having a varying degree of generality. An investigation was made of the manner in which oligophrenics utilize words used to designate the properties of objects which they have previously learned. Work has also been done in an attempt to clarify certain characteristic features of oligophrenic word usage.

In a study designed to investigate the manner in which students of the first five grades of an auxiliary school understand nouns having varying degrees of generality and used to designate objects (Shif, 1940), it was found that familiar terms having a wide general meaning (conventionally speaking, generic designations such as tool, berry, fruit, insect, animal, etc.) were considered by junior-grade auxiliary-school pupils to be "unsaid" words. That is, these pupils stated that these words are not used to name objects, but rather are "only written." These children sometimes exhibit a "narrowing down" in the meaning of these words, and believe, for example, that only a plane is called a tool, or only strawberries are called berries. By the time they reach the fourth grade, these children, as a result of exercises aimed at the development of speech, are able to comprehend that these terms are used as names for a group of objects. They do not, however, always use these terms properly. Only at a considerably later date do mentally retarded children recognize these terms as a second possible means for the designation of an object, a designation which includes its most important properties or characteristics.

Oligophrenics are also unable to catch the difference between qualifying designations such as "antonovka apple," "cabbage-butterfly," or "mongrel dog," and terms having a broader meaning, such as "apple," "butterfly," or "dog." [3] They characteristically consider that the former represent an unnecessary duplication of the latter. Normal third- and fourth-grade pupils were surprised when they were asked to explain the meaning of such specialized designations. They proposed the replacement of these words by terms having a more general meaning which they consider as being more adequate designations. This comprehension of specific terms was very poorly developed in oligophrenic children, even after five years of training. In contrast, normal children displayed, even in the junior grades, a differentiated attitude toward words having a varying measure of generality, and made rapid

3. *Editors' note:* The first three terms are, in Russian, one-word nouns, specifying instances of the second three terms.

progress over a period of three years in the comprehension of generic designations, and thereafter likewise in the comprehension of special terms used to designate specific "types."

A study of the manner in which oligophrenics utilize descriptive adjectives they have previously learned (Dul'nev, 1948) discloses even more clearly their peculiar attitude toward terms having special meaning. The study was conducted so that the meanings of adjectives were explained in detail to third-grade auxiliary-school pupils, while the adjectives themselves were learned by heart. After learning, the children had to use the adjectives to fill blanks in a text provided them. It was found in the task performance that these third-grade pupils used the terms "big" or "small" instead of the special designations of form which they had learned—designations such as "long," "narrow," and "high." The word "bad" was used instead of the many special designations required by the text (e.g., "dirty," "heavy," "malicious," "old," and "torn"). Similarly, the word "red" was used instead of the words "orange," "crimson," and "pink." In other words, it was established that, instead of the many special terms which the children had learned and, as experiments later showed, had not forgotten, these children used instead several familiar words having a general meaning, thereby unjustifiably expanding the sphere of their application.

A new stage in the study of vocabulary included an attempt to examine which terms are used by oligophrenics to recognize objects which they have examined. It also attempted to clarify which designations are used to establish various object properties during object analysis and comparison.

It was found that oligophrenics did not use terms having a broad, general, and appropriate meaning with which they were familiar during the examination and recognition of objects with which they were unfamiliar. Instead, they mistakenly used terms having a more specific meaning, terms used to designate objects familiar to them and resembling the objects which they examined. The sphere of diffusion of terms having a general meaning was found to be unreasonably narrow. Thus, they did not call a porcupine an "animal," but rather a "hedgehog." Similarly, they called an anteater a "mole," and an elk a "billy goat." At the same time, oligophrenics rarely used familiar terms which are used in a specialized and precise designation of objects. Thus, when the children compared various objects, it was found that they called a pharmaceutical vial a "bottle," the label on the vial a "paper," a cork, a "plug," the beak of a bird, a "nose," claws, "fingernails," and so on (Zvereva, 1948). In other words, instead of using special designations, oligophrenics very frequently and mistakenly had recourse to more familiar terms and sometimes to terms having a more general meaning. It should be added that they seldom use adjectives to which normal school children usually have recourse for the purposes of special designation during recognition, analysis, and comparison. Thus, in describing a small gold wrist watch or a thick red-faceted pencil, oligophrenics, in contrast to normals, did not use a special designation for the objects displayed, but merely called the objects by their simple designations—a "watch" or a "pencil" (Kudryavtseva, 1954). During the course of the analysis of object properties it was found that first- and second-grade oligophrenics frequently used the terms "large" and "small" as substitutes for many of the designations of form known to them. Similarly, the term "fat" was used not only in the correct manner, but also to convey the meaning of "broad." Oligophrenics did not use antonyms to designate opposite properties of a form, but frequently used such combinations as "not long" or "not thin." They also frequently used one name to designate similar colors: for example, orange was called "red." In the senior grades, a certain progress could be noted in the use of certain terms during the process of determining the properties of objects. Here terms appear which designate the form, weight, and the surface characteristics of objects (Lipkina, 1953). In the designation of color, senior-grade oligophrenics used the terms "light" and "dark" together with the names corresponding to the tone of the color. The words "pink," "azure," "lilac," and the like also appear in their speech. However, even in the senior grades, an insufficient degree of accuracy in the use of special terms is observed during the determination of closely related, difficult-to-differentiate properties (e.g., light–white, transparent–colorless, etc.). Also to be noted is a frequent recourse in these cases to the use of limited groups of terms (Shif, 1940).

During a study of peculiarities in the exposition of a story previously read (Feofanov, 1955), it was established that the operating vocabulary of oligophrenics, by the time they reach the fifth or sixth grade, is augmented to a certain extent by verbs having narrow, special meanings which previously were not found in their vocabulary. Whereas in the junior grades the children used such verbs as "rode," "walked," and "slept," in the senior grades, words with prefixes which stress shades of meaning make their appearance. Moreover, verbs are also used by this time in a figurative sense.

The same tendency is also observed in the use of adverbs. In junior grades, the number of adverbs used is limited and these adverbs are used in an unwarrantedly broad meaning. Prepositions, through which a wide variety of spatial relations are expressed, such as *pozadi* (back of), *vperedi* (in front), and *sboku* (on the side), are replaced in the oral and written speech of oligophrenics by the preposition *u* (near or by). Such an oversimplification is also observed when prepositions are used to express other groups of relations. The same observation applies to the manner in which conjunctions connecting principle and subordinate clauses are used.

At the present time, it can be considered an established fact that the scanty active vocabulary of the oligophrenic cannot be viewed merely as the result of difficulties in word recall. This is evident in those cases when an understanding of the meaning of certain words has been secured and the word firmly assimilated by the children due to frequent repetition in different contexts. Such words are not completely forgotten and are preserved in the children's passive vocabulary, and as has been shown, can be reproduced under certain conditions. This does not mean, however, that these particular words will be included in their active vocabulary.

In an attempt to explain the characteristics of the oligophrenic's active vocabulary, it should be noted first that the small number of words utilized and the insufficient differentiation of meanings are intimately connected with the undifferentiated and limited nature of their cognitive activity. The incompleteness and poverty of object perception when the objects perceived possess a wide variety of properties, present in a complex relation with each other, the drastic leveling of the features of these objects, and the defective nature of their mental analysis and synthesis, all result in the fact that oligophrenics are not in need of a rich and differentiated vocabulary. They are completely satisfied with having a limited number of words at their disposal although they are also familiar with many other words. The fact that these other words do not enter into their vocabulary indicates that, after making their appearance in oligophrenic speech, these words do not exert the proper effect on the improvement of their cognitive activity. Consequently, the *verbal designations acquired by these children do not play the same role in effecting a change in their sensory cognition as they do in the case of normals.* On the basis of certain observations, it seems that those special terms which are firmly assimilated in the course of everyday experience are included more rapidly in the active vocabulary of the mentally retarded. Observations have shown that oligophrenic children working in a sewing workshop applied the terms *"broad," "narrow," "long,"* and *"short"* to thread and cloth, that is, they used these terms in the context of a definite practical activity. However, these same children also used the terms "large" and "small." Thus, *the poverty of their active vocabulary is not due to difficulties in acquiring or learning words as such; rather, the limited nature of this vocabulary is due to an impoverished cognitive activity, on the one hand, and to the insufficiently active transformative role of words in the development of their thought process, on the other.* A change in the vocabulary used by oligophrenics in the senior grades constitutes an index of their mental development, occurring in combination with the development of their speech. This change is expressed in an increasing generalization and differentiation, and in an enrichment of the vocabulary's active word complement.

In recent years, the grammatical structure of oligophrenic speech has become a subject of serious attention on the part of psychologists and educators (Gnezdilov, 1959). It was found that violations of word order and omissions of principal parts in sentences are characteristic among junior-grade students. An inability to express relations of sequence or causality is frequently observed. It was also noted that case forms are not used to the fullest extent, but rather are used as an expression of a limited group of relations having a concrete character. Only in the fifth and sixth grades do children develop an ability to utilize several meanings of each form. At the same time, the verbal and written speech of the oligophrenic becomes richer and more coherent. Deficiencies in the use of words and word combinations are intimately connected with the peculiar features of the oligophrenic child's thinking process and are caused by these peculiar features.

Deficits in Thinking

Let us now attempt to illustrate certain features of the oligophrenic child's thought process, as well as the paths for its development. A study of the cognitive activity of auxiliary-school junior-grade students was conducted by Solov'ev and his associates (1953a). A special study of the development of analysis and synthesis by these children has shown that the cognitive decomposition of an object, that is, the analysis of its structure, takes place in a different way in junior-grade pupils than in normal school-age children. Oligophrenics are able to note a much smaller number of parts which make up the object. They omit parts which are of essential significance for the identification of the object, unless these parts possess specially noticeable or remarkable properties.

Observations of senior-grade auxiliary-school students have shown that, as a result of special lessons with objects, natural science lessons, and most importantly, properly organized work activity in agriculture and in workshops, an analysis of the structure of objects is somewhat richer and precise. This manifests itself in the difference between junior- and senior-grade pupils. The former demonstrate no definite connection between the parts of an object being examined while the latter show much more consistent performance both in the breakdown of an object as well as in improved synthesis.

A study of such object analysis has shown that oligophrenics note predominantly visual properties, and much less frequently are able to identify properties which can be perceived by touch. Consequently, in the mentally retarded school child, the cognitive analysis of properties is not based on the combined activity of all analyzers but rather rests predominantly on visual analysis. This results in a considerable one-sidedness of analysis, and consequently in the inability of the oligophrenic to identify the number of properties identifiable by normals of the same age.

Study of the characteristics of oligophrenic vocabulary used in designating the properties of objects has shown how difficult it is for them to perform this type of cognitive analysis. They have great difficulty in verbally differentiating shapes and sizes, can only imperfectly distinguish the wide variety of surface properties, and have difficulty designating the material out of which these objects are made. The designation or identification of colors is also very difficult. Words play an exceptionally important part in property designation. With the aid of words, it is possible to separate mentally the properties of an object from each other and from the object as a whole. During the normal development of the child, words are used very early and efficiently in analyzing the properties of objects. Also noteworthy is the fact that property analysis becomes more difficult for an oligophrenic, the more complex the structure of the object. By means of a carefully organized system of exercises, oligophrenics can be taught how to distinguish a definite group of object properties. In the senior grades, the identification of properties is clearly improved. By then they are capable of distinguishing not only the size, shape, and color but also the material out of which the object is made, its weight, characteristic features of its shape, surface, and so on.

Observations show that a knowledge of object properties is retained if this knowledge is constantly applied in the working activity of the child. However, if the knowledge obtained does not find a practical application in their everyday actions, this knowledge, although it is not completely forgotten, undergoes a change and "de-differentiation" takes place.

Study of the manner in which the process of object analysis develops in the oligophrenic child during the course of his school-age period has shown that the completeness and detailed nature of the analysis increase, and that he gradually learns how to identify the object's essential characteristics. However, the poverty of this analysis still makes older oligophrenics considerably different from normal school children.

During the course of assimilation of school knowledge, the students are faced not only with the analysis of graphic objects, but also, and to a much greater extent, with the analysis of data or materials presented to them in verbal form. Several studies have been devoted to the study of these processes in senior-grade oligophrenics (Nudel'man, 1949; Shif, 1959). These studies have shown that, if the reproduction of a story on a certain subject read by fifth-grade auxiliary-school students is based on a list of questions or a plan submitted to the students, then the reproduction is more complete by 40 per cent than in the case where this reproduction takes place without the help of questions (that is, when the analysis of the verbal information obtained in regard to the structure of the object and its properties must be performed independently by these students). Furthermore, it was shown that if the order of the questions in the plan presented to the children differed from the order of the material presented in the arrangement of the story, a search for the answer to these questions causes difficulties even for students of the sixth and seventh grades. Their answers are not sufficiently differentiated, since they do not always achieve the demarcation of the material necessary in order to answer the question. The above data indicate the difficulties encountered by oligophrenics while performing an analysis of information, even when the information has been offered in verbal form and the students helped in the process. If the material dealing with a problem or assigned topic must be extracted not from one text but from several texts, the difficulties encountered in the analysis increase further. It is natural to assume that the synthesis performed on the basis of a selective analysis of several texts is difficult and deficient. Seventh-grade students, after reading several stories describing different animals, had to tell only how all of the animals breathe. Instead of doing this they spoke not only about breathing, but also about the feeding and various other habits of these animals. In several individual cases, the problem of breathing was even omitted altogether (Nudel'man, 1949).

After reading three small stories describing a queen bee, a working bee, and a drone and after having been given the assignment of writing a story about a beehive, fourth- and fifth-grade auxiliary-school pupils identified the queen bee and the working bee with each other according to their external appearance and functions, and opposed these two types to the drone. This oversimplification during synthesis was related to an extremely defective analysis.

Confronted with the task of collecting information on three different birds found in three different textbooks, sixth- and seventh-grade pupils also exhibited a tendency (although not as sharply pronounced) to identify the characteristic features of these birds (Nudel'man, 1941). These students also failed to carry out a subtle and complex analysis necessary for the formation of a concrete image of each of the birds about which they had read, as a result of which they could have extracted special information from the texts. Their synthesis proved to be systematic and nonconcrete. They did not give the characteristics of a definite zoological species, but rather limited themselves merely to data by means of which the item described could only be referred to a broad zoological class, namely, to the class of birds.

The data showed that the knowledge they acquired from books was not sufficiently concrete and that they were much less enriched by this knowledge than was the case with normals. Apparently, object lessons which are not consolidated by the children's working activity do not result in the child's proper development, and prepare them poorly for the acquisition of knowledge from books.

The oversimplified and crude comprehension of reality, manifested during the recognition of objects, is also clearly observed during object comparison (Zvereva and Lipkina, 1953). A comparison requires a "correlative" examination and analysis of the objects being compared. During the course of comparison, statements about discrepant attributes are often observed in first- and second-grade oligophrenics. This makes the process of object comparison impossible or disturbs the course of this process. As a result of exercises in making comparisons, this ability is somewhat improved by the time the children reach the third or fourth grades, and the actual process of comparison becomes more systematic. However, the "correlative" analysis of objects being compared is not only poorer than in normal school children, but also exhibits a number of special features. Junior-grade students experience considerable difficulties in understanding that a similarity between objects represents a complex and varied relationship between these objects. Similar objects are frequently recognized as being either different or identical. A research study conducted by Petrova (1956) has shown that depicted objects having the same structure and color, but differing from each other in the size of their parts and in the arrangement of these parts, were considered as being identical by second- and third-grade pupils.

By the time children reach the third or fourth grades, the range of objects considered as being similar is expanded due to the development of improved analysis. The processes of comparison are considerably improved in these students and contribute to their general development, but neither in comparison or in recognition of objects do oligophrenics achieve the same degree of generalization, completeness, and concreteness which characterizes the normal child.

A study attempting to investigate the development of generalization in oligophrenics was performed with materials of different hues (Shif, 1940). The colors differed in both their brightness and their saturation. This study, involving junior-grade pupils, showed that the broad and undifferentiated grouping of objects having similar color gives way only gradually to a proper generalization. A proper generalization of hues of one and the same color is quite narrow in the medium grades, but becomes somewhat broader by the time the senior grades are reached. Oligophrenics differ to a considerable extent from normals in their behavior. Normals at the beginning of their school-age period no longer combine hues of adjacent colors and are characterized by a rapidly developing proper generalization of hues of the same color differing in brightness. The development of a graphic or descriptive thinking process was indicated by the fact that fourth- and fifth-grade pupils no longer group saturated hues of red, orange, blue, and violet together. However, they still continued to call an orange color "red," and a violet color "blue."

In recent years research has revealed that the mentally retarded's image formation is inadequate. This hinders his effectiveness in practical activity. Specifically, there was a discrepancy in younger children between objects which they drew or constructed (e.g., wall, fence) and those which had been presented to them (Pinskii, 1954). In the middle age group, planned training and assistance in explaining errors helped them greatly in overcoming these inadequacies.

Similarly, in a study of problem solving behavior in sixth-grade auxiliary-school students (Solov'ev, 1951; Kuz'mitskaya, 1957) it was shown that the children were unable to get an idea of the problems' objective content—that is, the data presented, relations between these data, and their connection with the questions formulated in the problem. This loss of objective content is manifested in a defective reproduction of the problem conditions, an incorrect selection of problem solving methods, and in an absurd arrangement of conditions. The data obtained in these studies are important for an understanding of language's role in oligophrenic cognitive activity. Reproductive representations, which are based primarily on language, are clearly impeded in the oligophrenic. This is one reason why a knowledge of history, geography, and natural science imparted in verbal form, without a proper reliance upon graphic materials, does not contribute to an oligophrenic child's development. Texts which have been read do not call forth imagery corresponding to the text material as readily as in the case of normals. This peculiarity is manifested both in junior- and in senior-grade pupils. A study conducted by Zankov (1935) has shown that the mentally deficient are able to identify simple causal relationships between phenomena occurring in inanimate nature when they are associated with their real life experience. However, it was also noted that the same children experience difficulties when they must imagine similar causal connections presented to them in verbal form.

It has been noted in many studies that oligophrenics experience a considerable difficulty in making actual use of acquired knowledge, that is, in selecting from known facts those facts which must be utilized in a given context. It has frequently been pointed out that acquired knowledge is "welded" to the form in which this knowledge has been learned. The intimate connection between assimilated pieces of knowledge, the conditions under which they have been acquired, and the form in which they have been learned deprive them of an indispensable mobility. If we consider also the lack of fullness and the breakdown of these pieces of knowledge, as well as the ease with which they can be mutually assimilated, one can readily understand the difficulties the oligophrenic child encounters when drawing upon and using this knowledge.

One must avoid the idea, however, that learned knowledge is not used by oligophrenics, for this knowledge is actually applied by them. They do not, however, use the knowledge available according to the requirements of the problem being solved. Rather, such knowledge is frequently utilized in its unchanged form, that is, in the form in which it was learned. Solov'ev (1953c) has suggested an explanation for a number of the peculiar features shown by the mentally deficient during the course of problem solution. He notes that oligophrenics, when drawing upon available knowledge, do not know how to modify this knowledge in order to adapt it to the conditions of a new problem; rather, they seem to do the opposite. They modify the problem so that it fits their previously acquired knowledge. For the fruitful use of knowledge which is drawn upon in order to solve a new problem, it is necessary that this knowledge be subjected to a creative modification and transformation.

The study of oligophrenic problem solving in the natural sciences, in geography, and in history indicates that even the mentally retarded of advanced school age show a profound break between mastered generalizations and information acquired in everyday life. They are incapable of independently subsuming everyday observations under generalizations which they have mastered. This inadequate unity of the general and the concrete inhibits their day to day activity.

All the material relevant to reasoning activity in the mentally retarded show these irregularities, but at the same time it has been noted by all researchers that a significant development in reasoning can occur with training, that the possibility of acquiring knowledge increases, that the development of memory and perception interact, and most importantly, that practical activity improves. Work in handicrafts and in agriculture is more fruitful as comprehension of the basic components of the activity increases.

One series of experiments was devoted to the study of structure and motivation in the activity of the mentally retarded child (Pinskii, 1962). Characteristic of the younger classes is a tendency immediately to attack a problem when presented with it. This "easy" approach to problems is due to an inadequate comprehension of the task. When difficulties arise, these pupils do not change their methods, due to their inertness. "Drifting" is often observed, as well as an uncritical relationship to the quality of the solution. Developmental studies indicate that this "easy" approach can be often overcome with proper training. Gradually they acquire the habit of starting a new task only after they have acquainted themselves with its content. This skill, combined with expansion of their areas of knowledge and the ability to differentiate and to apply this ability to their activity, enables them to compensate for slow thinking.

Summary

The results of much Soviet research on problem solving indicate that it is incorrect to speak of the destruction of this or that group of psychological processes in the retarded child. Inadequacy undoubtedly affects the oligophrenic's mind as a whole, and is more marked as cognitive activity becomes more complex.

The development of perception, memory, and certain aspects of reasoning was subjected to very detailed study. It was found that thought and speech defects are closely linked with peculiarities in perceptive cognition, retardation and inadequacy in differentiating perceptions, and incomplete retention of concepts and knowledge. With special education and training, mentally retarded children develop not only elementary skills and abilities, but to a certain extent master intelligent memory, voluntary attention, comparison, and generalization. Although these processes are weak, they yield to social influences such as training, thanks to the flexible cortex, and begin to play a leading role in the development of this category of child.

The view that the development of complex psychological activity occurs as a result of education seems paradoxical only on first glance. This position acknowledges that the development of the mentally retarded child is subject to exactly the same basic lawfulness as is the development of the normal child. To accept this position—and all facts speak in its favor—is to acknowledge that, despite the complexity of the defect, the oligophrenic has a foundation for significant development when placed in circumstances favorable to education and training.

But when we speak of the development of complex forms of psychological activity in these children, we must keep in mind the fact that their development is extremely peculiar in its course and results, and that it is conditioned by great complications which retard its course. It has already been noted that under favorable educational and training conditions oligophrenics can develop perception and memory. But the peculiarities of these processes remain extremely significant. Even in the most favorable circumstances it is characteristic for the oligophrenic to generalize weakly and display inadequate cognitive concreteness. Verbally acquired knowledge does not seem to have the same basic influence on the oligophrenic's development as it does in the normal child. Successes in sensory cognition and practical activity are inadequately interpreted in words. This, of course, limits the role played by words in the child's general development.

These peculiarities, so important in the mentally retarded child's development, must be considered in every possible way in their training and education. Material on a subject must be understood more precisely in order that it acquire a concrete pedagogical significance.

Soviet psychologists have focussed a great deal of attention on various aspects of training and education in the development of normal children (Vygotskii, Zankov, Bogoyavlenskii, Menchinskaya, Gal'perin, El'konin). The role of training in the development of the mentally retarded has been shown by all the material contained in *Peculiarities of Intellectual Development in the Participants of Auxiliary Schools,* published in 1965 and summarized in this chapter. This position must be extended and rendered more concrete in the future. For the moment, we must limit ourselves to only certain considerations.

The educator's role in assisting the mentally retarded to acquire knowledge, retain it, and to acquire the ability to utilize this knowledge is very great. His role in organizing, realizing, and stimulating the activity of these children is much more significant than with the normally developing child.

The relationship between stored knowledge and intellectual development in oligophrenics is much more complicated than it is in normal children. Despite intensive pedagogical influence, development proceeds slowly in the first years of training. Noticeable improvements in perception and retention occur in the third and fourth grades in the form of an increasing ability to acquire knowledge, and in the formation of certain skills. In the adolescent years these achievements are strengthened. However, there is a marked discrepancy between the accumulation of knowledge and the ability to use it independently. This is due to the fact that the mentally retarded child is prepared to undertake any task regardless of his inability to mobilize knowledge. A new level of intellectual activity is observed in the upper school age. To some degree the gulf between the accumulation and the use of knowledge is overcome. Sensitivity to contradictions is heightened, intellectual activity increases, and the work and social tendencies of personality are formed.

Training which depends primarily on verbal methods is not possible for these children, since it has an inadequate influence on their advancement. Oligophrenic development is also hindered when learned material is reinforced solely by monotonous repetition.

The Soviet auxiliary school has had noteworthy success in educating and training mentally retarded children, but we must not be content with these achievements. It must not be taken for granted that the methods hitherto utilized are the best for the development of the mentally retarded.

Psychological research and observation permit us to assert that the development of complex forms of cognitive activity is best achieved when training is closely associated with various kinds of practical activity. Observations indicate that if knowledge has roots in practical and work activity, in self-service work or in agriculture, thus acquiring definite significance, the children are able to use this knowledge with much greater ease.

References

Bein, E. S. Magnitude of distant objects in the perception of retarded and deaf-mute school children. In *Problems in the psychology of deaf-mute and mentally retarded children.* Moscow: Uchpedgiz, 1940.

Dul'nev, G. M. The significance of intention for accuracy and completeness in the reproduction of text (a comparative study of mentally retarded and normal school children). In *Problems in the psychology of deaf-mute and mentally retarded children.* Moscow: Uchpedgiz, 1940.

Dul'nev, G. M. Characterization of the use and comprehension of adjectives by mentally retarded children. In *Educational work in special schools.* Nos. 1–2. Moscow: Uchpedgiz, 1948.

Evlakhova, E. A. Characteristics of the perception of the representation of expressive movements in schools for the handicapped. *Dokl. Akad. Pedag. Nauk RSFSR,* 1957, No. 4.

Feofanov, M. P. Idiosyncrasies in the construction of phrases by children in schools for the handicapped. *Izv. Akad. Pedag. Nauk RSFSR,* 1948, No. 19.

Feofanov, M. P. *Essays on the psychology of Russian language learning in children from auxiliary schools.* Moscow: Izd. Akad. Pedag. Nauk RSFSR, 1955.

Gnezdilov, M. F. *Teaching Russian in younger classes of auxiliary schools.* Moscow: Uchpedgiz, 1959.

Kudryavtseva, E. M. Changes in the recognition of objects as a function of a child's development. Candidate's dissertation, Moscow: 1954.

Kuz'mitskaya, M. I. Fundamental difficulties in solving problems by students in auxiliary schools. *Izv. Akad. Pedag. Nauk RSFSR,* 1957, No. 88.

Leont'ev, A. N. Principles of the psychological development of children and mental deficiency. In *Problems of the development of mind.* Moscow: Izd. Akad. Pedag. Nauk RSFSR, 1959.

Lipkina, A. I. Analysis and synthesis in the recognition of objects by pupils in auxiliary schools. In *Characteristics of cognitive activity in pupils in auxiliary schools.* Moscow: Izd. Akad. Pedag. Nauk RSFSR, 1953.

Nudel'man, M. M. Changes in similar concepts in mentally retarded and deaf-mute school children. In *Problems in the rearing and education of deaf-mutes and mentally retarded children.* Moscow. Uchpedgiz, 1941.

Nudel'man, M. M. The ways children ask questions and its significance for development. In *Educational work in special schools.* No. 1. Moscow: Uchpedgiz, 1949.

Nudel'man, M. M. Certain peculiarities in the ideas of students of an auxiliary school. In *Peculiarities of the cognitive activity of auxiliary-school students.* Moscow: Izd. Akad. Pedag. Nauk RSFSR, 1953.

Petrova, V. G. Auxiliary-school students: discriminations of similar objects as a function of the nature of the combination of words and graphic properties. In *Psychological problems of the combination of words and graphic properties in the process of instruction used in auxiliary schools.* Moscow: Izd. Akad. Pedag. Nauk RSFSR, 1956.

Petrova, V. G. Discrimination of similar objects by pupils in auxiliary schools as a function of type of combination of word and visual representation. In *Proceedings of the Scientific Session on Problems of Defectology.* Moscow: Izd. Akad. Pedag. Nauk RSFSR, 1958. (a)

Petrova, V. G. Certain characteristics of text mastery by mentally retarded school children, *Spets. Shkola,* 1958, No. 3. (b)

Pinskii, B. I. Special features of remembering of students in schools for the handicapped. In *Educational work in schools for the handicapped.* Nos. 3–4. Moscow: Uchpedgiz, 1952.

Pinskii, B. I. Reproduction processes during incidental memorization and peculiar features of such memorization in auxiliary-school students (oligophrenics). *Izv Akad. Pedag. Nauk RSFSR,* 1954, No. 57.

Pinskii, B. I. *Psychological features of the activity of mentally retarded children.* Moscow: Izd. Akad. Pedag. Nauk RSFSR, 1962.

Shif, Z. I. The selection of similar shades of color and the naming of colors (a comparative study of deaf-mutes, mentally retarded, and normal children). In *Problems in the psychology of deaf-mute and mentally retarded children.* Moscow: Uchpedgiz, 1940.

Shif, Z. I. Certain special features of history instruction in auxiliary schools. In *Problems in the rearing and education of deaf-mute and mentally retarded children.* Moscow: Uchpedgiz, 1941.

Shif, Z. I. Analysis and synthesis of reading material by pupils in auxiliary schools. In *Proceedings of the Second Scientific Session on Problems of Defectology.* Moscow: Izd. Akad. Pedag. Nauk RSFSR, 1959.

Smirnov, A. A. Development of memory. In *Psychological science in the U.S.S.R.* Vol. 1. Moscow: Izd. Akad. Pedag. Nauk RSFSR, 1959.

Solov'ev, I. M. Changes in representations as a function of the similarity of objects. *Uch. Zap. Gos. Inst. Psikhol.,* 1940, *1.*

Solov'ev, I. M. Forgetting and its special features in mentally retarded children. In *Problems in the rearing and education of deaf-mutes and mentally retarded children.* Moscow: Uchpedgiz, 1941.

Solov'ev, I. M. Thinking of handicapped children during the solution of arithmetic problems. In *Educational work in auxiliary schools.* Nos. 3–4. Moscow: Uchpedgiz, 1951.

Solov'ev, I. M. (Ed.) Peculiarities of the cognitive activity of auxiliary school students. In *Psychological essays.* Moscow: Izd. Akad. Pedag. Nauk RSFSR, 1953. (a)

Solov'ev, I. M. The perception of reality by mentally retarded children. In *Characteristics of the cognitive activity of auxiliary school students.* Moscow: Izd. Akad. Pedag. Nauk RSFSR, 1953. (b)

Solov'ev, I. M. The thought process of mentally retarded pupils during the solution of arithmetical problems. In *Characteristics of the cognitive activity of auxiliary school students.* Moscow: Izd. Akad. Pedag. Nauk RSFSR, 1953. (c)

Stadnenko, N. M. Comparative characterization of the comprehension of thematic pictures by pupils in classes I and II of public schools and auxiliary schools. Candidate's dissertation, Moscow, 1958.

Vasilevskaya, V. Y. *Comprehension of text material by pupils in auxiliary schools.* Izd. Akad. Pedag. Nauk RSFSR, 1960. (a)

Vasilevskaya, V. Y. Pedagogical instruction of severely retarded children. In *The education and rearing of mentally retarded children.* Moscow: Izd. Akad. Pedag. Nauk RSFSR, 1960. (b)

Veresotskaya, K. I. Recognition of pictures of objects as a function of changes in their spatial position. In *Problems in the psychology of deaf-mute and mentally retarded children.* Moscow: Uchpedgiz, 1940. (a)

Veresotskaya, K. I. Problems of depth perception in students of auxiliary schools. In *Problems in the psychology of deaf-mute and mentally retarded children.* Moscow: Uchpedgiz, 1940. (b)

Zamskii, K. S. Variations in the repetition of teaching materials in auxiliary schools. *Izv. Akad. Pedag. Nauk RSFSR,* 1954, No. 57.

Zankov, L. V. The development of memory in the mentally retarded child. In *The mentally retarded child.* Vol. 1. Moscow, 1935, No. 1.

Zankov, L. V. *Psychology and the mentally retarded child.* Moscow: Uchpedgiz, 1939.

Zankov, L. V. *Memory*. Moscow: Uchpedgiz, 1949.

Zankov, L. V. (Ed.) Psychological peculiarities of junior grade students in an auxiliary school. *Izv. Akad. Pedag. Nauk RSFSR,* 1951, No. 37.

Zvereva, M. V. Characteristics of the process of comparison by mentally retarded school children. Candidate's dissertation, Moscow, 1948.

Zvereva, M. V., and Lipkina, A. I. Comparison of objects by mentally retarded school children. In *Characteristics of cognitive activity in auxiliary school students.* Moscow: Izd. Akad. Pedag. Nauk RSFSR, 1953.

11

Probabilistic Prognosis and Its Significance in Normal and Pathological Subjects

I. M. Feigenberg

EDITORS' INTRODUCTION

This chapter summarizes a decade of research on the experimental characterization of schizophrenic defects. The notion of an orienting reflex suggested by Pavlov has become an important component of Soviet physiological and behavioral analysis.[1] *I. M. Feigenberg adds to this concept evidence from new sources (e.g., perceptual illusions) and comes up with the idea of a "probabilistic prognosis." Although it is not yet carefully defined, the idea that disruption of "probabilistic prognosis" underlies schizophrenic defects is a controversial hypothesis in the Soviet literature and has found its way into translations into English (Lebedinskaya, Feigenberg, and Freierov, 1962).*

Feigenberg is presently on the staff of the Institute for Specialization of Doctors in Moscow. His laboratory is in the Institute of Psychiatry, Academy of Medical Sciences, in Moscow.

1. *Editors' note:* See the work of Sokolov, Vinogradova, and Anokhin in this volume, Chapters 23, 24, and 30.

Probabilistic Prognosis and the Orienting Response

At the present time neurophysiology has accumulated many facts which do not fit the concept of the reflex arc as a linear chain of neurons. The concept of the structure of the reflexive act is becoming more complex and precise. This chapter is devoted to only one aspect of this large problem—namely, to the question of probabilistic prognosis in the activity of the brain.

Current work on the orienting reflex clearly illustrates how complex the concept of a reflexive act has become. A characteristic trait of the orienting reaction is that it arises in response to sudden application of a stimulus and is extinguished when that stimulus is applied repeatedly. This extinction was explained by the development of inhibition (adaptation, exhaustion, fatigue) in the reflex arc, as reflected, for instance, in a rise in the response threshold. However, such an explanation gives rise to a series of major difficulties. If each reflex begins with the action of some kind of physical stimulus at the receptive end of the reflex arc, then how does one explain the orienting reaction?

Let us examine the orienting reaction to a tone which is repeated rhythmically at equal time intervals. Each repetition of the tone produces a weaker orienting reaction until it is entirely extinguished—that is, there is no reaction either while the tone is heard or during the pauses between sounds. But if one of the tones is omitted, the orienting reaction occurs all over again. Where is the physical stimulus which evoked the reflex? Where is the receptive end of that reflex arc? This question cannot be answered within the framework of the concept of the linear reflex arc. It is indeed strange to imagine how the orienting reflex can even arise when there is no physical stimulus at the receptive end of the reflex arc.

Difficulties also arise when one attempts to attribute the "law of strength" to the orienting reaction. The law states that the greater the physical energy of the stimulus which evokes a reflex, the stronger is the reaction, under equal conditions of the functional state of the reacting substrata. Let us suppose that we achieve extinction with a repeated rhythmical tone of 50 db. If the latter sound is replaced by one of the same pitch but of 75 db, the orienting reaction appears again. It would seem that this phenomenon can be explained by the traditional concept: extinction of the orienting reaction is produced by the development of inhibition in the reflex arc, which has developed to the point where the 50-db tone was unable to evoke a reaction but the stronger sound could evoke it. However, this explanation is not supported by experimental data. If the orienting reaction has been extinguished to a 50-db tone, it can also be evoked once more by substituting a softer sound of the same pitch—let us say, 25 db. In other words, the reaction is the same as it is when the original tone is replaced by a louder one. This fact indicates that extinction of the orienting reaction is by no means caused by the development of inhibition in a linear reflex arc. Moreover, this fact is not in accord with the "law of strength."

What, then, evokes the orienting reaction? The preceding description indicates that it arises in response to the appearance of a *new* situation. Under conditions of prolonged silence, the orienting reaction arises in response to a sound. Under conditions of prolonged sound, it arises in response to the cessation of sound or to a change in the nature of the sound (be it amplification or weakening of the physical strength of the sound, or change in the frequency of the sound). The concept of the orienting reaction as one which reacts to the *novelty* of the situation and which receives information by means of the sensory organs has gained wide acceptance among physiologists (Anokhin, 1941; Sokolov, 1960; Vinogradova, 1961).

"Novelty" does not imply that the reaction arises in response to a stimulus which the organism has never before encountered. It is understood as the *unexpectedness* of the change in the situation. The facts indicate that the orienting reaction is the organism's reaction to the discrepancy between the situation at a given moment (communicated by the sensory organs) and that situation which the organism expected (foresaw). Physiological observations force us to assume that in the brain there is a process of *prognosis* and a process of comparison of the actually occurring situation with the expected situation (Bernshtein, 1957, 1961, 1962). Pavlov's study of conditioned reflexes called the physiologist's attention to the numerous phenomena in which the organism's reaction is conditioned by the brain's ability to forecast the future course of events in response to a *signal* stimulus and to react in accord with events which have not yet occurred, to "anticipate" them. This kind of prognosis is biologically very expedient, since it prepares the organism to react. It prepares the organism for changes in the environment so that it will not take him "unawares." Thus the organism's reaction outstrips the development of events in the environment and enables the organism to survive.

The orienting reaction is the result of the development of the organism's adaptive acts. It is the result of the adaptation of the organism to chains of repeated events in the environment. Anticipatory reactions (i.e., the prediction of the development of the course of events) are characteristic of organisms even on the lowest levels of the evolutionary scale. Without them the organism would be unable to function actively.

As the organization of living organisms becomes more complex, the forms of prognosis become more complex and more perfect. They achieve the greatest perfection in the higher vertebrates. However, even in man prognosis may occur without conscious awareness.

How is prognosis formed in the brain? Its source is the brain's retention of the traces of temporal relations which occurred in the past, the traces of earlier acquired information. Suppose that event A logically preceded event B, to which the reaction C was evoked; then event A will become the signal for the organism to develop reaction C by forecasting the occurrence of event B, preparing for its occurrence in advance. The conditioned reflex is formed according to this scheme.

However, prognosis is not merely the blind utilization of past experience. The organism *extrapolates* the regularities encountered in its past experience. In other words, the organism discovers lawful characteristics of groups of phenomena. The process of extrapolating past experience which is found in various behavioral reactions has been studied both in man (Feigenberg, 1958) and in animals (Krushinskii, 1959).

In the life of organisms each event arises in various temporal combinations with other events. Among them are combinations which are not repeated and combinations which are statistically reliable in their repetitions. The very same event may enter into several stable repeated combinations, some of which occur more frequently than others.

Thus the occurrence of event A cannot be a completely *reliable* signal for the occurrence of a certain event B after a certain interval since in the organism's past experience event A preceded the occurrence of various events. By virtue of this, the biologically more expedient "strategy" of the organism is to react to event A in correspondence with the event which most often followed it in the past, in other words, to react in accordance with that event which *most probably* will occur after event A. Therefore, prognosis on the basis of past experience cannot be absolute and is always *probabilistic prognosis*. The organism's reaction based on such prognosis allows it to greatly reduce the number of incorrect reactions, that is, it is the most advantageous from the point of view of survival and adaptation to the surrounding environment.

This can be illustrated schematically in the following way. For event A to evoke the prognosis of event B in the brain and, correspondingly, reaction C to the as yet nonexistent B, it is not enough to merely have a certain number of combinations of these events. It is necessary to have a *statistically reliable predominance* of situations in which B follows A.[2] These must be dominant over the occasions on which A is not followed by B but by some other events. The brain chooses from among all the possible consequences of A those with the greatest probability of occurring. The

2. *Editors' note:* This statement seems to imply that Feigenberg is asserting the impossibility of conditioning with less than 50 per cent reinforcement. His formulation also neglects the effect of the significance of the stimuli. Conditioning with an intense UCS, a very significant stimulus, will be better than with a weak UCS even though the two are equally probable.

organism's active operations are structured in accord with this kind of prediction (Bernshtein, 1957, 1961, 1962). In the process of the evolution of the organic world the formation of this predicting mechanism corresponds to the lawfulness of the environment in which the organism lives and carries out its activities.

If event A always precedes event B and never occurs in other combinations (in other words, the conditional probability of event B in the presence of event A equals unity), a relatively small number of combinations of A and B is necessary to evoke reaction C, i.e., to develop a conditioned reflex. If event A precedes various events (B . . . N) but the conditional probability of the occurrence of event B following A is higher than that of other events (C . . . N), then a greater number of combinations of A and B is necessary to develop the conditioned reflex. The closer the conditional probability of other events is to A, the more difficult it is to develop the conditioned reflex and the greater the number of combinations needed. This is biologically expedient since in this case the occurrence of event A provides less basis to predict the occurrence of event B with greater probability than the occurrence of any other event.

One can find many examples of probabilistic prognosis in the behavior of man and animals. The swallow, catching an insect, does not catch it by following its flight. The swallow flies "along side" the insect (the stimulus) to a certain point in space where, according to past experience, it will *most probably* meet with the insect. When a man crosses a road, the sight of a moving automobile is a danger signal. However, the man does not run from the automobile. He either slows or quickens his pace in order not to be at that point in space in which he predicts the automobile will be. If the man has had little experience with automobiles in the past or if the automobile moves in an unexpected way (e.g., skids on ice), the man's chosen strategy may be unsuccessful and lead to catastrophe.

Activity is simply impossible without the probabilistic prognosis of external events and the results of the organism's own actions. Probabilistic prognosis is one of the most important components among those which have been studied from various points of view and described under different names: purpose (Uznadze, 1961), plan of motor tasks (Bernshtein, 1957), anticipatory arousal (Anokhin, 1962), images (Beritov, 1961), neural models of the stimulus (Voronin and Sokolov, 1958), "TOTE" (Pribram, 1961).[3]

All of these concepts are unified by the idea that the brain's work cannot be realized without "looking ahead," without comparison of the actual situation with the situation which is predicted as most probable or with the situation which should be achieved as a result of the organism's action

3. *Editors' note:* Discussions of the work of Uznadze, Bernshtein, Anokhin, Beritov, and Sokolov are to be found elsewhere in this volume.

(the neural model of the stimulus, the plan, the purpose). These two types of comparison are not identical, but they are nonetheless related.

Requiring the effectors to achieve a certain result cannot lead to the necessary outcome if the nervous system does not predict the development of external events. When birds soar for an express purpose (e.g., to retain the flight direction), the effective commands must move in accord with the prognosis of the most probable action of external forces (e.g., the force and direction of the wind). Only when good use is made of the predicted changes of external forces will the organism achieve the desired result in the most economical way, with a minimal expenditure of energy. Only when the brain collates the predicted with the available can it send signals to the working organs in order to achieve the necessary result, that is, to reduce as far as possible the discord between the predicted (or planned) and the actual situation. The signals of discrepancy always coordinate the course of the reaction, assuring that the organism's activity will be conditioned by the expected result of the action (i.e., in the final analysis, by the organism's past experience), despite the numerous accidental and interfering factors. If it were not for a system of comparisons, these accidental factors would distract the reaction from the correct path (Bernshtein, 1957, 1961, 1962; Grashchenkov, Latash, and Feigenberg, 1962). It is remarkable that the comparison of the actual situation with the one that should exist according to the program is one of the most important principles in the work of self-regulating, cybernetic systems created by man (Ashby, 1959); the apparatus of prognosis and comparison is the basic factor in these systems.

Probabilistic prognosis is an important factor in biologically useful activity, that is, in the activity which maximally suits the conditions in which the organism lives. As a result activity is much less a function of accidental, unforeseen factors.

The presence in the brain of mechanisms which react to "novelty," that is, to the discord between predicted and actual situations, is verified by electrophysiological studies of brain activity on the cellular level. Hubel, Henson, Rupert, and Galambos (1959) conducted experiments on unanesthetized cats using microelectrode probes of biopotentials in the auditory cortex. They discovered cells which do not react to all sounds, but only to new or significant ones (the calls and squeaks of mice) and often only in the presence of the behavioral orienting reaction. Adey, Walter, and Hendrix (1961) recorded electrical changes in the hippocampus during the early stages of the formation of a habit. When the habit became strong, these changes disappeared. They reappeared only when the animal made errors. Electrical changes have been recorded in the amygdala when the organism meets with new or significant situations associated with reward or punishment. These changes decrease when the situation becomes familiar.

However, when the hippocampal area of the limbic system has been removed, repetition of the same situation does not lead to reduction of reactions. Sokolov (1964) discovered neurons which react to the "novel" stimulus independently of its modality.

In the light of this information what is the significance of the arousal and extinction of the orienting reaction? When the organism finds itself in some kind of unvarying situation (e.g., silence), it predicts the continuation of this situation. If the situation changes (e.g., a tone occurs), there is discord between the predicted and the actual situation. The orienting reaction arises in response to this discord. If, in order to extinguish the orienting reaction, we repeat a tone separated by equal time intervals, *t,* the probabilistic prognosis undergoes a reconstruction and reformation. This reconstruction proceeds gradually. With each new tone the probability that it will occur again in interval *t* increases. Thus, with each new occurrence of the sound the degree of discord between the actual situation and the expected one decreases. The orienting reaction becomes weaker. Finally, when the probability of another occurrence of the tone in interval *t* becomes sufficiently great and, correspondingly, the discord becomes sufficiently small, the orienting reaction disappears entirely—it has been extinguished. Then, if the sound is not turned on after the regular interval of silence *t,* the discord between the predicted situation (the tone) and the actual situation (silence) arises again. And once again an orienting reaction arises.

Thus, the orienting reaction is not a reaction to the quantity of energy embodied in the physical stimulus, but a reaction to its novelty, unexpectedness, or significance. In other words, it is a reaction to the quantity and importance of the information which is provided by some signal to the organism. When the signal is repeated it carries less information to the organism and the orienting reaction is extinguished.

If the orienting reaction is viewed in this way it will be clear that the contradiction to the "law of strength" of which we spoke earlier is only an apparent contradiction. This law is retainable if we think of "strength" not as the *quantity of energy* in the signal, but as the *quantity of information* which the signal provides for the organism. The less probable the appearance of the given signal, the more information it bears. This approach is very important for the experimenter now that the quantity of information in the signal may be precisely measured by its physical characteristics.

The greater the discord between the actually occurring signal and the one that was predicted, the greater is the quantity of information provided by that signal. As the organism accumulates experience the predicted probability of the occurrence of various events following A becomes more varied. The "uncertainty" of the numerous possible events decreases, leading to the more expedient choice of reaction. If the brain is viewed as a system which receives and transforms information, the accumulation of experience reduces the informational entropy (i.e., the degree of chaos and uncertainty of choice) in that system. The accumulation of preliminary information (acquired through experience) organizes the brain as a system which transmits and retains information.

The orienting reaction is of great *biological significance* for the organism. It plays an essential role in the organism's ability to adapt to changes in the environment, for it is the reaction to a stimulus which utilizes the past experience of the given individual. The orienting reaction is expressed in the mobilization of the animal's analyzers, the desynchronization of the brain's bioelectrical activity, the increase of muscle tonus, the intensification of blood circulation, etc. In other words, the orienting reaction is expressed in the entire organism's preparation for prospective action (as distinct from the as yet uncertain conditioned reaction), or for a change in the organism's behavioral strategy. This preparation was evoked by unexpected changes in the organism's environment. The orienting reaction develops in response to these changes. Its biological value is that the organism prepares itself to react to some kind of future (but as yet undefined) changes. The nature of the action's form is still unclear. The reaction consists of an inclination for prospective activity in both the afferent systems, for the collection of supplementary information, and in the efferent systems for the production of a reaction adequate for the given situation.

Let us assume that the signal A which evokes the orienting reaction is repeated many times and precedes situation B. In this case the expedient preparation which follows A is for a completely defined activity—B—and is not a preparation for just any undetermined activity. In other words, it is not "general mobilization," which in this case would be a useless expenditure of great energy. And, in fact, we know that when repetition of A is a statistically stable predecessor of situation B, the orienting reaction is extinguished. This is due to the fact that as the quantity of information provided by A decreases, the nonspecific reaction to a signal decreases. Extinction of the orienting reaction to a repeated signal is an extremely valuable phenomenon, developed in the process of evolution, and represents economy of energy when the stimulus loses its "novelty." The orienting reaction's expensive energy is replaced by the more economical specific reaction C which responds to the signal B. This is the scheme for the formation of the conditioned reflex.

The formation of a conditioned reflex by means of repeated pairings of two stimuli without reinforcement may be considered a special case. The stimulus which is statistically stable precedes a situation of calm. The adequate response to this is inaction. It happens exactly in that way. The orienting reaction extinguishes and a state of sleep-calm ensues. It is like a conditioned reflex with reinforced calm. Thus, the orienting reaction and its extinction are highly expedient biologically, enabling the organism to adapt to a changing environment with the least expenditure of energy.

If the conditioned reflex is the anticipation of a *definite* situation and the preparation for action within it, then the orienting reaction arises as a prediction (based on past experience) of the *uncertainty* of the impending situation. In other words, the orienting reaction is the organism's preparation for action in an uncertain situation. The more complex the living organism, the more complicated will be the chain of processes through which it is necessary to pass in order to guarantee a response to the changing environment. Consequently, the probabilistic prognosis in preparation for the necessary and *timely* reaction would be more perfect.

Liberman (unpublished) provides an interesting confirmation of the occurrence of the orienting reaction in uncertain situations. Words and expressions which signify definite physical influences (cold, bell, etc.) scarcely evoke the orienting reaction. But words and expressions which warn of a possible influence, but which retain the indefinite character of the influence ("I will present the stimulus," "attention"), evoke a marked orienting reaction.

The processes of probabilistic prognosis and comparisons play a basic role in the arousal of certain *emotional reactions* which accompany somatic changes in the cardiovascular system, the respiratory system, etc. A good example is the occurrence of a sense of the comic and the reaction of laughter. The critical moment is when there is a discrepancy between the actual situation and the one which the listener or the viewer predicted as most probable on the basis of past experience. This is the basis for the humor of clowns. General laughter occurs when the clown, whose every movement has indicated awkwardness and clumsiness, suddenly executes a complicated acrobatic feat. In this situation the humor of the situation is determined by the total lack of correspondence of the clown's anticipated behavior with his actual behavior. If the same acrobatic feat is not preceded by awkwardness, it will not evoke laughter. A comical story or a funny anecdote are often structured so that the listener expects a certain outcome, but suddenly the outcome is completely unexpected.

Similarly, the reaction of fright arises in response to a sudden, unexpected stimulus: here the discord between the actual and the predicted situations also plays a role.

But emotion may occur in a somewhat different manner as well. For example, fear (as distinct from fright) occurs as the response to a stimulus which forces the organism to predict an undesirable (or dangerous) situation. In other words, fear is the result of the comparison between the predicted situation and one which corresponds to the organism's needs.

Thus, the arousal of the complex of somatic changes in emotion is related to the orienting response. It occurs as the result of comparison. Emotion and the orienting reaction are also related in their biological significance—the preparation for action.

The deviation of the course of events from that which the organism predicted leads to a series of changes which mobilize the organism for a change in the strategy of his behavior, and prepare it for action with the greatest possible expenditure of energy. Cannon's studies (1927) have shown how adrenalin is released into the blood and sugar is mobilized from the liver and enters the blood from whence it can be quickly utilized by any group of muscles. The work ability of the exhausted muscles is renewed, the size of the vessels changes, the heart rate and the blood pressure increase, the pupil dilates, the respiratory rhythm changes, the peristaltic movement of the intestines ceases and digestive juices are discharged, the coagulation of the blood is hastened if the vessels are damaged. This is the "general mobilization" of which we spoke in connection with the orienting response. It is a highly expedient adaptive reaction when the organism finds it necessary to prepare itself for action, but still does not know the precise nature of that action.

It is interesting to note that the usual behavior of people in certain complex situations is in full accord with the assumption that somatic changes during emotion depend on discrepancy. For example, when it is necessary to inform a weak aging person of some great misfortune, one "prepares" him. The preparation consists in helping him to predict, gradually, step by step, that which it is necessary to tell him. Then the fatal news will not seem to be so discordant with the predicted situation, and the stormy emotional reaction (in particular, a sharp rise in blood pressure) will not occur, despite the fact that the tragic meaning of the news is fully understood by the person.

Very little is known about the concrete physiological mechanism of probabilistic prognosis. Pavlov (1938) observed decorticated animals and found that the orienting response was unextinguishable, indicating the extremely important role of the cerebral cortex in the reshaping of the probabilistic prognosis under the influence of the individual's experience. The same conclusions were drawn by Hubel and others as we noted earlier. Electrophysiological data indicate that the reticular formation and the limbic system (in particular, amygdala, the hippocampal convolution) participate in the processes of probabilistic prognosis. The work of Anokhin on the "acceptor of action" (1941), Sokolov on the neural model of the stimulus (1959, 1960), and Pribram on the TOTE unit (1961) are interesting attempts to present a concrete concept of the physiological mechanism of behavioral acts involving the processes of prognosis.

Physiology is beginning to grope for this mechanism. However, if probabilistic prognosis is not even acknowledged, it is impossible to understand and analyze this important aspect of higher nervous activity which permits the organism to utilize its past experience in the changing conditions of its environment.

Pathological Changes in Probabilistic Prognoses

In the first part of this chapter it was shown that under normal conditions probabilistic prognosis plays a major role in various kinds of activity—in "simple (e.g., orienting) reactions" and in "complex" behavioral acts. It is to be expected that disturbance of probabilistic prognosis in pathological states will lead to disorders in those reactions and those forms of activity in which probabilistic prognosis usually plays a role. Since the orienting response is most accessible to study, it was examined by us in conditions of pathology. In this part of the chapter we shall examine the results of studies of schizophrenic patients. (The discussion which follows relies heavily on earlier articles: Feigenberg, 1960, 1963a, b; 1964a, b; Feigenberg and Levi, 1965.)

In order to determine the manner in which the orienting response is disturbed in schizophrenics, we conducted polygraphic recordings of various components of the generalized orienting response (EEG responses in various parts of the brain, galvanic skin responses, cardiac and respiratory activity, eye movements, motor responses) in schizophrenic patients. The study indicated that all components of the orienting response are disturbed in schizophrenics. It was also shown that the nature of the disturbance differed, depending on the clinical manifestations of the schizophrenia. In patients whose clinical records are dominated by schizophrenic defects but who have only "rudimentary" productive psychotic symptoms, or none, the orienting response is weakened. In patients with weakly manifested schizophrenic defects but with a predominance of productive psychotic symptoms,[4] orienting response extinction is disturbed. Extinction is retarded and sometimes fails to occur even after dozens of repetitions of the stimulus.

The correlation between the weakened orienting response and the degree of schizophrenic manifestations demanded verification on a large clinical sample of carefully selected clinical groups of patients. This experiment was conducted with 158 schizophrenics divided into the following groups:[5]

4. *Editors' note:* The term "productive symptom" describes a variety of behaviors which share the common attribute of activity (as opposed to passivity). Thus, delusions, hallucinations, and automatisms are examples of productive symptoms.

5. *Editors' note:* Dr. Feigenberg explains this classification system as follows:

(a) Simple schizophrenia is characterized by an uninterrupted malignant state. The process begins with negative symptoms and there is an absence of clearly expressed critical conditions.

(b) Paranoid is a general term used to describe the disorder in which delusions predominate. The three subtypes within this class are:

1. Early paranoid and hebephrenic. This disorder appears in late childhood or adolescence. It has a malignant course and rapidly manifested defects which increase in severity.
2. Paranoid. Begins in adulthood (25–30 yrs.) with a less malignant course than the early paranoid-hebephrenic type.

schizophrenia—simple form; schizophrenia—early paranoid and hebephrenic; paranoid; inertly expressed paranoid; and periodic. It turned out that, as the manifestations of schizophrenia weaken, beginning with the simple form and ending with the periodic, there is less and less disturbance of the orienting response (desynchronization of the EEG using a tone and a light). In the group of patients with simple schizophrenia whose defects were very sharply manifested, 53 per cent had no orienting response at all and only 6 per cent had a satisfactory orienting response. In the group of periodic schizophrenics with weak defects there were no patients with total absence of orienting response. In 39 per cent the orienting response was satisfactory (Lebedinskaya, Feigenberg and Freirov, 1962).

This research confirmed our hypothesis that the orienting response in schizophrenics is weaker in inverse proportion with the strength of the clinical schizophrenic defects.

Consequently, we have formulated the following hypothesis: *Disturbance of the orienting response in schizophrenic patients is the reflection of the disturbance of the ability to utilize past experience to organize future activity (probabilistic prognosis), and is also linked with the comparison of information of the ongoing probabilistic prognosis in the brain* (based on information received earlier). The development of schizophrenia is a sort of entropy (disorganization) of the brain as an information system: *differences in the probabilities of anticipated events are obliterated under these circumstances.*

In schizophrenics with mild defects, in whom the orienting response does not extinguish over a longer period of time, the ability to formulate a probabilistic prognosis is disturbed; the acquisition of new experience on the basis of earlier experiences is hampered.

This hypothesis permits us to explain not only the above-mentioned "physiological" disturbances in schizophrenics but certain clinical manifestations of schizophrenia as well. For example, one of the most characteristic traits of schizophrenia is weakened affective reactions, "emotional dullness." Earlier we said that unexpectedness is very important for the affective reaction, in any case its somatic manifestations, and for the orienting response. Thus, our hypothesis permits us to understand affective disturbances in schizophrenics. We should mention here these patients' frequent use of "unusual" words, that is, words which are rarely used by normal subjects in similar situations. The accumulation of vocabulary from past experience

---

3. Inertly expressed paranoid. Even less malignant than paranoid (one might even say "benign") and with an insignificant increase in the severity of the disorder.

(c) Paranoid. There are systematic delusions without hallucinations and a more or less benign course.

(d) Periodic. Alternating periods of schizophrenic attacks and normal conditions. Once an attack occurs the course of the disease does not get worse.

is retained by the patient, but his choice does not correspond to the structure of past experience.

Another asset of our hypothesis is that it provides the only unified explanation of the various disturbances which are observed in schizophrenics but which do not lend themselves to any other unified explanation.

The hypothesis still needed additional verification. The best criterion of the validity of a scientific hypothesis is its ability to predict the results of experiments other than those on which it was formed. In order to verify the predictive power of our hypothesis it was necessary to find a test which involves probabilistic prognosis but is not a manifestation of the orienting response. We chose the Charpentier illusion which involves a comparison of two objects equal in weight but not in volume. The smaller seems to be heavier. This illusion occurs in healthy people as the result of the lack of correspondence between the actual weight and the probabilistic prognosis which conditions the preparation of the proprioceptive-motor apparatus. If it is true that schizophrenics are defective in making such a preparation, then it is to be expected that the Charpentier illusion will be weak or absent: the stronger the schizophrenic manifestations, the more correctly the patient should be able to compare the weight of the objects.

We used a pair of cylinders of equal diameter (9 cm.) and different lengths (20 and 11 cm.), weighing 180 gr. The subjects were required to compare the weight of the cylinders. The identical diameters of the cylinders guaranteed the identity of the immediate sensation. Therefore the illusion had to occur as the result of the visual perception of the differing volumes. We compared the Charpentier illusion in three groups of schizophrenics: simple form (34 patients), paranoid (40 patients), and periodic (14 patients).

The study showed that in patients with simple-form schizophrenia in whom the defects were sharply expressed, the Charpentier illusion was disturbed in 73.5 per cent of cases and in 47 per cent the illusion was completely absent. In periodic schizophrenics the disturbance was observed in 43 per cent of the cases while only 14 per cent manifested no illusion at all.

Thus the data concerning the Charpentier illusion confirmed the hypothesis that in *schizophrenic patients probabilistic prognosis is disturbed.*

Some recent psychological experiments with schizophrenics conducted at the Institute of Psychiatry under the guidance of Polyakov yielded certain other facts which may be explained by the disturbance of probabilistic prognosis.[6]

Subjects were asked to say the first letter of the Russian alphabet that came to mind when presented with a signal. The normal person calls various letters with unequal frequency. Some letters are called frequently, others rarely. The frequency of a letter corresponds roughly to its frequency in the Russian language, that is, in the subject's past experience. Schizophrenics

6. *Editors' note:* See Polyakov's chapter in this volume, Chapter 12.

frequently call "rare" letters and more rarely call "frequent" letters, thus obliterating the probability of the various letters as they occur naturally (experiment by Bogdanov). Similar results were obtained when the subject had to quickly name a word using the first syllable pronounced by the experimenter, or to add a word to an unfinished phrase spoken by the experimenter (Kritskaya's data). In this situation normal people chose certain words more often. It is characteristic for schizophrenics to smooth out differences in the frequency of the presented words. The variety of answers in the patients was greater than for normal subjects.

In a special series of experiments Bogdanov studied the degree of focus on an image projected on a screen which was necessary for the subject to identify the image. At the beginning of a trial the image was out of focus, and was gradually brought into focus. Generally, the normal subjects recognized the image earlier than the schizophrenics, that is, while the image was still partly out of focus. Past experience helped them to pick out the light points which signify an object with a high degree of probability, although the image was very unclear. However, there were certain images which the schizophrenic was able to recognize earlier than the normal subjects; these were images of objects in very unusual situations, for example, an athlete at the moment of the jump over a hurdle. In this case, the probabilistic prognosis hindered the healthy person from correctly recognizing the image. This interference was less important in the patients, since they had less "help" from the probabilistic prognosis in the recognition of images of the first group. In Kritskaya's experiments it was necessary to recognize the last word of a phrase, against a noisy background, recorded on a tape recorder. The phrases differed according to the probability of the last (noisy) word, as determined by the context. The schizophrenics were less able to recognize the more probable words and more able to recognize less probable words than the normal subjects. All these data indicate poor use of the probability structure of past experience which, in situations of incomplete information, exert a fundamental influence on correct recognition.

Thus, the application of the idea of probabilistic prognosis to the analysis of pathological phenomena turned out to be productive, encouraging us to pursue further this line of research.

References

Adey, W. R., Walter, D. O., and Hendrix, C. E. Computer techniques in correlation and spectral analyses of cerebral slow waves during discriminative behavior. *Exper. Neurol.* 1961, *3,* 501–524.

Anokhin, P. K. Novelty as a special stimulus (disinhibition). *Trudy Inst. Fiziol. im. Pavlova.* Moscow-Leningrad, 1941.

Anokhin, P. K. Anticipatory reflection of activity. *Vop. Philos.,* 1962, No. 7.

Ashby, W. R. *Introduction to cybernetics.* (Russian edition.) Moscow, 1959.

Beritov, I. C. *Neural mechanisms in the behavior of higher vertebrates.* Moscow, 1961.

Bernshtein, N. A. Certain urgent problems of the regulation of motor acts. *Vop. Psikhol.,* 1957, No. 6.

Bernshtein, N. A. Recurrent problems in the physiology of activity. *Vop. Psikhol.,* 1961, No. 6.

Bernshtein, N. A. New lines in the developments in physiology and their relation to cybernetics. *Vop. Philos.,* 1962, No. 8.

Cannon, W. *The physiology of emotion.* (Russian edition.) Leningrad, 1927.

Feigenberg, I. M. Toward a methodology for investigating higher nervous activity in the clinic (research on the generalizing function). *Byull. eksper. Biol. Med.,* 1958, No. 1.

Feigenberg, I. M. Some electrophysiological data on the role of the reticular formation in the pathogenesis of schizophrenia. In *Materials of First Scientific Congress Concerning the Role of the Reticular Formation: Problems of Physiology, Morphology, and the Clinic.* Moscow: Pervii Moskov. Med. Inst., 1960.

Feigenberg, I. M. Probabilistic prognosis in the brain's activity. *Vop. Psikhol.,* 1963, No. 2. (a)

Feigenberg, I. M. Certain traits of the pathogenesis of schizophrenia in the light of physiological research. In *Fourth All-Union Congress of Neuropathologists and Psychiatrists.* Vol. 1. Moscow, 1963. (b)

Feigenberg, I. M. On the connection between physiological and psychopathological symptoms in the clinic. In *Tenth Congress of the Pavlov All-Union Society of Physiologists.* Vol. 1. *Abstracts of speeches and symposia.* Moscow-Leningrad, 1964. (a)

Feigenberg, I. M. Comparative electroencephalographic characteristics of various types of schizophrenia. *Zh. Nevropatol. Psikhol. im. Korsakova,* 1964, No. 4, 36–43. (b)

Feigenberg, I. M., and Levi, V. L. Probabilistic prognosis and its experimental investigation in pathological states (the Charpentier illusion in schizophrenia). *Vop. Psikhol.,* 1965, No. 1.

Grashchenkov, N. I., Latash, L. P., and Feigenberg, I. M. Fundamental problems in the structure of reflex action and their methodological evaluation. *Vop. Philos.,* 1962, No. 8.

Hubel, D. H., Henson, C. O., Rupert, A., and Galambos, R. "Attention" units in the auditory cortex. *Science,* 1959, *129.*

Krushinskii, L. V. The study of extrapolative reflexes in animals. *Probl. Kibernet.,* 1959, No. 2.

Lebedinskaya, E. I., Feigenberg, I. M. and Freierov, O. E. Generalized orientation responses in the defective stage of schizophrenia. *Soviet Psychol. Psychiat.* 1962, *1,* 51–57.

Pavlov, I. P. *Twenty years of experience in the objective study of the higher activity of animals.* Moscow-Leningrad, 1938.

Pribram, K. Toward a theory of physiological psychology. *Vop. Psikhol.,* 1961, No. 2.

Sokolov, E. N. The neuronal model of the stimulus. *Dokl. Akad. Pedag. Nauk RSFSR,* 1959, No. 2.

Sokolov, E. N. The neuronal model of the stimulus and the orienting reflex. *Vop. Psikhol.,* 1960, No. 4.

Sokolov, E. N. The orienting reflex as an information regulator. In *The orienting reflex and the problem of perception in normal and pathological states.* Moscow, 1964.

Uznadze, D. N. *Experimental foundations of the psychology of set.* Tbilisi, 1961.

Vinogradova, O. S. *The orienting response and its neurophysiological mechanisms.* Moscow, 1961.

Voronin, L. G., and Sokolov, E. N. Cortical mechanisms of the orienting reflex and its relation to the conditioned reflex. Speech at the International EEG Symposium, Moscow, 1958.

12

The Experimental Investigation of Cognitive Functioning in Schizophrenia

U. F. Polyakov

EDITORS' INTRODUCTION

The research reviewed here by Polyakov is representative of the experimental orientation of Soviet psychologists when they study problems of behavioral abnormality. This experimental approach has a long tradition in Soviet psychology. On the physiological side, both Pavlov and Bekhterev concerned themselves with problems of pathology. Bekhterev opened Russia's first experimental-psychological clinic in Kazan in 1885. The famous Russian psychiatrist Korsakov opened a similar clinic in Moscow the following year.

Following the Revolution, there was a significant expansion of clinical facilities and research. Clinical psychology was often viewed as one aspect of the psychology of work; mental as well as physical hygiene was required to insure healthy and productive workers.

In the 1930's and 1940's, two leading figures in the study of behavioral pathology were Vygotskii and Zeigarnik. Vygotskii's influence was exerted through the wide acceptance of his ideas on the relation between language and thought and the relation between the ontogeny and pathology of thought. (Vygotskii's ideas are discussed elsewhere in this volume; see especially Chapters 2 and 8, by Luria.) Zeigarnik, who is best known in the West for her research with Kurt Lewin on the recall of incompleted tasks, has for more than thirty years been conducting experiments on the psychopathology of thought. This research is summarized in a recently translated monograph (Zeigarnik, 1965).

U. F. Polyakov studied at Moscow University under the direction of the well-known psychological theoretician Rubenshtein. After completing his work at the University in 1951, he went to work in Zeigarnik's laboratory At present he is Director of the Laboratory of Pathopsychology in the Institute of Psychiatry of the Academy of Medical Sciences in Moscow. As the material in this chapter indicates, he is primarily concerned with the disruption of cognitive processes which accompany neurotic and psychotic states.

CONTEMPORARY FACTS about the structure and nature of psychological processes serve as the starting point for our analysis of schizophrenia. As the result of his sociohistorical development, man's higher mental processes form in the process of social intercourse. These mental processes constitute complicated "functional systems," which develop on the basis of a complex consisting of a brain structure and physiological mechanisms. Research being done in Soviet psychology increasingly clarifies the structure of various cognitive processes and precisely defines various factors, entering into their structure (Leont'ev, 1959; Luria, 1962, 1963; Teplov, 1961; and others).

Any complicated cognitive process can be changed with the disruption of any of its constituent factors (links). But when different links are disrupted, the whole process will be disrupted, and, accordingly, the manifestation of the disruption may vary. A brain disorder which involves changes in the brain's specific anatomical or physiological characteristics will result in a change in those cognitive processes, the structure of which depends on the affected region.

These considerations lead us to conclude that the changes in cognitive processes which are observed in schizophrenia are a function of changes in the relations among basic physiological parameters, which in turn are caused by a disturbance of more fundamental (biochemical) brain processes. Thus the unknown factors which disrupt the fundamental processes are the first link in a chain which leads to disruption of cognitive processes.

On the basis of this analysis it is possible to formulate the problems facing experimental research on the characteristics of cognitive processes in schizophrenia as follows:

1. What are the fundamental cognitive processes, and in what ways are they disrupted in schizophrenia?

2. Is there a relationship between the disruption of these processes and some feature of their structures?

3. Are there any general structural factors which underlie the lawful disruption of the various processes?

4. Can we find changes in these factors if they do exist?

The most essential feature of research based on these principles is that its success depends on clinical differentiation of the patients under study. The search for factors underlying the disruption of a series of cognitive processes is tied to the fact that we are concerned with a certain kind of brain disease which determines the nature of these factors. The factors will differ according to the character of the brain disease, and, consequently, the laws and scope of the disrupted cognitive processes will be different. Therefore it is important that the patients under observation be characterized by similar brain disorders.

Cognitive Activity in Schizophrenics

Our approach is distinct from various studies of schizophrenic disruption "in general," those studies which seek a solution to the question, What are the laws governing the disruption of the mind in schizophrenia "as a whole" (in all its clinical manifestations and varieties)? On the basis of the principles set forth by the workers at the Laboratory of Experimental Pathopsychology at the Institute of Psychiatry of the Academy of Medical Sciences of the U.S.S.R. (Meleshko, Kritskaya, Bogdanov, Monosova), a study was made of a group of hard-core schizophrenics. The 60 people under observation were all classified as having suffered from continuous, chronic schizophrenia since childhood. The main reason for this selection of patients is that the unique disruptions of cognitive processes typical of schizophrenic deterioration are more distinct in a long-standing defect which was formed in childhood and persists as chronic schizophrenia. The common clinical feature of the patients observed was the manifest negative symptoms of the disease (e.g., withdrawal, introversion) present in varying degrees. Productive symptoms such as delusions or hallucinations (in general, rudimentary in such patients) were at a minimum during the period of observation.

The actual direction and orientation of the investigation were determined by a working hypothesis, formed on the basis of previously obtained experimental and clinical data. The cardinal experimental facts, increasingly confirmed in the course of many studies (Cameron, 1939; Chapman and Taylor, 1957; Payne, Mattussek, and Georg, 1959) are the overinclusive utilization of stimuli and attributes, the ease of distraction by irrelevant stimuli, and the use of superfluous, irrelevant information in the thinking and perception of the schizophrenic. We believe that it is disturbance of these processes which underlies the schizophrenic disorder.

Our own experimental data, which were obtained in pilot work on less sharply expressed disruptions of the thinking in schizophrenics, also helped form the hypothesis. These data indicated that the change in the range of utilized attributes first occurs in a parameter provisionally designated as the "strength" of the attributes, that is, their meaning or probability of occurrence.

The comparison of experimental data with clinical indicators of the integrity of the patient's knowledge, his formal-operational abilities, and idiosyncratic changes in the way past experience influences his present activity allowed us to orient our studies more concretely toward an analysis of the way schizophrenics select information from the system of past experience and the role of information selection in the alteration of schizophrenic thought processes.

In our patients the thought processes of generalization and comparison were studied at the same time as the processes of auditory and visual perception. The investigation was composed of 19 specially designed experiments. A control group of 60 normal subjects of comparable age and education was run through the same complex of experiments.

To study generalization and comparison (Meleshko, 1965), two series of experimental problems were chosen. Problems making up the first series allowed for a great many solutions. An example was requiring the subject to compare two objects with no indication of the proper basis of comparison. Under these conditions, the selection of any attribute (the basis of comparison) from the numerous features of the given object essentially determines the meaning of the attribute according to the past experience of the subject.

The first experiment in the series involved the comparison of twelve pairs of objects. The experimenter named each pair in succession and instructed the subject as follows: "State what these objects have in common and how they differ." In this way the instructions allowed the subject complete freedom of choice, in no way influencing the basis of comparison. The twelve pairs of objects could be divided conditionally into two groups: relatively similar objects (for example: brass–gold, sparrow–nightingale) and different objects (for example: plate–boat, pencil–shoe).

In the second experiment 39 haphazardly chosen objects pictured on cards were shown to the subject, who had to divide the cards into any number of groups. As in the first experiment, the subject had complete freedom to choose the basis of classification.

In the third experiment a variation of the "the fourth one doesn't belong" classification was used in twelve problems. Four objects were pictured on cards or named aloud and the patient was supposed to generalize three of them in such a way as to exclude the fourth from the group.

Problems requiring a different kind of comparison and classification were included in a second series. The first experiment involved comparison within a set framework, for example, "Peter is taller than Nicholas, and Dmitri is shorter than Peter. Who is the tallest of all?" Here the conditions of the problem determined the basis (the attribute) on which the comparison must be made.

In the second experiment in this series the subject had to freely classify geometric figures, differing in shape, color, and size. Here the selection of a basis for classification is limited to three visually different features. These problems differ from those of the first series in that solving them does not depend on choosing the attribute on the basis of its significance in the patient's past history.

The results of the first series of experiments show that, if their logical, operational schema of activity is preserved, schizophrenics are able to abstract any attribute and on the basis of the attribute make a generalization as well as the normal person.

In comparing two different pairs of objects, the schizophrenics were able to make generalizations even more often than normal people. However, an essential difference between the normal and schizophrenic subjects was revealed in the basis or attributes they used to make generalizations and comparisons.

In view of the unstructured nature of the sorting task in the second problem, some indirect means had to be devised to characterize the attributes used by the two groups. We chose the frequency with which each group selected each attribute. We assumed that the typical attributes chosen by each group would reflect the qualitative characteristic of these attributes. Those features were conditionally accepted as standard which the normal group selected more often than would be expected by chance alone. The ratio of the frequency of standard features to the frequency of all features selected for comparison or classification characterizes the "standardness" of the normal group. To characterize the group of schizophrenics by this "ratio of standardness," the criterion attributes for the normal group were used and a new ratio computed. Using this measure, the larger the ratio, the more "standard" was the response of the group in question.

In addition to the relative frequency of occurrence of the attributes we thought it desirable to take into account the range of different attributes selected as the basis for comparison and classification. Thus, in addition to "standardness ratios," the number of non-standard features chosen by the members of each group is included in Tables 12–1, through 12–3. The results, according to each method, are reflected in the tables.

The data in the three tables indicate two essential differences between the groups. First, standardness ratio of the schizophrenic group is lower than that of the normal group in all three experiments. Second, the number of nonstandard attributes selected by the schizophrenics is considerably higher than the number of nonstandard attributes selected by the normal group.

Table 12–1 *Comparison of Objects*

Group	Type of object	Response measure: Standardness ratio	Response measure: Number of nonstandard attributes
Normal	Similar	75%	125
	Dissimilar	73%	63
Schizophrenic	Similar	62%	217
	Dissimilar	47%	206

Table 12–2 *"The Fourth Doesn't Belong"*

Group	Response measure: Standardness ratio	Response measure: Number of nonstandard attributes
Normal	75%	77
Schizophrenic	55%	187

Table 12–3 *Free Classification*

Group	Response measure: Standardness ratio	Response measure: Number of nonstandard attributes
Normal	85%	26
Schizophrenic	70%	53

In order to clarify the question, "How does the frequency with which a feature of an object is used reflect the qualitative nature of the relationship between objects?" it is necessary to determine those attributes which are frequently included as standard but which occur among the nonstandard features.

The analysis made on this basis showed that all standard attributes selected in classifying objects can be grouped as:

1. Inherent characteristics and characteristics pertaining to a species
2. The basic function
3. Exterior attributes, primarily shape
4. Meaning
5. Origin
6. Physical and chemical properties
7. Material

These are the attributes used most often by both groups in comparing and classifying, and therefore we grouped them with the standard attributes. The nonstandard attributes are those which are less significant from the point of view of social practice in the use of the object. Many nonstandard attributes chosen by the schizophrenics were never given by the normal group: for example, "leaves traces" (shoe and pencil), "moves along a closed circle" (clock and river), and so forth.

A special range of attributes selected by the schizophrenics can be related neither to the essential-conceptual nor to the sensual-concrete, nonsubstantial attributes. An attempt to analyze them in the same way as the responses already discussed did not help us to understand the peculiarities in the generalizations of these mentally ill people. This led us to search for other ways to view these attributes and we decided to examine them from the point of view of their social significance, as determined by the past experience of the person. On this plane these attributes can be classified as insignificant, "latent," "weak" attributes (Szekely, 1950) to distinguish them from conceptual and sensual-concrete attributes that are significant and practical. It is the tendency to select attributes which are "latent," "weak," and hardly dreamed of by the normal subjects that produces the uniqueness of the schizophrenic's generalizations.

On the basis of these results, we were led to predict that schizophrenics would be superior to normals on a problem in which it is necessary to pick out the "latent" attributes. To verify this prediction we used the following problem (suggested by Szekely, 1950).

Scales and an assortment of objects (small weights, a flashlight, a pencil, a saltshaker, etc.), among which there was also a candle, were placed before the subject. The problem was to balance the scales in such a way that after a while they would become unbalanced. After a balance was attained, the subject was not allowed to interfere from the outside. The subject's task was to analyze the problem and establish the necessary conditions for disruption of balance. The way to disturb the balance is of course to cause the loss of the weight by an object on one side of the scale. After reaching this conclusion the subject must find an object which decreases in weight in order to solve the problem. A burning candle is such an object. But the whole difficulty lies in the fact that the candle's capacity to lose weight while burning is a "weak" and "latent" attribute masked by the "stronger" attribute of giving light, and is therefore not immediately selected by normal subjects. The majority of normal adult subjects, rather than using the candle, would suggest an absent object. Objects were suggested for which a decrease in weight would be the strong attribute—above all, evaporating substances—ether, acetone, gasoline, spirits, and the like.

We obtained the following overall results: only 30 per cent of the normal subjects suggested the use of the candle immediately after establishing the cause and effect relationship. Of the remaining subjects, 60 per cent suggested other materials before using the candle, and 10 per cent never used the candle at all.

In the group of schizophrenics, 58 per cent immediately suggested using the candle. Forty-two per cent suggested using other objects before using the candle. In this group there was not a single subject who was unable to select the candle's attribute of weight loss through burning. The choices of objects other than the candle were idiosyncratic for the group of schizophrenics. The incorrect objects chosen by the schizophrenics were rarely chosen by the normals.

The results of these experiments support the conjecture that, under conditions which demand the choice of "weak" and "latent" attributes, schizophrenics can select them more quickly and easily than the normals.[1]

Auditory Perception in Schizophrenics

The study of auditory perception (Kritskaya, 1965) included two basic series of experiments in which conditions were arranged so that information presented in speech signals was incomplete.

Under these difficult conditions the signal cannot be unequivocally perceived; the situation only defines the range of possible outcomes and does not favor any of them. Therefore, the subject is in a signal-detection situation where he must use a system of hypotheses for the identification of the signal. The probability with which he applies the various hypotheses is essentially determined by his past experience. An important role must be played by statistical regularities of the speech process which reflect past speech experience. The so-called psychological (guessing) factor is conditioned by the subjects' earlier encounters with certain word patterns in which some speech units follow each other with greater regularity than others.

In the first series of experiments the subjects were presented sentences on a tape recorder in a certain sequence separated by 20-second intervals. White noise was imposed on the last word of each sentence.

The subject was instructed to identify the muffled word and write it down at once. The instructions indicated that in cases of uncertainty in the correctness of the identification, the word should be written down with a question mark; where identification was impossible, the examinee was supposed to make a dash. There were 33 sentences in all.

1. *Editors' note:* The preceding experimental results, as well as the results of other experiments to be reported, suggest from another point of view that, under certain circumstances, schizophrenics are more original than normals. They have relatively flat habit family hierarchies, so uncommon responses are more readily available. In any case, these are among the very few experimental studies that report schizophrenics performing in manner superior to normals. These interesting experiments are clearly in need of replication and extension.

In making up the sentences we relied on well-known laws of the statistical organization of speech, which state that the context of a phrase determines, on the basis of past speech experience, the probability of every possible ending. In a supplementary experiment we found that the probability of occurrence of each ending in different phrases varied through a wide range—from high-probability endings (phrases of the type: "Along the street sped a *car*." "The scouts sang a merry *song*."), to low-probability endings ("The photographer made a pretty *box*." "The capitol of our country is *large*.").

In those phrases where the probability of detecting the ending was close to 1.0, there were no noticeable differences between the two groups.

We selected signal-to-noise ratios such that the perception of the word was made difficult but possible. However, within the limits of this range, the ratio of the signal to the noise varied from phrase to phrase.

In addition, the noise hampered the perception of the words in different ways because their phonetic structure was different (white noise usually distorts the sound of the consonants more than the vowels).

The identifiability of phrase endings was checked on the control group, and the results showed that it is possible to divide all sentences into three groups, as shown in Table 12–4.

Table 12–4

Noise level	Percentage of correct identifications
Strong	0–10
Medium	10–50
Weak	50–100

In the first group of sentences, where the noise was too strong, there were scarcely any differences between the two groups under comparison. The relative weakness of the signal made it impossible to identify the word. The normal subjects correctly perceived 6 per cent, and the schizophrenics 4.5 per cent, of all the endings in this group of sentences.

In the third group of sentences, where the noise was weak and identification could result from adequate information, the results for the schizophrenics were only slightly worse than for the normals: in absolute numbers, the control group gave 499 correct identifications and the schizophrenics 476, that is, 5 per cent fewer correct answers.

Essential differences in the results of the identification between the schizophrenics and the normals became apparent in the perception of the second group of phrases, where there was an intermediate level of difficulty in detecting the signal. The normal subjects were the best at detecting the phrases with more likely endings, but for the phrases with the less probable endings the better result was achieved by the schizophrenics. If the result of the normal subjects for both groups of phrases is taken as 100 per cent, then the result of the schizophrenics for the phrases with more probable endings is equal to 80 per cent, and for the phrases with the less probable endings is equal to 130 per cent.

It appears that, within the limits of this experiment, the schizophrenics exhibit a tendency to perceive the more probable phrase endings which are based on past experience less accurately than normal people and to perceive the less probable endings more accurately.

The same tendency may also be seen in the following fact: in those cases where the indistinct phrase endings are perceived incorrectly, the schizophrenics were twice as likely as the normal group to name endings phonetically close to the word obscured by noise, largely ignoring the semantic probabilities, whereas normal subjects were more likely to name an ending which fitted better into the context.

The second basic series of experiments also involved incomplete information. However, a different method was used. Only the perception of one sound was hindered, that of the phoneme which controlled the meaning of the word in the sentence. Certain characteristics of the Russian language were exploited for this technique, such as the muffling of consonants at the end of a word, so that the word could be understood two different ways by the listener.

This second experiment was meant to expose still more precisely the dependence of perception on the probability of the given signal. In the first experiment, muffling the signals could lead to many different hypotheses of varying complexity. In the second experiment only two hypotheses were possible, and these were under our control. The context of the phrases made it possible to subtly vary the manifestation of each.

The method was as follows: The subjects were presented tape recorded sentences at intervals of 30 to 40 seconds. Experimental and neutral sentences were presented in an alternating order. The special point about the experimental sentences was, as mentioned above, that they could be understood in two ways, depending on the ambiguity of the word concluding each sentence (for example, "Under the tree lies a *plod* [fruit]/*plut* [raft]").

The correlation of the probabilities of identification of the two possible endings in each sentence was different. Within limits, all the experimental sentences could be divided into three groups:

1. The probabilities of the two possible endings were approximately equal.

2. The probability of one of the endings was close to zero, and the probability of the second was high.

3. The probability of one of the endings was higher than the other, but neither approached 1.0 or 0.0.

The speaker, in making the tapes of the sentences, slightly accented the significance-determining phoneme in the concluding word which corresponded to the less likely hypothesis on the basis of the context of the sentence.

The other conditions of the experiment were the same as in the first experiment. The subject was instructed to write down each sentence after listening.

The results for the control group indicated that perception is essentially determined by the probability of the signal on the basis of past speech experience. In those sentences where the probability of the alternatives was approximately equal (in the first group of sentences), half of the subjects identified the signal one way and half the other.

In the second group of sentences, where the probability of one ending was close to zero and the second ending was very high, in spite of the sound of the meaning determining phoneme, the subjects perceived the more likely variant of the signal in 247 out of 250 cases.

In the third group of sentences, where the probability of one of the variants was clearly higher than the second, an overwhelming majority of the control group perceived the more likely variant of the endings (211 out of 230).

The results obtained with the schizophrenics in the first two groups of sentences did not differ essentially from the data of the control group.

Essential differences did become apparent in the identification of the third group of sentences, where the probabilities of the endings were not equal and were not excessively far apart. The schizophrenics perceived the less likely variant of the ending significantly more often (4½ times) than the normal group; 85 less probable variants were chosen out of 230 signals given (whereas the normal subjects gave 19 out of 230).

In five phrases, one normal subject responded with less likely endings twice, and 18 people did so once each. By contrast, among the schizophrenics 14 did it once, 27 did it twice, and 6 did it three times.

Under the conditions of this experiment the schizophrenics perceived more accurately than normals when presented with unlikely signals.

To verify the relationship between habitual word contingencies and perception a task was devised to establish whether there would be any differences between the two groups when the probabilities of the verbal signals presented are as equal as possible, that is, when it is not necessary to determine the probability of each signal on the basis of past experience.

For this purpose five words selected at random were taped under noise, each word repeated three times. The subject was to identify these muffled words and write them down. Before the experiment the subject was shown a list of the words and was told that only these words would appear on the tape and each word might be repeated several times. Such instructions assured the equal expectation of each word.

In this experiment 30 normals and 30 schizophrenics were used.

As we might have predicted from the results of the previous experiments, there were no essential differences between the two groups: the normal subjects as a whole correctly identified 5.5 words, while the schizophrenics correctly identified 5.4.

Thus the data from this study indicate that the schizophrenics do not differ from the normal subjects in their ability to distinguish a signal from noise and to identify it under conditions where the expected probability of the signals is equal.

Differences appear only under conditions where there is incomplete information and the subject must make use of a system of hypotheses whose probabilities of application are determined by prior experience. Schizophrenics have a tendency to equalize the probabilities of their hypotheses, as manifested in a relative inability to identify more likely signals.

Visual Perception in Schizophrenics

A study of the idiosyncrasies of the visual perception of schizophrenics (Bogdanov, 1965) was also directed mainly toward the study of the influence of past experience. A series of five experiments was used (one basic series and four auxiliary ones). The overall goal was the creation of uncertainty, where the visual stimulus allowed the possibility of more than one identification. In such situations the resultant identification depends on the system of actualized "image hypotheses." The selection of the comparison hypothesis as a function of the incompleteness of the information in the stimulus is determined by past experience.

In the basic series of the experiments, blurred pictures of objects were presented, using images of animals, people, household goods, and the like.

The pictures were projected on a screen blurred in different degrees with their clarity measured on a conditional scale. Each image was at first presented maximally out of focus and then its clarity was increased gradually to complete visibility.

Each subject was presented 19 pictures to identify. Some of them showed common, standard, expected situations and positions of objects; in others, unusual situations and changes in perspective were used.

The subject was supposed to determine as early as possible what was on the screen and was repeatedly encouraged to voice his hypotheses.

The identification threshold was taken to be that point in the scale where the subject identified the image correctly for the first time. Records were kept on all the conjectures advanced by the subjects in the course of the experiment.

For some of the images the identification threshold of the schizophrenics was higher than that of the normal subjects. In some cases the thresholds were the same, and for a number of images the identification thresholds were lower for the schizophrenic group than for the control group.

After examining this data, it was not difficult to establish the rule which reflects the dependence of the schizophrenics' threshold changes on the character of the image. The images for which the schizophrenics' identification thresholds were highest were common, standard images. Those images for which the schizophrenics had thresholds the same as or lower than the thresholds of the control group were the unusual ones. For example, in one picture there was an unusual position of a man lying on his back and drawing a picture with his feet; in another, an unusual pose of a jumper crossing a plank; in another, an eagle was pictured upside down.

In real life a person encounters many images. Some figures are often repeated, some rarely. For example, a bird is more usually pictured right side up than upside down, although such a position is also possible in a picture (an eagle or parrot can hang on a ring upside down). Therefore, in a certain sense "usual" and "unusual" images represent different degrees of probability conditioned by past experience.

In schizophrenics a change in their identification threshold depends upon the probability of the presented object (picture). Schizophrenics recognize highly probable images worse, and unlikely images better, than normal subjects. The manifestation of this peculiarity depends on the completeness of information in the stimulus. When clear pictures were shown, there were no differences between the schizophrenic and control groups. Differences are apparent only in the early stages of stimulus presentation when the image is still very blurred and unclear. At this stage the normal subjects identify the highly probable images better than the schizophrenics, and the schizophrenics identify the less likely images better than the normals. (See Table 12–5.)

In our experiments involving inadequate information, identification is determined essentially by past experiences conditioning the actualization of the image hypotheses. According to the data of contemporary psychology, the identification of the image depends, to a great degree, on the system of image hypotheses that the subject is able to bring to bear on the identifi-

Table 12–5 *Results of Identification for Blurred Images*

	Percentage of normal examinees recognizing the picture	Percentage of schizophrenics recognizing the picture
Highly likely images	17	6.5
Unlikely images	12	27

cation of an actual stimulus. If a discrepant image is aroused by the stimulus, then this should make identification more difficult; if an image is actualized which really corresponds to the one pictured, then the process of identification is made easier. These facts allow one to conclude that, under conditions of inadequate information, where the process of perception is being built on the basis of a "choice" of hypotheses for comparison, the schizophrenics we have been studying have a peculiarity of perception tied to an alteration in the system of a priori probabilities of hypotheses based on past experience. Compared to normal people, schizophrenics, when they are perceiving, lower the expected probability of highly likely objects and increase the expected probability of unlikely objects.

This assertion is corroborated to a certain extent by an analysis of the distribution of hypotheses put forward by the subjects in the course of identifying the pictures.

We combined these hypotheses into the following groups: people, animals, birds, plants, household articles, instruments, constructions, and other objects. It turned out that the most probable hypotheses for the normal subjects were "people" and "animals." On the whole, the normal subjects responded thus in 67.8 per cent of the cases, the schizophrenics 50 per cent of the time.

A Theory of Schizophrenic Thinking

The results of these experiments clearly showed that for schizophrenics there is the tendency toward equalizing the a priori probabilities of the image hypotheses conditioned by past experience.

The significance of this study is determined in large part by the degree to which the experimental data can be correlated with clinical data. Also of importance is the extent to which the regularities in cognitive disruption help us to understand the area of psychopathological phenomena characteristic of the clinical picture of the particular disturbance under study.

In spite of the diverse and often contradictory evaluations and treatments of psychological deterioration in schizophrenia, numerous clinical descriptions agree on a set of characteristic psychopathological features, distinguishing this type of deterioration from psychological deterioration in all other mental diseases.

1. One difference between schizophrenic and other kinds of deterioration is the relative preservation of previously acquired knowledge by the schizophrenic. Even those most seriously afflicted can, in one way or another, demonstrate a wide range of previously assimilated knowledge while continuing to manifest an obviously disrupted intellect.

Attempts to explain this fact using various psychological concepts are to be found in such ideas as the following: "disunity" of past experience with present experience; disunity of different levels of personality; "loosening"; "splintering" of the chain of earlier associations while preserving their elements (Bleuler); disruption of "apperceptions."

It is possible to understand schizophrenic intellectual deterioration on the basis of the laws of disruption of the cognitive processes as manifested in our research.

Our results help to explain this psychopathological syndrome, showing how cognitive activity changes as a result of disruptions in the selection of information from past experience while the sum total of this information is preserved.

2. The uniqueness of schizophrenic deterioration is manifested in the unevenness of the disruption of thought, in the ability to carry out some intellectual tasks (tasks like construction activity, counting, chess, etc.) side by side with a clear deficiency in other cognitive activity. What is essential here is the absence of a direct relation between the disturbance and the complexity of the problem; more complex activity can be carried out without change at the same time as the fulfillment of elementary tasks is severely disrupted.

This feature of schizophrenic deterioration was particularly difficult to explain. Our experiments suggest that the best way to understand its nature is to consider peculiarities in the structure of activity. If the afflicted factor plays little or no part in the given cognitive process in schizophrenics, this process can continue without alteration. This is why, in spite of severely disrupted thinking, schizophrenics can carry out certain tasks quite well, independently of their complexity. We can now also understand the failure of such explanations of schizophrenic deterioration as a "potential preservation" of the intellect or "the machine is in order but not completely under control."

3. Closely connected with the aforementioned peculiarity of schizophrenic deterioration is the so-called "formal preservation" of thought, which led several authors to believe that, under schizophrenia, it is not the separate intellectual capabilities which suffer, but their utilization. Very often this peculiarity is explained as the preservation of "the prerequisite of the intellect," when it is the thought process itself that has been disrupted.

Our data lead us to interpret the nature of this psychopathological peculiarity in a different way. In the first place, it is true (as Meleshko's data showed) that the "operational" side of thought does not suffer under schizophrenia; analysis, synthesis, and abstraction can remain unchanged, if the critical factor is not part of the structure which carries out these activities. In the second place, one can see that the so-called prerequisites of the intellect are usually measured by tests of attention, memory, counting operations, construction capabilities, and the like—that is by exactly those types of activity (tasks) which are not connected with the factors we selected. The thesis of preservation of the "prerequisites of the intellect" appeared reasonable only because the tasks which tested these "prerequisites" require exactly those types of activity which are not disrupted in schizophrenia.

4. The distinctiveness of schizophrenic deterioration also produced the so-called problem of "abstraction" in the thinking processes of these people. The majority of clinical physicians have noted peculiarities in the way that schizophrenics abstract. However, even the qualitative analysis of these peculiarities seems to give rise to contradictions. Side by side with indications of a strong ability to think abstractly, there is also the widely held opinion that schizophrenics think more concretely than normal people. The view also exists that the thinking of schizophrenics is neither concrete nor abstract, but something qualitatively different—"pathological thinking."

It seems to us that the coexistence of such diverse views is conditioned to a large degree by a confusion of two different points: (1) the ability to abstract a given set of attributes and features of the object, and (2) the question of what attributes and features are attended to, and thus abstracted.

Meleshko's data show that the schizophrenic's ability to abstract does not differ from that of a normal subject. In looking at the second question, the data show a significant difference between the schizophrenic and the normal. With schizophrenics there is an increase in the probability of actualizing and generalizing insignificant, weak attributes of the objects which are rarely used by normal people. Obviously, there is a widening of the range of attributes which can be used for generalization among schizophrenics. If the problem is such that the answer is correct from the formal-logical point of view but does not correspond to actual human practice, the schizophrenic may actually be aided in his work. For example, if the subjects are asked to make comparisons of very heterogeneous, "unconnected" objects and phenomena, the schizophrenics may be expected to outperform the normal subjects, giving the impression of "greater abstractness" of their thoughts compared to normal people.

Our work has led us to believe that the "abstract-concrete" dichotomy represents an unfruitful way to formulate the problem.

5. Another feature of schizophrenic deterioration which requires explanation is the fact that there may be a disruption of thought but an absence of any definite clinical indications of the disruption of perception, which contradicts the idea of a unity of cognitive activity and the indivisibility of its components.

Our data clarifying the general rules of the disruption of thought and perception remove this contradiction. All evidence testifies to the fact that the disruption of the process of perception in schizophrenia manifests itself in a completely different way than is found if the brain is organically diseased.

References

Bogdanov, Y. I. The study of visual perception under conditions of incomplete information. In B. V. Zeigarnik (Ed.), *Problems of experimental psychopathology*. Moscow, 1965. 279.

Cameron, N. Deterioration and regression in schizophrenic thinking. *J. abnorm. soc. Psychol.*, 1939, *34*, 265.

Chapman, L., and Taylor, J. Breadth of deviate concepts used by schizophrenics. *J. abnorm. soc. Psychol.*, 1957, *54*, 118.

Kritskaya, V. P. The study of peculiarities of speech perception. In B. V. Zeigarnik (Ed.), *Problems of experimental psychopathology*. Moscow, 1965. P. 295.

Leont'ev, A. N. *Problems of the development of the mind*. Moscow, 1959.

Luria, A. R. *Higher cortical functions in man*. Moscow, 1962. (Also published in English, by Basic Books, New York, 1964.)

Luria, A. R. Man's brain and mental processes. Moscow, 1963. (Also published in English, as *The brain and psychological processes*. New York: Harper, 1966.)

Meleshko, T. K. A variation on the method of studying the process of comparison in schizophrenics. In B. V. Zeigarnik (Ed.), *Problems of experimental psychopathology*. Moscow, 1965. 288.

Payne, P., Mattussek, P., and Georg, S. An experimental study of schizophrenic thought disorder. *J. ment. Sci.*, 1959, *105*, 57.

Szekely, L. Knowledge and thinking. *Acta psychol.*, 1950, *7*, 1–24.

Teplov, B. M. *Problems of individual differences*. Moscow, 1961.

Zeigarnik, B. V. *The pathology of thought*. New York: Consultants Bureau, 1965.

13

Microsociology, Concrete Sociological Studies, and Psychiatry

O. V. Kerbikov

EDITORS' INTRODUCTION

Before his death in 1965, O. V. Kerbikov was one of the Soviet Union's leading psychiatrists. Kerbikov is best known for his monograph Acute Schizophrenia, *published in 1955. In his later work, however, he became interested in general problems of the origin of neuroses.*

The present chapter is of special interest because in it Kerbikov seeks to introduce social-psychological techniques into psychiatric practice. This is noteworthy not only because of the interest in the relation between social phenomena and individual psychological abnormalities, but because the careful distinction which Kerbikov draws between the empirical techniques, *which may legitimately be borrowed from Western science, and the* theoretical bases *of these techniques, which must be shunned, is now being echoed in many sectors of Soviet psychology. Thus, Kerbikov's discussion of microsociology may be considered a case study in how Soviet social scientists attempt to integrate a controversial area of Western research into Soviet theory.*

The Ideology of Sociometry

A characteristic of postwar Western sociology and social psychology is the shift in attention from the study of large social units to small ones—to small groups. Not only sociologists and psychologists, but also psychiatrists work in this area. Social psychology and psychiatry both claim leading roles in the study of society. The substitution of sociological laws for biological and psychological ones is typical of Western sociological and social psychological thought.

Microsociology is a prominent concept in sociological research. One of its main representatives is Moreno (1958) in the United States. In the course of his work on this new theory of society, which he named microsociology or sociometry, Moreno sought not only a scientific truth, but "also to preserve my own spiritual balance."

Moreno's work became widely known after World War II. The influence of his ideas is not as great or varied as, for example, that of Freud. All the same, Moreno, with much fanfare, proposes microsociology as a method for solving problems of universal dimensions. He asserts that sociometry must become "the principal theory of the social sciences," and he speaks of "the great theoretical achievements resulting from sociometry." In his opinion, these "achievements" will help "replace the theory of socialism with the theory of sociometry," and, furthermore, he promises, with the help of sociometry "to limit the expansion of the idea of Communism" (1958, p. 31).

In building his new social Utopia, Moreno dreams of creating and expanding a worldwide "psychiatric empire." Politicians and diplomats will take a back seat; first place in the leadership of humanity will go to psychiatrists, "sociometrically oriented socialists," and a psychiatrist will sit in the President's chair. With tragic irony Moreno asks: "Isn't the whole cosmos becoming more and more like a huge mental hospital with God as head doctor?" (1958, p. 226).

Consistent with this modern neo-Thomism, Moreno writes: "I postulated that the concept of divinity should rank above everything. It is primarily here that we must turn, because without it there can be no meaning to any living particle in the universe, whether man or protozoa" (1958, p. 263). And further, "The earlier abyss between science and theology has ceased to exist and is held on to only by aged theologians or ignorant scientists" (1958, p. 265). Moreno offers us the hope that the elaboration of sociometry "will give us the key to the best understanding of occult phenomena such as clairvoyance and telepathy" (1958, p. 192).

In all fairness, we should note that Moreno, like his French supporter,

Gourevitch, is an active participant in the peace movement. It is not without interest that Moreno speaks quite scornfully of Freud and of the neo-Freudians. "It is generally known," he points out, "that psychoanalysis has its roots in the French school of psychiatry led by Charcot. Even if he did bring some original ideas into medical psychology, that in itself does not make him a scientist" (1958, p. 146). Of Sullivan, a leading representative of the neo-Freudians, Moreno writes: "The late Harry Stack Sullivan, while recognizing the theory,[1] did so only partially and to some extent distorted it. Nevertheless he tried to make it acceptable for the psychoanalytical ideology of the West, so much in need of bolstering. Belief in the theory of psychoanalysis kept Sullivan from accepting all my ideas, although during his last years one can see in his work a gradual departure from official psychoanalysis toward group theory" (1958, p. 273).

The confused mixture of sociological idealism, political reaction, and infantile fantasy contained in Moreno's writings could not but repel Soviet researchers. In a series of papers, Bachitov (1958) and Chesnokov, Bekker, and Baskov (1961) exposed the methodological bases of microsociology to systematic criticism. Its unscientific and reactionary attitudes and its open hostility to Marxist teachings on society became obvious. Therefore, actual studies of small social groups carried out by microsociologists have been ignored in the U.S.S.R. However, several authors, among them Morozov (1964), have extrapolated this unfavorable judgment of Moreno's methodology into certain concrete sociological and psychosociological studies, for example, into research on the family. In the meantime it became clear, even to Moreno, that it is necessary to differentiate between microsociological theory and the specific sociometric method of research. "Sociometric method," he writes, "is not to be confused with sociometry as a general theory of the social sciences" (1958, p. 164). Recent studies by Soviet authors show that some sociometric methods can be useful if properly applied.

The Sociometric Method

When doing research on small groups, Moreno finds it necessary to begin by defining their external and internal structures. The outer structure is accommodation, the subordination of the members of one or another group according to their official position and functions. The inner structure consists of the interrelation of members of the group on the level of their mutual attractions and repulsions, sympathies and antipathies, respects and disrespects, attachments and estrangements, preferences and hostilities. Moreno calls the outer structure the *macrostructure* and the inner one the *microstructure*. Disorders in people's lives, conflicts with the life of society,

1. *Editors' note:* Of sociometry.

result from the disparity between the micro- and macro-structures of small groups, large human units, and society as a whole. In order to bring both structures together, methods must be found to perceive this hidden, inner microstructure.

The theory underlying the study of the sum total of these methods is called *sociometry* by Moreno. In his opinion, the study of the microstructure consists of several stages. In the first stage the complete confidence of all members of the group under observation is established. There should be openness among the members of the group and no fear that what is communicated to the investigator will become known to someone else. It takes time and effort to win this trust. More likely than not, it becomes necessary to include the investigator in the group under observation, for a period of time. The second stage of the investigation involves the acquisition of information from the group members. Usually the questionnaire method is employed. If, for example, a student group is being observed, the questionnaire will request such information as: With whom would you most like to be in an academic group? With whom not? and To whom are you indifferent in this matter? Similar questions are also formulated about sharing a room in a dormitory, participating in student activities, recreation, and so forth.

After receiving the information, a graph is drawn for each participant (in Moreno's terminology such a graph is called a *matrix*), as shown in Table 13–1. Matrices are compiled separately for each question and are then analyzed mathematically. After this a sociogram of the group is compiled. This is a graphic rendering of the results of the mathematical adaptation of the matrices. In the sample matrix the positive choices (+) are more

Table 13–1

CHOSEN \ CHOOSERS	G.	F.	D.	A.	P.
G.		+	+	—	0
F.	+		0	+	—
D.	0	+		+	—
A.	+	—	+		+
P.	0	+	+	+	

KEY: + = a positive choice, 0 = indifferent and — = a negative choice. Listed horizontally are the choosers (G. chose F. and A., was indifferent to D. and P.). Listed vertically are those chosen (G. was chosen by F. and D., rejected by A., and P. was indifferent to him, etc.).

numerous than the negative ones (–), indicating that there is adequate cohesion within the group. This is reflected in the matrix projection. On the basis of this graph P. enjoys the greatest authority in the collective. He has been chosen by the highest number and rejected by none. However, he is relatively isolated since he has rejected two, chosen one, and is indifferent to one.

One reads of some unquestionable successes in the works of microsociologists due to the application of sociometric methods. Thus, Moreno reports the successful assignment of people to a new housing project. Thirty-five houses had to be allotted to thirty-five families who had been living in a population center soon to be demolished. The selection of neighbors in the new settlement was carried out by sociometric methods. The problem of assigning boarding school students to rooms and dining tables was successfully decided, as were others. Moreno emphasizes that the most important stage in the process of sociometric observation is the last. Here the members of the group are distributed or redistributed with the purpose of bringing the outer structure into harmony with the inner structure.

Aisler (1961) writes that teachers and pedagogues, administrators of institutions and industrial empires, military men and workers in institutions for the re-education of criminals have all shown a practical interest in the study of "small groups." Although Moreno's unscientific approach and the inadmissibility of his theories are obvious to us, the attitude of Soviet authors toward the problem of studying small groups and toward the methods of such study is not so clear. Historically, the attitude of Soviet psychologists toward the study of small groups has depended upon the answer to a question having far broader significance: Does social psychology exist in its own right and is there a need to carry out sociopsychological research?

Historical Background

Sociopsychological research was begun in the U.S.S.R. shortly after the October Revolution. Several articles in this area were published in the proceedings of the First All-Union Congress on Human Behavior (1930). Later, however, concrete sociological research was curtailed and sociopsychological research was completely discontinued. During the cult of personality[1] the atmosphere was too unfavorable for such studies. Nevertheless, on a very limited scale, Soviet sociologists did conduct some sociological research. Soviet psychologists did not follow suit for a long time. In respected sources the very idea of social psychology was rejected, either on formal-logical grounds (Furst, 1957) or on the grounds that it was a

1. *Editors' note:* "Cult of personality" is the Soviet term applied to the years 1936 to 1953, during which time Stalin ruled the country without consulting the Communist party's other leaders.

reflection of Western psychological views and thus foreign to us (Rubinshtein, 1957).

The erroneous nature of this negative attitude toward sociopsychological research was convincingly discussed by Iliechev in a series of lectures at the All-Union Congress on the philosophical problems of the studies of neurological activity and psychology (Iliechev, 1963a). The problems of general psychology underwent detailed scrutiny (Parigin, 1963; Kuzmin, 1963; Shorokhova, Mansurov, and Platonov, 1963; Kovalev and Myasishchev, 1963; and Porshnev, 1963) in lectures at the Second Congress of the Society of Psychologists (June, 1963) and in the pages of *Problems of Psychology*. The first results of sociopsychological research done by Soviet psychologists were presented in the course of several lectures before the Congress. These were mainly studies of small collectives. After the acceptance of social psychology, a change also appeared in the attitude toward the study of small groups. The necessity of doing such research now arouses no suspicion whatsoever. We need hardly emphasize that we carry out these studies according to the scientific method. Their theoretical foundation is historical materialism.

From a practical point of view, the work of Soviet and Western investigators may have elements of similarity. These must not be exaggerated, however, for the essential difference in what is actually studied by certain methods can be hidden behind the outer resemblance of these methods. In this respect it is very interesting to compare studies of the causes for satisfaction and dissatisfaction of Soviet and United States industrial workers with their work. The studies of Zdravomyslov and Yadov (1964) show that the main reason for job satisfaction among Soviet workers is the content of the work, the fact that intellectual activity is incorporated in the work process. In the United States investigators find that a positive approach to work is determined in the first place by confidence in its stability, by guarantees against possible unemployment.

As yet there is no unity of opinion among Soviet sociologists and psychologists about the sociometric method. Kuzmin (1963), who applied the sociometric method in a study of industrial brigades in two Leningrad factories, concluded that it is definitely effective. On the other hand, Zotova, using the same method in conducting a group psychometric experiment at a Moscow factory, appraises it as labor-consuming and ineffective. Even investigators working at one and the same institution (the Institute of Philosophy, Academy of Sciences of the U.S.S.R.) arrive at diametrically opposed evaluations of sociometric methods. Zotova, mentioned above, gives it a negative evaluation; Valentinova (1964), who did sociopsychological research in another Moscow factory, was able to obtain interesting and instructive facts with the help of sociometric methods.

Much will probably be clarified in the near future, for concrete sociological and sociopsychological studies are attracting the attention of an ever increasing number of scientific groups. However, even now, the approximate boundaries of the possibilities of the sociometric method can be fixed. It seems adequate in research which tries to determine the interrelations among members of a group without probing deeper questions concerning the motivation and origin of these interrelations. Sociometric methods are apparently unable to help answer the latter type of question.

In the recent development of Soviet psychology, it should be noted that, side by side with the development of engineering psychology (to which the previous discussion was directed), increasing attention has been directed at social psychology. This increase is particularly noteworthy in studies of small groups and in the investigation of interrelations among individuals in families, industrial and academic collectives, and others.

"In this way it is the real world (practice) which plays the dominant role in the development of the sciences, raising the question of human interrelations to the level of the central problem of Soviet social psychology," writes Glatotchkin, who has carried out a major sociopsychological study of several military groups.

The selection of participants for small groups is very important, not only from the point of view of occupational preparation but also from the point of view of mutual compatibility. In the current press it was reported that the "problem of psychological compatibility" of people who will have to spend many months together in a spaceship cabin is taking on practical importance. Emerging as the leading principle of Soviet psychology is the idea that the study of personality and the study of the groups must be integrated as the principle of the study of the personality *in* the group.

Applications to Psychiatry

Can this rapidly developing branch of research in Soviet sociology and psychology have any meaning for the problems of psychiatry? There are reasons to take hope from the direction that sociopsychological research is taking. The vacuum resulting from the confusion between the fields of sociology and psychiatry may soon be filled.

Social influence has always played a major role in the genesis of mental illness, especially in the area of neurosis, pathocharacterological developments, psychopathic behavior, and the like. As an example, let us take neuroses. The origin of a neurosis is not to be found in the geographical environment or climate; in fact, it is not the result of the influence of nature on man at all. Neuroses arise in a social context, in the process of man's interrelations with man. This fact is significant not only in connection with the frequency and prevalence of neurosis, but also in connection with the clinical symptoms which are so full of social content. This becomes clear in an analysis of shyness, presented in Michaux' *Disturbances of Character* (1964).

Pathological shyness is widespread among neurotic disorders and particularly characteristic of psychasthenia. Shyness has something in common with fear but it is very different from, say, a fear of death or of physical suffering. Shyness does not arise in the face of such dire threats as fire, shipwreck, or a wild beast's attack. In such situations a shy person can display fearlessness and coolheadedness. Shyness is the fear of appearing foolish and ridiculous in the eyes of others, and is related to how much importance the person suffering its symptoms attaches to the opinions of others. Shyness cannot exist outside interpersonal situations. Siradoshch (1959) manifests a similar concept of neurotic symptoms when he asks: "Could Robinson [Crusoe] have had hysteria?" Corresponding questions with predictable negative answers could be asked about such neurotic symptoms as fear of blushing, pathological fear of obesity leading to an almost complete refusal of food, a morbid concern with one's supposed freakish appearance, and many others.

In the years immediately following the October Revolution a simplistic kind of sociology achieved some prominence in Soviet psychiatry. Several of its advocates tried to find a direct connection between membership in a certain social class and the psychotic symptoms of the patient. This primitivism was soon overcome. It became clear that it was impossible to establish direct connections between the social position of the patient and the symptoms of his illness. Productive relations, which are the foundation of our lives, influence the formation of the normal personality and pathological personality only indirectly, through many intermediate links. In one of his speeches Frantsev stated that, when working with the concepts of class and personality, one cannot avoid the middle link of the working collective. Its "anatomy" and "physiology" should be studied.

There never has been full clarity about this last factor. Therefore the views of Soviet psychiatrists about the social conditioning of mental illness remain, on the whole, ambiguous. Myasishchev (1960) did some interesting studies, based on historical materialism, concerning the system of relations in the personality and on the roles of these relations in the origin and clinical dynamics of neuroses. However, in his research Myasishchev is mainly concerned with the personality structure which the relationships establish and not with the social structure which establishes the relationships.

One of the complex tasks facing the general theory of neuroses is to supplement Pavlov's discoveries in the field of biological laws governing the development of neurosis (the mechanisms of the "nervous breakdown") with social doctrine. In this area the studies of Gilyarovskii (1934) are of great interest. He attributed the origin of neurosis to the disintegration of communications and of interrelations between the personality and the group. Unlike Adler, Gilyarovskii emphasized the significance of the inadequacy of the personality from the point of view of the group's demands, and not the biological inadequacy of the personality. The fear of appearing as a failure in the opinion of the group is what makes a neurotic. In talking of the disruption of interrelations within the group, Gilyarovskii specified that he did not mean an abstract understanding of society as a whole, but the actual group, the immediate environment of the individual. This includes his working and family surroundings, those circles which are socially most significant.

For the psychiatrist who deals with neurotics, these views are obviously sound. Mental traumas which give rise to neuroses in people with antecedent tendencies, or the pathological development of the personality, are not caused by society as a whole, by a Hobbesian Leviathan; they are born of the mutual relations within small social groups. It is noteworthy that, under Soviet conditions, traumatic experiences arising from work, industrial, or office situations are becoming rarer. Psychological disturbances linked to personal and family relationships still remain rather frequent.

Kharchev (1964) presents some results of concrete sociological studies of the family in the Soviet Union. One of the studies was devoted to families with children who became criminals. It turned out that of 500 juvenile delinquents only 200 had both parents; 267 of the remaining 300 had only a mother, 25 only a father, and 8 were brought up by a grandmother or another relative. The author concludes that "childhood amorality and crime have much more favorable conditions for development in broken families (where there is no father, no mother, or no parents) than in families which are intact" (p. 276). Further, of the 200 cases where a juvenile delinquent did have both parents, in 160 cases the intoxication of the father, or, more rarely, of both parents, was found to be a contributing factor. When the juvenile delinquent was brought up by his mother alone, in 234 cases out of 267 she was a hard drinker and led a promiscuous sex life. It follows that the intoxication and amorality of the parents have a destructive influence on the children. It is possible that the drunkenness of one of the parents was the most important cause for the dissolution of the family. Similar concrete sociological studies clarify several sources of psychopathology, as well as of crime. Workers at the Serbskii Institute carried out investigations analogous to Kharchev's (workers from a group directed by the present author participated). Minors registered at the juvenile division of the Moscow militia were studied by Morozov and Felinskii (Morozov, 1964). The group was divided into two subgroups: the first was made up of 124 minors without any symptoms of mental illness. The second subgroup consisted of 98 adolescents who displayed psychological defects in their mental makeup, such as mental illness, intellectual retardation, and psychopathic character structure. When both subgroups were analyzed it was revealed that, of 222 adolescents, only 56 came from secure family situations and 166 (74.8 per cent) had an unhappy family life.

In examining the different forms of unfavorable family conditions, the author recorded the alcoholism of the parents, fatherlessness, neglect (due to the occupation of the parents), and conflicts at home or in school. The author believes that in the first subgroup such conditions play the major role in the development of criminal or antisocial behavior of minors. In the second group it is a supplementary factor, although definitely important in the development of psychopathic traits.

According to Morozov and Felinskii, the role of the social elements should be understood in terms of microsocial relations. One may conclude that among young delinquents whose families were observed by Kharchev, medicopedagogic as well as pedagogic and general-upbringing measures are needed.

The family, as society's structurally smallest unit, lays the foundations of the character of its future citizens and transfers the values of society to the child. The overwhelming majority of Soviet families successfully cope with this task. The work of Kharchev convincingly shows that in a socialist society the housekeeping function of the family is gradually weakening while the educational function grows. Still, there are discrepancies between the way of life of a socialist society and the way of life of certain families which cling to the past. This discrepancy is the source of negative psychological and sometimes pathological, psychotraumatic influences on members of a family, especially on small children and adolescents.

In the case of pathological character development of a child, the school and work communities often have a beneficial influence. Clinical research shows that in the beginning stages of pathocharacterological development, when the possibilities of reversing the pathological traits of the personality have not been exhausted, the influence of a group other than the family can lead to a completely healthful balance of the personality. When a group which is exerting a bad influence on a personality is confronted by a positive group, the possibility of preventing personality disintegration arises.

In the origins of alcoholism a complex role is played by the interdependent influences of various small groups. Well known is the ruinous influence on some people of alcoholic parents, neighbors, or acquaintances. It is just as well known that a healthy job environment is a positive influence. However, it sometimes happens that alcoholism develops, not in the home, but, rather, in the working environment. Yanushevskii (1959) shows that the first desire for liquor and relapses after treatment are all too often due to the influence of fellow workers. He reports on some small groups, which, apart from common professional responsibilities, are bound together by almost obligatory daily drinking after work. The greenhorn who refuses to participate in such bouts is subject to various forms of ostracism. Yanushevskii observed similar situations among workers in grocery and provision stores.

It would be wrong to maintain that alcoholism lacks any social basis in our society. Social phenomena must have social origins. In our case, the peculiarity of alcoholism, hooliganism, sexual wantonness, and similar social phenomena is that their roots are not laid deeply in the very nature of society. Their source is not in the foundation of our society, but the peculiarities, maintained by small groups. Their sociopsychological nature lies in the traditions, habits, types, and forms of interpersonal relations, typical of some small groups.

Characteristic of a number of negative sociopsychological phenomena in our society is the absence of deep social roots in spite of the preservation of microsociological sources. In this sense they may be evaluated as survivals, the residue of earlier social patterns.

There are some foreign psychiatrists who are trying to use the laws established through the study of small groups in order to organize psychotherapy better. In mental institutions the primary concern is with organizing selected groups of patients in such a way as to encourage to the utmost the positive effects of one patient on another. Some institutions have achieved significant results using this method. Work with the mentally ill at the Belmont Hospital in London bears witness to this (Jones, 1952), as do the experiments at the medical center for the rehabilitation of neurotics in Lobchi, Czechoslovakia (Winid and Mitarski, 1959) and at the psychiatric clinic in Kharkov (Kepinski, Orwid, and Gatarski, 1960); and others can be added.

For Soviet psychiatrists the role played by social conditions in the spread of mental diseases is clear. Without a doubt the origins of mental disease are largely social. However, until recently there was no systematic approach to the connection between general theory and practical research on early clinical symptoms of mental illness and its pathogenetic mechanisms. Clinical methods did not make sufficiently clear which factors in the immediate social milieu gave rise to disease.

The study of small social groups gives rise to the hope that the missing link will be found in the border areas connecting sociology and psychiatry as more studies are initiated.

References

Aisler, A. W. In G. Bekker and A. Baskov (Eds.), *Contemporary sociological theory*. Moscow, 1961.

Bachitov, M. S. *The newest social utopia.* Moscow, 1958.

Chesnokov, D. I., Bekker, G., and Baskov, A. *Contemporary sociological theory*. Moscow, 1961. Epilogue.

Furst, J. B. *The neurotic, his surroundings and his inner world.* (Russian edition.) Moscow, 1957.

Gilyarovskii, V. A. *Moskov. med. Zh.,* 1926, No. 27, 55.

Gilyarovskii, V. A. *Sovet. nevropatol. Psikhiat. i Psikhol.,* 1934, *2–3,* 74.

Iliechev, L. F. *Kommunist,* 1962, No. 16, 13.

Iliechev, L. F. In *Philosophical problems of higher nervous activity and psychology*. Moscow: Izd. Akad. Nauk SSSR, 1963. (a)

Iliechev, L. F. *The social sciences and communism*. Moscow, 1963. (b)

Jones, M. *A study of therapeutic communities*. London: Tavistock, 1952.

Kepinski, A., Orwid, M., and Gatarski, L. *Kommunist,* 1960, No. 5, 697.

Kharchev, A. G. *Marriage and family in the U.S.S.R.* Moscow, 1964.

Kovalev, A. G., and Myasishchev, V. N. The psychology of personality and social practice. *Vop. Psikhol.,* 1963, No. 6, 23.

Kuzmin, Y. S. The subject matter of social psychology. *Vop. Psikhol.,* 1963, No. 1, 142.

Michaux, L. *Les troubles du caractère*. Paris: Hachette, 1964.

Moreno, J. *Sociometry*. (Russian edition.) Moscow, 1958.

Morozov, V. M. *Zh. Nevropatol. i Psikhol.,* 1964, *1,* 142.

Myasishchev, V. N. *Personality and neurosis*. Leningrad, 1960.

Parigin, B. D. Meeting on the problems of social psychology. *Vop. Psikhol.,* 1963, No. 5, 176.

Porshnev, B. *Kommunist,* 1963, No. 8, 94.

Rubinshtein, S. L. *Being and consciousness*. Moscow, 1957.

Shorokhova, Y. V., Mansurov, N. S., and Platonov, K. K. Problems of social psychology. *Vop. Psikhol.,* 1963, No. 5, 73.

Siradoshch, A. M. In *Neuroses and their treatment*. Moscow, 1959.

Valentinova, N. G. *Vop. Filos.,* 1964, No. 6, 90.

Winid, B., and Mitarski, J. *Zh. neur. neurokhir. Psikhol.* 1959, No. 6, 847.

Yanushevskii, I. K., *Zh. Nevropatol. Psikhol.* 1959, *6,* 693.

Zdravomyslov, A. G., and Yadov, V. A. *Vop. Filos.* 1964, No. 4, 72.

14

Consciousness and the Unconscious

F. V. Bassin

EDITORS' INTRODUCTION

The relationship between Freudian psychoanalytic theory and Soviet psychology has been a theoretical problem for Soviet psychologists during the entire history of the U.S.S.R.

In recent years the extreme proscriptions of the Stalin era against Western ideas have greatly relaxed. As this chapter by F. V. Bassin indicates, relaxation has by no means meant acceptance. However, real debate has begun and many sectors of Soviet psychology are being heard from. An earlier version of the present paper by Bassin (1960a) was subjected to a critique by Musatti (1960), a psychoanalytically oriented Italian psychologist and a Marxist, which prompted a further reply by Bassin (1960b). The controversy was spirited, critical, and suggests the beginning of an era of constructive theory and research on problems of conflict, unconscious motivation and symbolization without the psychoanalytic framework.

Russian terminology dealing with this problem is particularly difficult to translate because it provides several different words for different understandings of our notion of "unconscious." Bassin employs bessoznatel'noye *and related forms to refer to the Freudian unconscious; he employs* neosoznavayemii *and related forms to represent the Soviet understanding of unconsciousness. To obtain consistent discrimination these terms (and their related forms) are always translated by "unconscious" for* bessoznatel'nii *and* "noncognized" *for* neosoznabaemii.

The present chapter has been condensed from Bassin's presentation at the All-Union Conference on Philosophical Problems of the Physiology of Higher Nervous Activity and Psychology held in Moscow in 1962. The importance Soviet science attaches to the issues Bassin discusses can be inferred from the fact that his was one of thirteen major addresses at the conference.

Professor Bassin is one of a group of psychologists working at the Institute of Philosophy in Moscow.

THE PROBLEM of the "unconscious" is closely connected with the name of Freud. Actually, Freud and his followers wasted an enormous amount of effort in elaborating an explicit theory of the "unconscious." It was first conceived of as a narrow clinical concept intended to clarify the nature of hysteria and neurosis and, subsequently, as a doctrine which, finding wide acceptance abroad (especially during the last decade in the United States) spread its influence into the most diverse aspects of intellectual life. It took on the character of a unique philosophical system and closely approached directions of thought which are highly inimical to social and scientific progress.

In Russia, as early as the turn of the century, the traditions of an objective experimental-clinical approach to the functional syndromes and ideas of nervism, elaborated by Sechenov, Pavlov, Botkin, Vvedenskii, and their students, were opposed to Freudian teaching.

Abroad, however, the position of Freud's doctrine was quite different. Freudianism is one of the dominant currents in bourgeois psychology, sociology, and philosophy. Its influence is clearly revealed in so-called psychosomatic medicine. Work of the world psychiatric congresses of 1950 and 1961 and numerous other international meetings of recent years has been done under the aegis of its widespread acceptance. It is even looked on with favor in Catholic circles. In countless different forms its influence may be discovered in foreign belles-lettres, graphic arts, cinema, and theater. And even a scholar as far removed from psychoanalytic research as Norbert Wiener, the founder of cybernetics, not long ago asserted that Freudianism is consonant with contemporary concepts of physics.

Of course, the influence of Freudianism should not be overestimated. One of the most outstanding features of the development of foreign attitudes toward Freudianism in the last decade is a clear and progressive growth of ideological opposition to the movement. It is particularly indicative of contemporary foreign opposition to Freudianism that the most severe critics of psychoanalysis are just those persons who previously defended this point of view and later became convinced of its inadequacy as a result of their own research. This critical stream in the literature of recent years has convincingly demonstrated the scientifically primitive nature of psychoanalytic concepts, its lack of therapeutic productivity, and its reactionary role.

Furthermore, if we review an even larger field of studies coming into contact with Freudianism (works written neither by confirmed rivals, nor unconditional partisans of psychoanalytic doctrine), we then clearly see a very spotty array of different shades of opinion varying from a tendency to skeptical ridicule and disregard of the theory of psychoanalysis to an effort to make some sort of compromise with the theory and bring Freudian concepts into line with the traditions and ideas of Pavlovian physiology, applications of electrophysiological methods, the theory of the reticular formation, and so forth.

Even such great scientists as Bertrand Russell and Penfield have frequently defended this ideological compromise. Certain Indian neurologists friendly toward the U.S.S.R., and also some scientists from the United States, England, and France who are concerned with questions other than fundamentally materialistic convictions, are also inclined to favor this compromise. Even O'Connor, an extremely severe critic of Freudianism in many respects, considers it possible to pick out some valuable elements in this theory if one can clean off the "mystic fog," as he puts it, in which Freudianism embroils one. The notion that it was desirable to achieve a synthesis of psychoanalytic and Pavlovian approaches was very persistent and led to the International Conference in Freiburg in 1957, specially dedicated to consideration of the interrelation between Pavlov and Freud. To some extent this idea was also promulgated in the First Psychosomatic Congress in 1958, at the Montreal Psychiatric Congress in 1961, in some other international congresses in subsequent years, and also in many experimental and theoretical studies undertaken by researchers drifting in the psychoanalytic direction (Masserman, Hilgard and Marquis, Kubie, and others).

What principles induced so many researchers to strive for a compromise with Freud's teaching? The basic argument emerging from these efforts is that Freud's concept is the only theory recognizing the existence of a special type of brain activity, the so-called unconscious forms of complex mental activity, and that Freudianism is the only theory providing a method for revealing and acting upon this peculiar activity.

What is our principal position with respect to Freud's theory? First of all, it should be based on recognition of the unacceptability of any compromise whatsoever with psychoanalytic methodology which permits arbitrary interpretation of subjective experience. There should be no compromise with the frank appeal of some adherents of Freudianism (Brisset, 1961; and others) to substitute the results of introspection and intuition (which have no objective controls) for the data obtained by objective scientific analysis.

At the same time it is obvious that we should in no case skeptically ignore the problem of the "unconscious." We should be able to show the completely erroneous nature of any notion claiming the existence of non-cognizable forms of brain activity acting on behavior, a notion recognized only by Freudianism. We should be able to make clear exactly why the notorious problem of the "unconscious" can only be explained on the basis of dialectical materialist studies and the principles of Pavlovian teaching.

The foregoing throws light on circumstances which, again in recent years, have added a serious significance to the task of combating the most recent modifications of Freudianism. The resumption of discussions with the psychoanalytic school have been reflected in many ways: in studies of a special inter-institute meeting under the auspices of the Presidium of the Academy of Medical Sciences of the U.S.S.R. on questions of the ideological struggle with Freudianism (1958), in lectures of members of the Soviet delegation to the first Czechoslovakian Psychiatric Congress (1959) and at the Third World Psychiatric Congress (1961), in the publication of a series of discussion articles in the Soviet press, in the reading of Soviet lectures, and in reviews abroad. However, in spite of all this work the task of criticizing the basic principles of Freudianism from the viewpoint of Marxist-Leninist methodology is still far from concluded. In a resolution adopted several years ago by the above-mentioned meeting, sponsored by the Presidium of the Academy of Sciences of the U.S.S.R., it was quite correctly stated in this connection "We need a very extensive review from correct methodological positions of a series of important problems to which our psychologists, clinicians and psychiatrists have not devoted sufficient attention in recent years and which therefore have become quite incorrectly regarded abroad as monopolies of Freudianism."

A Critique of Freudian Theory

Why does Soviet psychology reject Freud's teachings? Above all, we have the incompatibility of the entire methodology of Freudianism with generally accepted methods for the establishment of scientific data, the arbitrary character of psychoanalytic dogmas, the therapeutic ineffectiveness of the psychoanalytic method, the harm done to public health by psychoanalysis as a result of deflecting attention from the true capabilities of medicine and prophylaxis, the demoralizing influences spread by psychoanalysis, especially in the younger generation, which give eroticism the place of a leading social principle and encourage the very worst forms of decadent literature and art. Other reasons for our rejection include the nonscientific interpretation of the role which the so-called unconscious plays in normal and pathological behavior, the grossly biological explanation which psychoanalysis gives for sociological problems and the reactionary role which this point of view plays by masking the true causes of social disasters with discussions of "displacement" instead of concentrating on the tasks related to the struggle against class exploitation and other negative aspects of the capitalistic system.

However, it would be a great mistake to think that Soviet critics of Freudianism are satisfied by simply making these condemnations. The very recognition of the existence of the "unconscious" obviously compels those who reject psychoanalysis to search for some other objective experimental means of studying cognitive processes which take place in the absence of awareness. In many discussions it has been shown that such means not only exist but have been used productively for a long time.

The first question which must be clearly answered in reviewing the problem of the "unconscious" is the following: Do there exist in man any cognitive activities influencing behavior and taking place, as it were, "beneath the threshold" of consciousness, processes which are subjectively not perceivable—or are there no special reasons to assume the existence of such processes? This question is not identical to the previously considered problem of different understandings of "consciousness" and "psyche," with which we must come to grips in analysis done from a phylogenetic basis. We are now concerned with the existence of noncognized cognitive processes, not in animals, but in a creature in which the development of consciousness is the most outstanding characteristic.

If we turn to the literature, we find a unanimously affirmative answer to this question. But the explanations for these noncognized forms of cerebral activity, understanding of their essential nature, methods of studying them and, most importantly, the roles they play in the organization of behavior, all prove to contain certain widely differing features. In point of fact, these differences of opinion constitute the subject of a bitter ideological struggle which has been going on for more than half a century in connection with the problem of the "unconscious."

One may truly state that the existence of noncognized forms of psychic activity and the important role of these in the behavior of man were never denied in Pavlovian teaching on higher nervous activity. On the contrary, Pavlov frequently stressed that analysis of psychological processes could not have full value without taking account of these important components. In the words of Pavlov: "We know quite well to what degree the mental psychic life is variously composed of both the conscious and the unconscious" (1951, p. 105). Referring to this citation, Rubinshtein goes on to say: "He [Pavlov] believed that one of the reasons for weakness in psychological research is that it is limited to conscious phenomena. Therefore, the psychologist finds himself in the position of a man proceeding in the dark with a torch in his hand which illuminates only a small area" (Rubinshtein, 1957). "With such a torch," writes Pavlov, "it is hard to study an entire locality" (1951, p. 108).

It is possible for various complex and psychologically rich experiences to be suppressed so that they are removed from consciousness but meanwhile remain intact in an inhibited condition so that, in the future, with weakening of inhibition, they will again enter consciousness. One may find numerous indications of this fact in the Pavlovian "Lectures on the Function of the Large Hemispheres," in "Pavlovian Clinical Wednesdays," and in many other sources.

Recognition of the existence of and efforts to study noncognized forms of complex cognitive activity can also be found in the foreign literature, done independently of Freud's work and even considerably prior to it. It is not without interest that the words "The key to psychology of the conscious will be found in the unconscious" were written by Karus as early as 1846, ten years before the birth of Freud. Efforts at systematic experimental and clinical study of noncognized nervous activity may be ascribed, in any event, to the period of the early works of Bernheim, which dealt with analysis of the phenomenon of so-called negative hallucinations under conditions of hypnotic sleep. In this research, repeated later by Janet, the following situation occurred: An individual receiving a posthypnotic suggestion did indeed fail to subjectively perceive a particular object for a specified period of time even though it was objectively differentiated from other objects by a number of complex visual characteristics, the perception of which was preserved wholly intact. Experiments showed that it is possible to retain extremely complex instructions for a long period of time in a posthypnotic state. These instructions remain completely noncognized but are still carried out when the objective conditions arise under which they should be executed according to the instructions of the hypnotist.

These observations show convincingly enough that undiminished interest in the problem of the noncognized nature of forms of psychic activity is by no means characteristic only of the psychoanalytic school and that it was, for decades, the stimulus for research having no ideological connection with the psychoanalytic school.

It is characteristic that even in recent discussions dealing with the problem of consciousness completely outside the psychoanalytic framework, the question of noncognized cognitive activity also arose consistently. In a book dealing with the practice and theory of theater, "The Actor Expresses Himself," Stanislavskii presents his own reflections on questions concerning the nature of artistic productivity. The last chapter is entitled "The Subconscious." In developing the theme of this chapter, the author states, "We must pay particular attention to this matter because therein lies the essence of productivity of the entire 'system' " (Stanislavskii, 1938). The offensive name of the chapter ("The Subconscious") of course does not mean that Stanislavskii is an advocate of Freudianism. He states that he does not use the term "subconscious" "in a philosophical but rather in a very simple everyday sense." Even so the problem of linkage between the "conscious" and the "unconscious" and the important role played by "unconscious" psychic processes in the process of theatrical productivity is explored in depth by this author, who was a great artist and a profound thinker.

In view of all this, it is no surprise that at the meeting called in 1958 by the Presidium of the Academy of Medical Sciences of the U.S.S.R. to consider questions related to the struggle with Freudianism, particular attention was paid to the necessity for research on noncognized forms of psychological activity. The importance of this problem was underlined by Anokhin:

> Up to this time we have unquestionably not paid enough attention to the processes of formation of what Freudianism calls the "subconscious." Carefully studying the reactions of the brain we forget that beyond the limits of the focus of the conscious there remains an enormous fund of knowledge which we may call the memory of the brain; this fund of knowledge accumulates throughout a lifetime and proves to be, as shown in certain hypnotic experiments, remarkably stable. But have psychologists studied in sufficient depth how these traces survive and in what way they emerge into consciousness? It must be recognized that we have studied these questions very little. As a result, the business of combating Freudianism has suffered (Anokhin, 1958).

In view of the above, we can scarcely take seriously the idea that the problem of noncognized forms of psychological activity was first investigated by Freud or investigated by his school alone. Freudianism neither monopolized nor illuminated the problem with its specific methodological approach or its theoretical treatment. But how can we approach the problem of noncognized psychological activity other than by the psychoanalytic method?

An Alternative Approach to the "Unconscious"

The experimental studies noted above, which aimed at revealing the features of various forms of noncognized psychological activity by objective methods, enable us to state at least one primary and important conclusion. Various types of complex stimuli may act on man as signals eliciting complex reactions without the subject's being clearly aware of them. These may be (1) active stimuli, (2) motives arousing the subject to completion of a reaction, and even (3) realization of the reaction itself. This peculiar "dissociation" of the signal effect of a stimulus from reflection of the changes elicited by it in consciousness is observed under conditions of clinical pathology and also under physiologically normal conditions.

This conclusion has an especially important significance for the correct approach to the entire problem of the "unconscious." Above all, it confirms the Soviet understanding of the nature of consciousness. "Cognitive processes not entering consciousness"—emphasizes Rubinshtein—"regulate the activity of man directly as signals. For consciousness the conditions of activity arise not only as signals regulating activity, but also as objective circumstances which are taken into account" (Rubinshtein, no date). Or, otherwise stated, the origin of consciousness is linked with isolation of the active subject from objective reality, with isolation of life from the reflex reactions to the environment, as knowledge about something found outside the subject (Rubinshtein, 1957).

This important point may be illustrated as follows. A man may perceive a complex sound stimulus and carry out complex instructions under the influence of this stimulus. This process may proceed in two ways psychologically. If a man in contact with a given signal separates himself from the environment and, consequently, perceives the environment as an objective reality opposed to himself, then he also perceives the sound signal as an element of this reality correlated with other elements thereof. The man in this case not only hears the signal but also knows that he hears. And this means that the signal is represented in consciousness which, in Rubinshtein's words, originates "separation of life from the reflexes therein," which gives rise to knowledge concerning something "which stands in opposition to" the subject of this knowledge.

But another possible variation is very widely observed under conditions of clinical pathology and was described for normal conditions by Ivanov-Smolenskii, Perel'man, and many others: A man hears a sound and acts in accordance with the sense of what he has heard in ignorance of the fact that he is being subjected to sound stimulation. In this case he does not "perceive" the signal; the signal does not enter into the structure of the man's perceived reflection of objective reality.

Of itself, the fact that a man reacts to noncognized stimuli is scarcely out of the ordinary. We need only recall that an overwhelming majority of the vegetative processes may be considered just such noncognized forms of physiological activity. The above-mentioned studies, which illuminated the phenomenon of "dissociation" (i.e., the phenomenon of dissociation between the objective effect of a stimulus, on the one hand, and consciousness of stimulation and effect on the other), are made more interesting by two factors. First, according to data from these studies, the signal function may be preserved without participation of consciousness, using stimuli of even the most complex second-signal type, which fall into the category of semantic (meaningful) structures embedded in speech. Secondly, the phenomenon of "dissociation" may be observed both under conditions of clinical pathology, and in the normal condition in various forms, because it may be expressed in varying degrees of intensity. Rubinshtein shows the meaning of the mildest level of such "dissociation." It may be observed, he says, under conditions which call forth complex emotions at certain stages of individual maturation. It may be seen during the first appearance of the young, hitherto unfamiliar feeling of love in boys or girls under those conditions which so frequently inspire the pen, the brush, and the sculpting chisel of the great masters of art. Inadequate perception of this new-born effect does not result from the fact that the sensation is not "experienced," but rather that the subject does not clearly recognize it as such, that is, it is not correlated, or not adequately correlated, with the objective world. A clearer form of "dissociation" may be observed in so-called impulsive acts. If the dissociation is not very marked then it results in an action which the man knows he carried out even though this action is not clearly enough correlated with its objective consequences; the action does not clearly enough "stand opposed" to the subject as an element of reality. Clinical hysteria, as frequently emphasized by Pavlov, is known to occur with such forms of reaction which are inadequately reflected in consciousness. Under conditions of seriously strained emotions, fatigue and so forth, similar patterns may be observed even in the normal subject.

The existence of various degrees of expression and various forms of the "dissociation" phenomena poses a number of complicated questions. The first concerns terminology. In those cases where "dissociation" is expressed in rather gross form we find ourselves dealing with very peculiar cerebral activity. On objective analysis this behavior appears, without any doubt, to be part of higher nervous activity—for it makes use of all individually acquired experience and the most complex forms of conditioned reflex circuits. Yet it is extremely difficult to determine to what degree it has the properties of cognitive activity, that is, to what extent it is accompanied by definite subjective sensations and experiences when it occurs. In all probability, under diverse degrees of "dissociation" the subjective tone must vary to some extent. It therefore seems to us that the cerebral activity displayed under conditions of "dissociation" should most properly be called, as suggested by Snezhnevskii, a noncognized form of higher nervous activity. This designation underlines the fact (extremely important in arguments with Freudianism) that the objective reactions elicited by it are the principal (if not the only) form of expression of this activity.[1]

The second question is the following: If unconscious forms of higher nervous activity are cerebral processes which do indeed exist, then how often do they appear? Are they only rare episodes arising under extreme condi-

1. By the expression "noncognized higher nervous activity," we imply processes of higher nervous activity which are not accompanied by consciousness of reality. This expression is only an abbreviated designation for a certain category of cognitive processes which regulate behavior but are not accompanied by consciousness of reality. For precisely this reason the expression "noncognized forms of higher nervous activity" seems to us to be philosophically more adequate and to set off the difference between our approach from that of the subjective treatment of the problems of the "unconscious" offered by Freudianism.

tions, under just those special experimental and true life situations which uniquely elicit them or, on the contrary, must we regard them as lawful components of common behavior, as elements of any adaptive activity? And, finally, a third question which is most important for the main dispute with Freudianism: What is the role of these peculiar forms of higher nervous activity, what is their relation to the activity of consciousness: are they factors which relate to the activity of consciousness, like the Freudian "unconscious," only as antagonists, or can there be observed here a relation of both functional antagonism and synergism? Are they subordinated in their dynamics to the activity of consciousness or, on the contrary, as the Freudians never tire of emphasizing with respect to the "unconscious," do they covertly control consciousness? Finally, how do the laws governing these peculiar forms of higher nervous activity differ under pathological and normal conditions?

It must be emphasized that it would be a gross error to consider noncognized forms of higher nervous activity as rare episodes in the working of the brain. In point of fact the situation is exactly the opposite. In support of this interpretation we have the widespread phenomena of automatization of habits, wherein forms of activity which started out under the control of consciousness gradually lose their conscious character although differentiation of their execution may even increase, notwithstanding the emergence of "dissociation." Confirmation of this interpretation also comes from an analysis of the functional structure of any activity: not one of a man's voluntary actions will be equally clearly conscious in all phases of its development and, consequently, in any voluntary activity there may be phases which are accomplished to a greater or lesser extent under conditions of "dissociation." And not infrequently almost the entire process of accomplishing a voluntary action, with the exception of its termination which achieves the goal of the action, falls completely outside of consciousness.

What is the function of these unconscious processes? Here we approach conditions, the analysis of which throws a particularly clear light on the basic difference between Freudian doctrine and that interpretation of the problem of the "unconscious" which prompts us to study it objectively.

One of the very greatest mistakes of Freudianism is gross simplification of the multiform and changing relations existing between noncognized higher nervous activity and the activity of consciousness. Freud and his followers ascribed the entire, almost unimaginable complexity of these relations to a single dynamic tendency, to functional antagonism of consciousness and the "unconscious." The doctrines of "displacement" and symbolization are employed as a means of overcoming this antagonism. There is not even a hint of the notion of functional synergism between the "unconscious" and the activity of the conscious in a detailed review of psychoanalytic theory. "Sublimation," like symbolization, is, according to

Freud, only a means to escape from the destructive consequences of antagonism between the conscious and "unconscious," but by no means an expression of actual removal of this antagonism.

How and why did such a simplification come to pass? The answer to this question will be in an unexpected form for those who accept Freudianism as the basis of a general theory of the "unconscious." Yet the thoughtful analysis of the psychoanalytic concept undertaken by Wells (1959) inevitably leads to an answer. Indicating specific features of the psychoanalytic doctrine which bring it into harmony with the ideology of contemporary capitalism, he states: "Freud did not give a detailed analysis of the application of his 'science of unconscious psychic processes' to the field of psychology" (Wells, 1959). In emphasizing this highly characteristic situation, Wells is absolutely correct. On the basis of his conception of the "unconscious" Freud tried to resolve only one problem of psychology, which seemed central to him, the fate of unsatisfied affective drive. Criticism of Freudianism has clearly shown how these efforts led to a conglomeration of myths and paradoxes. Freud never actually addressed himself to the general problem of the "unconscious" as a major problem of psychological theory.

The notion that psychoanalysis does not constitute a general psychological theory of the "unconscious" may be found, however, not only in studies by the critics of Freudianism. It is significant that the same point of view emerges on deeper analysis of some contemporary adherents of Freudianism. In this respect, interest attaches to statements made at a symposium, organized by the New York Academy of Science in 1958, for special consideration of some methodological problems of psychoanalysis, and, in particular, to the address of Bellak with which this symposium was opened. This eminent theoretician of contemporary Freudianism made a careful analysis of the concept of the "unconscious" and stated precisely in what ways this concept was important to psychoanalytic theory and in what ways it remains irrelevant. His statements were very significant with respect to exactly what psychoanalysis implies by the term "unconscious."

Bellak (1959) states that various things are meant by the "unconscious," under various circumstances, and as a result this concept emerges in a number of qualitatively diverse aspects. One of these aspects he proposes to call the "physiological," another the "structural." The physiological aspect of the "unconscious" represent noncognizance of the majority of the vegetative functions of the organism. According to Bellak, psychoanalytic theory has no relevance to this aspect because the noncognized somatic processes are not reflected in consciousness either directly or on the basis of symbolization. It should be noted that he is opposed in this respect to many theoreticians of the contemporary "psychosomatic" school who, by contrast, treat the idea of symbolic representation of somatic processes in consciousness as their fundamental thesis. The "structural" aspect of the unconscious represents, in his opinion, the noncognizance of automated actions and the neural activity on which the formation of any content of consciousness depends, activity which creates these contents but remains imperceptible after its task is accomplished. Many limitations on the possibilities of psychoanalysis are related, according to Bellak, to precisely this, that the psychoanalytic technique does not allow us to penetrate to this "structural" aspect of the unconscious. "I have never heard," he notes, "that any psychoanalyst uncovered, for example, the vanished memories of the process of learning to walk in early childhood" (Bellak, 1959, p. 1071). Therefore, the "structural" aspect of the "unconscious" likewise does not seem to be, according to Bellak, a feature of psychoanalytic theory. Then what is one of its features? Bellak clearly answers this question: There, is, he says, a third aspect of the unconscious—the "dynamic" aspect: unawareness of this results from the fact that its psychological content is not acceptable to consciousness but may struggle into consciousness by the roundabout route of symbolization. It is indeed just this aspect which is the basic, the specific, and the only feature of psychoanalytic theory.

These definitions leave no doubt that, even in the opinion of staunch supporters of contemporary Freudianism, this doctrine scarcely appears to be a general theory of the "unconscious." For the illumination of many sides of the problem of the "unconscious," Freudianism, as Bellak recognizes, has no general relevance. From these definitions it follows that "unacceptability" to consciousness is the main characteristic of this special form of the "unconscious" which psychoanalytic theory declares to be a basic feature of its study. Both of these conclusions are in good agreement with the above-mentioned opinion of Wells and with the tendency, which we noted, for psychoanalysis to exhaust the notion of relations between the conscious and the "unconscious" by the idea of "displacement."

We may, of course, say that if the psychoanalytic concept does not assume the role of a general theory of the "unconscious," it still has the right, in the last analysis, to choose any particular approach to the problem of unconscious processes which it prefers, and to carry that approach through to whatever depths it deems necessary. That, of course, is so. Criticism of Freudianism has quite convincingly demonstrated many reasons why the particular route chosen by Freudianism appears to be bankrupt when all accounts are summed up. We will not dwell too long on this bankruptcy but will stress only a typical inconsistency which is important to our further analysis, an inconsistency which Freudianism had already revealed in choosing the route by which it developed.

In the psychoanalytic literature, which willingly emphasizes Freud's struggle to provide a deterministic interpretation of mental life, one may often find an explanation of the reasons compelling him to create the bases of his concept. He studied neurotic symptoms, dreams, and slips of the tongue; as a result, making a causal analysis, he apparently found himself compelled to create a logical "bridge" to eliminate a seeming hiatus between affect and the clinical symptom, between experiences of sleep and of waking hours, between intentional and inadvertent actions. As a "bridge" of this sort we find his doctrine of the "unconscious" eliminating this seeming gap and permitting one to consider all events of the psychic life as causally interrelated.

In such an approach (no matter if it actually preceded the creation of psychoanalysis or was formulated *ex post facto*) there is one unequivocally rational element: the notion that noncognized psychic activity is a factor causally related to the activity of consciousness and to some extent preparatory to this latter activity. Actually, as indicated by analysis of the structure of very diverse forms of behavior, if there were no complex antecedent noncognized forms of cerebral activity then the activity of consciousness would be not only incomprehensible but, in many cases, impossible. If this is the case, then is it not obvious that the "structural" aspect of the "unconscious," which psychoanalytic theory refuses to investigate on principle, also has a direct bearing on this same problem of a "bridge," that is, on the problem of an uninterrupted causal chain between affect or intention, on the one hand, and behavior on the other? If we agree to this, then it becomes obvious that, excluding its "structural" aspect from the problem of the "unconscious," Freudianism falls into the contradiction that, by its own argumentation, it must face this entire problem.

Therefore, in choosing the "dynamic" aspect as the only aspect of the "unconscious" worthy of attention, Freudianism has no logical right to base this choice on the idea of a "bridge," for the role of a "bridge" is also fulfilled by those forms of the "unconscious" which psychoanalysis considers may be ignored completely.

It is to be anticipated that at some point in this dispute on principles which we are conducting with the psychoanalytic school our adversaries will object approximately as follows. It is fine, they will say, to let the problem of a "bridge" not be completely exhausted by the "dynamic" understanding of the "unconscious" and to let the Freudian "unconscious" be only one of the many mechanisms effecting a connection between affect and symptom, between intention and behavior. This mechanism has a direct relation to the psychological content of experience. At the same time the "unconscious," in its "structural" sense, is only an aggregate of the physiological, automatic performances needed for realization of behavior (and, therefore, also constitutes elements of the "bridge"), but is in no way connected with the thinking side of the situation. The "structural subconscious" is somewhat more like the "psychic automatisms" of Janet than the "Id" of Freud. In any case, this unconscious is something qualitatively different from the "unconscious" in its psychoanalytic sense. If this is the case, then, introducing the notion of the "noncognized form of higher nervous activity," do we not alter the topic of discussion and do we not abandon, in point of fact, the dispute with Freudianism, since we change over to a consideration of the physiological and neurological rather than the psychological aspects of behavior? But with respect to physiological and neurological doctrines the adherents of psychoanalysis might agree with us to a considerable extent without being forced thereby into abandoning their specific psychological ideas.

We can quietly and truthfully answer this serious objection of Freudianism. To do this, however, we need a more concrete explication of exactly what we mean by a noncognized form of higher nervous activity. In making this precise we will show that an objective approach to the "unconscious" means not an "alteration" of the object of the discussion, but on the contrary, a transfer of the dispute precisely into that field which is central to psychoanalysis, in which psychoanalytic thought for such a long time considered itself the only wholly worthwhile theoretical approach, and consequently in which Freudianism will be driven from its basic and ultimate position. The "unconscious" of Freud, actually, always assumed the role of a factor covertly effecting a link between some sort of initial experiences of the usual conscious type and the subsequent expression of these experiences, which allegedly (this is a specific element of psychoanalytic doctrine) appears only in the symbolic form of dreams, clinical symptoms, inadvertent behavior, and so forth. Were it not for the mediating function performed by Freud's "subconscious," the latter would actually not have provided a basis for construction of his entire peculiar concept and the "subconscious" would not have contained within it any reasons for its participation in forming behavior.

The Study of Set as an Objective Approach to the Unconscious

How does Freudianism represent this "unconscious" mediating mechanism? Uznadze was apparently one of the first who noted and understood the significant principle involved in the following most characteristic features of Freudianism. The theory of psychoanalysis represents the mediating mechanism of the subconscious, as it only can represent it, without any preliminary review of the psychological theory of this mechanism. The "unconscious" is represented as our usual thoughts, emotions, affects, and drives, which are simply deprived of the quality of consciousness; it is represented as experiences habitual to us, which simply escape into some sort of a sphere specially postulated by Freudianism, the content of which is inaccessible to consciousness. The "unconscious" of Freud is, thus, an aggregate of mental processes the peculiarity of which is only defined in a negative way. These processes are unconscious (their positive character is almost completely exhausted by indication of their tendency to be expressed mainly symbolically).

Analyzing this notion of the role and nature of the "unconscious," it is first necessary to make a sharp distinction between our relation to the basic task which is called for here and the proposed means of resolving this problem. Is this a real problem, that one for which Freud so persistently tried to find a solution? Does there really exist a problem of latent connections between various kinds of objectively perceived influences and subsequent reflection of the effects of these influences in behavior? There can scarcely be any doubt in answering this question. If such latent connections did not exist there would be no problem of the "unconscious" itself. As we have already seen, the existence of this problem is confirmed by a vast number of observations along various lines which lead us to one and the same phenomenon of "dissociation," that is, to the fact that noncognized forms of complex cerebral activity as well as conscious forms participate in the formation of behavior.

Thus, the task undertaken by Freud was completely reasonable. To be successful in a criticism of Freudianism this fact should never be obscured by the utter senselessness of the methodological route by which Freud traveled in his effort to resolve the problems which interested him.

If Freud and his school, having centered attention on the mediating function of the "unconscious," were unable to define the qualitative features of the complex forms of noncognized cerebral activity and therefore abandoned a scientific solution of the questions which interested them, then what indeed are the methods and theories which provide a satisfactory approach to all of this difficult problem?

Do there exist within the confines of Soviet psychological science or neurophysiology any attempts at systematic experimental review of the complex forms of noncognized cerebral activity determined by the concrete psychological content of an objective situation and influencing, in their turn, objective behavior? Unequivocally, yes. An example of such efforts is the experiments, conducted for many years at the Uznadze Institute of Psychology of the Academy of Sciences of the Georgian S.S.R., which made it possible to collect a large amount of factual material forming the basis for Uznadze's general theory of set. This theory is the only one, in fact, not only in the Soviet Union but also in the world literature, with a thoroughly developed conception of the "unconscious." It is not a method for studying noncognized forms of cerebral activity arising under the influence of isolated subthreshold stimuli, as takes place, for example, in the well-known experiments of Gershuni with subsensory stimuli. Rather, it is a method for studying a complex of superthreshold influences which act upon the subject from the whole experimental situation, arising under the influence of the situation's "meaning" for the subject. Therefore, in repudiating the psychoanalytic conception of the "unconscious" and making an effort to confront it with another view of noncognized forms of higher nervous activity which differs in principle, we should devote very serious attention to Uznadze's ideas.

The model experiment conducted in the Uznadze school to demonstrate the phenomenon of "set" consists in the following.[2] For several trials in a row a subject is given two spheres of equal weight but different volume, one in each hand, each always in the same hand. Then the subject is given spheres which are the same in both volume and weight. Asked which of these spheres is larger, the subject as a rule in this "critical" trial answers that the larger sphere is in the hand which previously received the smaller sphere. What is the nature of this illusion?

Underlying the weight illusion is a particular "internal state," according to Uznadze, or a peculiar change of the functional condition of the central nervous system, as we would prefer to say. Analysis of this "state" or functional disturbance makes it possible to throw some light on its characteristics.

This condition, first, is completely dependent on the series of trials preceding the critical trial; it usually fails to appear in the absence of those preceding trials. Therefore, in principle it appears to be a peculiar, extremely complex reflex reaction of the subject to an objective influence.

Second, having been formed, it is preserved over a given interval of time as a functional disturbance which may be objectively displayed by appropriate experimental measures (of the type described above for the critical trial) but which is not directly available to the subject's consciousness.

Third, notwithstanding its noncognized character, it influences succeeding conscious experiences, predetermining in certain respects their character and dynamics (in the model experiments described above, for example, predetermining the value of the influences in the critical trial and thereby eliciting the beginning of the illusion).

Fourth, it arises in response to stimulation of a complex character and itself appears as a change of a complex sort which is not localized within the limits of any one physiological system but is easily spread from one system to another in which, prior to the critical trial, the influence is not directly observable.

Fifth, it has primary central neural components, the physiological elucidation of which we now only approach by means of such research methods as electroencephalography, autocorrelation analysis, analysis of potentials

2. *Editors' note:* This work is illustrated extensively in Chapter 21 of this volume, by R. G. Natadze.

using computers, and so forth. Sets also have secondary peripheral components, the study of which by means of existing electrophysiological (particularly electromyographic and also conditioned reflex), biochemical, hemodynamic, and other objective methods is substantially more practicable than studying the central components. Research on this problem appears in many studies.

And finally, it is not equally connected with various cerebral systems, which makes it possible in principle to speak of a certain cerebral localization of these conditions. This is indicated by certain studies of Pribram and a number of other authors.

Uznadze used the term "set" for the peculiar unconscious change of the functional condition of the nervous system, which has, despite its noncognized character, important significance for the dynamics of succeeding conscious experiences.

It is self-evident that if the typical condition of a set was seen only in those model experiments noted above, or even more frequently, but still only under the special experimental conditions which elicit it, then it would have but limited interest. The entire significance of these states lies precisely in the fact that they are by no means developed only under the special conditions of laboratory experiments, but very much more widely. They form, in fact, the most important functional components of every adaptive action, of every goal-directed behavior.

Wherein lies the concrete role of sets as components of activity and factors which form behavior? Having been formed under the influence of external stimuli, as a definite reflex alteration of the functional condition of the central and peripheral systems, a set has further influence on the neurodynamic situation, predetermining the character of the development of the most diverse forms of psychological and physiological activity. This influence may appear in comparatively simple form, as in the model experiment with spheres, or it may appear in a very much more complex form. In the experiment with spheres the set arises as the sequel to closing a definite circuit between lateral stimulation (right vs. left hand) and the character of the elicited stimuli (which are mainly proprioceptive); the breakdown of this bond creates an illusion. The set, therefore, appears in this case to be the result of a certain gradually integrated organization of preceding experience, the expression of a certain internal concordance of past experiences which becomes a factor of behavior insofar as it creates a differentiated relationship, a selective preparedness toward impending experiences. And these special processes, the formation of sets by preceding experience and the regulating influence which these sets exert on succeeding activity, can be traced by analysis of the psychological structure of highly diverse simple and complex human actions.

For a deeper understanding of the role which noncognized sets play as a factor influencing conscious behavior one must take account of one more highly characteristic general feature of goal-directed activity. As is known, a necessary condition for the effectiveness of any form of such activity is comparative independence of the latter with respect to fortuitous external events. Without this comparative independence any organized behavior inevitably disintegrates, turning entirely into internally disordered direct reaction to all and sundry external influences, into a reaction whose structure is a mirror image of the processes of the external influence. What gives goal-directed activity this very necessary, relative independence from fortuitous external occurrences? Its conscious character? Obviously not only that, for, as has frequently been shown experimentally, goal-directed activity continues as such (and therefore retains its relative independence of fortuitous external events) even in those stages of partial completion in which it flows along completely noncognized.

In these stages of the formation of activity we again encounter a phenomenon with which we are already acquainted, "dissociation." In addition to what we already know about this phenomenon, we can now advance reasons why the lack of consciousness of a given phase of activity does not lead to dissolution of this phase as a fragment of goal-directed activity. Many arguments may be advanced to support the view that one factor precluding such dissolution is indeed the set which is integrated during the activity (or anticipating a given concrete activity). The set creates its own characteristic differentiated relation to various elements of the external situation: selective readiness for reaction to some stimuli, for inhibition with respect to others, for complete nonreactivity with respect to still others. With removal of such selectivity of reaction the goal-directed character of the activity is inevitably removed, and the presence of this selectivity is direct evidence for the regulating influence exerted on the activity by the set.

Noncognized sets, participating with the activity of consciousness, can add a highly adaptive and internally well-ordered character to behavior. But they may also, under certain circumstances, prevent the development of consciousness of regulated activity, being in such cases factors which directly facilitate disorganization and pathology in behavior.

In the foregoing pages we have made considerable use of Uznadze's notion of the noncognized set. This does not mean that we are in complete agreement with the interpretation advanced by Uznadze and his school.

The paramount aid which the ideas of Uznadze render for a critique of Freudianism consists in providing us with a notion which shows the very essence of the "subconscious" as a functional activity which, being in principle accessible to objective research, also comes to the fore as a factor determined by activity and in its turn, ultimately influencing activity in its most complex, "meaningful," and substantially psychological aspect. That is the main thing, and differences of opinion with respect to the nature of this activity, its relation to consciousness and to higher nervous activity in general, and so forth, will probably take place for a long time to come, but they will stimulate ultimate reinforcement of the network of ideas which destroy the last stronghold of psychoanalysis.

It has been shown by experimental studies of the Uznadze school that sets, noncognized by the subject, can nevertheless influence afferent and efferent processes, changing these processes in accordance with antecedent experience. As sets may be formed on the basis of a generalized perception of reality, they emerge as truly psychological factors called forth by the concrete content of preceding experiences and influencing the substantive aspect of forthcoming experiences. At the same time (we again recall that the Pavlovian conditioned reflex is a phenomenon simultaneously both physiological and psychological), they are the most important elements of unconscious higher nervous activity, dominated by many well-known neurophysiological laws as well as by some much less well understood relations. They are the elements which determine the dynamics of the second-signal forms of cerebral activity.

Unconscious sets thus fulfill the same role as the invisible "bridge" between certain forms of conscious experience and objective behavior which, according to Freud's conception, his "unconscious" should fulfill. We will now sum up what such a change in the nature of the "bridge" gives us.

Implications of a Theory of Set

The first advantage we get from such a change is emergence of the possibility of genuinely scientific research into the real and important field of the human mind. This research confirms the existence of a "subconscious." But it permits an interpretation of the unconscious which is not paradoxical and internally contradictory in its naive representation of thoughts and emotions which are not subjectively experienced by anybody. The concept of set provides an interpretation of the unconscious as objective changes in the functional condition of the nervous system, as a special form of higher nervous activity, reflexly defined by environmental factors and in its turn influencing the ultimate behavior of the subject.

The special feature of noncognized forms of higher nervous activity, particularly of noncognized sets, consists in the fact that they usually lead to behavior with an adaptive character, apparently requiring calculation and logical manipulation of a mass of complex features and thereby giving an impression of "reasonableness." It is just this fact which inspired Freud to depict the "unconscious" as something capable of intense aspirations, of symbolic reorganization of psychological content, of active searching for satisfaction—in short, to depict it as some sort of automatic psychic foundation inimically opposed to consciousness but differing little from consciousness with respect to peculiarities of psychological organization. Instead of this myth, the theory of noncognized forms of higher nervous activity emphasizes the generalized character of noncognized sets. That the quality of "reasonableness" arising as a result of the processes of generalization appears inherent in the effects of noncognized cerebral activity scarcely seems to present a paradox to those who live in an age of cybernetic systems where ultra-"reasonableness" of objective reactions is obtained not only without benefit of consciousness but in the absence of any neural activity whatsoever.

An approach to the problem of the "unconscious" from the position of the theory of noncognized forms of higher nervous activity creates, finally, one more advantage of great importance to methodology.

A basic principle of Freudianism is that there is an interaction between the conscious and "unconscious" which results in "displacement" and circumvention of this "displacement" by means of "symbolization." As a result of this interpretation all the multiform and heterogeneous aspects of links between conscious and unconscious forms of higher nervous activity are practically excluded from consideration. In the objective investigation of these forms, it is precisely in the study of the complexity of their interaction that we find the most important directions in their ultimate explanation from both clinical and experimental points of view.

There are many reasons to suppose that, in certain cases, the processes of noncognized higher nervous activity really do emerge as antagonists of consciousness, impeding this activity and, in turn, being disrupted by this activity. Clear examples of such a functional antagonism may be seen even in efforts consciously to reproduce the process of automatism due to frequent repetition. It is known that concentration of attention on such automated activity frequently disturbs it to a marked degree. Sometimes the basis of antagonism of the "conscious" and "noncognized," as Rubinshtein correctly emphasizes, is even the affective intensity of the experiences involved; sometimes other diverse factors play a role here.

Yet we have no basis for regarding such antagonistic relations as the basic and normal form of connection between consciousness and the "unconscious." Almost all the above-noted objective research on noncognized forms of higher nervous activity, all the material from the study of noncognized sets, convincingly supports the necessity of taking into consideration, when examining the relation between the conscious and "unconscious," the interactions produced by a type of functional antagonism of mutual inhibition. This functional antagonism may disrupt the coordination of conscious and noncognized processes of higher nervous activity and emerge most clearly in conditions of clinical pathology (and under certain special conditions as in affective tension, fatigue, under the condition of "stress," as well as in the normal state). They must also be considered interactions produced by a type of synergy predominating under usual conditions and facilitating adequate organization of the most diverse forms of behavior.

This instability of the functional relationships between consciousness and the "unconscious" leads to an instability which appears to be the concrete content of conscious and noncognized mental activity. This is stressed particularly from the clinical position by Snezhnevskii. For Freudianism, the "unconscious" is that which is unacceptable to the conscious because of its content. Such an interpretation tightly binds some contents to the "unconscious," others are linked to the conscious, and the line of demarcation between the conscious and "unconscious" appears simultaneously as an "iron curtain" between the two noncommunicating spheres of substantive experience. This far-fetched static and rigid psychoanalytic scheme of a theory of noncognized forms of higher nervous activity is opposed by a scheme with a directly opposite character, emphasizing the flexible instability of the relation which any concrete substantive experience bears to consciousness. That which at some point in time emerges in the form of a clearly conscious psychological phenomenon, may then, having lost the quality of consciousness, manifest itself in the form of noncognized process or set to then emerge again in its first psychological aspect, and so forth.

It is important from a methodological point of view to recognize this complexity, this polymorphous aspect and variability, of relations obtaining between consciousness and the "unconscious." An understanding of this sort, not rejecting problems of the noncognized, not denying the existence of the "unconscious" and the important role of the latter in behavior, at the same time annihilates the most poisonous ideological core of Freudianism, that which makes Freudianism so dear to reactionaries of every stripe. It destroys the root of the basic ideas of Freud: inherent antagonism of the conscious and the "unconscious" as two non-homologous essences standing opposed to one another; functional primacy of the "unconscious"; unresolvable subordination of consciousness to covert primitive appetites in the mind of man; the eternal rule of instincts over reason; hopelessness of the struggle against this, which is only shamefully veiled by a cover of civilization but which ineluctably continues to exist, eternally recalling man's bestial origin.

References

Anokhin, P. K. Stenographic record of meeting of the Presidium of the Academy of Medical Sciences, U.S.S.R., 1958.

Bassin, F. V. A debate on Freudianism: A critical analysis of Freudianism. *Soviet Rev.*, 1960, *1*, 3–14. (a)

Bassin, F. V. A debate on Freudianism: A rejoinder to Professor Musatti. *Soviet Rev.*, 1960, *1*, 27–44. (b)

Bellak, L. The unconscious. *Ann. N.Y. Acad. Sci.*, 1959, *76*, 1066–1097.

Brisset. C. *Rev. Méd. psychosom.*, 1961, Nos. 3–4.

Musatti, C. L. A debate on Freudianism: An answer to F. V. Bassin's criticism of Freudianism. *Soviet Rev.*, 1960, *1*, 14–27.

Pavlov, I. P. *Collected works*. 1951. Book 1, Vol. 3.

Rubinshtein, S. L. *Being and consciousness*. Moscow: Izd. Akad. Nauk, 1957. Pp. 272–273.

Rubinshtein, S. L. *Principles and trends of development in psychology*. (No date.)

Stanislavskii, K. S. *The actor expresses himself*. Moscow: *Goslitzdat*, 1938. P. 14.

Uznadze, D. N. *Experimental bases of the psychology of set*. Tbilisi, 1961.

Wells, H. *Pavlov and Freud*. Moscow: International Language Publishing House, 1959. P. 473.

PART III

GENERAL EXPERIMENTAL PSYCHOLOGY

15

On the Biological and Social Aspects of Human Development: The Training of Auditory Ability

A. N. Leont'ev

EDITORS' INTRODUCTION

This chapter was taken from A. N. Leont'ev's speech at the 16th International Congress of Psychology in Bonn, Germany, in 1960. It presents in brief but succinct form the basic characteristics of Leont'ev's work: emphasis on the specifically human forms of behavior (mental activity), an interest in their development, both social and historical, and concern with showing the relation between the facts of psychology and Marxist philosophy.

In 1963 Leont'ev was honored for his contributions to psychology, specifically for his book Problems of Mental Development, *with the Lenin Prize (the Soviet equivalent of a Presidential Gold Medal). This collection of articles includes material dating back to the 1930's, when Leont'ev, one of Vygotskii's most famous students, was chairman of the psychology sector at the Kharkov Institute of Psychoneurology.*

During World War II, Leont'ev, like many of his colleagues, worked on problems of restoring the health of soldiers injured in battle (Leont'ev and Zaporozhets, 1960). At present he is Chairman of the Department of Psychology, Moscow State University.

In recent years his laboratory has been concerned with the problem of information transmission and man-machine systems. However, to this traditionally quantitative area he has brought his lifelong theoretical orientation, a concern with the qualitative differences that distinguish human behavior from other systems, living or mechanical.

THE RESEARCH on which this chapter is based was devoted to a study of the features peculiar to man's sense of hearing. It might be asked: Why was it that in dealing with the biological and social aspects of development, we chose to investigate an area as specialized as that of auditory sensations?

By way of an answer, I will have to devote some time to discussing the ideas and hypotheses which guided us. We were principally concerned with the idea that the development of distinctly human psychological functions and abilities is a process which is altogether unique. It differs not only from the way in which biologically inherited behavior manifests itself, but also from the process whereby the individual acquires experience in life. Psychological functions and abilities which are intrinsic to man as a social being develop in an entirely unique way—through the process of learning and mastery.

I will try to explain what I mean by this. During the history of man as a social creature immense progress was made in the development of human psychological abilities. By comparison, thousands of years in the history of society produced far greater results than did the hundreds of millions of years which witnessed the biological evolution of animals.

To be sure, progress in the development of psychological functions and abilities came about gradually, achievements being transmitted from one generation to another. But what this means is that in one way or another these achievements proved to be firm and lasting. Had the situation been otherwise, the steady and continually accelerated progress that took place in human development would not have been possible.

But precisely how was it possible for these gains to become more secure and be transmitted to subsequent generations? Could they have become entrenched as morphological, biologically inherited modifications? Hardly, for while biological inheritance certainly exists on the human level, it has no direct effect on the achievements in the sphere of psychological development which mankind has made in the last forty or fifty thousand years, a period in which modern man reached his final stage of biological development and society evolved from a period of prehistory to history, a process fully governed by the operation of objective social laws.

From this point on, progress in the sphere of man's psychological abilities was established and transmitted from one generation to another in a unique form, one that was exoteric, that expressed itself through the phenomena of objective reality. The new form of accumulating and transmitting phylogenetic or, more precisely, historical experience emerged because of certain features which are typical of human activity—namely, its productive, creative aspect, which is most apparent in the basic human activity that work represents. The fundamental and, indeed, decisive importance of this fact was discovered over a hundred years ago by Marx, the founder of scientific socialism.

By effecting the process of production, both material and cultural, work is crystallized or assumes final form in its product. Whatever manifests itself as activity on the part of the subject takes the form of a potential quality in the product—that of existence or objectivity (Marx).

This process of conversion can be considered from various standpoints and in terms of a variety of relationships. One can consider it from the standpoint of the amount of labor expended in proportion to the amount produced, which is what political economists do. But it can also be viewed from the standpoint of the nature of the subject's very activity, without reference to other aspects and relationships. In this case the conversion of human activity into its product appears to be a process whereby man's activity, the activity of human qualities, is embodied in the product produced. The history of material and cultural development thus appears to be a process which, in its external objective form, gives expression to the growth of human abilities.

From this standpoint, the process of historical development—for example, the use of tools and instruments—can be thought of as expressing and consolidating the gains man has made with respect to the motor functions of the hand; the process by which the phonetics of languages has become more complex signifies improvements in articulation and the capacity to hear sounds; while progress in the sphere of artistic creation signifies the development of man's aesthetic abilities. Even when we consider industry, the production of ordinary material goods, we have, in the form of external things, "objectifications" of human ability (Marx).

This idea has decisive bearing on all aspects of scientific psychology. However, the full force of its significance emerges when we analyze the process from a different standpoint, when we consider it not in terms of the objectification of human abilities but in terms of the way these abilities are learned and adopted.

Before birth the individual is not a "nothing" in Heidegger's sense of the term, but rather an objective world reshaped by the activity of generations of people. However, the world of objects, of objects which embody the human abilities that were formed during the process of social and historical development, is not presented to the individual in *this* manner from the start. For the individual to discover the human aspect of the objects in his surrounding world, he has to relate to them through some activity which is adequate to those objects.

It stands to reason that this idea holds true also for the objective conceptual phenomena created by mankind—language, concepts, and ideas, as well as for works of music and the plastic arts. The individual, the child, is thus not "set" before a world of objects created by man; if he is to live in this world, he has to function actively and adequately in it.

But this amounts to only one of the conditions necessary for the specific process we have termed learning, acquisition, or mastery. Another necessary condition is that the individual's relationships to the world of human objects be mediated by his relationships with people, so that these relationships are included in the process of exchange. This is what one always finds to be the case; indeed, the notion of the individual, the child, face to face with the objective world, is a completely artificial construct. The child is not simply thrown into the human world; he is introduced and guided in this world by people in his environment.

The objective role and need for social contact in human development has been studied adequately enough in psychology so that there is no necessity for us to dwell on it here. Thus, exchange in its initial form, that of joint activity, or the form it assumes in the contact made through speech, constitutes the second necessary condition in the process whereby individuals learn to master the achievements made during the course of mankind's social and historical development.

To clarify further what I mean by this process, let me add that it represents one in which the individual reproduces the abilities which the species *Homo sapiens* acquired in its social and historical evolution. Hence what is accomplished, on the animal level, through the effect of biological inheritance is achieved on the human level through learning, a process which can be thought of as the humanizing of the child's psyche. I cannot help but agree with an idea suggested by our esteemed colleague, Professor Pieron, who, in a recent lecture on humanization, said: "At the moment of birth a child is merely a candidate for a human being, but he cannot become one in isolation; he has to be taught to be human through his contacts with people."

Indeed, whatever is distinctly human in the child's psyche takes shape during his lifetime. Even in the sphere of sensory functions, which one would think were so elementary, an actual restructuring occurs, with the result that completely new sensory abilities, as it were, are produced which are exclusively characteristic of man.

The development of new, and distinctly human, capacities in auditory perception was thus the subject we selected for experimental research.

Frequency and Tonal Discrimination

Animals have neither articulate tonal speech nor music. The world of speech sounds and of tones used in music are strictly human creations. As distinct from natural sounds, those of speech and music form distinct systems with special formants and constants that are intrinsic to them. These formants and constants must be of such a nature that they can appear distinct to human hearing.

As we know, specific timbres or tone qualities are the major formants and constants in speech sounds (I have in mind nontonal languages), or to put it differently, the characteristics of the speech sound's spectra. The basic frequency of these tones, however, does not perform a sense-discriminating function; when we comprehend speech sounds, we are generally not concerned with their frequency.

The situation with regard to musical tones is different, their chief formant being pitch, and their constants consisting of sound-pitch relationships. Accordingly, the kind of hearing used to comprehend speech sounds is based on a perception of timbre, while musical hearing is tonal, that is, it requires a capacity to distinguish pitch and pitch relationships in a complex of sounds.

It was precisely the latter type of hearing we studied in our laboratory. We began with a very simple task: we wanted to measure the thresholds of pitch discrimination for two successive tones that were presented to our subjects. But right at this point we ran into substantial difficulties. Successful measurements depended upon our subjects' comparing the two tones according to the desired parameter, which in this case was basic frequency. However, as was demonstrated numerous times, owing to certain physico-physiological causes, any tone, even a sinusoidal tone, is perceived as having a tone quality which changes with a change in pitch. For example, high tones were perceived as "clearer" and lower tones as "dimmer" or "heavier." Consequently, for our purposes, we could not confine the procedure to the classical method for measuring thresholds of tonal hearing. We had to find a new method which would eliminate the effect that minute shadings of tone color elements had on subjects' evaluation of the basic frequencies of the tones they were to compare.

We managed to devise such a method. This amounted to presenting for a comparison of pitch two successive tones with different sound spectra One of these, the constant, approximated the Russian vowel sound *u* in its spectrum; the other, the variable, resembled the long *e* sound. The sounds lasted for the duration of a second, the interval between them being 0.5 seconds, and the level of intensity 60 db. The experiments were carried out according to a scheme known as the "method of constant stimuli," with frequency zones ranging from 200 to 400 cps.

In the method described, which I will term a "comparative" method, a subject had to deal with a peculiar kind of task: he had to compare sounds of types *u* and *e* strictly according to their basic frequency, apart from their spectrum. A task such as this, which is characteristic of the processes involved in listening to music, in a certain sense, is antithetical to the kind of task related to hearing timbre in speech sounds.

We used this method after we had measured the thresholds according to the classical method, having subjects compare the pitch of tones having the same tone quality. Thus, we obtained two thresholds for each subject, one based on the customary method of testing, the other on the one we had devised. I will refer to the former by the conventional term, the "differential threshold," and the latter by the term "threshold of discrimination."

We began by measuring both these thresholds in 93 adult subjects who ranged in age from 20 to 35 years. Some of the results we obtained in this first series of experiments, in which we divided the subjects into three groups, are as follows. In the first group (which comprised 13 per cent of the subjects), the shift to experiments using sounds with different tone qualities did not produce a change in the thresholds. In the second and largest group (57 per cent of the subjects), the thresholds of discrimination increased by comparison with the differential thresholds. Subjects in the third group (30 per cent) proved to be totally incapable of performing the task of comparing the sounds *u* and *e* according to basic frequency; the sound *e* was always perceived as higher, even when it was actually more than an octave lower than the sound *u*. This held true despite our having gone through elaborate explanations of the task and demonstrated it to these subjects many times.

Subjects in the last group thus demonstrated a peculiar type of tone deafness which the classical method of measuring thresholds had completely masked, a fact which is clearly evidenced by the lack of correlation between the magnitude of the thresholds as measured by both methods. In experiments using the classical method, subjects in this last group apparently did not compare the sounds according to basic frequency (that is, according to musical pitch) but in terms of their general characteristics, including the minute tone-color elements which, it seems, were dominating factors for these subjects.

Let us turn now to the first group of subjects, who showed no increase in the thresholds when the shift was made to evaluating the pitch of the sounds *u* and *e*. These were subjects who had good tonal hearing; when we collected additional information on our subjects, it appeared that these were people who had a certain degree of musical ability.

The second group of subjects occupied an intermediate position between the first and third groups. For part of the subjects in this group the thresholds of discrimination were less than two times greater than the differential thresholds, which indicated that their capacity for tonal hearing had developed adequately. Conversely, the threshold of discrimination for other subjects in this group exceeded the differential thresholds by far; the results for these subjects approximated those of the group who revealed that they were tone deaf.

These were the results we obtained in the first series of experiments. They posed a number of questions on which we undertook to do further research.

Cultural Differences in Tonal Hearing

To begin with, we wanted to find out why a considerable number of the subjects had failed to develop a capacity for tonal hearing. Proceeding from the view that the ability to hear tone quality or timbre develops concurrently with mastering a language, and that tonal hearing develops in the process of learning music, we advanced the following hypothesis. It seems that if a child learns the tone qualities inherent in the sounds of his language at a very early age, this necessarily leads to a rapid development of his capacity to hear tone qualities of speech sounds. But this may have the effect of delaying the development of strictly tonal hearing. The latter idea seems even more probable when we consider that a highly developed capacity to hear verbal sounds can compensate, to some degree, for an inadequate development of tonal hearing. Hence, if the conditions of an individual's life are such that they do not require him to distinguish sound complexes according to their basic frequency, he may not develop a capacity for tonal hearing and will remain tone deaf.

But could this hypothesis be verified—even indirectly? We attempted to do this, assuming that if our hypothesis were correct, subjects whose native language happened to be one of the tonal languages (i.e., one in which purely tonal elements perform a sense-discriminating function) could not possibly be tone deaf, for in mastering their native language they would simultaneously have had to develop a capacity for tonal hearing.

Indeed, experiments conducted with twenty Vietnamese (Vietnamese is a tonal language) produced the following results: for 15 out of the 20 subjects in the experiment, the shift to comparing tones of different quality either did not result in any increase in the thresholds or merely produced an increase which was not significant. Only 5 of the subjects showed a more significant increase in the thresholds, but it happened that 4 of them were from the central regions of Vietnam, where the population speaks a language in which tonal elements play a less important role. *However, we did not encounter a single instance of tone deafness or a very sharp increase in the thresholds of discrimination in this group of subjects.*

These results, incidentally, are fully in agreement with a fact noted by Professor Taylor of Capetown. As he put it: "Despite the absence of any physiological defects, tone deafness proves to be a common phenomenon in England and America, but is practically unknown among African tribes whose languages entails intoning vowel sounds."

To be sure, the results we obtained in experiments with the Vietnamese subjects did not provide direct proof that our hypothesis was correct. But how is it possible to obtain direct proof that sensory abilities which meet the needs of dealing with the world of phenomena created by society are not innate in man but develop during his lifetime—that these sensory abilities result from having learned certain of the facts pertinent to these phenomena? Obviously, there is only one way this can be done: to attempt to develop an ability of this type under laboratory conditions. This, then, is what we undertook to do.

Training in Tonal Hearing

In order to develop a process, one has to have some preliminary notion about its structure, about the physiological mechanism it will entail. At present, there are, as we know, two points of view on the general mechanism of sensory processes. One of these, an earlier view, holds that sensation occurs when stimulation is transmitted from a receptor organ to sensory zones. The other, antithetical view, which was established in the nineteenth century by the eminent Russian physiologist Sechenov, holds that sensory processes necessarily include, as part of their structure, motor acts and their proprioceptive signalization. We adopted the latter view and were thus inclined to accept the idea Köhler proposed in 1915, to the effect that there is an intimate connection between stimulation of the auditory nerve and innervation of the organs used in vocalization. We therefore prepared to study the role of vocal motor activity in distinguishing the basic frequency of sounds, using this idea, as well as data from a number of contemporary research studies and some of our own observations as a basis.

We continued the experiments with our subjects, measuring their thresholds for "precision of vocalization" (intonation) of a given pitch within a range that was suitable for each subject. I will not dwell here on the techniques employed in these experiments but will note only that the measurements were obtained through the use of an oscillograph.

As a result of the measurements we had taken, we found that there was a high correlation (0.83 ± 0.03) between the magnitude of the thresholds of discrimination of basic frequency and the mean error of the vocalization of that pitch. What does this relationship signify? Does the degree of precision of intonation depend upon the degree to which basic frequency is discriminated precisely, or is the reverse true—that precise discrimination depends upon precise intonation?

Results of experiments which involved the following procedures supplied us with answers to these questions. We repeated experiments using the comparative method with those subjects who had not developed a capacity for tonal hearing, but included one additional feature. We asked subjects to intone the pitch of tones presented to them in full voice (they sang them aloud). As a result, every time we included the use of vocalization in the method, the threshold of discrimination dropped for all subjects.

Let me cite two of the most significant cases. Here are the results we obtained for subject 59 who belonged to the second, intermediate group. I will indicate the threshold values in *tsents* (*ts*) that is, units of the musical logarithmic scale which are equal to 1/200 of a tone.

In the first experiment (i.e., without singing) the threshold of discrimination was equal to 385 *ts*. In the second, when singing was introduced, the threshold dropped more than four times—to 90 *ts*. In the third experiment (without singing) the threshold was 385; in the fourth (with singing) it once again dropped to 90. Finally, in the fifth experiment (without singing) the threshold increased to 335 *ts*.

Let me turn now to the second case. This concerns results obtained on subject 82, one of the group of persons who were tone deaf. In the first, third, and fifth experiments, which were conducted without singing, this subject could not judge correctly the relative pitch of tones having different qualities, even when there was a difference of 1200 *ts* between them. However, in experiments using singing (the second and fourth), he was able to compare the sounds according to their basic frequency, and his thresholds were equal to 135 *ts* (which, given a range of 300 cps, amounts to about 22 cps).

Thus, the inclusion of vocal activity (singing) in the process whereby the basic frequency of a tone is perceived produced a distinct drop in the thresholds of discrimination. In order to confirm this hypothesis, we conducted several control and supplementary experiments which space will not permit me to discuss here. I need only say that they fully confirmed our conclusion about the decisive role played by the activity of the vocal apparatus in discriminating basic frequency of tones.

Using this idea as our point of departure, we moved on to experiments in which the aim was to develop strictly tonal hearing in those subjects who had failed to develop this capacity. Naturally, the subjects with whom we were dealing in these experiments exhibited various distinct features as individuals, the chief difference being that they did not all start out on the same level. To begin with, there were among them subjects who could not "tune" their voice correctly to a tone (using a calibrating device that was fed by an electric generator). We began by trying to "attune" them to this process. The experimenter would point out to a subject that he had not intoned a sound correctly, would encourage him in his attempts to alter the pitch of the tone in the right direction, and would, of course, point out to him the moment at which the pitch he had vocalized coincided with that of the tone coming from the calibrating device. Usually this type of "attuning" required two to six sessions; these training experiments were carried out with a total of 11 subjects.

The overall result of these experiments was that, once we had gone through them with the subjects, there were sharp drops in the thresholds of discrimination, particularly in those cases where subjects had learned to tune their voices correctly. Here are several instances of the results we obtained:

Subject 2: threshold of discrimination before the experiments—690 *ts;* after the experiments—60 *ts.*

Subject 7: before the experiments—1105 *ts;* after the experiment—172 *ts.*

Subject 9 turned out to be an interesting case. His initial threshold was also very high—1188 *ts,* and although he managed to attune his singing, nevertheless it appeared that after the experiments the value of his threshold remained at practically the same level—more than 1000 *ts.* However, when the experimenter suggested to him that in comparing the tones he use his ability to sing their pitch at full voice, his threshold of discrimination dropped five and one-half times.

Cases such as these are significant in that they allow us to single out another stage in the development of the individual's capacity for tonal hearing. A subject has to be able not merely to tune his voice to the tone he hears; it is essential, too, that he incorporate this procedure in the very act of perceiving the pitch of a tone. When a subject is given tones that are within his singing range and asked to sing them out loud, he can always manage to do this.

The next stage in the development of tonal hearing consisted of a shift to an experiment in which subjects had to discriminate pitch without singing the tones in full voice—that is, they had to remain silent while listening to tones that were beyond their singing range. By way of an example, let me cite the case of subject 9, whom I mentioned earlier. His threshold of discrimination dropped only when conditions permitted singing at full voice. Subsequently, we were able to obtain a sharp reduction in this subject's threshold (which initially was more than 1000 *ts*) under conditions which did not permit singing the tones aloud.

The basic method we used to shift subjects to this later stage consisted of the following procedures. After we had fully attuned a subject's voice to the pitch of the tone from the calibrating device and singing at full voice had been included in the process whereby subjects compared tones according to pitch, we suggested that they not begin to vocalize the pitch until the tone coming from the calibrating instrument had been cut off. As our analysis indicated, we had not simply excluded vocal activity at the moment a tone was heard, but merely delayed it, transforming it into an act whereby the subject, as a preliminary, soundlessly tuned his vocal apparatus to the pitch of the tone from the calibrator.

In this way we isolated from a process that was essentially one involving performance ("Sing the pitch given") a strictly orienting function ("What pitch?"). In fact, the process of modifying the functions of vocal motor activity constitute the key point in the development of tonal hearing. It also amounts to the act through which the ability to get some working notion of pitch is engendered.[1] As Teplov pointed out in his outstanding work on musical ability, this aptitude is always bound up with vocal motor activity.

We can say, then, that we succeeded in our attempt and managed to develop in subjects who earlier had proved incapable of distinguishing strictly musical pitch, the ability to do this. However, were we correct in attributing the results we had obtained to our having included vocal activity in subjects' perception of tones? As we know, thresholds of discrimination can be greatly improved simply by training subjects with sounds that have the same tone color.

Taking this into account, we undertook one additional series of experiments. We started a program of training with a group of subjects to try and get them to discriminate the pitch of simple sounds. As was true with other experimenters, we found this resulted in a sharp reduction of the thresholds for these tones. As for the values of the thresholds of discrimination measured before and after purely "sensory" training of this kind, it appeared that in seven out of nine cases they had not changed at all, and although in two cases there was a drop in the thresholds, this proved to be insignificant. The conclusion to be drawn from this is obvious: Unless vocal activity is included in the receptor system, the capacity to judge tones properly does not develop.

The Role of Feedback

During the course of the research I have described, we had an opportunity to obtain a more detailed conception of the actual mechanism involved in tonal hearing. For a person to be able to discriminate pitch, the effect of a sound complex upon the hearing organ has to produce not only unconditioned reflex reactions of an orienting and adapting type, but must also stimulate activity of the vocal apparatus. However, can this activity be generated through the mechanism of a simple sensory motor act? This idea seems unwarranted in that, as we have seen, it is not until either external or internal intoning is included in the perceptive act that the basic frequency of the sound complex is distinguished. In other words, the intoning of sounds does not merely reproduce the sounds or tones perceived, but becomes part of the intimate internal mechanism involved in the very process of percep-

1. *Editors' note:* This procedure is similar to the operant conditioning technique of fading. It is interesting to note that the effect of the technique here is ascribed in large part to its inducing the appropriate orienting responses rather than the shaping of an instrumental response.

tion. With respect to musical pitch, this activity performs the function of orienting a person so that he can discriminate pitch and make a comparative estimate of it.

We attempted to trace the dynamics of this process. Hence, when we measured the thresholds of discrimination, we recorded the frequency of the tone coming from the calibrator along one channel of the oscillograph and, along the other, the frequency sung by the subject. The high speed at which the film (on which the recordings were made) moved, allowed us to measure the frequency sung for minute segments of time (10 milliseconds each).

After processing the data we had obtained in experiments with 40 subjects, we found that the frequency intoned only gradually approximated that of the tone in effect at the moment. In some cases there was a considerable discrepancy observed—100 cps or more; in other cases the discrepancy was far smaller (e.g., 40 cps or, at times, only 10). The amount of time required to "tune" the voice to the frequency of the tone in effect also varied (1–0.1 seconds). The chief fact noted in these experiments was that, as soon as the frequency sung approximated that of the tone, it immediately stabilized itself.

Taking these and certain other data into account, one can conceive of the mechanism involved in tonal hearing as one which operates according to the system of the "comparator" MacKay described in 1957. This system provides for evaluating the incoming signal through the effect of a counter, "imitative" process which, as it were, "tests this out." According to this system, the mechanism that operates to compare the pitch of two tones can be illustrated in this way: after the process of intoning has tuned itself to the frequency of the first of the sound stimuli compared and become stable, the effect of a second stimulus changes the pitch intoned once again until it coincides with the frequency of the second stimulus. If the change involves a shift to a greater frequency, the second sound stimulus is perceived as higher; if it entails a shift in the opposite direction, the sound appears to the subject as a lower tone. It seems probable that the degree of change is basic to a subject's evaluation of the size of the interval.

The Training of Functional Perceptual Systems

I will now discuss the last experiments we did. Our intention was to create under laboratory conditions those functional systems of perception which do not develop under ordinary circumstances. We felt this was the only way we could obtain definitive experimental proof of our hypothesis. There were two tasks to be undertaken. One was to substitute another receptor organ for the auditory receptor used in tonal hearing. But in doing this it was essential that the effector apparatus which discriminates frequency, the apparatus used to intone sounds, continue its function. But what receptor could substitute for the organ of hearing? Obviously, only one which would respond to stimuli having the parameter of frequency. The organs which experience sensations of vibration are receptors of this type.

The sense of mechanical vibrations exhibits one peculiar feature that is particularly important for us: a change in another parameter, that of intensity (amplitude), influences the perception of frequency of vibrations. The greater the amplitude, the smaller the frequency appears to be, and vice versa. Hence, in comparing vibratory stimuli according to frequency, subjects usually do not become oriented strictly to the frequency of the vibrations but to the differences in the interval between them—to the "overall" quality of the vibrations. Thus, we were able to use our "comparative" method to measure thresholds of sensitivity to vibrations.

The conditions of the experiment were as follows. The vibrations of a rod from a noiseless vibrator were transmitted to the tip of the subjects' index finger; the surface of the rod in contact with the finger measured about 1.5 mm. in diameter. Measurements were carried out within a frequency zone ranging from 100 to 160 cps; the ratio of the amplitude of the vibrations in the measurement of thresholds of discrimination was 1:2.

First we measured the differential thresholds to stimuli having the same amplitude. Then, by comparing the frequency of stimuli having a different amplitude, we measured the "thresholds of discrimination." As one might expect, the latter were always two to four times greater than the differential thresholds.

The subjects' task was to include the activity of their vocal apparatus in gauging the frequency of mechanical vibrations, that is, according to the system of "comparison" I described earlier. All the subjects who participated in these experiments had adequate tonal hearing.

The experiments were carried out in the same order as those we did on hearing. At the same time, the process by which we were developing this new functional system of perception had several distinct features, the primary difference being that the most difficult stage was that of "attuning" the voice (the singing of the frequency of vibration acting upon the subject). This task struck the subjects at first not only as unexpected but as "unnatural"; some even thought it impossible. It proved even more difficult to include vocalization in the task of comparing vibratory stimuli, and this required a considerable number of sessions. However, by using some additional techniques, we were able to overcome these difficulties. The result of this work was that the thresholds of discrimination on the frequency of mechanical vibrations sharply declined. The following are some numerical data from the experiments:

Subjects 1 and 2: the initial threshold of discrimination (in *tsents*) was 700; after the experiments—246 (that is, almost three times less);

Subject 3: initial threshold 992; after the experiments—240 (four times less);

Subject 4: initial threshold 1180; after the experiments—246 (almost five times less).

Thus a new functional system had been formed and begun to "operate."

While the experiments I have just described were being carried out in our laboratory, A. Yoshpe performed another series of experiments. These had the reverse task of introducing another "comparator"—another effector apparatus—into the functional system of perception: namely, tonic stress of the arm muscles. But this had to be done without changing the receptor.

This proved to be a more complicated task. It not only required a special apparatus, but more important, an extensive period of work with each subject. The experiments were carried out with people who had clearly indicated they were tone deaf.

A device designed especially for the experiment was used. Pressure applied to the plate of this device (which, in fact was stationary) produced an even change in the frequency generated, which was then transmitted to a frequency gauge, an oscillograph, and ear phones. The amount of pressure on the plate and the frequency generated by the device were interconnected (within certain fixed ranges) by a linear function; this made it possible to indicate the amount of pressure on the plate by the number of vibrations generated, measured in cycles per second.

The task during this first stage of the work was to get subjects to form a conditioned link between the frequency of the sound operating and the level of static muscular stress in the arm muscles. Three subjects participated in the experiments.

The stimulus presented to the subjects was a pure tone (100–150 cps), to which they were supposed to react by pressing with their hands. The experimenter evaluated each reaction and encouraged the subject each time the amount of pressure he had applied coincided with the frequency of the tone that was conditionally linked with it.

As a result of these experiments (which were continued for twenty-five to thirty-three 40-minute sessions), the conditioned link "pitch of tone—degree of muscular stress" was developed in all of the subjects. A comparison of the mean error of muscular reaction after the first session and at the end of the experiments yielded the following (in terms of arbitrary units): subject K—65 and 1; subject B—65 and 5; subject L—25 and 10.

We also established that with the shift to tones of different timbre (*u, e, a*), the auditory-proprioceptive link which had been developed remained fully intact. This important phenomenon confirms that the muscular reaction and its proprioceptive signals were definitely related to the basic frequency of a tone. But was it the case that the muscular stress of our subjects was a function of pitch discrimination?

In order to determine this, we measured the thresholds of discrimination, and obtained the following figures:

Subject K: threshold of discrimination before training—1994 *ts;* after training—248 *ts.*

Subject B: before training—1615 *ts;* after training—248 *ts.*

Subject L: before training—828 *ts;* after training—422 *ts.*

Thus, after training, the thresholds of discrimination were lowered, although during the course of these experiments, subjects had not been given any practice in discriminating pitch. We were therefore inclined to explain the drop in the thresholds by the fact that the subjects' mechanism of perception had included a link between the pitch of a tone and the degree of muscular stress. At the same time we had to consider that, in the case of two of our subjects (K and L), given the high degree of precision of the conditioned muscular reactions they had achieved, the decrease in their thresholds of discrimination was not very great: altogether, it amounted to one-half the value it had earlier.

What was the explanation for this? We had begun to surmise that in the case of these two subjects, when the shift was made to the more complicated task of comparing tones of different timbre, something had gone wrong with the functioning of the link that had developed. Hence, we continued experiments with these subjects and found that, although there was no substantial change in their degree of precision of muscular stress, there were nevertheless sharp decreases in their thresholds of discrimination. Thus, subject K's threshold of discrimination was six times less and subject L's almost nine times less than what it had been earlier.

I attach considerable significance to this fact. It appears that after the "skeletal framework" of a given functional system is constructed, one other transformation must occur. The effect of this concealed, internal transformation is that, prior to the "performing" function it achieves, there is an orienting, reflecting function which substitutes for it, and the entire system thus becomes interiorized.

There remains for me now to bring up the last question this research raised: Could we really maintain that this experimental work had developed in our subjects an artificial mechanism of tonal hearing in which the arm muscles performed the role of the vocal apparatus? I will attempt to answer this by citing data we obtained from a control experiment.

In measuring the thresholds of discrimination for these control subjects, we required the subject to carry out an irrelevant task with the muscular apparatus of the arms in one case, and the vocal apparatus in another. It appeared that there was no question but that the former upset the subjects' discrimination of pitch, while the latter did not produce any noticeable change in the process. We could consider, then, that we had succeeded in developing this second functional receptor system.

This functional system, like the one I described above, is merely a product of laboratory conditions and apparently can only function for relatively simple tasks. The limited capacities of these artificial systems can be explained by the lack of certain necessary morphological elements. However, our experiments did not presume to indicate the possibility of developing capacities which generally are not characteristic of man. Our aim was merely to verify experimentally the mechanisms whereby functional systems of perception are formed.

Conclusions

Earlier scientific views invariably linked one or another psychological ability or function with the existence of correspondingly specialized, biologically inherited brain structures. This view was thought to hold also for those abilities which originated during man's social and historical development. Certainly it is essential to a scientific viewpoint that it maintain that every psychological function results from the activity of a distinct organ or organs. On the other hand, as I mentioned above, the abilities and functions which answer needs relative to distinctly human achievements cannot become fixed through morphological processes.

The controversy which has persisted on the nature of these abilities led us to advance the idea that specifically human abilities and functions are developed as the individual learns and masters the world of human objects and phenomena, that their material substratum is comprised of the stable systems of reflexes which take shape during one's lifetime. And while the development of complex reflex systems are to be found in animals, it is only in man that these become genuinely functional organs of the brain and are formed ontogenetically.

This fact has enormous significance. Were I asked what I consider to be the most important results of the humanizing of the brain, I would say it is *the transformation of the cortex into an organ which is capable of forming organs.*

The description I have given here deals with the formation of functional organs of only one relatively elementary type. Naturally, the process by which brain systems which perform the acts of "discerning" logical or mathematical relationships develop takes a different course. Nonetheless, as the material from an entire aggregate of research studies indicates, it is possible to isolate certain distinctive features common to all functional organs that develop ontogenetically.

The first is that, once these organs have developed, they function as a single organ. Hence, from a subjective, phenomenological standpoint, the processes they perform appear to manifest elementary innate abilities. Examples of processes such as these are to be found in the immediate grasp people have of spatial, quantitative, or logical structures (gestalts).

The second distinct feature these organs have is their stability. Although their development is the result of the closing of links established within the brain, these links do not become extinguished as do ordinary conditioned reflexes. It will suffice to point out by way of an example that the ability to visualize forms one has learned through touch—an ability which, as we know, develops ontogenetically—is not extinguished many years after the loss of sight, although there is no reinforcement of the corresponding links, this being impossible during blindness. This fact was recently demonstrated not only clinically but also through electrophysiological methods.

The third feature peculiar to the functional organs we have been discussing is that they develop differently than do simple chains of reflexes or so-called "dynamic stereotypes." The links which constitute them do not merely trace the order of external stimuli, but combine both the independent reflex processes and their motor effects in a single reflex act of a complex nature. At the start, "composite" acts of this type always have elaborate external motor components; subsequently these are deferred and, by changing its initial structure, the act as a whole becomes more contracted and automatic. As a result of these successive transformations, a stable constellation appears which functions as a complete organ—as though it were an innate ability.

Lastly, the fourth feature these functional organs exhibit is that, while they may perform one and the same task, their structures may differ. This feature was brought out with particular emphasis in the last series of experiments we did, and it can be explained by the almost unlimited possibility for compensation one finds in the development of distinctly human functions.

I think that introducing the concept of functional organs, as we have, makes it possible to shift the problem of the biological and social aspects of human psychological processes to the plane of precise facts which can be established under laboratory conditions. I also believe that the systematic research we started on developing these organs and the abilities related to them permits certain important general deductions even at this stage of investigation.

The main conclusion to be drawn from this work is that biologically inherited characteristics do not determine psychological abilities in man. In effect, the individual's capacities are not lodged in his brain. The brain virtually does not incorporate within it distinctly human abilities of one sort or another, but merely the capacity to develop these abilities. In other words, biologically inherited characteristics in man amount to only one of the conditions necessary for him to develop psychological functions and abilities—a condition, to be sure, which plays an important role. Thus, while these systems are not determined by biological characteristics they are nonetheless dependent upon them.

Another condition essential to the development of these functions is the world of objects and phenomena man finds himself in, a world which has been created by countless generations of people through work and struggle. *This world imparts to man that which is truly human.*

Thus, if, on the one hand, we distinguish the form of higher psychological processes in man—the purely dynamic features which depend upon their morphological "factor"—and, on the other, the content of these processes—their structure and the function they fulfill—we can say that the former are biologically determined and the latter socially. Surely there is no need to emphasize that it is the content which is decisively important.

In conclusion, I want to bring up another position that I strongly adhere to. As I mentioned several times, the process of mastering or learning the world of objects and phenomena created by people during the history of society is one in which the individual develops distinctly human abilities and functions. It would be a gross error, however, to regard this process as the result of conscious activity, or as the effect of "intentionality" in the sense that Husserl and others understand this. Learning takes place through the subject's very relationships with the world, and these do not depend either upon the subject or his conscious awareness, but are determined by the specific historical and social conditions in which he lives, and the way his life takes shape within them.

Thus the problem of the prospect of man's psychological development, of the development of mankind in general, is primarily one of providing for a sound, equitable way to structure human society so that in actual practice each individual has the opportunity of mastering what has been achieved by the progress of history, and of making his own creative contribution to these achievements.

I have devoted this chapter to the problem of the biological and social aspects of man's psychological processes and abilities not simply because I have been working on the problem for many years. My reason for selecting this subject is that even now views persist to the effect that the human psyche is directly, fatally, conditioned by biological inheritance. These views have engendered ideas of racial and national discrimination in psychology, and a sanction for genocide and wars of extermination. They are a threat to the peace and security of mankind. Hence, I considered it my duty to point out once again that such views blatantly contradict the objective data of scientific psychological research, and to add to the data already acquired that of the experimental work done in our laboratory.

Reference

Leont'ev, A. N., and Zaporozhets, A. V. *Rehabilitation of hand function*. New York: Pergamon Press, 1960.

16

Methods for Developing Physiology as Related to the Problems of Cybernetics

N. A. Bernshtein

EDITORS' INTRODUCTION

Before his death in 1966, Bernshtein was a leading patriarch of Soviet physiology. He is best known for his work on the physiology of movement, for which he won government recognition.

Bernshtein was a very early critic of the Pavlovian theory of conditioning and a forerunner of those contemporary psychophysiologists (such as Anokhin in the U.S.S.R. and Pribram in the United States) who emphasize the role of feedback mechanisms in the control of behavior. For many years this "cognitive" physiology was unpopular in the U.S.S.R. It is now widely accepted, although traditional psychophysiology has many powerful adherents.

In 1965 the competition of "cybernetic" and Pavlovian psychophysiology was symbolized by Anokhin's election to full membership in the Academy of Science, whereas Asratyan, the unofficial leader of more orthodox Pavlovianism, remained a corresponding member.

This chapter, which appeared as an article in Biological Aspects of Cybernetics *in 1962, represents Bernshtein's programmatic attempt to incorporate such concepts as "purpose" and "models of future consequences" into a materialistic physiology.*

His ideas, although framed in biological language, have been extremely influential in psychology.

THE TASK of this chapter is to examine generally the fundamental advances which physiology and all biological sciences are making in our time. To establish clearly the relations between these advances and ideas and interests and the already secure place occupied by theoretical cybernetics in science, we shall treat the term "cybernetics" not as the doctrine of Wiener, Shannon, and Ashby, but rather as a new branch of science, engendered in our times under the pressure of necessity, whose study is associated with the general problems of control theory, information theory, and communications theory. This new science must be developed from the strict postulates of dialectical materialism. We hope to indicate the many connections between theoretical cybernetics, as properly understood, and the most urgent problems of modern physiology.

The new problems arising from 1920 to the present mark the end of the nineteenth century as what may rightly be called the classical period of the development of physiology. Starting with the work of Flourens, Bell, and Magendie, before which almost nothing had been done, physiology was able to accumulate a huge storehouse of knowledge about all aspects of vital human and lower animal activity. By the end of its classical period, physiology had developed a well-thought-out scientific philosophy based on the natural, mechanical materialism of that period. This philosophy was progressive and successfully resisted attacks of idealists and vitalists.

But, inevitably, a scientific doctrine sooner or later finds itself unable to incorporate newer and deeper facts; the role of natural mechanistic materialism as a scientific methodology has died out in our times. The first approximations to scientific truth, which were achieved in the classical period of physiology, must now be replaced by new and more precise approximations that will in turn probably be superseded in the next century.

If we consider the chief area of interest and progress in modern physiology as compared with classical physiology, the most characteristic shift in interest has been from the lower to the higher animal organisms. Beginning with pigeons and frogs, physiology has gradually climbed all the way up the phylogenetic ladder from the cat to the dog, the monkey, chimpanzee, and finally to man. Human physiology was almost uninvestigated in the nineteenth century.

From the study of elements of organs and functions we have gone on to a study of entire systems of organs and even to the study of complicated behavioral functions and interactions with the environment. In classical physiology, a state of immobility was essential for an analysis of the atoms and elements of functions. This immobility was generally brought about by means that varied with the type of animal and the conditions of the experiment: for example, decapitation, decerebration, narcosis, or a restraining device. The new physiology is shifting its attention more and more toward the study of active working states. In accordance with the rough types of physical labor which were dominant at the beginning of our century, the first scientific achievements of the study of man's activity were expressed in the form of the energetics of labor, the hygiene of physical labor, biomechanics, the theory of physical training, and so forth. However, the rapid development of technology inevitably led to a situation in which these branches of applied physiology were replaced by the study of intellectual forms of human labor in relation to the machine; it is now necessary to investigate those activities which require a maximum mobilization of attention and self-control. For example, we now study the working conditions of the astronaut, the pilot of supersonic airplanes, and so forth.

One can readily see, even from this initial survey, the extent to which the problems arising in connection with these new trends in physiology are in keeping with the problems that confront theoretical cybernetics. This fact alone indicates the potential usefulness of the great array of concepts and mathematical methods—and the practical electronics—that have developed out of the current so-called weak communications technique that cybernetics brings to the service of important physiological investigations.

Critique of the Reflex Arc Conception

The leading principle of classical physiology was the reflex arc. Its positive methodological characteristics have long been fully appreciated: it permits a comprehensive, materialistic determinism and the clear formulation of the basic problem of physiology. This problem was defined as finding the laws of the input-output relationship of the organism and its environment, the formulation of what is now called the transfer function. This approach had, as its final objective, the precise treatment of an organism as a highly organized reacting machine.

The chief methodological fallacy of an arc terminating at the periphery was not perceived by the adherents of mechanistic materialism. Atomism, the firm belief that the whole is always the sum of its component parts and nothing more, made it easy to tolerate many simplifications which have not withstood the impact of new facts in modern methodology. Acceptance of atomistic philosophies made it possible to treat whole organisms as an assembly of cells (Virchov, 1928); the organism's vital activity and behavior were treated as assemblies or chance sequencings of reflexes. The natural materialists failed to recognize that a reflex *is not an element of an action, but rather an elementary action,* because they underestimated the decisive fact of the wholeness and systematic nature of an organism and its functions.

It may be said that, if we rank an organism's actions in order of increasing complexity and significance, then we shall find all reflexes at that end of the series which is associated with the most complicated actions.

It is now recognized that a feedback principle governs the regulation and control of all of an organism's functions. This fact compels us to admit the urgent need to replace the concept of the reflex arc by that of the *reflex loop,* which includes as an essential component a continuous stream of afferent signals that are vital for control and correction. The reflex arc must be regarded as a first approximation to the actual form in which nervous processes are regulated. This approximation once played a very significant role, but the idea has now been played out.

The important and fundamental significance assigned to the shift from the structural scheme of an arc to that of a loop is not limited to acknowledging the enormous role of a controlling and correcting afferent input. Still more important is the fact that the idea of an atomized chain of elementary reflexes connected only in a sequential order has been replaced in modern physiological thinking with the theory of a *continuous* cyclical process of interaction between the changing conditions of the external and internal environments, which develops and proceeds as a whole action to its actual completion. A loop process, which includes continuous participation of effectors and receptors, can, although it differs fundamentally from an arc process, begin with equal ease at any link of its block diagram. Thus it includes a far more extensive array of manifestations of vital activity. The same fundamental loop scheme is used to represent both the processes of active perception and the coordination of purposeful motor acts; apparently the larger part of the central brain process involves intellectual activity that falls into this category.

While the reflex arc inevitably provoked the concept of a living organism as some sort of reactive machine that responded to receptor signals and stimuli, the principle of a feedback interaction focussed attention, with no less force, on the active nature of vital processes that are dominant in all forms in which the loop occurs. We shall later illustrate briefly how the principle of activity is appearing more and more clearly as a general principle of biology; first we will concentrate on the motor functions of an organism.

Motor functions constitute a basic group of processes in which the organism not only interacts with the surrounding world, but also *acts* on this world, attempting to change it in accordance with its needs. If we analyze the basis for the formation of motor acts, we find that each significant act, whether reactive or spontaneous, is a solution (or an attempt at a solution) of a definite *problem of action.* But the problem may be considered to be the result which the organism is attempting to achieve, in the sense of something *which should be, but still is not, the case.* Thus, the problem of action is some sort of model of the required future, encoded or otherwise represented in the nervous system. It is obvious that an action which is useful or significant in life cannot be programmed or realized if the brain has not created guiding prerequisites in the form of such a model of the required future. It is essential to note that this principle is applicable everywhere within the framework of the more or less complicated requirements and functions that are characteristic of each living species—primate or worm.

Considering all factors, we have here two interconnected processes. One of them is a *probabilistic prognosis* based on the perceived, current situation, and this is some sort of extrapolation for a given interval of time in the future. We shall not dwell on a more detailed analysis of these extrapolating processes and the deep synthesizing process of simulation that unifies them. This has been done by the author in articles devoted to problems of the physiology of activity (Bernshtein, 1961a, b). This probabilistic extrapolation of the course of events in the environment is accompanied by a second process—the process of *programming* actions which should lead to realization of the required future event. This programming of actions now appears to be some sort of interpolation between the current situation and that which should be achieved in the interests of a given individual.

We shall discuss briefly still another fundamentally important feature of active, purposeful activities as they are understood in modern physiology. The fact that both programming and realization of an action usually take place under conditions of internal conflict between urgency and accuracy in forecasting necessarily introduces an element of randomness in all our actions. At the same time, the actual realization of the overwhelming majority of planned, purposeful actions is invariably accomplished as a struggle or active conquest of all sorts of changeable external obstacles: uncontrolled external resisting forces, the counteractions of an antagonist, diverse auxiliary, unexpected events, and so forth. This gives rise to a situation which probably would have caused surprise or misunderstanding among the classicists: instead of the stable, determined stereotypes which they used to describe the motor acts of reflex arcs and chains of reflexes, we are faced with phenomena that should be studied from the points of view of probability theory, the theory of games and strategy, and so forth. One cannot help but note here that the application of probability theory (which was developed in leisure hours by the great mathematicians of the eighteenth century to introduce clarity into games of chance) to the most important physical problems in the theory of gases and solutions came as an equally startling development in the last century.

Mathematics undoubtedly holds the key to all new types of problems and riddles in natural science; however, each new field will require the development of its own special key unless the new application turns out to be unexpectedly similar to the old, as in the example just given. The problems which stand before physiology and general biology urgently require the creation and development of new branches of mathematics. It is possible that these will include search theory, optimization, the theory of conflict, and many others which we cannot even name now. All these approaches are either directly or indirectly connected with the problems of activity.

To complete our discussion of this aspect of the problem, it is necessary to emphasize still another fundamental difference between the classical and modern ideas on the physiology of motor acts. Although, according to the reflex arc notion, each action by an organism is merely a reaction to a situation or to a meaningful signal element from the situation, it is now becoming increasingly obvious that an organism does not simply react to a situation, but *clashes with the situation,* which is dynamically changeable, thus compelling the organism to face the need for *choice*. The physiological theory of movements provides us with ever clearer indications that reactions to a situation or to stimuli do not constitute a reaction, but rather the *act of deciding* on an action, the technical realization of which is then entrusted to subordinate, lower coordinating systems of the brain.

We shall not dwell on the point that the concept of the forecast of the future, mentioned previously as a prerequisite to every motor act, is certainly not a hypothesis constructed on the basis of general observations of behavior or psychological considerations. Experimental physiology has accumulated a whole series of facts directly associated with this. From this viewpoint, even so-called nerve-muscle tonus, with its variety of manifestations, has turned out to be a system of mechanisms for readjusting the motor apparatus and various phenomena and processes in the nervous system. This notion is reflected in ideas such as the synchronism of Lapicque (1928), mastery of Ukhtomskii's "dominant" (1952), Sherrington's regulation of spinal cord irritability, the complicated function of the reticular formation (which is only gradually being revealed), the central system of the brain, and finally all manifestations accessible to experimental observation of the so-called nerve-muscle set (Uznadze, 1961). All these concepts turn out to be components of a vast apparatus whose role is always to anticipate a movement about to be made, to modify messages to the muscles in the necessary fashion, to activate some of them and inhibit others in accordance with the forthcoming element of movement, and so forth. Attempts at a more detailed description and analysis of this apparatus for "running into the future" have been made by the author in a number of articles (Bernshtein, 1961a).

We are witness to an ever growing number of indications that the principle of activity not only is manifested in the physiological functions of the individual but is an exceedingly general factor which penetrates all aspects and forms of vital processes and is the basis of various phenomena studied in general biology.

In contrast to the assumptions of the classical period, which treated the organism as a reacting and balancing self-regulating system, contemporary biological thought regards it as an organization characterized by two chief determining properties: In the first place, this is an organization which preserves its systematic identity with itself despite a continuous flow of energy and of the material of the substrate itself. Not a single atom is retained for longer than a very short time in a human or animal organism (except for the elements of the skeleton), but the organism still maintains its identity. In the second place, in spite of all this, an organism undergoes *directed changes* at all stages of its existence. This directedness is illustrated indisputably in individual development, beginning with embryogenesis, by the fact that a thousand individuals selected at random from one species develop into individuals which have the same basic characteristics in spite of very different external living conditions. It is particularly important to mention that this directed development—the realization of a definite program for morphogenesis which is ensured by this directedness—is based on a clear-cut *activity.* This activity alone permits an organism to overcome external influences, obstacles, and hindrances in its development, so that it can achieve the normal adulthood programmed in the genotype.

This conquering activity is clearly illustrated by experiments that involve significant damage to the embryo. These are well-known experiments in which complete excision of the central part from the growth bud of an extremity (corresponding to an adult forearm), followed by the transplantation of the end bud directly onto the base of the original bud, was nevertheless followed by the normal development of the extremity with all its parts. In turning from embryogenesis to the vital activities of an adult organism, we can see evidence of a similar conquering activity in the facts of regeneration, both morphological and functional. Extensive clinical data indicate that energetic activity is shown by an organism in its struggle to overcome a pathogenic factor; a manifestation of this conquering activity is also seen in the independence of mutations from environmental conditions, a fact which makes the very possibility of the inheritability of properties and characteristics acquired during life a questionable matter.

We shall omit the problem of chromosome codes in the program for morphological development, which is now [1] under intense investigation. This chapter is directly concerned with that problem only in that the encoded program is realized with the highest degree of nonreactiveness (if we may express it in this manner); that is, it always makes available abundant stores of energy for anti-entropic structuring and complication of an organism almost independently of external conditions.

---

1. *Editors' note:* As of 1962. This and the previous statement are symptomatic of the effect of the protracted Lysenko controversy on Soviet biology. Not until the 1960's did serious genetic research become acceptable after a twenty-five-year period of eclipse.

Directing our attention to embryogenesis and morphogenesis is important in still another respect. "Looking into the future" and "programming the required future," which we discussed in respect to motor actions of an individual, appear in the clearly tangible form of chromosome triplet codes. This fact indicates that it is possible that there may be material codes in the central nervous system (perhaps organized in an entirely different way) such that both forecasts and programs of the future may be programmed into the nervous system. This picture completely removes the coating of idealist finalism from such concepts as purposefulness, singleness of purpose, and similar notions by making it possible to treat them on an irreproachably materialist basis. Here one cannot help but see one of the great services rendered by cybernetics to scientific physiology, in the sense that cybernetics provides physiologists with an entire set of valuable concepts and postulates from the theory of codes and information theory.

Thus, the facts coming in from all sides indicate that the organism as a whole, and possibly each of its cells, struggles actively for its survival, development, and reproduction. The process of life does not "seek a balance with the environment," as the representatives of the classical period of mechanism thought, but to conquer this environment. This striving for conquest is not directed toward maintaining status or homeostasis, but toward an unceasing advance in the direction of the inborn program for development and security.

Here there arises an exceedingly interesting question, which apparently embraces the entire field of biology. We shall turn to it in the briefest outline. This question is closely connected with both the theoretical principles of biological simulation and with the facts previously touched upon concerning the directed development of the individual, for which the individual struggles. Both the question itself and its ramifications require comprehensive study.

We shall begin with a number of parallels between groups of phenomena that are, outwardly, exceedingly diverse, in order to attempt to formulate the features they have in common. An oak or a maple has several thousand leaves. One will not find two perfectly congruent leaves among them, and all possible metrical criteria for judging them always yield widely varying series. Nevertheless, there is never any doubt that each given sample leaf clearly belongs either to the oak or to the maple, according to the key criteria, in spite of all the difficulty involved in formulating the criteria mathematically.

The repeated habitual movements of people are seen in their most convenient form in handwriting, which is a visible documentation. A person may write many pages, he may sign his name a hundred times, he may write on paper with a pen or write in large letters on a vertical blackboard with chalk, and so forth; in these cases we do not encounter a single pair of congruent outlines, but nevertheless all these outlines retain a very important generality, defined as the handwriting. A man who withdraws money from his savings account on his signature encounters no difficulty even though that signature actually is not congruent with the sample signature kept with the account nor with any repetitions of the signature. We can establish the same patterns for repeated cycles of all possible habitual cyclic movements with the aid of a chronocyclograph. Our intuitive perception, which is not fixed by precise formulation, creates concepts analogous to handwriting, such as a person's walk, his bulk, the timbre of his voice, his accent and the like. The same limiting of criteria is applicable to all cases; they have an indisputable identity (equivalence) with respect to some of the criteria and, in this case, noncongruence with a set of metric criteria is distributed in a variational series, sometimes with very great scattering.

The third group, which is analogous in every way to the two described above, consists of phenomena connected with the perception and recognition of *shapes*. A person can recognize without hesitation the letters of the alphabet in any script scale and style precisely because their criteria (as a rule, not metric) include subsets of important distinguishing criteria which the brain has the capacity to separate from the whole mass of criteria and to utilize for identification. Other criteria which do not play a distinguishing role can form variational series at this time which are completely analogous to those in the case of the oak leaves. This capacity of the brain to separate important shape-determining criteria makes it possible to achieve recognition in a wide variety of cases. For example, recognition of a given leaf occurs in spite of the six degrees of freedom in the variation of its projections on the human retina; a small child unfailingly recognizes a dog or a cat as such in spite of the fact that individual differences in these animals and many other factors are added to all the above-mentioned changes in form on the retina caused by projective factors only. One cannot help but mention, incidentally, that the entire secret for designing effective reading machines may be in giving them the capacity for analytical classification of the criteria of the text matter presented to them into these two groups or types of criteria.

There can hardly remain any doubt that, with all the above-mentioned parallels, we have essentially a single set of phenomena, closely interconnected in their main outlines and principles of vital activity. This homogeneity emerges as a real generality, rather than a number of superficial analogies, if we examine more closely the behavior of an organism, in all the cases we have considered, according to some particular criterion.[2]

The mutual fertilization between cybernetics and physiology began with

2. *Editors' note:* There follows a discussion of how to characterize "organization" in mathematical terms. Work on this problem has been done by the Soviet mathematicians Gel'fan, Gurfinkel, and Tsetlin (1962).

the birth of scientific cybernetics, as soon as the close relation between the key problems of physiology and those problems which cybernetics was intended to solve was revealed. This mutual assistance and collaboration of the two sciences is still in existence today; it will be sufficient to mention the brilliant advances in bionics in recent years. The entire period, which began as long ago as the first decades of our century, considerably before Wiener's first publications, was permeated with the search for and the successful use of *analogies* between living and artificial systems. These analogies continue to be of help to physiologists in considering the systematic interrelationships of an organism with the environment and to technologists in developing new and valuable ideas for the design of automatic machines.

At the same time, questions opposing this direction have been appearing more and more frequently in the literature in the last few years: Is there any important and fundamental *difference* between living and nonliving systems? If there is, then where is it and what is the dividing line which forms the still impassable boundary between the two?

Of course, we are not speaking here of such trivial differences as those in construction materials or of such quantitative differences as make the model maker of our time helpless before the fifty billion cells in the cerebral cortex. At the same time, it is completely indisputable that this material difference, if it does exist, should be wholly contained within the fundamental framework of the materialist law of the unity of the forces which control the world.

The period of physiological classicism, the entire nineteenth century, saw no way out other than the complete denial of fundamental qualitative differences between living and nonliving nature; any and every attempt to trace such a difference appeared to the materialist of the nineteenth century to be an irreversible slide down into a nonmaterialist antiscientific world. But has the time not come for returning to this problem?

Great numbers of facts, phenomena, and laws have accumulated, to an extent that scientists of preceding generations would not have imagined could exist. Some of these facts could shed new light on that astounding transition from quantity to quality which we define as the beginning of life. Where this transition appears most distinctly—on the level of the cell, or its membranes, or on the molecular or atomic levels—is still difficult to say. But on one side of this problem we shall try to point out how close this question is to the field of the biology of activity, which is the chief subject of this chapter.

One of the most characteristic features of biological activity, as we have attempted to indicate, is the dominant directedness of development and actions which is shown at all times in life and in all processes of vital activities. This preprogrammed directedness is demonstrated by the fact that the organism, which responds to every external influence capable of disrupting the course of development nevertheless continues its development and that of each of its microelements under conditions of superstability, if we may use such a term.

The investigators of the classical period did not know any of the mechanisms which would be capable of ensuring such superstability. Now we have become aware, for example, of the enormous wealth of forms and processes of catalysis, the extraordinarily highly developed and varied activities of the enzymes which reliably control the synthesis of the most complicated organic compounds, in quantities many times exceeding the amount of the controlling enzyme, and so on. Our research thinking is merely beginning to penetrate, with the aid of powerful modern means for investigation, into the depths of matter, that is, into what may be called the electron-microscope processes of life and living structures and into interaction processes created by the motion of electrons in electric and magnetic fields. It is here, in the manifestation of the great dialectical principle of conversion of quantity into quality, that one can find explanations for that stability of the biochemical synthesizing processes and that anti-entropic directedness of development which are so characteristic of life in all its stages and which have not yet been reproduced by any attempts at simulation. In what processes we shall find the true explanation of the causes and mechanisms for the unique features of living matter depicted here, and what will turn out to be the deepest essential nature of the boundary between life permeated by activity and that which appears to us today to be nonliving nature, may perhaps be shown in the very near future.

References

Bernshtein, N. A. Paths and problems in the physiology of activity. *Vop. filos.*, 1961, No. 6. (a)

Bernshtein, N. A. Pressing problems of the physiology of activity. *Probl. Kibernet.*, 1961, No. 6. (b)

Gel'fan, E. M., Gurfinkel, V. S., and Tsetlin, M. L. Physiology and the tactics for controlling complex systems. In A. M. Kyzin (Ed.), *Biological aspects of cybernetics*. Izd. Akad. Nauk SSSR, 1962. Pp. 66–73.

Lapicque, L. *L'excitabilité en fonction du temps*. Paris, 1928.

Ukhtomskii, A. A. Lability as a precondition for speed and coordination of neural events. *Trudy Fiziol. Inst. LGU*, 1952, *17*.

Uznadze, D. N. *Experimental foundations of the psychology of set*. Tbilisi: Izd. Akad. Nauk GSSR, 1961. (Also available in English, as *The psychology of set*. New York: Consultants Bureau-Plenum Press, 1966.)

Virchov, R. *Vorlesungen über Zellularpathologie*. Berlin: 1928.

17

Problems in the Psychology of Memory

A. A. Smirnov and *P. I. Zinchenko*

EDITORS' INTRODUCTION

A. A. Smirnov began his career at the Institute of Psychology in Moscow in 1918. His early work was concentrated in the area of child psychology (his textbook Psychology of the Child and Adolescent *went through four editions in the late 1920's). Like many Soviet psychologists, he was called upon to teach and to do research in applied settings; consequently he worked in the Academy of Social Upbringing and the Institute of Physical Culture as well as at the Institute of Psychology.*

Unlike many Soviet psychologists, however, Smirnov did not enter the ideological debates of the 1920's and 1930's. Perhaps because of this rather eclectic neutrality, he was appointed Director of the Institute of Psychology in 1945 and remains in that post at the present time. For the last twenty-five years Smirnov's research has been concentrated on the problems of memory.

Smirnov's colleague P. I. Zinchenko is Chairman of the Psychology Department at Kharkhov University. He is best known for his doctoral research (Zinchenko, 1962). This work was reviewed by Berlyne (1964).

The present collaborative chapter presents an overview of traditional Soviet research related to memory, with a short section covering the more recent trend toward the application of information theory to the analysis of human information processing.

Basic Methods for the Study of Involuntary Memory[1]

A psychological description of involuntary memory flows from the very essence of the reflection theory of the mind. Memory, being a reflective process by nature, from the very beginning of its development functions to orient the individual in the context of its existence and to regulate his activity on the basis of previous experience. Sechenov wrote that memory "obviously serves the animal as a guide to purposeful action—without which it could not differentiate wood from food, would confuse a tree with an enemy and in general would be unable to orient itself among surrounding objects for one minute" (1952, p. 467). Ukhtomskii also emphasized this idea: ". . . the broader the capacity and facility of memory, the sharper the organism is in its current activity and the more cautious it is in its reactions" (1940, p. 46).

Zinchenko, who carried out an early research project on involuntary remembering (1939, 1961), proceeded from the view that this kind of memory is primarily the outcome of goal-oriented behavior. Hence, in order to determine its lawful characteristics, it was essential to incorporate the to-be-remembered material in some sort of activity and not to isolate it.

The first task in such a study was to prove experimentally that involuntary remembering is a function of activity. In order to accomplish this, subjects' activity had to be so organized that in one instance the material would be the object or goal of their activity, while in another it would amount merely to background stimulation. This being the aim of the experiment, the following method was devised: 15 cards, each containing a picture of an object, served as the material for the experiment; it was a simple matter for subjects to classify these objects into 5 groups according to specific features: apple, pear, raspberry, horse, dog, rooster, etc. In addition to the pictures, each card had a two-digit number on its upper right-hand corner in India ink.

Two experiments were performed with preschool-age children, schoolchildren from elementary grades, and adults. In the first experiment an activity with the objects depicted on the cards was organized for the subjects. With the preschool-age group the experiment was conducted as a game: the experimenter provisionally arranged space on the table for a "garden," a "yard," and so forth. The children were then asked to place the cards in the most appropriate places on the table, the idea being that they would put pictures of an apple, pear, raspberry in the "garden," those of a horse, dog, rooster in the "yard," etc. The schoolchildren and adults in

1. *Editors' note:* The Russian term *zaponenanie* is variously translated as "remembering," "recall," and "memory," depending on the context.

this experiment were given a cognitive task to perform: they were to arrange the cards in groups according to the nature of the object depicted on each card. After the cards had been arranged they were removed, and the experimenter then asked the subjects to recall both the objects and the numbers depicted on each card. The preschool-age children recalled only the objects. It was the author's assumption that in this experiment the objects would be recalled but not the numbers.

In the second experiment work with the numbers was organized for the subjects. A different group of subjects was asked to arrange the same 15 cards on a board so that the numbers written on them formed an ascending order numerically. In the experiments performed with preschool-age children, each card had one of 15 objects pasted on it. Each object consisted of a combination of three forms and five colors. The same objects were pasted on the 15 squares of the board. The subjects were asked to place the cards in the squares of the board so that the objects pasted on both the cards and the squares corresponded. After they had arranged the cards in numerical order, the adult subjects were asked to recall both the numbers and the objects. The preschool-age children recalled only the objects. It was the author's hypothesis that in this second experiment the numbers ought to be recalled but not the objects.

Each of the 354 subjects was run individually according to the method described above. The same method was also adapted for a group experiment, with the following changes: in the first experiment the subjects noted down on a piece of paper the names of the groups or classifications of objects—"garden," "yard," etc; as the experimenter showed the group one card after another, he called out ordinal numbers and asked the subjects to follow along and relegate the objects to a certain group as they also grouped the ordinal numbers. Thus, if a card containing a picture of a dog was presented as "fifth," the subjects wrote this number down next to the word "yard." In the second experiment, the cards were presented on a board to a group of subjects; they were asked to compare and note down the numerical order on sheets of paper. Not only was the nature of the task used in the individual experiments preserved in those conducted with groups of subjects, but a number of the conditions which were necessary to performing the tasks were also preserved.

The group experiments were carried out with pupils ranging from the second through seventh grades, as well as with adult students. Altogether, 1,212 subjects participated in these experiments. The individual and group experiments were so arranged that the first experiment was introduced as one intended to verify their ability to classify, while the second was supposed to test their attention span.

At the end of both experiments, when subjects were asked to reproduce both the pictures and the numbers, they were completely unprepared. This was true with regard to the objects of their activity, but even more so for the background stimuli (the numbers in the first experiment, the pictures in the second). The results of these experiments are presented in two tables. Table 17–1 contains results for experiments with individual subjects, Table 17–2 those for the groups.

Table 17–1 *Recall in Experiments with Individual Subjects* *

Experiment	Objects for recall	Group				
		Preschool	Older preschool	Young school-children	Older school-children	Adults
1. Classification of objects	Objects	9.6	11.1	13.0	13.4	13.2
	Numbers	—	—	1.6	1.1	0.7
2. Compiling a numerical order	Numbers	—	—	9.9	10.3	10.2
	Objects	—	3.1	2.5	1.3	1.3

* Mean number recalled out of 15.

Table 17–2 *Recall in Group Experiments* *

Experiment	Objects for recall	School Grades						
		II	III	IV	V	VI	VII	Adults
1. Classification of objects	Objects	10.3	10.6	11.6	12.8	12.9	13.0	13.2
	Numbers	2.0	1.9	1.7	0.9	0.9	1.6	1.4
2. Compiling a numerical order	Numbers	9.0	10.1	10.5	11.9	11.9	12.0	12.0
	Objects	3.1	2.7	2.3	2.5	2.2	2.0	1.1

* Mean number recalled out of 15.

Zinchenko relates the large differences in the recall of pictures and numbers in these experiments to the fact that in one case the material constituted the goal of the subjects' activity, while in the other it was merely background material. It was concluded that work with an object represents the most general and necessary condition for people to form an image of it and demonstrate involuntary recall of it. Involuntary remembering cannot be reduced to a direct imprint, to a product of the unilateral effect of objects on sense organs. The cases in which subjects remembered the objects and numbers which had functioned merely as background stimuli not only failed to contradict this conclusion but supported it, since an analysis of these cases indicated that such retention generally pertained to some chance orientation to the material (in the same way, that is, as subjects would normally orient themselves to an actual activity). Usually this chance orientation occurred at the beginning of an experiment when subjects first entered the task. A fact that at first glance seems paradoxical is that the retention of objects and numbers (when these constituted objects of activity) increased regularly with age, while the recall of background stimuli decreased among the older subjects (see Tables 17–1 and 17–2). Observations have shown that it takes more time for preschool-age children and younger pupils to become engaged in an experimental situation than it does for the school and adult groups. Thus, the numbers in the first experiment, and the objects in the second, attracted the attention of younger subjects more often and became the objects of some side activity. The younger children showed higher percentages of recall for every one of the background stimuli.

Zinchenko (1961, pp. 158–159) pointed out that these facts suggest two types of involuntary remembering. The first is a product of goal-oriented activity (subjects remember objects they have classified or numbers after they are arranged in numerical order). A second type of involuntary remembering appears to be the product of various, frequently chance orientations which are stimulated by objects that function in the background of the situation. It is precisely this type of retention which has been studied by many psychologists abroad and is now termed "incidental learning." There have been frequent attempts to reduce all involuntary remembering to this order of learning, and as such it assumes a predominantly negative aspect. However, "incidental learning," as it is called, is in fact not incidental; it is merely one form of involuntary remembering and not a fundamental one at that. The type of involuntary remembering which is the outcome of goal-oriented activity fulfills a major function in the lives of animals and people. For animals it amounts to the most fundamental and vitally important kind of memory. It is this form of memory which has been the subject of inquiry in the subsequent research on involuntary memory.

For instance, in research done by Smirnov (1945, 1948) his subjects (psychologists well versed in introspection) were asked to remember everything that had occurred on their way to work one day. They were questioned one and one-half to two hours after arriving at work. The inquiry, of course, came at an unexpected moment. Smirnov assumed that activity which forms material for involuntary remembering is always aimed at something; hence, the task of his experiment was to trace the role that focus or intention plays in recall. The experiment demonstrated that subjects' recollections of what had happened were related primarily to the main course of their activity—the business of getting to work—and that these memories pertained mostly to what the subjects *did* as well as to whatever required a certain effort of perception or comprehension.

Pinskii (1948) obtained essentially the same results in one of his experiments. Subjects were given 45 cards, each of which had a letter of the Russian alphabet written on it. There were 9 letters in all, and each one was repeated 5 times. The subjects had been given a handbook of the Morse code to use and were asked to break the cards down into 3 groups according to the number of symbols by which one or another of the letters could be signified in Morse code (two, three, or four symbols). After the cards had been so arranged, they were shuffled and arranged in groups once again. The subjects were not asked to recall either the letters or the symbols of the Morse code. After this training, they had no difficulty breaking the cards down into the 3 groups according to the number of Morse code symbols used, but they were at a loss to say precisely which symbols designated which letters.

In another experiment, subjects placed the cards containing letters on the squares of a chart in which the same letters were written in Morse code (the subjects had a code handbook). To carry out the task assigned them, they had to rely, not only on the number of symbols for each letter, but also on the nature and distribution of these symbols. In this experiment the number of coded letters correctly remembered increased significantly. Facts such as these clearly indicate that involuntary remembering of objects occurs in cases where subjects have had to deal actively with them. When there is no active involvement with the material, subjects are not too successful in remembering it. When some retention occurs, it is usually occasioned by phenomena that are difficult to take into account when designing an experiment; thus, there are fortuitous orientations on the part of subjects to aspects of the situation other than those needed to perform the task.

The facts described above were derived under conditions in which involuntary remembering took place on the level of the second signal system.[2]

Interesting facts concerning involuntary remembering, which occurs on the level of the first signal system, were obtained in a study by Rozanova (1959). Subjects seated in a darkened room were shown cards one at a time in various places on a screen and were asked to name the object which was pictured on the card and the species to which it belonged. The subjects remembered not only the objects and their shapes but also the location of the card on the screen and the color of the objects, despite the fact that the last two features were not unique features of the objects and were not isolated consciously or purposely by the subjects. The author hypothesized that memory for location and color occurred on the level of the first signal system only, and was related to the naming of the object only via its form.

---

2. *Editors' note:* "Second signal system" is a term introduced by Pavlov in discussing human behavior. All animals are said to share a "first" signal system in which environmental stimuli, through conditioning, come to signal other stimuli. Only man has the "second" signal system, by which Pavlov meant the symbolic representation of environmental stimuli. "Second signal system" may be used synonymously with "language."

The Nature of Activity and Its Implications for Memory

Thus the task of research on memory by Soviet psychologists has been to discover the specific features of activity which will ensure the most favorable conditions for a high degree of involuntary remembering. But this necessarily entails a distinctively psychological analysis of the nature of activity.

Rozanova did not specifically analyze the kind of activity that produces an imprint on the level of a first signal system. As she pointed out, such an analysis is bound up with a detailed study of the mechanisms of perception which were beyond the scope of her research. But one point is undoubtedly true: a first-signal-system imprint of specific objects cannot be caused by the unilateral effect of these objects on sense organs. Here, again, an imprint results from the interaction of subject and object, from the subject's manifesting some activity. This interaction can occur on various levels, and can emerge in various forms of activity by the subject: in the form of involuntary, unconscious, orienting reactions, elicited by various objects and their properties; in the form of conscious orienting activity, directed at discriminating objects which enter into the content of definite tasks; and, finally, in the form of conscious actions aimed directly at attaining definite goals.

However, working with an object is not a sufficient condition for involuntary retention. It is apparent that not everything with which a person works is recalled without fail. The important problem, then, from a standpoint of method, was to find tasks in which the same material would fulfill different functions in subjects' activity: in one case it would be the goal of such activity, in another, a means towards realizing that goal. This conceptual distinction is represented in the following two basic types of manipulations.

In the first manipulation, subjects were asked to solve 5 simple arithmetical problems using one arithmetical operation (addition or subtraction) and numbers ranging up to 100. In the second manipulation subjects were given the task of thinking up 5 problems using a single arithmetical operation and numbers up to 100. In the third (control) manipulation subjects were to think up 5 arithmetic problems of the type described above, but they were also given the numbers and the arithmetical operation to be used in each of these (for example, given the numbers, they were to create problems such as 97 minus 26, etc.). The numbers given to this group were the same as those used in the first experiment. In discussing the results of this experiment we will refer to the first manipulation as "problem solving," the second as "problem inventing," and the third as "partial problem invention."

After the subjects had performed the task, they were unexpectedly asked to reproduce the problems (with the numbers used) they had been asked either to solve or to think up on their own. There were 5 problems and 15 two-digit numbers to be recalled in each experiment. Each task was given to an independent group of subjects. The subjects were first- and third-grade pupils and college students.

The rationale for this experiment was based on the following assumptions: in the first group, subjects who had already acquired the skill of adding and subtracting two-digit numbers would find these operations merely means by which to solve a problem. In the second group the subjects had to think up numbers for themselves, and this required an independent operation, focussing on the numbers as the actual goal of the activity. The third (control) group (partial problem invention) provided an intermediate type of activity.

The number of correctly recalled numbers for all groups is shown in Table 17–3. The data given are the mean number of correct recalls out of the 15

Table 17–3 *Mean Recall of Numbers for Three Different Kinds of Incidental Tasks*

Experimental manipulation	Grade			
	I	II	III	College
Solving problems	11.1	7.6	4.0	3.8
Inventing problems	12.2	—	11.0	9.7
Partially inventing problems	11.5	—	5.6	4.7

items presented for learning. From the table, it is apparent that third-grade and college-students recall for numbers was much worse when they were given problems to solve than when they were asked to think up problems on their own. This can be explained by the fact that for third-grade pupils and, to a greater extent, for college students, addition and subtraction of two-digit numbers amounts to a general skill they have solidly mastered. Hence, the use of numbers as material for arithmetical operations did not demand any special, conscious effort on their part. But when subjects had to think up numbers themselves, this activity functioned as a special *goal,* a specific operation which in and of itself prompted a higher degree of recall of numbers.

The idea that material which is related to the goal of an activity is recalled more effectively than the same material used as a means of operating toward that goal was confirmed by data from the partial problem invention condition, in which subjects did not have to invent numbers (the very factor which made for a high degree of recall in the second experiment).

Quite different results were obtained for the first-grade pupils. Addition and subtraction of two-digit numbers represented self-contained, goal-oriented operations for this group: hence, the seemingly paradoxical fact that the recall of numbers by first-graders in problem solving is almost three times greater than the corresponding indices for third-grade and college students. This confirms the view that material which is related to the goal of an activity is recalled more effectively than material which functions as a means.

The same relationship was demonstrated in a study conducted by Smirnov (1945, 1948). Students were shown 8 pairs of phrases, each of which illustrated some rule of orthography. The subjects were to recall the rule to which each pair of phrases applied and then think up another pair of phrases illustrating the same rules. They were not asked to remember the phrases. The next day the subjects were asked to remember both the phrases the experimenter had given them and those they had thought up on their own.

It turned out that the phrases thought up by the subjects were recalled somewhat more than 3 times better than those provided by the experimenter (74 as opposed to 24). As Smirnov sees it, the basis for the difference in recall is "that in the first case (example phrases), the material which was recalled functioned as a means of achieving the goal and was given in a ready form, while in the latter case (produced phrases), it amounted to the actual goal the subjects might reach through independent, active work" (1945, p. 410). The phrases which had been provided at the start of the task functioned merely as means by which to achieve the primary goal of the activity—recalling the rules of orthography. This was precisely the reason, as the author notes, "that frequently, when subjects tried to remember the phrases the experimenter had given them they recalled the rule on which these phrases were based with no difficulty, but they were unable to remember the phrases themselves" (1945, p. 409). In the second case, the rules functioned merely as means for achieving what had now become the primary goal—thinking up phrases to fit the rules.

Thus, the different types of factual material described (the numbers in Zinchenko's research, the phrases in Smirnov's) produced the same results: material which is part of the content that forms the goal of an activity is recalled significantly better than the same material when it comprises the subject matter that serves as a means whereby a goal is achieved.

Leont'ev and Rozanova (1951) attempted to study the way associative connections fundamental to involuntary retention are formed and become effective. Sixteen cardboard circles, each with a familiar word written on it, were arranged on a square board. The experiment was carried out in a darkened room, and a lamp was used to light up each of the circles in succession.

In the first group, in which subjects removed the circles from the board at the experimenter's instructions, they did not recall a single element of the situation: neither initial letters of the words, nor the words themselves, nor the place on the board from which they had removed the circles. In the second group the subjects removed all cards containing words beginning with the letter *s*. These subjects remembered the initial letter of the words in the circles they had removed, as well as the places on the board where the circles had originally been. None of the other stimuli (including the words beginning with *s*) were recalled. For the third group, in which subjects had to determine which letter the majority of words began with, they remembered all the initial letters but did not recall any of the other elements in the situation.

Leont'ev and Rozanova attributed the differences in recall to the various activities the subjects had performed in response to instructions. The different instructions activated different systems of associations so that subjects developed different orientations to the elements of the experimental situation. Subjects showed good recall of elements which determined the outcome of an activity. Subjects might also recall certain other elements of the situation. The authors broke these down into two types of stimuli: those which formed part of the background and those related to achieving the desired end.

If we sum up the results of these investigations, certain conclusions appear tenable:

1. Material which forms an integral part of the subject matter that is the goal of a specific operation produces the most recall. In this situation, the subject's orientation to the material is sustained throughout the experiment.

2. Material related to conditions for achieving a goal produces less recall. These conditions affect the means of operating with material and, as such, amount to intermediate ends with respect to the primary goal. What appears to be generally true here is that objects which constitute conditions for achieving a goal necessarily produce some orientation on the part of the subject, since they are bound up with the material involved in the operation to be performed, or with the course this operation normally takes. However, the association formed from this type of orientation may become somewhat inhibited, since it is not directly connected with the goal of the task.

3. Neutral, background stimuli, which are not related either to the subject matter or the course a particular activity normally takes, are recalled least effectively. It appears that an orientation to "novelty" in a situation is a necessary condition for the recall of background stimuli.

These statements characterize involuntary remembering as a form of memory which is dependent upon the role that a specific material occupies in an activity. It is through activity that a subject develops an orientation to his material; this, in turn, helps him achieve his end in accordance with what he has learned earlier. Most importantly this process aids the subject in consolidating material he has encountered in the new experience. These characteristic features of activity also determine the dynamics of the neural processes; ultimately, the formation and durability of certain associative connections, and the inhibition of others, rests on the neural processes which occur. However, material may fulfill a different function, depending on its objective content. In one situation more substantial material may be part of the main goal, while material with less substance functions as an intermediate goal. In another situation just the reverse might be true.

As indicated by Zinchenko's research (1956, 1961), the success of involuntary remembering is determined not only by the position that material occupies in the structure of an activity, but by the content of this material. Subjects in his experiment were given 10 series of words containing 4 words each. In one group they were asked to select a word that might be linked to the first word in each series by some conceptual relationship (for example, house–building); in the second, the words were to be linked according to some concrete connection (house–window); in the third, subjects were to select a word unrelated to the one in the series in meaning (house–fish). It appeared that words which were linked by more cogent connections (even though this was not reinforced) were recalled more successfully than others which were reinforced but had less pointed and meaningful connections between them.

The Effects of Instructional and Motivational Variables on Involuntary Remembering

What role do motives play in involuntary remembering? Zinchenko (1961, pp. 222–241) investigated the hypothesis that the effect of motivation should be treated in close connection with the material, as well as the purpose involved in a given task. Consequently, he tried to set up an experimental situation in which it was possible to trace not only the influence of various motives on the performance of the same task, but also the effect one particular kind of motive has on the performance of different tasks.

His subjects were given 15 words which they were to match with a word they had thought up on their own (they were not asked to recall these). In the first task they were to think up words which would have some specific, meaningful connection with the words the experimenter had given them (e.g., hammer–nail); in the second, the words thought up were to denote some property, state, or function of the objects designated by the words the experimenter had provided (e.g., house–wooden); in the third, subjects were to think up words beginning with the same letter as those which had been assigned (e.g., pear–pigeon).

These three tasks were motivated in two ways. In one case the motive was to test subjects' ability to solve tasks similar to those outlined (the motive being of an academic nature). The experiments were carried out with two subjects at a time, thus creating a competitive relation between them. In the other case the same tasks were set up as a game (the motive here being one of play). This part of the experiment was also conducted with two subjects, and the subject who had made the fewest mistakes was said to have won the game.

The results in terms of mean number of items recalled out of 15 are presented in Table 17–4. As is evident from the table, apart from the variations

Table 17–4 *Involuntary Recall of Words as a Function of the Nature of the Task and the Motives for Performance.*

Tasks	Preschool group		Grade II		Grade V	
	Academic	Play	Academic	Play	Academic	Play
1. According to relations between them	3.5	5.0	8.6	5.5	10.8	8.3
2. Denoting "properties"	3.0	4.2	6.4	5.0	10.0	8.0
3. Beginning with same letter	—	—	2.8	2.7	4.1	4.0

for the different age groups, there were two types of differences found in recall: those caused by the specific nature of the tasks and those attributable to the special features of the motives operating.

The relationship which had least substance or meaning to it (pairing words beginning with the same letter) demanded the least amount of intellectual effort. Thinking up words signifying some relation between objects (cat–milk) was a more complicated task than finding words which would designate "properties" of objects (cat–gray). It required more independent and active work on the part of subjects to establish meaningful connections between two objects than between an object and one of its properties, with the result that the former produced a more permanent type of recall. Thus, the first task prompted the most active, meaningful type of intellectual effort on the part of subjects, the second task less so, while the third proved to be the least intellectually demanding of all. Accordingly, we note differences in the productivity of recall of each (Table 17–4).

What effect did the differences in motivation have upon retention? Second- and fifth-grade pupils were more successful in recalling words in the first and second tasks when the motivation involved learning rather than play (Table 17–4). The desire to put educational skills to use prompted pupils to concentrate on the actual process of thinking up words. The desire to demonstrate their ability *to think* intensified their efforts. When the motive was play, the job of thinking up words acted, to a great extent, as a means of winning; it lost its intrinsic value as subject matter. Furthermore, the heightened interest that subjects demonstrated in the outcome of the game proved too stimulating and thus distracted them from the actual subject matter of the tasks. This, too, led to discrepancies in the productivity of their recall of words.

Unlike the schoolchildren, the preschool group showed better recall when the motive entailed play rather than learning skills. For this group, demonstrating learning ability proved to be too weak an incentive. The children frequently lost interest and their efforts became haphazard. On the other hand, when play was the motive, it aroused greater interest in the act of thinking up words than in the outcome of the game. Thinking up words represented the goal of the activity, not just a means.

However, the learning motive did not appear to have any advantage over that of play for schoolchildren when they worked on the third task, which had little substantial content to it. This means that involuntary recall is not simply determined by either the tasks or the motivation but by the specific relationship a motive has to a task.

Involuntary remembering as a function of the means involved in an activity has been studied in a number of research projects conducted by psychologists in the U.S.S.R. These investigations have indicated that a certain amount of independent intellectual activity in working with the material in an assignment and in carrying out the necessary methods is an important condition determining the success of involuntary remembering.

Thus, the independent thought about a task led to more successful recall of numbers than solving ready-made assignments (Zinchenko, 1945); thinking up gave better recall than did the work with assigned phrases (Smirnov, 1945); in Zinchenko's experiments (1961) independent composition of the plan of the text led to more efficient recall of the text than did the use of a prepared plan, while work with a prepared plan was more effective than simply reading the text without a plan. Moreover, the active methods proved to be more effective the more difficult the text.

The success of involuntary remembering also depends on the extent to which the modes of activity are well structured. At the first stage in the formation of an act, the productivity of recall is low because the act has not taken shape; at the final stage, recall begins to diminish because the act becomes automatic (Zinchenko, 1939, 1945).

At all levels of motivation and ability, the dependence of involuntary remembering on the purpose of the acts involved is basic. These relationships indicate that the motives and abilities connected to activity fulfill a helpful role in recall (Zinchenko, 1948, 1961, pp. 208–241).

Studies of Voluntary Remembering

Let us turn now to studies that have been done on voluntary remembering as a special mnemonic activity having its own specific goals, motives, and means of operation.

Zankov and others (1940, 1949) studied the effect of mnemonic devices by giving subjects the following problems: (1) to recall and reproduce texts in as precise a way as possible; (2) to render the texts "in their own words"; and (3) to recall and reproduce these texts as fully as possible. When adults were given the task of remembering a story "point-by-point," they reproduced 35 per cent of the words in the text, but only 24 per cent when they were asked to render it "in their own words." Given the task of retaining as much of the text as possible, adults reproduced 12.5 per cent of the sentences; when they were not asked to do this, they were able to give only 8.7 per cent.

The effect of asking subjects to retain the sequence of material presented was also studied. In experiments on the recall of figures (some of which were similar to each other), adults who were asked to remember the order of the figures did so in 80 per cent of the cases; when they were not asked to recall order, they reproduced it only 43 per cent of the time. When recall was delayed 12 days, no appreciable decrement in recall occurred if the subject had been asked to remember order. When subjects were not asked to retain the order of presentation, their ability to reproduce it sharply declined.

Dul'nev (1940) noted that the plans that adults formed to facilitate retention of material changed with the specific features of a mnemonic task. Thus, when asked to recall as "accurately as possible," subjects developed an elaborate plan for recall, while those who had oriented themselves to reproducing the material "in their own words" did not employ such elaborate devices, but usually limited themselves to a general scheme.

Smirnov (1948) investigated the effect of various mnemonic goals on the nature of the *process* of recall itself. The subjects read the text independently and were not limited by any specified amount of repetition. It was shown that the task of *reproducing the text as accurately as possible* led to greater clarity and accuracy of perception of every part of the text on the first encounter. Without this task, much of the text was read superficially, as a result of which the subjects retained at most the general content of certain parts of the text and recognized only the most important and characteristic elements. The task of reproducing as accurately as possible stimulated mental repetition of various parts of the text connected with the comprehension of their content. The role of motor, and especially of motor-speech, elements increased markedly in "reciting" individual words and entire phrases aloud, in a whisper or "to themselves."

Another experiment involved a general, undifferentiated mnemonic task. In one group the subject (adults) read the text without a mnemonic task and only with the aim of understanding its content; in another they read the text with the purpose of remembering it. Isolating meaningful parts of the text improved the subjects' understanding and facilitated recall. The parts functioned as "landmarks of meaning" which helped subjects become better oriented to the content of the text when they were later asked to reproduce it.

These investigations showed that the role of a mnemonic task in recall cannot be reduced to the influence of the motive per se, as manifested in some form of mental effort. A different mnemonic task produces a different orientation to the material, to its content, its structure, its oral form, etc. It affects the selection of the material, and the selection of the specific means of remembering. All this to a greater or lesser degree activates the very process of recall itself.[3]

A study on the role of motivation in voluntary remembering was conducted by Istomina (1948). Children from 3 to 7 years old memorized and recalled words in variously motivated activities. In one experiment this was studied both under laboratory conditions and during play; in another experiment the children memorized and recalled words while executing definite, practical tasks (Istomina, 1953). Recall was especially efficient in the latter case: the problem of remembering was especially important to the children, and the achievement of positive results was most evident. The different motives which appeared in the experiments activated the subjects in different ways.

The Relationship Between Voluntary and Involuntary Memory

Studies of involuntary remembering have led to questions concerning the relationship between involuntary and voluntary types of memory. Research on this problem indicates that when involuntary remembering is based upon active and meaningful means of working with material, there is productive voluntary remembering (if analogous means have not been employed for the latter type of retention). Thus, when subjects have to classify objects depicted on cards they show better involuntary retention than when they use voluntary retention of the objects which is not based on classification (Zinchenko, 1939; 1961, pp. 245–289).

The subjects, adults and schoolchildren, were asked to perform various tasks: (1) to write words from dictation; (2) to free-associate to a word mentioned by the experimenter; (3) fixed associations, that is, to name a word in response to another word connected with the first in meaning; (4) to indicate orthographic errors, which were deliberately inserted into certain sentences presented to the subjects; and (5) to evaluate the logic and meaning of sentences. In none of these cases were the subjects warned that they would be asked to reproduce the words and sentences. However, after the assigned tasks were completed, the subjects were required to reproduce the

3. *Editors' note:* Luria's recent book, *The Mind of a Mnemonist* (Basic Books, 1968) presents unique material on the role of mnemonic devices in memory.

material. Then a test was conducted with each of the subjects on the voluntary retention of material, similar to the material with which they had just dealt. This made it possible to compare the efficiency of involuntary and voluntary remembering. In some subjects both immediate and delayed recall were checked.

The results of this experiment are presented in Table 17–5. The scores for voluntary retention were used as the standard (100 per cent). The results for involuntary retention are tabulated as percentages of the voluntary remembering scores (some tests were not conducted with all groups of subjects). Table 17–5 indicates significant differences in the relation of voluntary to involuntary remembering as a function of the activity whose completion served as the basis of involuntary remembering. It is also characteristic that, in delayed recall, the developmental differences were still more prominent.

Table 17–5

	Immediate test			Delayed test		
Activity during involuntary remembering	Grade II	Grade IV	College students	Grade II	Grade IV	College students
Writing words	108.6%	101.6%	83.5%	96.1%	—	55.1%
Free associations	100.0	92.7	76.8	—	—	121.1
Fixed associations	128.1	135.1	140.2	129.4	187.1%	307.4
Evaluation of orthography	—	—	45.6	—	—	—
Evaluation in terms of meaning:						
6 sentences	114.3	109.1	104.4	—	—	—
12 sentences	—	—	129.6	—	—	139.7

An explanation of the differences manifested in recall of material which is the object of different types of activity must be sought in the *degree of activity* which is required from the subjects in fulfilling the task. This, in turn, depends on the degree of *difficulty of the assignment.* Writing words from dictation, free association, or evaluation of sentences in terms of meaning did not present significant difficulties for adult subjects nor require special efforts from them. The objects of this activity were therefore remembered by the adults less successfully (relative to the objects of voluntary remembering) than by the children.

By way of contrast, thinking up words connected in meaning with the words named by the experimenter required great effort, especially in adults who tried to find the best possible semantic combination of words. Therefore retention, too, proved to be more efficient in them under these conditions.

Important results were obtained in a developmental study of involuntary and voluntary remembering in which subjects had to rely on identical methods of working with material for both types of memorization. Zinchenko (1961) performed the following types of manipulations, using small children, schoolchildren, and older students as subjects: In the first condition, subjects merely classified pictures of 15 objects they had been shown on cards (involuntary retention); in a second condition, a different group of subjects was asked to remember the pictures, but no mention was made of the possibility of using classification as an aid (voluntary remembering without classification); in a third condition (once again using a new group of subjects) subjects classified the pictures as a mnemonic device to aid them in recall (voluntary remembering with classification). The results of this experiment in terms of items recalled out of 15 are shown in Table 17–6.

Table 17–6

Conditions for remembering	Preschool mid-group	Preschool older group	Younger school-children	Middle school-children	Adults
Involuntary	9.6	11.1	13.0	13.4	13.2
Voluntary without classification	6.6	7.9	9.8	10.3	11.5
Voluntary retention with classification	4.8	8.7	12.4	14.3	14.1

Involuntary remembering which resulted from subjects who had classified objects turned out to be more productive for each group than did voluntary remembering which did not rely upon classification as an aid, although the advantages of involuntary recall decline with the older groups of subjects. However, when we compare the results of the first and third conditions, in which identical methods of working with the material were used (classification), it is evident that there are complex dynamics operating in the interrelationship of involuntary and voluntary remembering: with regard to the youngest group of subjects, the involuntary is twice as productive as voluntary. Involuntary remembering, however, does not have such an advantage among the older group of subjects.

In a study of pupils in grades 2, 4, 6, 7, and 9, Zinchenko found a similar relationship between involuntary and voluntary remembering for a text containing related parts (Zinchenko, 1961, pp. 289–367).

Summing up the results of his investigations, Zinchenko outlined the characteristics in the formation of cognitive and mnemonic activity (1961). In the first stage they are formed as a special purposive action and are not yet generalized; the fulfillment of these actions requires especially intensive conscious control. In the second stage, as a result of the transfer of actions to material of varying content, they begin to generalize. In the third stage, through further use, they become, to a certain degree, automatized and acquire the form of generalized skills.

The formation of mnemonic operations differs from the formation of cognitive processes in that it is always one stage behind cognitive processes when the latter are used as a means of remembering. Before a cognitive operation such as classifying remembered objects can become a means of remembering, it must be comparatively well formed. The initial use of a cognitive process for mnemonic ends becomes possible only when the individual can exercise a certain degree of freedom in operating with it.

What has been described here is the same general course of development as that formulated by Leont'ev (1959): cognitive operations which become the means towards another activity first develop as goal-oriented processes and only later assume the characteristics of a distinctly intellectual skill.

The way in which the development of mnemonic processes lags behind cognitive development is fundamental to the very nature of memory; it is this lag which creates the initial gap between voluntary and involuntary memory. Conversely, when an individual has achieved some ability to use cognitive operations as a means of mnemonic activity, voluntary remembering has a distinct advantage over involuntary.

The gap between mnemonic and cognitive processes, and the initial advantage of involuntary as opposed to voluntary remembering which is associated with this lag in *development,* manifest themselves in two ways:

1. As the law of the formation of these two processes and, more generally, as the law of the development of memory, of involuntary and voluntary remembering (Zinchenko, 1961, pp. 425–464). This has been confirmed by the research described above but also in other investigations dealing specifically with a study of the formation of logical, voluntary memory as it develops in preschool-age children (Zhitnikova, 1965).

2. As a law of the *functioning* of involuntary and voluntary remembering. This lag in mnemonic activity manifests itself *at every stage* in the development of memory when circumstances which are new or complex demand that a person employ a specifically goal-oriented procedure to grasp and retain material which has been presented to him. It is precisely under these circumstances that cognitive functions are subordinated to mnemonic ones as means—that is, if the former take the course of an independent, goal-oriented process, a cognitive process either becomes impossible or gives rise to serious difficulties.

Voluntary and Involuntary Remembering in Education

The relationships we have described are of great importance to an understanding of the development of memory as well as to an effective use of involuntary and voluntary memory in teaching. Certain aspects of these problems have been discussed by Zinchenko (1961, pp. 425–514). In dealing with the problem of memory and teaching, the author contends that one serious drawback in present pedagogical theory and its practical application is that students are oriented exclusively towards voluntary remembering. He argues at length on the need and the possibility of using involuntary memory as an effective aid in teaching. At the same time Zinchenko points out that if optimal use is to be made of the opportunities for involuntary memory in teaching, it is essential that there be a thoroughgoing reconstruction of subject matter and methodology. He contends that a special type of investigation is needed to explore these opportunities under the new conditions.

Just such an investigation was conducted recently by Sereda under conditions that had been set up specifically for experimental teaching (Zinchenko and Sereda, 1964). In this investigation experimental training of pupils in the early elementary grades was carried out, the stress being placed on an orientation toward the use of *involuntary memory* in mastering skills through the solution of problems requiring cognition.

The investigators' primary aim was to provide the most important condition for involuntary remembering of material; its inclusion, however, required a radical reconstruction of the subject matter and method used in teaching, since teaching by means of this procedure rules out the simple communication of knowledge in ready-made form so that it will be reinforced; instead it presupposes that a pupil will work through the material on his own, and by means of independent effort, discover the concepts to be mastered.

Conditions which would provide the kind of training outlined here were constructed according to Gal'perin's method for developing mental processes.[4] This type of training was set up for a number of academic subjects (morphology, Russian syntax, and mathematics).[5]

Convincing data were obtained in this research which confirm that there are considerable advantages to experimental training oriented towards involuntary remembering, since it ensures pupils' grasp and ability to operate with and retain skills they have acquired. The experiment showed that, with

4. *Editors' note:* See Chapter 7 of this volume, by P. Y. Gal'perin.

5. *Editors' note:* For some subjects, experimental programs were used which were developed in the laboratory headed by El'konin and Davydov, Institute of Psychology, Moscow. Without using the term, Smirnov and Zinchenko seem to be advocating the discovery method dear to the hearts of American educators.

a rational use of the laws of involuntary remembering in teaching schoolchildren, it is possible to guarantee successful recall of material such as poems, tables, etc.

Let us illustrate this by an example of involuntary remembering of multiplication tables by second-graders. As we know, multiplication tables have always been, and will continue to be, a classical case of voluntary remembering, for specialized memorization. A great deal of time and effort is spent learning them; nonetheless, learning the tables by heart does not guarantee that pupils will grasp the principles and laws of the multiplication table. Basically, it is this failure to understand concepts which hinders the development of pupils' skills in mathematics.

Sereda eliminated rote learning of products by memorizing mathematical tables. Pupils learned these products in the course of activities which had been specially organized with them; they had to construct a series in which the relation between the antecedent and consequent products constituted the basic end of the procedure, each product discovered becoming the basis for determining the one to follow. As a result, the entire series was mastered and memorized involuntarily.

At the same time, this research indicated that if recall is to be of a permanent nature, the inclusion of academic material as the subject matter of the goal of active, independent work is not in itself sufficient. Another condition is necessary: namely, that activity be organized so that at first the material to be learned functions as the *end* of a procedure, while in a later operation it becomes the *means*. When later tested, a group of students trained in the prescribed method outperformed a control group which had learned to multiply in the traditional way. They performed the task (recalling given answers) in less time and with fewer errors.

Particularly important were the results of another experiment in which the pupils had to do multiplication problems for which they had not learned tables. For example, in the work done constructing multiplication tables for "13," 15 per cent of the pupils in the experimental class made mistakes, while 62 per cent made mistakes in the control group. It took less time to achieve involuntary remembering of the tables in the experimental class than under the usual conditions.

Similar data were obtained for other courses. This confirms our belief that teaching which is oriented towards a rational use of involuntary memory has significant advantages not only for the recall of material, but most importantly, for the pupils' comprehension and ability to operate with the skills they have acquired. This is the kind of teaching which lays the groundwork for genuinely productive voluntary memory, since it ensures that cognitive functions will be sufficiently developed to be put to use as a valuable means in mnemonic activity.

Sereda (Zinchenko and Sereda, 1964) further confirmed the features of involuntary memory which earlier experiments had established. She also determined a new condition, which is particularly important for teaching and for productive work by involuntary memory, and which will not only ensure a pupil's grasp of skills but also the permanence of these skills. This can be achieved by organizing a system of activities in such a way that it is possible to make the subject matter, which is the end of one activity, the means to be used in the next activity performed.

Dynamic Processes in Memory

Soviet psychologists have long emphasized the active nature of the processes by which material is reproduced. Zankov (1949), for example, concentrated on one of the phenomena inherent in this activity—the sequence of material as reproduced; frequently this differs from the sequence in which the material was presented because there has been active intervention by memory processes. Thus, in Nudel'man's (1940) experiment (conducted under Zankov's direction), subjects were presented pictures with which they were asked to tell a story. When the cards were presented in a logical order, this order was retained in recall. However, when the pictures were presented in an illogical order, the logical sequence appeared in recall. This was true both for an immediate and a delayed (6-day) recall test.

Blonskii (1940) pointed out the active nature of voluntary reproduction and its connection with certain tasks. Memory "is always a reflection about a problem"; it includes "the use of certain definite techniques of recall . . . Recall is a volitional act determined by our needs and social requirements" (1940, pp. 4, 11).

A number of Soviet psychologists have studied various changes in the material which was reproduced. One example is an extensive study on the qualitative changes or reconstructions made in reproduction undertaken by Komm (1940) under the supervision of Rubinshtein. The main results of the investigation (using adult subjects) can be summarized as follows: Reconstruction in recall manifests itself in (1) the selection and sifting of material, (2) emphasis of the main points, (3) generalization of the content, (4) changes in the plan of the text, especially where the sequence of exposition does not correspond to the logic of its content, (5) the appearance of new content, (6) inferences, and conclusions, based on the text but not present in it, and (7) various substitutions of words and individual expressions, etc.

Reconstruction in recall is elicited by the objective properties of the material, the subject's emotional relation to it, and by the condition of the subject at the time of free recall. The nature of the reconstruction itself is the result of active cognitive processing of the content in the process of recall. The level of understanding also affects the nature of the reconstruction. The reconstruction of the material is the result both of unpremeditated and of conscious, purposive cognitive work. In delayed recall, reconstruction tends to intensify.

Another point that was also brought out was that the activity involved in reproducing some set of material often facilitated recall. The necessity of fulfilling a recall assignment and the molding of a certain definite content in speech stimulated cognitive activity and led to the recall of that which seemed "forgotten." This point found expression in one of Zinchenko's experiments (1961) which traced the forgetting of Archimedes' law over a protracted period of time (the subjects were fifth-graders).

The data manifest not only forgetting (a diminution of knowledge in pupils in the sixth grade in comparison with pupils in the fifth grade) but also frequent instances of restoration of this knowledge in seventh- and eighth-grade pupils, especially when they were solving problems connected with Archimedes' law. The restoration of knowledge occurred in the process of recollection of verbal formulas and especially in the process of reflection and the making of judgments, frequently conflicting ones, in solving a definite system of selected problems. The active, creative nature of reproduction, especially in eighth-grade pupils, led not only to the restoration of partially forgotten knowledge but also to a qualitative rearrangement of this knowledge.

Enikeev studied the various intrusions, inventions, and distortions which occur during reproduction (1946). He was able to determine certain conditions which produce changes in recall. With easy texts descriptive in nature, the interpolations in the first recall express visual impressions produced by the perception of the text. In subsequent recalls, these impressions expand, are supplemented and become concrete. Interpolations on repeated reproductions increase from 11 per cent in the first case to 52 per cent with the fourth reproduction.

In a difficult text the total number of interpolations increases; moreover, here, on first reproduction there are more (71 per cent) of them than on the fourth (52 per cent). The interpolations with the difficult text differ from those encountered with the easy text. They have a more generalized character. However, in neither type of text do the interpolations lead to a distortion of the basic content. Both visual images in easy texts and generalizations in difficult texts emerge as a means for transmitting the content of the texts, which are as accurate as possible.

Zal'tsman studied the nature of the cognitive processes which emerge as methods of reproduction (1949). He obtained the following basic results. The degree of activization of the cognitive processes depends on the nature of the recall assignment. For an assignment *to reproduce the text as completely and accurately as possible* the major method of remembering was association by similarity, and by visual representations. The task of repeating the main points of the text stimulated the use of the more complex and active techniques of analysis, comparison, generalization, and judgment.

Mnemonic means in recall varied as a function of the content and complexity of the material to be reproduced. The recall of literary, geometric, and even physical material was primarily by means of images. The image was frequently an initial strong point of recall. The recall of abstract material activated the processes of association, a search for formulas and definitions. Increasing the complexity of remembering material assimilated long ago activates cognitive processes. Usually, a plan is formed. With a plan toward the material to be recalled, even material assimilated long previously was reproduced quite exhaustively. In a number of instances it was reformulated on the basis of newly acquired knowledge. Material assimilated previously was subjected to a greater degree of reconstruction when it was recalled.[6]

Various motivational conditions affect both the direction of recall and the use of various cognitive skills. Thus, in the context of practical and classroom conditions, recall usually has an active character, with a clearly defined tendency toward a broad, complete, and exact reproduction which preserves the sequence of the original. There is an intensification of the search for a means of remembering and a mobilization of all knowledge for the evaluation of material which is being recalled.

Recognition and Recall

Several Soviet psychologists have studied recognition and its relations to recall. Solov'ev, investigating recognition (1943), noted its unity with perception and also its connection with the cognitive processes. The isolation of specifics in an object is necessary for recognition. Such isolation occurs most successfully in the process of practicing recognition of groups of objects of a certain type. On the other hand, recognition of the generic is connected with the processes of abstraction. Such recognition is a complex product of development.

Kudryavtseva studied alterations in the recognition of objects in relation to their specificity, fullness, and complexity, as well as the subjects' familiarity with the object (1954). Experiments were conducted on objects familiar, slightly familiar, and unfamiliar to the subjects.

Shekhter (1963) investigated the methods of learning which are funda-

6. *Editors' note:* The preceding interpretation possesses an obvious similarity to the general orientation of Miller, Galanter, and Pribram (1960). The types of problems studied and the variables and techniques studied by the Soviet investigators are in striking contrast to much of the research in verbal learning and complex processes conducted in the United States. It is hoped that despite the brevity of the descriptions of many of their experimental problems, they will nevertheless stimulate research along similar lines in the West.

mental to the spontaneous recognition of geometrical figures (signs, graphs, etc.). His work involved the recognition of figures of a "variable" nature, in other words, recognition of one or another class of figures having certain general properties (as well as others characteristic of a particular class).[7]

When an experimenter teaches an individual to recognize a variable figure, he generally points out to him a certain aggregate of "essential" features which he has singled out according to a logical, conceptual analysis of the figure. The striking fact noted in these experiments is that learning which is based on this complex of features inevitably requires conscious or unconscious fixation of all the essential features of the figure.

At the very start of training, in accordance with instructions given him, a person attends successively to the necessary features of the figure presented to him. However, we know that in time subjects no longer need resort to verifying the features they have recognized, since they know the figure "at once." The problem thus arises: Has spontaneous learning been achieved on the basis of the essential features which, after long training, rapidly and automatically ("subconsciously") are fixed in the objects, or is such learning based on other features?

In the experiments conducted by Shekhter, subjects had to distinguish a particular figure, which had been specially invented for the experiments from various other figures. The experimenter pointed out the complex of essential features and taught subjects to use these in recognizing the figure. After a lengthy period, training reached the stage of spontaneous recognition. In order to determine the features that subjects had used to orient themselves at this stage, a number of tests were carried out in which variants of the training figures were shown to the subjects.

An analysis of the results showed that spontaneous recognition does not involve an object's essential features, but rather a system involving certain other features. None of these happens to be a general characteristic of the diverse instances which make up a given class. On the contrary, each of these belongs to some specific variant ("subclass") of the given class, and any one of these represents a distinguishing feature; that is, one which occurs only in the instances of the class in question. Hence if a subject discovers some one of these features, it alone will suffice to identify the figure. Each one of these features is complete in itself; in the process of recognition it occurs not as a combination or system of several simple characteristics but as an indivisible whole. Features of this type, in particular, appear to subjects as the "general appearance," the figure, form, or entirety of a geometrical figure. Hence the number of operations used in making a comparison can be cut down to a minimum in such cases and recognition of a figure takes place much more rapidly.

---

7. *Editors' note:* A triangle is an example of a variable figure. It can be right-angled, acute-angled, obtuse-angled, etc.

The investigation thus indicated the following: (1) Spontaneous recognition is not a latent form of an elementary, sequential operation; it differs from this both by the nature of the features and processes it employs. (2) In addition to the "orthodox" method of learning (based on a complex of essential features), there are other quite valuable methods which are most effective with respect to the speed of learning.

Developmental Aspects of Memory

Issues related to the ontogenetic development of memory occupy a vital place in Soviet psychology. Earlier in this chapter we discussed a number of investigations that were carried out with children (studies by Leont'ev, Zinchenko, Smirnov, and others). Quite a number of other works have been devoted to exploring this problem as well. Particular attention has been given in these experiments not simply to quantitative indices of developmental changes in recall, but also to the qualitative aspects of memory at various stages in a child's development. It is data of this sort that Istomina, Barkhatova, and Samokhvalova, sought in experiments on memory in preschool-age children and elementary school pupils. On the basis of their results, it is possible to draw the following conclusions:

1. Recall increases irregularly with age; among preschool-age children a more significant increase is to be noted in the period from 4 to 5 years of age. In contrast to this, no significant differences are observed either between 3- and 4-year-olds or between 5- and 6-year-olds. Comparisons of pupils in grades 2 and 5 (8-to-9-year-olds and 11-to-12-year-olds) show that the difference in recall was greater than that in comparable performances by pupils in grades 5 and 7 (11-to-12-year-olds and 14-to-15-year-olds).
2. Not only speed, but also permanence of recall increases with age.
3. A qualitative analysis of recall and reproduction in preschool-age children made it possible to outline the levels at which these processes develop. These developmental levels may be described as:

   (a) A first stage in which children exhibit no purposeful behavior in remembering. The process proceeds, as it were, with no active participation on the child's part, so that it seems less a matter of the children's recalling material than that material presents itself to them for recall.

   (b) At the second level recall operates as purposeful behavior. The child sets himself the goal of remembering and actively tries to carry out his intention, even though he lacks the appropriate means to do this.

   (c) It is only at the third level that a child possesses means or methods which will facilitate recall. However, a child's stock of methods is still very slim, and it mostly amounts to repetitions of words which the child names "to himself" (by whispering); only in a few cases does he actually group material in any meaningful way.

The distribution of age levels and percentage of children at each is indicated below in Table 17–7. These were results obtained on the recall of pictures: Similar data were obtained in experiments on the recall of words. The qualitative aspect of the development of memory in school-age children is such that pupils show an increasingly greater mastery of rational devices or methods of recall. Children in second grade (8-to-9-year-olds) do not have any substantial reserve of devices, and their recall is largely spontaneous. But even when one or another method is tried, for example, grouping numbers by tens, linking words according to similarity of sense or sound, isolating the main points of texts, it is still far from adequate and sometimes proves unmanageable for children of this age. Further, such methods do not always facilitate recall as they are intended to. Frequently the method itself demands considerable intellectual effort and strain on the part of the child.

Table 17–7 *Percentage of Children Manifesting Various Types of Mnemonic Activity*

Levels	Age 3	Age 4	Age 5	Age 6
I	40	7	—	—
II	60	50	40	17
III	—	43	60	83

In fifth-grade pupils (11- and 12-year-olds), analysis of memory processes reveals that children at this age often use mnemonic devices. Their memory shows a marked increase in comprehension, active involvement with the subject matter, and willfulness in the way devices are used. Eighth-grade pupils not only use a greater number of devices but, more importantly, do so with more purpose and awareness. Their stock of devices, too, is richer.

Special research on the gradual mastery of certain means of cognitive processing of remembered material was investigated by Smirnov (1948). Of particular interest was the way schoolchildren come to use semantic groupings and semantic relationships when remembering verbal material.

In order to study the first of these processes, students from the second, fourth, and sixth grades were asked to remember texts with differing structures and lengths. The content of some of the texts could easily be divided into a series of sections (subunits) because the idea of each subunit followed directly from the previous subunit. Other texts were so constructed that it was difficult to group their contents; the ideas in each subunit were chosen at random. Reproduction of these texts, conversations with the subjects, and observations of the students led Smirnov to the following conclusions:

1. The conscious grouping of a text was not observed at all in second-graders and comparatively rarely in grades 4 and 6.

2. In memorizing school material assigned for homework, the students of upper grades used division into parts, but did not employ grouping as a general technique suitable for other cases.

3. For schoolchildren memorizing classroom material by division into parts, it is not a mental isolation of parts in order to outline the framework of the text. Its main purpose is to outline the order of memorizing the individual parts and to establish the amount that must be memorized in one sitting.

4. In those cases where a mental division is made, it is frequently observed in the retention of structurally formed ("grouped") texts, where such a division is easily accomplished. This is bound up with the fact that for children, grouping has a more immediate, unpremeditated and passive nature.

5. Recall is more frequently accompanied by semantic grouping than is recognition. A general rule is operative here: the need to recall induces an active search for methods facilitating this process to a greater extent than does mere recognition. The immediate perceptibility of the results of recall are basic, whereas the productivity of recognition is not always immediately clear.

6. The pupils fail to employ meaningful grouping to a sufficient degree, either by omitting it altogether or grouping elements in a way which shows that the children have not really grasped or thought through what they are about, but are simply going through the motions of classifying; they do not comprehend the difference between various degrees of structure in texts. Few pupils note the difference on their own; they usually become aware of structural differences only when carrying out a special assignment such as breaking a text down into parts.

7. While pupils fail to note structural differences between texts, they are aware of the various degrees of difficulty these texts present; most often, they regard those which are structurally well formed as the easier texts but are unaware what causes ease or difficulty with material.

8. While not grouping the material consciously, the pupils of all classes did reveal, however, a significant percent of "connected transitions" between ideas in reproduction, that is, they made the transition from one of them to another on the basis of semantic, content proximity. Contiguity as a condition of reproduction plays an insignificant role here. Its role is more significant only where it is combined with semantic proximity. Thus, while not grouping the material consciously, the pupils of all classes did group it, even though only in part, in an unconscious form.

9. As a deliberate process, accomplished in response to a special assignment, division into parts was not carried out at all by some second graders. In grade 4 a complete inability to group the material was noted only in isolated cases. In grade 6 it was not observed at all: all sixth graders could divide the text into sections, in one way or another.

10. The division of the text from memory is considerably more difficult than when the material is before one's eyes.

11. Transitions from one section of the text to another are not noted by the pupils who are in the initial stages of development of the ability to group in the process of reading and are recognized only later.

12. Division into parts is characterized in its initial stages by great detail. Even certain individual sentences are sometimes selected as independent parts. In phrases similar in content, the students frequently do not notice anything common at all.

13. Typical errors in the selection of labels for the parts in the early stages of this ability are the use of a part instead of a whole (abridged heading) and a simple summarization of the parts (summary heading).

14. If unable to find a heading independently, the pupils gladly accept correct headings suggested by the experimenter.

What do all of these features of grouping observed in children indicate? As noted in the investigation outlined, they point above all to the presence of a *significant discrepancy between what is rendered in a conscious form and what is performed unconsciously*. As a conscious process, semantic grouping in second-graders was completely lacking and even in upper grades (4 and 6) semantic grouping was observed only in a few pupils. More frequently (but even here only in grades 4 and 6) the structural differences between texts were recognized, yet even these were only independently noted in the process of reading by half of the students in grade 6. They were not noticed at all in grade 2. The degree of difficulty (structurally formed vs. ungrouped) is reflected in the performance of a number of pupils of all classes, but the source of the varying degrees of difficulty (presence or absence of structural formation) is not recognized. Thus, on the *conscious* level both semantic grouping itself and the structural differences between texts are inadequately grasped. At the same time, in an *unconscious* form, grouping by content (though not even covering all sentences of a section), is widespread: connected, intelligent transitions from one idea to another are observed in many cases even where what is being retained is a set of ungrouped texts; contiguity itself plays an insignificant role. The pupil does not see the structural formlessness of the text, but still he reorganizes it in reproduction. *Before becoming a conscious process, intelligent grouping occurs in unconscious form.* Pupils group ideas even before they note the absence of structural shape to the texts.

The second conclusion which may be drawn from the foregoing data is that *there is a discrepancy between what the pupils do and what they are able to do*. In conscious form, grouping of ideas, as has just been said, is inadequate. However, in response to an assignment to divide the material into parts, it is accomplished by a great number of pupils even including the second-graders. In the remembering of ungrouped texts grouping is less frequent than in the memorizing of grouped texts, but a special assignment to divide a text is performed in both cases in roughly the same way.

This same discrepancy between the possible and the actual is witnessed by the fact that, when asked to recall, the pupils often carry out a semantic grouping whereas when recollecting the text, they do not form semantic groups in a consciously recognized form.

All this means that, *although it is within the capacities of the schoolchildren, semantic grouping has not become a technique for remembering. It is performed as a special action and not as a part of some other, more complex intellectual activity.*

This is accounted for, in the first instance, by the fact that semantic grouping has not yet become *a habit, a solidly assimilated act.* Not only the second-graders but even upper-grade students (grades 4 and 6) do not accomplish it immediately. They sometimes take a long time to think over the division into parts. The transition from one semantic group to another is frequently observed to occur with a delay or to occur only after the major part of the following section has been read. Semantic grouping of ungrouped text is accomplished with exceptionally great difficulty and requires the help of the experimenter even for many older pupils.

With regard to pupils in eighth grade, one does not find among these 14- and 15-year-olds a considerable improvement over that noted for the age shifts from grades 2 to 5. On the whole, children in the eighth grade use the same devices as those in the fifth grade, but more eighth-grade pupils avail themselves of these and have greater mastery over them than do fifth-graders. It is indicative, too, that while pupils in the fifth grade use certain devices merely to reproduce material, pupils in the eighth grade have also learned to use these as aids in recall. These facts are fully in accord with the general view that a change in memory aids and the development of new and more perfect types of memory aids frequently take place in the very process of memorizing. *A memory aid functions first as a means for reproducing material and only later becomes a means for recalling it.*

The ontogenetic development of the way images and words are related in memory and recall at various stages of development has also been an area of considerable research. Blonskii developed a general theory of memory (1964) which relates to the data discussed here. One of his fundamental points was that the four types of memory (motor, emotional, pictorial, and verbal) are *genetic* stages of its development occurring in the given sequence. Pictorial memory is a much earlier and lower level of memory development than verbal memory.

The earliest type—motor memory—finds its initial expression in the first motor conditioned reflexes of children, above all in that original conditioned reaction which occurs when the child is taken in the arms in a feeding position. This reaction is observed in the first month after birth. The beginning of emotional or affective memory, expressed in the appearance of an affective reaction before the *direct* action of the stimulus, occurs sometime in the first half year of the child's life. The first rudiments of free recall which may be associated with the beginning of pictorial memory pertain, Blonskii says, to the second year of life.

The fact that a pictorial type of memory manifests itself earlier than verbal memory does not imply that it will subsequently disappear and be replaced by verbal memory. However, as Blonskii maintains, pictorial memory continues to be a lower form of memory than verbal. Vivid images are more inherently a part of childhood than adulthood. Ordinarily, images are merely episodes in the memory of an adult. Graphic memory may prove helpful only in extraordinary circumstances when there is a powerful or exceptional type of image. Usually, though, visual memory is rather poor, and thus another, higher form of memory—narrative memory—is of incomparably greater value; in its higher stages it merges with thought.

Though representing a higher level of memory, narrative memory does not immediately emerge in its most perfect form. It develops along a definite course which is characterized by the basic stages of development of narration. Originally, the narrative is just a verbal accompaniment of the action; then it is the words accompanying the action, and only then does it appear by itself as a live and pictorial message (Blonskii, 1964).

Because in the higher stages of its development it is narrative memory, human memory (verbal memory in the true sense) is socially conditioned. This social influence is expressed in the fact that verbal reproduction becomes more and more reliable and succinct. But memory, reproducing only the essence, already borders on thinking. Recognition and recall at a higher stage of memory development become thinking recognition and thinking recall. Concepts which provide the capacity to recognize and recall the most essential things, while forgetting all accidental things, play the greatest role. "Such memory," says Blonskii, "may be so nonspecific that not one word of the original will be found in the reproduced text." And, at the same time, this will be a correct rendition of the text. The process of remembering in these cases consists of the substitution of the concepts of the original by higher, equivalent or lower concepts. "This," says Blonskii, "is the process of reanalyzing the retained material in terms of concepts" (1964).

The selective, socially conditioned nature of reproduction in verbal memory does not appear all at once. According to Blonskii, three principal stages in its development can be distinguished: simple reproduction; socially conditioned, selective reproduction; and "literate" memory, which makes use of writing. The starting point for the ontogenetic development of verbal memory should be considered the second year of life, when reproducing verbal memory appears. This simple reproduction is most highly developed at the beginning of puberty, but its fastest development occurs at the preschool age. The reproducing memory, even in the 7-to-8-year-old, does not differ so sharply from the maximum of this memory. Beginning with adolescence this memory weakens.

Since simple reproduction, continues Blonskii, is the starting point for development of the child's verbal memory, under the stronger influence of social requirements this type of memory very rapidly is pushed into the background by a higher type—a selectively reproducing verbal memory. The development of verbal memory in childhood in essence is the development of this selective and socially conditioned memory. It is already developing in preschool childhood, but its most energetic "cultivation" occurs in school. This memory is most highly developed in late adolescence. It is developed in close connection with the development of thought and speech.

Finally, memory making use of writing develops, beginning with school age, and achieves the highest level only at maturity. Such are the basic points of Blonskii's conception of the correlation of pictorial and verbal memory in development.

This relationship of object image and verbal material was extensively investigated by Faraponova (1958). Her subjects, pupils of grades 2, 5, and 7, and college students, were asked to remember, in the first condition, visual material (pictures of objects); in the second condition, verbal material visually presented (names of objects); in the third condition, object material, but this time difficult to name (pictures of various types of fish, mushrooms); in the fourth condition, again verbal, but abstract material not presented visually (words designating abstract concepts).

Faraponova's results revealed the following: (1) In all age groups, better retention of visual material easily verbalized was observed; retention of material similar in content but verbal also yielded high, but somewhat lesser, results. (2) Under conditions of specifically limited activity of one or the other signal system (in the third and fourth condition), the results were lowest and at different ages they proved to be different: pupils of grade 2 retained visual material (third condition) better, pupils of upper grades and adults retained words (fourth condition) better. (3) In all series there was an increase in the retention of visual and verbal material with age; however, the increased recall of words was more significant than the increase for visual material. (4) The retention of abstract verbal material increased slightly more with age than the corresponding results of retention of concrete verbal material. (5) In tests, the increase of retention with age of various types of material showed up to a considerably greater extent for recall than in tests involving recognition. (6) Notable age differences were also observed in the qualitative features of memory processes; specifically, at older ages the use of semantic grouping of material, weakly displayed at an earlier age, increased.

A somewhat different approach to the developmental study of retention of material varying in content was employed in Lipkina's work (1958). She investigated the efficiency of recall of various types of classroom (geographic) material by pupils both in the school year in which this material was taught and in succeeding school years (up to grade 10). The following should be noted from the results of the investigation: (1) Various types of concrete and abstract material are remembered unequally. (2) Those types of concrete material which occur in the basic content of the academic subject and the retention of which depends on visual images (in a course in geography, for example, cartographical data) are retained in the memory better than is concrete material lacking any independent significance in the classroom subject in question and having to be remembered without recourse to distinct visual images (for instance, in geography—names, not connected with the map). (3) Various types of abstract material are also retained unequally: that which is closely connected with concrete material (explanation of facts) is remembered more firmly than what stands by itself, apart from the factual material (definitions). (4) The retention of both types of material to a great extent depends on the place the given material occupies in the academic discipline and on the relation of the abstract data with the concrete data. (5) With age the principle of reproduction of various types of academic material is changed substantially: the concrete is reproduced by young pupils on the basis of the concrete; the basis of reproduction of the concrete in older pupils is a general rule.

The problem of the correlation of the concrete and verbal in memory processes at various ages was raised in a different way in the work of Mal'tseva (1958). In this investigation the concrete and the verbal appeared not as the *object* but as the *means* of remembering.

Mal'tseva used the method of mediated retention, which had been suggested by Leont'ev and has already been described above. Whereas Leont'ev used only pictures as a support for retention, in Mal'tseva's work both visual (pictorial) and verbal material served as a support for retention. The task consisted in comparing the role of the two means as a method for facilitating retention. At the same time the role of *ready-made* supports (given by the experimenter) and of supports *devised by the subjects* themselves was investigated. The latter were necessary to reveal the capacity for independent use of supports by pupils of various ages. The subjects were pupils of grades 2, 4, and 8 and adults.

The experiment showed that both in immediate and in delayed recall, retention in all groups of subjects was higher in cases where subjects relied on visual material (pictures). However, the efficiency in cases where subjects relied on words increased more with age than it did in cases where subjects relied on pictures. Therefore, the difference in the use of the two supports decreases with age.

Tests for comparing the effectiveness of "ready-made" and independently devised supports revealed the following: the efficiency of remembering with independently devised (verbal) supports in subjects of all ages was higher than the efficiency of remembering with ready-made supports. There were no clearly expressed age differences in the relation between them.

A comparison of two other cases of remembering—with reliance on prepared pictures and on independently devised words—revealed that success was higher when independently devised words were used. Thus, in independent invention, verbal supports become a more effective means of remembering than ready-made pictures (which were of more significant help than ready-made words). Notable age differences in the effect on retention of independently devised verbal and ready-made visual supports were lacking.

Thus, all investigations discussed testify to one and the same thing: with age the role of the second signal system, emerging in studies on recall of verbal and abstract material, with use of verbal supports, increases, as a result of which the difference between retention of the two types of material and between the two types of support gradually diminishes; however, even in adults visual material is remembered more efficiently than verbal-abstract material, and visual supports display a more active effect than verbal supports. The best retention is observed in the joint operation of both signal systems.

Correlational Studies of Memory

An independent group of studies by Soviet psychologists has been concerned with the problem of correlation in the field of memory. A correlational analysis amounts to a special statistical way of studying the interrelationships of various types of psychological activities and personality characteristics.

No small amount of research has been done on this level of analysis, but the results have been quite disappointing. The data of a correlational analysis generally amount merely to a calculation of the coefficients of correlation (and a number of instances of inconsistent results), no attempt being made to arrive at a causal explanation of the quantitative indices obtained. The quantitative estimates of correlations are not linked up to any qualitative, psychological analysis of comparative processes and characteristics involved in personality study. Studies of this kind also fail to investigate whether the quantitative indices obtained are fixed (or, to be more exact, change within comparatively narrow limits), or whether they are largely dependent on the actual content of one or another type of psychological activity. Yet it is these very activities and the correlations between them that are the true object of study.

Research that we will take up at this point (studies supervised by Smirnov) was designed to fill in this gap by combining quantitative correlation indices with a qualitative description of the comparative types and components of psychological activity carried out by subjects. Correlations among the following were explored: involuntary and voluntary memory; effects on recall of the performance of various types of activity (both mnemonic and non-mnenomic); recall for various types of material; speed and permanence of recall—two important aspects of memory. Both adults and children were used as subjects, but the age range of subjects for each of the problems was limited.

The first two problems (involuntary or voluntary memory, and recall of various types of activity) were studied in experiments using preschool-age children as subjects (Istomina, 1964). The third problem (recall of various types of material) was studied among pupils in grades 2, 5, and 7 and college students (Samokhvalova, 1962; 1965). The last problem for study (speed and permanence of recall) was investigated in preschool-age children (Istomina) and schoolchildren in elementary grades (Barkhatova, 1964). There were 30 subjects in each age group so that when all of these studies are combined we have 11 groups and a total of 330 subjects in all.

In the experiments conducted with young schoolchildren and college students the objects for recall were: pictures (drawings of individual objects); series of individual words (both concrete and abstract); series of numbers (two- and three-digit numbers); and series of nonsense syllables. In addition, the school pupils were also given series of individual phrases as well as texts composed of related bits of material.

In the experiments performed with college students, learning continued until a completely accurate reproduction of each series had been accomplished (these were series of words, first names, names of pictures, and syllables). With schoolchildren the experiments limited the number of presentations of material, the total number of repetitions being dependent upon the nature of the material. After each presentation, subjects were asked to reproduce the material. When they had finished learning an entire series, questions were put to them to discover how learning had progressed at various stages.

For preschool children the material recalled involved activities such as games, work duties, listening to a story, and the ordinary laboratory-type experiments. In the first of these (recall of material presented in a game—"on a trip") one of the children (a different one each time) was asked, during the course of the game, to remember the names of things he had to get for his group from the director, who was in another room. Similarly, in the work activities (repairing toys) one of the children was asked to get from the kindergarten teacher a number of things that were needed by his group for their work. The child was to remember the names of these things.

In both cases the children were asked immediately to reproduce what had been named. In experiments in which they listened to a story, the child was asked (with no previous warning) at its conclusion to recall the names of animals and birds mentioned in the story. In each of these cases the children had 10 names to remember. The same number of words was used for recall in the usual laboratory-type experiments conducted with this group (individual words were presented once only and the children immediately asked to recall them).

The most general and important result of this research was the discovery of considerable variability, plasticity, and a dynamic aspect to the correlations obtained. The value of the correlations between the same types of recall appeared to vary considerably with the age of subjects, with their degree of learning, and with the differences in the indices of recall.

Thus, for the younger preschool group (3- and 4-year-olds) the coefficients of correlation for voluntary and involuntary remembering in different tasks were +0.87 and +0.69, respectively; for the older children in this group (5- and 6-year-olds) they were only +0.41 and +0.52. Statistically all these coefficients were quite significant and reliable.

In experiments on recall in which preschool-age children performed various types of activity all the coefficients were positive; for the 3- and 4-year-olds the mean values of the coefficients were equal to +0.44 and +0.46. For the older groups (5- and 6-year-olds) the mean values were +0.32 and +0.34, respectively. Once again, the correlation of results for the older children in the preschool group (5- and 6-year-olds) was lower than for the younger children (3- and 4-year-olds).

In experiments with schoolchildren the mean values of the coefficients of correlation between the recall of various types of material were +0.40 in grade 2, +0.21 in grade 5, and only 0.09 in grade 8; thus a steady reduction both of the value of the coefficients and their degree of reliability.

In experiments with adult students the mean value of the correlation was +0.26, which is evidence that there is somewhat of an increase in the correlation as compared with the results for the older group of elementary school students (pupils from the eighth grade). Thus, at first the correlation between the recall of different types of material decreases with age, but it increases again somewhat at a later point.

What were the results of the experiment in which Barkhatova investigated the degree of correspondence between speed and permanence of recall? First, we must note that there were two types of indices used to describe permanency of recall: (1) the absolute amount of material reproduced after a delay of 7 days; and (2) the ratio of delayed recall to immediate recall. The correlations based on the absolute amount retained were +0.70 in grade 2, +0.70 in grade 5, and +0.53 in grade 8. The correlations for relative recall were: +0.29 for grade 2, +0.25 for grade 5, and +0.07 for grade 8. Again, there was a drop in the correlation with age (although this was true only of the results obtained for age differences from grades 5 to 8).

In summing up the results of all three investigations, it can be said that from the preschool to the school groups there is a decrease in the correlation between various types and aspects of memory. In the adult student group these coefficients either increase somewhat, or, at the least, show no further tendency to decrease.

What can we conclude from these findings? The coefficients of correlation do not reveal the extent of *inter*individual, but of *intra*individual differences, that is, differences in the degree to which the same subjects have developed with respect to various aspects or types of psychological activity (here the frequency with which the same subject shows a coincidence or discrepancy between high, average, or low development in various types of memory).

How are the intraindividual differences for various age groups to be explained? Information derived through a qualitative analysis—an investigation of the activity of recall as performed by subjects of different ages—provides some answers to this question. This information reveals that higher coefficients are obtained when the mnemonic devices used by a subject in various experiments are somewhat similar in nature. Thus, in the experiment described above, the younger preschool-age children (particularly the 3-year-olds) more frequently behaved in identical ways for both voluntary and involuntary remembering; practically none of them used any special methods to aid them in recall in either case. Similarly, in voluntary remembering the 4-year-olds exhibited certain characteristic types of behavior which greatly resembled their behavior with material for involuntary remembering. Among the 5- and 6-year-olds there is a perceptibly greater difference in their behavior with voluntary and involuntary remembering as well as a greater variety of behavior in dealing with the former. They showed variety in the degree of active involvement, of forethought given to memory and reproduction, as well as to the amount of elaboration in the processes they had worked out. Also evident was a desire to rely upon some connection or other, to establish some logical relationship, however simple it might be. The same kinds of activity were noted for the group of 6-year-olds. The difference in behavior exhibited by the older children, given varied conditions of recall, also determined the greater number of cases in which there was a discrepancy in productivity of recall for the two situations described. The children who evidenced a high degree of *involuntary remembering* (when the basic structure of the experiment excluded the possibility of using special mnemonic devices) showed a *low* level of productivity in voluntary remembering. This was the case when they had not yet mastered (or had very poor mastery of) certain mnemonic devices needed for voluntary remembering. Conversely, those subjects who ranked as "average" or "poor" in the first instance (involuntary remembering) were able to make noticeable improvements in voluntary remembering if they had better mastery of some mnemonic device.

The same remarks hold true both for the dynamics of the coefficients of correlation in experiments in which preschool-age children performed various types of activity, and for the variations in the coefficients of correlation for the different age groups of school pupils in their recall of various types of material. Thus, as a rule, second-graders used a rather mechanical approach to recall; they linked several of the first and last members of a series, or a number of those in the middle of the list. Only with respect to separate parts of the material were there any attempts to group elements in a logical way. The children had been asked to recall the material, but they were not given any specific means by which to do this. Essentially what we find here (as with the younger preschool group) is immediate recall stimulated by the greater mass and difficulty of material, which required more complex methods than the younger children had at their disposal.

Among the fifth-grade pupils we noted distinct improvements in the type of mnemonic devices used. Pupils of this grade level attempt to find more reasonable means of recall than those implicit in the material itself (this was true, too, of the second-graders). However, active reworking of the material by fifth-graders still proved inadequate; they attempted to rework the material only with certain types of material. In some cases they treated material as though no special means of facilitating recall were possible and they simply had to "hammer it" into their heads. Clearly, this type of behavior tends to increase cases of discrepancy in the levels of recall when various types of material are being learned by the same group of pupils; consequently, it tends to lower the coefficients of correlation.

With the last group, pupils of grade 8, there is a growth in the variety of methods used in recall, but the pupils still indicate that they have not fully mastered them. Hence they are used only in a limited way—in recalling only certain parts of the material. This explains the subsequent decrease in the coefficients of correlation for the recall of various types of material and an increase in the intraindividual memory differences.

One finds quite a different picture with college students. Although they have no fewer means of recall available to them, and to some extent these are more varied than those employed by eighth-grade pupils, their use of mnemonic devices is more extensive (adult students use these for almost any type of material). Their mastery of these devices, too, is considerably greater, and consequently mnemonic processes for this group are less dependent upon the special characteristics of the material. All of these factors lead to greater consistency in the intra-individual differences of the subjects. Thus, it is possible for students to maintain their ranking when recalling various types of material, and this, in turn, produces a new increase in the value of the correlation coefficients.

In a study that Samokhvalova (1962) conducted with college students, she found that there was a marked difference between the coefficients of correlation computed for reproductions of the material at various times. Thus the first reproduction allowed for a breakdown of the material recalled into two groups: material that was simpler to recall—pictures, words, two-digit numbers; the more difficult material—three-digit numbers and nonsense syllables. The correlation coefficients for recall of all material used in the first group were fairly high on the first reproduction; recall of material in the second group did not correlate with that of the first, nor were there correlations between material recalled in the second group. Substantial changes, however, occurred with the third reproduction, and these became even more marked with succeeding reproductions, if one can judge by the coefficients computed for the total number of repetitions required to learn each of the experimental materials. The indices of the correlation of recall of material comprising the difficult tasks increased considerably in comparison with the rest of the material; this time the coefficients were higher than for materials which formed the easy tasks. Given the data for the entire number of repetitions, the correlations for the easy and difficult tasks turned out to be of the same order; all were positive and within a range of 0.40 to 0.60.

What is the relation between the data from the qualitative analysis of mnemonic devices used by subjects and the quantitative indices of correlation? According to accounts from the students themselves, when they recalled simpler material, they used various methods as aids from the start. On the other hand, in first attempting to recall more difficult material they frequently do not use auxiliary aids or, if they do, they are not too successful. However, once subjects become involved in the learning process, they make continually greater use of memory aids. The mnemonic activity in recalling material that varies in the degree of difficulty gradually tends toward greater conformity; this, then, increases the correlation between the recall of various types of material during subsequent reproductions (becoming more and more marked the further one gets from the type of perception and ability to reproduce material that students showed at the start of the learning period). That the correlation between the recall of various types of material depends upon the nature of mnemonic devices used is evident here as well.

In summing up the results of the experiments discussed above, Smirnov advances the following views: The interdependence of various aspects and types of memory which the correlative analysis revealed is not invariable; it changes quantitatively with the age of the subjects, the stage of their learning, and the conditions under which recall and reproduction take place. The characteristic features of the mnemonic devices subjects use for recall and reproduction are fairly important causes of the variability of correlations in memory work. Thus, once again (here using a special method) experiments have confirmed the highly important point about productivity of recall being dependent upon the very nature of mnemonic activity.

Information and Memory

Let us turn now to the studies on memory which have been stimulated by the development of cybernetics in engineering and psychology, attempts to provide optimal conditions for training, and the opportunities that apparently exist for applying information theory to the study of cognitive processes.

Of the Soviet studies that have explored problems of memory in conjunction with information theory, we should first point out a study which was carried out in the laboratory of Zinchenko and Nevel'ski (1965). This was designed to show that memory span is dependent upon the amount of information subjects have to deal with.

The investigation studied the recall of sequences of three-digit numbers which had been selected from different lists for the four experimental series: (1) 2 three-digit numbers; (2) 8 three-digit numbers consisting only of 3's and 4's; (3) 63 three-digit numbers made up of even numbers; (4) 512 numbers. These latter numbers represented all the possible three-digit numbers which do not contain the figures 0 or 1. A new selection was made from the table of random numbers for the series of numbers presented in each experiment. The only constant feature was the probability that the symbols for recall would appear. Fifteen subjects (college students) participated in the experiment; 10 sessions under each condition were conducted with each student. The sequence of conditions was also determined according to the table of random numbers. The experimenter read a series of 8 numbers at an even rate of speed and a subject repeated what he could remember of it. This procedure was repeated until the subject could render the entire sequence accurately. The average memory span for a single repetition was determined. Three measurements of memory span were considered: (1) absolute memory span in terms of symbols; (2) in bits; (3) relative memory span (the ratio of the material reproduced to that assigned).

According to the results of these experiments (Figures 17–1 and 17–2) memory span, in terms of symbols and percentages, decreases with an increase in the amount of information to be recalled (input information), the information provided by a symbol, and the length of the alphabet of symbols used; memory span in terms of bits, however, increases somewhat. It appeared that Miller's hypothesis (1956) that memory span is not dependent on the quantity of information but upon the number of symbols applies only to immediate memory. When the material to be recalled exceeds the limits of immediate memory, the reverse trend was evident: in this case memory span depends upon the amount of information and is closer to being a constant if measured by the number of bits rather than the number of symbols

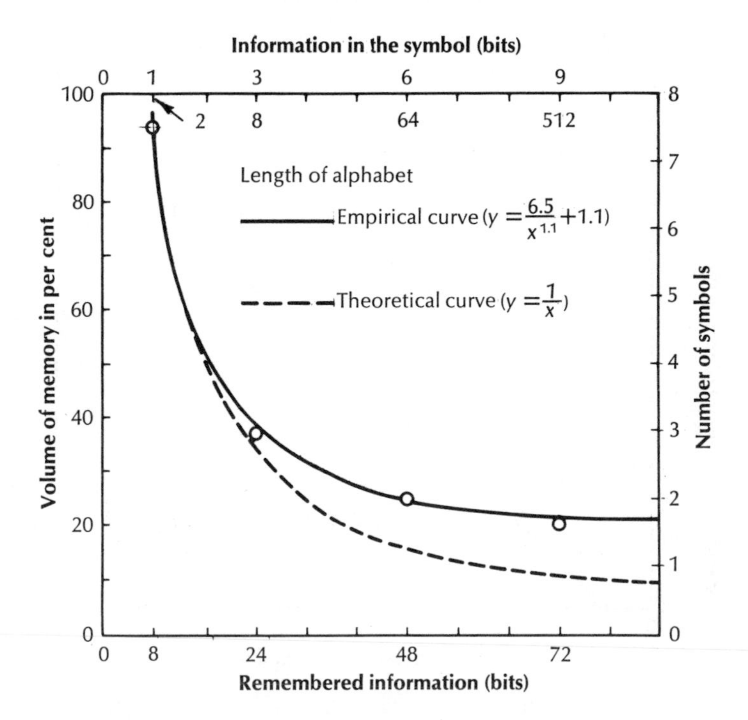

Figure 17–1. Relative and absolute memory span (expressed by the number of symbols) as a function of the amount of recalled information, information contained in a symbol, and length of the list of symbols, given equal probability that symbols from the various lists will appear. (Data obtained by Nevel'skii, 1965.)

reproduced. The same results were obtained by Zinchenko and Nevel'skii in experiments using words and artificial concepts (Nevel'skii, 1965).

A more extensive study of memory span's relation to the amount of information and the number of symbols recalled was conducted by Nevel'skii (1965). These experiments also tested the recall of sequences of three-digit numbers, selected from different lists so that they would have equal probability. Three conditions were investigated. In each condition, of the three parameters of the digit series (the number of symbols to be recalled, the amount of information contained in a symbol, and the entire amount of information for recall), one remained constant while the other two were varied. These experiments indicated that relative memory span depends upon the entire amount of information to be recalled (general uncertainty), but that absolute memory span depends upon information in a symbol. Insofar as the information in a symbol changes with any change in the length of the symbol list, when the symbols were equally probable (which was the

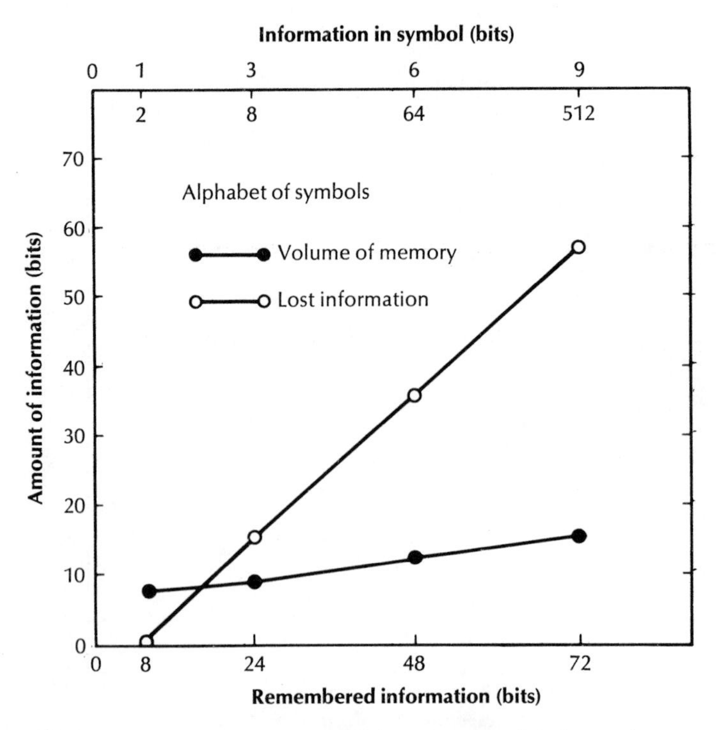

Figure 17–2. Memory span (expressed by amount of information reproduced and amount lost) as a function of the quantity of information recalled, information contained in a symbol, and length of the list, given equal probability that symbols from the various lists will appear. (Data obtained by Nevel'skii, 1965.)

case here), information may be presented either by the logarithm of the length of a list of symbols (log n) or the entropy of the set of probabilities ($-\Sigma p_i \log p_i$). One may then ask: On what does absolute memory span depend? On the nominal information in a symbol or on the length of the symbol list or on the entropy in the whole set of probabilities?

In an attempt to answer these questions, Nevel'skii (1965) and Barkhatova (1964) conducted an additional experiment which differed from the previous ones in that subjects were presented sequences of 15 three-digit numbers whose probability differed but which were selected from the same list. The experiment showed that when the average information in a symbol increases from 1.4 to 9.8 bits, memory span in terms of bits scarcely alters and remains at a level of 11 bits. Changes in memory span in terms of percentages and in symbols are shown in Figure 17–3. From these results it was possible to conclude that memory span in bits is directly dependent upon the nominal information in a symbol, and that memory span in terms of symbols is inversely dependent upon the average information contained in a symbol.

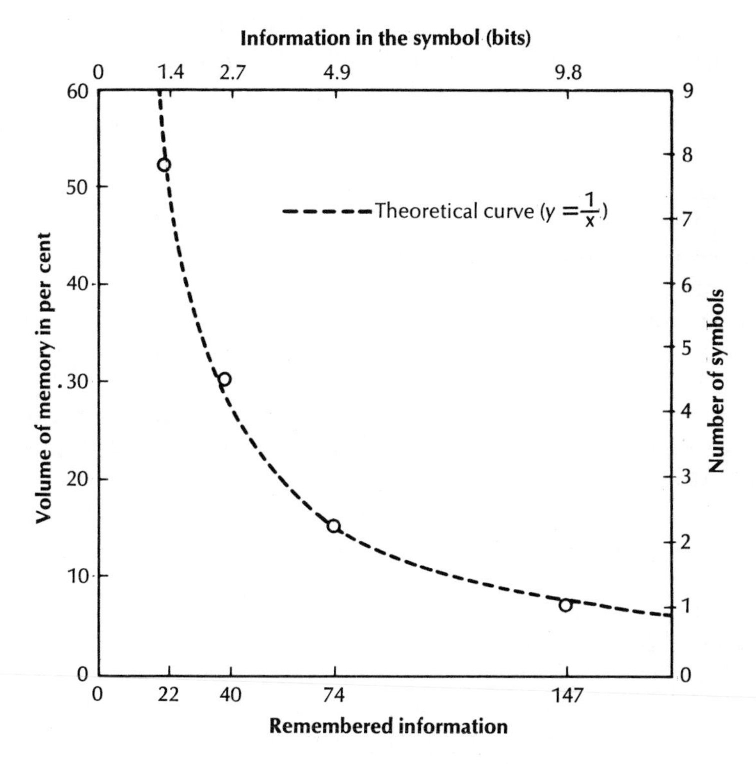

Figure 17–3. Relative and absolute memory span (expressed by the number of symbols) as a function of the amount of memorized information and the average information in a symbol, given equal probability that symbols from a list will appear. (Data obtained by Barkhatova and Nevel'skii.)

Thus, the concept of the amount of information represents three concrete factors which have various effects upon memory span: uncertainty, probability, and variety.

Nevel'skii's hypothesis that memory span is dependent upon the amount of information presupposes that there is a loss of information during recall. This has been borne out by certain facts such as the following: meaningful material is recalled better than nonsense material; verbatim recall is more difficult than recall of general meaning; recall is more difficult than recognition; grouped symbols are recalled better than ungrouped; etc. To reduce the amount of information means that one accepts all the information which has been transmitted but identifies a part of this with what the memory has already retained. For human memory the measure of recalled material is the amount of new information. The less new information there is (for a subject) in the material for recall, the easier it will prove for him to memorize it. Logical analysis of memorized material reduces the amount of new information. During recall a model is formed which reflects the sequential and repetitive events of the external world. The more information there is in an object which the model is to reflect, the longer it takes for this information to be assimilated. A reduction in the amount of information is related to (1) learning most or all of the elements of the model that are being formed from the beginning (repetition plays a major role in this), and (2) the formation of a model from elements that have been assimilated earlier (here understanding plays a major part: it requires fewer repetitions, since it takes advantage of what was learned earlier). The analysis and recoding of information which goes on during recall can be accomplished in two ways: the first is to reduce the amount of information in the symbols recalled by reducing the list of symbols while leaving the number of symbols actually presented unchanged; the second is to decrease the number of symbols by shifting to a new and longer list and replacing the symbols presented by a fewer number of newly learned symbols. The first of these methods represents a conclusion drawn from Nevel'skii's experiments (1965), the second a conclusion from Miller's experiments (1956).

At the same time both methods for increasing memory span, which are directly bound up with a variety of means for treating material to be memorized, have been widely explored by Soviet psychologists interested in problems of memory; at present these methods have become a subject of interest to psychologists abroad as well (Miller, Galanter and Pribram, 1960).

A study of operative memory[8] is important both from a practical and theoretical standpoint (cf. Zinchenko and Repkina, 1964; Repkina, 1965). The concept of operative memory is one which includes the memory processes that act as means whereby some concrete activity is accomplished, for example, when one has to memorize certain initial conditions, or when the conditions of a task (in the broad sense of the term) are such that a subject has to remember intermediate results, the sequence of operations he has performed. Under these circumstances, recall alone is not what matters; it is also important that at the right moment a subject forget information he has already used.

The first exploratory experiments specifically intended to discover some of the features characteristic of operative memory showed that the span, precision, plasticity, and resistance to interference displayed by operative memory depend on the nature of the particular task, as well as on the part these processes play in a subject's activity (that is, do they function as means to accomplish the activity or amount to independent operations in and of themselves?). In the case where they are independent operations, if the means of operative memory have not become automatic, subjects may use means that are not really adequate for the tasks at hand, with the result that the outcome of their work is jeopardized.

---

8. *Editors' note:* The short-term memory required to complete an operation.

In investigations designed to study the effectiveness of various ways of coding information which are necessary to the work performed by operative memory (Repkina and Rizhkova, 1965; Repkina, 1965), subjects were required to use a variety of symbols (numbers, letters, colors, geometrical figures, configurations) in their efforts to solve different tasks. It appeared that in solving these tasks (which taxed subjects' memory to a considerable degree) the most effective types of coding systems were those which made feasible the formation of larger units with which memory could operate, that is, "chunks" of material the memory might retain in solving a problem. The experiments showed that when subjects are required to recall material that is unfamiliar to them, such large units cannot be immediately formed.

In recent experiments by one of the authors (Zinchenko) in which subjects were required to use certain data as the first step toward establishing the sequence with which objects turned up at a designated point, the basic operations during the initial stages of training were extensive, goal-oriented procedures which subjects employed in a given sequence. However, during the course of training there was a shift from the sequential comparison of individual characteristics of objects to a simultaneous "grasp" of a complex of characteristics. Once the former type of operation had become automatic, it led to a change in methods employed by operative memory—to the formation of larger units for the memory to operate with.

All these changes had a distinct effect on the time required for an errorless solution of the task. In the beginning the amount of time required depended chiefly on the number of objects that had been organized into units and the variety of their attributes. During the last stages of training, when subjects were operating with larger units, the time required to solve problems depended simply on the number of objects.

These experiments also measured the formation of rudimentary operative memory units in the course of practice. It is possible that practice does not necessarily result in the formation of large operative memory units for all subjects. The marked improvement in performance shown by such subjects is related to their speeding up operations in which they explore and arrange the material into a good, workable order, rather than to any thoroughgoing restructuring of material. To evaluate this idea, Zinchenko estimated the probability of forming optimal units for memory to work with when the formation of these units is a goal of the subjects' activity. In order to determine this, he employed an activity such as transcribing material from a text. His experiments indicated that operative memory units take shape while a subject is mastering a particular activity. Fundamental to their formation are mnemonic devices; these, in turn, are the cumulative effect of the cognitive and perceptual procedures that have been employed during an activity. In the main, operative memory units are formed when goal-oriented procedures have been converted to automatic operations.

The experiments conducted by Rizhkova (Repkina and Rizhkova, 1965;

Rizhkova, 1965) for the purpose of doing a comparative study of various systems of coding employed a task in which subjects had to determine the location of an object on a panel.

The results indicated that when subjects had to determine the location of an object according to 2 to 4 parameters, or to indicate the position of 2 to 4 objects, they had no difficulty performing the task. But when there was a greater number of objects or more parameters to recall, subjects tended to make mistakes. With a shift from 4 to 5 parameters there was a sharp deterioration of results. This gives us some grounds for assuming that the span of short-term operative memory for a task such as this ranges from 4 to 5 units. The same results were exhibited for all the codes used, the differences in the span of operative memory for different codes being insignificant. However, if subjects rapidly broke the symbols down into groups, they had no trouble recalling them and were also able to retain them while performing an operation.

Experiments conducted by Repkina (Repkina and Rizhkova, 1965; Repkina, 1965) examined the effectiveness of codes using numbers, letters, colors, geometrical figures, and configurations in the solution of various tasks. It was found that when recognition of objects plays a major role (e.g., determining locations, number, or determining value), the comparative effectiveness of the codes was as follows: numbers, colors, geometrical figures, letters, configurations. Moreover, the absolute difference between the codes was not great (for speed, a range of from 4 to 6 seconds; for accuracy, a range of 2 to 15 per cent incorrect answers). In tasks which prove difficult mainly because of the load they place on operative memory (those in which subjects have to compare successive series of information on the basis of quantity, type, value, and the precise order for a particular group of objects), the order of effectiveness of the codes (with respect to their effectiveness) becomes the following: numbers, letters, colors, geometrical figures, configurations. There were sharp variations in the degree of effectiveness (for speed, a range of 4.45 to 10 seconds; for accuracy, a range of 0 to 62.5 per cent incorrect answers). Repkina links these variations to the fact that the different codes did not afford equal opportunity for memory to form operative units during the mnemonic analysis of the material.

The process by which a code is mastered has also proved to be an interesting subject for investigation. Experiments conducted by Rizhkova (Repkina and Rizhkova, 1965) studied the recall and reproduction of codes using letters and geometrical figures (in both their abstract and concrete forms). They found differences in the recall and decoding of symbols which were a function both of the physical terms in which a code was expressed and of the type of relationship between the symbol and the content of information being coded. There were more significant differences between the concrete and abstract variants of a code than between the various code systems (that is, letters and geometrical figures).

The indices of code learning did not always correlate with those of the short-term, operative recall of symbols, which means that, in and of themselves, indices of how well a code list has been learned are not an adequate basis upon which to evaluate a code. From the standpoint of memory, a fuller evaluation of a code would have to take into account both the characteristics peculiar to operative recall of a code and the fact that it is dependent upon the kind of activity performed. Rizkhova (1965) investigated the conditions under which a grouping of coded symbols would promote more effective recall. She found that groupings of coded symbols prove to be of positive value if they correspond to the logical structure of the information being coded. A grouping of signs which does not fit the objects contradicts the logical nature of memory and causes an interference between associations.

Lyaudis (1965) studied the overall operational structure of mnemonic activity and its makeup and the sequence of operative functions. The operations which are common to mnemonic activity were isolated in a number of experiments which analyzed the activity of subjects (adult students) while learning material that varied in content, organization, scope, and other parameters. The materials used were: word series (grouped according to various characteristics or ungrouped); numerical series such as one-, two-, and three-digit numbers; text passages which varied in their degree of logical organization. The results were analyzed in terms of the composition, number, and sequence of elements in each reproduction, the time and number of repetitions required, subject's accounts of the course of recall and reproduction, and so on.

From the analysis of the data, it was possible to draw up the following outline of the composition and sequence of operations performed in mnemonic activity: (1) a stage in which subjects become oriented to the material, assigning elements of it to categories; (2) subjects settle on a way to group the material based on similarity of symbols between the various elements; (3) they establish intragroup relationships of elements and a complex or group as units for use in reproducing material; (4) they set up intergroup relationships of elements and create an internal mnemonic scheme; this, in turn, regulates subsequent reproductions of material.

Other of Lyaudis' experiments studied the degree to which each operation is developed when the three most general features of the material for recall were varied (the length of a series, the type of relationships between elements in a series, the number and length of groups in a series).[9] The results

9. The nature of connections between elements was determined by the length of the "alphabet" from which the elements of the series had been selected: one list of words was taken from a long alphabet (plants and animals), the other from a short one (foliate trees).

indicated that the individual parameters of the material affect the development of operations used for recall in diverse ways. The functions performed by individual operations of the mnemonic process were also determined. The first two operations (categorizing and similarity grouping), which determine the logical, selective nature of recall, have the effect of regulating the performance of subsequent operations. Setting up intra- and intergroup relations (and thus a pattern for later reproductions) helps to ensure that the recall of material will be both complete and permanent.

A developmental study of mnemonic activity conducted by Zhitnikova (1965) is related to Lyaudis' research. Zhitnikova investigated the process by which preschool-age children master the ability to use classification as a means of voluntary remembering. In a training experiment based on Gal'perin's method, the stage-by-stage development of children's ability to classify objects and use this skill as a method of recall was studied.[10]

The stages at which the ability to classify develops in preschool-age children are as follows: (1) *the stage of elementary synthesis*—at this level a child can group objects correctly but is unable to name the group he has composed ($a + b + c$); (2) *the stage of graphic generalization*—the child still cannot designate the group by a generic term and substitutes for it the name of one of the objects of the group ($a + b + c = a$); (3) *stage of verbal generalization*—the child designates the group by a general term which subsumes the group of objects ($a + b + c = D$); (4) *stage of more advanced graphic generalization*—the child is able to designate the group, naming it according to one of its objects before he has gone through the entire process of grouping them ($a = a + b + c$); and (5) *stage of more advanced verbal generalization*—this is the highest stage of development, one in which the child, as a result of rapid orientation to the material, can label the group by a generic term before concluding any detailed classification of the objects ($D = a + b + c$). There are certain regular stages related to those described here at which mnemonic activity develops its individual operations and a child learns to master these. At the fifth stage a child is capable of an intricate type of orientation to the material and of ways of grouping; similarly, his memory can retain these separate groups and use them as an aid in reproducing material. The stages by which the ability to classify develops, as well as the special features that constitute the end product of these stages, may prove significant in dealing with a most difficult area in the field of memory—its modeling functions, and problems connected with the way memory selectively reproduces material it has patterned.

---

10. *Editors' note:* See Chapter 7 of this volume, by P. Y. Gal'perin.

References

Anokhin, P. K. The characteristics of the afferent apparatus of the conditioned reflex and their significance to psychology. *Vop. Psikhol.,* 1955, No. 6.

Baranov, T. P. Experimental phonetics and psychology in the study of a foreign language. *Uch. Zap. Moskov. Gos. Pedag. Inst. Inos. Yaz.,* 1940, No. 1.

Barkhatova, S. G. The relation between the speed and accuracy of recall. Communication 1. *Izv. Akad. Pedag. Nauk RSFSR,* 1964, No. 129.

Berlyne, D. E. Review of "Involuntary Remembering" by P. I. Zinchenko. *Contemp. Psychol.,* 1964, *9,* 323.

Blonskii, P. P. The psychological analysis of remembering. *Uch. Zap. Gos. Inst. Psikhol.,* 1940, *1.*

Blonskii, P. P. Memory and thought. In P. P. Blonskii, *Selected psychological works.* Moscow, 1964.

Borisova, M. N. Investigation of the phenomenon of relative predominance of the first or second signal systems in visual recall. In B. M. Teplov (Ed.), *Typological features of man's higher nervous activity.* Moscow: Izd. Akad. Pedag. Nauk RSFSR, 1956.

Borodulina, A. S. Reproduction in the course of studying from observations of second, fourth, and sixth-grade students. *Uch. Zap. Moskov. Gos. Pedag. Inst. Kaf. Psikhol.,* 1954, *36,* No. 2.

Dul'nev, G. M. The significance of motivation for the exactness and completeness in reproducing text. In *Problems in the psychology of deaf-mute and mentally retarded children.* Moscow, 1940.

El'kin, D. G. Forgetfulness as a conditioned reflex. *Vop. Psikhol.,* 1956, No. 1.

Enikeev, K. R. Intrusions, inventions, and distortions in recall. *Trudy Kaf. Psikh. Pedag. Bashkir. Gos. Pedag. Inst.,* 1946, No. 2.

Faraponova, E. A. Age differences in the recall of visual and verbal materials. In A. A. Smirnov (Ed.), *Problems in the psychology of memory.* Moscow: Izd. Akad. Pedag. Nauk RSFSR, 1958.

Golubev, Y. V. Problems in the psychology of teaching a new foreign language. *Uch. Zap. Leningrad. Gos. Pedag. Inst. im. Gertsena,* 1955, *112.*

Istomina, Z. M. Developmental and individual differences in the relation between incidental and intentional memory in preschool children. *Izv. Akad. Pedag. Nauk RSFSR,* 1946, No. 133.

Istomina, Z. M. The development of voluntary memory in the preschool period. *Izv. Akad. Pedag. Nauk RSFSR,* 1948, No. 14.

Istomina, Z. M. The development of memory by preschool-age children. *Doshkol. Vospit.,* 1953, No. 4.

Komissarachik, K. A. The order of recall of different types of material in high school children. In N. A. Ribnikova (Ed.), *Problems of the psychology of memory.* Moscow, 1958.

Komm, A. G. Reconstruction and reproduction. *Uch. Zap. Leningrad. Gos. Pedag. Inst. im. Gertsena,* 1940, *34.*

Korman, T. A. The psychology of reproduction (experimental research data from kindergartens). *Uch. Zap. Moskov. Gos. Pedag. Inst.,* 1954, *36.*

Krasil'shchikova, D. I. Reminiscence in reproduction. *Uch. Zap. Leningrad. Gos. Pedag. Inst. im. Gertsena,* 1940, *34.*

Krasil'shchikova, D. I. On the relation between recollection and reproduction. *Vop. Psikhol.,* 1955, No. 3.

Krasil'shchikova, D. I. The problem concerning the stability of elementary connections. *Vop. Psikhol.,* 1956, No. 6.

Kudryavtseva, E. M. Changes in the recognition of objects during the course of the development of a student. Candidate's dissertation, Inst. Psikhol. Moscow, 1954.

Leont'ev, A. N. The development of higher forms of recall. In *Problems in the development of the mind.* Moscow, 1959.

Leont'ev, A. N., and Rozanova, T. V. The dependence of association formation on the contents of activity. *Sovet. Pedag.,* 1951, No. 101.

Lipkina, A. I. The reproduction and forgetting of concrete and abstract material. In A. A. Smirnov (Ed.), *Problems in the psychology of memory.* Moscow, 1958.

Lyaudis, V. Y. The structure of mnemonic activity. *Probl. inzhen. Psikhol.,* 1965, No. 3.

Mal'tseva, K. P. Visual and verbal support for memory in school children. In A. A. Smirnov (Ed.), *Problems in the psychology of memory.* Moscow: *Izd. Akad. Pedag. Nauk RSFSR,* 1958.

Matlin, E. K. The influence of similarity on the learning of various material. In A. A. Smirnov (Ed.), *Problems in the psychology of memory.* Moscow: *Izd. Akad. Pedag. Nauk RSFSR,* 1958.

Mayants, D. M. Recall and reproduction of oral material by deaf-mute students. In *The education and training of deaf-mute and mentally retarded children.* Moscow, 1940.

Miller, G. A. The magical number seven, plus or minus two: Some limits on our capacity for processing information. *Psychol. Rev.,* 1956, *63,* 81–97.

Miller, G. A. Galanter, E. B., and Pribram, K. H. *Plans and the structure of behavior.* New York: Holt, Rinehart and Winston, 1960.

Nevel'skii, P. B. Volume of memory and the amount of information. *Probl. inzhen. Psikhol.,* 1965, No. 3.

Nudel'man, M. M. Changes in visual representations during forgetting in deaf and mentally retarded children. In *Problems in the psychology of deaf-mute and mentally retarded children.* Moscow, 1940.

Pinskii, B. I., Incidental learning in the course of repetition and its idiosyncracies in the mentally retarded. *Izv. Akad. Pedag. Nauk RSFSR,* 1948, No. 19.

Prangishvili, A. S. The problem of confidence in recall. *Trudy Inst. Psikhol. Akad. Nauk GSSR,* 1956, No. 10.

Razmislov, P. I. Developmental and individual differences in the recall of emotional-image and abstract material. In A. A. Smirnov (Ed.), *Problems in the psychology of memory. Izd. Akad. Pedag. Nauk RSFSR,* 1958.

Repkina, G. V. An investigation of operative memory. *Probl. inzhen. Psikhol.,* 1956, No. 3.

Repkina, G. V., and Rizhkova, N. I. An investigation of information coding. *Vop. Psikhol.,* 1965, No. 5.

Ribnikova, N. A. The comprehension and reproduction of complex material. In K. N. Kornilov (Ed.), *Problems of contemporary psychology.* Vol. 6. 1930.

Rizhkova, N. I. Various means of coding information. *Probl. inzhen. Psikhol.,* 1965, No. 3.

Rozanova, T. V. Incidental memory for various aspects of a situation as a function of their role in activity. *Vop. Psikhol.,* 1959, No. 4.

Samokhvalova, V. I. Individual differences in the recall of different kinds of material. *Vop. Psikhol.,* 1962, No. 4.

Samokhvalova, V. I. The relation between speed and accuracy in recall. Communication 3. *Izv. Akad. Pedag. Nauk RSFSR,* 1965, No. 138.

Saprykin, P. G. The mechanisms of forgetting. *Trudy Gos. Inst. mozg. im. Bekhtereva,* 1939, *9.*

Sechenov, I. M. *Collected works.* Vol. 1. Akad. Nauk SSSR, 1952.

Shardakov, M. N. Assimilation and preservation in learning. *Uch. Zap. Leningrad. Pedag. Inst. im. Gertsena,* 1940, *36.*

Shekhter, M. S. Some theoretical problems in the psychology of recognition. *Vop. Psikhol.,* 1963, No. 4.

Shvarts, L. A. The role of comparison in mastering similar material. *Izv. Akad. Pedag. Nauk RSFSR,* 1947, No. 12.

Smirnov, A. A. The conditions of retroactive inhibition. *Uch. Zap. Gos. Inst. Psikhol.,* Moscow, 1940, *1.*

Smirnov, A. A. The influence of set and the nature of activity on memory. *Trudy Inst. Psikhol. Tbilisi,* 1945.

Smirnov, A. A. *The psychology of memory.* Moscow: Izd. Akad. Pedag. Nauk RSFSR, 1948.

Sokolov, E. N. Some problems in the study of the memory. *Sovet. Pedag.,* 1954, No. 5.

Solov'ev, I. M. Changes in concepts depending on the source and difference of objects. *Uch. Zap. Gos. Inst. Psikhol.,* Vol. 1, Moscow, 1940.

Solov'ev, I. M. On forgetfulness and its characteristics in mentally retarded children. In *Problems in the education and training of deaf-mute and mentally retarded children.* Moscow, 1941.

Solov'ev, I. M. The psychology of learning. *Sovet. Pedag.,* 1943, Nos. 2, 3.

Ukhtomskii, A. A. What is memory? *Vestnik Znaniya,* 1940, No. 3.

Volkov, I. I. Distribution of practice in studying. *Uch. Zap. Moskov. Gos. Inst. Psikhol.,* 1940, *1.*

Zal'tsman, B. N. Thought processes in remembering. *Nauch. Zap. Inst. Psikhol. UkSSR,* 1949, *1.* (In Ukrainian.)

Zal'tsman, B. N. The role of words in the formation of voluntary reproduction in preschool-aged children. *Nauch. Zap. Inst. Psikhol. UkSSR,* 1956, *4.* (In Ukrainian.)

Zankov, L. V. *The memory of students, its psychology and pedagogy.* Moscow: Izd. Akad. Pedag. Nauk RSFSR.

Zankov, L. V. *Memory.* Moscow, Uch pedgiz, 1949.

Zankov., L. V., and Mayants, D. M. The recall and reproduction of objects in normal and deaf-mute preschool-age children. In *Problems of the psychology of deaf-mute and mentally retarded children.* Moscow, Uch pedgiz, 1940.

Zhitnikova, L. M. The genesis of the structure of mnemonic activity. *Probl. inzhen. Psikhol.,* 1965, No. 3.

Zinchenko, P. I. Problems of involuntary recall. *Nauch. Zap. Kharkov. Gos. Pedag. Inst. Inos. Yaz.,* 1939, *1.*

Zinchenko, P. I. Involuntary remembering. *Sovet. Pedag.,* 1945, No. 9.

Zinchenko, P. I. The dependence of involuntary remembering on the motive of activity. *Nauch. Zap. Inst. Psikhol. UkSSR,* 1948, *1.* (In Ukrainian.)

Zinchenko, P. I. Certain problems of the psychology of memory. *Nauch. Zap. Inst. Psikhol. UkSSR,* 1956, *6.* (In Ukrainian.)

Zinchenko, P. I. Involuntary recall. 1961.

Zinchenko, P. I. *Involuntary remembering.* Moscow: Izd. Akad. Pedag. Nauk, 1962.

Zinchenko, P. I. Nevel'skii, P. B., Rizhkova, P. I., and Sologub, B. V. The psychology of memory and the theory of information. In A. N. Leont'ev, V. A. Zinchenko, and D. U. Panov (Eds.), *Engineering psychology.* Moscow, 1964.

Zinchenko, P. I., and Repkina, G. V. Toward a formulation of the problem of operative memory. *Vop. Psikhol.,* 1964, No. 6.

Zinchenko, P. I., and Sereda, G. K. Incidental memory and learning. *Sovet. Pedag.,* 1964, No. 12.

18

Investigation of the Properties of the Nervous System as an Approach to the Study of Individual Psychological Differences

B. M. Teplov and *V. D. Nebylitsyn*

EDITORS' INTRODUCTION

B. M. Teplov, who died in 1965, was a psychologist of varied interests and talents. His early work on visual perception was conducted in the context of military research into effective means of camouflage. Just prior to World War II, Teplov began to publish articles on the theme that was to dominate the next twenty-five years of his work, individual human differences.

Like many Soviet psychologists, Teplov was influenced by the discussions occurring at the 1950 Pavlovian Sessions of the Academy of Science and the Academy of Medical Sciences. Following this meeting, Teplov's work took on its heavily Pavlovian flavor. However, as this chapter indicates, modifications of Pavlov's ideas on "typology" have been introduced in recent years.

V. D. Nebylitsyn, a student of Teplov's, has succeeded his teacher as Director of the Laboratory of Higher Neural Dynamics at the Institute of Psychology in Moscow; he is also Assistant Director of the Institute.

The research reviewed here indicates the new directions Soviet research is taking in an effort to escape the dead ends in which other typological approaches to human individual differences have found themselves.

The criticism of "testology" presented by Teplov and Nebylitsyn (see also the chapter by El'konin) is typical of such discussions in contemporary Soviet psychology and not unlike criticisms of testing which have appeared in the Western popular press in recent years.

A sign of the greater sophistication of Soviet investigators concerned with techniques involving multiple dependent variables is the increasingly heavy use of correlational and factor analytic techniques which are now a standard part of Nebylitsyn's experimental arsenal.

An extended review of the earlier work referred to in this chapter may be found in Gray (1964).

THE STUDY OF individual differences among people is one of psychology's most basic tasks. The importance of this problem has become especially marked since psychology set itself the task of becoming an applied science. Individual differences include, of course, differences in knowledge, skills, and habits, although the usual textbook discussion of individual differences deals with differences in temperament, character, and abilities.

At the present time, the situation in this highly important branch of psychology is clearly unsatisfactory, a fact recognized by Soviet psychologists.

In Western European and American psychology of the past few decades, individual differences have usually been studied by the so-called test method. There is a major difference of opinion between Soviet psychologists and adherents of "testology" concerning the usefulness of tests.

The word "test" is used to designate relatively short and strictly standardized experiments, the results of which can be expressed in a quantitative form and subjected to statistical analysis. There is no reason to object to "short tests" in principle or to oppose the standardization of the testing conditions. Nor can one object to attempts to express the results of the test in quantitative form, or oppose the statistical processing of the results. What must be objected to is the fact that the vast majority of tests are not based upon a firmly established scientific foundation.

Let us take as an example the Rorschach test, in which the subject is shown ink spots having a "random" design and asked to tell what he can "see" in these spots. Undoubtedly such a test can disclose certain features of the imagination and fantasy. But it is difficult to believe that this test can pretend to disclose the main properties of the human personality in all of its great variety. It is even more difficult to believe that tens of thousands of man-hours have been spent in developing techniques used in the preparation of these blots, that is, standard conditions for conducting the tests, methods for quantifying and analyzing the results. It is also difficult to believe that there are large numbers of people whose special field consists in the administration of Rorschach tests. And, finally, it is impossible not to protest against the fact that many types of "screenings," upon which the fate of human beings depends, are carried out with the aid of "Rorschach" and similar tests.

A significant number of tests represent "samples" obtained in a purely empirical way, whose significance must be established statistically. We believe, however, that if the physiological or psychological meaning of a test is not clear, if a test is "blind," then no statistical processing will be able to yield scientifically reliable results. "Blind tests" cannot acquire a sense of "vision" merely by the application of statistical methods.

This criticism also applies to those testological studies of the correlations between the results obtained with various tests. Since the publication of Spearman's book (1927) on the faculties of man, it has been believed that by using factor analysis it will be possible, solely by analyzing the intercorrelations among tests, to establish a "personality structure." An enormous amount of time and effort was spent on factor-analysis studies. The results obtained to date have been very modest. Neither factor analysis nor the theories based on everyday observation, such as the typologies of Jung or Kretschmer, have yielded anything basically new for an understanding of individual differences. These approaches were unable to provide scientifically valuable results, since they were based on the tacit assumption that one can begin the study of individual differences with a search for methods for the mathematical analysis of experimental results, without the prior investigation of the kinds of properties that should be tested and the methods suitable for testing these properties.

Individual tests have been proposed which are no doubt of scientific interest. These tests must be studied and used. However, "testology" as a whole has not opened up any new paths in the study of individual-psychological differences. In a scientific sense, it has proven itself barren, and in the sphere of practical application it has sometimes even been harmful.

This chapter will mainly describe the work done by the staff of psychologists who have been carrying out research work during the past few years in Teplov's laboratory at the Institute of Psychology in Moscow.

The aim of our staff is to achieve the most accurate possible study of individual differences, using as a starting point a study of the typological properties of higher nervous activity. Since the direction and character of our work has been described before (Teplov, 1955a, b, 1956, 1963), we will restrict ourselves to a review of the highlights of this research.

Types and Properties

Traditionally, there have been two approaches to a scientific characterization of individual differences. First, one can proceed from a quantitative description of certain properties (such as height, weight, sensitivity of each analyzer, memorizing speed, memory stability, etc.). Second, one can group individuals according to types (for instance, by body types—athletic, asthenic, and pyknic; or by types of memory—visual, auditory, motor or graphic, and verbally abstract).

It seems natural to call the first approach analytic, and the second synthetic. Neither approach, because of its one-sided nature, can provide a complete solution to the problem. By following the first approach, a considerable amount of useful empirical information has been obtained, which, by itself, is of no greater use than an incoherent "catalog" of individual characteristics. The second approach rapidly yields results which appear to be very effective and close to life, but which in the final analysis lead to a dead end. This second approach gave rise to such concepts as the introvert and extrovert (Jung) or of the cyclothymic and schizothymic types of Kretschmer, representing typologies which have at times been extremely popular in Western psychology. Attempts to conduct an objective study of individual differences, using such integrated types as a starting point, lead to the appearance of "irrational" methods—such as the Rorschach test mentioned above—which has a false appearance of objectivity resulting exclusively from the statistics used in processing the data, but which prove immune to scientific analysis.

Our staff follows the first approach, basing our work on the physiological concepts of typological properties of the nervous system suggested by Pavlov. Our final goal is the blending, or, more precisely, the meeting of the two research trends.

One of the decisive merits of Pavlov's theory is that Pavlov believed that the types of nervous activity represent "certain complexes of the basic properties of the nervous system" (1951, Vol. 3). The scientific importance and tremendous prospects offered by Pavlov's theory result from this interpretation.

Toward the end of his life, Pavlov became convinced that the basic properties of the nervous system which should be used as a foundation for the theory of animal types were the following: (1) the strength of neural processes, (2) their mobility, and (3) the equilibrium of excitation and inhibition. In his well-known work *General Types of Higher Nervous Activity in Animals and Man,* Pavlov summarized the experimental methods for determining these properties in dogs, using his classical salivary method. Concerning "types," Pavlov wrote the following:

> As a result of the possible fluctuations of the basic properties of the nervous system and possible combinations of these fluctuations, certain types of nervous system should occur; and, as an arithmetical calculation shows, there should be at least 24 such types,[1] but, as reality shows, there is a much smaller number of such types, namely 4 particularly sharp and striking types, which most important of all, differ from each other in their ability to adapt themselves to the surrounding environment and in their hardiness in resistance to harmful agents (1951, Vol. 3).

What are the criteria which Pavlov used to select precisely *four* types out of the twenty-four possible combinations of basic properties?

1. "Particularly sharp and striking." This argument stems from an understanding of type as a "model" of behavior. However, as Teplov has shown (1956, pp. 23–30), even in experimental dogs, typical pictures of behavior do not constitute direct and unambiguous evidence of types of higher nervous activity, understood as complexes of definite properties of the nervous system, a fact which was frequently noted and stressed by Pavlov himself.

2. "Ability to adapt themselves to the surrounding environment." This argument obviously cannot be transferred directly from dogs to man: the ability to adapt himself to the surrounding environment, in the case of man, is most decidedly determined by different factors than is the case for animals.

3. "Resistance to harmful agents." It is difficult to reject this reason. However, the following point deserves attention. Numerous attempts have been made to establish a connection between certain diseases and the types of higher nervous activity. If we examine carefully the studies conducted in this field, we find that the connection was observed not so much between the illness and the *type,* as a characteristic complex of properties, as between the illness and a definite *property* or properties of the nervous system. For example, Davidenkov has established a connection between the inertness of the nervous system and neuroses; people with the most inert nervous systems are more likely to develop neuroses (1947); Chernorutskii (1953) and Lang-Belonogova and Kok (1952) have observed a connection between hypertonic and ulcerous diseases, on the one hand, and weakness and imbalance of the nervous system, on the other. The question arises: would it not be more advisable, instead of attempting to classify patients according to "four types," to direct our work toward finding that property of the nervous system which plays a role in the appearance of a given disease?

The idea of "four types" and the analogy with four kinds of temperament was conceived by Pavlov prior to the maturing of the theory of basic properties of the nervous system. It is understandable, therefore, that the first serious attempts to apply Pavlov's theory of nervous system types to man

---

1. *Editors' note:* Presumably, this refers to the 4! combinations of the four basic properties.

were made not so much on the basis of the "properties" theory, as on the basis of the four types.

Between 1927 and 1935 the number "four" remained unchanged, as well as the tendency to correlate these "four types" with the designations of temperaments going back to ancient times. This tendency was very harmful to efforts to apply Pavlov's teaching on nervous system types to man.

A completely mistaken conviction arose, especially among those who attempted to use Pavlov's theory for practical purposes (in medicine or pedagogy), that the main problem is to divide people into the four types which correspond to the four traditional temperaments. It was often found that the majority of the individuals studied could not be classified under any one of these types; such people were then termed "intermediate."

The study of animals' nervous systems indicated the existence of types which are neither Pavlovian types nor intermediate types. For example: (1) a type characterized by very strong excitatory and very weak inhibitory processes, which is basically different (as admitted by Pavlov himself) from the usual "impetuous" (choleric) type, in which both inhibitory and excitatory processes are very strong and the excitatory process is only slightly dominant over the inhibitory process; (2) an unbalanced type, in which inhibition dominates excitation; (3) types which are unbalanced with respect to the mobility of excitation and inhibition.

There is not the slightest reason to doubt that these types may also be characteristic of human beings.

We understand the word "type" to mean a complex of the major properties of the nervous system. Thus, in order to know how many basic types exist, it is necessary to study the relation between individual properties and to determine which combinations of properties are the most natural and "typical." This problem has not yet been solved. The Pavlovian classification of types provides for a combination of inertness only with the strength and equilibrium of the nervous system (phlegmatic type). However, Teplov has obtained evidence which indicates that a combination of inertness with an imbalance or weakness of the nervous system is apparently more common and "typical" than a combination of inertness with strength and equilibrium (Teplov, 1956, pp. 94–96).

The task confronting us is not simply to preserve Pavlov's theory and to apply this theory to man, but rather to develop his ideas, clearly recognizing the basic foundation of his teaching.

We believe that it is wrong and harmful in practice to assume that the basic foundation of Pavlov's doctrine of types is the postulated existence of "four types," analogous to the four traditional temperaments, and "intermediates" between these temperaments. Using this idea as a starting point, it is impossible to go beyond purely descriptive "typology." This approach transforms the concepts of basic properties of the nervous system (conceived by Pavlov as accurate physiological concepts) into "metaphoric" concepts, which merely translate the features of the human character into a pseudophysiological language.

We believe that basic to Pavlov's doctrine of types is the search for those properties of the nervous system which make it possible to carry out a classification of types. We believe, therefore, that *one has to proceed from "properties" to "types," and not from "types" to "properties."*

The goal pursued by our staff is to study those central properties of man's nervous system which can be considered as "parameters" in the classification of nervous system types. We do not believe it possible to usefully study problems involving "complexes of these properties" until we have progressed sufficiently in the study of properties themselves.

Structure of the Nervous System's Basic Properties

Our analysis will begin with questions about the essence and content of one of the best known but perhaps most obscure of the Pavlovian parameters, namely, the equilibrium of the basic neural processes. We shall use the term "balance" as a synonym of "equilibrium."

It is well known that equilibrium of excitation and inhibition was the indicator underlying Pavlov's first typological clasisfication. In studying the evolution of this concept in Pavlovian typological conceptions, one notices a certain discrepancy between the concept of "equilibrium," as it was understood in the early period (approximately to 1930), and the meaning which it acquired in Pavlov's articles of the 1930's. In his early work Pavlov speaks simply of the equilibrium of neural processes or the predominance of this or that process. In the 1930's he speaks of the equilibrium of neural processes with respect to their strength and the correspondence between excitation and inhibition. Subsequently, properties of the nervous system and the structure of these properties were seen in the following way:

1. Primary properties: the *strength* of the nervous system in terms of excitation and inhibition, and the *mobility* of the nervous system.
2. Secondary property: the stability (balance) of excitation and inhibition as a function of the strength (endurance) of the neural processes.

In order to determine the type of nervous system present in any given case, a standard set of tests was devised (Podkopaev, 1952). To determine the level of excitation with respect to strength, the subject is given caffeine and then presented with an extremely intense stimulus. For evaluation of the inhibitory process, the subject is given a bromide and subjected to prolonged discrimination training. In certain recent studies (Ermolaeva-Tomina, 1963; Nebylitsyn, 1963) balance is understood not as a correlation based on strength, but as the correlation of neural processes according to the way in which positive and inhibitory conditioned reflexes function—in particular, according to rate of learning and amplitude. This approach is based on an interpretation of equilibrium which, while not excluding the existence of equilibrium based on strength, allows for the existence of equilibrium of neural processes according to a different physiological function: the dynamics of the formation of conditioned reflexes.

Thus, the concept of equilibrium has acquired two meanings in recent years. One—the historically older meaning—is equilibrium in terms of "absolute" strength, measured by determining the endurance of the nervous system for excitatory and inhibitory processes. The other, newer meaning is that equilibrium is measured primarily by the correlation of dynamic characteristics of positive and inhibitory conditioned responses in the process of conditioning.

Can it be that the two meanings are identical? It may be that the dynamic characteristics—in particular, the rate of conditioning—of a conditioned response (excitatory or inhibitory) is synonymous with the strength of the nervous system in its relationship to the neural process (also excitatory or inhibitory). In this case the question of two different interpretations of the concept of equilibrium would be unnecessary; those authors who base their typing on rate of conditioning would be correct. Therefore, it is necessary to examine the correlation between strength of the nervous system and speed of conditioning—the basic dynamic index of the process of the formation of temporal connections. There are various points of view on this subject.

Certain investigators (Biryukova, 1961; Krasuskii, 1963; Merlin, 1958) feel that it is possible to consider the speed of formation of positive or inhibitory conditioned responses as indicators of the strength of the nervous system, in accordance with relative excitation or inhibition.

However, experiments done with both animals and people indicate the reverse—that there is no connection between the speed of conditioning and the strength of the nervous system. Fedorov's study yields some extremely convincing data (1961). In quantitative studies of the properties of the nervous systems of mice, he established that there is no correlation between the average magnitude of a response during the formation of a conditioned reflex and responses on the caffeine test (which is a basic measure of strength). Equally low was the correlation between the mean magnitude of differentiation at the beginning of training and the two indicators of the strength of the nervous system in relation to inhibition—the magnitude of differentiation when the physical intensity of the inhibiting stimulus is increased and the effect of repeated discrimination training.

In her studies of conditioned reflexes in cows, Kokorina (1963) found a correlation close to zero between the strength of the nervous system (measured by the caffeine test) and the speed of conditioning.

Our own data, obtained by electroencephalographic methods (Nebylitsyn, 1963), indicate that the speed of formation of temporary connections and work ability (endurance) of the nervous system are two different, uncorrelated functions. Factor analysis of the average conditioned depression of the alpha rhythm in the initial period of conditioning produced a single factor. The tests of inhibition with reinforcement (an indicator of nervous system strength in relation to excitation) produced another factor of neural activity.

Thus, most of the experimental data obtained with various animals and with people indicate that the two forms of equilibrium of arousal and inhibition—in terms of work ability (endurance) and the speed of conditioning—are different parameters of nervous system activity.

It may be, however, that speed of conditioning is dependent on another basic property of the nervous system, namely, its mobility. This has been suggested by Asratyan (1939), Davidenkov (1947), and several other investigators. To answer this question it is first necessary to agree on the meaning of the concept of "mobility." We shall accept the definition as it appears in most contemporary studies—that the basic indicator of mobility is the speed of reconditioning.

The question is thus reduced to the relationship between speed of conditioning and the speed with which the signal meaning of the conditioned stimulus can be altered. If these measures are correlated and if, consequently, formation of temporary connections is a function of the mobility of the nervous system, then obviously we would have to acknowledge that equilibrium of the second (relative) type is nothing more than equilibrium of neural processes with respect to mobility.

But from the outset we must assert that there is no evidence of a correlation between the speed of conditioning and the speed of alteration in the experimental literature. There are descriptions of the rapidity of conditioning in dogs with clearly expressed inert nervous systems (Krasuskii, 1963), but there are no cases of slow conditioned reflex formation in animals followed by rapid alteration. Correlations between rate of conditioning and the alterations of conditioned reflexes are almost zero. Such data have been obtained by three groups of investigators: Borisova *et al.* (1963) using photochemical conditioned reflexes; Ermolaeva-Tomina (1963), using the galvanic skin reflex; and Ravich-Shcherbo (1956), using short-delay and trace photochemical reflexes. In Obraztsova's work with rabbits (1964), the correlation between the speed of the appearance of a stable reflex and alteration was only 0.12.

On the basis of all these data we must conclude that there is no relation between speed of conditioning and mobility of neural processes measured by the speed of alteration. We thus conclude that the speed of conditioning is not linked with either of the basic characteristics of the nervous system, that is, with its strength or its mobility.

On the other hand, the speed of positive and inhibitory conditioning is by no means an isolated function, unrelated to other functions of the central nervous system. Certain aspects of orienting reactions ("baseline" indicators of that physiological process which is involved in the formation of conditioned reflexes, in particular, the background activity of the EEG and a series of other functions of the nervous system) are linked with this function.[2]

There is no doubt that an important function is fulfilled by that factor in higher nervous activity which is correlated neither with the strength of the nervous system nor with its mobility, but which is linked with the success and rapidity of the formation of adequate reactions. Indeed, it is precisely this factor which determines the speed of the organism's primary adaptation to conditions which exist until the reaction can be maintained for a prolonged period at the normal level (the strength of the nervous system), or before there is a need to reverse the form of the activity (mobility of neural processes). We believe that this property of the nervous system, which determines its ability to form reactions adequate for the conditions of the experiment, should be examined as an independent factor of higher nervous activity, and as one of the most important of the basic neural properties.

We can call this property the "dynamicness" of the nervous system. Its basic feature is the ease and rapidity with which it generates the cerebral structures of a neural process in the course of the formation of excitatory or inhibitory conditioned reflexes. The system which is inclined to rapid formation of positive associations is said to be "dynamic" in relation to excitation; a system which rapidly forms inhibitory reflexes will be "dynamic" in relation to inhibition. In addition to these reference points, the property of dynamicness, as we have already stated, has a series of other manifestations.

Returning now to the problem of equilibrium and its interpretations, we conclude that equilibrium of neural processes (according to the interpretation which excludes the concept of balance in strength or mobility) is nothing more than equilibrium of excitation and inhibition defined by the dynamicness of these processes. The reference indicator of balance, as a function of dynamicness, is obviously the correlation between positive and inhibitory conditioned reflexes.

But if, by the term balance (or equilibrium), we mean not only the correlation of excitation and inhibition as a function of absolute strength but also mobility and dynamicness as well, then the concept of balance (or equilibrium) acquires a broader and more general sense than is usually attributed to it. It becomes a general principle of the organization of the properties of the nervous system.

2. *Editors' note:* One of us (I.M.) has repeatedly found this relationship between the orienting reflex and the speed of conditioning. However, the problem of response specificity or the generality of the relationship is still far from resolved.

Thus, in determining the characteristics of the nervous system of a given individual, it is necessary to foresee the "absolute" indicators of all primary properties. On the basis of the data thus acquired one may evaluate a series of secondary properties—the indicators of balance according to any of the properties of the nervous system. At the present time we have reason to speak of four basic properties—dynamicness, strength, mobility, and lability (see below for the latter). Our experiments show that a complete program of tests must consist of twelve quantitative measures, eight of which are primary and basic and four of which are secondary, which will permit an evaluation of balance for each of the properties. Each of these twelve properties may prove to be of special interest in the general picture of individual features of the nervous system in the sense that each of them may have—and apparently does have—its own circle of psychophysiological manifestations and correlates.

Psychological Manifestations of the Basic Properties of the Nervous System

Strength and mobility are properties of the nervous system, and not properties of personality. This means that, when a strong (or weak), mobile (or inert) nervous system is present, various psychological traits of personality may arise during the course of development under various living and educational conditions.

Still, a knowledge of these properties of the nervous system has a very important explanatory significance in the psychology of personality, or more accurately, in connection with individual personality differences.

Rubinshtein (1957) is quite right in distinguishing *two* basic aspects of personality: character and ability. Separation of these two aspects rests on psychological (and not physiological) criteria. From this viewpoint, temperament cannot be considered a special, third psychological characteristic. Temperament can only be considered a special problem within the framework of the problem concerned with character.

In working out the problem of the contents of the concept of "temperament," psychologists have been confronted with a sharp contradiction. On the one hand, psychology has a very long tradition according to which temperaments were characterized by definite psychological traits (although various authors used completely different traits as a basis for characterizing temperaments). On the other hand, as early as 1927, Pavlov identified temperaments with nervous system types: "We are fully entitled to transfer the types of nervous system established in dogs . . . to man. Apparently, these types represent that which we call 'temperament' in people. Temperament is the most general characteristic of each individual man, the most basic characteristic of his nervous system, which leaves an imprint of one type or another on the whole activity of every individual" (Pavlov, 1951, Vol. 3).

How is it possible to "superimpose" the psychological definition of temperament onto the Pavlovian interpretation of temperament as a type of the nervous system? We believe that this problem cannot be solved by a priori, theoretical considerations.

Least vulnerable and most correct are those definitions of temperament in which its psychological characteristic is not given, and where only its connection with a certain type of higher nervous activity is noted (Zaporozhets, 1953; Leites, 1956; Anan'ev, 1956). However, even the authors of such definitions were forced to touch on the psychological content of this concept.

Still, the concept of temperament should include those psychological manifestations, referring to character and not to abilities, which are connected with the properties of higher nervous activity. Probably, one can say that *the natural basis of character is most directly expressed in temperament.* However, it is still a long way from this essentially formal definition of temperament to a truly psychological characterization.

If we admit seriously, and not merely verbally, that "temperament is the psychological manifestation of a general type of higher nervous activity" (Yakusheva, 1956), a thesis which is presently acknowledged by the vast majority of Soviet psychologists, then *methods for determining the properties of a type must be available,* and *we must know both the psychological manifestations of individual properties and the type which is a definite combination of such properties.*

Rarely, however, is anyone concerned with this matter. It is tacitly assumed that these are evident and obvious things, or things which have been clarified by somebody at some time. Yakusheva, for example, has determined the temperament of schoolchildren by means of talks and observations, and makes some far-reaching basic conclusions in regard to the variability of temperaments (Yakusheva, 1956). However, a "diagnosis of temperament" in such studies is made by establishing certain definite psychological traits, either during the course of talks or by observation. But how can the author know that these traits are "psychological manifestations" of a general type of higher activity? The most surprising fact is that this question seems to be ignored by many researchers.

It is quite possible that the "psychological types" described in such studies deserve attention and that a study of these types is quite useful. But why should these types be "supported" by Pavlovian concepts concerning the properties of types of nervous systems? Would it not be better to forgo a "verbal" reliance on Pavlov, and to conduct the analysis on a purely psychological level?

These doubts apply even more strongly to the numerous studies which are not concerned with temperament, but rather with types of higher nervous activity, but in which these types are established only on the basis of so-called real life indices, that is, more or less complex psychological manifestations of personality. As a rule, it is also assumed to be a well-known fact that certain psychological traits are manifestations of the properties of a given type of nervous system.

Naturally, this does not mean that all studies concerned with the properties of a nervous system type or temperament, but conducted on the basis of "real life indices" (by means of observations, talks, "natural experiments," etc.) have no significance whatsoever.

Careful attention should be given to the "real life indices" of strength, equilibrium, and mobility, obtained on the basis of extensive clinical experience by leading workers in Pavlovian clinics (Birman, 1951; Davidenkov, 1947; Ivanov-Smolenskii, 1952b). The ideas expressed by these authors concerning the "real life indices" of the basic properties of the nervous system are carefully thought out hypotheses, of great importance for the direction of an experimental study of the properties of the nervous system.

Also of considerable interest are the studies conducted by Leningrad psychologists, under the direction of Samarin, which are based on prolonged observation and natural experiments with children of nursery, preschool and early school age (Gorbacheva, 1954a, b; Davydova, 1954; Samarin, 1954).

A different approach based on critical factors is the research work performed in our laboratory by Leites (1956). The purpose of this work was not to *use* certain psychological traits as indices of strength, equilibrium, and mobility because they have allegedly been scientifically approved sometime by somebody, but rather to *discover* "those psychological characteristics, which, although in a preliminary and hypothetical way, can still be considered indices of the basic properties of a type of nervous activity."

Special mention should be made of those still very rare studies, in which psychological characteristics, determined on the basis of "real life indices," are compared with experimentally established properties of a nervous system type.

For example, in the study conducted by Makogonova (1957), characteristics of the distribution of attention (the criterion of which was the successful work performed by students of radio schools during a switch to a rate of reception at which it is necessary simultaneously to receive a signal and record the preceding one) were compared with the indices of equilibrium and mobility obtained by the method of motor reactions with a preliminary instruction.[3]

---

3. *Editors' note:* Ivanov-Smolinskii's technique, which is discussed in Chapter 4 of this volume, by A. R. Luria.

Of a similar nature was the study conducted by Il'ina (1956), in which an attempt was made to isolate, in a character trait such as "sociability," that which may depend upon the properties of the nervous system (specifically, on mobility), and that which does not depend upon the properties of the nervous system type, but is determined by the general system of human relations. A similar study was conducted by Palei (1958), who compared manifestations of "restraint" in persons with a balanced and unbalanced type of nervous system, where excitation predominates over inhibition. In the studies of Il'ina and Palei, the properties of the nervous system type were determined both experimentally, using the GSR, and on the basis of real life indices.

Methods for Studying the Typological Properties of the Nervous System

At the present time methodology is probably the most important problem in the investigation of nervous system typology. How can we study the strength of the nervous system or its mobility and their psychological manifestations in the absence of accurate methods for determining these properties?

In the preceding section, we showed how it is possible, using observation, talks, and recollections, to study "psychological manifestations." However, following this course, it is only possible to construct hypotheses regarding what these "manifestations" represent. A truly scientific verification of the "real life indices" of the typological properties of the nervous system can be achieved only by *experimental means.*

The immediate object of our study is a physiological one (properties of the nervous system), even though the work is performed by psychologists and for a psychological purpose—the study of individual differences between people. The object of study becomes a psychological one only during the second stage of the investigation when we consider the problem of the "psychological manifestation" of an already established property of the nervous system.

However, in most cases, an experiment conducted with human subjects is, in its immediate content, a psychological experiment, although it may be a physiological experiment with respect to the object being studied. The fact that subjects' mental activity during the course of an experiment was often ignored, because of the false assumption that the "so-called" mental activity actually constitutes *merely* the dynamics of excitation and inhibition processes, has led to mistaken methods for studying the types of human higher nervous activity.

It is an indisputable merit of Ivanov-Smolenskii that, having consciously borrowed a number of methods from the field of experimental psychology, he analyzed these methods from the standpoint of their possible use for physiological problems, namely, for studying the higher nervous activity of man. Ivanov-Smolenskii's methodological book (1933) has retained its interest to the present day. In enumerating the dangers which confront a researcher engaged in developing a method for studying human higher nervous activity, he correctly pointed out the "danger of excessive methodological analysis of the already extremely complex neural processes" (1933, pp. 30–31).

It is not the technical complications which are dangerous, but rather psychological complications, for example, the creation of a situation in which the results of an experiment depend least of all on the natural characteristics of the subject's nervous system, but are determined, instead, mainly by complex psychological factors.

Ironically, the most typical methods, which have been "complicated" in this undesirable sense, are precisely those methods which are generally associated with the name of Ivanov-Smolenskii. I have in mind here the "motor method with spoken reinforcement" and the so-called "associative experiment." As early as 1917, Ivanov-Smolenskii started to use the motor method in its classical form, that is, with a preliminary instruction. In a study published in 1926, he first used a new variation of this method, in which the preliminary instruction was replaced by a "spoken reinforcement," that is, by the order "Press" given after the application of the stimulus which one desired to convert into a positive conditioned stimulus, and by the order "Do not press" given after those stimuli which one desired to convert into negative, inhibiting stimuli. By introducing this change in method, Ivanov-Smolenskii believed that he was simplifying, and not complicating, the method. In reality, the opposite occurred.

A situation was created which is very ambiguous from a psychological standpoint. When should the subject press? Should he press after getting the command "Press," or without waiting for this command? Should he press after the appearance of that signal which, during previous requests, preceded the command "Press"? Subjects, ranging from older children of preschool age to adults, are unavoidably confronted with this question and behave according to their own "self-instructions." Povorinskii, a student of Ivanov-Smolenskii's who used this technique, admits that in a number of subjects a conditioned reflex is not produced by spoken reinforcement. These subjects do not press upon receiving a signal, but only upon receiving the command "Press." He is also fully aware of the cause of this pheomenon: "Certain subjects told the experimenter that they 'decided' or 'considered' it necessary to press only when the command 'press' was given" (Povorinskii, 1954). However, strange as it might seem, he believed that these cases happen with experimenters "who are inexperienced in the method of spoken reinforcement" and are caused by a lack of "skill and persistence" on the part of the experimenter.

It is not by chance that Povorinskii uses the words "decided" and "considered" in quotation marks in the passage cited above. Even though he admits that people are actually capable of "deciding" and "considering," he still believes that these "decisions" cannot be the reasons for their actions. At the same time, he invokes (incorrectly) the authority of Sechenov: "it is well known that even Sechenov believed invoking thought as the primary cause of behavior was 'the greatest possible falsehood' " (1952, Vol. 1, p. 34). Povorinskii's misunderstanding lies in the fact that, in making such a statement, Sechenov laid an emphasis only on the word "primary." For Sechenov also wrote: "Our actions are directed not by phantoms such as various forms of the 'I,' but by our thoughts and feelings" (1952, Vol. 1, p. 267). To postulate the ineffectiveness of cognitive processes and to assert that the thoughts and decisions of a man cannot be the cause of his actions is to exclude the possibility of a scientific elaboration of methods for studying the higher nervous activity of man.

Human thought, reasoning, and decisions do not constitute an object of study in works devoted to typological properties of the human nervous system. But this does not mean that they should be ignored. It means that they should be carefully analyzed, in order to make corresponding tests as unambiguous as possible. *The absence of a preliminary instruction imparts a maximum degree of ambiguity to tests and therefore makes them most unsuitable for studying the typological properties of the nervous system.*

Luria, in whose laboratory this method was subjected to a prolonged and careful study, correctly noted that the so-called "production" of motor reactions by this method has a "complex, mediated character." "Tests involving the 'production' of a motor reaction according to the method of spoken reinforcement," writes Luria, "are actually transformed, in older children and adults, into tests involving the solution of a problem by analysis and generalization, which are carried out with the aid of the test's own speech connections, and in this respect such tests do not differ greatly from tests devoted to concept formation" (Luria, 1956). The questions as to which solution will be adopted by the subject and to what extent this solution will be "stable" has no direct relation whatsoever to such relatively simple (though sometimes complexly manifested) properties of the nervous system as strength and mobility.

In our previous work, we stressed the fact that in studying the properties of the nervous system, the methods of involuntary reactions and not the methods dealing with voluntary movement are of basic importance (Teplov, 1956). This thesis followed from an attempt to find methods which are relatively simple in a psychological sense and have a minimum degree of psychological ambiguity. We also seek indices that have a minimum degree of psychological ambiguity and that have the maximum possible direct relationship to the natural properties of the nervous system, accounting (or, even better, equalizing in different subjects) with relative ease for the influence of complex systems of verbal connections. These requirements, which were noted in our previous work, are still valid. However, the formula "methods of involuntary reactions" instead of "methods of voluntary reactions" now appears too simplified, yielding a poor picture of the actual state of affairs.

The first objection to this simple formula is that, in deciding whether a given method involves "voluntary" or "involuntary reactions," it is not so much the nature of the reactions themselves as the character of those processes which constitute the actual object of study which are of crucial importance. For example, the usual method of motor reactions is more or less a method of involuntary reactions if the dependent variable is the strength of a response immediately following some other response, because, under certain conditions, the subject cannot control this aftereffect. However, from a terminological standpoint, it is not advisable to designate the method of motor reactions as a method of involuntary reactions, no matter what indices the experimenter is interested in. Many methods cannot be subdivided at all on the basis of the "voluntary" or "involuntary" nature of the reactions.

Second, the experiments reviewed above show the many valuable possibilities involving typical methods of involuntary reactions. At the same time, only a few characteristic methods of voluntary reactions have as yet proven themselves useful for studying the typological properties of the nervous system. Without pretending to give a complete review of methods presently used in studying the typological properties of the nervous system, we shall discuss certain of these methods, which are now attracting the attention of research investigators.

Among the typical methods of involuntary reactions (or "autonomic" methods), we are using with increasing success the method of the so-called photochemical conditioned reflex (based on the conditioned-reflex variation in light sensitivity) which developed from a fact discovered for the first time by Dolin (1936).[4] Maizel' (1956) used this method to study the equilibrium of excitation and inhibition. Ravich-Shcherbo (1956) has shown that the rate of "transformation" of photochemical conditioned reflexes may be one of the indices of mobility. Rozhdestvenskaya (1956) found evidence in her early work that this method may be used to determine the strength of cortical processes. Recently, she has developed a special variation of this method, which, in our opinion, is one of the most direct and valuable meth-

4. *Editors' note:* The unconditioned response to a flash of light is pupillary constriction and temporary insensitivity of the retina. Soviet investigators have found a conditioned increases in threshold, due presumably to temporary insensitivity of the retina. This conditioned response is called a photochemical reflex.

ods for determining the strength of neural processes (1963). We shall talk in detail about this method in the next section.

Until quite recently, we believed that the photochemical reflex characterized the strength, mobility, and equilibrium of neural processes in the visual analyzer. However, Nebylitsyn (1957) showed that a photochemical conditioned reflex characterizes the typological properties of that analyzer to which the stimulus is addressed. Auditory stimuli were used as conditioning stimuli by Nebylitsyn; in this form, the photochemical method does not characterize the properties of the visual analyzer, but rather the properties of the auditory analyzer. It is possible, of course, to select visual stimuli as conditioning stimuli (either sufficiently weak stimuli, or, even better, red light). Conditioned photochemical reflexes in response to visual stimuli were first used by Ravich-Shcherbo (1956). They apparently characterize the properties of neural processes taking place in the visual analyzer.

It is obvious that conditioned photochemical reflexes can be produced in response to a stimulus from any analyzer. Moreover, as was demonstrated by Shvarts (1956), words (second-signal-system stimuli) may act as conditioned stimuli for a photochemical reflex. Thus, it is clear that the photochemical reflex involving the use of various conditioned stimuli may lead to a study of not only specific, but also of general typological properties of the nervous system.

The exceedingly laborious nature of this method still constitutes its basic defect; as a rule, several weeks, and sometimes even several months of work with each subject are required in order to answer any typological question.

Merlin (1958) and his associates have used the galvanic skin response (GSR) to determine the types of nervous system and individual typological properties. Among the significant defects of the GSR, the following might be mentioned: (1) considerable variations in the magnitude of both the conditioned and unconditioned GSR during the course of one and the same session; (2) instability of the positive reflex; (3) lack of clarity of a differentiation; (4) fading of the positive conditioned reflex, in spite of reinforcements. However, the results obtained using the GSR compared with the results obtained for the same properties on the basis of recollections and observation (according to "real life indices") have shown good agreement.

Ermolaeva-Tomina (1963) conducted a series of experiments in our laboratory in order to determine the potential of the GSR. The experiments were designed to compare GSR measures with each other and with certain proven indicators of the strength of the nervous system. Fourteen subjects were run in experiments involving the formation of conditioned responses and their differentiation, inhibition of the orienting and conditioned reflexes, alteration of the CS, increase of the intensity of the CS (both with and without caffeine), and the like. It is not possible for us to give a detailed description of the resulting comparisons. We will note here only her conclusion that the GSR may be useful in evaluating the balance of neural processes but is of doubtful use for determining the strength of the nervous system. The GSR method is, in essence, rather limited as an approach to the complex study of the properties of the nervous system. However, at the present time studies are being conducted which indicate that there may be new potential in the GSR which has not yet been discovered.

In our laboratory the electroencephalographic method, based on the measurement of the brain's reaction to various sensory stimuli, plays a major role in studying the nervous system. This approach is valued for its objectivity, for the fact that it can be used with any subject—in particular with very young children—for the relatively short duration of the tests necessary to obtain many measures, and finally, because it enables us to directly evaluate the dynamics of cerebral processes. It has been shown that alpha blocking of the occipital area either as orienting activity or as a conditioned response is a measure of the dynamics of excitatory and inhibitory processes (Nebylitsyn, 1964). The mean duration of the conditioned reflex blockade of the alpha rhythm, measured by presenting an isolated CS (usually a tone), is a basic measure of the dynamicness of excitation. The generally high correlation between speed of differentiation and the speed of inhibition of an earlier developed conditioned reaction is the basic measure of the dynamicness of inhibition. When the corresponding matrices of intercorrelations are factor analyzed, all three measures form a single factor which may be identified as the dynamicness of inhibition, separate from the dynamicness of the alpha index, that is, the amount of alpha activity. The alpha index is higher in people with high inhibition dynamicness and lower in people with high excitation dynamicness. Other EEG parameters (frequency and amplitude) also reveal a definite connection with the measures of dynamicness of either excitation or inhibition, although the corresponding correlations are often not statistically significant. Thus, a whole syndrome of measures grouped around the parameter of dynamicness may be revealed with the aid of electroencephalographic methods.

These methods have demonstrated the existence of still another property of the nervous system. We are speaking of lability. The first claim for its existence was made on the basis of the collective work of Borisova *et al.* (1963). Thirty-six measures, 34 of which were felt to be indicators of mobility, were subjected to comparison, correlation, and factor analysis. The resulting correlations bore witness to the fact that mobility can be divided into at least two unassociated characteristics of the nervous system.

One property, characterized by alteration of signs of conditioned stimuli, we shall call mobility, according to firmly established tradition. However, it should be noted that this property is still very poorly studied from the point of view of its physiological content.

The other property is characterized by the speed of the appearance and cessation of the neural (arousal) process. In the above-mentioned collective work of Borisova *et al.,* this property was manifested in adequate visual chronaxie, critical flicker-frequency, speed of recovery of light sensitivity after light presentation and several other indicators.

Study of the Strength-Weakness Parameter of the Human Nervous System

Strength is one of the most important properties of the nervous system. A study of this parameter is not only a problem of basic importance to an understanding of the typological properties of the nervous system, but a problem on which (until recently) little work has been done because of methodological difficulties.

The basic characteristic of the strength of the nervous system is the "work ability of the cortical cells" (Pavlov, 1951, Vol. 3, p. 344). The experience of the Pavlovian laboratories indicates that the best way to test the limits of work ability of the cerebral cells and, consequently, the strength of the nervous system, is to test their ability to endure intense excitation by stimuli under conditions of prolonged or repeated stimulation for short time intervals.

At the moment our laboratory divides its time between two methods designed to test the ability of the cortical cells to endure prolonged and oft-repeated arousal concentrated on the same "cortical point." In the first method the subject is conditioned to give a photochemical reflex, as manifested by a decrease in visual sensitivity in the presence of the CS. Concentration of excitation is obtained by going on to form a discrimination.

The second method, inhibition with reinforcement, was worked out by Nebylitsyn (1963), using the electroencephalographic method. In working out this method it was necessary to overcome one great difficulty—the extreme instability and lability of conditioned reflex blocking of the alpha rhythm.

Conditioned desynchronization is easily developed in many people (but by no means in all!), but is just as easily lost. The cause of this adaptation lies in the neutral nature of the light stimulus, usually applied as a reinforcement, which has no signal meaning. Nebylitsyn's solution was to present subjects with various reinforcing stimuli (not only light) with instructions to remember them and to be prepared to answer questions about them after the experiment. When this kind of reinforcement (which we have called "activating") was used, the conditioned blocking of the alpha rhythm was very stable in the majority of subjects. This gave us reason to assume that changes in the magnitude of conditioned reactions involved in extinction with reinforcement are not artifacts, but actually occur as a result of transfer of nerve cells to the state of excessive inhibition owing to exhaustion of the reserve of functional cells.

The technique of extinction with reinforcement using the electroencephalographic method is as follows. First, the orienting response to the CS is extinguished. A series of conditioning trials is then given and the subject develops a conditioned reflex. Then one isolated presentation of the CS evokes depressed alpha rhythms. In our experiments the CS was a 1,000-cps interrupted tone whose mean intensity was 50 db, and duration 4 seconds. The subject lay with his eyes open in a dark, soundproof chamber. Before his eyes was a white screen. Films were projected onto the screen through a hole in the chamber's wall. In the course of all 50 conditioning trials only one picture was presented on the screen. The instructions were that the subject attentively watch the screen until the end of the experiment and to try to remember the smallest details of the picture in order to answer the experimenter's questions. Bipolar occipito-temporal records were taken. The registration of brain waves was done with a four-channel electroencephalograph. We used 22 subjects between the ages of 20 and 26.

The use of active reinforcement led, in most cases, to extremely rapid (2 to 5 trials) and stable formation of a conditioned reflex, prior to extinction with reinforcement. After discrimination training with an interrupted tone of 250 cps, extinction with reinforcement was begun. The subjects were presented with 50 combinations of conditioned and reinforcing stimuli, with only a 4-to-5-second interval between trials (the interval in the ordinary experiment is 15 to 20 seconds. In order to observe the dynamics of the conditioned reaction, the sound was presented without reinforcement after trials 3, 7, 10, 15, 20, etc., 12 times in all. The entire procedure took about 15 minutes.

The results were analyzed in the following way. The duration of alpha-rhythm depression (in seconds) during the action of the CS served as a measure of the magnitude of the conditioned reaction. Inasmuch as the magnitude of conditioned reflexes sometimes changes considerably from measurement to measurement, it was decided to use the mean of three successive trials; for example, from 1–3, 4–6, 7–9, and 10–12. Since the first measurement was taken before the beginning of extinction with reinforcement, we used a ratio of the means of trials 4–6, 7–9, and 10–12 to those of trials 1–3 as a measure of the change in the strength of the response.

In one group of subjects the magnitude of the conditioned reaction did not really change or was lowered only slightly by the end of the experiment. In view of the work done with photochemical reflexes, this gave us reason to put all these subjects into the category of strong types of nervous systems. Another group of subjects manifested a marked decrease in the conditioned reflexes. These subjects must be considered as weak types. Finally, there was a group of subjects who occupied a middle position: we considered them of intermediate strength. Thus, it was assumed that a change in the conditioned reaction of less than 70 per cent of the baseline level is a sign of strength of the nervous system. A decrease of more than 50 per cent was considered an indication of weakness of the nervous system as it relates to excitation.

As we have already indicated, a more intense CS should, according to the logic of the experiment, raise the effectiveness of the test, that is, should lead to a greater decrease in the conditioned reflex as a consequence of massed trials, than is observed in the ordinary experiment. For this reason the loudness of the conditioned stimulus was varied in Rozhdestvenskaya's experiment (1963) using the EEG method. The curve for the group of "weak" subjects is lower than that which is found in the usual experiment. A fall in the conditioned reaction also occurs in "strong" subjects. This indicates the correctness of the assumption that the more intense conditioned reflex is more effective as a test of the excitatory strength of the nervous system. It follows, then, that we are justified in using extinction with reinforcement as a method for determining the strength of the nervous system. It is interesting that, while increasing the loudness of the CS led to lowered response magnitude with the "weak" subjects, the decrease was much less marked than the corresponding decrease for the "strong" subjects. This can probably be explained by the fact that individuals with weak nervous systems were already close to the limit in the previous session when the conditioned stimulus was less intense. Therefore, the louder stimulus could not exert additional influence on the transition to a state of excessive inhibition. Increasing the intensity of the CS brought each function to its physiological limit, but the magnitude of the decrement during the extinction with reinforcement varied as a function of distance from the limit of nervous system strength at the original intensity. These pilot data were then confirmed in a new series of experiments conducted in almost the same way (Nebylitsyn, 1965).

In 1955, Teplov advanced the hypothesis that a weak nervous system is characterized not only by a negative property, namely, a low limit in working ability, but also by a positive property, namely, high reactivity. On the basis of theoretical considerations, previously advanced by Pavlov, we stated the assumption that a low level of working ability can be considered the consequence of a high degree of reactivity (Teplov, 1955b).

The hypothesis of a connection between the weakness of the nervous system and high reactivity has made it possible for us to use a second technique—the study of sensitivity—for studying the strength-weakness parameter. The most natural and simple step in that direction was the study conducted by Nebylitsyn (1956), who has demonstrated the presence of a negative correlation between the strength of nervous processes in a visual analyzer and absolute visual sensitivity measured by the usual technique for determining the threshold using a verbal response.

Also significant in this context are facts concerning changes in sensitivity under the influence of caffeine. Nebylitsyn has shown that the consumption of caffeine by persons with a strong nervous system either does not cause any change in sensitivity or causes a slight increase in sensitivity, whereas the consumption of caffeine by persons with a weak nervous system causes either a strong increase in sensitivity or a drop in the sensitivity, even though the latter might be only a slight drop (Nebylitsyn, 1956). A method for determining the strength of the nervous system, based on these facts, is widely used in our laboratory.

The last group of methods used in studying the strength-weakness parameter of the nervous system is associated with the effect exerted by an additional distracting stimulus on the absolute visual sensitivity. Here, the reactivity of the nervous system assumes still another form, namely sensitivity to the action of distracting stimuli. This method is based on the following fact: the sensitivity of a dark adapted eye to a point-stimulus increases when an additional *weak* point-stimulus is present in the field of vision, and *drops* when an additional *strong* point-stimulus is present. The higher sensitivity can be explained by the irradiation of the stimulation from a focus corresponding to the weak stimulus; the drop in sensitivity can be explained as a result of the negative induction from a stronger, and consequently, a concentrated focus (Teplov, 1941). Let us recall the general law formulated by Pavlov: "During weak stimulation, irradiation takes place; during medium stimulation, concentration takes place; and during very strong stimulation, irradiation again takes place" (Pavlov, 1951).

Rozhdestvenskaya (1955) has shown that caffeine, as a rule, decreases sensitivity in the presence of strong irrelevant stimuli, and reduces, or even converts into the opposite effect, the increase in sensitivity in the presence of weak irrelevant stimuli. This action of caffeine is different in different people. The most interesting fact is that, in persons with a weak nervous system, or more accurately, with a weak stimulative process in the visual analyzer, only small doses of caffeine exert such an effect, whereas stronger doses (0.2 or 0.3 gm) have a paradoxical effect: strong irrelevant stimuli cause an increase and not a drop in sensitivity, that is, irradiation and not a negative induction.

These tests disclosed a further index of strength, which almost always coincides with the one just described above. Under normal conditions, that is, without the use of caffeine, an increase in sensitivity from a weak distraction is scarcely observed at all in highly reactive persons (i.e., persons with strong excitatory processes) whereas a decrease in sensitivity from a strong distraction is very clearly expressed. In persons with weak excitatory processes, on the contrary, an irradiation of stimulation (that is, an increase in sensitivity) from a weak distracting stimulus is very clearly expressed, and negative induction (a drop in sensitivity) from strong distractors is poorly expressed.

Let us examine the first index, the paradoxical effect of relatively strong caffeine doses in persons with a weak nervous system. Rozhdestvenskaya (1957) showed that an increase and not a reduction in sensitivity in the presence of a relatively strong distracting stimulus (for example, a stimulus which is a hundred times greater than the magnitude of the absolute threshold) can be obtained, without having recourse to caffeine, by two other methods:

1. By means of repeated trials (twenty trials in a row at one-minute intervals) and measurement of sensitivity in the presence of an extraneous stimulus. As a result of summation, this stimulus, it must be assumed, becomes, as it were, "very strong" (in the same way that it became "very strong" as a result of higher excitability caused by caffeine) and causes, not concentration and negative induction, but an irradiation of stimulation.

2. By means of repeated measurement of sensitivity (twenty times in a row at one-minute intervals) without any distraction stimulus. This results in a temporary weakening of the cells to which the main stimulus is addressed. The limit of the working ability is reduced, and sensitivity drops also. It was found that, in cells which have been brought into such a condition, a distractor stimulus, which usually causes a drop in sensitivity, now causes an increase in sensitivity. Descriptively, it can be said that, in relation to the debilitated group of cells, the distractor stimulus of medium strength acts as a "very strong stimulus." It should be recalled that such an effect can be obtained only in persons with a weak excitatory process in the visual analyzer, and therefore acts as one of the indices of weakness of neural processes in the visual analyzer.

We now believe that these two methods are even better indicators of the strength of neural processes than the caffeine test.

Let us now turn to the second index of this method: in persons with weak nervous systems there is a tendency toward an increase in visual sensitivity in the presence of another visual stimulus, while in persons with a strong nervous process there is a tendency toward a decrease in visual sensitivity in the presence of another visual stimulus.

Ermolaeva-Tomina (1957) used the same technique for measuring sensitivity of the eye as Rozhdestevenskaya did with the difference that in some cases the measurements were performed in complete silence, while in others the measurements were conducted in the presence of a clicking electric metronome.

It was found that, in some subjects, the clicking of the metronome increased the visual sensitivity, while in others it reduced this sensitivity. The effect of the click of the metronome at the time it is switched on or off, as well as in the very early tests (that is, when an orienting reflex plays a predominate role), may be different in different subjects.

The varied effect exerted by additional visual and auditory stimuli upon visual sensitivity has not yet been explained satisfactorily. At the same time, the diagnostic importance of this type of test from the standpoint of a study of the strength-weakness parameter is indisputably very great. A primary indication of this is the extremely sharp differentiation of subjects in such a test. Achieving a clear understanding of these complex and contradictory facts represents one of the most important tasks confronting our staff at the present time.[5]

References

Anan'ev, B. G. The development of abilities and character. In *Conference on Problems of the Psychology of Personality.* Moscow: Akad. Pedag. Nauk RSFSR, 1956.

Asratyan, E. A. The study of physiological lability of the higher nervous stages. *Uch. Zap. LGU,* 1939, No. 41.

Birman, B. N. Experimental clinical-physiological determination of types of higher nervous activity. *Zh. vyssh. nerv. Deyat.,* 1951, *1*, No. 6.

Biryukova, Z. I. *The higher nervous activity of athletes. Investigation of typological differences of the nervous system.* Moscow: Izd. Fizkult. Sport, 1961.

Borisova, M. N., Gurevich, K. M., Ermolaeva-Tomina, L. B., Kolodnaya, A. Y., Ravich-Shcherbo, I. V., and Shvarts, L. A. A comparative study of different measures of mobility of the nervous system in man. In B. M. Teplov (Ed.), *Typological features of man's higher nervous activity.* Vol. 3. Moscow: Izd. Akad. Pedag. Nauk RSFSR, 1963.

Chernorutskii, M. V. On the cortico-visceral pathogenesis of ulcers. *Zh. vyssh. nerv. Deyat.,* 1953, *3,* No. 1.

Davidenkov, S. N. *Evolutionary-genetic problems in neuropathology.* Leningrad, 1947.

---

5. *Editors' note:* It is of some concern that essentially the same kind of procedure with the addition of physiological measures has been used as evidence that the generalized orienting reflex facilitates perceptual sensitivity. The marked individual differences reported here limit the generality of the theoretical implications of the orienting reflex, and reveal a serious limitation in single subject research which ignores individual differences. Another matter of concern is that these individual differences, at least the ones determined in the threshold experiments, cannot unequivocally be ascribed to differences in sensitivity. Signal detection or forced choice procedures are needed to determine whether these individual differences might be a consequence of different criteria of certainty adopted by the subjects.

Davydova, A. N. An experimental study of children with different types of nervous system. *Izv. Akad. Pedag. Nauk RSFSR,* 1954, No. 52.

Dolin, A. O. New facts toward a physiological understanding of human learning (photochemical conditioned reflex in the eye). *Arkh. biol. Nauk,* 1936, *42,* Nos. 1–2.

Ermolaeva-Tomina, L. B. Certain features of attention connected with the intensity of nervous processes. *Dokl. Akad. Pedag. Nauk RSFSR,* 1957, *3.*

Ermolaeva-Tomina, L. B. Using the GSR to define the typological properties of the nervous system in man. In B. M. Teplov (Ed.), *Typological features of man's higher nervous activity.* Vol. 3. Moscow: Izd. Akad. Pedag. Nauk RSFSR, 1963.

Fedorov, V. K. A comparison of different tests for evaluating higher nervous activity. *Zh. vyssh. nerv. Deyat.,* 1953, *3,* No. 1.

Fedorov, V. K. Comparison of the results of different experiments in the evaluation of basic properties of the higher nervous activity of mice. *Zh. vyssh. nerv. Deyat.,* 1961, *11,* No. 4.

Gorbacheva, V. A. Experimental study of individual differences in three-year-old children. *Izv. Akad. Pedag. Nauk RSFSR,* 1954, No. 52. (a)

Gorbacheva, V. A. Formation of child behavior in a junior group of a kindergarten. *Izv. Akad. Pedag. Nauk RSFSR,* 1954, No. 52. (b)

Gray, J. A. *Pavlov's typology: Recent theoretical and experimental developments from the laboratory of B. M. Teplov.* London: Pergamon Press, 1964.

Il'ina, A. I. Sociability in school children as a function of the mobility of nervous processes. In *Conference on Problems of the Psychology of Personality.* Moscow: Izd. Akad. Pedag. Nauk RSFSR, 1956.

Ivanov-Smolenksii, A. G. Comparative study of the higher nervous activity of man and dogs. *Med. Biol. Zh.,* 1926, No. 3.

Ivanov-Smolenskii, A. G. *Methods for studying human conditioned reflexes.* (2nd ed.) Moscow: Medgiz, 1933.

Ivanov-Smolenskii, A. G. *Outline of the physiopathology of higher nervous activity.* (2nd ed.) Moscow: Medgiz, 1952.

Kokorina, E. P. The appetitive motor reflex as a method for measuring the fundamental neural process and type of nervous system. *Zh. vyssh. nerv. Deyat.,* 1963, *13,* No. 2.

Krasuskii, V. A. A method for the study of types of nervous system in animals. *Trudy Inst. Fiziol. im. Pavlova,* 1953, *2.*

Krasuskii, V. A. A method for evaluating the properties of nervous processes in dogs and the genetics of types of higher nervous activity. *Zh. vyssh. nerv. Deyat.,* 1963, *13,* No. 1.

Lang-Belonogova, N. S., and Kok, E. P. The significance of an amnesia in determining type of higher nervous activity and in clarifying the functional condition of the central nervous system preceding illness. *Trudy Inst. Fiziol. im. Pavlova,* 1952, *1.*

Leites, N. S. Typological differences in the aftereffect of excitation and inhibition. In B. M. Teplov (Ed.), *Typological features of man's higher nervous activity*. Moscow: Izd. Akad. Pedag. Nauk RSFSR, 1956. (a)

Leites, N. S. An experiment in the psychological characteristics of temperaments. In B. M. Teplov (Ed.), *Typological features of man's higher nervous activity*. Moscow: Izd. Akad. Pedag. Nauk RSFSR, 1956. (b)

Luria, A. R. Some problems in the study of the higher nervous activity of normal and abnormal children. In *Problems concerned with the higher nervous activity of normal and abnormal children*. Moscow: Izd. Akad. Pedag. Nauk RSFSR, 1956.

Maizel', N. I. Study of the typological differences in equilibrium of excitation and inhibition using the photochemical reflex method. In B. M. Teplov (Ed.), *Typological features of man's higher nervous activity*. Moscow: Izd. Akad. Pedag. Nauk RSFSR, 1956.

Makogonova, A. A. Distribution of attention in radio operators as a function of typological differences in higher nervous activity. In *Conference on Psychology (1–6 July 1955)*. Moscow: Izd. Akad. Pedag. Nauk RSFSR, 1957.

Merlin, V. S. The role of temperament in the emotional reaction toward school grades. *Vop. Psikhol.*, 1955, No. 6.

Merlin, V. S. Measuring the properties of a general type of higher nervous activity in man using the GSR. *Vop. Psikhol.*, 1958, No. 5.

Nebylitsyn, V. D. The relation between sensitivity and the strength of the nervous system. In *Typological features of man's higher nervous activity*. Moscow: Izd. Akad. Pedag. Nauk RSFSR, 1956.

Nebylitsyn, V. D. Individual differences in the visual and auditory analyzers with respect to the strength-sensitivity parameter. *Vop. Psikhol.*, 1957, No. 4.

Nebylitsyn, V. D. Electroencephalographic study of the strength of the nervous system and the equilibrium of nervous processes in man using factor analysis. In B. M. Teplov (Ed.), *Typological features of man's higher nervous activity*. Vol. 3. Moscow: Izd. Akad. Pedag. Nauk RSFSR, 1963.

Nebylitsyn, V. D. The problem of balance of nervous processes. *Vop. Psikhol.*, 1964, No. 6.

Nebylitsyn, V. D. Extinction with reinforcement of electrocortical conditioned reflexes as a test of excitation in the nervous system. In B. M. Teplov (Ed.), *Typological features of man's higher nervous activity*. Vol. 4. Moscow: Izd. Prosveschenie, 1965.

Obraztsova, G. A. The qualitative evaluation of the stability of nervous processes. In *Methods for the study of the typological features of higher nervous activity*. Moscow-Leningrad: Nauka, 1964.

Pálei, I. M. Individual peculiarities of restraint in connection with typological differences in regard to the equilibrium of the nervous processes. *Vop. Psikhol.*, 1958, No. 5.

Pavlov, I. P. *Complete collected works*. (2nd ed.) 1951–1952.

Podkopaev, N. A. *Methodology and the study of conditioned reflexes*. Moscow: Izd. Akad. Nauk SSSR, 1952.

Povorinskii, V. A. *Method for studying motor conditioned reflexes with spoken reinforcement.* Leningrad: Medgiz, 1954.

Ravich-Shcherbo, I. V. Study of typological differences in the mobility of nervous processes in the visual analyzer. In B. M. Teplov (Ed.), *Typological features of man's higher nervous activity.* Moscow: Izd. Akad. Pedag. Nauk RSFSR, 1956.

Rozhdestvenskaya, V. I. An experiment in the determination of the intensity of excitation as a function of its irradiation and concentration in the visual analyzer. *Vop. Psikhol.,* 1955, No. 3.

Rozhdestvenskaya, V. I. Certain cases in which it is impossible to produce a stable conditioned photochemical reflex. In B. M. Teplov (Ed.), *Typological features of man's higher nervous activity.* Moscow: Izd. Akad. Pedag. Nauk, 1956.

Rozhdestvenskaya, V. I. Measurement of equilibrium of nervous processes using the plethysmograph. In B. M. Teplov (Ed.), *Typological features of man's higher nervous activity.* Vol. 3. Moscow: Izd. Akad. Pedag. Nauk RSFSR, 1963.

Rubinshtein, S. L. Theoretical problems of psychology and the problem of personality. *Vop. Psikhol.,* 1957, No. 3.

Samarin, U. A. Experimental-psychological study of typological features of the nervous system of children. *Izv. Akad. Pedag. Nauk RSFSR,* 1954, No. 52.

Sechenov, I. M. *Selected works.* Vol. 2. Moscow: Izd. Akad. Nauk SSSR, 1952–1956.

Shvarts, L. A. On the typological significance of differences in the relation between the thresholds of appearance and disappearance of sensations. In B. M. Teplov (Ed.), *Typological features of man's higher nervous activity.* Moscow: Izd. Akad. Pedag. Nauk RSFSR, 1956.

Spearman, C. *The abilities of man.* New York: Macmillan, 1927.

Teplov, B. M. On the problem of inductive changes in absolute light sensitivity. *Prob. Fiz. Optiki.,* 1941, *1.*

Teplov, B. M. The theory of types of higher nervous activity and psychology. *Vop. Psikhol.,* 1955, No. 1. (a)

Teplov, B. M. On the concepts of weakness and inertness of the nervous system. *Vop. Psikhol.,* 1955, No. 6. (b)

Teplov, B .M. Certain problems concerning the study of generic types of higher nervous activity in men and animals. In B. M. Teplov (Ed.), *Typological features of man's higher nervous activity.* Moscow: Izd. Akad. Pedag. Nauk RSFSR, 1956.

Teplov, B. M. New data on the properties of the human nervous system. In B. M. Teplov (Ed.), *Typological features of man's higher nervous activity.* Vol. 3. Moscow: Izd. Akad. Pedag. Nauk RSFSR, 1963.

Yakusheva, T. G. On the variability of temperament in children and adolescents. *Vop. Psikhol.,* 1956, No. 4.

Zaporozhets, A. V. *Psychology.* Moscow: Uchpedgiz, 1953.

19

Studies of the Speech Mechanisms of Thinking

A. N. Sokolov

EDITORS' INTRODUCTION

The research summarized in this chapter represents more than twenty-five years of A. N. Sokolov's research as well as relevant material from other Soviet and foreign authors.

The experimental search for a material basis of thinking has been a persistent theme in psychology since the turn of the century. Sokolov indicates that it is a problem of theoretical and practical interest to Soviet psychologists, and from the very recent work of Hardyck, Petrinovich, and Ellsworth (1966) we can infer that it is a problem of contemporary interest for American science as well.

Introduction

The aim of this chapter is to present a short review and discussion of Soviet psychological and physiological studies devoted to the speech mechanisms and their relation to thinking. The theoretical point of departure for these studies is the monographs of Vygotskii (1934), Blonskii (1935), and Rubinshtein (1959), which present a detailed analysis of the socio-historical and ontogenetic development of thinking and speech proceeding from the principle of their unity and reciprocity in the process of human cognitive activity.

According to this principle, thought is not only expressed in speech but is formed and carried out in it. Language not only gives names to objects, but permits the abstraction of their properties and relationships. Language also leads to their generalization in the form of concepts and their objectification in the form of words and other symbols. It is therefore concluded that abstract thinking is impossible without language (in the broad sense of the word) and that "in man all thinking is based on language" (Rubinshtein, 1959, p. 106).

Each word is an indissoluble unit of *sound* (auditory forms) and *meaning* (generalization of objective content). Both are socially reinforced in the historical development of the language and acquire a relatively constant character. The word is assimilated by each person in the process of intercourse with other people in the given language community. As the individual assimilates the socially reinforced system of words and the grammatical rules of their changes and combinations in sentences, he also assimilates all the associated logical forms and thought processes.

This does not mean to imply that language and thinking are synonymous. The very same thought can be expressed in different words and in various grammatical forms. It follows then that the "thought-language" system is not rigid but extremely variable. It permits the substitution of some language devices for others and, in the same vein, for the replacement of words by various conditional symbols (e.g., in mathematics and other sciences).

A psychophysiological basis for this approach was provided by Sechenov and Pavlov. In his two famous books, *Reflexes of the Brain* (1863) and *Elements of Thought* (1878), Sechenov presented a detailed analysis of the development of thinking. He saw it as a process which begins with concrete (objective) associations and grows increasingly complex by means of "verbal symbolization of impressions." This concept was based on his discovery of central inhibition of reflexes (Sechenov, 1863). He treated the physiological mechanisms of thinking as the action of this general principle of the central nervous system. Thus, Sechenov arrived at his famous definition: *"Thought is the first two-thirds of a psychic reflex"* (1947, p. 155). In other words, thought is a reflex whose initial (receptor) and central (cerebral) components are present, but whose external (effector) expression is inhibited.

Sechenov illustrates his position with the example of thinking in the child. In the beginning the child becomes acquainted with his environment by means of various movements which are associated with visual, auditory, tactile, and other impressions. As the child masters speech, he develops the ability to hold back his movements and begins to express his thoughts in words ("the reflex remains only in the muscles of speech"). Subsequently, inhibition may extend to the external expression of words as well; then only "dumb speech" remains which is accompanied by soundless movements of the muscles of the tongue in the mouth cavity. Thinking in the form of words is then replaced by kinesthetic sensations ("verbal kinesthesis"). "It even seems to me," writes Sechenov, "that I never think directly in words, but always in muscular sensations which accompany my thought in speech form. In any case, I do not sing to myself only with sounds. I always sing with the muscles; then the recollection of sounds appears" (1947, p. 142).

Subsequently, Pavlov emphasized the role of speech-motor stimuli going from the speech organs to the cortex. He called them the "basal components" of the second signal system, that is, the system of verbal signalization of concrete stimuli by means of pronounced, heard, and seen words. "These new signals begin to designate everything that people perceive directly, both in the external world and in their own inner world as well. They were used not only for mutual intercourse but privately with oneself." Originally, Pavlov linked the second signal system mainly with the frontal lobes, but subsequently related it to the entire speech section of the cortex. The latter, when destroyed, produces various forms of aphasia (Pavlov, 1949, pp. 471–472).

The first (objective) signal system to which Pavlov attributed our perceptions and concepts does not simply transmit sensory material to the second signal system. It also performs initial, elementary forms of analysis and synthesis characteristic of clear thinking. As a result of the reciprocal influence of both signal systems, visual generalizations acquire an abstract-logical form which is characteristic of *"specifically human higher thinking"* with its two basic functions—abstraction and generalization (1949, p. 490). Thus, for Pavlov the second signal system refers simultaneously to speech and thinking and, as such, was investigated by him in relation to the physiological basis of their interconnections.

Obviously, the ideas of Sechenov and Pavlov diverged significantly from the "motor theory" of thinking. The latter, especially according to the early behaviorists, such as Watson (1919, ch. 9), reduces the entire thought mechanism to peripheral muscle processes (in the larynx or other organs). According to the reflex theory, thinking is a central, brain process, the highest integration of all the stimuli impinging on the cortex by means of speech (second-signal) associations. Therefore speech-motor stimuli acquire their integrative significance (abstraction and generalizaton) only as a result of their mutual associations in the brain, where their unification with all other stimuli occurs.

The presence of an interconnected system of motor, auditory, and visual components of speech corresponds to the linguistic and psychophysiological concept of the *phoneme* (the unit of audible speech), the *grapheme* (the unit of written speech), and the *articuleme* (the motor "schema" of speech sound), representing all of the elements of verbal and written speech as well as the means for all verbal-logical operations.

Owing to the uneven strengthening of connections between individual speech stimuli, the systems of words and connections vary considerably in both force and duration and may be represented by only a portion of their components: this leads to a decrease in the external (phasic) side of speech and to its conversion into so-called "internal speech" ("endophase"), that is, into concealed and reduced speech processes, which evolves into thinking "to oneself."

There is no doubt that the basic difficulties which arise in a discussion of the interrelationship between thinking and speech, frequently leading to erroneous, idealist statements about the existence of "pure" thought or to mechanist statements about the identity of thinking and speech, are caused by a completely inadequate study of the nature of internal speech—its genesis, semantic and grammatical structure, and physiological mechanisms.

Theories and Hypotheses Concerning Internal Speech

The initial Soviet investigations of internal speech were rather theoretical discussions of the genesis and semantic and syntactic structure of internal speech. Of greatest value were the works of Vygotskii (1934), Blonskii (1935), and Anan'ev (1960a), which emphasized greatly the importance of internal speech as a mechanism for verbal thinking and verbal-logical memory.

It was obvious to Vygotskii that "without proper understanding of the psychological nature of internal speech there is not and cannot be any possibility for explaining the relationship of thought to speech in all of its real complexity" (1934, p. 276). He was irresistibly drawn by the complexity of these questions; and though, in his struggle against simplified, mechanist understanding of internal speech, he did not always adhere to materialist positions, his theoretical analysis of this problem is still quite important. He was very critical of the concept of internal speech as merely verbal memory (retention of acoustic, optic, motor, and synthetic images of words). He justifiably repudiated the behaviorist concept of internal speech as simply a soundless form of external speech ("speech minus sound"). He felt that the most important factor of internal speech was its semantic features. In addition, Vygotskii repudiated both the idealist and spiritualist Würzburg school and Henri Bergson's concept of the total independence of speech and the word. According to Vygotskii, internal speech is a very special and unique psychological phenomenon: it is "the living process of the birth of the thought in the word" and, as such, reflects an extraordinarily complex interrelationship of thinking and speech.

On the basis of materials from child psychology, Vygotskii points out that speech "does not represent a simple mirror reflection of the structure of thought. Hence it cannot dress itself as thought, in a ready-made dress.

. . . Thought, converting to speech, is rebuilt and modified. Thought is not expressed, but is achieved, in the word" (1934, p. 271). The fallacy of the mechanist identity of thinking and speech is manifested in the fact that for children the semantic side of speech proceeds in its development from whole to part, from sentence to word, but the external side of speech proceeds from part to whole, from word to sentence. In general, the flow and movement of thought does not coincide immediately and directly with the development of speech: ". . . that which is contained in thought simultaneously, is developed into speech successively. Thought can be compared to a heavy cloud which is poured out in a rain of words. . . ." (1934, p. 313).

Vygotskii calls attention to the fact (also noted by Piaget) that grammar develops earlier than logic. "The child masters the subordinate clause, those forms of speech such as 'because,' 'since,' 'if,' 'when,' 'on the contrary,' or 'but,' long before he masters positive, temporal, conditional relationships, oppositions, and so on. The child masters the syntax of speech earlier than he masters the syntax of thought" (1934, p. 94).

Turning to the genesis of internal speech, Vygotskii hypothesized that it originates and is developed from the so-called "egocentric speech" of the preschool child. According to the writings of Piaget, egocentric speech is often a conversation of the child aloud with himself—observed during playtime—not directed toward a playmate. In this characteristic of egocentric speech Vygotskii saw its functional and structural convergence with internal speech and formulated his hypothesis on the evolution of egocentric speech into internal speech, all the elements of which he had already found in egocentric speech.

On the syntactic side, internal speech was characterized by Vygotskii as an extremely desultory, fragmentary, and abbreviated form in comparison with external speech. In the case of internal speech there is a "simplification of syntax, a minimum of syntactic analysis, expression of the thought in condensed form, a considerably smaller number of words" (1934, p. 295). This can take place owing to the strong emphasis on predicativeness in internal speech, a submerging of the subject and the parts of the sentence related to it while preserving the predicate and the parts of the sentence related to it. As for the thesis concerning the "absolute and complete predicativity of internal speech," Vygotskii argued that the subject of our internal deliberation is always present in our thoughts and is always implied by us without expression. "In internal speech, it is never necessary for us to name that about which we are speaking, i.e., the subject. We always limit ourselves only to that which is being said about this subject, i.e., the predicate. But this leads to dominance of pure predicativeness in internal speech" (p. 302). "The child speaks about that which occupies him at the minute, about that which he is now doing, about that which he has before his eyes. Hence, more and more, he de-emphasizes, abbreviates, condenses the subject and the words referring to it. Thus, he reduces his speech to predicates alone" (p. 303).

Vygotskii also believed that, as a result of this unique syntax, the semantics of internal speech must also change fundamentally: it must become more contextual and idiomatic, include not only the subject value of the words but all of the intellectual and affective content connected with it. This in turn leads to the dominance of the contextual idea of words over the subject value. Thus, Vygotskii sketched out a bold and broad plan for the psychological study of internal speech as a mechanism of verbal thinking which had great influence on all the subsequent research on this problem. However, much remained unclear and debatable in his schema.

The first criticisms of Vygotskii's concept of internal speech were made by Blonskii in his book *Memory and Thought* (1935), where he enunciated a number of his own ideas, which have exerted a great influence on the subsequent experimental development of this problem. In opposition to Vygotskii, who uncritically shared the view of Köhler and Bühler that thought and speech have different genetic roots, Blonskii stood solidly on the position that thought and speech originate from one source. "This common root is work: both speech and thinking are developed from work. Initial speech is soon action. Initial intellectual operations are actions and only gradually does true action become replaced by thought action: real planning is mental analysis" (1935, p. 200).

With regard to the genesis of internal speech, Blonskii held to the view that, owing to the limited study of internal speech, this question cannot yet be solved definitively. Vygotskii's hypothesis on the evolution of internal speech from egocentric speech was not considered authoritative by Blonskii because it moved the origin of internal speech to the school age (seven years), thus depriving the preschool age of internal speech.

Blonskii considered it more probable that internal speech originates simultaneously with spoken speech from a common source—communication between people, which presupposes not only that words are spoken but also heard. According to Blonskii's observations, hearing, particularly in early childhood, is always accompanied in the beginning by audible and later by soundless, internal repetition of the speech of the speaker, its "simultaneous reproduction," or "echolalia." "The hearing of speech is not simply hearing alone: to a certain degree we, as it were, speak together with the speaker. Of course, in this case there is not a complete repetition of his words, only an internal repetition. It is possible that right here we have the rudiments of internal speech" (1935, p. 154).

Blonskii did not specially analyze the syntactic and semantic side of internal speech, but his overall characterization of "thinking in everyday life" like Vygotskii's, pointed out the fragmentary nature of internal speech. It is so underdeveloped and incomplete that if we could in some way record the verbal expression of thoughts in internal speech we would derive the impression of something like the *Ideenflucht* of the psychotic: ". . . an extremely rapid and changing flow of thoughts, hard for the outsider to understand in its jumps and the incompleteness of deliberations and judgments, every now and then reverting to fragments of phrases and even to individual words" (1935, p. 181).

Further theoretical analysis of the problem of internal speech was made by Anan'ev (1960a). Anan'ev considers Vygotskii's and Blonskii's views inadequate in that they do not take into consideration the entire system of speech activity, which includes not only speaking and listening, but reading and writing as well; these too are a source of the formation of internal speech, particularly of its higher and more developed forms.

This thesis allowed Anan'ev to overcome Vygotskii's one-sided presentation concerning "absolute" and "pure" predicativeness of internal speech, and to confirm the proposition that the logical-syntactic structure of internal speech can be quite varied, depending upon the cognitive content of the thought. Internal speech can be both predicative and substantive. "Internal speech based on concrete thought is predicative. On the other hand, when the subject is not yet identified or recognized, not noted in thought, internal speech is substantive" (1960a, p. 366). Starting from certain properties of external speech, in particular the presence within it of single-component predicative and nominative sentences, Anan'ev (1946) and Podol'skii (1946) said that internal speech can be understood as a system of "null syntactic categories"—with "a null predicate" in the nominative sentence (of the type "night," "stars") and with "a null subject" in an impersonal predicative sentence (of the type "shines," "late"). From this point of view, the reduced quality of internal speech, its syntactic abbreviation and fragmentariness, can be explained by the effect of the indicated "null" syntactic categories.

Anan'ev also allows the possibility of a phonemic reduction of internal speech, the discarding of many phonemes, primarily the vowel sounds, of the type usually used in the written rendition of abbreviations (e.g., "L-d," "Lngr" instead of Leningrad, "D-r" instead of doctor, and so on). This reduction explains the sometimes observed "initiality" of internal speech, its functioning in the form of initial sounds or letters of words.

This discussion of the problem of internal speech permitted the generalization of the available psychological material and suggested a series of genetic and psychophysiological hypotheses for experimental verification. It showed that the psychological and semantic analysis of internal speech as a mechanism of thinking demands significant expansion in studies of the physiology of the nervous system and in the use of physiological methods. With this in mind, clinical observations were made of the disturbances of internal speech in patients with various forms of aphasia. The general results of these studies are cited below.

Thinking Under Various Conditions of Articulation: The Effect of Speech and Non-Speech Interference

The absence of a completely reliable method for recording internal speech makes it extremely difficult to answer experimentally questions connected with the speech mechanisms of thinking. As a consequence, experimenters are forced to work within rather narrow limits.

Most accessible to experimental study is the role of articulation and its associated "speech kinesthesis" in accomplishing various thinking actions: arithmetic computations, reading, writing, listening to foreign speech, and so on. In some cases, researchers resorted to the well-known methods of delay of external and internal articulation of words (using Binet's experiments of 1903). In other cases, the opposite strategy is used: strengthening articulation of words by requiring the subject to pronounce the experimental material aloud. These researchers could justifiably conclude that changes in fulfilling tasks reflect a functional dependence of cognitive activity on the degree to which it is expressed in verbal articulation.

The method of impeding and reinforcing external articulation was used successfully to investigate the role of speech kinesthesis on the initial stages of mastering such cognitive actions as occur, for example, in children's learning of reading and writing (Nazarova, 1952; Kadochkin, 1955) and particularly to investigate the role of articulation in patients suffering from various forms of aphasia (Luria, 1962). In these cases it was established that mechanical delay of articulation (e.g., by keeping the tongue and lips between the teeth) creates significant difficulties in verbal cognitive operations, principally because it hinders perception, comprehension, and recall of words and their logical-grammatical connections in word combinations and phrases. During the reinforcement of speech kinesthesis by "uttering" verbal material aloud, these difficulties disappear.

In laboratory experiments of a similar type, conducted with normal adults (Sokolov, 1941, 1956), however, it was found that, as the cognitive actions become automatic, mechanical impairment of articulation ceases to exert negative influence and may become a positive factor accelerating thought action. Reinforcement of articulation by uttering words aloud becomes a negative factor, impeding cognitive actions at this stage. In children the mechanical impairment of articulation exerts a negative influence over a longer period of time than in adults. The most probable explanation for this is that, for children, cessation of external articulation does not mean cessation of articulation in general, but only its transition into a concealed, internal form, accomplished by imperceptible movements of the speech apparatus which mechanical impairment of articulation is not in a position to prevent.

Indik (1958) used another, more complex variant of a method of speech interference. Various mental tasks were carried out during simultaneous, continuous enunciation aloud (without pause) of well-learned, extraneous series of words (for example, counting to ten, recitation of verses and so on) or of individual syllables (*ba-ba* or *la-la*). Continuity of pronunciation was controlled by means of laryngograms. It is obvious that speech interference of this type occupies not only the peripheral apparatus of the organs of articulation (lips, tongue, larynx, and so on), but also their representation in the cerebral cortex, loading the cortical portion of the speech-motor analyzer with extraneous speech impulses which create negative induction. An additional factor to consider is that recitation aloud of extraneous words or syllables, by demanding auditory control over the correctness of their recitation, to one degree or another must give rise to negative induction in the auditory zone of the cerebral cortex as well.

The results of this experiment showed that loading motor-speech and speech-auditing analyzers with extraneous speech stimuli initially gives rise to a state reminiscent of "sensory aphasia," when a word is heard as a word but the sense of the phrase as a whole is not discerned and, hence, carrying out of any verbal operations at that moment is made impossible. This state passes very quickly and is replaced by an "instantaneous amnesia," an extraordinarily rapid forgetting of the words of a heard or read text, which leads to a considerable lowering of the amount and precision of perception and memory and retards reading and the solution of problems. Later, as a function of an ever increasing automatization of the pronunciation of extraneous speech material, internal (concealed) articulation of words is gradually restored, and, regardless of the degree to which the speech apparatus is occupied with continuous pronunciation of words or syllables, subjects are able to discern and retain the sense of the perceived words and correctly manipulate them by means of concealed articulation of certain generalizing words. In this case, together with the rudimentary articulation of "stress words," all of the subjects experienced the appearance of clear, graphic forms which, under normal conditions, are usually absent and which they used here as a means for understanding and reinforcing meaning.

The basic theoretical value of these experiments is that they graphically demonstrate the possibility of stereotyped analytic-synthetic operations during maximum repression of speech motions and, hence, in the absence of developed pronunciation of words "to oneself." This fact poses a number of important theoretical and experimental problems for psychologists of thinking and speech.

First of all, starting from the principle of the unity and interrelationship of thinking and speech, it must be assumed that, under these conditions, there occur very involuted (reduced) speech processes, which are carried out with maximum abbreviation of the phonetic and syntactic structure of words and word combinations and a simultaneous reinforcement of graphic-image components of thinking. The existence of such conjoint graphic-speech complexes makes possible their "instantaneous" fixation, selection, connection, and comparison with each other and, on this basis, the construction of new thoughts in accordance with given premises, previous experience, and incident problems. The very process of reduced pronunciation of words "to oneself" in these experiments may be accomplished by those muscles of the speech apparatus which are unoccupied at the given moment.

Further, these experiments indicate a uniformly strong negative induction produced by motor-speech as well as speech-auditory interference (i.e., both by compulsory pronunciation of extraneous words and by the compulsory hearing of them), and also the fact of a reduction of the negative induction as a function of the decrease in auditory control over the pronunciation of the extraneous word. These facts obviously indicate the presence of a constant interaction of the motor-speech analyzer with the auditory analyzer. Hence, it is entirely possible that inhibition of the motor-speech component may not influence developed forms of thinking because, in this case, auditory and visual components of speech may function as well. This, then, gives reason to believe that all speech movements are "sounded" internally, that is, are connected with the speech-hearing stimuli, and the auditory and visual perception of words is connected with a speech kinesthesia. From the latter it follows that to characterize internal speech as "soundless" is valid only with regard to an external observer; for the one who is doing the thinking, internal speech remains connected with auditory-speech stimuli even if speech movements are maximally inhibited.

The last source of interference we shall consider is the effect of trace speech stimuli from all the components of speech. Speech stimuli, like stimuli in general, have a more or less prolonged trace or aftereffect, which can be aroused without the presence of speech stimuli only under the influence of object stimuli or visual forms related to them.

Experimental data obtained by Baev (1957) on this source of speech interference quite clearly indicate that participation of internal speech (internal pronunciation) is far from ubiquitous in the solution of problems of various types: problems of graphic content are solved with minimum participation of internal pronunciation whereas problems of abstract content, unconnected with any graphic property, may be solved only with the help of internal speech. Baev also points out the dependence of structural-grammatic properties of internal speech on the degree of "visualness" and abstractness of the thinking operations being conducted: "When there is a graphic support point for the thinking process, there is a tendency toward greater abbreviation of internal speech; with the absence of such a support point, there is a tendency toward greater use of internal speech since thinking in this case reduces to handling an exclusively verbal content and, hence, the range of utilization of speech facilities is greatly expanded."

Recently, Zhinkin (1960, 1964) attempted to interpret speech and non-speech (interference) in the light of information theory. As is known, one of the models on which information theory is constructed is that of communications, transmission of information along certain channels, taking into consideration channel capacity and the potentialities of mechanisms for converting and receiving information.

According to this model, it is possible to view speech as a combination of signals (sounds and letters), by means of which information is transmitted from one person to another. In this case, as in all lines of communication, various types of external and internal interference are possible. If the algorithmic nature of the interference (sequence of counting elements) approaches the speech algorithms, its effect will be maximal; if its algorithms diverge, its action will be minimal or generally will not be noted. Starting from this, Zhinkin applied methods of non-speech rhythmic interference to the study of the mechanisms of internal speech.

If, in the process of internal speech, talking does occur, then obviously the motor-speech analyzer must work out an algorithm of speech movement which corresponds to the elements of the pronounced words; this algorithm must be multirhythmic since words of the Russian language can have an accent at different points. By introducing an interference which upsets this algorithm, it can be judged whether speech movements actually participate in the process of internal speech.

The following method was used in experiments in Zhinkin's laboratory. While solving various problems, the subject had to tap with his hand in a certain constant rhythm. Thus, the constant tapping rhythm was designed to upset the variable rhythm of speech movements during the internal pronunciation of words. The rhythms were very simple. The accuracy with which the rhythms were executed was recorded by means of pneumatic transmission to a kymograph. The results generally coincided with the previously described experiments: for certain problems and certain subjects there was strong interference, while with other problems and other subjects, a lesser amount of interference occurred; sometimes it was almost absent and, in all cases, the effect of the interference gradually weakened with practice.

Zhinkin succeeded in finding one problem whose solution during the tapping of a rhythm was very difficult for all the subjects. The subject was asked to count sequentially the squares on one line of a sheet of folded writing paper (25–28 squares). His explanation for this is that, during counting, a word cannot be replaced by anything—it must be pronounced to oneself completely; whereas in other cases (e.g., in reading text or hearing extraneous speech), words may be replaced by graphic examples, diagrams, or whole groups of words can be replaced by one short word generalizing the sense of the entire phrase.

Later, Zhinkin, breaking down the mechanism of speech into two basic components—composition of a word from sounds and compilation of a communication from words—shows that reverse kinesthetic connections are necessary for the formation of the first member whereas in the second member (composition of communications from words) the feedback from the speech organs is weakened to a considerable degree as a result of the possibility of replacing the complete pronunciation of words by other (graphic) signals. However, toward the end of the process of composing a message out of words (the endpoint of the speech effector), interference begins to act with its previous strength. This means that complete words have been prepared for utterance.

In connection with this, Zhinkin distinguishes "complete" and "incomplete" words. By the latter he means any equivalents occupying the role of words in inner speech.

Conditioned-Reflex Methods

Conditioned-reflex methods were applied in the experiments which studied the "interaction of the first and second signal systems" (in the laboratories of Ivanov-Smolenskii and Krasnogorskii) and in those devoted to the interrelations of verbal stimuli (in the laboratories of Krasnogorskii and Kekche'ev). Internal speech (the hidden articulation of words) was not directly recorded in these experiments. But the formation of conditioned reflexes to words which are heard, seen, or pronounced by the subject either aloud or to himself definitely indicates that the "internal speech chains" (neural verbal connections) function in all the experiments. The fundamental facts established by these experiments are as follows:

1. *Conditioned reflexes which arise in response to concrete (non-verbal) stimuli subsequently occur when these stimuli are named. When they are replaced, verbal stimuli in such cases immediately evoke a conditioned reflex without preliminary reinforcement by an unconditioned stimulus.*

For example, Kapustnik (1930) developed a conditioned motor reflex to the sound of a bell in children. When the experimenter then pronounced the word "bell," the same conditioned reflex occurred. The same response occurred when the subject was presented with a card on which the word "bell" was written. The interchangeability of conditioned stimuli was observed in the development of inhibitory conditioned reflexes (Traugott, 1934) and in the development of conditioned reflexes to a sequential complex of stimuli. In Smolenskaya's experiments (1934), the positive signal complex was the sequential flashing of red, white, and yellow lights. The negative (inhibitory) signal was to flash them in the reverse order. After these conditioned reflexes were developed, the same effect was achieved by pronouncing the names of these colors in the required order.

Similar data were obtained concerning the formation of autonomic conditioned reflexes. Kotlyarevskii (1936) combined the sound of a bell with an Ashner ocular-cardiac reflex. The conditioned reflex to the bell was a decrease in heart rate. The same reflex then occurred without preliminary reinforcement when the word "bell" was pronounced. In another experiment, Kotlyarevskii (1935) developed a conditioned pupillary reflex by combining the sound of a bell with light. After the reflex was established, it could be evoked when the subject himself pronounced the word "bell" aloud, in a whisper, or to himself. In all cases the word "bell" evoked the same reflex as the sound of the bell itself.[1]

The authors of these works explain similar "special" replacements of non-verbal (first-signal) stimuli by verbal designations by the fact that verbal stimuli are usually firmly linked with concrete stimuli early in ontogenesis. Therefore, if a person forms a conditioned reflex to a first-signal stimulus (e.g., sound, light, etc.), subsequently the related verbal stimuli spread selectively along the neural pathways previously closed (in ontogenesis) and, thus, immediately evoke the reflex. Ivanov-Smolenskii (1953) called this phenomenon "selective irradiation" as distinct from the "diffused" or "broad" irradiation which occurs at the first stage of a conditioned reflex's development.

2. *When conditioned reflexes develop in response to complex stimuli of the first signal system whose components are of varying intensity, usually only the strong components are verbalized* (*transferred to the second signal system*).

Kotlyarevskii (1934) adequately demonstrated masking of weak first-signal stimuli by strong ones. The subjects were children from 8 to 12 years of age. They formed a conditioned motor reflex (squeezing a rubber balloon) in response to a momentary illumination of a green rectangle and a simultaneous slight increase in the illumination of the experimental room. The children responded with a motor response to each of these stimuli, but they noticed the connection of their responses, as a rule, only with the

1. *Editors' note:* Investigators in the United States have had much less success in pupillary conditioning and semantic conditioning of the kind described here. There may be several reasons for the discrepancy in results: Soviet investigators conduct conditioning over many sessions, utilizing far more trials than commonly employed in the West; they select subjects who are good conditioners and are generally more selective in their use of subjects; these studies are primarily with children while the Western studies have been conducted with college students. Finally, the Russian results may not be reliable, although we tend to doubt that this is the case.

strong stimulus (illumination of a green rectangle). On test trials with the weak stimulus (slight increase of illumination in the room), they squeezed the rubber balloon, but were unable to explain why they had done so. They could not clearly pick out the weak stimulus although they responded to it. It can be assumed that such "unnoticed" weak components are evoked by negative induction from the strong component. Negative induction may originate both within the bounds of the first signal system and in the paths for transmission of arousal from the first to the second signal system.

3. *Conditioned reflexes developed in response to definite verbal stimuli continue to function in response to other verbal stimuli if the latter have some kind of logical or semantic connection with the former.*

Examples of this are the experiments of Fedorov, which are described by Krasnogorskii (1954, pp. 307, 418, 467). In a 12-year-old child a firm association between six words was established by means of many repetitions. The words were "pigeon," "turkey," "hawk," "owl," "chicken," "swallow." Then, one of these words ("pigeon") was reinforced several times with a food stimulus (cranberries and sugar). Consequently, all the words of this complex turned into conditioned stimuli, each one evoking intensive salivary conditioned reflexes. At the same time, all other words designating animals (in this example) evoked the response, but trees and fruits did not evoke this response. The names of other birds which were not part of the original complex also did not evoke the conditioned response, but the general word "bird" did, all without any preliminary reinforcement. Later Volkova (1953) confirmed these observations with new, analogous experiments. She found that as the distance from the original verbal stimuli increased, the magnitude of the conditioned reflex decreased. Thus, if the original, specific bird evoked secretions of 708 drops of saliva and the general word "bird" 10 drops, then the word "flies" yielded only 4 to 5 drops. The even more distant word "lives" yielded only one drop.

Other examples of the influence of semantic associations on conditioned reflexes are the experiments using word substitutions in which conditioned reflexes are developed to synonyms and homonyms. In this connection the experiments of Shvarts (1948) are most significant. A conditioned photochemical reduction of visual sensitivity was developed by combining a verbal stimulus (e.g., the word *doktor,* which in Russian is a common synonym of the word *vrach*) with illumination of the eye. Then the conditioned reflex was tested with the synonym (in this case the word *vrach*). Without any preliminary reinforcement, the synonym evoked approximately the same conditioned-reflex reduction of visual sensitivity as the original word. A word similar in sound but different in meaning (e.g., the word *diktor*) barely evoked the conditioned reflex. If the conditioned reflex did appear, it quickly extinguished in subsequent trials. Our experiments with vascular conditioned reflexes yielded similar results.

Some extremely interesting experiments have been conducted that involve reflexes conditioned to verbal complexes (phrases and sentences). Shastin (1932) found that, in 11-to-12-year-old children, the subjects of sentences evoke a much stronger response than predicates and other parts of sentences. Changing the order of words in sentences evoked no significant changes in the strength of the conditioned reflex. However, in the later experiments of Matyukhina (1956) using the photochemical method, it seems that adult subjects respond to word order changes with sharp inhibition of the conditioned reflex. This, apparently, is due to the more subtle semantic differentiation of phrase structure by the adults. In addition, adult subjects uniformly developed strong conditioned reflexes not only to the subject of sentences, but to the predicate and, in some cases, depending on the previous context, to secondary parts of sentences.

4. *Conditioned reflexes to numbers.*

We shall consider this variant of "semantic" conditioned reflexes only because the action of numbers has a particularly marked connection with inner speech. Kryazhev (1955) conducted experiments on a large group of children aged 7 to 8 years. First a conditioned motor reflex (pressing a key with the hand or a pedal with the foot) was developed to the word "five." The unreinforced stimulus was the word "three." As the conditioned reflexes to these words were developed (in the first case, positive, in the second, negative), the numbers 5 and 3 were presented. They evoked the same conditioned reflexes as the words had, without additional reinforcement. Subsequently, in mental execution of arithmetical tasks, if the result was "five" ($3 + 2$; $10 \div 2$; $100 \div 20$), the positive conditioned reflex was evoked; if the number "three" appeared in the results ($5 - 2$; $9 \div 3$; 3×1), the negative (inhibitory) conditioned reflex was evoked.

These data were subsequently confirmed in Krasnogorskii's laboratory (1954). An 11-year-old child developed a conditioned salivary reflex to the word "ten" and differentiation to the word "eight" ("ten" was reinforced with food, "eight" was not reinforced). In control experiments, the child was asked to "add five and five." As the child solved the problem, the conditioned salivatory reflex appeared. In solving the second problem, "Subtract two from ten," there was no salivation. The more complex the arithmetical operation, the longer was the latent period of the conditioned reflex; in operations involving simple numbers, the latent period was 2 seconds, and with two-digit numbers it was 6 to 11 seconds. Generalizing the results of these experiments, Krasnogorskii concludes: "Due to the fact that, earlier, the word (ten) was associated with a food reflex (first signal system), the appearance of this word in the internal speech chain (second signal system) evoked conditioned salivation. This proves objectively the intimate interaction between the first and second signal systems."

Unfortunately, there are few additional experiments of this kind, and it is difficult to draw final conclusions about the dynamics of "internal speech chains" from them. To do so it will be necessary in the future to combine the conditioned-reflex methods with others.

Electromyographic Studies

The data concerning the hidden functioning of speech mechanisms in the form of internal speech were directly confirmed in electromyographic studies. The first recordings of an increase in the tonus of speech musculature during various forms of cognitive operation were reported by Jacobson (1932, 1956) and Max (1934, 1937). This fact was confirmed in Soviet electrophysiological laboratories where the prime concerns were the dynamics of speech-motor responses and their relationship to the nature and complexity of the mental tasks, the development of speech and cognitive stereotypes and the inclusion of visual and auditory components in cognitive operations, as well as the degree of retention and disturbance of speech functions. This research was carried out in Moscow on three groups: on normal children and adults, at the Institute of Psychology by Sokolov; on deaf mutes, in the Institute of Defectology by Novikova; and on aphasics, in the Institute of Neurology by Usevich, Bassin, and Bein.

The use of electrophysiological apparatus in all these experiments permitted recording of muscle potentials from 1 to 3 microvolts in a range of frequencies from 1 to 1,000 cps. Muscle potentials were recorded with the aid of surface (skin) electrodes. All of the usual conditions of electrophysiological research were observed (shielding the subjects and instruments from external electrical artifacts, preliminary extinction of orienting responses to the electrical apparatus, simultaneous recording of potentials from various areas of the speech and non-speech musculature, etc.).

In Sokolov's experiments the subjects were students, laboratory assistants, and young schoolchildren. Muscular tension of the tongue and lower lip (m. orbicularis oris) was recorded. In the control experiments tension of the scalp muscles (m. frontalis) and of the general extensor for the fingers (m. extensor digitorum communis) were recorded as well. Maximal relaxation of the musculature was achieved when the subjects were in a supine position on a bench or sofa and a bit less when they were sitting in a chair. In the latter case the involuntary relaxation of the speech musculature was enhanced if the subject fixated visually on a particular point on the wall opposite. The level of emotional arousal was measured by recording galvanic skin responses.

The electrical activity of the speech musculature in a state of relaxation is less than 5 microvolts. When the subject listened to the instructions, it usually increased to 10 to 15 microvolts. As the subsequent task was fulfilled (mental solution of various tasks), it increased even more and often reached 50 and more microvolts. Electrical activity was measured according to both maximal and average amplitude and was usually expressed as a percentage of the level of the "background" (state of calm) which easily converted to absolute magnitudes (in microvolts).

In addition to the electromyograms, a series of experiments was devoted to mechanical recording of micromovements of the tongue with the aid of a special pickup device which transduced mechanical movements into electrical readings (Sokolov, 1956).

In these experiments the subjects were given both verbal and nonverbal (visual) tasks. Basically, these tasks were as follows: mental arithmetic, reading "to oneself" in the native and in foreign languages, listening to and remembering selections of fiction and of scientific literature, solving visual matrix tasks (Raven, 1956), visual presentation of objects, and the like.

The first problem involved in these experiments was to explain the degree to which muscular tension of the speech organs and the dynamics of their micromovements are specific indicators of latent speech-motor responses and not simply the result of "general motor" tensions or emotion-like and positional reflexes. While the latter were reduced to the minimum by means of voluntary and involuntary relaxation of the musculature, it was still necessary to find other evidence of the speech specificity for the recorded muscle potentials.

It is interesting to compare the speech electromyograms when the same words are pronounced aloud or in a whisper and then when they are pronounced "to oneself" (soundlessly or mentally). Figure 19–1 shows electromyograms of the tongue and lower lip while the subject counts from one to five first in a whisper and then soundlessly ("to oneself"). As the electromyogram clearly shows, there are large groups of muscle potentials in the form of "volleys" or "bursts" of speech-motor impulses in the whispers and to a slightly lesser degree in the voiceless count only if the latter is sufficiently articulated. Unclear pronunciation of words "to oneself" produces muscle impulses which are less noticeable and which may even disappear entirely (when the muscle potentials are recorded by means of surface electrodes).

It is also characteristic for the bursts of muscle potentials to arise synchronously (or almost synchronously) in various sections of the speech musculature—in this case in the muscles of the tongue and lips.[2] A more

---

2. Faaborg-Andersen and Edfeldt (1958) also found a parallel activity of different speech muscles during phonation and silent reading. Their recordings were from the muscles under the tongue (m. mylohyoideus), the voice muscles of the larynx (m. vocalis). In the posterior celcoid muscle of the larynx (m. cricoarytenoideus), whose function is antagonistic to the voice muscle, the electrical activity during phonation and silent reading decreases.

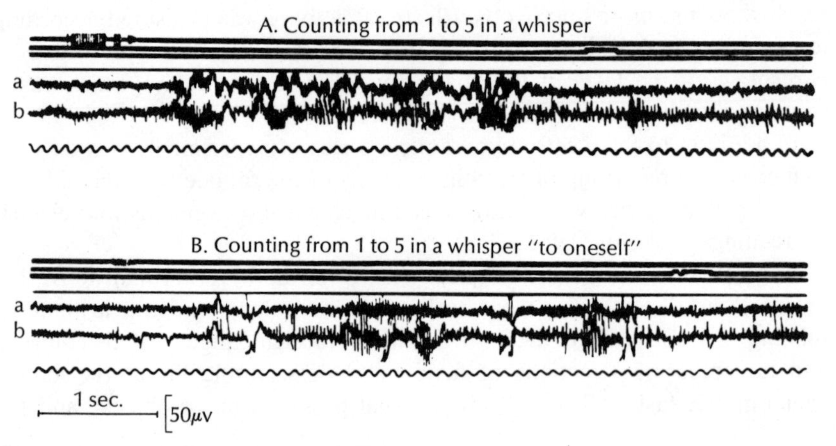

Figure 19–1. Simultaneous recording of electrical potentials in the muscles of the tongue (*a*) and the lower lip (*b*) while the subject is counting from 1 to 5 in a whisper (*A*) and "to oneself" (*B*). Muscle potentials were recorded on an eight-channel oscillograph. Silver electrodes were used. The beginning of the task is noted by the phonogram of the experimenter's words, "Begin to count" (upper line). The end is noted by the subject's signal (lightly tapping the finger on a pneumatic drum which was linked with one of the oscillograph's channels and evoked a spike on the second line of the oscillogram). Time is marked in 0.1-second intervals (lower line). The same order applies in the subsequent electromyograms with the exceptions as noted.

detailed analysis, however, indicates that in soundless pronunciation of separate speech sounds (labial and nonlabial Russian vowels), the difference between tension of the tongue and lips is retained because it corresponds to the differences in articulation of these sounds in voiced pronunciation (Figure 19–2).

Measures of the electromyographic activity in the various parts of the non-speech musculature are very important for establishing the speech specificity of the potentials recorded from the tongue and lips. Therefore, simultaneous control experiments were conducted to record the electrical activity of the scalp muscles and the muscles of the hands. The scalp muscle (m. frontalis) as well as the muscle of the hand (m. procerus) is generally very active. But their potentials synchronize to a greater degree with eye movements than with speech movements. During mental execution of verbal tasks their electroactivity increases relatively little. Similarly, in this case the electroactivity of the musculature of the hands increases relatively little, while at that moment very large bursts of electrical activity occur in the speech musculature (Figure 19–3).

When the hands are less calm, and primarily, during more prolonged mental activity, the tension of the musculature of the hands becomes more noticeable. Nevertheless, it is less intensive and occurs later than in the speech musculature. Thus it can be assumed that a certain increase in electroactivity of the non-speech musculature is a secondary result of the broad generalized arousal in the motor cortex or the result of general activation of

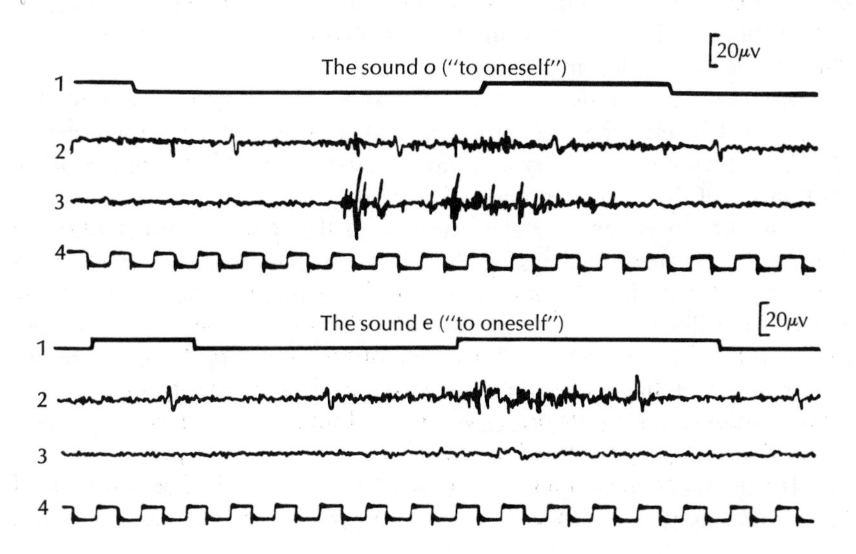

Figure 19–2. The difference in muscle potentials of the tongue (2) and lower lip (3) during pronunciation "to oneself" of labial and nonlabial Russian vowels. The potentials of the lip are more prominent in pronouncing "to oneself" the labial sound *o*. In pronouncing the nonlabial *e*, the potentials of the tongue are more prominent. (1) Markers of beginning and completion of the task. (2) Electromyogram of the tongue. (3) Electromyogram of the lower lip. (4) Time in 0.25-second intervals.

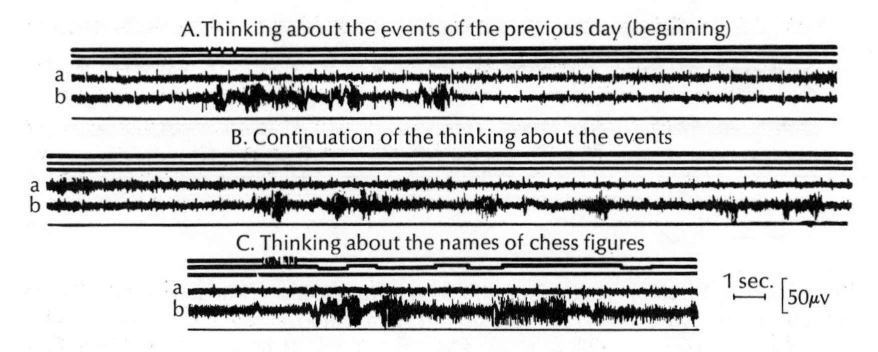

Figure 19–3. Electromyogram of general extensor of the fingers of the right hand (*a*) and the tongue (*b*) during mental recall: the events of the day (*A* and *B*) and the names of chess figures (*C*). The electromyogram (EMG) of the tongue clearly shows the intensive bursts of muscle potentials, while they are unclear on the EMG of the hand (both EMG's show the same rhythmically repeated electrocardiographic impulses).

the cortex from the reticular formation.[3] In people with speech disturbances (e.g., deaf mutes and aphasics), tension of the hands during verbal mental tasks becomes more noticeable and arises earlier than in the musculature of the tongue or lips. This occurs because the hands take upon themselves the functions of the speech organs (later in this chapter we shall discuss the experimental data relevant to this matter).

These data permit us to conclude that bursts of speech musculature activity which are recorded during mental activity are the expression of specific speech-motor activity and have a direct connection with the latent articulation of words in the process of thinking.

Let us turn to yet another characteristic of the speech-motor impulse: it quickly "attenuates" or stops, if the mental activity becomes *stereotyped and automatized.* It intensifies again if the automatization is disturbed. Figure 19–4 illustrates this point. The electromyograms show the recorded muscle potentials of the lower lip during ordinal counting from one to ten "to oneself," in three cases: the original count, a repeated count, and a reverse-order count. In the first case, bursts of muscle potentials corresponding to the general quantity of pronounced words are clearly seen, but it is possible to notice something else as well, namely, gradual attenuation of these bursts as each consecutive number is pronounced "to oneself." Even

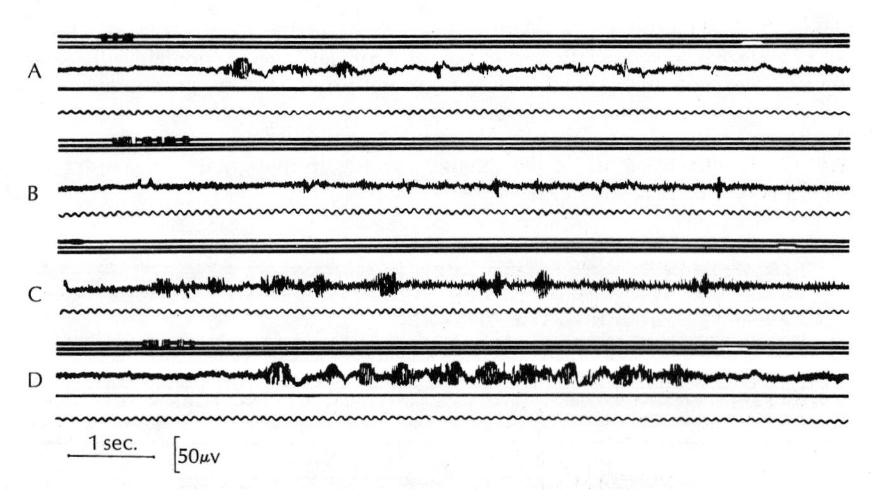

Figure 19–4. Electromyogram of the lower lip during sequential counting "to oneself" from 1 to 10: original count (*A*), repeated count (*B*), reverse count from 10 to 1 (*C*). *A* and *B* show gradual reduction of muscle potentials; *C* shows their increase. For purposes of comparison, *D* indicates ordinal counting in a whisper.

---

3. Canadian electromyographic research (Bartoshuk, 1956; Smith, Malmo, and Shagass, 1954; Wallerstein, 1954) has established a significant increase in the electrical activity of the musculature of the hands during attentive listening.

more noticeable is the attenuation of motor speech impulses during repetition of these numbers. However, during the mental counting of the same series in reverse order (from ten to one), the change from the previous order causes the potentials of the lip to increase significantly. It is obvious that the established mental stereotype results in weakened speech motor tension and that destruction of the mental stereotype (changing the order of the operation) evokes strengthened speech motor tension and the appearance of large bursts of electrical potentials in the speech musculature.

An analogous phenomenon was observed when the structure of the task was changed. For example, in the transfer from arithmetical operations with simple numbers to operations involving two- and three-digit numbers the speech motor impulses increase progressively (Figure 19–5). But in solving

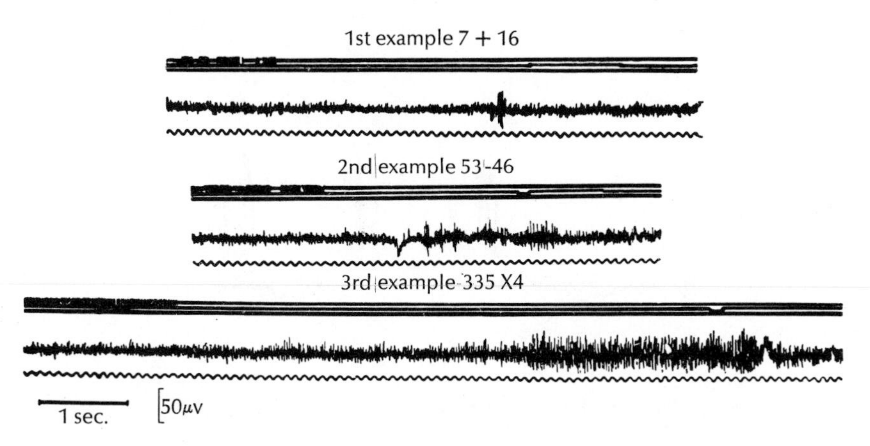

Figure 19–5. Increase of electrical activity of the muscles of the lower lip during mental solution of gradually more complex arithmetic problems.

arithmetical problems of a single type, they gradually decrease (Figure 19–6). Thus, it may be assumed that the speech motor impulses play the role of a "starting" or "controlling" mechanism which strengthens the arousal of the motor speech centers in the brain by means of "reverse afferentation" from the proprioceptive impulses, which arise during word pronunciation, including voiceless pronunciation in the process of internal speech. When automatization of mental operations occurs, the need for such speech motor control and for the strengthening of the brain mechanisms of speech is lessened. This leads to the reduction of electrical potentials of the speech musculature and to the abbreviation of the entire speech process.

Usually, bursts of speech motor impulses arise during speech memorization (internal pronunciation) of both the conditions of the problem and the results of intervening operations which are needed to keep them in the memory. Speech motor inhibition (reduction of the electroactivity of the speech

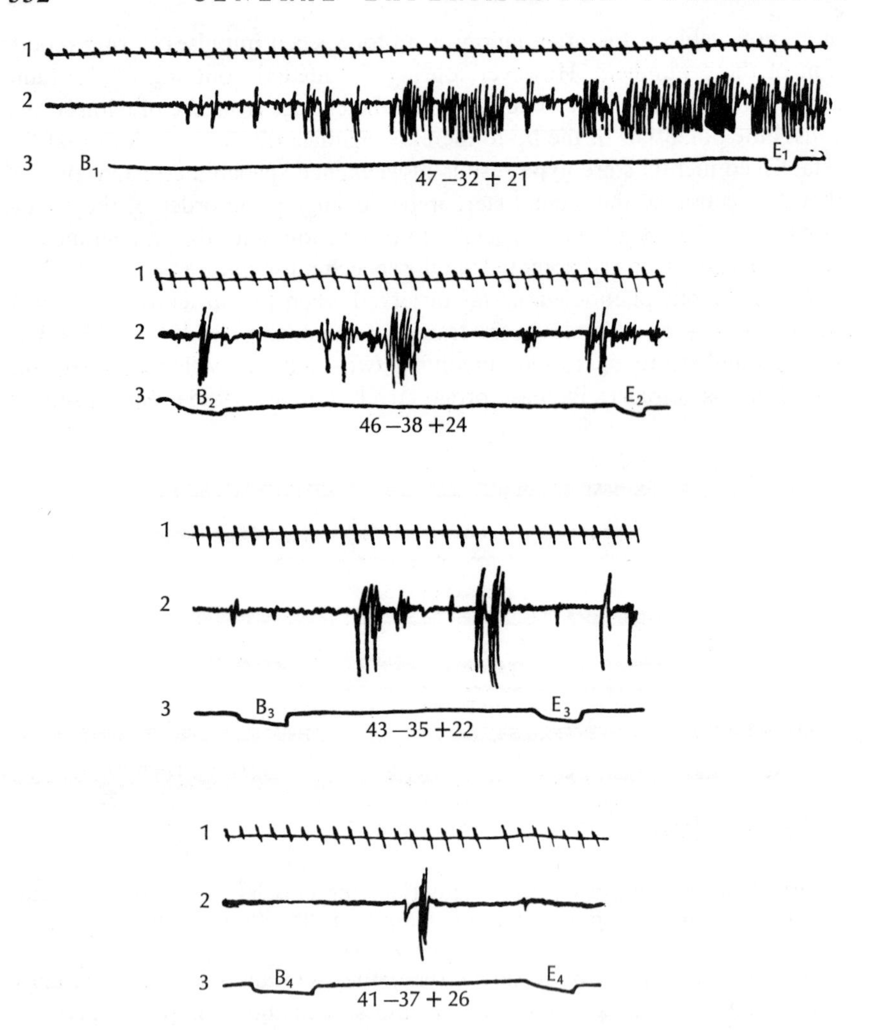

Figure 19–6. The mechanogram of micromovements of the tongue during the solution of a single type of arithmetical problem shows the gradual "attenuation" of these movements. The micromovements were recorded with the aid of a special pickup. (1) Time in 0.2-second intervals; (2) mechanogram of the micromovements of the tongue; (3) the beginning (*B*) and end (*E*) of the execution of the task.

musculature) arises in the pause between speech operations associated with visual fixation of the experimental material (e.g., during written presentation of the problem) or with reproduction of the contents of the problem in visual images (e.g., visual models of numbers in the solution of arithmetical problems). As a result, alternations of excitation and inhibition occur during the problem solving process, that is, increase and reduction of the electroactivity of the speech musculature. It is observed both in periods of generally high or low electroactivity (Figure 19–7). During the solution of very difficult problems, very strong speech motor arousal usually occurs in the beginning. It is then replaced by prolonged speech motor inhibition which leads to the subject's refusal to solve such problems.

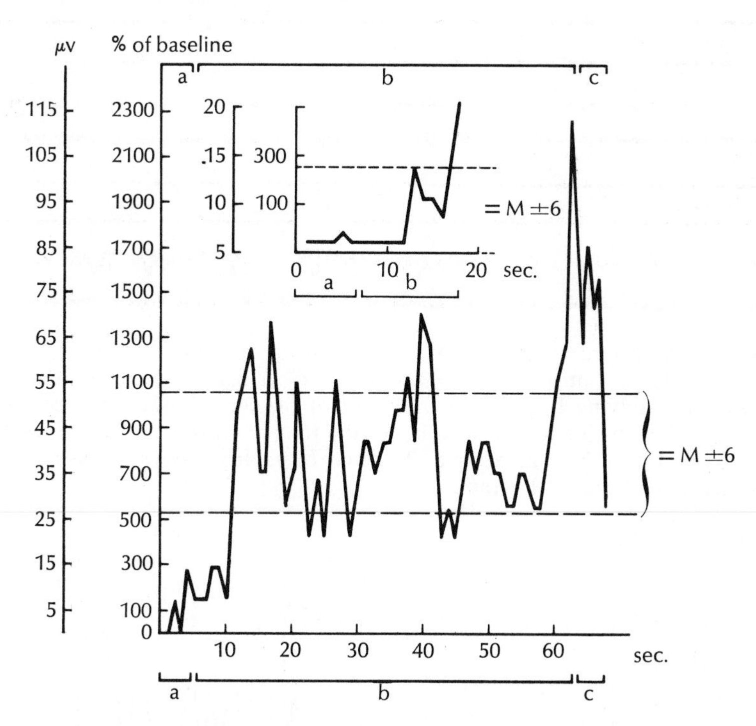

Figure 19–7. Graphs of electrical activity of the lower lip during mental arithmetic problems by two university students (the problem: $28 \times 13 \div 4$). The intensity of the recorded muscle potentials is shown along the ordinate in microvolts and percentages of the "baseline" (conditions of rest). The time in seconds and successive moments of solution are shown along the abscissa: (*a*) auditory perception of the task; (*b*) mental solution; (*c*) pronunciation of the solution aloud.

The analysis of speech electromyograms recorded during voiceless reading and listening is extremely interesting, since, to some degree, one may judge not only the role of the kinesthetic component of speech but, indirectly, the role of the visual component (in reading) and the auditory component (in listening) as well. According to the speech electromyograms, good readers visually perceive short phrases accompanied by very weak tonus of the speech musculature. When reading long and grammatically complex phrases, the tonus of the speech musculature increases and separate bursts of the speech motor impulses appear which are linked with micromovements of

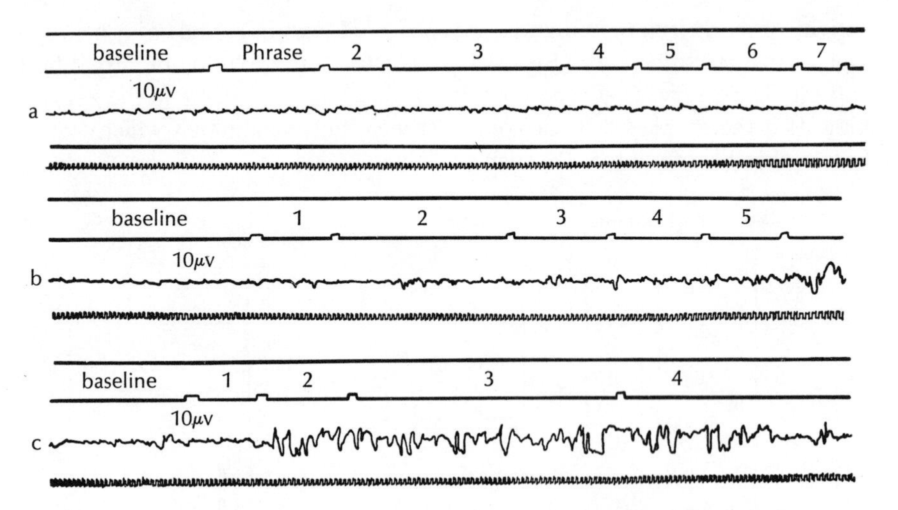

Figure 19–8. Micromovements of the tongue in reading "to oneself": (*a*) a Russian text; (*b*) an adapted English text; (*c*) a complex English text. (The subject was studying English.) Movements of the tongue were recorded with a horseshoe-shaped electrode placed under the tongue (inside the arc of the lower jaw). Time intervals, 0.25 second. The end of each phrase read is marked on the upper line of the oscillogram.

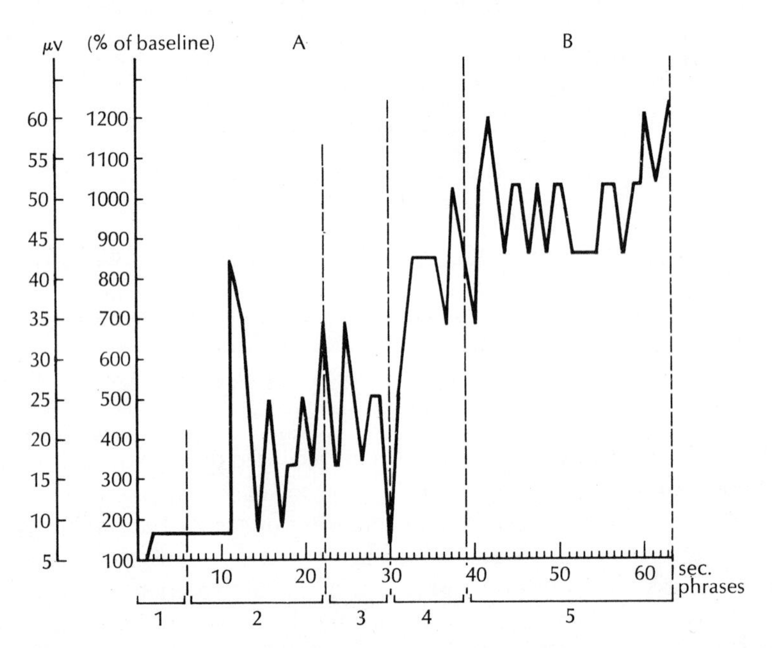

Figure 19–9. Graph of the electrical activity of the lower lip of one subject while reading a complex English text "to oneself" (an excerpt from "Squaring the Circle" by O. Henry). The reading of each phrase is designated by a vertical dotted line. Other indicators are the same as in Figure 19–7.

the speech organs. These movements become even more noticeable when the subject reads in a foreign language which he does not know well. In the latter case, both the electromyogram and the mechanogram of these movements are easily recorded (Figure 19–8). Characteristically, speech motor excitation and inhibition alternate during the reading of "difficult" texts, as they do in the solution of other difficult problems (Figure 19–9).

When listening to separate words in the native (Russian) language, speech motor impulses are not noticeable as a rule. They become noticeable only when the subject is asked to remember precisely words or phrases, or during subsequent recall (Figure 19–10). They also occur when the subject ana-

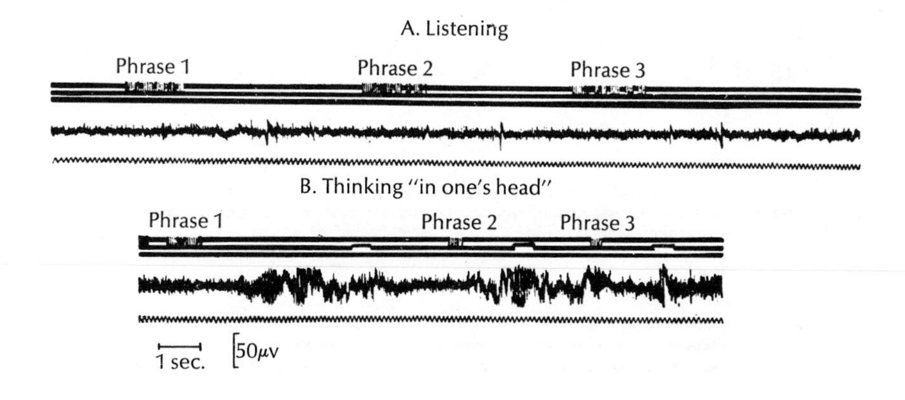

Figure 19–10. Electromyogram of the tongue: (*A*) while listening to separate phrases ("The sun is not very bright." "The trees have no leaves." "They are covered with snowflakes."); (*B*) while mentally recalling these phrases.

lyzes the meaning of perceived speech (e.g., in picking out the main point, in reformulating the sentence, etc.) or in listening to words and phrases in an inadequately mastered foreign language when it is necessary to mentally translate them into the native language (Figure 19–11). In general, all forms of thinking associated with the need to reason in a more or less complex fashion are accompanied by amplification of the speech motor impulses, and repeated mental action leads to its reduction (Figure 19–12).

All that has been said is also relevant to the fulfillment of visual tasks, in particular to Raven's "progressive matrices" (Raven, 1956). The most common outcome of the experiments with these tasks was as follows: with the exception of very few "self-evident" matrices, the matrix problems were solved with more or less significant tension of the speech musculature accom-

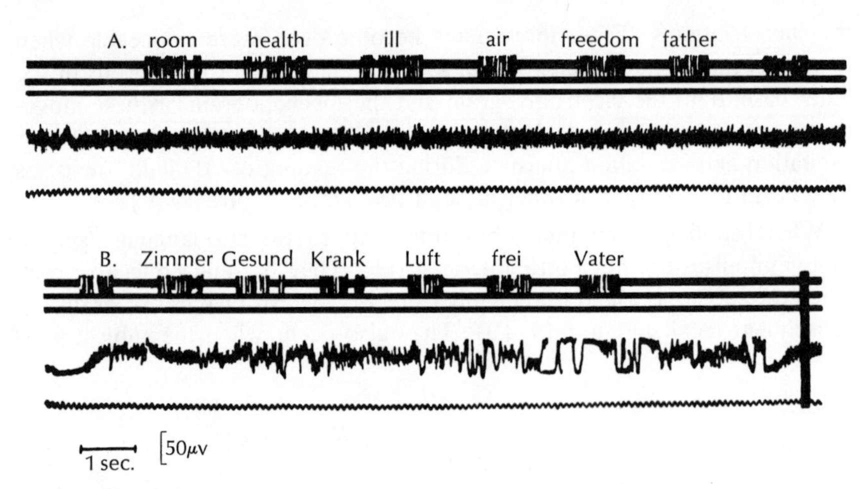

Figure 19–11. Electromyogram of the tongue: (*A*) listening to Russian words; (*B*) listening to German words. The latter situation evokes micromovements of the tongue.

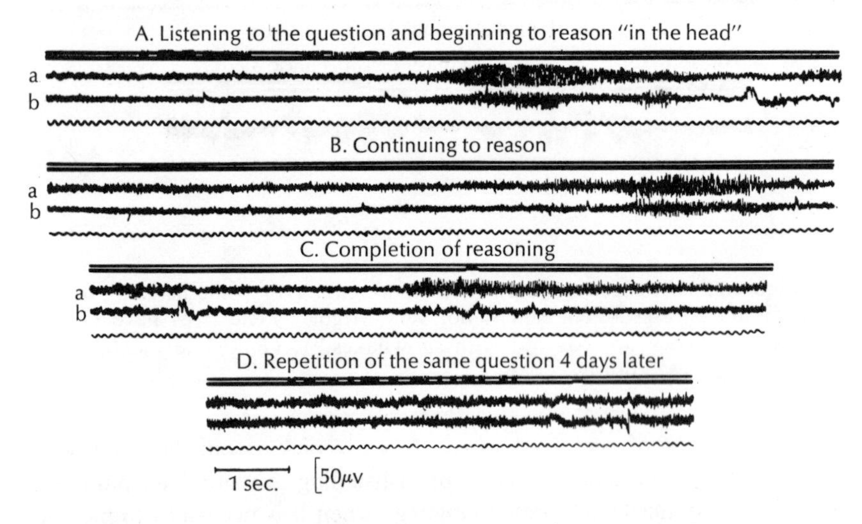

Figure 19–12. Electromyogram of the lower lip (*a*) and tongue (*b*) during mental deliberation of the following question: "Today is August 17. On what day of the week will September 10 of this year fall?" (*A, B, C*), and during repetition of the same question four days later (*D*).

panied by alternations of increase and decrease of electrical activity. This is clear on the electromyograms reproduced here. The more complex the matrix, the larger were the potentials of the speech musculature (Figure 19–13).

When the matrix task was very difficult, there were moments of pro-

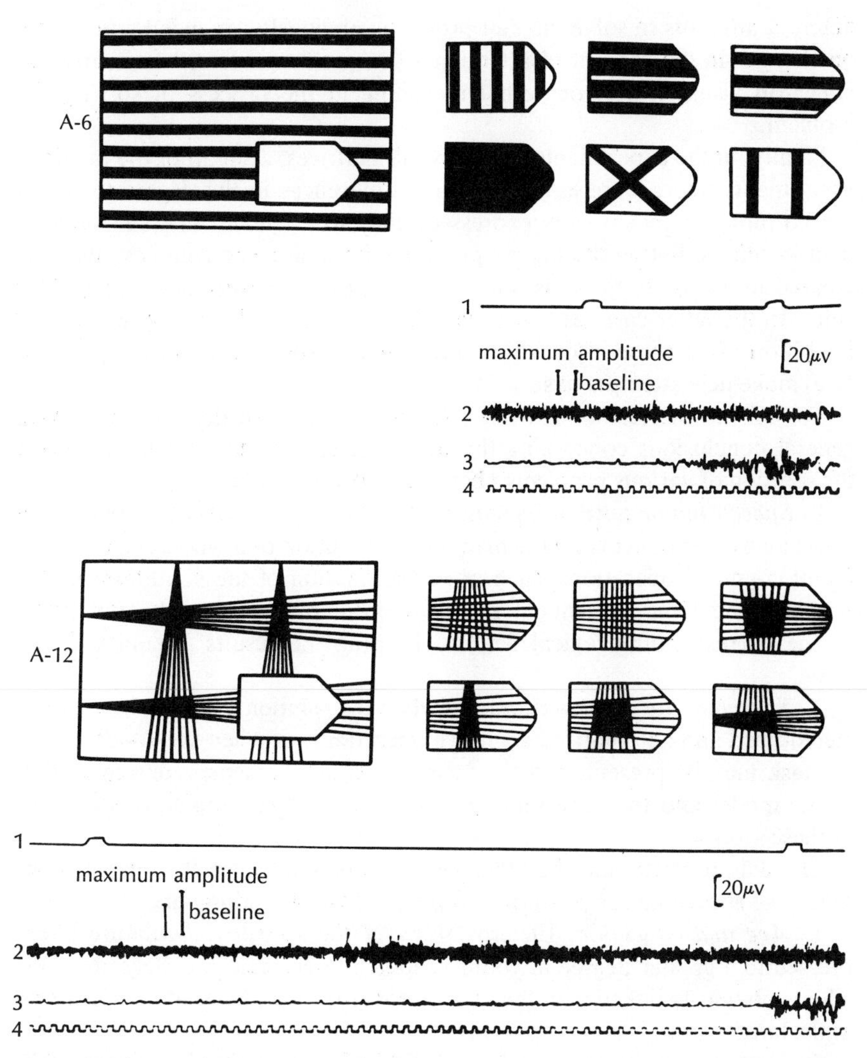

Figure 19–13. Electromyogram of the lower lip during the solution of two Raven matrices (*A*-6 and *A*-12). (1) Indication of the beginning and the end of problem solution; (2) Electromyogram of the lower lip; (3) Electromyogram of the right hand (at the moment that the chosen fragment was indicated); (4) Time intervals, 0.25 second.

longed speech motor inhibition followed by increased speech motor excitation. If the task was not solved on the first trial and speech motor activity was weak, the activity increased during the second trial, but again decreased during the third. On the other hand, if the speech motor activity was great during the first trial, it decreased during the second and again increased during the third. These successive intensity changes in the same person during different attempts to solve difficult problems obviously depended completely on changes in the "accent of attention"—on greater or lesser concentration either on visual search or verbal reasoning in the process of solving the problem.

Finally, in the experiments with Raven's matrices, as in all of the previous experiments, there were large individual differences in the degree to which speech motor impulses were expressed: they were greater in some subjects than in others, but as the matrix problems became more complex, they increased in all the subjects as long as these problems were not "super-difficult." In the latter case, as has already been noted, prolonged speech motor inhibition often arose after which the subject refused to solve the problem or to make new attempts to solve it.

To sum up the results of these experiments, we can draw the following general conclusions concerning the nature of speech motor tension during the solution of various problems (both verbal and visual):

1. *Speech motor tension increases* when the task is difficult, especially if it has many components and demands the execution of a whole series of different cognitive operations, such as verbal fixation of the conditions of the problem and their subsequent mental reproduction during the fulfillment of the corresponding logical actions, keeping the results "in mind," and so on.

2. *Speech motor tension decreases* when the solution of the tasks acquires stereotyped and automatized cognitive operations, or when the conditions of the task may be presented in the form of outlines, schemes, or some other visual model and the necessary operations consist of simple combinations of these models.

The data indicate that the other factors which influence the degree of intensity of speech motor potentials in the process of thinking are:

1. *Age and education:* Electroactivity of the speech musculature is expressed to a greater degree in young schoolchildren than in college students. This is obviously linked with the great automatization of cognitive operations in the latter.

2. *Interest and the emotional relationship:* When solving interesting problems, the electroactivity of the speech musculature increases. It falls when the emotional relationship is negative (e.g., during prolonged and unsuccessful attempts to solve a problem).

3. *The tendency to a particular type of verbal memory* (*motor, auditory, or visual*): Other things being equal, speech motor tension is greatest in people with a tendency to motor (speech motor) memory of words, somewhat less intense in those with a tendency to auditory memory, and still less intense in those who tend toward visual memory of words. In the latter subjects, speech motor tension is barely noticeable during solution of "easy" problems, but it rises during solution of more "difficult" problems. The

tendency to a specific type of memory in these experiments was established on the basis of the number of correctly perceived words and nonsense syllables under varying experimental conditions.

The data from experiments with deaf mutes and aphasics also indicate the complex nature of speech motor tension during mental activity. In the experiments by Novikova and her colleagues (1955) with deaf-mute children who had been taught oral and dactylic speech, simultaneous increases of potential from both the tongue and the hand muscles were observed during the performance of various thought operations. This not only indicates the presence of tongue kinesthesis in deaf-mute children who have been taught to speak, but also the existence of a single verbal functional system which includes tongue and finger kinesthesis.

Such a functional speech system is also created in persons with normal hearing who have learned dactylic speech; but in their case the leading role ("starting afferentation") of tongue kinesthesis is retained. As data (Figure 19–14) in this case have shown, with people of normal hearing who have

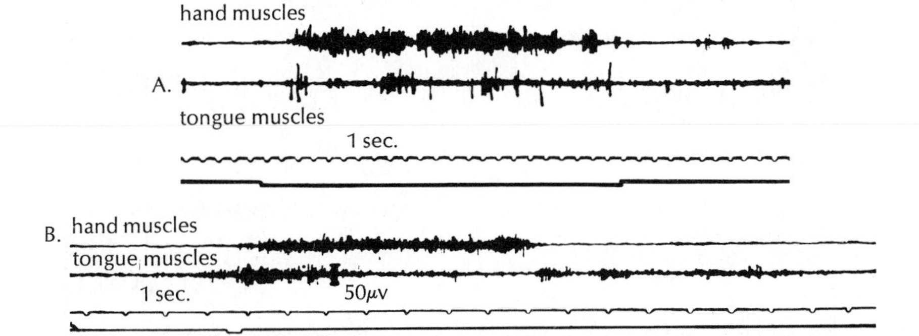

Figure 19–14. (*A*) Simultaneous appearance of a large burst of electrical potentials in the muscles of the tongue and hand in deaf-mutes trained in dactylic and oral speech (the deaf-mute signals the phrase: "Today the weather is fine."). (*B*) A series of impulses in the tongue appear earlier if the subject is dactylically perceiving the same phrase. (Data from L. A. Novikova.)

learned dactylic speech, tongue kinesthesis is evoked first and only later does the kinesthesis connected with hand motion occur; but in the case of deaf-mute children who have mastered oral and dactylic speech, the tongue and finger kinesthesis coincide almost completely.

The experiments of Yusevitch (1958) and of Bassin and Bein (1957) recorded the potentials of the speech musculature in people with organic speech disturbances (aphasics). These experiments indicate a generalized disinhibition of the lip EMG under conditions of rest (i.e., potential amplitudes higher than the normal magnitude). When aphasics work on a task which they are capable of handling, the amplitude of the potentials from the speech apparatus sharply increases (Figure 19–15), but when the problem exceeds their capabilities, depression of the lip muscle potentials results (the authors attribute this to the negative affective conditions aroused in the

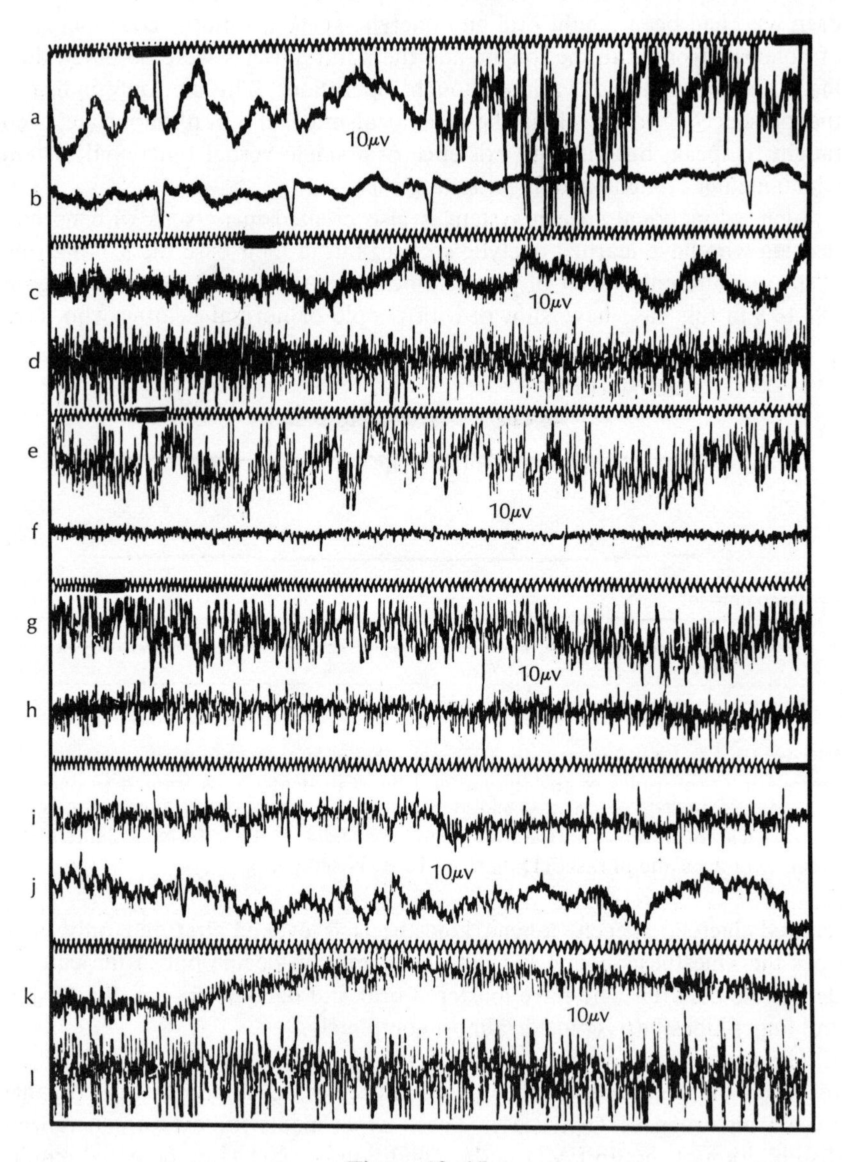

Figure 19–15.

subjects). On the other hand, the muscles of the hands show an immediately increased amplitude (Figure 19–16). When such patients regain their speech, the muscle potentials of the hand return to normal. It has also been observed that, for patients who use writing as a means of compensation for their defect, there is an increase in the muscle potentials of the hands during verbal tasks.

Clinical Observations

Clinical observations of speech and thought disturbances associated with various forms of aphasia are of great interest in the study of the speech mechanism of thinking. These problems have been treated in their fullest form in the monographs of Luria (1962), Lebedinskii (1941), Bein (1964), Blinkov (1948), and others. We shall discuss only one aspect of this problem—the disturbance of internal speech in motor and sensory aphasia.

It was noted in the early experiments of Soviet neuropsychologists and psychopathologists that both external and internal speech are disturbed in all the more pronounced forms of aphasia. The measure of the disruption of internal speech in aphasics is the fact that such patients perform various thought operations significantly worse to themselves than aloud. Aphasics better understand and remember material that is read aloud than material which they read "to themselves" and are obliged to translate all more or less complex deliberations into the spoken word. This has led to the conclusion that "there is no aphasia without disruptions of internal speech" (Lebedinskii, 1941). Disruption of internal speech becomes less pronounced in marginal forms of aphasia; in these cases the patient can read "to himself," solve

---

Figure 19–15. Electromyogram recorded during the execution of the same task by patients with various structural speech defects (motor, sensory, and amnesic aphasia). (*a*) and (*b*)—Electromyogram recorded from a patient with a *motor* aphasia syndrome from the common extensor of the fingers and lower lip during execution if a simple task (to find a given object in a picture. (*c*) and (*d*)—The same during execution of a difficult task (to repeat mentally a word pronounced by the experimenter). (*e*) and (*f*)—Electromyogram recorded from the common extensor of the fingers and the lower lip of a patient with sensory aphasia during execution of a simple task (to repeat mentally a word pronounced by the experimenter). (*g*) and (*h*)—The same during execution of a difficult task (to find a given object in a picture). (*i*) and (*j*)—Electromyogram recorded from the common extensor of the fingers and the lower lip of a patient with amnesic aphasia during execution of a simple task (find a given object in a picture). (*k*) and (*l*)—The same during execution of a difficult task (mentally name an object in a picture). Time intervals on the upper line of the electromyogram are at 0.02-second intervals. (Data from Bassin and Bein, 1957.)

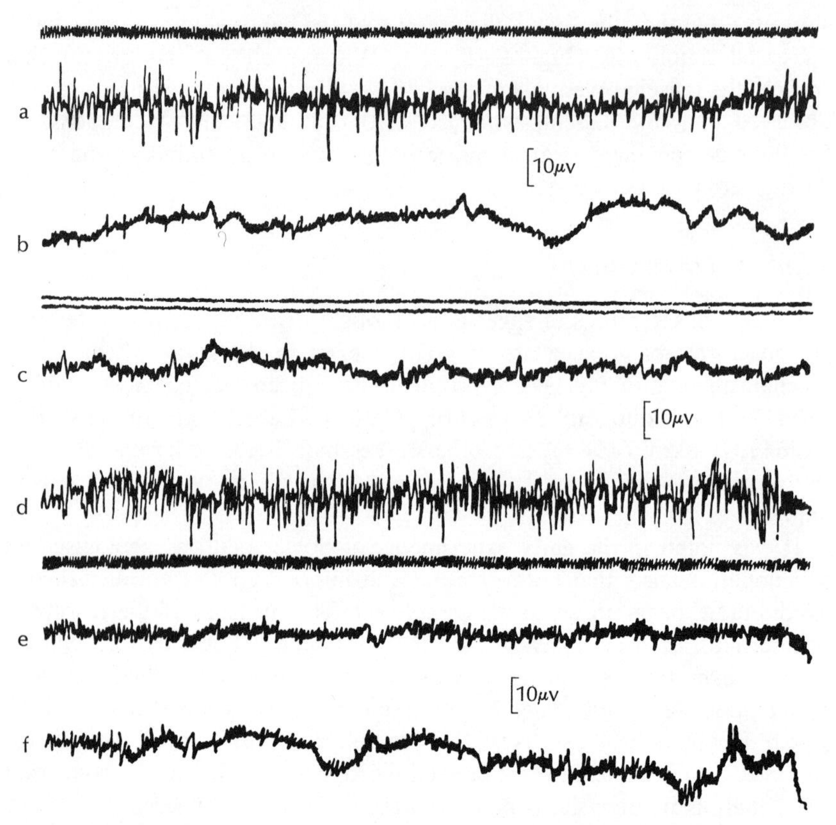

Figure 19–16. Electromyogram recorded from a patient with gross motor aphasia of vascular origin. (*a*) and (*b*)—Electromyogram of the lower lip and general extensor of the fingers in a functionally "undisturbed" state of rest. (*c*) and (*d*)—The same during attempts to execute difficult tasks (mental repetition of the experimenter's words) without preliminary training. (*e*) and (*f*)—The same during execution of this task after training. (Data from Bassin and Bein, 1957.)

arithmetical problems in his head, and perform similar thought operations, albeit slowly.

Subsequently, it was discovered that the greatest disruption of internal speech occurs in motor aphasia and not in sensory aphasia as had been assumed in earlier studies. By means of extremely simple methods it was established that motor aphasics are unable to understand grammatically complex phrases and sentences, to perform mentally more or less complex counting operations, to solve arithmetical problems, and the like, if external articulation is "disconnected," for example, by clamping the tongue between the teeth. This is due to the destruction of the function of fine speech kinesthesis in the motor aphasic. It is also relevant to the process of writing;

when the motor aphasic clamps his tongue between his teeth, his writing instantly deteriorates.

Since these facts have important implications, I will review several instances of similar findings from a study conducted by Luria (1963, pp. 279–292).

The patient, a thirty-year-old mechanic with a seventh-grade education, had suffered an injury to the premotor area of the cerebral cortex which had resulted in right lateral hemiplegia and motor aphasia, though with relatively little impairment to the temporal (auditory) cortex. In experiments designed to test the patient's understanding of speech, it was found that, given a fairly simple sentence, he experienced no appreciable difficulty in understanding it, even when external means of articulation had been cut off (by clamping his tongue between his teeth). The possibility of external articulation thus blocked, the patient was presented with a simple descriptive sentence, such as "Today there was a dense fog and driving was extremely difficult." After 15 seconds had passed, during which time his tongue remained clamped, the patient readily reproduced the sentence, saying: "I understood right away: I pictured to myself how hard it was to drive in the fog."

Under the same conditions, he needed considerably more time to grasp a sentence that was grammatically more complex. For example, he was asked to carry out instructions of this type: "Place the comb to the left of the pencil." With his tongue free, he repeated the instructions, saying: "That means put this . . . on the left . . . ," and solved the task in 7 seconds. But when conditions precluded normal speech kinesthesis, this process took far longer to carry out; the patient began to probe the objects, making trial attempts to arrange them, and spent 1 minute, 20 seconds solving the task (that is, 12 times longer than he had needed before). He then commented: "I figured it out with my hand; that's how I did it."

Experiments in which the patient was given sentences containing grammatical inversions proved to be even more indicative: when external articulation was impeded, these sentences were impossibly difficult for him. For example, he was given the sentence: "The girl is bigger than the boy," and was asked which of the two was smaller. His tongue compressed, the patient spent 1.5 minutes tracing the individual words with his finger and in the end refused to answer the question, saying: "I can read it and it seems I understand it, but somehow I just can't figure it out." Once his tongue was freed, he solved the same problem in 10 seconds, repeating: "The girl is bigger . . . the girl is bigger. That means the boy is smaller," adding, "I can picture it in my mind but, you see, it just doesn't work. I can't get it. But if I say it out loud, I understand. Then I can figure it out right away. I don't understand what it is that helps, but when my tongue is held tight it seems as if the words are being held back and I can't link them up."

Similar results were obtained with this patient in experiments using arithmetical operations. Under normal conditions the patient performed written operations using addition, subtraction, multiplication, and division of numbers up to ten, which he did slowly but nonetheless accurately. However, when external articulation was blocked, these same arithmetical processes proved to be impossible for him. Luria summed up the results of these experiments in the following table:

Table 19–1 *Mentally Adding and Subtracting Numbers up to Ten*

Experimental conditions	Percentage of correct answers	Average time in seconds
Tongue free	100	26
Tongue compressed, counting on fingers	100	15
Tongue compressed, counting on fingers not permitted	0	30
Use of eye blinking	100	6.5
Use of left hand clenched into a fist	100	8.4

It is apparent from the table that any disintegration of the patient's ability to perform these procedures is to be noted only when speech kinesthesis is weakened (or its operations impeded); this does not occur if the execution of a task is accompanied by other, auxiliary muscular efforts (blinking the eyes, clenching the fist, etc.).

Hence, these clinical observations and experiments indicate the important role that speech-kinesthetic impulses play in the performance of verbal tasks (and in many cases, of ocular and visual tasks as well) by motor aphasics, as well as the need that these patients have for enormously intensified speech kinesthesis in order to carry out cognitive processes. Nevertheless, motor aphasics are capable of performing elementary speech and thought processes (retention and comprehension of individual words and simple sentences, operations involving addition and subtraction of numbers up to ten, and other automatic procedures of a similar nature). The defective kinesthesis of the afferent impulses used in speech also accounts, apparently, for the genesis of a "conducting aphasia" in which the greatest damage is done to the patient's ability to pronounce individuual sounds and words in a loud voice, while his capacity for immediate comprehension of spoken phrases and for reading "to himself" is left relatively unimpaired.[4]

4. The relationship noted here between disturbed functioning of the speech motor impulses and a breakdown in motor aphasics' ability to grasp logical-grammatical relationships accords fully with facts described earlier on the negative effect that artificial speech motor impediments have on the performance of various thought processes.

Considering the need that motor aphasics have for intensified motor speech impulses in order to perform mental operations, it is fundamental that treatment aimed at restoring speech in these patients uses tasks which the patient accomplishes by speaking in a loud voice and then shifting to internal means by which he performs the tasks, as it were, "to himself." What takes place, then, is a kind of internalization of a system of external speech operations within an internal speech order, and this in turn becomes the basis upon which the patient will be able subsequently to utter detailed statements either orally or in writing (which is what one always encounters when mental or internal speech functions normally). In addition, attempts to restore the speech functions of motor aphasics must take into account a peculiar characteristic of these patients' speech, namely, the predominance of substantives and related words and the extremely poor stock of verb forms ("telegraphic style"). Consequently, special attention must be given in the treatment of motor aphasics to restoring the predicative aspect of internal speech.

In sensory aphasia, internal speech (as far as one can judge from the oral speech, reading, and writing of sensory aphasics) is less impaired than is the case with motor aphasia. Sensory aphasics retain the capacity for abstract operations and can grasp logical-grammatical relationships; but because of their disturbed "phonemic hearing" (distinguishing and recognizing the phonemes one hears), these patients frequently lose the ability to grasp the objective significance of words, which is the main reason they fail to understand what they hear. As a result, the speech of sensory aphasics differs from that of motor aphasics by being predominantly predicative and idiomatic while at the same time deficient in substantive forms (subjects). Thus, even though a sensory aphasic retains the ability for abstract operations, his thought is frequently interrupted, cannot be completed, and may be blocked altogether, because the direct associations between the words he hears and the objects these signify have broken down.

In addition, sensory aphasics' inability to differentiate speech sounds manifests itself in a "compensatory focusing on sense"; a patient begins to clutch at sounds, using any thought context that occurs to him, and this in turn produces the "verbal paraphrasia" which is typical of these patients (substituting words according to sound or some thought context). Because their ability to hear phonemes is impaired, patients suffering from sensory aphasia also have difficulty in writing a letter from dictation, even though they have the capacity to write. But because the mechanism for articulating speech in these patients remains relatively intact, as does their grasp of logical-grammatical relationships, the work of restoring their faculty of speech is greatly facilitated, and in the majority of cases the prospects for treatment are very good.

These findings on the antithetical types of speech disorders in motor and sensory aphasia may be regarded as evidence of the fact that the normal development of thought requires both of the brain mechanisms used in speech—motor and auditory—since the former provides that logical-grammatical relationships will be set up in speech, while the latter ensures that one can analyze acoustically what he hears spoken.

Data from Pedagogical Psychology

Through the works of Nazarova (1952) and Kadochkin (1955), the extremely important role of speech kinesthesis in the organization of writing and reading was established. They showed that the kinesthetic sensations arising during the articulation of words are a necessary condition for analysis of the sound structure of words in writing and reading and serve to refine and fix the composition and sequence of the sounds in a word. Since at the first stages of training the sound form of a word is still insufficiently differentiated, a considerable reinforcement of the external speech kinesthesis by way of separate (syllabified) pronunciation of words aloud is required. It was also established that reinforcement of speech kinesthesis has great significance for the formation of habits of the spelling of Russian orthograms, which are not controlled by orthographic rules (in particular, during the spelling of "unverifiable," unaccented vowels of the root of a word), and also in those cases when, by way of the syllabified pronunciation of words, there can be established a difference between "orthoepic" and "orthographic" standards. Later, with development of the habits of reading and writing, the necessity for syllabified pronunciation of words disappears, and speech kinesthesis gradually generalizes, abbreviates, and assumes the form of concealed internal articulation, which now emerges as the basic sense element of internal speech, organizing the processes of thinking in all acts of oral and written speech.

Pedagogical observations have also yielded very interesting material with regard to the logical-grammatical structure of internal speech during its transition to oral and written speech. Particularly great significance is attached to the study of young schoolchildren's errors in oral speech, which clearly testify to the many difficulties in the transition from internal design to external speech. A detailed description and classification of these errors are given in the Pomerantseva's dissertation (1953).

On the basis of these observations, Pomerantseva establishes that the speech of young schoolchildren, as a rule, "does not stick together, is not formed into well composed sentences." On the contrary, we frequently hear snatches of different sentences, attempts that involve errors and uncompleted phrases. In the speech of young schoolchildren there are frequently errors of anticipation, when the student pronounces some part of his speech earlier than it should be. For example, a little girl of the fourth grade says *gravnii gorod* instead of *glavnii gorod* (anticipating the second word in the first). Similarly, errors of speech inertia occur, in which the stimulus from one word is apparently combined with the word following; for example, having pronounced the word *ust'e,* the student then pronounces *rust'e* instead of *ruslo.*

Pomerantseva places these errors in the same category as errors resulting from the collision of thoughts, when, for example, in answer to a stern question from the teacher: *Ty pochemu tetrad' ne sdala?* the student replies, *U menya sdalas'* instead of . . . *konchilas'.* From *sdala* and *konchilas'* in this case, the author concludes, the ridiculous expression *sdalas'* was derived.[5] Analogous in nature are the "errors of shifting speech arrangement," occurring as a result of the fact that in the speaker's internal plan of speech there may occur some variation of design; in this case, there is a false combination in the outward expression. For example, there may occur a transition from a singular subject to plural. Thus, a fourth-grade student speaks of serf peasants: "The peasant may become whatever the landlord wishes: cook, hunter, artists, menials."

Some data relative to the mechanism of transition of internal plan into external speech are also contained in studies of the development of written speech in students. Of course, the internal complexity of the writing process remains concealed, but certain general tendencies in the development of internal speech during its transition into written speech nevertheless are manifested quite clearly. Thus, Zhinkin (1956), analyzing the compositions of third- and fourth-graders, distinguishes four basic elements which enter into the process of writing and are general elements of all speech, including internal speech, with which the process of writing begins. These elements are (1) selection of words in accordance with the subject for discourse, (2) selection of sentence structure in accordance with the distribution of subject symbols in a group of sentences, (3) separation of predicates by fixing the order of words and "internal intonation" of them during writing, (4) connection of sentences according to meaning.

Of particular interest is the relationship of subject and predicate in a sentence as a function of whether they are viewed within the limits of a separate sentence or in the context of several sentences, that is, in an interconnected system. In a separate sentence the main component is the predicate, that is, that new thing which is communicated concerning the subject of the expression; in a general context, however, the main thing is the subject of the expression which first emerges as an unknown, the properties of which are gradually revealed by the succeeding series of pronouncements.

The psychological side of this question consists in the fact that, during

5. *Editors' note:* This exchange would be approximated in English by: "Why didn't you give me the notebook?"—the response being: "I already gaved it!"

the writing of sentences, the subject of the expression must be inwardly retained by the writer. Only under this condition can a verbal series be synthesized into a definite system. There is "anticipation" of the imminent writing of a text both as regards normal sequencing of words and the logical sequence of the content. The concrete form assumed by the anticipation of future text in internal speech—in the form of finished phrases of separate, significant words—cannot, of course, be established from the analysis of compositions; but the very fact of the distinguishing of separate subject symbols—some as main, others as subordinate and co-subordinate—can, according to Zhinkin's data, be objectively established by contextual analysis of the intonation articulation of a text.

Since the writer speaks the text before writing it (electromyographic recording of motor speech pulses, as we have seen, definitely confirms this), the intonation articulation of a text in internal speech becomes a very important factor in determining the syntactic structure and the entire style of the text: by separating individual words or groups of words as logical predicates (by means of "internal intonation"), the writer determines the arrangement of the words and their syntactic connection within the sentence.

The presence of "internal intonation" in the process of writing is of interest in that it makes completely obvious the connection of the auditory and motor analyzers of speech not only in the case of external but also in the case of internal pronunciation of words, since "internal intonation" unequivocally presupposes "internal listening." From this we conclude that speech hearing is the most important condition for articulation of a sentence into thought parts and determination of the syntactic structure of the sentence and of the text as a whole.

Conclusions

Human thinking originates on the basis of actions with objects and gradually begins to abstract from them. It then becomes verbal speech activity, first in the form of "external" speech (aloud) and then in the form of "internal" speech (latent articulation), characterized by fragments of verbal expressions and often by the presence within them of individual symbols (figurative code).

From the psychophysiological point of view, internal speech is defined as latent and reduced articulation of words accompanied by heightened tonus of the speech musculature or by disconnected bursts of speech motor activity and sometimes by entirely obvious movements of the speech organs. By virtue of the connection of word articulations with auditory speech stimuli (while listening to speech) and visual speech stimuli (while reading), internal speech may also include auditory and visual representations of words. When the latter arise, the tonus of the speech musculature usually heightens as well.

Electromyographic research on latent articulation has indicated that its intensity depends on a series of factors. The most important factors are (1) the difficulty or novelty of a thought action, (2) the degree to which it is automatized, and (3) the inclusion of visual models in the thought activity. In the first case, speech motor responses increase, in the second and third, decrease. Accordingly, internal speech in some cases (during the solution of difficult problems) becomes extended and approaches external speech in structure. In other cases (during the solution of easier and stereotyped problems), it becomes very abbreviated.

An important aspect of the dynamics of internal speech is its discrete ("quantum") character. Latent articulation is not uninterrupted and not of uniform intensity, but sporadic and selective in accord with the content of the given thought activity. If this is so, then obviously the muscular tension of the speech organs during mental activity may be viewed not only as the result of the "passive" idea-motor act, in which the thought of the movement involuntarily evokes that movement but as a mechanism of *voluntary* regulation of thought activity as well, that is, as a purposive, selective mechanism which samples the perceived information in accord with the purpose of activity. This is even more probable in view of the fact that the "problem" itself, as a determining factor of thought, is usually fixated and reproduced in man's operative memory with the aid of internal speech (latent pronunciation of words). The same can be said of the "plan" for solution of the problem, which is also fixated in abbreviated form with the aid of internal speech.

Thus, we are better able to understand the great significance of word articulation in the child's mastery of various cognitive operations. It is well known that, in the beginning stages of the mastery of abstract material, the child must turn to intensive verbalization (pronouncing aloud, in a whisper and, finally, "to himself"). The necessity of external verbalization (pronunciation aloud or in a whisper) decreases as cognitive operations are mastered and automatized. It is replaced by reduced, abbreviated verbalization which becomes the basic, so-called "internalization" of cognitive operations—their execution on an "internal" (mental) plane with maximal abbreviation. This, however, does not exclude speech motor responses. Latent speech motor responses appear at moments of mental difficulty or in the transfer from one kind of cognitive activity to another and continue to fulfill their function in the verbal mechanism of thinking, even during maximal automatization of cognitive activities.

It seems to us that these facts permit us more accurately to evaluate the physiological functions of verbal kinesthesis in the process of cognitive operations. Its basic physiological function is, apparently, the proprioceptive activity of the cerebral mechanisms of speech by means of neuromuscular impulses according to the principle of feedback with the brain. This activating and controlling role of speech proprioceptive impulses may occur both by means of subcortical mechanisms of the reticular or "centro-encephalic" system (Penfield and Roberts, 1959) and by the direct action of the motor cortex which, according to contemporary notions (Buser and Imbert, 1961; Fessard, 1961; Mountcastle, 1961) is the polysensory region which receives and integrates neural impulses of the various modalities. Therefore, it is entirely possible that, with wide irradiation of the speech proprioceptive impulses throughout the cortex and subcortical structures, they can arouse visual and other kinds of images linked with speech.

We are aware that this account amounts only to a very broad schematization of the mechanism of verbal thinking, to the extent that it is possible to conceptualize it on the basis of the current level of development of psychology and neurophysiology. It is to be hoped that future investigations will lead to more detailed and concrete answers to these questions, especially in the area of the relationship of physiological action of reverse speech afferentation to the regulating mechanism of thinking.

References

Anan'ev, B. G. Toward a theory of inner speech in psychology. *Uch. Zap. Leningrad. Gos. Pedag. Inst. im. Gertsena,* 1946, *53.*

Anan'ev B. G. On the theory of internal speech in psychology. In *The psychology of sensory perception.* Moscow: Izd. Akad. Pedag. Nauk RSFSR, 1960. (a)

Anan'ev, B. G. A clinical-psychological analysis of the restoration of speech functions in motor aphasia. In *The psychology of sensory perception.* Moscow: Izd. Akad. Pedag. Nauk RSFSR, 1960. (b)

Baev, B. F. Some features of inner speech during solution of different thought problems. *Dokl. Akad. Pedag. Nauk RSFSR,* 1957, No. 3.

Bartoshuk, A. K. EMG gradients and amplitude during motivated listening. *Canad. J. Psychol.,* 1956, *10,* 156–164.

Bassin, F. V., and Bein, E. S. The application of electromyographic methods in the investigation of speech. In *Conference on Psychology* (*1–6 July 1955*). Moscow: Izd. Akad. Pedag. Nauk RSFSR, 1957.

Bein, E. S. *Aphasia and methods of overcoming it.* Leningrad: Izd. Meditsina, 1964.

Blinkov, S. M. The disturbance of writing during a temporal-lobe lesion. *Izv. Akad. Pedag. Nauk RSFSR,* 1948, No. 5.

Blonskii, P. P. *Memory and thought.* Sotsekgiz, 1935.

Buser, P., and Imbert, M. Sensory projections to the motor cortex in cats: A microelectrode study. In W. A. Rosenblith (Ed.), *Sensory Communication:*

Contribution to the Symposium on Principles of Sensory Communication. New York-London: M.I.T. Press and Wiley, 1961.

Faaborg-Andersen, K., and Edfeldt, A. M. Electromyography of intrinsic and extrinsic laryngeal muscles during silent speech: Correlation with reading activity. *Acta otolaryngol.,* 1958, *49.*

Faddeeva, V. K. Peculiarities of the interaction of the first and second signal systems in the formation of reactions to complex stimuli in children. *Zh. vyssh. nerv. Deyat.,* 1951, *1,* No. 3.

Fessard, A. The role of neuronal networks in sensory communication with the brain. In W. A. Rosenblith (Ed.), *Sensory communication: Contribution to the Symposium on Principles of Sensory communication.* New York-London: M.I.T. Press and Wiley, 1961.

Fonarev, A. M. Apparatus for electrical recording of micromovements of the tongue in latent articulation. *Izv. Akad. Pedag. Nauk RSFSR,* 1956, No. 81.

Hardyck, C. D., Petrinovich, L. F., and Ellsworth, D. W. Feedback of speech muscle activity during silent reading: Rapid extinction. *Science,* 1966, *154,* 1467–1468.

Indik, N. K. The role of speech kinesthesis in the recall of visual and verbal material. In *Problems of the psychology of memory.* Izd. Akad. Pedag. Nauk RSFSR, 1958.

Ivanov-Smolenskii, A. G. Experimental investigation of the interaction of direct and symbolic projections of the human cortex. *Arkh. biol. Nauk,* 1935, *38,* No. 1.

Ivanov-Smolenskii, A. G. An investigation of the combined work and interaction of the first and second signal systems as applied to medical problems. *Zh. vyssh. nerv. Deyat.,* 1953, *3,* No. 4.

Jacobson, E. The electrophysiology of mental activities. *Amer. J. Psychol.,* 1932, *44,* 677–694.

Jacobson, E. *Progressive relaxation.* (2nd. ed.) Chicago: Univer. of Chicago Press, 1956.

Kadochkin, L. N. The role of speech kinesthesis in the formation of certain orthographic habits. *Vop. Psikhol.,* 1955, No. 3.

Kapustnik, O. P. The relation between concrete conditioned stimuli and their verbal forms. *Trudy Lab. Fiziol. Patofiziol. Vyssh. Nerv. Deyat. Reb.,* 1930, *2.*

Kapustnik, O. P. The mutual relations between direct conditioned stimuli and their verbal symbols. *Trudy Lab. Fiziol. Patofiziol. Vyssh. Nerv. Deyat. Reb.,* 1934, *4.*

Kotlyarevskii, L. I. The reflection of direct conditioned associations in cortical symbolic projections. *Trudy Lab. Fiziol. Patofiziol. Vyssh. Nerv. Deyat. Reb.,* 1934, *4.*

Kotlyarevskii, L. I. The formation of pupillary conditioned reflexes and differentiation to direct and verbal stimuli. *Arkh. biol. Nauk,* 1935, *39,* No. 2.

Kotlyarevskii, L. I. Cardiovascular conditioned reflexes to direct and verbal stimuli. *Fiziol. Zh. SSSR,* 1936, *20,* No. 2.

Krasnogorskii, N. I. *Studies of higher nervous activity in man and animals.* Vol. 1. Moscow: Gosizdat, 1954.

Kryazhev, V. Y. *Higher nervous activity of animals in social conditions.* Moscow: Medgiz, 1955.

Lebedinskii, M. S. *Aphasia, agnosia, and apraxia.* Kharkov, 1941.

Luria, A. R. *Human higher cortical functions and their disturbance in local brain destruction.* Moscow: Izd. Moskov. Univer., 1962; New York: Basic Books, 1966.

Luria, A. R. *The human brain and psychic processes.* Moscow: Izd. Akad. Pedag. Nauk RSFSR, 1963; New York: Harper, 1966.

Matyukhina, M. B. The formation of a conditioned photochemical reflex to complex direct and verbal stimuli in man. *Izv. Akad. Pedag. Nauk RSFSR,* 1956, No. 81.

Max, L. W. An experimental study of the motor theory of consciousness: I. Critique of earlier studies. *J. gen. Psychol.,* 1934, 11, 112–125.

Max, L. W. Experimental study of the motor theory of consciousness: IV. Action-current responses of the deaf during awakening, kinesthetic imagery and abstract thinking. *J. comp. Psychol.,* 1937, *24,* 301–344.

Mountcastle, W. B. Some functional properties of the somatic afferent system. In W. A. Rosenblith, *Sensory communication: Contribution to the Symposium on Principles of Sensory Communication.* New York-London: M.I.T. Press and Wiley, 1961.

Nazarova, L. K. On the role of speech kinesthesis in writing. *Sovet. Pedag.,* 1952, No. 6.

Novikova, L. A. Electrophysiological studies of speech kinesthesis. In *Conference on Psychology (1–6 July 1955).* Moscow: Izd. Akad. Pedag. Nauk RSFSR, 1957.

Pavlov, I. P. *Pavlovian Wednesdays: Protocols and stenographic notes of physiological conversations* (1933–1934). Vol. 2. Moscow-Leningrad: Izd. Akad. Nauk SSSR, 1949.

Penfield, W., and Roberts, L. *Speech and brain mechanisms.* Princeton, N.J.: Princeton Univer. Press, 1959.

Podol'skii, L. I. On the interrelationship between internal and external speech. *Uch. Zap. Leningrad Gos. Pedag. Inst. im., Gertsena,* 1946, *53.*

Pomerantseva, D. G. The psychology of mistakes in the oral speech of young school children. Candidate's dissertation, Moscow, 1953.

Raven, J. C. *Guide to using progressive matrices.* London: H. K. Lewis, 1938. (Rev. ed., 1956.)

Rubinshtein, S. L. *Principles and paths of the development of psychology.* Moscow: Izd. Akad. Nauk SSSR, 1959.

Sechenov, I. M. Reflexes of the brain. In *Selected philosophical and psychological works.* Moscow: Gospolizdat, 1947.

Sechenov, I. M. On the mechanism of the frog's brain and the reflexes of the spinal cord. In *Physiol. Stud. üb. d Hemmungsmechan für d Reflexthätigk. d Ruckenm im Geh. d Frosch.* Berlin, 1963.

Shastin, N. R. On the physiology of verbal stimuli. *Fiziol. Zh. SSSR,* 1932, *15,* No. 3.

Shvarts, L. A. The problem of the word as a conditioned stimulus. *Byull. eksper. Biol. Med.,* 1948, *38,* No. 12.

Smith, A. A., Malmo, R. B., and Shagass, C. An electromyographic study of listening and talking. *Canad. J. Psychol.,* 1954, *8,* 219–227.

Smolenskaya, E. P. The verbal symbols of conditioned and differentiated stimuli. *Trudy Lab. Fiziol. Patofiziol. Vyssh. Nerv. Deyat. Reb.,* 1934, *4.*

Sokolov, A. N. Inner speech and understanding. *Uch. Zap. Gos. Inst. Psikh.,* 1941, *2.*

Sokolov, A. N. The speech mechanisms of mental activity. *Izv. Akad. Pedag. Nauk RSFSR,* 1956, No. 81.

Sokolov, A. N. Internal speech in the study of foreign languages. *Vop. Psikhol.,* 1960, No. 5.

Sokolov, A. N. Electromyographic analysis of internal speech and the problem of the neurodynamics of thinking. In N. I. Zhinkin and F. N. Shemiakin (Eds.), *Thinking and speech.* Moscow: Izd. Akad. Pedag. Nauk RSFSR, 1963.

Strokina, T. V. An experimental study of the interaction of the first and second signal systems in neurotic children. *Zh. Vyssh. Nerv. Deyat.,* 1951, *1,* No. 5.

Traugott, N. N. The interrelations of direct and symbolic projections in the formation of conditioned inhibition. *Trudy Lab. Fiziol. Patofiziol. Vyssh. Nerv. Deyat. Reb.,* 1934, *4.*

Volkova, V. D. Certain peculiarities of the formation of conditioned reflexes to speech stimuli in children. *Fiziol. Zh. SSSR,* 1953, *39,* No. 5.

Vygotskii, L. S. *Thought and speech.* Sotsekgiz, 1934.

Wallerstein, H. An electromyographic study of attentive listening. *Canad. J. Psychol.,* 1954, *8,* 228–238.

Watson, J. B. *Psychology from the standpoint of a behaviorist.* Philadelphia-London: Lippincott, 1919.

Yusevitch, Y. S. *Electromyographic studies in the mental diseases clinic.* Moscow: Medgiz, 1958.

Yusevitch, Y. S. *Electromyographia of the tonus of the human musculature in normal and pathological states.* Moscow: Medgiz, 1963.

Zhinkin, N. I. The development of written speech in third and fourth graders. *Izv. Akad. Pedag. Nauk RSFSR,* 1956, No. 78.

Zhinkin, N. I. Investigation of internal speech using the method of central speech obstacles. *Izv. Akad. Pedag. Nauk RSFSR,* 1960, No. 113.

Zhinkin, N. I. Code transfers in internal speech. *Vop. Yazik.,* 1964, No. 6.

20

Engineering Psychology in the U.S.S.R.

B. F. Lomov

EDITORS' INTRODUCTION

In the 1920's, Soviet engineering psychology was a thriving enterprise, with its own journals (such as Psychotechnics and the Psychophysiology of Work) *and the support of leading psychophysiologists such as Bekhterev and Bernshtein. However, in the 1930's, as part of the general crackdown on "psychotechnology" and "pedology," activity in engineering psychology was all but halted. Of particular concern to Soviet ideologists was the use of aptitude tests and interest inventories taken or borrowed from American and English testers. Whatever the specific concern, the whole field suffered.*

In the 1950's, increasing emphasis began to be placed on the rational use of human skills, especially as these skills interacted with newly developed machines. As one pair of influential psychologists put it, "The creation of complex, self-regulated technical systems has, so to speak, shifted the boundary between man and machine. Psychological functions, which only yesterday were carried out exclusively by man, came more and more to be considered machine functions" (Leont'ev and Panov, 1963, p. 399).

In the later 1950's, several conferences on engineering psychology were held. This activity increased, and during 1960–1965, several collections of articles on engineering psychology appeared (see References at the end of this chapter).

In 1959, the first university laboratory of engineering psychol-

ogy was opened at Leningrad University (under Lomov's direction). Shortly thereafter, laboratories opened at Moscow University, Kharkhov University, and the Institute of Psychology.

Today engineering psychology is one of the most energetic and sophisticated branches of Soviet psychology. For those who wish to pursue this topic further, the English translation of Lomov's monograph, Man and Technology, *is probably the most accessible source.*

Transmission of Information to the Human Operator

The study of transmission of information to the human operator is one of the most important tasks facing engineering psychology, owing to the widespread development of remote-control systems. It involves the practical task of investigating the interaction of sensory with other cognitive processes. Soviet psychologists and physiologists have accumulated significant experimental material revealing the characteristic features of sensations produced through the various modalities, their dependence on the physiological characteristics of stimuli, the interaction of sensations, the dynamics of the formation of the perceptual image, and the physiological mechanisms of the sensory processes.

These data provide a good foundation on which engineering psychology can build. It must be emphasized, however, that the transmission of information to the human operator cannot be reduced to the study of sensory processes in its classical form. Information transmission involves at least three basic aspects.

One of them concerns the *relationship of the physical signal, which conveys information, to "parameters" of the analyzer such as sensitivity, the dynamics of adaptation, etc.* This is the psychophysical aspect, associated with those characteristics of stimuli which can be used to transmit information. The worldwide accumulation of psychophysical data permits a rather detailed characterization of all the basic analyzers of man. However, they were obtained primarily in specially designed laboratory situations and cannot always be directly applied to the solution of problems arising in engineering psychology. Thus, there is a need for additional research.

The physical characteristics of signals must be maximally distinguishable. It is clear that the known magnitudes of difference thresholds cannot be the direct basis of evaluation. Consequently, the concept of "operative thresholds" was introduced (Bushurova and Tutushkina, 1964; Lomov, 1965). It has been repeatedly established that an increase in the discrimination interval of any sensory dimension of a signal increases the speed and accuracy of discrimination. The minimum divergence necessary for asymptotic speed and accuracy is defined as the "operative threshold," or, more accurately, "the threshold of optimal discrimination."

We shall discuss the data of Dmitrieva (1964) as an example. She studied the dependence of the speed with which a person processes information on the magnitude of the difference in length between pairs of lines (Figure 20–1). In her experiments, subjects were presented with pairs of

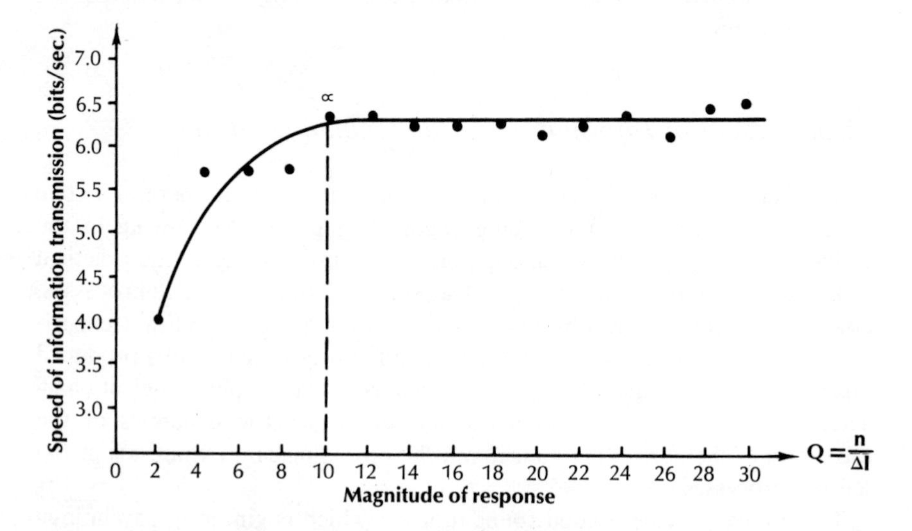

Figure 20–1. Function relating the speed of information processing to the size differences between lines. *On the ordinate*—speed of information processing in bits/sec. *On the abscissa*—size of the difference between stimuli in terms of the ratio $Q = n/\Delta i$, where n is the number of the interval and Δi is the size of the difference which corresponds to the difference threshold. The point marked *a* represents the "operative threshold." (Data from Dmitrieva, 1964.)

lines, equal or different in length, in random order. The magnitude of the difference varied from threshold to a magnitude 30 times greater than the threshold. If the subject considered the lines equal, he pressed one button. If he considered them different, he pressed another. The reaction time was recorded and the speed of information processing was evaluated. The speed of processing information measured in bits is the general measure which combines the separate measures of speed and accuracy of discrimination.

In various laboratories, work is being conducted on measurement of "operative thresholds" involving the discrimination of change in the speed of moving points (Vodlozerov, 1963) and of distinctions in the clarity of light stimuli (Chuprikova, 1964), in the angularity of simple geometric figures (Tutushkina, 1964), and in other attributes of unidimensional visual signals.

Another aspect of information transmission concerns the *maximum amount of information which a man can absorb and process in a given time.* This is the information-theory aspect of the problem, embracing such questions as determination of optimal length of the characteristics of signals, "saturation" of signals with information, evaluation of the number of attributes necessary for transmission of a given amount of information, distribution of incoming signals in time, and so on. In the Soviet Union research is being conducted on the capacity of the analyzers, especially the visual analyzer (Glezer and Tsukkerman, 1961; Lomov, 1963), as well as on the speed of information processing during the execution of various kinds of responses (Boiko, 1964). Many studies have been conducted to verify Hicks' well-known law, which posits a linear dependence of reaction time on the information content of the signal. These studies revealed a series of factors which influence this dependence.

Egorov (1965) demonstrated that this dependence manifests itself more or less markedly only after a certain level of training has been reached and only in certain states of work capacity. On the other hand, Hicks' law has no influence at a high level of training (Mowbray, 1960). At first glance these data contradict each other. However, they can be brought into accord if the *dynamics* of training are examined. It seems that early in training reaction time is determined by many different factors which mask the influence of the signal's probability; therefore, Hicks' law does not apply. In the middle range the law does function, but subsequently, if the experimental conditions do not change, the response mechanism undergoes a kind of reorganization: firm associative connections form between certain stimuli and certain responses and, as a result, the reaction time becomes independent of the number of possible stimuli or the probability of their appearance. Thus, a man who can read seems to identify letters instantly and directly on the basis of firm associative connections; he does not have to make a choice.

Other factors also influence the speed of information processing, such as discriminability of the signals (see Figure 20–1), their spatial position, and compatibility of stimulus and response (Prodan, 1964).

Leont'ev and Krinchik (1964) studied the influence of the "significance" of the signal on reaction time. In their experiments, one of a series of signals was given a special meaning: the subject was told that, if he responded to that signal more slowly than was necessary, the apparatus would be destroyed and the experiment rendered useless. Figure 20–2 shows the results of the experiment. The graph indicates that introducing the factor of significance led to a reduction in the reaction time. Significance also reduces the slope of the line which characterizes the dependence of the reaction time on the information content of the signal.

These authors attempted to define the psychological correlates of such

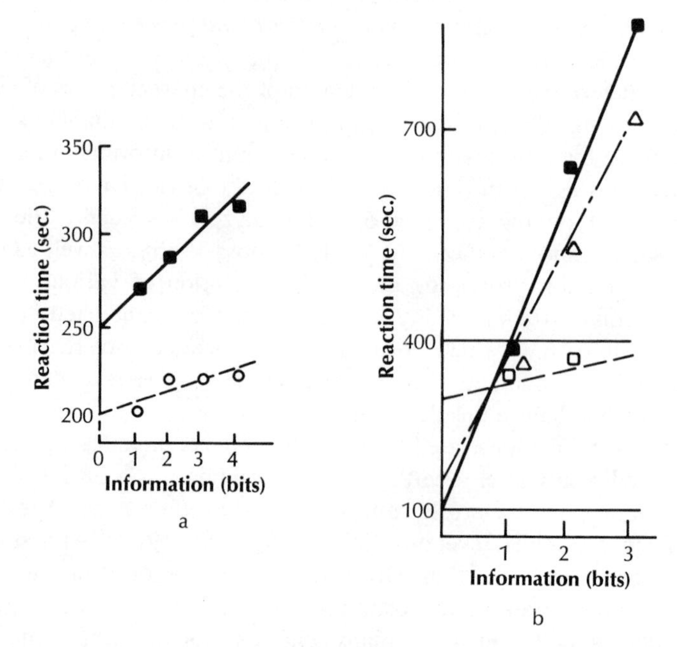

Figure 20–2. The influence of significance of a signal on the relation between reaction time and the amount of information. (*a*) The dependence of reaction time on the amount of individual information. The solid line is for the control condition, the broken line for the period when subjects were instructed so that all signals were made significant. (*b*) The dependence of reaction time on the amount of average information. The solid line is for the control condition. The broken line is for the instructed condition, and the dashed-dotted line is for a control condition following an instructed condition. (From Leont'ev and Krinchik, 1964.)

measures as probability of a signal and number of possible signals. Experiments were conducted to compare the dependence of reaction time on individual and average information. The former was defined by the formula $I_i = \log_2 p_i$; the latter, by the formula $H = -\sum_{i=1}^{K} p_i$. These dependencies turned out to be basically different (Figure 20–3). The authors concluded that the psychological correlates of these factors are the *degree to which the signal is unexpected* (probability of the appearance of a given signal, that is, on the amount of individual information) and the *degree of the complexity of the choice* (depends on the number of alternatives and the assessment of the probable appearance of its elements, that is, on the mean information).

Leont'ev and Krinchik's work showed that human information processing is not a passive reflection of the statistical structure of signals, but an active operation which leads to the most effective solution of a problem. In the course of training, the subject optimizes perception of information in such a way that, while he loses time in perceiving frequent signals, he gains in speed of perceiving infrequent signals.

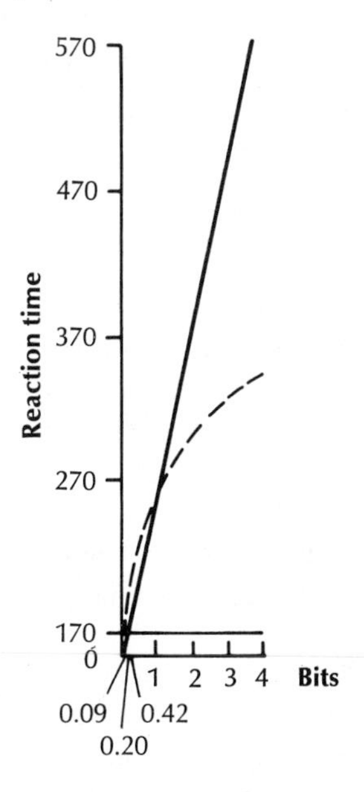

Figure 20–3. The dependence of reaction time on individual and average information. The dotted line is the function for individual information in the range from .09 to 4 bits. The solid line is an extrapolated straight line representing the dependence of reaction time on the average amount of information. (From Leont'ev and Krinchik, 1964.)

The influence of this active expectation in the speed of perceiving information was also found in Konopkin's experiments. He presented to his subjects consecutive signals of different length (4 cm. and 8 cm.) and measured the disjunctive reaction time to each of them. Then the subject was given instructions which formed a set (active expectation) that did not correspond to the true course of events. For example, in a series of experiments in which the signals were selected from a sequence of four alternatives (2 bits/signal in equal probability of their appearance), the subject was informed that he would be given signals from a sequence of eight alternatives (3 bits/signal). Under these conditions the reaction time was more in accord with the expected than with the actual information content of the signal, that is, it was determined by the *set*.

Dmitrieva (1964b) studied the dependence of speed of perception and of information processing on the nature of the functional associations between cues of the signals. The signal was composed of two cues. These cues had to be compared with a standard on each trial. In the first series the subject had to press a white button if both cues conformed to the standard and a black button if at least one of them did not conform to the model. In this condition the choice of white involved the grammatical connective "and"—conjunction. In the second series the subject had to respond to white if at least one cue of the signals conformed to the standard, and another way if neither conformed to the model, the connective "or"—inclusive disjunction. In the third series he responded one way if one and only one cue conformed to the model, and another way if both conformed or did not conform to the model, the connective "any"—exclusive disjunction.

In all three series, the subject was given exactly the same amount of information measured according to the probability of the appearance of the signals and demanding either one response or the other. However, the reaction time and the percentage of correct responses in all three series were different. The fastest information processing occurred in the first series of experiments. In the second series it was slightly less, and in the third series it was significantly less. These data indicate the dependence of speed of information processing on the nature of the problem to be solved and, consequently, on the type of choice operation.

In other experiments Dmitrieva measured the speed of information processing in the execution of separate elementary operations (comparison of pairs of number cues according to position, form, subtraction, and division of number pairs). Then the subjects were asked to do *several* elementary operations in a row with similar pairs. In this latter case the speed was noticeably higher than the mean of the speed of the elementary operations. This leads us to assume that, when a series of elementary operations are united in sequence, certain new ways of processing information are formed.

These studies indicate that it is impossible to evaluate the method and the speed of information processing without reference to the structure of the human being's activity. Therefore, the study of the structure of the human operator's activity is one of the most important tasks of contemporary engineering psychology.

To summarize this aspect of the problem of the transmission of information to the human operator, we shall note that there is no unanimity of opinion on the question of applying information measures in the study of psychological processes. Some researchers attempt to apply these measures everywhere, assuming that they can provide a basic means of quantitative analysis. Others regard them more cautiously (and sometimes even with hostility), pointing to the limitations of information measures and the necessity, above all, for qualitative analysis of psychological phenomena. It should be noted that so far the use of these measures has produced results only in the study of a very limited sphere of phenomena, basically, choice responses and acts of identification. Attempts to apply them to other kinds of human activity have met with significant obstacles.

At the present stage of development, information theory should not be limited to only one quantitative measure of behavior. The application of other contemporary methods of mathematical analysis is necessary. This becomes especially clear when we deal with the problem of reception and processing of information by the human being. Psychologists and mathematicians must work jointly in order to evaluate more fully the effectiveness and limitations of these methods in information theory.

This last aspect of this problem concerns the *study of those cognitive processes which man utilizes in the reception and processing* of information. We are speaking primarily of the formation of a subjective model of the signal and the decoding of the incoming information. Research in both general and engineering psychology indicates that the formation of a perceptual model goes through several phases. It can be traced clearly in experiments on visual perception. In the first phase the position of the object in the visual field is determined and a rough discrimination of its general proportions is carried out. This is followed by the phase of color and form "flicker." The apparent color and form turn out to be unstable, and the form sometimes seems "round," sometimes "star-shaped," and the color of the object changes. In the third phase discrimination of a clear overlap of the contours occurs. The fourth phase is characterized by globally adequate perceptions of the form. As a whole the form is adequately perceived, but without sufficient discrimination of the details. Finally, in the fifth phase there is optimal perception in the given concrete situation. At this point the model becomes differentiated: the contours are perceived in all their detail.

The duration of each phase depends on the complexity of the form presented. Knowledge of the sequence of the discrimination of the signal's cues and the formative dynamics of its model is important for the solution of certain engineering psychology problems, such as the choice of optimal outlines of the cues, determination of the number of lines in a televised image, the speed of signal transmission, the speed for replacing frames in projection systems, and the like. In this connection the problem of "interference tolerance" of perception also must be solved, that is, man's ability to reconstruct signals which are partially destroyed by interference.

The concepts which man forms (secondary model) in the process of his development play an important role in the organization of a perceptual model. According to the data of a series of authors, schematization of the model and an elementary level of generalization are characteristic of these concepts (Anan'ev, 1960; Lomov, 1963; and others). It can be assumed that the system of concepts, retained in man's memory, forms an individualized "subjective scale" with which this or that perceptual model is correlated. This significantly hastens the process of perception, but can also serve as the source of erroneous identification.

The problem of the formation of "subjective scales" and their utilization in perceiving signals must be studied. The results of such studies may be extremely useful in developing systems of optimal information coding and in training the operator.

The final and decisive moment in information reception is the *decoding*. Once the operator has perceived and identified the *signal* he must evaluate the condition of the *object*, that is, he must transfer the model of the former into the model of the latter or construct a "conceptual model" (Welford, 1962). This transformation may occur as a translation of the perceptual model into a concept through the mechanism of association, or by means of a more complex reformulation at the level of speech-thought processes. The character of the transformation, in the last analysis, is determined by the problem which the operator must solve.

Obviously, the speed, accuracy, and reliability of the transformation depend on the correlations which are established between the signals and the objects which they represent.

In this connection the first problem is that of the correlation of the number of cues of the object and the signal. This problem was studied by Tutushkina (cited in Lomov, 1963). She compared three groups of signals. In one group the number of cues in the signal corresponded precisely to the number of cues in the object; in another group the number of cues in the signal was greater than that in the object; in the third group, there were fewer cues in the signal (certain cues were combined). Maximal accuracy in decoding occurred in the first group. In the second group the subject sometimes attributed nonexistent cues to the objects, that is, the surplus of cues led to complexity of reception. The third group did not achieve the necessary completion of decoding, that is, unreliable information reception occurred. According to Table 20–1, which presents Tutushkina's data, the optimal system of coding seems to be one in which the number of cues in the signal equals the number of cues in the object.

A no less important question is the qualitative relationship between the

Table 20–1

Correlation of the signal's and object's cues	Accuracy of decoding (% correct)	Time of decoding (sec.)	Information reception (bits/sec.)
Insufficient cues	50	0.38	6.6
Equal cues	84	0.39	10.7
Surplus cues	80	0.44	9.1

cues of the signal and the object. In general, all signals may be divided into two large classes: *signal representations* (models), in which the nature of the signal in some way *reproduces* the nature of the object, and *signal symbols* which only *connote* the nature of the objects. The degree to which the model reproduces the object may vary from a more or less complete picture (e.g., televised color image) to diagrams (contour sketches, drawings).

Experiments have compared the time to decode signals of both classes. The subjects were first trained to emit elementary conditioned-reflex responses to simple objects. They were then presented with their representations (colored, tinted, and contour drawings) and with their symbolic, well-learned connotations. As might have been expected, the latent period of the response to representations was shorter (and more similar in time to the response to the object) than to the symbol. Average reaction time to the object was 0.4 second, to a colored drawing, 0.9 second, and to the symbol (a word), 2.8 seconds (Lomov, 1963). The previously mentioned experiments of Tutushkina also indicated that even signals which were only partially similar to the object in some way increased the speed of decoding.

In reception of information transmitted by signal representations, the processes of perception and decoding are combined, owing to association by similarity. This leads to a decrease in the time necessary for transformation. In the use of signal symbols these processes may diverge and thus, of course, require additional time to transform the image of the signal into a "concrete model."

This does not mean, however, that the signal representation is always the most efficacious. Using this type of signal, we gain in speed and interference tolerance, but we may lose in accuracy (the latter is completely determined by the analyzer's discriminative ability). In choosing the type of signal one must take into account the problems which the operator must solve. In most contemporary situations, signals which combine both the model and the symbol are used.

Recently the development of a specific variety of signal symbols of the cues of the object, which are transmitted in the form of a complete spatial structure ("space coding"), has attracted a great deal of attention. This graphic indicator is one of the most economical ways to transmit information regarding physical magnitudes (diagrams, graphs), produced electronically by informational-logical machines on the basis of the original information. Graphic indications allow for translation of almost any measure (including time, force, speed, tension, etc.), as well as dependencies between them which are not directly in the form of a spatial schema. Graphic indicators are not representations in the true sense of the word, in that they do not reproduce the properties of the object. The cues of the object are represented in the form of a complete conditional picture.

There is reason to believe that replacement of a mass of separate instruments, which transmit information regarding separate parameters of the object, by a complete spatial scheme (conditional picture) that changes its configuration in accord with reciprocally communicating changes of its constituent parameters, leads to increased speed and reliability of information reception by man. This kind of integrated coding system is based on man's ability to simultaneously and naturally evaluate a complex of parameters (Lomov, 1963).

These aspects of the problem of information transmission to the human operator involve certain *general* principles of optimal coding. The results of many studies may serve as a starting point for the development of methods of representation.

Any analysis of the work done on this problem would be incomplete without a description of the studies devoted to improving concrete forms of the indicators used. However, this topic is extremely specialized. For a general review of the types of indicators used and their various merits see Lomov (1963).

Investigations of Directive Actions of the Human Operator

In the process of receiving and processing information, the operator executes operations directed toward changing the object which he directs. In this way, information is transmitted from man to the machine. Spatial, force, and temporal characteristics of various types of actions have been studied in detail in physiology and biomechanics. The data may be applied to certain calculations regarding the organization of control instruments. However, they can be used to determine only the most general requirements of the control instruments (permissible amplitude of movement, speed, and resistance). They do not provide a basis for the choice of that organization which would ensure the necessary accuracy and reliability of the operator's actions. In this connection the problem of the *mechanism of mental regulation of work movements* arises. The majority of Soviet psychologists are of the opinion that various forms of mental reflection (perceptual models, concepts, conceptual models) are *regulators* of motor acts. This point of view was first advanced by Sechenov and later developed in the investigations of psychologists and physiologists.

Numerous physiological and psychological investigations have revealed certain concrete laws of the reflex mechanism of the motor act, the role of "sensory correction" and "reverse afferentation," certain characteristics of neurodynamics, etc. (Bernshtein, 1957; Anokhin, 1961; and others).

The human hand is a complex control system with reverse (feedback) connections in which kinesthetic and tactile analyzers play a basic role.

Accuracy and speed of hand movements are determined not only by muscle tissue and vascular structure, but primarily by the characteristics of the process of the circulation of the control information (the time of the regulatory cycle, the time of switching, the structure of the directing signal, etc.). The kinesthetic links become fully associated, and the movement coordinated, because in the synthesis of conducting signals, superfluous freedom of the moving organ is overcome. Even the simplest work action is formed from a more or less substantial mass of elementary movements, united by the regulatory mechanism into a complete structure. These movements may be divided into three groups according to their functions.

The first group consists essentially of *work* (execution) movements by means of which the object is influenced. The second group involves gnostic movements. As the designation implies, they are directed toward cognition of the object and the conditions of the action. These movements are extremely varied and include feeling, measuring, probing, and control movements. The third group consists of *adaptive* movements. There are adjusting movements (adjusting the work of the hand), correcting movements, which aid in correcting errors, and balancing or compensating movements, which ensure stability and plasticity of the working hand (Lomov, 1963).

The interrelationships between these forms of movement change in the process of habit formation. Gnostic movements are usually predominant on the first level. Later they are reduced and are so intimately merged with working movements that it is often difficult to separate them. These classes of movements were discovered in studies of the operations of hand work. Later they were observed in machine-directed operations. Roze (1963) studied manipulations with various organs of control (handwheels, hand grips, levers, pushbuttons). She showed (by analyzing each frame from a motion picture) that the motor act is composed of a mass of micromovements. The latency period depended on temporal characteristics of the adjusting movements. The earlier the hand assumes the necessary pose, the shorter is the latent period. The process of manipulation itself consists of many micromovements of the fingers, completed both with and without contact with the controlling apparatus. According to Roze's calculations, the fingers of the right hand execute more than 60 micromovements in the 0.75 second required to press a button. In the same time period, the fingers execute about 80 micromovements to turn a tumbler. A significant part is played by tactile micromovements which aid in discerning the form and resistance of the apparatus; this is important for the organization of grasp and the regulation of strength, as well as for compensation and balance. Usually the thumb and the middle and fourth fingers execute the work movement. The middle and fourth fingers often execute the gnostic movements, and the fourth and little fingers the adaptive movements. However, there is no simple relation between a type of movement and a certain finger.

Exchange of function and "transfer" of movements from one finger to another take place in the process of manipulation.

It can be assumed that each micromovement gives rise to an elementary kinesthetic signal necessary for regulation of the total act. As the motor act becomes more complete, the number of fractional movements increases and, consequently, the number of elementary kinesthetic signals increases. This is apparently important for the subsequent synthesis of movements and the formation of a complete, complex structure.

These data indicate that in constructing organs of control, it is necessary to consider the peculiarities not only of the work movements, but of gnostic and adaptive movements as well. Obviously, the instruments and organs of control most convenient for man will be those which ensure optimal correlation between the various forms of movement.

Since the controlling act responds to one or another signal appearing on the indicator, one must take into account the relationship of the control apparatus to the indicator. Pauzhaite (1965) compared the speed and accuracy of various responses for several combinations of scales and control apparatus; the task was to move a transfer pointer to a given position. The following variants were investigated: linear horizontal scale—circular handle (LC); circular scale—circular handle (CC); linear scale—linear moving handle (LL); circular scale—linear moving handle (CL). In all cases the form of the scale and control apparatus positively influenced the speed and accuracy of the movement. Table 20–2 shows the latent period and the duration of the motor component of the required response.

The influence of the compatibility factor appears, although insignificantly, in the size of the latent periods (at the stage of organization of movement) and, more markedly, in the magnitudes of the time required for the motor component (when the movement is being executed).

Table 20–2

Direction of movements	Combination	Latent period (sec.)	Duration of motor component (sec.)
Left to Right	CC	0.30	0.76
	LL	0.25	0.76
	CL	0.28	0.85
	LC	0.23	1.05
Right to Left	LL	0.24	0.71
	CC	0.17	0.77
	CL	0.23	0.81
	LC	0.18	0.92

Vekker and Surkov (1964) investigated the relationship between the sensory and motor fields of the operator. The subjects had to imitate the selection of the set of routes by a railroad dispatcher. In one of the conditions the control panel with switches was separated from the panel on which the railroad lines were depicted (in the form of arrows) and the distribution of switches coincided spatially with the distribution of arrows on the panel (Figure 20–4a). In another condition the control panel with switches was also separated from the panel depicting the rail lines and the switches were placed in a row (Figure 20–4b). In the third group the switches were distributed directly under the arrows (Figure 20–4c). The subjects had to transfer the "train" from one point to another (route) when certain paths were already occupied. The problem was solved most quickly and accurately by the third group. There were more errors in the second group than in the others and solution time was 2.5 seconds greater than in the third group. Solution time in the first and third groups was approximately equal. The authors concluded that the most important means of improving accuracy and speed is *structural conformity* in the distribution of signals and control apparatuses—not simply proximity, as is often assumed, but exact conformity.

Tracking is necessary in order to coordinate movements with signal changes. The study of tracking, therefore, is important if we are to understand controlling acts and the mechanisms of their mental regulation. Vodlozerov (1964) and Sukhodol'skii (1964) investigated the simplest variant of tracking a unidimensional visual signal. The subject had to keep the pointer on an evenly and rectilinearly moving mark by turning a handle. Analysis of the data indicated that the tracking operation is divided into two periods: transitional and fixed. A time lag is characteristic of the transitional period. As the speed of the marker increased from 1 to 4 mm. per second, the time lag decreased from 0.65 to 0.25 second, approaching the latency of simple sensorimotor responses. A great number of movements are faster or slower than the speed of the marker. The mean duration of pauses when the speed of the marker is slow (1–2 mm./sec.) is 0.5 second.

Two forms of the transitional process may be discerned: oscillation with extraneous movement (overregulation) and oscillation without extraneous movement. When the marker moves slowly (1–2 mm./sec.) the former predominates. When the marker moves more quickly (5–10 mm./sec.), the latter predominates. The transition period lasts 2 to 3 seconds.

In a given period, the number and duration of pauses decreases and the average speed of partial movements approaches the speed of the marker. In the first period, a leading role is played by the so-called external circuits (eye-hand) in regulating movements. The visual system measures the extent of the signal's movements, and the kinesthetic system the extent of the moving hand. When the visual and kinesthetic signals are commensurate,

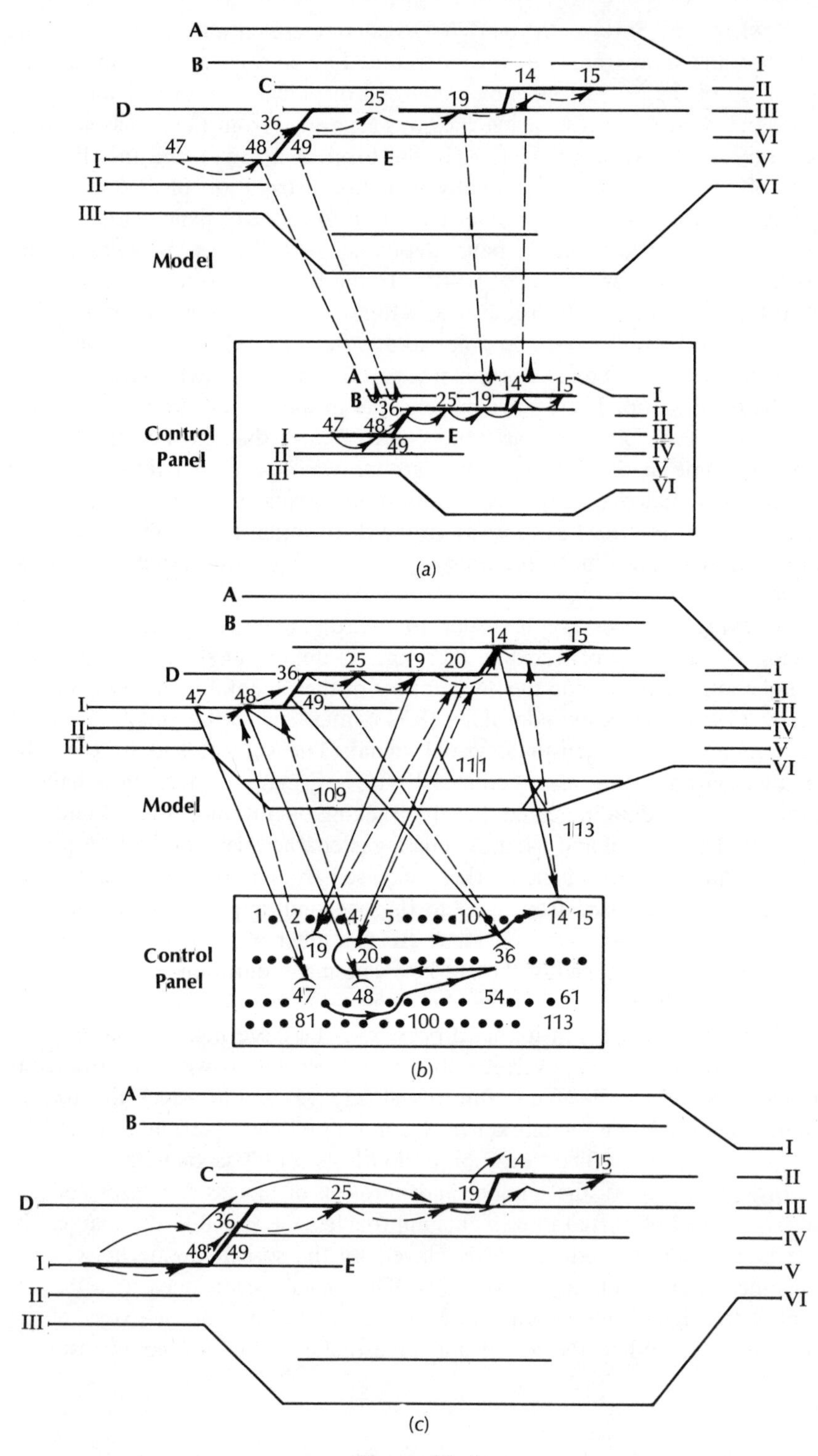
A
B
C
D
E
I
II
III
IV
V
VI
14
15
25
19
36
47
48
49
Model
Control Panel
(a)
20
109
111
113
1
2
4
5
10
54
61
81
100
(b)
(c)

Figure 20–4.

the relationship between the speed of the moving signal and the hand constitutes a sort of "gear ratio."

In the process of tracking, the model for regulation is reformulated and the hand movements become smoother and more stable (fixed period). As a result of comparison and averaging of the signals during the first period, it becomes possible to evaluate the *speed* of the marker. From regulation of hand movements by the position of the marker, the subject moves to regulating them according to speed. This in turn activates the mechanism of visual extrapolation.

Reformulation of the visual model creates the conditions for activation of the so-called internal circuits of regulation (kinesthetic analyzer of the hand-motor apparatus of the hand). As a result, movement becomes uninterrupted (although with changing speed) and smoother. The number and duration of pauses is decreased: the magnitude of errors decreases; "time of inertia" predominates. Control becomes the basic function of the visual system.

The motor component of the act includes all of the foregoing forms of movement. The internal circuits of regulation ensure optimal combinations of these movements and their reciprocal transmission at each given moment of time. In the process of tracking the hand is in a state of "dynamic equilibrium" which permits predominance of the evoked reactive force with minimal delay. This is one of the most important conditions of operative preparation for reformulation of motor behavior.

In the fixed period, despite the low level of accuracy, human activity is characterized by high dynamic stability and reliability which, obviously, is determined by the features of psychological regulation.

The problem of the transmission function of the human operator arises when we consider his control functions. Investigations indicate that a man is capable of working under various regimens and is not limited to one class of motor tasks (Vekker, 1964). He can function (within limits) as a simple amplifier, as a differentiating mechanism, a logical link, etc. Most characteristic of man is the ability to execute the very same action by several different means; there is no simple connection between systems of signals and responding movements. The number of possible "motor structures" is almost unlimited. The high degree of flexibility and adaptability of man's behavior

---

Figure 20–4. Differing layouts used for the study of the interrelationship between sensory and motor fields in the work of a railroad dispatcher. (*a*) Arrangement of switches on the control panel corresponds to arrangement of arrows on model panel. (*b*) Arrangement of switches on the control panel does not correspond to arrangement of arrows on model panel. (*c*) The switches are placed directly under the arrows on the model panel. The model represents various routes. The lines indicate the connection between arrows and switches. (From Vekker and Surkov, 1964.)

is explained, in the last analysis, by the specific cognitive regulation of movements. This mechanism is a multidimensional structure with a high degree of mobility from one level to another and is capable of reorganization.

Investigations of Operative Thinking

The need to solve problems which arise in the course of control processes occupies a central place in the operator's activity. The operator, participating in complex control systems, must deal with problem situations which he must interpret, analyze, and solve. Frequently, it is limited by time. Delay is tantamount to error and may result in additional complications, sometimes even to partial or complete destruction of an entire system. Operative thinking is understood as that process of solving practical tasks which results in the formation of a model of actions (plan of operations) which will ensure attainment of the requisite goal. It includes clarification of the problem situation and the system for its mental and practical solution. The problem of operative thinking was first discussed in detail by Teplov, using the activity of a military general as an example (1961). Teplov showed that the well-developed practical intellect is characterized by an ability to "quickly analyze a complex situation and almost instantly find the correct solution," by a process which is usually called intuition and which amounts to a unique combination of visual and verbal-logical thinking. The reflection of the general properties and basic interrelations between phenomena is combined with the predominance of visualness. The visual model of a situation absorbs the sum of that knowledge which is acquired by means of discursive thinking. Intuition assumes highly developed spatial and temporal concepts.

Teplov's conclusions are extremely interesting for engineering psychology because the operator's activity is in many ways analogous to the activity of the general (complex conditions, insufficient time, the need to evaluate opposing forces, great responsibility for every decision).

Zavalishina and Pushkin (1964) investigated operative thinking. They concluded that its basic components are the *ability to structure* (which appears in the formation of larger units of action on the basis of association of elements of the situation), *dynamic recognition* (recognition of parts of the final situation in the original problem situation), and formation of an *algorithm of solution* (development of principles and rules for problem solution in general as well as for any concrete situation—the determination of the sequence of actions).

The authors discerned three stages in the process of problem solving. On the first level there is the attempt to act only with one element of the situation; each element emerges as a single dimensional component. On the second level the elements are grouped in a definite way. The third level consists of the creation of more general principles of solution: the principle of unification of elements into invariant subgroups and the separation of unsatisfactory elements. A basic role is played by image-bound or visual thinking, that is, the conception of the actual situation based on received and decoded information. It was noted in studies by Pushkin (1960a, b) and Vekker (1963) that with concrete, practical experience, concepts may achieve an extremely high degree of accuracy, stability, and structure.

While investigating the properties of representation it is important to bear in mind that the operator's functions are not limited to the reception of information; the critical moment of his activity is the solution of some sort of problem. Therefore, information must be transmitted in a manner which will facilitate the operator's analysis of the problem situation, dynamic recognition, and formation of an algorithm for solution. It is important to know the form which the course of solution will take. If it takes the form of an operative conception then it is important to provide forms of information transmission which will ensure quick and accurate translation of signals into a visual "thought picture" of the situation.

Investigations of the Operator's Memory

All of the basic types of memory appear in some form or other in the activity of the man who controls machines with instruments. The interrelationship between these forms depends on the problems to be solved by the "man-machine" system and on the structure of the operator's activity. In some cases a leading role is played by momentary (spontaneous and operative) memory, and in other cases, by long-term memory.

The problem of the operator's memory is being intensively and productively investigated in the Kharkov University laboratories (Zinchenko and Zinchenko, 1965).

Repkina (1965) studied the characteristics of operative memory (volume, flexibility, accuracy, and interference tolerance) in relation to the solution of relatively simple problems. Operative memory is understood as the momentary retention of information necessary for successful solution of problems of *current activity and the achievement of its goal.*

In one of a series of experiments, Repkina compared the effectiveness of different codes used to transmit information to man: numbers, letters, color, geometric figures, configurations. These experiments confirmed Hitt's conclusions (1961) regarding the dependence of the effectiveness of codes on the nature of the operative problems. In addition, Repkina's data indicated that different cognitive functions predominate in the solution of various problems. In some cases the leading role is played by processes of perception, in others—by operative memory, and in still others—by thinking processes. This is no doubt due to the fact that a code, optimal for one process, may not be optimal for another.

In another series of experiments Repkina investigated the solution of problems requiring the subject to determine the sequence in which a group of objects had to be attended to. In solving such problems the load on the operative memory is especially great. The number of objects was varied from 5 to 35, as well as the number of their parameters (e.g., speed, height, type of object, etc.). The mean time of solution of the problem was measured and the time spent on each object was calculated. The following formula was used to fit the data:

$$t_{xy} = 0.174xy + 0.056x - 0.28y + I$$

where t_{xy} represents time spent on one object, x, the number of sequential objects, y, the number of parameters, and I is a constant.

For a given number of parameters the dependence of t on x is expressed in a straight line. The slope of a straight line changes in a predictable manner when the number of parameters is increased (see Figure 20–5). With training, the influence of the number of parameters on the solution time

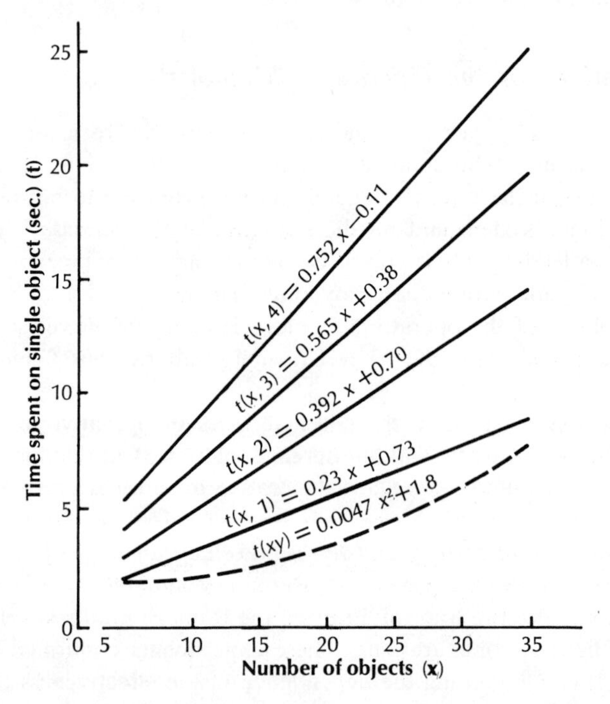

Figure 20–5. Changes in the time spent on each object as a function of the number of objects and the number of parameters of each object when the subject has to attend to the objects in a given order. y = the number of parameters of an object to be evaluated. The solid lines represent functions for different values of y. The dotted line represents data from well-practiced subjects responding to objects with 1 to 4 parameters. (From Repkina, 1965.)

may be eliminated. More detailed analysis of the training process indicated that more economical routes of search and sequence are discoverd by the subject and automatization of both perceptual and mnemonic actions occurs. In the course of such training larger and larger units of memory are formed.

In solving operative problems which place a significant burden on memory the most effective codes are those which permit formation of larger memory units. Ryzhkova (1965) conducted a study comparing ease of assimilation, speed, and accuracy of symbol recognition for one-, two-, and three-dimensional methods of coding. The subject was required to search for objects on a flat surface. The number of objects which he had to find was increased, thus increasing the load on operative memory. The experiments indicated that the volume of operative memory is in the 4-to-5-unit range. The number of symbol changes did not seem to have any essential influence. It was also found that the volume of operative memory depends on the degree to which the remembered material yields to quick logical processing. This processing is expressed in the grouping of symbols and recoding of the groups, that is, in the formation of larger units.

As Liaudis (1965) subsequently showed, reorganization of the remembered material occurs in two basic ways. The first is associated with a decrease of the indeterminancy of the material through *discovery* of its organization (redundancy). The second means of decreasing indeterminancy is the *introduction* (by the subject) of organization on the basis of correlation of objects according to some chosen parameter.

Nevel'skii (1965) attempted to evaluate both the operative and the long-term volume of memory. In a series of experiments using numbers, words, and artificial concepts the number of remembered symbols and remembered information (in bits) was determined. The process of transmission of material into long-term memory in the course of repetition was viewed as progressive "exhaustion" of the original information. These experiments indicated that Miller's hypothesis (1956) that memory depends only on the number of symbols and not on the amount of information which they contain is correct only for immediate memory. Nevel'skii formulated his conclusions in the following way: "The size of immediate memory is closer to invariant if it is measured by the number of remembered symbols and not by the amount of remembered information; the volume of long-term memory is closer to invariant if it is measured by the amount of reproduced information and not by the number of reproduced symbols" (1965, p. 59). Figure 20–6 shows the results of Nevel'skii's experiments as compared with Hays' data (as reported by Miller, 1956).

Nevel'skii's experiments also indicated the significance of grouping material for memory. His criterion of grouping is the ratio of the number of groups formed to the number of elements in the group. The optimal group was one in which the ratio approached unity. Deviation from unity leads to reduced size of the memory store and creates difficulties in establishing intergroup and intragroup associations in the material.

Analysis of the Operator's Activity

The research described in the previous paragraphs is of an analytical nature. It investigated separate processes and aspects of the operator's activity. The results can only provide a basis for solving certain specific problems

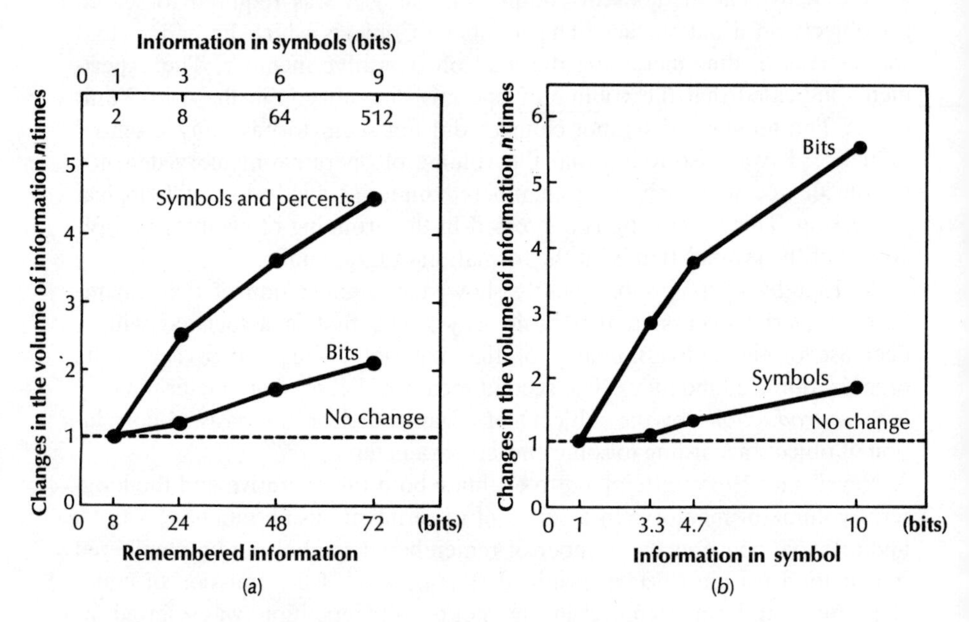

Figure 20–6. Comparison of the amount of long-term and operative memory. (a) The amount of long-term memory expressed in the number of remembered symbols and in bits. (b) The amount of short-term (operative) memory expressed in the number of remembered symbols and in bits. (Data from Hays, cited in Miller, 1956.) The dotted line is a constant. (From Nevel'skii, 1965.)

involved in bringing the nature of the machine into accord with human peculiarities in control systems. Engineering psychology has now reached the stage where it is clear that *general* concepts of the operator's activity must be formulated. The creation of a theoretical model of activity revealing its structure and mechanisms would permit a new evaluation of the analytical data and help to determine the most effective methods of their utilization.

One of these approaches is to construct algorithms of the operator's activity (Liapunov and Shestopal, 1957; Dmitrieva, 1964a, b). The idea is to pick out the elementary operations performed by the operator and to describe the entire activity in sequence; this indicates the logical conditions necessary for the transfer from one operation to another.

On the basis of the algorithmic description of activity and in order to evaluate it, Zarakovskii (1962) proposed introduction of a coefficient of stereotypy of the work process and a coefficient of logical complexity.

The application of these coefficients permits integrated evaluation of the activity and determination of the "tight spots" in the work process. Zarakovskii, using the example of activity with a wheel, showed that for man the greatest difficulty involves those points in the algorithm which involve an uninterrupted sequence of more than four logical conditions.

The algorithmic description of activity may be useful for the development of "man-machine" systems; however, it still does not reveal the psychological contents of that activity. Zinchenko and Zinchenko (1965) approached the problem in another way. In their opinion, the most essential aspect of the operator's activity is that it occurs not with actual objects, but with their information models. The information model is "organized in accord with a definite lawful system and arranged to represent the actual environment" (p. 4). It may include information about the external environment, the controlled objects, and the assembly of the control system itself. Such a model is a source of information for the operator, on the basis of which he can make decisions and ensure that the whole system will function properly.

Zinchenko and Zinchenko (1965) described the stages of the operator's activity. In the first stage, the information is received and decoded, the significant information is separated from the totality of signals, changes in the condition of the objects to be controlled are perceived—especially those which deviate from the preliminary regime. In the second stage the information is processed, i.e., it is transformed in such a way as to make a solution possible. Here the operator evaluates the environment, determines the problem and determines the urgency of the problem. In the third stage, decisions are made about the necessary operations. The decisions are made both on the basis of data obtained from an analysis of the information model and from previously known information. Finally, in the last stage, the decision leads to action. The operations of the first two stages are called the information search and are viewed as preparation for action; the operations of the last two stages are united under the concept of "service."

There are two possible types of relationships between these groups of operations: (1) information search with fast service, and (2) information search with delayed service. The dynamics of activity and the cognitive processes involved are different for these two cases. For example, in the first case the load on operative memory is not great and compatibility between stimulus and response is very important. In the second case very great demands are made on operative memory, but compatibility between stimulus and response is not so esssential. Sometimes it is more expedient for the control apparatus to be distributed in accord with the executed operations and not in accord with distribution of the signals.

Detailed analysis of the structure of activity is required to determine the principles governing the formation of an information model.

Generally, *groups* of people participate in large systems of control. Therefore data acquired in the study of individuals is often insufficient. Engineering psychology must also be concerned with the problem of group activity. Gorbov and his colleagues (1964) devoted a series of investigations to this problem.

The investigations are conducted in a specially constructed apparatus called the "homeostat," in which several pointer instruments are connected. Each group of subjects (2 to 3 men) work only with one instrument. The subject's task is to manipulate the handle in order to place the pointer on zero. Since all the instruments are linked, the action of each subject results in changes not only on the indicators of his instrument, but on all the others as well. The problem is solved only when the actions of all the participants in the group are in accord. The experimenter can change the coefficients of the instruments and thus create problems of varying difficulty. Because all movements of the handle and the pointers are continuously registered on an oscillograph, it is possible to trace the nature of the actions of the group as a whole as well as the tactics of each of its members.

Preliminary experiments were conducted to study the individual typological peculiarities of each subject. The results indicated that many subjects behave differently in a group situation than they do as individuals. For this reason it is impossible to predict group activity on the basis of the isolated study of each of its participants. It was necessary to work out a system of special tests in order to evaluate groups. The concept of "psychophysiological combination of operators" was introduced to express the possibility of reciprocal actions. A scale was developed to make quantitative evaluations of this combination.

Gorbov traced the dynamics of group training by increasing the difficulty of the successive problems. Some of the groups mastered only problems of a certain difficulty and were unable to go beyond that point despite extensive training. Other groups, less successful in the beginning, mastered more and more difficult problems in the course of time.

In order to compare groups, it was necessary to distinguish the qualities of learning capacity and learning. Learning capacity is associated primarily with the prognosis of the group's activity in new conditions. It is important to note that the learning capacity of the group is not the simple sum of its participants' individual qualities. In certain experiments one member of the group was temporarily removed. The remaining members and the experimenter were able to solve a problem which previously they had been unable to do. The group did not lose this ability when the missing member returned.

In this case the two members who had learned to solve the problem "transmitted" the skills to the third (the group consisted of three people). However, the mechanism of this "transmission" is still not clear.

The problem of group activity is very significant for solving organizational problems concerning the interrelations of operators in control systems. Thus, observations of the activities of two aviators in emergency situations indicated that the outcome depends on how their interrelations are organized. If the older, "slower" aviator has a quick and decisive man as his assistant, a conflict situation arose, the younger interfering in his attempts to force his own line of behavior. The outcome of emergency situations in a series of cases was associated with the degree of suggestibility of one of the operators.

Comparison of the results of experiments with real group activity (especially in prolonged group isolation) has shown a high degree of predictability.

Reliability of the Human Operator

It is obviously impossible to ensure high reliability of control systems without taking into account the peculiar activity of the human operator. Yet this is a very difficult task. Applying existing methods of evaluating reliability, the impression is that man is an extremely unreliable link in the man-machine system. He is incapable of working at a task for a long period of time without making errors, he is quickly exhausted, he is easily distracted, and it is difficult to predict his behavior, since it is influenced by many factors.

At the same time man is significantly better than any existing machine. He can cope with the unexpected, he can foresee the course of events, find optimal solutions in complex situations, and transform the method of activity in new conditions. Engineers who construct control systems strive to include man in them in order to ensure the necessary reliability.

Thus, there are opposing concepts which may be designated "the paradox of the reliability of the human operator": on one hand, he is less reliable, but on the other hand he is more reliable than existing machines.

In engineering psychology experiments there are several approaches to the study of the reliability of the human operator. Some investigators focus on the reasons for those moments in his activity which determine unreliability. The question is formulated in the following way: why is a man unable to work with 100 per cent reliability even in the most favorable conditions? Inaccuracies are divided into lawful (so-called systematic error) and accidental (which cannot be explained by any apparent reason). The study of accidental errors forces the attention on the erratic nature of man's activity.

In other investigations, the most important question concerns the factors which ensure reliable work even under unfavorable circumstances. This question involves the great flexibility of man's behavior, his reserves, and the mechanisms of compensation for destroyed or hindered functions (Anan'ev, 1963; Asratyan and Simonov, 1963). In this connection there is interesting data on the correlation of accuracy and stability in human behavior. Investigations by several authors show that the stability of man's actions is extremely high; difficult conditions may reduce accuracy, however the general strategy of behavior is retained for a prolonged period of time. It is as if man "sacrifices" accuracy for the sake of stability (Kozerenko, 1965).

Certain investigators feel that reliability is the same as work ability (Tochilov, 1964). In this connection, careful investigations are being conducted on the dynamics of work ability and the characteristics of its basic phases, the transitions between phases and the correlations between work productivity, the organism's capabilities at a given moment and the level of emotional-volitional tension in each phase (Derevianko, 1959).

The next approach to this problem consists of investigating specifically cognitive regulation of the human operator's activity (Vekker and Lomov, 1960, 1961; Lomov, 1963). It is claimed that various forms of mental reflection regulate actions: perceptual models, concepts, conceptual models. Their features determine man's highly adequate behavior in the surrounding conditions. Thus, the structure and unity of the perceptual model ensure a certain freedom in the choice of the course and sequence of work movements as well as their adaptability. The general and global nature of concepts is the source of the variety of work methods and the transfer of actions from one set of conditions to another.

Still another approach to the problem is the study of individual-typological traits of men (Nebylitsyn, 1964). These investigations show that man's work ability and his "interference tolerance" (the ability to work in a concentrated fashion despite distractions) are based on one of the fundamental traits of the nervous system, that is, its strength. The mobility and steadiness of neural processes also have a definite influence on man's activity and are manifested in the flexibility and adaptability of his behavior. It is hoped that this approach will lead to the rational selection of operators with the goal of increasing the reliability of man-machine systems.

All these approaches to the problem of the operator's reliability have a rational core. However, each of them touches upon only one aspect of the problem. The task for the future is to systematize and generalize these data, to construct a unified theory of human reliability and to develop criteria for evaluating it.

Summary

The work described in this chapter in no way exhausts the field of engineering psychology in the U.S.S.R. It gives only an idea of the kinds of problems which generally concern engineering psychologists in our country.

In conclusion, it is important to note that at the present time there is a strong tendency toward complex investigations of man. In particular, engineering psychology is passing from the solution of individual problems and analytical investigations of separate aspects of man's activity in control systems to the development of general concepts of its structure and dynamics. In this connection it is inevitable that the contacts between engineering psychology and related sciences will be increased.

The complex approach to the study of man transforms the special problem of engineering psychology—"man as the cornerstone of control systems"—to more general problems of "man as the subject of work, cognition, and generalization."

References

Anan'ev, B. G. *The psychology of sensory cognition.* Moscow: Izd. Akad. Pedag. Nauk RSFSR, 1960.

Anan'ev, B. G. Bilateral regulation as a mechanism of behavior. *Vop. Psikhol.,* 1963, No. 5.

Anokhin, P. K. Physiology and cybernetics. In *Philosophical problems of cybernetics.* Moscow: Sotsekgiz, 1961.

Asratyan, E. A., and Simonov, V. P. *Reliability of the brain.* Moscow: Izd. Akad. Nauk SSSR, 1963.

Bernshtein, N. A. Some fundamental problems concerning the regulation of motor acts. *Vop. Psikhol.,* 1957, No. 6.

Bodrov, V. A., Genkin, A. A., and Zarakovskii, G. M. Certain lawful responses of man to test problems involving one of two possible solutions. Communications 1, 2, 3. *Dokl. Akad. Pedag. Nauk,* 1961, No. 2, 1962, No. 4.

Boiko, E. I. *Reaction time in man.* Moscow: Izd. Meditsina, 1964.

Bushurova, V. E., and Tutushkina, M. K. The problem of perception and recognition of sign indicators. In B. F. Lomov (Ed.), *Problems of general and engineering psychology.* Leningrad: Izd. Leningrad. Gos. Univer., 1964.

Chuprikov, N. I. Constants characterizing the optimal conditions for the detection of suprathreshold differences. In *Fifteenth International Congress of Applied Psychology. Liubliana,* 1964. (Abstracts.)

Derevianko, E. A. The interrelations between certain physiological and psychological factors in the development of exhaustion during work activity. In *First Congress of the Psychological Society.* Moscow: Izd. Akad. Pedag. Nauk RSFSR, 1959. (Abstract.)

Dmitrieva, M. A. A psychological analysis of the activity of the airplane dispatcher. In B. G. Anan'ev and B. F. Lomov (Eds.), *Problems of general and engineering psychology.* Leningrad: Izd. Leningrad. Gos. Univer., 1964. (a)

Dmitrieva, M. A. Speed and accuracy of information processing and their dependence on signal discrimination. In B. F. Lomov (Ed.), *Problems of engineering psychology*. Leningrad, 1964. (Abstract.) (b)

Egorov, V. A. The operator's capacity as an indicator of training potential and complexity of executed work. *Vop. Psikhol.*, 1965, No. 1.

Glezer, V. D., and Tsukkerman, I. I. *Information and vision*. Moscow-Leningrad: Izd. Akad. Nauk SSSR, 1961.

Gorbov, F. D. The individual and the group in experimental group psychology. In B. F. Lomov (Ed.), *Problems of engineering psychology*. Leningrad, 1964. (Abstract.)

Hitt, D. W. *Human factors*, 1961, *3*, No. 2.

Kozerenko, O. P. The interrelations of accuracy and stability in "living systems" using the example of static adaptation. In V. P. Zinchenko, P. I. Zinchenko, and B. F. Lomov (Eds.), *Problems of engineering psychology*. Leningrad, 1965, No. 2.

Leont'ev, A. N., and Krinchik, E. P. Human information processing in choice situations. In V. P. Zinchenko, A. N. Leont'ev, and D. Y. Panov (Eds.), *Engineering psychology*. Moscow: Izd. Moskov. Gos. Univer., 1964.

Leont'ev, A. N., and Panov, D. Y. The psychology of man and technical progress. In P. N. Fedoseev (Ed.), *Philosophical problems of the physiology of higher nervous activity and psychology*. Moscow: Izd. Akad. Nauk SSSR, 1963.

Liapunov, A. A., and Shestopal, G. A. The algorithmic description of control processes. *Matemat. Prosv.*, 1957, No. 2.

Liaudis, V. Y. The structure of mnemonic activity. In V. P. Zinchenko, P. I. Zinchenko, and B. F. Lomov (Eds.), *Problems of engineering psychology*. Leningrad, 1965, No. 3.

Lomov, B. F. *Man and technology: Studies of engineering psychology*. Leningrad: Izd. Leningrad. Gos. Univer., 1963. (English translation: U.S. Department of Commerce, Office of Technical Services, Joint Publication Research Service. Washington, D.C., 1963.)

Lomov, B. F. Certain criteria for the evaluation of signals transmitting information to the human operator. In V. P. Zinchenko, P. I. Zinchenko, and B. F. Lomov (Eds.), *Problems of engineering psychology*. Leningrad, 1965, No. 2.

Miller, G. A. The magical number seven, plus or minus two. *Psychol. Rev.*, 1956, *63*, 81–97.

Mowbray, G. H., Choice reaction times for skilled responses. *Quart. J. exp. Psychol.*, 1960, *12*, 193–202.

Nebylitsyn, V. D. The reliability of the operator's work in complex control systems. In V. P. Zinchenko, A. N. Leont'ev, and D. Y. Panov (Eds.), *Engineering psychology*. Moscow: Izd. Moskov. Gos. Univer., 1964.

Nevel'skii, P. B. The volume of memory and the quantity of information. In V. P. Zinchenko, P. I. Zinchenko, and B. F. Lomov (Eds.), *Problems of engineering psychology*. Leningrad, 1965, No. 3.

Pauzhaite, S. A. *The correlation of sensory and motor in regulatory responses.* Leningrad: Leningrad. Gos. Univer., 1965. (Dissertation abstracts.)

Prodan, V. T. The problem of human choice responses. In B. F. Lomov (Ed.), *Problems of engineering psychology.* Leningrad, 1964. (Abstract.)

Pushkin, V. N. Features and methods of rationalizing the dispatcher's control panel. *Vop. Psikhol.,* 1960, No. 6. (a)

Pushkin, V. N. Some problems of controlling the production processes in railroad transport. *Vop. Psikhol.,* 1960, No. 6. (b)

Repkina, G. V. A study of operative memory. In V. P. Zinchenko, P. I. Zinchenko, and B. F. Lomov (Eds.), *Problems of engineering psychology.* Leningrad, 1965, No. 3.

Roze, N. A. Experimental investigation of finger micromovements in manipulating control apparatus. In B. G. Anan'ev and B. F. Lomov (Eds.), *Problems of general and industrial psychology.* Leningrad: Izd. Leningrad. Gos. Univer., 1963.

Ryzhkova, N. I. Several ways of coding information. In V. P. Zinchenko, P. I. Zinchenko, and B. F. Lomov (Eds.), *Problems of engineering psychology.* Leningrad, 1965, No. 3.

Sukhodol'skii, G. V. The formation of the skill of tracing a moving object in the human operator. In B. G. Anan'ev and B. F. Lomov (Eds.), *Problems of general and engineering psychology.* Leningrad: Izd. Leningrad. Gos. Univer., 1964.

Teplov, B. M. *Problems of individual differences.* Moscow: Akad. Pedag. Nauk RSFSR, 1961.

Tochilov, K. S. The problem of reliability (work capacity) in men working with control systems. In B. G. Anan'ev and B. F. Lomov (Eds.), *Problems of engineering.* Leningrad, 1964. (Abstract.)

Tutushkina, M. K. Dependence of speed and accuracy of perception and recognition of cues on changes in their angle dimensions. In B. F. Lomov (Ed.), *Problems of engineering psychology.* Leningrad, 1964. (Abstract.)

Vekker, L. M. Restructuring sensory and motor functions in the remote control of railroad transport. In B. G. Anan'ev and B. F. Lomov (Eds.), *Problems of general and industrial psychology.* Leningrad: Izd. Leningrad. Gos. Univer., 1963.

Vekker, L. M. Perception and the fundamentals of modeling it. Leningrad, 1964.

Vekker, L. M., and Lomov, B. F. The structure of work activity. In *Problems of psychology.* Erevan, 1960.

Vekker, L. M., and Lomov, B. F. The sensory image as a model. *Vop. Filos.,* 1961, No. 4.

Vekker, L. M., and Surkov, E. N. Toward a comparative characterization of the sensory motor components of the operator's activity in various control systems. In G. B. Anan'ev and B. F. Lomov (Eds.), *Problems of general and engineering psychology.* Leningrad: Izd. Leningrad. Gos. Univer., 1964.

Vodlozerov, V. M. The problem of visual discrimination of acceleration. In

B. G. Anan'ev and B. F. Lomov (Eds.), *Problems of general and industrial psychology*. Leningrad: Izd. Leningrad. Gos. Univer., 1963.

Vodlozerov, V. M. Certain characteristics of the operator's work in tracking a unidimensional signal. In B. G. Anan'ev and B. F. Lomov (Eds.), *Problems of engineering psychology*. Leningrad, 1964. (Abstract.)

Welford, A. T. On the human demands of automation: Mental work, conceptual models, satisfaction, and training. *Industrial and business psychology*. Munkegaard, 1962.

Zarakovskii, G. M. An analysis of man's controlling work based on a logical scheme of the algorithm of the work process. *Dokl. Akad. Pedag. Nauk RSFSR*, 1962, No. 4.

Zavalishina, D. N., and Pushkin, V. N. The mechanism of operative thinking. *Vop. Psikhol.*, 1964, No. 3.

Zinchenko, V. P., and Zinchenko, P. I. An investigation of memory in connection with the problems of engineering psychology. In V. P. Zinchenko, P. I. Zinchenko, and B. F. Lomov (Eds.), *Problems of engineering psychology*. Leningrad, 1965, No. 3.

21

Experimental Foundations of Uznadze's Theory of Set

R. G. Natadze

EDITORS' INTRODUCTION

The research reviewed in this chapter is unique among the contributions in this volume because for twenty-five years it was the exclusive concern of a small group of Georgian psychologists headed by D. N. Uznadze. Beginning with explanations of the classic psychophysical illusions, Uznadze and his students (notably Prangishvilii, 1963, and Natadze, 1963) have developed a general theory of cognition based on the concept of "set" outlined in these pages.

For many years this work went unrecognized, even in the Soviet Union. Part of the explanation for this arises from the fact that the original monographs were all written in Georgian, a language few outside Georgia can read. Further, the general unpopularity of strictly psychological theories in the postwar period, especially of non-Pavlovian theories, restricted the dissemination of Uznadze's findings. However, in recent years the theory of set has become a part of Soviet psychology. An entire program at the 18th International Congress of Psychology, Moscow, 1966, was devoted to a discussion of the concept of set. A comprehensive monograph reviewing the state of this subject at the time of Uznadze's death has recently been published in English (Uznadze, 1966).

R. G. Natadze is presently Director of the Department of Psychology at Tbilisi State University and Director of the Department of Developmental Psychology at the Uznadze Institute of Psychology.

THE PURPOSE of this chapter is to trace the origin and development of Uznadze's conception of the psychology of set. Uznadze's work on this topic began in the mid-1920's, occupied his attention until his death in 1950, and continues now under the direction of his many students.

Although the roots of the theory of set, elaborated by Uznadze, can be traced in his experimental studies during the period of 1923–1926 (Uznadze, 1923, 1926, 1927), in some of these studies the concept of set is used as an explanatory concept. A systematic experimental study of set itself, as a definite phenomenon, and the experimental substantiation of the conception began with the experimental study of perceptual *illusions* in various modalities. The main laws governing the manifestation of set were established during the course of these studies. Therefore, we shall begin our presentation of the experimental foundations of the theory of set from the period of the experimental study of perceptual illusions (Uznadze, 1930, 1931).

The First Stage of Research: Establishing the Phenomenon

As early as 1860, Fechner published work on the illusion of weight resulting from a preliminary repeated raising of objects of different weights. Several decades later Muller and Schumann published an experimental study in which they attempted to present a theoretical interpretation of this illusion. The explanation proposed by these authors has been adopted on such a wide scale that it can be considered the most typical explanation in the field of traditional foreign psychology.

This explanation is based on the concept of a "motor set." After a pair of objects of different weight has been raised with both hands, a pair of objects of the same weight is raised in a different manner: the hand which was used in the previous test for raising the heavier object is now raising the object with a *greater motor impulse,* and therefore this object is easily lifted above the table and "flies upwards," as a result of which it gives the impression of lightness. In contrast, the object (of the same weight) which is lifted by the other hand is raised with a smaller motor impulse (since in the previous test this hand raised a lighter object), and therefore this object appears to "stick" to the table—it is detached from the table with greater difficulty and gives the impression of being heavier.

The magnitude of the motor impulse with which the critical object is raised represents the manifestation of a "motor set," which is conceived by the authors as a muscular phenomenon, which in the final analysis is the cause of the illusion of heaviness.

Toward the end of the last century, Charpentier published his well-known "illusion of Charpentier": of two wooden cylinders of the same weight which are raised by means of a cord, the larger cylinder is perceived as being *lighter* than the smaller cylinder.

In order to explain this new weight illusion, Muller used the same basic theory: the larger object, upon being raised, elicits a greater motor impulse, while the smaller object, on the contrary, elicits a smaller impulse; in the first case, a greater heaviness is expected, and in the second case a smaller heaviness. Otherwise, this illusion represents the same psychological effect ("the flying up" of one object and "the sticking" of the other object). Following such an explanation of Charpentier's illusion, Muller's theory was almost universally accepted as the theory of "the illusion of heaviness" in general.

As early as 1925, Uznadze, proceeding from an integral-personal conception of human activity, expressed doubts concerning the validity of the theory of "motor set" and "expectation," which was widely accepted abroad. In particular, he expressed doubts concerning the fact that such experiences as "a flying upwards" or "a sticking to the table" underlie Charpentier's illusion. He believed that this illusion is based upon a deep-seated and more integral condition of the subject than the motor phenomenon. In order to check this hypothesis, it was necessary to obtain experimentally a similar illusion of perception, but one which was not motor in nature. Uznadze and his associates set up a number of tests aimed at causing similar illusions in those modalities which do not involve kinesthetic perception.

In one such experiment the subject, while visually perceiving a pair of boxes of the same weight but of different sizes, compared their weight according to the pressure exerted by these boxes upon his hands by means of a so-called Wundt balance. The result was found to be entirely positive: the subject exhibited an illusion similar to Charpentier's illusion. In spite of the fact that the motor impulse of lifting various weights and the phenomenon of "flying upwards" of one hand are excluded by Uznadze's procedure, the weight was perceived in a tactile manner in the form of a pressure exerted by the corresponding lever of the Wundt apparatus upon the surface of the hand of the test subject, with the hands in an immobile position.

It was found that during the first weight comparisons, 71 per cent of the test subjects exhibited a contrast illusion, which was completely analogous to the illusion of Charpentier: the larger box was perceived as being lighter, and the smaller box as being heavier; 15 per cent of the test subjects exhibited an assimilative illusion, and 14 per cent exhibited an adequate perception. When the test was repeated many times, the percentage of illusions was considerably reduced.

The following demonstration of a successive illusion of pressure was devised by Adamashvili. In control tests, the experimenter applied two consecutive pressures, at first a strong pressure and then a weak pressure, to the hand of the subject. The subject had to compare those two pressures according to their intensity. After 15 repetitions of the control (set) test, two equal pressures were applied successively to the hand of the subject (critical tests). The following results were obtained: 45 per cent of the subjects exhibited a *contrast* illusion of pressure (the first pressure appeared to be weaker); 25 per cent exhibited an *assimilative illusion;* and 15 per cent exhibited an adequate perception.

Studies conducted by Khmaladze (1938) show an analogy to Fechner's illusion of weight during *haptic* ("grasping") perception of the volume of balls. The main variation of these tests consists in the following: the subject, with eyes closed, must compare the volume of two wooden balls which the experimenter places simultaneously for a moment in the hands of the subject. These balls differ considerably in their size. After each size estimate by the subject, the experimenter again gives him the same balls for comparison. This is repeated 15 times, and each time the larger ball is placed in the same hand. This represents the first stage of the experiment—namely, the "control (set) tests." At this stage, the subject is supposed to develop and then "fix" a specific internal readiness, that is, a set for the perception of the larger ball in a definite position (on the right or on the left).

After these control (set) exposures, the experimenter immediately and without notice switches over to the "critical" tests: the subject, who continues to sit with eyes closed, is again given for a size comparison a pair of balls, but these now have the same volume. As a result of these tests, it was found that the vast majority of subjects (up to 97 per cent) perceive these "critical" balls as being of unequal size: one ball appears larger and the other one smaller. At the same time, as a rule, during the first perception, the illusions have a *contrast* nature, that is, a ball is perceived as being larger on the side where the smaller ball was perceived during the control (set) tests.

It must be stated that an analogy with Charpentier's illusion in regard to the volumes of balls was also established by Khmaladze. During the haptic perception of balls of objectively *different weight* (280 grams and 880 grams) but of the *same size,* an illusion of volume was observed: the heavier ball was perceived as having a smaller volume, and the lighter ball was perceived as having a larger volume (Khmaladze, 1938). This illusion, which is the opposite of Charpentier's illusion, was called by Uznadze an "illusion of weight-volume" (Charpentier's illusion is usually called "an illusion of volume-weight").

In the context of the problem of interest to us, this experiment is remarkable in view of the fact that, in this test, the illusion of volume arises in spite of the fact that a moment of "flying upwards" and "sticking" of the raised object is excluded from the perception; the subject does not raise any objects.

In the research done by Khmaladze, an illusion of volume was obtained not only during a simultaneous, but also during a *successive* perception by one hand of balls having a different volume. During control (set) tests, the subject, after closing his eyes, was asked to hold in his hand successively, for comparison purposes, two balls—first a large one, and then a small one (or vice versa) up to 15 times in a row. Then, during critical tests, balls of equal size ("first" and "second") were also given to the subject successively. As a rule, the balls were perceived in a contrasting manner. For example, if, during control tests, the large ball was given to the subject first, then in critical tests the first ball was perceived as being smaller.

In all of the tests listed above, the illusion is based, in the final analysis, on a *kinesthetic-tactile* perception: a passive perception of pressure, an active perception of weight, a haptic perception of volume, etc. This raises the question of the possibility of obtaining similar illusions in modalities from which a kinesthetic-tactile perception is excluded, and consequently, from which the Muller-Schumann explanation of an illusion of heaviness is also excluded.

The study of a *visual* illusion of volume, which was conducted for the first time by Khmaladze and which was further developed in detail by Uznadze, provides an answer to this question.

With the aid of a tachistoscope, the subject is shown simultaneously, for purposes of a comparison according to size, two circles (with a diameter in the range of 20 to 30 mm.), one of which is clearly smaller than the other. This control (set) trial is repeated 10 to 15 times. Within a single experimental session, the larger circle is always presented on the same side. During critical tests, circles of equal size were presented in place of the control (set) stimuli.

During the first critical exposures, the majority of subjects exhibited a contrast illusion. Of two circles of equal size, the circle which is located on that side on which a smaller circle was perceived during control exposures, is perceived as being of greater size. A certain number of subjects (5 to 9 per cent) gave an assimilative illusion (the circle is perceived as being of greater size on that side on which it was perceived as a larger circle in control tests).

Thus, analogously to classical illusions of weight, there occur illusions in the visual perception of *small* objects, which fit completely into the center of the field of vision, and therefore do not require a sweeping motion of the eye for the perception of their size. Consequently, a kinesthetic basis for the perception of size is excluded.

However, since the visual tests still involve a comparison of volumes, which we associated with kinesthetic-tactile sensations, the question arises of whether it is possible to obtain similar illusions during the perception of properties of objects and qualities, the perception or representation of which is alien to these modalities of sensation.

An answer to this question is supplied first of all by tests involving a perception of auditory intensities (Adamashvili, 1941). A pair of tones is presented consecutively to the subject, sitting with his back turned toward the apparatus, who is supposed to compare the intensity of these stimuli. The first stimulus is clearly louder than the second. After this control test has been repeated 15 times in a row, a pair of tones of equal intensity is presented to the subject during critical tests.

The result was found to be positive: an illusion was experienced in 76 per cent of the cases (accurate perception was recorded in only 21 per cent of the cases) in spite of the fact that the illusion is usually less widespread with a successive than a simultaneous comparison.

The perception of various degrees of brightness of a gray color has nothing in common with the perception of volume. However, Adamashvili established an analogy with Fechner's illusion of weight during the visual perception of the degrees of brightness of squares shown to the subjects in a tachistoscopic manner, dark on one side, light on the other. During control tests, a dark and light square are shown 15 times in a row for comparison. During critical tests, two squares of equal brightness are shown. The following results were obtained: over 73 per cent of the subjects exhibit an illusion in the perception of brightness; 56.6 per cent of these subjects exhibit a contrast illusion (i.e., these subjects perceive the square as being darker on the side where a lighter square was shown during control tests), 16.6 per cent of the subjects exhibit an assimilative illusion, and 21.6 per cent of the subjects perceive the critical objects correctly.

And, finally, a similar illusion was established (Khachapuridze, unpublished) in the perception of a group of elements, that is, a direct, rather diffuse perception of a greater and smaller quantity. During these tests, two circles of equal size filled with dots were exposed tachistoscopically. The number of dots in one circle was clearly greater than the number of dots in the other. The subject was required to establish which circle had the greater number of dots. This control (set) test was repeated up to 15 times. In the critical tests, circles with an equal number of dots were shown.

The result was analogous to the result obtained in the other tests: the majority of the subjects exhibited a contrast illusion in the perception of a group of elements.

The results of all these tests entitled Uznadze to draw the conclusion that the theory of a "motor set" developed by Muller-Schumann and others was wrong. It is clear that a different motor impulse, or a different speed in raising an object, can have no relation whatever to the illusion in the perception of the intensity of sound, brightness of color, and to the illusion of the perception of a number of dots.

Apparently, the essence of this phenomenon does not consist in a "motor" or a "sensory" set, that is, not in peripheral processes taking place in the "motor" or "sensory" system and, specifically, not in a change of the motor impulse itself during the raising of weights. The phenomena discussed here suggest that a set is an integral state, an integral "modification" of the individual, a certain "degree of mobilization" of the individual as a whole, which expresses itself in a wide variety of perceptual modalities and therefore cannot be reduced to the features of motor impulses.

Transfer of an Illusion (Irradiation of a Set)

If the various illusions described above are really based upon a single, integrated state of mobilization of an individual—a general set of the individual—then this set, which has been developed during the course of control (set) tests in one modality, because it is an integral state of the individual, must also manifest itself in other modalities, that is, in the process of perceiving "critical" objects in another modality.

In 1932 Uznadze experimentally established the following facts: first, control (set) tests with a successive haptic perception of balls of different volumes were established with one hand, and critical tests with a successive perception of objectively equal balls were presented to the other hand. Transfer of the illusion to the other hand was observed in 83.5 per cent of the cases (a contrast illusion in 60 per cent, and an assimilative illusion in 23.5 per cent) while an absence of illusion was observed in 16.5 per cent of the cases.

A transposition of the illusion also took place in regard to different modalities: balls of different size are placed in the hands of the subject, whose eyes are closed. After these control (set) tests have been repeated 15 to 25 times, circles of equal size are presented *tachistoscopically* to the subject as critical objects. A set illusion was observed in 56.4 per cent of the cases (a contrast illusion in 48 per cent of the cases, and an assimilative illusion in 8.4 per cent of the cases). Thus, a set, which was developed during the process of a haptic perception of the balls, expressed itself in a *visual* perception of circles. The same thing takes place in the reverse direction. A set, developed during the course of a comparison of circles, perceived tachistoscopically, expresses itself in an illusion involving a haptic perception of objectively equal wooden balls.

This intermodal irradiation of a set indicates the "central" nature of the set underlying the above-mentioned perceptual illusions, regardless of the modality in which these illusions manifest themselves. Once a set has been developed in the subject (e.g., a set to a larger object on the right side), regardless of the way in which it is developed—whether by means of a visual perception of miniature circles having a diameter of about 20 mm. or by means of grasping large wooden balls—this set will manifest itself to a greater or lesser extent during almost every kind of perception of two magnitudes. Illusions in different modalities constitute essentially a common and single illusion which manifests itself in different modalities. More precisely, it is the consequence of a single generic condition of the subject —of a single set, expressing itself in different modalities.

As a result of special tests conducted by Khodzhava (1941), it was shown that a set developed during the process of size comparison of objects having a certain definite shape (e.g., circles) expresses itself in relation to the perception of the size of objects having an entirely different shape. It is interesting to note that a similar result was obtained and published by Piaget and Lambercier (1945). This property of a set was called *generalization* of a set by Uznadze. Strong irradiation of a set together with its generalization discloses the integral character of this condition in the subject. Following the establishment of all these facts, the theory of Muller-Schumann must be rejected. This theory is based on facts which are specific to one subspecies of a general perceptual illusion, namely, facts concerned with an illusion in the perception of weight.

However, in traditional foreign psychology, another theory is also rather widespread—the theory of "an unjustified" or "deceived expectation," which, as Uznadze points out, can claim to provide an explanation for all types of illusions of perception of the type described above. According to this theory, or more precisely, according to this poorly developed point of view, during early (control) tests, that is, during a multiple perception of various objects (e.g., of objects of different weight), the subject develops "an *expectation*" of the further perception of these same objects, or more precisely of the same differences; for example, the subject expects a heavier object (or an object with a larger volume) on the right side than on the left side, and when in reality (during critical exposures) an object is encountered which does not correspond to the subject's expectation, the subject's expectation is not fulfilled, and therefore a contrast illusion takes place: the object appears to be even lighter than it actually is. Thus, the principal factor which is responsible for the illusion, according to this theory, is the moment of "expectation" which is developed during the course of control (set) tests.

To what extent is such an explanation of these illusions of perception acceptable? Uznadze (1936) conducted a special experiment to clarify the role of the "expectation" factor in the illusions described above. Control tests involving a haptic perception of balls of different size were performed on the subject who was in a state of hypnotic sleep, that is, two balls of different size were placed in the hands of the subject 15 times in a row for comparison purposes. The subject was exposed to a special suggestion that he should forget everything which occurred during his sleep. The subject was then awakened and subjected (already in an alert state) to critical tests; that is, two balls of equal size were placed into his hands for comparison purposes. It was found that the subjects perceived the balls in an illusory way, namely, in a contrasting manner. In a hypnotic condition, an *expectation* of the perception of unequal objects could not arise. In view of the fact that a posthypnotic amnesia is characteristic for persons arising from a state of hypnosis, and in the tests conducted by Uznadze this amnesia was intensified, as was noted above, by an additional special suggestion, *the factor of expectation was therefore completely excluded in these tests.* The subjects could not *expect* a particular perception of the balls, since they did not remember what happened to them during their sleep. Hence, Uznadze concluded that no expectation at all is required for the appearance of a set illusion. He considers it an obvious fact that a set toward the perception of the larger and smaller ball arose during the course of repeated perceptions. This set—an internal, integral, and dynamic state of readiness toward such a perception of degree of magnitude in a definite direction—was formed as a result of multiple repetition (in this case, in a state of hypnotic sleep) of a corresponding "setting" perception of a larger and smaller ball. Uznadze emphasizes that the set, which arose during the condition of sleep, is a factor which determines the activity of the subject in a critical test.

Insofar as the factor of expectation is excluded in the test described above, the theory of "a deceived expectation" is unable to explain this illusion. A set, which is not itself a phenomenon of consciousness, can also arise during sleep and can be responsible for, or can regulate, the course of corresponding phenomena of consciousness, and, specifically, the illusory perception of critical objects. The reasons why "set tests" (or control tests) constitute an indispensable condition for the appearance of an illusion of perception is that, during the course of these tests, a specific state (set) is developed and "fixed" (see the next section), which, though it is not a content of consciousness, is responsible for the course of processes of consciousness and which, in the tests described above, is responsible for a certain definite distortion of the subsequent perceptions.

Experimentally Established Characteristics of a Set

The Concept of a Fixed and Non-Fixed Set

According to Uznadze, a sharp distinction should be made between two types of expression of a set. The first type includes a set which, as is usually the case during conditions of normal activity (and during the process of perception specifically), is adequate to a given situation. It causes not an illusionary perception, but, on the contrary, an adequate perception of the objective situation and in general is responsible for a human activity which is adequate to the given situation. This state of mobilization of the subject as a whole is always conditioned by an identity of the need manifested by the subject and the objective situation. Such an adequate set represents a necessary mediating link in the behavior of the human individual.

The situation is different in regard to the so-called *fixed* set, which arises when a set corresponding to a given situation becomes fixed and firmly established, which most frequently takes place as a result of repetition of a definite activity, and, specifically (as in the majority of the tests described above) as a result of repeated perception of one and the same situation, or as a result of an exceptionally strong impression produced by even one single perception of a given situation. As a result of such a fixation, or consolidation, a given set to a certain extent loses its potency. It loses its ready faculty of adaptation to the slightest changes in the situation (which is a characteristic feature for a non-fixed set). In view of this fact, it does not have time to adapt itself to *insignificant* changes in the objective situation (e.g., to a change in the size of balls during critical tests), and accordingly distorts the perception of this changed situation. For example, balls of equal size are perceived as being of unequal size in view of the fact that their perception was preceded by fixation of the set towards the perception of a larger and a smaller ball. Then, under the action of the properties of this new situation, the subject gradually shifts to an adequate perception; that is, the fixed set loses its fixed nature and is converted into an adequate set.

It should be emphasized that a fixed set is responsible for an adequate perception if there is a constant objective situation (i.e., a situation which corresponds to this set), and even facilitates a corresponding perception or another activity, for example, a perception under difficult conditions (in darkness), an automation of actions, the effect exerted by a habit, and so on.

An interesting experimental fact showing the positive effect exerted by a fixed set upon perception was observed during tests conducted by Khodzhava (1941) in connection with the reading of a "neutral script" (see below under "Set Formed to a Quality"): when a subject, in whom no fixed set toward reading of any kind was developed, was shown tachistoscopically meaningless sets of "neutral" letters (i.e., letters, the configuration of which is common to both the Russian and the Latin alphabets), the subject became confused by these letters and could not read them; on the other hand, when meaningless written words were shown to a subject in whom a fixed set towards a reading of either Latin or Russian letters had been previously developed, the subject was able to read these words freely and easily under conditions involving the same tachistoscopic exposure.

In regard to the fact that an experimental study of set takes place mainly by way of the discovery of laws governing a *fixed* set, this can be explained by the fact that laws of set can be established much more easily and accurately in an experimental manner following its fixation, and, specifically, during the course of a distortion of perception.

It should be noted that during "control (set) exposures," that is, during the period of exercise which precedes critical tests, not only does there take place a fixation of the set which has arisen, but also a process of *differentiation* and concretization of an initial diffused set. The relatively diffused set, which has arisen during the very first perceptions and is not fully adapted to the given situation, assumes a final shape, becomes differentiated, and assumes a concrete form during the course of the recurrence of the perception of the same situation.

Indispensable Conditions for the Formation of a Set

As we have seen, every experiment involving set begins with set or control tests, during which the subject is given the assignment of *comparing* objects (set [control] objects) in regard to their size, weight, brightness, etc. The fact that such an assignment is given at the beginning of the experiment is no accident. A central place in the conception of Uznadze is occupied by the principle according to which a set is a modification of the subject as a whole, created exclusively by the interaction of two factors, namely, the need of the individual (which, as is known, in general constitutes the basis of an activity) and a corresponding situation (which can satisfy this need); in this sense, a set represents the unity of a need and an objective situation.

Under experimental conditions, a situation, reflected in the set, is provided in the form of objects which are shown to the subject for comparison, while the need is provided in the form of an urge, formed under the influence of the instruction, to compare and to establish the mutual relationship between the given objects, or more precisely, between definite properties of the objects being compared (Uznadze, 1949).

It has been established experimentally that if it is possible, via distraction of attention by irrelevant stimuli, to achieve a truly indifferent attitude on the part of the subject toward the two objects of different size which are being perceived, then as a rule a set is not formed.

The Phasic Nature of the Manifestation of a Fixed Set

During the course of tests conducted by Khachapuridze (1938), it was established that, in the process of transition from a set illusion to an adequate perception of critical objects, the transition from a fixed set to an adequate set has a phasic nature. If, after switching over from set tests to critical tests, one does not limit oneself to one or two critical exposures of equal objects but continues to show critical objects until the subject finally reaches an adequate perception, then one finds that the evaluation (perception) of critical objects passes through several phases, or periods, of differing evaluations of the critical objects. Uznadze has distinguished three main phases. In the first phase, objectively equal critical objects are evaluated by the subject in a *contrasting manner;* that is, the object is perceived as being larger on that side in which during the training tests a smaller object was perceived; in the second phase, a disintegration of the fixed set already begins along with disintegration of the contrast illusions. With the development of this phase, the frequency of assimilative illusions increases, and, finally, only assimilative illusions occur. In the third phase, adequate perceptions make their appearance. (Limitations of space do not permit an examination of the discussion which has arisen concerning the necessity of an act of comparison for the formation of set. Experimental investigations of this problem are now being conducted in Tbilisi and Moscow.)

It was found that characteristic features of the transition from a set illusion to an adequate perception, that is, peculiarities of the transitional phases to an adequate perception, disclose great individual differences. The establishment of the phasic nature of a fixed set marks the beginning of a new trend in research work in which the differential psychology of set and the psychopathology of set are important areas of research.

On the basis of individual differences in the phasic course of a set, a number of typological characteristics of set were experimentally established, and thus a new field of research was opened up, namely, a differential psychology of set. A number of properties of set were found to have an extremely significant differential-psychological importance.

Main Properties of a Set

It was found, first, that individuals differ to a considerable extent in the ease with which a fixed set can be developed.

Thus, for example, during the course of basic ("classical") experiments, (the haptic and tachistoscopic tests) it was possible to establish a number of gradations in the ease of fixation which fluctuate between the following extremes: on the one hand, subjects in whom a fixed set arises after one or two setting exposures, and on the other hand, subjects in whom such a set arises or is developed only after 20 or more control (set) exposures.

An important property of a fixed set is its *"static nature"* or, *"dynamic nature."* These terms were used by Uznadze to designate the following contradictory properties of a fixed set. Individuals with a static set, in spite of prolonged (up to 50 exposures) repetitions of equal objects, do not pass through all phases of the set and are unable to reach an adequate perception; this type of person freezes at a *certain phase, not necessarily at the first phase.* On the contrary, persons with a dynamic set, under the influence of critical objects, are sooner or later able to reach an adequate perception of critical objects during the course of the experiment. They pass through the various phases of manifestation of the set.

Regardless whether a set is static or dynamic, it may be *plastic* (flexible) to a smaller or greater extent, or, on the contrary, *inert*. Plasticity is a special property of a set, which manifests itself in a gradual transition from one phase to another. For example, a dynamic set will be plastic if, prior to switching to an adequate perception (before a fixed set disappears completely) the subject gradually passes through all of the phases. A *static* set will be plastic when, before freezing at a certain phase, it gradually passes through all the preceding phases. Conversely, an inert set is one which skips intermediate phases. It jumps from the first to the last phase, from a contrast perception to an adequate perception during a dynamic set.

An important typological property is the degree of *irradiation* of the set. In spite of its integral character, a set may irradiate to such a small extent that, developed through one organ, it does not extend even to the other paired organ (from one hand to another). In many subjects, a fixed set developed in the sphere of one modality manifests itself easily in the sphere of another modality. In the first case, we are dealing with a poorly irradiated, relatively "local" set, and in the second case with a strongly irradiated set.

Individual differences were observed in the degree of *generalization* of the set, that is, in the manifestations of a fixed set toward objects of a differing form.

Differences are also found in the degree of *constancy* or *variability* of the set. If, for example, in experiments conducted at different times with the same subject, one and the same type of set manifests itself, we are dealing with a constant set; if, on the other hand, at different times, one and the same subject discloses a different type of set, we are dealing with a variable set (Avalashvili, 1941).

A further property of a set is its degree of *stability* or *lability*. This property indicates the degree of preservation of a fixed set in time without the action exerted by an exposure of critical objects. Extreme cases of stability have been established experimentally, in which a set fixed in the usual experimental way manifested itself in a subject two to three months after it had been developed (Khachapuridze, 1938).

When a fixed set is preserved for a long time in an unchanged, or constant, form, we are dealing with a constant-stable set, and on the contrary, when a set is preserved for a long time but in a changed form, we are dealing with a variable-stable set. A set which fades rapidly, a labile set, also manifests itself in two forms: if it remains constant prior to fading, it is called a constant-labile set; if, on the other hand, prior to a final fading, this set undergoes a change, then it is called a variable-labile set.

An important property of a set is its degree of stability during the perception of critical objects. It has been demonstrated experimentally that certain subjects, after as few as 2 or 3 critical exposures, are able to achieve an adequate perception, that is, the set illusion in these subjects extends only to 2 or 3 critical exposures. Another extreme case includes subjects in whom the set illusion extends over more than 50 critical exposures ("infinite illusion"). Between these extreme cases, a wide variety of degrees of stability are observed.

Set Formed to a Quality

We have become familiar with the principal properties of a set. However, these properties have been established in relation to a set which has been developed towards *quantity,* namely, in response to quantitative differences, such as size, heaviness, degree of brightness, and so on. The question arises as to the properties of a set which has been developed in response to quality.

In order to answer this extremely significant question, it was necessary to develop a new test in which a set would be developed not in response to quantitative relations, but in response to the quality of objects. First we should recall that, in tests conducted in relation to a set towards quantity, a a study was conducted not only of a set toward a difference—that is, toward an inequality—but also of a set toward an equality, which led Uznadze to note that "an equality also refers in a certain sense to the category of a quality." Nevertheless, a set towards an equality should not be considered as a set towards a quality, since the equality of magnitudes is primarily a quantitative ratio. In a study conducted by Natadze (1941) the fact of the development of a fixed set towards an equality was established, as a result of which unequal objects (circles, squares) were perceived as being equal during critical tests.

Among the special experimental research studies of a set toward quality, special attention should be given to the research work done by Khodzhava (unpublished). Khodzhava used the so-called method of neutral script. Basically, this method consists of the following: German words written in Latin print are shown successively by means of a tachistoscope to the subject in order to establish a set. When a set toward the reading of Latin script is fixed in the subject, he is shown tachistoscopically, as critical objects, a succession of several Russian words, which are selected in such a way that they consist exclusively of "neutral" letters, that is, letters the configuration of which is found both in Russian and Latin type, as in *nevod, topor, pochva, neva, porcha,* etc.,[1] which are written out by hand. How will the subject perceive these words, how will he read them: in Russian or Latin transcription? For example, will the first word be read as

1. *Editors' note:* These words appeared to the subjects as follows: *neboq, monop, noчba, neba, mopчa.*

the Russian word *nevod* or as the word *neboq?* If, as is usually the case, the subject will read a number of Russian words in Latin transcription, as meaningless words or as foreign words unknown to him, we are obviously confronted with a set illusion, caused by a preliminary reading of the German words in Latin transcription, or, more precisely, a fixed set toward the reading of foreign words caused by this initial reading.

Later, other methods were also used for studying a set toward quality (Eliava, 1964; Chkhartishvili, 1964; and others). The methods used by Eliava consist basically in the following: during set tests, the subject is shown colorful pictures several times (e.g., a picture showing a number of sailboats near the shore), while in the critical tests a brief exposure is made of a picture having a different content (e.g., a lotus flower), but which is selected in such a manner that this picture has something in common with the first picture in the configuration of certain lines and in the coloration of certain spots.

If, during the first exposures, the subject perceives the second picture in a manner similar to the first one (e.g., if he perceives the petals of the lotus flower as representing the sails of the sailboats), then, according to the author, we will be confronted with a set illusion: the set, fixed upon the perception of sailboats, has distorted in a corresponding manner the perception of the second picture: a sail was perceived instead of a lotus flower.

In the test conducted by Chkartishvili (1964), following a highly emotional talk about snakes, the drawer of a table is opened to reveal a brightly colored scarf which test subjects, as a rule, perceive as a snake.

Experimental data obtained by these methods have shown that, under the proper conditions, a set established to a quality is evoked in virtually all subjects. In addition, its functional properties do not differ from a set established to quantity. A number of peculiar features of a set toward quality were also found. It should be noted in particular that a set toward quality always manifests itself in an assimilative, and not in a contrast, manner. Uznadze sees in this factor a new proof of the fact that the action of a fixed set is generally an assimilative action by nature. He believed that the contrast illusion, which is frequently expressed in the action of a set toward quantity, "is a phenomenon caused by the peculiar feature of a quantitative ratio," that "it does not constitute the specific character of set itself."

It was found that a considerable number of subjects continued to read a disjointed text without noticing a lack of correspondence; in one example, the second half of the text, which had no relation to the first half, was completely assimilated by the fixed set, which had developed during the reading of the first half of the text. (Obviously, a selection of appropriate texts is of crucial importance in order to obtain the necessary effect.)

The Phylogenesis of Set

Thus, the data obtained during the tests examined above indicate the integrity of the state of a set, and also that this integral dynamic state of the subject precedes the appearance of conscious processes. From these experimental data, we learn a great deal about the properties of set: its excitability, its stability and dynamism, its plasticity or inertness, etc. However, the question arises as to whether this state is specific to man or whether it also plays a role at lower stages of phylogenesis. Tests were conducted with lower apes, dogs, white rats, and birds (hens). In all of these animals, a fixed set was established experimentally.

In the research work performed by Adamashvili (1948) with monkeys, two variations of the experiment were used. In the main (second) variation, which was conducted with two Capuchin apes, the experiment was preceded by a "training period" of one and a half months. The purpose of the training was to produce in the apes a different reaction toward food balls or cakes, which were either of the same or different size. At the end of this training period, the monkey reacted to the balls of food offered to it in the following manner: when balls of different sizes were handed to the monkey, it always took only the larger ball; when the monkey was offered balls of the same size, it took both of them, in succession, but always in one impulse. The set-establishing tests were conducted only after these habit-forming sessions were completed. During the set-establishing tests, the monkey received food only in the form of balls or cakes of different size, after which, during critical tests, food was given only in the form of small balls or cakes of the same size.

The definite existence of set illusions was established as a result of this training. During critical tests, when balls of equal size were handed to the monkeys, they always took only one ball and not both, as they did when they perceived balls of unequal size. It is clear that such behavior is based upon an illusion of volume caused by a fixed set: one of the objectively equal balls was perceived as being larger.

Contrast illusions were observed most frequently in monkeys, although assimilative illusions were also observed rather frequently.

During the same tests, the *excitability* of the set in monkeys was also studied. In some cases, it is extremely high; a set is developed after two and even sometimes after only one exposure, while in other cases it is extremely low. In general, the excitability of the set in monkeys is extremely variable. The persistence of the set in monkeys is also highly variable; sometimes it extends only over 1 to 2 critical exposures and sometimes over 9 exposures. According to the data obtained by Adamashvili, it must be assumed that the set of monkeys is characterized by a low plasticity and a high variability and dynamism. The *stability* of the set in monkeys is also characterized by great variability: a fixed set sometimes manifests itself even after a week's interval, and sometimes does not manifest itself after one day. The fading of a fixed set in monkeys also has a phasic character.

In tests conducted by Adamashvili with dogs, after the animal had been "trained" to look for food in the larger of two boxes of different sizes, the set-establishing tests were conducted, which were similar to the "classical" set-establishing tests. The larger box was always made available on the same side. During critical tests, boxes of equal size were always placed in front of the dog. In this situation, the dog at first always approached that one of the two boxes of equal size which was standing at the place occupied by the smaller box, that is, it clearly exhibited a contrast illusion; later during the tests, the dog started to hold back and hesitate, and sometimes even came to a dead stop, without approaching either one of these two boxes—thus exhibiting a clear fading of the illusion.

In tests conducted by Chrelashvili with rats (1963), a fixed set was developed towards the degree of brightness of the gray color of the door of a maze. The same author developed a set towards the slope of the path followed by the animal. The track taken by the rats was movable. When a rat followed a path with an upward (rising) slope of 70 degrees, upon reaching the next fork, it turned to the right, whereas when the animal was following a path with a downward slope of 70 degrees, it turned to the left; when following a horizontal path, the rat did not turn either to the right or to the left, but proceeded straight ahead through the choice point. The horizontal path was used in critical tests.

After completion of the set-establishing trials, the rats, when following an objectively horizontal path, in most cases turned to the left; it must be assumed that the horizontal path was perceived as having a slope, under the influence of the set towards a slanted path, which had become fixed during the preceding (setting) tests.

In these tests, the excitability of the set was found to be very high, since the set was formed in 2 to 3 setting tests. Contrast illusions predominated at the beginning of the critical tests. The stability of the set was considerable.

Experiments with hens were also conducted by Chrelashvili. A set was developed in the hens to pick up grains from the dark half of a board. During the critical tests, both halves of the board were of the same gray color, but nevertheless the hen picked grains only from one half. It must be assumed that this half of the board was perceived by the hens as being darker.

The main result obtained during this study was the establishment of the fact that a fixed set can be developed in hens. In addition, a number of peculiarities in the manifestation of this set were established during this study: low excitability, the predominance of assimilative illusions, etc.

Thus, as was to be expected according to Uznadze's conception, a set is also inherent in animals; it is not a specifically human characteristic. According to Uznadze, the ability to react to the influences of the external world primarily by means of a set, that is, by an integral modification of the individual and by a readiness to action on the part of the individual as a whole, constitutes the most basic characteristic property of the organism. It is the most primitive form of a reaction of the organism against the influence of the external environment. However, in animals, set has a considerably less differentiated character than in man. This lower degree of differentiation expresses itself in the variable character of the manifestations of a fixed set; at various times, this set manifests itself in differing forms of activity.

The Characteristics of Set Specific to Man

The fact that the manner of reacting towards the action of the external world is also expressed in animals by means of a set, as an integral dynamic state of the entire individual, does not at all mean that the behavior of animals and man belongs to the same stage of development or that their behavior is conditioned by identical factors. On the contrary, Uznadze attributed considerable importance to the problem of the specific peculiarities of human behavior by advancing his theory of so-called objectification.

According to this conception, the specific nature of human behavior is due primarily to the fact that man is a social being. In the context of social life, man develops the ability of "objectification," which, according to Uznadze (1949) constitutes the most characteristic feature of man. It is precisely because of his ability to "objectify" that a set, which is directly conditioned by a given situation, no longer plays a major role in a man's life and activity. Such a set exists, "in a displaced form," and the leading role is assumed by "thought activated on the basis of an objectification" and by objectified reality, which is the basis for the appearance of a set.

Man is not "a slave of a given situation"; his behavior is not conditioned directly by a given situation. He can react to the action of his environment even after he has realized, thought over, and "objectified" the given situation. Man can act, not impulsively as animals do, but voluntarily according to his judgment. Such specifically human activity is designated by Uznadze as the "second plane" of the operation of the mind, the higher level of behavior, and contrasted with man's impulsive actions, which he calls the "first plane."

As a result of objectification, man perceives the object as a thing, rather than simply reacting to it, and the object becomes a part of consciousness. We see here a special process as a result of which the relation between the subject and the object becomes conscious. Uznadze termed this "theoretical behavior." (Interesting experimental investigations on objectification in children have been conducted by Mosiava, 1945, 1948).

As a result of the process of objectification "on the second plane," that which on "the first plane" remains unnoticed is noted, and therefore man develops a set also toward those factors which, on "the first plane," could not occasion the appearance of a set.

According to Uznadze, objectification constitutes an indispensable psychological basis for the appearance of speech and thought. A man acts according to the reality reflected in speech. Words represent an important factor of objectification, and that which is designated by a word is thereby objectified.

The most specific feature of a human set is that it can arise on the basis of a consciously realized, *objectified* situation, that is, in behavior belonging to "the second plane." In the case of man, a set arises not only during the action of a specific concrete situation, but also according to a merely imaginary situation, a situation given only on a "verbal plane"; in other words, man can act according to an imagined situation, and this fact constitutes the basic specific feature of a human act.

Thus, according to Uznadze, we must distinguish two levels of mental life: (1) the level of the set (setting level), at which behavior is completely conditioned by the set; the set directly controls behavior, so that the subject does not objectify either the situation or his actions; his behavior has an impulsive character; and (2) the level of objectification—or the level of objectified behavior. At this level a subject acts on the basis of an objectification of the situation and of his own actions. The behavior of an animal takes place entirely on the first level, while the second level is characteristic for human behavior.

Uznadze believed that experimental studies of set based on psychological representations lying outside the range of perception explore a form of set specific for man, based on "the second plane" of activity. The basic data obtained in those research studies (summarized by Natadze, 1958a, b, 1960, 1962) can be summarized as follows: (1) it has been experimentally established that a fixed set can be developed by merely *imagining* grasping balls of different volumes with the hands, or by means of a visual *representation* of circles of different size, or by the *imaginary* raising of loads of a different weight; (2) it has been experimentally established that a fixed set can be developed on the basis of an *imaginary* comparison of weight or volume during the course of an actual perception of sensory contents *opposite* to what is being imagined (e.g., the imaginary notion of grasping balls of different size while actually holding balls of equal size); and (3) a high degree of correlation between the ability to role play and the ability to easily develop a fixed set on the basis of imagination has been experimentally established (Natadze, 1962).

According to Uznadze, it is a set elicited by an "ideational" or "speech" situation which is being studied in these experiments. The objective factors of a set in these tests include not an actually given, not a perceived situation, but rather an "ideationally" given situation, that is, "an imaginary situation, expressed by means of words," which is conceived or imagined.

We believe that the decisive factor in the formation of a set under these conditions is the ability to evoke in oneself a specific active relation to the imaginary, and that this factor is not due to any particular features of that which is imagined.

What is important is the subject's skill at eliciting in himself a specific active attitude or relation towards the imaginary set situation (a skill which involves the development of a specific active attitude towards that which is imagined) and not the peculiar features of the images proper (Mosiava, 1948; Natadze, 1958b).

Psychopathology of Set

If set is really such a deep-seated, integral factor in the internal life of an individual and his behavior, as it appears to be in the data presented here, then we must assume that those deep-seated changes which take place in the internal life of a personality during a mental illness must also affect the manifestations of set; the expressions of a fixed set during a mental illness of the subject must undergo a substantial change. The experimental study of set during such diseases as schizophrenia and epilepsy and during such states as psychasthenia and hysteria do indeed produce a significantly changed picture of the manifestations of a fixed set: every type of psychosis and neurosis was found to be characterized by a form of expression of the set which is specific for that disease and is associated with the characteristic course of the disease.

A characteristic feature of schizophrenics was an extremely high excitability of the set, an extraordinary irradiation, and a sluggishness and staticness of the set; as a rule, schizophrenics exhibit an infinite illusion, without ever perceiving critical objects in an adequate manner. It is particularly remarkable that in tests with a haptic perception, a schizophrenic, after opening his eyes, continues to perceive the balls in an illusory manner. Even a visual interference is incapable of disturbing the set illusion which has arisen in the haptic sphere. The set of schizophrenics is characterized by a high stability (stable in time) and constancy. According to data obtained by Bzhalava (1958), the set of an epileptic is also easily stimulated, sluggish, static, constant, and stable, but in contrast to the schizophrenic, the set of an epileptic is a local set, that is, its irradiation is extremely limited and does not extend to another modality, not even to the corresponding organ (for example, from one hand to another).

The most characteristic features for hysterical patients were a great variability and lability of the set. A fixed set during hysteria, with the course of time, is readily and rapidly weakened and disappears (Mdivani, 1936, unpublished). Characteristic features of set in psychasthenics are the low excitability of a fixed set, a low stability, a weak plasticity and sluggishness, a great dynamism, a weak irradiation and lability. However, a typical feature for a psychasthenic is the sluggishness of his set; in this respect, it is the complete opposite of the set observed during hysteria (Mdivani). Problems concerned with the psychopathology of set are systematically presented by Uznadze (1949).

References

Adamashvili, N. G. Intermodal transfer of the perception illusion. [In Georgian.] *Trudy TGU,* 1941, *17.*

Adamashvili, N. G. Fixed set in lower apes. [In Georgian.] *Trudy Inst. Psikhol. GSSR,* 1948, *5.*

Avalishvili, A. G. On the problem of an intermodal constancy in fixed set. [In Georgian.] *Trudy TGU,* 1941, *17.*

Bzhalava, I. T. The nature of the contrast illusion. *Vop. Psikhol.,* 1958, No. 4.

Chkhartishvili, S. N. The localization of optical illusions caused by set. *Vop. Psikhol.,* 1964, No. 5.

Chrelashvili, N. V. The experimental study of the effect of a fixed set in animals. In *Experimental studies on the psychology of set.* Tbilisi: Izd. Akad. Nauk GSSR, 1963.

Eliava, N. L. *Problems of set in the psychology of thinking.* [In Georgian.] Tbilisi, 1964.

Khachapuridze, B. I. The phasic character of a change in set. [In Georgian.] In *Data on the psychology of set.* Tbilisi, 1938.

Khmaladze, G. The illusion of volume. [In Georgian.] In *Data on the psychology of set.* Tbilisi, 1938.

Khodzhava, Z. I. The role of configuration in the action of a set. [In Georgian.] *Trudy TGU,* 1941, *18.*

Mosiava, A. N. Data concerning the problem of the objectification process. *Trudy Inst. Psikhol., GSSR,* 1945, *3.*

Mosiava, A. N. On the problem of the objectification of speech in connection with the beginning of instruction in grammar. [In Georgian; resumé in Russian.] *Trudy Inst. Psikhol. GSSR,* 1948, *5.*

Natadze, R. G. The problem of set in relation to equality. [In Georgian.] *Trudy TGU,* 1941, *17.*

Natadze, R. G. On certain factors concerned with the development of set on the basis of an imaginary situation. *Vop. Psikhol.,* 1958, No. 3. (a)

Natadze, R. G. *The set-forming effect of imagination.* [In Georgian.] Tbilisi: Izd. Akad. Nauk GSSR, 1958. (b)

Natadze, R. G. Some factors in the formation of a set to an imagined situation. *Vop. Psikhol.,* 1958, No. 3. (Also in *Brit. J. Psychol.,* 1960, *51.*)

Natadze, R. G. On the psychological nature of stage impersonation. *Brit. J. Psychol.,* 1962, *53,* 421–429.

Natadze, R. G. *Memory.* Tbilisi: Izd. Akad. Nauk GSSR, 1963.

Piaget, J., and Lambercier, M. An essay on an effect of set intervening in the course of successive visual perceptions (Uznadze effect). *Arch. Psychol.,* 1945, *30,* No. 118.

Prangishvilii,A. S. *Phychology.* Tbilisi: Izd. Akad. Nauk GSSR, 1963.

Uznadze, D. N. Psychological foundations of designation. [In Georgian.] *Nasha Nauk,* 1923, Nos. 2–3.

Uznadze, D. N. Perception and representation. [In Georgian.] *Trudy TGU,* 1926, *6.*

Uznadze, D. N. On the grasping of meaning. [In Georgian.] *Trudy TGU,* 1927, *7.*

Uznadze, D. N. On the problem of the basic law of a change in set. *Psikhol.,* 1930, *3,* No. 9.

Uznadze, D. N. On the weight illusion and its analogue. *Psychol. Forsch.* 1931, *14.*

Uznadze, D. N. Toward a theory of post-hypnotic suggestion. [In Georgian.] *Trudy Inst. Funk. Nerv. Zabol,* 1936, *1.* (Also published in Russian, in *Experimental investigations on the psychology of set.* Tbilisi. Izd. Akad. Nauk GSSR, 1963.)

Uznadze, D. N. Experimental foundations of the psychology of set. [In Georgian.] Tbilisi, 1949. (Also published in Russian, in *Experimental research studies on the psychology of set.* Tbilisi: Izd. Akad. Nauk GSSR, 1958.)

Uznadze, D. N. *The psychology of set.* New York: Consultants Bureau, 1967.

PART IV

HIGHER NERVOUS ACTIVITY

22

Concerning Psychoneural Activity of Animals

I. S. Beritashvili

EDITORS' INTRODUCTION

The research summarized in this chapter represents more than a half-century of investigation on the physiology and neurophysiology of higher nervous activity. Beritashvili, born in 1885, began his academic career in 1909 at St. Petersburg University, where he studied with the well-known physiologist Vvedenskii.

Following his initial research on the physiology of central coordination, Beritashvili [1] *began his study of conditioned reflexes in 1916 while a lecturer at Odessa University (this work is summarized in Beritoff, 1924). This research was motivated by a disagreement with Pavlov concerning the physiological basis for the formation of a conditioned reflex. In the late 1920's, Beritashvili came to the conclusion that the Pavlov-Bekhterev conditioning situation, with the great restrictions that it places on the animal's behavior repertoire, was not a proper model for the study of higher nervous activity. Instead, Beritashvili came to prefer the "method of free movements" which he describes in this chapter. The theory generated by this work (Beritov, 1965) bears a strong resemblance to the "cognitive learning" theory developed by Tolman*

1. *Editors' note:* Beritashvili is a Georgian name. The Russian version of this name is spelled variously as Beritov and Beritoff, depending upon the source.

(1932), with the important addition of a physiological theory for the "cognitive map."

Although severely criticized for his unorthodox (vis-à-vis Pavlov) theories in the early 1950's, Beritashvili is now considered a patriarch and leader among Soviet neurophysiologists. He is Director of the Institute of Physiology, of the Georgian Academy of Sciences at Tbilisi.

General Characteristics of Conditioned-Reflex and Image-Guided Feeding Behavior

Early studies of higher nervous activity dealt with single components of animal behavior: salivary secretion during conditioned feeding behavior (Pavlov, 1932) and leg flexion associated with conditioned defense behavior (Bekhterev, 1925; Beritov, 1927, 1932). The theoretical concepts emerging from these studies may be very important for an understanding of the total pattern of feeding and defense behaviors, those complete behavioral networks which reflect the animal's adaptation to his external environment. This is why we undertook a study of total feeding behavior under conditions where the animal's movements were not restrained.

Our method of studying the behavior was as follows. An animal was habituated to lying quietly in a cage or on a wooden shelf approximately 10 cm. high in a definite place in a large experimental room. The animal was then trained to run to one of a number of feeding boxes located several meters from his home base when some sort of auditory or visual signal was given. These feeding boxes were opened and closed by means of the experimenter's pulling a cord or automatically by means of an electric motor. The experimenter sat at an experimental table 5 to 6 m. in front of the cage. His table was usually concealed by screens. Observations of the animal were made through a slit in the screens. The auditory and visual stimuli used for signals were located either at the feeding box, in the feeding cage, or on the experimental table (Figure 22–1). The results of observations of the behavior of the animal were recorded in detail by cinematography.

Usually the experiments began by leading an animal to a given bowl and feeding it there while presenting some neutral auditory or visual stimulus. After several repetitions of this procedure, the stimulus involved became a conditioned signal for the feeding behavior and the animal ran to the particular food box voluntarily. After eating, the animal at first had to be forced back to its cage when the call "To your place" was given. After several such trials the animal, having eaten, returned to his cage when he heard the call "To your place," or even returned without the call.

By this method we studied conditioned-reflex behavior in birds (pigeons, chickens, and emu from the lower Struthioniformes), in mammals (rabbits, cats, pigs, puppies, dogs, and monkeys), and in people (children, adults, microcephalics, and adult idiots). Experiments were also done on amphibia (frogs, axolotls, and newts) and on fish.

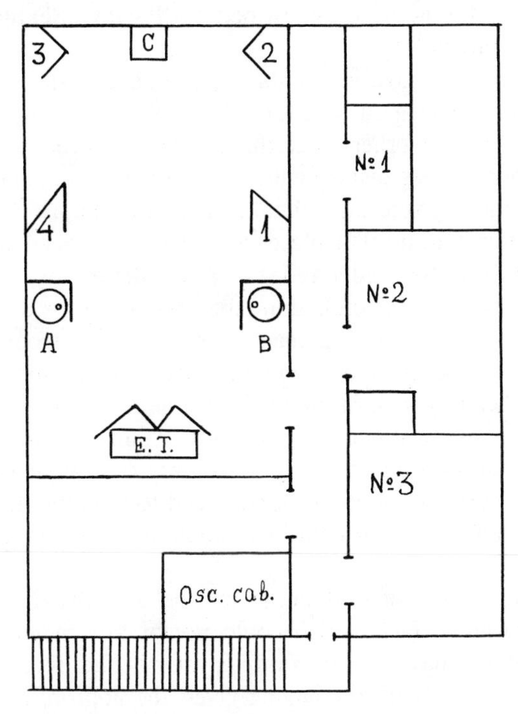

Figure 22–1. Schematic diagram of experimental room for studying behavior. The room, 13.4 m. long and 6 m. wide, is divided into two sections by a barrier: the larger for free-movement behavioral experiments, the smaller (Osc. Cab.) for oscillographic study of the electrical activity of the cerebral cortex. In the larger section there are an animal cage (*C*), four screens (*1, 2, 3, 4*) behind which food may be given, two feeders (*A, B*), and an experimental table (*E.T.*) shielded by screens. Cage and feeder are opened and closed automatically. All these articles are movable. Some experiments were designed under the conditions shown in the figure. In other experiments these articles were moved about. When necessary, particularly during movie making, the barrier was moved so that photography could take place from the small section. The animals live across the corridor.

We observed all known conditioned-reflex behavioral relations: the formation of conditioned feeding behavior on one signal paired with one food box and on another signal paired with another food box, differentiation between the two, extinction, interaction, influence of unanticipated stimuli, and so forth (Beritov, 1932; Beritov and Bregadze, 1929, 1930; Bregadze, 1930, 1946). We consider feeding behavior to be a conditioned chain reflex, where each link of the behavior is a conditioned reflex act in response to exteroceptive and proprioceptive stimuli arising at the time of the antecedent links. We must examine the cortical activity which takes place during this behavior to find an explanation of all the relationships of conditioned-reflex activity established by Pavlov, Bekhterev, their co-workers, and by ourselves.

That we do indeed have involuntary movement in the form of a chain conditioned reflex during such automatic activity is clearly seen from the following fact (among others). If the feeder is moved to another place about one to two meters distant while the animal is watching, then, when the habitual signal is given, the animal runs first to the usual position of the feeder. Only after sniffing that place does it turn its head in the direction of the new location of the feeder and run up to it there.

That all environmental stimuli along the route from the cage to the feeder actually became conditioned signals is clearly seen from the following experiment with a dog. A metronome was placed on the route to the feeder. As the animal, heading toward the feeder, came to the metronome, it began to tick. After numerous pairings the tick of the metronome became a conditioned signal. If, after onset of the primary conditioned signal, the dog moved to the feeder and the metronome failed to tick, the dog stopped near the metronome and waited for the tick, continuing its run only after onset of the metronome.

But at the very outset of studying animal behavior by the free-movement method we also noted facts which could not by any means be considered conditioned-reflex behavior. For example, after its first feeding a dog ran to a particular feeder without our having given the appropriate signal. It ran there when hungry, a minute or so after eating, several hours later, and even after several days. Furthermore, it ran to this feeder not only from its usual living place but from another part of the experimental room and also from a different room if it had been removed to that place and liberated (Beritov, 1934b, 1935b).

These and other facts noted in mammals and birds led me to the conclusion that, when higher vertebrates first perceive food in a particular place, an image or concrete representation of the food and its environmental location is formed. This image is retained, and each time it is reproduced on perception of a given environment or part thereof the animal produces the same orienting movement of head and eyes as with the perception itself; then it runs to the food location and sniffs it even if no food or remnants of food are there (Beritov, 1934b, 1935b, 1939).

Originally we termed such behavior, thus directed by an image, psychoneural behavior, but now we call it simply image behavior. We find that this behavior is voluntary, and characteristic to an equal degree of both higher vertebrates and very young children. We maintain that, during formation of feeding behavior to a neutral stimulus by the free-movement method, this behavior is first under the control of an image of the location of the food. The same sequence occurs during formation of Pavlovian conditioned salivary reflexes. When, in the first period of generalization, nonhabitual stimuli elicit salivary secretion and orienting movement of the head toward the food location, reproduction of an image of the location of the food is the cause.

We know that, when a hungry dog goes through searching movements and sniffing of the familiar food location, saliva is necessarily secreted (Beritoff and Kalabegashvili, 1944). But when saliva is differentially secreted only in response to a given conditioned stimulus, then we are dealing with saliva secretion under the control of temporary connections with the food center, connections which were developed by numerous pairings of the stimulus with feeding.

With formation of conditioned-reflex feeding behavior, reproduction of an image of the signal feeder does not disappear. This image arises every time there is a feeding signal, but it does not have primary force in regulating feeding behavior if the behavior can be more rapidly and economically guided by the action of temporary connections. The presence of the image of the location of the feeder facilitates establishment of the conditioned-reflex behavior because the image of the feeder projects at that same place in the cortex which directs the animal's conditioned-reflex route. That the image of the location of the feeder is actually produced under the influence of the food signal can be very easily shown. If the route to the feeder is blocked by a screen 2 m. long, then, when the conditioned signal is on, the animal goes up to the screen and immediately passes around it, reaching the feeder without delay. Movement up to the screen undoubtedly takes place by the conditioned-reflex route, but going around the screen is guided by an image of the location of the food. Or, if the cage is taken into another room across the corridor, the dog placed therein, and the feeding sound signal given at this place, the dog then runs from the cage at first in the same direction as it did in the experimental room; but after going one or two meters it stops for a second, then rapidly turns to the door and runs across the corridor to the experimental room to precisely that feeder from which it received food with this particular signal.

Thus, feeding behavior under the control of food-location images appears to be a fundamental, higher form of behavior for the higher vertebrates. On the basis of this image behavior, conditioned-reflex behavior is established and carried out by means of temporary connections developed by numerous occurrences of identical image behavior in a constant environmental situation.

Image psychoneural activity is characteristic of all the highest vertebrates and man. It appears to be the higher form of psychological activity in animals and very young children. For adult humans with logical verbal speech, specific conscious psychological activity regulates work behavior by preliminary verbal planning of the objective of behavior and all stages of movement for attainment of this objective. This behavior is primarily based, not only on the experience of the given individual, but also on the historic experience of the entire society to which he belongs (Beritov, 1934a).

Image and conditioned-reflex forms of behavior are produced by the central nervous system and are determined by definite external and internal conditions. But they are, qualitatively, absolutely different phenomena of the active life of the organism and must be accomplished by means of qualitatively different neural substrates; the activity of these substrates takes place in accordance with laws which are common to both as well as in accordance with laws which are specific to each.

Neural Substrate of Image Psychoneural Activity

On the basis of contemporary understanding of the cerebral cortex, it may be assumed that the basic neural substrates of subjective experience (sensations, perceptions, images) are those neural complexes in the primary zones of the projection areas of the cerebral cortex in which specific thalamic routes from the receptors terminate. In these neural complexes, located largely in layer IV of the primary zones, we find a predominance of stellate cells with a pericellular neural net, and it has therefore been proposed that these stellate cells are the sensory elements which produce sensations of light, color, sound, taste, odor, touch, warmth, and cold when stimulated.

Definite morphological, physiological, and psychological facts support this conviction (Beritashvili, 1963b). The principal mass of stellate neurons with short axons is located in layer IV of the primary projection areas. There are definitely fewer stellate neurons in the secondary zones and between zones. The more weakly developed the perceptive function of a particular receptor, the more weakly developed is layer IV with its stellate neurons in the corresponding perceptual area of the cortex. For example, in the visual area of the cerebral cortex of the hedgehog, which has poor sight, the stellate neurons are significantly fewer than in the rabbit (Shkol'nik-Yaross, 1954, 1958).

With phylogenetic development of the cortex the number of stellate neurons with short axons is markedly increased, mainly in the primary zones. There are substantially more of them in monkeys and man than in cats and dogs. In primates and man, layer IV in the primary zones occupies a substantial portion of the cortex and is divided into three sublayers consisting mostly of stellate neurons (Sarkisov and Polyakov, 1949; Polyakov, 1956). On this basis, Lorente de Nó (1922) and later Sarkisov and Polyakov (1949) suggested that the predominance in man of stellate cells with short axons in layer IV of the primary perceptual zone is an anatomical reflection of the refinement and higher development of brain functions.

Stellate neurons with short axons are united into a functional system by means of internuncial and association pyramidal neurons. This functional system accounts for perception and images of the outer world. There are grounds for supposing that union of stellate neurons of the primary zone of one perceptual area for production of a given perception is accomplished with the participation of pyramidal neurons of the primary zone, but for elicitation of an image from a given perception and for preservation and reproduction of this image, pyramidal neurons of the secondary zone must participate. For example, in visual perception this union must be accomplished primarily by association and internuncial pyramidal neurons of primary-zone field 17, whereas visual figures arise with participation of similar neurons in fields 18 and 19, which are secondary zones.

This position gets direct support from experiments with people. Penfield (1958) discovered that stimulation of the human visual cortex in the area of the calcarine fissure (field 17) of one hemisphere elicits sensations of diverse types of light, color, and dark indeterminate figures moving in the contralateral visual field, and at the same time the subject is blinded in this visual field. Stimulation of the visual area outside the calcarine fissure (in fields 18 and 19) brings forth the same visual effects but they are more structured and appear to move in both visual fields. In the latter case blinding is less severe and does not always occur.

Penfield and Jasper (1954) suggest that field 17 is the primary representation area for elicitation of visual sensations and that fields 18 and 19 have the function of organizing visual perceptions and also have a relation to binocular vision.

There can be no doubt that the primary zones are a terminal station for afferent impulses moving from the receptors along a specific system. But here, probably, they not only elicit sensations from all active components of the outer world but also produce primary perception of an object, that is, the union of a large complex of sensory stellate cells into one functional system which produces the subjective reflection of a given object. It may be assumed that the numerous internuncial and association neurons with recursive collaterals in layers V, IV, and III of the primary zone, where they terminate, in particular, on sensory stellate cells (Shkol'nik-Yaross, 1961), must serve as a most important structural basis for integration of excited sensory cells into a functional system of perception.

As any given object is perceived in a definite external environment, perception of this environment enters into the above-mentioned functional system. As a result the perceived object is projected in its environment.

From this functional system, the impulses of excitation must be transmitted across association pyramidal neurons to the secondary zones. Here they terminate on association neurons which, in their turn, send impulses to the given functional system of the primary zone.

Furthermore, it is now known that afferent impulses move from each receptor not only to the primary zone, but also to the secondary zone. In the latter zone these impulses arrive not only along the nonspecific system but also across a specific system; for example, they go into the visual area via the pulvinar (Shkol'nik-Yaross, 1961). Simultaneous excitation of primary and secondary zones certainly must create a particularly favorable environment for the establishment of bilateral connections between these two zones, that is, connections for the development of closed neural circuits in which there is reverberation of excitation impulses. In these circuits excitation may reverberate for some time at the high rate of 50 to 100 impulses per second and thereby may structurally reinforce these circuits to the extent that they become the basis for preservation of an image of an object for a long period of time. After this, any component of the object or of its environment may serve to reproduce an image of the object.

The formation of an image of complex objects of the environment with participation of several perceptual areas must be accomplished with pyramidal neurons of association fields lying between these areas. This explains why electrical stimulation of human temporal areas between the auditory and visual perceptual areas elicits concrete visual and auditory images as visual and auditory memories (Penfield, 1958).

Finally, observations on people show that stimulation of receptors coincides with the appearance of primary electric potentials in the primary zone and the subjective feelings of stimulation which these potentials elicit. And in those cases where, as a result of diversion of attention or absorption in intellectual work (e.g., solution of an arithmetic problem), primary potentials in the cortex weaken in response to a given peripheral stimulation, the subjective experiences from these peripheral stimuli also diminish (Hernandez-Peon *et al.,* 1959; Hernandez-Peon and Donoso, 1959).

Jung (1959, 1960) demonstrated parallels between electric potentials and subjective sensations in extracellular monitoring of different cortical neurons of the primary zone. Specifically, Jung compared the electrical activity of cortical neurons of the primary visual zone of a cat with subjective experiences of a man given the same visual stimulus and found twelve different types of parallel phenomena. For example, during increase of light stimulation the intensity of light sensation in man grows according to the well-known Weber-Fechner law. Correspondingly, discharges of *B*-neurons in the visual cortex of the cat, when excited by light, become more frequent approximately in accordance with the logarithm of the intensity of illumination if light adaptation is held constant. Also, subjective fusion of a flickering light in man takes place at a frequency of approximately 50 per second. In the cat too this limiting rhythm of excitation of visual neurons during flickering light occurs at approximately 50 per second. Specifically, when light intensity increases there is an increase in both the subjective threshold of flicker and objective discharge of visual neurons. Other psychophysiological parallels set forth by Jung are also rather convincing.

Apparently, in each functional system of cortical neurons excited by a given external influence, the activity of sensory elements depends on the number of neural circuits which participate in this system and on the frequency of excitation of the latter. Also, the number of reacting neural circuits and the frequency of their excitation depend on the number of excited receptor elements and on the number, frequency, and intensity of stimuli acting on them. This is what produces parallels between psychological and physiological phenomena.

The facts set forth above clearly indicate that stellate neurons in layer IV of the primary zone of the perceptual areas are apparently the only neural elements which produce differential sensations for perception of the external world and for reproduction of images. These stellate neurons are termed sensory and therefore the primary zone may also be termed sensory.

Structural and Physiological Characteristics of Stellate Neurons

Stellate neurons with short axons may be divided into two groups on the basis of their external appearance. One group is characterized by more or less thick branching of the axon in the area of the dendrites of the neuron. Furthermore, the dendritic and axonal branching is sometimes so interlaced around the body of the cell and so fine and thick that it is almost impossible to distinguish one from the other. Such neurons with thick pericellular network are termed arachnoid or Golgi cells of type II. Neurons of this sort are most frequently found in layers IV and III of the primary zone (Figure 22–2).

One group of sensory neurons does not have axonal branchings going out from the pericellular network which might activate other neural cells. Lorente de Nó (1943) gave a characteristic picture of stellate neurons with a pericellular axonal net. The axon emerges from the area of dendrites, then, bypassing this area, gives collaterals exclusively lateral to these dendrites. Another group of neurons with a pericellular net has axonal branchings going out from it which emerge from the dendrite area and terminate immediately or somewhat further along on pyramidal or stellate cells. Frequently these axonal branches terminate on the nearest stellate neurons,

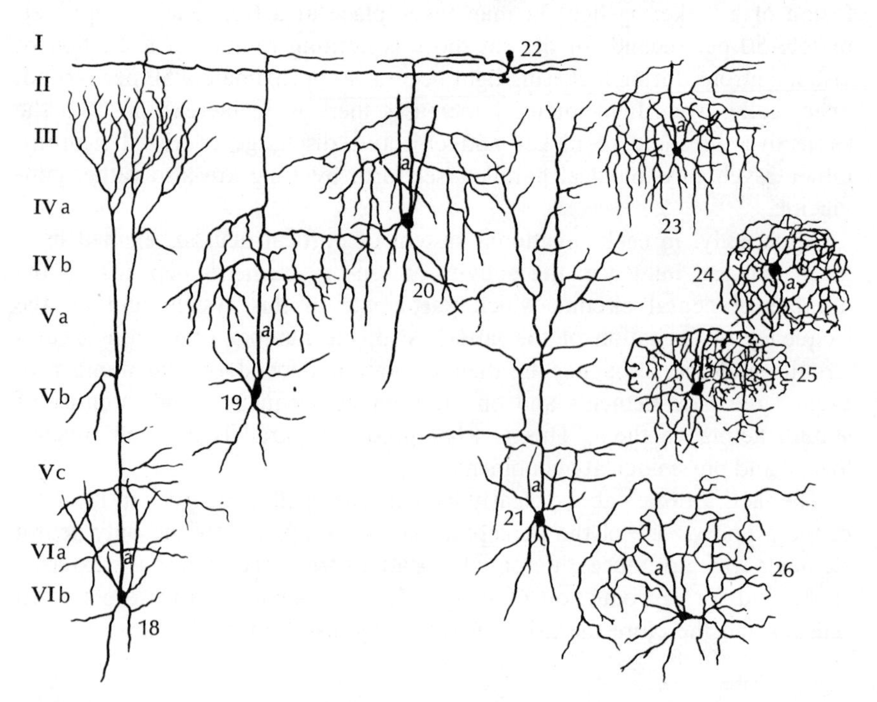

Figure 22–2. Types of neuron with intracortical axons. Stellate cells with ascending axons (18, 19, 20, 21). Cell with horizontal axon (22). Stellate ceils, axons of which form a thick nexus within the limits of dendritic branching (24, 25). Stellate cells, the axons of which are branched both in the area of dendrites and external to it (23, 26). (From Lorente de Nó, 1943.)

thereby forming separate individual nests (Shkol'nik-Yaross, 1955). These peculiar glomerules are united by branching efferent thalamic fibers (Figure 22–3). According to Lorente de Nó, in each of these glomerules there are several tens of stellate cells in close proximity (Lorente de Nó, 1922). Apparently these cells are united among themselves both by means of axodendritic and axosomatic synapses as well as by dendrito-dendritic synapses (Estable, 1961). Stellate cells of any one nest appear to be sensory cells of a single modality.

Let us make a comparison of various forms of stellate neuron. In man and in monkeys, according to data of Sarkisov and Polyakov (1949) and Shkol'nik-Yaross (1954) (see Figure 22–4), the situation is not that shown in lower mammals (rabbits and mice) by the drawings of Lorente de Nó (1943) and O'Leary and Bishop (1938) (Figure 22–5). It is suggested that, in both man and monkeys, in layer IV of the cerebral cortex there predominate cells with a pericellular neuron net without supplementary axonal branching outside of this net or outside of the clustered interlacing

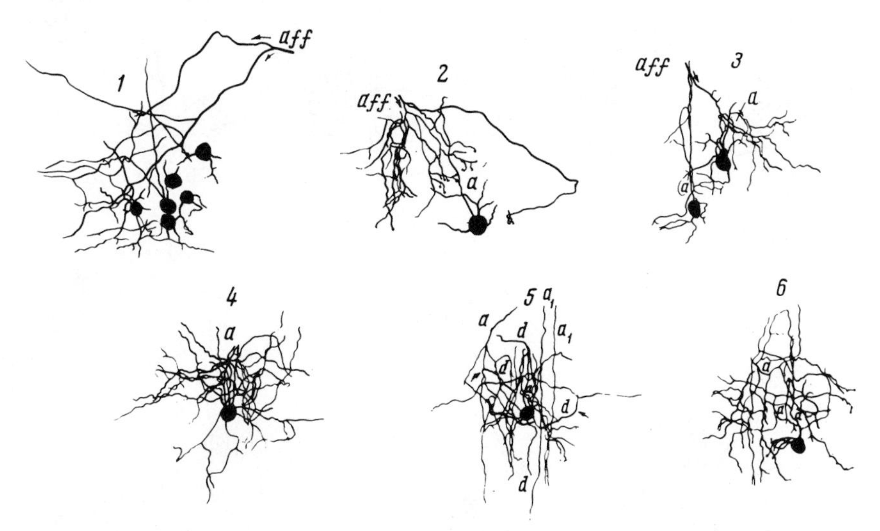

Figure 22–3. Stellate cells with afferents in layer IV of the green monkey. With afferents (*Aff.*) (1, 2, 3). Stellate cells with well-developed pericellular net (4, 5, 6): *a*—axon; *d*—dendrite; a_1—transmission axons. (From Shkol'nik-Yaross, 1955.)

of these cells; while in mice and rabbits, apparently, these cells in most cases have supplementary axonal branching outside the pericellular network, which apparently terminates both on neighboring stellate cells and on internuncial pyramidal cells. For example, according to the drawings of O'Leary (1961), field 17 of the cat cortex has very few stellate cells with a pericellular network without axonal branchings issuing therefrom. According to the data of Sholl (1955), such stellate cells are found principally in the area of distribution of the thalamic fibers of the specific system.

Axonal branchings around a stellate cell not only interlace the dendrites of this cell many times but also terminate thereon as well as on the body of the cell in synapses (Figure 22–6). Such a structure makes it possible for these neurons to effect a closure of the cellular excitation onto itself. This must guarantee that with each activation of a stellate neuron there will be numerous excitations of that neuron.

The above-mentioned structural feature of stellate neurons has its characteristic physiological feature. To wit, in the experiments of Li, Cullen, and Jasper (1956), Li (1959), and others, independent perceptual neurons in the sensorimotor zone (posterior sigmoid gyrus of the cat) usually respond to some degree with a prolonged rhythmic discharge of peak impulses of excitation on a background of prolonged slow potentials. This is observed during extracellular monitoring from layer IV during stimu-

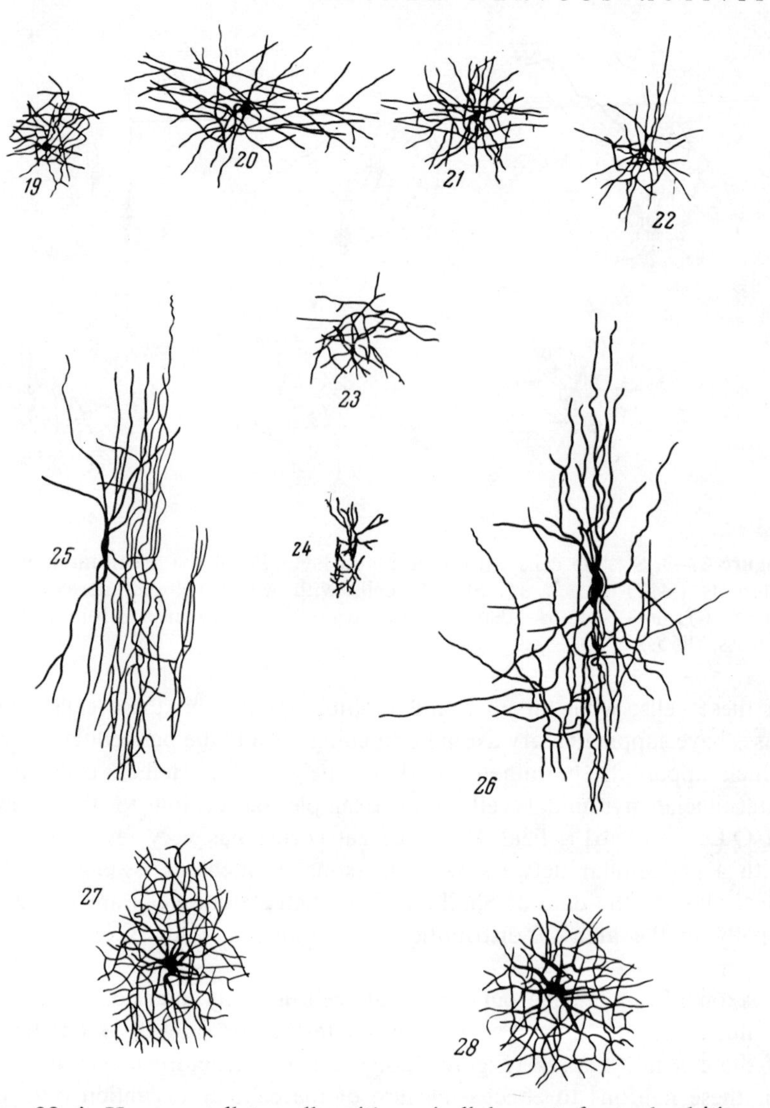

Figure 22–4. Human stellate cells with pericellular net from dendritic and axonal branching. From layer II (24). From layer III (25). From layer IV (23, 27). From layer V (20, 21, 22, 26). From layer VI (19, 28). (From Polyakov, 1958.)

lation of a relay nucleus of the thalamus, or a sensory nerve of an extremity with separate electrical shocks (Figure 22–7a).

The prolonged flow of slow potentials of about 50 milliseconds results from a summation of local potentials from cell bodies and dendrites and apparently depends upon prolonged repeated impulsation from the region

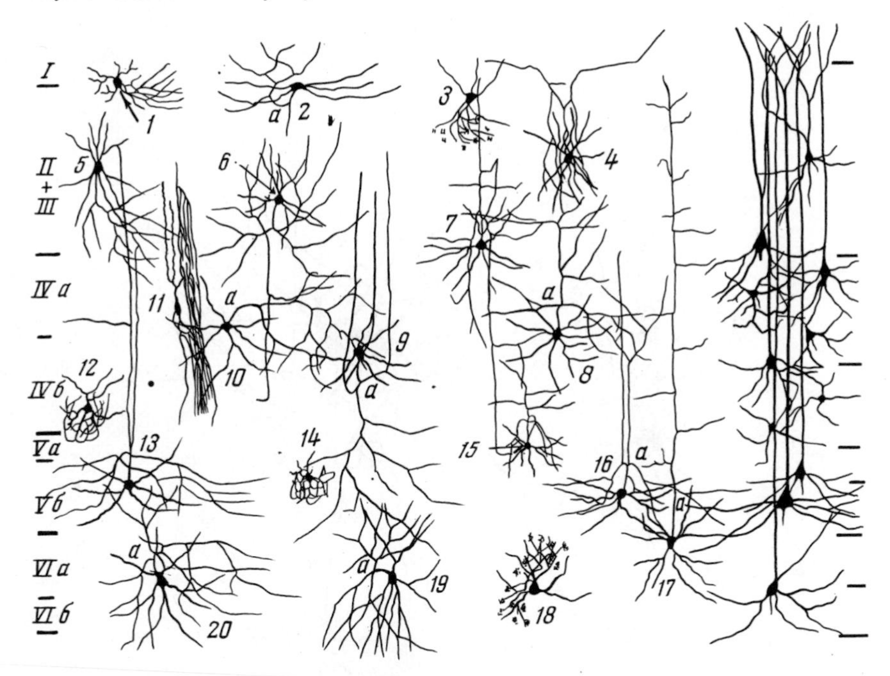

Figure 22–5. Distribution of stellate cells with short axons and pyramidal neurons from the medial surface of the visual analyzer of a cat. Stellate neurons with pericellular net without axonal branches (12, 14). Stellate neurons with pericellular net and branching (13, 15, 16). Stellate cells without pericellular axonal net (2, 10, 17). (From O'Leary, 1961.)

of their own axons. The rapid potentials on the slow potential background arise from stimulation of the axonal branchings due to the excitational action of the above-mentioned slow potential on the beginning parts of the axons. The higher rhythm at the outset, during the slow, strong potential and the gradual falling of this rhythm with weakening of the slow potentials, are evidence of stimulation of the axonal biocurrents under the influence of the slow cellular-dendritic potential.

Characteristically, after local strychnine poisoning of the sensorimotor zone, one observes a speeding up and lengthening of axonal discharges along with strengthening and lengthening of the slow potentials (Li, 1959) (Figure 22–7b). The discoverers of this phenomenon consider these cortical elements a separate type, I, consisting of cells which relate to cortical functioning of dermomuscular sensations. They claim that along with these cells there appear "stellate pyramidal cells" and an abundance of Golgi type II cells on which afferent endings make synaptic contact (Li *et al.,* 1956).

It may be assumed that these neurons, which produce long rhythmic discharges in response to a single peripheral impulse, are stellate neurons

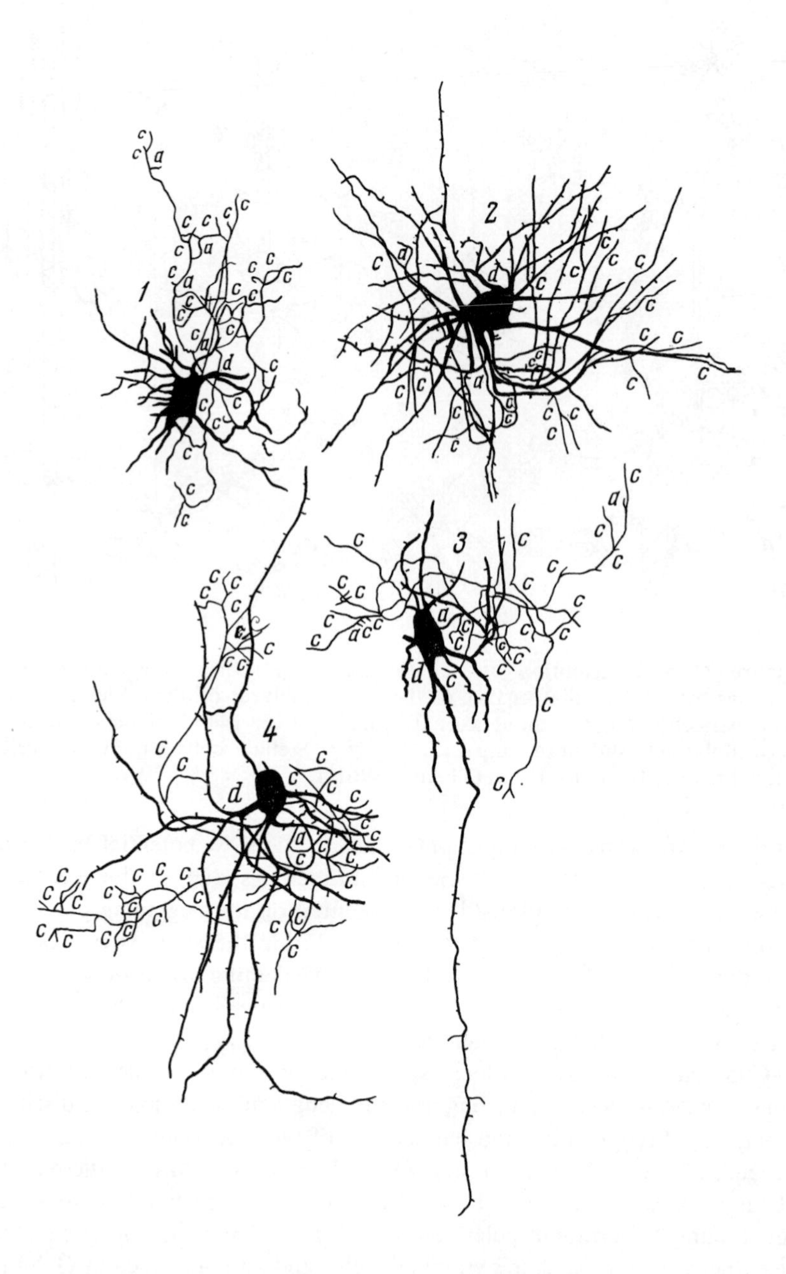

Figure 22–6. Stellate neurons from human cerebral cortex. Branching of an axon with terminations on dendrites and on the cell body (*a*). Free axonal collaterals (*c*); they also terminate on dendrites, which are not represented. (From Polyakov, 1956.)

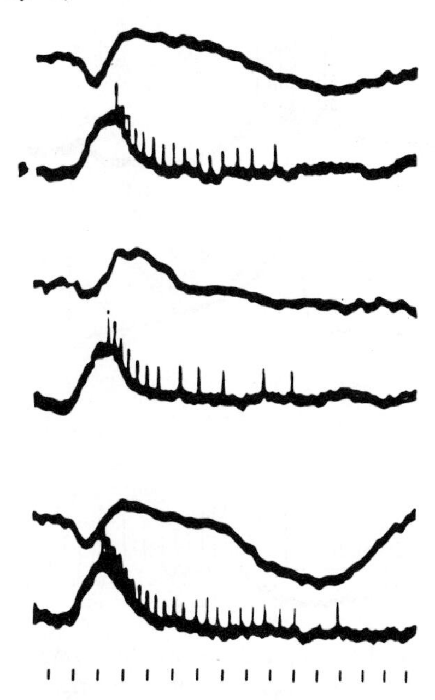

Figure 22–7a. Potentials obtained from cells of the sensorimotor cortex of a cat brain. In each pair of oscillograms the upper figure was produced with plate electrodes on the surface of the cortex and the lower ones from a depth of 1.12 mm. with microelectrodes from the surface of a perceptual cell. Radial nerve stimulated with single electrical charge. Time: 5 millisec. (From Li, Cullen, and Jasper, 1956.)

with a pericellular axonal network or nests uniting them. Therefore such discharges should be characteristic for all perceptual areas and not only for the sensorimotor area. They serve everywhere for the production of sensations under the influence of impulses from the receptors along specific thalamic routes. Apparently these stellate neurons, under the influence of their own axonal discharges, reach such an active condition that they begin to produce the subjective sensations of light, sound, touch, and so forth (Beritov, 1961).

However, on the basis of current data it is known that afferent impulses from the receptors moving along direct ascending routes (i.e., over the specific system) are not sufficient for stimulation of sensory stellate neurons. This is also substantially dependent on impulses from the reticular formation, that is, from the nonspecific system. It has been demonstrated by electrophysiological research that afferent impulses from both the specific and nonspecific systems terminate on stellate cells (Creutzfeldt and Akimoto, 1958). Afferent impulses from the vestibular apparatus also converge on them (Jung, 1959). Probably this takes place also via the nonspecific system.

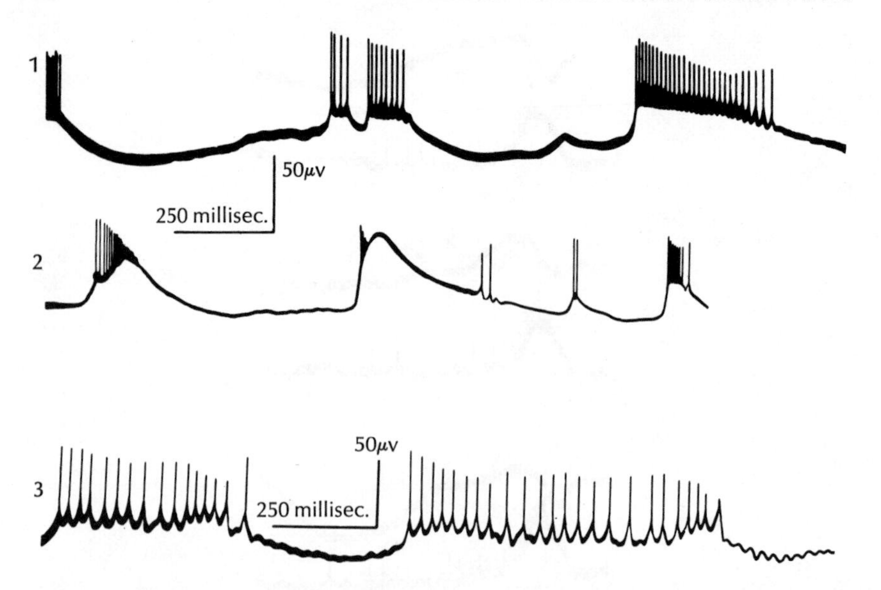

Figure 22–7b. Potentials of perceptual cell of this same area after local strychnine poisoning: (1) Spontaneous discharges during intracellular monitoring over ten minutes. (2) Over 15 minutes. (3) Over 40 minutes under high-speed exposure. Fast potentials arise when the level of the slow potential reaches 20 millivolts and higher up to 35 millivolts. (From Li, 1959.)

Further, it has been demonstrated that when the reticular formation is stimulated the slow electrical activity characteristic of the sleeping condition changes into a rapid activity and desynchronization occurs (Moruzzi and Magoun, 1949). With chronic implanted electrodes, when the reticular formation of a sleeping animal is stimulated the animal wakes up (Segundo, Arana, and French, 1955). When the reticular formation is damaged or narcotized, on the other hand, slow synchronized electrical activity appears in the cortex and during this the animal falls asleep: peripheral stimulations fail to elicit primary electrical potentials (Lindsley, Bowden, and Magoun, 1949; Lindsley, Schreiner, Knowles, and Magoun, 1950).

From all this it follows that the level of arousal of the sensory elements of the cortex, which is necessary for their arousal with a subjective phenomenon, depends upon tone-maintaining excitation from the reticular formation.

A second group of stellate neurons is found in all layers of the cortex. These neurons have a small number of short dendrites and the axons go out from the cell horizontally or vertically into other layers and terminate there in numerous collaterals. According to Polyakov (1958), very frequently the branchings of such a stellate neuron entwine around the bodies of a great number of pyramidal cells. It is assumed, therefore, that stimulation of each such cell should lead to simultaneous stimulation of a large number of pyramidal cells. Apparently, stellate cells of the second group serve for transmission of impulses of stimulation from afferent thalamic fibers to internuncial, association, and projection pyramidal neurons (Beritov, 1961).

There is some basis for assuming that sensory neurons with a pericellular axonal net and dendrites without spurs are not directly inhibited. They intermittently cease activity, due to inhibition of the association and internuncial pyramidal neurons with which they are united or due to inhibition in subcortical relay nuclei of neural routes of the specific and nonspecific systems (Beritashvili, 1956).

Thus, stellate neurons of one definite type (those with the pericellular axonal net characteristic for the fourth layer of the perceptual areas in higher vertebrate animals) are, in our opinion, sensory neurons producing the most highly differentiated sensations. But this attribute should not by any means be considered a function of the above-mentioned external construction, which is adapted for the greatest possible repetition of excitation of a neuron under the influence of short-term impulses acting upon it. It is for this reason that such arachnoid stellate neurons exist even in other sections of the brain and not only in the cortex. One must assume that the production of differentiated subjective sensations is a phylogenetically developed property of neural cytoplasm. It is only as a result of the peculiarity of the molecular and submolecular construction of cytoplasm, most probably of ectoplasm, that particular neurons became the basis of psychological activity, which is the highest form of adaptation. There is no doubt that the external form of sensory neurons varies extensively. Probably the arachnoid form of stellate neurons with pericellular axon net is the most highly developed form of sensory neuron found in the higher vertebrate animals and man.

The fact that sensory stellate neurons are arranged in united groups, forming nests, between which direct axonal links have not been found, has deep biological significance. The stellate neurons of layer IV must perceive, mirror the outer world; they must enter an active condition simultaneously under the influence of the external environment in order to create concrete images of it. Irradiation of stimulation in the stellate neuron system could only disturb such image perception of the outer world and the rapid change of images in connection with changing external conditions.

The fact that some of the arachnoid stellate neurons also do not have axonal links with the pyramidal cells must indicate that not all sensory neurons participate in direct transmission of stimulation to pyramidal cells for production of even so much as the orienting movement of the head. Their basic and only function is to produce subjective reflection (mirroring) of the outer world, to create images.

Characteristics and Production of Images of the Outer World

In people, subjective elements of an image are, in general, like perceptions. But even in animals an image of an object may include all the necessary elements for perception. We demonstrated that in a dog the image of food, perceived in a definite location, includes not only the quality of the food but also its amount and geographic location. For example, if a hungry dog is shown meat behind one screen and bread behind another and then they are removed without being noticed, subsequently the dog goes first to the location of the meat, and, not finding it there, then goes to the location of the bread. Or, if one shows the dog a small piece of meat in the first place and many pieces of meat in another place, subsequently the dog will go where it saw the larger amount of meat.

If the dog is shown bread behind one screen at a distance of two to three meters and meat behind another screen at a distance of four to five meters, the dog will go first to the near food location (to the bread) but without eating will then proceed to the meat. After eating the meat, it will return to the bread. Or the dog may even take the bread in its mouth, take it to the location of the meat, drop the bread, eat the meat, and then eat the bread (Beritov, 1934b, 1939). Finally, if the dog has eaten all the meat or seen an empty bowl in some spot, it will not go quickly to that place at a later time. All these facts clearly indicate that the dog has images of the outer world which contain as concrete a composition as there would be in perception of the outer world.

Images of perceived objects are created during the first perception. Apparently, the sensory stellate cells, which produce sensations in one or various modalities, are combined into a single functional system immediately after they have been stimulated simultaneously. These images are preserved for a long time; sometimes they last for months or years after the perception. They are reproduced every time there is a repetition of the influence of the given object, a part of it, or the environment in which it occurred at the moment of perception. However, the uniting of sensory stellate neurons into one functional system during perception proceeds in a different way from the establishment of the temporary bonds of a conditioned reflex. In perception the bonds between sensory neurons arise immediately on the first influence of an object and are later preserved, making possible the reproduction of images for a long time, sometimes almost the entire lifetime. These images actually do not extinguish with time, even when repeatedly reproduced without a new perception. Apparently the neural bonds between the sensory neurons are qualitatively different from the temporary bonds (formed with projection pyramids) on which the development of a conditioned reflex depends. Bonds of the latter sort require numerous repetitions for their formation and strengthening; moreover, they rapidly extinguish if they are not practiced.

As indicated above, images of perceived objects are obtained by uniting stellate neurons with association pyramidal neurons of the secondary zones. These zones characteristically differ in their microstructure from the primary zones. In the primary zone, layer IV is most strongly developed and contains many more stellate cells with pericellular axonal net than there are in layer IV of the secondary zones; and the secondary zones show a considerable increase of layer III, in which internuncial and association pyramidal neurons are accumulated to a greater extent than in the other layers (Figures 22–8 and 22–9). With respect to the visual perception area it is known that the area of the secondary zones (fields 18 and 19) is increased relatively more than the primary zone as a function of phylogenetic development (Filimonov, 1948). Fields 18 and 19 are phylogenetically younger structures than field 17 (Sarkisov and Polyakov, 1949). Ontogenetically, field 17 matures sooner than fields 18 and 19 (Preobrazhenskaya, 1948) (Figures 22–8 and 22–9).

All these facts indicate that the development of the secondary zones should be connected with a higher integration of cortical activity, with its psychological activity.

The functional peculiarities of the primary and secondary zones have also been subjected to physiological research with respect to vision. Thus Bonin, Carol, and McCulloch (1942) locally poisoned various fields in monkeys with strychnine and observed the resulting changes of electrical activity in other fields. It was discovered that when field 17 was poisoned, spasmodic discharges appeared in fields 17 and 18, and when field 18 was poisoned they arose in field 17 of both hemispheres and even in ipsilateral field 19; when field 19 was poisoned they appeared in field 19 only. From this the authors concluded that field 18 receives impulses from field 17 and, in turn, sends impulses to field 17, to ipsilateral field 19, and to contralateral field 18. From field 19 strychnine impulses do not transfer to other fields; on the contrary, the authors noted an inhibition of electrical activity in this field which slowly spread to both hemispheres. Apparently, association fibers from field 19 terminate in other fields of the cortex, for the most part in the first layer on dendrites of pyramidal neurons and therefore, as we understand the situation, they produce general inhibition of the cortex (Beritov, 1960, 1961).

From these physiological observations we may make one very important conclusion: fields 17 and 18 are closely and bilaterally connected with one another and, therefore, during stimulation of the retina they are activated as a single formation producing visual images of external objects. Field 19,

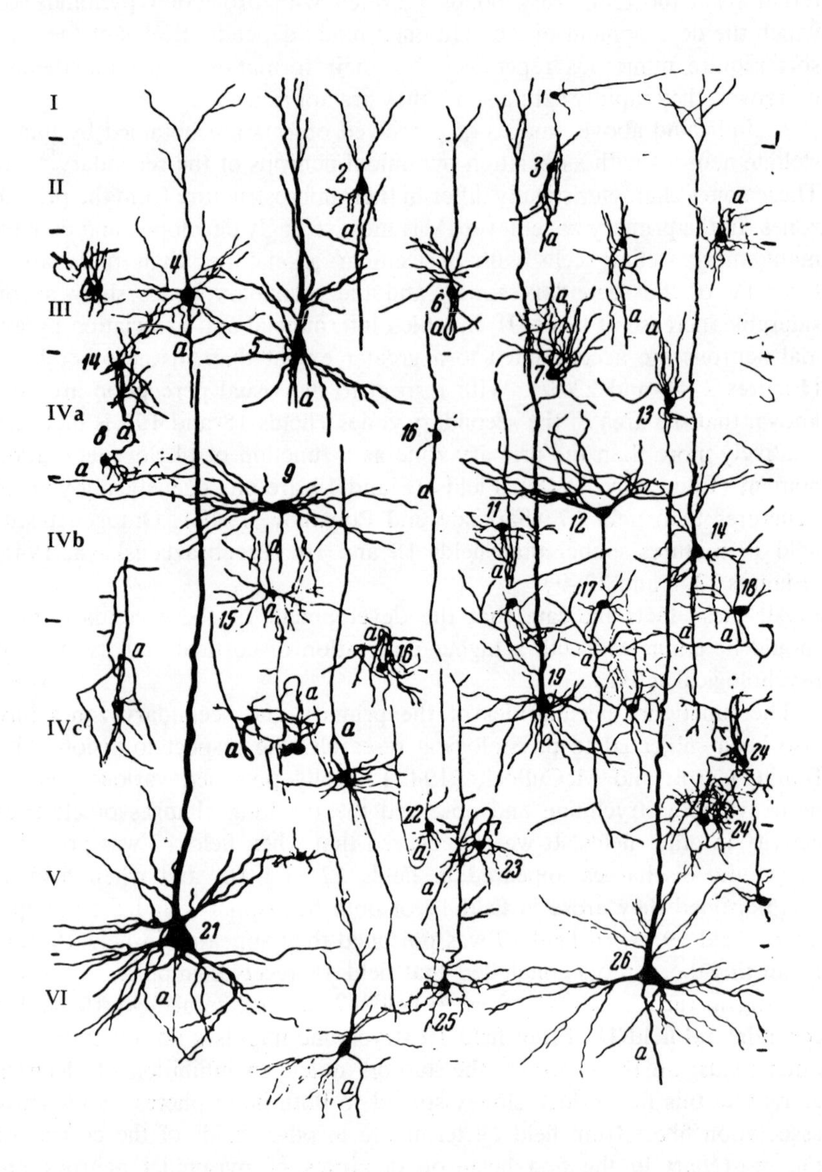

Figure 22–8. Neurons of field 17 of the visual analyzer of the monkey (*Cercopithecus*). Pyramidal cell layer II (2). Pyramidal cells of layer III (4, 5, 6). Small pyramidal cell of sublayer IVb (14). Cajal stellate cells of sublayer IVb (9, 12). Stellate cells of sublayer IVa (7, 8, 13). Fine stellate cells of sublayer IVb (11, 15, 17, 18). Stellate cells of sublayer IVc (16, 20, 24). Pyramidal cell of sublayer IVc (19). Gross pyramidal cells of layers IV and V (21, 26). (From Shkol'nik-Yaross, 1950.)

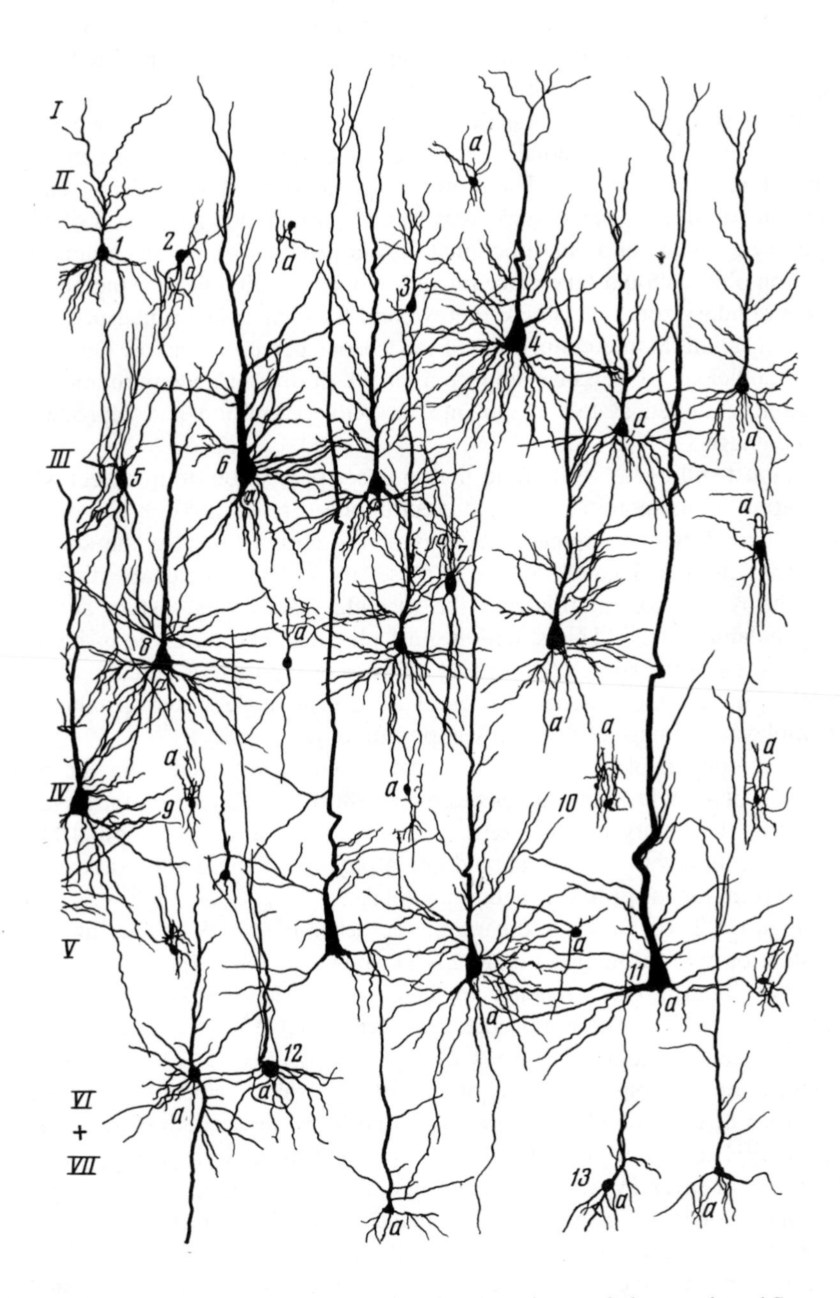

Figure 22–9. Neurons of field 19 in the visual analyzer of the monkey (*Cercopithecus*). Pyramidal cells of layer II (1, 3, 4). Pyramidal cells of layer III (6, 8). Brush-shaped cells of layer III (5, 7). Stellate cells of layer IV (9, 10). Pyramidal cells of layer V (11). (From Shkol'nik-Yaross, 1954.)

activated at this time from field 18, produces general inhibition of the cortex and preserves the local and complete nature of a given visual image apart from simultaneous influence of other objects.

We have considered production of an image based on visual perception of a given object. In actuality an external object is usually perceived by almost all sense organs. Therefore, in perception of an object, sensory neurons of various perceptual areas should participate. The union of these sensory elements into one functional system producing a complete image of a given object should take place by means of association fields lying between the secondary zones. It is here that we find those association neurons which serve as bilateral interconnection of the various perceptual areas. Obviously, it is sufficient to perceive any component of the outer environment for the entire united system to go into an active condition and reproduce a given image.

It must still be borne in mind that in every perception of an object which is important to an animal's life, afferent impulses reach not only the primary and secondary zone perceptual areas of the cortex but also the so-called association areas located outside of these zones. These areas are stimulated by the reticular formation and the ascending activating system and also via thalamic nuclei. This situation must play an important role in bilateral unification of the stimulated sensory neurons of the various perceptual areas with neurons of the association areas to form a single system producing a complex total image of the vitally important object.

Development of image psychological activity considered from the point of view of a phylogenetic series of animals must first depend on the development of the ability to unite sensory elements of various perceptual areas. In connection with this one should find a phylogenetic growth of association areas from the lower to the higher mammals.

Figure 22–10 shows a diagrammatic scheme of the united functional system of a visual image. Figure 22–11 shows the same thing for a visual-auditory image. These schema are based on present-day knowledge of the construction of the cerebral cortex. Afferent thalamic routes terminate on sensory and pyramidal neurons of layer IV; axons of the primary zone association neurons terminate on internuncial and association pyramidal neurons of the secondary zones. Axons go from the secondary zone to the primary zone, and here they terminate first on internuncial pyramidal neurons of layer IV and then close neural circuits between secondary and primary zones; then they are terminated on similar neurons of layers III and IV and also on transmission stellate neurons. The axons of these neurons run to layer IV, where they must be terminated on sensory stellate neurons. All these structural data are in accordance with researches of Roman y Cajal, Lorente de Nó, Chang, Polyak, Polyakov, Shkol'nik-Yaross, and others.

The structural bases for general inhibition are also represented on these diagrams. The neural circuits of a given image put out collaterals terminating on the basal and apical dendrites of neighboring pyramidal neurons both directly and via Martinotti cells, through which they produce general inhibition around the excited neural circuits.

It is further seen from these diagrams that sensory neurons with pericellular axonal networks do not enter into the neural circuits of an image. They are activated from circuits of association neurons by collaterals directly or via internuncial pyramidal neurons and stellate transmission neurons.

A series of experiments was carried out for experimental clarification of the functional significance of the primary zone (field 17) and the secondary zone (fields 18 and 19) of the visual perceptual area in psychological activity of the dog. To determine the role of these zones in perception of external objects and in subsequent creation and maintenance of visual images, we first established the maximum delay in normal dogs and then one or another zone of the cortex of the larger hemispheres was removed. Thus, Beritashvili, Aivazashvili, and Ordzhonikidze (1965) demonstrated that, if a normal dog confined in a cage is shown meat and this food is then removed several meters and concealed behind a screen while the dog is looking, and if bread or an empty bowl is then shown, removed to another location, and placed behind a screen, the dog reacts adequately not only immediately after the demonstration but also after many minutes. Thus, for example, a normal, quiet dog, on opening of the cage, ran to the preferred food (meat) not only immediately but also after 10 to 25 minutes; and it did not go to the location of the bread and the empty bowl, or only went there after eating the meat.

From the foregoing it may be concluded that a functional system of neurons producing an image of external objects and their location can be maintained in an excited condition or in a condition of heightened excitability for a period of many minutes. But we know that if the dog is taken to some new location and shown food there, it can go directly to this place not only after several minutes but even on another day or after a week. It must not be concluded, therefore, that the functionally united system of neurons of a given visual image was constantly in an excited condition, that this image survived for the entire time. It is known that every functional system consists of closed neural circuits of varying complexity, but excitation cannot reverberate in them for the entire time that the stimuli activating them are no longer in effect. Such a postaction condition of excitation may continue for seconds, in rare cases for minutes. As is now almost universally accepted, in the cortex of the larger hemispheres the activity of each functional system of neurons is combined with general inhibition of all the other neurons of the cortex, more especially all of the nearest association

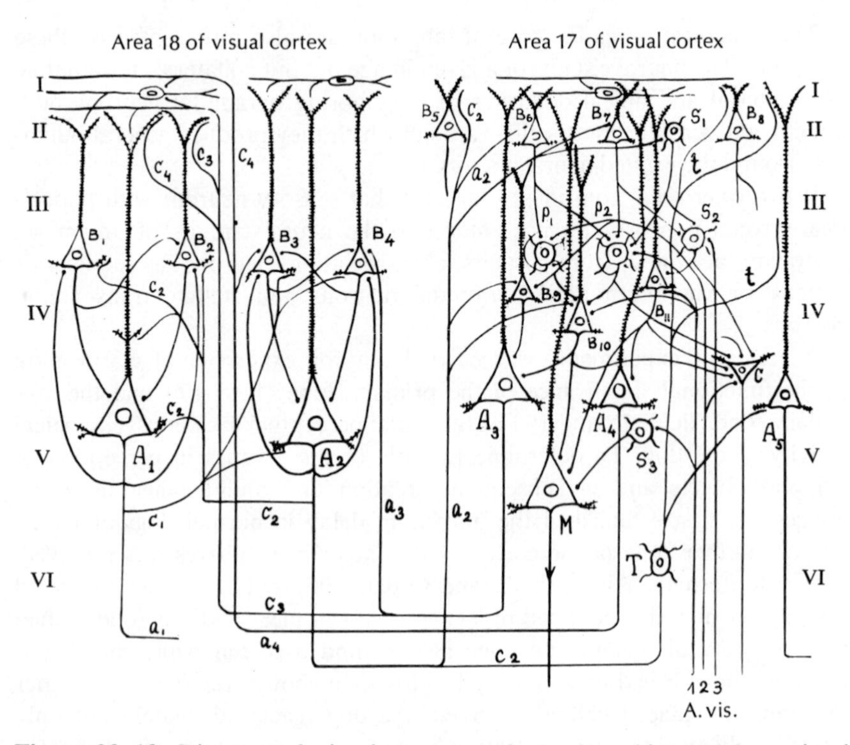

Figure 22–10. Diagram of visual area neural circuits which produce visual perception and orienting reactions. Sensory stellate neurons (P_1, P_2). Transmission stellate neurons (S_1, S_2, S_3). Internuncial neurons (B_1–B_2). Association neurons (A_1–A_4). Pyramidal projection neuron of Meynert (M). Projection oculomotor neuron of Cajal (C). Internuncial neuron of Martinotti (T). Neurites of association neurons (a_1–a_4). Collaterals of the preceding (c_3–c_4). In field 17 afferent visual fibers (*A. vis.*) from the thalamus are terminated on cells of stellate and internuncial neurons of layer IV and also on a cell of an oculomotor neuron. These stellate and internuncial neurons are linked with cells of association neurons (A_3 and A_4) and with a Meynert cell (M); the latter cell is also linked with a thalamic fiber via stellate cell S_3. During excitation of visual thalamic fibers this system of neurons produces, on the one hand, perception of an object, and, on the other hand, orienting reaction of head and eyes directed toward fixation of the eyes on the object.

Axons from association neurons A_3 and A_4 of field 17 proceed to field 19 and terminate there on cells of internuncial neurons B_3 and B_4, which, by their axons, converge on association cell A_2. An axon of this cell goes to field 17 and terminates there on cells of internuncial neurons of layer IV and then to an even greater degree on internuncial cells of layer II. Axons of the latter cells are terminated on stellate neurons of layer IV. During visual perception all these neural links are also activated and in this way a functionally united system is created which is preserved for a greater or lesser length of time and serves for reproduction of images of the entire object when only a portion of the object acts on the eyes.

Collateral C_2 of the axon of association neuron A_2 is terminated in field 17 neurons. Therefore, one must suppose that, during constantly changing environmental conditions, when one behavioral act is replaced by another, reverberation of excitation in the neural circuits of one image must necessarily be terminated when the neural circuits of another image are activated. Therefore we must not be dealing with prolonged preservation of images due to uninterrupted reverberation of excitation in the appropriate neural circuits.

In recent years the idea has frequently been expressed that the basis of the mechanism of image preservation lies in some constant intracellular molecular change in the cortical cells which participate in the neural circuits excited during perception (Hyden, 1960; Schmitt, 1962; and others). Molecular reorganizations must take place, particularly in the synaptic portions of the cell, and they must somehow facilitate transmission of excitation to specific neural circuits. When, later on, some link of those circuits becomes active under the influence of some part of a perceived object or its environment, this active condition may be distributed throughout the entire complex of these neural circuits. But the very activation of the sensory neurons which reproduce the image must take place secondarily under the influence of impulses from the activated neural circuits.

The view has also been expressed that the basis of fixation of the functionally united system lies in firm plastic changes in the structure of the synaptic apparatus (Konorski, 1961; Hebb, 1961). Such changes in the synapses undoubtedly must take place during excitation as changes of form or increase in size and number of synaptic endings (Plechkova, 1961; Kuparadze, 1964). But in order that such changes become permanent, lasting over many days and months, excitation must be frequent over a period of many days. The development of temporary bonds during formation of conditioned salivary or defense reflexes must depend on such plastic changes (Beritashvili, 1964).

Be this as it may, preservation of an image must depend upon preservation of a unique molecular and structural change in some system of association pyramidal neurons. Activation of this system by any action of the environment leads to excitation of the sensory neurons connected with it, that is, formation of an image of some object.

Figure 22–10 (*continued*)

on internuncial cell *T*, the axon of which is related to dendrites in the upper layers. In a precisely similar way the axons of association neurons A_3 and A_4, going to field 19, put out collaterals C_3 and C_4, which are terminated primarily on dendrites of the upper layers. Via these collaterals, activation of dendrites of neighboring internuncial and association neurons takes place and thereby produces general inhibition. This guarantees localization of excitation in a given functional system. In the diagram, bonds between the cortex and nonspecific thalamic fibers are not shown.

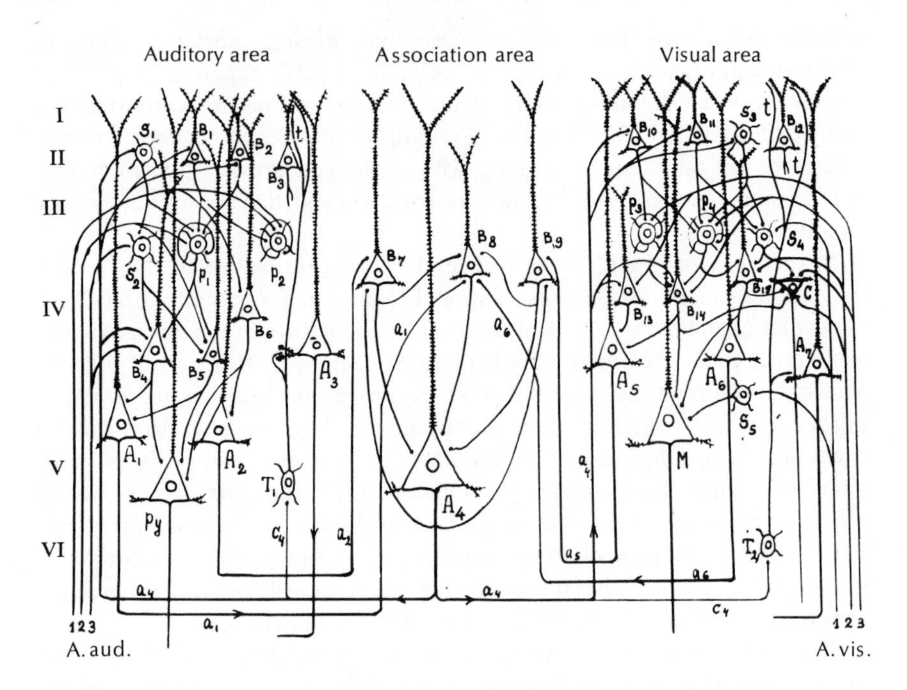

Figure 22–11. Diagram of neural circuits uniting auditory and visual perceptual areas of the cortex for perception and creation of an image of an object which makes noise. (Notation is the same as on Figure 22–10.) From the influence of a given object the thalamic fibers *A. aud.* and *A. vis.* in corresponding perceptual cortical areas activate sensory stellate neurons of layer IV (P_1–P_4), and also internuncial neurons (B_3–B_5, B_{12}–B_{14}). Through these neurons are activated association neurons (A_1–A_2, A_5–A_6), the axons of which go to an association field and converge on internuncial neurons B_7–B_9. The latter activate cells of association neurons A_4, from which axons go to auditory and visual perceptual areas and terminate there on internuncial neurons of layers II and IV. Via these neurons there is a supplementary excitation of both sensory neurons (P_1–P_4) and projection neurons of Meynert (M) and Cajal (C). Activation of this entire system of neurons produces perception and creates a visual-auditory image of a given object. This functional system is preserved for a more or less extended period of time. Therefore, under the influence of some portion of an object on the organs of hearing or sight there is an excitation of the entire system of neurons mentioned above with reproduction of a complete image of the perceived object and occurrence of the appropriate orienting reactions of the head.

In Figure 22–10, elicitation of perception and an image is represented thus: when an object acts on the eyes afferent impulses along neural routes 1, 2, and 3 stimulate sensory neurons P_1 and P_2. This produces a perception of the object. The afferent impulses also stimulate internuncial pyramidal neurons B_9, B_{10}, and B_{11}. These latter in their turn activate association neurons A_3 and A_4. The axons of these latter go to the secondary zone and, via internuncial neurons B_3 and B_4, stimulate association cell A_2. An axon of the latter, on the other hand, goes to the primary zone and via internuncial neurons B_6 and B_7 additionally stimulates the same sensory neurons, reinforcing perception of the object.

When afferent impulses emanate from part of an object, say via neural route 1, this stimulates only sensory neuron P_2, and a perception of the given part is obtained. But simultaneously stimulated internuncial neurons B_{10} and B_{11} activate association neurons A_3 and A_4. Impulses are transmitted via these latter to the secondary zone, stimulating neuron A_2; its impulses go to the primary zone and activate both sensory neurons P_1 and P_2. A subjective reflection of the entire object (i.e., its image) is produced. In Figure 22–11 there is a similar schematic picture of perception and the elicitation of an image from an object acting on hearing and sight.

We conducted a series of investigations on dogs to clarify experimentally the roles of primary and secondary zones in the elicitation and preservation of an image. After preliminary study of the behavior of a dog we removed one or another zone of the visual perceptual area. Our coworker Sikharulidze (1962a, b) in one series of experiments removed all three fields (17, 18, 19) that is, all of the occipital lobes. As expected, adequate visual perception disappeared and the animal began to bump into obstacles. If one placed a bowl with meat at a distance of more than a meter in front of the animal's eyes it did not go to the food. By special experiments we were convinced that the animal could distinguish light from dark and we were able to teach automatic feeding behavior to a lighted screen and developed differentiation to a dark screen. It is known that such automatic feeding behavior can be developed also in animals lacking the neocortex (Ordzhonikidze and Nutsubidze, 1961).

In another series of experiments, field 17 was removed. When one hemisphere was removed the animal's reaction to visual stimulation was in general unchanged. But changes were noted after removal of field 17 in both hemispheres. The first experiment was done after one week. The animal bumped into obstacles. It recognized the cage or the feeder after bumping into it. After two weeks it bumped into things rarely, and later on it stopped bumping into things; food, cage, and feeder were recognized at a distance.

Prior to operation Sikharulidze taught a dog to make a specific response when it perceived figures of an animal projected on a screen. To the figure of a rabbit, for example, the animal went to the right-hand feeder, and to the figure of a chicken it went to the left-hand feeder. The feeders were 5 m. from the cage. Immediately after bilateral removal of field 17 this behavior was destroyed: the dog came out of its cage upon projection of the figure, went right up to the screen, but did not go to the appropriate feeder.

After two weeks with several sessions with figures and feeders appropriately paired, the animal began to go to the correct feeders. But it made a great many mistakes; it went first to the place where it had last eaten food. Regular, accurate movement was established with a great deal of difficulty at the end of two months after a considerably greater number of feedings than were needed for primary establishment of this behavior prior to the operation. Under these circumstances the animal went to the appropriate feeder not only during presentation of the figure but also several minutes after this. Differentiation of an entire figure from its parts, which was established prior to operation, was not re-established despite many trials over a period of many months. On projection of a part of the stimulus (e.g., the head) the animal went to the feeder even though it was not fed under this condition.

Thus, after bilateral destruction of field 17, we observe a certain defect of vision. This defect is expressed primarily in disruption of perception and in making it more difficult to establish temporary bonds between this perception and the projection pyramidal cells which produced the movements of the dog. This explains both the difficulty of establishment of differential movement to the feeders and the increased difficulty of differentiation of an entire animal picture on the basis of its parts. But however defective the images of the feed object and of its location, they arise immediately after first perception and are retained a long time.

This is apparently explained by the fact that, in these particular experiments with removal of cortex in the area of the primary zone of the visual perceptual area, some of the visual sensory neurons were preserved. As is known, the ascending visual routes also terminate in fields 18 and 19. Furthermore, some part of the primary zone might have escaped destruction.

In a third series of experiments, fields 18 and 19 were removed. After removal of these fields in one hemisphere, perception did not suffer to any measurable extent and automated activity was normal. But after removal of these fields in both hemispheres there was a very peculiar disorganization. The dog saw the feeder (bowl with meat) even at a considerable distance. If the bowl with food was removed to four or five meters and set in sight of the dog, the animal went to it. Note that it had the food in view constantly. But if the bowl was taken and placed behind a screen, the animal went there only for delays of no more than 10 or 15 seconds. After a more extended period of time, it did not go there. Characteristically, if the dog was led behind the screen and shown the food, it went there itself when liberated, even after several minutes. Otherwise stated, in a dog with bilateral removal of fields 18 and 19, orientation in space by means of visual images was seriously disrupted, but we found that orientation in space by means of an image of a traveled route on the basis of labyrinth (vestibular) reception was completely preserved. It is known from our experiments that images of spatial relations between the subject and external objects, and also between these objects, is established both in higher animals and in children not only by visual perception but also by vestibular perception. This latter occurs when the individual moves between the objects. It was also established that removal of fields 18 and 19 did not influence delayed reactions to auditory stimuli and that orientation in space by auditory perception was not destroyed.

After bilateral removal of fields 18 and 19 from a dog, we could soon re-establish previously formed conditioned-reflex movement to particular feeders on perception of particular animal figures. And dogs reacted correctly at the time of perception, immediately thereafter, or after ten or fifteen seconds. Later on, when the cage was opened, they went out and wandered around the room in search of food. From this it follows that the functional union of the sensory neurons necessary for achievement of perception takes place in the primary zone. Creation and preservation of visual images capable of regulating behavior a long time after perception are apparently accomplished with the indispensable participation of secondary-zone association neurons.

From these observations, it follows that prolonged preservation of the images of perceived objects depends essentially not on peculiarities of sensory neurons or neurons of the primary zone in general but on their connections with the secondary zone. Therefore we must not consider the phenomenon of emergence and preservation of images as a manifestation of trace processes in sensory neurons. It apparently depends primarily on peculiarities of more or less permanent intracellular molecular reorganizations in association pyramidal neurons which somehow facilitate transmission of excitation at synaptic parts of the cell. It must be considered that creation of a functional system of neurons of some image or other depends on the above-mentioned molecular and functional changes in the synaptic regions and that these changes arise after one volley of excitation impulses is transmitted across them.

However, it is now known that in reproduction of an image substantial importance attaches not only to the secondary zones but also to the prefrontal association area (Konorski, 1961; Lawicka and Konorski, 1959; Beritashvili *et al.*, 1965). In our experiments, under bilateral removal of gyrus proreus memory suffers in visual, auditory, and vestibular perception. And in this case we observed memory disorganization for several weeks; moreover, it took place simultaneously in visual, auditory, and vestibular perception. It was gradually re-established after several months. Apparently, an image of some object is normally created and preserved as a firm system of reverberating neuronal circuits with simultaneous participation of secondary zones and the prefrontal area. Summated impulses of these circuits acting on sensory neurons of the primary zone call forth the reproduction of an image of an object. Gradual re-establishment of memory after operation appears to depend on training with maximum delay, as was established in our experiments. For example, on showing food to each animal the maximum delay at first consists of several minutes, and after numerous repetitions from day to day the maximum delay reaches twenty or thirty minutes (Beritashvili *et al.,* 1965).

Motor Activity of Reproduced Images

Sechenov accorded reproduced images of the outer world considerable significance in the vital activity of the organism (1952). He believed that they regulated behavior and suggested that images of vitally important objects might elicit the same external reaction (some act of adaptation to the environment) as would perception of these objects itself.

We can now give a similar explanation of this phenomenon. During perception of the outer environment an orienting reaction is always elicited. This produces head turning and fixation of the perceived object with the eyes to improve perception of the object. The appropriate structural mechanism must exist in layer IV of the primary zone of the perceptual area which receives afferent fibers from the receptors. Thus, in the visual primary zone the structural mechanism of the orienting reaction must include Meynert's pyramidal cells and so-called Cajal stellate cells. Their axons leave the cortex and go to the midbrain, terminating in the anterior corpora bigemina. Thence the neural route from the Cajal cells is continued to the oculomotor nucleus, and therefore it must serve for fixation of the eyes; from these Meynert cells the route goes to the spinal cord and apparently elicits movement of the head. Afferent fibers terminate on Meynert and Cajal cells either directly or via transmission neurons, group II stellate cells and internuncial pyramidal neurons (Figure 22–12). Consequently, Meynert and Cajal cells are stimulated with every perception of the environment, eliciting orienting movements of the head and eyes. It must be assumed that the cortical neural complex responsible for perception of the environment is united with Meynert and Cajal projection neurons of the corresponding orienting reaction so that each time an image of the external world is reproduced there may also be an appropriate orienting movement of head and eyes (Figures 22–10 and 22–11).

Perceived external objects are projected outwardly into those very places of the external environment from which they acted effectively. The capacity to project perceived objects outward is an inherent capacity of the whole functional neuron system by means of which external objects are perceived. Therefore, neonate animals (colts, shoats) orient themselves in space in the first hours after birth. For example, the first time a shoat leaves the mother for any distance, it runs back to her grunting call. If the neonate shoat is attached to a particular nipple of the mother and is then taken away from that nipple and led aside, on return to the mother it reattaches itself to the very same nipple (Beritov, 1935a).

Reproduced images also are projected in the same location from which they acted effectively. As established by Sechenov, with respect to a process in the neural apparatuses it is actually all the same whether one sees a given object or remembers it (Sechenov, 1952, p. 91).

We are now in a position to state the morphophysiological basis of this equivalence of perception and image. During perception of any object we find participation of receptors, relay sensory nuclei in the brain stem and, finally, the cerebral cortex. It has now been established that the cortex, relay nuclei, and receptors are excited even during reproduction of an image. From the cortex and also from relay nuclei, efferent routes go to the receptors where they terminate on perceptual or on relay neural elements. In the retina, for example, they terminate on amacrine and bipolar cells (Polyak, 1957; Granit, 1955; Shkol'nik-Yaross, 1961). Accordingly, relay nuclei and receptors are excited during reproduction as well as during perception. Characteristically, when efferent routes are stimulated the receptor ceases to react to appropriate stimuli. Thus, when efferent routes to the organ of hearing are stimulated the individual grows deaf in the ear which is involved (Galambos, 1956). Apparently, this results from refractivity of the excited perceptual elements of the receptor.

It follows from these facts that, if there is excitation of cortex, relay nuclei, and receptors during image reproduction, the subjective effect must be the same as during perception itself. On this basis Bekhterev (1926) suggested that the efferent system of neurons fulfills the specific function of projecting reproduced images outwardly. Outward projection of reproduced images creates the same capacity for orienting movements adaptive to the environment as is the case during perception of the outer environment. In both cases, animal and man establish not only spatial relations between objects but also represent to themselves the quantitative and qualitative peculiarities of these objects.

Activation of the functionally united system of sensory and pyramidal neurons producing an image of a vitally important object is always accompanied by emotional excitation and its subjective and external expression. These emotional conditions are connected with both formation and satisfaction of the organism's biological needs: food and water, protection against harmful agents, reproduction, and so on.

Experiments on animals with removed neocortex clearly indicate that these animals are not deprived of all emotional reactions. Thus, for example, in the experiments of Ordzhonikidze and Nutsubidze (1961) cats without neocortex demonstrate a feeling of hunger and satiation. In the hungry condition they become restless, mew, and even cry furiously. When they are

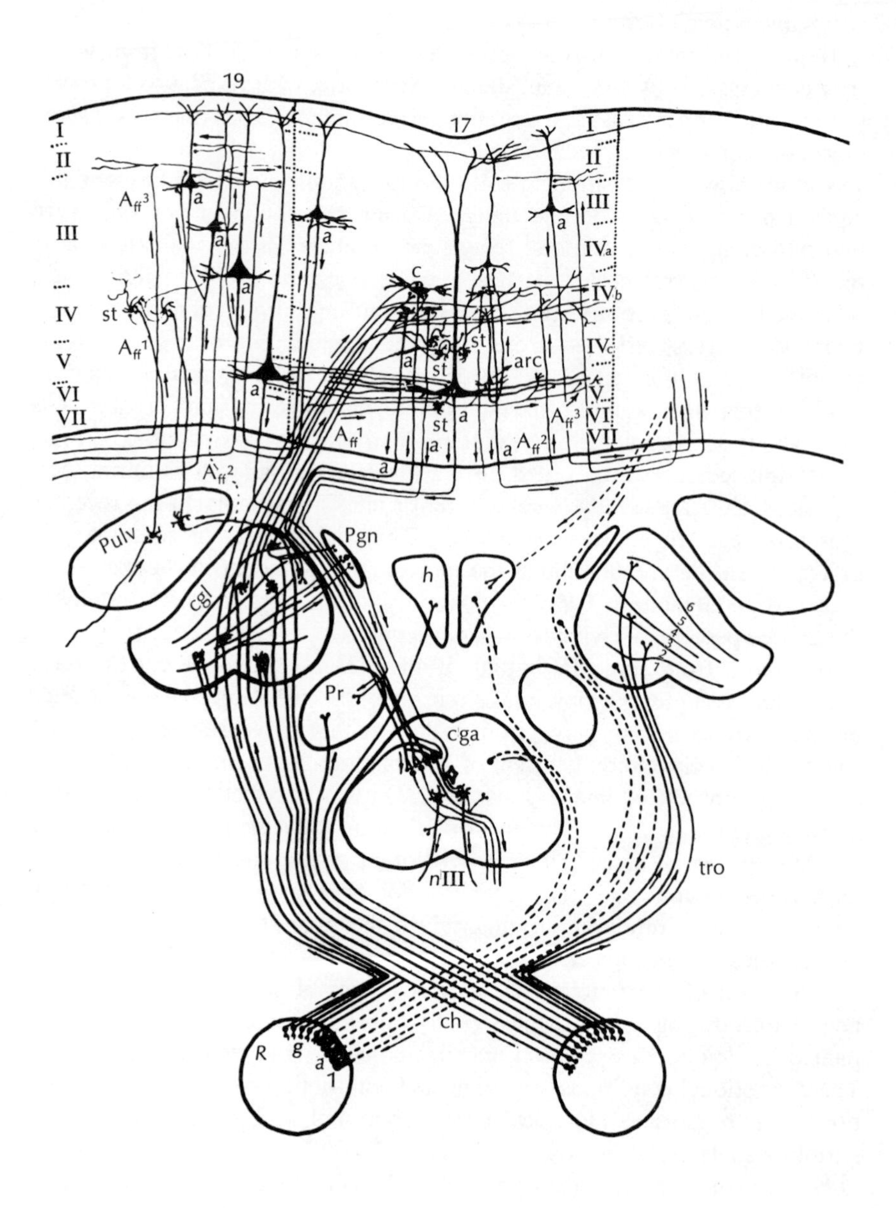
19
17
I
II
III
IV
V
VI
VII
IVa
IVb
IVc
a
c
st
arc
A_{ff}^1
A_{ff}^2
A_{ff}^3
Pulv
cgl
Pgn
h
Pr
cga
nIII
tro
ch
R
g
1

Figure 22–12.

satisfied they stop being restless and also stop mewing. Cats without neocortex easily enter into a rage during irritation of the skin. They are terrified by situations where they are subjected to painful stimulation (Beritov, 1961).

Furthermore, it is now known that during stimulation of certain parts of the archipaleocortex with live electrodes one can obtain all types of emotional reaction. During certain liminal stimulations of the amygdala there is a reaction of pricking up the ears, which changes to an orienting reaction and finally into terror expressed by retreat from the situation in which the stimulation is produced. During stimulation of another part of the amygdala there is a feeding reaction in the form of sniffing, approach, chewing, salivation, change of respiration, and so forth (Ursin and Kaada, 1960). Apparently, the amygdala is one of the central formations participating in integration of both defense and feeding behavior. Reactions of fear and rage are also elicited during stimulation of the cingulate gyrus (Nutsubidze, 1963). During stimulation of the piriform lobe, the animal gets up and begins to sniff for food and, not finding any, licks the floor and walls of the cage. It does this even in the satiated condition and, given food at this time, it will begin eating. When this stimulation is terminated, eating stops immediately, and the animal turns away from the food (Oniani, 1965).

It is generally accepted that some particular organic need underlies every emotional reaction. This organic need arises as a result of activation of definite nuclei of the archipaleocortex when the hormonal or metabolic condition of the internal milieu is altered. Accordingly, normal emotional reactions occur in the presence of corresponding organic needs. However, during direct stimulation of these nuclei the emotional reactions occur even

---

Figure 22–12. Diagram of neuronal bonds in the visual perceptual area. Schematic representation of cortical fields 17 and 19. Roman numerals indicate layers of the cortex: *left,* field 19; *right,* field 17. Borders between fields indicated by dotted line. Field 18 is not represented in the diagram. In the central portion of the diagram are given subcortical formations, below retina of the eye. Stellate Cajal cells (*C*). Short-axon stellate cells (*St.*). Specific afferents from geniculate body ($Aff._1$) Vertical afferents of unknown origin ($Aff._2$) Association afferent ($Aff._3$). Pyramidal Meynert cell (*M*). Pyramidal cell with arc-like axon (*Arc.*). Axons of pyramidal cells (*a*). Pulvinar of optic tubercle (*Pulv.*). Lateral geniculate body (*cgl.*) Pregeniculate nucleus (*Pgn.*) Hypothalamus (*h*). Pretectal nucleus (*Pr.*). Superior colliculi (*Cga.*) Oculomotor nerve (*n II*). Chiasma (*ch.*). Retina (*R*). Ganglion cells of the retina (*g*). Amacrine cells (a_1). Visual tract (*tro.*) Roman numbers indicate layers of lateral geniculate body. Dashed lines indicate efferent system of fibers which begins in the cortex and other sections of the brain and terminates in the retina on amacrine cells. (Diagram of Shkol'nik-Yaross prepared on the basis of his own data and data from Minkovskii, Le Gros Clark, Polyakov, Cajal, and Novokhatskii *et al.*)

in the absence of the appropriate need. But, characteristically, in both cases these emotional reactions easily form a basis for the establishment of individually acquired reactions to neutral sound or light stimuli after one or several pairings. It is occasionally sufficient to elicit some emotional reaction under given circumstances only once to obtain at least a fraction of it under the influence of all or part of the same conditions at a later time (Beritashvili, 1961). This occurs in normal animals as well as in animals with bilateral removal of the neocortex (Ordzhonikidze and Nutsubidze, 1961). This capacity disappears in totally decorticate animals, that is, after removal of both neo- and paleocortex. It follows that individual emotional reactions to neutral stimuli can be formed in the presence of the archipaleocortex only. It is known that stimuli act on the archipaleocortex via the reticular formation and also outside of it via nuclei of the diencephalon and that any neutral stimuli influence the paleocortex, eliciting electrical potentials. Consequently, any extraneous stimulation may be linked with emotional sensory elements of the archipaleocortex and its integrating mechanisms.

We suggest that in the archipaleocortex some complexes of sensory stellate cells produce a sense of hunger when excited, others a sense of satiety, others a sense of fear, and so forth. These sensory complexes are linked with definite integrative mechanisms of the pyramidal neurons by means of which the somatovegetative reactions of a corresponding emotional excitation are elicited (Beritashvili, 1961).

It may be assumed that, during the first effective influence of a vitally important object on the organism, a perception by means of the neocortex as well as an emotional excitation by means of the archipaleocortex is produced. As a result of the coincidence of these neuropsychic processes, differential neural bonds are first formed between excited sensory complexes of the neocortex and the archipaleocortex by means of association pyramidal neurons. Therefore reproduction of an image of a given object should lead not only to orienting reactions via the neocortex but also to emotional excitation of the archipaleocortex with its subjective experience and overt somatovegetative expression (Beritashvili, 1961).

Thus, higher animals and little children, under the control of reproduced images, can move about in the environment toward or away from vitally important objects according to their emotional character. This is the scientific basis for concluding that image-guided mental activity is the principal regulator of behavior in higher vertebrate animals and little children.

Voluntary Movements and Conditioned Reflexes

We consider the goal-oriented behavior controlled by images of the environment to be the voluntary movements characteristic of animals and young children. Adults are directed by conscious voluntary movements produced during definite work behavior in accordance with a previously set up plan of action.

However, as Sechenov suggested, goal-directed orienting movements are not necessarily regulated by psychological activity in the form of images of important objects or conscious planning of a behavioral act, that is, they are not always voluntary movements.

Well-learned automatic animal feeding behavior as well as skilled human behavior may flow along without participation of the mind. At the time of each link of the learned behavior, ascending afferent impulses from stimuli of the muscles and the labyrinth receptors and from stimuli of exteroceptors under the influence of the environment ineluctably elicit the link of the learned behavior which follows them in the chain.

Pavlov considered these automatically flowing learned movements to be a conditioned chain reflex. They may even flow without any subjective sensation because stimuli of the proprioceptors and labyrinth receptors under such conditions are not felt subjectively. Therefore, the term voluntary movements should not be applied to conditioned reflexes. As is known, Voronin and other authors try in every way to equate psychological activity with conditioned-reflex activity and do not recognize the qualitative differences between them. For example, they consider that the "focus" of excitation in the cortex and the "image" are identical phenomena, that all movements emanating from the cortex of the hemisphere are voluntary (Voronin, 1962), and that every conditioned reflex is at the same time a psychological act (Shustin, 1962, cited in Beritashvili, 1963a).

We have frequently proven with various kinds of facts that not every cortical activity is mental or voluntary. In the *Journal of Higher Nervous Activity* for 1962 and again in the *Symposium on Philosophical Questions of Higher Nervous Activity* in 1962 we examined critically and in detail all the incorrect conclusions which follow from an identification of a mental act with a conditioned reflex, and we will not repeat ourselves here. We shall only advance a few very persuasive facts which served as the basis for assuming qualitative difference between a mental act, a voluntary movement, and a conditioned reflex.

Usually, to establish conditioned-reflex feeding behavior, we lead the dog from the cage to the feeder by a short route on a given signal. After the first feeding the dog itself runs to the food location without a signal. We consider this phenomenon to be a voluntary act dependent on reproduction of an image of the food location. After the dog has frequently been led from the cage to the feeder during a given signal and fed, it begins to run just on the signal. We consider this running on signal a conditioned reflex, where the signal gives the impetus to leave the cage and the ultimate behavior is accomplished according to the principle of a conditioned chain reflex, because the proprioceptive, labyrinth, and external stimuli during each link of the behavior become conditioned signals for the succeeding link of behavior. It is not difficult to substantiate this inference experimentally. If one transported the feeder and the signal which was always located at the feeder to another location while the dog is watching, it would run on signal to the usual place of food and only then go to the new food location. Apparently, the neural circuits of the entire reflex chain in the cortex of the hemispheres produced such a general inhibition of the cortex that the regulatory influence of the mental act (the image of a new location of the feeder) was ineffective. Initially, prior to complete formation of a conditioned reflex, after transfer of the feeder and signal to a new location the dog went directly to the new spot. We knew this thirty years ago (Beritov, 1934b).

Not long ago even more persuasive facts were obtained. A fellow worker in our institute, Aivazashvili (1965), while sounding a bell led a dog to a feeder by a complicated route, not by a short route. First they went left for 4 or 5 meters to feeder 1, where the bell was located; not showing food and not feeding here, they immediately proceeded right for two meters up to feeder 2; and then they backtracked for 5 or 6 meters to feeder 3, and only here was food given. After eating, they returned by the same route, first to feeder 2, then to feeder 1, and finally to the cage. In the backward route the dog was not shown food in these feeders. Now, after one single feeding from feeder 3, the dog itself ran directly to this feeder and not by the route over which it had been led out. Obviously, this took place as a result of reproduction of an image of the food location in the third feeder. On the run to feeder 3 by the short route the dog was not fed. Forced leading on the sound of a bell by the complex route for feeding from feeder 3 was accomplished many times each day. But in the first days the dog ran on the sound signal directly to feeder 3, that is, by the short route. The first evidence of the formation of conditioned behavior appeared only on the fourth day after 40 to 45 leadings. On signal the dog first ran forward 3 to 3.5 meters and then ran directly to feeder 3. In cases of this sort the dog was not fed. Only after 80 to 100 feedings with leading by the complex route did the dog begin approximately to repeat this complex route.

However, the conditioned running of the complex route, despite hundreds of feedings, was rather unstable and was not repeated frequently. On the very best experimental day after five trials the dog completed the complex route, but on the eighth and ninth trials with the conditioned signal it went to the feeder by the shortest route. Frequently, in precisely this same way, at the beginning of an experimental day on the first signals, the dog ran to feeder 3, only partially repeating the complex route, and after an interruption of two or three days, the dog began to go to the feeder by the shortest possible route.

All these facts indicate that, after one feeding from feeder 3, an image of the food location is created and feeding behavior is regulated by this image.

Then, only after repeated leadings by the complex route, a conditioned chain reflex was formed. But on the conditioned signal not only was this conditioned reflex elicited but, also, an image of the location of the food was reproduced. Because of this the dog frequently turned its head toward the food location and ran to it, abandoning the complex route.

If the dog was fed on this complex route from each of the three feeders, first from feeder 1, then from feeder 2, and, finally, from feeder 3, it began to run to all these feeders, running the route in the same order as during directed feeding after just one trial. This means that under this condition an image of the food and its location is projected to the feeders and apparently in that order in which feeding was accomplished. Characteristically, the dog ran this complex route voluntarily even when it did not receive food from the feeders. Clearly, such behavior resulted from serial reproduction of images of the food location.

These observations show that in the voluntary feeding movements there is an image of the food location created immediately after the first perception of this location. In this the animal uses both inherent and individually acquired or learned movements, that is, conditioned reflexes. In a conditioned reflex chain such as automated feeding behavior, a leading place is occupied by temporary connections established for each link of behavior in response to the external and internal stimuli regularly repeated before this link.

These observations clearly indicate that emergence of an image of the food location only facilitates formation and strengthening of conditioned behavior vis-à-vis this place if this conditioned behavior is produced along the same route as movement by image. If there is no such correspondence then we get an opposite effect, that is, reproduction of an image of the food location significantly impedes automatization of conditioned behavior because the neural circuits of the psychoneural process of the image of the food location, strengthening with every repetition, elicit strong general inhibition of the cortex and thereby depress the temporary bonds of the conditioned behavior which have been established.

This action of the image psychoneural process of food location which negates conditioned reflex running may be explained thus: the neural circuits of the psychoneural process, consisting primarily of internuncial and association pyramidal neurons, by their collaterals activate the uppermost dendrites of pyramidal neurons in the upper layers of the cortex. In accordance with the dendritic hypothesis of inhibition, this activation of dendrites produces general inhibition of the corresponding pyramidal cells (Beritov, 1961). As a result of this the excitability of these pyramidal cells falls; this must be the principal reason for difficulty in formation of temporary bonds involving participation of these cells. Afterward, when these temporary bonds, consisting again primarily of pyramidal neurons, are sufficiently firmed up after hundreds of trials, they may also elicit general inhibition of the cortex, due to activation of the uppermost dendrites by collaterals of the aforementioned pyramidal neurons. It must be the case that, in its turn, this depression acts on the pyramidal neuron composition of the psychoneural complex producing the image of food location, which leads to weakening of the motor activity of the reproduced image. This explains why, when the temporary bonds have been sufficiently strengthened, the dog runs to feeder 3 by the complex route and not by the shortest route under control of the image.

Summary

Behavior of higher vertebrate animals aiming at satisfaction of natural needs for food, self-defense, reproduction and so forth is of two types. The lower type, inherited and instinctive behavior, appears immediately after birth or during the ensuing stages of ontogenetic development, and is entirely based on inherited organization of the central nervous system. It flows through each of its links according to the stimulus-response principle. The higher type of behavior is individually acquired behavior based on reorganization of the central nervous system after one or many perceptions of the outer world. It is regulated by an image or by a concrete representation of vitally important objects (such as food or an enemy). In the case of the image of food location the animal tries to approach, and in the case of the image of an enemy it avoids the place or runs in the opposite direction, depending on the conditions which obtain at the time of perception.

The image of an external object is always created in a definite situation. This image is so closely connected with the situation that it is reproduced and projected onto the outer environment under the influence of part of the appropriate object as well as during perception of some component of the situation in which the object was originally perceived.

An image of an external object is created immediately on the basis of sensations elicited by this object which stimulate the various receptors; it is preserved for a long time, for a matter of days or months. However, it is improved with every new perception of the object. Reproduction of the image of the vitally important object may elicit the same goal-directed behavior as does perception of the object itself.

Individual behavior directed by images or, otherwise stated, image psychoneural activity, is the highest form of behavior for vertebrate animals and also for very young children. Adults are characterized by still another higher form of behavior (conscious work behavior), which is characterized by the fact that, prior to onset of the behavior, a verbal plan of this behavior is set up in accordance with previously noted behavioral objectives, that is, as a result of creation of an abstract image of the results of behavior.

With frequent repetition, image behavior directed by an image of a vitally important object, as well as conscious work behavior, under the very same conditions, are substantially altered, they begin to flow automatically. Each link of behavior, one after the other, follows the conditioned-reflex, route by means of established temporary bonds. In the meantime there is also a reproduction of the outwardly projected image of a vitally important object in animals or, in man, knowledge of the results of behavior. But this psychological activity begins to regulate behavior only if changes of the environment or internal milieu of the individual take place in such fashion that the conditioned-reflex neural bonds cease to be influential.

On the basis of contemporary knowledge of the structure and physiology of cortical neurons and also on the basis of clinical observations, we conclude that stellate neurons with pericellular axonal networks, which compose the basic mass of neurons in layer IV of the primary perceptual areas of the cortex, are sensory in nature. On being excited, these neurons produce the elementary subjective sensations of light, color, sound, taste, odor, touch, warmth, and cold. These modalities of sensing are determined not by the form of the stellate cells but by the nature of cytoplasm, which has evolved phylogenetically.

A large number of sensory neurons in one or several of the primary zones are involved in perception of external objects. Simultaneously, a multitude of internuncial and association pyramidal neurons are excited in both primary and secondary zones and in this way all excited sensory neurons are combined into one functional system. This functionally unified system is fixated, apparently, by means of more or less firm molecular reorganization in the cytoplasm of association pyramidal neurons of the secondary zones and association areas. Apparently, on repeated perception of a portion of a given object or of the environment in which this object occurs, there is an activation of these same pyramidal and sensory neurons and the same perception is reproduced. This reproduced perception is an image or a concrete representation.

With many repetitions of image behavior, conditioned-reflex or learned behavior appears which must be based on formation of temporary bonds resulting from a stable plastic change of the synaptic endings on association neurons. When this occurs it must be the case that there are changes of form and increase in size and number of synaptic terminations, which facilitate synaptic transmission.

During each perception the animal turns its head and fixates the perceived object with its eyes. This takes place by means of excitation of particular efferent neurons in the primary zones which are also activated when an image of the external object is reproduced. The reproduced image is also projected outwardly to that very same portion of the environment where the perceived object was actively influential in the first place. Sechenov has already demonstrated that these two psychological processes (perception and image representation) are substantially equivalent. We now find that their structural and physiological bases are completely identical. In both these processes the cortex, relay nuclei, and receptors participate. But during reproduction of an image the relay nuclei and the receptors are excited after the cortex by efferent routes.

Each behavioral act occurs with emotional excitation reflecting the creation or satisfaction of some organic need. Nuclei of the archipaleocortex constitute the structural basis of emotional excitations. Subjective emotional experiences and integrations of overt emotional reactions take place in this area. Under the influence of a vitally important object the nuclei of the archipaleocortex are activated simultaneously with the neocortex. The neural complexes excited in these nuclei are united into one complete system with initial onset of excitation and, therefore, when an image of a vitally important object emerges, a particular emotional condition is also produced.

References

Aivazashvili, I. M. The role of the image in feeding behavior of animals. *Zh. vyssh. nerv. Deyat.*, 1965.

Bekhterev, V. M. *General bases of reflexology in man.* Moscow-Leningrad, 1925.

Bekhterev, V. M. *The spinal and cerebral conducting pathways.* (3rd ed.) Leningrad, 1926.

Beritashvili, I. S. The role of emotional excitation in the behavior of higher vertebrate animals. *Trudy Inst. Fiziol. Gruz. Akad. Nauk,* 1961, *12,* 19–53.

Beritashvili, I. S. Les bases structurales et physiologiques de l'activité psychique. *Neuropsychologia,* 1963, *1,* 104–143. (a)

Beritashvili, I. S. The characteristics and origin of voluntary movements in higher vertebrates. *Prog. Brain Res. Brain Mechanisms,* 1963, *1,* 340–348. (b)

Beritashvili, I. S. The characteristics and origin of memory in mammals. In *All-Union Congress of Physiologists, Erevan (27 October 1964).*

Beritashvili, I. S., and Aivazashvili, I. M. On the effects of g. proreus ablation on delayed reactions in dogs. *Byull. Akad. Nauk GSSR,* 1965.

Beritashvili, I. S., Aivazashvili, I. M., and Ordzhonikidze, T. A. On the origin of delayed reaction in dogs. In *Modern problems of the activity and structure of the central nervous system.* Tbilisi, 1965.

Beritoff (Beritashvili) I. S., and Kalabegashvili, S. Salivary secretion caused by imagining food. *Uch. Zap. Tbilisi Univ.,* 1944, *26,* 41–60.

Beritoff (Beritashvili), I. S. On the fundamental nervous processes in the cortex of the cerebral hemispheres. *Brain,* 1924, *47,* 109–148; 358–376.

Beritov (Beritashvili), I. S. Über die individuel-erworbene Tätigkeit des Zentralnervensystems. *J. Psychol. Neurol.,* 1927, *33,* 113–335.

Beritov (Beritashvili), I. S. *Individually acquired activity of the central nervous system.* Tbilisi, 1932.

Beritov (Beritashvili), I. S. On the psycho-nervous principles of labor behavior of man. *Travaux Biol. Acad. Sci. USSR, Filiale Transcauc. Section Georgienne,* 1934, *1,* 41–76. (a)

Beritov (Beritashvili), I. S. Studies on individual behavior in dogs. Communication 7. *Fiziol. Zh. SSSR,* 1934, *17,* 912, 1186. (b)

Beritov (Beritashvili), I. S. Inherent food behavior in newborn puppies and pigs. In *Problems of biology and medicine.* (L. S. Stern memorial volume.) Moscow-Leningrad, 1935. P. 69. (a)

Beritov (Beritashvili), I. S. Studies on individual behavior in dogs. Communication 8. *Fiziol. Zh. SSSR,* 1935, *18,* 994. (b)

Beritov (Beritashvili), I. S. Comparative study of individual behavior in higher vertebrates. *Byull. Akad. Nauk SSSR,* 1939, *84,* No. 10, 1.

Beritov (Beritashvili), I. S. On the Nervous Mechanisms of Animal Spatial Orientation. *Symp. Soc. Exp. Biol.,* 4, 1950, Cambridge.

Beritov (Beritashvili), I. S. On the origin of the inhibition of nervous elements in the cerebral cortex. *Acta neurol. Latino-Amer.,* 1960, *6,* 137–162.

Beritov (Beritashvili), I. S. Nervous mechanisms of behavior in higher vertebrates. *Byull. Akad. Nauk SSSR.* Moscow, 1961.

Beritov (Beritashvili), I. S. *Neural mechanisms of higher vertebrate behavior.* Boston: Little, Brown, & Co., 1965.

Beritov (Beritashvili), I. S., and Bregadze, A. N. Zur Physiologie des Verhaltens der Tiere auf eine Komplexreizung: III. Mitteilung. *J. med. Biol.* 1929, No. 4, 83–101.

Beritov (Beritashvili), J., and Bregadze, A. On the physiology of behavior in response to complicated stimuli. *J. med. Biol.,* 1930, *3,* Nos. 1–2, 104–126.

Bonin, G., Carol, H. W., and McCulloch, W. S. The functional organization of the occipital lobe. *Biol. Sympos.,* 1942, *7,* 165.

Bregadze, A. N. Zur Physiologie des Verhaltens der Tiere auf eine Komplexreizung: V. Mitteilung. *J. med. Biol.,* 1930, *3,* No. 6, 483–498.

Bregadze, A. N. A study of individual behavior in cats. *Byull. Akad. Nauk GSSR,* 1946, *7,* 475–484.

Creutzfeldt, O., and Akimoto, H. Konvergenz und gegenseitige Beeinflussung von Impulsen aus der Retina und den unspezifischen Thalamuskernen an einzelnen Neuronen des optischen Cortex. *Arch. Psychiat. u. Z. Neurol.,* 1958, *196,* 520.

Estable, C. Considerations on the histological bases of neurophysiology. In J. F. Delafresnaye (Ed.), *Brain mechanisms and learning.* Oxford: Blackwell, 1961. Pp. 309–334.

Filimonov, I. N. Basic laws of evolution of the mammalian cerebral cortex. In *Third United Scientific Conference on the Problems of the Structure and Development of the Cerebral Cortex.* Inst. Neurol. Med. USSR, 1948, 3.

Galambos, R. Suppression of auditory nerve activity by stimulation of efferent fibers to cochlea. *J. Neurophysiol.,* 1956, *19,* 424.

Granit, R. *Reception and sensory perception.* New Haven: Yale Univer. Press, 1955.

Hebb, D. O. Distinctive features of learning in the higher animals. In J. F. Delafresnaye (Ed.), *Brain mechanisms and learning.* Oxford: Blackwell, 1961. Pp. 37–53.

Hernandez-Peon, R., Dittborn, J., Borlone, M., and Davidovich, A. Changes of spinal excitability during hypnotically induced anaesthesis and hyperesthesia. *Int. Congr. Physiol. Sci.* Vol. 21. Buenos Aires, 1959. P. 124.

Hernandez-Peon, R., and Donoso, M. Influence of attention and suggestion upon subcortical evoked electric activity in the human brain. In *Proc. I Int. Congr. Neurol. Sci.* Vol. 3. 1959. P. 385.

Hyden, H. Neuron. In J. Brachet and A. E. Mirsky (Eds.), *The cell.* Vol. 4, Part I. New York: Academic Press, 1960. Pp. 215–323.

Jung, R. Microphysiology of cortical neurons and its significance for psychophysiology. *Ann. Tac. Med. Montevideo,* 1959, *44,* 323.

Jung, R. Korrelationen von Neuronentätigkeit und Sehen: Neurophysiologie und Psychophysik des visuellen Systems. Symposium in Freiburg, 1960. P. 410.

Konorski, J. The physiological approach to the problem of recent memory. In J. F. Delafresnaye (Ed.), *Brain mechanisms and learning.* Oxford: Blackwell, 1961. Pp. 115–132.

Kuparadze, M. P. Plastic properties of the brain axons. Doctoral dissertation, Tbilisi, 1964.

Lawicka, W., and Konorski, J. Physiological mechanisms of delayed reactions: The effects of prefrontal ablation on delayed reactions in dogs. Comm. 3. *Acta Biol. Esper.,* 1959, *19,* 221–231.

Li, C. L. Cortical intracellular potentials and their responses to strychnine. *J. Neurophysiol.,* 1959, *22,* 436.

Li, C. L., Cullen, C., and Jasper, H. H. Laminar microelectrode studies of specific somatosensory cortical potentials. *J. Neurophysiol.,* 1956, *19,* 111.

Lindsley, D. B.., Bowden, K. W., and Magoun, H. W. Effect upon EEG of acute injury to the brain-stem activating system. *EEG clin. Neurophysiol.,* 1949, *1,* 475.

Lindsley, D. B., Schreiner, L. H., Knowles, W. B., and Magoun, H. W. Behavioral and EEG changes following chronic brain-stem lesions in the cat. *EEG clin. Neurophysiol.,* 1950, *2,* 483.

Lorente de Nó, R. La corteza cerebral del raton. *Trab. Lab. invest. Biol. Univer. Madrid,* 1922, *20,* 41.

Lorente de Nó, R. Cerebral cortex. In J. F. Fulton (Ed.), *Physiology of the nervous system.* Oxford, 1943. P. 274.

Moruzzi, G., and Magoun, H. W. Brain stem reticular formation and activation of the EEG. *EEG clin. Neurophysiol.,* 1949, *1,* 455.

Nutsubidze, M. A. Emotional reaction of cat evoked by stimulation of g. cinguli. *Trudy Inst. Fiziol. GSSR,* 1963, *13,* 103–111.

O'Leary, J. L. Structure of the area striata of the cat. *J. comp. Neurol.,* 1961, *75,* 131.

O'Leary, J. L., and Bishop, G. H. The optically excitable cortex of the rabbit. *J. comp. Neurol.,* 1938, *68,* 423.

Oniani, T. The role of the lobus pyriformis and hippocampus in emotional reactions of cat. *Byull. Akad. Nauk GSSR,* 1965.

Ordzhonikidze, T. A., and Nutsubidze, M. A. The role of the archicortex in emotional reactions of the cat. *Trudy Inst. Fiziol. GSSR,* 1961, *12,* 95–104.

Pavlov, I. P. *Twenty years' experience of objective investigation of higher nervous activity in animals.* (5th ed.) Leningrad, 1932.

Penfield, W. *The excitable cortex in conscious man.* Liverpool Univer. Press, 1958.

Penfield, W., and Jasper, H. *Epilepsy and the functional anatomy of the human brain.* Boston: Little Brown, 1954.

Plechkova, E. K. *Response of the nervous system of an organism to chronic lesion of peripheral nerves.* Moscow, 1961.

Polyak, S. *The vertebrate visual system.* Univer. Chicago Press, 1957.

Polyakov, G. I. On the ratio of main types of neurons in the cerebral cortex of a man. *Zh. vyssh. nerv. Deyat.,* 1956, *6,* 469–478.

Polyakov, G. I. Recent data about neurons and interneuronal connections in the central nervous system. *Tez. Dokl. VI Kongr. Gistol Embryol.,* 1958, 78–83.

Preobrazhenskaya, N. S. Postnatal ontogenesis of the occipital region. *Trudy Inst. Mozga SSSR,* 1948, *6,* 44.

Sarkisov, S. A., and Polyakov, G. I. Neurons and interneuronal connections in the cerebral cortex. In *Cytoarchitecture of the human cerebral cortex.* Medgiz, 1949.

Schmitt, F. Psychophysics on molecular and submolecular levels. In *Horizons in biochemistry.* (Albert Szent-Gyorgyi dedicatory volume.) 1962. Pp. 338–354.

Sechenov, I. M. Brain reflexes. *Selected works.* 1952, 7–128. Remarks on Kavelin's book, *Problems of psychology, ibid.,* 129–171; By whom and how is psychology to be worked out, *ibid.,* 172–268; Elements of thought, *ibid.,* 272–426.

Segundo, J. P., Arana, R., and French, J. D. Behavioral arousal by stimulation of the brain in the monkey. *J. Neurol. Neurosurg. Psychiat.,* 1955, *12,* 601.

Shkol'nik-Yaross, E. G. On the morphology of the visual analyzers. *Zh. vyssh. nerv. Deyat.,* 1954, *4,* 289.

Shkol'nik-Yaross, E. G. The question of the structure of the brain ending of the visual analyzer in primates. *Probl. fiziol. Optik.*, 1955, *11*, 162.

Shkol'nik-Yaross, E. G. Efferent pathways of the visual cortex. *Zh. vyssh. nerv. Deyat.*, 1958, *81*, 123–136.

Shkol'nik-Yaross, E. G. Some forms of interneuronal connections in the visual system. *Zh. vyssh. nerv. Deyat.*, 1961, *11*, 680.

Sholl, D. A. The organization of the visual cortex in the cat. *J. Anat.*, 1955, *89*, 33.

Shustin, N. A. Speech made on I. Beritashvili's report at the Symposium of All-Union Conference on Philosophical Questions of Higher Nervous Activity. Moscow, 1962.

Sikharulidze, N. I. Some data on the study of the 17th field in dogs with removal of visual analyzer. *Byull. Akad. Nauk GSSR*, 1962, *28*, 725. (a)

Sikharulidze, N. I. Some data on the study of partial and complete removal of the visual analyzer in dogs. *Byull. Akad. Nauk GSSR*, 1962, 725. (b)

Tolman, E. C. *Purposive behavior in animals and men.* New York: Appleton-Century-Crofts, 1932.

Ursin, H., and Kaada, B. Functional localization within the amygdaloid complex in the cortex. *EEG. clin. Neurophysiol.*, 1960, *12*, 1–25. (a)

Ursin, H., and Kaada, B. Subcortical structures mediating the attention response induced by amygdala stimulation. *Exper. Neurol.*, 1960, *2*, 109–122. (b)

Voronin, L. G. On the problem of the mechanisms of voluntary movements. *Zh. vyssh. nerv. Deyat.*, 1962, *12*, 569–577.

23

The Modeling Properties of the Nervous System

E. N. Sokolov

EDITORS' INTRODUCTION

Among the most influential lines of research pursued in Soviet psychology and psychophysiology of recent years has been the study of the reflex basis of attention carried on by E. N. Sokolov and his associates at Moscow University. Sokolov's interest in the "orienting reflex" grew out of work he had been conducting in Kravkov's laboratory on sensory interaction; he found that in some cases the effect of one sensory system on another weakened with repeated trials. From 1952 to 1956 he studied this "extinction" effect as the sensory component of the orienting reflex (a term borrowed from Pavlov), using electrophysiological techniques (Sokolov, 1963). This research received wide attention in the U.S.S.R. and later in the West, where both translations (Voronin, Leont'ev, Luria, Sokolov, and Vinogradova, 1966) and new research on the orienting reflex (Maltzman and Raskin, 1965) were undertaken.

Most recently Sokolov has concentrated on a search for the neural mechanisms of the orienting reflex, which he views as being closely related to the problem of the neural basis of memory. His quest for the material basis of the neural model of the stimulus has led to micro-electrode studies on mollusks and other lower organisms. Given the trend of his research, a combination of psycho-

physical, neurophysiological, and biochemical techniques can be expected in Sokolov's future research.

This chapter was taken from a recent collection of essays on the application of cybernetic principles to the study of cognitive processes (Berg, 1964). The interested reader is referred to Sokolov's (1963) monograph.

Models and the Nervous System

The theory of reflex activity, which regards behavior as a system of regular responses by an organism to environmental agents, has become an established part of the literature dealing with learning theory. Unfortunately, some analyses of the reflex principles of behavior amount to highly oversimplified accounts of reflex activity. It thus happens that ideas fundamental to a dialectical materialist theory of learning (such as the concepts of an image of the external world, of reflection) are not fully developed in certain cases, but are equated with the simple reflex. One reason for this state of analysis is that writers have failed to deal adequately with that part of the reflex which Sechenov (1863) termed the central part of the reflex arc. Yet the neurophysiological processes which take place in the central divisions of the nervous system are of primary importance in all reflex activity. Study of these is necessary if we are to discover the processes through which images are formed, and to demonstrate the laws that govern the way in which the human mind mirrors the external world.

Cybernetics has proved valuable in this work in that it has provided investigators with a focus for studying the formation and function of images through a comparison of the complex behavior exhibited by living organisms with that of self-adapting automatons.

One possible approach to analyzing the process of reflection is to consider the nervous system as a mechanism which models the external world by specific changes that occur in its internal structure. In this sense a distinct set of changes in the nervous system is isomorphic with the external agent that it reflects and resembles. As an internal model that develops in the nervous system in response to the effect of agents in the environment, the image performs the vital function of modifying the nature of behavior, allowing the organism to predict events and actively adjust to its environment.

The use of models, which is based on a mathematical analogy between a model and a system under study, presupposes that a model in some distinct way represents the behavior of an object or a process in nature. Operations with models in physics do not make use of all points of similarity between nature and a model but only of those which are relevant to relationships the investigator wishes to study. A description of the physical processes that occur in a model allows us to arrive at mathematical solutions to problems affecting the system under study. Further, in many cases the resemblance of the model to nature enables us to obtain a fairly good correspondence of functions through a simple change in the scales; when plotted graphically, these functions simultaneously describe processes being examined both in the model and in nature.

We may assume that the nervous system, which possesses a great many neurons capable of preserving traces of excitation, itself produces a model or imprint of agents from the external world. From this standpoint, changes occurring in the nervous system ought to resemble the agents which induced them. We should emphasize, however, that the resemblance will be partial rather than complete, apparently affecting only those relationships of interest to the organism in adapting to its surroundings. As understood here, then, the central nervous system can be thought of as a modeling system, whose complexity may characterize the complexity of the problems it has to cope with.

In this chapter I will consider certain types of neural activity as examples of the way in which neural models of external agents function to regulate behavior.

The Neural Model of a Stimulus and Its Properties

My first encounter with phenomena which indicated that the higher divisions of the central nervous system form models of external agents involved the study of reactions to "novel" features in the stimulus relating to research on the so-called *orienting reflexes.* The peculiar feature of the orienting reflex is that after several applications of the same stimulus (generally five to fifteen) the response disappears (or, as the general expression goes, "is extinguished"). However, the slightest possible change in the stimulus is sufficient to reawaken the response. The disappearance of the orienting response cannot be explained in terms of decreased excitability, since a radical reduction of the stimulus to a value close to the absolute threshold of excitation will also revive the reaction. The selective nature of the extinction we have obtained can be demonstrated by recording a number of the components of the orienting reflex, such as eye movement, galvanic skin reflex, and depression of brain-wave rhythms. No matter how we alter the parameter of a stimulus after a response is extinguished, the orienting reflex inevitably recurs (the most striking expression of this being changes in brain-wave rhythms in humans and animals).

Research on the orienting reflex indicates that it does not occur as a direct result of incoming excitation; rather, it is produced by signals of discrepancy which develop when afferent signals are compared with the trace formed in the nervous system by an earlier stimulus. Within a certain range of amplitude and duration, the orienting response is proportional to the difference between the trace (as measured in units for the stimulus administered) and the stimulus operating at a given moment. When the effect produced in the nervous system by the stimulus operating upon it coincides with a trace that has formed earlier, the orienting reflex does not appear. Insofar as the magnitude of the orienting reflex depends upon the degree to which the stimulus coincides with the trace process, we can determine the entire "configuration" of the trace left in the nervous system from repeated applications of a stimulus by administering specially selected test stimuli. Research indicates that the trace left in the nervous system by a frequently administered stimulus has a certain resemblance to the stimulus itself. This gives us some grounds for regarding the trace of a stimulus in the nervous system as its unique neural model.

The formation of a neural model of a stimulus is analogous to the use of models in technology in that both the neural and the technological models describe processes taking place in the environment.

Let us consider a typical experiment used to study the neural model of a stimulus. A light of fixed duration, intensity, color, dimension, and location in space is presented repeatedly, and at equal intervals, to a subject who sits quietly and in total darkness before a screen. A continuous record of the electrical activity of the subject's brain makes it possible to observe the effect of each presentation of the stimulus. During the course of repeated applications of the stimulus, the subject's reactions to it (which consist of a depression of the regular electrical fluctuations of brain waves) grow fainter and subsequently cannot be detected. At this point a critical trial is employed: one of the constant parameters of the stimulus is altered and a changed stimulus is presented to the subject. If the change in the parameter of the stimulus reaches the threshold of discrimination, the extinguished reaction recurs, thus indicating that the nervous system has detected a difference between the signal which had been presented and the new stimulus. The reaction appears precisely when the external stimulus fails to match the established trace, that is, when it first appears distinct from the neural model which has been formed.

The diagrams in Figure 23–1 are examples of reactions to a signal under the following conditions: when the signal is intensified, weakened, lengthened, or shortened; when it is presented before the usual time; when it has been omitted at the usual time; when the nature of the signal has been changed. The orienting response also appears if, along with the light stimulus, we add a signal of another kind, such as a tone; similarly, it will be elicited if we exclude one of the elements in a complex of stimuli, for example, in that of light and sound.

Since the orienting reflex appears after a change in any parameter of a

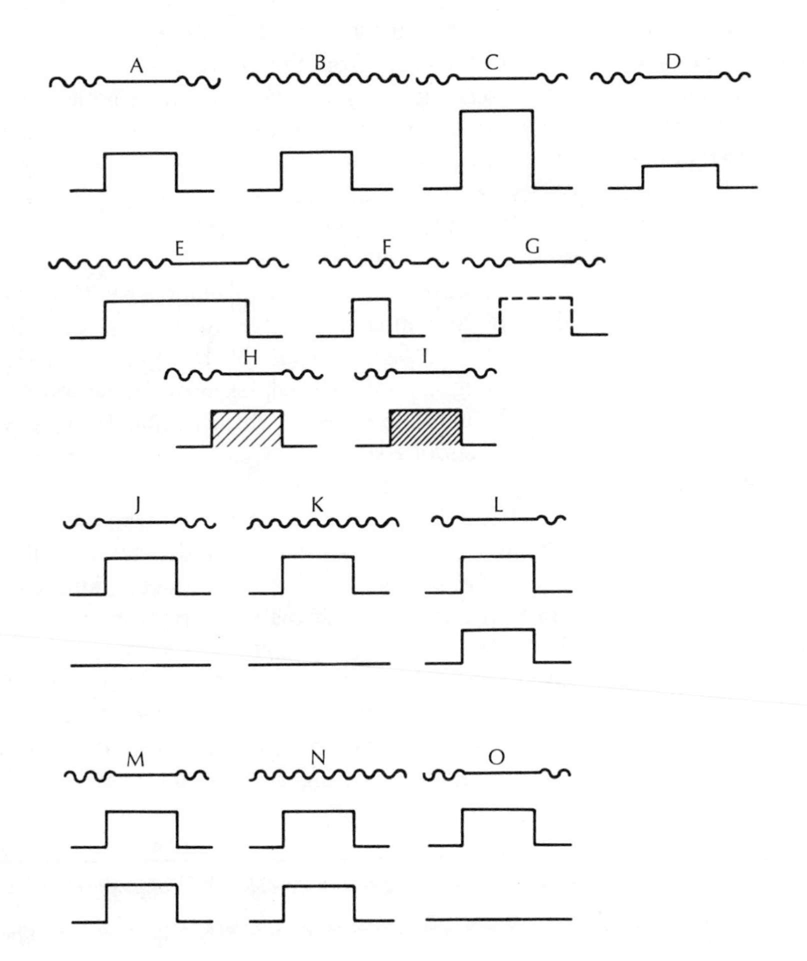

Figure 23–1. Diagram of a typical experiment to disclose trace processes. For each set (*A–O*), the top line presents a diagrammatic view of the alpha rhythm or its depression, and the bottom gives a diagram of the stimulus. (*A*) The first presentation of a stimulus produces a depression of brain waves. (*B*) After a number of presentations, the stimulus having a fixed parameter, it ceases to elicit a reaction. The reaction occurs when a stimulus is (*C*) intensified; (*D*) weakened; (*E*) lengthened; (*F*) shortened; (*G*) omitted; (*H, I*) qualitatively changed. (*J–O*) Here it should be noted that if a stimulus is lengthened or shortened, a reaction will occur precisely when the former meaning of the trace no longer coincides with stimulation actually in effect at the moment. (*J, K*) Experiments with complexes of two stimuli operating simultaneously. (*M, N*) These demonstrate the extinction of alpha blocking to one component of the complex. (*L*) When a second component is added, the reaction occurs. (*M, N*) When the reaction to the complex of stimuli has been extinguished, omitting one of the components (*O*) will also elicit a reaction.

stimulus (color, magnitude, form, duration, or rhythm), it follows that the model is a manifold image of the agent from the external world.

The neural model also accounts for complicated interrelations among stimuli affecting various sense organs. The so-called method of subtraction is one way to study the neural model of complex stimuli (that is, stimuli which simultaneously affect a number of receptors). This method involves the following procedure. Once the orienting reflex to a complex of stimuli disappears, the experimenter omits one element of the complex, and the orienting response is elicited again. The only explanation for this is that there is some mechanism which compares the stimulus operating upon the organism with a neural model (in short, signals of discrepancy are developed). Since experiments using a stimulus complex provide the most convincing demonstration of the intricate ways in which attributes of external objects are modeled by the nervous system, let us consider a specific instance of this type of research.

The first time a light stimulus is presented to a subject, who has his eyes open but is confined to a completely darkened room, a distinct alteration of the brain-wave rhythms in the occipital region is produced. This change involves both a decrease in the amplitude of the alpha rhythm (brain-wave fluctuations with an 8-to-12-cps frequency) and an increase in the basic frequency of brain-wave fluctuations, which are detected by means of an electronic frequency analyzer (see Figure 23–2).

The main part of the experiment begins once the light stimulus has been administered many times and the orienting reflex fully extinguished. A

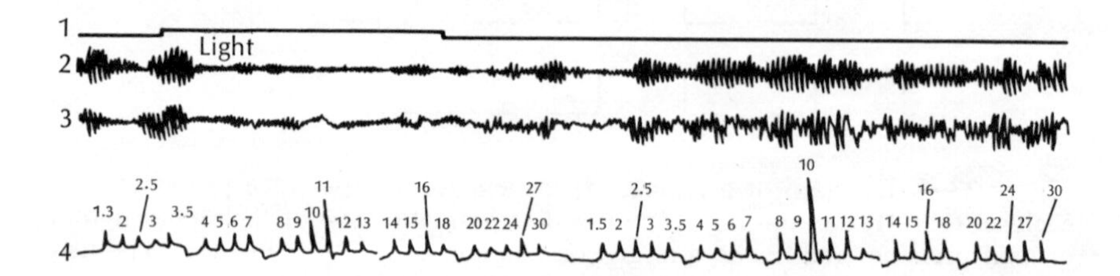

Figure 23–2. The first presentation of a light stimulus causing a local depression of alpha rhythm in the electroencephalogram of a human subject. The amplitude of the oscillations of the pen indicate the energy stored by the integrator during the 10 seconds of analysis. The numbers signify the frequency to which each filter was adjusted. It is apparent from the figure that the light causes a reaction in the occipital region, consisting of a depression of the alpha rhythms having a frequency of 10 cps, and a simultaneous transformation of the alpha rhythm to 11 cps but reduced in amplitude. When stimulation is discontinued, the basic alpha rhythm (a frequency of 10 cps) is restored. (1) Represents the light stimulus. (2) Alpha rhythm produced by means of an electronic filter adjusted to 10 cps. (3) Electroencephalogram of the occipital region. (4) Index of activity obtained from the Walter analyzer.

sound is then introduced simultaneously with the light stimulus. As a result, the orienting reflex reappears in the form of a brief depression of the alpha rhythm, both at the initial moment the stimulus complex is introduced and throughout the time it continues to operate. However, after the light-sound complex has been repeated a number of times, the reaction to this combination of stimuli disappears entirely. At this point, instead of presenting the subject with the light-sound complex, which his nervous system has already become accustomed to, the light stimulus is presented unaccompanied by sound, a change which elicits the orienting reflex once again. If we then introduce the light-sound complex again, it will prove effective for a certain period of time (see Figure 23–3).

Analogous experiments conducted with three different stimuli (light, sound, touch), operating one after the other (a sequential complex), indicate that the neural model of a stimulus not only reflects the coincidence of various stimuli, but also the temporal order in which they occur (Voronin and Sokolov, 1960).

The Neural Model of a Stimulus and the Nervous System's Capacity to Extrapolate Information

We have assumed that the orienting reflex is elicited by impulses which signify a discrepancy. When afferent stimulation fails to coincide with the neural model of a stimulus, we should expect the orienting reflex to continue as long as the difference holds—that is, throughout the period during which the stimulus is being compared to the trace in the nervous system. But in fact this is not what we find. The reaction appears only at the initial moment when the discrepancy is noted and disappears as the new stimulus continues to operate, although in relation to the model the stimulus still appears changed. If we are to explain this phenomenon, we must assume that during the time the new stimulus is operating the previous neural model has already been replaced by a new model which corresponds to the new stimulus. Thus, the neural model of a stimulus cannot be thought of as some static imprint. Rather, it constantly undergoes revisions in order to account for the characteristics of the stimulus which is operating at a given moment.

The dynamic aspect of the neural model has also been observed in experiments on the extinction of the orienting reflex, in which strict uniformity of the time intervals between presentations of stimuli was maintained. Selective extinction of the orienting response was obtained with respect to the temporal order of stimuli, but the response was elicited again when the sequence was disturbed—for example, by omitting a stimulus. Since this result is of particular importance for the material we will be dealing with

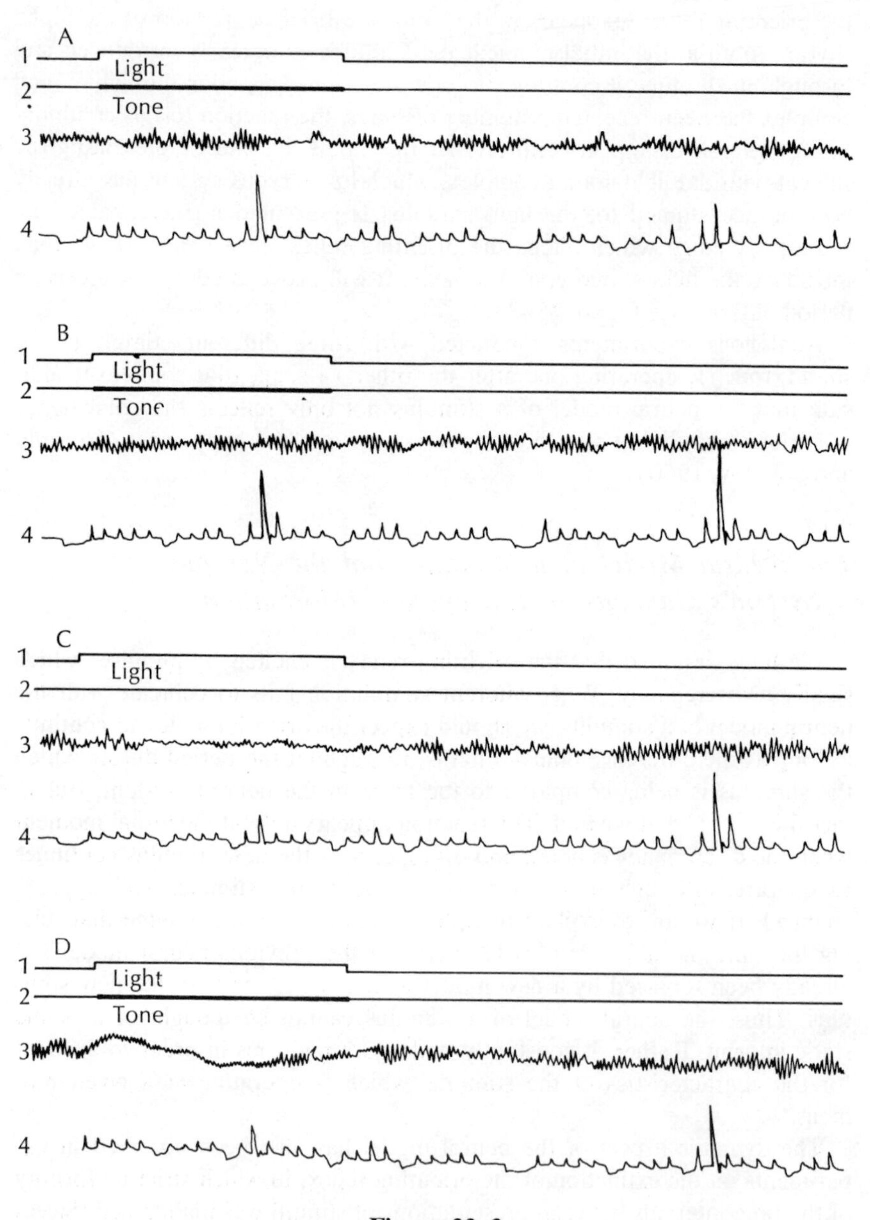
A
1
Light
2
Tone
3
4
B
1
Light
2
Tone
3
4
C
1
Light
2
3
4
D
1
Light
2
Tone
3
4

Figure 23–3.

later in this chapter, let us consider a specific case in which the EEG reaction was extinguished.

At first a light presented to the subject repeatedly at 20-second intervals produced a depression of the alpha rhythm. Subsequently the reaction diminished and then disappeared altogether. However, it was elicited again when the regularity of the sequence was disrupted by omitting a stimulus at the "usual" time. After the omission, there was recovery of the response to the stimulus which followed (see Figure 23–4).

In this experiment there was no external stimulus operating. The source of the reaction was a neural trace corresponding to the frequency with which stimuli were being presented. The absence of a stimulus at the regular time failed to conform to the neural model which had formed, producing excitation in the nervous system and a reaction in the form of a depression of the EEG. A change in the time interval at which signals were presented led to a restructuring of the neural model and, consequently, the production of a response, even though the next stimulus which elicited it appeared at the earlier frequency rate.

In this case it is possible to speak of a neural model of the distribution of a stimulus in time. In order to explain this phenomenon we must assume that the nervous system takes an exact reading of time intervals and develops impulses signaling the operation of an expected stimulus. Thus, when the stimulus starts to operate, afferent stimulation and the signal of anticipation (extrapolation) coincide. If the impulses developed by the nervous system and those caused by a stimulus operating at a given moment happen to coincide, there is no discrepancy signal and the orienting response does not appear. When these two types of impulses fail to coincide (as in the example cited in which a stimulus was omitted, thus giving rise to a

---

Figure 23–3. The orienting response which occurs after omitting one component of a complex of stimuli that had been operating simultaneously. Reading from top to bottom, each set (*A–D*) of diagrams: (1) Light stimulus. (2) Sound stimulus. (3) EEG of the occipital region. (4) Indices of the EEG frequency analyzer.

(*A*) After the reactions to light and sound were extinguished separately, the combination of these stimuli still elicited a weak reaction which could be detected only as a brief depression of the alpha rhythm. Changes in the spectrum of the brain-wave rhythms are within the range of possible fluctuations. (*B*) After a number of repetitions of the complex (light-sound) all reactions are extinguished. (*C*) With the exclusion of the sound, which was part of the complex, the light (operating in isolation) gives rise to a local depression of the alpha rhythm; this is observed in the change of the spectrum of brain wave rhythms (apparently a depression of brain waves having a frequency of 10 cps). (*D*) Following the presentation of one isolated component of the complex (the light), there is a recovery of the reaction to the complex (light-sound), although this reaction had previously been extinguished.

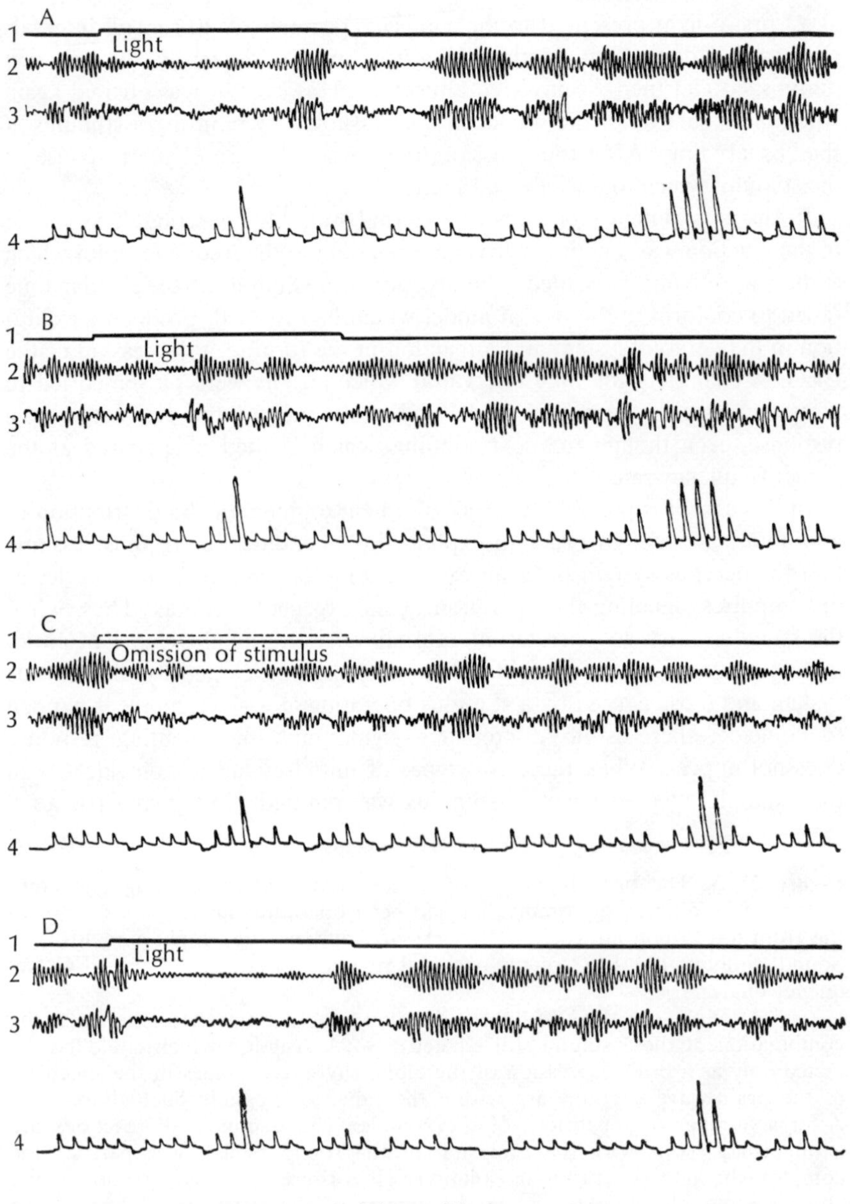
A
1
Light
2
3
4
B
1
Light
2
3
4
C
1
Omission of stimulus
2
3
4
D
1
Light
2
3
4

Figure 23–4.

situation in which the impulses of extrapolation were not attended by afferent impulses), the discrepancy signal, and the orienting reflex linked to it, occur.

How the Neural Model of a Stimulus Functions to Regulate Behavior

There is a unique biological regulator bound up with the phenomenon of the neural model of a stimulus which unifies the mechanisms of the orienting and the conditioned reflexes. Briefly outlined, this regulator may be conceived of as having the following elements: a mechanism for perception; a device which models images of external stimuli; a mechanism for comparing afferent stimulation with signals from the modeling component; an organ which controls the orienting reflex; and a component for carrying out the conditioned reflex, using signals from the modeling structure (see Figure 23–5). The impulses which control the orienting reflex can penetrate to the motor centers by two different paths: through the collaterals of the axons of specific paths, and through paths from the gray matter in the cerebral hemispheres which function to compare a trace with incoming afferent stimulation. With repeated presentations of a stimulus, those paths which lead through the collaterals and the system of supplementary neurons (so-called interneurons) to mechanisms which carry out the orienting reflex are

---

Figure 23–4. The orienting response which occurs when a light stimulus is omitted at the usual time. Reading from top to bottom, each set of diagrams (*A–D*) indicates: (1) Light stimulus. (2) Indices of the filter adjusted to 10 cps. (3) EEG of the occipital region of the brain. (4) Indices of the frequency analyzer.

(*A*) The reaction to the first presentation of the light in this experiment is weakened, owing to the influence of repeated extinction of the response in previous experiments. (*B*) After the light stimulus has been presented a number of times (after 20-second intervals that are strictly adhered to), the reaction disappears. (*C*) Indicates a disruption of the frequency with which stimuli are presented (by omitting a stimulus). The reaction occurs at the interval when the stimulus should have appeared; it differs in that it has a somewhat longer latency than it had when the stimulus was in fact operating. That there is a reaction at the moment when the stimulus should have been operating confirms the hypothesis that the nervous system takes a fairly accurate reading of time. (*D*) After a stimulus is omitted, we note a reappearance of the reaction to the stimulus which usually occurs, the reaction being significantly greater than it was when the signal was omitted. This indicates the existence of two mechanisms that participate in generating the orienting response: impulses which signal a discrepancy (seen in pure form when the stimulus was omitted) and disinhibition of the direct path of excitation to the performance mechanisms of the orienting reflex (expressed in terms of an intensified reaction to the stimulus which follows the one omitted).

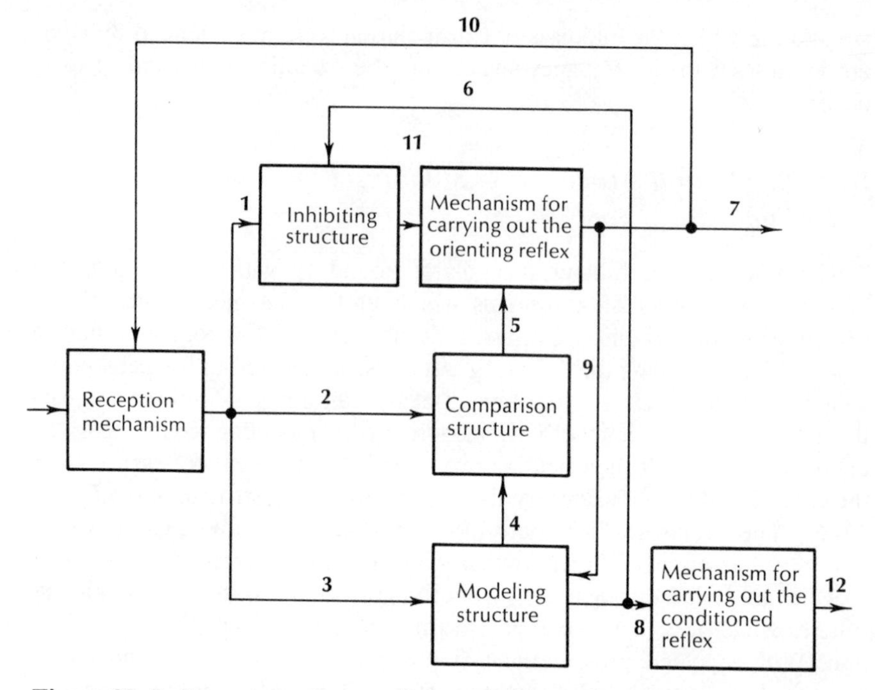

Figure 23–5. Structural schema of the orienting reflex. (1) Specific afferent stimulation proceeding through the collaterals to the efferent mechanisms across the inhibiting structure. (2) Specific afferent stimulation proceeding to the comparison structure. (3) Specific afferent stimulation proceeding to the modeling structure which contains the mechanism of extrapolation. (4) Impulses developed by the extrapolating mechanism and which enter the comparison structure. (5) The discrepancy signal that occurs when afferent stimulation is compared with the signal extrapolated. (6) Impulses of extrapolation used to inhibit afferent signals proceeding through the collaterals to the afferent mechanisms of the orienting response. (7) Efferent impulses of the orienting reflex. (8) Impulses of extrapolation which function in the mechanism of the conditioned reflex. (9) Feedback of the orienting reflex on the mechanism by which the neural model of a stimulus is formed. (10) Feedback of the orienting response on receptors. (11) Impulses which have bypassed the inhibiting structure. (12) Efferent impulses of the conditioned reflex.

blocked. This inhibition might be thought of in the following way. Any prolonged activity of a stimulus will, with the aid of the interneurons, lead to the development of an inhibitory process. When a stimulus is presented repeatedly, this process operates as an unconditioned reflex and forms a conditioned-reflex link with the stimulus presented. Once this conditioned inhibitory link has formed and a stimulus begins to act upon the organism, it functions as a signal for the inhibitory process to develop. Consequently, the path which conducts excitation through the branches is already closed when the stimulus to which the organism has become accustomed begins to operate. As for the path which has an indirect effect on the orienting reflex (through the mechanism of comparison), this remains. If it happens that afferent stimulation and the impulses extrapolating the meaning of a signal occur simultaneously, there will be no impulses to signify a discrepancy, and the investigatory response will not occur. But if a stimulus is either changed or suddenly omitted, afferent impulses no longer agree with the extrapolated meaning of the signal; hence, impulses signaling a discrepancy are elicited, as is the orienting response. Simultaneously, there is disinhibition of the path which leads directly through the collaterals and the interneurons to the centers of the orienting response. The reason for this is that the neural model of the stimulus breaks down and its effect on the conditioned-reflex mechanism of inhibition is weakened. This disinhibition is evident in that a single change in a stimulus which had been administered earlier (and to which reactions had been completely extinguished) will elicit the orienting reflex again.

One of the essential features of a neural model is that it anticipates the future significance of afferent impulses based on the past flow of impulses. Nervous impulses which anticipate the meaning of a stimulus are used by the nervous system in two ways: first, to arouse a positive conditioned response while a stimulus is in operation; second, to inhibit impulses approaching the centers which carry out the orienting reflex. Impulses which anticipate the meaning of afferent signals are constantly being checked against afferent signals which are actually operating. The discrepancy signal that appears is proportional to the difference between the extrapolated and the actual meaning of a signal.

When we consider the orienting reflex as a unique biological regulator, we should take note of the fact that it belongs to a group of negative feedback regulators. Wiener (1948) illustrates this type of regulation in the following simple example. While out hunting a man aims at a flying duck; in so doing, he tries to reduce the possibility of error to a minimum while aiming his rifle at the moving target. However, he may err in predicting the position of his target at the moment the charge from his rifle should strike it. On the next shot, he uses information about his previous attempt to improve his aim. The effectiveness of this feedback mechanism is determined primarily by the degree to which the position of an object has been inferred correctly. One way to improve the quality of extrapolation is to secure additional information; another method is to change the principles by which such information is handled, so that the process of regulation will prove more effective. In the example above, it was the information actually being received that needed regulating, and in this sense the feedback mechanism may be thought of as a regulator of information. From this standpoint, the orienting reflex is a regulator which corrects an extrapolation, influencing the way new information is secured, selected, transmitted, and handled.

The investigatory movements made by the eye searching for objects are an example of reactions of this type, which are aimed at obtaining new information.

The increased rate at which simple nervous processes operate in the analyzers, due to the activating mechanism of the orienting response, illustrates how the transmission of information is regulated in the nervous system. By influencing the selection, transmission, and, apparently, the analysis of information, the orienting reflex guarantees that the organism will be in the best position to predict the operation of stimuli and thus produce highly effective conditioned responses that are directly related to its adjustment to the environment.

The Orienting Reflex as a Regulator of Information

The possibility of anticipating external signals through the use of a neural model of the stimulus rests upon a process whereby any external stimulus may be recognized by its assignment to a distinct category of stimuli. Until this recognition has been made, the orienting response, which involves a hierarchy of receptors and general searching movements, provides the organism with processes for collecting and effectively transmitting the information it needs to recognize an unfamiliar object correctly.

The important features of the orienting reflex as a system of reactions aimed at securing and transmitting information about external objects to the proper nerve centers can be illustrated by an analysis of the so-called *tactile component* of the orienting reflex in human subjects. By "tactile component" we mean the distinct movements a subject makes with his hand or finger in order to probe an unfamiliar object when the experimental conditions are such that they exclude the use of sight. The regularity of these tactile movements is similar to the investigatory movements of the eyes. However, since tactile movements have to be carried out slowly, so that the response takes longer to perform, experiments involving the use of touch allow for a better study of the orienting reflex. Further, the use of tactile movements makes it possible to study a single-channel receptor system.[1]

With this aim in view, we constructed the image to be perceived by subjects (letters of the alphabet) in our experiments by spreading the pattern of the letter on a checkerboard with individual checkers whose size was equivalent to that of the first segment of the index finger. The same dimensions held for the distances between the checkers. The subject was allowed to use only the tip of his index finger in movements he made to try to

1. *Editors' note:* It remains to be demonstrated that physiological and performance measures of the orienting reflex co-vary as closely as implied by this statement. It also remains to be demonstrated that the orienting reflex measured to stimulus change is the same as the orienting reflex generated by cognitive hypotheses.

recognize the figure formed by the checkers laid out on a board containing 25 squares in a 5-by-5 array. The conditions of the experiment were such that we were able to calculate all the information the subject had obtained about the figure, since he could not determine the nature of the design from an element, being unable to shift his finger about in space. The path of his finger movements reflected the system of orienting responses through which he managed to gather information necessary for recognizing the figure (see Figure 23–6).

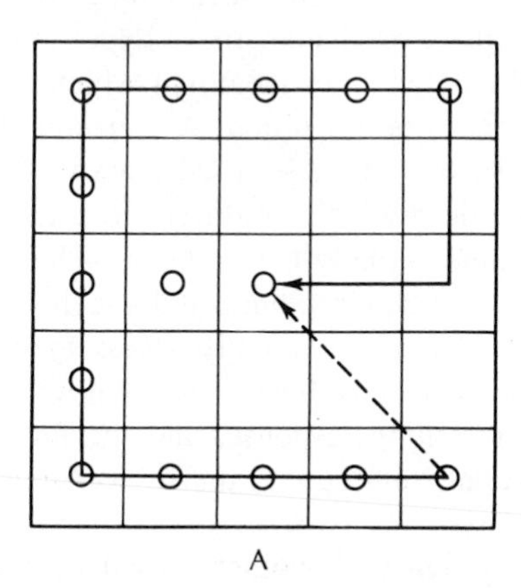

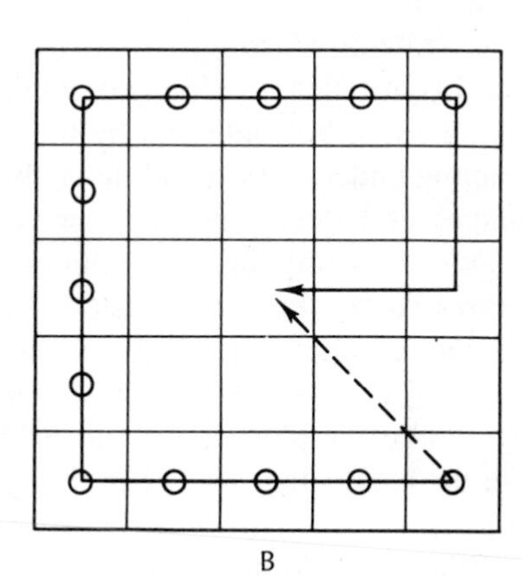

Figure 23–6. Diagram of the tactile perception of letters. Diagram *A* represents the probes of the letter *E;* diagram *B,* probes of the letter *C.* These letters were laid out with checkers on a square containing five rows of five squares each. The figures show probing carried out at different stages of training: The unbroken line corresponds to the point in the experiment at which probing of just the contour of the letters had superseded probings of all the points of the square. The dotted line indicates the path of probes at the final stage of training.

The presence or absence of a checker in a particular square served as an elementary sign about the letter represented. In the course of the experiments, analysis of the process by which figures are recognized led us to conclude that the orienting response represents a system of active "questions" addressed to an object, the answer being the information obtained by way of elementary signs from the object. Each successive finger movement (each successive "question") was the result of information the subject had obtained and reworked after probing the previous squares. The time spent by a subject in carrying out the entire set of movements characterized the duration of the orienting reflex, and the number of squares probed—the information obtained through the act of probing.

By means of experiments conducted in collaboration with Arana to study the process by which an individual uses touch to recognize different types of figures presented to him (letters, or outlines of Chinese ideograms), we were able to link the process of recognizing complex figures with the part played by the neural model of the stimulus in regulating the orienting reflex (Sokolov, 1960). In particular, it appeared that the length of the path formed by the tactile movements depends upon the system of neural models (hypotheses) used by a subject in attempting to recognize an object. The greater the number of hypotheses employed, the longer it takes for the subject to carry out his probing operations. The squares he elects to probe are determined by the system of hypotheses used and by the results he obtains in the course of probing, his initial set of hypotheses being revised according to the rate at which figures actually turn up. In particular, those hypotheses (in this instance, the forms of letters in the individual's memory) which are not likely to be confirmed by the experiment are not tested. As a result of training under stable conditions, the number of hypotheses used (that is, the shapes of letters considered in verifying) is gradually reduced so that it begins to correspond to the number of letters actually being shown. This is expressed by the shorter period of time spent in probing, and the fewer number of squares probed—up to a point which is minimally necessary for the subject to recognize the letters presented. The fewer the number of hypotheses employed, the shorter is the orienting response, and the fewer are the elementary acts of probing individual squares that the subject must perform.

When new forms are introduced, the system of hypotheses used by the subject becomes far more extensive, so that the number of hypotheses is considerably greater than the number of figures actually presented. Hence, the length of time required for the orienting response increases, as does the number of squares probed. When a new set of figures is presented, the system of hypotheses used is transformed until once again it corresponds to the set of figures presented.

An analysis of the path that these tactile movements form reveals the following peculiarity about the way in which figures are recognized by means of touch: The presence or absence of a checker in a particular square (which, as was pointed out, represents a sign of the particular letter) alters the probability that a given neural model will correspond to the figure being shown. When, after a number of probes, the probability of one of the hypotheses reaches the threshold value and becomes significantly greater than the probability of other hypotheses, recognition takes place; that is, the particular figure is assigned to one of the neural models. This can be accomplished long before the subject has probed all the squares.

The correct assignment of a figure to a specific neural model is fundamental to processes involved in extrapolation, since it allows the subject to predict the arrangement of unknown elements in a figure. Thus, the process by which a figure is recognized is closely related to the mechanism of extrapolation. As indicated above, the system of investigatory movements, which form a path of probes, can be thought of as a unique system of "questions" addressed to an object. The image that appears contains answers to these questions. However, if the subject correctly identifies the figures, it also provides answers to other questions about the same object which might have been, but were not, raised.

The regularities we have noted with regard to the tactile component of the orienting response might apply when figures recognized through touch involve a perception of temporal sequences. As an intermediate step, to prepare a subject for the transition from experiments such as those described above to others in which he has to deal with temporal sequences of stimuli, we could present a figure (which he would have to perceive through touch), such as a sequence of checkers and of "empty" spaces spread out on a line —elementary signs amounting to "yes" and "no." We might also discover that, among subjects who perceive figures by means of touch, the system of hypotheses is reduced owing to the fact that those hypotheses whose probability has dropped below a certain level are eliminated. Simultaneously, we may find that the process of recognizing a figure goes on until the subject has perceived all the elements spread out across the line.

The amount of time spent in the probing movements depends upon the same factors which hold for other components of the orienting reflex (eye movements, depression of alpha rhythm) in experiments designed to test differentiation of sequences of light and sound.

It is possible, then, to extend the laws relating to the tactile component of the orienting reflex to its other components, and on this basis construct a general descriptive scheme of the course of the orienting reflex.

The model which seems reasonable for the process of recognizing figures provides one possible scheme which implies a number of the regular features of the orienting reflex. Fundamental to such a schematic outline is the idea that the nervous system contains detailed traces of complex signals which it used to calculate the probability of their occurrence under the conditions of a given experiment. It is assumed that, to the degree that a complex stimulus is in operation, the probabilities of the hypotheses being used by the organism are continually undergoing refinement. This refining process, which makes the hypotheses more precise, is based on observations of changes occurring in a signal at each moment of time, changes which are represented in the nervous system by groups of nerve impulses. According to this view, recognition involves relating an unfamiliar figure (signal) to an already established memory trace and thus is based on: (1) incoming impulses; (2) a system of traces in the memory about signals the subject has dealt with in a previous experiment; (3) the probability that each of these signals can appear under the conditions of the present experiment; (4) the probability that there will be an elementary sign from the signal currently operating which is represented in the nervous system by a group of impulses having a certain frequency.

In this case it is assumed that the nervous system registers traces (neural models) $A_1, A_2, \ldots, A_n$, which represent a system of hypotheses. In dealing with stimuli such as temporal sequences, it might be held that at a given moment in time each neural model is characterized by the presence or absence of a sign K_j, represented by a group of neural impulses of a certain frequency. The probability that each neural model will be realized in a given experiment—that is, that the unknown object will fit it—can be signified by the probability $P(A_i)$. The appearance of the sign K_j for the corresponding neural model A_i is expressed by the conditional probability $P(K_j \mid A_i)$.

Recognition of the sign K_j alters the probability that a figure will pertain to each of the neural models. This change can be expressed by means of the following set of transitions:

$$P(A_1) \rightarrow P(A_1 \mid K_j);$$
$$P(A_2) \rightarrow P(A_2 \mid K_j);$$
$$\cdots\cdots\cdots$$
$$P(A_n) \rightarrow P(A_n \mid K_j).$$

According to this view, the processes of recognition, as they take place in the nervous system, can be represented by Bayes' theorem, which allows us to evaluate quantitatively the change in the probabilities of the hypotheses as the result of distinct signs which occur from an object. According to this theorem,

$$P(A_i \mid K_j) = \frac{P(A_i)P(K_j \mid A_i)}{P(K_j)}$$

where $i = 1, 2, \ldots, n$—the index of the number of hypotheses
$j = 1, 2, \ldots, m$—the index of the number of signs
$P(A_i)$ = the *a priori* probability that a signal in the experiment which pertains to group A_i will occur (the term "*a priori* probability" is used in a relative sense here; it indicates the probability of the appearance of a signal, which has been determined by the organism on the basis of past experience at the moment the sign K_j is perceived).

$P(A_i \mid K_j)$ = the *a posteriori* probability that the signal presented actually belongs to group A_i, given the occurrence of the sign K_j. It should be stressed that the *a posteriori* probability derived from the observation of a certain sign is *a priori* in relation to the next observation of a sign.

If the neural model A_i is linked to a reaction by the organism, it is possible for the organism to react to a given signal before it has observed all the signs about an object. The condition under which a reaction may occur before a subject has perceived all the signs about an object can be formulated as $P(A_i \mid K_j) \geqq a$, where a represents the threshold of recognition.

Thus, the possibility of recognizing an object before all its signs have been examined allows the organism to prepare and react early. This also explains the possibility of a conditioned reaction in response to indirect signs about an object, that is, signs which provide no definitive information about the object but signify that it is highly probable.

The various forms of the orienting response (probing movements, eye movements, changes in alpha rhythm, etc.) are reactions to the indefiniteness of a situation. The reaction occurs when a situation lacks clarity and continues as long as the situation remains indefinite. The orienting response is intended to eliminate the lack of clarity in a particular situation by securing additional information about it, or by changing the way in which information is handled.

It is logical to assume that the scope of the orienting response can be estimated by the entropy that holds for the range of probabilities of the hypotheses. If there are a great many hypotheses which are equally probable, there is a high degree of entropy in the system of hypotheses. The orienting response which emerges then, and which is aimed at acquiring knowledge of the situation, increases the probability of one of the hypotheses so that the entropy of the entire system of hypotheses decreases. The lack of clarity in the situation is eliminated and the orienting response dies out.

The scope of the orienting response is characterized by the entropy of the system of hypotheses as follows:

$$\mathrm{R} = k\,[H(A_{1,2,\ldots,n}\,K_j) - a],$$

where $H(A_{1,2,\ldots,n}\,K_j)$ represents the entropy of the system of hypotheses after the sign K_j has been observed; a—the threshold value of entropy; R—the scope of the orienting response; and k—the coefficient of proportionality.

The orienting response occurs as soon as the entropy exceeds the threshold value of a and continues as long as this condition holds. Insofar as the observation of specific signs increases the *a posteriori* probability of one of the hypotheses the entropy of the entire system of hypotheses decreases. The orienting response terminates as soon as the probability of one of the hypotheses has become significantly greater than that of the others, and the entropy of the system decreased to a point below the threshold value. Since the orienting response depends upon the entropy of the entire system of hypotheses, what group a stimulus is assigned to is inconsequential. What is important is the fact of recognition. However, the moment a new stimulus is presented, there is less probability that it will pertain to the previous neural model; for a period of time, then, all the hypotheses are equally probable. In this case the amount of entropy increases and the orienting response is elicited, terminating only when the new stimulus has been recognized.

Since the amount of entropy depends upon the number of hypotheses being used, a reduction in the system of hypotheses (which occurs when those that are not likely to be confirmed under the conditions of the experiment are excluded) leads to a decrease in the scope and duration of the orienting response. This corresponds to the extinction of the orienting response with repetitions of the same stimuli. When new figures are introduced in the experiment the system of hypotheses is expanded, and the amount of entropy increased; this coincides with the disinhibition of the orienting response after a new stimulus has been put into operations. To the extent that repeated applications of a stimulus cut down the system of hypotheses, the maximal amount of entropy is lowered; concurrently, there is a lessening, or even total extinction, of the orienting reflex.

According to the view outlined here, the formation of a neural model of the stimulus entails a notation about a signal in the nervous system and some calculation of its probable occurrence.

Figures 23–7 and 23–8 present a diagrammatic view of the part played by the neural model of the stimulus in regulating the orienting reflex and in recognizing a stimulus which has been administered. The sequence of nervous impulses entering the central nervous system is checked against a number of the neural traces which represent the system of hypotheses being used by a subject.

Let us consider a case in which, owing to the activity of a stimulus, the

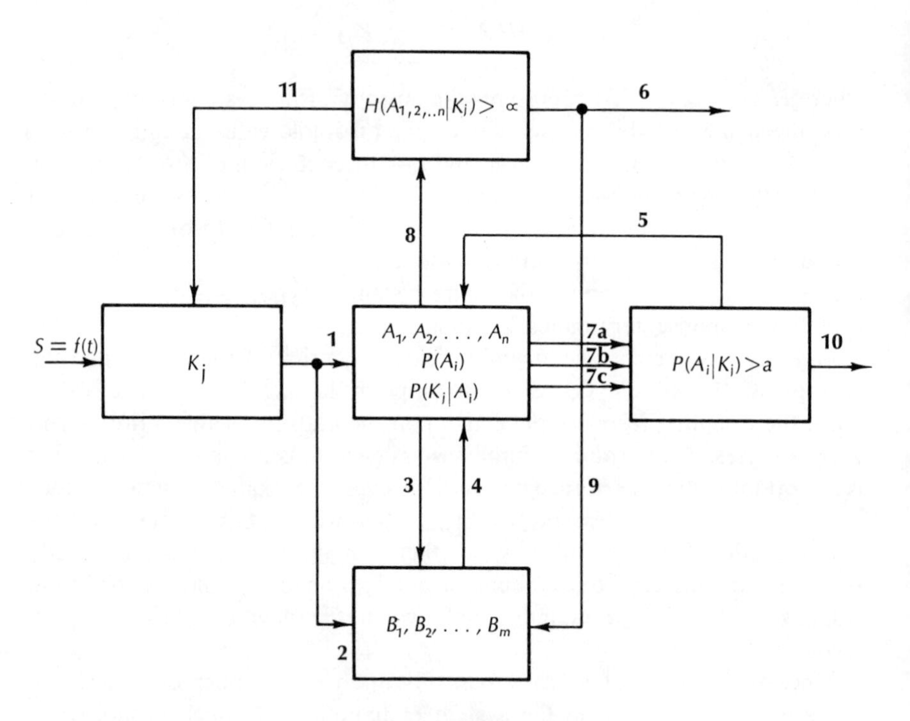

Figure 23–7.

Figure 23–7. Structural outline of a model which includes recognition of a stimulus, regulation of the orienting response, and execution of the conditioned reflex.

Groups of nervous impulses which code afferent stimulation proceed (1) to the system for determining the *a posteriori* probabilities of the hypotheses, and (2) to the mechanism of the long-term memory which contains a notation about all of the possible images (hypotheses) $B_1, B_2, \ldots, B_m$. The sign K_j indicates the presence of nervous impulses at a certain moment of time. The system of hypotheses $A_1, A_2, \ldots, A_n$, used in the act of recognition, forms a block which is linked to the long-term memory by a two-way connection, hypotheses that seem unlikely being excluded from the system of hypotheses subject to verification (3), whereas new hypotheses can be introduced into the system from the long-term memory (4).

The conditions under which the image is deduced from the system of hypotheses being tested is represented by $P(A_i) < \gamma$, where γ equals the threshold value of the *a priori* probability that a given image will appear. Each image (hypothesis) is characterized by certain probabilities with regard to the appearance of the sign K_j—that is, by $P(K_j|A_i)$. The block for calculating the *a posteriori* probabilities of the hypotheses is related to the threshold structure which guarantees the occurrence of the conditioned response (10) through 7a, 7b, and 7c. When the *a posteriori* probability amounts to the threshold value $P(A_i|K_j) > a$, the object is recognized.

If a given hypothesis is related to a distinct reaction, the hypothesis appears in advance as a conditioned response (10). If a given hypothesis is not related to a reaction, the process ends with recognition. The block for calculating the *a posteriori* probabilities of the hypotheses is related (8) to the block for determining the entropy of the given system of hypotheses and the orienting response (6). As long as the amount of entropy exceeds the threshold $H(A_{1,2,\ldots,n}|K_j) > \alpha$, the orienting response continues uninterrupted. But as the *a posteriori* probability of one of the hypotheses increases, the entropy of the whole system decreases and the orienting response fades. This occurs not only when an object is recognized but also when there is a conditioned response to it. Each recognition is used to make the *a priori* probability that a given object will appear more precise (5). In turn, the correlation between the hypotheses of the operative and long-term memory in the block of *a posteriori* probabilities depends upon the orienting response (9). When it is extinguished, hypotheses with a low degree of *a priori* probability are excluded from the system of hypotheses being checked. With the emergence of the orienting response, new hypotheses enter this block from the long-term memory. An important component of the system is the channel of a counter connection between the block for calculating entropy and the mechanism of the receptor (11). This connection indicates the influence of the orienting response on the afferent systems. Thus, the fact that the activity of a stimulus results in its being assigned to a distinct category before all the sequences of impulses have been presented allows the organism to predict subsequent stimulation. The system described works in conjunction with anticipation, and permits the organism to extrapolate the meaning of stimuli in the future. A calculation of the entropy, which increases with the activity of any new stimulus, makes it possible for us to characterize the orienting response quantitatively. A decrease of entropy, which can be noted when there is prolonged activity of a stimulus or repeated presentations of the same stimulus, allows for a description of the effect produced by the extinction of the orienting response.

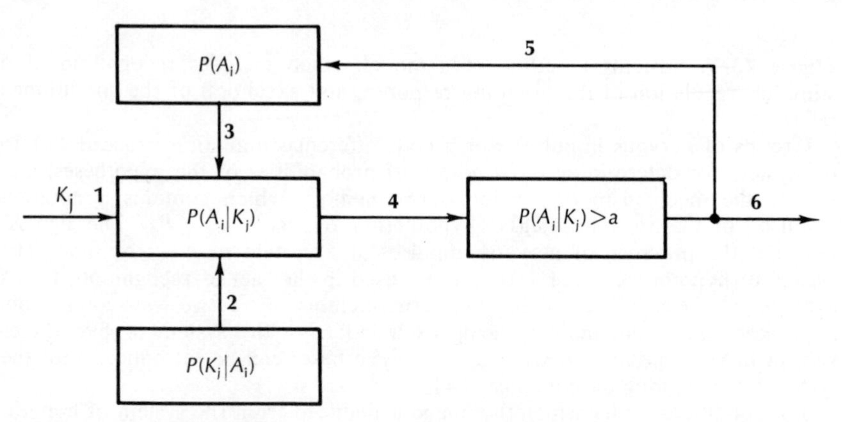

Figure 23–8. Diagram of the checking of a hypothesis. Incoming signals (K_j) are compared with a trace of the probabilities of the sign $K_j|A_i$ of the hypotheses $A_1, A_2, \ldots, A_n$ by taking into account the probability that a given hypothesis $P(A_i)$ will be confirmed. As soon as the *a posteriori* probability of the hypothesis $P(A_i|K_j)$ equals the threshold (4), recognition takes place. If this hypothesis is linked with subsequent activity, a conditioned response (6) follows. The fact of recognition alters the *a priori* probability (5) of the hypothesis $P(A_i)$. With the next occurrence of the same signal, the calculation $P(A_i|K_j)$ takes this new *a priori* probability into account.

a posteriori probability of one of the hypotheses is close to 1 (which, as we know, expresses the fact that the stimulus has been recognized and the orienting response terminated). Under these conditions let a new stimulus be put into operation. As soon as it starts to act, there is less probability that it will be identical to the preceding stimulus, and the entropy of the system of hypotheses temporarily increases; the orienting response appears, aimed at securing information that will eliminate the uncertainty which has developed. However, as the stimulus continues to operate, the *a posteriori* probability of another hypothesis gradually increases—until the probability is such that it amounts to the threshold of recognition. Subsequently, the entropy of the system of hypotheses drops sharply, the orienting response rapidly diminishes, and then ceases. When the system of hypotheses is reduced, the range and length of time required for each orienting response also decrease; recognition takes place sooner, and the latency period of the conditioned response is reduced. This corresponds to what we have observed experimentally when, given a strong conditioned reflex, the range of the orienting response decreases, or the response extinguishes completely. If, while stimuli continue to operate, we introduce a new stimulus, all the hypotheses will be equally probable for a time and the amount of entropy will increase. This agrees with the experimental evidence that the orienting response emerges as a reaction to a new stimulus and persists until the new object has been recognized.

With reference to what has been said above, it can be assumed that two types of memory participate in the mechanism which produces the orienting response: (1) operative memory, which stores the system of hypotheses that are being verified in the experiment; and (2) a more permanent type of memory consisting of a stable set of notations about the figures that have been depicted. If the probability that a given figure will turn up decreases to a certain level, the hypothesis is excluded from the operative memory, which consists of those hypotheses to be subjected to verification, but it is retained in the nervous system as a trace. Hence, a calculation of the frequency with which different figures actually turn up is most important in regulating the group of hypotheses to be used. Further, it is possible that new hypotheses drawn from a more permanent type of memory process will be introduced into the set of hypotheses that are being verified. The process of recognition presupposes, too, that the memory retains a record of the probabilities of signs occurring from each of the figures that have been shown.

The scheme we have developed makes it possible to link the process whereby figures are recognized: (1) with the occurrence of the conditioned reflex in situations involving a complicated choice; (2) with an extrapolation about the significance of a stimulus in the future; and (3) with the dynamic course of the orienting reflex. This view, in particular, provides an explanation of the following: the extinction of the orienting reflex and the intensification of the conditioned reflex when the same stimulus is repeated; the emergence of an intensified orienting reflex when a new agent is introduced, and the increased latency period of the conditioned reflex when the complications of diverse stimuli intensify the orienting response. How effective extrapolation will prove in the future is determined by the extent to which an unfamiliar stimulus has been correctly assigned to one of the trace processes—one of the neural models.

The Modeling Process on the Neuronal Level

Research on the orienting response through experiments on the visual cortex, thalamus, and the reticular system of dogs with chronically implanted electrodes indicates that all the basic patterns that hold for the extinction of the orienting reflex in humans are reproduced in animals. Karimova and Bowden carried out research that I supervised on the extinction of the orienting response to simple and complex sound stimuli, as well as to stimuli directed to different analyzers (Bowden, Sokolov, and Karimova, 1964). This was an attempt to discover the anatomical structures which are linked to the neural model of a stimulus. Various experimental treatments were used on these dogs in whom (a) the reticular formation had been blocked by nembutal; (b) the auditory region of the cortex had been severed from the cortical projections of other analyzers by an incision through the gray matter of the brain; and (c) the basic mass of the auditory region of the cortex had been removed surgically. In these experiments with animals who were in a state of sleep induced by nembutal, the investigators were interested in discovering whether: (1) the many components of the orienting response would be preserved under the conditions of the experiments; (2) there would be a cortical EEG reaction; and (3) a selective extinction of the reaction to simple and complex stimuli would occur.

The experiments indicated that when dogs are in a sleep induced by nembutal the multiple components of the orienting response fade out, primarily the somatic components (the animals' ear movements), but that there is local activation of the auditory cortex in response to the effect of sound stimuli. Further, extinction of the response in the auditory cortex

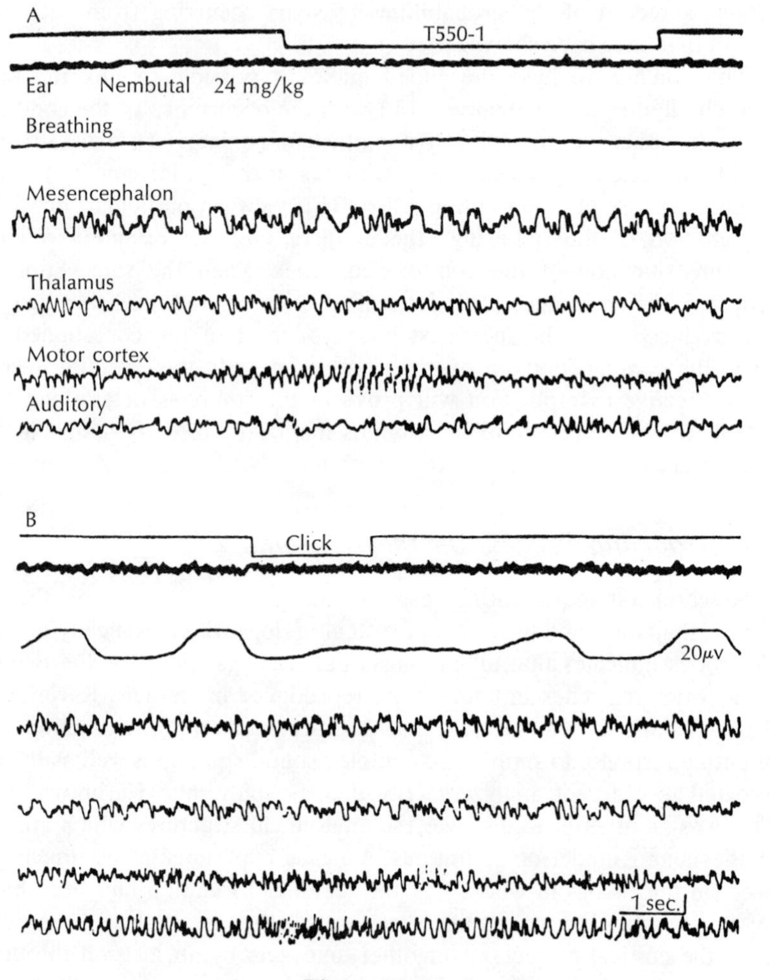

Figure 23–9.

is related specifically to the parameters of the stimulus (see Figure 23–9). This indicates that the formation of a neural model of the stimulus, the development of discrepancy signals, and activation may take place on the cortical level and not in the reticular system of the brain.

Separation of the auditory section of the cortex from the rest of the area indicates that the transcortical connections have no bearing either on the number of components of the orienting response, or on the specific nature of the extinction of cortical activity evoked by simple and complex stimuli, even when these are applied to different analyzers. These results indicate that the transcortical connections are not of vital importance in the formation of a neural model, a fact which holds true even when the model reflects stimulation that is applied to a number of sense organs. The fact that the many components of the orienting response are preserved when the auditory cortex has been extirpated further suggests that the mechanism of efferent integration does not require the assistance of transcortical connections. Bilateral extirpation of the basic mass of the auditory cortex also fails to disrupt the many components of the orienting response. If, under these conditions, stimuli are directed to different analyzers, the processes by which these stimuli are integrated are not disrupted, and the specific type of extinction is still obtained. However, when the basic mass of the auditory part of the cortex has been removed, there is appreciable

---

Figure 23–9. The orienting response of local activation of brain-wave rhythms of the auditory cortex of a dog to the presentation of a stimulus—the dog's name. The dog is in a state of sleep induced by nembutal. Reading from top to bottom within each set (*A* and *B*), the diagrams indicate: the sound stimulus acting upon the dog (its name, Vernie); the EMG of the ear muscles; respiration; EEG recorded from the midbrain; EEG recorded from the thalamus; EEG recorded from the motor area of the cortex; EEG recorded from the auditory region of the cortex.

(*A*) After prolonged extinction of the orienting response to a sound having a frequency of 500 cps and an intensity of 60 db, a change in the frequency to 550 cps (introduced 15 minutes after sleep had been induced by nembutal) did not elicit the orienting response. Slow waves were visible in all the EEG channels. (*B*) The dog's name, spoken by the experimenter through a microphone attached to the dog, who was in a soundproof room, elicited the following type of reaction. While the dog was in a continuous sleep induced by nembutal, the stimulus (which was given 51 minutes after the onset of sleep) produced a distinct group of rapid fluctuations localized in the auditory region, and a simultaneous delay in the dog's breathing. There was no somatic reaction in the way of ear movements, and the dog did not awaken. The possibility of local activation of the auditory cortex under the effect of nembutal, which suppresses the functioning of the reticular system, indicates that a specific path for conducting excitation to the auditory part of the cortex remains open, and that during sleep the cortical mechanism by which afferent stimuli are checked against the neural model of a stimulus continues to operate. The fact that there was cortical activity and no activation of the brain stem indicates that the cortex may have its own internal mechanism for local activation.

damage to the selective extinction of the orienting response to auditory signals arranged in a distinct order.

These experimental results offer grounds for the following conclusions. The efferent mechanism of the orienting reflex, which ensures that the reaction will retain its many components, appears to be linked with the brain stem reticular formation. On the cortical level, the mechanism which produces a neural model of a complex stimulus entering the brain from different analyzers does not require transcortical connections; it is introduced into many points of the cortex, apparently through the assistance of special "integrating" neurons which receive nervous impulses from different sense organs (Kogan, 1961). What appears to be most important is that a local reaction is registered in the cortex when there is suppression of the reticular formation. The fact that there is a local response of activation allows for the assumption that all the mechanisms required for eliciting and extinguishing the orienting response are present on the cortical level. Hence, there should be mechanisms which perform the following functions: (1) conduct afferent signals; (2) extrapolate information; (3) compare afferent signals with those used in extrapolation; and (4) produce the activation which is one of the components of the orienting response.

A comparison of the patterns exhibited by the extinction of the orienting response with data in the literature concerning the types of neurons present in the cortex suggests that each of the specific operations performed by the orienting reflex system is linked to special types of neurons. Specific afferent neurons represent one type of neuron involved in the orienting reflex. The peculiar feature displayed by these neurons is that their reactions are not extinguished. Neurons which belong to this category are those which respond with a discharge to light (so-called type B neurons) and to darkness (type D neurons), which Jung (1962) discovered in the visual cortex of the brains of cats. Another type of neuron is responsible for the mechanism of extrapolation. These do not respond to stimulation at first; however, when stimuli are repeated regularly, they begin developing signals, doing this in advance, so to speak—that is, before the next regular stimulus occurs. Morrell (1962) observed a similar response by a neuron to repeated activity of a light stimulus. In his experiments on the neuron Morrell found that there was a reaction while the stimulus was operating, even though rhythmic stimulation had ceased.

A third type of neuron is represented by those involved in comparison; "comparator" neurons is a term that may be used to designate neurons about which there is some ground for assuming that they perform a process in which afferent impulses are compared with the impulses extrapolated. Nervous impulses are generated by a neuron of this type when the meaning of a stimulus does not coincide with what has been extrapolated about it. The so-called attention cells, discovered by Galambos and Hubel in the auditory cortex of cats, may be regarded as the equivalent of comparator neurons. The peculiar feature exhibited by comparator neurons is that they cease to respond to repetitions of a stimulus and react again only when the stimulus has been changed. In 1963, under my direction, Vinogradova and Lindsley studied responses by individual neurons of the visual cortex of a rabbit to light flashes and clicks of sound. The purpose of this research was to learn how neurons are organized in modeling the characteristics of a stimulus in the orienting reflex system (Vinogradova and Lindsley, 1963). A considerable number of the neurons which responded were specific visual afferent neurons, whose reactions did not alter during the course of lengthy repetitions of a stimulus (see Figure 23–10). The experiments confirmed

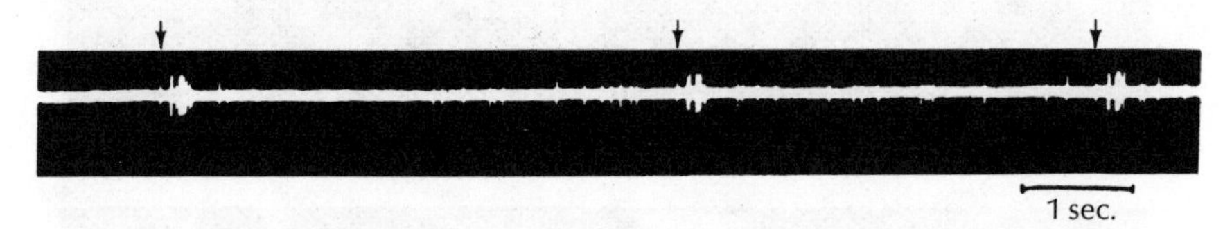

Figure 23–10. An example of responses by a specific afferent neuron of the visual cortex of a rabbit to a flash of light. After hundreds of applications of the stimulus, the reaction occurs with no sign of its being extinguished. The arrows indicate the moments when stimulation was in effect, each of them followed by a group of high-amplitude impulses. Impulses with a lower amplitude (which does not change during the activity of the light flash) belong to another neuron, which does not react to the given type of stimulation. What is striking here is the rigid structure of the volley of impulses of the specific afferent neuron: a brief burst of impulses; then a more prolonged discharge; and intervals between the two.

the existence of attention cells in the visual cortex of rabbits. These cells respond with a volley of impulses to a novel stimulus but, subsequently, as the stimulus is repeated, they gradually cease to react (Figure 23–11).

It was found that in addition to the neurons described above there are neurons in the cortex which build up an inhibiting effect when a stimulus is repeated. The inhibition developed by these neurons manifested itself in a depresssion of their spontaneous rhythm (up to a point at which the rhythm faded entirely) (Figure 23–12). At the same time, any change in the stimulus reduced the inhibitory effect and led to a restoration of the spontaneous rhythm of the neuron. Impulses of extrapolation are apparently the source of inhibition for neurons of this type (which accords with our assumption concerning the way extrapolation is used to block the paths of the cortex which lead to the centers of the orienting response).

In addition to the reactions of neurons which are directly engaged in the orienting reflex system, we should consider the effect of their response on

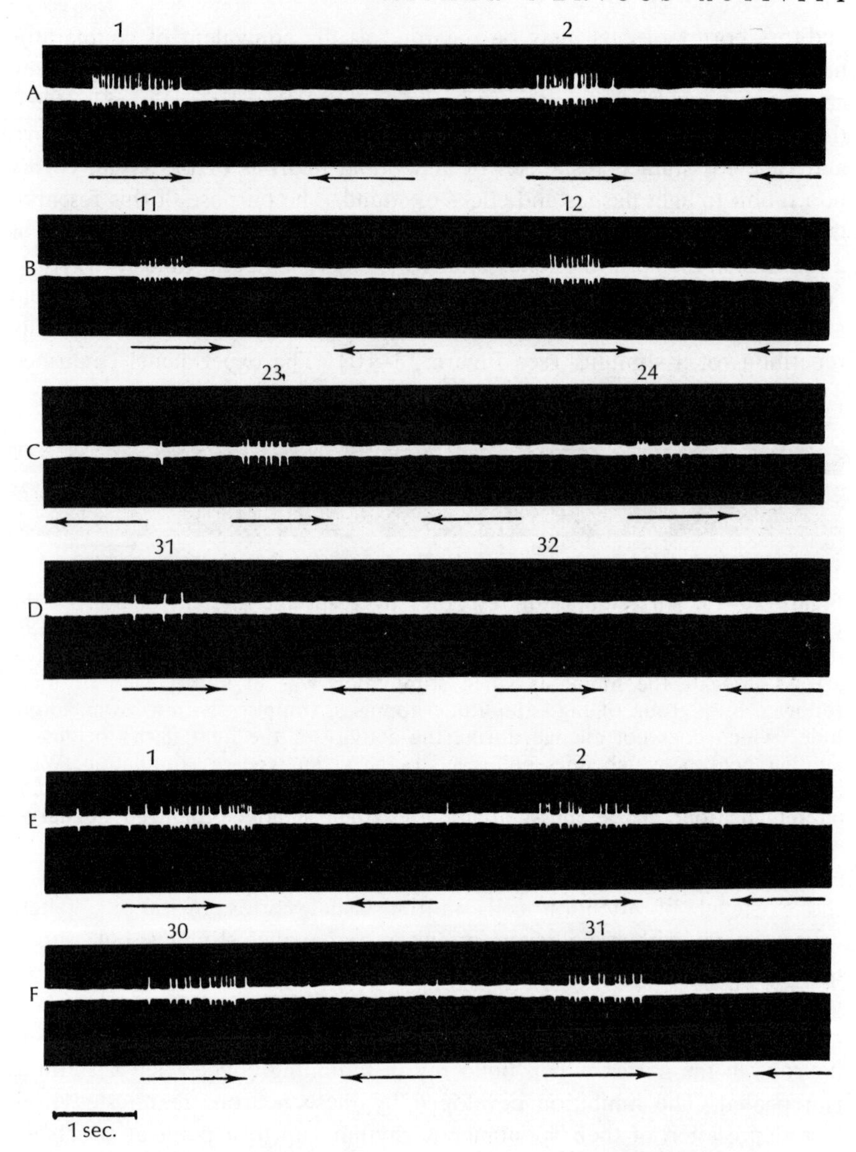

Figure 23–11. An example of the reaction of an attention neuron in the visual cortex of a rabbit. The numbers above the oscillograms indicate individual presentations of the stimulus. The directions of the movement of the light stimulus in the rabbit's field of vision are designated by the arrows. The neuron is not capable of spontaneous activity; the discharge occurs only when there is a movement of light in the field of vision in one of two possible directions (*A, B*). When the same stimulus is repeated, the density of the impulses in the burst, as well as the total number of impulses, decreases (*C*); finally, the reaction fades entirely (*D*). The introduction of a new visual stimulus leads to a recovery of the reaction if the light is moved in the same direction (*E, F*).

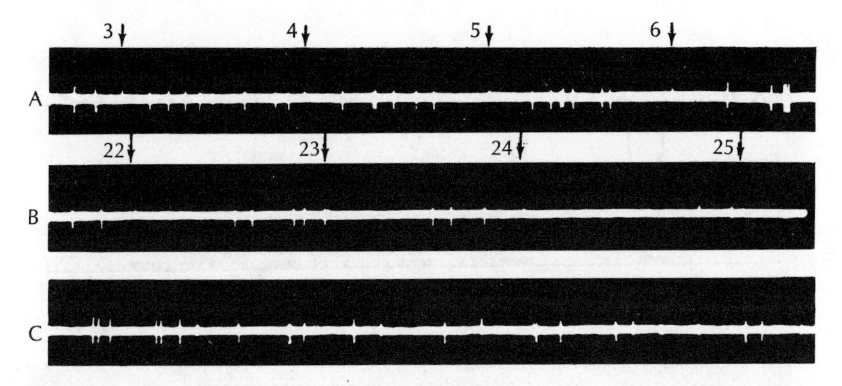

Figure 23–12. Example of the inhibitory response of a neuron in the visual cortex of a rabbit to repetitions of a light stimulus. The arrows designate the activity of the stimulus, the numerals indicate the number of times it has been presented. The first presentations of the stimulus do not give rise to a noticeable change in the background activity (*A*); gradually, however, the zone of quiet in the spontaneous activity that follows each presentation of the stimulus increases until all the intervals give evidence of discharges (*B*); when the stimulus stops, the background rhythm is gradually restored (*C*).

specific afferent neurons, and on those which fail to respond to stimuli, given the conditions of a particular experiment.

The orienting reflex has a different effect on "responsive" and "unresponsive" neurons. When the orienting response occurs, "responsive" neurons reduce background activity so as to heighten the signal to noise ratio. Under the same circumstances, "unresponsive" neurons intensify the spontaneous discharges thereby leading to a reduction of the signal to noise ratio. In accordance with the laws which hold for macroscopic extinction of the orienting response, these changes in the frequency of the spontaneous discharges decrease with repetitions of a stimulus (see Figure 23–13). It is particularly interesting to compare these reactions with those consisting of a depression of alpha rhythm characteristic of the phenomenon of activation. A depression of alpha rhythm and the change in the spontaneous rhythm of neurons are phenomena unique to the orienting response. The first is apparently related to heightened activity of the cells of the neurologia which are responsible for supplying energy to the neurons; the second, with a change in the synaptic transmission of neurons. It is possible that neurons which do not require information at a given moment reduce the signal-to-noise ratio. Conversely, those neurons for which such information is vitally important increase the ratio.

If we take into account all the data relative to a neural organization of the orienting reflex, it is possible to set up the descriptive scheme of Figure 23–14. This outline includes the specific receptors which transmit information to neurons of extrapolation, to neurons of comparison, and to

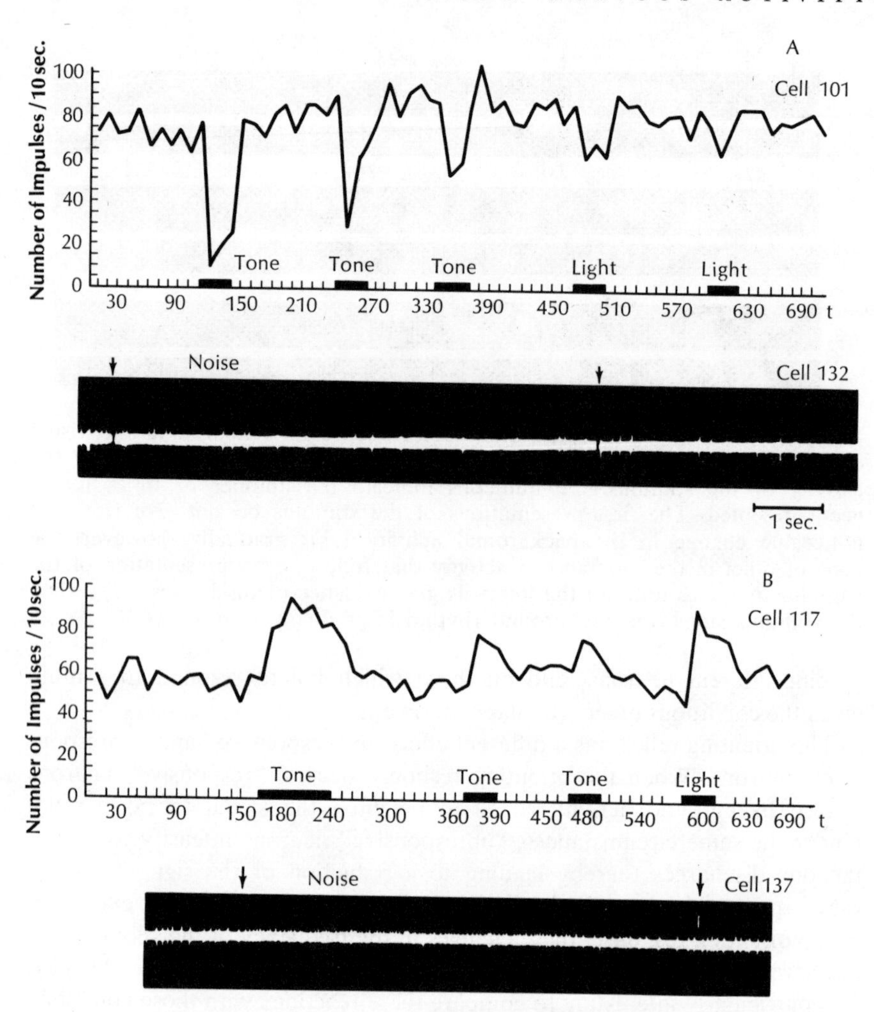

Figure 23–13. Example of two ways in which the orienting reflex affects spontaneous activity of neurons. (*A*) A neuron responding with a burst of impulses to a flash of light. (*B*) A neuron which does not respond to the flash.

The figure illustrates two ways of analyzing tonic changes in the rhythm of a neuron: a method for calculating the number of impulses for each 10 seconds by using an integrating device and a photographic record of the oscilloscope's reactions. The activity of a lengthy sound and light produced a decrease in the intensity of the spontaneous activity of cell 101. As the stimulus was repeated, the reactions habituated in a way that is typical for reactions of the orienting reflex on a macroscopic level (GSR, the vascular system, and others). In the case of cell 132, a decrease in nerve impulses was noted when there was a background of noise. In cells 117 and 137, which did not respond with a burst of impulses during the activity of light and sound, there was a reaction which took the form of an increase in spontaneous activity. There is a decrease in spontaneous activity as the stimulus continues, which reveals the effect of extinction characteristic of the orienting reflex on a macroscopic level.

the performing cells of the orienting reflex. Impulses developed by extrapolating neurons are used (1) to create a mechanism for a positive conditioned reflex to time, and (2) actively to inhibit those neurons which are not involved in the reaction. The inhibition of afferent impulses entering the afferent cells of the orienting reflex is an instance of the latter type of inhibitory action. Neurons of comparison are linked to cells of the neuroglia and function to change the level of activation in certain parts of the brain.

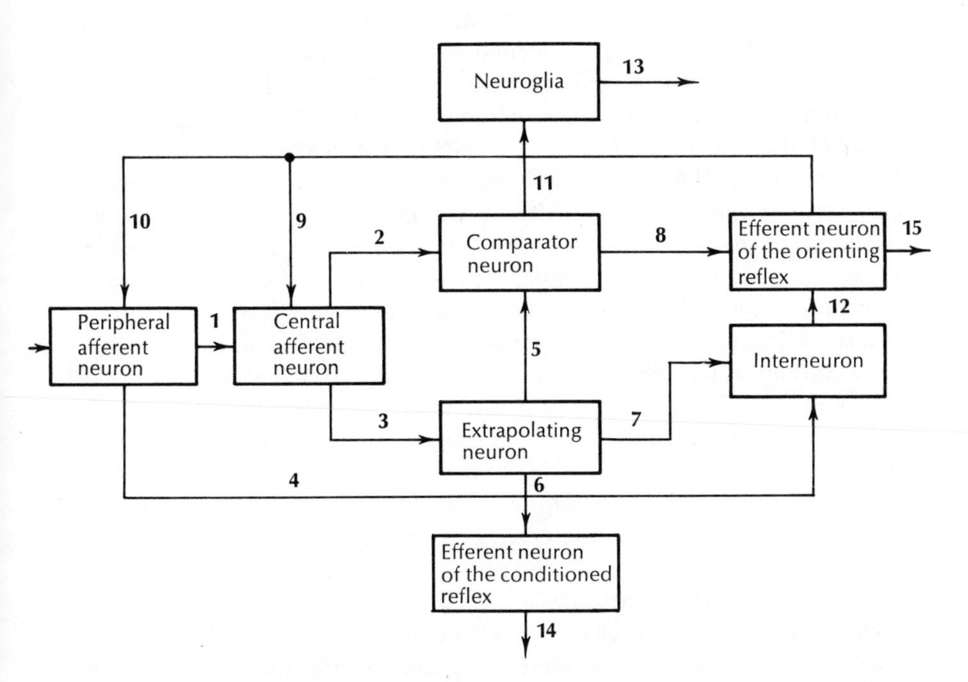

Figure 23–14. Diagram of the neural organization of the orienting reflex. (1) Axon of the peripheral afferent neuron. (2) Axon of the cortical afferent neuron leading to the comparator neuron. (3) Axon of the cortical afferent neuron leading to the extrapolating neuron. (4) Collaterals of the peripheral afferent neuron leading to efferent neurons of the orienting reflex through an interneuron. (5) Axon of the extrapolating neuron leading to a comparator neuron. (6) Axon of an extrapolating neuron leading to the center of the conditioned reflex. (7) Axon of an extrapolating neuron with a system of hyperpolarizing synapses which produces the conditioned-reflex inhibition of impulses along the path to the efferent neurons of the orienting reflex. (8) Axon of a comparator neuron transmitting a discrepancy signal to an efferent neuron of the orienting reflex. (9, 10) Axons of an efferent neuron of the orienting reflex which are correspondingly bound up with regulating the spontaneous activity of a cortical afferent neuron (the mechanism for altering the signal/noise ratio), and with regulating the peripheral afferent neuron. (11) Axon of a comparator neuron which influences the cells of the neuroglia. (12) Axon of an interneuron. (13) A reaction of cells of the neuroglia. (14) Efferents of the conditioned reflex. (15) Efferents of the orienting reflex.

By regulating the signal-to-noise ratio, the orienting reflex directs the selection of signals and thus fulfills one of the main functions of an information regulator.

The schema we are considering for the interrelation of neurons presupposes the existence of the following basic types of neurons: afferent neurons, neurons of extrapolation, neurons of comparison, afferent neurons of the orienting reflex, and interneurons which develop an inhibitory action. It is assumed that the neuroglia functions as an activating mechanism. If we maintain that neurons of extrapolation terminate at interneurons which have hyperpolarizing synapses, it follows that the mechanism of extrapolation can be used not only for conditioned excitation but also for conditioned inhibition of impulses and for inhibiting the action of other neurons. The effect of the orienting reflex on the cells of the glia, as well as on other neurons, ensures that there will be tonic reactions by way of either reduced or increased spontaneous activity of the slow fluctuations of bioelectric potentials of the cortex, and a change in the activity of individual neurons. However, it may be that comparison and extrapolation are effected by mechanisms consisting of aggregates of interacting neurons which are formed in a special way, and not just by individual, specialized neurons.

According to the scheme we have proposed, the following occurs when a stimulus is administered repeatedly. First, the future significance of a signal is anticipated; this is the basis upon which the conditioned reflex develops for a time, either arousing or actively inhibiting a reaction. Second, there is a coincidence of afferent and extrapolating impulses, as a result of which impulses signaling a discrepancy disappear and the orienting response terminates. Consequently, the effect of the response on the synaptic transmission in the afferent neurons dissipates, altering the selection of information. When there is a change in a stimulus, extrapolation breaks down, impulses appear that signal a discrepancy, and the orienting reflex is elicited, changing the conditions whereby signals are transmitted to the afferent neurons.

Summary

An analysis of the experimental data indicates that reflex activity is mediated through complex mechanisms in the central divisions of analyzers which function to reflect the external world. By measuring the scope of the orienting reflex while administering highly controlled test stimuli, it is possible to describe the characteristics of the neural trace and draw some conclusions about its resemblance to a stimulus which has been repeatedly applied. This trace constitutes the "neural model of the stimulus," which simultaneously registers the intensity, duration, location in space, dimensions, qualitative features, and rhythm of the stimuli as well as stimulation applied to other sense organs. From this point of view, the nervous system reflects the external world by creating an internal model of its environment. By accurately reflecting the external world, the neural model amounts to a system which anticipates the future meaning of a stimulus (extrapolating effect). Whether or not an internal neural model corresponds with objective reality is determined by how effective the interaction of the organism with its environment proves to be. The mechanism which checks the meaning of a stimulus extrapolated by the nervous system with afferent signals actually entering from the sense organs is most vital in continually refining the process of reflection.

The idea of reflection as a way in which the nervous system model's images of the environment leads us to conclude that reflection is, by nature, an active process. Practical activity is the criterion for judging how adequately a particular neural model has reflected its material.

References

Berg, A. I. *Cybernetics, thought, life.* Moscow: Izd Mysl', 1964.

Bowden, D., Sokolov, E. N., and Karimova, M. M. Selective extinction of the orienting reflex to complex auditory and multi-modality stimuli. *Zh. vyssh. nerv. Deyat.*, 1964, *9*, No. 4, 608–617.

Jung, R. Neuronal integration in the visual cortex and its significance for information in W. A. Rosenblith (Ed.), *Sensory communication.* Cambridge, M.I.T. Press, 1962. Vol. 4, p. 627.

Kogan, A. B. On the structure of the circuit-closing apparatus of the conditioned reflex. *Zh. vyssh. nerv. Deyat.*, 1961, No. 4, 654–659.

Maltzman, I., and Raskin, D. C. Effects of individual differences in the orienting reflex on conditioning and complex processes. *J. exp. res. Pers.*, 1965, *1* (1), 1–16.

Morrell, F. The effect of superficial anodal polarization on the motor reaction and on the discharges from individual cells in the cortex. *Fiziol. Zh. SSSR,* 1962, *46*.

Sechenov, I. M. *Reflexes of the brain.* Moscow, 1863. (English translation by S. Belsky, published by M.I.T. Press, Cambridge, 1965.)

Sokolov, E. N. A probabilistic model of perception. *Vop. Psikhol.*, 1960, No. 2, 102–116.

Sokolov, E. N. *Perception and the conditioned reflex,* New York: Macmillan, 1963.

Vinogradova, O. S., and Lindsley, D. B. Extinction of reactions to sensory stimuli in a single nerve cell of the cortex of the visual regions of a rabbit which had not been anesthetized. *Zh. vyssh. nerv. Deyat.*, 1963, No. 2.

Voronin, L. G., Leont'ev, A. N. Luria, A. R. Sokolov, E. N., and Vinogradova, O. S. *Orienting reflex and exploratory behavior*. Washington, D.C.: Amer. Inst. Biol. Sci., 1966.

Voronin, L. G., and Sokolov, E. N. On the mechanism of the investigatory reflex: Its interrelation with the conditioned reflex. In *Gagra Discussions*. Vol. 3. Tbilisi, 1960, 213–239.

Wiener, N. *Cybernetics*. New York: Wiley, 1948.

24

Specific and Nonspecific Response Systems in the Formation of Conditioned Responses in Man

O. S. Vinogradova

EDITORS' INTRODUCTION

As the chapters by Feigenberg and by Sokolov, as well as an additional extensive literature, indicate, any change in stimulation may evoke a nonspecific orienting reflex (OR). One of the measures of the OR, the GSR, has been frequently employed as the dependent variable in studies of conditioning and stimulus generalization. But until recently the GSR, as a measure of the OR and as susceptible to elicitation by stimulus change, has been neglected in America. Much of the data and hypotheses concerning conditioning of physiological responses such as the GSR must be re-evaluated in terms of the implications of the concept of the OR and related principles. Stimulus generalization is one such phenomenon. Of necessity, a stimulus change is involved in the generalization test situation in that conditioning is first accomplished with a specific stimulus and then new stimuli are introduced. A test stimulus may evoke a GSR which in part is a function of stimulus changes per se, resulting in an "unconditioned OR" and generalization of associative strength or of the conditioned connection. Because of the elicitation of an unconditioned OR to the new test stimulus, initial generalized responses may be even larger than the conditioned response (CR).

This phenomenon, obtained by Hovland (1937) in some of his classic studies of stimulus generalization of the GSR, led Hull to formulate his unduly complex theory of inhibition of reinforcement, implying that the CR was actually depressed during acquisition. Introduction of the test stimulus resulted in disinhibition of the previously accumulated inhibition. The alternative interpretation is that the test stimuli initially evoke an OR which then habituates with repeated test trials. Stimulus-generalization gradients of conditioning are thus confounded by generalization of the associative connection and the OR with opposed effects generated by the two variables. Magnitude of the OR would be directly related, while associative strength would be inversely related, to the difference between the conditioning and generalization test stimuli.

One way to avoid the confounding is to induce generalization of habituation or the OR in the absence of prior conditioning. Repeated presentation of an auditory stimulus of a given frequency results in habituation of the OR to that particular stimulus. Introduction of auditory stimuli of varying frequency evokes manifestations of the OR where the greater the stimulus change, the larger the OR as manifested by such measures as the GSR and alpha blocking. Sokolov (1960) has reported such a gradient of habituation of the OR. More recently, Williams (1963) has confirmed the effect.

The following chapter by Vinogradova describes a procedure for investigating stimulus generalization following conditioning, where the effects of the OR and generalization of the associative connection can be differentiated. It involves the use of measures which differentiate the OR from the defensive reflex (DR). The GSR does not effectively do this, but the vasomotor pattern of peripheral vasoconstriction (OR) and cephalic vasoconstriction (DR) does provide such a differentiation. The procedure is to establish a conditioned DR before beginning tests for generalization. Occurrence of cephalic vasodilation would then indicate an OR evoked by the change in stimulation per se, while cephalic vasoconstriction would indicate generalization of the conditioned connection.

The results reported by Vinogradova, admittedly on few subjects, and based on hypotheses still lacking substantial support, nevertheless are of great importance. They suggest the gross inadequacy of much of current American data and theory concerning the complexities, details, and truly important nature of the phenomena of classical conditioning, particularly at the human level.

O. S. Vinogradova was a student of Luria's in the 1950's. She collaborated with Luria on his work on verbal-process-defective children (see, e.g., Luria and Vinogradova, 1959). In the latter 1950's she began a decade of collaboration with E. Sokolov. Most recently Vinogradova has been studying the mechanisms of attention at the neuronal level, following a well-established Russian tradition of seeking to identify the physiological (i.e., material) foundation of psychological processes. She is presently employed by the Institute of Higher Nervous Activity and Neurophysiology in Moscow.

INVESTIGATION OF the "arousal reaction," as one of the organism's nonspecific responses (Sharpless and Jasper, 1956; Jouvet, 1956; Lissak, 1956; Jansen, Andersen, and Kaada, 1956; Gangloff and Monier, 1956; and others) has made it possible to identify this reaction with the "attention," or orienting, reflex first discussed by Pavlov. Investigations carried out in the last few years have shown that vasomotor changes constitute one of the essential and constant components of the "arousal reaction" (Wang and Ranson, 1939; Ackner and Pampiglione, 1957; Bonvallet, Dell, and Hiebel, 1954; Ingvar and Soderberg, 1956; and others). Change (increase) in peripheral sympathetic tone was always viewed as parallel to the electroencephalographic and motor expressions of the "arousal reaction."

The restricted extent to which direct methods can be used for investigation of excitation and its qualitative analysis in man has compelled the use of certain indirect methods. Sokolov and Vinogradova (1957) have demonstrated that the vascular components forming part of orienting and specific thermoregulating and defensive reflexes can be qualitatively differentiated from each other. On the basis of this differentiation, qualitative analysis of the character of the excitation arising during the formation of a conditioned connection has been carried out.

Our approach to this was based on an examination of the spatial irradiation of nervous processes, a phenomenon well known from the works of the Pavlov school. The characteristic feature of this irradiation is revealed by the general methodological procedure of forming a conditioned reflex to one stimulus and testing response to others more or less close to it.

In our experiment, conditioned defense reflexes were formed to a pure tone of 500 cps, at 60 db. After acting alone for 10 to 15 seconds, this tone was reinforced by three brief shocks of 50 to 75 volts, alternating current, delivered to the index finger of the subject's right hand. The conditioned and unconditioned stimuli terminated simultaneously. The long duration of the conditioned stimulus was necessary in order for the character of the conditioned response to be clearly seen before the onset of shock.

The 500-cps tone was always reinforced; but other tones, from 200 to 2000 cps (in one series, from 100 to 4000 cps), were also used, and these were never reinforced. The latter also acted for 10 to 15 seconds. The interstimulus interval varied from 15 to 90 seconds. The tones were delivered through earphones, only the right one being active; the left earphone was disconnected.

The vascular reactions recorded from a finger of the left hand and from the left temporal region of the subject's head constituted the response measures. Analysis of the results is based on the fact that the vascular components of the orienting and defensive reflexes differ in character. The vascular component of an orienting reflex manifests itself in reciprocal constriction of the hand vessels and dilation of the head vessels, whereas a defensive reaction is a concurrent parallel constriction of the vessels (Vinogradova and Sokolov, 1957; Vinogradova, 1958).

The experiment started with the presentation of *all* the stimuli in the tonal scale used (including the 500-cps tone, the future CS) in random order without reinforcement. This was done to extinguish orienting responses to the tones. When general extinction had been achieved and the stimuli no longer produced vascular reactions, defensive conditioning was begun. Only the 500-cps tone, reinforced by electric current, was used at this stage of the investigation.

A conditioned defense reflex, constriction of the vessels of the head and hand during the 500-cps tone, appeared after 15 to 30 pairings of the CS and UCS. The main tests were carried out after the conditioned response was stable. Higher and lower tones were used at this stage. The trials were repeated in this form *10 to 15* times on each subject. Since measurement of differential thresholds was not the principal purpose of this study, the threshold values are only approximate in a number of cases. The vascular reactions were recorded by means of a photoplethysmograph. The pure tones were delivered from an audiofrequency generator; the source of the electrical skin reinforcement was a generator of rectangular pulses. Sessions were conducted every other day. The investigation was carried out on four subjects, from 20 to 25 years old, with normal hearing.

After consolidation of the conditioned defense reflex to the 500-cps tone, all the tones, from 200 cps in the lower part of the scale to 2000 cps in the higher part, at first caused changes in the vascular curve. The responses to tones at different distances from the main tone were not the same in character. A fairly wide band of frequencies around the basic stimulus (300 to 350 cps on the one side and 900 to 1300 cps on the other) produced reactions of the same character as the 500-cps CS, parallel constriction of the vessels in the head and hand. The reactions to tones beyond these limits took the form of constriction of the hand vessels with dilation of the vessels in the head, that is, they constituted the vascular component of an orienting reflex.

With increasing remoteness from the extreme points on the scale there was a gradual increase in the intensity of the orienting reactions. The same gradual increase in strength could be seen for the group of stimuli causing defensive responses as the positive CS was approached. At the boundary between the "orienting" and "defensive" zones there was a group of stimuli which produced reactions of an intermediate transitional type. These stimuli continued to produce pronounced vasoconstriction in the hand, while, at the same time, the responses of the head vessels were feeble, reduced, or generally absent. These responses were apparently the result of mutual interference between the defensive and orienting reflexes, which have opposite signs in the vessels of the head (Figure 24–1).

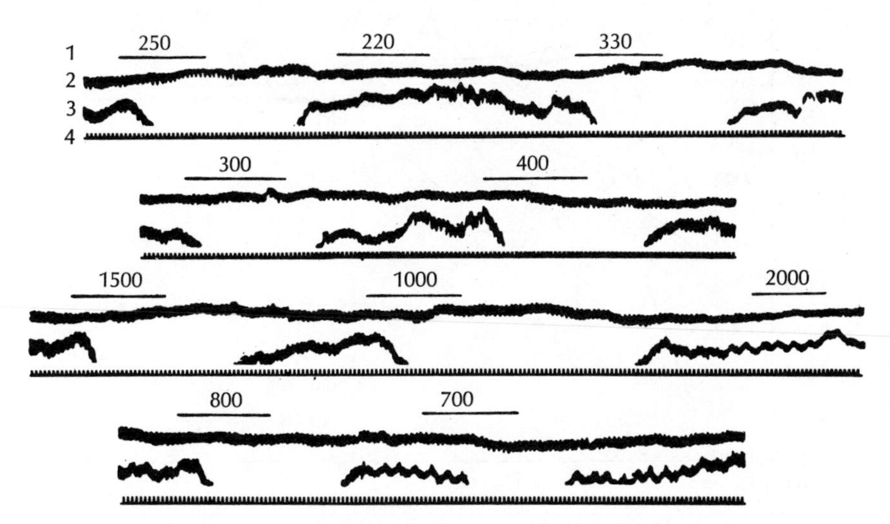

Figure 24–1. Initial state of concentration (subject L. A., session No. 4). The stimuli most remote from the basic tone (500 cps) in both the lower and higher part of the scale did not produce any changes in the vascular curves (220 and 2000 cps). Closer tones (250–330 and 1500–1000 cps) evoked pronounced "split" reactions. Tones of 350 and 800 cps produced reactions of a transitional character (no pronounced dilation in the cephalic vessels). Tones of 400 and 700 cps were accompanied by vasoconstriction of the same type as the reaction to the basic tone. (1) Lines denoting stimuli. (2) Plethysmogram of the cephalic vessels. (3) Plethysmogram of the peripheral vessels. (4) Time in seconds.

As the same procedure was repeated, the successive sessions revealed progressive narrowing of these zones. After only two or three alternations the stimuli at the extremes of the frequency scale employed failed to evoke any vascular response. Orienting responses were elicited at frequencies of 250 to 300 cps on one side and at 1200 to 1700 cps on the other. A corresponding shift toward the positive CS was also seen in the zone of tones producing a defensive reflex (up to 380 to 400 cps and 750 to 800 cps).

Subsequently, progressive narrowing of both zones was obtained with each successive test throughout the course of the experiment.

The narrowing of the zones of active stimuli, which proceeded very rapidly during the first 5 to 6 trials, later acquired an exceptionally slow character so that all the curves ran almost parallel to the abscissa.

Figure 24–2, showing the progressive changes in the vascular reactions during a series of sessions, reveals that the zone of active tones in the high part of the scale was much wider and contracted more slowly than the

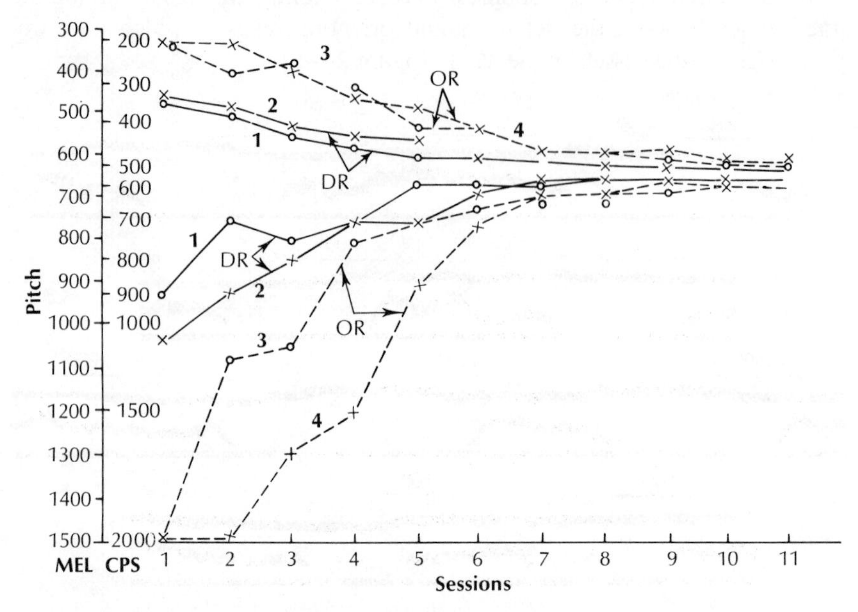

Figure 24–2. Changes in the boundaries of the orienting and defensive reactions in the course of 11 sessions on two subjects (A. C. and L. A.). Thresholds for the defensive reactions: (1) Subject A. C. (2) Subject L. A. Thresholds for the orienting reactions: (3) Subject A. C. (4) Subject L. A.

corresponding zone in the lower part. In this connection it should be pointed out that it was noted in an earlier work (Burmakin, 1909) from Pavlov's laboratory dealing with the problem of auditory generalization in the dog that "additional reflexes to the action of tones extended less downward than upward."

In the course of repeated trials, the actual group of stimuli which produced reactions of different types became more clearly defined. The "intermediate" zone between the "defensive" and "orienting" zones contracted and the transition became sharper. A similar steplike character was also assumed by the transition from the zone of inactive tones to the zone of orienting responses.

In the last stage of the experiment, when only a very narrow band of frequencies surrounding the positive conditioned stimuli (20 to 30 cps on either side) retained their activity, sharp differences were observed in the character of the effect of very closely adjoining stimuli on both sides of the signal tone of 500 cps. Tones right up to 470 to 475 cps on one side and down to 530 to 525 cps on the other did not produce reactions. Further approximation of 5 to 10 cps to the positive CS led to the sudden development of a very pronounced, prolonged, and intense orienting reaction. One more shift of 5 to 10 cps in the same direction elicited a sharp change in the nature of the reaction of the head vessels: there was constriction instead of dilation of the vessels, that is, the reaction assumed a defensive character. These relationships remained unchanged during a series of sessions (Figure 24–3).

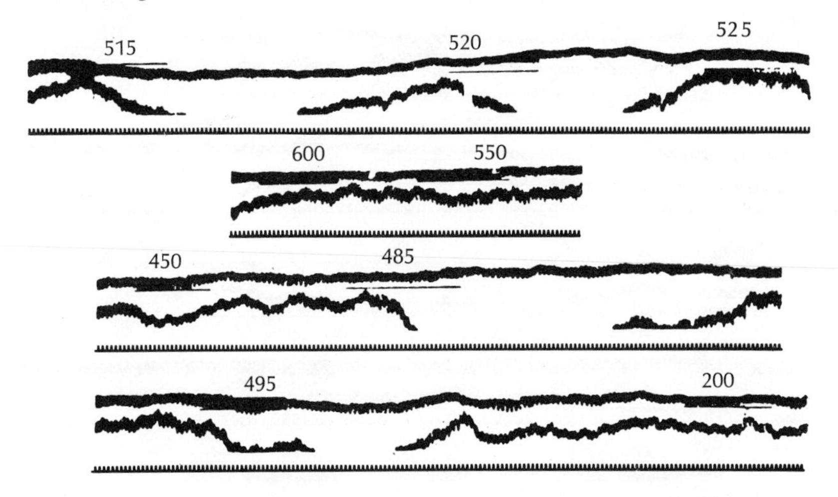

Figure 24–3. Terminal stage of concentration (Subject L. A., session No. 11). Defensive reactions were produced by tones of 515 and 495 cps. Tones of 520 and 485 cps were accompanied by reactions of orienting type. More remote tones did not produce reactions.

During the relative stability of the effect of the "central" group of stimuli seen at this stage in the experiments, there were changes in the effect of the very disparate stimuli. For a considerable period of time, commencing from the second and extending to the seventh or eighth session, the use of these stimuli did not, as we have stated, lead to changes in the vascular curve. It was observed in the last experiments of this series that the tones remotest from the positive CS again began to produce orienting reactions. This zone expanded slowly from session to session and embraced previously inactive stimuli lying ever nearer to the conditioned stimulus. During this period it could be seen quite clearly that, as the distance from the conditioned tone (and from the band of inactive tones lying close to it) increased, the reactions became more intense and more pronounced (Figure 24–4).

Certain additional changes were introduced in the last sessions in order to elucidate special features in the dynamics of the reactions being

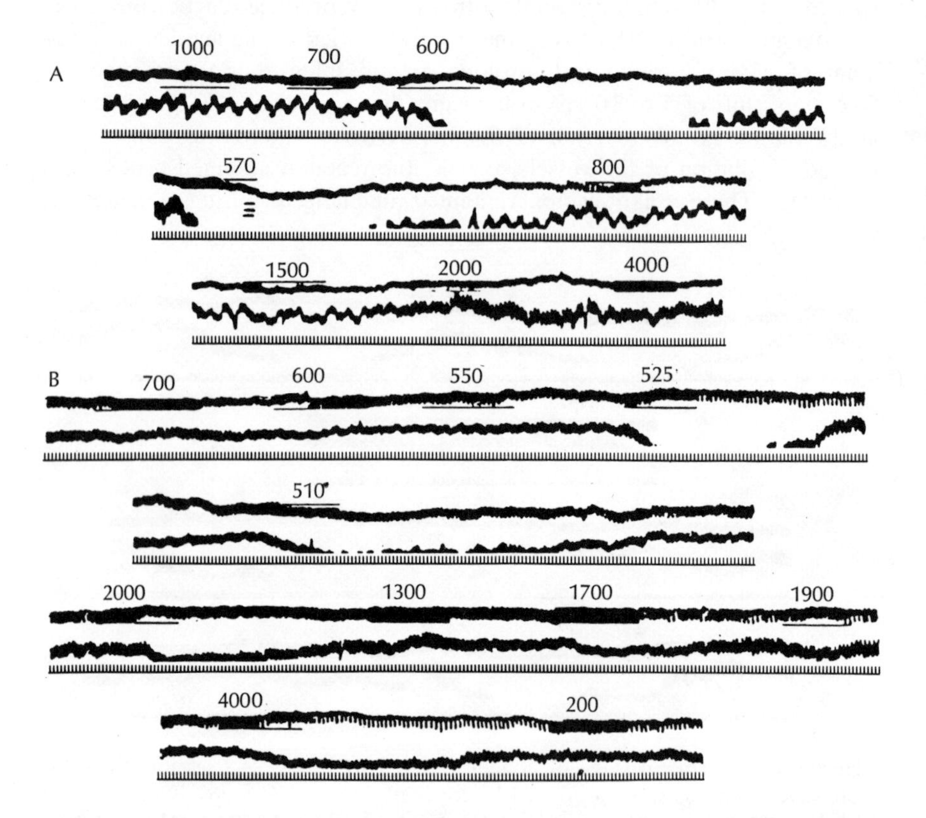

Figure 24–4. (*A*) Subject A. S., session No. 8. Stage of concentration. There was no reaction to tones remote from the basic tone (from 700 to 4000 cps). (*B*) The same subject, session No. 11. The sounds most remote from the basic tone (from 1700 to 4000 cps or more) began again to evoke reactions of the split type. The more remote the tone, the more intense was the reaction.

investigated. It has already been stated that the sounds were delivered through earphones to the right ear in all the main sessions of this series. Later, without warning, the side of delivery of the sound was changed; in all other respects the sessions were conducted exactly as before. With this change the boundaries of the two zones of reactions (of orienting and defensive types) were changed but the extent of these changes differed markedly. The zone of defensive reactions was expanded only slightly, but by 5 to 10 cps above the previous measurement with delivery of the sound to the usual right ear. The zone of orienting responses was sharply extended in both directions, by 200 to 700 cps (Figure 24–5, *A,* columns I and II). Control measurements at the end of the session with delivery of the sound to the usual right ear gave the same readings as in the initial measurement at the commencement of this experiment.

Binaural delivery of the sound was tried in the subsequent sessions. In this, as compared with the preceding application of the sound to the left

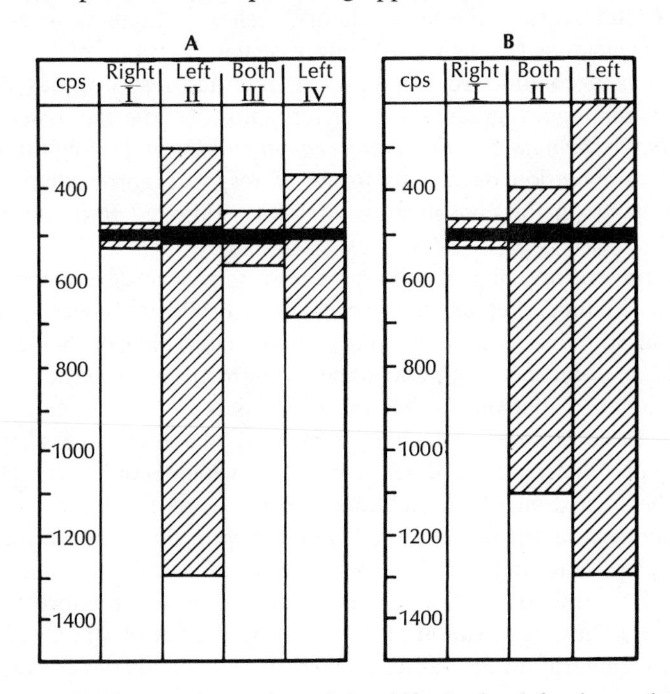

Figure 24–5. Graphic representation of the shifts in the defensive and orienting reactions when the conditions of tone delivery are changed. The zone of defensive reaction is shown in black; the zone of orienting reactions is shaded.

ear, both zones were reduced, the defensive zone only very slightly and the orienting fairly markedly (column III). This sharp reduction could have been entirely due to contraction of the zone of active stimuli as a result of repetition of the altered conditions of the experiment. The next control test showed, however, that this explanation was only partly true. Repeated trials with delivery of the sound to the left ear on a background of continuing contraction of the defensive zone revealed an unexpected shift of the boundaries for the orienting reaction. These were, it is true, much narrower than on the first delivery of sound to the left ear, but they were more than twice the width with the binaural application of the sound (column IV).

That this was not a chance occurrence was confirmed by a variation of this manipulation, which is illustrated in Figure 24–5, *B*. In this variation the sounds were applied first binaurally (II) and then to the left ear (III). Even in this case the binaural presentation of the sound produced a narrower band of restored orienting responses than the delivery of the tone to the left ear.

This work is a continuation of a series of investigations carried out in Sokolov's laboratory dealing with the relationship between orienting and specific (defensive and thermoregulatory) reflexes. In these investigations it has been demonstrated by recording vascular reactions that, during the formation of a conditioned response, an orienting response develops first and later undergoes gradual conversion into the *specific reaction corresponding to the nature of the reinforcement employed.* During this process, the gradual evolution of various forms of response corresponding to the different stages in the consolidation of the conditioned response could be observed.

In the present investigation the same process is seen developing in space as well as in time. Let us, in accordance with Pavlov's views, regard a differential stimulus as a compound stimulus consisting of elements some of which are coincident with and some different from the basic CS; it may then be assumed that the further the stimulus is in its physical properties from the basic stimulus, which is reinforced, the fewer the elements of similarity and the smaller will be the part of it which is indirectly reinforced during the formation of a conditioned response to the basic signal. The actual connection of this remote stimulus with the reinforcement will, therefore, be weak and unstable. A closer stimulus will be more intensely reinforced via the basic CS; its connection with the reinforcement will be stronger. Thus, observation of the effect of a series of stimuli of varying degrees of similarity to the basic signal should reveal a series of conditioned connections in various stages of elaboration.

Whereas adjacent stimuli evoked the same defensive reaction as the positive CS, remote stimuli produced nonspecific orienting responses (independent of the quality of the reinforcement). The nature of this effect was evident in an analysis of the response to a stimulus at the boundary between the two zones; this reaction is particularly clear in the terminal stages of concentration. It is distinguished by its considerable intensity both in the hand (constriction) and the head (dilation), by its prolonged latent period, and its considerable duration. Reactions of this type have already been described (Vinogradova and Sokolov, 1955) in relation to the presentation of stimuli of various intensities. In this case, prolonged and intense responses developed to threshold stimuli.

The "threshold reaction," with a differential (frequency) threshold of auditory sensitivity rather than an absolute one, was encountered again in this investigation. It is interesting that the zone of specific (defensive) responses, which in the course of the initial sessions underwent concentration parallel to that of the zone of orienting responses, was not subject to analogous parallel shifts when the delivery of the signal was changed; it was merely slightly extended. The change in the locus of delivery of the signal, all its basic signal properties being preserved, did not affect the conditioned defensive reflex. The phenomenon of bilateral symmetrical formation of the conditioned response in the auditory analyzer was apparently operating here. But the response to a new specialized stimulus, i.e., the orienting reflex, displayed a sharp shift when the conditions of the experiment were changed.

The comparison between responses to tones presented monaurally to the left ear and those to binaural presentations, which gave less expansion of the zone of orienting response, was somewhat unexpected in this respect. The delivery of the sound to the left ear, which had never hitherto been used in the experiments, apparently involved a greater element of novelty than the delivery of sound to the right and left ears simultaneously, in which case there was, along with the element of novelty, complete retention of the constant, usual components.

There is, of course, the quite separate question of the nature of the "second zone of orienting reactions," separated from the first zone by a wide band of "inactive" stimuli which appears only at a certain stage in the concentration of nervous processes. The exact nature of the effect of stimuli which do not produce any vascular reaction in the zone of reduced excitability is not quite clear.

It may be stated that any sufficiently intense focus of excitation which has a specific unconditioned effect (as in the former experiments with Sokolov) or a specific conditioned effect (as in the experiments of this series) is surrounded peripherally by a special zone of increased excitability. A stimulus addressed to this zone does not produce a specific reaction, but neither is it indifferent. It produces an orienting response in the same way as differential stimuli close to the positive CS produced such reactions.

Any shift in the effect of constant stimuli which does not affect their special signal properties leads to activation of a considerable zone of nonspecific excitation. When these shifts involve the signal properties of the CS, they disturb the structure of the conditioned response itself as well as the zone of nonspecific excitation extended to the central focus, inhibiting its specific manifestations.

Undoubtedly this schematic description of the dynamic changes in these processes is very much simplified. Facts identical with those described here have also been obtained using a system of verbal stimuli linked together by meaning (Vinogradova and Eisler, 1957), the spread of excitation here being of a complex selective character. It is obvious that in our more easily interpreted case it was a question not of "foci" of excitation but of complex functional systems, the structure of which was gradually changed in the course of repeated action of the stimuli and the reversible reactions in the organism.

If it is accepted that an orienting response, as a general nonspecific activity of the organism, depends on the reticular formation in the diencephalon and midbrain, then, on the basis of the evidence of these experiments, one must recognize the leading role of the orienting reaction in the structural formation of reversible corticoreticular connections. These connections provide for accurate readjustment of the analyzer and the very delicate qualitative analysis of adjacent stimuli.

References

Ackner, B. and Pampiglione, G. *J. Neurol. Neurosurg. Psychiat.*, 1957, *20*, No. 1.

Bonvallet, M., Dell, P., and Hiebel, G. *EEG clin. Neurol.*, 1954, *6*, No. 1.

Burmakin, V. A. *The process of generalization of an auditory conditioned reflex in the dog.* St. Petersburg, 1909.

Gangloff, H., and Monier, M. *EEG clin. Neurol.*, 1956, *8*, No. 4.

Hovland, C. I. The generalization of conditioned responses: IV. The effects of varying amounts of reinforcement upon the degree of generalization of conditioned responses. *J. exper. Psychol.*, 1937, *21*, 261–276.

Ingvar, D., and Soderberg, U. *EEG clin. Neurol.*, 1956, *8*, No. 3.

Jansen, J., Andersen, P., and Kaada, B. *Yale J. Biol. Med.*, 1956, *28*, Nos. 3–4.

Jouvet, M. *J. Psychol. norm. pathol.*, 1956, *53*, No. 2.

Lissak, K. *Z. ärztl. Fortbild.*, 1956, *50*, Nos. 7–8.

Luria, A. R., and Vinogradova, O. S. An objective investigation of the dynamics of semantic systems. *Brit. J. Psychol.*, 1959, *50*, 89–105.

Sharpless, S., and Jasper, H. *Brain*, 1956, *79*, No. 4.

Sokolov, E. N. Neuronal models and the orienting reflex. In Mary A. B. Brazier (Ed.), *The central nervous system and behavior.* New York: Josiah Macy, Jr., Foundation, 1960. Pp. 187–276.

Sokolov, E. N., and Vinogradova, O. S. *Residual hearing in deaf and deaf-mute children.* Moscow, 1957.

Vinogradova, O. S. *The orienting reflex and orienting investigatory activity.* Moscow, 1958.

Vinogradova, O. S., and Eisler, N. A. *Proceedings of a Conference on the Joint Activity of the First and Second Signal Systems.* Moscow, 1957.

Vinogradova, O. S., and Sokolov, E. N. *Vop. Psikhol.*, 1955, No. 2.

Vinogradova, O. S., and Sokolov, E. N. *Fiziol. Zh. SSSR*, 1957, *43*, No. 1.

Wang, S., and Ranson, S. *J. comp. Physiol.*, 1939, *71*, No. 3.

Williams, A. Novelty, GSR, and stimulus generalization. *Canad. J. Psychol.*, 1963, *17*, 52–61.

25

The Application of Electronic-Computer Techniques to the Analysis of Bioelectric Processes in the Brain

M. N. Livanov

EDITORS' INTRODUCTION

M. N. Livanov is Director of the Laboratory for the Electro-encephalographic Investigation of Conditioned Reflexes at the Institute of Higher Nervous Activity and Neurophysiology in Moscow. Beginning with the study of relatively simple reflexes, Livanov has extended his studies of EEG activity to human problem-solving and the behavior pathologies. This latter work, although not discussed in this chapter, is available in Snezhnevsky's interesting description of Soviet studies of disturbances of higher nervous activity accompanying schizophrenic states (Snezhnevsky, 1961). Most recently, Livanov has been collaborating with Luria on the study of disturbances caused by local brain lesions. His techniques are held in high esteem in the U.S.S.R., where they are being applied in an ever increasing number of basic and applied research settings.

ATTEMPTS TO APPLY analytic methods to make possible precise quantitative calculations of particular response functions appeared early in the study of electroencephalography. We may cite the work of Dietsch

(1932), Livanov (1938), and Bernshtein (1927); somewhat later, there appeared the work of Shpil'berg (1941), Drohocki (1948), Grass and Gibbs (1938), and other investigators in which methods of frequency analysis were applied.

Interest in these problems has been growing in recent years. This is connected largely with the development of electronic-computer techniques, which have opened new possibilities. Here the works of Brazier (1960), using autocorrelation and cross-correlation analysis, and of Barlow (1961), Adey (1961), and a number of other investigators are well known. Moreover, numerous attempts were made to separate weak rhythmic potentials from background noise (Kozhevnikov, 1960, and others).

In recent years our laboratory has also turned to the problem of correlational analysis of biopotentials in the brain. In 1956 we worked with Anan'ev to develop a multichannel system which permitted us to record information from 50 to as many as 100 points on the cerebral cortex (Livanov and Anan'ev, 1960). Here we encountered a difficulty—the eye could not record everything produced by this system. We needed a precise evaluation of the material obtained. Analyzing the data by hand meant literally to "destroy life" in order to analyze only a few trials. This inadequacy brought about the need for electronic-computer techniques. We believe that the further recording methods are improved, the more essential it will be to utilize electronic computers.

Our work has involved different methods of analysis. In the first stage we were faced with the problem of correlating points in the cerebral cortex with respect to time in order to detect synchronicity.

We physiologists are specially interested in this problem, for if there is synchronicity, the points are interconnected. Putting aside the difficult problem of how this interconnection occurs, we emphasize that even simply hypothesizing interconnections among points on the cortex influences our methods for processing the data.

In our work (carried out with the cooperation of Glivenko, Kuznetsova, Korol'kova, Tsypina, and Trubnikova), we have had to be satisfied with hand methods from the very beginning and still use such methods in the first stages of data processing. Processing begins with a visual reading of discrete amplitude values for each point and tabulating their changes. This data is then read into an electronic computer (we are now developing apparatus for automatic encoding).

Figure 25–1 shows a typical example of this visual reading. The points are numbered from 1 to 33 inclusive; the results for each point under study are given by 1½-second segments. An increase in amplitude is designated by a plus, a decrease by a minus, and absence of change by a zero. This procedure is repeated for all 33 points.

These data were read into an electronic computer, which compared the signs of the first time derivative (increase, no change, or decrease) for each

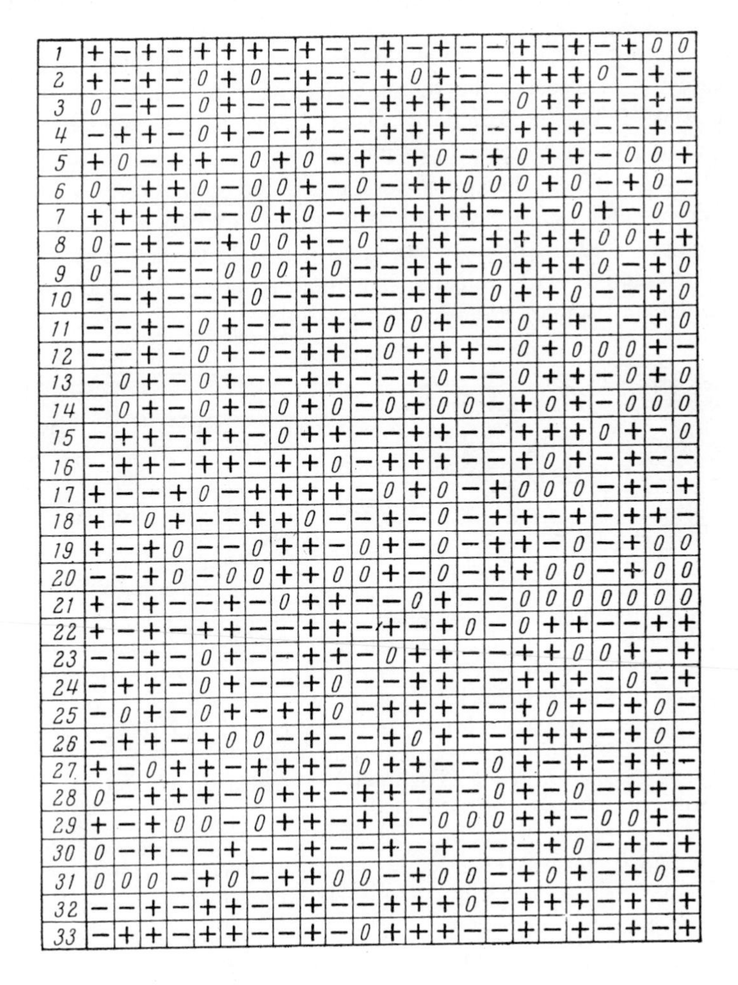

1	+	−	+	−	+	+	+	−	+	−	−	+	−	+	−	−	+	−	+	−	+	0	0
2	+	−	+	−	0	+	0	−	+	−	−	+	0	+	−	−	+	+	+	0	−	+	−
3	0	−	+	−	0	+	−	−	+	−	−	+	+	+	−	−	0	+	+	−	−	+	−
4	−	+	+	−	0	+	−	−	+	−	−	+	+	+	−	−	+	+	+	−	−	+	−
5	+	0	−	+	+	−	0	+	0	−	+	−	+	0	−	+	0	+	+	−	0	0	+
6	0	−	+	+	0	−	0	0	+	−	0	−	+	+	0	0	0	+	0	−	+	0	−
7	+	+	+	+	−	−	0	+	0	−	+	−	+	+	+	−	+	−	0	+	−	0	0
8	0	−	+	−	−	+	0	0	+	−	0	−	+	+	−	+	+	+	+	0	0	+	+
9	0	−	+	−	−	0	0	0	+	0	−	−	+	+	−	0	+	+	+	0	−	+	0
10	−	−	+	−	−	+	0	−	+	−	−	−	+	+	−	0	+	+	0	−	−	+	0
11	−	−	+	−	0	+	−	−	+	+	−	0	0	+	−	−	0	+	+	−	−	+	0
12	−	−	+	−	0	+	−	−	+	+	−	0	+	+	+	−	0	+	0	0	0	+	−
13	−	0	+	−	0	+	−	−	+	+	−	−	+	0	−	−	0	+	+	−	0	+	0
14	−	0	+	−	0	+	−	0	+	0	−	0	+	0	0	−	+	0	+	−	0	0	0
15	−	+	+	−	+	+	−	0	+	+	−	−	+	+	−	−	+	+	+	0	+	−	0
16	−	+	+	−	+	+	−	+	+	0	−	+	+	+	−	−	+	0	+	−	+	−	−
17	+	−	−	+	0	−	+	+	+	+	−	0	+	0	−	+	0	0	0	−	+	−	+
18	+	−	0	+	−	−	+	+	0	−	−	+	−	0	−	+	+	−	+	−	+	+	−
19	+	−	+	0	−	−	0	+	+	−	0	+	−	0	−	+	+	−	0	−	+	0	0
20	−	−	+	0	−	0	0	+	+	0	0	+	−	0	−	+	+	0	0	−	+	0	0
21	+	−	+	−	−	+	−	0	+	+	−	−	0	+	−	−	0	0	0	0	0	0	0
22	+	−	+	−	+	+	−	−	+	+	−	+	−	+	0	−	0	+	+	−	−	+	+
23	−	−	+	−	0	+	−	−	+	+	−	0	+	+	−	−	+	+	0	0	+	−	+
24	−	+	+	−	0	+	−	−	+	0	−	−	+	+	−	−	+	+	+	−	0	−	+
25	−	0	+	−	0	+	−	+	+	0	−	+	+	+	−	−	+	0	+	−	+	0	−
26	−	+	+	−	+	0	0	−	+	−	−	+	0	+	−	−	+	+	+	−	+	0	−
27	+	−	0	+	+	−	+	+	+	−	0	+	+	−	−	0	+	−	+	−	+	+	−
28	0	−	+	+	+	−	0	+	+	−	+	+	−	−	−	0	+	−	0	−	+	+	−
29	+	−	+	0	0	−	0	+	+	−	+	+	−	0	0	0	+	+	−	0	0	+	−
30	0	−	+	−	−	+	−	−	+	−	−	+	−	+	−	−	−	+	0	−	+	−	+
31	0	0	0	−	+	0	−	+	+	0	0	−	+	0	0	−	+	0	+	−	+	0	−
32	−	−	+	−	+	+	−	−	+	−	−	+	+	+	0	−	+	+	+	−	+	−	+
33	−	+	+	−	+	+	−	−	+	−	0	+	+	+	−	−	+	−	+	−	+	−	+

Figure 25–1. Table of the first time derivatives (increased or decreased activity, or no change) obtained by comparing the amplitude of the EEG in adjacent time samples.

1½-second segment for each pair of leads (first and second, first and third, up to first and thirty-third). Then the second point was compared, beginning with the third, and ending with the thirty-third, and so on. Thus, the machine made paired comparisons of all the points, giving the result in percentages of the 1½-second intervals spent in synchronous activity for the entire sample.

The results of this sort of quantitative processing can be represented either in the form of distribution curves or in the form of a diagram mapping the points on the cerebral cortex. This latter procedure can be seen in

Figure 25–2, where the hemisphere of a rabbit brain is shown in two such diagrams.

Both diagrams deal with individual points, each denoted by square cross-hatching. These are the points which were used in the pair-by-pair comparisons. Points indicated by black areas were correlated with the first point in 70 to 100 per cent of the time segments studied. When points denoted by horizontal hatching were compared with points denoted by square cross-hatching, they yielded correlations in 43 to 69 per cent of the time segments studied. Blank white areas generally do not yield significant correlations. Points with diagonal hatching are negatively correlated with points which have square cross-hatching.

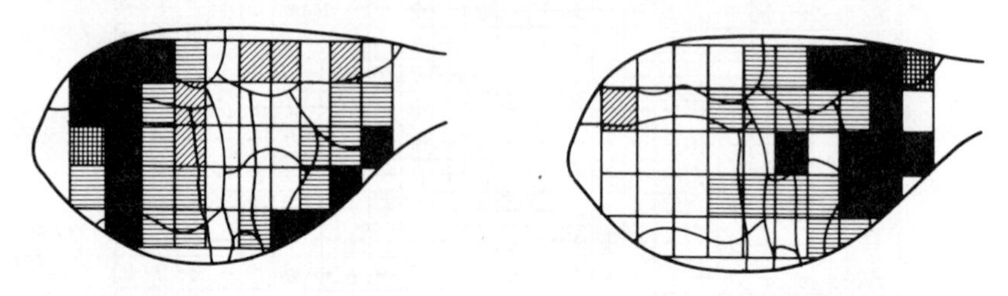

Figure 25–2. Correlation between one brain segment of a rabbit (square cross-hatching) and all other points in that hemisphere. On the contour of the left hemisphere we have indicated the borders of the cytoarchitechtonic fields distinguished by Rose (1931). Each square represents the field of one electrode. The black squares correlate with the reference point 70 to 100 per cent of the time. The squares with horizontal lines correlate 43 to 69 per cent. The unmarked squares are uncorrelated with the reference point, and the obliquely hatched squares are negatively correlated.

The second stage in data processing also involved electronic computers. At this stage, the signs of the first time derivatives were read into the machine, not for all the points, but only for those points which yielded high correlations in the preliminary pair-by-pair processing. The machine has now given us those points which operated with the same sign for no less than 70 per cent of the time under study. This permitted precise separation of synchronous systems of points in the brain cortex. We shall call such points constellations, that is, these are constellations of points which are interconnected by mutual influences.

What sort of regularities are found in these systems? Figure 25–3, *A* shows a compact constellation, a system formed by a number of synchronously acting points, compactly arranged. It turned out, however, that synchronicity did not by any means require a compact arrangement of the points. Synchronously working points may be separated from each other by areas of the brain cortex that do not participate in this synchronous activity (Figure 25–3, *B*).

The question then arises: How are various points in the brain synchronized? As a first guess, we turn to the subcortex as the system which may cause this selective, remote synchronicity. However, we still cannot answer this question; it is a matter for future resolution. Let us consider the case presented in Figure 25–3, *C,* which is still more interesting and is encountered fairly often. Here several synchronized systems are present in the cortex at the same time: the first system—shown in black; the second system—by shading; and the third—by horizontal hatching. Each system

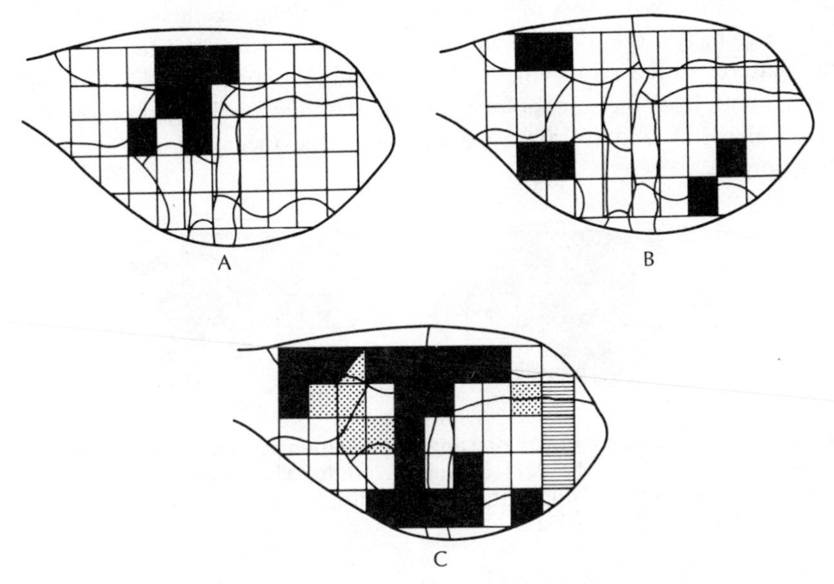

Figure 25–3. Example of constellations found in the rabbit cortex. For interpretation of this figure, see the legend to Figure 25–2.

is synchronized within itself for 70 per cent of the time under study, but they are not synchronous with each other. Thus, we find that several independent systems with synchronized biopotentials can exist simultaneously in the cortex.

There is still one other detail here. Note that one square in Figure 25–3, *C* is partially shaded and partially black. This point is remarkable, because insulated constellations of synchronicity come together in it. Thus some points in the cortex work simultaneously with more than one synchronized system. It will now be possible to investigate where such interstratification takes place most easily in the cortex and what structural features distinguish these areas. Again, there are as yet no answers to these questions.

Of course, all these synchronized systems in the cortex change rapidly. But if there were no sort of constancy in them, it is questionable whether they would be of interest. As it turns out, there is constancy in these constellations. In spite of constant fluctuations, they do show significant similarity in their arrangement in the brain cortex.

Figure 25–4 shows diagrams of the brain cortex with superimposed synchronized constellations in two different rabbits. The constellations were arrived at by averaging results from three experiments on each animal. In spite of certain differences in the constellations, both of them are located in approximately the same areas of the cerebral cortex. Adjacent to them are areas of the cerebral cortex which rarely participate in synchronized systems. What sort of areas are these? What are their peculiarities? This, again, is a question we cannot answer today. But the fact that there are patterns in the arrangement of constellations shows that they are interesting, both from the standpoint of finding the functional organization of the cerebral cortex and from the standpoint of the theory of localized brain functions.

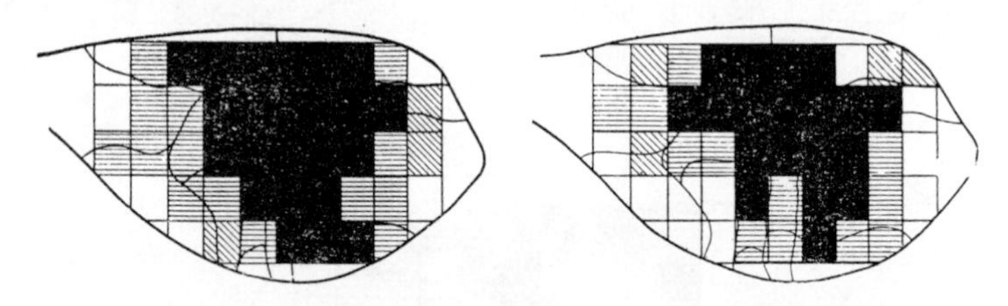

Figure 25–4. Examples of long-lasting constellations in the rabbit brain. Each square corresponds to the field of one electrode. The black squares correlate with each other 69 to 100%; the horizontally hatched squares are negatively correlated. (After Rose, 1931.)

We have already noted that synchronized systems constantly fluctuate and change. We must add that they can be disorganized by all sorts of stimuli. It was emphasized earlier that these systems are said to exist when the bioelectric oscillations of different points in the cortex are similar for 70 per cent of the time under study. Then the question is, what goes on in the remaining 30 per cent of the time? One may assume from an analogy with technology that noise processes play a role here and that 30 per cent of the time is spent by the cerebral cortex in "making noise."

Here we encounter a curious fact. It turns out that the brain is poor at making "noise" and this 30 per cent of the time is spent in the formation of new constellations. Figure 25–5 shows a table in which data are presented from a synchronized system consisting of seven points in the cerebral cortex. It can be seen that all signs are the same in the majority of columns. In some columns we see what appears to be a random deviation of one (or maximum of two) signs, but these cases are not numerous and the course of the total synchronized system is not disrupted. At times, however, several points go out of phase at once (for example, in columns 1, 8, 15, and 21); then the constellation is destroyed.

This shows that 30 per cent of the time is not spent on random "noise" processes, but in systematic "going out of phase," apparently connected with some factors we have not taken into account, possibly some stimuli. In fact, these constellations are exceedingly responsive to different stimuli.

Limitations of space do not permit us to illustrate this proposition. We shall say only that constellations can change in three ways:

1. The first case is one in which the synchronized system does not disappear under the influence of a stimulus, but, on the contrary, is reinforced; the amplitudes of the biopotentials participating at its points are increased.

2. The second case is one in which a constellation is completely dissolved and can be replaced by a new constellation.

5	−	−	+	+	−	−	+	+	+	−	+	+	−	−	+	−	+	+	−	−	0	+	−	+	−	+	−	−	+	−	+	+
16	+	−	+	+	−	−	+	0	+	−	+	+	−	−	−	+	+	+	−	−	−	+	−	−	+	+	−	+	+	−	+	+
7	−	−	+	+	−	−	+	+	+	−	+	+	−	−	−	+	+	+	−	−	−	+	0	+	−	+	−	−	+	−	+	+
17	+	−	+	+	−	−	+	+	+	−	+	+	−	−	−	+	+	+	−	−	−	+	0	−	−	+	−	−	+	−	+	+
24	0	−	+	+	−	−	+	+	+	−	0	+	−	−	+	+	−	+	−	−	−	+	−	+	−	+	−	−	+	−	+	+
27	+	−	+	+	0	−	+	0	+	−	+	+	−	−	−	+	+	+	−	−	0	+	−	+	−	+	+	−	+	−	+	+
36	+	−	+	+	−	−	+	−	+	−	+	+	+	−	+	+	+	+	−	−	0	+	−	+	−	+	−	−	+	−	+	+
		−	+	+	−	−	+		+	−	+	+	−	−		+	+	+	−	−		+	−	+	−	+	−	−	+	−	+	+

Figure 25–5. A table of the sign of the first time derivatives from points in a single synchronized system.

3. The third case, which is encountered most often, is one in which a constellation changes, is modified, without being completely dissolved and retains a part of its previous features.

A single stimulus does not exert a particularly strong influence. Changes are effected only by combinations of stimuli, as, for example, in the development of conditioned reflexes.

Figure 25–6 shows the changes in constellations during the development of a defensive conditioned reflex in response to a stereotype of stimuli consisting of light followed by a tone. Figure 25–6, *A* presents the background of synchronized systems prior to the development of a conditioned reflex in a rabbit. Here one can see several systems, denoted by point shading, square cross-hatching, diagonal hatching, black, and horizontal hatching. They are scattered and there is no established contact among them. Then, a total of 12 CS-UCS presentations is given. There still is no conditioned reflex, but the synchronization changes sharply (Figure 25–6, *B*). It now includes extensive areas in the cortex, but not all the cortex is involved in a single synchronized system.[1] A motor conditioned-reflex appears within 20

1. We are speaking of data obtained from rabbits. This should be taken into account since the process may go on in different ways in different animals.

to 60 combinations. It can be seen from Figure 25–6, *C* that after 60 trials there is a reduction in the concentration of constellations; here different synchronized systems begin to be differentiated. After 90 combinations the previous diffuse synchronization disappears completely, but separate areas which work in a synchronous manner are retained in the cortex. The pattern approaches the original picture.

We have spent a great amount of time in investigating the phenomenon of synchronization of biopotentials in the cortex. Still, one can ask: What is synchronization from a physiological standpoint?

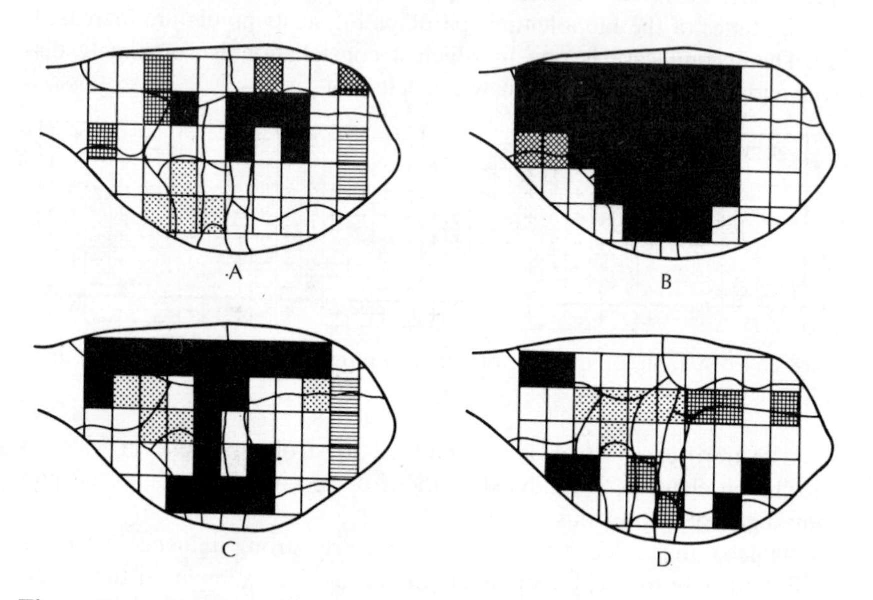

Figure 25–6. Changes in the degree of synchronization of cortical biopotentials during the development of a conditioned reflex: (*A*) initial level; (*B*) after 12 trials; (*C*) after 60 trials; (*D*) after 90 trials.

We believe that synchronization reflects that state of the cortical substrate in which irradiation of the nerve processes is facilitated. This is the basis for generalization of conditioned reflexes.

One can better interpret this from the standpoint of present ideas concerning the origin of biopotentials in the cerebral cortex in the following manner. The most widely accepted idea at present is that the biopotentials recorded from the surface of the cortex reflect postsynaptic potentials of the *apical* dendrites. These potentials regulate the irritability of the nerve cells. From this standpoint their synchronization should lead to synchronous oscillations in the irritability of a set of neurons. This is, then, the substrate of irradiation.

Finally, we turn to interconnections of cortical areas in man. This work was done in collaboration with Kaganova, Gavrilova, and Aslanova.

Most investigators who have studied changes in the EEG during mental work have used alpha depression as the criterion of changes in the EEG. For instance, Penfield and Jasper (1958) considered a depression of the alpha rhythm to be a manifestation of "higher mental processes and acute emotional states." Walter (1957) attempted to associate thinking with the dynamics of alpha depression. He took the further step of dividing people into groups in whom verbal or visual forms of thinking predominate on the basis of the dynamics of their alpha depression.

However, there is no unanimity of opinion on the relation of the EEG to thinking. Bujas, Peitz, and Kzkovic (1953) used the so-called alpha index as an EEG measure during mental work and found a marked depression of alpha activity only at the onset of a task. Some investigators have failed to obtain alpha depression during mental work (De Lange, Storm van Leeuwen, and Veere, 1962), and Barlow even observed an increase in alpha activity during emotional states (Barlow, 1962).

Genkin (1961) concluded that the alpha rhythm is a manifestation of more primitive processes, probably neurohumoral in nature. Sokolov (1958) has shown that alpha depression can be caused by noncognitive factors as one of the components of the orienting response.

We felt that this absence of agreement and the relative scarcity of results concerning the role of EEG changes during mental work were caused in part by the fact the methods used in these investigations were somewhat limited. Recordings were made from at best a very few areas so that neither the functional state of the cortex as a whole nor the interrelation among different areas could be determined. By the same token, our recording techniques, described above, seem well suited for a study of this problem.

For our own study of EEG changes during mental activity we used seven healthy adult subjects. Each subject was first given 5 minutes of dark adaptation in a dark, sound-proof chamber, after which a 10-second recording of cortical activity was made. Then the subject was asked to calculate the answer to a multiplication problem (the numbers were two- or three-digit, depending on the subject's educational level). Recording of the EEG began 4 to 5 seconds after assignment of the task and continued for 25 seconds. A 25-second sample of EEG activity was taken every other minute until the subject produced an answer or gave up. Each subject was tested 3 to 10 times on different days. During each session he was asked to do three or four problems.

In our analysis of the data, we examined time segments which varied in length from 3 to 9 seconds. Analyses were carried out separately for the background EEG level (recorded at the beginning of each session) and for the 25-second samples taken at various stages of problem solution.

With the cortex at rest, about half of the points recorded from operated independently, that is, showed no significant positive correlations. Points were considered independent if they showed correlated activity less than 44 per cent of the time (100 per cent correlation would mean that the points in question changed in the same direction throughout the entire period analyzed). Independent cortical points were located diffusely, with no tendency to appear in any particular cortical region.

Many cortical areas produced correlations 45 to 75 per cent of the time. We have termed this a group of cortical points with a low percentage of correlations. The correlations in this group may occur in adjacent or widely separated areas, even between different hemispheres.

We also found cortical regions whose biopotentials were correlated more than 75 per cent of the time. During rest these regions represented only 2.5 to 3 per cent of the total. As a rule, only adjacent points yielded such a high percentage of intercorrelations. It should also be noted that none of these points is ever highly correlated with many cortical points, but only with two or three.

This picture changes radically during mental work. A marked increase in the number of correlations between different cortical areas takes place. Points correlated 75 per cent of the time or more now begin to predominate.

Such a shift in the pattern of cortical activity was recorded in five of our seven subjects. The number of areas with a low percentage of correlations decreased while the number of independently functioning areas increased.

We will make a detailed analysis of those cortical points which are correlated a high percentage of the time during mental work. The changes in activity associated with these points are shown in Figure 25–7.

Prior to assignment of the problem (Figure 25–7, *A*), there is very little correlated activity and that which exists occurs primarily between adjacent points. During execution of mental arithmetic, nearly all of the cortical points show some correlated activity (*B* and *C*). At certain times a fluctuation in activity may reduce the number of correlations below the resting level, but such periods are only one-third as frequent as the more active periods. In four of our seven subjects no such reduction was observed.

A second feature of the activity observed during mental arithmetic is an increase in the number of points that each cortical point is correlated with. From a dominance of very few correlations during rest, the picture changes to one of multiple correlations (*B* and *C*).

The topography of activity also changes during the course of problem solving. During the height of mental activity, the frontal lobes show the highest density of correlated points, while the central gyrus is most active once the problem has been solved.

Table 25–1 shows the number of correlations in different cortical areas for different subjects during rest and during mental arithmetic. The entries

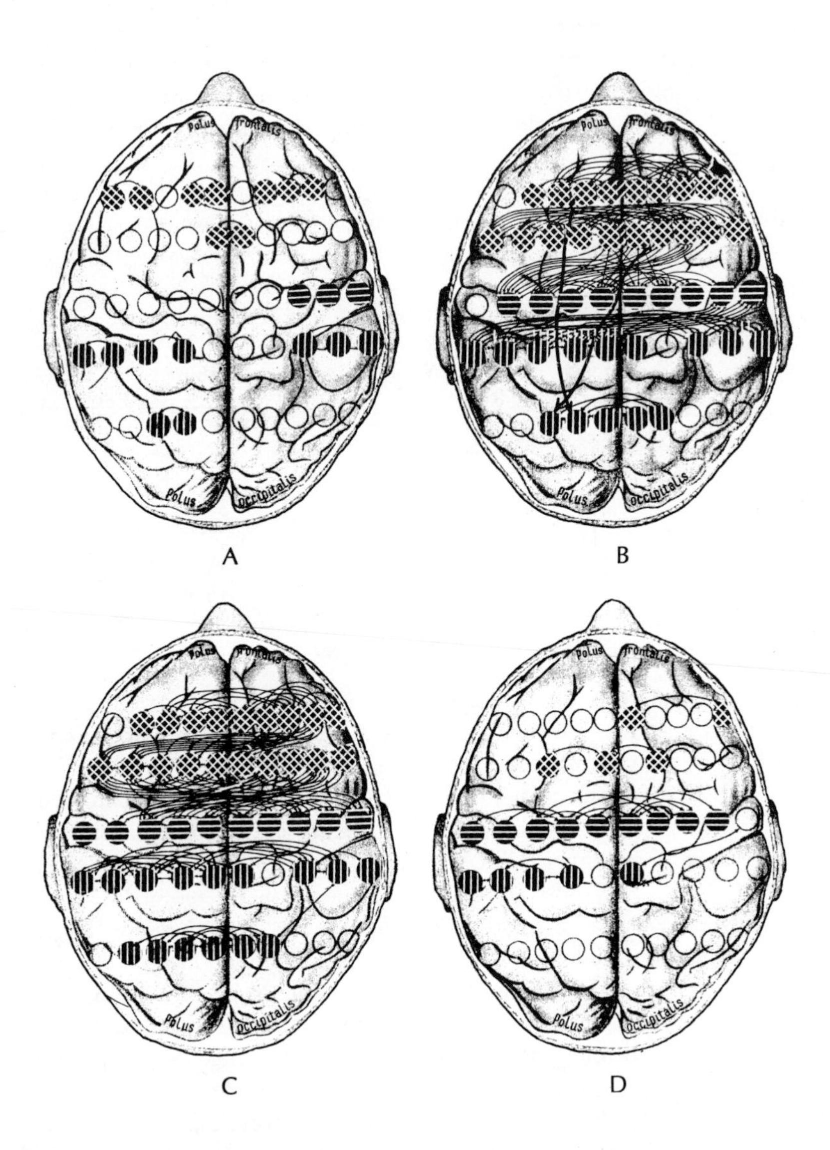

Figure 25–7. Temporal correlations between points on the human brain during mental work. The circles on the map of the cortex represent points where electrodes were placed. Circles with cross-hatching represent points in the frontal lobes; circles with horizontal lines—points in the frontal, central gyrus; circles with vertical lines—points in the parietal region. The arrows represent the presence of correlation between the two designated points 70 to 100 per cent of the time: (*A*) prior to presentation of the task; (*B*) 15 sec. after solution is begun; (*C*) 30 sec. after solution is begun; (*D*) after completion of the task.

in the tables are from time segments which exhibited the maximum activity for the rest and work periods.

As is seen, the number of "connections" is greatest in the frontal lobes, where, for example, for subject A. S. they amount to 74 (for a given interval of time) while in posterior regions of the parietal area there are only 21, and in the occipital area, 9.

Table 25–1 *Number of "High-Percentage" Correlations in Different Cortical Areas During Rest and During Mental Arithmetic*

Subject	Anterior frontal regions		Motor area		Posterior parietal region		Occipital area	
	Rest	Mental activity	Rest	Mental activity	Rest	Mental activity	Rest	Mental activity
1. N. G.	12	86	12	48	11	42	5	36
2. A. S.	5	74	2	32	6	21	2	9
3. B. E.	2	82	1	57	2	36	2	30
4. A. A.	0	11	0	2	0	4	0	2
5. V. A.	9	102	6	43	5	33	5	9
6. Y. C.	7	36	5	4	6	10	4	3
7. A. M.	4	4	6	23	15	13	18	14

It appears that correlations occur most easily between the areas localized along the frontal line. However, not only adjacent points become interconnected but the remote ones as well (Figure 25–7).

In all the subjects, correlations occurred between areas situated in opposite hemispheres. Special analysis is being carried out at present to elucidate which hemisphere, left or right, is more involved in mental processes.

There were very few correlations of biopotentials from the areas localized in the parietal and occipital regions, that is, sagittally through the whole cortex. As an illustration we can take points 3 and 44 or 16 and 43 (Figure 25–7, *B*), which are each connected by a heavy line.[2] A constellation formed by the areas with correlations in a high percentage of time is very dynamic. It does not remain permanent but changes its structure from one moment to another (Figure 25–7). In time period *C*, EEG correlations occurred not only between the points situated along the frontal line but also between the points in the rostral parts of the right frontal region and caudal parts of the frontal zone of the left hemisphere, whereas in the preceding one and a half seconds (*B*) only the frontal-line correlations were observed.

Of interest are the EEG correlations of the motor analyzer area. Nearly

2. *Editors' note:* Cortical points are numbered left to right and top to bottom, ten points to a row. (See Figure 25–7.)

all the points of this area gave a great number of intercorrelations (Table 25–1). The structure of the functional connections here is also very unstable and dynamic. Correlations were recorded not only between the points within the motor analyzer area but also between the motor analyzer and other cortical areas, especially in the anterior frontal zone. In the latter case correlations were mostly directed crosswise. Here we should take into consideration the fact that not all the motor neurons are localized in the anterior gyrus centralis. A great many scattered elements of the motor analyzer are situated in other cortical zones, for instance, in anterior frontal regions (Dzugaeva, 1960). These data point to a close functional connection between the anterior parts of the frontal cortex and the motor analyzer proper. Constant participation of the anterior gyrus centralis in EEG changes caused by mental activity is indicative of the presence of ideomotor acts.

Besides the intercorrelations of high-percentage EEG changes (75 per cent of the time and above) during mental activity, we have also recorded an increase in the number of correlations with a lower percentage of interaction (45 to 75 per cent of the time). Such an increase took place in five out of seven subjects. These correlations are observed not only between adjacent cortical areas, but often between quite remote areas, for example, the frontal and occipital regions. During mental activity such a dense "network" of "weak" correlations appears that the only way to estimate these changes is to analyze separately the connections of each point.

Figure 25–8 illustrates a characteristic of mental activity; an increase in correlations between the points whose EEG changes agree for 45 to 75 per cent of the time. It demonstrates the correlations of the second, third, and tenth points. When resting, the second point was correlated with only 8 other points (Figure 25–8, *A*), whereas during mental arithmetic it developed 44 connections (*C*); point 3 (*B*) was correlated with 12 points during rest and with 41 during mental work (*D*). A similar increase of intercorrelations between cortical areas has been observed in other regions as well.

As regards the predominance of one or another area in these correlations, we tend to think that the areas producing correlations in the low-percentage time intervals are situated diffusely through the whole cortex. These connections obviously reflect the appearance of a higher (as compared to the state of rest) functional level against whose background EEG correlations in a high percentage of the time intervals appear during mental activity. Table 25–2 presents the changes in percentages of correlations during rest and mental work for high and low degrees of synchronization as well as the change in the number of independently functioning points.

Table 25–2 shows the increase of correlations for both kinds of synchronization and the decrease in the number of points functioning independently in five subjects out of seven. Subjects N. G., A. S., and A. A. show this most clearly. In subjects Y. C. and A. M. such changes were not observed. The

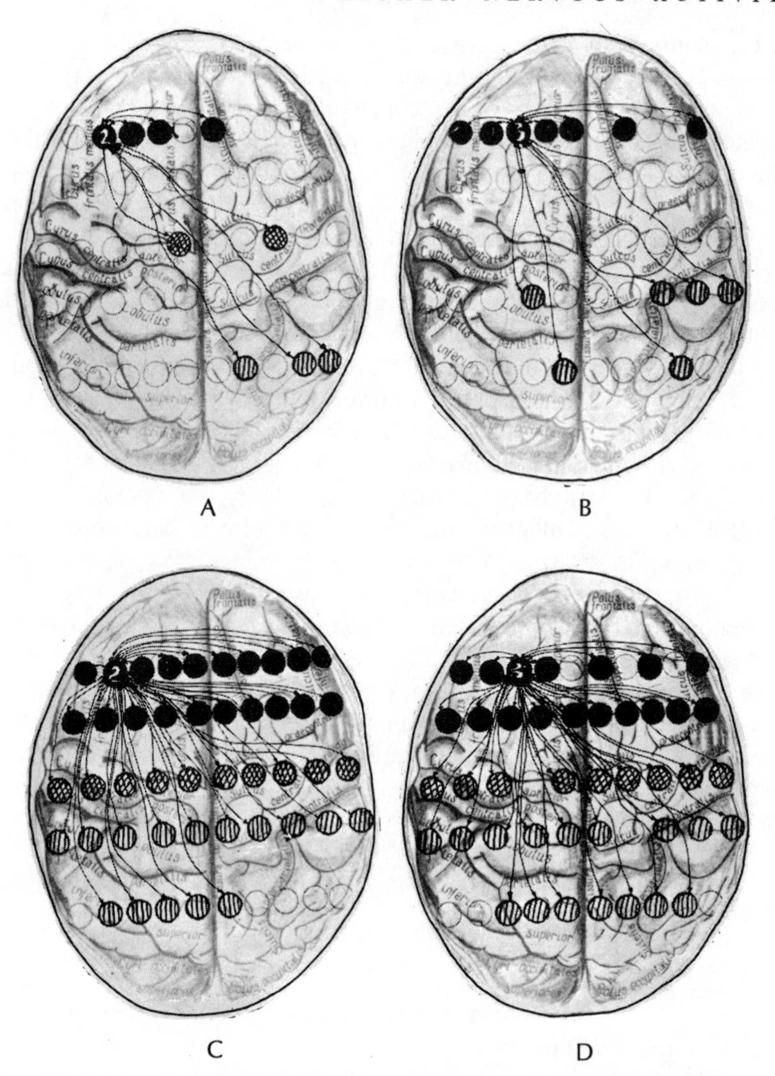

Figure 25–8. Correlations for single points that are correlated 45 to 75 per cent of the time. The cortical maps in the upper half of the figure represent activity in the resting state; the maps in the lower half were obtained during mental arithmetic.

stablest pattern is that of A. M. She was asked to code a number of figures for a computer. This seemingly very difficult task proved to be very simple. She said she performed it momentarily without any strain—"just automatically."

We believe that the increase of EEG correlations (mainly in the high-percentage points) is markedly pronounced only in those cases where the

Table 25–2 *Number of "High-Percentage" Correlations During Rest and Mental Activity as a Function of Degree of Synchronization*

Subject	High percentage of correlations		Low percentage of correlations		Independently functioning points	
	Rest	Mental activity	Rest	Mental activity	Rest	Mental activity
1. N. G.	4	19	58	72	37	8
2. A. S.	3	8	36	59	57	32
3. A. A.	3	14	43	68	51	16
4. E. B.	3	10	67	69	29	21
5. V. A.	0	2	37	63	61	35
6. Y. C.	2	3	34	29	62	62
7. A. M.	4	4	42	43	50	50

subjects are given rather difficult tasks. Presentation of easy tasks evokes either no correlation at all, or an increase of the "connections" with a low degree of synchronization. This hypothesis remains to be proved.

It was interesting to follow up the changes of correlation during mental activity after administration of aminasine, the drug which mostly affects the reticular formation and anterior parts of the brain.

Figure 25–9 illustrates the "connections" of different brain areas of the intact subject N. G. during mental arithmetic (multiplication of two-figure numbers). Figure 25–9, *A* gives the resting level; Figure 25–9, *B* shows the abundance of correlations among different cortical areas (in high percentage of time) during the multiplication. Figure 25–9, *C* shows the "connections" in the same subject performing a similar task, 1 hour 15 minutes after administration of 25 mg. of aminasine. The frontal regions of the brain now have no EEG correlations whatsoever. At the same time, the synchronism in the activity of different points is preserved in other cortical areas, for example, in the parietal area.

In discussing the data obtained the following question may arise: cannot the changes observed during mental work be the result of the orienting reaction? If this were so, then the increase of correlations between different cortical areas would be most pronounced during the first seconds of mental arithmetic with a subsequent diminution. In reality, however, the changes observed during mental activity fluctuate and may be more pronounced in the subsequent periods of the activity than at the beginning. Besides, the experiments were performed repeatedly, which would facilitate the extinction of the orienting reaction to the environment and to the problems presented. No decreased correlation with repetition was observed. Further, if the increase of EEG correlations were caused by the orienting reaction, it

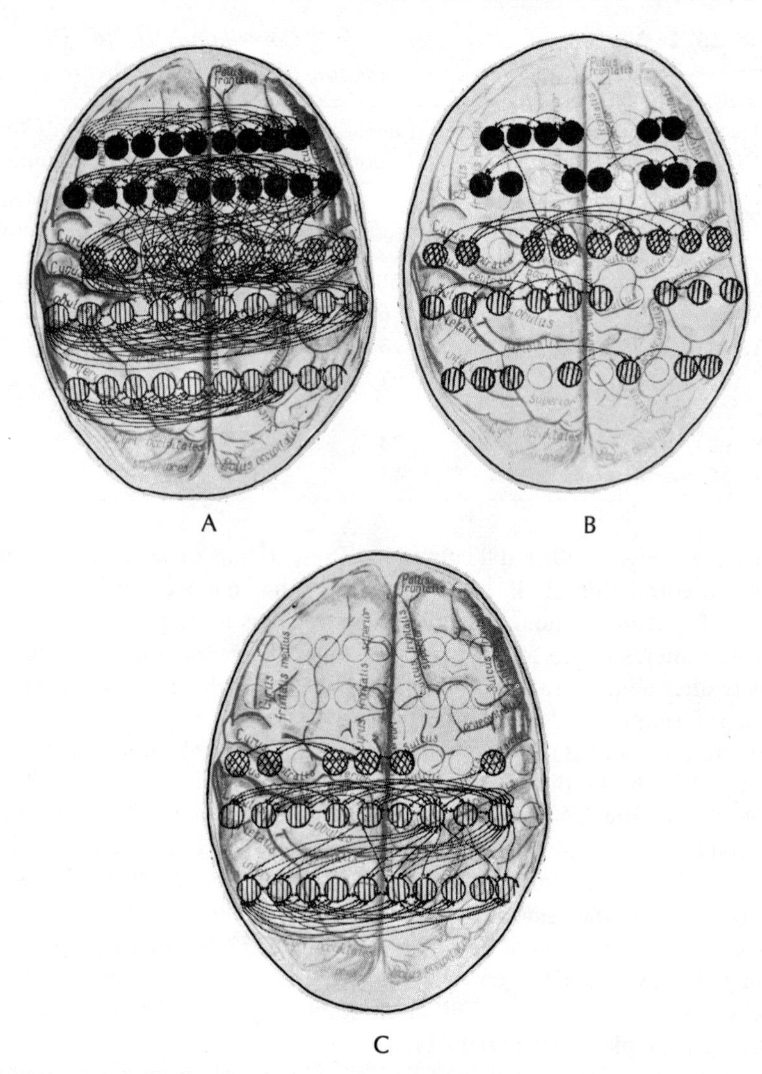

Figure 25–9. The effect of aminazine on temporal correlations during the solution of an arithmetic problem for cortical points showing correlated activity 75 to 100 per cent of the time: (*A*) prior to presentation of the problem; (*B*) during mental arithmetic; (*C*) during mental arithmetic 75 min. after administration of 25 mg. of aminasine.

would be equally observed in trained and untrained subjects for these particular kinds of mental activity.

These research examples show what wide horizons have been opened before investigators with the aid of electronic computers. Quantitative processing of electroencephaloscopic data is making it possible to approach the study of very complicated processes taking place in the cerebral cortex. Such investigations will be interesting in various cases of pathology, in various functional states, and so forth. However, it must be borne in mind that the connections we have been discussing are merely correlations of cortical areas. The extent to which they reflect, or whether they do reflect, associative processes in general is not known.

References

Adey, W. R. Brain mechanisms and learning processes. *Federation Proceedings,* 1961, *20,* No. 2.

Barlow, J. S. Autocorrelational and crosscorrelational techniques in EEG analysis. *EEG clin. Neurophysiol.,* 1961, Suppl., *20.*

Barlow, J. S. Cited by J. W. M. De Lange, W. Storm van Leeuwen, and P. S. Veere. In *Electroencephalography of higher nervous activity.* Moscow: Izd. Akad. Nauk SSSR, 1962.

Bernshtein, N. A. Zur Analyse der aperiodischen Trigonometrie schen reihan. *Ang. Mathematik,* 1927.

Brazier, M. Some uses of computers in experimental neurology. *Exper. Neurol.,* 1960, *2.*

Bujas, Z. Peitz, B., and Kzkovic, I. A. Electricna aktivnost mozga u toku duzec interektualnog rada. *Arkiv zu Higj. Rada,* 1953, *4.*

De Lange, J. V. N., Storm van Leeuwen, W., and Veere, P. F. Correlation between psychological and encephalographic events. In *Electroencephalography of higher nervous activity.* Moscow: Izd. Akad. SSSR, 1962.

Dietsch, G. Fourier Analyse von Electroencephalogramm in dem Menschen. *Pflüg. Arch. ges. Physiol.,* 1932, *230.*

Drohocki, Z. Sur l'emploi des filtres-electroniques en elektrospectro graphie du cerveau. *C. R. Soc. biol.,* 1948, *100.*

Dzugaeva, S. B. Topography of the pyramidal pathway. In *Problems of the morphology of the nervous system.* Moscow: Medgiz, 1960.

Grass, A. M., and Gibbs, F. A. Fourier analysis of the EEG. *J. Neurol.,* 1938, *1.*

Kozhevnikov, V. A. Automatic methods for analyzing brain waves and their use for the study of weak electrical responses of the brain. Doctoral dissertation, 1960.

Livanov, M. N. Analysis of the brain waves in the mammalian cortex. *Trudy Inst. Mozga,* 1938, *3–4.*

Livanov, M. N., and Anan'ev, B. M. *Electroencephalography.* Moscow: Medgiz, 1960.

Penfield, W., and Jasper, H. *Epilepsy and the functional anatomy of the human brain.* Moscow: Foreign Languages Publishing House, 1958.

Rose, M. Cytoarchitektonischer Atlas der Grosshirnrinde des Kaninchens. *J. Psychol. Neurol.*, 1931, *43*.

Shpil'berg, P. I. Harmonic analysis of the electroencephalogram of man. *Fiziol. Zh. SSSR*, 1941, *30*.

Snezhnevsky, A. V. Psychopharmacology, the pathophysiology of higher nervous activity, and clinical psychiatry. *Ann. N.Y. Acad. Sci.*, 1961, *92*, 1077–1097.

26

The Formation of Conditioned Place Reflexes

P. S. Kupalov

EDITORS' INTRODUCTION

P. S. Kupalov, who died in 1964, was for many years Pavlov's closest collaborator. From 1925 until Pavlov's death in 1937 he was second in command of Pavlov's laboratory at the Institute of Experimental Medicine. From 1937 to 1964 he headed the Physiological Laboratory at the Institute.

During his fifty years of research on higher nervous activity, Kupalov's interests ranged over a wide variety of problems. For many years he worked on the problem of the formation of "functional mosaics" in the cortex. A functional mosaic is defined as a complex relation between excitation and inhibition, a reflection of the environmental influences consisting of excitatory and inhibitory agents which constantly bombard the organism. This problem in turn led to a study of the effect of the general tonus of the cortex on the formation of conditioned reflexes.

Another of Kupalov's important contributions in the area of neurophysiology dealt with the question of local states of excitation and inhibition built up in the cortex as a result of specific experiences. This work on "cortical tonus" is described in two of Kupalov's articles available in English (1960, 1961). It is similar in many respects to the research by Romanovskaya and Tchilingaryan described in Asratyan's chapter in the present volume.

The chapter that follows is taken from a posthumously published monograph, Conditioned Place Reflexes in Normal and

Pathological Dogs. *It represents a summary of research conducted over a twenty-year period by Kupalov and his colleagues on the application of Pavlovian theory to situations in which the movements of the animal are less restricted than in the typical salivary conditioning experiment and the tasks generally more complex.*

The reader will perhaps be struck by the general similarity of the "place" reflex to what American psychologists term a discriminated operant. Although Kupalov's work is liberally sprinkled with references to Western neurophysiological studies, he makes no references to the work of those Western behaviorists, such as Skinner and Spence, whose work is in many ways quite similar to that reported here.

THE PRESENT INVESTIGATIONS were carried out on dogs in a large, specially equipped room with an area of 7.5 by 5 m. The room contained two tables with ordinary mechanical food boxes (Figures 26–1

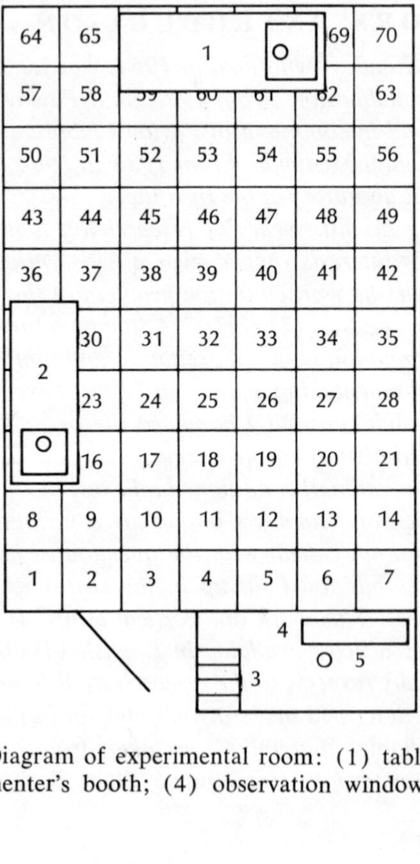

Figure 26–1. Diagram of experimental room: (1) table 1; (2) table 2; (3) experimenter's booth; (4) observation window; (5) experimenter's table.

and 26–2) and various devices for delivery of conditioned stimuli. The food boxes were not rigidly fixed to the tables; they could easily be placed on the floor when necessary. A number of studies used an electrical food box with a rotating food dispenser.

Externally, the tables differed little from each other and had the following dimensions: table 1, 250 (length) by 100 (width) by 75 cm. (height); table 2, respectively 215 by 85 by 75 cm. In order to facilitate jumping onto the tables, supports were placed in front of them: in front of table 1, a bench, and in front of table 2, portable steps (Figure 26–2).

Figure 26–2. Steps and bench placed by tables with food boxes.

Three rows of lights were placed on the ceiling; klieg lights were fastened along the walls. This made it possible to vary the illumination of the entire room as well as that of its individual parts within a wide range. The windows of the room were curtained with closely woven black fabric, which eliminated the effect of stimuli difficult to control, such as alteration of natural lighting.

During the experiment the investigator was in a special booth directly adjoining one of the walls of the room. This wall contained a glass-covered window (4, Figure 26–1) with an area of 200 by 70 cm., through which the animal was observed. The window could be completely covered by a lightproof curtain; in that case observation was done through a small opening in the curtain. The booth was 1 m. above the floor of the experimental room; it contained a control panel, a switchboard for switching on fixtures, rubber bulbs connected via pneumatic transmission with the mechanical food boxes and devices for stimulus delivery, electrical metronomes, an audiofrequency oscillator, a kymograph, and a table and a chair for the experimenter.

Various auditory and visual stimuli were used as conditioned stimuli: bell, buzzer, tones of varying frequency and loudness, bubbling sound, light (continuous, flickering, and reflected), appearance of geometrical figures (e.g., circle, square, cross), and others. The apparatus for delivery of conditioned stimuli was located at a certain spot in the room, but its location could be changed as required by the purpose of investigation. Isolated action of each conditioned stimulus usually lasted from 3 to 5 seconds. The intervals between conditioned stimuli varied between 30 seconds and 1 to 2 minutes. From 8 to 15 conditioned stimuli were presented in each session.

Formation of conditioned reflexes was reinforced by meat-biscuit powder moistened with water or milk (1:1), little pieces of meat, or a mixture of both. A single reward of powdered meat-biscuit was 15 to 20 gr. by weight, that of meat, 10 to 20 gr. A bowl with water was on the floor of the experimental room at all times.

Observations of the animal's behavior were recorded during the course of an experiment. The location of the dog and hence its movements could be described precisely at any given movement owing to the fact that the room's floor was divided into 70 squares (Figures 26–1 and 26–2). In individual experiments the animal's movements were represented as an uninterrupted line on a diagram of the experimental room prepared beforehand. Whenever necessary, a kymograph record was made of the length of time the dog spent in the individual parts of the room and of latencies and rates of motor reactions. For this purpose, contact plates connected in series with an electric marker and a direct-current source were placed underneath the mats in front of the food boxes and in some other places in the room. Documentation of experiments by means of photography and cinematography was widely used.

An experimenter usually began by training the dog to run from the door of the experimental room to one of the food boxes. Before the start of the tests, pieces of meat were therefore scattered in the area between the door and the food box. Let into the room, the dog picked up the meat pieces and thus approached the food box, an open bowl which also contained meat. The "meat path" was covered 3 to 5 times during an experimental day. On the days following, the distance between the separate meat pieces was increased each time. Finally, the meat was placed only in the open bowl of the food box. Let into the room now, the dog ran at once to the food box and ate the first portion of food reinforcement.

After the dog's reflex run from the door to the food box had become consolidated, elaboration of a conditioned reflex to clatter (noise), which accompanies a change of bowls when the food box is set in operation, was begun. As soon as the animal consumed the first meat portion in the food box, a second one was delivered, then a third, and so forth. After the food-box clatter became a positive stimulus, the change of bowls was made only when the animal was at some distance from the food box.

Upon consolidation of the reflex to food-box noise, elaboration of a conditioned reflex to one of the usual exteroceptive stimuli, such as a light or a bell, began. Each conditioned stimulus was at first tested with respect to neutrality; then it was combined with the food-box noise and food reinforcement.

Following consolidation of the conditioned reflex to an exteroceptive stimulus of some kind, there began elaboration of a reflex to a certain place in the experimental room. A rug was usually placed on this spot. This time the conditioned stimulus was presented only when the animal passed over the rug by chance or when it lingered upon it. As soon as the reflex of standing on a certain spot became consolidated, there would begin elaboration of positive and negative reflexes to new stimuli.

Thus, with the conclusion of this part of the investigation, the first component of conditioned-reflex activity was always a run from the door toward the table, to the food box; standing on the mat constituted the second component; and the third was a run to the table toward the food box in response to the positive, visual (or auditory) conditioned stimulus. During the operation of an inhibitory conditioned stimulus a run to the food box did not take place.

This is the procedure for forming a conditioned place reflex which is most often used in our laboratory. In a few studies, conditioned place reflexes were elaborated in a somewhat different manner. Sometimes the meat path was traversed only once; and following consumption of the first food reinforcement, the remaining dishes containing food were immediately presented.

A conditioned reflex to a certain location sometimes became established immediately following the formation of a conditioned reflex to the clatter of the food box. In some studies a separate conditioned reflex was not elaborated to food-box clatter; in those experiments food-box clatter was delivered simultaneously with presentation of one of the usual conditioned stimuli, such as ticking of a metronome.

When necessary, elaboration of a new system of reflexes was carried out; conditioned stimuli were reinforced from a food box located on another table. The methods of elaboration of reflexes remained the same. In a special series of experiments, formation of motor conditioned reflexes was carried out on the basis of imitation.

As stated above, the animal's behavior during an experiment was meticulously recorded, special attention being paid to the following indices of conditioned reflexes: duration of the animal's stay in a certain place in the experimental room (on the rug, next to the conditioned stimulus, etc.); latency of the motor reaction; time of food-box run; duration of the consummatory behavior; and time required to return to the dog's place. The dog's general behavior during the intervals between the operation of conditioned stimuli also was described in detail. As a rule, the experiments were conducted at the same time of the day or night.

The experimental animals received their daily food ration once every 24 hours and at a specific time, usually after the termination of a session. The animals were periodically weighed and observed by a veterinarian. The studies continued for more than 100 days.

As mentioned above, formation of conditioned place reflexes involves several stages; we shall dwell on each of these in greater detail. In the initial experiments, *in the course of training the animal to run from the door to the food box,* all the animals displayed, by virtue of an inborn exploratory reflex, a well-defined orienting reaction to the experimental setting. Having entered the room, the animals start walking or running around the room in a haphazard manner, examining and sniffing the floor and the objects placed on it; occasionally they jump onto the tables. Finding pieces of meat scattered over the floor in a direct line between the door and the food box in the form of a meat path, they eat them. In the first tests the animals perform many additional irregular movements throughout the room, away from the meat path, before picking up all the pieces of meat. The amount of additional movement gradually becomes smaller, so that at last, having entered the room, the animal walks from the door toward the food box only along the meat path; the majority of the animals do this on the first day of experimentation, if several trials are given. From the second or third test day on, the distance between the individual pieces of meat is increased with each trial; finally, meat is placed only in an open dish in the food box.

By the third to fifth day the positive reaction to the sight of the food box becomes firmly established in a majority of the animals: when let into the room the dog runs at once toward the food-box table and eats the first food reinforcement. At this time a conditioned connection not only to a certain location of food within the experimental room but also to the experimental setting as a whole is formed and becomes consolidated in the animals. This is manifested in the fact that some of the animals run from the vivarium, where they are usually kept, to the experimental room even without the attendant's intervention.

The formation of a conditioned reflex *to the clatter of the food box* takes place in the following manner. To the initial food-box noise caused by the replacement of dishes, the majority of the animals respond with a simple orienting reaction: catching sight of meat in a new bowl, they first look at it and then start eating it calmly. Others cautiously take the meat in their teeth from the dish, step away from the food box, and only then begin eating it. Still others display a passive-defense reaction: they move away from the food box or jump to the floor, trying to remove themselves as far away from the table as possible; some time later, however, they again jump onto the table and eat the food reinforcement. By the fifth to tenth day of experimentation all the animals usually eat the food reinforcement calmly from the other dishes as well. From the fifth to eleventh day on, a majority of the animals run at once toward the table with the food bowl when they hear the clatter of the food box, regardless of what place in the room they find themselves at the moment; that is, from this time on the food-box noise acquires signal significance.

In elaborating a conditioned reflex *to the first exteroceptive* (*visual or auditory*) conditioned stimulus, each stimulus was at first tested for neutrality. On the first presentation of a stimulus a well-defined orienting reaction is usually observed: most often the dog turns his head toward the stimulus and looks at it; less frequently he approaches it, and if the stimulus is located on the floor, some of the animals sniff at it, touch it with a paw, or lick it. Still less frequent are the cases when the animal runs toward the food box upon the first delivery of a stimulus. A stimulus was considered neutral if the dog did not run to the food-box table upon its presentation. Following the test for neutrality the stimulus would be combined with the food-box noise, to which a running reflex to the table had already been formed.

Initially, the dog runs to the food box only in response to the clattering noise. After a few combinations of a conditioned stimulus with the food-box noise followed by food reinforcement, however, the animal runs to the food box in response to presentation of a conditioned stimulus alone. A conditioned motor reflex was considered established when the dog ran toward the table with the food box as soon as the stimulus was presented. The speed of formation of the first conditioned motor reflex to exteroceptive stimuli varied widely (Table 26–1), depending upon the physical intensity

Table 26–1 *Elaboration of Positive Motor Conditioned Reflexes Involving a Run Toward One Table*

Animal's name	Speed of formation of conditioned reflex to:			
	bell I	rug II	M-120 [a] III	light IV
Jack	14	35	9	2
Dozor	10	24	9	2
Tobik	8	23	5	1
Rex	12	27	12	2
Rhzhiy	9	20	5	3
Zhan	48	23	3	4
Tarzan	7	21	5	2
Jim	18	30	9	7
Pisklya	28	81	8	5
Baron	15	48	5	2

NOTE: Roman numerals denote the sequence of establishment of conditioned reflexes; Arabic numerals, the number of trials.

[a] Stands for "metronome beating at 120 times per minute."

of the conditioned stimulus, the individual peculiarities of the animal's nervous system, and a number of other factors which will be considered in detail below. We shall note here only that the speed of formation of the first conditioned reflex to auditory stimuli most frequently fluctuates within a range of 5 to 25 pairings; that to lights, from 25 to 60 pairings; and that to geometric figures, from 35 to 40 pairings (Table 26–2).

Table 26–2 *Mean Speed of Formation of Conditioned Motor Reflexes in Response to Various Stimuli*

Conditioned stimulus	Pairing after which reflex	
	Appeared	Became consolidated
Bell (loud)	2–10	5–15
Tone (600 cps; moderate intensity)	8–20	18–25
Light (55 watts)	20–30	35–60
Light (150 watts)	10–20	25–40
Moving figure (circle)	10–20	35–40

During the intervals when the conditional stimulus is inactive, the intersignal interval, the animals move around the room, occasionally stopping on one square or another, mostly lingering either near the table with the food box or close to the conditioned stimuli.

Formation of a conditioned reflex *to the animal's location within the experimental room during the intersignal intervals* occurs in the following manner. To start with, a conditioned stimulus is presented only if the animal passes by chance a certain square or lingers upon it; after a few pairings of the conditioned stimulus with the dog's position on a given square, he starts to settle with increasing frequency precisely on this square. The conditioned reflex to location is established more rapidly if the selected spot on the floor is covered with a rug.

During the first 1 to 1½ weeks from the day of establishment of a conditioned reflex, the animals, having jumped from the table after the end of the meal, perform many irregular movements within the room (Figure 26–3), sometimes standing upon the rug for several seconds but then leaving it again and walking or running around the room, often jumping onto the table and approaching the food box. Gradually the number of intersignal runs to the table becomes progressively smaller; in the end they disappear altogether. The rate of extinction of intersignal runs to the table is different in different animals (Figure 26–4). When the reflex to place becomes firmly established, the animal goes to the rug as soon as he has consumed the reinforcement, places himself on it and assumes a certain posture: he either

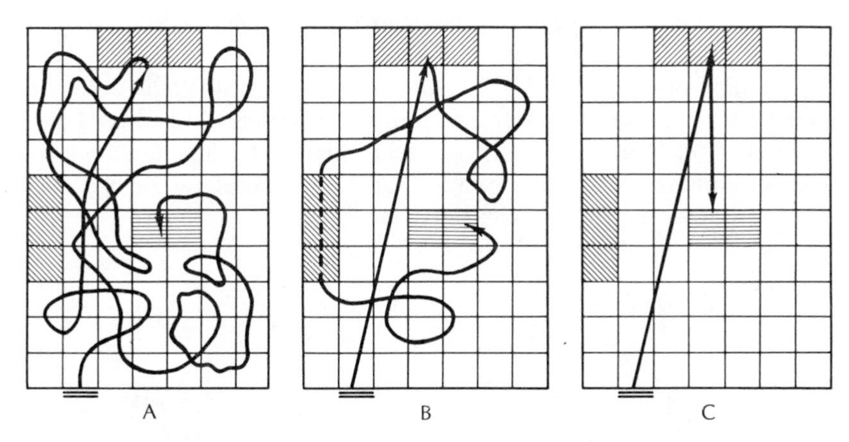

Figure 26–3. Schematic representation of the dog Sharik's movements over the experimental room from the moment of his entrance into the room to the moment of settling on the rug on different test days: (*A*) session No. 3: the dog reached this position on the rug after 4 min. 19 sec.; (*B*) session No. 10: position reached after 2 min. 12 sec.; (*C*) session No. 32; position reached after 45 sec. Oblique lines denote tables; horizontal lines, the rug.

stands, sits, or lies down on the rug, with his head and trunk usually oriented toward the table upon which reinforcement is given, or toward the location of the conditioned stimulus. A certain place in the room thus turns into a positive conditioned agent, the animal comes to this place actively and independently, assumes a certain posture (Figure 26–5), and stays there until the presentation of the next positive conditioned stimulus.

Establishment of *subsequent conditioned reflexes with reinforcement involving one table* is carried out in accordance with the same scheme that applied to the first conditioned reflex. These reflexes are usually formed more rapidly than the first conditioned reflex (see Table 26–1).

The latencies of conditioned reflexes to auditory stimuli are usually somewhat shorter than those to visual stimuli, and the rate of motor reactions is greater in the case of auditory stimuli than it is with visual ones. As the training progresses, however, the speed with which reflexes are formed (see Table 26–1), their latencies (Figure 26–6), and the speed of the motor reactions themselves may be identical for conditioned stimuli of different physical strengths (Kupalov and Pravosudov, 1959; Popova, 1960; and others). The latencies of conditioned reflexes under prolonged training most frequently range between 0.1 and 1.0 seconds; the time of the run from the rug to the food box fluctuates between 2 and 5 seconds, depending on the characteristic properties of the individual animals' higher nervous activity, the rate of their motor reactions, and the distance of the rug from the food box. The eating time is 5 to 30 seconds, depending on the amount and quality of reinforcement and on the degree of the animal's alimentary excitability.

Formation of *conditioned reflexes involving runs to two tables* offers the animal a special case of stimulus differentiation, which we shall consider in more detail below. Here we note only that training of differentiation among positive conditioned stimuli reinforced at different tables was carried out by us in two ways—successively and simultaneously.

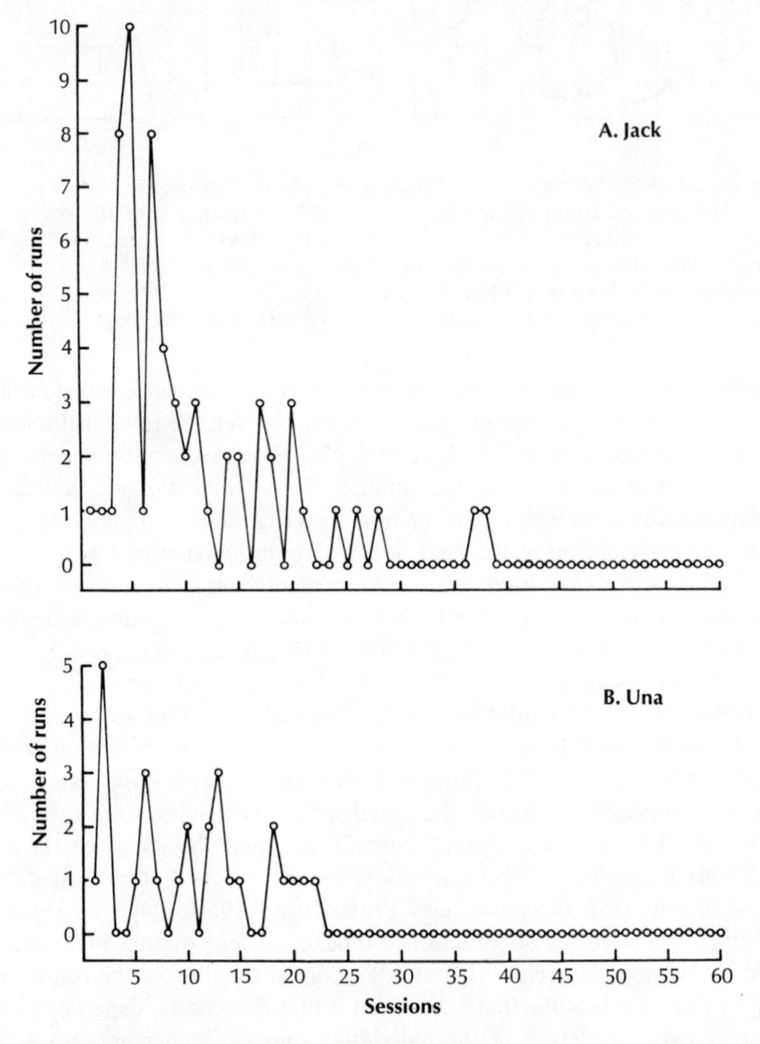

Figure 26–4. Rate of extinction of intersignal runs to the table with the food box in dogs Jack (*A*) and Una (*B*). The abscissa represents the number of sessions; the ordinate, the number of runs during each session.

For successive conditioning of differential reflexes, conditioned reflexes are first elaborated and reinforced at one table; it is only after their consolidation that conditioned reflexes to new—to-be-differentiated—stimuli, reinforced at another table, are trained.

Figure 26–5. Location and posture of the dog Akkord within the experimental room during the intersignal intervals.

Formation of a conditioned motor reflex in the form of a run toward food box 2 occurs in exactly the same manner as in the case of food box 1; that is, a meat path is laid out first, followed by elaboration of a conditioned reflex to the noise of the food box. The first conditioned motor reflex involving a run to the second food box appears (from the fourth to tenth pairing on) and is consolidated more rapidly than the run to the first food box. This period requires approximately 3 to 8 trials. When runs to the second food box are being established, those conditioned stimuli in response to which a reflex run to food box 1 was trained are temporarily omitted in the experiment. After the conditioned reflex runs to food box 2 become firmly established, conditioned stimuli reinforced from the first food box come into use in the experiment.

When two food boxes are used in the experiment, their differentiation is found to be disrupted at first, that is, conditioned signals in response to which a run to food box 1 had previously been trained elicit a run to food box 2, and vice versa. For several days there is observed simultaneously a disinhibition of inhibitory differentiations (if they had been established) and individual cases of animals inexactly positioned upon the rug. Soon afterward, however, inhibitory discrimination and the precise position on the rug are reinstated; disturbance of discrimination between the two food boxes lasts longer.

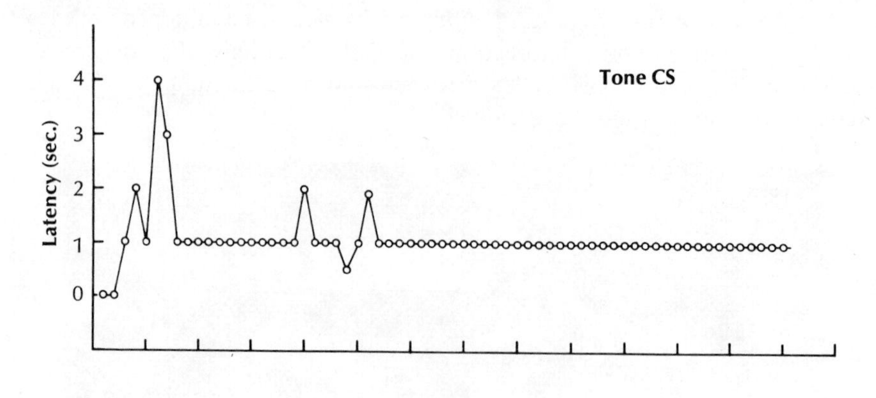

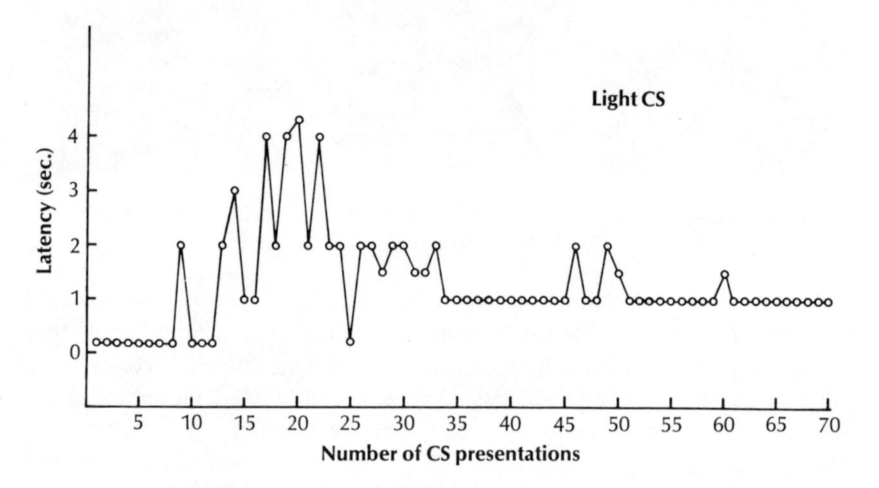

Figure 26–6. Change in latencies of conditioned motor reactions of dog Una with consolidation of reflexes. The abscissa represents the number of presentations of conditioned stimulus, the ordinate, latencies of the conditioned reflexes in seconds.

For simultaneous conditioning of differential reflexes, stimulus differentiation is trained by means of a concurrent—parallel—establishment of conditioned reflex runs to both food-box tables. In the beginning, meat paths are laid out to both tables, and reflexes to the noise of the food boxes are established. Then, during a single test day, training of two conditioned reflexes to various auditory or visual stimuli with reinforcement at different tables is begun.

In collating the results of these experiments, it was apparent that successive differential conditioned reflexes are more readily elaborated than simultaneous differential reflexes. Furthermore, it was observed that in order for the movement toward a certain table after the presentation of a conditioned stimulus to be correct, the animal's previous location within the room, its posture (orientation of its head and trunk), and location of conditioned stimuli are significant (Kupalov, 1946; Yakloveva, 1947, 1949; Gordeladze, 1953; Kudryashova, 1955, 1958; Khananashvili, 1956; Kupalov and Khananashvili, 1958, 1960; Syrenskii, 1961, 1962; and others).

Studies of the Law of Strength

In the initial investigations on the animals' conditioned-reflex activity, attention had already been directed toward the dependence of the conditioned reflexes on the physical intensity of the conditioned stimuli (Zelenii, 1907; Kupalov and Gantt, 1928; Krasusskii, 1954; and several others). Using salivary conditioning, these studies established a direct relationship between the magnitude of a conditioned alimentary reflex and the physical intensity of conditioned stimuli. This was what provided Pavlov with grounds for formulating the "law of strength."

Kas'yanov and Fruktov (1952), using athletes as subjects, investigated the effect of the intensity of a conditioned stimulus on the speed of motor acts. Their results demonstrate that, when a physically intense stimulus is used, the latent period of excitation and the time it takes to run a standard distance are shorter than they are when a physically weaker stimulus is used.

The study carried out by Kupalov and Pravosudov (1959) investigated the effect of the physical strength of a conditioned stimulus on the animals' motor conditioned reflex activity established by the method of conditioned place reflexes.

At first, a conditioned reflex was trained in the dog Lis in response to food-box clatter, and the dog's location on a rug placed in square 18. Next, a conditioned reflex was elaborated in response to a metronome ticking with a frequency of 120 clicks per minute and to a "soft noise." Conditioned stimuli were placed on the wall (upon a shelf) to the right and in front of the rug (above squares 42 and 49). The physical intensity of the metronome was 65 db; that of noise, 55 db. The conditioned stimulus was paired from 10 to 12 times with reinforcement at table 1 in this experiment. The distance between the rug and the food-box table was 4.5 to 5 m. By the time the conditioned reflex to the metronome had become firmly established, the latency of the motor reaction usually equaled 2 seconds, the time of the run to the food-box table, 3 to 5 seconds, and the time of eating, 15 to 20 seconds. After his meal the dog returned immediately to the rug and stayed there until presentation of the metronome (Table 26–3).

A conditioned reflex to noise made its appearance at the seventeenth pairing. The latency and the time of run to the table with the food box were

Table 26–3 *Response Characteristics to a Constant Strong Stimulus*

Number of trials	Conditioned stimulus (beats/min. metronome)	Duration of conditioned stimulus (sec.)	Latency of conditioned reflex (sec.)	Time of run from rug to table with food box (sec.)	Eating time (sec.)	Time of staying upon table after eating (sec.)	Time of return to rug (sec.)	Time of standing upon rug (sec.)
114	M-120	10	4	3	20	0	10	15
115	M-120	10	2	3	15	0	15	15
116	M-120	10	2	3	20	0	10	15
117	M-120	10	2	3	15	0	3	15
118	M-120	10	2	3	25	0	2	15
119	M-120	10	2	3	20	0	3	15
120	M-120	10	2	4	20	0	5	15
121	M-120	10	2	4	15	0	3	15
122	M-120	10	2	5	20	0	3	15
123	M-120	10	2	5	25	0	3	15
124	M-120	10	2	3	20	0	3	—

initially greater than they were during the action of the metronome. In subsequent experiments the above-mentioned latencies for noise began to shorten gradually. From the 175th application of noise the conditioned reflexes evoked by the noise and the metronome became identical.

Following consolidation of the conditioned reflexes, the motor activity of dog Lis was made more complex in the following manner. A barrier (a tight net) was placed 1.5 to 2 m. from the rug; the dog had to jump over this barrier in the course of his run toward the table with the food box and when returning to the rug. Initially, the height of the barrier was 40 cm. A barrier of this height did not in any way alter the dog's conditioned reflex activity; the animal would overcome it with ease.

In subsequent sessions the height of the barrier was raised by 5 cm. every 3 to 4 tests. With an increase in the height of the barrier from 45 to 60 cm. the time of run toward the table with the food box in response to noise increased, and so did the time of the dog's return to the rug after the reinforcement (see Table 26–4).

Here the following was observed. Whereas previously, having finished his food, the dog would immediately jump down from the table and, easily overcoming the barrier, return to the table, now he would often stop directly in front of the barrier and start walking around the room, urinating, drinking water, then jumping again upon the table, turn himself to face the barrier; after 5 to 10 minutes he would again jump down from the table,

Table 26–4 *Differential Effects Strong and Weak Stimuli When an Obstacle Is Introduced* [a]

Number of trials	Conditioned stimulus	Duration of conditioned stimulus (sec.)	Latency of conditioned reflex (sec.)	Time of run from rug to table with food box (sec.)	Eating time (sec.)	Time of standing in place after eating (sec.)	Time of return to rug (sec.)	Time of staying on the rug (sec.)
486	M-120	8	0.5	3	18	2	10	65
466	Noise	8	0.5	4	20	2	28	67
467	Noise	8	0.5	4	20	3	57	65
487	M-120	7	0.5	3	20	1	7	60
468	Noise	10	0.5	5	16	1	35	60
488	M-120	8	0.5	4	15	1	90	60
469	Noise	15	0.5	10	15	1	58	—

REMARKS: After the meal walks around the room, urinates, drinks water, and only then jumps over the barrier and runs to the rug.
[a] Barrier raised to a height of 60 cm.

and only then surmount the barrier. In other words, following an unsuccessful attempt at overcoming the barrier, the dog would go through his routine motor stereotype in order to achieve that goal.

When the barrier was raised to 65 cm. at the end of an experimental day for the first time, the dog, responding to a conditioned stimulus (noise), headed toward the barrier but did not surmount it; however, the dog jumped over the barrier with ease in response to a stronger auditory stimulus (metronome). The dog's behavior underwent a slight simultaneous change: he began to display restlessness and shortness of breath. Further investigations were carried out on this dog after a two-month rest. Experiments were resumed with a 50-cm.-high barrier. The dog easily overcame this height, both during the action of conditioned stimuli and after a reinforcement. When the height of the barrier was raised to 65 cm., there again appeared the dependency of the motor reaction on the intensity of conditioned stimuli, that is, the dog would continue to jump over the barrier in response to a strong stimulus (metronome), whereas he was unable to overcome the obstacle when responding to a weaker stimulus (noise).

By the fourth day of training with the 65-cm. barrier, however, the dog began to jump over it in response to the noise as well, that is, as the training progressed, the dependency of conditioned motor reactions on the physical intensity of stimuli was reduced.

When the height of the barrier was further increased to 85 cm., the following was observed: whereas, at the beginning of the experiment before the presentation of conditioned auditory stimuli, the dog would ordinarily jump over the barrier at once and approach the food box, now he would enter the room and start running along the barrier, often whining, urinating, and only then overcoming the barrier. With a barrier height of 90 cm., the dog ceased altogether to jump over it at the very beginning of a test; he would overcome it only when affected by the action of auditory conditioned stimuli. The dog was unable to cope with this height following reinforcement, that is, when returning to the rug. This was accompanied by the simultaneous appearance of symptoms of disturbances in higher nervous activity: the dog became very excited and whined. To avoid an exacerbation of these disturbances in the subsequent sessions, one edge of the barrier net was raised so that the dog could go back to his initial location without having to jump over the barrier after eating his food reinforcement.

The results obtained thus indicate that the "law of strength" is also valid within the context of conditioned-reflex activity when the animals' movements are unrestricted.

The effect of a change in alimentary excitability on the manifestation of the "law of strength" was investigated in the same dog. Alimentary excitability was altered by feeding the dog prior to the start of the experiment or by substituting pure meat for the meat-biscuit powder in the food boxes. In those cases when the dog's alimentary excitability was altered by feeding him prior to investigation, the tests were conducted twice a day, in the morning and in the evening. The evening experiment was performed after the animal had received one-half of its daily food ration. By way of an illustration we shall consider one such experiment (Table 26–5), performed with Lis. The height of the barrier was 67.5 cm. During the morning test (11:50 A.M.) the dog overcame the barrier with ease and after the reinforcement quickly went back to his rug. The second test was carried out at 3:50 P.M., the dog having previously been fed. At the start of the experiment, there was an increase in the time of run to the food box in response to a weak conditioned stimulus (noise); subsequently the dog was unable to overcome this barrier at all when this stimulus was presented; at the same time, he jumped over the barrier with ease in response to an intense auditory stimulus (metronome).

This relationship was demonstrated even more clearly in experiments involving a change in the quality of unconditioned reinforcement. When reinforcement was switched to meat, the dog, in response to the action of unconditioned stimuli, easily overcame the barrier heights of 90 and 95 cm. and went back to the rug very quickly through a passage made in the net (Table 26–6). It can be seen from the session in Table 26–6 that, with meat reinforcement, the dog surmounted a barrier 95 cm. high in response to both weak and strong conditioned stimuli.

Table 26–5 *The Effect of Deprivation Level on the "Law of Strength"* [a]

Number of trials	Conditioned stimulus	Duration of conditioned stimulus (sec.)	Latency of conditioned reflex (sec.)	Time of run from rug to table with food box (sec.)	Eating time (sec.)	Time of standing on table after eating (sec.)	Time of return to rug (sec.)	Time of standing on rug (sec.)
547	M-120	8	0.5	4	18	2	15	88
547	Noise	10	0.5	5	20	4	30	90
548	Noise	12	5	3	28	2	7	87
548	M-120	10	1	4	20	2	5	87
549	Noise	15	Listens, remains seated on rug.					
550	Noise	15	Stood up, approached barrier, then went back to rug.					
549	M-120	8	0.5	4	Overcomes barrier, jumps onto table with food box, but refuses to eat. Here test was terminated.			

[a] Height of barrier, 67.5 cm.

Table 26–6 *Effect of Increased Reinforcement Quality on the "Law of Strength"* [a]

Number of trials	Conditioned stimulus	Duration of conditioned stimulus (sec.)	Latency of conditioned reflex (sec.)	Time of run from rug to table with food box (sec.)	Eating time (sec.)	Time of standing on table after eating (sec.)	Time of return to rug (sec.)	Time of standing on rug (sec.)
642	M-120	8	0.5	3	15	15	12	93
654	Noise	9	0.5	4	14	4	8	92
655	Noise	8	0.5	3	15	2	8	92
643	M-120	8	0.5	3	13	2	8	94
656	Noise	8	0.5	3	12	8	12	90
644	M-120	8	0.5	3	14	2	9	91
657	Noise	9	0.5	4	10	—	Test ended	

[a] Height of barrier, 95 cm.

On the next day meat reinforcement was replaced with meat-biscuit powder. This immediately affected the animal's conditioned-reflex activity. At the start of the experiment and in response to the first presentation of the metronome the dog overcame a barrier 95 cm. high, but was unable to do so in response to the two subsequent presentations of noise and the second presentation of the metronome (Table 26–7).

Table 26–7 *Effect of Decreased Reinforcement Quality on the "Law of Strength"* [a]

Number of trials	Conditioned stimulus	Duration of conditioned stimulus (sec.)	Latency of conditioned reflex (sec.)	Time of run from rug to table with food box (sec.)	Eating time (sec.)	Time of standing on table after eating (sec.)	Time of return to rug (sec.)	Time of standing on rug (sec.)
645	M-120	8	0.5	4	18	4	8	91
658	Noise	15	Orienting reaction; goes to the net, then returns to the rug.					
659	Noise	15	Same.					
646	M-120	15	Runs to the barrier but comes to a standstill immediately in front of the barrier, walks back and forth along it, tries to penetrate underneath the net, whines. In view of the fact that the dog started to show anxiety and shortness of breath, and began to whine, the experiment was terminated.					

[a] Height of barrier, 95 cm.

It follows from these experiments that both an increase and a decrease in alimentary excitability alter the animal's conditioned reflex activity; in one case (when alimentary excitability is lowered) the dependence of the motor reaction on the physical intensity of conditioned stimuli becomes increasingly evident; in another case (when alimentary excitability is raised) this relationship weakens. Apart from this, the dependency of the motor reaction on the physical strength of conditioned stimuli was brought out in a distinct manner. The law of strength also operates when conditioned signals were delivered against a background of extraneous stimuli (random noise, a tone, etc.). As a rule, the latter inhibited the motor reaction evoked by a weak conditioned stimulus (noise), without affecting a strong stimulus (metronome).

Under these conditions the animal's conditioned-reflex activity depends on the functional state of the cerebral cortex, which is determined, to a considerable extent, by the intensity of both conditioned and unconditioned stimuli.

Khananashvili investigated the manifestation of the law of strength in response to visual and auditory stimuli. Initially, firmly established conditioned reflexes were trained in Jack in response to a tone of 800 cps and to light from bulbs of 40, 96, and 150 watts. All the bulbs were located on a support which was placed on square 47. When those stimuli were turned on, the dog ran from his rug to the support standing next to table 1, jumped on it, then jumped on the table and went to the food box. After the reflexes became consolidated, in the overwhelming majority of cases the dog's run toward the food box was completed with an identical latency and an identical speed, regardless of whether a 40-watt or a 96- or a 150-watt bulb was switched on (Table 26–8).

Table 26–8 *"Law of Strength" for a Simple Motor Act*

Intersignal intervals (min.)	Number of trials	Conditioned stimulus	Duration of conditioned stimulus (sec.)	Latency of conditioned reflex (sec.)	Reaction to conditioned stimulus
1.5	58	Light (96 watts)	5	1	Runs to table 1
1.5	50	Light (150 watts)	5	1	Runs to table 1
2.0	60	Light (40 watts)	5	1	Runs to table 1
2.0	51	Light (150 watts)	5	1	Runs to table 1
2.0	41	Tone (800 cps)	5	1	Runs to table 1
1.5	42	Tone (800 cps)	5	1	Runs to table 1

NOTE: The stand is located next to table 1.

Subsequently the setting was altered: the support was moved away from the table to a distance of 1 m. Now, in order to obtain food, the dog had to perform a more complex motor act—a jump to overcome the distance separating the table and the stand. This complication resulted in a lengthening of the latency of conditioned reflexes and of the time of running toward the food box in response to weak visual stimuli (Table 26–9). When the support was moved 120 cm. away from the table, the dog continued to overcome the obstacle only in response to a strong, 150-watt light stimulus, whereas in response to weak light (40 watt) he only ran to the stand, climbed it, and then went back to the rug. Similar results were subsequently obtained with Jack in response to auditory stimuli of varying physical intensity.

Table 26–9 *"Law of Strength" for a Complex Motor Act*

Intersignal intervals (min.)	Number of trials	Conditioned stimulus	Duration of conditioned stimulus (sec.)	Latency of conditioned reflex (sec.)	Reaction to conditioned stimulus
2.0	69	Light (150 watts)	5	1	Runs to table 1
2.0	81	Light (40 watts)	10	6	Runs to table 1
2.5	70	Light (150 watts)	5	2	Runs to table 1
1.5	82	Light (40 watts)	10	9	Runs to table 1
1.5	63	Tone (800 cps)	5	1	Runs to table 1

NOTE: The stand is located at a distance of 100 cm. from table 1.

Discrimination Phenomena Associated with Place Learning

The process of discrimination has been studied in our laboratory ever since the methods of conditioned place reflexes came into use, so that at the present time we have at our disposal voluminous factual material which enables us to establish the principles governing discrimination among stimuli under the conditions of free motor activity. We have investigated variations of conditioned-stimulus discrimination based both on a discrimination between positive stimuli reinforced at different tables and on differential conditioning contrasting a positive (reinforced) and a negative (nonreinforced) conditioned stimulus.

Discrimination of visual stimuli located in different areas of the room and reinforced at different tables was carried out on Blek, Sharik, and Ruslan (Khananashvili's experiments).

At first Blek was trained to make a positive conditioned reflex to a bell, a circle, and light from a 55-watt bulb, involving a run to table 1. The bulb was located on a support on square 47. During the intervals between stimuli the dog stood on a rug (square 26). Following consolidation of the reflexes mentioned above, there began conditioning to the light from a 200-watt bulb located on the left shelf (above square 36) with reinforcement at table 2. This discrimination between two visual stimuli situated in different places within the room and reinforced at different tables was elaborated as follows. During the first six daily sessions only the left visual stimulus was used with reinforcement at table 2 while presentation of all the conditioned stimuli reinforced at table 1 was omitted. A conditioned reflex to this stimulus appeared for the first time at the thirty-seventh combination and became consolidated with the fifty-fourth combination.

Thereafter, application of all the conditioned stimuli reinforced at table 1 was resumed. The very first test revealed that the dog developed a clear-cut discrimination with respect to the above stimuli. Whenever light from the 55-watt bulb was presented, the dog always ran to table 1, and in response to light from a 200-watt bulb he ran to table 2. Ruslan had initially been conditioned to the light from a 55-watt bulb (in square 47) and a circle, which were reinforced at table 1; then inhibitory differentiation with respect to a cross was elaborated in the dog (Table 26–10).

Table 26–10 *Performance of a Conditioned Discrimination to Table 1*

Intersignal interval (min.)	Number of trials	Conditioned stimulus	Duration of action of conditioned stimulus (sec.)	Latency of conditioned stimulus (sec.)	Reaction to conditioned stimulus
1	109	Circle	4	1	Runs to table 1, eats food, returns to the rug.
1	110	Circle	4	1	Same.
1	46	Cross	20	—	Continues to stand on the rug.
1	111	Circle	4	1	Runs to table 1, eats food, goes back to the rug.
1	47	Cross	20	—	Continues to stand on the rug.
1	112	Circle	4	1	Runs to table 1, eats food, returns to the rug.
1	113	Circle	4	1	Same.
1	48	Cross	20	—	Continues to stand on the rug.
1	114	Circle	4	1	Runs to table, eats food, returns to the rug.
1	19	Light (55 watts)	5	1	Same.

Following consolidation of reflexes involving the animal's run to food box 1, elaboration of conditioned reflexes involving a run to table 2 was begun. For this purpose all the conditioned stimuli reinforced at table 1 were omitted for several days, and a meat path was laid out toward table 2.

Under these conditions the dog continued to jump frequently onto table 1 at the start of an experiment and in the intervals between conditioned stimuli (noise of food box 2), but with the fourth application of noise from food box 2 a clear-cut move toward table 2 was observed; on the fifteenth combination, the reflex became firmly established. After the consolidation of the conditioned reflex elicited by the noise of box 2, elaboration of a conditioned reflex to the light from a 200-watt bulb (square 36) began. A conditioned reflex was formed on the seventh combination (Table 26–11).

Table 26–11 *Performance of a Conditioned Discrimination to Table 2*

Inter-signal interval (min.)	Number of trials	Conditioned stimulus	Duration of conditioned stimulus (sec.)	Latency of conditioned reflex (sec.)	Reaction to conditioned stimulus
1	6	Light (200 watts)	10	—	Runs to table 2 in response to food-box noise only.
1	7	Light (200 watts)	5	1	Runs to table 2, eats food, and goes back to the rug.
40 sec.	8	Light (200 watts)	5	1	Same.
1	9	Light (200 watts)	6	1	Same.
1	10	Light (200 watts)	5	1	Same.
1	11	Light (200 watts)	6	2	Same.

Following consolidation of the reflex evoked by the 200-watt light, involving a run to table 2, use was again made of the previously elaborated conditioned reflexes involving a run to table 1. The very first experiment using conditioned stimuli which were reinforced at both tables showed that the dog discriminates between the sites of reinforcement for the various stimuli (Table 26–12). Some changes in the animal's conditioned-reflex activity were observed, however, during the initial period: for instance, the latencies of the conditioned reflexes became longer; the conditioned reflex to the light of a 55-watt bulb was sometimes unstable. These changes occurred during the initial three sessions, whereupon the conditioned-reflex activity was fully reinstated.

Syrenskii (1962) investigated discrimination of positive auditory stimuli which were located in different places in the experimental room and which were reinforced at different tables. Una was at first conditioned to respond to a metronome beat of 60 per minute with reinforcement at table 1, then to a metronome beating at a rate of 120 per minute with reinforcement at table 2. Conditioned stimuli were not delivered in a stereotyped manner.

Table 26–12 *Double Discrimination to Stimuli Associated with Tables 1 and 2*

Inter-signal interval (min.)	Number of trials	Conditioned stimulus	Duration of conditioned stimulus (sec.)	Latency of conditioned reflex (sec.)	Reaction to conditioned stimulus
1	12	Light (200 watts)	6	2	Runs to table 2.
1	13	Light (200 watts)	6	2	Runs to table 2.
1	12	Light (200 watts)	6	2	Runs to table 2.
1	21	Light (55 watts)	10	—	Runs to table 1 in response to food-box noise only.
1	22	Light (55 watts)	6	3	Runs to table 1.
1	21	Light (55 watts)	4	1	Runs to table 1.
1	53	Light (200 watts)	6	2	Runs to table 2.
1	24	Light (55 watts)	5	2	Runs to table 1.
1	126	Circle	4	1	Runs to table 1.
1	56	Cross	20	—	Stands on rug.
1	127	Circle	4	1	Runs to table 1.
1	16	Light (200 watts)	6	2	Runs to table 2.
1	25	Light (55 watts)	4	1	Runs to table 1.
1	17	Light (200 watts)	6	2	Runs to table 2.
1	26	Light (55 watts)	6	3	Runs to table 1.

A conditioned reflex to the metronome at 60 beats per minute was formed on the thirtieth combination, and one to the metronome at 120 beats per minute—on the twentieth combination.

The facts adduced thus demonstrate that positive discrimination of visual and auditory conditioned stimuli which are separated in space and reinforced at different tables is established by animals with comparative ease.

Extinction of Place Responses

The phenomenon of extinction of conditioned reflexes became an object of comprehensive study in Pavlov's laboratory almost at the very start of investigation of higher nervous activity. The neural mechanism of this phenomenon and the laws which govern it, as well as the processes of reinstatement of conditioned reflexes, have been studied by many authors (Babkin, 1904; and others).

It is well known that extinction of conditioned reflexes occurs when any conditioned stimulus which is repeatedly presented without being reinforced by an unconditioned stimulus gradually loses its conditioning effect.

Our experiments, which involved different kinds of extinction of motor conditioned reflexes, alternated in the course of several weeks and occasionally months with routine experiments in which all the conditioned reflexes previously elaborated in an animal were tested, among them also the reflex under consideration. Positive conditioned reflexes to a rug placed in square 47, the 55-watt light, and metronome beat of 120 per second were first elaborated in Alma; this was followed by extinction of the conditioned reflex to light (Khananashvili's experiments). When extinction began, the conditioned stimulus (light) had been used 247 times, and the metronome 30 times (Table 26–13). The conditioned reflexes were stable; their

Table 26–13 *Performance at the Start of Extinction*

Inter-signal interval (min.)	Number of trials	Conditioned stimulus	Duration of conditioned stimulus (sec.)	Latency of conditioned reflex (sec.)	Dog's behavior during the action of conditioned stimulus
1	244	Light	5	0.5	Runs to the food box, eats food, then goes to and stands on square 47.
1	245	Light	5	0.5	Same
1	246	Light	5	0.5	Same
2	28	Metronome	5	0.5	Same
0.2	29	Metronome	5	0.5	Same
1	30	Metronome	5	0.5	Same
1	247	Light	5	0.5	Same

latencies did not exceed 1 second. Extinction of the conditioned reflex was obtained by withholding food reinforcement until a complete cessation of the dog's movements toward the table took place.

Partial extinction of the conditioned reflex to light occurred on the very first day (Table 26–14). In response to the fifth trial on that day the dog approached the table but did not jump onto it; and at the ninth trial the dog remained standing in his usual place—square 47. By using the metronome occasionally, with a varying time interval since an acutely extinguished conditioned reflex to light, it was possible to ascertain that nonreinforcement of a visual stimulus did not affect the conditioned reflex established in response to the metronome, that is, extinction of a reflex to a weak visual stimulus exerts no inhibitory influence on the conditioned reflex established with respect to a stronger auditory stimulus. The dog's

Table 26–14 *Initial Extinction Session*

Inter-signal interval (min.)	Num- of trials	Conditioned stimulus	Duration of conditioned stimulus (sec.)	Latency of conditioned reflex (sec.)	Dog's behavior during action of conditioned stimulus
1.5	31	Metronome	5	0.5	Runs to food box
1.5	I	Light	20	0.5	Runs to food box
1	II	Light	20	0.5	Runs to food box
2	III	Light	20	0.5	Runs to food box
2	IV	Light	20	0.5	Runs to food box
1.5	V	Light	20	—	Approached table and stopped
1	32	Metronome	5	0.5	Runs to food box
1.5	VI	Light	20	0.5	Runs to food box
1	VII	Light	20	1	Runs to food box
1.5	VIII	Light	20	—	Approached table and stopped
1	IX	Light	20	—	Remains sitting in place
1	33	Metronome	5	0.5	Runs to food box

NOTE: Number of nonreinforcements of photic stimulation is expressed by Roman numerals.

behavior during the intersignal interval did change, however: having finished his food, the dog would linger for minutes on the table, sometimes lying down on it; having left the table, he would run around the room, approach the door, or jump onto the second table, without placing himself upon square 47. The nonreinforcement of the conditioned stimulus (light) with the dog's location at square 47 evidently evoked a negative reaction to square 47, or, possibly, to the entire segment of space in front of the table with the food box. This might also explain the dog's prolonged lingering on the table after eating.

After the light began to be reinforced again, the dog ceased to linger on the table and placed himself with increasing frequency on square 47 during the intersignal interval. Shortly after the reinstatement of the conditioned reflex to light the dog's behavior would become the same as it had been prior to the onset of extinction.

Thus the experiments carried out on Alma showed that extinction of the conditioned reflex to light did not affect the conditioned reflex formed to the metronome, but it did distinctly alter the spatial conditioned reflex determining the dog's location within the experimental room during the intersignal intervals.

Other experiments were carried out on Jack and Una, in whom a stereotype was elaborated for conditioned reflexes to two positive (bell and light) stimuli and one differential (metronome) stimulus. Each conditioned stimulus was in operation for 5 seconds. The intervals between stimuli were 1 minute each. By the onset of extinction, the bell had been used 1,215 times, and the light, 1,205 times, for Una; and the bell 1,210 times and the light 1,201 times for Jack. Extinction began with the second conditioned reflex, within the stereotype to light. It was carried out by means of repeated presentation of light alone (at 1-minute intervals) without reinforcement in the experiment until this stimulus failed to evoke a conditioned reflex in the course of three successive applications.

With the initial two to three applications of a nonreinforced conditioned stimulus, the animals ran at once toward the table with the food box (latency, 0.5 to 1.0 seconds) but, not finding any food, jumped to the floor and placed themselves upon the rug. Then they often left the rug and entered the adjacent squares or performed circular movements on the rug. After 4 to 5 nonreinforcements the latencies of the conditioned reflexes increased, the speed of the run toward the table with the food box diminished; during the intersignal intervals the animals often lay down on the rug or next to it; occasionally they approached the exit. Thereafter the reflexes would become unstable, in the end extinguishing altogether.

In Una the reflex to light became unstable from the eleventh trial on and extinguished at the twenty-second trial; in Jack the reflex to light became unstable from the nineteenth trial on and extinguished at the twenty-fourth trial.

Then, following a series of routine sessions involving use of the entire stereotype, extinction of the first conditioned reflex within the stereotype, elaborated in response to the bell, was carried out in an identical setting. In Una the reflex to the bell became unstable from the nineteenth trial on and extinguished at the thirty-fifth trial; in Jack the reflex to the bell became unstable from the twenty-third trial and extinguished at the thirty-seventh trial.

Thus in both animals the reflex to light extinguished more rapidly than did the reflex to the bell, in spite of the fact that the bell was subjected to extinction after the extinction of the reflex to light. Taking into account the fact that in both Jack and Una the conditioned reflexes to light and bell had been consolidated to an approximately equal degree, this might be explained by the fact that the rate of extinction of conditioned motor reflexes depends on the physical strength of the conditioned stimulus: the stronger the conditioned stimulus, the slower the extinction.

These facts show that conditioned place reflexes are learned and extinguished according to the laws of extinction which had been found in Pavlov's laboratory on the basis of salivary conditioned reflexes.

References

Babkin, I. S. An experiment on the systematic study of complex neural psychological phenomena in the dog. Dissertation, Leningrad, 1904.

Gordeladze, L. K. Defining parts of a rocm as positive and negative conditioned stimuli. *Tez. Dokl. Nauch. Konf. Molod. Uch. IEM Akad. Med. Nauk SSSR,* Leningrad, 1953, 11–13.

Kas'yanov, V. M., and Fruktov, A. L. Influence of the strength of a sound stimulus on the speed of motor acts in man. *Fiziol. Zh. SSSR,* 1952, *6,* 681–687.

Khananashvili, M. M. New data on the differentiation of spatial conditioned stimuli. In *Yearbook IEM Akad. Med. Nauk SSSR,* Leningrad, 1956. Pp. 36–40.

Krasusskii, V. K. The significance of the physical strength of a component in a complex stimulus. *Zh. vyssh. nerv. Deyat.,* 1954, No. 1, 104–107.

Kupalov, P. S. The organization of the nervous processes of the brain during conditioned reflex activity. *EEG clin. Neurophysiol.,* 1960, Suppl. No. 13, 3–11.

Kupalov, P. S. Some normal and pathological properties of the nervous processes of the brain. In N. S. Kline (Ed.), *Pavlovian Conference on Higher Nervous Activity. Ann. N.Y. Acad. Sci.* 1961, *92,* 1046–1053.

Kupalov, P. S., and Gantt, V. K. On the relationship between the strength of the conditioned stimulus and the magnitude of the conditioned reflex. *Trudy Fiziol. Lab. im. Pavlova,* 1928, *1,* No. 2, 5–12.

Kupalov, P. S., and Khananashvili, M. M. Complex motor responses to inhibitory stimuli. *Zh. vyssh. nerv. Deyat.,* 1958, No. 5, 629–636.

Kupalov, P. S. and Khananashvili, M. M. Discrimination of spatial conditioned stimuli. *Zh. vyssh. nerv. Deyat.,* 1960, No. 3, 305–312.

Kupalov, P. S., and Pravosudov, V. P. Factors influencing the duration of conditioned motor reflexes, *Vestnik Akad. Med. Nauk SSSR,* 1959, No. 1, 19–26.

Popova, N. S. Certain features of the formation of conditioned reflexes to auditory and visual stimuli in dogs (the method of free response). *Zh. vyssh. nerv. Deyat.,* 1960, No. 1, 80–87.

Syrenskii, V. I. The influence of pharmacological agents on the behavior of dogs with extirpated frontal lobes. In *Yearbook IEM Akad. Med. Nauk SSSR.* Leningrad, 1961. 45–47.

Syrenskii, V. I. The significance of certain positions of the head and body of an animal for correct discrimination of auditory conditioned stimuli in conditions of free movement. *Byull. eksper. Biol.,* 1962, No. 7, 6–10.

Yakloveva, V. V. Dependence of a dog's position in the room on the conditions of stimulation. *Tez Dokl. S'ezda Fiziol. Biokhim. Farmakol.*, 1947, 250.

Yakloveva, V. V. Analysis of voluntary movements in the dog (dependence of the dog's position and posture on the conditioned food stimulus). *Probl. sovrem. fiziol. Biokhim. Farmakol.*, 1949, No. 1, 163–165.

Zelenii, G. P. Materials on the problem of the dog's reaction to auditory stimuli. Dissertation, Leningrad, 1907.

27

Classical Conditioning Research and Theories

E. A. Asratyan and *Associates*

EDITORS' INTRODUCTION

Classical conditioning research conducted at the Institute of Higher Nervous Activity and Neurophysiology, headed by E. A. Asratyan, and the theories developed by him are of considerable importance for psychology. Asratyan is one of the few remaining physiologists who studied with Pavlov, and is one of the outstanding proponents of the classical Pavlovian point of view in the area of physiological and behavioral studies of conditioning. He has been slow to accept revisions of Pavlovian theory based on analogies from the computer and information sciences (the acceptor of action proposed by Anokhin, 1961, or Miller, Galanter, and Pribram's TOTE mechanism, 1960, both of which have become enormously popular concepts in Soviet psychophysiology). However, the experimental research stemming from his Institute reflects an ingenuity and flexibility in the use of classical conditioning procedures generally lacking in the American use of the method. Results from experiments conducted in his Institute highlight some of the shortcomings in current American behavioral theories and the limited conditions under which these theories apply. Some of the research conducted in Asratyan's Institute further demonstrates the fruitfulness of combining physiological and behavioral methods in approaching theoretical problems of interest to physiology and psychology.

The present chapter has been compiled by the editors from

several sources in order to provide sufficient depth of presentation to make the material useful for Western psychologists unfamiliar with Asratyan's terminology and techniques. In addition to Asratyan's monograph (1965), a collection of articles edited by Gutmann and Hrik (1963) is recommended to the interested reader.

TWO THEORETICAL PROBLEMS have been the principal concern of Asratyan and his associates: (1) the locus of inhibition in the conditioned-reflex arc and (2) the effects of stimulus strength and sequence or temporal order on the elaboration of conditioned reflexes.

Asratyan's Theory of Inhibition and Related Research

Asratyan believes that the inhibition developed during extinction initially occurs in the temporary connection itself, physiologically, in the internuncial cells connecting the foci of the CS and the UCS. This theory is contrary to Pavlov's (1927), that inhibition accumulates in the cortical focus of the CS. It is also contrary to Anokhin's (1932) theory that the cortical focus of the UCS is where inhibition develops. All three of the foregoing theories may be contrasted with a behavioral theory such as Hull's (1934), which implies that reactive inhibition accumulates in the effector system. Asratyan also asserts that in the later stages of extinction the inhibition may spread to the cortical foci of the CS and the UCS. It is the subsequent spread of inhibition after extended or chronic extinction that has misled other investigators into assuming that inhibition is initiated in the cortical projection area, or focus, of the CS or UCS.

Switching Experiments

A distinctive feature of switching experiments is that the same stimulus serves as the CS for such widely different conditioned responses as salivation and leg flexion, large and small conditioned responses, and so on. The same CS paired with different UCSs in different stimulus contexts or at different times will evoke different CRs under different physical or temporal conditions. One of the first experiments of this type was conducted by Shitov and Yakovleva (Asratyan, 1961a).

In the morning one experimenter paired a metronome with food for the elaboration of a conditioned salivary response. In the afternoon a second experimenter using the same dogs and experimental room paired the metronome with electric shock to the paw, producing a conditioned defense reflex. In the mornings the metronome typically evoked only the salivary CR while in the afternoon it evoked the defense CR and inhibited the salivary CR.

Struchkov (Asratyan, 1961b) developed a more complex transswitching reflex. He first elaborated a salivary CR to a buzzer CS and a flexion defense response to a tactile CS. Using a different room, Struchkov then reversed the CS-UCS pairings presented to the animals. Tactile stimulation was followed by food while the buzzer now served as the CS, paired with electric shock to the paw. Eventually, in one room the buzzer elicited only the defense reflex and the tactile stimulus elicited only a salivary CR while in the other room the tactile stimulus evoked only a defense CR and the buzzer evoked a salivary CR.

Asratyan theorizes, by a process of elimination, that Struchkov's results imply that the locus of inhibition must be in the temporary connection, the internuncial cells connecting the cortical foci of the CS and the UCS. Inhibition cannot be concentrated in the focus of the CS since in each room it evokes one of the two conditioned reflexes while the other is inhibited. Inhibition cannot be concentrated in the cortical focus of the UCS since a given UCS effectively elicits its UCR and permits the elaboration of a CR in each room.

Another problem studied in Asratyan's Institute is the possibility of elaborating switching conditioned reflexes where a given conditioned stimulus would evoke two conditioned reflexes of the same type but of different magnitudes or latencies.

Switching conditioned reflexes of different magnitudes was demonstrated by Yan Wei-jin (Asratyan, 1961a, 1965). In one experimental room she developed conditioned salivary responses to auditory, visual, and tactile stimuli, reinforcing each of these stimuli with 20 grams of food while using a 15-second CS-UCS interval. When these conditioned reflexes were stable another experiment was started in a second room, using the same conditioned stimuli but a UCS of 60 grams. Experiments were alternated daily in the two experimental rooms. In the first room, with a relatively small UCS, relatively small conditioned reflexes were acquired. In the second room, with the relatively large amount of reward, large conditioned salivary responses developed.

Zhu Zi-jiao (Asratyan, 1961a, 1965) conducted an analogous experiment, switching conditioned reflexes of different latencies. In one experimental chamber conditioned salivary responses to auditory, visual, and tactile stimuli were elaborated, using a UCS of 60 grams of dry food. Delayed conditioning with a 15-second CS-UCS interval was employed. When these conditioned reflexes were stable another experiment was started in a second experimental chamber, using the same conditioned stimuli and reinforcement but with a longer CS-UCS interval, 1 to 2 minutes. Experiments were alternated daily in the two chambers. In the first room with the relatively short CS-UCS interval, relatively short latency conditioned responses were acquired. In the second with the relatively long CS-UCS interval, long-latency conditioned salivary reflexes developed to the same conditioned stimuli. In one dog, for example, latencies to the tactile stimulus were 7 seconds in the first room and 25 seconds in the second room while for the visual stimulus the latencies were 4 and 34 seconds, respectively.

In both kinds of experiments (using different amounts of reinforcement or different CS-UCS intervals) extinction of one conditioned reflex resulted in marked inhibition of the other conditioned reflex elicited by the same conditioned stimulus in a different room.

Asratyan concludes from these experiments that the same neural structures are involved in the two conditioned reflexes of the same type elicited by the same conditioned stimulus. However, exactly what the common neural structures are has not been specified. The extinction results do not provide any particular support for Asratyan's theory concerning the locus of inhibition. The experiments do demonstrate that it is possible to elaborate difficult discriminations between stimulus complexes, and fine differentiations between conditioned responses.

According to Asratyan (1961a, 1965) the constant features of the environment, which initially are relatively neutral, become continuously acting conditioned stimuli that evoke tonic conditioned reflexes, an hypothesis counter to the common assumption in American behavioral theories that constant environmental stimuli become inactive. These tonic reflexes establish a heightened background of cortical excitability for the phasic conditioned response. The tonic conditioned reflex is the differential factor responsible for determining which phasic conditioned response will occur in the switching experiments.

Sakhyulina (Asratyan, 1961a, 1965) has obtained some evidence supporting the hypothesis that switching is dependent upon tonic conditioned reflexes by recording the EEG during the elaboration of switching reflexes. In the morning an auditory CS was paired with electric shock to the left hind leg. In the afternoon the same CS was paired with shock to the right hind leg. Appropriate conditioned reflexes were established: an anticipatory flexion of the left leg to the CS in the morning experiment, and an anticipatory leg flexion of the right leg in the afternoon experiment. Electroencephalogram records showed that, as soon as the animal was prepared for a given experiment, the cortical focus of the appropriate unconditioned reflex showed heightened bioelectric activity. In the morning when the left hind leg was to be stimulated, the parietal area in the right cortical hemisphere showed the increased activity while the left parietal area showed the increased activity in the afternoon. A phasic stimulus, the CS, applied in the presence of the dominant focus established by the tonic conditioned reflex increased the excitability of the tonic reflex still further but also increased excitability in other areas of the cortex. The EEG data thus indicate that two conditioned reflexes are established, the tonic CR evoked by the constant stimuli of the particular experimental environment, and the phasic CR evoked by the relatively brief CS which summates with the tonic reflex. The particular tonic reflex evoked by the constant stimuli characterizing a specific experimental situation determines the type of conditioned reflex evoked by the phasic conditioned stimulus.

In the terms of behavior theory developed in the United States, effects ascribed to the tonic reflex would be interpreted in terms of the fractional anticipatory goal response, r_g-s_g (Hull, 1934; Spence, 1956). Effects of different amounts of reward, delays of reinforcement, CS-UCS interval, although not of course investigated in the context of switching connections, could all be interpreted in terms of the r_g-s_g concept. The concept of the tonic reflex, however, has a basic advantage over that of the r_g-s_g. The latter, like most theoretical terms in current behavior theory, has limited significance, and is often quite redundant, since it is defined in terms of the same behavior it is designed to explain. The concept of r_g-s_g lacks generality. The advantage of a concept such as the tonic reflex is that it may be defined in terms of EEG measures and is used to explain the behavior of phasic conditioned responses defined in terms of a behavioral response. It could be argued that the tonic reflex and the r_g-s_g are equivalent abstract concepts, which to some extent is correct. But at least the Soviet investigators have looked at appropriate correlated physiological variables, activity in the brain and not licking of the lips. As a consequence there is a relatively large amount of physiological information and concepts which can be related to the tonic reflex but not to the r_g-s_g.

The correspondence between the usage of the tonic reflex by Asratyan and the r_g-s_g by behavior theorists may be more evident in an experiment conducted by Khachaturian, described by Asratyan (1961a, 1965). The amount of saliva consistently evoked by a 10-gram portion of bread and meat was first determined. Portions were then increased to 50 grams, which evoked a larger salivary reflex. Feedings with the larger amount continued for at least one week before the amount was reduced once more to 10-gram portions. A greater amount of saliva was secreted to the 10-gram portion following a week of feeding with 50 grams than prior to the feeding with the larger amount. After several days of feeding 10-gram portions, the amount of saliva secreted returned to its initial value.

Khachaturian's results could be accounted for in terms of the conditioning of a larger r_g-s_g to the 50-gram portion which persisted for some time in the presence of the 10-gram portion before extinguishing to its original level. An implication of this interpretation is that the amount of saliva initially elicited by the 50-gram portion in the early sessions, those immediately following the 10-gram sessions, would be less than the amount evoked by 50 grams after several sessions. Data reported by Asratyan (1961a, 1965) indicate that such was the case. The amount of saliva elicited by 50-gram portions increased with repeated feeding sessions. These results are also interpretable in terms of Asratyan's concept of a tonic reflex, and the data are presented by him as support for the conception, which is formulated in accordance with current neurophysiological conceptions.

He assumes that the intensity of a neural process corresponds to the number of activated neural cells. The strength of conditioned and unconditioned reflexes is therefore determined primarily by the number of activated cortical cells in the foci stimulated by the CS and the UCS. The strength of the temporary connection formed between the foci of the CS and UCS will be determined by the number of activated cells in the foci. Thus a change in the amount of reward, that is the magnitude of the UCS, is accompanied by changes in the number of cells activated in the cortical focus of the UCS, and therefore by a change in the strength of the conditioned reflex.

In the same experimental situation the relatively small 10-gram portion of food excites fewer cells in the cortical focus of the UCS than does the relatively large 50-gram reinforcement. Repeated feeding of the 50 grams produces a tonic conditioned reflex to the experimental situation proportional to the large number of cells activated in the focus of the unconditioned alimentary reflex. With a switch to a smaller food portion, 10 grams, the larger number of cortical cells of the tonic reflex conditioned with 50 grams produces a larger response to the 10-gram portion than before the feeding with the larger portion. Because of the decrease in reinforcement, the tonic reflex gradually diminishes. The number of cells activated in the focus of the UCS is eventually reduced.

Switching experiments with different amounts of reward are interpreted in the following manner. The number of cells in the focus of the UCS is greater when stimulated by the larger UCS in a given experimental room at a given time than when stimulated by a relatively small UCS in another room or at a different time in the same room. Two types of conditioned reflexes corresponding to the amount of reward become established in each experimental room, tonic conditioned reflexes to the static cues of the experimental situation and phasic conditioned reflexes to the specific, relatively momentary CS. A large or small CR is appropriately evoked by the same CS paired with two different UCSs because of the different amounts of cortical excitability induced by the tonic conditioned reflexes. When the same phasic CS is presented in the presence of a large tonic reflex it evokes a larger conditioned reflex than when it is presented in the presence of a smaller tonic reflex, a smaller focus of excitability.

Asratyan has emphasized that the conception of a tonic reflex as the critical factor in switching conditioned responses, especially in switching delayed responses, is a tentative hypothesis. However, the effects of tonic reflexes are not peculiar to switching. They occur in most if not all standardized experimental situations and represent the conditioned background cortical excitability upon which the phasic conditioned response is elaborated.

The theoretical conception of tonic conditioned reflexes is testable, as already indicated, and should be of fundamental importance in the analysis of human classical conditioning and learning generally. The context of the experimental situation, "status" of the experimenter, social characteristics of the experiment, and attitude of the experimenter as well as that of the subject may all establish conditioned tonic reflexes that profoundly modify the conditioned response that may be elaborated to the phasic conditioned stimulus.

Two-Way Connections

"Two-way connections" refers to the simultaneous development of forward and backward conditioned reflexes. At least two experimental conditions are necessary for their establishment. First, the stimuli, each of which serves as a CS and a UCS, must be approximately equal in physiological strength. Exactly how equality of physiological strength is determined is not always entirely clear. One procedure would be to determine the rates of forward conditioning with each of the stimuli serving as a UCS with an "indifferent" stimulus as CS. Apparently, the procedure used seems to be to estimate the physiological strength of the stimuli, and determine *post hoc* whether they were in fact equivalent by comparing their effectiveness in the experiment establishing two-way connections. This procedure is possible since the stimuli are each used as the preceding and subsequent stimulus either on alternate trials with the same animal, or if given in a constant order, different animals would receive the stimuli in each of the two orders.

A second critical requirement for the demonstration of simultaneous forward and backward conditioned reflexes is the elicitation of different recordable unconditioned responses by each of the stimuli. The use, for example, of a tone and an electric shock as CS and UCS, each of which evokes the GSR where only this response is recorded, as is often the situation employed in the study of backward conditioning in the United States, meets neither of these essential requirements.

Demonstration of the establishment of two-way connections appeared quite early in the conditioning literature and for many years has been a subject of investigation by Beritov and his associates (1924). Studies of the conditions necessary for the elaboration of two-way conditioned reflexes are of general significance because of the information they provide concerning the conditions affecting the establishment of conditioned reflexes and the possible implications for the neurophysiology of the underlying temporary connections.

An innovation introduced by Asratyan and his associates in the study of two-way connections is particularly relevant to the problem of the locus of inhibition during extinction. If forward and backward conditioned reflexes can be elaborated simultaneously, then it is possible to study the effects of extinguishing one reflex on characteristics of the other.

Varga and Pressman, associates of Asratyan, have been particularly active investigators of the phenomenon of two-way connections (Pressman and Varga, 1963; Varga and Pressman, 1963). Stimuli typically employed in their studies using dogs are an airpuff to the eyes and passive leg movement of a hind limb. The latter response is elicited by the experimenter, using a string and a pulley system. Prior to the start of conditioning a base rate of unconditioned responses to each of the stimuli was obtained. The airpuff and passive leg movement were presented individually in varying orders 10 to 50 times with an interstimulus interval ranging from 1 to 5 minutes. The airpuff always elicited an eyeblink and occasionally a *reduction* in action potentials and relaxation of the extensor gastrocnemius muscle. Passive raising of the limb induced an *increase* in action potentials but was often accompaned by an eyeblink.

When the sequence of stimuli during conditioning was, passive leg movement–airpuff, conditioning in the forward direction reached the 100 per cent level. Passive leg movement by means of the pulley system was always accompanied by an eyeblink. Backward conditioning was much weaker. On 23 per cent of the test trials, presentation of the airpuff elicited an *increase* in action potentials in the limb.

Different animals were given the stimuli in the order airpuff–passive leg movement. Forward conditioning here again was very strong, the airpuff eliciting leg flexion or an increase in action potentials in the limb. The test for backward conditioning was passive movement of the leg 1 second after the airpuff. Eyeblinks occurred on 53 per cent of the test trials with two dogs, indicating formation of a backward connection. The higher rate of backward conditioned responses with these dogs as compared to the previous animals is assumed to be due to the sequence of stimuli. Presenting the relatively noxious airpuff first rather than the leg movement favors development of backward conditioning, since the airpuff is the UCS for the reverse connection. Evidence obtained by Lyan Chi-an, which will be described shortly, supports this implication of stimulus sequence. A study such as Kimmel's (1959), which found that the weaker the CS intensity with a shock UCS the better was the forward conditioning, might well find, with appropriate response measures, just the opposite effect in terms of backward conditioning. Within limits, the greater the intensity of the "CS," the better the backward conditioning.

Although Asratyan (1961a, 1961b, 1963) believes that the results obtained by Varga and Pressman represent the simultaneous elaboration of forward and backward conditioned reflexes, these investigators do not entirely agree. They emphasize a number of differences between the two kinds of conditioned responses in addition to the obvious difference in strength. Manifestations of backward conditioned responses tend to be grouped in series of 2 or 3 responses. Two or three successive tests might evoke backward conditioned reflexes, a series of failures might occur, and then another brief run of backward CRs would occur. This is contrasted with the consistent occurrence of forward conditioned responses. The general picture of a weak temporary connection suggests to Varga and Pressman that, at least in their experimental situation, backward connections are not true conditioned reflexes of the same nature as forward connections. Backward connections are a manifestation of summation reflexes which lie somewhere between sensitization and true forward connections. Summation reflexes may be conceived of as an initial state which may subsequently develop into a true temporary connection, or the physiological state underlying the conditioned reflex (Kupalov, 1961).

However, whether backward connections are summation reflexes or true conditioned reflexes is largely irrelevant to the problem of the locus of inhibition in the conditioned reflex arc. Given the stimulus sequence airpuff–passive leg movement, the leg movement CR elicited by the airpuff is extinguished by presenting the airpuff while omitting passive leg movement. Isolated passive leg movements, test trials for the backward connection, were interspersed among 100 unreinforced presentations of the airpuff, extinction trials for the forward connection. Extinction of the forward connection did not affect the frequency of occurrence of the backward conditioned reflex. Findings of this kind indicate that the UCS for the forward connection, passive leg movement in this case, does not function as the locus of inhibition. If it were a locus of inhibition, then the backward connection in which it serves as the CS should show some decrement.

Comparable results for backward conditioned reflexes were obtained with a pair of dogs receiving the sequence of stimuli in reversed order, passive leg movement–airpuff. Passive lifting of the leg was followed in 1 to 2 seconds by an airpuff to the eye. Only partial extinction of the eyeblink to the leg movement could be obtained after more than 100 extinction trials (CS elicitations of passive leg movements unaccompanied by the airpuff). Evidence for the conclusion that the cortical locus of the CS is not a center of inhibition is that electromyographic recordings of the leg movements did not show a decrement during extinction of the conditioned eyeblink. As a test for backward conditioning, the airpuff alone was presented at different stages of extinction of the forward connection. In some cases it evoked increased action potentials in the limbs as well as an eyeblink. The backward connection was not affected by the extinction of the forward conditioned reflex, again indicating that the UCS is not an initial locus of inhibition. The results of extinction with both sequences of stimuli also indicate that the effector response is not a locus of inhibition as implied by Hull's theory of reactive inhibition.

In contrast to the study of Varga and Pressman, who used two "indifferent" or relatively weak stimuli, Lyan Chi-an (Asratyan, 1961b) studied two-way connections using what ordinarily would be considered two unconditioned stimuli. Electric shock and food were employed as preceding-subsequent stimuli with some animals while other dogs received food–electric shock. Both stereotyped sequences of stimuli produced strong forward CRs more rapidly than the "indifferent" stimuli employed by Varga and Pressman. Reverse or backward CRs, however, were still weak and unstable, similar to the reverse connections obtained by Varga and Pressman with indifferent stimuli. Using two strong stimuli apparently results in a greater difference in the strength of forward and backward CRs than in the case of two relatively weak stimuli.

Lyan Chi-an introduced a number of variations in the strength of the preceding and subsequent stimuli that revealed the importance of the stimulus sequence in establishing two-way connections. The subsequent stimuli more readily evoked the backward CR if the strength of the preceding stimulus, the UCS for the backward CR, was increased or if the excitability of the cortical focus of the preceding stimulus was increased. A similar result was obtained when the excitability of the cortical focus of the subsequent stimulus was decreased or the intensity of the stimulus was weakened. For example, in the stereotyped sequence electric shock–food, a backward CR was facilitated if presentation of the food was preceded by a stronger shock than usual.

On the other hand, an increase in excitability of the cortical focus of the subsequent stimulus or an increase in its intensity resulted in inhibition of the backward conditioned reflex. Similar results were obtained by a decrease in excitability of the cortical focus of the preceding stimulus or a decrement in its strength.

Thus, in the stereotyped sequence electric shock–food, presentation of food does not elicit the backward CR of leg flexion if the animal is in a hunger state, or if it is given a preferred food at the start of the experiment, or if it is initially stimulated by a weak shock.

Struchkov (1963) has also been actively engaged in the investigation of two-way connections. He has employed what is ordinarily considered a UCS, food, as the preceding stimulus and in some dogs passive leg movement as the subsequent stimulus. In other animals cooling of the skin on the trunk was employed as the subsequent stimulus. What ordinarily would be considered a backward conditioning paradigm was employed. The important difference between Struchkov's experiments and the procedure of backward conditioning employed in the United States is that he obtained measures of the UCR evoked by the preceding as well as the subsequent stimuli, salivation evoked by the food and pneumographic recordings of leg movements and skin temperature changes recorded by thermocouples. Seven dogs were employed in the experiments.

The preceding stimulus or "CS," food, was given to the dog, and 5 to 20 seconds after the start of feeding a passive leg movement was elicited in some animals while in others a cold stimulus of 5 to 7°C was applied to the skin of the trunk. The second stimulus was continued until feeding ceased. Thus there was overlap of the preceding and subsequent stimulus.

For one group of dogs, after a relatively small number of trials, leg movements were evoked as soon as feeding began, prior to the passive leg movement elicited by the experimenter. In the second group of animals, in which the cold stimulus was the subsequent stimulus, "UCS," conditioned anticipatory vasoconstriction was elicited shortly after the onset of feeding and prior to the application of the cold stimulus. These results are interpreted as indicating that a forward conditioned reflex can be established between the cortical focus of a strong stimulus, food, and the cortical focus of a weak excitation, the motor or vasomotor focus. A forward conditioned reflex may be established despite the greater relative strength of the preceding stimulus.

In addition to the forward connection, Struchkov found backward conditioned reflexes. When the leg of the dog was passively moved a salivary response occurred. Application of the cold stimulus also evoked a conditioned alimentary reflex, salivation, licking, and the like. Struchkov believes that, in all cases where conditioned reflexes are established, backward as well as forward connections are formed. The frequently reported finding by Soviet investigators that the subsequent stimulus eventually acquires inhibitory properties when it is preceded by a strong stimulus is probably due to the lack of reinforcement the subsequent stimulus receives during test trials. Given that the backward connection is relatively weak to begin with, it extinguishes quickly with repeated test trials.

Struchkov also found that after complete extinction of the forward connection the backward conditioned reflex remained intact, further support for Asratyan's theory that independent forward and backward connections are formed and that inhibition is localized initially in the temporary connection itself. Struchkov also found that tests for the backward connection act as a disinhibitor for the forward connection, since the previously extinguished forward conditioned reflex reappears for a time following the test for the backward conditioned reflex. Struchkov obtained better backward conditioning with the stimuli that he employed than did Varga and Pressman, and therefore believes that backward connections represent true conditioned reflexes.

Struchkov's evidence of forward conditioning with food as the preceding stimulus is contrary to the assumption that the subsequent stimulus must be stronger than the preceding stimulus for the reliable elaboration of forward classical conditioned reflexes. His results on forward conditioning provide support for Asratyan's hypothesis that the sequence of stimuli in classical conditioning is more critical than the relative strengths of the stimuli. Struchkov and Asratyan assert:

> During the elaboration of a conditioned reflex it is important to note that excitation reaches the point of the subsequent stimulus twice during each connection: once from the focus of the conditioned (preceding) stimulus and a second time from the reinforcing (subsequent) stimulus. Consequently excitation is raised in the focus of the subsequent stimulus and is connected with the conditions of the experiment and is later reproduced by them. When the wave of excitation induced by the preceding (conditioned) stimulus reaches the focus of increased excitability (the point where the reinforcing stimulus is applied), then subthreshold excitation becomes suprathreshold and a conditioned reflex appears (Struchkov, 1963, p. 295).

According to this scheme, a relatively strong forward conditioned reflex connection is formed from the preceding to the subsequent stimulus because the cortical focus of the subsequent stimulus is always acted upon by two sources of excitation, the conditioned and after that the unconditioned stimulus. The focus of the subsequent stimulus becomes the dominant focus, in Ukhtomski's terms, because it has two sources of excitability while the cortical focus of the preceding stimulus has only one source of excitability. It is this sequential effect on the focus of excitability which permits various stimuli to be used interchangeably as the "UCS." This interchangeability of stimuli in the role of a subsequent "UCS" rather than the absolute intensity or amount of reinforcement is analogous to Premack's (1959) analysis of reinforcement in operant conditioning. Asratyan's interpretation may provide a theoretical basis, with corresponding physiological evidence for the reinforcing effects obtained by Premack. It may also be noted that the theoretical interpretation of the effect of stimulus sequence is opposed to the hypothesis of Kimble (1961) and Kimmel (1966) that the CS develops inhibitory properties over the UCR. Subsequent experiments that we shall review (Romanovskaya, 1963; Tchilingaryan, 1963) contradict in a more direct manner the conception that the CS inhibits the UCR.

Both Varga and Pressman and Struchkov found that a variable sequence of stimuli produced poorer forward conditioning than a constant sequence of stimuli. This difference in the efficacy of constant versus variable sequence is taken as further evidence for the advantage accruing to the subsequent stimulus in the sequence. With a constant stimulus sequence, a high level of conditioned responding can be attained when the subsequent stimulus is an innocuous condition such as passive leg movement or cooling of the skin. Elaboration of conditioned reflexes under such reinforcement conditions poses a problem for traditional theories of reinforcement, particularly drive-reduction theory.

In addition to its usefulness in the analysis of the locus of inhibition, the conception of concurrently developing two-way connections has theoretical significance for the persistent problem of the relationship between classical and instrumental conditioning. Asratyan (1966) believes that the differences between instrumental and classical conditioning are differences in performance and not differences in the basic conditions of learning. The basic physiological condition necessary for learning, the closing of a temporary connection, is the same in classical and instrumental learning.

> Pavlov not only drew attention to the specific nature of this (instrumental) type of conditioned reflexes, but also advanced his well-known view of the functional peculiarities of the cortical apparatus of the motor system underlying this specific nature. We refer to his view that kinesthetic cortical neurons become connected during instrumental conditioning with afferent nerve cells of any other cortical areas, by bilateral conditioned connections capable of conducting excitation both from kinesthetic neurons to these cells and from these cells to kinesthetic neurons. In the case of food instrumental reflexes, for example, such a bilateral connection is formed between cortical points of the "working" paw and the food reflex. And if after this, some extraneous stimulus also becomes a conditioned food signal, it can excite the food centre and through it also activate nervous elements of the "working" paw and evoke its movement. The same can happen if the food centre is stimulated by endogenous factors (Asratyan, 1966, p. 36).

Binary Connections

Experiments by Daurova (1963) on the formation and extinction of binary conditioned reflexes were also designed to investigate the problem of the locus of inhibition. Establishment of binary conditioned reflexes involves the conditioning of two different reflexes to the same CS by pairing a given CS with two different unconditioned stimuli which evoke different reflexes. Daurova employed the alimentary reflex, salivation, and a defense motor reflex, a leg flexion response to electric shock. Two variations of the procedure were employed. In one procedure the CS was paired with only one UCS on a given trial, but different UCSs were presented on different trials in a random order. On one trial, for instance, the light CS was paired with food while on another trial the light was paired with electric shock to the limb. The second procedure involved the simultaneous presentation of both UCSs with the same CS on every trial. Switching reflexes also may involve pairing a given CS with qualitatively different UCSs, but it is not done simultaneously or within the same acquisition session.

For the salivary response the UCS was 30 grams of dry meat powder dissolved in milk. An electric shock above threshold intensity delivered to the front leg was used as the UCS for the defense response. In some animals the CS was a 1100-cps tone while for other animals a light from an electric bulb was used as the CS. A delayed conditioning procedure was used, the onset of the CS preceding the UCSs by about 20 seconds. In many of the experimental sessions the CS and the electric shock were continued for as long as the animal ate the food, thereby equating the duration of the two UCSs in the presence of the CS.

Graphic data presented in Figure 27–1 (obtained by Daurova) clearly indicate that it is possible to establish both reflexes simultaneously. During the period in which the CS occurs prior to the onset of the UCSs the dog shows anticipatory salivation and leg flexion. One conditioned reflex does not consistently appear before the other, indicating that response chaining did not occur.

An experimental variation designed to produce supramaximal inhibition was conducted in order to test the hypothesis of localization of inhibition in the temporary connection. The intensity of the auditory CS was greatly increased. This procedure resulted in inhibition of the salivary conditioned

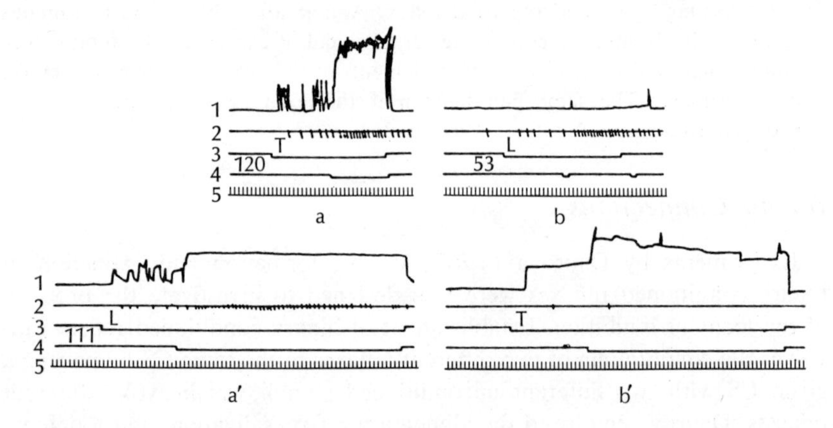

Figure 27–1. Binary (*a* and *a′*) and ordinary (*b* and *b′*) conditioned reflexes: (1) leg movement; (2) salivation; (3) conditioned stimulus; (4) unconditioned stimulus; (5) time (sec.). Numbers on the record of the conditioned stimulus indicate number of conditioning trials with tone (*T*) and with light (*L*), respectively.

response while the conditioned defense response persisted for some time. Continued occurrence of the conditioned defense response in the absence of the conditioned salivary response indicated the independence of the two conditioned reflexes with respect to the locus of inhibition. With continued trials using the high-intensity CS, the conditioned defense response was also finally inhibited.

When both UCSs were omitted, the two CRs extinguished, but at different rates. The salivary CR extinguished before the conditioned leg flexion response. It is argued that if the afferent cortical cells receiving the CS were the locus of inhibition developing during extinction, the two CRs would have to extinguish at the same rate.

When one UCS was omitted while the other continued to be presented, the CR based upon the omitted UCS extinguished. However, the other CR which was followed by its UCS did not show extinction effects. An illustration of this effect is seen in Figure 27–2. These results are also taken as

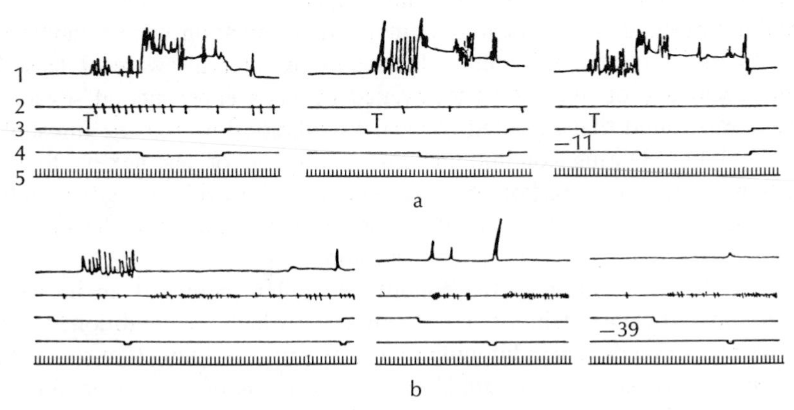

Figure 27–2. Extinction of one component of the binary reflex independently of the second component: (*a*) extinction of the alimentary component; (*b*) extinction of the defense component.

contrary to the hypothesis proposed by Pavlov that the cortical focus of the CS develops inhibition. Daurova further reports that if both CRs are extinguished by omission of their UCSs, and then one of the UCSs is reintroduced, only the corresponding CR is reinstated. Once more, this result is taken as a demonstration of the functional independence of the two conditioned reflexes evoked by the same CS.

Measurement of Cortical Excitability

Romanovskaya (1963) studied changes in excitability in the cortical projection area of the unconditioned reflex during the elaboration and extinction of a classically conditioned leg flexion reflex. A measure of the excitability of the cortical focus was obtained by determining the threshold for an electric current necessary to elicit leg flexion before conditioning, during the development of a conditioned flexion defense reflex, and during extinction of leg flexion.

Chronic experiments were conducted with seven dogs. Silver EEG electrodes reaching to the dura mater were inserted through a small opening in the skull. Three to five electrodes were inserted in the motor region of each hemisphere at points having the lowest thresholds for eliciting responses in the front and hind legs. After recovery from surgery the thresholds of reflex excitability were determined by cortical and cutaneous stimulation. Flexion of the limbs served as the response measure in both cases. Within-subject variability was slight; cortical thresholds varied from 0.1 to 0.2 milliampere for a given animal. Between-subject variability was relatively great, varying from 0.3 to 1.5 milliamperes. Thresholds for cutaneous stimulation were lower, ranging from 0.04 to 0.3 milliampere.

Stable thresholds for cortical and cutaneous stimulation were established prior to the start of conditioning. Interstimulus intervals were at least 2 minutes and one or more days intervened between experimental sessions, since it was found that repeated cortical stimulation lowered the threshold of excitability. During conditioning and extinction of leg flexion to the cutaneous shock, the threshold intensity necessary for evoking leg flexion by a current applied cortically and cutaneously was determined at the start of, during, and the end of an experimental session.

During the elaboration of the conditioned reflex there was an irregular increase in cortical excitability up to the point at which the conditioned connection was formed. Reconditioning following previous extinction showed a marked increase in cortical excitability at the focus of the unconditioned reflex. These increases in cortical excitability during the elaboration of a conditioned reflex are changes to be expected on the basis of the conception of the orienting reflex (Sokolov, 1963).

There were considerable individual differences in the dogs, presumably due to typological characteristics, in the degree to which extinction could be obtained. In all the dogs in which extinction occurred, excitability to cortical and cutaneously applied current was determined. Cortical excitability did not change during the early stages of extinction when the CS continued to evoke intermittent leg flexions and when responses occurred during the intertrial interval. There was a gradual fall in the cortical excitability of the focus of the motor reflex with continued extinction. The most pronounced decrease in cortical excitability occurred when extinction was relatively complete, when repeated presentations of the CS did not evoke a response and intertrial responses did not occur. These changes in cortical excitability are depicted in Figure 27–3.

In one experiment the threshold of cortical excitability increased fourfold following chronic extinction. The threshold for cutaneous excitability increased by a factor of two. Romanovskaya found that in some dogs the cortical foci showed some loss of excitability for at least a day following repeated extinction sessions.

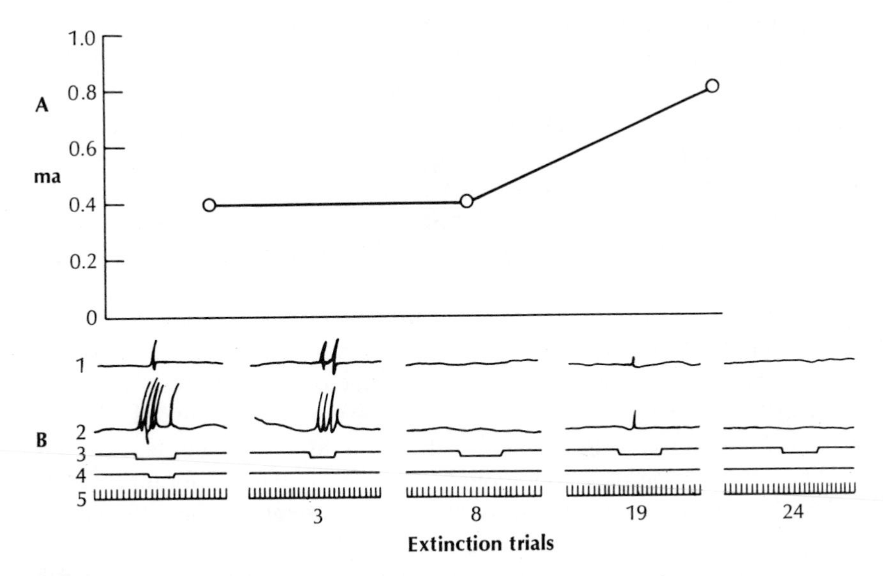

Figure 27–3. Changes in threshold of excitation of a cortical point in the motor area during extinction of a conditioned reflex formed to stimulation of that point. (*A*) threshold values for movement evoked by cortical stimulation (ma); (*B*) selected extinction trials: (1) movement of right leg; (2) movement of left leg; (3) conditioned stimulus; (4) unconditioned stimulus; (5) time.

Romanovskaya interprets these experimental results in accord with Asratyan's theory. Inhibition developing during the course of extinction initially develops in the cortical cells corresponding to the temporary connection. With continued extinction trials inhibition spreads to the cortical focus representing the UCS, and presumably the inhibition also spreads to the cortical focus of the CS.

Romanovskaya (1963) employed a standard classical defense conditioning procedure with the innovation of tests of cortical excitability in the motor cortex using the unconditioned response, leg flexion, as the dependent measure of cortical excitability. Tchilingaryan (1963), on the other hand, used stimulation of the motor cortex as the UCS for leg flexion defense conditioning as well as for tests of cortical excitability.

Chronic experiments lasting 2 to 10 months were conducted with six dogs. Silver EEG electrodes were implanted in the motor cortex to the level of the dura mater in the area corresponding to the front legs. The experiment proper began 3 to 4 weeks after the operation.

The CS was a 300-cps tone. The UCS was electrical stimulation of the motor area inducing a definite motor response. The CS-UCS interval varied from 5 to 10 seconds, employing a delayed conditioning technique. The UCS was a direct current at 50 pulses per second.

The unconditioned response elicited by stimulation of the motor cortex varied somewhat among the animals, in part undoubtedly due to variations in electrode placement. The complex response usually elicited included lifting the leg and moving backward with a more pronounced response in the leg contralateral to the area stimulated. In a given animal the response pattern evoked by cortical stimulation was usually quite consistent, and was reproduced by the conditioned reflex. The conditioned response usually appeared after 15 to 20 sessions and was well established after 20 to 40 sessions.

Excitability of the motor cortex was measured under a number of different conditions. It was determined at the start and the end of an experimental session, and it was determined in the presence of the conditioned stimulus prior to the establishment of a conditioned response, after conditioning was established, and following extinction of the conditioned response.

After elaboration of a conditioned reflex, excitability determined at the point of stimulation of the motor cortex was consistently higher at the end of an experimental session than at the start of the session. At the very beginning of conditioning the CS appeared to inhibit the effects of stimulating the motor cortex in that a suprathreshold intensity was needed to evoke an unconditioned reflex. The situation changed as soon as the CS became an effective signal stimulus. When conditioned reactions began to appear there was an increase in excitability. Subthreshold intensities of the current acting in the presence of the CS now evoked motor activity. These and the similar results obtained by Romanovskaya (1963) are contrary to the hypothesis proposed by Kimble (1961) and by Kimmel (1966) that the CS progressively inhibits the UCR during the course of conditioning.

Once extinction sessions were introduced a decrease in excitability occurred. Excitability in the cortical focus of the unconditioned response was greater at the start of an extinction session than at the end. However, in the early stages of extinction when there were only intermittent lapses in the CR, no change was found in the excitability of the cortical focus of the unconditioned reflex. After extinction progressed to the point where there were consistent omissions of the CR, excitability decreased. The threshold was raised twofold. The fall in excitability was localized in the region of the electrode stimulating the UCR. Other areas in the motor cortex did not show a change in their level of excitability. Some of these changes in cortical excitability during extinction are illustrated in Figure 27–4. The loss of

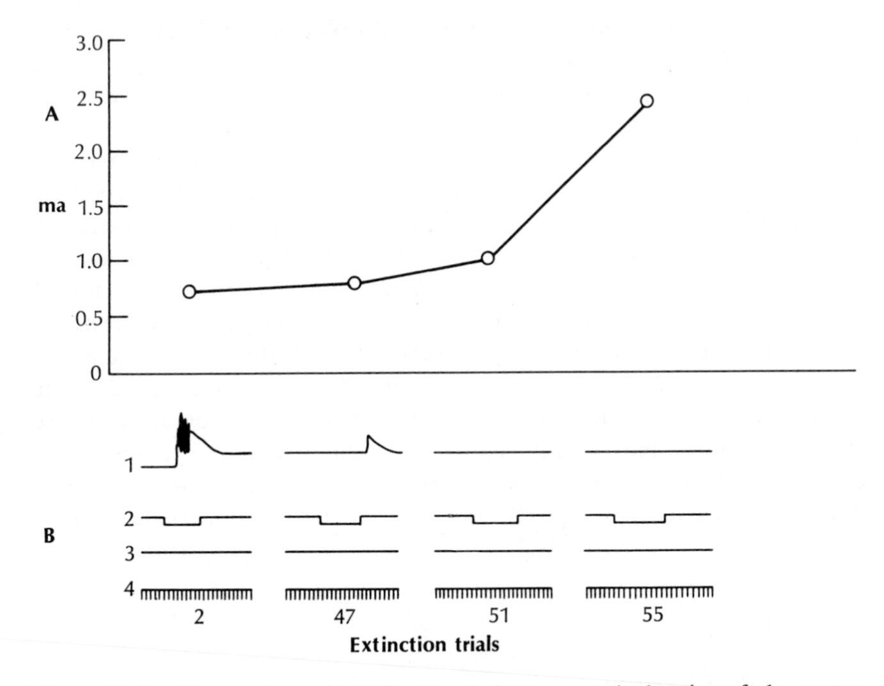

Figure 27–4. Changes in excitability threshold in a cortical point of the motor area during extinction of a conditioned defense reflex. (*A*) threshold values for movement evoked by cortical stimulation (ma); (*B*) selected extinction trials: (1) leg movement; (2) conditioned stimulus; (3) unconditioned stimulus; (4) time.

excitability in the focus of the UCS was particularly pronounced in the presence of the extinguished CS. Following reconditioning, excitability in the presence of the CS returned to approximately its original level.

The fact that a localized decrease in excitability occurred and, according to Tchilingaryan, there were no pain reactions to cortical stimulation, indicates that changes in drive level were not induced by the presence or absence of cortical stimulation. Nevertheless, an implication of drive theory must still be considered. The localized loss of excitability may be due to a decrease in primary or secondary drive owing to the absence of the stimulating current during the extinction phase of the experiment. As a control for such a contingency, Tchilingaryan introduced delays during conditioning equal to the time involved in the extinction sessions. Tests of excitability following the absence of conditioning trials failed to show a decrease in cortical excitability. The latter result again fails to support a drive interpretation of the changes in cortical excitability. It provides further evidence that classical conditioning with cortical stimulation serving as the UCS can be obtained in the apparent absence of a primary pain drive, contrary to a drive-reduction theory of reinforcement. Negative results obtained by Loucks (1935), a failure to find such conditioning, appear to have been due to procedural deficiencies in his experiment (Doty and Giurgea, 1961; Kupalov, 1961; Tchilingaryan, 1963).[1]

Each of the four types of experimental procedure employed by Asratyan and his associates has provided some evidence in support of his hypothesis that the inhibition developing during extinction is initiated in the temporary connection. Obviously, further behavioral and neurophysiological research is needed before the hypothesis can be considered completely substantiated. However, the experimental procedures used, such as switching reflexes and binary and two-way connections, lend themselves to the study of a variety of important problems that have not been adequately investigated in the United States, such as the relationship between discrimination or perception of signal stimuli and conditioned-response differentiation, parameters of stimulus sequences and intensity necessary for conditioning, and the utilization of concurrent physiological and behavioral measures of conditioning.

References

Anokhin, P. K. Active secretory method for the study of the dynamics of higher nervous activity. *Gorki med. J.*, 7–8.

Anokhin, P. K. Features of the afferent apparatus of the conditioned reflex and their importance for psychology. *Vop. Psikhol.*, 1955, No. 6, 16–38. (Reprinted in N. O'Connor [Ed.], *Recent Soviet psychology*. London: Pergamon Press, 1961.)

Asratyan, E. A. The initiation and localization of cortical inhibition in the conditioned reflex arc. *Ann. N.Y. Acad. Sci.*, 1961, *92*, 1141–1159. (a)

Asratyan, E. A. Some aspects of the elaboration of conditioned connections and formation of their properties. In J. F. Delafresnaye (Ed.), *Brain mechanisms and learning*. Oxford: Blackwell, 1961. Pp. 95–113. (b)

Asratyan, E. A. The localization of the cortical inhibition in the conditioned reflex arc. In E. Gutmann and P. Hrik (Eds.), *Central and peripheral mechanisms of motor functions*. Prague: Publishing House of the Czechoslovak Academy of Sciences, 1963. Pp. 113–122.

Asratyan, E. A. *Conditioned reflex and compensatory mechanisms*. London: Pergamon Press, 1965.

Asratyan, E. A. Functional architecture of instrumental conditioned reflexes.

1. *Editors' note:* A recent study by Wagner, Thomas, and Norton (1967) on this issue offers an alternative interpretation of the processes involved. They suggest that reinforcement from postural adjustments can account for the learning.

In *Symposium 4, Classical and instrumental conditioning, Eighteenth International Congress.* Moscow, 1966. Pp. 35–53.

Beritov, I. S. On the fundamental nervous processes in the cortex of the cerebral hemispheres. *Brain,* 1924, *47,* 109–148, 358–376.

Daurova, F. K. Binary conditioned reflex. In E. Gutmann and P. Hrik (Eds.), *Central and peripheral mechanisms of motor functions.* Prague: Publishing House of the Czechoslovak Academy of Sciences, 1963. Pp. 161–166.

Doty, R. W., and Giurgea, C. Conditioned reflexes established by coupling electrical excitations of two cortical areas. In J. F. Delafresnaye (Ed.), *Brain mechanisms and learning.* Oxford: Blackwell, 1961. Pp. 133–151.

Gutmann, E., and P. Hrik. *Central and peripheral mechanisms of motor function.* Prague: Publishing House of The Czechoslovak Academy of Science, 1963.

Hull, C. L. The concept of the habit-family hierarchy and maze learning. *Psych. Rev.,* 1934, *41,* 33–54, 134, 152.

Kimble, G. A. Discussion. *Ann N.Y. Acad. Sci.,* 1961, *92,* 1189–1192.

Kimmel, H. D. Amount of conditioning and intensity of conditioned stimulus. *J. exp. Psychol.,* 1959, *58,* 283–288.

Kimmel, H. D. Inhibition of the unconditioned response in classical conditioning. *Psychol. Rev.,* 1966, *73,* 232–240.

Kupalov, P. S. Some normal and pathological properties of nervous processes in the brain. *Ann. N.Y. Acad. Sci.,* 1961, *92,* 1046–1053.

Loucks, R. B. The experimental delineation of neural structures essential for learning. The attempt to condition striped muscle responses with faradization of the sigmoid gyri. *J. Psychol.,* 1935, *1,* 5–44.

Miller, G., Galanter, E., and Pribram, K. *Plans and the structure of behavior.* New York: Holt, Rinehart and Winston, 1960.

Pavlov, I. P. *Conditioned reflexes.* London: Oxford Univer. Press, 1927.

Premack, D. Toward empirical behavior laws: I. Positive reinforcement. *Psychol. Rev.,* 1959, *66,* 219–233.

Pressman, Y. M., and Varga, M. Y. The mechanisms of extinction of motor conditioned reflexes. In E. Gutmann and P. Hrik (Eds.), *Central and peripheral mechanisms of motor functions.* Prague: Publishing House of the Czechoslovak Academy of Sciences, 1963. Pp. 275–278.

Romanovskaya, Y. A. Changes in excitability in cortical foci of the motor analyser during elaboration and extinction of the conditioned defence reflex. In E. Gutmann and P. Hrik (Eds.), *Central and peripheral mechanisms of motor functions.* Prague: Publishing House of the Czechoslovak Academy of Sciences, 1963. Pp. 161–166.

Sokolov, E. N. *Perception and the conditioned reflex.* New York: Macmillan, 1963.

Spence, K. W. Behavior theory and conditioning. New Haven: Yale Univer. Press, 1956.

Struchkov, M. I. Concerning the mechanism of formation and functioning of a motor conditioned connection. In E. Gutmann and P. Hrik (Eds.), *Central and peripheral mechanisms of motor functions.* Prague: Publishing House of the Czechoslovak Academy of Sciences, 1963. Pp. 289–296.

Tchilingaryan, L. I. Changes in excitability of the motor area of the cerebral cortex during extinction of a conditioned reflex elaborated to direct electric stimulation of that area. In E. Gutmann and P. Hrik (Eds.), *Central and peripheral mechanisms of motor functions.* Prague: Publishing House of the Czechoslovak Academy of Sciences, 1963. Pp. 167–176.

Varga, M. Y., and Pressman, Y. M. Some forms of relationship between two temporarily connected motor reflexes. In E. Gutmann and P. Hrik (Eds.), *Central and peripheral mechanisms of motor functions.* Prague: Publishing House of the Czechoslovak Academy of Sciences, 1963. Pp. 279–288.

Wagner, A. R., Thomas, E., and Norton, T. Conditioning with electrical stimulation of motor cortex: Evidence of a possible source of motivation *J. comp. physiol. Psychol.,* 1967, *64,* 191–199.

28

Defense Conditioning and Avoidance

G. V. Skipin, I. G. Ivanova, I. B. Kozlovskaya, and *R. L. Vinnik*

EDITORS' INTRODUCTION

This chapter is a composite of several articles by their respective authors, which have previously appeared in various Soviet sources.

It summarizes one of the major lines of research which occupied the efforts of the Laboratory of Conditioned Motor Reflexes at the Institute of Higher Nervous Activity and Neurophysiology in Moscow during the late 1950's and early 1960's.

The chapter is included in this volume as an example of Soviet research strategies in an area that has been intensively investigated in the West using quite a different approach.

Until his recent death, Skipin was Director of the Laboratory of Conditioned Motor Reflexes. His co-authors are presently co-workers in that laboratory.

PROTOPOPOV (1909), working in Bekhterev's laboratory, was one of the first investigators of conditioned motor defensive reflexes. With his technique, an exteroceptive conditioned stimulus is accompanied by electric shock even after a conditioned reflex has been elaborated. If reinforcement with the unconditioned stimulus is terminated, the conditioned defensive reflex of lifting the paw under stimulation will gradually cease as a consequence of the development of extinctive inhibition. These techniques were subsequently widely used by physiologists (Erofeeva, 1912; Beritov, 1932;

Zelenii, 1929; Fursikov, 1926; Asratyan, 1953; Gambaryan, 1952). Research using this technique, commonly called classical defense or aversive conditioning, is frequently employed in the United States, particularly in eyelid and GSR conditioning.

However, Protopopov's method of classical defense conditioning is not a satisfactory method for the investigator of higher nervous activity. The decisive importance of conditioned reflexes elaborated to various stimuli lies in the signal role of the latter. With the appearance of a signal warning of the imminent action of a noxious stimulus from the external environment, the animal avoids, through an established movement, the potential action of the painful stimulus. Herein lies the basic biological significance of conditioned defense reflexes, by means of which the animal adapts itself to the conditions of his environment.

In using Protopopov's techniques, which require reinforcement of the conditioned stimulus (CS) with an unconditioned defensive stimulus (UCS), the animal's movements do not attain their chief purpose—avoidance of a painful stimulus.[1] Stimuli to which temporary connections are formed by this method can in no sense be called signal stimuli; reflexes established to these stimuli cannot have adaptive, defensive significance. It is therefore understandable that experimenters have made further efforts to develop more adequate methods for investigating motor conditioning. Thus, Staritsyn (1926), and later Petropavlovskii (1927), modified Protopopov's technique. In Petropavlovskii's method, the animal's paw was tied to a lever; by moving it, the animal could break the circuit and thereby avoid electric shocks. Neither the author of this technique nor later experimenters have expressed their opinion as to the nature of the underlying mechanism responsible for the formation of conditioned reflexes with this latter experimental variation (avoidance conditioning).

Skipin (1957) employed Petropavlovskii's method of avoidance conditioning as well as variations of that method. In the initial investigations with Shirokova and Vasil'eva, dogs were placed in a stand and restrained with straps. The right front paw was tied to a lever which recorded movements. When the paw was lifted to a certain height the UCS was terminated by means of a contact breaker located on the lever. The motor reaction was recorded on a kymograph placed outside the isolated chamber. Electrodes connected to an induction coil were attached to the same paw of the dog. Exteroceptive stimuli, a light, and a bell which came on 10 seconds prior to the UCS were used as CSs.

The CS overlapped the action of the UCS, which remained on for 15 seconds. Note that an unconditioned response (UCR) does not terminate the trial. Any lowering of the leg during the 15-second period in which the

1. *Editors' note:* This distinction is equivalent to the distinction commonly made in the American literature between classical and instrumental conditioning.

UCS is in effect would result in shock. Conditioned reflexes to the exteroceptive stimuli usually were established rather quickly, within the first ten pairings.

Such an experimental arrangement, where the signal precedes reinforcement by a UCS and then coincides with it for a certain time, would seem to be the most elementary one. Yet the results obtained were complex and difficult to analyze. An example is the data obtained from the dog Orlik in the process of defense conditioning to a bell. This animal was characterized as possessing an inert nervous process, according to the common practice of Pavlovian typing of nervous systems.[2] The experiments were conducted by Vasil'eva.

The formation of a CR was retarded in this animal. It can be seen that the conditioned avoidance reflex to the bell is still absent on an early conditioning trial where presentation of the bell was reinforced with shock (Figure 28–1, *A*). When the UCS is turned on, however, the animal attempts to lift his paw high so as to escape pain through these movements.

But these attempts cannot be called successful because, through jerking paw movements, the dog repeatedly reinforces himself with shocks. From subsequent pairings it is evident (Figure 28–1, *B*) that there is still no CR to the bell; however, with the very first shock the animal reveals the development of a motor response in that he immediately lifts his paw to a height sufficient to switch the current off, and holds it in this position for the possible duration (15 seconds) of the UCS. It is only later (at the fifty-sixth pairing) that the dog begins to show a clearly detectable CR to the auditory stimulus (Figure 28–1, *C*).

The establishment of a CR to an exteroceptive stimulus (e.g., the light and bell) is evidently preceded by formation of a CR to the electrodermal stimulus, a process illustrated by another excerpt from the kymogram (Figure 28–2). It can be seen that in response to the auditory stimulus there is a clearly manifested CR, albeit small in magnitude. But in addition, at the tenth second, i.e., when the UCS is usually delivered, the dog energetically lifts his paw to the height at which the shock is switched off.

Thus, Figure 28–2 shows three distinctly expressed learned reactions: a preparatory reaction to the conditioned auditory stimulus; a CR to the time of delivery of the painful stimulus, and a CR to the 15-second period during the course of which the animal turns off the current and avoids a possible electric shock. The complexity of the CR thus formed necessitated a further simplification of the experimental conditions which permitted the investigation of the animal's reaction to electrodermal stimulation alone.

For this purpose five naive dogs were used (experiments by Shirkova) that had as yet not been subjected to defense conditioning using shock.

---

2. *Editors' note:* See Chapter 18 of this volume, by Teplov and Nebylitsyn.

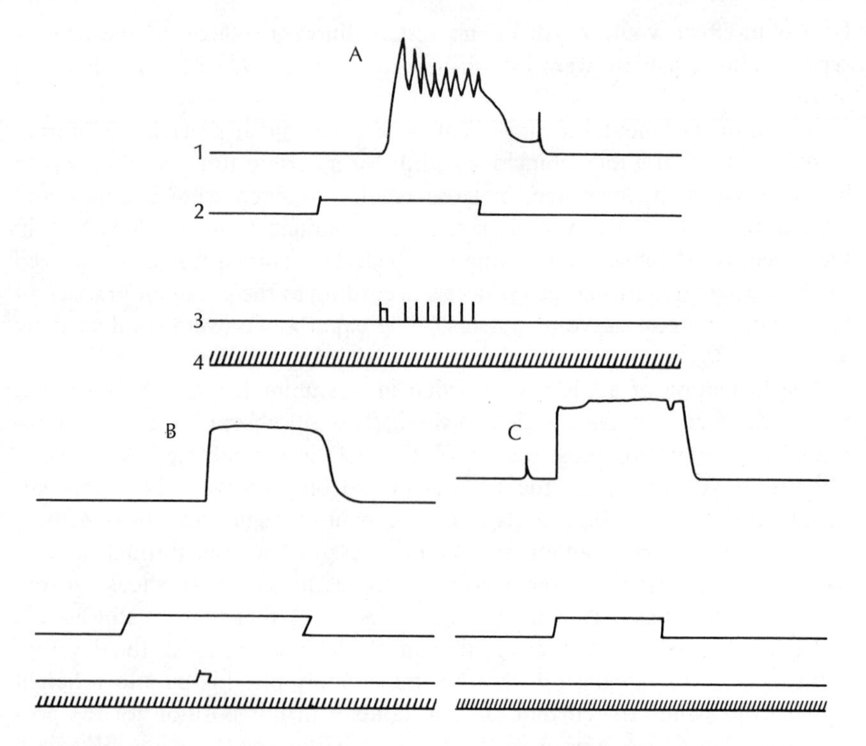

Figure 28–1. Orlik: (*A*) session 6, 17th trial; (*B*) session 14, 45th trial; (*C*) session 18, 56th trial. (1) record of right front paw movements; (2) presentation of CS (bell); (3) presentation of UCS; (4) time marked in seconds.

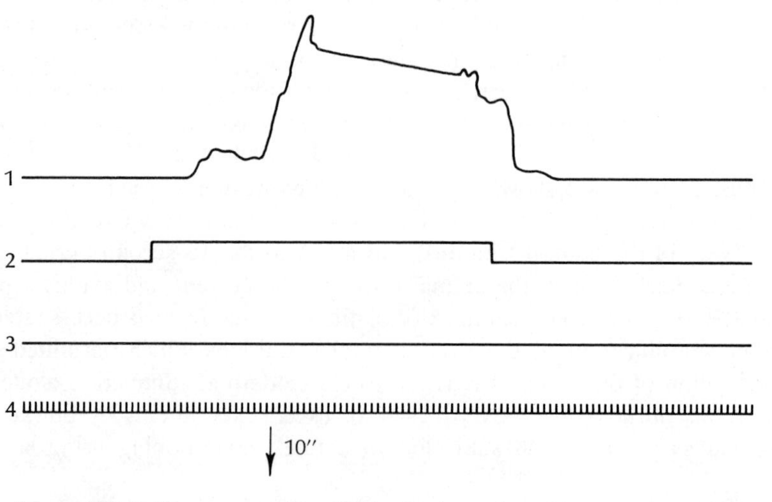

Figure 28–2. Tsygan: session 68. Legend numbers: same as in Figure 28–1.

Their right front paws were tied to levers and electrodes were attached to the surface of the metatarsus of the same paw. In some dogs, the intervals between repeated presentations of shock were kept constant; in others they were varied during the entire experiment.

With the first presentations of shock the animals performed a series of jerking movements with the stimulated paw. Whenever the paw was lifted sufficiently high, the shock was switched off, but as soon as the dog let its paw drop, it received an electric shock to the paw again.

A series of such jerks are called "phasic" movements (Figures 28–1, *A* and 28–3, *A*). According to prevailing concepts of the nature of reflex acts, it is necessary to characterize such a motor reaction as an unconditioned reflex to an unconditioned defense stimulus.

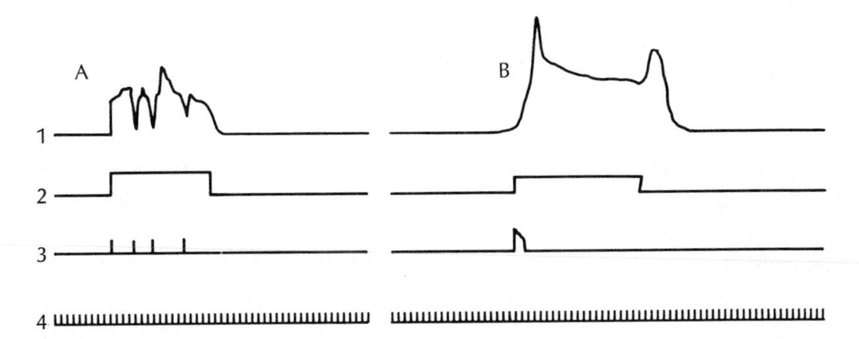

Figure 28–3. Chebak: (*A*) session 17, 65th trial; (*B*) session 104, 476th trial. (1) record of right front paw movement; (2) time of electrodermal stimulus (UCS); (3) closing of electrodermal stimulus circuit; (4) time in seconds.

With repeated applications of the shock, elements of a "tonic" motor defense reflex appeared in the stimulated leg. The tonic reflex is said to be present when the animal lifts his paw (thereby switching off the shock) and holds it in that position for a certain period of time. As the number of presentations of the UCS increases, the tonic movement becomes even more distinct, so that eventually the dog will lift the stimulated paw immediately to a certain height and hold it raised during the entire period (15 seconds) during which the current can operate (Figure 28–3, *B*).

It is quite clear that the animals developed a conditioned motor defense reflex to unconditioned electrodermal stimulation. What is the electrodermal stimulus in this situation, a CS or a UCS? We believe that it has become transformed into a CS. But this raises the question: What was going on in the higher segments of the central nervous system during the transformation of the UCR into a CR, as a consequence of which the UCS became a CS?

Investigations into the basic laws of higher nervous activity provide data concerning this question. Studies by Erofeeva (1921) dealt with the conversion of a defense UCS into a food CS; in the work of Savich (1913) and of Varga (1955), defense UCS became the CS for a food stimulus and vice versa: reinforcement with food could act as a signal for a defense reflex. These examples indicate that under certain conditions nerve impulses arriving at the cortical representation of the UCR may switch over in new directions, whereas the effector portion of the unconditioned reflex arc finds itself either partially or completely inactive, inhibited.

This raises the following question: What physiological mechanisms underlie the conversion from a defense UCR to a defense CR? When using Petropavlovskii's techniques a clear-cut answer to this question could not be given because both the CR and UCR were implemented by means of one and the same effector apparatus, that is, muscles of the shocked leg. By modifying Petropavlovskii's method, new data were obtained which permitted a better approach to the problem. Experiments by Vinnik illustrate the new procedure.

The modifications of technique were as follows: As usual, the dog was strapped to the stand. The shock electrodes were fastened to the skin of the metatarsus of the right hind paw, which was also attached to the lever which recorded the movements of that paw. The left front paw was tied to another lever connected to the circuit breaker for the shock (Figure 28–4). The right hind leg was stimulated with an electric current of such strength as to elicit, from the region of the central nervous system receiving nociceptive stimuli from the skin of the right hind extremity, irradiation of excitation over the central nervous system, as a result of which all the dog's extremities would be activated. The UCS remained in effect for 15 seconds.

Upon the first presentations of electrodermal stimuli the naive dogs

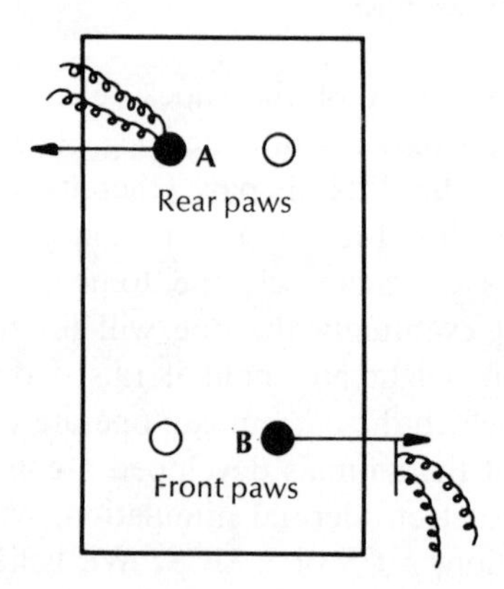

Figure 28–4. Diagram showing location of electrodes and response levers on the animal's paws: (*A*) stimulating electrodes; (*B*) circuit breaker for UCS.

manifested jerking movements of all the extremities, including the left front one, the lifting of which to the height of 11 to 12 cm. from the stand disconnected the shock circuit. These movements had a phasic character (Figure 28–5, *A*). There is not the slightest doubt that the electrodermal stimulus functioned as a defensive UCS and that the general motor reaction evoked by it is a complex inborn defense reflex.

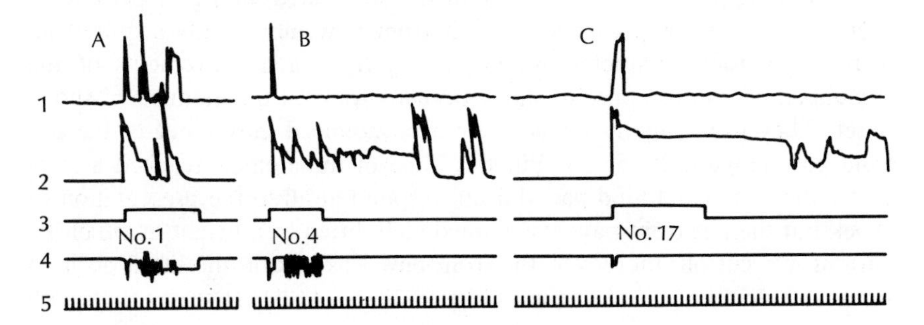

Figure 28–5. Likhoi: (*A*) session 1, 1st trial; (*B*) session 1, 4th trial; (*C*) session 4, 17th trial. (1) movement of stimulated rear paw; (2) movement of left front paw; (3) delivery of UCS; (4) closing of electrodermal stimulus circuit; (5) time in seconds.

With repeated trials, the movements of the hind left (nonstimulated) as well as those of the front right (nonfunctional) paw gradually disappeared. Only the movements of the hind right and front left paws remained during the shock, although their movements still manifested a phasic unconditioned-reflex character; of all paw movements, only those which bore a direct relation to the onset and disappearance of nociceptive stimulation were preserved.

From the physiological standpoint it is to be assumed that excitation initiated by painful stimulation, on reaching the afferent part of the cutaneous analyzer in the cortex, irradiates throughout that analyzer. As a result of repeated terminations of the painful stimulus effected by front-paw movements, the excitation over the cutaneous analyzer started to change its direction. There arose, if one may express it this way, a selective irradiation of nervous process from the part of the analyzer controlling pain sensitivity from the hind right paw skin toward the cells of the cutaneous analyzer for the left front leg.

This limiting of excitatory irradiation can be implemented only because of interference produced by an active inhibiting process. The origin of an active, conditioned inhibition process which eliminates movements that are superfluous for the implementation of a defense response indicates that this process develops in the cerebral cortex; one of the specific physiological properties of the cortex is its capacity for developing active inhibition.

On the other hand, the motor reflexes to which the developing inhibition does not extend continue to retain their unconditioned (phasic) character. The presence of conditioned inhibition on the one hand, and retention of reciprocal responses of the unconditioned inhibitory types on the other, imply that these processes develop in the cortical cutaneous analyzer, which evidently comprises the cortical projection of the defense UCR.

As training progressed, the lifting of the stimulated hind paw became of ever shorter duration, whereas the left front paw movements acquired an increasingly tonic character (Figure 28–5, *B*). Later movements of the stimulated paw in response to shock occurred only at the moment of shock onset. They were rapidly replaced by a pronounced movement of the left front paw (Figure 28–5, *C*). Finally, some of the animals reached a state where the stimulated hind paw did not respond at all to the presentation of shock but the left front paw was immediately lifted to a height at which he current was cut off; moreover, the front paw was held in the lifted position for a considerable period of time (Figure 28–6, *A, B*). It seems that, with

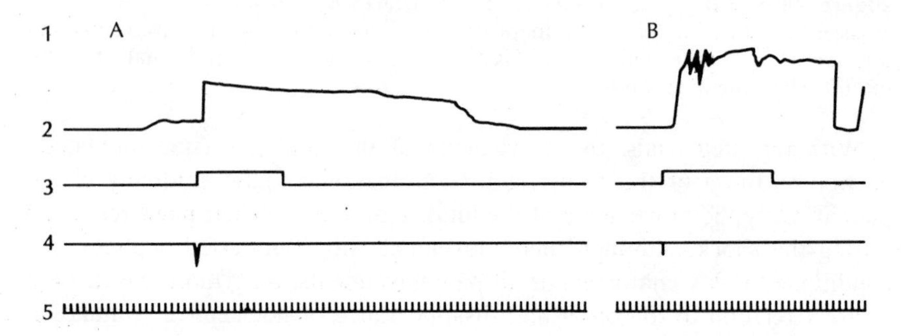

Figure 28–6. Tsezar': (*A*) session 25, 149th trial. (*B*) Nord: session 22; 100th trial. Legend numbers: same as in Figure 28–5.

repeated presentations of the defensive UCS applied to the hind paw, increasingly fewer impulses were reaching the muscles of the hind extremity via the nervous representation of the cutaneous analyzer (from the receptor part to the affector part of the unconditioned-reflex arc). Instead, the waves of excitation being set up in the afferent portion of the unconditioned reflex arc start to switch over, coming in, from another direction, at that part of the cutaneous analyzer whose cells are associated with the functioning of the front leg which terminates the electric current.

From these experiments it can be seen that the unconditioned electrodermal stimulus that once elicited an irradiated defensive UCR ceases, under certain conditions (termination of painful stimulus through a chance leg movement), to evoke this defense UCR, acquiring the significance of a

CS. In contrast, the phasic unconditioned motor reflex of the left foreleg acquires the features of a tonic defense CR.

On the basis of data obtained from experiments using separate recordings of concurrent or successive unconditioned and conditioned defense reflexes, unequivocal as to their biological significance, and on the basis of data furnished by the literature, the following assumptions may be made concerning the physiological mechanisms underlying the conditioned motor and so-called voluntary defense reflexes which we observed. Upon application of an electrodermal (unconditioned) stimulus, excitation from cutaneous receptors reaches the corresponding segments of the spinal cord and arrives, along the ascending pathways of the spinal cord via the optic thalamus, at the projection of the cutaneous analyzer in the cerebral cortex. In the course of executing unconditioned reflex acts involving the participation of the cutaneous analyzer, the latter is to be regarded as the cortical representation of the unconditioned defense (including the electrodermal) reflex. Nerve impulses travel from the receptor cells of the cutaneous analyzer into the effector part in the lower fifth layer of the same analyzer, rich in pyramidal cells (Adrianov, 1953). From the latter the nervous excitation is transmitted, via the extrapyramidal system (Protopopov, 1931), to the motor neurons of the spinal cord, and further to the appropriate groups of muscles implementing the unconditioned reflex at the periphery.

In the course of execution of an unconditioned motor defense reflex, series of afferent proprioceptive nerve impulses, whose destination is the kinesthetic analyzer of the cortex, are initiated in the receptors located in the contracting muscles.

With a certain degree of muscle contraction in the left front leg (and hence with a certain intensity of excitation in the kinesthetic cortical cells for this leg), the electric current is cut off and the nociceptive excitation starts to weaken and disappear within the cutaneous analyzer. Consequently, excitation is directed from the receptor cells of the cutaneous analyzer toward the excited group of more reactive kinesthetic cells (Konorski and Lubinska, 1939), as a result of which a new neural connection begins to form between two cortical analyzers. The excitation, in this case, moves from the cortical projection of the UCR (the cutaneous analyzer) toward the kinesthetic analyzer, to which a new connection is being formed.

With repeated applications of the electrodermal stimulus, the developing pathway becomes increasingly well worn so that the passage of nerve impulses from the sensory cells of the cutaneous analyzer to the cells of the kinesthetic analyzer becomes facilitated. The latter in turn are functionally linked with the giant pyramidal cells located in the fifth layer of the analyzer, whence the nerve impulses arrive, along the pyramidal paths and via the spinal cord, at the operative muscular apparatus to activate it. Thus the pattern of the movement is formed by those types of muscle contraction which took place during execution of the UCR. The character of this unconditioned-reflex activity (the intensity and duration of muscle contractions) which turned out to be favorable for the animal's existence became fixed in the kinesthetic cells of the cortex.

During the formation of a conditioned connection an inhibitory state in the effector part of the cutaneous analyzer probably arises. This can be surmised from the fact that the incoming excitation from the cutaneous receptors is not transmitted from the higher segments of the central nervous system to the effector portion of the unconditioned-reflex arc. The inhibition that develops facilitates the conversion of the nerve impulses from the historically established, well-trodden pathways of the unconditioned-reflex arc to new directions. As a result, the UCS properties are transformed to that of a conditioned, signal stimulus.

The process of converting the nerve impulses from an unconditioned-reflex arc to new directions seems to require a great effort from the dog's nervous system; not all animals cope with this task equally well. Some of the dogs, in spite of the considerable number of trials, nevertheless lift the stimulated paw briefly at the onset of painful stimulation and, having dropped it quickly, next lift the "conditioned" paw which terminates the electric current. Yet in other dogs a total inhibition occurs in the effector portion of the unconditioned-reflex arc.

Subsequently, experiments by Vinnik with defense conditioning to distant stimuli—light from an electric bulb and bell—were carried out on these same dogs. The new stimuli were presented for 10 seconds, whereupon a shock was applied to the skin of the right hind leg. After several reinforcements of light and bell with shock, the animals who used to respond with a left foreleg movement, to the shock only, would now also lift the left forepaw in response to conditioned distant stimuli, thus altogether avoiding reinforcement by electric current (Figure 28–7). Despite the absence of

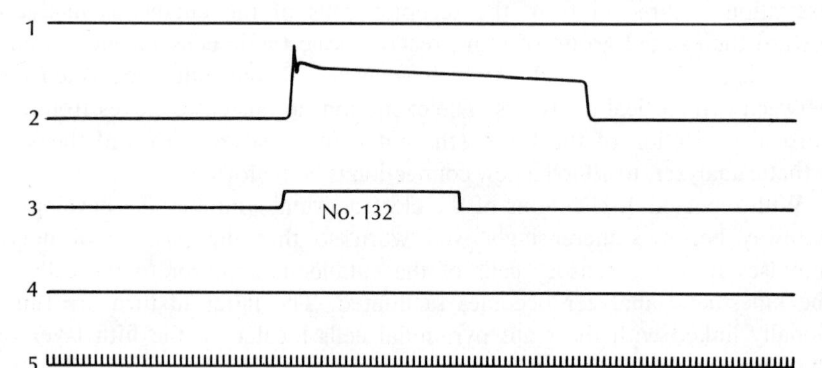

Figure 28–7. Tsezar': session 51, 132nd trial with bell. Legend numbers: same as in Figure 28–5.

shock reinforcement, the conditioned left foreleg movement established in response to light or bell was reproduced, without extinction, in the course of a prolonged period of testing.

In this case, a new nervous connection is established, apparently of a conditioned-reflex type, between the auditory or visual cortical analyzers and the cells of the kinesthetic analyzer associated with the functioning of the foreleg. However, the possibility that a temporary connection also forms between the distant CS and the cells of the cutaneous analyzer, which were receiving the effect of the cutaneous stimulus, cannot be excluded. Further investigations may provide an answer to this question.

The relationship between cortical "centers" linked by a temporary connection has been studied via the interaction of conditioned and unconditioned reflexes. The functional state of the "linked" nervous centers was inferred from the magnitude of the conditioned and unconditioned responses. Experiments performed with stable CRs have established the existence of antagonistic relationships between the centers of conditioned and unconditioned reflexes (Perel'tsveig, 1907; Asratyan, 1934; Stroganov, 1945). It has also been shown that interaction between two excitation centers existing simultaneously in the cortex may produce either induction or summation (Asratyan, 1941; Kupalov, 1941, 1951; Fedorov, 1938, 1950). Podkopaev (1941) discovered that these interrelations constantly change, depending on the stage of formation and stabilization of the temporary connection: the antagonism observed at the beginning of reflex formation is replaced by synergism as a synthetic functional complex form.

It has been established that the magnitude of the response is affected by the induction and summation observed when one reflex precedes the other (Asratyan, Kupalov, Fedorov) or when they are performed simultaneously.

All of these investigations of the interrelation between centers of conditioned and unconditioned reflexes were exclusively concerned with CRs repeating the UCRs on the basis of which they had been elaborated by Protopopov's method. Such conditioned and unconditioned responses are performed by the same effector. Consequently, we decided to study cortical "centers" in the arc of "multieffector" conditioned motor defense reflexes (i.e., CRs which do not mirror the UCR).

Experiments were performed on four dogs, using Skipin's method, which permitted separation of the conditioned and unconditioned reflexes constituting the single functional complex of the elaborated defense reaction. The animal's left forelimb and right hind limb were attached by sleeves to light metal rods moving freely in a vertical plane. A shock was administered through silver electrodes applied to the back of the lower third of the leg; the current intensity was selected so as to elicit a generalized motor reaction (0.4 milliampere above the excitation threshold).

Pain stimulation of the hind limb automatically ceased when the animal raised its left forelimb (which was not stimulated) to a certain height (this height depended in each case on the size of the animal). The functional state of the cortical representation of the UCR was evaluated by the movements of the stimulated hind limb, and the degree of excitation of the CR "center" was estimated by measuring the forelimb's movements.

Motor reactions of the hind and forelimb were recorded on a kymograph. The range of the movements of the pen along the paper was directly proportional to the height to which the limb was raised. The magnitude of motor reflexes was expressed in relative units (Skipin and Sharov, 1955). Analysis of the experimental data took into account the motor reflexes performed during the isolated application of the signal stimuli. Movements performed during the same lapse of time were taken into account in the analysis of extinction and differentiation.

The CSs, a 60-watt electric light and a bell, were employed with a 5-second CS-UCS interval. The animals began to raise their forelimb in response to these signals, thereby avoiding pain stimulation to their hind limb.

Application of the distant CSs revealed the functional interrelation between the conditioned (upward movement of forelimb) and unconditioned (upward movement of hind, stimulated limb) reflexes, which were combined in the structure of a single defense reaction. Additional tests used were the elaboration of differentiation to a CS (experiments on Ryzhik and Krasavets) and extinction of the signal meaning of the CS (experiments on Radzh and Tsezar').

At first, two motor CRs to the signal stimuli were formed in the animals, an upward movement of the stimulated limb and a "tonic" flexion of the forelimb which broke the electric circuit.

When one of these motor reactions was performed in response to the signal, the other was either completely omitted, or its magnitude was reduced. As shown in Figure 28–8 (Radzh), a response of the hind limb to the CS was usually elicited when the reflex of the forelimb was either omitted or weak; this was also noted in the other three animals (Ryzhik, Tsezar', Krasavets). In the case of Ryzhik, for example (Figure 28–9, *A*), the second presentation of the light elicited a conditioned reflex of the forelimb, while the hind limb remained motionless. In contrast, only upward movements of the hind limb were recorded at the third to eleventh presentation of the light. At the twelfth stimulus presentation only the forelimb reflex was observed. This animal responded to the signal on certain days (16th, 17th, and 22nd to 24th light trials) by moving both its left front and its right hind leg. In these cases the conditioned movements of the left foreleg had a shorter latent period and usually a greater magnitude than the responses of the hind leg.

In the case of Krasavets, one response rarely suppressed the other com-

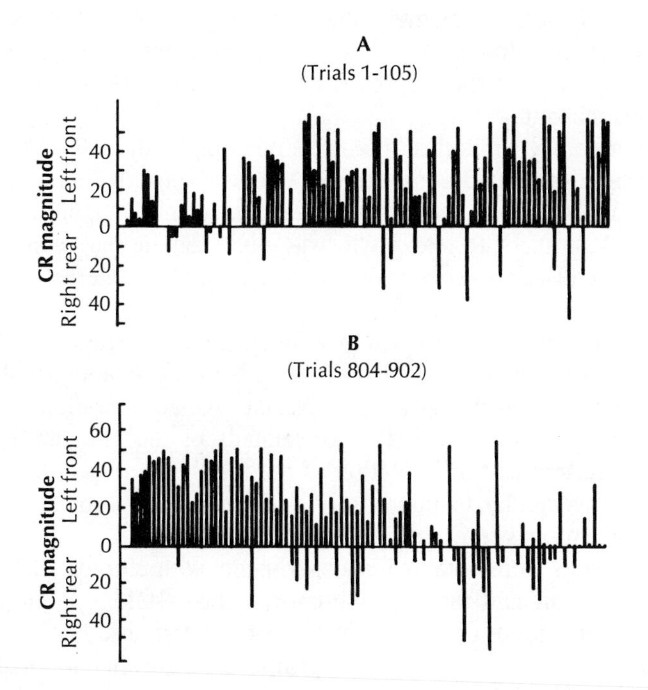

Figure 28–8. Formation of a motor defense CR to a bell (*A*) and extinction of the response to the auditory stimulus (*B*) in the dog Radzh. Responses of the left front leg are indicated along the upper part of the abscissa; those of the right rear leg are shown in the lower part.

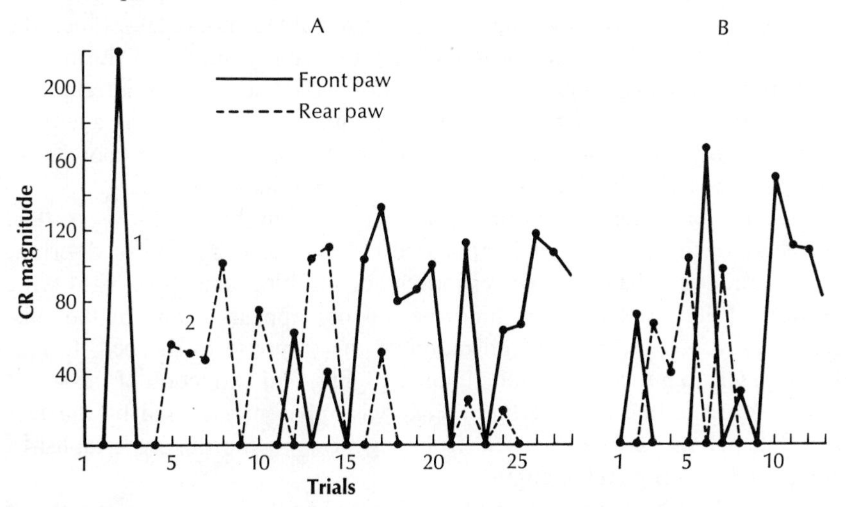

Figure 28–9. Interrelationship of motor defense CR in Ryzhik during the formation of a positive conditioned reflex (*A*) and of differentiation (*B*).

pletely; this animal performed simultaneous movements of both legs for a long time; the magnitudes of the reactions were inversely proportional. However, synergism of the responses could also be observed side by side with their distinct antagonism.

As the temporary connection became more stable, the CR of the stimulated hind leg disappeared completely in all cases, and the animals reacted to the CS only by raising the left front leg. The same antagonism between the "centers" of the CR and UCR was observed in the sessions when extinction and discrimination training, which involve internal inhibition, were carried out.

Acute extinction (achieved within a single session, May 18, 1960) of Radzh's CR to the bell revealed that the previously inhibited CR of the hind leg reappeared on the baseline of partial or total inhibition of the CR of the forelimb (Figure 28–8, *B*). Movements of the hind limb became more and more frequent as inhibition of the forelimb's response increased. This picture was similar to that observed during reflex formation, but the sequence of events was reversed (see Figure 28–8, *A, B*).

Identical results were obtained in experiments with chronic extinction of the CR to the light and the bell, the entire process taking approximately two months. Fluctuations in the extinction of the response of the front leg were regularly accompanied by the appearance of movements of the hind leg, which coincided with a decrease in the excitatory phase in the neural structures involved in the first motor act.

Identical relations were also observed when discrimination training was carried out. Figure 28–9, *B* which includes data on the formation of a discrimination to an intermittent light, clearly shows that movements of one limb were performed only when the other remained motionless. Since the movement of the hind limb was the first to become inhibited during the formation of the discrimination (at the ninth presentation of the intermittent light), performance of the two reactions and their antagonism could be observed only during this short initial period. The animal then responded to the positive discriminative stimulus by lifting only its left front leg.

Tsezar' constituted a special case. Antagonism between the cortical "centers" of the CR and UCR appeared only at the beginning of discrimination training, when the two responses (of the hind and front legs) were performed. The reflex of the hind leg did not appear in any of the subsequent sessions involving stabilization of the response to the bell, formation of a CR to a second distant stimulus (light), and extinction of the signal meaning of the bell and the light. This was apparently caused by the fact that the defense CR of the left front leg became thoroughly established and the UCR completely inhibited.

The method by which different movements could be used as indices of the functional state of the cortical representation of the CR and UCR revealed that mutual induction exists between these cortical centers.

One of the basic laws of higher nervous activity, discovered in Pavlov's laboratory, is the "law of strength," according to which the magnitude of the CR is determined by the intensity of the CS, all other conditions being equal. This law was first formulated by Pavlov in 1906, and was confirmed by a great number of experiments made by Pavlov's co-workers and students, indicating its importance in conditioning.

At the same time the Pavlovian school discovered certain facts which could not be explained by the "law of strength," and which limited its generality. In 1910, Babkin showed that the physiological intensity of the CS changes during reinforcement or partial extinction of a CR although its physical intensity remains constant. Consequently, Babkin complemented the "law of strength" by introducing the concept of a "law of relative strength," according to which the animal can group stimuli not by their physical intensity, but by the importance which they have in its life. Similar data were later obtained by Nikitin (1933), Kleshchev (1936), Petrova (1937), Pavlova (1941), Troshikhin (1945), Airapetyants (1955), and others, who studied the changes in intensity of a salivary CR when the intensity of the UCS was altered.

Although the data found in all these works are most convincing, the relationship between strength of conditioning of the CS and of the UCS at various stages of conditioning still remains unclear; this is also true with respect to the role of each of these factors in the formation of a CR when the CS and UCS are of different intensities. In the opinion of several researchers the absolute intensity of the CS is important only in the initial stage of conditioning, after which the strength of the CR is determined by other factors, particularly by the qualitative and quantitative characteristics of reinforcement. These authors usually point out the great biological expediency of this law, enabling the organism to differentiate stimuli by their importance and to adapt its reaction to the magnitude of the UCS. Most of the studies on this question have used methods in which the correspondence of CR magnitude to UCS intensity was undoubtedly biologically appropriate, such as increase of the amount of saliva when large amounts of food are given (Kleshchev, Petrova, Pavlova and others) or large amounts of acid are poured into the animal's mouth (Fedorov), or an increase in the number of food-seeking movements when the amount of food used in appetitive reinforcement is increased (Aslanova), and the like.

The present experiments studied the role of the UCS when the increase or decrease of the CR which follows the change in intensity of the reinforcing stimulus is not clearly appropriate from the biological point of view. In order to achieve this state, Skipin's method was used, in which pain stimulation by electric current applied to one of the animal's hind legs is switched off when the contralateral front leg is lifted to a certain height. The change in magnitude of the CR in such experiments is not clearly appropriate, since the level to which the front limb must be raised in order to switch off the UCS has been previously established by the experimenter.

After the defense response to the shock had been learned, responses to distant stimuli were elaborated. The CSs were a bell of medium strength and the light from an 82-watt bulb, 0.7 meter from the animal's head. This choice of stimuli was not accidental. According to most of the data, a visual stimulus is considerably weaker than an auditory one, from the physiological point of view. Some investigators (Zachinyaeva, 1949; Adrianov and Mering, 1955; Popova, 1960) explain this by the more extensive cortical representation of visual function, others (Denisov and Kupalov, 1933; Makarychev, 1947) by the inhibition of the CR to the light, because the light of the chamber constitutes an external stimulus. Nevertheless, the difference in intensity of the physiological effect of visual and auditory stimuli is a fact accepted by all.

The UCS in our experiments was shock, applied to the animal's hind leg for 10 seconds. A previously conditioned movement of the front leg (raising it above a certain level determined by the experimenter) terminated the shock. Visual and auditory stimuli were introduced simultaneously, and in the case of two dogs (Barsik and Pushka) the bell (strong stimulus) was reinforced from its first presentation by a weak shock (0.2 to 0.4 milliampere above threshold) and the weaker stimulus (light) by a strong shock (0.2 to 2.5 milliamperes). When the threshold is 0.2 to 0.6 milliamperes, a stimulus 5 to 10 times stronger than threshold is considered to be extremely strong. In the first 18 sessions on the dog Dzhul'bars, the pairing of stimulus and reinforcement was reversed. After the normal relationship between the response to the bell and the light was established, the CS-UCS pairings were changed; in all the other experiments it was the same as for the other animals.

The stimuli were applied in a haphazard order, the intervals between them varying from 1.5 to 3 minutes. The time of isolated presentation of the CSs was always constant (5 seconds); the period of simultaneous presentation of the CS and UCS was 10 seconds. Movements of the hind (stimulated) and front (conditioned) legs were recorded on a kymograph.

The experiments showed that when the CS and UCS were of different intensities, the UCS played a leading role in determining response magnitude. In all experimental animals the visual stmulus, when it was reinforced by a strong pain stimulus, clearly exhibited all the signs of increased physiological intensity.

The CR to the visual stimulus was usually much greater than the response to the bell (see Figures 28–10, 28–11, 28–12). The magnitude of Barsik's CR to the bell varied between 20 and 40 units, infrequently reaching 60 units, while to the light it reached 60, 80, 100, and more units (Figure 28–10, *B, C*). In 15 tests with isolated presentation of the CS for 15 seconds,

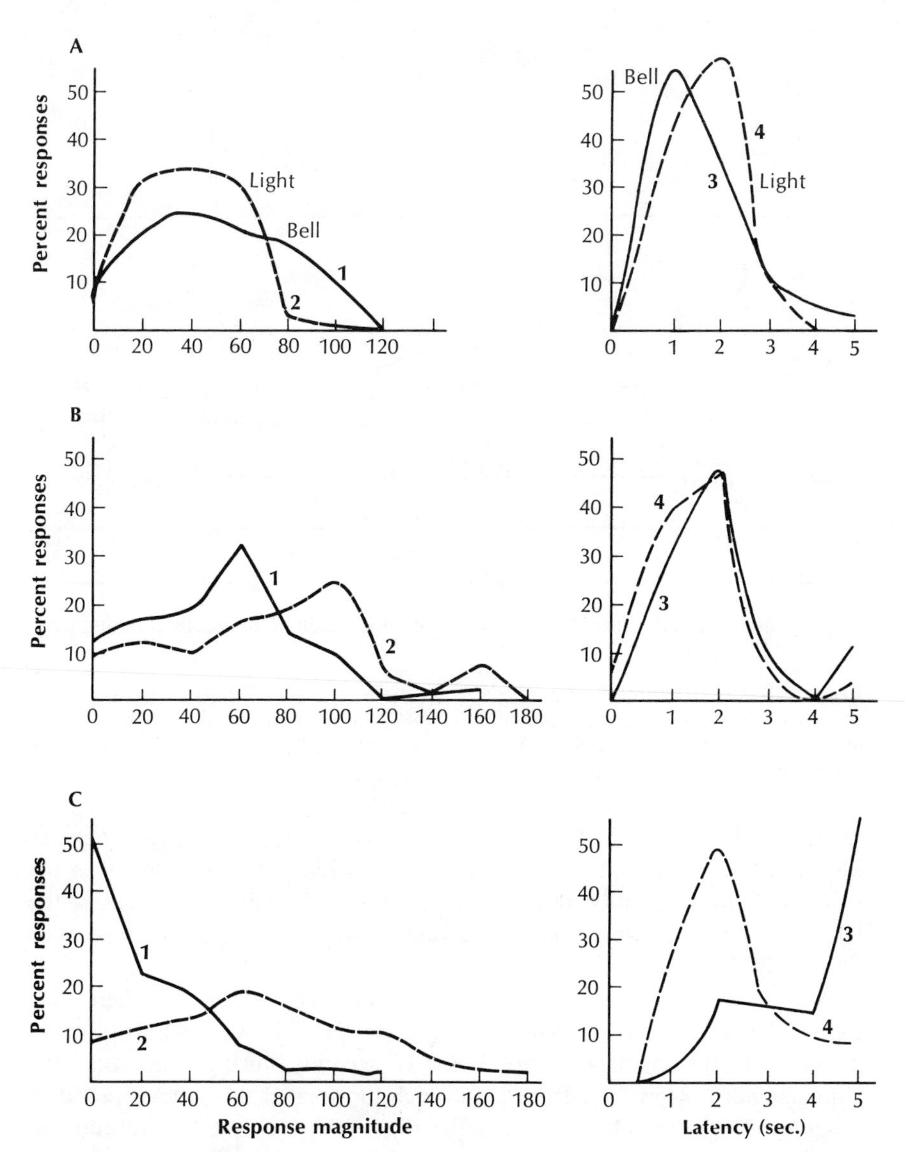

Figure 28–10. Change in magnitude and latent period of CRs during paradoxical reinforcement of the CS (Barsik). (*A*) sessions 1 to 15; (*B*) sessions 16 to 36; (*C*) sessions 40 to 60.

Barsik's CR to the light was stronger than his CR to the bell, with an average increase of 70 to 90 per cent; in some cases the difference reached 150 to 200 per cent (Table 28–1).

In the majority of cases the latency of the CR, which is usually closely

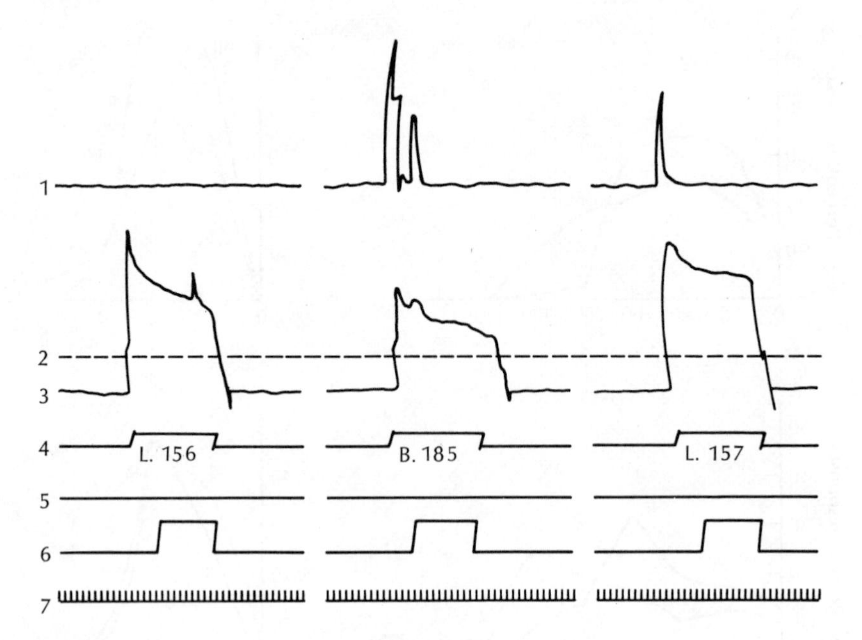

Figure 28–11. Fragments of records of January 5, 1960 (Pushok): (1) movement of stimulated leg; (2) cut-off level; (3) movement of the "conditioned" leg; (4) application of CS; (5) application of UCS; (6) period of possible action of current; (7) time in seconds.

related to the intensity of the UCS, was also shorter to the light (Figures 28–10, 28–11, and Table 28–1). In Barsik, while response latency to the bell was 2 to 4 seconds, reaching 5 seconds in 50 per cent of cases, the latency to the light was usually 2 seconds, and less often 1 and 3 seconds (Figure 28–10, *C*).

A distinct difference between CR magnitudes was also found when comparing the duration of responses elicited by the CS. As we have already pointed out, the shock was applied for 10 seconds, during which time the animals had to keep their front leg (which terminated the shock) raised to a certain height in order to avoid the reinforcement; but the duration of the conditioned response was not always adequate. As the kymographs show (Figure 28–12), in the case of Dzhul'bars the period during which the front leg was maintained at the given level never lasted 10 seconds, and was usually 2 to 6 seconds, depending on the strength of reinforcement. This same phenomenon was occasionally observed in other animals.

Table 28–2 and Figure 28–12 show that the number of reinforcements resulting from short duration responses was always considerably smaller during the light than during the bell. In other words, excitation arising when the visual stimulus is switched on remained at a high level for a long time,

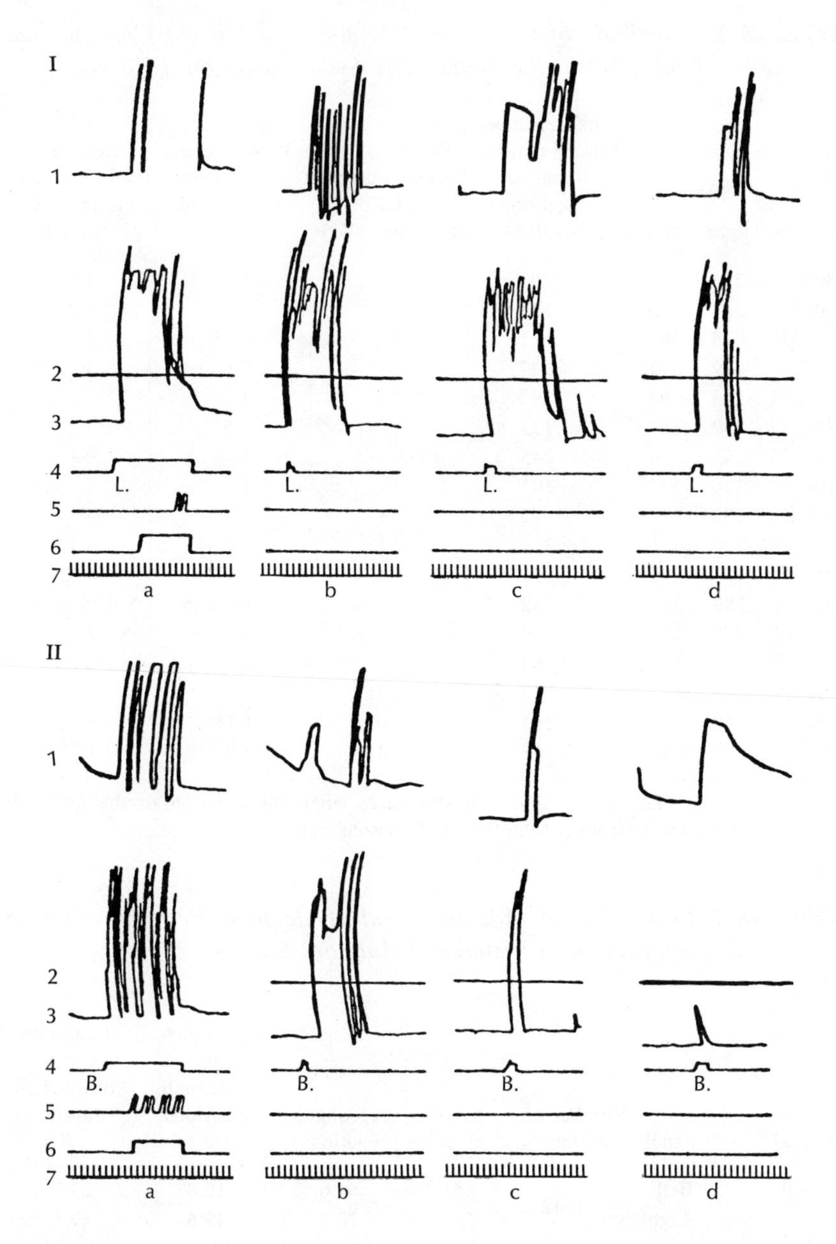

Figure 28–12. Dynamics of changes of motor CRs to auditory and visual stimuli when the time of application of the conditioned stimuli is shortened (Dzhul'bars). (I) Visual stimulus: (*a*) baseline; (*b, c, d*) second, fourth, sixth tests with the shortened visual stimulus, respectively. (II) Auditory stimulus: (*a*) baseline; (*b, c, d*) first, second, and third tests with the shortened auditory stimulus, respectively. Legend numbers: same as in Figure 28–11.

Table 28–1 *Magnitude of Conditioned Motor Reaction (in Conventional Units) When the Signals Are Switched on for 15 Seconds*

Date	Stimulus		Difference between magnitudes of conditioned reactions	Difference between magnitudes of reactions (%)	Latent period of reactions to the light (sec.)	Latent period of reactions to the bell (sec.)
	light	bell				
Nov. 16	283	180	103	57	1.5	1.5
Nov. 17	523	400	123	30	1	1.5
Nov. 18	678	567	111	20	0.75	1
Nov. 19	439	212	227	107	0.6	1
Nov. 21	284	92	192	208	1	2.5
Nov. 23	337	214	123	57	1.5	1.5
Nov. 24	245	0	245	—	1	—
Nov. 27	330	534	−203	−61	1	2
Dec. 2	392	380	12	3	1.5	1
Dec. 4	300	521	−221	−73	1.75	1.75
Dec. 9	151	0	151	—	2.1	—
Dec. 10	589	357	232	65	Not measured	Not measured
Dec. 14	449	159	290	188	2	2
Dec. 17	169	100	69	69	2	2.25
Dec. 19	269	202	67	33	3	3
Dec. 23	358	143	215	150	1.75	6
Dec. 26	423	406	17	4	1.5	1.75

NOTE: The minus sign indicates cases when the reaction to the auditory signal was stronger than that to the visual signal.

Table 28–2 *Proportion of Adequate and Inadequate Responses during Application of Visual and Auditory Stimuli*

Animal	Signal	Number of sessions	Number of cases	Adequate reactions	Incomplete or inadequate reactions (%)	Reactions of insufficient (duration) (%)
Pushok	Bell	31–42	55	64.0	12.8	23
	Light		55	70.4	19.6	9.8
	Bell	46–60	60	60.0	29	11
	Light		60	85.8	9	5.2
Barsik	Bell	1–15	70	50.7	35.2	14.1
	Light		70	70.0	27	3
	Bell	46–60	75	40.3	23.6	36.1
	Light		75	54.3	18.6	27.1

while excitation induced by the auditory stimulus tended to disappear rapidly. This assumption is also confirmed by experiments in which the CS occurred for only 1 to 1.5 seconds instead of the usual 5 to 10 seconds (see Figure 28–13) just as in those of Kupalov and Lukov (1933). In such conditions the duration, magnitude, and latency of the response to the light did not differ from those of CRs observed in the usual experimental conditions. In contrast, the strength and duration of the CRs to a 1-second bell decreased by the second and third tests, and the response resembled intertrial responses rather than conditioned ones. In other words, the stimulating (physiological) strength of the visual stimulus was so great that a short application led to the appearance of the whole complex system of the defense CR. In contrast, the physiological strength of the auditory stimulus was slight, and prolonged application of the signal was necessary in order to elicit a CR. The CRs to the light were also much more resistant to inhibition.

When stimuli acting as external inhibitors were applied, CRs to the bell totally disappeared, while the CRs elicited by the visual signal were maintained and did not differ significantly from the reactions on normal experimental days. The CRs to the light were also highly resistant to internal inhibition.[3] Data given in Table 28–2 and in Figure 28–10 show that as the sessions progressed CR latency began to increase, and the percentage of omissions of the movement increased during the whole period of isolated CSs. In the first 15 sessions with Barsik (Figure 28–10, *A*) we found almost no failures to respond when the bell was delayed for 5 seconds; in the second period the CR was absent in 15 per cent of the cases (Figure 28–10, *B*), and in the third period there was no response on half the trials (Figure 28–10, *C*). When the movement did occur, its latency was 2 to 4 seconds instead of the initial 0.5 to 1.5 seconds. This was also observed in the other dogs (Table 28–2).

Thus, a strong UCS undoubtedly increases greatly the effectiveness of a weak CS; it becomes a particularly effective stimulus and is singled out from the entire complex of stimuli reaching the animal's nervous system.

But a study of the development of this process shows that a change in physiological intensity of stimuli constitutes a strain on the animal's CNS. In all the dogs, three stages in the course of forming such relationships were clearly observed: at first, the magnitude of the CRs, despite paradoxical reinforcement, corresponded to the physiological intensity of the CSs (Figure 28–10, *A*); during the second stage there was a gradual increase in response to the light, with a simultaneous decrease in responses to the bell.

As in Petrova's experiments, there were fluctuations and variations, clearly indicating the complexity of the situation. From day to day reversals were observed in the magnitude and latency of the CRs and of the other parameters of conditioned excitation. The main role in determining the

3. *Editors' note:* For example, extinction.

intensity of the CR in this stage was played sometimes by the physiological strength of the signal, and at other times by the intensity of UCS. The duration of the second stage varied for the different animals between 16 (Barsik) and 30 (Pushok) sessions.

In the third stage the intensity of conditioned excitation usually corresponded adequately to the experimental conditions, more so when the light was switched on, less so when the bell rang. But again, in sessions during this last period the magnitude of the CR did not always correspond to the strength of UCS. In some sessions the law of strength of the stimuli again stood out clearly.

Even after a great number of reinforcements with a strong shock Dzhul'bars' response to the light never reached the intensity observed in sessions where strong pain stimulation reinforced the stronger CS (Figure 28–13). Correspondingly, the CR to the bell never decreased to the same extent when its reinforcement was weak, as had been observed when the light had been weakly reinforced.

These facts are contrary to Makarychev's (1947) assumption that the intensity of the CS is important only in the initial stages of conditioning, and show that the law of strength also applies to a system of firmly elaborated connections; it is apparently masked in certain situations by other factors which have a greater effect on the organism.

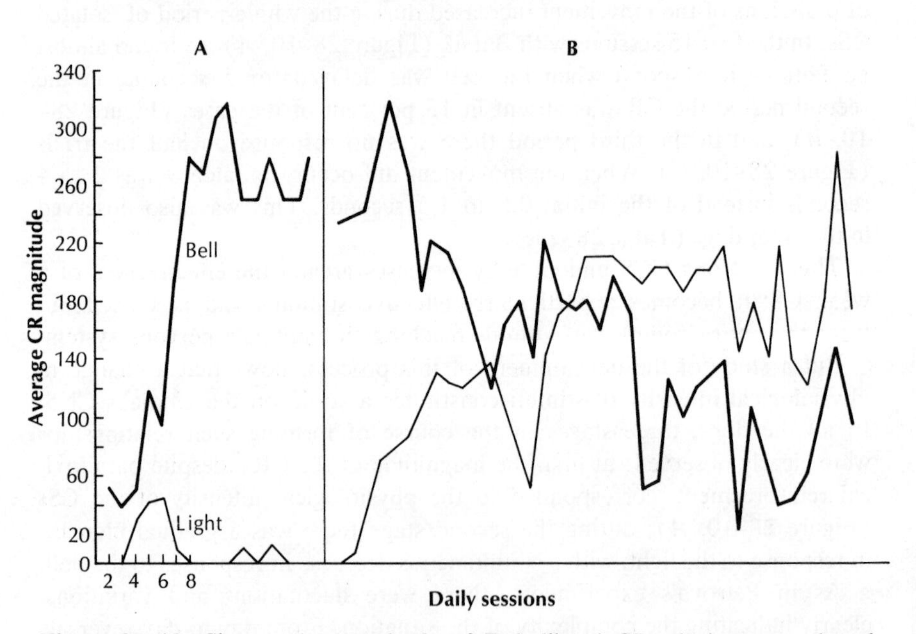

Figure 28–13. Changes in magnitude of Dzhul'bars' CRs during normal and paradoxical reinforcement of the CSs: (*A*) sessions 1 to 18 (the bell is reinforced by a strong current, the light by a weak one); (*B*) sessions 19 to 60 (the bell is reinforced by a weak current, the light by a strong one).

On the other hand, the data also fail to confirm the opinion of Zachinyaeva and Popova, who think that the difference in intensity of auditory and visual stimuli inevitably exhibits its effect under any experimental conditions. This conclusion may be correct for the method used by these authors, running toward the food box. It may be assumed that, in Zachinyaeva and Popova's experiments, the failure of the reactions to change when the UCS is modified was a consequence of a highly automatized running response which was connected to a great extent with the auditory function, which has less cortical representation and is more generalized in the subcortical structures.

In the present experiments the change in physiological intensity of the visual and auditory stimuli was very distinct, although the experimental method did not impart any apparent biological utility to the correspondence between the strength of the motor response and the strength of reinforcement. The increase of the CR above the level required for terminating the shock is difficult to explain from the point of view of utility. The difficulty is even greater with respect to the decrease, and even the total disappearance, of the CR, but the law of the strength of reinforcement applies also in these cases.

It is still impossible to draw definite conclusions about the intimate mechanisms of these phenomena, but several assumptions are possible.

It is well known that at the beginning of conditioning the temporary connection is generalized both in the afferent and in the efferent link. Because of this, both stimuli are initially a part of the same complex of structures participating in the defense UCR, and, in accordance with the physiological strength of the auditory and visual signals, the level of excitation during the bell is higher. When the reflex later becomes localized, the light, coinciding with the strong generalized defense reaction, acquires the capacity to elicit the activity of the entire complex including the cortex because of the conditioned connection. In its turn, the bell, coinciding with a weak defense reaction limited to the effector link only becomes associated with the limited number of elements participating in the reaction, and the reaction to the bell becomes less intense.

The gradual oscillating decrease in CR magnitude to the weakly reinforced stimulus, increasing latencies and decreasing durations, points to the active participation of inhibition producing the correspondence between the intensity of the CR and the weak reinforcement.

Kupalov (1952), Makarychev (1947), and Troshikhin (1945), who studied the changes in physiological strength of the CS which occur when the UCS is weakened, have already come to the conclusion that the decrease in the CR occurs because it is partially extinguished. It is possible that in the present experiments also, when weak reinforcement modified the strength of the signal which had previously been reinforced by a strong UCS (experiments on Dzhul'bars), the decrease in the CR was partly caused by the development of extinction.

But it is just as possible that, in all the experiments using the combination of one weakly reinforced and one stronger UCS, discrimination of stimuli according to their physiological strength occurred, and that the inhibition arising in these cases was a result of this discrimination. The presence of differential inhibition is supported by the fact that the strength of the weak shock (0.2 to 0.4 milliampere above threshold) is usually considered an optimal strength in normal experiments, and no decrease in the magnitude of the CR is noted when working with such a current. A gradual decrease in response magnitude is observed only when other considerably stronger shocks are introduced into the experiments.

The difference between the discrimination observed in these experiments and the classical discrimination studied in Pavlovian laboratories consists only in the fact that in the present case the discrimination is not developed by applying or withholding reinforcement, but only by varying its amount. As shown by the first session with Dzhul'bars, in which the auditory signal was reinforced by a strong shock and the light by a weak one, such a discrimination is not a difficult task for the animal. The difficulty in the other sessions is apparently explained by the fact that, because of its physiological peculiarities, the auditory stimulus immediately becomes, independently of reinforcement, a stronger stimulus for the CR than the light; the discrimination involves a transformation in the course of which differential inhibition overcomes the strength relationships inherent in these stimuli.

Finally, one must not exclude the possibility that, when the strength of the reinforcing stimulus changes, a change in excitability of the elements of the analyzer which receives the CS also occurs. This assumption, already expressed by Pavlov in 1934, has been confirmed by Sokolov (1958), Gershuni (1957), and Jouvet and Hernandez-Péon (1955), who discovered an increase in sensitivity in the structures of the analyzer when a previously indifferent stimulus is reinforced by any unconditioned activity.

It is highly probable that all these factors act together in the intact organism, ensuring discrimination and perfect adaptation of the CR to the external medium, in this case to the strength of reinforcement.

References

Adrianov, O. S. and Mering, T. A. *Tez. Dokl. Vsesoyuz. S'ezda Fiziol. Farmakol. Biokhim.*, 1955.

Adrianov, O. S. *Zh. vyssh. nerv. Deyat.*, 1953, *3*, No. 3.

Airapetyants, M. G. *Trudy Inst. Vyssh. Nerv. Deyat. Ser. Fiziol.*, 1955, *1*.

Asratyan, E. A. *Dokl. Akad. Nauk SSSR, Nov. Ser.*, 1934, *3*, No. 1.

Asratyan, E. A. *Trudy Fiziol. Lab. im. Pavlova*, 1941, *10*.

Asratyan, E. A. *Physiology of the central nervous system*. Akad. Med. Nauk, 1953.

Beritov, I. S. *Individually acquired activity of the nervous system*, 1932.

Denisov, P. K. and Kupalov, P. S. *Arkh. biol. Nauk*, 1933, *33*.

Erofeeva, M. N. Electrical stimulation of dog's skin as a conditioned stimulus for the functioning of the salivary glands. Dissertation, St. Petersburg, 1912.

Fedorov, V. K. *Trudy Fiziol. Lab. im. Pavlova*, 1938, *8*.

Fedorov, V. K. *Fiziol. Zh. SSSR*, 1950, *36*, No. 5.

Fursikov, D. S. *Proceedings of Second All-Union Conference of Physiologists*. 1926.

Gambaryan, L. S. *Trudy Inst. Fiziol.*, 1952, *1*.

Gershuni, G. V. *Zh. vyssh. nerv. Deyat.*, 1957, *7*.

Jouvet, A. and Hernandez-Péon, R. *Colloque de Marseille*, Paris, 1957.

Kleshchev, S. V. *Trudy Fiziol. Lab. im. Pavlova*, 1936, *6*.

Konorski, J., and Lubinska, L. *Acta Biol. Exper.*, 1939, *13*, 143.

Kupalov, P. S. *Arkh. biol. Nauk*, 1941, *61*, No. 3.

Kupalov, P. S. *Zh. vyssh. nerv. Deyat.*, 1951, *1*, No. 6.

Kupalov, P. S. In *Fifty years of Pavlov's teaching on conditioned reflexes*. Moscow-Leningrad: Izd. Akad. Nauk SSSR, 1952.

Kupalov, P. S., and Lukov, B. N. *Arkh. biol. Nauk*, 1933, *33*.

Makarychev, A. I. *The law of strength of higher nervous activity*. Izd. Akad. Nauk SSSR, 1947.

Nikitin, N. N. *Arkh. biol. Nauk*, 1933, *33*.

Pavlova, A. M. *Trudy Fiziol. Lab. im. Pavlova*, 1941, *10*.

Perel'tsveig, I. Y. Material on the theory of conditioned reflexes. Dissertation, St. Petersburg, 1907.

Petropavlovskii, V. P. *Med.-biol. Zh.*, 1927, No. 2.

Petrova, M. K. *Trudy Fiziol. Lab. im. Pavlova*, 1937, *7*.

Podkopaev, N. A. *Fiziol. Zh. SSSR*, 1941, *30*, No. 1.

Popova, N. S. *Comparative characterization of the dynamics of the nervous processes in the auditory and visual analyzers of dogs with respect to specificity of their structure*. Dissertation, Moscow, 1960.

Protopopov, V. P. *On the combinative-motor responses to auditory stimulation*. Dissertation, St. Petersburg, 1909, Sourem. psikhoneurol.

Protopopov, V. P. *Sovet. Psikhiat.*, 1931, No. 1.

Savich, A. A. *Additional material on the problem of the mutual effect of alimentary reflexes on each other*. Dissertation, St. Petersburg, 1913.

Skipin, G. V. *Zh. vyssh. nerv. Deyat.*, 1957, *7*.

Sokolov, E. N. *Perception and conditioned reflexes*. Izd. MGU. 1958.

Staritsyn, S. E. In *Collection of essays dedicated to B. M. Bekhterev's 40th year of professional activity*. Leningrad, 1962.

Stroganov, V. V. *Trudy Fiziol. Lab. im. Pavlova,* 1945, *12,* No. 2.

Troshikhin, V. K. *Trudy Fiziol. Lab. im. Pavlova,* 1945, *12*.

Varga, M. Y. *Zh. vyssh. nerv. Deyat.*, 1955, *5*.

Zachinyaeva, I. A. *Problems of higher nervous activity*. Moscow: Medgiz, 1949.

Zelenii, G. P. *Zh. eksper. Biol. Med.*, 1929, *12,* No. 31.

29

The Ecological-Physiological Approach to Problems of Animal Behavior

A. D. Slonim

EDITORS' INTRODUCTION

Since the 1920's, when Pavlovian theory attained widespread recognition among psychologists and neurophysiologists, the name Pavlov has generally represented a theory of conditioning (or learning). When the question of unlearned, "innate" behaviors has been raised in this context, the purpose has usually been to set the stage for showing some sort of behavior modification or stimulus substitution which follows from Pavlovian theory.

The following chapter represents contemporary Soviet thinking on the problem of "innate versus learned" behavior. Pavlov viewed instinct as an inborn, hereditarily determined act, distinguished from a simple unconditioned reflex by the complexity of its structure and the number of links required for its completion. More recent research in the Pavlovian tradition (Bykov and Slonim, 1960; Slonim, 1961) has viewed instinct as a combination of inborn and acquired activities which form at different stages of prenatal and, especially, postnatal development.

The center for this research in the U.S.S.R. is A. D. Slonim's Laboratory of Ecological Physiology at the Pavlov Institute of Physiology in Leningrad. Very little of this work has appeared in English. Perhaps the best single source is the Proceedings of

Symposium No. 1, 18th International Congress of Psychology (*Moscow, 1967*). *The symposium, brief accounts of which were published in English, represents a cross section of Soviet, as well as American, ethological research.*

CONTEMPORARY KNOWLEDGE of animal and human behavior is based on the accomplishments of biological, sociological, humanistic, and (in connection with the development of cybernetics) several physical sciences. However, the large amount of available data has not yet been subject to systematization and generalization. Indeed, this is hardly possible; precise sciences have as yet barely penetrated biology, and, therefore, any investigator must limit his approach to his subject. The study of behavior is an integral part of problems concerning the physiology of work and sport, zoötechnical physiology, the genetics of behavior, the structure of a species, the dynamics of the number of species on given territories, the harmful activity of various species, and so on.

The strict dependence of an organism's behavior on external environmental factors, and the conditioned and unconditioned reflexes based on these factors, and on internal stimuli, including those that emerged in the course of evolution, allow us to predict many elements of an organism's behavior and to program "much of its behavior."

From this point of view, the recording of behavior as a whole and the subsequent analysis of the separate elements of this whole (motor behavior and regulation of physiological functions) are necessary. This allows one to understand many aspects of an animal's subtle adaptation to factors in the environment.

This presentation of the issue, which is based upon Bykov's teachings concerning corticovisceral physiology, differs radically from the system of behavior (the so-called ethograms) widely used by ethologists, who reject the reflexive character of these dependencies and by so doing advocate the indivisibility of behavior as a whole. Recognition of the indivisibility of behavior does not guarantee physiological analysis and does not allow one to understand its formation during ontogenesis and phylogenesis.

Ecological physiology, which fully retains and expands the methods of subjective and objective investigations of behavior in natural environments and experimental settings, pays special attention to the internal environmental state of the organism (to homeostasis in the broad sense of the word; to physiological mechanisms of motor and vegetative processes).

It is clear that all of the accomplishments of the ecolo-physiological experimental approach to the study of behavior cannot be described in this brief chapter. Most important are different forms of adaptive behavior, developed during the evolutionary process and during ontogeny. Analysis of these forms of behavior is sometimes very difficult, and it is not accidental that presently there is no generally agreed upon definition of the term "instinct" as a characteristic of the specific behavior of the organism. Thus Tembrock (1962) cites a series of definitions of "instinct" which, although not mutually exclusive, characterize this phenomenon from various points of view. Let us examine some of them:

All actions of an animal which are not dependent on training are called instinct.

Instinct is inborn behavior.

Instinctive behavior is constructed on the basis of unconditioned reflexes.

Instinctive behavior is based on the species-specific rate of movement (endogenous automatisms) and also on the species-specific rate of responding.

Instinct is a neural integration of internal and external elements of arousal under the influence of training.

Contemporary ethology defines instinct approximately as follows: "Instinctive behavior is species-specific behavior which must be examined from the same points of view as the species-specific construction of the body and its functions" (Tembrock, 1962).

At the international colloquium conducted in Paris in 1956 on the topic of the study of instinct, no common understanding was reached concerning those causes and conditions, that is, stimuli, which evoke instinctive activity in an animal. Piéron (1956) differentiates the following stimuli capable of eliciting instinctive responses:

1. Stimuli which elicit (realize) reflexes or partial reactions.
2. Stimuli directly eliciting directional behavior (tropisms according to Leba), possibly based on galvanotaxis.
3. Conditioned stimuli which do not show any external effect but which elicit a state of arousal in the animal.
4. Stimuli eliciting avoidance or increased speed of departing from an object.
5. Warning stimuli eliciting avoidance or flight.
6. "Releasers" (Lorenz, 1957), releasing species-specific instinctive movements.
7. Concluding stimuli eliciting an adequate termination of the instinctive act.
8. Combinations of stimuli acting as "signals" or "symbols" (e.g., the "language" of bees).

Thorpe (1956) suggests three criteria for defining the instinctive form of behavior: instinctive activity has to emerge spontaneously (endogenously), be inherited, and organized from within. Thus many ethologists view instinct not as a reflexive activity but as a spontaneous one in the most direct sense of the word.

Craig (1918) was the first to introduce the concept of an accumulation of specific energy within the organism which provides for the flow of reactions in instinctive behavior. According to Craig, an enabling situation leads to the liberation of this energy and the behavior acquires direction and is concluded by a consummatory act.

Lorenz (1937) introduced the notion of specific hereditary coordinations —instinctive movements. Tinbergen (1955) views these movements as hierarchically subordinate to specific nervous centers. According to him, there are higher as well as lower instincts. For the manifestation of an instinct the external stimuli corresponding to the instinct are necessary (matching like a key to a lock).

Ethologists evaluate the significance of external stimuli for the manifestation of an instinct in different ways. Lorenz ascribes particularly important meaning to the "vacuum reaction" (*Leerlaufreaktion*), that is, reaction in the absence of stimuli. Armstrong (1950) views instinct as a separate form of reaction—"overflow" of energy. Bastock, Morris, and Moynihan (1953) view the appearance of the reaction as a result of subliminal-suboptimal stimuli (a lowering of the threshold).

From the physiological point of view, it is hardly worth examining the rather complex transitions between directed behavior, inclinations (*Triebe*) and, finally, motives, or as Tembrock calls them, tendencies. All of this terminology can hardly be used in a physiological analysis of instinct; however, the great divergence in terminology permits us to contrast the data of various authors. We shall attempt to present certain comparisons of terminology used in the physiology of higher nervous activity and by ethologists. It is clear that the correspondence between some of them is highly tentative, but they all enable one to familiarize oneself with those aspects of the study of animal behavior which are being objectively investigated.

Table 29–1

Terminology in area of higher nervous activity	Terminology in area of contemporary ethology
Dominant	Appetition
Adequate stimulus	Inborn releasing mechanism
"Natural" reflex	Imprinting
Unconditioned reflexes	Inborn behavior, instinct
Natural conditioned reflexes	Obligatory learning
Artificial conditioned reflexes	Optional training
Level of arousal, tonus of the nervous system	Charging of the centers
Return afferentation	Reafferentation

One cannot fail to note that many differences between individual investigators are of a purely terminological nature. These concern, for example, questions of training and the formation of conditioned reflexes, the formation of durable conditioned reflexes and the so-called phenomenon of imprinting, manifestations of dominance and direction, and terminology pertaining to conditioned-reflex ("intelligent") and unconditioned-reflex (instinctive) behavior. These terminological distinctions differ only slightly with respect to their understanding of the phenomena. However, this overlap hinders comparison of facts obtained under similar methodological conditions when there are important methodological differences. An example is the problem of the so-called vacuum reaction (*Leerlaufreaktion*), meaning a reaction not elicited by any internal or external factors, for which terminological comparisons are obviously quite useless. This position is held by many ethologists (Lorenz, 1937, 1957, 1960; Tinbergen, 1955; Eibl-Eblsfeldt and Kramer, 1958) and must be recognized as final.

Viewing behavior as a whole as activity directed toward the preservation of the individual or species, it is necessary first of all to focus on basic ways of investigating behavior in nature as well as experimentally. In the latter case, it is again necessary to isolate those forms of behavior having adaptative significance.

It is hardly necessary to point out that all complex forms of animal behavior in natural environments are a result of a combination of inborn behavioral elements (inherited coordinations), closely bound up with natural conditioned reflexes and complex stereotypes (elements of obligatory learning), and more specific elements characterizing a given person or a given species. In essence, ecolo-physiological investigation concerns each one of these elements of behavior, but is especially interested in the characteristics and analysis of species and populational elements. As a rule, the investigation is conducted on the basis of a study of daily and seasonal rhythms or more complex stereotypes: diving, receiving and obtaining food, defensive activity (for example, digging holes and hiding places), activity connected with the nurture of the young, and so forth. We shall examine three basic means for investigating behavior in natural settings: the qualitative and quantitative characteristics of behavior and the study of individual reflex acts which are necessary for understanding the behavior of a given species.

Quantitative Characteristics of Behavior

Motor Activity

Attention has been paid to this aspect of the question in connection with the 24-hour rhythm of motor activity. Included here are the study of the cumulative motor activity of an animal during a given period of time and the distribution of this activity over a 24-hour period (Szimansky, 1918,

1920; Shcherbakova, 1937, 1938, 1949; Kalabukhov, 1938, 1940, 1950; Cherkovich, 1950; and others).

A large amount of factual material, accumulated in our laboratory, enables us to assert that common cumulative motor activity (walking, running, jumping) and its energy equivalent constitute a relatively stable indicator, characterizing a given species and even a given individual. With higher monkeys (chimpanzees) and with lemurs similar relationships were established by Person and Myarkovskaya (1953).

The constancy of the cumulative energy value of the muscular work carried out by an animal in 24-hour periods led us to study the influence of imposed muscular loadings on the spontaneous activity of the animal. The first investigation of this topic was the work of Maizelis (1953), conducted with the great gerbil. It was found that involuntary muscular work, even of short duration, considerably reduces the spontaneous activity of the animal. This reduction in activity may continue for several 24-hour periods; reduction in gas exchange and weight reduction during the days of the reduced motor activity are also noted.

With the reduction of general motor activity, certain of its accompanying characteristics became apparent. During the 24-hour periods it was possible to observe distinctive cycles of such movements as running and walking, feeding, and grooming. The interchange of these elements remained unaltered and only a shortening of their duration and an increase in intermittent periods of rest were observed. Certain elements of activity connected with feeding, urination, and defecation essentially did not change. Subsequently, Ponugaeva (1953, 1960) and Sklyarchik (1963) established the same kind of behavioral changes following muscular loadings in relation to cycles of play in young golden hamsters. Consequently, in the behavior of an animal it is possible to distinguish obligatory as well as optional elements for each species. The obligatory elements cannot be changed even quantitatively (referring, of course, to the normal individuals of a given species); they are characterized not only by a qualitative feature, but also by a quantitative one, that is, their specific weight in the animal's general motor activity. Apparently, nutritive reflexes and food seeking cannot always be counted as obligatory elements of behavior. This is evident from the experiments of Chernigovskii, Kassil, and Ugolev (Chernigovskii, 1962), which established that the amount of a solution consumed depends on the concentration of the solution, its composition (8 and 40 per cent glucose solutions), and also the condition of nutritive arousal. In this study the 40 per cent glucose solution was used as a nutritive substance. Consequently, the act of drinking can vary with the state of nutritive arousal.

This proposition, however, does not change the fact that the temporal characteristic of the eating act (as a more important element of behavior) is quite constant for a given species, and the time involved in food intake (in relation to percentage of total time in a 24-hour period) is a stable species characteristic. As the special chronometric observations of Makarova (Slonim, 1958) in the Leningrad Zoological Garden have shown, general eating time for the carnivorous animals (e.g., the families Felidae and Canidae) ranges from 8 to 28 minutes in a 24-hour period. This comprises from 0.55 to 1.98 per cent of the total time. In the herbivorous species, a sharp distinction exists between grain-eating and grass-eating species. In the former, the time in the 24-hour period for eating ranges from 21 to 48 minutes (1.45 to 3.3 per cent of the total period); in the latter (hoofed animals and kangaroo) this time takes up from 155 to 435 minutes during the 24-hour period (from 13 to 30 per cent of the total 24-hour period). In grass-eating rodents (white rabbit and great gerbil), this time is 142 and 234 minutes (i.e., 9.85 and 16.2 per cent of the 24-hour period). In the omnivorous species (wild boar, badger, armadillo), belonging to quite different families of mammals, the time for food consumption was very similar, from 3 to 40 minutes, which makes up from 0.2 to 2.8 per cent of the total 24-hour period (Slonim, 1962).

Thermo-regulation

Other data indicate that an inverse relationship exists between the duration of the eating period and the caloric content of the consumed food. The lower the caloric value of the food, the greater was the eating time. Per 1 kg. of body weight of herbivorous, grass-eating species, 0.04 to 0.14 kcal./kg. per minute is consumed; for carnivorous animals, 1.03 to 9.66 kcal./kg. per minute; and for omnivorous, 1.4 to 5.5 kcal./kg. per minute is consumed. Such are the energy factors characterizing nutritive behavior from a quantitative point of view. It is clear that these relationships, obtained under conditions of confinement, completely exclude natural food-seeking activity. However, observations in the pasture also show definite relationships in the time spent searching for food of different species under different conditions (for details see Tribe, 1959; Slonim, 1962).

Consequently, the quantitative aspect of behavior is determined by the energy relationships of the body surface and this, apparently, determines the species-specific constancy mentioned above. The quantitative characteristic of behavior, of a general (motor) as well as specific (nutritive, food-seeking) nature, depends largely on the temperature of the external environment. This is adequately shown in numerous investigations of grazing in domestic animals (Tribe, 1959). Under laboratory conditions, changes of such inborn aspects of behavior as digging and gnawing with changes in the temperature of the external environment were reported by Ponugaeva (1960) and Shcheglova (1958a). For the gnawing activity of the great gerbil, an optimal temperature at which the animals gnaw the largest amount of wood is 20–22°C. High temperature inhibits the digging reaction for rodents of different types. Thus in the case of general motor activity, as well as in its specialized forms, there is an optimal temperature zone. What physiological mechanism lies at the base of this optimum? Numerous investigators have observed a shortening of the time for total food-seeking activity in domestic animals under environmental conditions of high temperature. This is generally explained by the need to lower heat production under warming conditions, which is achieved by reducing food consumption. It is also possible that increased heat production during motor activity is a factor elevating the body temperature and, as a result of the regulation of heat balance, overflowing inhibition appears in the central nervous system which limits motor activity.

Apparently, more complex relationships exist between the temperature of the external environment and the magnitude of motor activity of a homeothermal organism. However, before examining these relationships, it seems necessary to examine the reaction to changing temperature of the environment with reference to the ontogenetic development of thermoregulation as one of the more important aspects of homeostasis.

In investigations conducted in our laboratory (Alimukhamedov, 1960; Ivanov and Alimukhamedov, 1963) it was established that the thermal reaction appears earlier than the development of thermoregulation. Newborn rodents, taken from the nest where they were with the mother, react to a slight cooling first by an increase and then by a decrease in voluntary motor activity. In the days following birth the picture changes considerably. The initial phase in response to cooling is lengthened, and warmth, which during the first days and hours after birth elicited arousal in the animal, begins to depress it. This latter reaction, characteristic of the adult homeothermal animal, enters as a necessary component in the maintenance of bodily temperature (thermoregulation) under natural living conditions. Some investigators (Hart, 1960; Scholander, 1955) have argued that the ability to maintain body temperature during cooling must be viewed as a phenomenon of adaptation only if the animal is in a complete state of rest. In practice many homeothermal organisms do not remain at rest for long periods of time (e.g., mice-like rodents, shrews). For many species a small background of motor activity appears to exist. Therefore, heat production during muscular activity, especially moderate activity, constantly enters into general energy balance of the organism as an inevitable structural component.

Play

From this point of view, the study of the effect of environmental temperature on the so-called spontaneous activity of the young animal, well known even to the casual observer as play or play activity, is of considerable interest. Ponugaeva (1960) showed in a quantitative study that the intensity of play (time of play/hour) in the developmental process displays a characteristic curve. Play begins in the young golden hamster on the fifteenth to eighteenth day, reaches a maximum on the twenty-sixth to twenty-eighth day, and drops sharply on the thirty-sixth day.

For other types of rodents these events are somewhat prolonged. As a comparison of data obtained in our laboratory by Ponugaeva and Rashevska indicates, the intensity of play activity in ontogeny corresponds to the utilization of oxygen, as well as to the magnitudes of the systolic and momentary volume of the heart. The last two were directly determined by the Fick method, as well as by estimates of the oxygenated pulse.

Ponugaeva also showed that by maintaining a litter of hamsters at an environmental temperature of 10–15°C, approximately 85 per cent of the total experimental time was devoted to play activity; in a litter of hamsters maintained at 23–25°C, the percentage of play time was only 65 per cent. Interesting data were obtained from a comparison of animals maintained in a thermograded apparatus. It was found that "cold" hamsters, maintained at a temperature of 10–15°C played in a thermal zone of 12–16°C. "Warm" hamsters, maintained at 23–25°, played in a zone of 17–34°C. It is interesting to note that following muscular work—play—the "warm" as well as the "cold" animals stretched out and fell asleep in the thermograded apparatus at the same temperature (22–23°C). Consequently, initial containment of the young in different temperatures not only shows an influence on the level of spontaneous activity, but also allows one to detect essential differences in thermal preference in these animals. The executed muscular work sharply reduces the thermal sensitivity of the organism. This view has been elucidated in a series of previous reports (Slonim, 1952, 1962). Consequently, low environmental temperature (a certain thermal gradient of heat exchange) is one of the important factors stimulating muscular activity. And while certain investigators hold that muscular tremors in terms of their calorigenic effect are more effective than voluntary muscular movements, muscular tremors are only utilized by the animal in cases of extremely intensive cooling. Would anyone—and here we have in mind a human being required to spend some time in the cold—consciously lead himself to the point of trembling and then refuse to execute a few energetic movements? Man and animals begin to move under these conditions and the lowering of thermal sensitivity in this case apparently plays an important role.

The data cited above, as well as special investigations of the relationships between bodily temperature and the appearance of fatigue during muscular activity (Sklyarchik, 1963), enable us to formulate an hypothesis concerning thermostatic regulation of muscular work ability and the intensity of the motor activity of animals. In all instances, for the general quantitative evaluation of an animal's motor behavior, the temperature of the external environment is of primary significance at the time of investigation, as well as during the period preceding the investigation (thermal adaptation).

However, stimulation and inhibition of general motor activity is not observed only with changes in environmental temperatures. In the investigations of Shcheglova it was shown that limiting water intake and water content in food materials sharply increases motor activity in the desert rodent, the great gerbil. Under these conditions the distribution of motor activity during 24-hour periods does not change (the great gerbil is an animal with a daily activity cycle). In the nocturnal species, the southern great gerbil, maintenance on food with little water content elicits a significant reduction in activity. The same findings were obtained by Shcheglova with experimental mice. Limitation of motor activity with a dry diet was observed in our laboratory by Filatova (1944) with the yellow gopher.

Thus, such a nonspecific stimulus as a change in the osmotic concentration of blood evokes quite different behavioral changes in animals with different ecological specializations. If the limitation of movement, as in the case of the yellow gopher, is a passive adaptation, evoking economy of water loss, then an increase in the diurnal activity of the great gerbil, to the contrary, is apparently connected with migration or with an increase in digging activity leading to the acquisition of plant roots containing water. These questions and their physiological study are in need of supplementary investigations.

Consequently, the quantitative study of an animal's behavior, conducted under different sets of conditions, may itself contribute a great deal to an understanding of the biological significance of its separate forms, and sometimes may even uncover specific physiological mechanisms underlying it. However, the quantitative characteristic alone does not allow one to discover the series of behavior dependencies of different species of animals which are related to their ecological specialization. In this area, investigations of the structure of the separate elements of behavior-reflexive acts, including movements as well as vegetative functions, are of considerable help.

Qualitative Characteristics of Behavior

In our laboratory, the question of the significance of the structure of the peripheral component of the complex reflex act initially occurred during the study of the natural conditioned salivary reaction in female cats stimulated by food or by the sight of a live prey (Ugolev, 1950, 1953).

Inhibition of salivation at the time of stimulation, subsequent salivation after cessation of stimulation, the presence of salivation in domestic female cats and kittens in their first weeks of life—all of this shows that the natural nutritive conditioned reflex in a female cat is quite different in its structure, which includes separate effectors (muscular, secretional, cardiovascular, etc.) from that of the dog. This difference was interpreted in terms of methods of food seeking in these two types of predatory mammals; data supporting the interpretation were obtained in subsequent investigations (Daniyarov, 1952; Chechulin, 1955; Liberman and Uzhdavini, 1959). Investigations of the electrical activity of the skeletal musculature of female cats were also very illuminating. As recently obtained data of Yakimenko (unpublished) indicate, the appearance of muscle potentials, connected with the movements of the ears, is observed in female cats stimulated by the sight and smell of food, but no increase of muscular electrical activity in masticatory muscles and muscles of the extremities is observed. Only after the termination of stimulation is it possible to see the emergence of electrical activity in these latter muscles. Thus, the investigation of arousal, emerging in different muscles, when contrasted with salivation, the formation of gastric juices, and pulse rate, indicates a significant overflow of inhibition accompanying the first stage of the food-seeking act of the female cat—a predatory animal with a characteristic means for obtaining food (Zernov, 1937). Among other mammals (e.g., rabbit) stimulation by the sight and smell of food evokes the appearance of gradually increasing activity in the areas of the nose, muscles of the ear, masticatory muscles, and also in the muscles of the extremities.

Consequently, utilization of electromyography as a method for studying the arousal of individual muscular groups when to external appearances the animal is quiescent presents unlimited opportunities for studying qualitative aspects of muscular activity and its structure in connection with the ecological specialization of the animal. This has been especially apparent in studies of orienting reflexes. Thus, for example, in a rabbit following brief light stimulation (30 seconds) it is possible to observe the sequential inclusion of muscles of the nose, masticatory, and ear muscles and, thereafter, muscles of the hip. With stimulation by sound, the muscles of the ear, then masticatory muscles, and finally muscles of the nose and extremities are activated. This stable picture of the distribution of arousal in different muscles presents evidence for different response structure in different species to the same stimuli. Yakimenko also points to the significance of the strength of the stimulus in the spreading of the process to various muscular groups. Thus, for example, the reaction of a rabbit to a bell is always expressed more distinctly than to pure tones of even greater intensity. All of this suggests numerous possibilities, beginning with the study of the peripheral component of the structure of the reflex in various species with different ecological specialization.

We had already concluded in 1949 (Slonim, 1949), on the basis of comparisons with nutritive, defensive and other reactions, that orienting reactions of animals of different species may be quite varied. Apparently, the orienting reaction itself may consist of the initial undifferentiated phase as well as a subsequent phase, specific for each type of organism. The extent to which these phases correspond to humoral and tissue movements, identified as an alarm reaction, must be shown by future studies.

Clear differences between orienting reflexes to olfactory stimuli have been obtained in investigations by Rashevska (unpublished). The action of orienting stimuli directed to the olfactory analyzer (smell of mint or camphor) never evoked increases in gaseous exchange in dogs. Also absent was any kind of electrical activity in the hip muscles. An entirely different picture was observed with goats: an increase in gaseous exchange and the appearance of considerable electrical activity in the hip muscles were produced by olfactory stimulation. These differences can be explaïned by the different reactions of animals to so-called higher and lower scents. In hooved animals the former is connected with moving and smelling of the air while moving. In dogs the lower scent is connected with fixating an animal. Herein lie the differences in the character of what appear to be very simple reflexive responses to olfactory stimulation.

Some interesting aspects of skeletal muscular reactions were found with natural, well-compensated-for hypoxia in diving animals—seals. According to data obtained by Davydov and Makarova (unpublished), submerging an animal's head in water evokes a sharp lowering of the muscle tonus, which is expressed by the lowering of electrical activity of the skeletal musculature. The lowering of the electrical activity of the skeletal (locomotor) muscles has also been found by Davydov (1960) in a hedgehog during curling. The hypoxia emerging under these conditions is accompanied by the lowering of gaseous exchange (Filatova, 1946, 1958) and simultaneously by a sharp lowering of the muscle tonus. Future investigations must refine the topography of this original reflex, which depresses the muscle tonus. It has already been found that in the hedgehog clearly expressed reciprocal relationships exist between powerful skin muscles (m. orbicularis dorsi) and the skeletal musculature. It is thought that particular reactions which ensure the existence of the diving animals and of those which curl into a ball (defensive reaction) under conditions of sharp hypoxia also include a specific distribution of muscle tonus which favors a reduction in the need for oxygen.

The Structure of the Reflexive Act and Its Specialization

Along with the highly specialized reactions of animals cited above, there are also more general reactions, characteristic not only of a given order but also of classes of vertebrates. To the number of such general reactions one can undoubtedly assign homeothermy and its accompanying reflexes of thermoregulation. There is no doubt that thermoregulation is a reflexive act; this assertion is not disputed by investigators whether within this country or abroad. From premises formulated in our laboratory concerning the peripheral structure of the reflex, we have every reason for assuming that the thermoregulatory reflex also has its own structure, which apparently is more or less common to different mammals. Reality has substantiated these assumptions. It was found that any cooling elicits the appearance of electrical activity in certain groups of muscles. This reaction begins with the muscles of the neck, then the masticatory muscles, then the muscles of the humeral area followed immediately by the muscles of the pelvic area. Data concerning the scheme of drawing into the reaction those muscles which support the increased exchange during chemical thermoregulation are based on numerous investigations conducted in our laboratory by Ivanov, Biserova, Ruttenburg, and Chusov. All animals investigated, from mice to human beings, develop reactions according to this scheme. Of particular interest in the above-stated sequence is the physiological significance of heightened heat production occurring in the musculature. It is apparent that while the thermoregulatory musculature is static (antigravitational), skeletal (locomotor) musculature is brought into the reaction of thermoregulation (in a state of muscular quiescence) as the last step in the sequence—during a sharp cooling.

The accumulated facts permit one to study mutual relationships between phasic contractions of the musculature in the form of thermoregulatory tonus and trembling as well as the interrelationships between the degree of skeletal muscle arousal and the appearance of "spontaneous" activity. Along these lines, data obtained by Labas (unpublished) in the study of masticatory muscles are of interest. It was found that the frequency of contractions of masticatory muscles in small animals (rodents, mice, etc.) is considerable and may reach 10 to 15 contractions per second. These frequencies exceed those previously encountered in mammals, and for recording them it was found necessary to use a special transducer which was inserted under the animal's skin in the area of the lower jaw. It is important to note that in animals with great heat loss (and corresponding heat production), overt sequential movements of the jaw following completion of the act of eating are observed. Also of considerable interest is the quiescent state of the masticatory muscles in these animals. It is always accompanied (in conditions of moderate environmental temperatures) by intensified electrical activity. Contractions of the masticatory muscles, in addition to a volley of electrical activity, are accompanied by perseverating thermoregulatory activity of the tonus type. One can never succeed in observing these phenomena in the area of the quadriceps muscle of the hip, for example, where muscle contraction alternates with relative muscle quiescence (absence of thermoregulatory tonus). In small animals, alternation between attacks of trembling and thermoregulatory tonus is observed only under conditions of extreme cooling.

Consequently, masticatory muscles, in the full sense of the word, are muscles which are constantly included in thermoregulatory activity. It is possible that other muscles supporting the posture of small animals are also capable of alternating contracting and thermoregulatory arousal. These are questions for future investigations.

The data presented above concerning the qualitative as well as the quantitative characteristics of behavior enable us to view behavior as an effector which lawfully responds to complex stimulation which is a part of the environmental conditions of an animal's life.

It is clear that this simplified application of reflex theory to the study of animal and human behavior, although frequently applied in the past, by no means served to uphold naturalistic views of behavior. Therefore, there is presently no lack of critical comment on the view that the reflex underlies behavior, even from a physiological point of view. It is possible in this connection to refer to Bernshtein's (1948, 1962) remark concerning the necessity of examining life phenomena, including the work of the effectors, as a circular process; this concept is similar to propositions concerning reverse afferentation by Anokhin and the views of ethologists concerning reafferentation as a system of internal signals connecting the effector with the central nervous system. This regulating, self-guiding system is not only capable of reacting to an external stimulus, but itself changes under the influence of external stimulation and the executed reactions (Ashby, 1962). Obviously, the problem of the construction of the adaptive mechanisms of behavior is not exhausted by these interrelationships of "effectivity" and "receptivity" (Bernshtein, 1962). An explanation proposed by Bernshtein (1962) concerning the "problems of activity" as forms of the reactions of the animal to the external environment, as means for attaining that "which has to be, but is still lacking," may undoubtedly be studied best in terms of the formation in ontogeny of reflex activity at stages when it is still possible to make a fairly adequate distinction between the inborn and the acquired.

Especially interesting and demonstrative is the specific significance of certain environmental factors for the appearance of individual and specialized forms of the behavior of animals at different stages of ontogeny. In this case —without any formation of the conditioned reflex—the appearance of a purely unconditioned reflex is possible, and such an adequate stimulus is in the specific sense of the word the releasing mechanism referred to by ethologists.

The above-cited investigations of Ponugaeva concerning the formation of play activity in a golden hamster indicate that the appearance of this form of inborn activity at a predetermined stage of ontogeny does not depend on the external environment but, at the same time, it may be reinforced by the formation of corresponding conditioned reflexes and may be reinforced and inhibited by external thermal influences. Thus, even though in essence the "releaser" of this form of inborn activity is solely the partner in play, the preceding stimuli (e.g., thermal), conditioned reflexes to the surroundings (e.g., systematic placing into the cage for play), and the time of the experiment are undoubtedly significant factors. However, in terms of these investigations one cannot reject the fact of the existence of a certain "change" in the centers, which presumably reflect the accumulated energy potential. Even if the proposition concerning the accumulation of energy in the centers is only hypothetical and does not explain anything, the state of heightened arousal and the ability to perform work of the central and peripheral mechanisms which fulfill this form of activity are unquestionable.

On the basis of numerous investigations conducted in our laboratory by Ponugaeva (1960), Rakhimov (1958), Uzhdavini (1955, 1958), Shcheglova (1958a, 1958b) and Shepeleva (1961, 1963), it can be stated that definite periods in postnatal development exist when instinctive reactions are elicited by weak (subliminal) external environmental stimuli or even occur "spontaneously." In the latter case there is no opportunity to determine the nature of the external stimulation which elicits a reflex reaction formed prior to this period of development. However, this obviously concerns only external stimuli which are relatively easy to record and study. Internal stimulation, including stimulation arising in the neuromuscular apparatus, obviously remains unaccounted for. Furthermore, there are many facts which compel one to become concerned with this neglected aspect of the matter.

We would like to recall an incident in connection with the work of our teacher, Academician Bykov. In 1936 Professor Bykov arrived in Sukhumi, where our laboratory was located at the time. His attention was attracted by the play of young monkeys and he spent several days at the large open-air cage occupied by the young animals. At that time Professor Bykov expressed the thought that play is an expression of an animal's growth, a result of a particular and intensified exchange of substances in the muscles. Almost thirty years have elapsed since that time and our knowledge concerning the origin of the "spontaneous" activity of animals has been little expanded or refined.

Recently in our laboratory Labas, while studying electromyograms of masticatory activity in mice, discovered that each chewing movement and each volley of impulses is preceded by heightened electrical activity of the muscles. In addition to the constant background of heightened electrical activity of the masticatory musculature, described above, increased intensification of this activity leads to the apparent contraction of the muscle. This phenomenon can only be observed with the masticatory muscles. Simultaneous recording with the deltoid muscle failed to produce the effect. Thus the motor act is accomplished as a result of the heightened activity of separate muscular tissues and it is preceded by this heightened activity. There is every reason to assume that the study of the effector structure of motor acts, reflexive as well as "spontaneous" (where the stimulus remains unknown), may become quite useful in the investigation of this problem.

The elevated level of the exchange of substance could be observed in various types of young rodents in the nest just prior to the beginning of an animal's play activity (Ponugaeva, 1953). We still know nothing about the significance of the state of arousal of individual muscle groups and the distribution of muscle tonus in the posture-tonic (antigravitational) and locomotor (phasic-tonic) musculature. Are these individual muscle groups effectors as well as the basis for maintaining "spontaneous" activity (reversed afferentation according to Anokhin or reafferentation according to Holst)? Presently, we cannot answer these questions; however, they arise from the data presented above. A great deal of information still remains hidden within the structure of the effector muscles during voluntary activity. Yet this hidden information is very important for understanding the problem of maintaining those forms of activity which cannot be defined in terms of direct external environmental influences.

References

Alimukhamedov, A. A. The role of motor activity in the formation of thermoregulation in early ontogeny. *Tez. Dokl. 1-i Konf. Fiziol. Sred. Azii.* Frunze, 1960.

Armstrong, E. A. The nature and function of displacement activities. *Symp. Soc. Exp. Biol.,* Cambridge, 1950, *4.*

Ashby, W. R. *Construction of the brain.* Moscow, 1962.

Bastock, M. A., Morris, D., and Moynihan, M. Some comments on conflict and thwarting in animals. *Behaviour,* 1953, *6.*

Bernshtein, N. A. *Concerning the construction of movements.* Moscow, 1948.

Bernshtein, N. A. Directions in the development of physiology-related questions of cybernetics. In *Biological aspects of cybernetics.* Moscow, 1962.

Bykov, K. M., and Slonim, A. D. *Investigation of complex reflex activity in animals and man under natural conditions.* Moscow-Leningrad: Izd. Akad. Nauk SSSR, 1960.

Chechulin, A. S. Some new data concerning physiology and pathology of gastric secretion in female cats. *Tez. yub. Nauch. Sessii posv. 200-Litiu 1-i Moskov. Med. Inst.* Moscow, 1955.

Cherkovich, G. M. The experimental study of the 24-hour cycle of certain physiological functions in monkeys. Dissertation, Leningrad, 1950.

Cherkovich, G. M. An attempt to induce neurosis in monkeys via experimental manipulation of the 24-hour cycle. *Byull. eksper. Biol. Med.,* 1959, *47,* No. 8.

Chernigovskii, V. N. *The interoceptors*. Moscow, 1962.

Craig, W. Appetites and aversions as constituents of instincts. *Biol. Bull.*, 1918, 34.

Daniyarov, S. B. Natural nutritive reflexes in connection with distance. *Trudy Inst. Fiziol. Akad. Nauk SSSR*, 1952, *1*.

Davydov, A. F. *The investigation of motor activity and pasture regime of the caribou*. Dissertation, Leningrad, 1960.

Eibl-Eblsfeldt, Y., and Kramer, S. Ethology, the comparative study of animal behavior. *Quart. Rev. Biol.*, 1958, *33*.

Filatova, L. G. *Ecolo-physiological investigations of mammals—inhabitants of Kirgizian semi-desert*. Dissertation, Frunze, 1944.

Filatova, L. G. Aspects of pulmonary breathing and physiological hypoxia in the hedgehog. *Byull. eksper. Biol. Med.*, 1946, *22*, Series 5, No. 11.

Filatova, L. G. Reactions to hypoxia in mammals with different ecological specialization. *Tez. Dokl. Sov. Ekol. Fiziol.*, Vol. 1, Moscow-Leningrad, 1958.

Hardy, J. Physiology of temperature regulation. *Physiol. Rev.*, 1961, *41*.

Hart, J. S. in *Cold industry, Trans. Sixth Conf. Josiah Macy Jr. Foundat.*, New York, 1960.

Hart, J. S. Heat production mechanisms. *Proc. Internat. Union Physiol. Sci., Vol. 1,* Twenty-second intern. Congr., Leiden, 1962.

Ivanov, K. P., and Alimukhamedov, A. A. Concerning physiological mechanisms of thermoregulation in ontogeny. *Fiziol. Zh. SSSR*, 1963, *49*, No. 4.

Kalabukhov, N. I. Certain ecological aspects of closely related types of rodents. *Zool. Zh.*, 1938, *17*, No. 3.

Kalabukhov, N. I. The 24-hour activity cycle in animals. *Usp. sovrem. Biol.*, 1940, *12*, No. 1.

Kalabukhov, N. I. Ecolo-physiological aspects of animals and environmental conditions. In *Divergence of some ecolo-physiological signs of closely related mammals*. Kharkov, 1950.

Liberman, V. B., and Uzhdavini, E. R. Changes in pulse and breathing with unconditioned and conditioned nutritive reflexes in some types of carnivorous animals. *Tez. Dokl. Sov. ekol. Fiziol.* Moscow-Leningrad, 1958.

Lorenz, K. Über die Bildung des Instinktbegriffes. *Naturwiss*, 1937, Bd. 25.

Lorenz, K. Methoden der Verhaltensforschung. *Handb. Zool.*, 1957, Bd. 8, T. 10.

Lorenz, K. Methods of approach to the problem of behaviour. *The Harvey Lectures 1958–1959*. New York, 1960.

Maizelis, M. P. The influence of muscular activity on the 24-hour activity cycle of rodents. In *Experimental studies of the regulation of physiological functions in the natural environment of organisms*. Vol. 2, Moscow-Leningrad, 1953.

Person, R. S., and Myarkovskaya, N. E. Materials concerning the 24-hour activity cycle of certain primates. In *Experimental studies of the regulation of physiological functions in the natural environment of organisms*. Vol. 2.

Piéron, H. *L'instinct dans le comportement des animaux et de l'homme.* Paris, 1956.

Ponugaeva, A. G. Reflexive regulation of gaseous exchange in groups of rodents in the nesting period of development. *Trudy Inst. Fiziol. Akad. Nauk SSSR,* Vol. 2, 1953.

Ponugaeva, A. G. *Physiological investigations of instinct in mammals.* Moscow-Leningrad, 1960.

Rakhimov, K. R. The study of inborn and natural conditioned nutritive reflexes in the ontogeny of ruminant animals. In *Experimental studies of the regulation of physiological functions in the natural environment of organisms.* Vol. 4, 1958.

Scholander, P. F. Evolution of climatic adaptation in homeotherins. *Evolution,* 1955, *9.*

Shcheglova, A. I. A physiological analysis of the gnawing activity of a great gerbil. In *Experimental studies of the regulation of physiological functions in the natural environment of organisms.* Vol. 4, 1958. (a)

Shcheglova, A. I. Unconditioned nutritive salivary reflexes and aspects of water exchange in the muskrat. In *Experimental studies of the regulation of physiological functions in the natural environment of organisms.* Vol. 4, 1958. (b)

Shcherbakova, O. P. Materials concerning the study of the 24-hour cycle of physiological processes in higher mammals. The normal 24-hour cycle of physiological processes. *Byull. eksper. Biol. Med.,* 1937, *4,* No. 4.

Shcherbakova, O. P. Materials concerning the study of the 24-hour cycle of physiological processes in higher mammals. *Byull. eksper. Biol. Med.,* 1938, *5,* No. 2.

Shcherbakova, O. P. The 24-hour cycle of physiological processes in certain orders of mammals. In *Experimental studies of the regulation of physiological functions in the natural environment of organisms.* Vol. 4, 1958.

Shepeleva, V. K. Some data concerning the development of reflexive activity of female cats (*Felis*) in early postnatal ontogeny. *Tez. 3-i Sov. evol. Fiziol.,* Leningrad, 1961.

Shepeleva, V. K. Concerning some aspects of inborn reflexes in young caribou. In *Physiological basis of complex forms of behavior.* Moscow-Leningrad, 1963.

Sklyarchik, E. L. The effects of muscular loadings on play activity of golden hamsters. In *Physiological basis of complex forms of behavior.* Moscow-Leningrad, 1963.

Slonim, A. D. Concerning unconditioned and conditioned reflexes in phylogeny. In K. M. Byka (Ed.), *Collection of papers dedicated to the 100th anniversary of I. P. Pavlov.* Leningrad, 1949.

Slonim, A. D. *Animal warmth and its regulation in mammals.* Moscow-Leningrad, 1952.

Slonim, A. D. Concerning the investigations of specialized reflex acts in mammals. In *Evolutionary function of the nervous system.* Leningrad, 1958.

Slonim, A. D. *Foundations of the general ecological physiology of mammals.* Moscow-Leningrad: Izd. Akad. Nauk SSSR, 1961.

Slonim, A. D. *General ecological physiology of mammals.* Moscow-Leningrad, 1962.

Szimansky, J. S. Die Verteilung von Ruhe und Aktivitätsperioden ben einigen Tierarten. *Pflung. Arch.,* 1918, Bd. 172.

Szimansky, J. S. Aktivität und Ruhe bei Tieren und Menschen. *Z. allg. physiol.,* 1920, Bd. 18.

Tembrock, G. *Grundlagen der Tierpsychologie.* Berlin, 1962.

Thorpe, W. H. *Learning and instinct in animals.* London, 1956.

Tinbergen, N. *The study of instinct.* Oxford, 1955.

Tribe, D. E. Behavior of grazing animals. In *New developments in the physiology of domestic animals.* Vol. 2. Moscow-Leningrad, 1959.

Ugolev, A. M. *Conditioned salivary reflexes in female cats and means of procuring food.* Dissertation, Leningrad, 1950.

Ugolev, A. M. Conditioned salivary reflexes in female cats. In *Experimental studies of the regulation of physiological functions in the natural environment of organisms.* Vol. 2, 1953.

Uzhdavini, E. R. *Concerning the formation of natural nutritive reflexes in the ontogeny of the dog.* Dissertation, Leningrad, 1955.

Uzhdavini, E. R. Concerning the formation of natural nutritive reflexes in the ontogeny of the dog. In *Experimental studies of the regulation of physiological functions in the natural environment of organisms.* Vol. 4, 1958.

Zernov, S. A. *General Hydrobiology,* Ch. 10. Moscow-Leningrad, 1937.

30

Cybernetics and the Integrative Activity of the Brain

P. K. Anokhin

EDITORS' INTRODUCTION

From the extensive references to his work in the other chapters in this volume, it is clear that P. K. Anokhin is one of the Soviet Union's most influential physiological psychologists. This was not always the case. During the Pavlovian Sessions in 1950, Anokhin was severely criticized for his deviations from orthodox Pavlovian theory. But Anokhin, who fought in the Revolution and worked for several years with Pavlov, went on with his work. At the time when his public record was being chastised, Anokhin was busy absorbing the new findings on the role of the reticular formation which were to play an important role in his later work.

In recent years Anokhin's style of research and theorizing has become immensely popular in the U.S.S.R. The affinity of this approach with the "computer language" theories of Pribram, Sokolov, and others has been remarked on elsewhere in this volume.

Anokhin is presently Director of the Sechenov Institute of Physiology in Moscow and a full member of the Soviet Academy of Sciences. The interested reader is referred to his 1961 articles for further examples of Anokhin's work. This chapter appeared as an article in Voprosi Psikhologii, *1966,* 12, *No. 3, and represents Anokhin's report at the 18th International Congress of Psychology, held in Moscow in August, 1966.*

THE PRIMARY RELATION between cybernetics and neurophysiology is to be found in the use of cybernetic models of the basic laws of the brain's functions. Two other ways in which cybernetics has affected neurophysiology are (1) the use of analogies based on the principle of self-regulating systems by neurophysiologists who thus seek to study the brain as a whole and (2) the application of cybernetic principles in data analysis, the use of mathematical thinking, and the like. These tools borrowed from cybernetics have become the constant and necessary tools of neurophysiologists seeking to understand the regulated adaptations of the entire organism.

Conversely, cybernetic models of brain activity have gradually been improved. Newly designed machines have a higher "intelligence level," with features approximating the operation of the brain itself.

The success of a model in reproducing brain activity is directly dependent on the degree to which actual brain functions, as determined by neurophysiologists, are accurately reflected in the model. The success of neurophysiology is measured in the degree to which the true structural elements of the function of the entire brain are reflected in the mechanical system.

It now seems clear that the usefulness of cybernetics depends on our success in creating an adequate logical model of the work of the whole brain. Such a model would not only facilitate the analysis of any act as an integrated unit, but would also help formulate new research projects as well.

The contacts between neurophysiology and cybernetics have resulted in the need to construct a neurophysiological model of the brain's integrative activity that will meet two basic requirements: (1) It must be substantiated by experimental data from neurophysiological studies. (2) It must be a sufficiently extensive cybernetic structure to account for all the subtle results obtained in the study of particular brain structures. For this reason, we must discover the structure of the behavioral act itself before proceeding to specific neurophysiological mechanisms underlying it. At the 17th International Congress of Psychology, I discussed a possible physiological structure which, in our opinion, meets the requirements mentioned above and which was based on our earlier concepts of a self-regulating functional system involving reverse afferentation (see Figure 30–1).

However, during the intervening five years my colleagues and I have obtained new data which we believe provide a deeper understanding of those universal mechanisms that, acting as a unit, support the many components of that functional system which mediates the final adaptive effect. The integrated brain mechanisms which we hypothesize in order to account for the structure of the behavioral act are very similar to the principles of self-organization and model formation which are presently being developed in neurocybernetics.

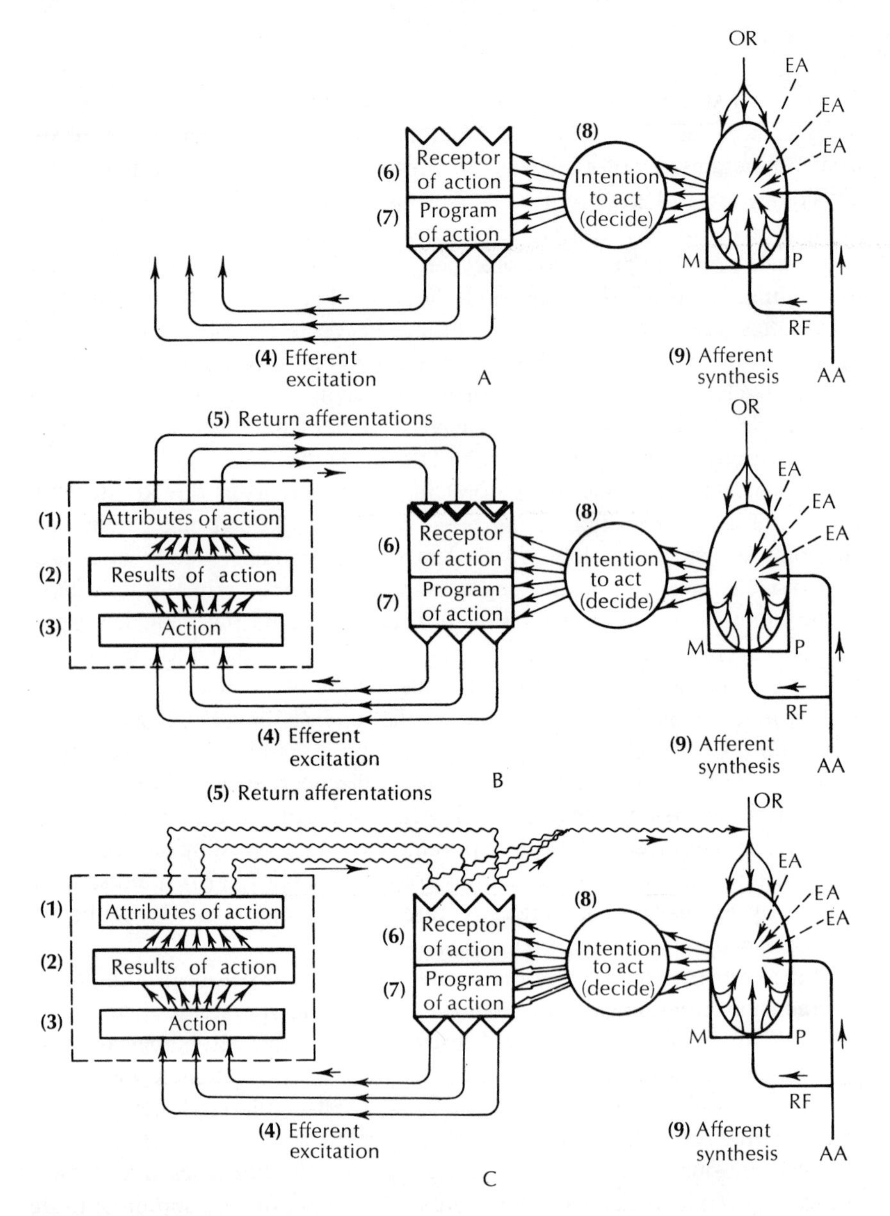

Figure 30–1. Basic diagram for the model of a behavioral act shown in three stages of development.

Key:
1. Attributes of action
2. Results of action
3. Action
4. Efferent excitation
5. Return afferentations
6. Receptor of action
7. Program of action
8. Intention to act (decide)
9. Afferent synthesis

The physiological structure of integrated brain activity described below is developing significance beyond its role as a model explaining the mechanisms of activity and is becoming a method for formulating new research projects involving the most subtle, analytical neurophysiological methods. This model is presently guiding our search for the overall structure of behavioral acts and even determines the neurophysiological conditions which we choose to study.

We shall outline below the key mechanisms of this physiological model which we have found useful for analyzing any behavioral act and which, in conjunction with other structural models, constitutes a general model of behavioral acts.

The Stage of Afferent Synthesis

The neurophysiological significance of the stage of afferent synthesis is that it permits the thorough processing, comparison, and synthesis of all the data which the organism needs in order to perform that adaptive action which is most adequate to the given circumstances. Afferent synthesis is the most important moment in integration. It is the key mechanism of the functional system in the fullest sense of the word. It assists in the solution of three fundamental problems involved in every behavioral act: what to do, how to do it, and when to do it. We will speak of these problems as parameters of the behavioral act.

These three parameters establish the adaptive relationship of the animal to its environment. Afferent synthesis permits the animal to determine its constantly changing need with a certain degree of accuracy and to match its need states with the infinitely varying effects from the external world. From a historical viewpoint it seems that afferent synthesis is absolutely necessary in order to allow for the incredible number of variables which can determine any behavioral act. The simultaneous presence of numerous influences upon the organism has made afferent synthesis the universal factor in all living matter; life even in its most primitive form must establish an adequate relation between the organism's requirements and the sum total of external influences.

Another factor relating to the nature of afferent synthesis is that it must invariably precede decision making. It is hardly necessary to dwell on the fact that the moment of "decision making" is the physiological Rubicon in the formation of behavioral acts. As we have already said, afferent synthesis is required to determine what to do, how to do it, and when to do it. If one considers these three questions in relation to decision making it will become clear that they each involve a factor of choice, that is, the exclusion of surplus degrees of freedom which are the inevitable result of the organism's anatomical and physiological structure.

For instance, let us analyze the problem, *what to do*. By virtue of the location and innervation of separate and often rather fractional, muscular structures, the animal is so constructed that at almost any given moment it is potentially capable of performing millions of possible movements. For instance, a person may point his finger at some object, he may rise from a chair, he may turn his head toward the window, and so on. He may perform millions of such specific motor acts. In the given example, however, suppose he extends his hand toward a pencil and picks it up. A natural question arises: On what physiological basis did stimuli for precisely this motor act proceed to the muscular apparatus with the exclusion of all of the other millions of possibilities? On the other hand, in a different sequence of behavioral acts that same pencil might be picked up at a precise moment when picking up the pencil is the consequence of a completed afferent synthesis. If the pencil were picked up much later than that moment it would probably not have led to a positive adaptive effect. Consequently, the problem, *when,* must also be adequately decided as a result of afferent synthesis, for example, as the result of comparison and coordination of all afferent signals from the external world at that given moment with respect to the object of the act. It seems obvious that this limitation of freedom in the choice of afferent signals is determined by the basic needs of the organism at the given moment.

From all this it follows that the problem of forming an afferent synthesis is an extremely complex one from the physiological viewpoint, and consequently we must analyze the problem further in order to consider both the composition of afferent synthesis and its intimate neurophysiological and neurochemical mechanisms, as well as the general neurodynamics of afferent synthesis.

From all that we have said it should be apparent that afferent synthesis is the most crucial aspect of brain activity, involving most of the specific properties of the brain as a whole. Pavlov long ago expressed a similar point of view when he said that the afferent aspect of central nervous system activity is the "creative" one, whereas he ascribed a merely "technical" role to efferent functions. Pavlov's assertion reflects the role of afferent synthesis rather colorfully and at the same time quite adequately. As we have already said, afferent synthesis invariably concludes with decision making, but this is essentially a creative act since the decision to select one act out of millions of possibilities is made on the basis of thousands of bits of heterogeneous information.

We know that there is a tremendous variety of afferent information which must be reliably processed, collected, and compared with previous experience before the critical event which has been expressly named "decision making" can occur (Bishop, 1960; Bullock, 1959). It is our view that no instance of decision making, no matter how elementary the adaptive act, can occur without some sort of preliminary afferent synthesis. This is why it is necessary to determine the composition and mechanisms which underlie afferent synthesis. Hopefully, using this material, basic problems of psychology bordering on those of neurophysiology can be moved toward a solution.

Composition of the Stage of Afferent Synthesis

What is the composition of afferent synthesis with respect to the quantity and quality of information which must be processed in order for decision making to occur? Physiological analysis using conditioned-reflex techniques shows that its structure includes the following qualitatively different components:

DOMINANT MOTIVE

The dominant motive may be created either (1) as a result of hormonal or metabolic conversion in the organism or (2) as the result of previous sequences of behavioral acts. An example of the first type of motivation is hunger; an instance of the second type of motivation might be the desire to enroll in a higher educational institution to acquire certain objects or to fulfill certain other "basic drives." Both types of motivation, when they are dominant, are capable of processing data entering the brain in accordance with their energy potential. Of course, formation of the second type of motivation requires more extensive collection and processing of a vast quantity of information, which is frequently received over a long period of time, but the fundamental structural elements of this stage are identical in either instance. What physiological mechanisms initiate and establish the dominating motivation in the cortex? Electrophysiological experiments on deprivation of animals conducted in our laboratory by Sudakov and others have shown that motivation, that is, the state prevalent at the given moment, has a very interesting effect on the cerebral cortex. Ascending stimuli related to biologically different motivations selectively mobilize only those synaptic structures in the cortex which have been associated with the satisfaction of this same condition in the past experience of the animal. Owing to the selective distribution of stimuli in the cerebral cortex, energy conditions are created which promote a functional dominance of those cortical associations which had promoted the arousal and satisfaction of the given need in the past. This amplified stimulation via the synapses of those cortical cells associated with a particular biological function is the basis on which the surplus information entering the central nervous system (primarily the cerebral cortex), in huge quantities, begins to be selected on the basis of this prevalent or dominant motivational state which is distinctively represented in almost every cortical neuron.[1]

1. *Editors' note:* These problems are related to a variety of issues in traditional Hullian drive theory. This work indicates the fruitfulness of a neurophysiological and pharmacological approach to problems originally considered solely at the behavioral level. For psychology undoubtedly the most fruitful approach to problems of irrelevant

It is apparent that the mere presence of a dominant motivational state greatly facilitates decision making by the organism. At the level of the very first synaptic organizations in the cortex an inhibitory process (an assisted shunting) occurs with respect to all information which lacks a constructive functional association with the motive that controls the organism at the given time. A diagram of this hypothetical mechanism is shown in Figure 30–2. A natural question arises: How is every motive which possesses a certain biological utility able to exert such a selective influence on the synaptic organization at the cortical level? Using intravenous injections of various neuropharmacological and neurochemical agents, we were able to discover rather interesting, detailed mechanisms of the selectivity with which various

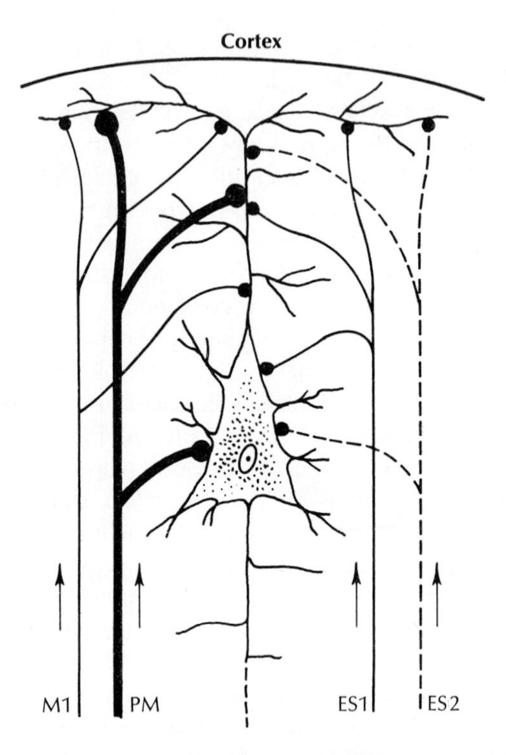

Figure 30–2. Schematic representation of convergent stimuli interacting in the cortex. The diagram shows that the prevalent motive (*PM*) arriving at the cerebral cortex occupies a dominant position with respect to all the other motives which lack actual significance at the given moment (*M*). External stimuli (*ES*) are partitioned in relation to this dominant motive depending on whether or not they bear some relationship to it.

---

and relevant needs, the selectivity of drive and the associative and nonassociative components of drive stimuli and generalized drive would be a combination of behavioral and physiological and pharmacological approaches.

ascending stimuli move into the cortical level. It turned out that different biological modalities of ascending stimuli operate synapses of differing chemical natures. This probably constitutes the primary mechanism for the selective distribution of stimuli throughout the cerebral cortex. We were surprised by the variety and specificity of the mechanisms which assist in the selective influence of ascending subcortical stimuli on the cortex. For example, a cat which has been deprived of food for only one or two days shows noticeable desynchronization of cortical electrical activity, primarily in the frontal areas of the cortex. At the same time other areas of the cortex remain in a typical sleep state with slow baseline activity (see Figure 30–3, *A*). Controlled experiments involving coagulation, polarization, and

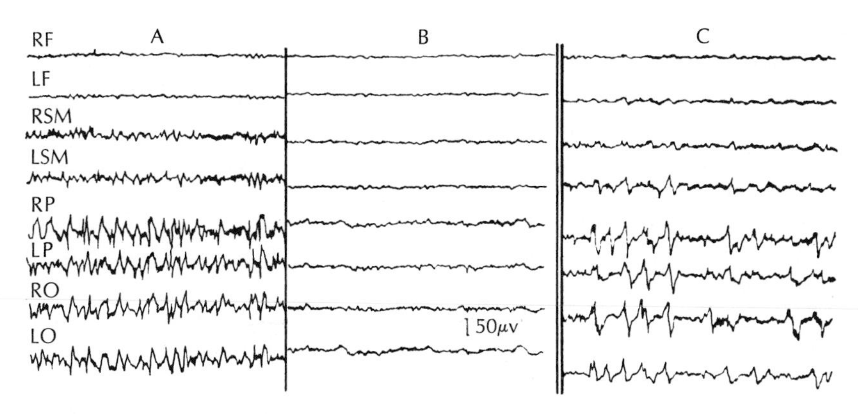

Figure 30–3. Electroencephalogram records of a cat under varying degrees of deprivation. In the case of one day's food deprivation (*A*), activity arises only in the frontal lobes. With four days of deprivation (*B*), activity becomes generalized throughout the cortex. Application of aminazine under these conditions eliminates desynchronization in the posterior areas, but leaves it unchanged in the frontal lobes (*C*).

Key:
- RF Right frontal
- LF Left frontal
- RSM Right sensory motor
- LSM Left sensory motor
- RP Right parietal
- LP Left parietal
- RO Right occipital
- LO Left occipital

the like indicated that the source of this rising activity is the hypothalamus (Sudakov). However, the picture changes radically after five days of deprivation. Now the entire cerebral cortex is found to be in a state of desynchronization (see Figure 30–3, *B*). It would appear that this generalized desynchronization is the result of the extensive spread of the same stimuli for the modality concerned with food throughout the cerebral cortex and that they are spread from the same source, namely, the hypothalamus. However, this turned out not to be the case although desynchronization itself remains outwardly the same. Direct investigations showed that the neurochemical nature of the subcortical and cortical synaptic organizations involved in the formation of these two activity states are different. Knowing from our previous research (Shumilina, Gavlichek) that chlorpromazine blocks pain activation at the subcortical level, we decided to use it during that stage of the cat's food deprivation when local activation of the frontal areas of the brain develops into general activation of the entire cortex. The result was quite informative. Chlorpromazine eliminated the activating effect of five days' deprivation completely in the posterior sections of the brain but did not at all affect the local activation in the frontal area of the brain nor the primary activation which had arisen at the onset of deprivation (Figure 30–3, *C*). In addition, direct application of amizil to the area of primary activation showed that this activation takes place with the aid of cholinergic mechanisms (Turenko, 1965).

From these experiments it seems clear that the initial stages of hunger are primarily the result of localization of cholinergic mechanisms in the cortex and subcortex, while in the case of deprivation for a number of days the activity, that is, the formation of motivated behavior, begins to be carried out primarily by adrenergic mechanisms.

It is interesting that microelectrode research involving the application of various pharmacological substances to the surface of the cortex showed that even a single cortical cell can receive ascending influences in the form of a convergence of different biological motives, the ones for food and defense (Fadeev, 1965; Kotov, 1966). What remarkable ability the brain has to operate dynamically, including everything that is in any way adequate to the present motive while excluding everything which is not suitable for it!

The question arises: Via what specific mechanisms does the cortical cell accomplish this remarkable acceptance and classification of a tremendous quantity of converging stimuli differing in origin and neurochemical properties? As we have seen, the keynote in this selective mobilization of cortical elements which correspond to the dominant motivation is the widespread convergence of stimuli on the neuron.

In order to obtain a better understanding of this vital mechanism we have worked out a special research method. The purpose of these studies is as follows: if an evoked response is electrically recorded from one and the same point on the cortex, it will still almost certainly be composed of cells which are receiving essentially different types of excitation. The differences may involve sensory modality (Fessard, 1960) or biological modality (Fadeev, 1965). In these experiments we were able to compare evoked potentials with themselves as well as the cell discharges occurring at the same point in response to stimuli of different qualities and origins. Once set up for these multiple comparisons, various pharmacological substances were applied to the cortical surface at the point of electrode contact. Then, by comparing the effect of these substances upon the various components of the elicited potential and upon the discharge of the nerve cells, we were subsequently able to reach conclusions about the chemical nature of the synaptic formations, in particular of the subsynaptic membranes. For example (Figure 30–4), at a single point of the cortex we were able

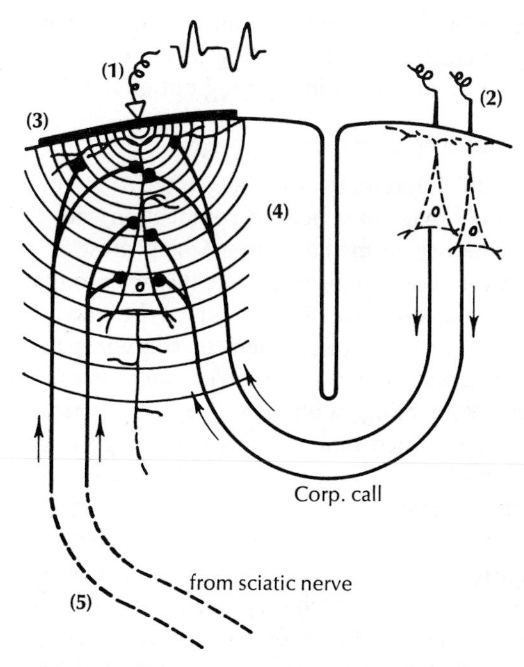

Figure 30–4. Diagram of the arrangement of stimulating and recording electrodes when recording potentials of differing origins.
Key: 1. Recording electrode
2. Stimulating electrode
3. The black line under the recording electrode represents the tissue paper soaked with a pharmacological agent.
4. Concentric circles represent presumed propagation of applied agent.
5. From the sciatic nerve

simultaneously to record evoked potentials of various types: those of interhemispheric origin, those from the sciatic nerve, and those from other areas of the brain. These potentials usually differed according to the origin of stimulation. A tremendous variety in chemical sensitivity was discovered in externally identical negative components of the above potential which had been elicited by stimuli arriving from different areas of the body (Chupina, 1965). Thus it seems that motivation acts to speed the process of afferent synthesis and rid the brain of surplus information. The apparatus and mechanisms involved are related to the structural features of the nervous system as well as to the differences within it among subtle metabolic processes. This fact determines the great selective sensitivity of cortical synapses to the arrival of various ascending stimuli. Because of these properties all sensory information lacking significance for the motive dominant at a given moment are immediately excluded from active participation in integrated activity (see Figure 30–1). This line of research, which has only been barely begun by our laboratory, can undoubtedly provide an infinite number of very interesting results relating to the properties of the location and role of motivational stimuli in carrying out afferent synthesis.

ENVIRONMENTAL AFFERENTATION

By environmental afferentation we mean the sum total of all external influences upon the organism which, in conjunction with the initial motivation, indicate to the organism that action which must be selected in order to correspond to the motivation present at the given moment. The physiological role and behavioral significance of environmental afferentation is that it creates a broad integrated system of stimuli in the central nervous system, a kind of neural model of the environment because of its relatively constant nature. Remaining subliminal for long periods of time, these systems can be transformed into an active state by the presentation of an "activating stimulus" (see below), that is, they can perform a behavioral act integrating the interests of motivation and the possibilities of the environment. The significance of environmental stimuli as a special type of afferent data is particularly clear in the classical experiment using the conditioned reflex. In this case, the animal, finding itself repeatedly in its accustomed experimental environment, turns out to be completely prepared for a salivary response, that is, it possesses all the central processes necessary for the response to take place. However, we know from experience that the conditioned salivary response of the animal does not occur in the intervals between stimuli until the conditioned stimulus is applied. At the moment when the animal is quietly standing in the chamber, in the intervals between presentations of conditioned stimuli, the nervous system contains a complex of previously organized heterogeneous excitations which we at one time called "preactivity integration" (Anokhin, 1949). The presentation of a conditioned stimulus integrates the subliminal state and forms a behavioral act.

What then are the factors establishing this harmony between the processes determining "what to do," and the processes determining "how to do it"? Special experiments carried out in our laboratory by Shumilina showed that during the animal's rest period, between presentations of conditioned stimuli, a complex equalizing of environmental and activating stimuli which are responsible for the great distribution in time of the separate elements of the behavioral act (standing in the stall, running to the food box, and conditioned salivary response) does indeed occur. It is well known that removal of the frontal lobes impairs discrimination between environmental and activating stimuli: the animal no longer remains at rest in the stall but runs alternately from one food box to the other, obviously having lost the proper discriminatory routine for these forms of afferent signalization. In the past, physiologists have exaggerated the role of the conditioned stimulus in the conditioned reflex. It was thought to be self-evident that the conditioned stimulus is an absolute and sole cause of the conditioned response. Now with the discovery of the laws governing the dynamic stereotype (Pavlov) it is becoming more and more clear that the visible conditioned response is the result of extensive afferent synthesis which includes external as well as internal factors in varying sequences. The role of the third component of afferent synthesis, namely, the activating afferentation, follows from a comparison and analysis of the previous components.

ACTIVATING AFFERENTATION

A characteristic feature of the activating stimulus is that it precisely times transitions of the integrated neural condition already formed in the brain on the basis of previous motivational and environmental afferentation. While the dominant motivational state determines what the organism must do and environmental afferentation determines how it must do it in a given situation, the activating stimulus determines the third important attribute of a behavioral act—when to do that which has been suggested by both the motivational state and the environment. What are the specific physiological mechanisms by which the activating stimulus translates the "concealed" integration of the behavioral act into a visible, manifest form? What is the locus of this meshing of excitation from the activating stimulus and the subliminal model of stimuli created by motivation and environment? These questions must inevitably become the subject of research because the process of afferent synthesis itself has obviously become the decisive stage in the formation of a behavioral act.

It might seem that afferent synthesis can be completely accounted for by the components analyzed above and that the entire structure of a behavioral act could thus be placed in operation. However, there is hardly a single behavioral act which can be formulated unless all the molecular traces, conditioned connections, and associations accumulated in analogous or similar situations by the organism can be extracted from its memory, that is, the organism's previous experience.

MEMORY AS A COMPONENT OF AFFERENT SYNTHESIS

It would hardly be prudent of me to review all of the notions concerning the nature of memory that have been developed in recent years by Hyden, McConnell, Gaito, and others in connection with afferent synthesis. We are presently concerned only with the mechanisms of memory insofar as they contribute to afferent synthesis and to decision making which leads to the performance of one of millions of behavioral acts. In recent years, on the basis of results from neurochemical research (see above), we have constructed a working hypothesis of the so-called convergent circuit of the conditioned reflex. The core of this hypothesis is the subsynaptic membrane process which apparently constitutes the starting point on the basis of which the elements of previously fixated life experiences are extracted from the neural cell molecules.

As is often pointed out, the problem of memory consists of understanding the moment of memorization of a given physiological system's experience and the moment of retrieval of this fixed life experience—in a word, retrieval. Although we are presently able in some degree to form a hypothetical notion of the process by which past experiences are laid down, we are still unable to say anything about how retrieval occurs, that is, through what mechanisms the extraction of a fixed experience is accomplished exactly at that moment and to that degree in which it promotes decision making most adequate for the given situation. Based on the idea of molecular fixation of past experience, we can hypothesize that the chains of chemical reactions originating on the subsynaptic membrane continue in the axoplasm as well. Here they must surely possess high enzyme specificity. It seems to us that it is precisely along this enzyme chain originating at the subsynaptic membrane that the impressions of past experience are able to "stretch" in precise correspondence to the requirements of afferent synthesis at the given moment. Only the chemical specificity of enzyme processes is able to explain the speed, accuracy, and timing of retrieval which is characteristic of the frequent extractions of information from memory in the process of forming a behavioral act.

Following Hyden, we considered it quite reasonable to assume that, at some stage of these processes between the subsynaptic membrane and the generator of the cell's axon discharges, nucleic acids may become incorporated into the process. One must visualize for a moment all the dynamic diversity of the processes described above in order to comprehend the immense amount of activity involved in the synthesis. As you have seen, it includes not only the problems of correlating various types of afferent forces acting on the nervous system, but also the internal processes involved in forming our inclinations and motivations and even memory processes as well. We must only keep in mind that memory and retrieval from memory can be of interest to us only in the sense that they assist in the formation of goal-oriented behavior.

The General Dynamics of Afferent Synthesis

The complexity of afferent synthesis lies not only in the fact that it contains a vast number of processes and components but also in the question

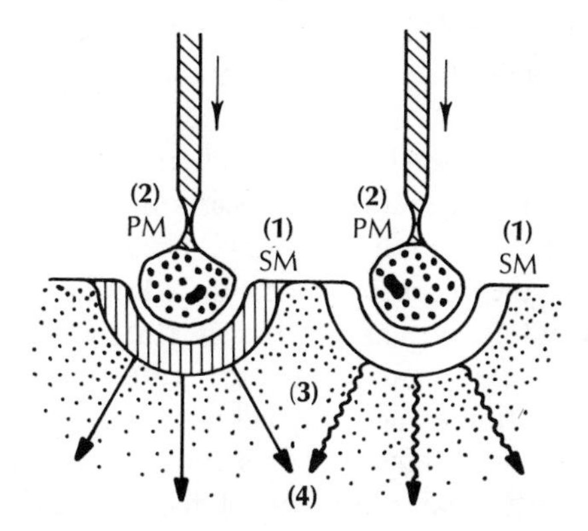

Figure 30–5. Schematic representation of two synapses on the membrane of a single cell with differing subsynaptic membranes.
Key: 1. Subsynaptic membranes (SM)
2. Presynaptic membranes (PM) surrounding bulbous ends of incoming axons
3. Axoplasmic area of the neuron (dotted)
4. Different arrows show chains of specific enzyme processes beginning at the subsynaptic membrane.

of how these components interact with each other. They are all constantly performing comparisons of one process to others until the time that the decision is made and an afferent model of the expected results has been constructed. In other words, the problem of the neurodynamics of the interaction between the numerous processes of afferent synthesis and, more importantly, the active "fitting" of these processes to the moment of decision making are first and foremost. All these brain operations are performed by two very vital elements which facilitate interaction between rather distantly removed nerve elements in the brain. These factors are the analytic orienting reaction and the centrifugal activating and restraining effects which act upon the intermediate stages as well as on the sensitivity of peripheral receptor apparatuses (Mescherskii, 1966).

The analytic orienting reaction is manifested in the fact that the ascending activating influence from the hypothalamus and the reticular formation on the cortex is present for almost the entire process of afferent synthesis. Consequently, the cortical neurons acquire a state which significantly facilitates the "investigation" of favorable connections between various synaptic organizations which are adequate to the given motive. Actually the selective mobilization of cortical synaptic connections which we mentioned in the section on motivation turns out to be considerably more extensive in the analytic orienting reaction, and consequently the probability of making the correct decision is maximized. Afferent synthesis may be considered the interaction of the components of the analytic orienting reaction, but an interaction taking place at a high energy level of cerebral activity supported by the hypothalamus and the reticular formation through continuous reverberation.

As research by Hernandez-Péon and others has shown, the process of activating the peripheral receptors also assists in the evaluation of external data. According to the research of Granit, Lindsley, and others, the centrifugal influence on the receptors leads to a lowering of their sensitivity thresholds and ascending activation promotes a significant increase in the discriminability of stimulation arriving at the cortex.

This general description of neurodynamic situations arising in the course of afferent synthesis completely accounts for the role of analytic orienting reactions and the centrifugal activation of the receptors in the process of afferent synthesis. However, a vast number of questions still remain to be qualified. For example, ascending activation accompanying the analytic orienting reaction unquestionably assists in the retrieval of elements of past experience from memory. But how does it accomplish this? What are the intimate molecular processes that are brought into play at the approaches to these storage areas?

True, we do have reasons to suspect that the subsynaptic membranes through which the stimulation of the orienting reaction is transmitted to the nerve cell possess their own chemical specificity. Perhaps this specificity consists of the fact that a process initiated on the subsynaptic membrane causes the acceleration of all types of enzyme reactions in the nerve cell axoplasm. Perhaps this new chemical state in the nerve-cell membrane and the cell axoplasm is actually that favorable situation which promotes the speediest and most correct contact among the various bits of information (see Figure 30–5). These are all still only tentative hypotheses, but they are hypotheses not nearly as improbable as they might have seemed ten years ago before the period of quite rapid expansion in our knowledge of the near dynamics and near chemistry of synaptic processes.

The Predictor Apparatus and the Formation of Acts

Afferent synthesis inevitably leads to decision making, that is, to the selection of a certain activity from among the millions of possibilities. It is clear that this selection process indicates the beginning of a selective distribution of stimuli throughout the afferent portion of the nervous system. Just how this decision making and selection of an adequate act are accomplished is one of the most intriguing questions facing behavioral neurophysiology. One thing seems certain: a moment must inevitably come in the process of afferent synthesis when the brain determines, by using some sort of indicators, that afferent synthesis must be completed and the appropriate decision must be made. One might think that the moment of decision is caused by the convergence of stimuli on the cortical neurons which is accompanied by a comprehensive comparison of afferent stimuli of various origins. We agree with Bishop that at the moment of decision making all brain processes must somehow become specially condensed in time and space (Bishop, 1960). The same hypothesis is asserted by Bullock, who devoted special attention in one of his works to the problem of decision making (Bullock, 1959).

How and where does this highly integrated process of forming a behavioral act occur? We do not yet have an answer to these questions which, in fact, have only been raised in recent years in great measure because of the influence of cybernetics. However, the very fact that this question has now been stated in a clear-cut form represents a tremendous achievement in the study of the brain's integrative activity.

Shumilina's experiments involving removal of the frontal lobes suggest to some degree that the most integrated and economical process in decision making is formed in the frontal lobes. We can conclude that the results of afferent synthesis must be represented there in some form. We can be considerably more definite about the formation of another important stage which concludes with the construction of afferent elements. These elements as a unit comprise the most important parameters of the future results of an act. As indicated by an analysis of behavioral responses and any physiological regulation, this apparatus which we call the acceptor of effect [2] (i.e., the process which perceives information about the results of an action) is a most important structure for the regulation and correction of inadequate human and animal behavioral acts. The direct observation of an ordinary conditioned response to food, where meat is substituted for the usual bread reinforcer, resulted in the discovery that a conditioned stimulus in combination with other components of afferent synthesis does indeed form an afferent model which quite accurately reflects the characteristic symptoms of the subsequent reinforcement. This is why the sudden replacement of bread for which an afferent model has been prepared with the new reinforcer, meat, creates a special "discord" between the previously formed attributes of the effect (reinforcement by bread) and the actual sum total of afferent systems from reinforcement by meat (Anokhin and Strezh, 1933).

Similar experiments, involving the sudden replacement or elimination of reinforcing factors in other types of experiments, for example, in the self-stimulation situation used by Olds, invariably show the same results. In the latter instance, the new sum total of afferent attributes of the new effect (switching off of the excitatory current) turns out to be inadequate for the previously formed predictive model suggested by the afferent synthesis.

In order to understand the function of the acceptor of effect, it is important to remember that the mechanism by which it is formed is a universal

2. *Editors' note:* This translation of Anokhin's concept seems more accurate than the usual translation "acceptor of action."

one. It occurs anywhere in the nervous system where an established functional system causes commands to be sent to the periphery and where any kind of adaptive effect occurs. In this sense even such an automatic act as breathing involves the participation of the acceptor of effect, although the physiological structure is a distinctive one.

Thus, for example, it has been shown that before a command from the breathing center to inhale 400 cc of air is carried out at the periphery, an afferent apparatus is formed in the respiratory center itself, prior to actual inhalation (in 1.5 to 2 seconds). The task of this afferent apparatus is to receive information from the lungs indicating whether the 400 cc were actually inhaled, or whether the command was improperly fulfilled (see Figure 30–6).

These speculations were confirmed by Polyantsev (1961), working in

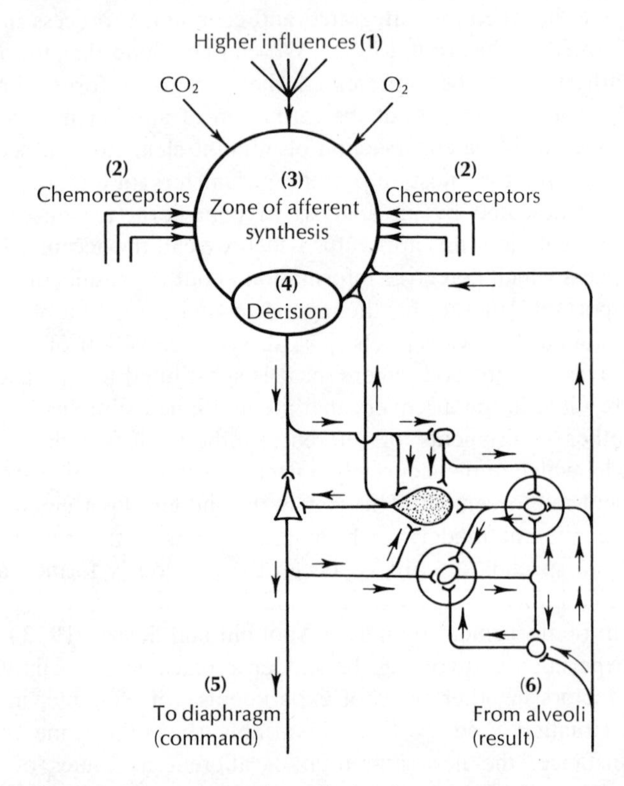

Figure 30–6. Diagram representing all the key mechanisms of a functional system applicable to respiration. Diagram includes efferent synthesis, decision making, and the sending of efferent stimulation to the diaphragm. In the center of the diagram among the collateral mechanisms is a mechanism for prolonged reverberation of stimulation to which return afferentation from the lung alveoli is directed. This system can serve as a universal model for the structure of the receptor of action.

our laboratory. Polyantsev devised a preparation whereby impulses from the phrenic nerve were transformed in an electronic device which transmitted the transformed impulses to an artificial breathing device. This latter device fed air into the lungs in accordance with the amounts determined by the output of the transformed impulse unit. By altering the information transmitted to the respiratory unit via the electronic transforming unit, we were able to introduce whatever volume of air the lung required in accordance with experimental considerations rather than the volume needed by the organism. For example, instead of 300 cc encoded in impulses from the respiratory center, only 100 cc were introduced into the lung for the experiment; a discrepancy was created between the command and the result.

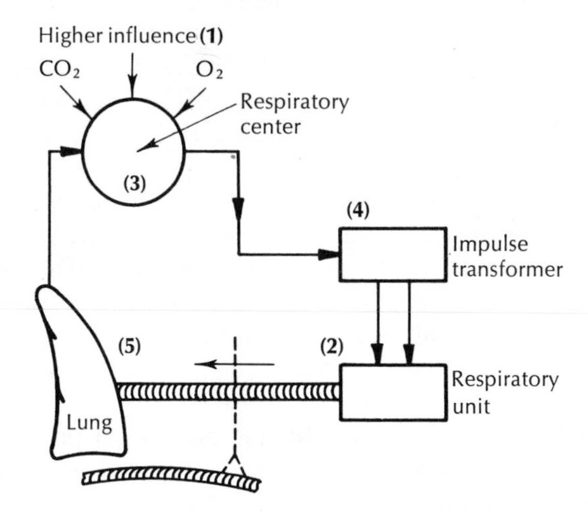

Figure 30–7. Diagram of device for intervening in the respiratory process with the aid of an electronic impulse transformer and a respiratory unit.

This discrepancy serves as a stimulus for the formation of a new compensatory action as a result of which considerably more air is taken in on the next inhalation.

Using this and similar experiments we have repeatedly shown that every instance of decision making intended to produce results is invariably accompanied by the formation of an acceptor of effect. In its physiological nature the acceptor of effect is a diffuse system of neural processes in the afferent section of the brain which reflects all the essential attributes of future results.

I cannot describe the formation and composition of this apparatus in detail at the present time. It undoubtedly includes not only the afferent attributes of the final results (which reflect the purpose of the act in question) but also all of the intermediary stages in the performance of the behavioral act which lie, so to speak, on the way to achieving its goal. Here, too, any discrepancy between an intermediary result and its return afferentation, and the already formed acceptor of effect, leads to the correction of the inaccuracies and errors. This is the mechanism that makes all of our actions generally harmonious and expedient.

In recent years, taking advantage of the great simplicity with which we could simulate the respiratory function, we have attempted to use microelectrode techniques in order to determine the changes occurring in individual neurons of the respiratory center during the formation of the apparatus which predicts the future effects of an act. Some preliminary remarks can be made about the way in which the acceptor of effect is formed, based on these microelectrode studies.

It is certain that at the moment when "decision making" takes place and the decision is beginning to be carried out, a branching off of efferent stimulation takes place in the efferent collateral axon pathways; this constitutes an entire "copy of the command" to perform an act. The complex of collateral efferent stimulation, in contact with afferent synthesis processes, constitutes the original nucleus of the acceptor of effect. This nucleus remains in a constant state of excitation until the arrival of signals from the periphery indicating the achievement of the goal.

Our microphysiological research indicates that the respiratory center contains many diverse types of cells and that several of these fully correspond to the logic of our hypothesized process.

These studies justify our belief that the problem of prediction of effects is a part of the realm of precise neurophysiological research at the present time. We believe that the numerous axon collaterals, particularly of cortical neurons, are the specific neural substratum involved in the transmission of a "copy of the command" to the acceptor of effect. Although the acceptor of effect is the key mechanism of the behavioral act, it is not the only mechanism forming a closed-circuit process at the completion of a behavioral act; the act must also satisfy the afferent synthesis and decision process by obtaining useful results.

The Results of Action as an Independent Physiological Category

One of the most significant aspects of the history of the study of the brain as an integrative mechanism has been the concentration on the act itself, rather than on its results. Thus, for example, we speak of the "scratching reflex," "grasping reflex," "blinking reflex," and so on. What do these expressions mean? As a rule they refer only to reflex action, without even hinting at the results. The term "scratching reflex" means only that scratching has taken place; it does not indicate what results were obtained by scratching. The same applies to the other terms mentioned. In fact, one can survey the entire vocabulary of reflex theory and thus be assured that the results of action have been completely excluded from the habitual thinking of the physiologist. This is of course a serious defect in the methodology of studying the integrative activity of the whole brain; it is precisely the results of action which are the final goal of behavior.

Because reflex theory has failed to cross the barrier in so many years, it is not easy for it to include the results of action as a full-fledged link in the development of reflex action. This is why even today there are many researchers who limit themselves to the concept of the reflex arc. This concept naturally excludes the mechanism of afferent synthesis and the acceptor of effect because it conceives of neural process as being linear in nature.

Isolating activity from its results is not a defect in reflex theory alone, but extends a great deal further, permeating philosophy as well. For example, Bunge (1959) writes in his interesting monograph, "Confusion of cause and basis and confusion of action and result is also prevalent in our own speech." It is for this reason that the concept of the reflex arc has historically developed with respect to action and therefore has remained "open"; it could be closed only by the inclusion of the results of action and by the inclusion of a mechanism to inform the brain of these results, that is, return afferentation.

In the course of research, the "results of action" are assumed to be something self-evident, but this "something" has not been represented in the organic continuity of the behavioral act. The failure to include the results of the act in the researcher's consideration also resulted in a failure to take account of the mechanism for evaluating the result of the act, that is, return afferentation.

Using the examples of reflex acts cited above, we might say that the result of the "grasping reflex" is not grasping as an act, but the sum total of afferent stimulation corresponding to the attributes of the grasped object (result of act). The movement of this stimulation in the direction of the brain is what creates the final stage, the comparison of these afferent stimuli in the acceptor of effect. If our example is the grasping of a pencil, the acceptor of effect will include an aggregate of the pencil's attributes (many-sidedness, weight, temperature, etc.).

It seems to me that it is in this concept that we must seek the cause of the extreme stability of the concept of the "reflex arc" which has for many years held the attention of physiologists on the act performed, thus placing an impenetrable screen between them and the evaluation of the obtained results, which are an organic consequence of action.

Return Afferentation

The concept of return afferentation fills the gap between the act and its central effect; it turns the behavioral act into a harmonious structure, an integral unit which is completed with an evaluation of the results of the acceptor of effect.

Some authors prefer the term "corrective afferentation" to the term "return afferentation." The former expression is incorrect, owing to its own physiological nature. Afferent signalization from the results of an act is unable to correct anything since it is always the passive consequence of the results of any act, even an incorrect one. Return afferentation arises even when an error occurs, because it can always arise as the result of the organism's encounters with environmental factors. Only the acceptor of effect, which contains all of the afferent attributes of the purpose suggested by afferent synthesis, can exert a corrective effect.

The acceptor of effect does not exert this corrective influence directly on the result obtained. Rather it excites the whole activating apparatus of the central nervous system, which then brings about a more delicate afferent synthesis and a more precise program of action in the form of a comparison between the presently available attributes of the result with the attributes encoded in the return afferentation.

One of the most fundamental problems in evaluating return afferentation is that it almost always involves many attributes of the result. For example, the result of an act might consist of the arrival of return afferentation through visual channels, skin receptors, auditory receptors, and the like. This means that each attribute of the result may be localized in its own projection zone. Consequently, a set of attributes characterizing a particular result must be based on an extensive system of connections encompassing the entire cerebral cortex.

This fact in turn raises the question: How is it possible for such a vast system to form connections with the acceptor of effect, which also contains afferent parameters? It seems natural to conclude that, if the return afferentation is projected into various areas of the cerebral cortex, which are frequently distinct from one another, the acceptor of effect must also be an extensive, dispersed physiological structure.

This conclusion seems logical, but it is unlikely that the brain operates on such a principle. I am inclined to the view that when they first arrive in the cerebral cortex the dispersed afferent stimuli become collected into a more compact form in some elements of the cortex and subcortex, perhaps even in individual neurons. In any event, some kind of compact kernel is formed. If this were true, the physiological contradiction between the dispersion of afferent attributes of the results throughout the cortex, the decision-making process, and the acceptor of effect would be eliminated.

Divergence Between the Goal and the Result

One of the remarkable moments in the operation of the functional system of a behavioral act occurs when the afferent prediction of results which is condensed in the acceptor of effect is compared with the nerve impulses arriving at the acceptor of effect as signals about the results obtained. This moment is undoubtedly critical for the formation of future behavioral acts in a continuous sequential series.

During this comparison the acceptor of effect appears to be a constant, direction-giving element (motivational model), whereas the return afferentation about the results may vary constantly, depending on the success of the results. This variable relationship is particularly prevalent in behavior formed by "trial and error."

The mechanism for comparing the integrated attributes of future results with the signals about results already attained includes one other important element—the emotional component, satisfaction and dissatisfaction. It is clear that this factor serves as an additional stimulus to search for new programs of afferent activity that are more adequate to the purpose. The connection between discrepant processes and the emotional nature of the entire reaction is especially pronounced when the discrepancy is caused by the complete absence of biologically positive return afferentation (e.g., from the act of eating). In these cases a discrepancy occurs between the acceptor of effect, which includes the attributes of the food substance, and the absence of real stimulation from the food substance itself (gustatory, olfactory, tactile, etc.).

A typical example of such divergence occurs during the extinction of a food response. Even the first instance of nonreinforcement of the acceptor of effect evoked by the conditioned stimulus is enough in some cases to elicit a sharply aggressive reaction and energetic attempts to obtain food from the food box (Anokhin, 1925).

Essentially similar human behavior can occur if the same situation arises. We know that in man such discrepancies lead to rather pronounced negative emotional states. One might hypothesize that in the process of evolution a discrepancy between a goal and results of an act helped to generate negative emotion if the discrepancy occurred owing to a failure to obtain vitally important goals. Conversely, in the case of an absence of return afferentation signaling a biologically negative action, the divergence leads to positive emotions.

The connection between the mechanism for evaluating the final result of a behavioral act and the emotional apparatus can be considered a rather progressive and expedient acquisition in the long-range biological plan.

In seeking the mechanism that evaluates this instant of discrepancy (or coincidence) in the acceptor of effect, we must once again point out the great importance of the analytic orienting response. Wherever there is a discrepancy between the acceptor of effect and the results of an act, the analytic orienting response is automatically aroused. This leads to an immediate expansion and mobilization of afferent information leading to an emphatic analysis of the environment.

This is a lengthy process. It involves a continuous flow of central-peripheral cycles of stimulation in the afferent systems. As a result, a new program of action is created which is to attain those final results at the periphery which correspond to the previously established acceptor of effect.

As we have seen, the neurodynamics of the formation of efferent synthesis depend on the analytic orienting response, which creates two basic conditions for supplying afferent synthesis with increasingly greater amounts of afferent information.

This is accomplished on the one hand by the extraordinarily powerful energizing influence of the reticular formation and the hypothalamus on the cerebral cortex. As a result of this influence, the necessary conditions are created in the cortical neurons to facilitate interaction of cortical cellular elements located in various and frequently quite disparate points in the cortex.

On the other hand, the analytic orienting response also assists the centrifugal effects on the peripheral receptors. This leads to a significantly decreased sensitivity threshold for the analyzer that is switched into the analytic orienting response at that moment; this increases the success of afferent synthesis and leads to a more successful program of action.

Among the neurodynamic activities which take place immediately after a discrepancy between a result and the acceptor of effect's model of the result, is that of the acceptor of effect as an important stimulus triggering a new search which involves a new afferent apparatus and creates a new program of action.

Conclusion

The material discussed above represents a completed structure of a behavioral act; all of its key mechanisms have been neurophysiologically and behaviorally demonstrated many times.

This physiological structure represents a quite heterogeneous picture with respect to the qualities of integrative processes; the interaction between these processes is itself a specific property of an integrative whole. For example, the occurrence of the acceptor of effect is unthinkable without preliminary afferent synthesis or the processes involved in the evaluation of signals from the periphery concerning the results achieved.

It is obvious that each of these key mechanisms involves an infinite number of dependencies and interactions of stimulation and inhibition; identical as well as different patterns of stimulation occur repeatedly in each mechanism. But this is precisely the point of a universal model of behavioral acts. Although the structure of its processes and mechanisms is quite complex, it nevertheless represents a logically complete entity which determines the place of each process and mechanism in this immense system.

From the standpoint of cybernetics this model of brain function is particularly convenient because it is based on the most detailed neurophysiological laws but at the same time suggests great possibilities for model building and for mathematical processing of data concerning its individual mechanisms. By correlating the work of these individual mechanisms with the entire structure, electronic and mechanical equipment can be designed and cybernetic models constructed.

I have been concerned here with demonstrating the physiological structure of the behavioral act as a whole for psychologists because I believe that the behavioral act constitutes the connecting link between neurophysiology, higher nervous activity, and psychology. As one can readily see, we are now in possession of definite results concerning a number of key elements of this physiological structure which were obtained by precise neurophysiological investigations.

Fessard, in accepting our fundamental theses on the physiological structure of the behavioral act, once remarked that the time has come when we must reveal, by a precise neurophysiological experiment, the mechanisms and process involved in causing this behavioral structure to remain a unified, integrative whole (Fessard, 1961). We believe that we have clarified many aspects of this problem, but a great deal remains to be done before we completely understand this amazingly expedient organization which has formed in the course of millions of years.

We are now close to understanding the mechanisms of afferent synthesis down to and including the molecular level. We have considered the physiological components of the acceptor of effect and have understood the tremendous role that the result plays as an independent component of the entire structure. Two key mechanisms which we understand from a logical, but not a physiological, viewpoint are "decision making" and the "discrepancy" between actually obtained results and the afferent model of these results reflected in the acceptor of effect.

However, I have no reason to suspect that these complex questions are insoluble. For example, we can point out that the role of the "copy of the command" in the performance of any afferent act is becoming increasingly clear. As shown by microelectrode research, afferent stimulation, branching off along the collaterals of thousands of axons, remains active for a long time in the closed "stimulus traps" discussed by Lorente de Nó. This stimulation is apparently cyclical and remains active through the entire structure until the moment when the return afferentation of the results arrives.

I have no doubts that the detailed act of evaluating the results takes place somewhere at the junction of the still fresh, energy-charged traces made by the efferent commands to action and the subsequently arriving signals about the result obtained.

We are presently striving, with the aid of various research techniques ranging from the study of molecular processes to higher nervous activity and psychology, to unite all of the levels of knowledge into a single theory of the brain's integrative activity.

The task is undoubtedly a difficult one, but we are well aware of the fact that there has never been an instance in the history of science when fear of difficulties has promoted scientific progress.

References

Anokhin, P. K. The role of conditioned reflexes in the work process. *Chelovek i priroda,* 1925, *9,* 9–28.

Anokhin, P. K. *The problem of the center and the periphery in the physiology of higher nervous activity.* Gork. Izd. Gorkii, 1935.

Anokhin, P. K. *Problems of higher nervous activity.* Moscow: Izd. Akad. Med. Nauk SSSR, 1949.

Anokhin, P. K. The multiple ascending influences of the subcortical centers on the cerebral cortex. In Mary A. B. Brazier (Ed.), *Brain and behavior.* Washington, D.C.: Amer. Inst. Biol. Sci., 1961. Pp. 139–168. (a)

Anokhin, P. K. Electroencephalographic analysis of cortical-subcortical relations in positive and negative conditioned reactions. *Ann. N.Y. Acad. Sci.,* 1961, *92,* 899–938. (b)

Anokhin, P. K. Physiology and cybernetics. In *Philosophical problems of cybernetics.* Moscow, 1961, pp. 262–305. (c)

Anokhin, P. K. Integration: free discussion. *Proceedings of the International Congress of Physiology,* 1962, vol. 3, pp. 358–360. (a)

Anokhin, P. K. *The theory of the functional system as a prerequisite for the construction of physiological cybernetics.* Moscow: 1962. Izd. Akad. Nauk SSSR. 1962. (b)

Anokhin, P. K., and Strezh, E. F. Investigation of the dynamics of higher nervous activity, III. Disruption of active choice as the result of changing the unconditioned stimulus. *Fiziol. Zh. SSSR,* 1933, *16,* No. 1, 280–298.

Ashby, R. W. *Design for a brain.* London: Chapman & Hall, 1960.

Asmayan, N. V. Mechanisms for regulating a dog's behavior when he is hungry or thirsty, with free choice of the reinforcing stimulus. *Twenty-first Meeting on Problems of Higher Nervous Activity.* Leningrad, 1966. (Abstracts.)

Ata-Muradova, F. Certain features of the synaptic organization of the cortex of the newborn rabbit. *Fiziol. Zh. SSSR,* 1963, *49,* No. 7, 783–789.

Beritov, I. S. *The structural and functional foundations of psychological activity.* Moscow: Izd. Akad. Nauk SSSR, 1963.

Bishop, G. H. Self-organizing systems. In S. Cameron and M. Yovits (Eds.), *Proc. of Inter-displ. Conf.,* 5 May 1959. New York and Paris: Pergamon, 1960.

Bullock, T. H. Neuron Doctrine and Electrophysiology. *Science,* 1959, *129,* No. 3355, 997–1002.

Bunge, M. *Causality.* Cambridge, Mass.: Harvard University Press, 1959.

Chupina, L. Electrophysiological analysis of the chemical features of components of the evoked potential. *Fiziol. Zh. SSSR,* 1965, *51,* No. 9.

Cossa, P. La cylbernetique. *Du cerveaux humain aux serveaux artificiels.* Paris, 1957.

Fadeev, U. A. *Fiziol. Zh. SSSR,* 1965, *51,* 1169–1176.

Fessard, A. Le conditionnement consideré à l'echelle du neurone. The Moscow Colloquium on Electroencephalography of Higher Nervous Activity. H. H. Jasper and G. D. Smirnov (Eds.), No. 13, *EEG clin. Neurophysiol.,* 1960.

Gavlichek, V. The electrophysiological characterization of a conditioned defensive dominant. *Fiziol. Zh. SSSR,* 1958, *44,* No. 4, 305–315.

Gordon, P. Learning machines. Survey paper at Second IFAC Conference, Basel, 1963.

Granit, R. *Receptors and sensory perception.* New Haven, Conn.: Yale University Press, 1956.

Hernandez-Péon, R., Guzman-Flores, C., Alcaraz, M., *et al.* Habituation in the visual pathway during "attention" in unanesthetized cats. *Acta Neurol. Latinoamer.* 1957, *3,* 1–8.

Hyden, H., and Egyhazi, E. *Proc. Nat. Acad. Sci.,* 1964, *52,* No. 4, 1030–1055.

Jung, R. In G. Moruzzi, A. Fessard, and H. Jasper (Eds.), *Progress in Brain Research.* Elsevier Publ. Co., 1963, vol. 1.

Klauss, G. *Kybernetik in Phylosophischer Sicht.* Berlin: Dietz. Verlag, 1962.

Kotov, A. The neurophysiological analysis of pain activation at the cortical level. *The integrative activity of the brain.* Leipzig, 1966.

Lindsley, D. B. Attention, consciousness, sleep and wakefulness. In *Handbook of Physiology,* Sec. 1, Neurophysiology, vol. 3, pp. 1553–1593, Washington, Am. Physiol, Soc., 1960.

Livingston, A., and Phillips, C. G. Maps and thresholds for the sensorimotor cortex of the cat. *Quart. J. Exp. Physiol.,* 1957, *42,* 190–205.

Luria, A. R. *The human brain and psychological processes.* Moscow: Izd. Akad. Ped. Nauk RSFSR, 1963.

Magoun, H. W. *The waking brain.* Springfield, Ill.: Charles C Thomas, 1963.

Minsky, M. Personal communication, 1964.

Pavlov, I. P. The dynamic stereotype of the higher section of the brain. In *Twenty years' experience in the objective study of the higher nervous activity (behavior) of animals.* Leningrad, 1932.

Pavlov, I. P. A physiologist's answer to psychologists. In *Twenty years' experience in the objective study of the higher nervous activity (behavior) of animals.* Leningrad, 1932.

Polyantsev, V. A. A method for the self-regulation of artificial respiration. *Path. fiz. i eksper. terap,* 1961, *5,* No. 4.

Pribram, K. Toward a theory of physiological psychology. *Vop. Psikhol.,* 1961, No. 2, p. 183.

Shumilina, A. I. *Conditioned reflexes of de-efferented extremities.* Moscow: Izd. Akad. Med. Nauk, 1949.

Shumilina, A. I. Characterizing the conditioned reflex activity of dogs during the application of aminazine. *Zh. Neuropat. i psikh. im. Korsakova,* 1956, *56,* No. 2, 116–120.

Shumilina, A. I. Comparative characterization of the retina and the cortex during elaboration of a conditioned defensive reflex. *Fiziol. Zh. SSSR,* 1959, *45,* No. 10, 1177–1187.

Shumilina, A. I. Functions of the frontal cortex in the conditioned reflex activity of dogs. In A. R. Luria and F. D. Homskaya (Eds.), *Frontal lobes and regulation of physiological processes.* Moscow, 1966.

Sudakov, K. V. Neurophysiological mechanisms of food excitation. Doctoral Dissertation, Moscow, 1965.

Turenko, A. I. Functional relations between the hypothalamus and forebrain areas during hunger. *Materials of the conference on the physiology and pathology of cortico-visceral inter-relations and functional systems,* vol. 2. Ivanovo, 1965.

Wiener, N. *Cybernetics.* Moscow: Izd. Sovet. Radio, 1958.

NAME INDEX

SUBJECT INDEX